# Professional School Counseling

## A Handbook of Theories, Programs & Practices

*Edited by Bradley T. Erford*

CAPS Press
An independent imprint of

PRO-ED
An International Publisher
8700 Shoal Creek Boulevard
Austin, Texas 78757-6897

© 2004 by Pro-Ed, Inc.
8700 Shoal Creek Blvd.
Austin, TX 78757-6897
800/897-3202 Fax 800/397-7633
www.proedinc.com



ISBN 1-4164-0043-5

This book was developed and produced by CAPS Press, formerly associated with ERIC/CASS, and creator of many titles for the counseling, assessment, and educational fields. In 2004, CAPS Press became an independent imprint of PRO-ED, Inc.

Printed in the United States of America

1 2 3 4 5 6 7 8 9 10 08 07 06 05 04

## Table of Contents

## *Section 2:Techniques and Approaches to Counseling in Schools*

## *Section 3: Comprehensive School Counseling Services*

## *Section 4: Assessment in School Counseling*

## *Section 5: Clinical Issues in School Counseling*

## *Section 6: Serving Special Populations*

## *Section 7: Special Issues in School Counseling*

## Preface

On almost a daily basis, professional school counselors and counselor educators encounter situations that call for authoritative information on a variety of topics. Typically, they must seek information from multiple sources, often of variable quality and applicability. The task can be time-consuming and the results less than what is needed or expected. This handbook was developed to address this problem by providing a single source that will meet most of the professional school counselor's information needs.

A review of the table of contents will reveal the exceptional breadth and comprehensiveness of this publication. In fact, it is so broad and the articles so authoritatively written that it would suffice as an excellent source and resource for all of the many topics covered in an accredited school counselor education program. For the practicing counselor, it will provide a highly useful resource for the myriad questions a counselor must respond to in a typical day.

Whatever your position, be it counselor, counselor educator, administrator, or interested citizen, this handbook provides an excellent means to update your knowledge about the school counseling profession.

Dr. Bradley Erford is a highly respected leader in counseling; and, as such, he was able to assemble a body of writers of exceptional counseling expertise and writing skill. It is a book that provides a quick (but authoritative) study, and it does so in an interesting and non-pedantic fashion. Unlike some large and impressive-appearing tomes which are used only once, this book will "hook" the reader and he/she will want to refer to it again and again. We predict that eventually almost everyone in or interested in professional school counseling will want to have his/her own copy of this handbook. Why not begin now and reap the benefits of having the all-encompassing resource you've always needed and wanted?

*Garry R. Walz and Jeanne C. Bleuer*

## About the Editor

Bradley T. Erford, Ph.D., is the Director of the School Counseling Program and an Associate Professor of Education at Loyola College in MD. He is the recipient of the American Counseling Association's (ACA) Professional Development Award and the ACA Carl Perkins Government Relations Award. He has received the Association for Counselor Education and Supervision's (ACES) Robert O. Stripling Award for Excellence in Standards and the Maryland Association for Counseling and Development's (MACD) Maryland Counselor of the Year, Professional Development, Counselor Visibility, and Counselor Advocacy Awards. His research specialization falls primarily in development and technical analysis of psycho-educational tests and has resulted in the publication of 3 books, numerous journal articles, numerous book chapters, and 8 psycho-educational tests. He is Past Chair of the American Counseling Association (ACA) - Southern (US) Region; Past President of the Association for Assessment in Counseling and Education (AACE); Past President of the Maryland Association for Counseling and Development (MACD); Past President of the MD Association for Counselor Education and Supervision (MACES), Past President of the MD Association for Mental Health Counselors (MAMHC), and current President of the MD Association for Measurement and Evaluation (MAME). Dr. Erford is the current Chair of ACA's Task Force on High Stakes Testing, Past Chair of ACA's Task Force on Standards for Test Users, Past Chair of ACA's Public Awareness and Support Committee, and Past Chair of ACA's Interprofessional Committee. Dr. Erford is a Licensed Clinical Professional Counselor, Licensed Professional Counselor, Nationally Certified Counselor, Licensed Psychologist and Licensed School Psychologist. He teaches courses primarily in the areas of assessment, human development, school counseling, and stress management.

## About the Authors

**Patrick Akos**, Ph.D., is a former elementary and middle school counselor and current assistant professor of school counseling at the University of North Carolina at Chapel Hill. He is a National Certified School Counselor, serves on the editorial board for *Professional School Counseling* and the *Journal for Specialist in Group Work*, and is the coordinator of the Research Triangle School Partnership (RTSP) School Transition project (http://www.unc.edu/depts/ed/rtsp/proj_st.html). His current research centers on school transitions, promoting development as a school counselor, middle school counseling, and school counselor training.

**Antoinette L. Banks** is a graduate student in school counseling at Bowling Green State University, Bowling Green, OH.

**Jan R. Bartlett**, Ph.D., is an assistant professor in Educational Leadership and Policy Studies, Counselor Education, at Iowa State University. Her K-12 professional school counseling experience was in a rural mountain school district in Arkansas. Her research interests include the role of intergenerational connections in youth development, body image issues in youth, and professional school counselor preparation and advocacy.

**Patricia L. Barton**, M.S., LCPC, is a 1990 graduate of the Johns Hopkins University School of Continuing Studies. Currently, she is an Anne Arundel County Public Schools (AACPS), Maryland principal. As a counselor specialist, Ms. Barton developed a family resource center for AACPS. She has written grants to increase parent involvement and is a trainer/co-author for *Parenting for Success* and *Reaching All Parents*.

**Dorothy Breen**, Ph.D., is Associate Professor of Counselor Education at the University of Maine. She attained her master's degree in Counselor Education and doctorate in Counseling Psychology from the University of Wisconsin. Dr. Breen is conducting research with rural counselors nationwide, with the intent of asking counselors to tell their stories and define the area of inquiry in terms of their perspectives and meanings. In general, she wants to develop an in-depth understanding of the realities and challenges associated with counseling practice in rural settings.

**Vicki Brooks** is the Department Chair of School Counseling in the Graduate School of Education at Lewis & Clark College in Portland, Oregon. Prior to higher education, she was a public school educator and a professional school counselor in Colorado. She is also a National Fellow with MetLife and consultant for the Education Trust's National School Counselor Initiative to provide training for school districts across the nation in school counseling reform.

**Lela Kosteck Bunch** is assistant professor in the Division of Counseling & Family Therapy at the University of Missouri – St. Louis. Prior to taking her current position, she was the Director of Guidance and Placement for the Missouri Department of Elementary and Secondary Education. During her tenure in that position, she was instrumental in developing *The Guidelines for Performance-Based Professional School Counselor Evaluation* as well as a major revision of the *Missouri Comprehensive Guidance Program Manual*. Her leadership also helped bring to fruition the *Missouri Standards for Teacher Education Programs in School Counseling*. In the past she has worked as a professional school counselor, a supervisor of adult education, an outpatient therapist, and a psychoeducational consultant. She has also been very active in the Missouri School Counselor Association.

**Tonya Butler** is a school psychology doctoral student at Mississippi State University. Her research interests include behavioral consultation, Functional Behavior Analysis, and behavioral interventions.

**Peggy S. Byrer** is a Nationally Certified Psychologist and employed as a psychologist in Indiana. She earned a bachelor's degree in Sociology from Purdue University, and holds graduate degrees in educational and school psychology, school counseling and secondary education from Indiana State University. She is a member of several boards of directors for community agencies that address the needs of youngsters.

**Laurie Carlson**, Ph.D., NCC, NCSC, is an assistant professor in the counseling/career development program at Colorado State University. Dr. Carlson holds a doctorate in counselor education from the University of Arkansas and is a member of many professional associations including the honor societies Kappa Delta Pi and Chi Sigma Iota International. Dr. Carlson's professional experience includes ten years of experience in public schools, four of those years as a K-12 professional school counselor in Minnesota.

**David J. Carter** received his Ph.D. from the University of Nebraska at Lincoln. He is an assistant professor and clinical supervisor in counselor education at the University of Nebraska at Omaha. His private practice work is with children and adolescents. He is a past-president of the Nebraska Counseling Association.

**John "Jack" R. Charlesworth**, Ph.D., is a counselor education and educational psychology faculty member at the State University of West Georgia. He received a master's and doctorate in Educational Psychology with a minor in Counseling from Mississippi State University and has completed an APA-Approved Post-Doctoral Clinical Psychology Internship. Dr. Charlesworth has experience as a professional school counselor and practicing licensed psychologist in a wide variety of settings. He also has experience providing workshops and consulting services for schools and universities. His research interests are improving teacher and counselor effectiveness.

**James R. (Jamey) Cheek**, LPC, is an assistant professor of counselor education at St. John's University, New York. Dr. Cheek's background as an educator includes experience as an elementary school teacher, a professional school counselor, and a community-based counselor working with children and adolescents and HIV/AIDS populations. He earned a master's degree from Texas Woman's University, and a doctorate degree from Texas Tech University. Dr. Cheek's research interests include the development of school counseling programs, brain-compatible learning, counselor supervision, and using expressive arts in counseling children and adolescents.

**Stuart Chen-Hayes** is Assistant Professor and Coordinator, Counselor Education/School Counseling at Lehman College of the City University of New York, Bronx, NY.

**Gayle Cicero** is a Licensed Clinical Professional Counselor and 1994 graduate of the Loyola College of Maryland with an M.Ed. in Guidance and Counseling. She is currently employed as a Pupil Personnel Worker for Anne Arundel County Public Schools, Maryland. In that role she combines experience as a teacher, professional school counselor and developer of an interagency team to serve families with complex needs. Ms. Cicero is an active member of the Maryland Association of Counseling and Development and the International Association of Pupil Personnel Workers.

**Mary Ann Clark**, Ph.D., NCC, is an assistant professor in the Department of Counselor Education at the University of Florida, Gainesville, Florida. She has been a professional school counselor and administrator in stateside and overseas schools for twenty years prior to her university work. Dr. Clark has served as a consultant and speaker to school and community groups on topics including student assessment, school safety and violence prevention and small group counseling. Her areas of special interest include family/school collaboration, character education, university/school partnerships, and career development.

**Dr. J. Kelly Coker** is an assistant professor in the school counseling program at the University of Nevada, Las Vegas. Dr. Coker has worked as a counselor in school, agency, and college settings. Her primary areas of interest and expertise are creative arts in counseling, the use of technology in counseling and supervision, and substance abuse counseling.

**Doris Rhea Coy**, Ph.D., is an Associate Professor at the University of North Texas where her areas of expertise are school counseling and career development. She is past-president of the American Counseling Association and the American School Counselor Association. She has published over 100 articles and chapters and is the co-editor of three books. She is a former school counselor and teacher.

**Carol Dahir** is the primary author of *Sharing the Vision: The National Standards for School Counseling Programs* and *Vision Into Action: Implementing the National Standards For School Counseling Programs*. Dr. Dahir has coordinated the national standards initiative from its inception in 1994 and serves as a consultant to organizations and state departments of education for the dissemination, implementation and evaluation of the national standards nationwide. She is actively involved in program development, research and educational reform initiatives for school counselors, administrators and student services personnel. Before joining the faculty at the New York Institute of Technology to coordinate the graduate level counseling programs, she worked as an elementary school teacher, school counselor, and coordinator of school counseling and guidance services and director of pupil personnel services.

**Joyce A. Devoss**, Ph.D., NCC, is an assistant professor and school counseling program coordinator in the Educational Psychology Department at Northern Arizona University at Tucson. She is a licensed psychologist and a certified school guidance counselor in Arizona and has experience as a school counselor/educationally handicapped specialist, consultant and outreach specialist and has developed prevention, early intervention and professional development programs in schools. She is a Metlife Fellow for the National School Counselor Training Initiative. Dr. DeVoss serves as co-president of the Adlerian Society of Arizona and secretary of the Arizona Educational Research Association and the University of Arizona Chapter of Phi Delta Kappa.

**R. Anthony Doggett**, Ph.D., is an Assistant Professor in the school psychology program at Mississippi State University. Dr. Doggett received his Ph.D. in school psychology from the University of Southern Mississippi. He completed a pre-doctoral internship and a one-year post-doctoral fellowship in behavioral pediatrics at the Munroe-Meyer Institute for Genetics and Rehabilitation in Omaha, NE. His professional interests include applied behavior analysis, functional behavioral assessment, behavioral consultation, parent training, instructional interventions, and behavioral pediatrics.

**Deborah L. Drew**, M.Ed., NCC, LCPC, has spent a career of twenty-seven years working in areas of rural and small town Maine as a professional school counselor and clinical counselor. She is currently employed as Director of the School Counseling program for the Millinocket, Maine, School Department. She also has a private practice providing counseling and supervision services, and is a student in the doctoral program in Counselor Education at the University of Maine. Her primary area of interest is in ethical issues in rural counseling.

**Brad A. Dufrene** received his master's degree in psychology from Louisiana State University in 1997. Currently, he is a Ph.D. candidate in school psychology at Mississippi State University. His research interests include functional behavior assessment, habits and tics, and direct behavioral consultation.

**Ruth B. Ekstrom** recently retired as a principle research scientist in the Higher Education Research Division of Education Testing Service (ETS). Her work at ETS included studies of test use, guidance and counseling, student achievement, and women's education and employment. Ekstrom holds a master's degree from Boston University and a doctorate from Rutgers University. She is the co-editor of *Assessing Individuals with Disabilities in Education, Employment, and Counseling Settings*, published by the American Psychological Association in 2002, and co-author of *Education and American Youth: The Impact of the High School Experience*, published by Falmer Press in 1988. She serves on the editorial board of *Measurement and Evaluation in Counseling and Development.* In 1996, Ekstrom received the American Counseling Association's Extended Research Award for her career accomplishments.

**Grafton Eliason**, Ed.D., M.Div., is a licensed professional counselor and coordinator of the school counseling program and assistant professor in the departments of Counseling Psychology and Education at Chatham College in Pittsburgh, PA. His research interests include existential personal meaning, death anxiety, and spirituality.

**Cyrus Marcellus Ellis** is currently a professor of Counselor Education at Governors State University in University Park, Illinois. Dr. Ellis earned a Ph.D. in Counselor Education from The University of Virginia. Dr. Ellis is the recipient of the Lincoln Scott Walter Award in Counseling from Rider University and the William Van Hoose Memorial Award from the University of Virginia. Dr. Ellis directs the Counseling and Clinical Psychology section for the Association for the Advancement of Educational Research. Dr. Ellis is an active member of the American Counseling Association, presenting at national conferences concerning counselor instruction, culture and race.

**Patricia B. Elmore** is Associate Dean in the College of Education and Human Services and Professor in the Department of Educational Psychology and Special Education at Southern Illinois University-Carbondale (SIUC). She received her Ph.D. in 1970 in educational psychology with a specialization in educational measurement and statistics. She is a past-president of the Association for Assessment in Counseling and the 1994 recipient with Ruth B. Ekstrom and Esther E. Diamond of the American Counseling Association Research Award. She is editor of *Measurement and Evaluation in Counseling and Development,* and co-author with Paula L.Woehlke of *Basic Statistics*, published by Addison Wesley Longman in 1997.

**Bradley T. Erford**, Ph.D., LCPC, LPC, NCC, is associate professor of education and director of the school counseling program at Loyola College in Maryland and the 2001 Maryland Counselor of the Year. A graduate of the University of Virginia, he has authored nearly 50 publications and served in numerous leadership capacities in state and national professional associations. He maintains a private practice specializing in assessment and treatment of children and adolescents with behavior, educational, adjustment, and anxiety disorders.

**Mardi Kay Fallon** is a doctoral student in the counseling program at the University of Cincinnati. She has been working in the field of Social Work and Counseling for the past 17 years and is an Adjunct Instructor at University College (a part of the University of Cincinnati). Ms. Fallon also works as a therapist in private practice.

**Teesue H. Fields** is Associate Professor and program coordinator of counselor education at Indiana University Southeast in New Albany, IN. She is a nationally certified counselor and worked for 10 years in K-12 schools before coming to IUS. Her research interests include group work and the role of the professional school counselor in raising academic achievement. She is a past-president of the Indiana Counseling Association.

**Nancy Foster** is a predoctoral intern at Girls and Boys Town in Omaha, NE. She will receive her Ph.D. in School Psychology from Mississippi State University in 2004. Her interests include consultation, functional assessment, and time-out.

**Nadine E. Garner**, Ed.D., NCC, LPC, is Director of School Counseling and an assistant professor in the Psychology Department at Millersville University, Millersville, PA. She is co-author of the book *A School With Solutions: Implementing a Solution-focused/Adlerian-based Comprehensive School Counseling Program*. She is editor of *PCA, Inc.*, the Pennsylvania Counseling Association newsletter and an editorial board member for the *Journal of the Pennsylvania Counseling Association*. She is a recipient of the Outstanding Article Award from the *Journal for Specialists in Group Work*. As a professional school counselor at Scotland School for Veterans' Children, Dr. Garner created a comprehensive conflict resolution/peer mediation program.

**Donna Gibson** is an assistant professor of school counseling at The Citadel in Charleston, South Carolina. She has worked in public schools, hospitals, private practice, and clinics as a counselor and psychologist, working with families and children.

**Gary Goodnough**, NCC, LCMHC, is the coordinator of the counselor education program at Plymouth State University in New Hampshire. He is a former elementary school teacher and professional school counselor. Dr. Goodnough publishes and presents regularly on issues related to school counseling and counselor education.

**Brenda S. Hall**, Ed.D., is an assistant professor of counseling at North Carolina A&T State University and a Nationally Certified Counselor. Brenda is an active member in state and national professional organizations. She has authored articles on collaborative practices in school counseling, technology in counseling, and counselor education pedagogy.

**Henry L. Harris** is a former secondary school counselor and military vetcran. He received a master's degree in counseling from UNC Chapel Hill and his doctorate from the University of Virginia. He is currently an Assistant Professor in the Counseling Program at the University of North Texas and also a Licensed Professional Counselor.

**Trish Hatch**, Ph.D., is the co-author of *The ASCA National Model: A Framework for School Counseling Programs* (ASCA, 2003). She served as vice-president of ASCA from 2001-2003, and is an appointed member of the National Panel for Evidenced-Based School Counseling Practices. She has served as an expert representative to the National Board for Professional Teaching Standards (NBPTS) National Teacher Assessment Development Team, and is a Trainer of Trainers for the Ed Trust MetLife Transforming School Counseling Initiative. Dr. Hatch was a school counselor before moving into administration, working at both the site and district level as the coordinator of student services. Awarded as ASCA's administrator of the year, Dr. Hatch is well known as a passionate and engaging keynote speaker, conference presenter, academy trainer, adjunct professor and consultant. Dr. Hatch is the Director of the School Counseling Graduate Program at San Diego State University.

**Carlen Henington**, Ph.D., is an Associate Professor in the school psychology program at Mississippi State University. She received her doctorate in educational psychology with an emphasis in school psychology from Texas A&M University. She completed her internship at the Meyer Institute at the University of Nebraska Medical Center in Omaha, NE. Her current professional interests include academic skills assessment and intervention, behavioral pediatrics, and early childhood assessment and intervention.

**Peggy LaTurno Hines** is Associate Professor and school counseling program director at Indiana State University. She was the Principle Investigator of ISU's Wallace-Reader's Digest Funds Transforming School Counseling Initiative Grant. Dr. Hines helped develop ASCA's National Model for School Counseling Programs and is a consultant with The Education Trust's National School Counselor Training Initiative. She is a former elementary and middle school counselor.

**Suzanne M. Hobson**, Ed.D., is an Associate Professor in the Department of Leadership and Counseling at Eastern Michigan University where she specializes in school counseling. She holds credentials as a teacher, professional school counselor, Licensed Professional Counselor, National Certified Counselor, and Doctoral Limited Licensed Psychologist in the State of Michigan. Dr. Hobson is currently President of the Michigan Counseling Association.

**Nick Hoda** is a school psychology doctoral student at Mississippi State University. His research interests include pediatric psychology, functional behavioral analysis, and behavioral interventions.

**Cheryl Holcomb-McCoy**, Ph.D., is Assistant Professor in the Department of Counseling and Personnel Services at the University of Maryland at College Park. Her areas of research and scholarly interest include multicultural competence of professional school counselors, multicultural counseling training, and urban school counselor reform. Dr. Holcomb-McCoy is a former public school teacher and professional school counselor and is currently involved in the implementation of the first professional development school for professional school counselors in the Washington, DC area.

**Jill Holmes-Robinson** received her Ph.D. in counselor education from the University of Virginia. Dr. Holmes-Robinson is a Nationally Certified Counselor and an Adjunct Assistant Professor of Pastoral Counseling at Loyola College in Maryland. She holds Primary Certification in Rational Emotive Behavior Therapy from the Albert Ellis Institute for Rational Emotive Behavior Therapy. A former higher education administrator, Dr. Holmes-Robinson is the former Director of Ithaca College's Opportunity Programs, which provided academic support and scholarships to low-income/at-risk and minority first-generation college attendees.

**Susan Norris Huss**, LPC, is an assistant professor in the guidance and counseling program at Bowling Green State University, Bowling Green, OH. She received her Ph.D. in counselor education from the University of Toledo after being a professional school counselor for 23 years. Dr. Huss has extensive experience in working with bereavement in schools. For twenty years she led loss support groups for students who experienced a death. She has presented at local, state, and national levels in the area of bereavement and legal and ethical issues and has conducted research related to the efficacy of school-based loss support groups for parentally bereaved students. Dr. Huss is a past-president of the Ohio Counseling Association and currently serves as Ethics Chair for the Ohio School Counselor Association.

**C. Marie Jackson**, Ed.D., LPC, NCC, is a counselor education faculty member at State University of West Georgia. She has a master's degree in counseling from Jacksonville State University and a doctoral degree in Counselor Education from the University of Alabama. She has experience in public schools as a teacher, psychometrist, and a school counselor, K-12. She has been program leader for school counseling training programs in three university settings. In addition to her school counseling credentials and experience, she is a Licensed Professional Counselor and a Nationally Certified Counselor, and has worked in a psychiatric hospital outpatient setting as a therapist.

**Gregory R. Janson** is an assistant professor of Child and Family Studies at Ohio University, Athens, OH. He is a Professional Clinical Counselor, a National Certified Counselor, and a Certified Family Life Educator. He has worked extensively both in community mental health and in private practice as a family counselor with severely disturbed children and adolescents and their families. A former therapeutic foster parent, he has published in the areas of ethics; gay, lesbian, bisexual, and transgender issues; and the impact of repetitive abuse such as bullying on victims and bystanders.

**Gerald A. Juhnke**, Ed.D., LPC, NCC, MAC, CCAS, ACS, is an Associate Professor and Clinic Director in the Department of Counseling and Educational Development at the University of North Carolina at Greensboro. Juhnke is the President-elect of the International Association of Addictions and Offender Counselors, past-President of the Association for Assessment in Counseling, and past-editor and current Review Board Member of the *Journal of Addictions and Offender Counseling.*

**Carol J. Kaffenberger** is assistant professor at George Mason University in Fairfax, Virginia, in the Counseling and Development Program. Dr. Kaffenberger teaches counseling skills and theories classes, principles and practices of school counseling, and supervises field experience for master's students seeking school counseling licensure. A professional school counselor and special education teacher, Dr. Kaffenberger's research interests include school re-entry for children with cancer and chronic illness, the impact of the cancer experience on family members, and the transformation of professional school counselors.

**Tracy C. Leinbaugh**, NCC, is an assistant professor of counselor education and coordinator of school counseling in the Department of Counseling and Higher Education at Ohio University. She has over 20 years of experience working with children with disabilities and their families as a developmental specialist, primary therapist, school psychologist, and elementary school counselor.

**Dana Heller Levitt** is Assistant Professor of Counselor Education at Ohio University. She received her master's and doctoral degrees from the University of Virginia. In addition to eating disorders and body image, Dr. Levitt also focuses on training and supervision for counselors across settings.

**Lynn Linde** is the Branch Chief for Pupil Services at the Maryland State Department of Education. Currently a representative to the ACA Governing Council, she is a Past-Chair of ACA-Southern Region and the Maryland Association for Counseling and Development (MACD).

**Estes J. Lockhart** is a psychotherapist in private practice with Harper Associates in Frederick, MD, and teaches couples and family therapy in the Department of Counseling and Human Services at Johns Hopkins University in Baltimore, MD. He is a retired director of student services for Howard County (MD) Public Schools.

**Larry C. Loesch**, Ph.D., NCC, is a professor in the Department of Counselor Education at the University of Florida, Gainesville, Florida. He is a former president of the Association for Measurement and Evaluation in Guidance, Southern Association for Counselor Education and Supervision, Chi Sigma Iota, and the Florida Counseling Association. He was a co-recipient of the American Counseling Association's Research Award and of its Hitchcock Distinguished Professional Service Award. He has served for more than 20 years as an evaluation and research consultant for the National Board for Certified Counselor.

**David J. Lundberg**, Ph.D., is an associate professor of counseling at North Carolina A&T State University and a Nationally Certified Counselor. He has published articles on multicultural counseling and technology in counseling.

**Patricia Jo McDivitt** has over 15 years of test development experience, including overseeing the item development of multiple and complex assessments for various statewide standards-based programs. She began her career as an educator, serving as a classroom teacher for 12 years, and has received several awards for outstanding service for the guidance profession, including merit awards from the Alabama Counseling Association and outstanding service award from the National Career Development Association. She is past-president of the Association for Assessment in Counseling (AAC), a division of the American Counseling Association (ACA), and is currently serving as a member of the Joint Committee on Standards for Educational Evaluation (JCSEE).

**Adriana McEachern** is an associate professor in counselor education and Chair of the Department of Educational and Psychological Studies at Florida International University in Miami, Florida. She was awarded the Ph.D. in Counselor Education from the University of Florida in 1989. She is a licensed mental health counselor in Florida and National Certified Counselor. She is a Past-President of the Florida Counseling Association. Her research interests include exceptional students and exceptional student education, child abuse, and multicultural family issues.

**Jennifer A. McKechnie**, M.Ed., LCPC, is a professional school counselor at Centennial High School in the Howard County Public School System, MD. She is a graduate of Loyola College's school counseling program, a trained bereavement counselor (Edinburgh University, Scotland), and co-author of several therapeutic games and book chapters.

**Gail Mears**, Psy.D., is a counselor educator at Plymouth State College, Plymouth, NH. She is a licensed Clinical Mental Health Counselor, teaches mental health counseling courses, and supervises practicum and internships. She has 25 years' experience as a psychotherapist with a broad range of clients. In addition to her work as an Assistant Professor of Education, she provides counseling services to college students through the Plymouth State College Counseling and Human Relations Center. She is the current president of the New Hampshire Mental Health Counselors Association.

**Amy Milsom**, NCC, is an assistant professor at the University of Iowa. She earned her D.Ed. from Penn State University and is a former middle and high school counselor. Her primary research interests are in the areas of students with disabilities, group work, and school counselor training.

**James L. Moore III** is an assistant professor in counselor education at Ohio State University. He received his B.A. in English Education from Delaware State University and earned both his M.A. and Ph.D. in Counselor Education at Virginia Polytechnic Institute and State University (Virginia Tech). Dr. Moore has numerous publications on counseling African Americans (particularly males), academic persistence and achievement, and counseling student-athletes.

**Cheryl Moore-Thomas** received her Ph. D. in counselor education from the University of Maryland. She is a National Certified Counselor. Currently, Dr. Moore-Thomas is an assistant professor of education in the school counseling program at Loyola College in Maryland. Over her professional career, Dr. Moore-Thomas has published and presented in the areas of multicultural counseling competence, racial identity development of children and adolescents, and accountability in school counseling programs.

**Joel Muro** is a doctoral student in the counseling program at the University of North Texas.

**Sally Murphy**, Ph.D., is an Assistant Professor and Clinical Coordinator in the Counseling and Development Program, Graduate School of Education at George Mason University, Fairfax, VA. Sally has worked in a variety of educational settings and roles over the past 30 years: professional school counselor, university professor, and elementary school teacher. She has given numerous presentations and workshops to educators, parenting groups, and school community leaders on a variety of issues including bully/victim relationships, conflict resolution, sexual harassment, substance abuse, school counseling leadership, and the transformation of school counseling.

**Kelly M. Murray**, Ph.D., is Assistant Professor of Clinical Psychology and Director of Ph.D. Clinical Education in the Pastoral Counseling Department at Loyola College in Maryland. Dr. Murray is a clinical psychologist whose treatment and research interests are in the area of women's health and trauma. She served as a Navy Psychologist for seven years, and was on staff at both the National Naval Medical Center and the United States Naval Academy. Along with being on the full-time faculty at Loyola, she is also a Visiting Scientist at the Center for the Study of Traumatic Stress. Her research interests have been broad and she has published empirical research on topics such as women and personality styles in relation to success, and health and psychological states during trauma and crisis.

**Amy Newmeyer** completed a post-doctoral fellowship at the Kennedy-Krieger Institute at Johns Hopkins University School of Medicine upon completion of her medical degree from Ohio State University and residency from Akron Children's Hospital. She is double boarded in Pediatrics and Neuro-Development Disabilities and currently on faculty at Cincinnati Children's Hospital.

**Mark D. Newmeyer**, M.Ed., is a second-year doctoral student in the counseling program at the University of Cincinnati. He has over ten years of extensive work in the schools providing behavioral evaluation, testing and assessment.

**Debbie Newsome**, Ph.D., LPC, NCC, is an assistant professor of counselor education at Wake Forest University, where she teaches courses in career counseling, appraisal procedures and statistics, and supervises master's students in their field experiences. She also serves as an adjunct clinician at a nonprofit mental health organization, where she counsels children, adolescents, and families.

**Spencer G. Niles** is a Professor of Education and the Professor-in-Charge of Counselor Education at Penn State University. He served previously as Professor and Assistant Dean in the Curry School of Education at the University of Virginia. He is currently the editor of the Career Development Quarterly. He has served on the Board of Directors of the National Career Development Association and was twice the President of the Virginia Career Development Association. He is currently the President-elect of the National Career Development Association.

**Ralph Orsi** earned an M.A. in community counseling from the University of Nebraska at Omaha (UNO). He works as a counselor in the Employee Assistance Program at Methodist Health Systems. He is Past-President of the UNO Chi Sigma Iota chapter.

**Cheryl Ann Phillips**, M.A., is a professional school counselor at Franklin High School in Livonia, MI. A graduate of Eastern Michigan University, Ms. Phillips is credentialed both as a professional school counselor and as a Limited License Professional Counselor in Michigan. She served as the Editor of the Michigan Counseling Association newsletter and frequently provides guest lectures at Eastern Michigan University.

**Ralph L. Piedmont** is an associate professor of pastoral counseling at Loyola College in Maryland as well as the Director of the Institute for Religious and Psychological Research. His research interests include the Five-Factor Model of Personality and its relationship to spiritual phenomena. He has also developed a motivationally-based measure of spirituality, Spiritual Transcendence, and is interested in documenting its predictive validity in a number of applied contexts.

**Mark Pope**, Ed.D., is an associate professor in the Division of Counseling & Family Therapy at the University of Missouri – St. Louis. He is the 2003-2004 American Counseling Association President and 1998-1999 National Career Development Association President. He is a Fellow of the National Career Development Association, and was previously the Director of Psychological Services at the Native America AIDS Institute in San Francisco. His research interests include multicultural career counseling; lesbian, gay, and bisexual issues; assessment; and the history of the counseling professions.

**Tarrell Awe Agahe Portman**, Ph.D., LMHC, NCC, is an Assistant Professor in the Department of Counseling, Rehabilitation, and Student Development at The University of Iowa. She teaches in the M.A. school counseling program and the Ph.D. counselor education program. She is a licensed teacher and K-12 professional school counselor in Missouri and Iowa. Dr. Portman is a member of the NBPTS School Counseling Standards committee and an ASCA National Trainer. Her research agenda is in the area of school counseling, supervision and multiculturalism.

**Inez G. Ramos** is a professional school counselor at the High School for Health Opportunities, Bronx, NY.

**Michael Rankins**, M.Ed., is a doctoral student in the Division of Counseling & Family Therapy at the University of Missouri – St. Louis. He has held positions at the Masters and Johnson Institute, St. Louis Effort for AIDS, Victim Service Council, and Hyland Behavioral Health.

**Vivian V. Ripley**, NCC, is an assistant professor at Old Dominion University, Norfolk, VA, in the Department of Educational Leadership and Counseling. She received an M.Ed. and Ed.D. from the University of Virginia. Dr Ripley is a former middle and secondary school teacher, secondary school counselor, Director of Guidance, alternative education counselor and site supervisor for master's level interns. Her areas of interest include group counseling in schools, conflict resolution, and school counselor supervision. She served previously as associate director of the school counseling program and assistant professor at the University of Scranton and co-coordinator of the Education Trust Companion School Project for Transforming School Counseling.

**Gabrina Schneider** is the professional school counselor at Babies Prep School in Manhattan, NY.

**Susan Jones Sears** is an associate professor and coordinator of the school counseling program in the College of Education at the Ohio State University. Dr. Sears is director and principle investigator of OSU's Transforming School Counseling Initiative (TSCI). She has published extensively, including four books and eight book chapters. Dr. Sears is the recipient of 12 national and state awards for outstanding leadership and service to the counseling profession.

**Carl J. Sheperis**, Ph.D., NCC, LPC, is an Assistant Professor in the Department of Counseling, Educational Psychology, and Special Education at Mississippi State University. His research interests include reactive attachment disorder, parent-child relationships, and peer conflict.

**Shelly F. Sheperis**, Ed.S., is a doctoral candidate at the University of Florida and an instructor at Mississippi State University. Her research interests include family-school interventions and peer mediation.

**Jo Ellen Smith**, M.S., is a graduate of the Counseling Psychology program at Chatham College and has 17 years experience in the counseling field.

**Brent M. Snow** is a Professor and Chair of the Department of Counseling and Educational Psychology at the State University of West Georgia. He is the Principle Investigator of one of the six national transforming school counseling grants funded by the Dewitt-Wallace Reader's Digest Fund administered through the Education Trust. Previously, he was a faculty member at Oklahoma State University and the University of Idaho. He received his Ph.D. from the University of Idaho, his M.S. from Oklahoma State University, and his B.S. from Brigham Young University.

**Fran Steigerwald**, Ph.D., is Assistant Professor in Counselor Education at Radford University in Radford, VA. In 2000, she received her doctorate in Counselor Education from Ohio University in Athens, Ohio. Her master's degree was from Cleveland State University in Community Mental Health. She is a Licensed Professional Clinical Counselor (LPCC) in Ohio. She has taught in the Counselor Educational and Family Studies programs at Ohio University and was Clinical Director of the Counselor Education Clinic at Emporia State University. She has worked as an administrator and clinician in community agencies, private practice, and a college counseling center. Her teaching and research areas of interest include multicultural-diversity, family, and crisis issues and human and counselor development.

**Carolyn Stone** is an Associate Professor at the University of North Florida where she teaches and researches the legal and ethical implications for working with minors in schools. Prior to becoming a counselor educator, Dr. Stone was a Supervisor of Guidance, an elementary and secondary teacher, and elementary and high school counselor.

**Dawn M. Szymanski**, Ph.D., is an assistant professor in the Division of Counseling & Family Therapy at the University of Missouri – St. Louis. Her professional interests include lesbian, gay and bisexual issues, feminist therapy and supervision, multicultural counseling, and counselor and research training. She is currently serving on the editorial board for the ACA *Journal of College Counseling*.

**Mei Tang**, Ph.D., is an associate professor in the counseling program at the University of Cincinnati. Dr. Tang coordinates the school counseling program and teaches and publishes in the areas of school counseling, counseling children, career development, testing and assessment, and cross-cultural issues. She serves on the editorial boards of *Journal of Career Development*, *Journal of College Counseling*, and various committees of ACA and APA.

**Barbara Thompson** is Assistant Professor of Education at Indiana University Southeast where she teaches classes in elementary literacy, children's literature and ESL methods. Prior to joining IUS, she taught grades K-7 in Colorado, California and Arizona.

**Jerry Trusty** is Coordinator of the Secondary School Counseling Program in the Department of Counselor Education, Counseling Psychology and Rehabilitation Services, Pennsylvania State University. Dr. Trusty has experience as a middle school and high school counselor. He has published numerous works on adolescents' educational and career development. Dr. Trusty is currently the Associate Editor of Quantitative Research for the *Journal of Counseling and Development*.

**Lawrence E. Tyson**, Ph.D., NCSC, is an assistant Professor in the Department of Human Studies, Counselor Education Program at the University of Alabama at Birmingham. He is the school counseling advisor and also an American School Counselor Association Trainer for National Standards for School Counseling Programs.

**Joe R. Underwood**, Ph.D., is coordinator of the school counseling program at Mississippi State University and Director of MSU Summer Scholars, a summer residential program for gifted/talented junior and senior high school students. He is former state president of the Mississippi Association for Counselor Education and Supervision, Mississippi Counseling Association, and Mississippi Association for Gifted Students. A National Certified Counselor and Licensed Professional Counselor, Dr. Underwood often teaches staff development workshops for professional school counselors and classroom teachers.

**Nancy B. Underwood**, M.S., teaches art for gifted/talented students at Armstrong Middle School in Starkville, MS. She holds a Class AA License in gifted education and language arts. During the past twenty years, Ms. Underwood has taught university, high school, and middle school students. During summers, she is the creative writing instructor for a university residential theater camp for students in grades 7-12. For the past 15 years, Ms. Underwood taught art and creative writing to 7th-9th grade students. She also co-teaches a graduate course in counseling the gifted.

**Ann Vernon**, Ph.D., NCC, LMHC, is Professor and Coordinator of Counseling at the University of Northern Iowa and a therapist in private practice where she works extensively with children, adolescents, and their parents. Dr. Vernon is the Director of the Midwest Center for REBT and Vice-President of the Albert Ellis Board of Trustees. She is the author of numerous books, chapters and articles, including *Thinking, Feeling, Behaving* and *What Works When with Children and Adolescents*.

**Jose Arley Villalba** has a Ph.D. in counselor education. He currently is an Assistant Professor in the Department of Counseling at Indiana State University. He was a certified school counselor in Florida and has presented at several state, regional and national conferences for a variety of organizations, including ASCA and ACES. His research interests include the development of counseling interventions specifically designed for limited-English proficient children, and school counselor attrition rates. His teaching specialties include assessment in counseling, multicultural counseling, introduction to school counseling, and supervision.

**Suzy Mygatt Wakefield**, Ph.D., C.D.F., a retired high school counselor, worked in two states (Michigan and Washington) in three school districts since 1970, when she earned her Master's Degree in Education from the University of Washington. In 1978, she earned her Ph.D. in Education from the University of Michigan. She was a part-time program coordinator for the Washington Pre-College Program (1981-85) in Seattle, served as President of the Washington School Counselor Association (1988-89) and helped to pass the *Fair Start Bill* to fund elementary counseling (1992). She is a certified Career Development Facilitator and has taught in the Career Development Certificate Program at the University of Washington.

**Janet Wall** has experience in assessment at the state and national levels. At present she operates her own consulting business, is President of the Association for Assessment in Counseling (AAC), and co-chair of the Joint Committee on Testing Practices (JCTP). She has authored numerous publications and has co-edited a book titled *Measuring Up: Assessment Issues for Counselors, Teachers, and Administrators*.

**T. Steuart Watson** is Professor of School Psychology at Mississippi State University. Dr. Watson received his Ph.D. from the University of Nebraska in 1991 with a major in school psychology and a minor in applied behavior analysis. He has conducted research on the treatment of habits and tics and on the effects of environmental stimuli on habits and tics. He is currently involved in designing anti-crime and anti-corruption curricula for schools in the Republic of Georgia, Mexico, El Salvador, Guatemala, Colombia, and Nigeria.

**Adam D. Weaver**, M.S., is a school psychology doctoral student at Mississippi State University. His research interests include behavioral consultation and the effects of rewards on academic performance and behavior. Prior to graduate school, he was a teacher for three years.

**Nancy H. Whitlatch**, M.A.Ed., NCC, is a former elementary school teacher and has worked as a professional school counselor at both the elementary and middle school levels.

**Robert E. Wubbolding**, Ed.D., is the director of the Center for Reality Therapy in Cincinnati, Ohio, director of training for the William Glasser Institute and professor emeritus of Xavier University. A former elementary school and high school counselor and adult basic education instructor, he is the author of 10 books on reality therapy, including *Reality Therapy for the 21st Century*. He has taught reality therapy in North America, Asia, Europe, and the Middle East and has received the Marvin Rammelsberg Award, the Herman Peters Award, the Mary Corre Foster Award, and outstanding alumnus of the University of Cincinnati College of Education.

**Teresa Yohon**, Ph.D., assistant professor at Colorado State University, is a Business and Marketing Education educator. Prior to this position, Dr. Yohon taught and managed a community college-level applied management program where she counseled students and business people in career decision-making. She has a master's degree in counseling, master's degree in management, and Ph.D. in community resources.

**Anita A. Young** is a Ph.D. student at Ohio State University. She earned an M.Ed. in counseling from Boston University and a B.S. in Psychology for the University of Southern Mississippi. Previously, she served as a professional school counselor and high school guidance director with the Fairfax County Public School System in Fairfax, Virginia. Her primary research areas are school counselor leadership and resiliency counseling for at-risk students.

# Professional School Counseling: A Handbook of Theories, Programs & Practices

# *Section 1*

# The Foundations of School Counseling

# Chapter 1

## Professional School Counseling: Integrating Theory and Practice Into an Outcomes-Driven Approach

*Bradley T. Erford*

### Preview

This chapter provides the rationale for necessary changes in the way professional school counselors operate in contemporary practice. The focus of the transformed role is to build on the broad-based theoretical and practical counseling skills that have become the core of a professional school counselor's training and expand into a more systemic orientation in order to meet the needs of all students. The systemic approach highlights comprehensive services, social advocacy and accountability dimensions in order to remove barriers to student performance and promote a system of equity and access for all students.

Society, in general, and school systems, in particular, continue to change. As a result, the school counseling profession necessarily undergoes a continuous evolution as well. This evolution involves both the traditional roles and functions of professional school counselors, as well as the comprehensive school counseling programs that professional school counselors strive to implement - a program that serves the academic, career and personal-social needs of every student. The task before us is ominous:

- Dryfoos (1994) and Lockhart and Keys (1998) reported that substance abuse, poverty, and community and domestic violence are on the rise.
- SAMHSA (1998) indicated that significant emotional disorders could be found in 15-22% of school-aged students to a degree that treatment is required for a healthy adjustment. Unfortunately, only about 20% of these impaired students in need of treatment actually get help.
- Up to 50% of students with significant emotional impairments drop out of school (Institute of Medicine, 1997).
- Between 3 million and 6 million students experience clinical depression (American Psychiatric Association, 1992).
- More than 2,000 adolescents commit suicide annually, while between 10,000 and 20,000 adolescents attempt suicide annually. Suicide continues to be the third leading cause of death among the adolescent population (Brown, 1996).
- Up to 50% of all students referred to mental health clinics can be diagnosed with behavior disorders, including Conduct Disorder and Attention-Deficit/Hyperactivity Disorder (AD/HD) (Erk, 1995).
- Nearly 5 million students receive special educational services (Kupper, 1999).
- Government funding for community mental health services has not kept pace with need, nor has affordability of mental health services available in the community (Keys & Bemak, 1997; Luongo, 2000).

As has often been the case in the past, society and governments turn to schools for help in meeting the needs of students. Unfortunately, the professional school counselor to student ratio is currently 1:513 (Institute of Medicine, 1997) and has remained near that level throughout much of the past decade – substantially higher than the 1:250 recommended by the American School Counselor Association (ASCA) – with no real hope of dramatic improvement in the near future.

Given that the problems continue to mount and service availability remains stagnant, what is the solution? While the answer is in no way simple, the transformed role of the contemporary professional school counselor requires that counselors became agents of social change, school reform and accountability, as well as experts in the traditional theory and practice of individual and small group counseling (Erford, House & Martin, 2003). This shift from an individual, student-centered focus to a systemic intervention focus stems from the realization that, while essential in some cases, "fixing" students one at a time is akin to sticking one's finger in a dike:

> A look to the left and right will often show other professionals using their fingers to plug a hole. By joining with other professional counselors...and speaking with a united voice in advocating for the needs of students, they are seeking solutions not only for the students they are working to help, but for all students – those that colleagues are seeking to serve, and those that will seek help in the future. (p. 14)

## Transforming the Professional School Counselor's Role: Five Guiding Realizations

Erford et al. (2003) discussed five realizations that can spawn changes in the ways professional school counselors approach program implementation and service delivery:

1. *Professional school counselors receive extensive training in consultation, collaboration, and team/relationship building.* Professional school counselors can use these skills to reach beyond the counseling office, think systemically, and build partnerships with other educators, mental health resources, community organizations, parents and others to provide needed services to ALL students, but especially those who have been marginalized or oppressed.
2. *Professional school counselors cannot do it all!* The "lone ranger" approach of a single, autonomous professional school counselor "hanging out a shingle" and providing the equivalent of "private practice services" to a select few will perpetuate the "finger in the dike" phenomenon. Thinking systemically and building partnerships with valuable internal and external resources will help far more students in the short- and long-term.
3. *Comprehensive developmental school counseling programs are efficient and effective.* Face it. If a professional school counselor does not implement a comprehensive developmental school counseling program, one will not exist in that school! Professional school counselors who spend most of their time engaged in a single activity (i.e., individual counseling, paperwork, or classroom guidance) are not implementing a comprehensive program.
4. *All professional school counselors have strengths and weaknesses; thus, each provides services of varying quality to varying clientele.* The key here is to know what one is proficient at and use these strengths to benefit all students, while developing strategies and partnerships with other resource providers to cover the other areas of a comprehensive program.
5. *Many students are not getting what they need from our educational and mental health systems.* Professional school counselors need to become skilled social

advocates and develop effective referral procedures through partnerships with community organizations. The training of professional school counselors is broad by design so that one can serve in the "triage role," allowing the professional school counselor to prioritize the allocation of services in the most efficient manner. This often means that professional school counselors can best serve the greatest number of students by making referral arrangements for the neediest students or those most able to afford services available in the community, thus freeing the professional school counselor to focus on the students for whom the counselor is the last and perhaps only hope for effective treatment.

A helpful metaphor for understanding the complex interplay of the services provided by a professional school counselor was explained by Chen-Hayes and Erford (2003) through the metaphor of various-sized nets:

> A comprehensive developmental school counseling program with its focus on large-group guidance and prevention-based programs is the first and highest net attempting to catch students and keep them on track developmentally. But as fate would have it, some students' needs are more serious and not necessarily developmental in nature, thus requiring intervention services. The next level of netting attempting to catch students in need may be group counseling with students or consultation or collaboration with parents and teachers. While many students are put back on track through effective implementation of these services, some require additional interventions (nets) that are more individualized. Individual counseling, or referral to qualified mental health professionals when lack of time or skill requires it, serve as that next level of nets. However, even after individualized services, some students will still present with unmet needs. These students are the ones who in the past have been described as "falling through the cracks" and require a more systemic service delivery approach. This is where school-community-agency partnering and social and academic advocacy come in. These systemic interventions (nets) are essential to ensure that the needs of all children in our society are addressed. (p. 451)

## Ten Current and Emerging Roles and Practices of the Professional School Counselor

The realizations described above give rise to potential changes in how professional school counselors function. Erford et al. (2003) proposed ten roles or functions that should be adopted by professional school counselors. Some of these roles and functions are traditional; some are less so, but of equal importance. They include the professional school counselor as a/an:

1. Professional.
2. Developmental classroom guidance specialist.
3. Career development and educational planning specialist.
4. School and community agency collaboration specialist.
5. Provider of individual and group counseling services.
6. Safe schools, violence prevention, at-risk specialist.
7. Agent of diversity and multicultural sensitivity.
8. Advocate for students with special needs.
9. Advocate for social justice.
10. School reform and accountability expert.

While there are those who will argue about which of these ten roles and functions is most important, each is an essential component of a comprehensive program designed to meet the needs of ALL students. Please note, however, that all subsequent components flow from the first one! "Professional school counselors use effective techniques and practices implemented through legal, ethical, and professional means. Belonging to a profession requires one to adhere to the highest standards of that profession...[because] how one behaves, good or bad, reflects on all" (Erford et al., 2003, p. 14). All professional school counselors should belong to local, state, and national counseling organizations so that the profession can speak as one voice. Advocacy sometimes is accomplished most effectively with one's pocketbook – paying your membership dues could be one of the best advocacy actions of your career – and the future of your profession!

Furthermore, one cannot overemphasize the importance of accountability and outcomes-driven decision-making in the implementation and continuous improvement of any comprehensive developmental school counseling program. A number of comprehensive reviews have been conducted, resulting in moderate to strong support for the effectiveness of school counseling services (Borders & Drury, 1992; Sexton, Whiston, Bleuer, & Walz, 1997; Whiston, 2003; Whiston & Sexton, 1998). Several chapters in this handbook address these studies more directly. The critical issue remains, however, that outcomes research in the school counseling field lags behind that of other counseling specialties, and what research indicates is effective or not effective is frequently not known by the average practitioner in the field. The uneven application of an outcomes-driven approach by school-based practitioners presents one of the greatest challenges to a profession that strives to meet the academic, career, and personal-social needs of every student. The school counseling profession must strive to: 1) conduct more outcomes research to determine which services and strategies are effective and which are not, and 2) disseminate this information to school-based practitioners, supervisors, and counselor educators so that practitioners' theoretical orientation and practice can be driven by an understanding of what is and is not effective. In many ways, the purpose of this handbook is to provide a resource that is not just accessible and understandable to the practicing professional school counselor or counselor-in-training, but is informed by outcomes research, thereby providing a wealth of information for practitioners regarding what is and is not effective in our work with students.

## The Future of School Counseling

The school counseling profession has been shaped by numerous events and initiatives, including: *Sputnik,* Wrenn's "The Counselor in a Changing World," ASCA's *National Standards for School Counseling Programs* (Campbell & Dahir, 1997), The Education Trust's "Transforming School Counseling Initiative," and *The ASCA National Model: A Framework for School Counseling Programs* (ASCA, 2003). Throughout the past century the profession has evolved to meet changing societal and school system demands.

For some time now, doomsayers have predicted the demise of the school counseling profession. Well, the reports of our demise are premature! Perhaps Ed Herr (2003), eminent counseling historian and scholar, said it best:

> The historical roots that have spawned the need for counselors in schools and future issues that remain to be fully resolved at the beginning of the 21st century suggest that the role of the professional counselor is not a rigid and static set of functions. Rather, it is in a constant state of transformation in response to the changing demands on American schools and the factors and influences that affect the growth and development of America's children and youth.
>
> Across the one hundred years or so that comprise the history of school counseling in the United States, the questions and issues have changed. However, there is no longer the question of whether professional school counseling will survive or whether it is relevant to the mission of the school. The questions today are how to make its contribution more explicit, how to distribute its effects more evenly across school and student groups, and how to deploy these precious

> professional resources in the most efficient and effective manner. These are the challenges that the future professional school counselor will face. (p. 38)

Undoubtedly, the school counseling profession will continue to evolve and thrive so long as professional school counselors strive to meet the academic, career and personal/social needs of all students.

## Summary/Conclusion

The school counseling profession has a rich history of evolving in new and necessary directions to address societal, systemic, and student needs. The current phase of evolution, or transformation, must be driven by outcomes research that identifies effective practices. In addition to the traditional emphasis on counseling theoretical orientations and practices, the contemporary professional school counselor must emphasize accountability, social advocacy, and systemic interventions, all within the umbrella of a comprehensive developmental school counseling program that removes barriers to student success and addresses the academic, career, and personal-social needs of ALL students!

## References


American Psychiatric Association. (1992). Childhood disorders [Brochure]. Washington, DC: Author.

American School Counselor Association. (2003). *The ASCA national model: A framework for school counseling programs.* Alexandria, VA: Author.

Borders, L. D., & Drury, S. M. (1992). Comprehensive school counseling programs: A review for policymakers and practitioners. *Journal of Counseling and Development, 70,* 487-498.

Brown, A. (1996, Winter). Mood disorders in children and adolescents. *NARSAD Research Newsletter.*

Campbell, C., & Dahir, C. (1997). *The national standards for school counseling programs.* Alexandria, VA: ASCA.

Chen-Hayes, S., & Erford, B. T. (2003). Living the transformed role. In B. T. Erford (Ed.), *Transforming the school counseling profession* (pp. 449-454). Columbus, OH: Merrill/Prentice-Hall.

Dryfoos, J. (1994). *Full-service schools: A revolution in health and social services for children, youth, and families.* San Francisco: Jossey-Bass Publishers.

Erford, B. T., House, R., & Martin, P. (2003). Transforming the school counseling profession. In B. T. Erford (Ed.), *Transforming the school counseling profession* (pp. 1-20). Columbus, OH: Merrill/Prentice-Hall.

Erk, R. R. (1995). The evolution of attention deficit disorders terminology. *Elementary School Guidance and Counseling, 29,*243-248.

Herr, E. L. (2003). Historical roots and future issues. In B. T. Erford (Ed.), *Transforming the school counseling profession* (pp. 21-38). Columbus, OH: Merrill/Prentice-Hall.

Institute of Medicine. (1997). *Schools and health.* Washington, DC: National Academy Press.

Keys, S. G., & Bemak, F. (1997). School-family-community linked services: A school counseling role for the changing times. *The School Counselor, 44,* 255-263.

Kupper, L. (1999). *Questions often asked by parents about special education services.* National Information Center for Children and Youth with Disabilities (4th ed. Briefing paper), Washington, DC.

Lockhart, E. J., & Keys, S. G. (1998). The mental health counseling role of school counselors. *Professional School Counseling, 1,* 3-6.

Luongo, P. F. (2000). Partnering child welfare, juvenile justice, and behavioral health with schools. *Professional School Counseling, 3,* 308-314.

Sexton, T. L., Whiston, S. C., Bleuer, J. C., & Walz, G. R. (1997). *Integrating outcomes research into counseling practice and training.* Alexandria, VA: American Counseling Association.

Substance Abuse and Mental Health Services Administration. (1998). *National expenditures for mental health, alcohol and other drug abuse treatment.* Washington, DC: SAMHSA, Department of Health and Human Services.

Whiston, S. C. (2003). Outcomes research on school counseling services. In B. T. Erford (Ed.), *Transforming the school counseling profession* (pp. 435-447). Columbus, OH: Merrill/ Prentice-Hall.

Whiston, S. C., & Sexton, T. L. (1998). A review of school counseling outcomes research: Implications for practice. *Journal of Counseling and Development, 76,* 412-426.

# Chapter 2

## The History of School Counseling

*Mei Tang & Bradley T. Erford*

### Preview

Reviewing the history of a profession generally serves two purposes. One is to answer the question of how our profession came into being and how it reached its current status? The other is to look for a direction for the future. This chapter will focus on the first goal: to explore the roots and developmental stages of school counseling as a profession. As Herr (2003) argued, counseling in schools did not arise in a vacuum, it is necessary to review the development of school counseling in the historical context. "The historical moment must be right for the ingredients of change to take root and begin to flourish" (p. 22). This chapter will chronicle school counseling developmental periods through four dimensions: historical context, external forces or significant events that have had momentous impact on the growth and direction of the school counseling profession, theoretical frameworks that have influenced professional school counselors' work, and roles and functions professional school counselors have performed.

### Emerging Years [1900–1915]

*Historical Context*

At the beginning of the 20th century, American society went through a vast change as a result of the Industrial Revolution. The Industrial Revolution resulted in a concentration of the work force, a demand for skilled workers, uncertainty in the labor market, and consequently a growth in secondary school enrollment and a challenge to the classical education that was not preparing skilled workers (Dixon, 1987). The other societal and contextual factors for the change during the early 1900s included urbanization, a large influx of immigration, the abuse of child labor, city ghettos and neglect of individual rights and integrity (Herr, 2002; Minkoff & Terres, 1985; Schmidt, 1999).

Brewer (1942) identified four important economic and social conditions (division of labor, technological innovations, vocational education, and modern democracy) that influenced the rise of educational reform and vocational guidance; while Traxler and North (1966, p. 6) pointed to "philanthropy or humanitarianism, religion, mental hygiene, social change, and the movement to know pupils as individuals." These changes forced schools to address the needs of students and respond to the social, economic and educational problems. Bookish learning and impractical instruction were criticized for failing to prepare students adequately to enter the growing opportunities in the work force. At the same time, because the labor division was so differentiated and comprehensive, family and friends could no longer provide essential information and assistance for occupational choice (Herr, 2003). Therefore, it became necessary for schools to provide vocational guidance for these youngsters. Vocational guidance, as the root for school counseling, has been well documented in the literature (Baker, 2000; Gysbers, 2001; Herr, 2003; Minkoff & Terres, 1985; Schmidt, 1999) as a response to the effects of industrial growth in the late 19th and beginning of the 20th century. "Vocational guidance was not only viewed as assisting the development of individuals, but also seen as a means for achieving social goals" (Dixon, 1987, p. 112).

*External Forces/Significant Events*

The pioneering work by early practitioners laid out a foundation for vocational guidance and career education that is still useful in present day. Important figures emerged: George Merrill developed the first systematic vocational guidance program in San Francisco in 1895; Eli W. Weaver authored *Choosing a Career* and organized guidance services for New York City; Frank Goodwin developed a system-wide guidance program for Cincinnati, OH; Meyer Bloomfield and Anna Reed established a guidance program with a focus on employability of students and the ethics and practice of business; Jesse B. Davis and Frank Parsons were acknowledged in the literature for their significant ground-breaking work in incorporating vocational guidance programs into school systems (Gysbers & Henderson, 2001; Herr, 2003).

From 1889 to 1907, Jesse B. Davis was a school administrator and counselor in Detroit, and was greatly concerned with students' vocational and social needs. When he became the principal of the high school in Grand Rapids, MI in 1907, Davis introduced the first guidance course as a part of the school's English curriculum, for the first time making guidance an accepted part of the school program (Beale, 1986).

Frank Parsons, known as the "Father of Guidance," founded the Vocation Bureau of Boston in 1908 and authored a major book, *Choosing a Vocation,* in 1909. Parsons was concerned about the transition from school to the world of work and society's failure to develop resources and services for human growth and development (Schmidt, 1999). His work at the bureau aimed to help young students make appropriate choices for a vocation using a scientific approach (Gysbers & Henderson, 1994). Parsons also designed training programs for young men to become vocational counselors. His work was instrumental in creating the first counselor certification program in Boston and was eventually adopted by Harvard University as the first college-based counselor education program (Miller, 1968). His book "laid out the principles and methods of implementing vocational guidance, collecting and publishing occupational information, conducting a group study of occupations, carrying on individual counseling, and processing individual assessment" (Herr, 2003, p. 23), which also set the tone for the trait and factor approach that later became a major school of career development theories.

In 1913, the National Vocational Guidance Association (NVGA) was founded in Grand Rapids, MI. This particular organization was one of the founding divisions of the American Personnel and Guidance Association (APGA) in 1952 (later renamed the American Association for Counseling Development [AACD], and now called the American Counseling Association (ACA). NVGA was also the original publisher for two current major journals – *Career Development Quarterly* and *Journal of Counseling and Development* (Schmidt, 1999). The significance of NVGA is its instrumental role in the unification and identification of what has become the counseling profession, and particularly the school counseling profession.

*Theoretical Framework*

Parsons (1909) articulated the principles and methods of providing vocational guidance in the most influential theoretical work of that time and for many decades to come. He specified three essential factors in choosing an appropriate vocation: clear self-understanding of one's aptitudes, abilities, interests, resources, limitations and other qualities; understanding of the requirements and conditions, pros and cons, compensation, opportunities and prospects of different jobs; and understanding of the relationship between the two groups of factors. The goal of the early guidance movement was to prepare students for the world of work.

*Roles and Functions*

In the early 1900s, there were no job titles such as "professional school counselor" or "guidance counselor." The implementation of guidance was accomplished by appointed teachers who provided guidance and counseling without relief from their regular teaching loads or additional pay (Gysbers & Henderson, 2001). These teachers were given a list of activities relating to vocational guidance but no organized structure in which to work.

## Formative Years (1915–1930s)

*Historical Context*

In the years following the early vocational guidance movement in the 1900s, there was a continual emphasis on vocational guidance within education; however, educational reform and concerns about the dignity and rights of children emerged (Gysbers & Henderson, 2001, Herr, 2003). The National Education Association (NEA) supported guidance activities for education but not for vocation or employment, believing that vocational guidance was irrelevant to the needs of college-bound students (Minkoff & Terres, 1985). In the next two decades, the school counseling focus was shifted from job-oriented counseling to personal counseling and academic advisement. A number of movements (e.g., mental hygiene, measurement, developmental studies of children, introduction of cumulative records, and progressive education) influenced the changing purpose of vocational guidance (Gysbers, 2001). A broader focus including issues of personality and human development beyond vocational guidance started to emerge.

During this period, World War I and the Great Depression were two major events that affected the development of the school counseling profession. WWI affected the development and growth of testing. During the Great Depression, many young people were out of school or work and needed guidance to address livelihood needs.

*External Forces/Significant Events*

The mental hygiene movement, which reformed mental health services, was influenced by Clifford Beers, a former patient with a mental illness, and his book, *A Mind That Found Itself.* Published in 1908, this book was instrumental in reforming the treatment of patients with mental illness. The mental hygiene movement contributed to the acceptance and understanding of mental illness by society (Dixon, 1987). It also brought rising attention to students' personality and maladjustment issues (Herr, 2003). As a result, a clinical model of guidance and personal counseling began to dominate practice.

Psychological testing and measurement, another contributing force for counseling development, experienced a tremendous growth during this time. During WWI, the U.S. military began to use group training and testing procedures to screen and classify draftees (Schmidt, 1999). This classification provided impetus for further development of aptitude and interest measurement for the subsequent decades. The testing movement served to provide a conceptual strength and methodology to guidance.

Progressive education in the schools, introduced by John Dewey, emphasized the school's roles in guiding students' personal, social, and moral development (Nugent, 1994). Guidance activities were incorporated into the school curriculum to help students develop skills for living (Schmidt, 1999). While progressive education was criticized for not attending to the fundamentals of education, the most significant influence of progressive education was supporting the establishment of the guidance counselors.

Several other significant events followed. In 1926, New York became the first state to require certification for guidance workers. In 1938, a Guidance and Personnel branch was created in the U.S. Division of Vocational Education. Finally, in 1939, the first edition of

*Dictionary of Occupational Titles* was published by the U.S. Department of Labor, providing a reference for job descriptions and related job titles (Beale, 1986; Herr, 2003).

*Theoretical Frameworks*

Guidance was less concerned with social and industrial issues than personal and educational issues during this period. Yet there were no major theories or models of school counseling (Herr, 2003). The rapid development of measurement and subsequent availability of numerous tests saw an increased use of the trait and factor approach. Williamson (1939) developed a directive, or counselor-centered, approach which stated that counselors should enlighten students through exposition. In this direct approach, counselors were expected to collect data, synthesize data, and deliver the results with the purpose of motivating students.

Burnham, referred to as the "Father of Elementary School Guidance," (Stone & Bradley, 1994) authored *Great Teachers and Mental Health* which advocated for the necessity of guidance in elementary schools. He emphasized the critical role of classroom teachers in the mental health of children and the importance of developmental and preventive guidance programs.

*Roles and Functions*

The work of the pupil personnel, the organizational framework of the time, focused on bringing the pupils of the community to the educational environment and enabled them to maximize their desired development (Meyers, 1935). Personnel involved in pupil personnel work included attendance officers, visiting teachers, school nurses, school physicians and vocational counselors. Herr (2003) summarized the roles and functions of professional school counselors in the 1920s to 1940s as: 1) helping students gain more personalized educational experience (counteract the insensitive education system); 2) helping students sort through educational positions and create a unified course of instruction to discover the student's talents and locate the resources to develop these talents; and 3) coordinating the student personnel services to provide integrated support rather than compartmentalized assistance.

## Professional Identity and Growth (1940s–1950s)

*Historical Context*

The onset and end of World War II increased government involvement in the counseling profession. During the war, many psychologists and counselors were needed to help screen and train military and industrial specialists. After the war, many veterans needed services to readjust to civilian life. One particular governmental influence was the George-Barden Act of 1946, which provided funds to develop and support guidance and counseling activities in schools (Schmidt, 1999). "For the first time in history, school counselors and state and local supervisors received resources, leadership, and financial support from the government. This action fueled the start of a period of rapid growth for guidance and counseling services in schools" (Schmidt, 1999, p. 12).

The problems in school counseling, such as limited preparation of professional school counselors, lack of advocacy for professional school counselors, no systematic professional organization, and little legislative support for school counseling, began to change (Herr, 2003). Renewed hope also came from the emergence of person-centered counseling developed by Carl Rogers, and the first national school counselors organization.

*External Forces/Significant Events*

Carl Rogers published his monumental books, *Counseling and Psychotherapy: New Concepts in Practice* (1942), and *Client-Centered Therapy: Its Current Practice, Implications, and Theory* (1951). Most importantly, Rogerian influences emphasized a growth-oriented counseling relationship as opposed to an informational and problem-solving approach (Dixon, 1987; Schmidt, 1999).

In 1948, the *Occupational Outlook Handbook* was first published. In 1949, Robert Mathewson published *Guidance Policy and Practice*, a pioneering work on planning and implementing developmental guidance programs in schools (Beale, 1986).

In 1952, professional school counselors formed their own professional organization, the American School Counselor Association (ASCA). The impetus for the new organization stemmed from school counselors' belief that the National Vocational Guidance Association no longer served the needs of school counseling adequately, given that the professional school counselor's role and responsibilities extended beyond merely vocational guidance (Minkoff & Terres, 1985). ASCA became the fifth division in APGA in 1953. As professional school counselors became more recognized in schools across the country, ASCA reinforced the unique role professional school counselors performed and provided a forum for communication among professional school counselors (Herr, 1979).

*Theoretical Frameworks*

Rogers (1942; 1951) developed one of the most widely used counseling frameworks in history. He encouraged counselors to attend to the person in the process, and his ideas transformed counseling from medical and problem-solving models to a personal growth model. This theoretical approach fit naturally with the gradually emerging theme since the 1920s – individual counseling that focused on the personal and emotional needs of students.

The pupil personnel work structure continued to dominate guidance and counseling in schools (Gysbers, 2001). Counseling services were a subset of services to be delivered by professional school counselors. The clinical model of guidance made individual counseling emerge as the central part of guidance. The nature and scope of counseling services expanded compared to earlier decades, but there was still no unified, systematic, standard framework for what professional school counselors did. As a result, counseling services depended to a large extent on the mandates of local school districts.

*Roles and Functions*

Professional school counselors started to provide more than just vocational and personal counseling. Their responsibilities included orientation, individual appraisal, information, placement, follow-up, individual and group guidance, and consultation with parents and teachers (Schmidt, 1996).

## Booming Years (Late 1950s, 1960s & 1970s)

*Historical Context*

The late 1950s through the 1960s produced legislation initiatives that served to define school counseling's importance throughout the second half of the 20th century. The 1960s saw the expansion of school counseling across the nation. More training programs for professional school counselors were developed and professional school counselors hired. Interestingly, the school counseling movement occurred primarily as a result of the Cold War. After WWII, the U.S. and Soviet Union became world superpowers representing two very different ideological frameworks. When the Soviet Union launched Sputnik in 1957, the first man-made earth satellite, the U.S. was alarmed. A serious concern arose as to whether the U.S. had the scientific and technological capability to compete with the Soviet Union in space programs and eventually win the Cold War. A series of initiatives in the late 1950s and throughout the 1960s increased the competitive ability of the United States (Herr, 2003). As a result of federal funding and legislative support, school counseling positions expanded to unprecedented levels as did the quantity and quality of professional school counselor training programs.

*External Forces/Significant Events*

The passage of the *National Defense Education Act* (NDEA) in 1958 was one of several legislative initiatives to counteract the perceived threat of the Soviet Union. The NDEA provided funding to enhance school counseling programs in public schools, aiming to identify and encourage talented students to enter science and engineering careers. The funding also benefited new and existing counselor education programs, as the need for training professional school counselors was enormous. Most important for the school counseling profession, the counselor training programs became more systematic and integrated, state certification requirements were established, and many more students were served (Herr, 2003).

In 1964, the NDEA *Title V-A* was passed to extend guidance and counseling for all students, including elementary schools and various types of post-secondary schools (Herr, 1979). Despite this addition, elementary school counseling was not yet readily accepted within school systems or by the public. In the mid-1960s, several national studies investigating the functions and roles of elementary school counselors gave visibility, clarity and direction to elementary school counseling, resulting in more counselors becoming employed in that setting (Schmidt, 1996).

In 1966, the U.S. Department of Education established the Educational Resources Information Center (ERIC) to provide for education the same systematic acquisition and dissemination of relevant, quality information which had already been established for the physical sciences. A key feature of the ERIC system was its decentralization in which individual clearinghouses carried the responsibility of insuring that the ERIC database included the important literature and met the information needs of its designated scope area constituents. Fourteen clearinghouses were established with scope areas such as math and science, reading, early childhood education, etc. A proposal by Dr. Garry R. Walz at the University of Michigan led to the establishment of an ERIC Clearinghouse on Counseling and Personnel Services. This assured that all relevant counseling journals and publications, and particularly the school counseling literature, were processed for input into the national database.

At the same time, numerous pieces of legislation were being passed to address social issues such as unemployment, poverty, and civil rights. In response to the *Elementary and Secondary Education Act of 1965* and the *Vocational Education Amendment of 1968*, school counseling services incorporated attention to school dropouts, the economically and academically disadvantaged, and students with disabilities. The myriad legislation enacted in the 1960s also created vocational guidance, career education, and other career-related projects, emphasizing the role of professional school counselors in preparing students for transition from school to work (Herr, 2002; 2003; Minkoff & Terres, 1985).

In the 1970s, two important pieces of legislation had significant impacts on professional school counselors. The first was the *Education for All Handicapped Children Act of 1975* (known as Public Law 94-142), which involved professional school counselors in program planning, counseling, consulting and curriculum monitoring for exceptional children (Schmidt, 1999). The other was the *Family Educational Rights and Privacy Act of 1974* (known as the Buckley Amendment), which limited access to a student's records.

Other significant events during this period included the emergence of two important and widely read publications. In 1959, *The American High School Today,* authored by James Conant, inspired the idea that all students should have access to counseling, and advocated for one full-time professional school counselor for 250 to 300 students (Baker, 2000; Herr, 2002; 2003). This student:counselor ratio is still valid today, but is not fully implemented in most states.

Importantly, C. Gilbert Wrenn (1962) wrote *The Counselor in a Changing World* in which he strongly stressed the importance of building a developmental elementary and secondary school counseling program rather than a crisis-oriented, remedial program.

*Theoretical Frameworks*

Even though there was still no unified and systematic school counseling theory *per se*, the 1960s saw the rise of several counseling and career development theories (Brown & Srebalus, 1996; Nugent, 1994). Many counseling theories (e.g., Ellis' Rational-Emotive Therapy, Glasser's Reality Therapy, Behavioral Counseling introduced by Wolf and Krumboltz, Super's career development theory, Holland's theory of occupational types) familiar to contemporary counselors across practice settings were developed in this period.

Other influential approaches to school counseling included Keat's (1974) multimodal counseling approach which promoted examining and treating the student across several dimensions rather than on presenting problem only, and Egan's (1975) concept of stages in the counseling process, which provided professional school counselors a road map for how to counsel.

*Roles and Functions*

One of the primary goals of increasing the number of professional school counselors was to identify and encourage talented students to pursue science and engineering careers. In addition to the coordination role which assisted students in achieving educational and vocational goals, professional school counselors continued to provide individual counseling to students, albeit generally in reaction to events or circumstances. Baker (2001), in reviewing his professional school counselor job in the 1960s, stated:

> There was not enough time for proactive guidance programming. [Time was spent] scheduling all students over the summer (without pay) and making schedule adjustments in the fall — all by hand, lunch-room monitoring, student council advising, junior and senior proms, senior-class awards day, and graduation. (p. 76)

Nonetheless, the literature during and following the 1960s emphasized broader programmatic roles and functions for professional school counselors. Preferred services included developing comprehensive guidance programs to incorporate into the school curriculum, individual and group counseling, student assessment, and consultation with parents and teachers (Schmidt, 1996). Much of this focus on services stemmed from efforts by the National Association of Guidance Supervisors and Counselor Trainers which, in 1959, began a five year project to construct educational standards for preparing high school counselors.

## Challenge and Opportunity (Late 1970s – present)

*Historical Context*

The years after the boom (between the late 1970s and 1990s) observed several significant events in the U.S. and world. In U.S. society, these decades observed the movements of civil rights, women's liberation, school desegregation, a sharp rise in drug abuse, an AIDs epidemic, and the end of the Cold War. Problems of inner-city schools, high drop-out rates, diversity of student populations (in terms of racial/ethnic, cultural and socioeconomic backgrounds), readiness to learn, violence in schools and homes, teenage pregnancy, peer pressure, and limited resources have presented enormous challenges to school counseling professionals and educators in general (Baker, 2002; Rye & Sparks, 1999).

In the 1970s, a decade of enrollment decline in schools along with a depressed economy forced local school districts to reduce the numbers of professional school counselors (Baker, 2000; 2001). The fact that professional school counselors are often the victims of budget cuts in school systems has caused the profession to focus on two pertinent issues: role clarification and accountability. The debate about the definition and direction of roles, functions and responsibilities of professional school counselors has centered on the training, capabilities, and certification of professional school counselors compared to counseling in other settings (Aubrey, 1977; Paisley & McMahon, 2001; Schmidt, 1999). The focus on accountability has provided evidence of the effectiveness of school counseling services (Baker, 2001).

*External Forces/Significant Events*

The *Career Education Incentive Act of 1978* and the *Carl Perkins Vocational Education Act of 1984* steered the development of career education programs in schools. The *School to Work Opportunities Act of 1994* "has endeavored to create new models of collaboration between schools, transition mechanisms designed to facilitate the successful movement of students between school and employment, and employers" (Herr, 2002, p. 228).

By 1970, all states had professional school counselor certification (Stone & Bradley, 1994). The department of education in each state regulates the requirements of training and experiences for school counseling certification. In 1982, The National Board of Certified Counselors (NBCC) was developed to certify counselors across the states (Stone, 1985). NBCC provided a consistent credentialing process across the country.

Starting in the 1980s, the comparison between students produced through American education and other developed countries alarmed educational professionals, politicians and the public. In 1983, the National Commission on Excellence issued the publication *A Nation at Risk* to advocate for more rigorous standards for high school graduation (Herr, 2002). As the 21st century approached, ASCA called for professional school counselors to take action to help students be academically competitive and productive citizens.

Throughout the 1980s and early 1990s federal funds for school counseling programs were provided primarily through the *Carl D. Perkins Vocational Education Act of 1984* and the *Carl D. Perkins Vocational and Applied Technology Act of 1990* (Herr, 2003). *The Elementary School Counseling Demonstration Act of 1995* provided federal grants to local school districts to make counseling services available to all students. Counselor preparation programs began to collaborate with K-12 schools to provide assistance to students in school settings. According to Herr (2003), this act provided the impetus for orienting school counseling to include more than just career guidance.

ASCA published the *National Standards for School Counseling Programs* in 1997 (Campbell & Dahir, 1997) and later the *Vision into Action: Implementing the National Standards for School Counseling Programs* (Dahir, Shelton, & Valiga, 1998). A draft of *The ASCA National Model for School Counseling Programs* was published in 2002, followed by the final document, *The ASCA National Model: A Framework for School Counseling Programs*, in 2003 (ASCA, 2003). The *Standards* aimed at providing guidelines and a framework for professional school counselors to develop and implement comprehensive developmental counseling programs for all students in the personal/social, academic, and career development areas. It emphasized the importance of assessment of students' needs and evidence-based research to make the school counseling program accountable.

During the 1970s to the present, the ERIC database grew to be the most used education database in the world, eventually containing over one million documents. In 1993, Dr. Garry Walz and Dr. Jeanne Bleuer moved the ERIC Clearinghouse on Counseling and Personnel

Services (ERIC/CAPS) from the University of Michigan to the University of North Carolina at Greensboro. At that time, the name was changed to the ERIC Clearinghouse on Counseling and Student Services (ERIC/CASS). Although the U.S. Department of Education abolished the decentralized structure of ERIC and closed the sixteen ERIC Clearinghouses in December of 2003, during its 38 years of existence, ERIC/CAPS(CASS) acquired and processed over 25,000 counseling-related documents, indexed and abstracted over 50 journals, and published over 250 books and 200 ERIC Digests. In addition, the Clearinghouse conducted 25 heavily-attended national workshops devoted to cutting-edge topics relevant to school counseling, e.g., assessment and testing, use of computers and technology in guidance programs, life/career development, and leading and managing comprehensive school counseling programs.

Although the ERIC/CASS Clearinghouse has closed, Drs. Walz and Bleuer have established a new organization, Counseling Outfitters, to continue and, in fact, expand many of the services and products which had been offered by the Clearinghouse. This handbook is an example of the new line of resources produced by CAPS Press, the publishing division of Counseling Outfitters.

*Theoretical Frameworks*

The concept of comprehensive developmental school counseling programs, rather than a professional school counselor providing an ancillary set of services, has evolved since the 1970s and become an adopted guideline by ASCA for all professional school counselors to follow. Gysbers and Henderson's innovative work (1988) provided a conceptual and practical guide for the profession to develop and manage a school guidance program. "The emergence of developmental guidance and counseling in the 1970s and 1980s provided a central organizing structure for counselors and counselor educators to reframe their work" (Sink, 2001, p. 157).

Recently, a particular counseling approach has gained popularity in the school counseling profession - brief, solution-focused counseling (Davis & Osborn, 2000; Sklare, 1997). The reason for this approach's appeal to professional school counselors lies in the promise of efficiently solving the problem in a short time frame. Traditional approaches may be effective, but professional school counselors simply do not have time for long-term therapy.

*Roles and Functions*

Despite the debate about the roles and functions of professional school counselors (Schmidt, 1996), in the past three decades professional school counselors have performed duties widely perceived as "traditional" - i.e., academic advising, vocational planning, personal/individual counseling, reactive/crisis-oriented counseling, participating in Individual Education Programs (IEP), testing administration and scoring, and scheduling. At the same time, professional school counselors were torn between providing direct services or working as social change agents to provide a better school environment for students (Whiston, 2001). It was recommended that professional school counselors need to function as counselor, consultant, facilitator and coordinator to successfully develop and implement a comprehensive developmental school counseling program (Baker, 2000; Erford, 2003; Paisley & McMahon, 2001; Schmidt, 1999).

## Summary/Conclusion

School counseling was rooted in vocational guidance at the beginning of the 20th century as a response to the needs of students in transition from an agricultural to an industrial economy. In close to a century, the direction of school counseling was often shaped by social reform, school reform and the national welfare (see the timeline provided in Figure 1). The school counseling profession has evolved from "a peripheral, ancillary role in schools to a more central one" (Herr, 2002, p. 230).

**References**

Aubrey, R. (1977). Historical development of counseling and guidance and implications for the future. *Personnel and Guidance Journal, 55*, 288-295.

American School Counselor Association. (2003). *The ASCA national model: A framework for school counseling programs*. Alexandria, VA: Author.

Baker, S. B. (2000). *School counseling for the twenty-first century (3rd ed.).* Upper Saddle River, NJ: Prentice-Hall.

Baker, S. B. (2001). Reflections of forty years in the school counseling profession: Is the glass half full or half empty? *Professional School Counseling, 5,* 75-83.

Beale, A. V. (1986). Trivial pursuit: The history of guidance. *The School Counselor, 34,* 14-17.

Bowers, L. J., & Hatch, P. A. (2002). *The national model for school counseling programs.* Alexandria, VA: American School Counselor Association.

Brown, D., & Srebalus, D. (1996). *Introduction to the counseling profession (2nd ed.).* Boston, MA: Allyn & Bacon.

Campbell, C. A., & Dahir, C. A. (1997). *The national standards for school counseling programs.* Alexandria, VA: American School Counselor Association.

Davis, T. E., & Osborn, C. J. (2000). *The solution-focused school counselor: Shaping professional practice.* Philadelphia, PA: Accelerated Development.

Dahir, C. A., Shelton, C. B., & Valiga, M. J. (1998). *Vision into action: Implementing the national standards for school counseling programs.* Alexandria, VA: American School Counselor Association.

Dixon, D. N. (1987). From Parsons to profession: The history of guidance and counseling. In J. A. Glover, & R. R. Ronning (Eds.), *Historical foundations of educational psychology* (pp. 107-119). New York: Plenum.

Egan, G. (1975). *The skilled helper.* Monterey, CA: Brooks/Cole.

Erford, B. T. (2003). *Transforming the school counseling profession.* Columbus, OH: Merrill/Prentice-Hall.

Gysbers, N. C., & Henderson, P. (1994). *Developing and managing your school guidance program (2nd ed.).* Alexandria, VA: American Association for Counseling and Development.

Gysbers, N. C., & Henderson, P. (1988). *Developing and managing your school guidance program.* Alexandria, VA: American Association for Counseling and Development.

Gysbers, N. C. & Henderson, P. (2001). Comprehensive guidance and counseling programs: A rich history and a bright future. *Professional School Counseling, 4,* 246-256.

Gybers, N. C. (2001). School guidance and counseling in the 21st century: Remember the past into the future. *Professional School Counseling, 5,* 96-105.

Herr, E. L. (1979). *Guidance and counseling in schools.* Falls Church, VA: American Personnel and Guidance Association.

Herr, E. L. (2002). School reform and perspectives on the role of school counselors: A century of proposals for change. *Professional School Counseling, 5,* 220-234.

Herr, E. L. (2003). Historical roots and future issues. In B. T. Erford (Ed.), *Transforming the school counseling profession* (pp. *21-38).* Columbus, OH: Merrill/Prentice-Hall.

Holland, J. L. (1985). *Making vocational choices: Theory of vocational personalities and work environments.* Englewood Cliffs, NJ: Prentice-Hall.

Keat, D. B. (1974). *Fundamentals of child counseling.* Boston, MA: Houghton Mifflin.

Miller, G. (1968). *Guidance: Principles and services.* Columbus, OH: Merrill.

Minkoff, H. B., & Terres, C. K. (1985). ASCA perspectives: Past, present, and future. *Journal of Counseling and Development, 63,* 424-427.

Myers, G. E. (1935). Coordinated guidance: Some suggestions for a program of pupil personnel work. *Occupations, 13,* 804-807.
Nugent, F. A. (1994). *An introduction to professional counseling (2nd ed.).* New York: Merrill.
Paisley, P. O. & McMahon, H. G. (2001). School counseling for the 21st century: Challenges and opportunities. *Professional School Counseling, 5,* 106-115.
Parsons, F. (1909). *Choosing a vocation.* Boston, MA: Houghton Mifflin.
Rye, D. R., & Sparks, R. (1999). *Strengthening K-12 school counseling programs: A support system approach (2nd ed.).* Philadelphia, PA: Accelerated Development.
Rogers, C. R. (1942). *Counseling and psychotherapy: Newer concepts in practice.* New York: Houghton Mifflin.
Rogers, C. R. (1951). Client *centered therapy.* Boston, MA: Houghton Mifflin.
Schmidt, J. J. (1996). *Counseling in schools: Essential services and comprehensive programs (2nd ed.).* Boston, MA: Allyn & Bacon.
Schmidt, J. J. (1999). Counseling *in schools: Essential services and comprehensive programs (3rd ed.).* Boston, MA: Allyn & Bacon.
Sklare, G. B. (1997). *Brief counseling that works: A solution-focused approach for school counselors.* Thousand Oaks, CA: Sage Publication.
Sink, C. A. (2001). In search of the profession's finest hour: A critique to four views of 21st century school counseling. *Professional School Counseling, 5,* 156-163.
Stone, L. A. (1985). National Board for Certified Counselors: History, relationships, and projections. *Journal of Counseling and Development, 63,* 605-606.
Stone, L. A., & Bradley, F. O. (1994). *Foundations of elementary and middle school counseling.* New York: Longman.
Whiston, S. C. (2001). Response to the past, present, and future of school counseling: Raising some issues. *Professional School Counseling, 5,* 148-155.
Williamson, C. G. (1939). *How to counsel students.* New York: McGraw-Hill.

**Figure 1. Timeline of Significant Events in School Counseling History**

| Time Line | Significant Event and Impact |
|---|---|
| Emerging Years (1900s-1915) | |
| Late 19th century | Industrialization, urbanization, influx of and early 1900s immigrants, classification of labor – demand for skilled work force and need for employment guidance |
| 1908 | Frank Parsons founded the Vocational Bureau of the Civic Services in Boston – pioneer work in schools to help students |
| 1908 | Jesse Davis introduced the first guidance course as part of the English curriculum in Detroit – making guidance accepted as part of the school curriculum |
| 1908 | Clifford Beers authored *A Mind That Found Itself* – brought the treatment of mental patients to public attention |
| 1909 | Parsons' book *Choosing a Vocation* published one year after his death – laid out principles and methods of providing vocational guidance |
| 1913 | Founding meeting of National Vocational Guidance Association in Grand Rapids, MI – first professional counseling organization which later became a founding division of ACA |
| Formative Years *(1915-1930s)* | |
| 1920 | Mental hygiene, measurement movement, progressive education |
| 1926 | Burnham published *Great Teachers and Mental Health* – first to advocate for elementary school counseling |
| 1926 | New York requires certification for guidance workers |
| 1938 | A Guidance and Personnel Branch was created in the Vocational Education division in the US Office of Education |
| 1939 | First edition of *Dictionary of Occupational Titles* (DOT) was published |
| Professional Years (1940s-1950s) | |
| 1942 | Carl Rogers published *Counseling and Psychotherapy* |
| 1948 | *The Occupational Outlook Handbook* was first published |
| 1952 | American School Counseling Association (ASCA) was founded |
| 1953 | ASCA became the fifth division in the American Personnel and Guidance Association |
| 1958 | National Defense Education Act was passed expanding the training and hiring of school counselors |
| 1959 | James Conant published the *American High School Today* – suggesting 1:250 to 1:300 school counselor to student ratio |

| | |
|---|---|
| Booming Years<br>*(1960s-1970s)* | |
| 1962 | Wrenn published *The Counselor in a Changing World* – influential guide for the school profession in the years to follow |
| 1964 | NDEA Title A – legislation to extend counseling to elementary schools |
| 1966 | The U.S. Department of Education established the ERIC Clearinghouse on Counseling and Personnel Services (ERIC/CAPS) at the University of Michigan |
| 1976 | Career Education Incentive Act – infusion of career education in schools |
| Challenge and<br>Opportunity Years<br>*(Late 1970's-Present)* | |
| 1988 | Gysbers and Henderson published *Developing and Managing your School Guidance Program* |
| 1993 | ERIC/CAPS moved to the University of North Carolina and became ERIC/CASS (Counseling and Student Services). |
| 1994 | School to Work Act was passed reinforcing career guidance and counseling |
| 1995 | Elementary School Counseling Demonstration Act provided $20 million to assist schools to have counseling services available |
| 1997 | ASCA publishes The National Standards for School Counseling Programs – aims at providing benchmark for school counseling programs to promote student competency |
| 2003 | ASCA publishes *The ASCA National Model: A Framework for School Counseling Programs* |

# Chapter 3

# Current and Future Perspectives on School Counseling

*Joyce A. DeVoss*

## Preview

> Professional school counselors face numerous current and future challenges: clarifying role definition, obtaining optimal training, integrating programming, defining delivery systems, deciding on generalist versus specialist roles, attaining reasonable student-to-counselor ratios, accepting leadership, advocacy and public relations roles, developing technological competencies, and continuing involvement in professional development. This chapter addresses these challenges. The school counseling profession is challenged to define and enunciate its roles and functions more clearly as social changes and socioeconomic pressures influence the changing directions of school programs. The next generation of counselors has an opportunity to be significant contributors to the responses the schools make to these demands (Baker, 2000, p. v).

Professional school counseling's origins go back over a hundred years. Its development was influenced by a variety of forces, including the industrial revolution's exploitation of children, population immigration and migration, the educational reform movement at the turn of the 20th century, the evolution of counseling theory, and the national agenda. At the turn of the current century, educational reform once again has become a primary source of influence on the evolution of this profession.

Several authors have identified and discussed current and future challenges for professional school counselors (Baker, 2000; Gysbers, 2001; Paisley & Borders, 1995; Paisley & McMahon, 2001; Sandhu, 2001; Sears & Granello, 2002). In addition, a group of about 300 counselors, counselor educators, central office personnel and state-level personnel who attended a national conference, Leading & Managing Comprehensive School Guidance Programs, in February, 2002, in Greensboro, North Carolina, listed 10 critical issues in school counseling (American School Counselor Association (ASCA, 2002b). These key challenges and issues facing school counselors are addressed within this chapter and are organized by the following topics: school counselor role definition, school counselor preparation, school counseling programming, school counseling program delivery system, generalist versus specialist, reasonable student-to-counselor ratios, leadership/advocacy/public relations, technological competencies, and professional development.

## Professional School Counselor Role Definition

The professional school counselor's role definition has been a frequently identified challenge for the school counseling profession and one that has caused considerable difficulty in daily practice, limiting credibility for the profession. Perceptions of professional school counselor roles vary widely even within the same school district. Some professional school counselors reported experiencing a lack of administrative support, confusing expectations, and lack of respect

(ASCA, 2002a). Sears and Granello (2002) noted that professional school counselors struggle with role definition. Paisley and Borders (1995) stated that professional school counselors experience a lack of control over day-to-day duties and, sometimes, competing expectations from principals and counseling directors.

Baker (2000) stated, "School counseling, long viewed by some as an ancillary service in the schools, remains unclearly defined both within and outside the profession" (p. v). It is important for professional school counselor roles to be clear, yet broad-ranged, and not so demanding as to limit effectiveness.

In the early stages of the National Transformation of School Counseling Initiative (NTSCI), House & Martin (1999) outlined the new vision school counselor role and compared it to the traditional role of professional school counselor. The new vision professional school counselor is expected to be a proactive leader who is committed to quality education and equity of access to higher education for all students. The professional school counselor is envisioned as an assertive advocate and social activist on behalf of students, parents, schools and the school counseling profession. The Education Trust (1999) defined school counseling as:

> ...a profession that focuses on the relations and interactions between students and their school environment with the expressed purpose of reducing the effect of environmental and institutional barriers that impede student academic success.

In an effort to assist professional school counselors in defining their roles more clearly, ASCA adopted position statements regarding the profession. In one statement concerning the use of non-school-counseling-credentialed personnel, ASCA (1994) emphasized that professional school counselors should be looked upon to lead in creating, organizing and implementing school counseling program activities for both credentialed and non-credentialed personnel. Quality graduate training programs prepare professional school counselors for leadership of their school counseling programs.

## Professional School Counselor Preparation

In order to effectively carry out the mission of schools and function optimally as part of school leadership teams, professional school counselor trainees must receive adequate training. Potential professional school counselors have choices from diverse training programs. With information about criteria of quality graduate training, they should be able to locate graduate programs which meet national standards of the Council for the Accreditation of Counseling and Related Educational Programs (CACREP, 2001). Many state departments of education are adopting CACREP standards as minimum standards for certification or licensure (Baker, 2000; Sears & Granello, 2002).

Even with CACREP standards, there has been little consistency across school counseling training programs. In 1992, although 195 graduate programs in 72 institutions were CACREP accredited (Kandor & Bobby, 1992), the curriculum varied considerably from one graduate school counseling program to another. CACREP standards (2001) for master's level school counseling programs require a minimum of 48 semester hours of graduate study including the following eight areas: professional identity, social and cultural diversity, human growth and development, career development, helping relationships, group work, assessment and research and program evaluation. In addition, CACREP specifies that professional school counselor trainees must successfully complete a 100-hour practicum and a 600-hour internship in school settings. These are considered minimal standards for counselor preparation.

ASCA (2000) developed a list of professional school counselor competencies which fall in three domains: knowledge competencies, skill competencies, and professional competencies. Some examples of the knowledge competencies are: human development theories and concepts, career decision-making theories and techniques, and program development models. Some of the skill competencies include: diagnosing student needs, career and educational counseling and planning, and conducting inservice for staff. Professional competencies include: conducting a self-evaluation to determine strengths and areas needing improvement, advocating for appropriate state and national legislation, and adopting a set of professional ethics to guide practice. In order for new professional school counselors to be truly competent, it is in the best interest of prospective professional school counselors to seek graduate preparation programs that, in addition to being CACREP accredited, have been continuously updated and aligned with national standards and the Transformation of School Counseling Initiative.

In addition to the professional school counselor competencies, ASCA (2000) identified a list of personal attributes of successful professional school counselors. Some of the characteristics are: a genuine interest in the welfare of others, openness to learning, willingness to take risks, a strong sense of self-worth, caring and warmth, and a keen sense of humor. Certain of these characteristics can be acquired during the course of training while others are brought with the trainee to the program. The complete list of effective professional school counselor skill competencies and personal characteristics is available from ASCA.

## School Counseling Programming

Hart & Jacobi (1992) identified six problems with school counseling programs. In a presentation at the Education Trust Summer Academy, 2002, in Chicago, Kuranz reminded participants of those six problems: lack of basic philosophy, poor integration, insufficient student access, inadequate services for some students, lack of counselor accountability, and failure to utilize other resources.

### *Basic Philosophy*

Kuranz (2002) noted, with a sense of urgency for the continued existence of the profession, that in Iowa elementary school counselors were eliminated because their focus was not clearly tied to academic achievement. If school counseling programs in K-12 settings are going to survive, it is imperative that they be systematically planned and focused on academic results instead of the traditional basis of services offered. The basic philosophy and mission of a school counseling program should be tied directly to the school's mission. Examples of desired results might include improved national and state test results, improved graduation rates, improved attendance, decreased drop-out rates, increased enrollment in postsecondary education programs, and increased enrollment of poor and minority students in high level math and advanced placement (AP) courses.

### *Integrated, Longitudinal Developmental Counseling*

Integration is a key characteristic of an effective school counseling program. An effectively integrated program needs to be truly longitudinal (Herr & Cramer, 1996) and should span from elementary school through secondary school. Sandhu (2001) stressed that, starting with elementary school, counseling programs need to emphasize the interconnections among cognitive, physical and social development of children. Gysbers & Henderson (2000) described in detail the steps in designing a comprehensive guidance program for a school building or district. The process involves concretely describing the content, organizational framework, time allotted, and resources needed. It is a time-intensive process but well worth the investment for the program.

For maximum effectiveness and relevance to all students, Sandhu (2001) recommended that school counseling programs be proactive and positive in approach. It is reasonable that these programs be comprehensive and well integrated into the mission of the school. Gysbers & Henderson (2000) reported that comprehensive guidance programs are becoming a reality in school districts across the U.S. These programs are staffed by professional school counselors concerned with serving all students instead of focusing only on high and low achieving students and providing less-than-adequate services to all others.

*Student Accessibility and Services For All Students*

ASCA has developed national standards for school counseling programs (Campbell & Dahir, 1997). These standards are the essential elements of an effective school counseling program at any level of K-12 education. They address program content and expected knowledge, attitudes, and skill competencies for all students in schools with comprehensive school-counseling programs. Three content areas include: academic, career and personal/social development. Under each of these headings are three standards, which describe the outcomes for students of an effective school-counseling program. For example, under the career development domain, standard B states, "Students will employ strategies to achieve future career success and satisfaction" (Campbell & Dahir, 1997, p. 92). The trifold developmental focus, including career development, should start in the elementary school and continue through 12th grade (Sandhu, 2001).

Gysbers & Henderson (2000) described in detail how to adapt a school counseling program model to meet the specific needs of a school district or a school building and to balance the use of the professional school counselor's time according to predetermined priorities. The use of established steering and school-community advisory committees is recommended throughout the decision-making process. This collaborative approach ensures that the school counseling program adopted by the decision makers will adequately address the systemic needs of the district or school.

Recently, ASCA (Hatch & Bowers, 2002) developed *The National Model for School Counseling Programs* to create a common vision for professional school counselors. This model includes four major components: foundation, delivery system, management system and accountability. The model integrates an emphasis on advocacy, leadership and systemic change in keeping with themes of the school counseling reform movement. It provides professional school counselors with a framework for the development of school counseling programs while allowing flexibility for responsiveness to local community needs.

School counseling programs are faced with responsibility for guidance of all students. This means that counselors in the 21st century must be prepared to provide appropriate school counseling services to students and families of diverse cultural and ethnic backgrounds, learning disabilities, various sexual orientations, emotional and physical disabilities, and diverse religious beliefs and practices (Sandhu, 2001). It also means that professional school counselors need to meet the challenge to become assertive advocates for all students, especially disadvantaged and minority students, in the important work of closing the achievement gap between these students and their peers.

Gysbers (2001) contended that professional school counselors can reach all students through comprehensive school counseling programs with planned guidance activities in the classrooms. He cited research indicating that comprehensive guidance programs do benefit students academically, in career development, and in school climate.

Currently, stage models of development are the foundation for school counseling programs. Some question the adequacy of these models for this purpose (Green & Keys, 2001; Sears & Granello, 2002). The models may not sufficiently take into account issues of diversity and other contextual factors important to consider when developing a comprehensive developmental school counseling program.

To address these concerns, Green and Keys (2001) recommended use of a development-in-context paradigm in school counseling program design. This model takes into consideration contextual factors such as culture, values and living environment that impact student development. Professional school counselors operating from this model facilitate student awareness of self-in-context, an awareness of the multiple contexts impacting the student's life.

While the profession emphasizes the role of school counselors in delivery of comprehensive guidance programs, it has been noted that there are many obstacles (Sandhu, 2001). Although the comprehensive guidance approach is preplanned, proactive and comprehensive in nature, in practice the professional school counselor must constantly strive to achieve and maintain balance in the school counseling program. Despite the best planning efforts, there continues to be many demands on the professional school counselor's time and effort. Sears and Granello (2002) noted that professional school counselors get pulled in different directions as they attempt to conform to the national reform agenda. For better or worse, professional school counselors respond to more school-based crises and intervene on behalf of both more and more intensely emotionally disturbed or troubled students. Baker (2000) acknowledged many demands to which counselors in schools are expected to respond. The national model and standards as well as the national, state and local school counseling organizations are resources available to help professional school counselors meet the challenges of setting and assertively maintaining priorities for their comprehensive, developmental school counseling programs.

*Accountability*

Baker (2000) explained the difference between the terms evaluation and accountability. "Evaluation is the act of gathering information about one's services; accountability is the act of reporting the results of the evaluation" (p. 300). He described basic professional school counselor accountability competencies, such as how to do a needs assessment and how to assess cost-effectiveness.

Accountability is expected of educators, including professional school counselors. Data from schools is readily available for professional school counselors to use in evaluating the impact of school counseling programs. Professional school counselors have made progress and will continue to be expected to access and disaggregate data for developing data-driven school counseling programs. When professional school counselors report the outcomes of their interventions on achievement data, other educators begin to understand the connection between counseling programs and the mission of schools. In 1970, in the midst of economically hard times, Arbuckle (as cited in Baker, 2000) wrote an article entitled, "Does the School Really Need Counselors?" The article challenged the profession to become more accountable. In response, some individuals developed models of accountability, others reiterated the need for accountability, and some state legislation mandated accountability of school counseling programs and professional school counselors. Yet many professional school counselors resisted instituting evaluation measures. Since that time, the pressure for accountability has mounted to an all-time high.

In the face of current educational reform and *No Child Left Behind* legislation that mandates educational accountability, professional school counselors can no longer afford to resist. With the economic stresses and decreased educational funding following the events of September 11, 2001, some school districts are again asking Arbuckle's question. Professional school counselors are challenged to advocate for their survival. Advocacy via use of data indicating the impact of school counseling programs on achievement can be powerful and gives the profession credibility.

*Other Resources and The Need for Collaboration*

Considering the challenge for professional school counselors to meet the needs of all children, success in serving students may best be achieved through a team effort. Because typical school student-to-counselor ratios are far in excess of the ideal of somewhere between 200 and 300 to 1 (Baker, 2000), professional school counselors cannot adequately meet those needs on their own. A recent ASCA study (2002a) reported that in 1999-2000, the national average student-to-counselor ratio was 490 to 1. This data lends support to professional school counselor efforts to collaborate with others in delivering services to students.

Paisley and McMahon (2001) believed that professional school counselors must foster collaborative relationships with other school personnel, parents, professionals and other community members in order to combine efforts to meet student needs. By doing so, professional school counselors enlarge the pool of talent and resources available to the school community. In one example, some teachers have effectively delivered guidance curriculum in the classroom. And while involvement of others besides professional school counselors in the counseling program can be beneficial to students, ethical and professional practice requirements (ASCA, 1998) dictate that counseling-related activities performed by non-credentialed personnel be supervised and coordinated by credentialed school counselors.

## School Counseling Program Delivery System

The National Model for School Counseling Programs (Hatch & Bowers, 2002) outlines the delivery system for school counseling programs. Based on this current national model, professional school counselors must be competent in the following areas in order to meet basic practice standards of the profession: implementing developmental guidance curriculum, providing individual planning, offering responsive services to meet immediate needs, and performing systems support administration and management activities.

Currently, there is considerable consensus in the field of school counseling that the resources of the professional school counselor can best be utilized with a proactive developmental approach (Sandhu, 2001). The professional school counselor is looked upon to coordinate the design, planning and implementation of the school counseling program with care and flexibility to adequately meet the needs of students, parents, teachers, administrators and other school community stakeholders.

## Generalist Versus Specialist

Professional school counselors must decide on the extent to which they are generalists or specialists. This decision may be made best according to the needs of the school district or school building and may be influenced based on the degree to which teams are utilized. If the school building has a counseling department, the professional school counselors may be expected to be part of the departmental team. In the new vision role (House & Martin, 1998), the professional school counselor is likely to be a member and/or leader of one or more school leadership teams, e.g., staff development planning, suicide prevention, crisis response.

Such teams can operate in a variety of ways. In some settings, the most efficient teamwork occurs when members are specialists who continuously hone specific knowledge bases and related skills. In the case of a counseling department team, the counselors might divide the departmental responsibilities depending on the specialities of its members. In other settings, professional school counselor team members work optimally as generalists and provide an array of services to pre-assigned caseloads of students. And, in other environments, a department may operate most efficiently with some specialists and some generalists.

When a school building has only one counselor assigned, that counselor is most likely to function as a generalist. This is frequently the case for elementary school counselors. These professional school counselors can become isolated if they are not proactive in assuring involvement on leadership teams and in other collaborative relationships.

## Reasonable Student-to-Counselor Ratios

Reasonable student-to-counselor ratios are essential for professional school counselors to become adequately familiar with students and their needs. Because of the amount of variation in type and intensity of needs in student populations and in expectations of professional school counselors, it is difficult and unrealistic to determine a standard ratio of students to counselor to fit all settings.

However, generally, caseloads of 300 or less are seen as optimal (Baker, 2000). According to Shaw (as cited in Baker, 2000), these ratios are determined primarily by financial conditions and secondarily by the perceived value of the school counseling program. Gysbers & Henderson (2000) offered a formula that calculates approximate student-to-counselor ratios in an optimal school counseling program. The ratio varies depending on the pre-arranged counseling program activities for the school and, therefore, the professional school counselor's availability to provide the program activities.

## Leadership/Advocacy/Public Relations

Professional school counselors must successfully articulate to policy makers, media, and the public about essential contributions of professional school counselors to the mission of schools. In order to effectively educate the community about the important role of school counseling, professional school counselors must actively promote the profession and its mission. Baker (2000) suggested that social activism is the approach needed to accomplish recognition of the preferred identity for professional school counselors. The Education Trust (n. d.) outlined "the new vision" role of the professional school counselor as leader, advocate, collaborator and consultant.

> The profession fosters conditions that ensure educational equity, access, and academic success for all students, K-12. ...the trained school counselor must be an assertive advocate creating opportunities for all students....The school counselor serves as a leader as well as an effective team member working with teachers, administrators and other school personnel to make sure that each student succeeds. The school counselor as consultant empowers families to act on behalf of their children... as well as access available resources.

With a clearer definition of school counseling and the roles of professional school counselors, the local and national community can have a better understanding of key contributions made by professional school counselors in achieving educational equity for all children. Baker (2000) believes that professional school counselors and their supporters need to join local and national professional organizations like the American School Counselor Association (ASCA), Association for Counselor Education and Supervision (ACES), and American Counseling Association (ACA), and initiate grassroots efforts to achieve dramatic educational change on a national level. He expressed concern that less than half of all professional school counselors are members of any professional organization.

## Technological Competence

Competence in the use of technology for professional school counselors is clearly an expectation (Sandhu, 2001). ACES's Technology Interest Network (1999) established twelve technological competencies for counselors that should be included in counselor education. These competencies, which are expected to need updating every three years, are summarized here.

Counselors need to be able to:

- use productivity software to develop Web pages, group presentations, letters, and reports;
- use audiovisual equipment such as video recorders, audio recorders, projection equipment, videoconferencing equipment, and playback units;
- use computerized statistical packages;
- use computerized testing, diagnostic, and career decision-making programs with clients;
- use e-mail;
- help clients search for various types of counseling-related information via the Internet, including information about careers, employment opportunities, educational and training opportunities, financial assistance/scholarships, treatment procedures, and social and personal information;
- subscribe to, participate in, and sign off of counseling-related listservs;
- access and use counseling-related CD-ROM databases;
- know strengths and weaknesses of counseling services provided via the Internet;
- know the legal and ethical codes that relate to counseling services via the Internet;
- use the Internet for finding and using continuing education opportunities in their profession;
- evaluate the quality of Internet information.

Sabella and Tyler (as cited in Sandhu, 2001) provided a detailed description and discussion of each of these competencies. Current technology skills are necessary tools supporting effective school counseling services.

## Professional Development

Due to the rapidly changing educational environment, professional development is a priority for counselors in schools. Professional school counselors can utilize professional development opportunities to stay current in the profession. Professional school counselors can participate in professional development to maintain their professional identity. Furthermore, professional school counselors can view professional development as an opportunity to network and exchange innovative ideas in the profession. Hatch (2001) strongly urged professional school counselors to become actively involved in professional development and reminded them of state requirements to maintain certification.

Professional school counselors are encouraged to become members of at least one professional organization. Less than half of professional school counselors take advantage of such a membership. The benefits may include subscriptions to the publications of the organization, liability insurance, notices of professional development or networking opportunities, as well as discounts on conferences and professional publications. These organizations offer potential leadership roles for professional school counselors along with the opportunity to make a difference at a systemic level. ASCA is the national school counselor professional organization and each state also has a state school counselor association.

## Summary/Conclusion

School counseling in the United States has evolved over more than a century of rapid social, political and economic change. The profession has been impacted by a myriad of influences, including: social reform efforts, immigration, economic changes, national defense issues and the advancement of psychological and developmental theory. The impact of its meandering evolutionary process left the school counseling profession with numerous challenges at the end of the 20th century including: clarifying role definition; identifying and obtaining optimal preparation; integrating programming; clearly defining program delivery systems; deciding on a generalist versus specialist role; attaining reasonable student-to-counselor ratios; accepting leadership, advocacy and public relations roles; developing technological competencies; and participating in relevant professional development.

The role of the professional school counselor in the 21st century remains fluid and constantly changing in response to changing demands of our schools and our local and national communities. However, as the profession continued its transformation process begun at the end of the last century, it has sought to become an active participant in the educational reform movement, unlike its limited, if any, role in past reform movements. Counselors have begun to address the challenges and issues discussed in this chapter and are encouraged to continue this important work. In the process, professional school counselors have begun to speak as advocates with one voice towards insuring that all students have equal access to quality education and that, in reality, no child is left behind.

## References


American School Counselor Association. (1994). Position statement: The professional school counselor and the use of non-school-counseling-credentialized personnel. *ASCA membership directory and resource guide.* Gainesville, FL: Naylor Publishing.

American School Counselor Association.(1998). *Ethical standards for school counselors.* Alexandria, VA: Author.

American School Counselor Association. (2000). *School counselor competencies* [Brochure]. Alexandria, VA: Author.

American School Counselor Association. (2002a). ASCA study examines counselor-to-student ratios. *ASCA School Counselor, 39*(5), 50.

American School Counselor Association. (2002b). Hot topics for school counselors. *ASCA School Counselor*, *39*(5), 51.

Association for Counselor Education and Supervision (ACES) Technology Interest Network. (April, 1999). *Technical competencies for counselor education students: Recommended guidelines for program development* [On-line]. Available: www.chre.vt.edu/thohen/competencies.htm.

Baker, S. (2000). *School counseling for the twenty-first century.* Upper Saddle River: Prentice-Hall.

Campbell, C. A., & Dahir, C. A. (1997). *The national standards for school counseling programs.* Alexandria, VA: American School Counselor Association.

Council for the Accreditation of Counseling and Related Educational Programs (CACREP). (2001). *CACREP accreditation standards and procedures manual.* Alexandria, VA: Author.

Education Trust. (1999). *Transforming school counseling initiative* [Brochure]. Washington, DC: Author.

Education Trust. (N. D.) *What we do. Transforming school counseling. Working definition of school counseling*. Retrieved June 20, 2002 from: http://www.edtrust.org

Green, A., & Keys, S. (2001). Expanding the developmental school counseling paradigm: Meeting the needs of the 21st century student. *Professional School Counseling, 5,* 84-95.

Gysbers, N. C. (2001). School guidance and counseling in the 21st century: Remember the past into the future. *Professional School Counseling, 5,* 96-105.

Gysbers, N. C., & Henderson, P. (2000). *Developing and managing your school guidance program.* Alexandria, VA: American Counseling Association.

Hart, P. J., & Jacobi, M. (1992). *From gatekeeper to advocate: Transforming the role of the school counselor.* New York: College Entrance Examination Board.

Hatch, T., & Bowers, J. (2002). The block to build on. *ASCA School Counselor, 39* (5), 13-17.

Herr, E. L., & Cramer, S. H. (1996). *Career guidance and counseling through the lifespan.* (5th ed.). New York: Harper-Collins.

House, R. M., & Martin, P. J. (1998). Advocating for better futures for all students: A new vision for school counselors. *Education, 119,* 284-291.

Kandor, J. R., & Bobby, C. L. (1992). Introduction to a special feature. *Journal of Counseling and Development, 70*, 666.

Kuranz, M. (2002, June). *The New ASCA National Model for School Counseling Programs.* Presentation at the Education Trust 2002 Summer Academy, Chicago, IL.

Paisley, P. O., & Borders, L. D. (1995). School counseling: An evolving speciality. *Journal of Counseling and Development, 74,*150-153.

Paisley, P. O., & McMahon, G. H. (2001). School counseling for the 21st century: Challenges and opportunities. *Professional School Counseling, 5,* 106-115.

Sandhu, D. H. (Ed.). (2001). *Elementary school counseling in the new millennium.* Alexandria, VA: American Counseling Association.

Sears, S. J., & Granello, D. H. (2002). School counseling now and in the future: A reaction. *Professional School Counseling, 5,* 164-171.

# *Chapter 4*

# Outcomes Research on School Counseling

*Patrick Akos*

## Preview

A continuing trend in mental health and education is a push for evidence-based practice and accountability. Professional school counselors have limited outcome research available for practice, which presents both a challenge and an opportunity. A summary of current outcome research in school counseling as well as implications and recommendations for practicing professional school counselors are offered.

The school counseling profession has seen a great deal of reform in the past decade. Comprehensive school counseling programs (Gysbers & Henderson, 1994) have helped to organize and professionalize the services that professional school counselors provide, while the American School Counselor Association's (ASCA) National Standards (Dahir, 2001) have prescribed types of student outcomes school counseling programs should produce. More recently, the *Transforming School Counseling Initiative* has suggested a stronger focus on academic achievement and increased leadership and advocacy roles (Sears, 1999). The emergence of ASCA's National Model (Hatch & Bowers, 2002; ASCA, 2003) builds on these previous efforts and consolidates a comprehensive system of advocacy, collaboration, systemic change, and leadership towards the ASCA National Standards. Accountability, a familiar word to all school personnel, is a core part of the new ASCA National Model. The accountability theme endorses program evaluation, appropriate performance evaluation, and results reports. Within the recommended results reports, effectiveness data for immediate, intermediate, and long-range results serve as tools for advocacy for students and school counseling programs.

In addition to school counseling, research and professional trends in psychotherapy and education have also focused more attention on effectiveness and results. Using rigorous scientific methodology, empirically validated treatments (interventions proven to be effective) are promoted for psychotherapy and at times are the only accepted treatments for managed care. At the same time, the field of education is focused on accountability. While the process or means of determining academic accountability has been debated, the demand for results is inescapable. Many teachers and schools are now measured by student performance on state mandated standardized achievement tests. In fact, funding and teacher incentives are tied to the outcomes on student tests in many states.

As therapists, teachers, and schools are measured by client or student outcomes, professional school counselors are not far behind. In 1993, Fairchild found that 67% of professional school counselors were involved in some type of accountability effort. Professional school counselors must increasingly describe their contributions to student achievement and validate their time spent with students. This push for counseling science or school accountability requires professional school counselors to measure and determine the effectiveness or outcomes of interventions. Along with the responsibility for accountability comes an ethical duty of making informed decisions about interventions (Lambert, 1991). Professional responsibility and the direction of education and counseling reform beg an important, yet difficult question: What school counseling services or interventions work to create desired student outcomes? This chapter provides a brief summary of the outcome research, puts the findings in perspective, and suggests several implications for professional school counselors.

## Major Findings in School Counseling Outcome Research

In general, research has demonstrated that psychotherapy with children and adolescents is effective (Kazdin, 1993). Although school counseling has the least amount of empirical evidence to support practice as compared to other types of counseling (Sexton, 1999), several meta-analytic reviews of the outcome research in school counseling have suggested moderate to positive results (Baker, Swisher, Nadenichek, & Popowicz, 1984; Nearpass, 1990; Prout & DeMartino, 1986; Prout & Prout, 1998; Sprinthall, 1981). Qualitative reviews of school counseling have demonstrated generally positive impacts (Borders & Drury, 1992; Whiston & Sexton, 1998) and positive effects specifically for low achieving students (Wilson, 1986), elementary school students (Gerler, 1985), and middle school students (St. Clair, 1989). Reviews of research are particularly helpful in that many studies help evaluate the multitude of duties performed by professional school counselors (Whiston, 2003).

Considering the content areas in the ASCA national standards, evidence exists to show that professional school counselors have been effective in promoting career, personal/social, and academic development in students. Career development seemingly has the most depth and breadth of outcome or effectiveness evidence. Both meta-analysis (Whiston & Sexton, 1998) and narrative reviews (Palmer & Cochran, 1988) have supported the effectiveness of career interventions, especially through individual counseling. Students have also benefited from parent consultation about career development. Gysbers (1988) described various benefits of classroom guidance in outcomes related to developing career goals, college attendance, and career-planning skills. The outcome research has also revealed that career services have been useful to a wide variety of students including ethnic minorities, the academically gifted, and students with disabilities (Sexton, Whiston, Bleuer, & Walz, 1997).

In terms of personal/social development, group counseling was found to be effective for elementary students in helping students adjust to family difficulties (Whiston & Sexton, 1998). Social skills training has also been found to produce results in helping students (Whiston & Sexton, 1998). Borders and Drury (1992) suggested that students who received counseling improved their behavior and attitudes toward school, and that small group counseling helps improve student attendance, classroom behaviors, self-esteem, self-concept, and attitudes towards themselves and others. Additional studies have shown classroom guidance activities to be effective in improving school behavior, attitudes toward school, attendance, and coping skills (Bundy & Boser, 1987; Gerler & Anderson, 1986; Myrick, Merhill, & Swanson, 1986). As with career development, these outcomes for personal and social development were found to generalize across widely varying groups of students.

For academic development, research (Whiston & Sexton, 1998; Wilson, 1986) has concluded that guidance activities, while not efficacious to promote self-esteem, exhibit trends of positive influence on academic achievement. Borders and Drury (1992) also suggested that students who received counseling improved their academic performance.

Research has suggested that a variety of factors might affect school counseling outcomes. For example, outcomes vary depending on school level (elementary, middle, high) (Nearpass, 1990; Prout & Demartino, 1986; Prout & Prout, 1998), although it is clear the least amount of research exists for middle school counseling (St. Clair, 1989; Whiston & Sexton, 1998). In addition, while some research has suggested that student factors like gender and referral status (self vs. other) affect outcomes (Wilson, 1986), other research suggests that a variety of demographic and school factors are unrelated to counseling outcomes (Hagborg, 1993).

A review of research shows that certain types of interventions are more frequently the topic of research and/or have more positive outcomes than do other types of interventions. Although not conclusive, it seems that more outcome research has examined and supported group counseling as compared to individual counseling. Additionally, while some outcome studies have found positive outcomes for classroom guidance, the research is very limited (Whiston, 2003). Furthermore, investigation of typical professional school counselor led activities (e.g., peer mediation, family education, and consultation) produced mixed findings and conclusions were difficult to draw because of the variance of professional school counselor involvement and functioning. In turn, the comprehensive guidance movement has been propelled by research that supports better student outcomes (e.g., grades, positive environment) and program improvement (Lapan, Gysbers, & Sun, 1997).

## Outcome Research in Perspective

It is important to remember that research on school counseling is based on probabilities, rather than assurances of effectiveness or prescriptive directions (Martin & Hoshmand, 1995). Additionally, most of the research is correlational, which does not suggest causality (Gelso, 1979). So, although research is available to support school counseling effectiveness, the research is neither vast nor methodologically strong.

In the comprehensive review of published school counseling literature from 1988 to 1995, Whiston and Sexton (1998) found no consistent type of outcome targeted, no consistent measure or instrument used, and most research focused on responsive services rather than preventative or developmental activities. With only 22% of the studies incorporating experimental design and the majority focused on remediation, research has not proved the effectiveness of school counseling services nor focused on the preventative or proactive nature of helping (Sexton et al., 1997). Whiston and Sexton's (1998) review suggested no clear trend in the research favoring one method over another (individual, group, classroom). Disturbingly, the review also suggested that the many flaws with the existing research limits confidence in results (e.g., lack of experimental design, convenience samples, non-standard outcome measures). Even the psychotherapy literature was often based on laboratory research (Sexton, 1999). In fact, most of the research on children and adolescents is conducted in clinical or research settings (Kazdin, 1993).

Additionally, it is a challenge for practicing professional school counselors to keep up with outcome research articles as they appear in a variety of journals (Sexton, 1996). Often results are difficult to decipher and it is a challenge to find results pertinent to practice (Whiston, 2003). Furthermore, choosing interventions from a list often inhibits innovation, dehumanizes students, and puts too much attention on technique (Waehler, Kalodner, Wampold, & Lichtenberg, 2000). This approach of matching treatment/intervention to remedial need dismisses many influences important to professional school counselors, including diversity, career counseling, psycho-educational, and developmental concerns, and prevention/proactive programs. Additionally, the counselor must have the knowledge and ability to assess presenting concerns and apply these treatments (Sexton, 1999).

## Implications for Professional School Counselors

### *Be An Active Consumer of Outcome Research In School Counseling*

Although reports of evidence-based interventions for professional school counselors are not conclusive, it is important to be an astute consumer and incorporate research into practice. Research has shown that some practices are more effective than others and some client problems are helped most by specific counseling models (Sexton, 1999). Professional school counselors must examine a diverse set of published research in a variety of journals and read each study with caution. Therefore, professional school counselors must examine effectiveness research as one step in the decision making process to determine an appropriate intervention.

*Keep Grounded in Core Conditions of Effective Helping*

In reality, the great majority of what works will be determined by efforts related to, but distinct from, determining an appropriate intervention. Research has suggested that the specific psychological technique accounts for only 15% of the outcome (Lambert, 1991). Lambert (1991) has suggested that 30% of the outcome in counseling is related to common factors evident in therapy regardless of type of theory or intervention. These common factors include: (a) the supportive value of a collaborative counseling relationship; (b) the value of learning (through affective experiencing, corrective emotional experiences, or skills acquisition); and (c) action (through behavior change, successful experiences, behavioral regulation, and mastery) (Sexton, 1999).

As a professional school counselor, improving the outcome of helping occurs when working with these common factors. For example, professional school counselors often see challenging students who may be referred by teachers or parents. Many counselors scour the research literature for a solution using the newest technique, but often fail first to focus on and establish a collaborative counseling relationship. Research would suggest that the type of counseling relationship established would dictate the student's value of learning from the counselor and the action taken. Historically, demographic factors, professional identity, and even experience have all been thought to be influential in the effectiveness of the counselor. Current evidence suggests that when all other factors are equal, these three factors are unrelated to the counseling outcome (Sexton, 1999). Instead, level of skillfulness (competence), cognitive complexity (ability to think diversely and complexly about cases), and an ability to relate and relationally match with the clients with whom they are working are important to outcomes (Sexton, 1999).

Lambert (1991) further suggested that 15% of the outcome of counseling depends on client expectations. Students come to see professional school counselors with varying levels of expectation for change. Again, students referred by others often have limited desires or expectations for change. Client expectations are shaped by the student's experience, background, and relationship with counselors. Professional school counselors are again challenged to create expectations for change when determining what works (much like how solution-focused counseling builds with the miracle question). Beyond the relationship and client expectations, various factors outside of the counseling dynamics influence outcomes.

In terms of counseling or therapy in general, Lambert (1991) proposed that 40% of outcomes in therapy are attributed to factors outside of the counseling relationship. For professional school counselors, two influential aspects "outside of counseling" include the systems involved in student's lives and the context or culture of the school and the student. An element that is perhaps unique to the professional school counselor role (as compared to other types of counselors or therapists) is that professional school counselors often have access to and can influence many of the factors "outside of counseling." In an ecological framework, this element is where a variety of helping services (consultation, collaboration, coordination, leadership, advocacy, and parent education) may be influential to outcomes in school counseling.

*Consider Multiple Systems, Culture, and School Context*

Most outcome studies published on school counseling examine a specific school or district sample, so it is important for professional school counselors to consider how to apply the research to their own individual context and students. Schools are stratified by a number of context issues including, but not limited to, structural factors (urban/rural, public/private, academic grouping, disability services), instructional factors (teacher expectations, qualifications, behavioral management), and relational factors (peer rejection, peer influence, school/class social dynamics) (Farmer & Farmer, 1999). All of these factors influence the outcomes of a professional school counselor's efforts to help students. For example, the way a professional school counselor helps a student who has a learning disability and exhibits behavioral problems may be differentially effective depending on whether the student is mainstreamed in the regular classroom or in a self-contained classroom. In the same way, school climate may dictate the effectiveness of a peer helping program.

The multiple systems involved in a student's life can reinforce or inhibit professional school counselor practice. Students do not live in a laboratory, nor do they operate only in one type of school. Although scientific research on professional school counselor intervention does not always account for multiple influences inside and outside of the school, professional school counselors can use their understanding of the school context.

Essential to both the school context and the student culture is the consideration of the developmental forces occurring in children and adolescents. Students experience a great deal of developmental change independent of professional school counselor intervention. For example, a professional school counselor group intervention to promote healthy body image will be greatly influenced by the developmental level of the participants. Whereas a mixed gender group of elementary school students may focus on generalized self-esteem, a gender- specific middle school group may focus on the messages of popular culture to women/girls. Although both of these groups would be described as a group intervention for personal/social development, the outcomes will be greatly influenced by the developmental stages and needs of the students.

Even as multiple systems and contexts are considered in determining interventions that work, professional school counselors also have a responsibility to serve all students in the school. Most of the research about effectiveness or best practices is centered on helping students who demonstrate problems. An effective professional school counselor, when selecting what works, should also consider the effectiveness of proactive activities targeted toward normal or optimal development.

*Implement Action Research on Your Own Developmental, Preventative, and Proactive Interventions*

At the point where much of the school counseling research leaves off, professional school counselors can research their own programs. Relevant, simple research designs may not immediately prove useful to the field of school counseling as a whole, but a wealth of information can be maintained by practicing professional school counselors about what works in their own schools. Piecing smaller studies together in a systematic way can go a long way to showing effective school counseling services (Myrick, 1984).

One particularly useful research design includes action research. Action research is varied, but is used for immediate, local needs and application rather than generalization of results (Allen, 1992). For example, a middle school counselor may choose to understand what interventions help English as Second Language (ESL) students feel connected and perform well academically in school. Determining a research design (e.g., comparison study), treatment or interventions (e.g., group vs. classroom guidance), data collection (e.g., connectedness measure, grades, and test scores), and data analysis (e.g., t-test between groups) may allow the professional school counselor to make an informed choice about providing services to ESL students. Collaborative designs with others (i.e., professional school counselor educators, educational or psychology professionals inside and outside of the school) also hold great promise. Many school-university partnerships produce fruitful research and provide both professional school counselors and university faculty a means for professional development.

## Summary/Conclusion

Several authors (Allen, 1996; Deck, Cecil, & Cobia, 1990) have suggested that professional school counselors have little interest in the research or science of school counseling or see it as beyond their responsibility. Although reforms and national models are useful, professional school counselors cannot establish or maintain an important role in the school without science to validate their presence. At the extreme, several states and districts may have already cut school counseling positions because they are viewed as ancillary services.

"The outcome-based knowledge is currently not, and may never be, refined to the point that it will dictate specific treatments for an individual client" (Sexton, 1996, p. 598). There is no exact study that will dictate how a professional school counselor can best help students. An idea of what works needs to be contextualized within the student, professional school counselor, school, family, and community framework. Selecting what works is also highly dependant on student needs. Making choices on what works will involve a combination of knowledge and use of current research, a commitment to actively researching what works, and continuing to be an inner-critic to choice of interventions.

> For additional resources on outcome research please consult Prout and DeMartino (1986), Sexton, Whiston, Bleuer, & Walz (1997), Whiston (2003), and Whiston and Sexton (1998).

## References


Allen, J. (1992). *Action-oriented research: Promoting school counseling advocacy and accountability*. (Report No. EDO-CG-92-11). Washington, D.C.: Office of Education Research and Improvement. (ERIC Document Reproduction Service No. ED 347477).

Baker, S., Swisher, J., Nadenichek, P., & Popowicz, C. (1984). Measured effects of primary prevention strategies.*The Personnel and Guidance Journal, 62*, 459-464.

Borders, L., & Drury, S. (1992). Comprehensive school counseling programs: A review for policymakers and practitioners. *Journal of Counseling and Development, 70*, 487-498.

Bundy, M., & Boser, J. (1987). Helping latchkey children: A group guidance approach. *School Counseling, 35*, 58-65.

Dahir, C. (2001). The National Standards for school counseling programs: Development and implementation. *Professional School Counseling, 4*, 320-327.

Deck, M., Cecila, J., & Cobia, D. (1990). School counselor research as perceived by ASCA leaders: Implications for the profession. *Elementary School Guidance and Counseling, 25*(1), 12-20.

Fairchild, T. (1993). Accountability practices of school counselors: 1990 National survey. *The School Counselor, 40*, 363-374.

Farmer, E., & Farmer, T. (1999). The role of schools in outcomes for youth: Implications for children's mental health services research. *Journal of Child and Family Studies,8*, 377-396.

Gelso, C. (1979). Research in counseling: Methodological and professional issues. *The Counseling Psychologist, 8*(3), 7-36.

Gerler, E. (1985). Elementary school counseling research and the classroom learning environment. *Elementary School Guidance & Counseling, 20,* 39-40.

Gerler, E., & Anderson, R. (1986). The effects of classroom guidance on children's success in school. *Journal of Counseling and Development, 65,* 78-81.

Gybers, N., & Henderson, P. (1994). *Developing and managing your school guidance program.* Alexandria, VA: American Counseling Association.

Gysbers, N. (1988). Major trends in career development theory and practice: Implications for industrial education and guidance personnel. *Journal of Industrial Teacher Education, 25,* 5-14.

Hagborg, W. (1993). Middle-school student satisfaction with group counseling: An initial study. *Journal for Specialists in Group Work, 18*(2), 80-85.

Hatch, T., & Bowers, J. (2002). The block to build on. *ASCA School Counselor, 39(*5), 12-19.

Kazdin, A. (1993). Psychotherapy for children and adolescents: Current progress and future research directions. *American Psychologist, 48,* 644-657.

Lambert, M. J. (1991). Introduction to psychotherapy research. In L. E. Beutler, & M. Crago (Eds.), *Psychotherapy Research: An international review of programmatic studies* (pp. 1-23).Washington, DC: American Psychological Association.

Lapan, R., Gysbers, N., & Sun, Y. (1997). The impact of more fully implemented guidance programs on the school experiences of high school students: A statewide evaluation study. *Journal of Counseling and Development, 75,* 292-302.

Martin, J., & Hoshmand, L. (1995). Research on psychological practice. In L. Hoshmand & J. Martin (Eds.), *Research as praxis: Lessons from programmatic research in therapeutic psychology* (pp. 48-80). New York: Teachers College Press.

Myrick, R. (1984). Beyond the issues of school counselor accountability. *Measurement and Evaluation in Counseling,16,* 218-222.

Myrick, R., Merhill, H., & Swanson, L. (1986). Changing students' attitudes through classroom guidance. *School Counselor, 33,* 244-252.

Nearpass, G. (1990). *Counseling and guidance effectiveness in North American high schools: A meta-analysis of the research findings* (Doctoral dissertation, University of Colorado at Boulder, 1989). Dissertation Abstracts, 49,1948-A.

Palmer, S., & Cochran, L. (1988). Parents as agents of career development. *Journal of Counseling Psychology, 35*(1), 71-76.

Prout, H., & DeMartino, A. (1986). A meta-analysis of school-based studies of psychotherapy. *Journal of School Psychology, 24,* 285-292.

Prout, S., & Prout, H. (1998). A meta-analysis of school-based studies of counseling and psychotherapy: An update. *Journal of School Psychology*, 121-136.

Sears, S. (1999). Transforming school counseling: Making a difference for students. *NASSP Bulletin, 83,* 47-53.

Sexton, T. L. (1996). The relevance of counseling outcome research: Current trends and practical implications. *Journal of Counseling and Development, 74,* 590-600.

Sexton, T.L. (1999). Evidence-based counseling: Implications for counseling practice, preparation, and professionalism. ERIC Document.

Sexton, T.L., Whiston, S.C., Bleuer, J.C., & Walz, G.R. (1997). *Integrating outcome research into counseling practice and training*. Alexandria, VA: American Counseling Association.

Sprinthall, N. (1981). A new model for research in the science of guidance and counseling. *The Personnel and Guidance Journal, 59,* 487-493.

St. Clair, K. (1989). Middle school counseling research: A resource for school counselors. *Elementary School Guidance and Counseling, 23,* 219-226.

Waehler, C., Kalodner, C., Wampold, B., & Lichtenberg, J. (2000). Empirically supported treatments (ESTs) in perspective: Implications for counseling psychology training. *The Counseling Psychologist, 28*, 657-671.

Whiston, S. (2003). Outcome research on professional school counseling services. In B. Erford (Ed.), *Transforming the school counseling profession.* Upper Saddle River, NJ:Merrill/ Prentice Hall.

Whiston, S., & Sexton, T. (1998). A review of school counseling outcome research: Implications for practice. *Journal of Counseling and Development, 76*, 412-426.

Wilson, N. (1986). Effects of a classroom guidance unit on sixth graders' examination performance. *Journal of Hispanic Education and Development, 25*(2), 70-79.

# Chapter 5

## Applying Outcome Research to School Counseling

*Tarrell Awe Agahe Portman*

### Preview

Education reform encourages data-driven intentionality in school counseling programs. Key factors in data-driven programs include measuring student successes and evaluating program effectiveness. These factors may be directly related to reliance on research. A framework for applying outcome-based research is presented.

Professional school counselors are responsible for school counseling program decisions which affect the development of students on a daily basis. Student development is systemic in nature, and problems may be manifested as the need for interventions in areas such as personal growth, career decision making, or attaining appropriate academic potential. These and other issues require professional school counselors to be knowledgeable of empirical evidence which is supportive of the primary or secondary interventions they select to use with students. This knowledge provides the foundation of accountability for the school counselor, the school counseling program, and ultimately the school district. This concept is the basis for applying outcome research in school counseling programs.

Comprehensive school counseling programs have been upheld as "results-based systems that construct essential counselor roles around critical student outcomes to be achieved by all students" (Lapan, 2001, p. 289). Effective professional school counselors rely on data-driven research in conducting on-going evaluation of student outcomes and seek out research prior to implementing interventions with students. When outcome research is applied within the school counseling program, counselor accountability and effectiveness is increased through the creation of data driven programs (Lapan, Gysbers, & Sun, 1997).

Outcomes-based research provides an approach for utilizing experimental or quasi-experimental research findings to address counseling efficacy (Heppner, Kivlighan, & Wampold, 1999; Perry, 1993). The conceptual diagram presented in Figure 1 offers a triadic framework for the application of outcomes research to the daily functioning of school counseling programs. The base of the triangle represents outcomes-based research. Student success is represented by the diagonal side of the triangle. The perpendicular side of the triangle represents the effectiveness of the school counseling program. The interior area of the triangle represents the degree to which interventions and service delivery are based upon outcomes-based research. Theoretically, *increased* reliance on outcomes-based research *increases* the effectiveness of the school counseling program, thus *increasing* individual student success.

This greater use of outcomes-based research to determine counselor practice facilitates student success with interventions such as small group or large group counseling, classroom guidance, individual planning, and system support. Tangible evidence of school counseling program effectiveness is provided through data collected on student successes and failures. Reporting the results of effective school counseling programs enhances the value of school counseling interventions while increasing accountability and the perceived worthiness of the program by community stakeholders. This requires professional school counselors to be intentional in their application of outcomes-based research.

**Figure 1. Conceptualization of Outcome-Based Research within Data-Driven School Counseling Programs (Portman)**

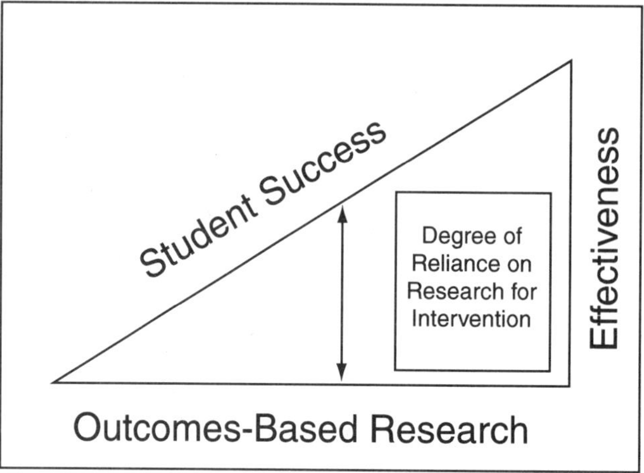


## Intentionality in Applying Outcomes-Based Research

*Intentionality* implies aiming at a goal, targeting an issue, and/or creating an action plan. For example, setting a goal that each freshman will begin a career portfolio in his/her first semester of high school, targeting peer refusal skills with 8th graders in a middle school, or planning a "red ribbon week" for an elementary building are all goals intended to increase student success. Each of the goals can be strengthened by incorporating empirically-based research in a rationale statement. The selection and implementation of interventions with students that have proven to be effective with other students in similar situations reinforces the intentionality of the professional school counselor. Therefore, students benefit from the professional school counselor's knowledge and awareness of research findings which support outcome results for specific interventions. Consider the following case:

> Jan is employed as the only counselor in a K-12 rural school with 450 students. Recently, Jan has identified eight girls, ages 15 – 18, who are involved in high risk relationships with friends, boyfriends, or family members. Jan is considering the best intervention approach for meeting the needs of these students. The school counseling program has limited time allotted for individual counseling sessions. A school counseling peer at a neighboring school remembered reading a research article from *Professional School Counseling* (Zinck & Littrell, 2000) that may be helpful to Jan. Using an electronic library search on the Internet, Jan finds the article. She is amazed at the similarities between the research participants and the girls she has been seeing on an individual basis. The outcome results of the research study indicate group counseling with at-risk adolescent girls is effective in promoting changes in attitudes and personal relationships. Now, Jan has a foundation to help her in selecting appropriate interventions with these students. Her rationale for group counseling is supported by the research findings and can be presented to the principal.

In this case scenario, the professional school counselor consulted with a peer about possible interventions. Both the consultation and the action taken to locate the research-based article were intentional and led the professional school counselor to a possible delivery strategy to help these students. In the process, the professional school counselor increased her professional awareness of other outcomes-based research for working with at-risk secondary students that dealt with counselor characteristics (Esters & Ledoux, 2001). Intentionality in this scenario lead to greater potential impact on student success. If Jan had not consulted with a peer, the interventions she selected may or may not have been effective for the students. Her rationale for selecting the interventions would not have been based on empirical evidence and therefore may not be acceptable to her principal or community.

## Suggestions for Incorporating Outcomes-Based Research

Practicality in the everyday life of professional school counselors requires efficiency of time in meeting the needs of students. In reality, a professional school counselor is pulled in numerous directions and often must select interventions quickly. Six suggestions are provided in the next section to help professional school counselors incorporate outcomes-based research: 1) Establishing goals; 2) Identification of outcomes-based research resources; 3) Gathering and managing resources; 4) Selecting prevention and intervention strategies based on research; 5) Comparing populations; and 6) Evaluating findings.

### *Establishing Goals*

Goals that encompass the use of outcomes-based research are established through the school counseling profession, viewed through the lenses of the local school district, and made public in the school counseling program's mission statements. Mission statements may include wording similar to the following:

- Enhance student achievement.
- Identify best practices in school counseling.
- Advocate for retaining or reforming school policies.
- Promote professionalism.
- Highlight school counseling program accountability.

Goals can be written acknowledging the importance of the school counseling program's reliance on outcomes-based research and data-driven objectives. A sample goal statement might read as follows:

> Student achievement will be enhanced by school counseling that centers on outcomes-based research related to the influence of a positive school climate on the academic performance of middle school students.

This type of goal statement increases the visibility of research as a foundational component of the school counseling program.

### *Identification of Outcomes-Based Research Resources*

Application of outcomes-based research within a school counseling setting involves the professional school counselor identifying available research resources. Most research is circulated through professional journals in the form of research articles. However, a variety of papers, monographs, and research reports may be obtained from places such as ERIC or professional conference proceedings. For the majority of professional school counselors, journal articles and electronic databases are the most accessible tools for identifying outcomes-based research findings.

A significant benefit of professional membership in the American School Counselor Association and the American Counseling Association is receiving the professional journals relevant to the counseling profession. Current research and evaluation of programs and interventions are presented in these journals. Reviewing the tables of contents of journals will help the professional school counselor develop an awareness of outcomes-based research. Systematically reading the research articles for findings will increase the professional school counselor's knowledge base and prevent professional stagnation. For professional school counselors, *Professional School Counseling* is considered the primary source of outcomes-based research.

Another resource for gathering outcomes-based research is through attending professional development workshops. These workshops may be presented at state, regional, or national levels. The intentional counselor will particularly seek workshops which present research findings related to counseling efficacy or program effectiveness.

*Gathering and Managing Resources*

Obviously, professional school counselors cannot use resources they do not have. For this reason, it may be necessary for them to gather and manage outcomes-based research information relevant to their school populations' needs. At the elementary level, for example, maintaining a file on outcomes-based interventions with children of divorce is more appropriate than maintaining a file on job placement or transitioning from high school to work. Organization of outcomes-based research in topical files, whether paper copies or electronic copies, can be beneficial in building a solid foundation of reliance on research findings. An ongoing electronic bibliography is an example of gathering and managing resources. An example is provided at the end of this chapter.

*Selecting Prevention and Intervention Strategies Based On Research*

School counseling programs require planning and implementation for proactive and reactive service delivery. The optimum situation would be for professional school counselors to provide prevention activities relevant to the skills needed in all aspects of each individual child's life; however, this is not a utopian world. Therefore, professional school counselors can be intentional in creating developmentally appropriate program components which are preventive in nature. Outcomes-based research should be used and properly cited in curriculum plans, system-wide programs, individual planning, and group counseling. Individual counseling research related to common concerns of students in the school can also be acknowledged and collected prior to counseling sessions. For instance, elementary school children often exhibit adjustment issues when transitioning to a new school or new family situation.

The professional school counselor can have specific activities or strategies based on outcomes research prepared and accessible in the counseling office to work individually with these children. However, caution is required not to develop a "one size fits all" mentality. The individual students or population groups served may have varying needs based on ability, cultural background, or socioeconomic status. School counselor awareness of the population or individual dynamics in their schools is necessary when selecting outcomes-based research as a foundation for selection of interventions.

*Comparing Populations Found In Outcomes-Based Research*

Not all empirically-based outcomes research can be generalized to every school counseling situation. When applying outcomes-based research, the context (people, place, and procedures) of the research setting and the school setting must both be considered. First, determine the characteristics of the people who participated in the research study. Were the research participants similar in age, gender, grade level, and ability level to the students targeted for intervention? Second, compare the context in which the study took place. Did the study take place in a similar school setting or was it a mental health setting? And third, what procedures did the researchers use to determine if the outcomes were effective? Answering these questions may help the professional school counselor determine if the outcomes from the research study are *generalizable* (meaning the similarities in population are greater than the differences) or *transferable* (meaning there is enough information to warrant implementing the intervention in the school setting with appropriate monitoring and continued data collection). Monitoring through data collection brings the use of outcomes-based research full circle and stands as the basis for incorporating action research into the school counseling program.

*Evaluating Findings After Outcomes-Based Research Has Been Implemented*

Simply using outcomes-based research in a school counseling program is not sufficient for determining student success. Ongoing data collection is necessary to determine if applying outcomes-based research in a particular situation was effective. This requires evaluating or engaging in action research within one's school counseling program. Action research can be formal or informal and may be a joint endeavor. As leaders and advocates in the profession, intentional professional school counselors will develop skills and establish relationships with school counseling researchers to add new outcomes-based research to the field of counseling. This continues the empirical evidence cycle leading to validating school counseling program effectiveness. Whiston (2003) provides an excellent overview of outcomes-based research specifically targeting school counseling services. Her overview is organized under three headings related to the effectiveness of professional school counseling: 1) student benefits obtained as a result of school counseling interventions; 2) effective service delivery methods; and 3) characteristics of effective school counseling programs.

Outcomes-based research disaggregates into three methodological categories; longitudinal reviews, qualitative inquiry, and quantitative analysis. Longitudinal reviews provide a historical research perspective and encompass school counseling literature published over an extended period of time. The cumulative reflections from these studies indicate the effectiveness of school counseling. Examples of such reviews include compilation of works reviewing the professional literature related to school counseling interventions on student academic and personal/social competencies (Borders & Drury, 1992; Whiston & Sexton, 1998).

Qualitative inquiry involves the gathering of data through interviews, document reviews, and examination of personal reflections (student, faculty, school counselor, etc.). These findings may focus on specific populations and the effects of school counseling interventions related to a particular group of students (Gerler, 1985; St. Claire, 1989; Wilson, 1986). Some examples of this would include Jackson and White's (2000) study on referrals to the professional school counselor. This qualitative study found there was a disadvantage to using a medical model approach in school counseling programs and encouraged professional school counselors to examine their own assumptions about helping relationships with students.

Research that evaluates findings from outcomes-based school counseling investigations using quantitative methodology is also present in the literature. For example, Kraus and Hughey (1999) examined the impact of a career intervention with 1,625 high school students in the Midwest. Findings indicated there were no differences between the two groups in the experiment on career indecision; however, gender made a difference in career decision-making self-efficacy - an important finding for selecting interventions in the career domain in school counseling programs.

## Summary/Conclusion

Professional school counselors are required to make decisions regarding interventions with students on a daily basis. These decisions promote the personal, academic and career aspirations of students. Therefore, these decisions must be supported by empirically-based research to be effective. School counseling reform focuses on data-driven responses within educational settings. Thus, school counseling programs are accountable to students, parents, faculty, administration, boards of education, business leaders, and the school counseling profession. The conceptual diagram presented in this chapter provides professional school counselors with a common language and framework for applying outcomes-based research in school counseling programs. Professional school counselors are intentional in providing help to students by incorporating outcomes-based research into their programs.

## Bibliography on Outcomes-Based Research


Constantine, M. G., & Gainor, K. A. (2001). Emotional intelligence and empathy: Their relation to multicultural counseling knowledge and awareness. *Professional School Counseling, 5*, 131-137.

Kottman, T., & Ashby, J. (2000). Perfectionistic children and adolescents: Implications for school counselors. *Professional School Counseling, 3*, 182-188.

Krentz, A., & Arthur, N. (2001). Counseling culturally diverse students with eating disorders. *Journal of College Student Psychotherapy, 15*, 7-21.

Lapan, R. T., Kardash, C. M., & Turner, S. (2002). Empowering students to become self-regulated learners. *Professional School Counseling, 5*, 257-265.

Lehr, R., & Sumarah, J. (2002). Factors impacting the successful implementation of comprehensive guidance and counseling programs in Nova Scotia. *Professional School Counseling, 5*, 292-297.

Littrell, J. M., & Peterson, J. (2001). Facilitating systemic change using the MRI problem-solving approach: One school's experience. *Professional School Counseling, 5*, 27-33.

Prout, S. M., & Prout, H. T. (1998). A meta-analysis of school-based outcome studies of counseling and psychotherapy: An update. *Journal of School Psychology, 36*, 121-136.

Rowell, L., & Hong, E. (2002). The role of school counselors in homework intervention. *Professional School Counseling, 5*, 285-291.

Sexton, T. L., Whiston, S. C., Bleuer, J. C., & Walz, G. R. (1997). *Integrating outcome research into counseling practice and training*. Alexandria, VA: American Couneling Association.

Tobler, N. S., & Stratton, H. H. (1997). Effectiveness of school-based drug prevention programs: A meta-analysis of the research. *Journal of Primary Prevention, 18*(1), 71-128.

Wagner, E. F., Dinklage, S. C., Cudworth, C., & Vyse, J. (1999). A preliminary evaluation of the effectiveness of a standardized student assistance program. *Substance Use & Misuse, 34*, 1571-1584.

Wahl, K. H., & Blackhurst, A. (2000). Factors affecting the occupational and educational aspirations of children and adolescents. *Professional School Counseling, 3*, 367-374.

Whiston, S. C., & Sexton, T. L. (1998). A review of school counseling outcome research: Implications for practice. *Journal of Counseling & Development, 76*, 412-426.

Yeh, C. J. (2001). An exploratory study of school counselors' experiences with and perceptions of Asian-American students. *Professional School Counseling, 4*, 349-356.

## References


Esters, I., & Ledoux, C. (2001). At-risk high school students' preferences for counselor characteristics. *Professional School Counseling, 4*, 165-170.

Gerler, E. R. (1985). Elementary school counseling research and the classroom learning environment. *Elementary School Guidance and Counseling, 20,* 39-40.

Heppner, P., Kivlighan, D. M., Jr., & Wampold, B. E. (1999). *Research design in counseling* (2nd ed.). Belmont, CA: Wadsworth Publishing Company.

Jackson, S. A., & White, J. (2000). Referrals to the school counselor: A qualitative study. *Professional School Counseling, 3,* 277-286.

Kraus, L. J., & Hughey, K. F. (1999). The impact of an intervention on career decision-making self-efficacy and career indecision. *Professional School Counseling, 2,* 384-390.

Lapan, R. T. (2001). Results-based comprehensive guidance and counseling programs: A framework for planning and evaluation. *Professional School Counseling, 4*, 289-299.

Lapan, R. T., Gysbers, N. C., & Sun, Y. (1997). The impact of more fully implemented guidance programs on the school experiences of high school students: A statewide evaluation study. *Journal of Counseling and Development, 75,* 292-302.

Perry, N. S. (1993). School counseling. In J. C. Bleuer & G. R. Walz (Eds.), *Counselor efficacy: Assessing and using counseling outcomes research* (pp. 37-49). Ann Arbor, MI: ERIC Counseling and Personnel Services Clearinghouse.

St. Claire, K. L. (1989). Middle school counseling research: A resource for school counselors. *Elementary School Guidance and Counseling, 23,* 219-226.

Whiston, S. C. (2003). Outcomes research on school counseling. In B. T. Erford, *Transforming the school counseling profession* (pp. 435-447). Columbus, OH: Merrill/Prentice-Hall.

Wilson, N. S. (1986). Counselor interventions with low-achieving and underachieving elementary, middle, and high school students: A review of literature. *Journal of Counseling and Development, 64,* 628-634.

Zinck, K., & Littrell, J. M. (2000). Action research shows group counseling effective with at-risk adolescent girls. *Professional School Counseling, 4*, 50-59.

# *Chapter 6*

# Codes of Ethics and Ethical Issues for Professional School Counselors

*Lynn Linde*

## Preview

One of the hardest challenges facing all counselors today, and particularly professional school counselors, is how to determine the best and most appropriate way of working with students who present a myriad of complex problems. While federal and state laws apply in some situations, many of the issues with which counselors deal fall into a gray zone. This means that there is no clear guideline for handling the situation. Fortunately, the American Counseling Association (ACA), the American School Counselor Association (ASCA), and the National Board for Certified Counselors (NBCC) have developed codes of ethics that provide guidelines for ethical behavior. Each of the sections of these codes applies to different situations that counselors face.

Whenever supervisors for school counseling programs or professional counselor associations survey members regarding topics for professional development, ethics and legal issues always rank at or near the top of the list. Schools and school systems are no longer immune from the litigious society in which they operate. Parents are much faster to complain and hire lawyers when they feel that their rights have been violated or when they question the way the school or a staff member has handled a situation. Professional school counselors often feel overwhelmed by the variety of problems the students with whom they work present each day and struggle to find the best—legal or ethical—way to work with students. They strive continually to balance the needs of the students with the needs of the school or family.

Some situations are clearly defined by federal or state law or by local policy; however, many are not. Local boards of education are hesitant to pass policies or procedures for controversial issues. And it is likely if they did create such policies, they may significantly limit the ability of professional school counselors to operate without informing parents about everything. Fortunately, the professional associations for counselors have developed codes of ethics and standards that provide a framework for professional conduct. In order to understand the applicability of the codes of ethics to professional school counselors, it is helpful to understand something about the organizations that create the codes.

## Professional Associations

The American Counseling Association (ACA) is the professional association for all counselors. The mission of the association is to promote public confidence and trust in the counseling profession. Organizationally, ACA is a partnership of associations representing professional counselors who enhance human development. It is comprised of 18 divisions that represent specific work settings or interest areas within the field of counseling; 56 state or affiliate branches, which are divided into 4 regions representing major geographical areas; and several organizational affiliates, which enhance member services. Through its activities and entities, ACA influences all aspects of professional counseling. These areas include the credentialing of counselors and the accreditation of counselor education programs, developing and promulgating ethical standards, offering professional development, offering professional resources and services, and influencing public policy and legislation.

ACA has 14 standing committees that address much of the professional business of the association. One of those committees is the Ethics Committee, which is responsible for updating the ethical standards for the association and investigating and adjudicating ethical complaints. When joining ACA, one must sign a statement agreeing to abide by the Code of Ethics and Standards of Practice. Additional information about ethics, ethical issues, and professional behavior is available through a number of services and resources offered by the association. ACA and its entities offer a variety of training and professional development opportunities. Some of these are offered at state, regional, and national conferences; others are workshops and learning institutes offered throughout the year.

The journals published by ACA and its divisions provide current research, professional practices, and other information valuable to the practicing counselor. Articles and information about professional behavior is frequently covered in these sources. ACA's monthly newsletter, *Counseling Today*, includes valuable information about general counseling topics as well as covering special topical issues. ACA publishes many books about counseling and current trends and topics in the field; these are frequently used as texts in counseling courses. One example is the *ACA Ethical Standards Casebook* (5$^{th}$ ed.) (1996) written by Herlihy and Corey. This book is a valuable resource for all professional counselors and is an excellent addition to the *Code of Ethics* (ACA, 1995). ACA staff is available for consultation on a variety of issues, including legal and ethical questions. In summary, ACA touches all counselors' lives, from the training they receive, the requirements they must achieve to be credentialed, the way in which they conduct themselves across all counseling specialty areas, and the professional development in which they engage. Further information about the American Counseling Association is available on their webpage: http://www.counseling.org.

The American School Counselor Association (ASCA) became a division of ACA in 1953. During the past few years it has become a more autonomous organization, but still remains a division. ASCA supports professional school counselors' focus on the academic, personal/social, and career development of all students. According to ASCA (2003), its members assist in the growth and development of each student and "uses his/her highly specialized skills to protect the interests of the counselee within the structure of the school setting" (p. 1). ASCA targets its efforts to professional development, publications and other resources, research, and advocacy for school counseling.

The structure of ASCA is similar to that of ACA. ASCA has a number of committees, one of which is the Ethics Committee. This committee is responsible for the development of the *Ethical Standards for School Counselors,* the code of ethics for professional school counselors that will be discussed in the next section. ASCA sponsors a national conference and offers a number of professional development activities for professional school counselors. One of the topics covered at some of these events concerns ethics and professional behavior. More information about the American School Counselor Association is available on their webpage: http://www.schoolcounselor.org.

The National Board for Certified Counselors (NBCC) began as a corporate partner of ACA and is now an autonomous organization. While the link between ACA and NBCC remains strong, it was necessary to separate the certifying entity from ACA to eliminate any potential conflicts of interest. Headquartered in Greensboro, NC, NBCC is the only national credentialing organization for professional counselors. All other licenses and certifications for counselors are obtained through state agencies and local organizations. NBCC has established the National Certified Counselor (NCC) credential and several specialty area certifications. Counselors must pass the National Counselor Exam (NCE) as part of the process to become nationally certified. Many states use the NCE as the exam required for professional counselor licensure or certification; and in some states, counselors may be eligible for certification by the state board of education if they are an NCC. The NBCC has also developed a code of ethics that must be followed by counselors who hold this certification. More information about this association and certification is available on their webpage: http://www.nbcc.org.

## Purposes of Ethical Standards

Ethical standards are usually developed by professional associations to guide the behavior of a specific group of professionals. According to Herlihy and Corey (1996), ethical standards serve three purposes: educate members about sound ethical conduct, provide a mechanism for accountability, and serve as a means for improving professional practice. Codes of ethics are updated periodically to ensure their relevance and appropriateness and all associations insure stakeholder input in the process. Codes of ethics are based on generally accepted norms, beliefs, customs and values (Fischer & Sorenson, 1996). Codes of ethics also serve another important function—they protect and educate the public about the standards for the behavior they should expect from counselors.

The ACA *Code of Ethics* and *Standards of Practice* (1995) are based on five general moral principles (Herlihy & Corey, 1996) which guide counselors' behavior. Autonomy refers to the clients' ability to choose and to make decisions about their behavior and choices for themselves. Nonmaleficence means to do no harm. Counselors always need to ensure that they operate in ways that neither result in harm nor potentially result in harm. Beneficence is the opposite of nonmaleficence; it means to always promote that which serves the growth and good of their clients. Justice refers to fairness in counselors' relationships and includes fair treatment and consideration of clients. The last principle is fidelity, which refers to honesty in the counselor-client relationship, honoring one's commitment to the client and establishing an accepting relationship.

Within ACA there are multiple codes of ethics. ACA has a *Code of Ethics* (1995) to which members must adhere. Additionally several divisions, specifically the American School Counselor Association (ASCA), the American Rehabilitation Counseling Association (ARCA) and the International Association for Marriage and Family Counseling (IAMFC) have their own codes. The Association for Specialists in Group Work (ASGW) has developed *Best Practice Guidelines* to supplement ACA's Code of Ethics.

These codes of ethics parallel ACA's *Code of Ethics*, but speak more directly to the specialty area. For example, ASCA's *Code of Ethics* discusses what ethical behavior consists of in a school setting. Additionally, in 1999 the ACA Governing Council approved guidelines for the use of electronic communication over the Internet, such as online counseling. These guidelines also supplement the ACA *Code of Ethics*.

Many counselors belong to multiple organizations, some of which have their own code of ethics. Professional counselors may also hold credentials from organizations or state credentialing boards that either have their own code of ethics or require that a particular code of ethics be followed. It is sometimes confusing and difficult to discern which code takes precedence. While all professional counselors need to make that decision for themselves, there are two general guiding principles. First, in what type of setting is the professional counselor practicing and is there a designated code that applies or is required for that setting? Second, what is the professional counselor position in that setting? The reality is that all codes of ethics are very similar, are based on the same general principles, and serve the same general functions.

All codes of ethics concern behaving in an appropriate and professional manner, always functioning in the best interests of the client or student, and always practicing within the scope of one's education, training and experience. Counselors who behave ethically should not be concerned about multiple codes of ethics.

## ACA *Code of Ethics* and *Standards of Practice*

The ACA *Code of Ethics* (ACA, 1995) delineated the responsibilities of professional counselors towards their clients, their colleagues, their workplaces, and themselves by describing the ideal standards for counselors' behavior. All ACA members are required to abide by the *Code of Ethics* and *Standards of Practice*. Any violation of ethical behavior will result in action taken against the member. Unfortunately, there is little action that can be taken by ACA against professional counselors who are not members. However, as these are the standards of the profession, all professional counselors are held to these standards, regardless of their professional association membership status. Failure to be familiar with, use, or comprehend the *Code of Ethics* is not a legally valid excuse for unethical or inappropriate behavior. In the absence of any law or written policy or procedure, courts will use the *Code of Ethics* as the standard for all professional counselors.

The *Code of Ethics* (ACA, 1995) is divided into eight areas:

- Section A: The Counseling Relationship – covers all areas related to the nature of the relationship with the clients. It includes the following subtopics: client welfare, client rights, clients served by others, personal needs and values, dual relationships, sexual intimacies with clients, multiple clients, group work, fees and bartering, termination and referral, and computer technology. In general counselors must always put the best interests of their clients first and ensure that clients understand the extent and limitations of counseling.
- Section B: Confidentiality – covers all areas related to the confidentiality rights of the client(s) and discusses the limits to confidentiality. It includes the following subtopics: right to privacy, groups and families, minor or incompetent clients, records, research and training, and consultation.
- Section C: Professional Responsibility – covers counselors' responsibilities towards their clients, themselves, other professionals and the public. It includes the following subtopics: standards of knowledge, professional competence, advertising and soliciting clients, credentials, public responsibility, and responsibility to other professionals.
- Section D: Relationships with Other Professionals – covers work setting issues and includes the following subtopics: relationships with employers and employees, consultation, fees for referrals, and subcontractor arrangements.
- Section E: Evaluation, Assessment, and Interpretation – covers standards related to the assessment of clients, the counselor's skills, and appropriateness of assessment. It includes the following subtopics: general appraisal issues, competence to use and interpret tests, informed consent for appraisal, releasing information, proper diagnosis of mental disorders, test selection, conditions of test administration, diversity in testing, test scoring and interpretation, test security, obsolete tests and outdated test results, and test construction.
- Section F: Teaching, Training, and Supervision – covers issues related to training counselors and counselor education programs. It covers the following subtopics: counselor educators and trainers, counselor education and training programs, and

students and supervisees.

- Section G: Research and Publication – covers issues related to the ethical treatment of subjects and ethical research procedures. Subtopics include research responsibilities, informed consent, reporting results, and publication.
- Section H: Resolving Ethical Issues – covers the procedure professional counselors should follow when they suspect another counselor of unethical behavior. Subtopics include: knowledge of standards, suspected violations, and cooperation with the ethics committee.

The *Standards of Practice* are the minimal behavioral expectations for the Code of Ethics. Each of the eight sections of the Code of Ethics has at least one parallel standard that describes what that ethical behavior would actually look like in practice. There are 51 *Standards of Practice.* Many counselors find this section very helpful because it is more concrete than the *Code of Ethics.*

*Guidelines for Internet Counseling*

As previously mentioned, the Governing Council of ACA approved guidelines for the use of electronic communications, including online counseling, in response to the growing use of technology in counseling. These guidelines are intended to be used in conjunction with the *Code of Ethics* and *Standards of Practice.* The guidelines cover confidentiality, specifically privacy information; the limitations concerning the use of technology in counseling; informational notices; client waivers; records of electronic communications; the electronic transfer of client information; the on-line counseling relationship and its appropriateness; counseling plans; continuing coverage; boundaries of competence; and minor or incompetent clients. This is an area that is still relatively new and counselors can expect to see continued discussion about the use of technology in counseling. Further information can be found in two recent publications co-published by the American Counseling Association and the ERIC Clearinghouse on Counseling and Student Services, *Cybercounseling and Cyberlearning: New Strategies for the Millennium* Bloom & Walz, 2000) and *Cybercounseling & Cyberlearning: An Encore* (Bloom & Walz, 2004).

## ASCA Ethical Standards for School Counselors

ASCA has developed a parallel set of ethical standards that specifically address professional school counseling. As described by ASCA (2003), the *Ethical Standards for School Counselors* is based on ten tenets that delineate each person's right to respect and dignity, self-direction and self-development, choice and responsibility, and privacy and adherence to all aspects of confidentiality. As in the ACA standards, these standards discuss putting the student's best interests first, treating each student as an individual and with respect, involving parents as appropriate, maintaining one's expertise through on-going professional development and learning, and behaving professionally and ethically. A summary of each of the eight sections follows.

- Section A: Responsibilities to Students – covers the professional school counselor's responsibilities to treat each student as a unique individual; maintain confidentiality as appropriate in the relationship; develop counseling plans; make appropriate referrals; utilize appropriate evaluation and assessment techniques, information, and technology; and ensure the welfare of students in peer helper programs.
- Section B: Responsibilities to Parents – covers parents' rights and responsibilities regarding the professional school counselor's behavior and confidentiality.
- Section C: Responsibilities to Colleagues and Professional Associates – covers relationships with other professionals, including sharing information.

- Section D: Responsibilities to the School and Community – covers the professional school counselor's responsibility to identify any situations in the work that may be adverse for students, only working in settings for which qualified, assisting with developing programs to meet students' needs, and working with outside groups and agencies.
- Section E: Professional Competence – covers the professional school counselors' responsibility for maintaining their professional growth and multicultural skills and monitoring their effectiveness.
- Section F: Responsibilities to the Profession – covers ethical behavior and involvement with professional associations.
- Section G: Maintenance of Standards – covers the process for dealing with concerns about potential ethical violations.
- Section H: Resources – lists a number of resources for professional school counselors to increase their knowledge and information.

One question that professional school counselors frequently ask is what should be done when it appears that laws and ethical standards are in conflict. Both laws and ethics are based on the same standards generally accepted by society. However, there are some differences. Laws are written into statute and therefore carry sanctions for failure to follow them. Usually the most significant penalty an association can impose on a professional counselor is to revoke membership. Both laws and ethical standards are created to protect the public or society by outlining behavioral expectations for the practitioners. When laws and ethical standards conflict with each other, the professional counselor must attempt to resolve the issue. Since penalties are associated with breaking laws, professional school counselors will generally choose the legal course of action, assuming doing so does not harm the client. Ethical standards recognize that laws, policies, and procedures must be followed and recommend that professional school counselors advocate changes to any requirements that are not in the best interests of their clients.

## Summary/Conclusion

One of the most important sources of information for professional school counselors to use in their practice to ensure appropriate behavior is the code of ethics from professional associations. ACA, ASCA, and NBCC have all developed codes of ethics that cover counselors' responsibilities to themselves, their clients or students, colleagues, other staff in their workplace, and communities in which they work. Counselors must become familiar with the specifics of which code they deem most appropriate for them and implement its standards in their practice. When professional school counselors behave ethically, they ensure quality services to their students and limit the possibility of getting into legal difficulty.

## References

American Counseling Association. (1995). *ACA code of ethics.* Alexandria, VA: Author.

American School Counselor Association. (2003). *Ethical standards for school counselors.* Retrieved on January 30, 2003 from http:/www.schoolcounselor.org.

Bloom, J. W., & Walz, G. R. (Eds.) (2000). *Cybercounseling and cyberlearning: Strategies for the millennium.* Alexandria, VA: American Counseling Association.

Bloom, J. W., & Walz, G. R. (Eds.) (2004). *Cybercounseling and cyberlearning: An encore.* Greensboro, NC: CAPS Press.

Herlihy, B., & Corey, G. (1996). *ACA ethical standards casebook* (5th ed.). Alexandria, VA: American Counseling Association.

# Chapter 7

## Ethical and Legal Considerations for Students, Parents, and Professional School Counselors

*Carolyn Stone*

### Preview

This chapter discusses the rights and responsibilities of minors and their parents and the implications of these rights on the professional school counselor's work. Ethical codes, federal statutes, state laws, and court cases that involve student and parental rights are examined. Addressed are the complications for professional school counselors as they work to protect students' rights while remaining vigilant that their obligations extend beyond the minor student to their parents.

The legal and ethical complexities of working with minors in schools require that professional school counselors remain vigilant as to the rights and responsibilities of minors and their parents and the implications of these rights on the counselor's work. The legal and ethical landscape in a school is complicated as a professional school counselor's obligation extends beyond the minor student to the parents who have considerable rights. Private and agency counselors who work with minors usually do so because parents seek their help. Students are sent to school for academics so the dynamics are quite different when they show up at the professional school counselor's door through teacher or self-referral. A professional school counselor's multiplicity of responsibility to parents, students, administrators, teachers, and others in a setting designed to deliver academic instruction complicates the legal and ethical world of school counseling (Arthur & Swanson, 1993; Fisher & Sorenson, 1996; Remley & Herlihy, 2001; Stone, 2001).

The very nature and function of school (i.e., to provide a free and appropriate quality education) creates immediate conflict when a student seeks a professional school counselor's help for emotional or social needs. When a student approaches a professional school counselor without parental knowledge or consent, immediate tension arises between the student's right to privacy and the parents' right to be the guiding voice in their child's life. Generally, the younger the child, the more rights are vested in the parents. The conflict between a parent's right to be informed as to what is happening in the child's personal life and the child's need and right to privacy is a decided challenge for professional school counselors who are charged with protecting the rights of both students and parents (Arthur & Swanson, 1993; Fisher & Sorenson, 1996; Remley & Herlihy, 2001; Stone, 2001).

This chapter examines some of the ethical codes, federal statutes, laws, and court cases that involve student and parental rights and should be augmented by some of the texts that address the legal rights of students and parents and ethical behavior of professional school counselors. Remley and Herlihy (2001), Fisher and Sorenson (1996), and other authors (see reference list) have texts that more thoroughly address legal and ethical issues. Professional school counselors are encouraged to also attend legal and ethical workshops and university courses to increase their comfort level and competence in student and parental rights. Consulting with other professionals and seeking guidance is paramount when addressing issues of student and parental rights.

*Ethical Codes*

The American School Counselor Association (ASCA) *Code of Ethics and Standards of Practice* (1998) for professional school counselors is an attempt by the profession to standardize professional practice for the purpose of protecting students, parents, and the professional school counselor. ASCA's *Ethical Standards* are a guide to help meet the needs of individual situations, but are rarely appropriate for rote application, as it is the context of the dilemma that determines appropriate action.

It is only the professional school counselor, in consultation with other professionals, who can determine how to apply an ASCA ethical code to further the best interest of the student. "Codes are not intended to be a blueprint that removes the need for judgment and ethical reasoning" (Welfel & Lipsitz, 1983, p. 6).

Standards A and B of the ASCA *Ethical Standards* (1998) give professional school counselors guidance in respecting students while still encouraging counselors to accept their obligations to parents. Confidentiality for students is an area that is tough to negotiate while protecting both student and parental rights. Confidentiality is a cornerstone of individual counseling and facilitates a trusting relationship between students and professional school counselors. The ASCA code forwards the philosophy that professional school counselors have a primary obligation and loyalty to students. However, confidentiality is far from absolute for minors in a school setting. Parental rights must also be considered in any value-laden work, such as individual counseling, that a professional school counselor does with a student. Parents are continually vested by our courts with legal rights to be the guiding voice in their children's lives (Bellotti v. Baird, 1979; H. L. v. Matheson, 1982).

Standard A.1. discusses informed consent and instructs professional school counselors to give the meaning and limits of confidentiality in developmentally appropriate terms when a student enters into a counseling relationship. The professional school counselor explains that he/she will try to keep confidences except when the student is a danger to self or others, the student or parent requests that information be revealed, or a court orders a counselor to disclose information.

Standard A.2. explains that the professional school counselor must understand that loyalty to students is at the heart of the profession and that professional school counselors must provide a safe and secure environment in which trust can be established and maintained. Professional school counselors must keep information related to counseling services confidential unless disclosure is in the best interest of students, or is required by law.

Standard B.1. requires that the professional school counselor respect the inherent rights and responsibilities of parents for their children and endeavors to establish, as appropriate, a collaborative relationship with parents to facilitate the student's maximum development. Professional school counselors must be sensitive to cultural and social diversity among families and recognize that all parents, custodial and non-custodial, are vested with certain rights and responsibilities for the welfare of their children by virtue of their role and according to law.

Standard B.2. instructs professional school counselors to: 1) inform parents of the counselor's role with emphasis on the confidential nature of the counseling relationship between counselor and counselee; 2) provide parents with accurate, comprehensive, and relevant information in an objective and caring manner as is appropriate and consistent with ethical responsibilities to the counselee; and 3) make reasonable efforts to honor the wishes of parents and guardians concerning information that he/she may share regarding the counselee.

Codes give professional school counselors guidance in their ethical responsibility to students and parents but do not propose or attempt to provide complete answers. Ethics are situational and have to be considered in context of institutional and community standards, school board policy, and the circumstances surrounding each individual ethical dilemma. It is ultimately the responsibility of the professional school counselor to determine the appropriate response for individual students who put their trust in the security of the counseling relationship (Stone, 2001).

*Students' Rights and Responsibilities*

The legal status of minors is complicated. Salo and Shumate (1993), in the American Counseling Association (ACA) Legal Series, discussed the difficulties of working with minor students in schools and pointed out the inconsistencies in juvenile and tort law.

> Minors generally cannot be bound by their contracts, but they can be held liable for intentional and negligent injuries inflicted on others. Once minors reach teenage years and display increasing capacity for rational decision making, both the common law and statutory law recognize this capacity by providing more legal autonomy for minors in carefully prescribed areas. (pp. 73-74)

Minors are emancipated or free from parental or guardian control when they reach the age of 18, enter the military, marry, or are declared emancipated by the Circuit Court. Emancipated minors do not enjoy all the rights of the age of majority. For example, they cannot buy, sell, or consume alcohol until they reach the age of 21. These inconsistencies affect the professional school counselors' ability to rely on clearly stated principles of legal policy.

Students' rights and responsibilities are far reaching and differ by states (consult your state's statutes). However, in most states there are similar student responsibilities while on school grounds or under school supervision. Students must avoid unlawful activity, including sexual behavior, using profanity, drinking alcohol, gambling, using dangerous drugs or tobacco, or causing damage or injury to persons or property. Infractions may result in suspension, expulsion, or financial restitution. Students and their parents or guardians are liable for damages they cause to persons or property of the school district, and for all property such as books that have been lent to them and not returned (Florida s233.47, 2000).

What happens when a student gets involved in the Juvenile Justice System? The Juvenile Justice System (JJS) is a term devoted to a number of legal entities, such as the Juvenile Division of the Circuit Court and the State Attorney's Office, designed to address issues for youth less than 18 years of age. Juvenile Court is a special branch of the Circuit Court whose judges hear cases in which minors are believed to have violated the law (delinquency) or when they need help because of family or personal problems (dependency).

When a student becomes part of the Juvenile Justice System, his/her case may be handled judicially or non-judicially. The State Attorney decides whether or not to handle a minor's case judicially or non-judicially, which means the case may be dismissed, go to Juvenile Arbitration, or be referred to a diversionary program. If the State Attorney decides to handle the case judicially, it may be transferred to Adult Court or it may be referred to Juvenile Court for an adjudicatory hearing (a non-jury trial). If, at the adjudicatory hearing, a minor is found not guilty, then he/she will be released. If the minor is found delinquent or if adjudication is withheld, the case will be disposed of in one of three ways: commitment, community control, or other alternative judicial services. Commitment includes direct release and post-placement services such as aftercare, post-commitment community control, or furlough. Community control includes probation. Alternative juvenile services include work restitution, community service, or judicial warnings. Minors are released from the JJS when they have successfully completed their commitment, community control, or alternative services (Santa Rosa County Public Schools, 2000).

An area of student and parental rights that has far reaching ramifications for professional school counselors involves the value-laden areas of abortion and sexual activity, which often involves a family's religious beliefs, values about sexual conduct, and parental rights to be the guiding voice in their children's lives. Professional school counselors need to be advocates and a source of strength for the individual student who comes to them for help in confronting and dealing with areas such as sexual activity and abortion, but principles of law and school board policy must be considered.

Currently there are 42 states that have laws on the books which require varying degrees of parental involvement before their child can obtain an abortion (Planned Parenthood, 2002). The laws determining the right of parents to be involved in their children's abortion decision impact how professional school counselors must behave when a student confides in them that they are pregnant and considering abortion. Generally speaking, unless there is a school district policy that forbids discussing abortion, contraceptives, etc., a professional school counselor, in the course of fulfilling his/her job responsibilities, may assist students with value-laden issues such as abortion if he/she is competent to give such advice and if he/she proceeds in a professional manner.

Under what circumstances might a counselor be held liable for giving abortion advice? In Arnold v. Board of Education of Escambia County (1989), Jane and John, two high school students, filed suit along with their parents against the School District of Escambia County, Alabama, alleging that the professional school counselor, Kay Rose, and the Assistant Principal, Melvin Powell, coerced and assisted Jane into getting an abortion (Arnold v. Board of Education of Escambia County, 1989; Zirkel, 2001b). During the process of discovery, the trial court concluded that the students were not deprived of their free will, had chosen to obtain an abortion, had chosen not to tell their parents, and that there was no coercion on the part of school officials (Arnold v. Board of Education of Escambia County, 1989; Zirkel, 2001). However, the outcome of the trial would likely have been very different if the courts had found that Rose and Powell had coerced this student to have an abortion. Professional school counselors must always consider that their responsibilities extend beyond the student to parents and guardians and take great care in value-laden issues such as abortion counseling. Fisher and Sorenson (1996) stated:

> If an immature, emotionally fragile young girl procures an abortion with the help of a counselor, under circumstances where reasonably competent counselors would have notified the parents or would have advised against the abortion, liability for psychological or physical suffering may follow. The specific facts and circumstances must always be considered. (p. 60)

Students who give birth and decide to abandon the baby can do so anonymously in some states. For example, in Florida parents can abandon a baby at a hospital or fire station within 3 days of its birth. The courts assume that the abandonment means the mother is consenting to terminate parental rights (Florida Statute 188, 2000.213).

*Parents' Rights and Responsibilities*

The *Family Educational Rights and Privacy Act (FERPA)*(1974) a federal law that governs the disclosure of information from educational records, gives parents the right to talk to teachers and school administrators about their children, see their children's educational records, and decide if their child will participate in a questionnaire, survey, or examination regarding a parent's personal beliefs, sex practices, family life, or religion. *FERPA* allows parents to request that information that they believe to be inaccurate or misleading be purged from their child's educational record.

*Educators' Rights and Responsibilities Regarding Students and Parents*

Educators have a responsibility to provide students with an environment conducive to learning in which sexual harassment is not allowed. The U.S. Supreme Court in *Davis v. Monroe County Board of Education* (1999,) in combination with Title IX of the Education Amendments of 1972, established that public schools may be forced to pay damages for failing to address student-on-student sexual harassment. Sexual harassment can no longer be ignored or given cursory attention by school districts. The Davis case (1999) demands advocacy against known sexual harassment. According to the Supreme Court, liability may be imposed when the school district is deliberately indifferent to sexual harassment of which the recipient has actual knowledge (Biskupic, 1999). The harassment must be severe, pervasive, and deprive the victim of access to an equal educational opportunity.

Most states have statutes giving educators the right to conduct searches of students on public school property, school buses, and at school events based on reasonable suspicion of criminal activity. School officials can question students without informing them of their constitutional rights. The constitutional rights of minors are not equated with that of adults in most states. For example, school officials can establish dress codes and grooming requirements as part of the student code of conduct.

## Application of Student and Parental Rights through Case Studies

The following cases are presented to highlight additional legal and ethical principles in an effort to raise awareness, reduce risk, and transfer the principles of these cases to other situations.

*Rights For Non-Custodial Parents I: Working Through A Case Study*

> *A student's mother, who is incarcerated, requested copies of her son's educational records. Are you legally required to provide her with education records?*

Non-custodial parental rights are often misunderstood. *FERPA* makes it clear that both parents have equal access to education records. Even incarcerated parents, parents who have refused to pay child support, and abusive parents have rights to educational records under *FERPA* unless there is a court order expressly forbidding a parent to have educational records.

*Rights for Non-Custodial Parents II: Working Through A Case Study*

> *Sharon, a nine-year-old student, occasionally seeks your help with relationship issues with her mother, the custodial parent. Sharon's parents are divorced and generally at war over everything including how to raise Sharon and her sister. Sharon describes her mother as being very strict. A teacher expressed concern that Sharon's grades have been plummeting and that she seems distracted and withdrawn, a marked contrast to how Sharon usually behaves. After meeting with Sharon, you believe you need to involve her parents. Sharon begs you to call her father instead of her mother. You believe Sharon's mother will be upset that you contacted Sharon's father instead of her. Can you consult Sharon's father without seeking permission or notifying her mother, the custodial parent?*

Professional school counselors can find guidance in the court case *Page v. Rotterdam-Mohonasen Central School District* (1981). John Page had visitation rights for his son, Eric, but repeated requests to the school district to provide him with educational records went unheeded. Mikado Page, Eric's mother, sent a statement to the school (at what was believed to be the school's request) explaining that she has legal custody of Eric and that she did not want John

Page to have Eric's education records, participate in teacher-parent conferences, or in any way engage in the education of Eric. The court found that John Page was not trying to alter custodial rights but simply participate in his son's educational progress. The court found that school districts have a duty to act in the best educational interest of the children committed to their care which means providing educational information to both parents (Fisher & Sorenson, 1996; Huey & Remley 1988; *Page v. Rotterdam-Mohanasen Central School District*, 1981). Parents, whether or not they have legal custody, do not have to give up their rights to be involved in their children's education or psychological care. Consulting with your building level supervisor and/or your district level supervisor of guidance can help answer the legal rights of noncustodial parents and also shed light on what is in Sharon's best interest and the best interest of the family.

*Students Right to a Public Education and the Right to Privacy: Working Through a Case Study*

> *An autistic preschool handicapped student entered your school. You accidentally acquire information that this four-year-old child is HIV+. The principal has warned you that you are not to reveal the child's HIV+ status to the teacher. This four-year-old is not potty trained and is a biter. It is inconceivable to you that this information is being withheld from the teacher. You are seriously considering dropping some hints to the teacher such as, "This school year you need to be especially careful to use your rubber gloves when cleaning up after your students." Is there an ethical dilemma here? Is there a legal dilemma here?*

The *Family Educational Rights and Privacy Act* (1974) bestows on parents the privacy rights of their minor children regarding education records. Professional school counselors can find guidance in *FERPA* if their state does not have a statute addressing the privacy rights of HIV+ children in schools. *FERPA* gives parents the authority to release records to third persons; therefore, it follows that parents can decide who in the school will know that their child is HIV+ or has AIDS. Most states have statutes protecting the privacy rights of HIV+ people to protect them against the fear and prejudice directed toward them (McGuire, Nieri, Abbott, Sheridan, & Fisher, 1995). Schools need protective safeguards in place to keep sensitive information from being acquired accidentally.

Additional guidance can be found in *Martinez v. School Board* in which a Federal Court of Appeals ruled that a 7-year-old boy who had AIDS could not be excluded from his Trainable Mentally Disabled (TMH) class. The court would not exclude the student from school in the face of theoretical possibilities. The court ruled that the overwhelming medical evidence is that AIDS is not transmitted in schools through casual contact and, therefore, the court would not exclude a student from a free appropriate public education (*Martinez v. School Bd.* 1988). The *Individuals with Disabilities Education Act* (IDEA) and *Section 504 of the Rehabilitation Act of 1973* guarantee this student a free education in the least restrictive environment. Supported by legislation and recommended by the Centers for Disease Control, students who are HIV+ should be afforded a free, appropriate public education.

> For most infected school-aged children, the benefits of an unrestricted setting would outweigh the risks of their acquiring potentially harmful infections in the setting and the apparent nonexistent risk of transmission of [HIV]. The children should be allowed to attend school and after-school day-care and be placed in a foster home in an unrestricted setting (Centers for Disease Control, 2002).

*Runaway Children: Working Through a Case Study*

> *You have been counseling Whitney for several months. You believe Whitney's parents emotionally abuse her and you have reported this suspicion to the Department of Children and Family Services twice during this time. Emotional abuse has never been established. You recognize how hard it is to determine emotional abuse, and you believe that Whitney will never find relief from authorities. You believe that, at 15 years-of-age, Whitney's best course of action is to flee the abuse. You have never suggested to Whitney that she leave home, but she has brought it up several times and you do not encourage or discourage this course of action. You have listened and asked questions about her plans. Whitney finally leaves home and you learn from her friend that she is safe with friends. Whitney's parents call the school inquiring if school officials would ask Whitney's friends and teachers and counselor if they had any information about her whereabouts. When asked, you remain quiet. Have you acted illegally?*

In most states it is unlawful to aid an unmarried or minor runaway. If anyone who is not authorized by the Department of Juvenile Justice or the Department of Children and Family Services knows a child has left home without parental consent and knows that the child is being provided shelter and does not report this to law enforcement authorities, then that person is guilty of a first degree misdemeanor in most states (*Children and Families in Need Services Act*, 2000; *Delinquency – Interstate Compact on Juveniles Act*, 2000).

## Summary/Conclusion

The ASCA codes dictate that professional school counselors have a primary obligation and loyalty to students, but that parents need to be involved, as parents are continually vested by our courts with legal rights to guide their children (*Bellotti v. Baird*, 1979; *H.L. v. Matheson*, 1980). Community standards, a counselor's own personal values, school board policy, the school setting, state and federal statutes, all contribute to the complex nature of working with minors in schools.

The rights and responsibilities of students and their parents have considerable implications for all educators, but in many ways are even more complicated for professional school counselors because their work involves the personal/social arena. The multiplicity of responsibility to parents, students, administrators, teachers, and others in a setting designed to deliver academic instruction requires a vigilance to not only protect the rights of students but also consider parents and others who have rights to influence students.

Professional school counselors must be constant consumers of legal and ethical information by seeking counsel of colleagues, administrators, supervisors, school attorneys, and Title IX officers. Such supervision and advice make the legal and ethical world of professional school counselors less daunting.

## References

American School Counselor Association. (1998). *Ethical standards for school counselors.* Alexandria, VA: Author.

Arnold v. Board of Education of Escambia County, 880 F. 2d 305 (Alabama 1989).

Arthur, G. L., & Swanson, C. D. (1993). Confidentiality and privileged communication. *The ACA Legal Series.* Washington, DC: American Counseling Association.

Bellotti v. Baird, 443 U.S. 622 (1979).

Biskupic, J. (1999, May 25). Davis v. Monroe County Board of Education et al. *The Washington Post*, A1:1.

Centers for Disease Control. (2002). *HIV+ children and schooling*. Retrieved January 20, 2002 from http://www.cdc.gov/

Children and Families In Need of Services Act, 984.085, (2000). Florida Statutes. Retrieved September 30, 2002 from http://www.leg.stat.fl.us

Courses Of Study And Instructional Aids Act, 233.47 & 233.061, (2000). Florida Statutes. Retrieved September 30, 2002 from http://www.leg.stat.fl.us

Davis v. Monroe County Board of Education et al. 120 F.3d 1390. (Supreme Court, May 24, 1999).

Delinquency; Interstate Compact On Juveniles Act, 985.2065, (2000). Florida Statutes. Retrieved September 30, 2002 from http://www.leg.stat.fl.us

Family Educational Rights and Privacy Act (20 U.S.C.ß1232g) (1974).

Fischer, G. P., & Sorenson, L. (1996). *School law for counselors, psychologists and social workers* (3rd ed.). White Plains, NY: Longman.

Florida Statute 188, 2000.213 (2000).

H. L. v. Matheson, 101 S. Ct. 2727 (1982).

Huey, W. C., & Remley, T. P., Jr., (1988). Confidentiality and the school counselor: A challenge for the 1990's. *School Counselor, 41*, 23-30.

Martinez v. School Bd., 861 F2d 1502 (11th Cir. 1988), on remand, 711 F. Supp. 1066 (M.D. Fla. 1989)

McGuire, J., Nieri, D., Abbott, D., Sheridan, K., & Fisher, R. (1995). Do Tarasoff principles apply in AIDS-related psychotherapy? *Professional Psychology: Research and Practice, 26* (6), 608-611.

Page v. Rotterdam-Mohonasen Central School District 109 Misc. 2d 1049, 441 N.Y.S.2d 323 (1981).

Planned Parenthood. (2002). Retrieved September 30, 2002, from http://www.plannedparenthood.org/LIBRARY/ABORTION/StateLaws.html

Remley Jr., T., & Herlihy, B. (2001). *Ethical, legal, and professional issues in counseling.* Upper Saddle River, NJ: Merrill/Prentice-Hall.

Salo, M. M., & Shumate, S. G. (1993). Counseling minor clients. *The ACA Legal Series, 4,* 73-78.

Santa Rosa County Public Schools. (2000). *Know the law: A guide for adolescents and their families.* Santa Rosa, FL: Santa Rosa District Schools.

Stone, C. (Speaker). (2001). *Legal and ethical issues in working with minors in schools* [Film]. Alexandria, VA: American Counseling Association.

Welfel, E. R., & Lipsitz, N. E. (1983). Wanted: A comprehensive approach to ethics research and education. *Counselor Education and Supervision, 23,* 123-129.

Zirkel, P. (March, 2001). A pregnant pause? *Phi Delta Kappan, 82*, 557-558.

# Chapter 8

## Professional Credentials in School Counseling

*Brent M. Snow & C. Marie Jackson*

### Preview

Due to the confusion and differential requirements relative to certification, licensure, and accreditation in the field of school counseling, this chapter is dedicated to helping clarify these issues. In addition to a brief history of credentialing, state certification in school counseling, national certification in counseling, and licensure in professional counseling will be discussed.

School counseling, along with other specialty fields in education, has a long history of requiring practitioners to meet certain requirements to work with children in public schools. In addition to teachers, administrators, and other specialists, stakeholders in school counseling have developed standards in every state requiring a credential to work in the schools as a professional counselor. In addition to state certification in school counseling, school counselors with appropriate training and education are eligible for licensure as professional counselors in most states and for national certification in counseling.

Many counselors in training and those just graduating from master's programs (in addition to those contemplating a career in school counseling) can become very confused about the whole issue of credentialing including licensure and certification. Bloom and Clawson (1992) indicate that, "credentialing is probably the most complicated issue for most new professional counselors. . . " (p. 4). Most experienced counselors and counselor educators would agree based on many years of answering and fielding questions on this topic.

Because of the lack of standardization of terminology and differential requirements found between states and credentialing bodies, this chapter is dedicated to helping clarify this confusion. In addition to a brief history of credentialing, state certification in school counseling, national certification in counseling, and licensure in professional counseling will be discussed.

*Why All the Confusion with This Credentialing Stuff?*

Until the 1970s, there was very little, if any confusion in the field of counseling about credentials. That's because until that time there were basically only two credentials that had any effect on counselors: state certification in school counseling (administered by a state department of education or similar body) and licensure as a psychologist (administered by a state licensure board). The first controlled who could be a school counselor in a public school and the second controlled who could practice "psychology" (which included counseling and psychotherapy) independently or in private practice ("hanging up a shingle"). If a professional, then, wasn't interested in working in a school or in private practice, credentials weren't an issue. State and private agencies and other employers of counselors simply developed their own requirements for hiring counselors. At that time, counselors with doctoral degrees were routinely licensed as psychologists (Snow, 1982). While school counseling wasn't particularly affected, Snow (1981) indicated that:

> There has been considerable dialogue in recent years alluding to difficulties between psychologists and counselors regarding who should or should not be licensed (as psychologists) and who can do what to whom. The problem seemed to magnify in the early 1970s as state psychology licensing boards became more restrictive in just who they were willing to identify as psychologists." (p. 80)

With licensure as a "psychologist" (led by the American Psychology Association) becoming more restrictive, "counselors," led by the American Personnel and Guidance Association (APGA), now called the American Counseling Association (ACA), began to advocate for separate licensing laws governing private, independent practice. In 1976, Virginia became the first state to enact a separate licensure law for counselors, and today most states license counselors separately as "professional counselors." During this same time, other specialties represented by professional associations such as the American Association for Marriage and Family Counseling began to push for separate licensure as well. Today, most states now separately license psychologists, counselors, marriage and family therapists, and social workers, thus adding to the confusion surrounding licensure relative to private practice in the helping professions.

*State Certification in School Counseling*

According to Gladding (2000) certification is a professional, statutory, or nonstatutory process by which an agency or association grants recognition to an individual for having met certain predetermined professional qualifications. State certification for professional school counselors is a statutory process and is a requirement in all states, according to Randolph and Masker (as cited in Schmidt, 1999). The procedures and requirements for obtaining certification vary from state to state but all do require a minimum of some graduate education for initial certification in school counseling. Even the training program requirements outlined by state agencies vary across states with some state education agencies reviewing and approving university programs. A few states continue to require teaching experience prior to certification. Previous teaching experience as a prerequisite is a long-debated issue in the field of school counseling even though research does not indicate a link between teaching experience and successful counseling practice (Baker, 1994). Counselor educators (professors who train professional school counselors at colleges and universities) agree that professional school counselors do not need prior teaching experience to be successful (Smith, 2001).

According to Paisley & Hubbard (1989), a majority of states allow counselors to become certified before they complete all requirements, and some states offer provisional certification allowing counselors in training to be placed in school counseling positions prior to finishing degree requirements. Often, provisional certifications have a limited time frame during which degree requirements must be completed and full certification earned. An overview of state certification requirements in school counseling as of 2000 can be summarized as follows (ACA, 2000): all states required graduate education in guidance and counseling with 39 requiring a master's degree in guidance and counseling; 12 states required supplemental graduate education in addition to counseling; 28 states required completion of a school based practicum or internship; 21 states required previous teaching or related experience; 23 states utilized standardized examination as part of the certification process; and 35 states required a criminal background check.

Once received, certification must be kept in effect through gaining the appropriate required continuing education as designated by each state agency. Renewals must be applied for periodically, usually every 5 - 8 years. Additional coursework can serve as continuing education for recertification purposes. According to Clawson (as cited in Wittmer, 2000), credentialing of professional school counselors is for the purpose of protecting the school counselor as well as protecting the general public. State certification allows the school counselor to practice as a school counselor and, theoretically, prohibits those without appropriate credentials from legitimately being employed in those positions (although Clawson reported that exceptions are common practice). He also suggested that credentialing protects the professional school counselor in the case of salary equity questions and adds to the potential for a clearly defined counselor role. State school counseling certification is meant to insure the public (parents, teachers, students, community members) that those hired in these positions have had the minimum training required, no character defects, and other necessary qualifications to provide the designated services to students.

*National Certification in School Counseling*

Unlike state certification, which is mandatory for professional school counselors, national certification is a voluntary professional credential and is not required to practice in the schools, in other agencies, or in private, independent practice. Rather, it indicates that a professional counselor meets national standards developed by counselors for counselors (rather than by legislators or education departments). While it does not or cannot substitute for state credentials, it is an avenue for identifying those who meet nationally set standards.

At the present time, there are two national organizations that certify school counselors: the National Board for Certified Counselors (NBCC) and the National Board for Professional Teaching Standards (NBPTS). Of these two, the largest and most well known at this time is the National Board for Certified Counselors, which was created in the early 1980s. This credentialing body certifies "general" counselors who, when certified, are referred to as a National Certified Counselor (NCC). Additionally, the organization also credentials three counseling specialties known as the National Certified School Counselor (NCSC), Certified Clinical Mental Health Counselor (CCMHC), and Master Addictions Counselor (MAC). Requirements (NBCC, 2002) for becoming a nationally certified or "general" counselor include a combination of education (at least a master's degree), supervised experience, and passing an examination known as the National Counselor Examination for Licensure and Certification (NCE). There are several options that allow for a variety of combinations of education and experience, including benefits associated with graduating from a program accredited by the Council for Accreditation of Counseling and Related Educational Programs (CACREP). Requirements for obtaining the National Certified School Counselor credential from NBCC include completing a graduate degree in counseling with 48 semester or 72 quarter hours of coursework covering eight content areas and including two academic terms of field experience; three years of post-master's supervised experience as a school counselor; and passing the National Certified School Counselor Examination (NCSCE). It is possible for applicants to just take the school counseling examination and obtain both the general (NCC) and school counseling certification (NCSC).

In recent years, propelled by calls for educational reform and accountability, the National Board for Professional Teaching Standards (NBPTS) has developed a strong presence in certifying teachers at the national level. One of the major thrusts pushing this movement, in addition to acknowledging quality and excellence, is the willingness of states and school systems to financially reward teachers who gain such certification. Incentives for teachers becoming nationally certified exist in many states and have resulted in a large number of teachers becoming nationally certified with a trend suggesting many more to follow. Professional school counselors have obviously desired to be included in these incentives encouraging national certification and, hopefully, resulting in improved student academic performance and in reducing achievement gaps.

In 2002, the National Board for Professional Teaching Standards adopted 11 standards of accomplished practice for professional school counselors that serve as the basis for certification.

The resulting credential is referred to as the Early Childhood through Young Adulthood/School Counseling (ECYA/School Counseling) certificate. Recently developed eligibility requirements include: a baccalaureate degree; three years of school counseling experience; and state certification/licensure in school counseling. After meeting the above requirements, an additional assessment process involves presenting a portfolio with work samples, videotapes, and other evidence demonstrating effectiveness in meeting the eleven standards. The assessment also includes a "test" demonstrating knowledge in human growth and development, school counseling programming, diverse populations, theories, data and change, and collaboration.

There were early attempts to unify certification between NBCC and NBPTS and create one national credential and process. While many had hoped (and perhaps assumed) that the National Board of Professional Teaching Standards would adopt the requirements already in existence with the National Board for Certified Counselors and the National Certified School Counselor credential, this never occurred, leaving these two national certification bodies competing with each other. It remains to be seen which credential (or if both credentials) will stand the test of time in influencing national recognition in school counseling.

*Licensing in Professional Counseling*

All but five states currently license professional counselors (ACA, 2002). Terminology varies some but the most common titles for those licensed are "professional counselor," "professional mental health counselor," "clinical professional counselor," or "clinical mental health counselor" (ACA, 1997). Licensure laws are passed by state legislatures and generally regulate, through state statute, the title and practice of counseling. Essentially, licensure laws govern the independent (private) practice of counseling and generally exclude those working in government agencies and schools. The American Counseling Association (ACA) has developed model legislation for states to use in developing counseling licensure laws and many have followed these guidelines. Some states, of course, have not done so, resulting in licensure laws involving varying requirements to become licensed and differing definitions of counseling practice. The model law includes the following definition in the scope of practice of professional counselors (ACA, 1995):

> The practice of professional counseling includes but is not limited to: individual, group, and marriage and family counseling and psychotherapy; assessment; crisis intervention; diagnosis and treatment of persons with mental and emotional disorders; guidance and consulting to facilitate normal growth and development, including educational and career development; utilization of functional assessment and counseling for persons requesting assistance in adjustment to a disability or handicapping condition; consulting; research; and referral.
> Assessment shall mean selecting, administering, scoring, and interpreting psychological and educational instruments designed to assess and individual's attitudes, abilities, achievements, interests, personal characteristics, disabilities and mental, emotional and behavioral disorders and the use of methods and techniques for understanding human behavior in relation to coping with, adapting to, or changing life situations. (p. 3)

Most states require a master's degree, supervised experience, and the passing of an examination, which is most often the National Counselor Examination for Licensure and Certification (NCE). This exam is the same exam used and developed by the National Board for Certified Counselors. All states exempt school counselors from the requirement of becoming a licensed professional counselor to practice counseling. Many professional school counselors, however, qualify and are eligible for state licensing should they chose to do so. School counselors who have private, independent practices outside of their employment in the schools must be licensed in those states with licensure laws.

## Summary

With a brief background and understanding of credentialing in the field of counseling, professional school counselors in practice and aspiring school counselors can better assess the value of the various certifications and licenses to be acquired. This chapter provided information to help sort out licenses, certifications, and program credentialing in the field of school counseling. All professional school counselors must become state certified in order to practice in the schools. In order to practice outside of the school in an agency or private practice, most states require an additional license as a professional counselor. Becoming a Nationally Certified Counselor (NCC) or a Nationally Certified School Counselor (NCSC), or receiving an Early Childhood through Young Adulthood/School Counselor (ECYA/School Counselor) certificate identifies the counselor as having achieved professional standards and qualifications at the highest level. Graduating from a nationally accredited program in school counseling, such as those approved by the Council for Accreditation of Counseling and Related Educational Programs (CACREP), adds an element of distinction to one's degree and can be a benefit when seeking national certifications. Professional school counselors can add to their professionalism and credibility through the credentialing process.

## References


American Counseling Association. (1995, April). *Counselor credentialing laws: Scopes of practice, language and tiers.* [Document] Alexandria VA: Author.

American Counseling Association. (2000, March). *A guide to state laws and regulations on professional school counseling.* [Document} Alexandria, VA: Author.

American Counseling Association. (2002). A guide to state laws and regulations on professional school counseling, *Journal of Counseling and Development, 80*, 2, 233-236.

Baker, S. B. 1994. Mandatory teaching experience for school counselors: An impediment to uniform certification standards for school counselors, *Counselor Education & Supervision, 33,* 314-326.

Bloom, J.W. & Clawson, T.W. (1992). Sorting through the Credentialing maze: NBCC, NACCMHC, CRCC, and CACREP, *INFOCHANGE, 67*, 4-5.

Gladding, S. T. (2000). *Counseling: A comprehensive profession.* (4th ed). Columbus, OH: Merrill/Prentice-Hall.

Harris, A. D. (1997) *Licensing requirement. Licensing requirements: Includes Scope of Practice* (2nd ed.). Alexandria, VA: American Counseling Association.

Hollis, J. W., & Dodson, T. A. (2000). *Counselor Preparation: 1999-2001 Programs, Faculty, Trends.* Philadelphia, Pa: Accelerated Development.

National Board for Certified Counselors (NBCC). (2002). *General information: The national certified counselor (NCC) credential.* Retrieved June 28, 2002, from http://www.nbcc.org/cert/ncc.htm

Paisley, P. O., & Hubbard, G. T. (1989). School counseling: State officials' perceptions of certification and employment trends. *Counselor Education and Supervision, 29,* 60-70.

Schmidt, J. J. (1999). *Counseling in schools.* (2nd ed.). Needham Heights, MA: Allyn & Bacon.

Smith, S. L. (2001). Teaching experience for school counselors: Counselor educators' perceptions, *Professional School Counseling, 4*, 216-224.

Snow, B. M. (1981). Counselor licensure as perceived by counselors and psychologists, *The Personnel and Guidance Journal, 60,* 80-83.

Snow, B. M. (1982). Counselor licensure: What activities should be allowed? *Counselor Education and Supervision*, *21*, 237-244.

Wittmer, J. (2000). *Managing your school counseling program: K-12* developmental strategies (2nd ed.). Minneapolis, MN: Educational Media Corporation.

**Table 1. Additional information.**

**State School Counselor Certification Requirements**:
The American School Counselor Association website contains State Certification and Continuing Education Requirements within the section on Career Roles.
URL: http://www.schoolcounselor.org
Ph: 1-800-306-4722

**State Professional Counselor Licensure Requirements:**
The American Counseling Association Website contains information on licensure and certification.
URL:http://www.counseling.org/site/PageSaver
Ph: 1-800-347-6647

**National Board for Certified Counselors (NBCC) Requirements:**
The National Board for Certification website provides information about the various certifications available through NBCC.
URL: http://www.nbcc.org/
Ph: 336-547-0607

**National Board for Professional Teaching Standards (NBPTS) Requirements:**
The NBPTS website provides information about various teacher certifications available and also includes information about the certification of school counselors.
URL: http://www.nbpts.org/
Ph: 703-465-2700

# Chapter 9

## Professional Training and Regulation In School Counseling

*Sally Murphy*

### Preview

The purpose of this chapter is to highlight the federal regulations that authorize the training of professional school counselors, review current research and practice, and offer the specific training recommendations and vision needed for professional school counselors in the 21st century.

Professional school counselors have the opportunity and responsibility to influence the academic achievement and success of every child within a school community. They have an obligation to take the leadership role to become advocates for all students, especially for those who need special services or assistance. Professional school counselors are uniquely situated to positively influence the learning environment of their school community, thus making it possible for all students to establish and achieve their academic goals.

But, all too often, professional school counselors are hindered in their job by two key factors. First, the local school district and site administrators frequently are the ones who define the role and responsibilities of professional school counselors (Muro & Kottman, 1995). Many times, professional school counselors are required to perform administrative and non-counseling related tasks (e.g., test coordinators, discipline, substitute teaching, clerical assignments). While teachers may also have additional duties, it is not during the time teachers should be in the classroom teaching. Not so for counselors. Their extra duties cut into the precise time that should be spent with students, taking counselors away from focusing on the academic, career and personal/social developmental issues of their student populations.

Second, professional school counselors have not always been adequately trained for the demands and needs of the society in which they currently live and work. They do not have the required knowledge and skills needed to provide their school communities with the necessary vision and leadership for addressing issues relevant in today's society.

In order to fully understand the training requirements for pre-service professional school counselor education, it is important to first review the statutory regulations that form the requirements for professional school counselor training. Against that background, one can examine current research and practice to include new educational reform initiatives that seek to transform the role of professional school counselors. Building from the 21st century vision contained in the reform initiative, one can then examine the implications for counselor training requirements.

### Federal Regulations in School Counseling

Professional school counselors have been in school communities for over 100 years. They started out working with students on vocational issues, advising them on career choices and educational decisions. Then, in 1957, the Soviet Union launched Sputnik, and the response by the United States was the passage of the 1958 National Defense Education Act (NDEA). Along with other education initiatives, NDEA dedicated funding for secondary school counseling programs and for colleges and universities for counselor education programs. The United States made school counseling a national priority. This was further emphasized in 1965, when the United States Congress passed the Elementary and Secondary Education Act, mandating school counseling programs and the training of professional school counselors. This subject has been of high interest to recent Congresses.

Additional legislation introduced to Congress underscores the importance of professional school counselors within school communities. A total of seventeen pieces of legislation were introduced into the 108th Congress (Library of Congress, 2004). These bills covered several key areas: additional recruitment, training, and hiring of more professional school counselors to serve as school-based resource staff; establishment or expansion of elementary and secondary school counseling programs; school safety; student-counselor ratios; and crisis intervention for students at risk of high school drop-out.

While only two of these federal legislative initiatives have yet been passed and signed into law, the numbers alone indicate that the legislative environment surrounding school counseling programs can be expected to continue to evolve. Counselor education faculty will need to also check separate state school counseling legislation and regulations and incorporate that information into the training of pre-service professional school counselors.

## Training in School Counseling

The federal mandate to establish school counseling and counselor education programs is well documented. But how do counselor education programs determine what should be included in training for those programs?

### *American School Counselor Association*

The American School Counselor Association (ASCA), the national association for professional school counselors, provides the structure and standards for professional school counselors and school counseling programs (ASCA, 2002a) and describes the role of the professional school counselor (ASCA, 1999b). The structure for school counseling programs, which should be part of the counselor education curricula, is found in The ASCA *National Model: A Framework for School Counseling Programs* (Hatch & Bowers, 2002; ASCA, 2003). The *National Model* presents an organized approach to program foundation, delivery, management, and accountability - four major elements for school counseling programs. The *National Model* incorporates ASCA's four overarching professional school counselor role description themes of leadership, advocacy, collaboration and teaming, and systemic change.

ASCA's model incorporates three standards (Campbell & Dahir, 1997) for student development: academic, career, and personal/social development. It reflects current education reform initiatives, including the *No Child Left Behind* legislation and builds upon its philosophy of *One Vision One Voice* (ASCA, 2002b). Thus, ASCA provides all professional school counselor educators with a professional, organized, and consistent framework for school counseling programs. By integrating ASCA's national model within a professional school counselor education program, pre-service school counselors graduate with the skills and knowledge necessary to work with diverse school communities and student populations.

ASCA provides the ethical framework needed to clarify the nature of ethical responsibilities that govern school counseling professionals (ASCA, 1998). Counselor education programs teach the ethical standards that govern the basic tenets of the counseling process, addressing counselors' responsibilities to parents, colleagues, professional associates, school, community, self, and to the profession. But the professional school counselor's foremost ethical responsibility is to the students. The three primary ethical responsibilities pertaining to students are do no harm, respect issues of confidentiality, and avoid dual relationships.

## Council for Accreditation of Counseling and Related Educational Programs

ASCA supports the professional school counselor standards developed by the Council for Accreditation of Counseling and Related Educational Programs (CACREP), which require standards-based graduate level education and training (ASCA, 1999a). Since 1981, CACREP has been the primary professional counseling accreditation organization (CACREP, 2002). It defines a counselor education program as a structured sequence of curricular and clinical experiences for which accreditation is sought. CACREP provides the foundation for graduate level school counseling programs to achieve and maintain a high level of quality and integrity based on rigorous national standards.

CACREP standards require counselor education programs to have a minimum of two full academic years of graduate study to include 48 semester hours of credit. It stipulates eight academic common-core areas: human growth and development, social and cultural foundations, helping relationships, group work, career development, appraisal, research and evaluation, ethical and professional issues and specialized studies in school counseling. Its clinical instruction requirements mandate that students obtain 600 hours of internship with 240 hours of direct services to students, to include supervised individual and group work, and 100 hours of practicum experience.

While all school counselor education programs do not offer a CACREP-accredited program, most university programs are aligned with CACREP's core curriculum requirements. These academic common-core curricula requirements are frequently the basis that states use to regulate certification or licensure requirements of graduate level school counseling education programs.

Currently, 44 states and the District of Columbia require a master's degree in school counseling. The remaining six states require a bachelor's degree in education with a minimum of 30 hours in graduate-level work in school counseling (ASCA, 2002a).

## Current Research and Practice

### *Education Reform's Effect on Training*

Over the last few years, counselor education professionals, professional school counselors, and other education experts began to examine the role of the professional school counselor in the school reform movement (Bemak, 2000; House & Hayes, 2002). The educational reform for professional school counselors not only examines the role of the counselor within the school community, but also addresses the training of pre-service school counselors based on professional standards and regulations and on current research and practice. While a more comprehensive discussion of this reform is covered in other chapters, it is important to understand the integral role it has in the training of professional school counselors.

Although CACREP provides the guidelines for core curriculum requirements within a school counselor education program, these core areas only begin to address the training needs of the professional school counselor for the 21st century. The Education Trust, funded by the DeWitt Wallace-Reader's Digest Foundation, has played a significant role in the research and ensuing dialogue and training to improve school counseling by focusing particularly on the graduate-level preparation of school counselors (Perusse & Goodnough, 2001). Its focus has helped define a new role for professional school counselors, one they believe is more relevant to the needs of 21st century school communities.

The Education Trust's new vision for professional school counselors "describes school counseling as a profession that focuses on educational equity, access, and academic success, with a concentration on interventions that will close the achievement gap between poor and minority children and their more advantaged peers" (Perusse & Goodnough, 2001, p. 100). It highlights five domains intrinsic to the role of the professional school counselor: leadership, advocacy, teaming and collaboration, counseling and coordination, and assessment and the use of data. Note these are closely aligned with the ASCA overarching themes.

The Education Trust (2002) delineates eight essential elements for school counselor education change: (1) criteria for selection and recruitment of candidates for counselor preparation programs; (2) curricular content, structure and sequence of courses; (3) methods of instruction, field experiences and practices; (4) induction process into the profession; (5) working relationships with community partners; (6) professional development for counselor educators; (7) university/school district partnerships; and (8) university/state department of education partnerships. Prospective graduate students in counseling should weigh these program components against their professional goals as they consider what counselor education program best fits their needs.

The Education Trust (2002) challenges school counselor education programs to expand beyond the basic training to include specific counseling skills necessary to transform the role of the professional school counselor. In addition to its focus on leadership and social advocacy skills, The Education Trust promotes specific training in multicultural counseling and cross-cultural communication skills to better serve increasingly diverse school communities.

The Education Trust (2002) also stresses the need for pre-service counseling students to have training in the use of technology for monitoring student progress and student career planning, and in acquiring and accessing data needed to inform decision making on individual students. The use of quantitative data is critical if professional school counselors are to effect changes within school communities.

The Education Trust (2002) stresses the need for school counselor education programs to incorporate program development and management within their curricula. Equally important, school counseling students should be taught effective presentation skills appropriate with multiple audiences (e.g., students, parents, administrators, staff, school community members, etc.).

## Incorporating the Transformation of School Counseling Initiative into a Counselor Education Program: A Case Study

An example of a counselor education program that incorporates the transformation of school counseling initiative into its training program is found at George Mason University, Graduate School of Education, Fairfax, Virginia. The Counseling & Development (C&D) faculty re-designed its entire school counseling program to reflect the goals and needs of the professional school counselor in the 21st century. They developed their new program based on current research and practice, infusing standards directed by many of the professional school counseling associations and initiatives (e.g., ASCA, CACREP, The Education Trust). This is evident in its mission statement, course curricula, and clinical field experiences (George Mason University, 2002). These standards are also included in the doctoral program and in its post-master's school counseling leadership and administration certificate program.

The content, structure, and sequence of courses represent the new vision for professional school counselor preparation. GMU's C&D program maintained the basic course content requirements suggested by CACREP, but expanded the focus to include training in leadership, multiculturalism, social justice, and advocacy. The counseling & development program requires that professional school counselors be taught to assume leadership roles, be proactive change agents, and become advocates for social, economic, and political justice.

GMU views these topics as integral to the preparation of professional school counselors. For example, it hired two faculty members, experts in multicultural and diversity issues, to ensure that C&D faculty and students understand the changing demographics in Northern Virginia and the implications of those changes for counselor skills and knowledge. It also hired two faculty members who were experienced practitioners in school counseling and had strong working relationships with area school district administration. Their previous work as professional school counselors provides a seamless link between the theoretical perspectives and authentic practical applications within the program. Their solid associations with school district leadership provide the open communication needed for collaborative partnerships.

Based on recommendations from ASCA's *National Model* (ASCA, 2003) and The Education Trust (2002), GMU's new school counselor education program reflects fundamental changes in all aspects of its program. For example, the criteria for the selection and recruitment of potential students are more rigorous than in previous years. Goal statements are carefully examined. Letters of recommendation are given more consideration, with subsequent follow-up phone calls placed if further clarification about an applicant is needed. After a thorough review of the application packets, selected candidates are invited to an extensive faculty panel interview appointment. Candidates are then asked to submit a writing sample reflecting on the C&D program's mission statement. This provides the faculty a written narrative of how prospective students hope to integrate the GMU C&D's program philosophical purpose into their program of studies.

The GMU Counseling & Development program established strong working relationships and partnerships with all of the local school districts. These partnerships have resulted in significant improvements in many aspects of the program, especially in the quality of placements for practicum and internship students. They have also resulted in stronger supervision by school district site supervisors.

Another example of the two-way partnership with one of the school districts is the development of a post-master's school counseling and administration certificate program. In collaboration with Fairfax County Public School's coordinator for counseling, other school district administrators, and the C&D faculty, a program was developed and implemented to provide intensive preparation for experienced secondary school counselors to assume counseling leadership roles. Its field-based courses emphasized experiential learning and the cohort-training model.

One last example of GMU's adoption of the school counseling educational reform initiative is demonstrated in the C&D faculty's belief that it has a responsibility to provide continuous professional development opportunities to counselor educators, professional school counselors, and other mental health counselors in their area. This was evident when GMU hosted an all-day workshop on "Choice Theory" (Glasser, 1998) with Dr. William Glasser. Well over 300 C&D students, colleagues, professional school counselors, mental health professionals, and area school district personnel were in attendance.

## Recommended Actions for Change

The training of pre-service school counselors is a tremendous responsibility, one that graduate schools do not take lightly. An opportunity now exists to improve the quality of counselor education programs. University counselor educators have a professional responsibility to examine and re-structure current programs that are outdated and incompatible with current research and practice. The following recommendations are offered as steps to address these changes:

1. Incorporate ASCA's *National Model for School Counseling Programs* into the school counselor education program.
2. Integrate specific educational reform changes, i.e., *Transformation of School Counseling Initiative* (Education Trust, 2002), into the training of pre-service school counselors.
3. Form and/or strengthen partnerships with local school districts in order to establish authentic and collaborative relationships.
4. Help school districts understand, accept, and implement the school counseling reform initiatives of the professional school counselor.
5. Help school district leadership understand the importance of integrating theory and practice, and thus link what is taught in graduate programs to the real world of the professional school counselor.

## Summary/Conclusion

Counselor educators have the federally mandated requirements to train pre-service school counseling students to become professional school counselors who can effectively work with students and adults within school communities. ASCA and CACREP provide the necessary training requirements to achieve this responsibility. ASCA's *National Model* and The Education Trust initiatives have laid the groundwork for the implementation of improved standards and competencies. Each offers specific examples needed for the training and education of pre-service school counseling students and for professional school counselors working in school communities. The challenge now lies within counselor education programs and local school districts to implement these initiatives. Educational leaders must be serious about training student counselors and professional school counselors to help all students achieve academic success and to ensure that no child is left behind.

## References

American School Counselor Association. (1998). *Ethical standards for school counselors.* Retrieved on July 8, 2002 from http:/www.schoolcounselor.org/content.cfm?L1=1&L2=15.

American School Counselor Association. (1999a). *The professional school counselor and credentialing and licensure.* (Adopted 1990; revised 1993, 1999). Retrieved on July 8, 2002 from http://www.schoolcounselor.org/content.cfm?L1=1000&L2=14.

American School Counselor Association. (1999b). *The role of the professional school counselor.* Retrieved on July 8, 2002 from http://www.schoolcounselor.org content.cfm?L1=1000&L2=69.

American School Counselor Association. (2002a). *Certification requirements.* Retrieved on July 8, 2002 from http://www.schoolcounselor.org/content.cfm?L1=1000&L2=81

American School Counselor Association. (2002b). *American School Counselor Association: One vision one voice.* Retrieved on July 8, 2002 from http://www.schoolcounselor.org/

American School Counselor Association. (2003). *The ASCA national model: A framework for school counseling programs.* Alexandria, VA: Author

Bemak, F. (2000). Transforming the role of the counselor to provide leadership in educational reform through collaboration. *Professional School Counseling, 3,* 323-331.

CACREP. (2002). *Council for Accreditation of Counseling and Related Educational Programs (CACREP): The 2001 standards.* Retrieved on July 8, 2002 from http://www.counseling.org/cacrep 2001standards700.htm

Campbell, C. A., & Dahir, C. A. (1997). *The national standards for school counseling programs.* Alexandria, VA: American School Counselor Association.

The Education Trust. (2002). *Transforming school counseling: The national initiative for transforming school counseling.* Retrieved on July 8, 2002 from http://www.edtrust.org/main/main/school_counseling.asp

George Mason University. (2002). *Counseling & Development Program.* Retrieved on July 8, 2002 from http://gse.gmu.edu/programs/counseling/

Glasser, W. (1998). *Choice theory: A new psychology of personal freedom.* New York: Harper-Collins.

Hatch, T., & Bowers, J. (2002). The blocks to build on. *School Counselor, 39*(5), 13-19.

House, R. M., & Hayes, R. (2002). School counselors: Becoming key players in school reform. *Professional School Counseling, 5*(4), 249-256.

Library of Congress. (2004). *Thomas legislative information on the Internet: Bill summary & status for the 108th Congress.* Retrieved on February 18, 2004 from http://thomas.loc.gov

Muro, J., & Kottman, T. (1995). *Guidance and counseling in the elementary and middle schools – A practical approach.* Madison, WI: WCB Brown & Benchmark.

Perusse, R., & Goodnough, G. E. (2001). A comparison of existing school counselor program content with The Education Trust initiatives. *Counselor Education and Supervision, 41, 100-110.*

# Chapter 10

## Professional School Counseling Advocacy: Marketing and Beyond

*Laurie A. Carlson & Teresa I. Yohon*

### Preview

This chapter introduces and supports the concept of professional advocacy for professional school counselors. Professional advocacy is essential to the continued strength of the school counseling profession, and professional school counselors themselves play a critical role. The main sections of this chapter include essential concepts, public awareness and marketing strategies for the professional school counselor, advocacy beyond marketing, and public policy and legislation.

School counseling is a continuously evolving profession. This continuous evolution has lead to confusion and debate regarding the definition of professional school counseling. As a result, for too long the professional school counselor's role has been defined by those outside of the profession (Paisley & Borders, 1995; Paisley & McMahon, 2001). This enforces the critical need for professional school counselors to advocate for themselves and their profession.

Professional school counselors often struggle when trying to help others learn about the school counselor's role within the school community. Because of this, formal training and supervised practice in the skills of professional advocacy are extremely important. There is a need to train school counselors in the skills of professional advocacy, including public and political policy awareness and development (Carlson, 2002; Tysl, 1997). This chapter reviews the concepts of advocacy and political/public policy development, introduces concepts and effective marketing strategies as an essential foundation of public awareness, and identifies resources available to professional school counselors.

### Essential Concepts

Several organizations have taken a vested interest in education and the profession of school counseling. The Education Trust is one such organization. Since 1997, the Education Trust has been working towards a new vision for 21st century school counseling practice. To realize this vision, professional school counselors "will need to learn leadership skills and advocacy skills as well as skills needed to promote change in already established systems" (Sears & Haag-Granello, 2002, p. 169). Schools can characteristically be closed systems, difficult to permeate; and young professional school counselors need to be trained in the skills required for infusing change. Rye and Sparks (1999) offer many helpful strategies to professional school counselors for weaving a school counseling program into an existing school system. Identification and inclusion of community values into the school counseling program is the most foundational concept. Strong and insightful program planning utilizes the American School Counseling Association's (ASCA) *National Model* guidelines (Bowers & Hatch, 2002; ASCA, 2003) to represent best practice, while core values from the community provide both a marketable program and an accepting market.

Program marketing is one essential component of professional advocacy. Much of the current school counseling literature supports the need for professional advocacy, including documentation of impact upon student success and systemic educational change (Bowers & Hatch, 2002; Erford, House, & Martin, 2003; Whiston, 2003) and forming collegial relationships with the community and other school personnel to further the mission of the comprehensive school counseling program:

> Both external and internal publics are important in the ongoing dialogue about the role and function of professional school counselors. Part of the professional school counselor's essential role in schools is to ensure that professional school counselors are defined and affirmed as supporting the academic, career. And interpersonal success of all learners in a school...A strong internal and external public relations effort is essential to ensure that professional school counselors are seen as central to the school's mission of educating all students effectively. (Bailey, Getch, & Chen-Hayes, 2003, p. 429)

## Public Awareness and Marketing the School Counseling Program

Gysbers and Henderson (2000) included marketing as an essential component of effective, comprehensive guidance program implementation. Effective marketing relies on strong public awareness strategies. Public awareness can be achieved through accountability, professional service, professionalism, publicity, student activities and events, and visual display within the school (VanZandt & Hayslip, 2001).

There are many resources available for professional school counselors looking for ideas concerning public awareness. One resource is the American Counseling Association's (ACA) *Public Awareness Ideas and Strategies for Professional Counselors.* Information regarding this material can be found on ACA's website at http://www.counseling.org. ASCA also offers the *School Counselor's Resource Kit* from their website at http://www.schoolcounselor.org.

VanZandt and Hayslip (2001) offer professional school counselors the following suggestions: (a) submit an annual report to the school board demonstrating how well you have addressed the goals of your comprehensive plan; (b) meet regularly with building administrators; (c) serve on the advisory committee of a local community service organization; (d) be an advisor for a school club; (e) present a workshop at a state counseling conference; (f) be a model of mental and physical wellness; (g) regularly send out a school counseling program newsletter; (h) share program activities through the local cable TV station; (i) celebrate National School Counseling Week [always the first full week of February]; (j) develop a Step-Up Day for students who will be entering or leaving the school the following year; (k) develop attractive bulletin boards that focus on the themes from the guidance curriculum; and (l) wear lapel pins with counseling messages on them.

## From the Marketing Field to Professional School Counselors

The key to successful marketing is consumer satisfaction that occurs when one understands consumers and then meets their needs. A marketing "mix," consisting of pricing, product, distribution, and promotion, is developed for marketing tangible products. These marketing mix components are also important for services such as professional school counseling, but since counseling services are intangible, a special marketing approach is required.

In professional school counseling, satisfaction for the student and the educational community is dependent upon the interplay between the student and the counselor. In other words, the student participates in and affects the outcome of the service. Because of this interplay, there is variability in the success of counseling experiences. Additionally, the need for counseling varies depending on the time of year and special needs (i.e., school violence, death in student body or faculty, etc.). This variability means that the marketing mix developed by professional school counselors must pay special attention to the consumers, the process of counseling, and physical evidence of successful counseling experiences (Zeithaml & Bitner, 1996).

*The Marketing "Mix"*

Professional school counselors need to perform three types of marketing activities to reach three different audiences: internal marketing (marketing between counselors and faculty, administrators, and staff), external marketing (marketing between the counseling program and the community), and client marketing (marketing between the counseling program and students). Internal marketing is crucial to a successful school counseling program. In fact, the promotion of the school counseling program to administrators, teachers, and staff including secretaries, janitors, or security personnel should be done before external or client marketing. Internal marketing ensures that people who come in contact with students are aware of the help available through the counseling program.

External marketing is directed toward people outside the school. Parents, business people, and community agencies such as child protection and health agencies are among the targets of external marketing. These groups support the school counseling program by sharing knowledge about the school counseling program to students and families who may use their services and through extended services that aren't being provided internally through the school counseling program. External marketing is part of external advocacy, a topic covered later in this chapter.

Client marketing makes certain that students, the end user of school counseling services, are familiar with available counseling services and know that professional school counselors possess the skills and attitudes that make students feel "safe" in using the counseling service. Typical client marketing activities include brochures about services offered, information workshops, bulletin boards about the counseling services, and classroom visitations.

Counseling "quality" involves the technical and functional quality of the counseling experience. The technical quality is essentially concerned with whether or not the counseling process helps students. The functional quality relates to the degree to which professional school counselors within the program showed concern, were nonjudgmental, and inspired more successful student behavior. A needs assessment is an essential tool for listening to all audiences and developing a well-rounded program that matches the needs of the local community. These audiences also should evaluate the counseling program based on the goals and mission of the school counseling program. Evaluation should include quantitative data such as the number of students served or a documented decrease in negative behavior, and qualitative data that may include student narratives via focus groups or case studies. Evidence collected about the counseling program's effectiveness should be shared with the counseling program's audiences and is part of internal advocacy as outlined later in this chapter.

## Marketing Plan for a Professional School Counseling Program

A professional school counseling program's marketing plan focuses on the program's audiences and what messages these audiences need to hear. These messages may include: (a) goals and objectives of the counseling program, (b) research or evaluation information about the program, (c) available services, (d) new programs, and (e) state and national school counseling initiatives.

A professional school counseling program marketing plan should be developed every year.

Program goals and audiences change. Therefore, the marketing plan should be updated as well. To develop a marketing plan, the professional school counselor must first identify the audiences. Second, a decision regarding what message to send to each audience is made. To help determine the message, it is useful for the professional school counselor to ask questions like, "What does a parent, an administrator, or businessperson need to know about the school counseling program?" After determining what information is important to each audience, one must determine what action is desired from the audience upon hearing the message. Actions include students coming to the counseling office, business leaders supporting a career development workshop, or internal support for a crisis management team. The final task is to determine how to most effectively deliver the message to the audience. A school counseling program can provide workshops, develop a website describing services and providing online career information, or host a parent night. To help in the organization of the marketing plan, a marketing plan worksheet is provided in Table 1.

## Beyond Marketing to Advocacy

Marketing and public awareness are merely the beginning. Advocacy goes beyond public relations and marketing in that it seeks to influence, not merely inform (Lenhardt & Young, 2001). Professional school counselors have a long and rich history in advocacy, especially advocacy surrounding student and social issues (Borders, 2002; Gysbers, 2001). But professional school counselors need to go beyond advocating for students and take an active role in advocating for their profession (Lenhardt & Young, 2001; O'Bryant, 1992; Paisley & McMahon, 2001; Sears & Haag-Granello, 2002).

### *Internal Advocacy*

Internal advocacy measures are those that are essentially local in scope. Lenhardt and Young (2001) outlined the following internal advocacy strategies: (a) provide accountability for your program, (b) conduct research on the efficiency of school counseling, (c) establish a networking system with influential community members, (d) complete an annual needs assessment, (e) market your program, (f) join your school's site-based management team, (g) join outside community organizations, and (h) keep abreast of legislative issues.

As indicated earlier, program accountability begins with strong program planning that is based on meaningful goals and objectives developed from an understanding of professional and community core values and identified needs. Sample needs assessment instruments can be found in the needs assessment chapter of this book and in several school counseling texts including Erford (2003), Rye & Sparks (1999), and Wittmer (2000). From the basis of strong program planning, appropriate and meaningful program evaluation can be carried out. It is important for school counseling programs to institute both formative and summative evaluation. Many leaders in the field have devoted much effort to advancing the skills of program evaluation. For some guidelines on program evaluation see Erford (2003), Gysbers & Henderson (2000), Rye & Sparks (1999), VanZandt & Hayslip (2001), and the new national model developed by ASCA (Bowers & Hatch, 2002; ASCA, 2003). Program evaluation and program accountability are related but not synonymous. Program accountability requires that evaluation results and other similar information, such as research findings, be shared with the stake-holders in the school district. Modes of dissemination of information include, but are not limited to, district newsletters, local newspapers, community service bulletins, and public forums.

For too long, professional school counselors have ascribed to the notion that research is just for counselor educators and other academicians. Practice-based research is essential not only for individual program accountability, but also the advancement of professional practice. It

**Table 1. Marketing Plan Development Worksheet.**

| | Internal Audiences | | | External Audiences | | |
|---|---|---|---|---|---|---|
| | **Administration** | **Teachers** | **Staff** | **Business/ Community** | **Help Agencies** | **Students** |
| Summer<br><br>Overall Goal: Program information | Message<br>Changes in counseling program staff, etc., which enhance student support<br><br>How delivered:<br>e-mail<br><br>Action to be taken:<br>Feedback on e-mail | Message:<br>Changes in counseling program, staff etc., which enhance student support<br><br>How delivered:<br>e-mail; updated website information<br><br>Action to be taken:<br>Use of new services and staff in the school year | Message:<br>Changes in counseling program, staff etc., which enhance student support<br><br>How delivered:<br>e-mail; updated website information<br><br>Action to be taken:<br>Student referrals to counseling center | Message:<br>School counseling program's goals and objectives; how business and whole community can participate in the program<br><br>How delivered:<br>Brochures; scheduled future presentations<br><br>Action to be taken:<br>Business and community leaders involved in school counseling program as mentors, job interview coaches, etc. | Message:<br>School counseling program's goals and objectives<br><br>How delivered:<br>Brochures; schedule future presentations or meetings with their staff<br><br>Action to be taken:<br>List of agencies that will provide support services to students and school staff | Message:<br>School counseling's program's goals and objectives; staff list; available support services<br><br>How delivered:<br>Prepare for school year by developing multiple message formats, i.e. brochures, bulletin boards class presentations, etc.<br><br>Action to be taken:<br>Students use counseling services more frequently |
| August<br><br>Overall Goal: Develop community resources and increase knowledge on bullying | Message:<br>Bullying resources available for student and staff use<br><br>How delivered:<br>e-mail<br><br>Action to be taken:<br>Use information when teachers have problems with bullying in their classrooms | Message:<br>Bullying resources available for student and staff use<br><br>How delivered:<br>e-mail; workshops; updated website<br><br>Action to be taken:<br>Recognize students who are being bullied; help students themselves or refer them to the counseling office | Message:<br>Bullying resources available for student and staff use<br><br>How delivered<br>e-mail<br><br>Action to be taken:<br>Recognize students who are being bullied; refer them to the counseling office | Message:<br>You are a valuable resource for students; ways to support students' career development<br><br>How delivered:<br>presentations; brochures; personal contacts<br><br>Action to be taken:<br>Develop lists of businesses where students can have job shadowing experiences | Message:<br>Valuable partner in student counseling support<br><br>How delivered:<br>Presentations<br><br>Action to be taken:<br>Develop list of "advocate" agencies with specific contact people where students can be referred | Message:<br>School counseling program's goals and objectives; staff list, available support services<br><br>How delivered:<br>Prepare for school year; develop multiple formats for message, i.e., brochures bulletin boards, class presentations, etc.<br><br>Action to be taken:<br>Students use counseling services more frequently |

is imperative that professional school counselors understand that the parameters surrounding research are extensive. Research designs can range from descriptive to experimental, qualitative to quantitative, and single case study to large samples. A single intervention with one student can be carefully documented and analyzed to provide meaningful practice-based research. It is also important to regularly read the professional literature. Not only does the literature provide insight and new strategies for practice, it also gives the professional school counselor a guide for research sought after in professional publications.

Establishing a strong community network and joining outside community organizations are closely related. Professional school counselors cannot passively expect the community to know and understand the school counseling profession. They must demonstrate their skills through active leadership not only in school-based collaborative programs, but also in community-based programs (Green & Keys, 2001; Paisley & McMahon, 2001). There are many organizations that can benefit from the expertise of professional school counselors and that can offer a valuable connection to community leaders. Examples of such organizations include child protection teams, corrections advisory boards, early childhood programs, service organizations such as Jaycees, and community arts councils. Marketing and needs assessments were covered earlier in this chapter, and legislative issues will be covered later in a special section. Some of the internal advocacy strategies discussed in this section are closely related to those in the next section, and at times, advocacy strategies straddle the line between internal and external advocacy.

*External Advocacy*

External advocacy strategies typically are more regional or national in scope. According to Lenhardt and Young (2001), external advocacy strategies include (a) membership in professional organizations; (b) state and national credentials; (c) organization of a guidance task force or advisory committee; (d) regular meetings with local businesses and service agencies; (e) repeated contact with legislators; (f) applications for local, state, and federal grants; and (g) appointment of legislative liaisons within professional organizations.

Many professional school counselors are exposed to professional organizations during their training programs. The image of the counseling profession rests on the shoulders of both professional organizations and individual counselors themselves (VanZandt & Hayslip, 2001). Active membership in professional organizations can provide professional school counselors with an opportunity to demonstrate a dedication to the profession, and with many other professional advantages. Networking and connection with other professional school counselors is the most direct benefit of membership. This professional connection manifests through not only meetings and conferences, but also through newsletters, journals, and other print materials. Local and state organizations typically provide extensive opportunities for networking, and regional and national organizations have the fiscal and staffing resources to provide valuable support resources. Professional school counselors who are tempted to seek membership in only local/state school counseling associations should seriously consider the benefit of joining not only ACA and ASCA, but also other related professional organizations.

The National Career Development Association (NCDA) and the Association for Counselor Education and Supervision (ACES) have both done much to support school counseling (Paisley & Borders, 1995). Because so much of what professional school counselors do is related to career planning and life skills throughout student development, NCDA is an extremely valuable resource. The most readily available resources from NCDA can be found on the organization's website at http://www.ncda.org. Here, the organization offers material for elementary, middle and senior high school level professional school counselors. The support emerging from ACES tends to be more indirect. ACES is committed to addressing training and supervision issues for professional school counselors. Perhaps one of the greatest influences on the profession is the training accreditation program, the Council for the Accreditation of Counseling and Related Educational Programs (CACREP).

Many professional counselors are familiar with the work of CACREP; however, most are unaware that the council was first formulated by ACES to govern the training of professional school counselors in particular (Wittmer, 2000). Accreditation is a voluntary process that training programs dedicate themselves to for various reasons, including a demonstration of commitment to professionalism. Just as accreditation is a programmatic commitment to professionalism, seeking certification is the individual professional's commitment to professionalism. The National Board for Certified Counselors (NBCC) offers not only the Nationally Certified Counselor (NCC) credential, but also the Nationally Certified School Counselor (NCSC) credential. Information regarding the acquisition of the NCSC credential can be found on the internet at http://www.nbcc.org/cert/ncsc.htm.

In October of 2002, the National Board for Professional Teaching Standards (NBPTS) developed national standards for the certification of professional school counselors. General information regarding the pursuit of certification from the NTBS board can be found at http://www.nbpts.org/standards/nbcert.cfm, and specific information regarding the school counselor certification can be found at http://www.nbpts.org/candidates/guide/whichcert/27SchoolCounseling.html. Despite which certification is achieved, the pursuit of national certification is a strong statement by professional school counselors regarding their dedication to professionalism, and this dedication is an important component of effective professional advocacy.

Unfortunately, sometimes a lack of financial resources can hinder both the marketing and outreach of school counseling programs as well as the involvement of professional school counselors in the leadership of professional organizations. Enter the importance of grant writing. Regrettably, many professional school counselors are not exposed to training related to specific skills necessary for successful grant writing. Grants usually come from two places: national or state agencies and foundations. National or state grants usually require extensive writing, often 20 to 25 pages of narrative plus various appendices. Foundations tend to require a brief project statement and a budget, usually about five pages in length. No matter to what agency or group the grant proposal will be sent, five key strategies should be followed in writing the proposal:

1. Follow the grant's writing directions exactly. This includes number of pages, font size, and table format. The narrative should be organized in the exact sections indicated in the grant's Request for Proposal (RFP). Use of the exact section titles allows grant reviewers to find needed information quickly and increases the chances of maximum points in each section.
2. Review what past grants have been funded by the agency or foundation. Understanding prior funding history increases ones understanding of what types of projects the agency funds and how the proposed project is unique from past-funded projects.
3. Clearly state the problem the grant proposal is designed to solve. In most cases, the problem needs to be stated in both local and national contexts. The local context provides the reason for the grant request while the national perspective provides a funding rationale if the grant activity presents a model that can be applied to a more universal problem.
4. Understand who the grant readers will be. Grant readers have their own "lenses" and interpretations of the grant guidelines and what the important "problems" are that can be solved via grant monies. Call the grant program director or foundation liaison to clarify what types of projects are most likely to be funded and from where grant readers will be solicited.
5. Write measurable outcomes for the grant project, then write the evaluation plan to

measure these outcomes. Evaluation plans are hard to write so think about evaluation through the grant writing process.

These are just a few basic strategies for professional school counselors to consider when writing successful grant proposals. It is also wise to seek the counsel of other professionals who have a history of success. Grants are often linked in one way or another to public policy and legislation. This enforces the fact that informed political involvement is a key to effective professional advocacy.

## Public Policy and Legislation

Professional school counselors need to help shape education through active involvement and leadership regarding local, state, and national policy that leads to stronger legislative support of guidance and counseling programming (Gysbers, 2001). Gaining legislative support for the profession at local, state, and national levels is paramount to the future of professional school counseling (Lenhardt & Young, 2001; Roberts, 1996). The school counseling profession has a longstanding and essential relationship with legislative action. From the National Defense Education Act of 1958 and the Elementary and Secondary Education Act of 1965, to the Elementary School Counseling Demonstration Act of 1995, federal legislation has significantly influenced the creation and definition of the school counseling profession (Paisley & Borders, 1995). Beyond federal legislation, state licensing laws and mandates have further defined and influenced the profession of school counseling. It is imperative that professional school counselors individually take responsibility for understanding and influencing legislation at all levels.

Writing to a state or United States legislator is an important tool in political advocacy. In writing a letter or sending e-mail to legislators, keep the communication brief, ideally only one-page in length. Discuss only one bill or issue per correspondence. The correspondence should include: (a) an introduction of yourself or the organization on whose behalf you are writing; (b) a straightforward introduction to the issue, which may be support of a bill; (c) the bill number if available; (d) a concise explanation of why you support or oppose a particular bill or issue (bullet points are very effective); (e) how the bill or issue will affect your local situation; (f) specific facts or an example to illustrate your point; and (g) contact information for follow-up if the legislator desires. E-mail is just as effective as a letter and may be received more promptly by a legislator since posted letters are undergoing a more stringent review before going to the legislator.

Both ACA and ASCA offer professional school counselors valuable resources related to legislation and political advocacy. At http://www.counseling.org/public, professional school counselors have access to the public policy page of ACA's website. Here, professionals will find links to the ACA Legislative Action Center, Washington Update Archives, Library of Congress Legislative Information, and other important links. Through ACA's important links for public policy at http://www.counseling.org/public/links.htm, one can find links to such legislative sources as (a) the ARCA/Alliance Legislative Page, (b) The White House, (c) the U.S. Senate, (d) the House of Representatives, (e) Thomas (a searchable database concerning the U.S. Congress and the legislative process where one can search bills, by topic, bill number, or title), and (f) a link to help send a message to Congress. The ACA Legislative Action Center and these web-based resources are extraordinarily valuable to professional counselors committed to making a difference through public policy.

In addition to ACA's resources, ASCA also offers comprehensive resources for public policy and legislative issues in school counseling. At http://www.schoolcounselor.org/content, the professional school counselor will find a link entitled "Legislative Affairs" that will provide members with an opportunity to sign up for legislative updates delivered electronically through e-mail, and links similar to those offered by the ACA site.

## Summary/Conclusion

The topics and specific strategies presented in this chapter provide a foundation and starting point for professional school counselors as they embark on the critical road to professional advocacy. The future of school counseling rests squarely on the shoulders of professional school counselors who possess the skills and passion to advance the profession through effective marketing, thoughtful program planning, program delivery that enlists the cooperation of numerous stakeholders, leadership at multiple levels, program enhancement through successful grant-writing, and legislative involvement.

## References

American School Counselor Association. (2003). *The ASCA national model: A framework for school counseling programs.* Alexandria, VA: Author.

Bailey, D. F., Getch, Y. Q., & Chen-Hayes, S. (2003). Professional school counselors as social and academic advocates. In B. T. Erford, *Transforming the school counseling profession* (pp. 411-434). Columbus, OH: Merrill/Prentice-Hall.

Borders, L. D. (2002). School counseling in the 21st century: Personal and professional reflections. *Professional School Counseling, 5*, 180-185.

Bowers, J. L., & Hatch, P. A. (2002). *The national model for school counseling programs.* Alexandria, VA: The American School Counselor Association. Available at http://www.schoolcounselor.org/library/modeltext.pdf.

Carlson, L. A. (2002). *Project CARE: A student exercise in learning professional advocacy.* Available on-line at http://ericcass.uncg.edu/brag/carlson.html.

Erford, B. T. (Ed.) (2003). *Transforming the school counseling profession.* Columbus, OH: Merrill/Prentice-Hall.

Erford, B. T., House, R., & Martin, P. (2003). Transforming the school counseling profession. In B. T. Erford, *Transforming the school counseling profession* (pp.1-20). Columbus, OH: Merrill/Prentice-Hall.

Green, A., & Keys, S. (2001). Expanding the developmental school counseling paradigm: Meeting the needs of the 21st century student. *Professional School Counseling, 5*, 84-95.

Gysbers, N. C. (2001). School guidance and counseling in the 21st century: Remember the past into the future. *Professional School Counseling, 5*, 96-105.

Gysbers, N. C., & Henderson, P. (2000). *Developing and managing your school guidance program* (3rd ed.). Alexandria, VA: American Counseling Association.

Kuranz, M. (2002). Cultivating student potential. *Professional School Counseling, 5*, 172-179.

Lenhardt, A. C., & Young, P. A. (2001). Proactive strategies for advancing elementary school counseling programs: A blueprint for the new millennium. *Professional School Counseling, 4*, 187-194.

O'Bryant, B. J. (1992). *Marketing yourself as a professional counselor* (Report No. EDO-CG-92-26). Ann Arbor, MI: ERIC Clearinghouse on Counseling and Personnel Services. (ERIC Document Reproduction Service No. ED 347 492).

Paisley, P. O., & Borders, L. D. (1995). School counseling: An evolving specialty. *Journal of Counseling and Development, 74*, 150-153.

Paisley, P. O., & McMahon, G. (2001). School counseling for the 21st century: Challenges and opportunities. *Professional School Counseling, 5*, 105-115.

Roberts, W. B., Jr. (1996). Research in action: Using survey results on the Elementary School Counseling Demonstration Act as a communication tool with members of Congress. *Elementary School Guidance and Counseling, 30*, 275-281.

Rye, D. R., & Sparks, R. S. (1999). *Strengthening K-12 school counseling programs: A support system approach* (2nd ed.). Philadelphia: Accelerated Development.

Sears, S. J., & Haag-Granello, D. (2002). School counseling now and in the future: A reaction. *Professional School Counseling, 5*, 164-171.

Tysl, L. (1997, January). Counselors have a responsibility to promote the counseling profession. *Counseling Today*, pp. 40-42.

VanZandt, Z., & Hayslip, J. (2001). *Developing your school counseling program: A handbook for systemic planning*. Belmont, CA: Wadsworth.

Whiston, S. C. (2003). Outcomes research on school counseling services. In B. T. Erford (Ed.), *Transforming the school counseling profession* (pp. 435-447). Columbus, OH: Merrill/Prentice-Hall.

Wittmer, J. (2000). *Managing your school counseling program: K-12 developmental strategies* (2nd ed.). Minneapolis: Educational Media Corporation.

Zeithaml, V. A., & Bitner, M. J. (1996). *Services marketing*. New York: McGraw-Hill.

# *Section 2*

# Techniques and Approaches to Counseling in Schools

# Chapter 11

## Using Cognitive Behavioral Techniques

*Ann Vernon*

### Preview

The purpose of this chapter is to provide an overview of cognitive behavioral principles, with specific emphasis on practical applications of CBT and REBT that professional school counselors can use in working with students in individual and small group counseling. In addition to an intervention focus, the author discusses how to develop a preventative approach that integrates cognitive principles in classroom guidance lessons. Further applications with parents and teachers are also highlighted.

Rational emotive behavior therapy (REBT), founded by Dr. Albert Ellis, was the first of the cognitive behavior therapies (CBT) and has been in existence since 1955 (Ellis, 1957). After Ellis originated REBT, Beck developed his approach, known as cognitive therapy (CT), and Meichenbaum followed suit with another alternative, cognitive behavior modification (CBM), which focused on changing clients' self-verbalizations (Corey, 2001). These three forms of cognitive behavior therapy (CBT) encompass a variety of strategies and procedures, but they "all share the tenet that learning plays a central role in the acquisition and maintenance of behavior, whether adaptive or dysfunctional—and that learning involves the manner in which the individual processes information cognitively" (Finch, Nelson, & Ott, 1993, p. 5).

Cognitive-behavior therapies emphasize how emotional and behavioral problems can be addressed most effectively through cognitive restructuring - showing people how their irrational beliefs or cognitive distortions upset them and how they can modify this inaccurate thinking using a variety of methods. Cognitive therapies emphasize the present and strive to be time limited (Corey, 2001).

Although REBT and CBT share this common philosophical basis concerning the effect of beliefs on feelings and behaviors, REBT is considered more comprehensive and integrative than most other cognitive therapies because, unlike the other CBT therapies, REBT has very strong emotional and behavioral components in addition to the cognitive components. As such, it is considered more multimodal in nature (Ellis & Poppa, 2001).

Today, cognitive therapies are increasing in popularity and are used extensively throughout the world, not only with adults, but also with children and adolescents (Corey, 2001). Meichenbaum's self-instructional training program (SIT) was originally designed to teach impulsive children to identify verbal self-commands that would help them regulate their own behavior (Finch et al., 1993). Beck's cognitive therapy initially focused on the treatment of depression, and Kovac modeled the *Children's Depression Inventory* (CDI), the most commonly used measure of childhood depression, on the *Beck Depression Inventory* for adults (Finch et al.).

REBT has a long-standing history of application with children, most notably through The Living School that Ellis established in 1971 to help young people learn rational principles. Since that time, it has been applied to children of all ages for a variety of problems, including school phobia, depression, anger, underachievement, acting out, anxiety, perfectionism, and procrastination, as well as typical developmental issues (Bernard, 1991; Ellis & Wilde, 2002; Vernon, in press; Wilde, 1992).

An integral part of REBT is its strong emphasis on prevention and emotional education. Several programs have been designed to help children and adolescents apply rational thinking skills to promote emotional and behavioral well-being (Bernard, 2001; Knaus, 1974; Vernon, 1989a, 1989b, 1998a, 1998b, 1998c). These programs can be used in classroom and small group counseling settings to teach rational principles.

The purpose of this chapter is to describe practical applications of CBT and REBT that professional school counselors can use in individual and small group counseling. Classroom guidance applications that emphasize prevention will also be addressed, as well as how to employ these principles with parents and teachers.

## Cognitive Theory: A Brief Overview

"What we feel is what we think" is a simplistic way of describing the philosophic basis of the cognitive behavior therapies. Maladaptive thoughts affect how people perceive activating events and result in distressing emotions. Beck (1988), Burns (1999), Ellis (2001a), and Meichenbaum (1977) all identified overgeneralizing, "awfulizing," and "musturbating" as key dysfunctional beliefs, as well as mind reading, focusing on the negative, dichotomous thinking, personalizing, magnification, arbitrary inference, and perfectionizing (Beck, Rush, Shaw, & Emery, 1979; Ellis, 2001b). According to these experts, dysfunctional beliefs have to be challenged or restructured in order for individuals to experience less intense negative emotions, behave in more self-enhancing ways, and think more functionally and rationally.

Cognitive restructuring can be accomplished in a variety of ways, depending on the counselor and the specific orientation. Ellis, for example, favors a very active-directive, and oftentimes confrontive, method of disputing (Ellis & Dryden, 1997; Ellis & MacLaren, 1998). However, Ellis himself acknowledged that the degree to which you are active-directive is a choice (Dryden & Ellis, 2001), and practitioners working with children and adolescents would be well advised to be flexible and less directive, in addition to employing a wide range of disputing strategies (Vernon, in press). Beck used more of a reflective questioning process that helped the clients discover their own misconceptions, while Meichenbaum's self-instructional therapy helped clients gain awareness of their own self-talk (Corey, 2001).

This overview of the basic premises of CBT is obviously overly simplistic, but given the nature of this chapter, the major focus is on practical applications with children and adolescents. Readers are encouraged to engage in further study and training in the theory and practice of these therapies.

## Effectiveness with School-Aged Populations

Cognitive behavioral therapies are very effective with children and adolescents for several reasons:

1. They are easily understood and can be adapted to children of most ages, cultures, and intelligence levels.
2. They are short-term problem-solving forms of counseling, which makes them particularly applicable in school settings where time for counseling is often limited.
3. The fact that these are briefer forms of counseling is especially important for young clients whose sense of time is so immediate; they need something to help them *now*.
4. The teachable concepts readily lend themselves to skill acquisition.

5. They teach behavioral and emotional self-control by helping children understand the connection between thoughts, feelings, and behaviors.
6. They help children deal realistically with what they can change in their lives and help them cope more effectively with what they can't change.
7. The cognitive principles empower children to deal not only with present concerns, but also give them tools to use for solving future problems.
8. They are particularly effective with children in the concrete operational stage of development, since children in this developmental stage have a natural tendency to think dichotomously and lack the ability to reason logically. Teaching them to challenge their cognitive distortions helps minimize cognitive deficiencies.

Cognitive therapies promote skill acquisition; they help children acquire practical coping skills. More importantly, they teach children how to *think* better. As a result, youngsters don't just "feel better," but they also "get better" because they correct the faulty thinking that creates and perpetuates problems. For this reason, as well as for those previously mentioned, professional school counselors will see that using cognitive behavioral approaches with children and adolescents is an efficient and effective approach for problem remediation and prevention.

## Individual Counseling Applications

Children and adolescents have to deal with typical developmental problems, and many have to deal with more serious situational problems stemming from dysfunctional family environments, death, illness, or other major issues. Because their sense of time is more immediate and their array of coping skills may be limited, it is critical to employ developmentally-appropriate strategies that address the specific problem. Accurate problem assessment is the first phase of this process.

*Problem Assessment*

Problem assessment consists of assessing cognitive distortions and irrational beliefs, as well as negative feelings and problematic behaviors. Since children, and many adolescents as well, may not be verbally adept and will struggle to label their feelings or articulate their thoughts, professional school counselors have to be creative and use a variety of methods in the assessment process. Inviting younger clients to draw, role-play, or use puppets to describe the problem may be necessary. Likewise, using techniques such as feeling flash cards, unfinished sentences or feeling games may be good assessment strategies.

After getting a sense of the problem and how the child feels and behaves, it is important to determine the frequency, intensity, and duration of the problem: How long has it been going on, how often does it occur, and how intense is it? It may be helpful to ask students to fill out a feeling/behaving chart, in which they rate the frequency of the problematic feeling or behavior every hour of the day for a week. This visual record is an excellent way for the student, as well as the young client, to better understand what the problem is.

After establishing what the problem is, how the student feels and behaves, and how intense the problematic emotions and behaviors are, it is time to assess the beliefs. Keep in mind that not all beliefs are dysfunctional or irrational. For example, it is perfectly normal for a 10-year-old student to feel worried about her grandmother who is sick. One would detect the presence of irrational beliefs by asking her what she is thinking about her grandmother's situation. If she says that all she can think about is that her grandmother might die and that if that happens she would want to die too because she couldn't stand to live without her, you would know that this client was awfulizing since she is thinking that *she* can't go on living if her grandmother dies.

On the other hand, if she is thinking that her grandmother could die, that she would be very sad, and that it would be very difficult to deal with, there is nothing irrational or dysfunctional about her thinking. The same holds true for an adolescent who didn't receive the scholarship he thought he would get. He naturally would feel disappointed, but if he were devastated, he would be telling himself that this was the worst thing that could ever happen to him, that it proves he is worthless, and that it will do no good to ever apply for scholarships again because he will never get one. These cognitive distortions contribute to his extreme emotional reaction.

In assessing irrational and cognitive distortions, the professional school counselor needs to detect musts (I must always do well; others must treat me as I deserve to be treated), awfulizing and blowing problems out of proportion (this is so awful; nothing could be worse), low frustration tolerance (things should come easily to me; I shouldn't have to work too hard at anything), dichotomous thinking (it's either this way or that way), overgeneralizing (she will always be mean), or personalizing (it's all my fault she ignored me) and self-downing (I'm only good if I perform perfectly).

*Individual Interventions for Children*

As previously noted, cognitive interventions can address a wide array of childhood problems ranging from typical developmental problems such as fighting with friends to more serious situational problems such as coping with the death of a parent. Following is an intervention that helps children understand the cognitive theory concepts.

*Don't Blow It Out of Proportion.* To help children understand the concept of dichotomous thinking, put a long strip of masking tape on the floor. Use a typical example such as assuming you will fail a test. On an index card write "fail the test," and put this card at one end of the masking tape strip. Then involve clients in helping you identify at least 4-5 other points along strip: for example, "getting a super good grade on the test" could be at the other end, "missing only a few," could be somewhere in between, and so forth. Process this by pointing out to children that there are more than two ways of looking at most situations. Have them give you examples as they apply this process to personal situations.

In addition to employing interventions that help children understand the general cognitive concepts, interventions such as the one that follows can be developed for a variety of typical childhood problems.

*Adios Anxiety.* This is a concrete way to help young students deal with their anxiety. You will need a plastic tablecloth with a large hopscotch board drawn on it. When students describe things they are anxious about, such as taking a test, swimming in the lake, riding in an airplane, or doing something new for the first time, indicate that you will be their secretary and you will write down all the thoughts they have about one of these anxious events. Next, invite them to stand on the first square of the hopscotch board and you will read off something they are anxious about. If they can identify something they can think of to tell themselves to be less anxious, they can hop to the next square. Then read the next item, ask them to think of something they could think of to tell themselves to be less anxious, and hop to the next square. You may have to offer suggestions if they don't understand the concept, such as if they were anxious about swimming in the lake, they could say to themselves that if they wear a life jacket they will probably be very safe, that they could stay in shallow water, that they could wear shoes if they were afraid they would get bitten by a fish, and so forth. Introduce the idea of *rational coping statements*. These are things they can say to themselves to counter a fear. For example, if they were afraid they would drown in the lake, a rational coping statement might be, "If I don't go past the rope, I should be safe; I can always yell for help." The purpose is to help students identify less anxious self-talk and more effective coping strategies.

*Individual Interventions for Adolescents*

To help adolescents learn the principles of cognitive behavior therapy, the following intervention has proven effective.

*Thoughts and Feelings* (Vernon, 1989b). To help adolescents learn that emotional problems are caused by their thoughts, invite them to write their responses to questions such as the following:

a. The principal announces there will be no junior-senior prom this year. How do you feel and what are your thoughts about this?
b. The person you are going with starts dating someone else. How do you feel and what are your thoughts about this?
c. Your mother announces you will be moving to a different town and next week is the last time you will attend your present school. How do you feel and what are your thoughts about this?

After they have written their responses, give them a blank copy of the situations and have them ask a friend to complete it (without seeing how your student responded). After your student has both sets of responses, have him or her compare them to see if they are similar, and if not, what the differences are. Help the student understand that the reason there might be differences is that people think differently, and how they think affects how they feel. For example, if your student felt angry about the prom being cancelled, he or she would have been thinking things such as "This isn't fair; this will ruin my whole year." In contrast, if he or she had felt mildly irritated, the thoughts would be something like: "It's not that big of a deal; I can find something else to do." Continue to help the student see how thoughts cause feelings.

Cognitive therapies embrace a variety of methods and strategies to help young clients deal with their concerns. The following intervention illustrates how to help adolescents deal with depression.

*When You Need a Helping Hand.* This intervention helps adolescents remember that they can control their thoughts that contribute to depression and sadness. To implement this intervention, first invite them to identify a specific depressing situation and help them identify the thoughts that contribute to the depression. For example, if they broke up with a significant other, they might think that it was the end of the world, that they would never be in another relationship, or that there is something wrong with them. Ask students to draw around their hand, and help them identify how to dispute the irrational beliefs and cognitive distortions, such as thinking: "This isn't the end of the world;" "There will probably be other relationships," and "This doesn't mean there is something wrong with me." As they successfully identify disputes, have them write these on the fingers of their hand as a visual reminder of how to overcome the negative thoughts.

There are numerous other cognitive behavioral techniques that can be used to help young people learn to change their maladaptive thinking and consequently cope more effectively with problems they encounter. Role playing, rational emotive imagery, rational role reversal, assertiveness training, bibliotherapy, self-help materials, and homework assignments can all be employed and readily adapted depending on the developmental level of the child (Bernard, 2001; Vernon, in press).

## Small Group Counseling

Cognitive behavioral techniques are also very effective in group counseling situations. There are two formats that are generally employed: a homogeneous group, in which all group members have a similar problem, and an open-ended group, in which group members take turns presenting problems they would like help with (DiGiuseppe, 1999).

Homogeneous groups can focus on typical developmental problems, such as getting along with friends or dealing with the emotional ups and downs of adolescence. They might also emphasize skill development, such as anger management or study skill groups. They could also address specific situational stressors, such as divorce or living in an alcoholic family. Regardless of the focus, this type of group would have more structure than the open-ended group in that various activities would be introduced to help participants learn more about the topic and develop effective coping skills. The emphasis would be on introducing cognitive behavioral principles such as the connection between what they think and how they feel; the connection between how they think and feel to how they behave; and ultimately, helping them apply these principles to the specific issue so that they have less intense negative emotions and more adaptive behavior. An advantage of the group approach is that participants can help each other develop the cognitive behavioral skills and apply them to their individual situation.

To illustrate, the leader of a divorce group for children would elicit feelings from participants about how their family situation is affecting them. In turn, the leader would probe for children's beliefs about this situation that could pertain to overgeneralzing, awfulizing, demanding, catastrophizing, and low frustration tolerance, such as: "This is the worst thing that could ever happen, it is unfair," "Nothing will ever be the same again," "They will never get over it", "It is too painful to deal with," and so forth. Utilizing a variety of techniques such as bibliotherapy, journaling, rational role reversal, and feeling games, the leader would help children see that divorce can be a very upsetting circumstance, but wouldn't it be worse if one of their parents died? And even though it is painful, is it possible that in time they will adjust and feel somewhat better at least? The ultimate goal would be to help children deal with this unfortunate circumstance by recognizing that they can reduce the intensity of their negative emotions by changing their thinking about this event. Through the group format, children help each other challenge their irrational beliefs and identify effective coping strategies.

In an open-ended group, individuals bring present-day problems to the table and the leader integrates cognitive behavioral principles into the discussion to help them think more clearly about the situation, experience more moderate as opposed to intensely negative emotions, and develop an array of coping strategies. For example, an adolescent might introduce the problem of feeling anxious about calling someone for a date. With the assistance of other group members, the leader would help this student identify his or her disturbing thoughts, such as "What if I get rejected?" "What if I stumble over my words?" "What if they laugh at me or hang up?" They would then help the client learn to dispute them. Again, different techniques such as role playing, continuums, or writing rational coping statements could be used.

## Classroom Applications

Of the cognitive therapies, REBT in particular has been psycho-educational in nature from its inception. From 1971 to 1975, The Institute for Advanced Study in Rational Psychotherapy (now called the Albert Ellis Institute) ran an elementary school in the building. The focus was on teaching rational thinking as a preventive mental health program in addition to the regular subjects (DiGiuseppe, 1999). The staff developed activities to help teach children effective thinking, feeling, and behaving strategies, and from these activities, Knaus (1974) developed a curricula that would educate children in the ABC's of RET. Since that time, other curricula (Vernon, 1989a, 1989b) have been developed that teach children to develop critical thinking skills, differentiate between facts and assumptions, distinguish between thoughts and feelings, link thoughts and feelings, identify what leads to emotional upset, distinguish between rational and irrational beliefs, and learn to challenge irrational beliefs. Vernon (1998a, 1998b, 1998c) also developed curricula to help children apply rational thinking concepts to typical developmental problems, and Bernard (2001) developed a comprehensive program that applies rational thinking concepts to improving school achievement.

The purpose of introducing these concepts in the classroom is to teach children principles they can apply to problems of daily living as well as to give them tools to use in solving future problems. A wide variety of cognitive behavioral methods are employed in delivering these lessons, including rational role reversal, self-help materials, worksheets, rational emotive imagery, thinking, feeling and behaving games, music and art activities, and didactic approaches. The primary focus is on prevention.

## Applications with Parents and Teachers

Parents and teachers can also benefit from cognitive behavioral therapy in several ways. First, they can learn to apply the principles to their own issues, irrespective of their parenting or teaching. Second, they can recognize how cognitive distortions affect their parenting and teaching and learn to function more effectively by challenging these distorted thoughts. Finally, they can serve as rational role models for their children and the students they teach.

Parents and teachers unwittingly fall victim to a number of dysfunctional beliefs, including the following (Vernon, in press):

*Uncertainty* (anxiety). It is not uncommon for parents and teachers to be uncertain about what to do in certain situations involving children. Adults often think they should know exactly what to do and what the outcome will be.

*Self-condemnation.* When children have problems at home or in the classroom, adults often blame themselves. For example, if Juan did poorly on his basic skills tests, his teacher might put herself down, thinking that this reflects on her poor teaching. Parents of children who turn to drugs condemn themselves for their poor parenting. In reality, parents and teachers cannot be totally responsible for a child's behavior or performance.

*Demanding.* Oftentimes parents and teachers demand that children must behave a certain way, and if they don't, it is awful. These adults are often very authoritarian and have little tolerance for children who don't always put forth their very best effort. Needless to say, this has a negative effect on their relationships with children.

*Low frustration tolerance.* Low frustration tolerance is related to the idea that children, as well as adults, should not have to experience any frustration or discomfort. These adults consequently try to make life easy for children, which means rescuing them and failing to follow through with reasonable consequences for misbehavior.

Professional school counselors can assist parents and teachers by helping them identify these cognitive distortions, as well as others such as overgeneralizing or awfulizing, tunnel vision (only seeing the negative), and the like. Concepts can be presented through parent group meetings and teacher inservices.

## Summary/Conclusion

This chapter presented a brief overview of cognitive behavioral therapy, which has successfully been employed with children and adolescents in school settings. Perhaps the most compelling reason for using a cognitive-behavioral approach is that it can be used both for remediation and prevention, and because it teaches children to identify and challenge the thoughts that create and perpetuate problems. Long-lasting change is more likely than with other theoretical approaches.

## References

Beck, A. T. (1988). *Love is not enough.* New York: Harper & Row.

Beck, A. T., Rush, A. J., Shaw, B. F., & Emery, G. (1979). *Cognitive therapy of depression.* New York: Guilford.

Bernard, M. E. (Ed.). (1991). *Using rational emotive therapy effectively: A practitioner's guide.* New York: Plenum.

Bernard, M. E. (2001). *Program achieve: A curriculum of lessons for teaching students how to achieve and develop social-emotional-behavioral well being, Vols. 1-6.* Laguna Beach, CA: You Can Do It! Education.

Burns, D. D. (1999). *Feeling good: The new mood therapy.* New York: Morrow, Williams, & Co.

Corey, G. (2001). *Theory and practice of counseling and psychotherapy.* Belmont, CA: Wadsworth/Brooks/Cole.

DiGiuseppe, R. (1999). Rational emotive behavior therapy. In H. T. Prout & D. T. Brown (Eds.), *Counseling and psychotherapy with children and adolescents: Theory and practice for school settings* (p. 252-301). New York: John Wiley & Sons.

Dryden, W., & Ellis, A. (2001). Rational emotive behavior therapy. In K. S. Dobson (Ed.), *Handbook of cognitive behavioral therapies* (p. 295-348). New York: The Guilford Press.

Ellis, A. (1957*). How to live with a neurotic: At home and at work.* New York: Crown.

Ellis, A. (2001a). *Feeling better, getting better, staying better.* Atascadero, CA: Impact Publishers.

Ellis, A. (2001b). *Overcoming destructive beliefs, feelings, and behaviors.* Amherst, NY: Prometheus Books.

Ellis, A., & Dryden, W. (1997). *The practice of rational emotive behavior therapy* (2nd ed.). New York: Springer Publishing.

Ellis, A., & MacLaren, C. (1998). *Rational emotive behavior therapy: A therapist's guide.* Atascadero, CA: Impact Publishers.

Ellis, A., & Poppa, S. (2001). Interview with Albert Ellis: The "cognitive revolution" in psychotherapy. *Romanian Journal of Cognitive and Behavioral Psychotherapies, 1* (1), 7-16.

Ellis, A., & Wilde, J. (2002). *Case studies in rational emotive behavior therapy with children and adolescents.* Columbus, OH: Merrill-Prentice Hall.

Finch, A. J., Nelson, W. M., & Ott, E. S. (1993). *Cognitive-behavioral procedures with children and adolescents: A practical guide.* Boston, MA: Allyn & Bacon.

Knaus, W. (1974). Rational-emotive education: A manual for elementary teachers. *New York: Institute for Rational Living.*

Meichenbaum, D. (1977). *Cognitive-behavior modification.* New York: Plenum.

Vernon, A. (1989a). *Thinking, feeling, behaving: An emotional education program for children.* Champaign, IL: Research Press.

Vernon, A. (1989b). *Thinking, feeling, behaving: An emotional education program for adolescents.* Champaign, IL: Research Press.

Vernon, A. (1998a). *The passport program: A journey through social, emotional, cognitive, and self-development (grades 1-5).* Champaign, IL: Research Press.

Vernon, A. (1998b). *The passport program: A journey through social, emotional, cognitive, and self-development (grades 6-8).* Champaign, IL: Research Press.

Vernon, A. (1998c). *The passport program: A journey through social, emotional, cognitive, and self-development (grades 9-12).* Champaign, IL: Research Press.

Vernon, A. (in press). *What do you do after you say hello: Individual counseling interventions for children and adolescents.* Champaign, IL: Research Press.

Wilde, J. (1992). *Rational counseling with school-aged populations: A practical guide.* Muncie, IN: Accelerated Development, Inc.

# Chapter 12

# Development and Implementation of Behavioral Interventions in Schools: A Function-Based Approach

*R. Anthony Doggett, Carl J. Sheperis & Tonya S. Butler*

## Preview

School personnel are increasingly faced with the responsibility of teaching students important social and behavioral skills in addition to providing instruction in traditional academic material. In fact, government agencies have mandated proactive interventions be developed and implemented for students with disabilities who display problematic behavior. Such suggestions have also been strongly recommended for individuals without documented disabilities who have long histories of displaying problem behavior. This chapter reviews the motivating factors for engaging in problem behavior, methods for identifying the purpose of problem behavior, and intervention development, implementation, and monitoring guidelines for teaching proactive, replacement behaviors.

Professional school counselors often interact with teachers, administrators, parents, and other applied personnel in designing interventions for students displaying problem behaviors in the school setting. Traditionally, professional school counselors have been encouraged to generate interventions based on the topography of the behavior (i.e., how the behavior looks) rather than the function of the behavior (i.e., the purpose that the behavior serves for the individual). Because the interventions developed to teach important behavioral skills need to be as idiosyncratic as the students displaying the problem behaviors, this chapter will take a functional approach to intervention development. Readers interested in more traditional approaches to the implementation of behavioral techniques (e.g., group contingencies, token economies, Premack principle, overcorrection, response cost, time-out) should refer to the chapter *Setting Up and Managing a Classroom* in this book. Specifically, this chapter will discuss the motivating factors associated with problem behaviors, best practices in functional behavioral assessment, and proper methods for intervention development, implementation, and monitoring. Such knowledge will enable the professional school counselor to serve as a vital resource to schools and families and assist in improving the behavioral and academic skills of the children they serve.

Currently, school professionals are faced with the increasing responsibility of providing safe school environments in addition to providing academic instruction. As a result, schools have developed zero-tolerance policies, implemented "target hardening" procedures (e.g., controlled access entrances, metal detectors, body searches), and utilized segregation procedures (e.g., suspension, expulsion, alternative placements, self-contained classrooms) as methods for trying to control the display of disruptive behavior on school grounds (Kenney & Watson, 1998; Sprague, Sugai, & Walker, 1998). Unfortunately, such restrictive or "get-tough" responses have proven ineffective, and the continued display of problematic behavior has served to threaten the process of schooling for all children (Walker, Colvin, & Ramsey, 1995). As such, representatives of government agencies (e.g., Department of Education, National Institutes of Health) have advocated for more emphasis on the development of proactive procedures designed to provide social and academic skill acquisition (Drasgow & Yell, 2001; Vollmer & Northup, 1996). In addition, these representatives have opposed methods solely designed to reduce or eliminate the display of disruptive behavior without an alternative or replacement skill development component. In an effort to promote best practice among professional school counselors related to behavioral problems in children, we discuss potential reasons for the display of problem behavior, assessment strategies for discovering the purpose of problem behavior, and intervention strategies for both reducing the display of disruptive behavior and promoting the occurrence of more adaptive behaviors.

## Reasons For the Display of Problem Behavior

Understanding assessment of disruptive behavior and the implementation of proactive interventions requires a discussion about potential functions of problem behavior. Function refers to the purpose that the behavior serves for the student (Gresham, Watson, & Skinner, 2001). A student can choose to engage in any given behavior in a classroom setting (Martens, 1992). However, the particular behaviors that the student chooses to engage in are greatly affected by "learning history" or the previous interactions that one has had with significant others or events in their environment (Martens, Witt, Daly, & Vollmer, 1999). For example, one student may immediately begin working on a new math assignment once it has been passed out by the teacher because completing similar academic assignments in the past has led to social praise from teachers. However, another student may look out the window, flip through pages of a book, or walk around the classroom before beginning the math assignment. Eventually, the teacher redirects this student to his seat and provides assistance in completing the worksheet. As such, this student conceivably avoids working on the worksheet until social attention is provided in the forms of redirection and assistance. Both students obtained and were reinforced by social attention from the teacher. In addition, both students were faced with the same set of choices when given the worksheet. However, their responses to the worksheet were greatly influenced by their prior history with similar academic demands.

Potential functions of behavior have previously been divided into five general categories: a) positive social reinforcement (e.g., social attention from teachers or peers); (b) material or activity reinforcement (e.g., access to preferred items or activities; (c) negative reinforcement (e.g, escape or avoidance of aversive instructional tasks or activities, (d) negative social reinforcement (e.g., escape or avoidance of nonpreferred individuals; and (e) automatic or sensory reinforcement (e.g., internal stimulation) (Carr, 1994). Of these potential functions, obtaining social attention from teachers or peers and/or avoiding or escaping instructional demands appear to be the most common motivators for engaging in disruptive behavior in classroom settings (Vollmer & Northup, 1996). In addition, previous researchers have revealed that a particular problem behavior could serve only one function or could serve multiple functions (Iwata, Pace, et al., 1994). Furthermore, several behaviors may serve the same function or each could serve a different function (Doggett, Edwards, Moore, Tingstrom, & Wilczynski, 2001). The task of the professional school counselor is not only to obtain detailed information about the problem behavior, but more importantly, to obtain information about the motivation for performing the problem behavior.

## Reasons For Failed Behavioral Interventions

Teachers and other school personnel often report that they spend a significant amount of time and effort trying to reduce the occurrence of problem behavior exhibited by students in their classrooms. Traditionally, treatment efforts aimed at reducing the problem behavior have focused more on the topography of the problem behavior rather than on the function or purpose of the behavior (Lewis, Scott, & Sugai, 1994). In other words, textbook interventions have been universally applied to individuals who have demonstrated similar behaviors or been diagnosed with the same or similar disorders. However, reported research results have indicated that many universally applied school-based interventions have proven ineffective (DuPaul, Eckert, & McGoey, 1997; Elliott, Witt, & Kratochwill, 1991; Ysseldyke & Mirkin, 1982). Although several reasons for ineffective intervention results could be identified for a student, treatment selection without reference to the behavioral function of the problem behavior has been identified as a significant limitation. According to Vollmer and Northup (1996), at least four problems may arise when behavioral interventions are selected without reference to behavioral function. First, the problem behavior may inadvertently be strengthened through positive reinforcement. An example includes the use of reprimands delivered by a classroom teacher in an effort to reduce disruptive behavior. In fact, research has demonstrated that the increased use of reprimands by teachers often leads to a direct escalation in problem behavior by students whose behavior is maintained by obtaining teacher attention (Broussard & Northup, 1995; Doggett et al. 2001; Moore, Doggett, Edwards, & Olmi, 1999; Northup et al., 1995; Umbreit, 1995). Second, the behavior may inadvertently be strengthened through negative reinforcement (e.g., avoidance or escape).

A commonly used classroom management strategy that may strengthen problem behavior through negative reinforcement is the use of time-out. Studies have shown that time-out or the removal of demands or attention may negatively reinforce problem behaviors by allowing students to escape tasks or other individuals viewed as aversive or nonpreferred (Carr, Newsom, & Binkoff, 1980; Moore, Edwards, Olmi, & Wilczynski, 2001). Third, the intervention may be functionally irrelevant to the problem behavior. For example, an intervention aimed at reducing teacher attention for problem behavior would be functionally irrelevant for a student whose behavior is primarily maintained by escape from academic demands. Finally, an intervention may not provide alternative sources of reinforcement for more proactive replacement behaviors. For example, in-school suspension, out-of-school suspension, and detention are commonly used punitive procedures designed to reduce problem behavior. However, such procedures do not teach alternative behaviors nor do they provide reinforcement for the display of proactive behaviors.

Because approaches based solely on topography or diagnosis have proven ineffective in leading to positive outcomes, recent literature has been proliferated with assessment strategies that focus on identifying the function of problem behavior (Cone, 1997). One such procedure is functional behavioral assessment (FBA). FBA has been defined as a collection of methods for gathering information about target behaviors, events in the environment that precede the target behaviors (antecedents), and events in the environments that follow the target behaviors (consequences). This information is then used to determine the reason for the performance of problem behavior (Gresham et al., 2001). Federal law requires FBA for students verified with disabilities who display problem behaviors at school (Individuals with Disabilities Education Act Amendments of 1997; PL 105-17). Furthermore, FBA is strongly recommended for individuals without disabilities who have a history of displaying disruptive behavior that impedes learning in the school environment (Drasgow & Yell, 2001). Finally, the primary goal of FBA is to identify the specific environmental events associated with the performance of problem behavior in order to enhance the probability of treatment effectiveness and prevent a series of ineffective interventions based on best guesses and unconfirmed hypotheses (Iwata, Dorsey, Slifer, Bauman, & Richman, 1994).

## Best Practices in Functional Behavioral Assessment

Best practice in FBA occurs in a four-phase process: (a) description, (b) interpretation, (c) verification, and (d) intervention development, implementation, and monitoring phase (Ervin et al., 2001; Sterling-Turner, Robinson, & Wilczynski, 2001).

*Phase I: Description*

The descriptive phase involves both indirect and direct procedures and is used to generate hypotheses about the environmental events that may be triggering and/or maintaining problem behavior. Indirect methods are utilized to obtain information from archival data and/or important others (e.g., teachers, administrators, parents) about the display of problem behavior and the potential functions of problem behavior. Traditionally, indirect methods have included record reviews, rating scales, and interviews. When evaluating student records, professional school counselors should review grade reports, group/individual standardized test results, discipline records, attendance records, medical history, individualized educational plans, and previous interventions. Appropriate use of rating scales requires individuals familiar with the student to rate the perceived impact of specific environmental events (i.e., antecedents and consequences) on the performance of problem behavior. Some of the more commonly used rating scales include the *Motivation Assessment Scale* (MAS; Durand & Crimmins, 1988), the *Problem Behavior Questionnaire* (PBQ; Lewis et al., 1994), and the *Functional Analysis Screening Tool* (FAST; Goh, Iwata, & DeLeon, 1996). Other indirect methods for gathering information about the functional relationship between problem behaviors and environmental events are teacher and student interviews. Examples of structured or semi-structured interviews include the *Functional Assessment Interview* (FAI; O'Neill et al., 1997), the *Preliminary Functional Assessment Survey* (Dunlap et al., 1993), the *Functional Assessment Information Record for Teachers* (FAIR-T) (Edwards, 2002; Doggett, Mueller, & Moore, 2002), and the *Student Assisted Functional Assessment Interview* (Kern, Dunlap, Clarke, & Childs, 1994).

The second aspect of the descriptive phase in FBA involves the use of direct methods. Direct descriptive assessment involves the collection of data on the performance of target behaviors and environmental events via direct observation. The most common type of direct observation technique used to obtain data about behaviors and functional relationships is an A-B-C assessment or contingency analysis (Bijou, Peterson, & Ault, 1968; Cooper, Heron, & Heward, 1987). A-B-C observations require that the observer record data on the occurrence of antecedent events (e.g., potential triggers), target behaviors, and consequent events (e.g., potential reinforcers). Direct descriptive data can be collected through narrative recording, event recording, or through time-sampling procedures. Review of these procedures is beyond the scope of this chapter and professional school counselors are encouraged to consult Alberto and Troutman (1995) or Miltenberger (1999) for additional information about these observation methods.

*Phase II: Interpretation*

Data obtained from the indirect and direct methods are used during the second phase, or interpretive phase, to develop hypotheses about functional relationships between the problem behaviors and the events that precede or follow the behaviors. In fact, O'Neill and colleagues recommended that summary statements be developed for each hypothesis (O'Neill et al., 1997). To illustrate, consider the student described earlier who had difficulty attending to the math assignment. One potential summary statement could be: "When the student is given a math work sheet (antecedent event), he or she will look out the window, flip through pages of a book, and walk around the room (observable behaviors) in order to obtain attention from the teacher and/or briefly escape the task (consequent events)." It is important to remember that information collected during the descriptive assessment phase is only correlational in nature. In other words, the school-based professional can only make informed suggestions about potential relationships between environmental events and problem behaviors. However, definitive statements about the specific events that occasion or maintain the occurrence of problem behavior cannot be made at this stage. In order to make statements about causal relationships, progression to the third phase must occur.

*Phase III: Verification*

Verification of hypotheses developed during the interpretation phase occurs via experimental or functional analysis or through implementation of a function-based intervention. A functional or experimental analysis is a brief experiment designed to confirm or disconfirm prior suggestions made about potential functional relationships between environmental events and problem behaviors. In other words, predictable changes are purposely made in the student's environment to see how those changes affect the performance of problem behavior. As in the case described earlier, the teacher may be instructed to attend to the student every time he or she engages in problem behavior (usually through reprimands or redirections) during a 10-minute functional or experimental analysis condition to evaluate the effect of teacher attention on problem behavior. In another condition, the teacher may be instructed to only attend to appropriate behavior (usually through praise statements) during a 10-minute condition to see if teacher praise, in fact, does increase the display of appropriate behavior.

Most functional analysis research has been based on the work of Iwata, Pace et al. (1994) or Carr and Durand (1985) and has been expanded for proper use in classroom settings (Radford, Aldrich, & Ervin, 2000). Functional or experimental analysis conditions can be conducted in analogue settings (i.e., contrived settings designed to approximate the typical classroom setting) or in naturalistic settings (i.e., the child's actual classroom during regular academic instruction). Furthermore, functional or experimental analysis conditions have included manipulation of both antecedent conditions (e.g., level of task demand, amount of attention, presence or absence of peers) and consequent conditions (e.g., social attention for disruptive behavior, removal of task contingent upon the display of problem behavior). For a complete review of school-based experimental analysis conditions, professional school counselors are referred to Radford et al. (2000).

A primary advantage of experimental analysis is that it is the only method for demonstrating a causal relationship between target behaviors and antecedent and consequent events. Major disadvantages include the effort, time, and professional expertise required to implement such procedures (Miltenberger, 1999). In fact, researchers have suggested that many school-based professionals proceed to intervention after completing record reviews, rating scales, interviews, and direct observations if a clear relationship can be hypothesized from the descriptive methods (Doggett et al., 2001). Furthermore, recent researchers have demonstrated that function-based interventions can be used to validate the hypotheses generated from descriptive methods making functional or experimental analyses unnecessary (Doggett et al., 2002).

*Phase IV: Treatment Development, Implementation, & Monitoring*

The last phase of FBA involves treatment development, implementation, and monitoring. Treatment should not consist of a single technique that is designed to simply eliminate the problem behavior. Instead, the behavioral intervention should be comprised of a set of antecedent- and consequent-based strategies designed to reduce the problem behavior and, more importantly, increase the performance of alternative, replacement behaviors (O'Neill et al., 1997). Such interventions have been referred to as positive behavioral supports and are mandated by federal law for students with disabilities and strongly encouraged for non-disabled students with histories of problem behavior (Drasgow & Yell, 2001). O'Neill et al. (1997) posited that interventions should match the values, resources, and skills of those persons who would be required to implement the procedures. They also emphasized that positive behavior supports should make the display of problem behaviors irrelevant, inefficient, and ineffective such that the student is highly motivated to engage in the alternative behaviors that serve the same function or purpose as the problem behaviors.

*Treatment development: Linking assessment to intervention.* As mentioned previously, positive behavior supports or proactive interventions will be composed of intervention elements designed to increase the display of appropriate behavior. These elements will include both antecedent- and consequent-based strategies. Recently, more attention has been given to antecedent strategies that could serve to prevent the problem behavior from occurring (Dunlap, Kern, & Worcester, 2001). Typically, variables that often trigger the display of inappropriate behavior are broadly defined as the curriculum (Dunlap & Kern, 1996). Once the curricular variables that occasion the occurrence of problem behavior have been identified through FBA methods, changes can be made to increase the probability that appropriate behavior will be displayed. While not exhaustive, modifications to the curriculum have included changing task difficulty, modifying task size or duration, changing the instructional media, incorporating the student's personal interests in the task, allowing the individual to choose the order of the tasks, changing the pacing of the instruction, and interspersing different tasks (e.g., short versus long, varied versus repetitive, long versus short) over the academic period.

In contrast to antecedent strategies, consequent-based interventions have typically focused on contingencies of reinforcement (i.e., positive and negative reinforcement) in order to increase the display of appropriate behavior. Reinforcement, by definition, increases the probability that a certain behavior will be performed in the future (Skinner, 1953). Positive reinforcement refers to the presentation of a stimulus or event that increases the likelihood that a target behavior will be performed at a later time. Negative reinforcement refers to the removal of a stimulus or event that increases the likelihood that a target behavior will be performed in the future. Thus, both positive and negative reinforcement increase the probability that some target behavior will be displayed over time. Furthermore, it is important to note that negative reinforcement is not punishment (which decreases the probability that a behavior will be displayed in the future).

The most common classroom applications of positive reinforcement include differential reinforcement of alternative behavior (DRA) or differential reinforcement of other behavior (DRO) (Martens et al., 1999). DRA involves reinforcing the alternative behavior and ignoring or extinguishing the inappropriate behavior. Using the same example of the student engaging in the math assignment, a teacher using DRA would increase her social praise for working on the math assignment and systematically ignore the off-task behaviors. Conversely, DRO is used to provide reinforcement for a set interval of time that the problem behavior has not been displayed. In this case, the teacher using DRO would calculate the time between distributing the math assignment and initial off-task behavior. If the student gets out of his desk within approximately five minutes after being given the assignment, then the teacher would set the interval at five minutes. Positive social attention (e.g., verbal and physical praise) would be provided to the student after the five minute interval only if he worked on the assignment for the entire interval.

Thus far, the discussion of differential reinforcement has focused on providing attention contingent upon the display of appropriate behavior. However, differential reinforcement can be used to reduce the occurrence of escape-maintained behavior and increase the occurrence of working on a task or interacting with a nonpreferred individual. When negative reinforcement is applied, the terms "differential negative reinforcement of alternative behavior" (DNRA) and "differential negative reinforcement of other behavior" (DNRO) are used (Vollmer & Iwata, 1992). DNRA or DNRO could be used so that the problem behavior no longer produces escape from or avoidance of task demands or nonpreferred individuals. In other words, the contingencies could be arranged such that longer periods of on-task behavior, work completion, or social interactions lead to escape from the demand. For example, the student who avoided the math assignment could be taught to request a break after working on the worksheet for an appropriate period of time.

Another form of differential reinforcement that is gaining attention in the literature is noncontingent reinforcement (NCR), which refers to the delivery of reinforcers on a fixed schedule independent of the display of problem behavior. For attention-maintained behavior, the teacher could provide social attention at set periods throughout the day regardless of the display of problem behavior. For escape-maintained behavior, the teacher could provide scheduled breaks throughout the day that are noncontingent on the display of problem behavior. Martens and colleagues suggested that NCR could serve as a viable intervention alternative for two reasons (Martens et al., 1999). First, NCR reduces the student's motivation to engage in the problem behavior because he or she is obtaining the desired reinforcer (e.g., attention or escape) on a predictable schedule. Second, NCR disrupts the contingency between the problem behavior and the maintaining consequence because the reinforcer is delivered independent of the display of problem behavior. One caution is that NCR procedures have not been researched as thoroughly as other differential reinforcement procedures, and the effectiveness of such a procedure is not as well established.

Finally, the implementation of traditional behavioral techniques can be very useful in managing student behavior as long as the interventions are related to the function of the problem behavior. For example, group-oriented contingencies can be very effective procedures for reducing peer attention for problem behavior and increasing peer attention for appropriate behavior, especially if the students earn free time together for following classroom rules. Furthermore, behavioral charts and school-home notes can often serve to provide social attention or other desired activities to students for engaging in appropriate behavior. Additionally, response cost and time-out procedures can be useful additions to differential reinforcement for managing problem behavior maintained by social attention. Finally, other punishment-based procedures, such as overcorrection, can be a useful addition to curricular changes in the environment for reducing escape-maintained behaviors. For more guidance on implementing these traditional behavioral techniques, the interested reader should consult the classroom behavior management chapter in this edition.

*Treatment implementation and monitoring: Increasing treatment integrity.* After the target behaviors and alternative behaviors have been clearly defined, the functions of the problem behavior have been verified, and the treatment protocol has been developed, the professional school counselor will have to work closely with other school personnel to ensure that the intervention procedures are implemented properly (Sterling-Turner et al., 2001). The amount of time devoted to ensuring that the intervention is implemented properly will vary with each student and teacher. However, proper training is crucial for proper intervention implementation (Sterling-Turner et al., 2000). When interventions are not implemented properly, the true impact of the intervention remains unknown. In other words, it will be difficult to determine if the FBA results were incorrect and led to inappropriate intervention design or if improper treatment implementation led to the failed efforts. If the results of FBA were incorrect, then the professional school personnel need to review the FBA data in order to generate and test other hypotheses. If the treatment was implemented with poor integrity, then the professional school counselor needs to determine if the teacher lacked the skills to implement the intervention or the motivation to implement the procedures (Watson & Robinson, 1996).

In order to ensure proper treatment implementation, direct behavioral consultation (DBC) has been suggested (Sterling-Turner et al., 2001). Although Watson and colleagues discuss the procedures involved in DBC elsewhere in this edition, the procedures will be briefly reviewed here. First, the teacher should be provided with a rationale for implementing the treatment that is linked directly to the results of the FBA. Second, the intervention should be modeled for the teacher, and the teacher should be allowed to practice implementation of the intervention while receiving reinforcing and corrective feedback. Once the teacher becomes more proficient in implementing the intervention, then assistance can be faded. However, it would still be important to have the teacher monitor his or her own integrity in implementing the intervention over time.

**Table 1.**

*Phase I: Description*

Step I: Conduct record reviews, interviews, and complete rating scales.
Step II: Identify and clearly define problem behaviors.
Step III: Conduct A-B-C observations or other direct observations.

*Phase II: Interpretation*

Step I: Review all data obtained from the FBA.
Step II: Develop hypothesis statements about antecedent events that could be setting off or triggering the problem behavior.
Step III: Develop hypothesis statements about consequent events that could be maintaining the problem behavior.

*Phase III: Verification*

Step I: Conduct experimental or functional analysis conditions, if necessary.
Step II: Implement function-based interventions, if satisfied with results from the preceding phases.

a. Identify and clearly define replacement behaviors.
b. Identify antecedent strategies.
c. Identify consequent strategies.
d. Provide training and feedback to teacher.

*Phase IV: Treatment Development, Implementation, and Monitoring*

Step I: If you did not implement treatment in the verification phase, then implement it here following the steps above.
Step II: Monitor the treatment for proper implementation through direct observations and treatment integrity checklists.

## Summary/Conclusions

Functional behavioral assessment seeks to answer the questions, "What is triggering the problem behavior?" and "What is maintaining the problem behavior?" Once these questions are answered, function-based interventions can be developed that increase the display of appropriate, replacement behaviors and decrease the display of problem behaviors by making them ineffective, inefficient, and irrelevant. Interventions or positive behavior supports are not composed of one simple technique but include both antecedent- and consequent-based strategies for increasing the display of appropriate behavior. Finally, intervention implementation and monitoring are also crucial components for ensuring treatment success. Table 1 reviews the steps in conducting FBAs and implementing function-based interventions.

## References


Alberto, P. A., & Troutman, A. C. (1995). *Applied behavior analysis for teachers* (4th ed.). Columbus, OH: Merrill.

Bijou, S. W., Peterson, R. F., & Ault, M. H. (1968). A method to integrate descriptive and experimental field studies at the level of data and empirical concepts. *Journal of Applied Behavior Analysis, 1*, 175-191.

Broussard, C. D., & Northup, J. (1995). An approach to functional assessment and analysis of disruptive behavior in regular education classrooms. *School Psychology Quarterly,10,* 151-164.

Carr, E. (1994). Emerging themes in functional analysis of problem behavior. *Journal of Applied Behavior Analysis, 27*, 393-400.

Carr, E., & Durand, V. M. (1985). Reducing behavior problems through functional communication training. *Journal of Applied Behavior Analysis, 18*, 111-126.

Carr, E., Newsom, C. D., & Binkoff, J. (1980). Escape as a factor in the aggressive behavior of two retarded children. *Journal of Applied Behavior Analysis, 13*, 21-39.

Cooper, J. O., Heron, T. E., & Heward, W. L. (1987). *Applied behavior analysis.* Columbus, OH: Merrill.

Cone, J. (1997). Issues in functional analysis in behavioral assessment. *Behavior Research Therapy, 35,* 259-277.

Doggett, R. A., Edwards, R. P., Moore, J. W., Tingstrom, D. H, & Wilczynski, S. M. (2001). An approach to functional assessment in general education classroom settings. *School Psychology Review, 30,* 313-328.

Dogget, R. A, Mueller, M. M., & Moore, J. W. (2002). Functional assessment informant record for teachers: Creation, evaluation, and future research. *Proven Practice: Prevention & Remediation Solutions for Schools, 4*, 25-30.

Drasgow, E., & Yell, M. L. (2001). Functional behavioral assessments: Legal requirements and challenges. *School Psychology Review, 30*, 239-251.

Dunlap, G., & Kern, L. (1996). Modifying instructional activities to promote desirable behavior: A conceptual and practical framework. *School Psychology Quarterly, 11,* 297-312.

Dunlap, G., Kern, L., dePerczel, M., Clarke, S., Wilson, D., Childs, K., White, R., & Falk, G. (1993). Functional analysis of classroom variables for students with emotional and behavioral disorders. *Behavioral Disorders, 18,* 275-291.

Dunlap, G., Kern, L., & Worcester, J. (2001). ABA and academic instruction. *Focus on Autism & Other Developmental Disabilities, 16,* 129-136.

DuPaul, G. J., Eckert, T. J., & McGoey, K. E.(1997). Interventions for student with Attention-Deficit/Hyperactivity Disorder: One size does not fit all. *School Psychology Review, 26,* 369-381.

Durand, V. M., & Crimmins, D. B. (1988). Identifying the variables maintaining self-injurious behavior. *Journal of Autism and Developmental Disorders, 18*, 99-117.

Edwards, R. P. (2002). Functional assessment information record for teachers (FAIR-T). *Proven Practice: Prevention & Remediation Solutions for Schools, 4,* 31-38.

Elliot, S. N., Witt, J. C., & Kratochwill, T. R. (1991). Selecting, implementing, and evaluating classroom interventions. In G. Stoner, M. R. Shinn & H. M. Walker (Eds.), *Interventions for achievement and behavior problems* (pp. 99-135). Silver Spring, MD: National Association of School Psychologists.

Ervin, R. A., Radford, P. M., Bertsch, K., Piper, A. L., Shrhardt, K. E., & Poling, A. (2001). A descriptive analysis and critique of the empirical literature on school-based functional assessment. *School Psychology Review, 30,* 193-210.

Goh, H. L., Iwata, B. A., & DeLeon, I. G. (1996, May). *The functional analysis screening tool.* Poster presented at the meeting of the Association for Behavior Analysis, San Diego, CA.

Gresham, F. M., Watson, T. S., & Skinner, C. H. (2001). Functional behavioral assessment: Principles, procedures, and future directions. *School Psychology Review, 30,* 156-172.

Individuals with Disabilities Education Act, 20 U.S.C. 1401-1485.

Iwata, B. A., Dorsey, M. F., Slifer, K. J., Bauman, K. E., & Richman, G. S. (1994). Toward a functional analysis of self-injury. *Journal of Applied Behavior Analysis, 27,* 197-209. (Reprinted from *Analysis and Intervention in Developmental Disabilities*, 1982, 2, pp. 3-20.)

Iwata, B. A., Pace, G. M., et al. (1994). The functions of self-injurious behavior: An experimental-epidemiological analysis. *Journal of Applied Behavior Analysis, 27,* 215-240.

Kenney, D. J., & Watson, T. S. (1998). *Crime in the schools: Reducing fear and disorder with student problem solving*. Washington, D.C.: Police Executive Research Forum.

Kern, L., Dunlap, G., Clarke, S., & Childs, K. E. (1994). Student-assisted functional assessment interview. *Diagnostique, 19,* 29-39.

Lewis, T. J., Scott, T. M., & Sugai, G. (1994). The Problem Behavior Questionnaire: A teacher-based instrument to develop functional hypotheses of problem behavior in general education classrooms. *Diagnostique, 19,* 103-115.

Martens, B. K. (1992). Contingency and choice: The implications of matching theory for classroom instruction. *Journal of Behavioral Education, 2,* 121-137.

Martens, B. K., Witt, J. C., Daly, E. J., & Vollmer, T. R. (1999). Behavior analysis: Theory and practice in educational settings. In C. R. Reynolds & T. B. Gutkin (Eds.), *The handbook of school psychology* (pp. 638-663). New York: Wiley & Sons, Inc.

Miltenberger, R. (1999). *Behavior modification: Principles and procedures* (2nd ed.). Pacific Grove, CA: Brooks/Cole.

Moore, J. W., Doggett, R. A., Edwards, R. P., & Olmi, J. (1999). Using functional assessment and teacher implemented functional analysis outcomes to guide intervention for two students with Attention-Deficit/Hyperactivity Disorder. *Proven Practice: Prevention and Remediation Solutions for Schools*, *2*, 3-9.

Moore, J. W., Edwards, R. P., Olmi, D. J., & Wilczynski, S. M. (2001). Using antecedent manipulations to distinguish between task and social variables associated with problem behaviors exhibited by children of typical development. *Behavior Modification*, *25*, 287-304.

Northup, J., Broussard, C., Jones, K., George, T., Vollmer, T. R., & Herring, M. (1995). The differential effects of teacher and peer attention on the disruptive classroom behavior of three children with a diagnosis of Attention Deficit/Hyperactivity Disorder. *Journal of Applied Behavior Analysis, 28,* 227-228.

O'Neill, R. E., Horner, R. H., Albin, R. W., Sprague, J. R., Storey, K., & Newton, J. S. (1997). *Functional assessment and program development for problem behavior. A practical handbook.* Pacific Grove, CA: Brooks/Cole.

Radford, P. M., Aldrich, J. L., & Ervin, R. A. (2000). An annotated bibliography of 102 school-based functional assessment studies. *Proven Practice: Prevention & Remediation Solutions for Schools*, *3*, 24-43.

Skinner, B. F. (1953). *Science and human behavior*. New York:Macmillan.

Sprague, J., Sugai, G., & Walker, H. (1998). Antisocial behavior in schools. In F. M. Gresham & T. S. Watson (Eds.), *Handbook of child behavior therapy* (pp. 451-474). New York: Plenum Press.

Sterling-Turner, H. E., Robinson, S. L., & Wilczynski, S. M. (2001). Functional assessment of distracting and disruptive behaviors in school settings. *School Psychology Review, 30,* 211-226.

Sterling-Turner, H. E., Watson, T. S., & Moore, J. W. (2000). The effects of direct training and treatment integrity on treatment outcomes in school consultation: Applications of direct behavioral consultation. *School Psychology Quarterly, 17,* 47-77.

Umbreit, J. (1995). Functional assessment and intervention in regular classroom setting for the disruptive behavior of a student with Attention Deficit/Hyperactivity Disorder. *Behavioral Disorders, 20,* 267-278.

Vollmer, T. R., & Iwata, B. (1992). Differential reinforcement as treatment for behavior disorders: Procedural and functional variations. *Research in Developmental Disabilities, 13,* 393-417.

Vollmer, T. R., & Northup, J. (1996). Some implications of functional analysis for school psychology. *School Psychology Quarterly, 11,* 76-92.

Walker, H. M., Colvin, G., & Ramsey, E. (1995). *Antisocial behavior in schools: Strategies and best practices*. Pacific Grove, CA: Brooks/Cole.

Watson, T. S., & Robinson, S. L. (1996). Direct behavioral consultation: An alternative to traditional behavioral consultation. *School Psychology Quarterly, 11,* 267-278.

Ysseldyke, J., & Mirkin, P. (1982). Assessment information to plan instructional interventions: A review of the research. In C. Reynolds & T. Gutkin (Eds.), *The handbook of school psychology* (pp. 395-409). New York: Wiley.

# Chapter 13

## Adlerian Therapeutic Techniques for Professional School Counselors

*Mardi Kay Fallon*

### Preview

Adlerian theory has been used for decades to help counselors and educators to understand the inner world of the student. By exploring how a student understands and experiences the world, the professional school counselor can develop effective interventions that teach the child how to adapt to and cope with life's difficulties in a cooperative and socially responsible manner. Misbehavior is seen as a learning issue and all students are seen as desiring to belong and to interact in a healthy and beneficial manner with others. Adlerian interventions seek to help the student understand his misbehavior and to learn how to develop greater self-control. Professional school counselors can use a variety of interesting and creative techniques to help the student to achieve this level of self-awareness. Adlerian therapy is very appropriate to today's multicultural schools and can be adapted to work with special needs populations.

The Adlerian school of psychology has developed several principles regarding students and student behavior that are of practical use to the professional school counselor. These principles are also applicable to students with special needs and from diverse backgrounds, making Adlerian theory a viable option for today's school populations.

A basic tenet of Adlerian theory is that all behavior is purposeful. A student is a social being, someone who observes her environment, forms opinions about how things work, and acts upon those (often faulty) assumptions. Therefore, every behavior, no matter how unusual or dysfunctional, has a goal and a purpose. If one can understand the goal and purpose of a student's behavior, then one is able to understand the motives of that student. Understanding a student's motives helps the professional school counselor to understand how best to help the child to change her problem behavior (Pryor & Tollerud, 1999).

Because children are social beings, they have a need to belong and to live cooperatively with others. Indeed, Adlerians consider the ability of a child to have a positive social interest (such as sharing, showing concern for others, and developing empathy) as a measure of that child's mental health. However, because of the natural conditions of childhood, all students experience a sense of inferiority and being weak and vulnerable. Thus, they strive to achieve superiority, which is seen as working to obtain a sense of mastery and self-control (Carlson & Sperry, 2001).

Children live within a subjective world and tend to distort what they see and experience in order to fit that world-view. They develop a form of "private logic" which helps them to make sense of themselves and their world (Sapp, 1997). Students begin by observing their families and developing a set of beliefs and expectations based upon those experiences. This sets up a paradigm through which the student seeks to find meaning as well as ways to belong and achieve superiority (Ehly & Dustin, 1989).

In essence, these tenets set up a belief that students choose their behaviors as a means to obtain goals. However, the assumptions upon which the student's decisions were made may be faulty, leading to misbehavior that is problematic. Misbehavior, then, is viewed as more as a learning difficulty than a character flaw. Indeed, misbehavior is seen to arise from discouragement, from a student not being able to find a way to meet his needs and goals in a cooperative and beneficial manner (Dreikurs & Soltz, 1964).

*Understanding Misbehavior*

There are essentially four main goals of misbehavior. Each has specific qualities and attributes that can alert the professional school counselor to which particular intervention may be most beneficial to the student in question. The four goals of misbehavior are: attention, power, revenge, and inadequacy.

The goal of attention is very common with students in a school setting. Here, the student feels that she is only of value if the student can get others to notice or serve her (Sweeney, 1981). When a student is seeking attention, an adult's tendency is to feel annoyed. This is, in fact, one way to assess what a student's motives may be, to determine from the beleaguered adult just what feelings the student's behavior has elicited. The student seeking attention will initially tend to stop misbehaving when first corrected, then begin repeating the attention-seeking soon after (Dinkmeyer, Pew & Dinkmeyer, 1979). Corrective action for attention-seeking would be to withhold attention until the student behaves appropriately (Pryor & Tollerud, 1999). Eventually, the student should learn that the best way to obtain positive attention is to act appropriately and cooperatively.

The goal of power is the most likely misbehavior to result in a student being referred to the professional school counselor for intervention. With a power motive, the student is feeling that she only counts if the student can force others to do what she wants (Sweeney, 1981). Students acting out of a goal for power elicit in the adult a sense of being challenged and wanting to engage in a power struggle with that student. The adult will want to show the student that he can't get away with that kind of behavior. If the motive is indeed power, the student's behavior will tend to worsen as corrective action is taken (Dinkmeyer et al., 1979).

The way to correct power misbehavior is to avoid engaging in a power struggle. The professional school counselor will need to set clear limits (such as not hurting self, others, or acting destructively). No limits should be set upon the student's speech, however, since the goal of therapy is to help the child to express his thoughts and feelings. When limits are set, the professional school counselor must be careful not to convey a sense of being punitive or judgmental. If a student continues to misbehave, the professional school counselor can give the child choices regarding which appropriate behavior he/she can engage in. Otherwise, the professional school counselor could decide to use logical or natural consequences (Kottman & Johnson, 1993).

Logical consequences are statements of an expected outcome for a student's misbehavior that is fair and consistent. These consequences must be related to what a student actually has done and be geared to help the child to understand her misbehavior and to see the benefits of behaving properly. The student needs to feel that she is respected and approved of despite the student's misbehavior. Punishment and rewards are to be avoided as the student needs to learn to behave properly for the intrinsic value of cooperating with others. This will teach the student to learn responsibility and cooperate with others without seeking to be rewarded for good behavior (Pryor & Tollerud, 1999). Examples of logical consequences would include: a student who throws a tantrum over a candy bar will not get that candy bar; having others pick up one's clothes means they may put them where the child cannot easily find what she wants; or a student who won't cooperate with other students will have to leave the game until she can agree to play cooperatively.

Natural consequences are those events that can be expected to happen if the adult doesn't intervene. These are the things from which the adult seeks to protect the student; but allowing a student to experience a natural consequence allows him to learn how to grow and prepares the student for the realities of life. If adults try to protect a student from these natural consequences, the student can get the message that he is inferior and unable to cope on his own (Dreikurs & Soltz, 1964). Examples of natural consequences would be that a student who goes outside in the rain without raingear gets wet, or a student who forgets his lunch money misses lunch, or a student who doesn't put his bike away has a rusty or stolen bike.

The final two goals of misbehavior are revenge and inadequacy. Both of these misbehaviors may indicate significant problems/issues, and the professional school counselor may wish to refer these students to community counseling where more time and attention can be spent on the students (Kottman & Johnson, 1993).

With the goal of revenge, the student believes that she must hurt others because the student does not feel likeable (Sweeney, 1981). The goal of revenge is common among students who are the victims of physical and/or sexual abuse (Kottman & Johnson, 1993). When a student is acting out of a goal for revenge, the adult will feel hurt and outraged. Initially, any attempt to correct this student will result in violent behavior (Dinkmeyer et al., 1979). Corrective action would involve setting fair and clear rules and imposing natural consequences. The adult needs to take care not to give the student a sense of being disliked. This student will tend to respond better to encouragement, persuasion, and a sense that she is liked by others (Pryor & Tollerud, 1999).

Finally, the student who misbehaves due to a goal of inadequacy has learned to feel that he does not matter to others due to being too stupid or hopeless. This student feels too discouraged to try, believing that he would fail and that then, everyone would know just how inadequate he really is (Sweeney, 1981). Often, this type of student has experienced some history of abuse (Kottman & Johnson, 1993). Adults working with this kind of student often feel like giving up on the child. Any attempt to correct this student's behavior is likely to be met with futile, insincere attempts to change or try things (Dinkmeyer et al., 1979). A way to correct the misbehavior of inadequacy is to use a lot of encouragement and to help the student to see that he is valued (Pryor & Tollerud, 1999).

Encouragement is a specific technique geared to help a student to understand that she is likeable and helps a student change her motivation to misbehave. Adlerians believe that a student will learn better in an accepting, democratic environment where the setting optimizes that student's ability to grow and develop. In such a nurturing setting, the student will tend to automatically seek to change her misbehavior into something more acceptable and constructive (Pryor & Tollerud, 1999). Encouragement does not refer to simple praise or reward, but rather to statements that convey to the student a sense of respect and recognition that she is a competent, acceptable person. Encouragement can be used to build rapport with a student by showing the student that the professional school counselor has faith in the student's ability to do things. An Adlerian-style counselor will allow a student to do things on her own that the student is capable of doing. If the professional school counselor believes the student cannot do a task, the counselor can suggest that the student agree to do it together with the counselor. This is an opportunity to show the student how to problem solve. As the student works on a task, the professional school counselor can acknowledge the effort and improvements she is making and encourage the student to continue to try (Kottman & Johnson, 1993).

Through encouragement, a student who misbehaves learns to put forth effort to change and to be motivated to remain on task. Providing praise before the student has learned these steps may not help the student to learn these necessary skills (Ehly & Dustin, 1989). Allowing a student to do things on his own and encouraging the student to accept the problems inherent in doing difficult things helps him to grow and develop in a healthy manner. Since students often have trouble separating what they do from who they are, they tend to judge their value by how competent they are. If a student is allowed to develop competence and to learn to deal with life consequences, that student develops a positive sense of self. Students cannot be effectively shielded from life consequences and need to be taught how to cope with them rather than to be kept from them (Dreikurs & Soltz, 1964).

*Goals of Counseling*

The goals of counseling involve helping the student to develop a healthier way of being involved with others, to develop greater self-awareness, and helping the student to challenge and change her faulty goals and assumptions about life. Counseling involves a form of re-education in which the student learns new ways to act, to feel self-esteem, and to decrease a sense of being inadequate or inferior. As the student learns to identify her own mistakes in thinking and behaving, she will be able to self-correct and start behaving more appropriately (Carlson & Sperry, 2001).

These goals involve developing an empathic relationship where the student feels understood and accepted by the professional school counselor. This provides an environment where the student can be led to explore and understand his beliefs, feelings, motives and goals regarding life. This exploration helps the student to develop insight into his own mistaken attitudes regarding goals, as well as how he has been acting in a self-defeating manner. Finally, the student learns to identify and consider new, viable ways to change his problem behaviors and to commit to actually changing his misbehavior (Dinkmeyer et al. 1979).

*Therapeutic Techniques*

Adlerian therapy uses a multitude of techniques to aid the student to explore his behavior. Some of these techniques are appropriate to therapy in general and others are more appropriate for individual or group settings. Some explanations of general techniques follow.

*Tracking.* As a student moves about the room, the professional school counselor tells the student what she is doing, such as, "You are picking up the truck and taking it over there." This can be used to develop a relationship with the student and to convey to the student that what she does is of importance. This technique works well in play therapy (Kottman & Johnson, 1993).

*Restatement.* Restate the content of what the student says. If the student says, "The doll wants to hug you." The professional school counselor can respond with "The doll wants to hug me." Restatement would be most appropriate in play therapy and is a way to convey interest, develop rapport, and help the student to develop self-awareness (Kottman & Johnson, 1993).

*Reflection.* Reflect the emotion of the student to help him become more aware and understand his own feelings. The professional school counselor should seek to reflect both the surface level of the emotion as well as underlying feelings. An example might be a student throwing down a broken toy, kicking it and saying, "That always happens to me!" The professional school counselor might say "Sometimes you feel angry because things don't work and you feel like that often happens to you" (Kottman & Johnson, 1993).

*Early recollections.* This technique requires the student to recall several early life events (which usually come from the time the student was four to six years old). These recollections help the professional school counselor to identify what the student has come to believe about the world, herself, and others. These recollections can reflect themes as well as specific emotions that are important to understanding the student. The professional school counselor can identify if the student conveys a sense of being safe, cared for, able to control things, etc. (Kottman & Johnson, 1993).

*Therapeutic metaphors.* Students will often use metaphor and symbolism in play and the professional school counselor can use the student's metaphor to understand the child and help the child understand herself. This can be used in play therapy, where a student will spontaneously use a metaphor, such as "Here's the daddy doll. He comes home and turns into a monster and eats up the whole family" (Kottman & Johnson, 1993). Obviously, this example provides the professional school counselor with a great deal of information about how the student feels and perceives the world.

*Mutual storytelling.* The student's metaphors can also be used to help a student understand his beliefs and views of life. The professional school counselor can have a child tell a story with a beginning, middle and end. The student's story may contain some mistaken beliefs or perceptions and the professional school counselor can take the opportunity to retell the story in a more positive and adaptive light to help the student develop a new perspective (Kottman & Johnson, 1993). The Mutual Storytelling Game (Erford, 2000a), a Windows-based CD-ROM program, helps facilitate student storytelling by providing backgrounds and diverse characters.

*Therapeutic games.* Older students often do not wish to attend counseling or are unwilling to either discuss their emotions or to change their behaviors. Games, both ones that are bought in the stores and special games designed for counseling, such as the series developed by Erford (2000 b-e; 2001 a-c; 2002 a-c), can be used to engage the reluctant student. Playing games can afford the professional school counselor an opportunity to observe the student's behavior and to identify some of the student's attitudes about herself and others. Game playing in groups, particularly, can provide information regarding social skills, ability to wait, taking turns, coping with disappointment, etc. The professional school counselor can use these opportunities to help the student explore her thoughts, feelings and behaviors, develop a sense of competence, and build her self-esteem. Sometimes a student may talk while playing the game and provide more information than in a formal face-to-face session (Kottman, 1990).

*Role-play and simulation.* Using creative dramatics can work to motivate older students in a group setting. Group members can use role-play to explore different behaviors and to observe how these behaviors affect others. Role-play and simulation can also help group members develop empathy for others, develop social skills, explore their inner world with others, develop listening and attending skills, cooperate with others, learn decision-making skills, and develop the ability to observe and evaluate both self and others (Kottman, 1990).

*"Could it be" questions.* "Could it be" questions involve the professional school counselor being aware of the feelings a student's misbehavior is eliciting and help the student to identify his misbehavior. So, if a professional school counselor is feeling annoyed by a student's obvious attempts to get the counselor to watch him, the counselor could say, "Could it be you are keeping me busy with you because you want me to pay attention to you?" This would help the student become more aware of the goals of his misbehavior (Poppen & Thompson, 1974).

*Paradoxical intent.* As an experiment, the professional school counselor can have the student do the opposite of what the student would expect to emphasize the symptoms or misbehavior. This could help the student develop a greater awareness of the consequences of her misbehavior if she does not resist doing it, but deliberately does it. For example, if a therapist tells a student, as an experiment, to deliberately not do her homework for one night, this might help the student become aware of the fact that she chooses her own behavior, that not doing homework is less attractive when it is permitted, and help the student see how silly or ridiculous that misbehavior may be (Dinkmeyer et al., 1979). This technique must be used carefully, for a limited time, with the appropriate student (and with the approval and support of the student's teacher) to work effectively.

*Spitting in the client's soup.* This technique refers to an old boarding school activity where a student would spit in another child's soup in order to get that child to give up the soup. Here, the professional school counselor identifies the purpose of, and payoff for, a certain misbehavior and spoils the fun for the student by decreasing the pleasure he may derive from misbehaving. For example, the counselor may reflect to an older student that his drinking problem may be a way for the student to keep connected to the father he claims to hate, because the father is an alcoholic and that is something they can share (Carlson & Sperry, 2001).

*Acting "as if."* The professional school counselor can have the student, as an exercise or assignment, act the way she would like to act. The student may initially resist, saying that it's just pretending and not real. However, the counselor could relate it to trying on a new outfit or suit of clothes. The student could try it on and see if it works. If the student does try and feels better, she may decide to behave differently. This can be done for a certain time span, then the student can return to the counselor to discuss the results (Dinkmeyer et al., 1979). An example would be that a shy student could act as if she was friendly and say "hi" to everyone she meets.

*Catching oneself.* As the student becomes more aware, the professional school counselor can suggest that the student catch himself doing something the student wants to change. At first, the student will tend to catch himself too late to do anything. As the student practices, he learns to anticipate and avoid certain situations or to change his behavior. This can be done with a sense of humor and works well if the student can laugh at himself (Dinkmeyer et al., 1979).

*Creating movement.* Sometimes, a student needs to be motivated to change. This tactic must be used carefully and in light of a sense of trust and a relationship the professional school counselor has developed with the student. To create movement, the counselor can use surprise to jar a student out of inaction. For example, if a student decided she wanted to give up, the professional school counselor may agree with her (Dinkmeyer et al., 1979). If used properly, not saying the expected thing could result in a moment of deeper self-awareness.

*Avoiding power struggles.* Often, a child will try to fit the professional school counselor into a role based upon that student's expectations and beliefs about the world. Thus, a student may try to provoke the counselor into validating that the student is unlovable. The counselor must avoid falling into this trap, or risk confirming to the child that he is, indeed, unlovable. The counselor must keep aware of the feelings the child is attempting to elicit and avoid giving in to feelings of being hurt or discouraged. In particular, the counselor needs to avoid any power struggles with the child (Dinkmeyer et al., 1979).

*Task setting and commitment.* Here, the professional school counselor helps a student to identify what she can do about a problem and commit to doing it for a specific time period. If the student is successful, she may feel encouraged and continue to change. If not, new behaviors could be explored and the student could try again (Dinkmeyer et al., 1979).

*Push-button technique.* Students need to understand that they are responsible for both the good and bad feelings they experience. Humans create their own moods. In this technique, the student could be directed to mentally re-experience something that gave him/her a very good feeling. Then, the student could visualize an experience that made him/her feel very bad. As the child does this, the professional school counselor could help the student to learn to connect how one's thoughts about an experience lead to one's feelings about that experience (Carlson & Sperry, 2001).

### *Group-Specific Techniques*

In groups, the group member gets to interact with peers in such a way as to be able to work on specific ideas and issues. To do this in a safe environment, group members must develop acceptance for each other (have respect and empathy). Acceptance could be modeled by the group leader who could also help specific group members develop their own ability to accept others.

Altruism is the natural tendency in humans to seek to help each other. Group could provide an opportunity for group members to extend help to each other. This can be modeled by the group leader, who can also encourage altruism and provide the group opportunities to use and develop this skill.

*Spectator therapy* refers to the observation that some group members may interact little with the group, but may still be listening and developing a greater understanding of him/herself. Just listening to others in a group situation can help a group member to see himself in others and to develop self-awareness.

*Universalization* involves helping group members to understand that their problems are not all that unique, that they are not as alone as they thought. To understand that they share problems with others can help group members feel less alienated and lonely and able to look at various solutions. This sharing can be used to encourage exploration and discussion.

*Feedback* helps group members understand how others experience them. This can help develop insight and greater self-awareness. It also helps the group member challenge her faulty beliefs and perceptions. Honest, authentic feedback can also convey to a group member that she is important to others and that others care and are concerned about the student.

*Ventilation* provides group members the opportunity to express normally inhibited emotions. It also provides an outlet for internal pressures, promotes the expression and exploration of feelings and helps the group member to develop greater insight.

*Reality testing* helps a group member test a faulty perception or belief within the group setting. For example, if a boy has developed a belief that girls are enemies and that he could never get to understand them, he could test this theory in the group by learning to talk to girls in the group. As he develops an ability to accept that his first assumptions were wrong, the boy may learn to look at other misperceptions or faulty assumptions and develop an ability to be self-aware (Dinkmeyer et al., 1979).

## Consultation

Adlerian principles also apply to consultation with teachers and parents. Parents need to understand their child's behavior and can benefit from learning about the four goals of misbehavior and ways to intervene with difficult behaviors. Weekly face-to-face consultations are optimal, but not usually practical. Therefore, the professional school counselor may have to seek some other way to consult with the parents (such as via phone). Contact with parents is an important way for the counselor to gather more information regarding the student and to suggest to the parents ways to deal with the student's misbehavior (Kottman & Johnson, 1993). Teachers, also, often can benefit from learning about the goals of misbehavior and identify new, creative ways to intervene with problem behaviors.

Adlerians also avoid assigning blame for a student's problems (as so often happens when parents blame schools, schools blame parents, and the student escapes responsibility for her behavior). Sometimes, a meeting with all parties (student, parents and teachers) is advisable in order to improve communication and cooperation to deal more effectively with the student's misbehavior. Adlerian counselors also avoid using labels or overestimating evaluations and test scores. Each student is seen as an individual and not compared with others (Dinkmeyer et al., 1979).

## Special Topics

Adlerian theory seeks to understand the individual within a social context, therefore, it is conducive to ethnic/multicultural issues. A student with a diverse background may develop a sense of inferiority and become pessimistic about being able to meet his life goals. Adlerian techniques could be used to help that student understand his own innate worth and status and to raise that student's self-esteem (Herring & Runion, 1994).

Adlerians focus on understanding a student's subjective view of the world, respecting the individual student, believing that each student can learn and grow, and developing a student's ability to be cooperative and socially responsible. All of these tenets work well with multicultural and special needs issues. Many cultures value community and social cooperation, but the professional school counselor must operate from a sound understanding of the student's background as well as a sensitivity and respect for that student's culture in order to be responsible and effective in helping that student (Sapp, 1997). Children with special needs may also suffer from feelings of inferiority or faulty beliefs about how the world works and can also benefit from the Adlerian focus on self-worth of the individual student without comparing children.

## Summary/Conclusion

The professional school counselor will find that Adlerian theory and therapeutic techniques are very applicable to the work that they do. This chapter has provided a brief review of some of the basic tenets of Adlerian theory and how they apply to counseling children within a school setting. The professional school counselor can use the ideas presented in this chapter to identify the goal of a student's misbehavior and to develop an intervention that is specific and appropriate to the needs of that individual student. Some guidelines for consultation were also provided, with a special emphasis to avoid placing blame and keeping the child responsible for his/her own behavior. The scope of this chapter was such that a more comprehensive review was not possible. Therefore, this chapter can provide only a brief overview of Adlerian theory and techniques and the interested reader is advised to consult the reference section for further readings.

## References


Carlson, J., & Sperry, L. (2001). Adlerian counseling theory and practice. In D. C. Locke, J. E. Myers & E. L. Herr (Eds.), *The handbook of counseling* (pp. 171-179). Thousand Oaks, CA: Sage Publications.

Dinkmeyer, D. C., Pew, W. L., & Dinkmeyer, D. C., Jr. (1979). *Adlerian counseling and psychotherapy*. Monterey, CA: Brooks/Cole Publishing Company.

Dreikurs, R., & Soltz, V. (1964). *Children: The challenge*. New York: Hawthorn.

Ehly, S., & Dustin, R. (1989). *Individual and group counseling in schools*. New York: Guilford Press.

Erford, B. T. (2000a). *The mutual storytelling game: CD-ROM*. Shrewsbury, PA: Counseling Innovations.

Erford, B. T. (2000b). *Psychotherapeutic game: Changing families*. Shrewsbury, PA: Counseling Innovations.

Erford, B. T. (2000c). *Psychotherapeutic game: Conflict resolution*. Shrewsbury, PA: Counseling Innovations.

Erford, B. T. (2000d). *Psychotherapeutic game: Anger management*. Shrewsbury, PA: Counseling Innovations.

Erford, B. T. (2000e). *Psychotherapeutic game: Good grief*. Shrewsbury, PA: Counseling Innovations.

Erford, B. T. (2001a). *Psychotherapeutic game: Solving problems*. Shrewsbury, PA: Counseling Innovations.

Erford, B. T. (2001b). *Psychotherapeutic game: Social skills.* Shrewsbury, PA: Counseling Innovations.

Erford, B. T. (2001c). *Psychotherapeutic game: Studying skillfully.* Shrewsbury, PA: Counseling Innovations.

Erford, B. T. (2002a). *Psychotherapeutic game: The ADHD game.* Shrewsbury, PA: Counseling Innovations.

Erford, B. T. (2002b). *Psychotherapeutic game: Perfectionism.* Shrewsbury, PA: Counseling Innovations.

Erford, B. T. (2002c). *Psychotherapeutic game: Self-concept.* Shrewsbury, PA: Counseling Innovations.

Herring, R. D., & Runion, K. G. (1994). Counseling ethnic children and youth from an Adlerian perspective. *Journal of Multicultural Counseling and Development, 22,* 215-226.

Kottman, T. (1990). Counseling middle school students: Techniques that work. *Elementary School Guidance & Counseling, 25,* 138-145.

Kottman, T., & Johnson, V. (1993). Adlerian play therapy: A tool for school counselors. *Elementary School Guidance & Counseling, 28,* 42-51.

Poppen, W. A., & Thompson, C. L. (1974). *School counseling: Theories and concepts.* Lincoln, NE: Professional Educator's Publications, Inc.

Pryor, D. B., & Tollerud, T. R. (1999). Applications of Adlerian principles in school settings. *Professional School Counseling, 4,* 299-304.

Sapp, M. (1997). *Counseling and psychotherapy: Theories, associated research, and issues.* Lanham, MD: University Press of America, Inc.

Sweeney, T. J. (1981). *Adlerian counseling: Proven concepts and strategies.* (2nd ed.) Muncie, IN: Accelerated Development.

# Chapter 14

## Using Gestalt Counseling in a School Setting

*J. Kelly Coker*

### Preview

Professional school counselors are faced with the challenges of large caseloads, large workloads, and not enough hours in the day to address those challenges. Identifying theoretically-based approaches that are conducive to school settings is one way to make school counselors more effective and efficient. Gestalt counseling, while not traditionally viewed as a school-based approach to counseling, has some developmentally appropriate techniques that work well with children and adolescents in brief counseling environments.

*I do my thing and you do your thing.*
*I am not in this world to live up to your expectations,*
*And you are not in this world to live up to mine.*
*You are you and I am I*
*And if by chance we find each other, it's beautiful.*
*If not, it can't be helped* (Gestalt Prayer, Perls, 1969)

Not long ago, a student at the institution where the author teaches embarked on a small-scale inquiry regarding the theoretical orientation of practicing professional school counselors. The student surveyed 13 professional school counselors in a local school district, and asked, among other things, what the counselors considered to be the primary theoretical orientation that guided their practice. Three counselors identified Reality therapy, two identified Adlerian approaches, and seven counselors labeled themselves "eclectic" without much description of what that meant to them. The remaining counselor labeled her style as "from the gut."

While these results, such as they are, cannot be used to make any inferences about the theoretical orientation of professional school counselors in general, they do provide an interesting jumping off point for this chapter on Gestaltian approaches in school counseling. It is not unusual during our counselor training programs to be grilled about the importance of learning about and adhering to theories of counseling and psychology during our professional practice, even though the integration of "theory into practice" was not something always at the forefront of reconciling schedules or wading through sophomore credit checks.

Theoretical approaches and techniques in general, and Gestalt approaches and techniques specifically, do play a significant and potentially useful role in the professional practice of school counseling. Many of the original concepts of Gestalt therapy and counseling continue to be utilized in therapeutic settings, and some have been modified to work more effectively with children. In addition to sharing these original ideas as they relate to work with children, the chapter will also present a brief history on Gestalt Therapy and its founder, Fritz Perls, the major tenets of the theory, considerations for adaptation with younger populations, and specific Gestaltian techniques appropriate for a school setting.

## Historical Perspective

In his book *Gestalt Therapy Verbatim*, Fritz Perls (1969) wrote, "One of the objections I have against anyone calling himself a Gestalt Therapist is that he uses technique. A technique is a gimmick. A gimmick should be used only in the extreme case. We've got enough people running around collecting gimmicks, more gimmicks and abusing them" (p. 1). To do an empty chair technique without first grasping Gestaltian principles such as the importance of the development of a sense of self, the significance of the interaction between client, environment, and relationships, and the relevance of the here-and-now experience to meaningful growth would be, in Perls' view, irresponsible.

Perls spent 12 years in South Africa where he formulated all of the basic ideas of what would become Gestalt therapy. Once he moved to New York in 1946, Perls began traveling throughout the United States presenting on his new theory. It wasn't until the mid-to-late 60's, however, shortly before Perls' death, that Gestalt Therapy became a significant force in the field of psychology. Perls developed the Gestalt Institute of Canada in 1969, and died of pancreatic cancer in March of 1970. Gestalt therapy was still considered "in progress" at the time of Perls' death, and many of Perls' writings were published posthumously.

## Major Tenets

While some contemporaries of Perls have specifically looked at the application of Gestalt counseling with younger populations, many of the original ideas of Gestalt theory may resonate with professional school counselors. In his work, *The Gestalt Approach & Eye Witness to Therapy*, Perls (1973) described some key concepts (see Table 1) that shape both Gestaltian theory and practice. Professional school counselors might consider how the examples in Table 1 fit in their work with children and adolescents.

The theoretical tenets can be examined in the context of the school setting with the following example. An 8-year-old boy is referred to the professional school counselor by his teacher for sucking his thumb during class. The teacher reports that the student will suck his thumb three or four times a day, and seems to "zone out" or lose focus when he does so. The professional school counselor first observes the student and notices the same behavior. During thumb sucking, the boy's eyes seem to glaze over, and he seems unaware of what's happening around him.

From a Gestalt perspective, the student is engaging in attempts to withdraw from his environmental field through thumb sucking. Since the Gestalt perspective does not assume all withdrawal behavior is unhealthy, the professional school counselor's first order of business would be to explore with the student *how* he feels when sucking his thumb, and *how* sucking his thumb in class is serving him in the here and now. A Gestalt approach might include the counselor first trying to gather some key information about the student's perspective of his environmental field. For example, through experiential approaches such as drawing his family or drawing himself at school, the professional school counselor can gain insight into the student's reality. Then the professional school counselor might bring the thumb sucking behavior into awareness when it is occurring. So instead of talking about the behavior ("Why do you suck your thumb in class?"), the counselor might "catch" the child in the act of sucking his thumb and say, "I notice you are sucking your thumb right now, can you tell me how that feels? Does it make talking to me easier to suck your thumb? Do you notice that it makes being in class easier when you suck your thumb?" This line of questioning serves two purposes: 1) to bring the problem behavior into awareness in the here-and-now, and 2) to begin to link the here-and-now behavior to other contexts.

The professional school counselor then might work with the student to link the thumb sucking behavior to other events or contexts. For example, does the thumb sucking occur only

**Table 1. Key Concepts of Gestaltian Theory and Practice.**

1. No person is totally self-sufficient; the person can only exist in an environmental field.
2. In relationship to this field, people will engage in either *contact* or *withdrawal.*
3. *Contact* refers to a person's attempts to reach out towards those people and things in the environmental field that are desirable or reinforcing.
4. *Withdrawal* refers to a person's attempts to remove or separate from people or things in the environmental field that are perceived as harmful, threatening, or otherwise negative.
5. Not every contact is healthy and not every withdrawal is unhealthy.
6. The contact with and withdrawal from the environmental field are the most important functions of the total personality. They are the positive and negative aspects of the psychological processes by which people live.
7. Therefore, people are both an individual and a function of the environmental field.
8. The focus of Gestalt counseling is not on *why* behavior problems or neuroses exist or came to be, but on *how* the individual experiences her issues in the here and now.
9. The goal of Gestalt counseling is to give the client the means with which he can solve his present problems or issues and any that might arise in the future.
10. Gestalt counseling is largely experiential vs. verbal with the goal of helping the client experience herself as much as she can in the here and now.
11. Increased awareness of here and now attempts at contact and withdrawal as well as interpreting success and failure of these attempts leads to new insight into more effective ways of interacting with the environmental field.

at school, or at home as well? Is the thumb sucking tied to particular feelings such as being anxious, or to particular events, such as being called on in class? The professional school counselor might also explore with the student his attempt to make contact with his environmental field. "When does it feel comfortable in class and with your teacher? What kinds of things do you do or say when you feel comfortable?" Ultimately, the goals might not be to stop the problem behavior (thumb sucking), but instead to increase positive interactions between the student and his environment, also increasing healthy contact attempts, which should naturally decrease the unhealthy withdrawal attempts.

## Working With Children

Violet Oaklander, a Gestalt therapist who works primarily with children, suggested that using the Gestaltian approach with children provides a process-oriented experience that focuses attention on the healthy, integrated functioning of the total child (Oaklander, 2000). Oaklander defined healthy *contact* as a child's ability to be fully present in a particular situation. Students who are anxious, worried, grieving, scared, or angry pull themselves inward (withdrawal) and block healthy contact with their environment and the people in it. Resistant behavior in students, however, is not always negative. Children, like adults, will engage in self-protecting behavior which is sometimes a healthy response, particularly when the environment the student is withdrawing from is unhealthy.

## Process of Counseling

Gestalt counseling can be ideal for short-term work because it is both focusing and directive (Oaklander, 2000). The therapeutic process involves several steps that can be accomplished in brief counseling sessions.

1. **Establishing the therapeutic relationship**. The Gestaltian counselor sees this process as key. Establishing trust, boundaries, limits, and an independent "I/Thou" relationship sets the stage for further change. Since a key function in Gestalt counseling is to use the here-and-now experience, the ability for the student to view the counselor as a person worthy of trust is paramount.
2. **Contact functions**. As indicated above, contact involves the student's ability to be fully present in the interactions. Resistance, or breaking contact, is viewed as a way of coping with pain or stress, and is respected and valued during the interaction.
3. **Building self-support**. This process involves helping students strengthen their sense-of-self through personal expression. The use of a variety of experiential and creative techniques (i.e., clay, imagery, drawing, sandplay) are suggested to facilitate building self-support. Gestalt counselors often refer to this process as establishing a sense of self instead of building self-esteem. From a Gestalt perspective, it is the awareness of the total self, good and bad, that is important; not just making the student "feel better." Interventions that encourage the student to make choices, allow her to experience mastery, and allow her to experience a sense of power are useful in building self-support.
4. **Emotional expression**. Once the student experiences self-support, helping the student to experience blocked emotions is a key step in the process. Often students get the message from adults in their lives that particular feelings are "bad." "You shouldn't be angry!" is a phrase many students might hear. The Gestalt approach honors the feelings as neither good or bad, just real; and then allows for safe expression of those feelings. In the counseling process, first talking about feelings to help students understand what different feelings are, and then expressing feelings through creative expression are strategies in dealing with emotions. Finally, learning skills for dealing with feelings when they occur is a part of the process.
5. **Self-nurturing work**. In this stage of counseling, the professional school counselor works to reinforce the student's ability to reframe negative, external and internal messages about the self. The student is encouraged to actively nurture the self through ongoing creative expression (journal writing, drawing, self-talk, imagery).
6. **Dealing with process**. It is not unusual for students to continue to use ineffective coping mechanisms in an effort to get their needs met. Dealing with process helps to build the bridge between the counseling process and strategies for coping with the outside environment. This includes taking responsibility, experimenting with new behaviors, obtaining environmental support, and confronting self-defeating behaviors (V. Oaklander, personal communication, November 1998).

In addition, family work and parent education are key components to the therapeutic process. For professional school counselors, teacher education might be equally important. Parents and teachers can be asked to experiment with new behaviors and to allow for student experimentation with new behaviors. If a student periodically throws things at other students in a teacher's class, the teacher might agree to allow the student to retreat to a corner of the room with some paper and crayons if the student is feeling particularly angry. This honors the child's feeling of anger while providing a safer outlet for an expression of that anger.

*The Use of Language*

An important step in using the Gestalt approach with a student is to examine the language used in counseling interactions. Some language methods in working with students include:

*Using "I" language.* "I" language is used to help the student take responsibility for his own behaviors, feelings, and thoughts. It is not unusual for students to engage in blaming, and to use "you" or "they" language (e.g., "They just don't listen to me!" or "You just don't understand!"). Using "I" language, the student would be encouraged to say, "I feel frustrated when I don't think I'm being heard or understood." The professional school counselor can certainly model the use of this language as well. Instead of saying, "You got in trouble again with your teacher which is why you are back in the principal's office," the professional school counselor might say, "I'm aware of the situation with your teacher, and I'm sorry it resulted in more time spent with the principal."

*Using "what" and "how" instead of "why."* As discussed above, the "why" question is generally one to be avoided in the Gestalt approach. "Why" questions can put students on the defensive, and do not generally open the door for further communication. Instead of asking, "Why won't you listen to your teacher?" you might ask, "What are you usually doing when your teacher is talking? How do you feel when your teacher is talking?"

*Using "won't" instead of "can't."* In order to increase personal responsibility, students can be encouraged to substitute the word "won't," which implies more responsibility, for the word "can't," which relinquishes responsibility. So the statement, "I can't do my homework!" would be re-stated as, "I won't do my homework" (Thompson & Rudolph, 2000).

Sentence completion exercises are one way to help students use language differently to gain a different perspective on their problem. One such exercise has been used by the author when working with students (see Figure 1). This exercise encourages students to first visualize the issue or problem, and then to finish the sentences as written. The second step of the exercise is to make word substitutions for the existing leads. For example, the lead, "I had to..." becomes "I chose to..." and "I can't..." becomes "I won't...." The other substitutions are listed in Figure 1. The use of this exercise encourages both personal responsibility and the concept of choice. It is suggested that the exercise be presented as a possible view of the problem, not an absolute. After all, there might be some problems or issues that the student has no real control over or choice about. For example, if the problem is that the student's parents have gotten a divorce, it would not be realistic to have the student change a sentence from, "I had to live with my Dad" to "I chose to live with my Dad."

**Figure 1. Sentence completion exercise.**

1. I had to ______________________________________________ .
   (I chose to)
2. I can't ______________________________________________ .
   (I won't)
3. I need ______________________________________________ .
   (I want)
4. I'm afraid to ________________________________________ .
   (I'd like to)
5. I'm unable to________________________________________ .
   (I'm willing to try to)

## The Use of Gestalt Counseling in a School Setting

While several authors have discussed the use of Gestalt counseling with children (Oaklander, 1988; 2000; Thompson & Rudolph, 2000), little has been written about the use of Gestalt counseling and techniques in a school setting. Most textbooks focusing on school counseling, for example, usually devote one chapter to individual counseling and one to two pages to different theoretical approaches, such as Gestalt counseling. The author examined four school counseling textbooks widely used in counselor education programs (Baker, 2000; Gibson & Mitchell, 1999; Muro & Kottman, 1995; Schmidt, 1999). Only two of the books addressed Gestalt counseling as a viable approach in working with children in schools, but these books talked about the approach in less than one page. The other two books did not mention Gestalt counseling at all. This is not a criticism of the works or authors, but rather a commentary on how Gestalt theory and practice has been relatively absent from the school counseling literature.

One example of Gestalt counseling being used effectively in a school setting was described by Alexander and Harman (1988). These authors discussed the application of Gestalt counseling as a means of dealing with the aftermath of a student suicide at school. From a Gestalt perspective, the professional school counselor at a middle school where the suicide had occurred worked with students both in classroom and small group settings. Starting in the classroom, the counselor worked with the 150 students with whom the suicide victim, Jason, had daily contact. She went into each classroom informing the students she was there to help them say goodbye to Jason. She then asked where he had sat in the room, and using the empty chair technique, invited students to tell Jason anything about how they felt, what they would have done for him if they had known he was in trouble, and what they would like him to know. They all ended their statements with, "and goodbye, Jason" (Alexander & Harmon, 1988). Out of the large class experiences, the professional school counselor began some small groups for those students most directly affected by Jason's death. Again using a Gestaltian approach, the counselor encouraged participating members to reflect on Jason and his death, and then express their feelings on large sheets of paper using whatever colors, symbols, shapes, and lines they wished. In describing their drawings to the rest of the group, feelings of emptiness, loneliness, confusion, and students' own suicidal fears emerged (Alexander & Harman, 1988). This one example illustrates the potential power of this approach for dealing with other crisis situations. One of the techniques listed above, the *Gestalt Empty Chair*, also has utility for other issues not as severe as suicide, including communication issues, relationship issues, and unresolved issues with others.

### *Gestalt Empty Chair Technique*

Perls (1969) referred to the empty chair as the place to implement the client's personality and other interpersonal encounters. Perls would use the empty chair technique both for dialogue with significant others, either living or dead, and for dialogue with other sides of the self. The author has used this technique with both children and adolescents, and has found that, while both age groups can benefit from dialogues with others, adolescents are more developmentally able to engage in dialogue with sides of the self. Both approaches will be described below.

*Dialogue with others.* The professional school counselor arranges the room so there are two chairs facing one another. The client is invited to sit in one chair, and describe to the professional school counselor the person he/she is having a conflict or issue with. The counselor helps to develop the picture of the person by repeating back key descriptors, i.e., "So your Dad is a tall man with dark hair, very skinny, with big, strong hands. Is that right?"

The student is then invited to imagine the person (Dad) is in the other chair. The professional school counselor then says, "I'd like you to tell your Dad anything you would like. You might talk to him about how you feel about being grounded this weekend, or anything else you'd like to say. Remember that you can say anything you want to Dad right now without having to worry about what he might say or do in return." The counselor intentionally "pulls back" from the experience at this point, not engaging in eye-contact with the student so the student can have an uninterrupted discussion with Dad. Further prompting is appropriate if the student does not know how to start, but efforts should be made to keep the client from turning back to the counselor. For example, "Okay, that's very good, but now turn around and say that to your Dad, not to me."

Once the student has spoken her piece, the counselor can focus processing on here-and-now experiences such as, "How did it feel to say those things to your Dad?" "I noticed you raised your voice when you were talking about being grounded. What were you feeling then?" "You balled your fist up several times. Do this again now. Do it again. Now release your fist and relax your hand. Now say what you said again to Dad, but with a relaxed hand instead of a fist." "How was that different?" Notice the questions are geared toward bringing into awareness all of the elements of the student's process during the exercise.

Variations of the activity could include having the student then move to the other chair and speak back as the person identified, or discussing with the student the pros and cons of actually having this discussion with the "real" person, if that person is still living or available. This technique can be particularly powerful when there are things left unsaid between the student and someone no longer available to them either through death or absence. The empty chair technique can allow for true expression of feelings of loss, anger, sadness, and remorse.

*Dialogue with self.* Another way to use this technique, with adolescents in particular, is to encourage the student to have a dialogue between two sides of the self. One often sees female adolescents, for example, who are experiencing trouble due to the recent end of a relationship. These girls often have conflicts between their "head" (I knew it was right to end it) and their "heart" (but I still love him so much). The variation on the empty chair would be to have the "heart" in one chair talk to the "head" in the other. The student would first talk from the heart. The heart would have lead sentences like, "What I feel about the breakup is...". Then physically moving to the other chair, the student would talk from the head. The "head" might start with something like, "What I think about the breakup is...." The student can then explore the two sides, and see which is stronger. She can also examine pros and cons of listening to the "heart" over the "head" and vice versa.

## Summary/Conclusion

For other useful Gestalt techniques tailored for use with children, a recommended reading is *Windows to Our Children* by Oaklander (1988). Building on Gestalt underpinnings, Oaklander describes experiential games and interventions designed to help children experience their true feelings, their relationship with their environment and the people in it, their sense of responsibility for their actions and behaviors, and their sense of power and ownership in their world. While professional school counselors are responsible for a myriad of duties, none would argue that helping students cope with painful situations and solve difficult problems is a significant part of the role. Gestalt counseling provides professional school counselors with a theoretically based approach that is conducive to brief interactions and both insight and behavior change.

## References

Alexander, J. C., & Harman, R. L. (1988). One counselor's intervention in the aftermath of a middle school student's suicide: A case study. *Journal of Counseling and Development, 66,* 283-285.

Baker, S. B. (2000). *School counseling for the twenty-first century* (3rd ed.). Upper Saddle River, NJ: Merrill/Prentice-Hall.

Gibson, R. L., & Mitchell, M. H. (1999). *Introduction to counseling and guidance* (5th ed.). Upper Saddle River, NJ: Merrill/Prentice-Hall.

Maples, M. F. (1999). Gestalt theory. In D. Capuzzi & D. R. Gross (Eds.), *Counseling and psychotherapy: Theories and interventions* (pp. 231-259). Upper Saddle River, NJ: Merrill/Prentice-Hall.

Muro, J. J., & Kottman, T. (1995). *Guidance and counseling in the elementary and middle schools: A practical approach.* Dubuque, IA: WCB Brown & Benchmark.

Oaklander, V. (1988). *Windows to our children.* Highland, CA: The Gestalt Journal Press.

Oaklander, V. (2000). Short-term Gestalt play therapy for grieving children. In H. G. Kaduson & C. E. Schaefer (Eds.), *Short-term play therapy for children* (pp. 28-52). New York: The Guilford Press.

Perls, F. S. (1969). *Gestalt therapy verbatim.* Lafayette, CA: Real Person Press.

Perls, F. S. (1973). *The Gestalt approach and eyewitness to therapy.* New York: Bantam.

Schmidt, J. J. (1999). *Counseling in schools: Essential services and comprehensive programs* (3rd ed.). Needham Heights, MA: Allyn & Bacon.

Thompson, C. L., & Rudolph, L. B. (2000). *Counseling children* (5th ed.). Belmont, CA: Wadsworth/Thomson Learning.

Tucker-Ladd, C. E. (1996). *Psychological self-help.* Retrieved September 17, 2001, from http://mentalhelp.net/psyhelp/chap15/chap15e.htm

# Chapter 15

# Using Rogerian Theory and Techniques

*Grafton Eliason & Jo Ellen Smith*

## Preview

Person-centered counseling offers professional school counselors a humanistic philosophy that incorporates basic helping skills essential for all counseling relationships. Roger's therapeutic skills and counseling attributes are particularly applicable to the school setting (Eliason, Hanley, & Leventis, 2001; Rogers, 1951; 1969; Schmidt, 1999).

## Historical Perspective

As the director of the Rochester Guidance Center at the Society for the Prevention of Cruelty to Children, Rogers (1980) experienced situations that significantly affected his theoretical understanding of the importance of following the client's lead. Rogers began to counsel a child displaying serious behavior problems. Both Rogers and another colleague determined that the primary issue was the mother's rejection of her son. After many sessions with the mother and child with no change, Rogers decided to terminate therapy. The mother then asked if he provided adult counseling, wherein she shared with Rogers her personal story and her authentic desire for help. At this point, Rogers' role was primarily that of an active listener. As a result of this experience and the influence of Otto Rank, Rogers determined that by trusting the client's potential for self-awareness and positive growth in therapy, and by providing the right conditions, the individual would move naturally toward actualization. Rogers eventually began teaching classes in the Department of Sociology at the University of Rochester and wrote *The Clinical Treatment of the Problem Child* in 1939. In 1942, he accepted a full-time position at Ohio State University and wrote the unique and controversial book, *Counseling and Psychotherapy* (Rogers, 1980; Thompson & Rudolph, 1992).

## Non-Directive Therapy

Rogers' theory, developed in the 1940's, was initially a reaction to psychoanalysis used by his contemporaries. Rogers believed that the medical model was biased and prejudicial, so he eliminated diagnosis, interpretation, and advice-giving. Instead, Rogers emphasized the feelings that the client expressed through reflection, summarization, and clarification, with the aim of facilitating greater insight and self-awareness. This theory of counseling was called non-directive therapy (Rogers, 1980).

## Client-Centered Therapy

Rogers' approach continued to evolve as he began to develop a rigorous theory of therapy and compile personal attributes that a counselor should possess in order to foster a healthy therapeutic relationship with the client. He also began to understand that his philosophical underpinnings were actually a "homegrown" variety of existentialism. When providing a climate comprised of the specific counselor attributes of genuineness (congruency), unconditional positive regard (acceptance), and accurate empathic understanding, people become more flexible, autonomous, self-accepting, and self-actualized. As a result, they begin to experience more positive relationships and personal mental health. In 1951, Rogers wrote *Client-Centered Therapy*, which shifted the focus from non-directive methods to the phenomenological world of the client and her personal frame of reference. The actualizing tendency becomes the primary motivation for change, and by providing the appropriate environment, positive change will occur (Rogers, 1951).

### Person-Centered Therapy

Person-centered therapy is a theoretical orientation that expands upon aspects of existential philosophy and phenomenological humanism. The etymology of phenomenology originates in the Greek, *phainomenon*, referring to a "phenomenon," or "that which appears or shows itself." Rogers held the view that the counselor-client relationship was the basis of his theory. He believed that establishing an atmosphere in which the relationship can grow facilitates the individual's move toward greater self-direction, self-awareness, and positive change. The optimal situation focuses on a combination of the counselor's attitude and the client's perception. There needs to be trust, confidence, acceptance, and a democratic style of equality. Goals are oriented to the personality, rather than to symptoms, diagnoses, and the curing of a disease. The client must feel that he is being heard in a non-judgmental manner. It is not enough for the conditions to exist, they must be successfully communicated as well.

### Therapeutic Attributes

As a professional school counselor builds a relationship with the student based on Rogers' therapeutic attributes, change is facilitated by the student's growing trust, the feeling that he is accepted and understood. As the student's awareness grows, it enhances his ability to learn, adapt to the present environment, better cope with life stressors, and choose more socially appropriate behavior. Congruence, also known as genuineness or "realness," is the therapeutic stance when the professional school counselor presents his real self, rather than taking the position of a professional or expert. The professional school counselor has the ability to maintain his own self-identity and convey this to the student (Thompson & Rudolph, 1992).

> The term "congruent" is one that I have used to describe the way I would like to be. By this I mean that whatever feeling or attitude I am experiencing would be matched by my awareness of that attitude. When this is true, then I am a unified or integrated person in that moment, and hence I can *be* whatever I deeply *am*. This is a reality which I find others experience as dependable. (Rogers, 1961, p. 51)

A professional school counselor who is perceived as "real" provides the student with the conditions to experience, tolerate, and accept feelings and emotions that cause difficulty in his or her interpersonal interactions in the school, family, and community. It is often very rare for a student, or any individual for that matter, to experience such a genuine response. The student then reacts positively when she perceives congruence, which enhances trust in the relationship and promotes growth and change.

The second attribute, unconditional positive regard, or acceptance, implies that the professional school counselor believes in the student's innate possibility for positive growth. It includes the willingness to accept whatever feelings or emotions are present, resulting in a decrease in defenses and resistances, while promoting constructive change (Thompson & Rudolph, 1992).

> As a second condition, I find that the more acceptance and liking I feel toward this individual, the more I will be creating a relationship which he can use. By acceptance I mean a warm regard for him as a person of unconditional self-worth – of value no matter what his condition, his behavior, or his feelings. It means a respect and liking for him as a separate person, a willingness for him to possess his own feelings in his own way. (Rogers, 1961, p. 34)

Cochran & Cochran (1999) found that the counseling relationship, which includes the Rogerian attribute of acceptance, facilitates change in students with conduct disorders. In the most difficult situations, students with conduct disorders display negative behaviors resulting from the student's maladaptive beliefs concerning self and how he or she fits into his or her phenomenological world. Ongoing experiences of rejection or non-acceptance by others lead to feelings of emptiness, depression, and existential non-being. Behavioral responses result in a disruption of learning, inappropriate social interactions, or aggressiveness. This behavior not only impacts individuals, but other students and teachers as well, further alienating them from the love and acceptance they need. This may result in the creation of labels such as "trouble maker" and a cycle that perpetuates the growing gap between the student and peers. Placed in a counseling environment that emphasizes unconditional positive regard and acceptance, the students' assumptions that they are unloved or uncared for are challenged. New awareness and acceptance are accompanied by a motivation for positive change.

Finally, accurate empathic understanding is the characteristic that a professional school counselor displays when accurately communicating the feelings and personal meaning that the student is phenomenologically experiencing. The result of these factors enables the student to increase self-awareness, congruence, and a more caring attitude toward self. Positive growth and greater freedom to become oneself is the outcome. Experiencing empathy in a counseling relationship not only facilitates the students' acceptance of self, but can also enhance understanding of people different from themselves, thus decreasing tension and conflict in the school setting.

## The Motivation for Change

Change is inherent in individuals, yet positive and lasting change may be more difficult if there are blocks which the individual is unable to overcome without a supportive environment and helping relationship. Rogers believed that a counseling relationship possessing appropriate attributes can facilitate renewed movement and growth. Each student possesses his own specific personal motivations for change. Being able to correctly identify the student's phenomenological motivation, genuinely engage the student in dialogue, accept the student's feelings and subjective reality unconditionally, and communicate accurate empathic understanding reinforces the initial motivation and provides the atmosphere necessary for further personal awareness and growth.

## Real Self and Ideal Self

Rogers (1959b) believed that individuals are motivated to realize their innate possibilities, leading to the actualizing tendency, or self-actualization. An integral part of actualization is the process of differentiation, which generates a concept of the self (a symbolic representation of who one is) and an ideal self (a representation of who one wishes to be). If there is a large discrepancy between the real self and the ideal self, incongruency results and the student experiences anxiety. Individuals need warmth, support, and positive regard from others. When a student begins to experience positive regard independently of others, she develops a need for self-regard. In imagining the ideal self, conditions of worth are interpreted in relation to self-regard. Experiences are avoided or sought after based on their possible contributions to self-regard. Theoretically, a fully functioning individual has no need for conditions of worth or defenses. She is open to experiences and there is congruency between the real self and the ideal self (Engler, 1984; Tomer & Eliason, in press).

Students struggling with incongruency between the real self and the ideal self may hold distorted perceptions of their phenomenological self or who they think they "should" be. They may use defenses to protect themselves against experiences not fitting their conditions of worth. Defenses may also include selective perception, distortion of an experience, or denial. Person-centered counseling helps to lower these defenses and draw attention to the student's subjective reality. As the student gains self-awareness, distorted perceptions of self are reevaluated and goals related to the ideal self are reassessed. Eventually, the real self and the ideal self will benefit from a healthy subjective reality and move closer to congruency, lowering anxiety and raising personal functioning (Tomer & Eliason, in press).

## The Continuum of Change

Movement and growth can be seen along a continuum identified by three characteristics: fixity, movement, and fluidity (see Table 1). The continuum of change begins with a fixed state resulting in distress, anxiety, and an inability to function at one's optimal level. The student experiences incongruity in his encounter of the world and his perception of self. Interpretations of events are viewed in a rigid manner and perceived as external facts. There is an unwillingness to communicate "self-to-self" resulting in conflict between the real self and the ideal self. Although there is significant distress, there is little desire for movement and the individual is not aware of his or her personal issues. This results in alienation and withdrawal from others, particularly relationships that are perceived as being risky or dangerous (Rogers, 1961).

Indicators of movement along the continuum can be described as a process of becoming. Each new and individual experience has unique meaning as a result of the loosening of cognitive maps established from past experiences. The student's responses are no longer dictated by distorted perceptions of events based on previous history. Current perceptions of reality are interpreted more accurately and based more fully in the present. Previous conceptions are modified with each new experience. Through the counseling relationship, personal defensiveness is decreased and an awareness of previous inaccuracies between the real self and ideal self is increased. This allows the student to open his or her self to discovery and change, and to focus in the present. Through the process of change, the student recognizes that issues negatively affecting his or her optimal health do exist and are not entirely the result of external forces. With this awareness, the student discovers personal freedom and, in turn, a stronger sense of responsibility. Through the safety of the counseling relationship, the student develops a tolerance for personal vulnerability. This willingness to take personal risks is generalized to his or her daily life experiences and interpersonal relationships outside of the counseling environment (Rogers, 1961).

The third characteristic on the continuum of change is fluidity. This is not a static stage, but rather an ongoing process in which self-awareness, self-actualization, congruity, and a sense of peace continue to evolve. Fluidity is recognized by the experience of "being" and an ability to live more fully and genuinely in the present. Through the reorganization of self-concept, there is a narrowing discrepancy between the real and ideal self. The student addresses current issues and problems with flexibility and personal responsibility. Behaviors and interactions are based on immediate experiences and are appropriate to the social environment. Relationships are approached honestly, resulting in a more gratifying outcome (Rogers, 1961).

**Table 1. The continuum of change.**

| Fixity | Movement | Fluidity |
|---|---|---|
| Experience of incongruity and distress | Becoming | Experience of congruence, peace, and self actualization |
| Understanding experience in a rigid manner, perceived as external facts | Loosening of the cognitive maps established from past experience;<br>Meaning is modified with each new experience | Being;<br>Focusing on the present |
| Conflict between real self and ideal self. Unwillingness to communicate self to the self, or gain personal awareness | Decrease in defensiveness;<br>Increased awareness of the previous inaccuracies of the real self and ideal self;<br>Openness to discovery and change | Reorganization of self-concept, with little discrepancy between the real self and the ideal self |
| Problems are unrecognizable and there is no desire for change | Recognition that problems exist, not entirely the result of external forces | Increased self-responsibility, lives with problems subjectively |
| Avoids close relationships that are perceived as being too risky or dangerous | Increase in appropriate risk taking in interpersonal relationships, and an increased tolerance for personal vulnerability | Living openly with others, behaviors are in relationship to immediate experience |

## Counseling Methods (Techniques)

Rogers was opposed to the general concept of "techniques," feeling that they detracted from the genuiness of the counseling experience. However, there are basic methods of interactive communication including: active listening, reflection of thoughts and feelings, clarification, summarization, confrontation of contradictions, and open-ended statements that facilitate self-exploration. These basic methods have become an integral component of Rogers' person-centered theory (and many others) and are briefly described below (Thompson & Rudolph, 1992).

1. Active listening, or "being there," refers to the full attention of the professional school counselor and the use of appropriate responses.
2. The professional school counselor uses reflection to convey the essence of what the student has communicated so that he or she can hear what has been expressed.
3. Clarifying is used by the professional school counselor to focus on key underlying issues and to sort out confusing or conflicting feelings. It can also be used to make

sure that the professional school counselor is "on the right track." Summarizing points out themes for the student. The student can also summarize his own experience.

4. In order to empathize, the professional school counselor must have an accurate understanding of the student's subjective world. It is the ability to grasp another's experience while maintaining one's separateness.
5. Gentle confrontation of the student's personal contradictions can be used to facilitate awareness.
6. Open-ended statements are used by the professional school counselor to facilitate dialogue and thought. The student cannot respond to these with a simple "yes" or "no" answer. He or she must respond in more detail, or in a narrative style. (Corey & Corey, 2002a; 2002b)

## Group Counseling and Collaboration Contexts

Person-centered counseling is very conducive to both group work with students and collaboration with other professionals. The counseling attributes are a good starting point for the establishment of group trust and cohesion. Rogers' methods (techniques), such as active listening, models appropriate group interaction and communication. Professional school counselors will also find benefits when using these attributes in any professional relationship or dialogue, including consultations and collaborations with parents, teachers, administrators, or individuals in the community (Corey & Corey, 2002a).

## Multicultural Counseling

Diversity in our schools and communities is now measured in terms that are broader than race and ethnicity (Paisley & McMahon, 2001). Socioeconomic status, disabilities, sexual orientation, and differences in lifestyle impact students' attitudes, values, and behavior. As schools become more culturally diverse, professional school counselors must attend to the unique needs of students, addressing both their personal characteristics as well as the context in which they live. Rogers has made considerable contributions to the field of multicultural counseling. His work has reached over 30 countries and his writings have been translated into twelve languages. Rogers' approach has been used to develop mutual understanding and reduce tension among antagonistic groups (Corey, 2001a).

One of the primary benefits of person-centered theory is increased self-awareness, which promotes the students' ability to adapt to the multiple contexts in which they find themselves. Multidimensional factors influence students' self-views, which are sometimes congruent and sometimes incongruent. These influences include culture, family, media, peers, teachers, gangs, and others. There is a parallel between Rogers' attributes for positive counseling relationships and the basic components recommended for counseling culturally diverse students. Genuineness, acceptance, and empathy become the foundation for building any trusting therapeutic relationship (Sue & Sue, 1990). Constantine (2001) found a correlation between feelings of concern, warmth, and empathy, and the counselor's ability to work effectively with culturally diverse students.

Though it may be difficult for professional school counselors to always communicate in such a direct way due to cultural differences, this limitation can be overcome through respect and sensitivity to the rich diversity that exists in our world. Some professional school counselors may also find it helpful to provide more structure to the counseling session than is usually needed in a person-centered framework. In addition, some cultures may view counseling, or asking for help, in a negative light. One way of reducing this stigma is to provide a supportive and open counseling environment. Both the professional school counselor and the student will grow from the cultural dialogue and counseling experience (Corey, 2001a; Sue & Sue, 1990).

## Case Example

Jim was a junior high school student who presented for counseling resulting from anxiety, dropping grades, and feelings of depression. The professional school counselor, Ms. Gomez, provided a safe environment and used active listening skills. She listened closely to Jim's subjective reality and self-report. He described anxiety due to a perception that he was not living up to his parents' expectations. He experienced feelings of "letting them down," as well as loneliness and isolation from his peers.

The professional school counselor was empathic and accepted Jim with unconditional positive regard. Jim felt that this could be a trusting therapeutic relationship. Through the use of reflection, clarification, summarization, confrontation, and open-ended statements, Ms. Gomez was able to help Jim become aware of conflicting aspects about himself. By establishing a relationship based on Rogers' theory, the professional school counselor provided Jim with the conditions for movement toward growth and self-actualization.

Jim came from a family of doctors and grew up with the belief that he was obligated to follow the family path. During the counseling session, Jim came to discover that medical school was not his true interest or goal. Although he displayed a strong aptitude for science, his real interest was in environmental science and the politics involved in protecting the environment. He told the professional school counselor of his experiences of community service and volunteerism with a focus on ecology. He reflected a sense of belonging and worth. Within the successful counseling relationship, Jim became increasingly aware of the discrepancy between his real self and his ideal self. He became less influenced and motivated by external factors and focused more clearly on his personal experiences and needs. He was able to accept himself and his feelings, and reorganize his self-concept. He was also able to express his true feelings to his parents. This allowed him to follow his personal and educational goals, lowering his anxiety and depression. With increased self-awareness and feelings of congruence, Jim gained confidence in his decision making ability, which facilitated movement, or "becoming."

## Summary/Conclusion

Rogers' counseling attributes and therapeutic methods are particularly applicable to the school setting. Person-centered theory offers professional school counselors a humanistic theory that incorporates basic helping skills that become the foundation for most counseling relationships. Facilitation of movement, self-awareness, and growth occurs through a positive relationship between the professional school counselor and the student. Positive change is a result of congruence and self-actualization (Eliason, et al., 2001; Rogers, 1951; 1969; Schmidt, 1999).

## References


Cochran, J. L., & Cochran, N. H. (1999). Using the counseling relationship to facilitate change in students with conduct disorder. *Professional School Counseling, 2*, 395-403.

Constantine, M. (2001). Theoretical orientation, empathy, and multicultural counseling competence in school counselor trainees. *Professional School Counseling, 4*, 342-348.

Corey, G. (2001a). *Theory and practice of counseling and psychotherapy* (6th ed.). Pacific Grove, CA: Brooks/Cole.

Corey, G. (2001b). *Student manual for theory and practice of counseling and psychotherapy* (6th ed.). Pacific Grove, CA: Brooks/Cole.

Corey, M. S., & Corey, G. (2002). *Groups: Process & practice* (6th ed.). Pacific Grove, CA: Brooks/Cole.

Eliason, G., Hanley, C., & Leventis, M. (2001). The role of spirituality: Four theoretical orientations. *Pastoral Psychology, 50,* 77-91.

Engler, B. (1984). *Personality theories* (3rd ed.). Boston: Houghton Mifflin Co.

Paisley, P. O., & McMahon, H. G. (2001). School counseling for the 21st century: Challenges and opportunities. *Professional School Counseling, 5*, 106-115.

Rogers, C. R. (1951). *Client-centered therapy: Its current practice, implications, and theory.* Boston: Houghton Mifflin Co.

Rogers, C. R. (1959). *A therapist's view of personal goals.* Wallingford, PA: Pendle Hill.

Rogers, C. R. (1959). A theory of therapy, personality, and interpersonal relationships, as developed in the client-centered framework. In S. Koch (Ed.), *Psychology: A study of a science* (Vol. 3) (pp. 184-256). New York: McGraw-Hill.

Rogers, C. R. (1961). *On becoming a person: A therapist's view of psychotherapy.* Boston: Houghton Mifflin Co.

Rogers, C. R. (1969). *Freedom to learn.* Columbus, OH: Merrill.

Rogers, C. R. (1980). *A way of being.* Boston: Houghton Mifflin Co.

Schmidt, J. J. (1999). *Counseling in schools: Essential services and comprehensive programs* (3rd ed.). Boston: Allyn & Bacon.

Sue, D. W., & Sue, D. (1990). *Counseling the culturally different: Theory & practice* (2nd ed.). New York: John Wiley & Sons.

Tomer, A., & Eliason, G. (in press). Theoretical approaches concerning death attitudes. In J. Wittkowski (Ed.), *Sterben, Tod und Trauern (Dying, death, & bereavement).* Stuttgart, Germany: Kohlhammer Verlag.

Thompson, C. L., & Rudolph, L. B. (1992). *Counseling children* (3rd ed.). Pacific Grove, CA: Brooks/Cole.

# Chapter 16

## Solution-Focused Brief Counseling: An Approach for Professional School Counselors

*John R. Charlesworth & C. Marie Jackson*

### Preview

Solution-focused brief counseling (SFBC) is presented as an efficient and effective model that professional school counselors can use to meet the needs of students in light of current school counseling program limitations. A general overview, the structure of the model, its basic steps, and techniques are presented.

In recent years, more and more emphasis has been placed on the professional school counselor's role in insuring high student achievement (Hart & Jacobi, 1992). This changed role focus has reduced the amount of time counselors have available to provide traditional individual counseling services, although the need and demand remains high. In order to continue to meet the individual counseling needs of students, counselors have had to seek more efficient and effective counseling approaches. Solution-focused brief counseling (SFBC) is one approach that has shown great promise, and that allows counselors to provide effective counseling to more students in less time.

### So What Is Solution Focused Brief Counseling?

SFBC is a counseling approach based upon a newly evolving resource-oriented constructivist theory. It is an outgrowth of a wellness system to counseling rather than one based on mental health disorders or dysfunctional behaviors. This method builds upon existing "positives"—the strengths of the individual, the present resources, and the solutions already occurring for these individuals. It is solution-focused rather than problem oriented, and brief in terms of the number of sessions required from the initial meetings to termination.

This counseling model has been deemed appropriate for schools for several reasons:

- SFBC is simple in concept and easy to learn.
- It is perceived as more effective and more practical since the focus is on "what works" rather than "why" something is a problem.
- Its emphasis on strengths, successes, resources, and hope is an element useful for schools.
- The model spotlights small changes and reasonable co-constructed goals.
- SFBC encourages the acceptance and accommodation of diverse opinions and beliefs, which is appropriate for today's professional school counselors who operate in complex arenas with diverse student bodies.
- According to Murphy (1997), drawing upon past successes, existing positive attitudes, and effective working behaviors is more practical and less time consuming than attempting to teach new behaviors.

- A brief approach is crucial for the professional school counselor who has little time to give to individual counseling and must out of necessity make a difference quickly or refer a student to an outside resource who will have more time available for individual counseling.

## Development of the SFBC Model

The development of the SFBC model has been attributed to many counseling and psychology practitioners. Among them are Berg and Miller (1992), deShazer (1985), O'Hanlon and Weiner-Davis (1989), and Walter and Peller (1992). Applying the model in schools has been the subject of numerous writers in professional journals, (see Bonnington, 1993; Bruce, 1995; Downing & Harrison, 1992; La Fountain, Garner, & Eliason, 1996; Littrell et al., 1992; Murphy, 1994). Books for the professional school counselor are also available. Murphy (1997) has written for middle and high school counselors, while Sklare (1997) has provided an easy and readable text explaining a solution-focused approach for professional school counselors. He provided a step-by step model based on the work of deShazer (1985).

According to Sklare (1997), it was deShazer who first developed the SFBC approach. Sklare pointed out that the SFBC model encompasses techniques learned in other counseling approaches, thereby making it easier to master than the more traditional approaches. Techniques utilized in SFBC common to many other counseling theories are listening, responding with empathy, asking open-ended questions, supporting, reinforcing, identifying goals, and applying scaling methods. These techniques are not new with SFBC. For example, scaling has been attributed to Wolpe & Lazarus (1966).

Professional school counselors have reported that often the counseling models learned in their university training programs require longer term counseling than is possible to provide in today's busy schools. Learning SFBC and utilizing previously learned counseling skills makes the model more amenable for adoption by professional school counselors.

## Central Philosophy and Basic Assumptions

For professional school counselors to "own the model" and accept it as clearly effective, understanding the basic rules and the assumptions on which the model is based is crucial.

### *Central Guiding Philosophy*

As cited in Sklare (1997), DeShazer and Berg and Miller proposed three basic SFBC rules as the central guiding philosophy for the model. These rules are: 1) "If it ain't broke, don't fix it" (p. 8); 2) "Once you know what works, do more of it" (p. 8); and 3) "If it doesn't work, don't do it again" (p. 9).

### *Assumptions*

Walter and Peller (1992) presented 12 assumptions of SFBC, and Murphy (1997) presented six assumptions. Sklare (1997) presented five assumptions, but added four guiding concepts. After reviewing all of the foregoing, the most obvious commonalties among them are:

1. Counseling should focus on solutions rather than problems for beneficial change to occur.
2. An effective counseling strategy is to find and transform "exceptions" (i.e., those times when the problem is not present) into solutions.
3. Small changes lead to bigger changes.

4. Counselees have all the necessary resources to resolve concerns.
5. The counselor should focus on developing meaningful counselor/student co-constructed goals with emphasis upon what the counselee wants rather than on the counselor's ideas/opinions.

*Guiding concepts*

Sklare's (1995) addition of guiding concepts is useful to the SFBC beginner. One might refer to these as rules for the professional school counselor to follow. The first one reminds the counselor to avoid exploration of the problem. A second reminder, to be efficient with interventions, suggests that the counselor should get the most accomplished with the fewest number of interventions possible. Another concept is that insight does not provide solutions. Sklare reminded the counselor that it is more important to take action than to discuss how counselees "got to be the way they are." The final guiding concept presented by Sklare is to focus on the present and the future. Having students think about what will be different in the future when the solutions are in place builds a belief that things will be better. Acknowledging the times in the present when solutions already exist increases the student's self-efficacy.

## SFBC Is Working for Professional School Counselors

Professional school counselors are being trained in SFBC and responding to its use in training programs and in the schools quite favorably (Charlesworth & Jackson, 2002). Research supporting successful SFBC outcomes is increasing. Gingerich and Wabeke (2001) focused on the issue of the need for more empirical validation of solution-focused approaches while reporting empirical studies that lend support to its efficacy. Much of the school-based research is reported in anecdotal and case study format and indicated successful outcomes. Gingerich and Wabeke listed a number of writers who have provided detailed discussions and case examples of the successful use of solution-focused models in schools. Two case studies in a public school setting were presented by Williams (2000). McKeel (1996) reported various research studies (see Lafountain, Garner, & Eliason, 1996; Littrell, Malia, & Vanderwood, 1995) as indicative of SFBC's effectiveness in schools.

## An SFBC Counseling Model

There are several approaches to brief counseling found in the literature. These various models generally contain the same elements, although there may be slight differences in the terminology and sequencing of steps. The general organization of Sklare's (1997) approach has been selected to acquaint the reader with implementing solution-focused brief counseling.

*Initiating the First Session*

Since SFBC counselors assume rapport with the student exists from the moment they meet, little time is spent attempting to develop it, unless it doesn't appear to be present. In those instances, additional time is spent developing rapport before proceeding.

Once good rapport has been established counselors provide their students with an overview of how the sessions will proceed. Sklare (1997) included the following information:

- The student will be asked a lot of questions, some a little strange and others challenging.
- The counselor will be taking notes during the session.
- Near the end of the session, the counselor will move to another part of the room to write the student a message.

- The counselor will return and read the message to the student, then provide the student with a copy of the message, while keeping one for the records.
- The counselor will insure the student's understanding of the purpose of the message and its contents, and provide the student an opportunity to ask questions and make comments.

*Identifying Student Goals*

One of the most significant predictors of success in any counseling approach, including SFBC, is the ability to help the student formulate clear goals. According to Sklare (1997), well-established goals add to the efficiency and effectiveness of SFBC. The goals established in this approach must, of necessity, be stated in small steps of obtainable, observable, measurable, behaviorally specific actions that the students are to "begin doing." Because of SFBC's focus on goals, when students present with problems, rather than pursuing the "how and why" of the problems, SFBC counselors help reframe the problems as goals.

The emphasis in SFBC is on helping students develop positive goals rather than negative "stop doing" goals. SFBC counselors initiate goal-oriented thinking by asking questions such as, "What is your goal in coming for counseling?" or "What would need to happen for you to consider your counseling sessions with me a success?" Questions such as these frequently lead to student goal statements that Sklare (1997) has classified as: (a) positive, (b) negative, (c) harmful, or (d) "I don't know" goals.

*Positive goals*. These goals are stated as what the student wants to achieve, and in an observable, behaviorally specific, measurable, and attainable manner. When a student presents with a vague, general positive goal such as "I want to behave better in class," the counselor must use appropriate questions to define the goal in more specific, concrete terms. Questions such as "What would you be doing that would indicate you are behaving better?" or "What would your teacher say you are doing when you are behaving better in class?" help produce concrete, explicit descriptions of what the student will be doing when making progress toward goals. The student will create clear images of the desired solutions. By continuing to emphasize "what the student will be doing" when they are moving toward goals, the counselor is implicitly suggesting to the student that success is possible. For additional detail for the goal picture, follow-up questions can be asked related to what the achieved goals will look like to the student or significant others.

*Negative goals*. Sklare (1997) defined negative goals as those stated as the "absence of something." They typically refer to the student wanting self or others to stop doing something. Examples of these two types of negative goals are: "I want to stop making bad grades," and "I want my teacher to quit making me stay in during recess." Such goals are very difficult to accomplish and in most instances are unattainable. To reframe negative goals into positive ones, the student must replace the "stop doing" behaviors (negative goals) with the presence of desired behaviors. Questions that assist students in reframing what they don't want into what they do want include, "If you stopped getting bad grades, what would you be doing?" and "What would you rather be doing instead of staying in at recess?" When the student has responded with a positive goal statement, counselors will frequently need to use additional "What else would you be doing?" questions to elicit more specific details of the positive goal.

When a student presents with a negative goal that expresses the desire for others to change or stop doing something, the student is placing the responsibility for achieving the goal on someone other than himself or herself. Frequently the student is either requiring the other person to initiate change, or expecting the counselor to "fix things." When presented with a negative (others) goal, such as the one previously stated ("I want my teacher to quit making me stay in during recess."), the counselor must assist the student to reframe the goals into positive ones in which the student assumes responsibility for change. Questions that can help counselors understand the student's motivation for wanting others to change include: "If they did change, what would that do for you?" and "How can I help you with this?" Such questions may lead a student like the one with the negative goal above to respond that he would like to be able to go to recess to play with friends. With that as the student's positive goal, the counselor could begin to obtain specific details of what the student would be doing to achieve that goal.

*Harmful goals*. Sometimes students respond with harmful goal statements involving behavior that would be illegal, harmful, or not in their best interest. Such behaviors as becoming a prostitute, stealing, quitting school, taking and/or selling drugs, hurting others, damaging property, and the like would not be supported by ethical school counselors. When helping students to modify destructive goals into productive positive goals, counselors need to uncover how these destructive goals are symptoms of students' unmet needs. Once the need is identified, counselors help students establish healthy, attainable positive goals to better meet needs. As an example, if a student presents with a goal of "wanting to sell some drugs," the counselor could attempt to identify the student's unmet need by using a question such as "What will selling drugs do for you?" If the student responds with the explanation, "I want to get money so I can go to the prom," the counselor could then use this information to help the student identify more appropriate behaviors to attain the positive goal. When students present with impossible goals, such as wanting their separated parents to reunite, counselors address these goals in a similar fashion as when working with negative goals.

*"I don't know" goals*. Quite frequently students come to counseling not because they made the choice, but because parents, administrators, teachers, or others have referred them. Sklare (1997) insisted that for change to occur, the student must be the customer. When the student is other-referred, the real customers are the ones who made the referral. Other-referred students are often difficult and resistant, acting as if they are merely visitors to the counselor's office. When these students are asked for their goal in coming to counseling they commonly respond with the phrase, "I don't know." Other-referred students will typically identify the reason for their referral when the counselor uses hypothetical "if" questions, such as "If you did know, (or, If you could guess), why do you think you've been referred?" In some instances, obtaining from the student an underlying reason for being sent for counseling may require the use of repeated "if" questions. Using the "if" questions allows the student to "not know" and, in essence, to appear to guess the answer.

Some students have little, if any, motivation for counseling even when they have been able to identify why others have referred them for help. To convert such students from being reluctant to more cooperative generally requires that the counselor "sell" them on the benefits they will receive from counseling. For example, a student may have little motivation to "get along better with a teacher" even though the consequence of undesirable behaviors is repeated stays in in-school suspension. A question to the student such as, "If we could help you get along better with your teacher so that you wouldn't have to spend so much time in in-school suspension, would that be something you would like to work on?" can be effective in increasing motivation for counseling. The success of this intervention depends upon the counselor's ability to recognize what students want and to help them to understand how counseling can help them get what they want.

Sklare (1997) described another approach for dealing with a reluctant student who believes the reason for being referred was due to an inaccurate assessment by the person making the referral. He identified this approach as the "They're wrong, you're right" technique. When a student strongly stresses that the referring person has made a mistake and that no problem for which the student needs help exists, the counselor should respond, "So you're convinced that you don't need help with getting along with your classmates. If we could find a way to prove that your teacher was wrong about you needing help in getting along with other children and that you were right about not having a problem all along, would that be something you would like to work on?" When a student indicates that he would like to correct the teacher's wrong impression, the counselor can then help the student establish positive goals. By having the student elaborate on "What would the teacher need to see you doing that would convince her that she was wrong and you were right?," positive goals are likely to evolve.

Even though the focus of the early phases of goal identification is to clearly outline measurable goals, it is not always accomplished at this phase. Other techniques such as the "Miracle Question" are used to build a picture of how the solution(s) might look and thereby aid the development of concrete behavioral goals.

*Using the Miracle Question*

During the student goal identification process, the emphasis is on helping the student identify positive goals and the "doing" behaviors needed to accomplish the desired solutions. Frequently, hypothetical questions are needed to help students fully develop specific, observable, concrete, behavioral goals and to gain a clear vision of what life will be like when they have attained these positive goals. According to Sklare (1997), because of its success, the "Miracle Question," developed by deShazer, is one of the more frequently used hypothetical questions. Following is an example of a "Miracle Question:"

> Suppose you go to sleep tonight and while you are sleeping a miracle happens without you knowing about it. When you awaken the problem that brought you here has been solved. What's the first thing you would notice that would tell you the problem has been solved, what would be different? (p. 31)

Sklare (1997) suggested using an alternative hypothetical question with younger children who may not understand the concept of "miracles." One example is as follows: "Suppose I had a magic wand and waved it over your head and your problem was solved, what would be different? What would you see yourself doing differently?" (p. 31). Another alternative hypothetical question is: "Imagine that it is six months from now and you have solved the problem that brought you for counseling. What would you notice that was different, and what would tell you that you no longer needed help with that problem?"

Whichever hypothetical question the counselor uses, the student's responses need persistent clarification, using the student's own words or "language" to ultimately form detailed, specific, well-developed goals. Often students respond to one of the hypothetical miracle questions with a vague response, such as "I'd wake up and I'd be nicer to my brother." A question using the student's own words, such as "And when you are being nicer to your brother, what would you see yourself doing?" is likely to lead to a more specific goal. Further questioning about how others might react to these changes helps students to see how making little changes may produce favorable changes in others. For example, asking the question "If you started being nicer to your brother by helping him with his chores, how do you think he would respond?" might help the student to recognize the benefit of a simple change in his own behavior and also might help increase the student's motivation for change.

Sometimes students answer miracle-type questions by stating impossible goals, or goals that have little chance of being attained. They may want their parent's chronic illness to be cured, to have their lost pet returned, or to have a favorite relative move to their city. Frequently, students realize the counselor can't produce these results, but if a miracle could happen, that is what they would want. By responding to the student's impossible wishes with questions such as "How would things be different for you if your miracle happened?" counselors can discover the student's real desires and help identify realistic goals.

*Identifying Instances and Exceptions*

After using the miracle question and constructing a clear vision of a successful resolution of a problem, the counselor's next task is to help the student identify instances when she has been successful or partially successful at solving the problem. SFBC counselors believe that, regardless of the presenting problem, there are always times when the problem is either absent or less severe. These times are referred to as "exceptions." Because students are often unaware of these occurrences, the counselor must help them recall these exceptions and identify what they were doing that led to them.

Students' language often provides cues as to when these instances or exceptions have occurred. For example, when students use words or phrases such as "generally," "sometimes," "almost always," and "most of the time," it suggests there are times when the solution is already occurring to some degree. For example, if a student remarks that he almost always has trouble getting along with Mrs. Jones, it suggests that there are times when he does get along with her. The counselor can help the student become more aware of these unrecognized successes through responses such as "Tell me about the times you were getting along better with Mrs. Jones," or by using questions that imply some degree of success.

*Mindmapping*

After counselors have helped students to identify their unrecognized successes, the next step is to help students identify what they were doing that contributed to those successes. Students' responses to counselors' questions about what they did to accomplish a goal provide the counselor with specific behaviors the student has used successfully in the past. By continuing this process, counselors help students develop mindmaps, which are like roadmaps that guide students' approaches to solving their problems. Mindmapping is one of several techniques useful to the SFBC counselor.

*Cheerleading*

Another technique characteristic of SFBC is cheerleading as a way to acknowledge students' success and encourage more of it. Professional school counselors sincerely praise or cheerlead any success students demonstrate, no matter how small. The cheerleading helps educate students about what they did to make things better. It also provides encouragement and support for continued success, and increases a sense of personal control and self-esteem. Counselors are cheerleading when they praise students, using genuine enthusiasm shown in their voice inflections, facial expressions, and bodily movements. For example, a student might report an instance in which she went to bed without her mother having to "make her." The counselor could cheerlead by responding with comments such as "You mean you went to bed without your mother even having to tell you?" or "How did you manage to do that?"

*Scaling*

Professional school counselors use scaling questions with students for a number of reasons, including establishing a baseline to determine students' progress towards their goals. Students are asked to imagine or are shown a scale from zero (lowest) to ten (highest) and asked to rate their perceived level of goal attainment at that time. Students generally provide a rating greater than zero, which indicates that things have been worse. Questioning the student about what they did to progress from zero to their current position helps students realize unrecognized personal resources and builds their confidence that they can make progress towards their goal(s).

Even when students report their current position on the scale as a zero or a one, counselors can provide complimentary feedback that highlights students' strengths and bolsters their hope. For example, if a student initially responds that his position on the scale is a zero, the counselor could comment "Considering what you have been facing, how have you managed to avoid being at a minus ten?" Such a response highlights the student's ability to cope with a difficult situation. For a student providing a low initial rating of one or two, the counselor might respond with "That's great! What did you do to move from a zero to a two?"

Once an initial baseline is determined, counselors can encourage a student's further progress by asking, "What would you need to do to move up one number?" Through follow up questions, counselors can help students clarify what behavior or behaviors are needed to make various degrees (i.e., 10% or a 7 to an 8) of improvement toward their goals. The scale ratings also provide the student and counselor with feedback about progress and reinforce both the student and counselor for their continued efforts for improvement.

*Identifying and Overcoming Obstacles to Student Success*

To prevent students from becoming discouraged as they pursue their goals, professional school counselors help them identify possible obstacles they might experience. Once obstacles are identified, possible courses of action to avoid or overcome them are explored. Counselor questions, such as "What have you used successfully in the past to keep from getting off track?" are useful in initiating solution-focused discussions.

*Concluding the Initial Session*

*The message.* The initial (SFBC) session is concluded by informing the student that the counselor is going to move to another part of the room for a few minutes in order to reflect on and review the session notes before writing the student a brief message. The message is an extremely important step in SFBC, and is comprised of three parts: compliments, bridging statements, and task assignments.

Effective messages include a minimum of three compliments that recognize and reinforce the student's strengths, resources, and accomplishments that were identified during the initial session. Using the student's own words which were used during the session makes the message powerful and meaningful. These compliments frequently address a student's desired behaviors, efforts, commitments, attitudes, thoughts, decisions, and attributes. The following is an example of the compliments part of a message: "Your decision to seek counseling demonstrates your maturity and genuine desire to learn how to express your anger in appropriate ways. I'm really impressed with your effort and ability to identify ways you have effectively expressed your anger appropriately in the past. Your insights, intelligence, and flexible thinking all reflect your desire and commitment for positive change."

*Bridging statements.* The second part of the message is comprised of bridging statements, which connect the compliments to the task part. Bridging statements provide students with a rationale for engaging in tasks that relate to the accomplishment of their goals. The following is a bridging statement that connects what the student wants (goals and solutions) to homework tasks: "Because of your strong desire to express your anger more appropriately, I would encourage you to (engage in identified, assigned tasks)..."

*Tasks.* The final part of the message contains task statements. Sklare (1997) recommends that the student's assigned homework tasks be intentionally vague, thereby, indicating confidence and trust in the student's ability to make responsible decisions about what tasks need to be completed to attain the goal(s). If concerns exist about a student's ability to benefit from vague tasks, the counselor assigns tasks that make reference to the student's successful behaviors that were previously mentioned in the compliments portion of the message. Referring back to the compliments portion of the message written for the student with the anger management problem, the appropriate task portion of this message might include the following: "Because of your strong desire to express your anger more appropriately, I would encourage you to use more of the strategies that you identified that have worked for you in the past, and notice and continue to do what has been working for you."

Before the initial SFBC session ends, the counselor asks the student if there is any additional information he would like the counselor to know. Counselors conclude the session by having the student assess the need for any additional sessions to accomplish the identified goals.

*Subsequent SFBC Sessions*

Sklare used EARS, an acronym for a sequence of steps attributed to Berg (as cited by Sklare, 1997), to guide the second and succeeding sessions: *E*licit, *A*mplify, *R*einforce, and *S*tart. Counselors begin these sessions by *eliciting* or asking "What's better or different since the last session?" When students respond by identifying what is better, the counselor *amplifies* these improvements by asking questions that help students recognize how changes in their behavior have favorably impacted the behaviors of others. The letter *R* in EARS reminds the counselor to *reinforce* or cheerlead the student for the changes in their behaviors that "made things better." The last step in the EARS sequence is *starting* over again by attempting to elicit, amplify and reinforce additional student changes that have enabled the student to make progress toward their counseling goal(s).

Following the EARS sequence, *scaling* is once again used to assess progress toward a goal that was achieved since the last session. Students should not be reminded of their previous session scaling responses in order to obtain the most objective assessment of current position.

The additional session's assessment is once again used to determine the need for other meetings. The counselor should begin to spread the sessions and plan for ending sessions completely. The message format continues to be the method for concluding sessions and, if follow-up sessions are necessary, the counselor will continue to utilize the SFBC approach as outlined in this chapter.

## Summary/Conclusion

This chapter has provided an overview of solution-focused brief counseling concepts for the professional school counselor. A quick look at the steps in SFBC has been presented to encourage professional school counselors to try this approach with students. It is efficient, effective, and versatile. According to Sklare (1997), SFBC acknowledges the power of focusing on the solution rather than the problem.

## References


Berg, I. K., & Miller, S. (1992). *Working with the problem drinker*. New York: Norton.

Bonnington, S. B. (1993) Solution-focused brief therapy: Helpful interventions for school counselors. *The School Counselor, 41,* 126-128.

Bruce, M. A. (1995). Brief counseling: An effective model for change. *The School Counselor, 42*, 353-364.

Charlesworth, J. J., & Jackson C. M. (2002). *Solution focused brief counseling research.* State University of West Georgia (unpublished manuscript.).

deShazer, S. (1985). *Keys to solution in brief therapy*. New York: Norton.

Downing, J., & Harrison, T. (1992). Solutions and school counseling. *The School Counselor, 39,* 327-332.

Gingerich, W. J., & Wabeke, T. (2001, January). A solution-focused approach to mental health intervention in school settings. *Children & Schools*, *23*, 33-41.

Hart, P. J. & Jacobi, M. (1992). *From gatekeeper to advocate: Transforming the role of the school counselor*. New York: The College Board.

LaFountain, R. M., Garner, N. E., & Eliason, G. T. (1996). Solution focused counseling groups: A key for school counselors. *The School Counselor, 43,* 256-267.

Littrell, J. M., Malia, J. A., Nichols, R., Olson, J., Nesselhuf, D., & Crendell, P. (1992). Brief counseling: Helping counselors adopt an innovative counseling approach. *The School Counselor, 39*, 171-175.

Littrell, J. M., Malia, J. A., & Vanderwood, M. (1995). Single-session brief counseling in a high school. *Journal of Counseling and Development, 73,* 451-458.

McKeel, A. J. (1996). A clinician's guide to research on solution-focused therapy. In S. D. Miller, M. A. Hubble, & B. L. Duncan (Eds.), *Handbook of solution-focused brief therapy* (pp. 251-271). San Francisco: Jossey–Bass.

Murphy, J. (1994). Working with what works: A solution-focused approach to school behavior problems. *The School Counselor, 42*, 59-65.

Murphy, J. J. (1997). *Solution-focused counseling in middle and high schools.* Alexandria, VA: American Counseling Association.

O'Hanlon, W. H., & Weiner-Davis, M. (1989). *In search of solutions: A new direction in psychotherapy*. New York: Guilford.

Sklare, G. B. (1997). *Brief counseling that works: A solution-focused approach for school counselors.* Thousand Oaks, CA: Corwin Press, Inc.

Walter, J. L., & Peller, J. E. (1992). *Becoming solution-focused in brief therapy.* New York: Brunner/Maxel.

Williams, G. R. (January, 2000). The application of solution-focused brief therapy in a public school setting. *Family Journal, 8*(1), 76-78.

Wolpe, J., & Lazarus, A. (1966). *Behavior therapy techniques*. Elmsford, NY: Pergamon.

# Chapter 17

## Using Family Systems Interventions in Schools

*Estes J. Lockhart*

### Preview

This chapter describes family systems concepts and strategies useful to the professional school counselor. Strategies are illustrated by actual school cases. A four-step initial family systems interview model is presented that is specifically designed to allow for an integrated use of strategies drawn from diverse family systems models.

When families come to me for help, I assume they have problems not because there is something inherently wrong with them but because they've gotten stuck—stuck with a structure whose time has passed and stuck with a story that doesn't work. To discover what's bogging them down, I look for patterns that connect (Minuchin & Nichols, 1998, p. 43).

Professional school counselors understand that students bring the problems of life outside the school into the school where they can negatively influence the educational process (Keys, Bemack & Lockhart, 1998; Lockhart & Keys, 1998). Professional school counselors can employ brief family interventions with students and their families to address educational issues that are linked to the home (Hinkle, 1992; Kraus, 1998; Lockhart, 2002). Conceptualizing a school problem by its connections to the family system and using family systems techniques to address the problem offers a practical set of strategies for helping students.

### Four Categories of Family Adjustment

Family systems interventions are helpful when the student's behavior is a response to stresses and changes with which the family is attempting to cope. When this is the case it does not necessarily mean there is anything wrong with the family. Rather, it means that the family finds itself in a tough patch on its journey through life. Pittman (1987), in a book on treating families in crisis and transition, described four categories for thinking about the ways families get stuck in tough patches. First, a family can get stuck trying to cope with a normal task of family development. For example, maybe the family was doing well before the first child had to go to school, but the transition to school for the child is proving a difficult challenge for the family. Second, a family can become stuck trying to use a structure with rules that are outdated for the challenges they face. For example, when children enter adolescence, the family faces the task of having to reorganize their rules. Third, a family may be hit with one or more "bolts from the blue," unexpected stresses, traumas or discontinuities. For example, a family member may be lost through death, divorce may occur, or the family may be overwhelmed through job loss or illness causing the family to have trouble coping. A family may find itself in trouble through the stress of having to be a caretaker for another family member with a disability or illness.

Whenever stress affects a family system and requires a change to the system's usual repertoire, a crisis can result. Such a crisis can cause nonspecific changes in the family, such as the loosening of boundaries, changing of rules, relaxations of expectations and prohibitions, loss of goals and values, revival of unresolved conflicts, and heightened tension between family members (Pittman, 1987). A student may carry the stress and tension from any of these nonspecific changes resulting from a family crisis into the classroom where a crisis for the student may result.

*Example 1: An Eating Disorder and Decreased Academic Performance*

The author intervened with a young girl in elementary school who began exhibiting eating problems and decreased academic performance. Her classroom problem was directly related to living alternating weeks in the homes of the two blended families of her divorced, and subsequently remarried, biological parents. The systems intervention was to bring in both biological parents with their new mates, who were now stepparents for the girl, and help the two sets of parents to align their discipline systems. The student was experiencing high anxiety by switching each week from a set of very loose family rules to a set of very rigid family rules. Also, the student was attempting to relate to new stepparents and new stepsiblings. To intervene, the student was informed of the new procedures by both sets of parents in front of the professional school counselor. The school counselor then followed up with the girl and checked in by telephone with the two families.

*Example 2: A Divorce and Anticipation of Decreased School Performance*

At times, the family may inform the professional school counselor of a crisis that is either anticipated or ongoing in the home and the counselor then can work proactively and collaboratively with the family to prevent the crisis from seriously affecting the student at school. For example, consider a case in which a parent contacted the school counselor seeking help and worried that her child in middle school might be experiencing academic or social problems at school because the student's mother had divorced the student's father. The counselor met with the student using a family systems perspective to address the issue. Together the father and mother assured the student that he didn't cause the problem and couldn't cure the problem, but he could cope with it. Coping is a standard message that is helpful for students to hear from divorcing parents. Both the father and mother reassured their son they would be there to support him. The school counselor also obtained agreement from both parents not to use the student in any way as a pawn, message carrier, or person upon whom to vent on issues related to the failed marriage and divorce. The father arranged his schedule to meet regularly with the son. The purpose of this intervention was to make the changing complexity of the family crisis into a more specific, manageable reality allowing the student to focus on schoolwork.

*Example 3: Loss of a Father Through the Catastrophic Illness of AIDS*

Sometimes the professional school counselor can help the student by simply conceptualizing a student's dysfunction at school as not residing solely within the student and by providing resources, including referral information, to the family. For example, this author encountered a bright, very talented student who began to shut down and even become verbally aggressive when given negative feedback in school. The student had lost his father first to marital separation and then to death from AIDS. Prior to the parents' separation, the student felt they blamed him for much of their anger. During the final days of helping his mother take care of his father, the student experienced renewed fights between the three of them along with negative interactions with his dying, bedridden father, e.g., statements of his failure as a son. The student viewed his situation as one in which he was constantly on edge, feeling rejected by a parent whom he mourned and whom he also felt he had failed at the worst possible moment. The student was helped by having his mother seek his assistance in the grieving process and by her helping him to see that much of the rejection and failure he felt resulted from the failed marriage and his father's depression and pain as he approached death. Feeling blame in the home led to the student acting out at school. There was caretaker stress, bolt from the blue stress, and the structural stress of a family that reduced conflict by *triangulation*, in this case forming an *alliance* between two members to blame a third. It was helpful to have the mother clarify that the son did not cause the divorce. Further, it was helpful for mother and son to understand that classic psychiatric syndromes such as dementia, anxiety, depressive and psychotic disorders are commonly associated with HIV-related disorders (Kaplan & Sadock, 1998). This made some of the loved one's behaviors understandable and helped explain the mother's and son's stressful relationships with him near the end of his life. In this complex case, it was important for the counselor to refer the mother to a family therapist in the community. The professional school counselor then became a case manager serving as a liaison between school staff, mental health counselor, student and family. Importantly, the professional school counselor's initial family session led to the referral to an outside counselor. At home, in therapy, and at school the same message was reinforced, "Don't play the blame game with self or others."

*Example 4: The Power of Context in Racial Victimization at School*

The unique *context* in connection with *family beliefs,* in this case forces operating within the school, can lead to problems in school. For example, the author once intervened with a young African American male high school student who was being racially victimized by a group of white students in a school that had only a few minority students. The African American student refused to report verbal assaults against him by the white students and instead let verbal insults continue until they reached the level of physical confrontation. When the student's family was contacted, it was learned that the parents had told the son that racial victimization was simply a fact of life in the United States. They instructed him that in their family the way to handle racial victimization is to pay no attention to it and walk away. The student had been trying to follow his family beliefs. Unfortunately, the white students continued to name-call. The African American student, unable to take it any longer, stood his ground and prepared to fight. Luckily the principal intervened.

A single session intervention with the African American student's family helped them to see that their response of putting up with racial victimization would not work in the context of their son's school. Unlike the context in their youth, their son had little to no support from peers and was assaulted by students who didn't respect the boundaries of others. The intervention was to *challenge family assumptions* in an appropriate and respectful way. The family changed their belief. The son was encouraged to contact administrators and professional school counselors who then intervened.

## The Family Systems Process

The family system is a *self-organizing system,* which adapts to the stresses the family faces by sometimes having to reorganize its rules significantly. An example would be the death of a grandmother who had parented the kids while both parents worked long hours. It is a system in which various members are connected more or less closely in *subgroups*, for example the parental subgroup or the sibling subgroup. It is a system that draws *boundaries* to control the degree to which those outside any subgroup will communicate or interact with those inside the subgroup. For example, parents might tell their children not to go to a certain place or not to talk with certain people. It is a system in which family members set emotional boundaries to protect individual autonomy, which if too open or too closed can lead to problems. Where boundaries are too open or loose, relationships can be dysfunctionally cohesive (*enmeshed*). For example, parents of a child with a serious mental health disorder or disability, in an effort to protect the child, may become enmeshed, fearing to set more open boundaries that allow for the child to be independent. The family is a system in which the leadership *hierarchy,* whether weak or strong, rigid or flexible, structured or chaotic, affects all members. Since *family rules* are not always explicit and may be very complex, professional school counselors can not assume anything about the family.

Also, the family is a system that the student can't ever really leave completely in the sense that we can leave a job. We may attempt to disengage, separate or *cut off* from the family in some way, but we will never completely escape all of its influences. In fact one of the major challenges that adolescent students in America face is learning how to begin to leave the family appropriately. The families of adolescents may have difficulty helping their children to leave, and this can lead to struggles for power, with ramifications in the schoolhouse. Also, *cultural issues* must be taken into account. For example, a family from South America or Turkey may be sad that their child would even want to think about leaving the family prior to marriage.

The family organizes itself to adapt to environmental challenges and, subsequently, transcends the separate characteristics of individual family members. In one family this might mean individuals would engage in *complementary relationships*, strengthening each other and the family as a whole by providing that which each of the individual members attempting to adjust alone would have trouble providing for themselves. In another family, the attempt to adapt might lead to them getting stuck in a power struggle or some other dilemma.

*Example 5: Preparing to Leave Home Influencing Student Achievement*

Consider the case of a student whose family complained that their daughter wanted to be on her own and was no longer committed to the educational goals she once shared with her family, nor did she want to follow family rules. In this case, there was another issue combined with the normal developmental task of preparing to leave home. The girl served as a *parental child*, spending much time after school taking care of her younger siblings. This girl felt undervalued by her parents because she felt they continued to treat her as a child, making rules for her as though she was just another one of their children when she was on the verge of adulthood and parenting the other children. She wanted the freedom of an adult both at home and at school since she took on a parental role at home. Not getting what she expected led to a loss of commitment to the expectations of her parents and a desire to find a way out of the home so that she could be her own person. The student showed lack of motivation in school and began having conflicts with authority figures. The family reorganized positively in several ways. The family changed communication styles with the girl to more resemble those with their adult friends. The family *renegotiated family rules.* The parents remained in charge of the family *hierarchy,* leadership and decision-making, but adjusted the rules to recognize their daughter's developmental needs. They also took her out of the role of a parental child so that she was able to enjoy a normal life as an adolescent without the stress of intense parenting responsibilities.

*Example 6: Student Violence Ignited by an Extended Family Member*

Increasingly, those who take the family systems view address other contexts in the student's life besides the nuclear family. These may include, but are not limited to, in-laws, peer-networks, and welfare, health, cultural, racial, ethnic, political, social, legal, sports, and school systems. Consider the following rare and unusual example of the power of an in-law to affect the student's behavior at school. The student would violently attack other students at the drop of a hat. The student had been referred to the county neurological clinic where the examining physician determined that he appeared to have a seizure disorder that would need to be evaluated in a residential center. While waiting for a bed in the residential program, the student was enrolled in an alternative school for troubled youth for part of the day and his regular school part of the day. The widowed mother of the student, who allowed an uncle to live with them, was never able to attend meetings at the school. One day, a social worker at the school dropped by the mother's home, explaining that she just happened to be in the neighborhood. During the visit, she learned that the uncle was a psychopath whom the mother had taken in as a deathbed request from her husband. This student went to school everyday wondering if his mother would be alive when he returned home and wondering what stress the evening would hold for both of them. Once the mother was helped to report the psychopathic uncle's behavior to the police, he was removed from the home, and the student ceased the violent attacks on other students. The student returned to his regular school full time without ever needing to attend a residential program. While this example is a rare case, it is not rare for the professional school counselor to intervene with "acting-out students" who live in stressful homes where alcohol, substance abuse, physical abuse and severe mental health issues of family members produce high anxiety and affect student school performance.

*Example 7: A Substance Abusing Home Affecting School Performance*

An elementary student was refusing to do class work and reacting in a hostile way when anyone attempted to make him work. This young elementary student lived with his mother and father in public housing where the parents were doing illegal hard drugs and the young boy was being intimidated daily. He was not able to do well at school because he sat wondering if he would return home to find his parents arrested and removed from the home and his favorite possessions removed from the house. Poverty and illegal drug activity are but two powerful influences in *the larger system,* outside home and school, that the school counselor had to deal with in order to help the student address educational issues. In this case, the counselor first *joined* with the family so that the family respected the professional school counselor as a trusted family member. Joining was a major family systems intervention in that it represented the first time this family, in serious violation of the law, had trusted anyone in the school system. Communication with the family and the school administration had resulted in angry conflicts. The counselor helped the family to agree to *shelve their issues* temporarily with the school administration in order to do what was needed for their child. Next the professional school counselor suggested local resources the family could trust in helping them address their substance abuse issues, realizing that any progress in this area would likely take much time. A collaboration between family and counselor led to the student moving in with a nearby relative for a short-time.

*Example 8: Student Refusal to Attend School*

There can be many possible forces driving a student's dysfunctional behavior. For example, a student may be refusing to attend school because he wants to avoid the stress of work. On the other hand, the student might be experiencing anxiety about separation from a major attachment figure, or worrying about harm befalling a major attachment figure while the student is at school. The student might even fear attack from a gang, or simply find the long day or interactions with classmates anxiety-producing. There are many and varied reasons which might influence a student's refusal to attend school, and they might work in combination. The father of the student may have recently been diagnosed with cancer or there may be an impending parental divorce or loss of income. Any of these family systems dynamics might cause a reorganization of the family that results in anxiety for the student and can be inseparable from other forces working against the student attending school.

For example, consider a case in which a high school student's deceased grandfather had lived in the student's home. The student's father had a heart attack a few months prior to the student complaining of intense fear upon trying to enter the high school. This was a student who wanted to be in school. He was a high school senior with a high grade point average, a girlfriend at school, and a position on the varsity basketball team. He complained of desperately wanting to be at school, but being terrified by a feeling that all the energy in his body was leaving him as he tried to walk from his car into the school. He said that this had been coming on slowly in other settings like restaurants, and he had been coping by ceasing to visit settings that made him anxious. Now the problem had generalized to his school. The school counselor carried out individual desensitization and relaxation training with the student, combined with strengthening the family hierarchy and setting boundaries with his mother, who was enmeshed emotionally with the student. In this case school refusal was driven by separation anxiety. The student feared that if he left home and became locked into a full day of school, something might happen to someone he loved away from school that would be catastrophic, i.e., his father might suffer another heart attack or his mother with whom he was enmeshed might become ill. He could say that he knew these were irrational fears, but that didn't stop him from having them. His fears led to panic resulting in a catastrophic feeling of a loss of all the energy in his body. It was important that he be given permission to leave class at any time and check in with parents and that he be allowed to go to the counselor's office as needed to listen to a relaxation tape.

## Family Members in Attendance During a Family Systems Intervention

Although it is often helpful to bring in other family members when carrying out a family systems intervention, it is not necessary. One reason that it can be helpful to bring in other family members is that people have difficulty reporting accurately on their own social situations (Haley, 1976). Another reason is to engage significant others directly in the support of the student. However, family systems interventions do not require the attendance of a family member. Also, taking a family systems perspective does not mean that the professional school counselor stops thinking about the individual student as an individual, with an individual's own heart, mind, temperament, will, and dreams. One can work individually while using a systems perspective.

For example, if the professional counselor wishes to encourage the student to respond more appropriately in an individual session, the counselor may use the family system intervention of asking the student how his or her deceased grandmother would advise the student if she were here. In this family systems intervention without any family members present, the influence of a deceased family member can hold great power. This type of family intervention could be referred to as an *invocation of significant others*, and is powerful with students who might otherwise resist or detour challenging issues. Obviously, the counselor could ask, "If your mother and father or sister or brother were here, would they agree with you?" These are the kinds of questions that allow for the family systems perspective to influence the intervention without any family member present.

## Three Models of Family Systems Interventions

There are a wide variety of family systems intervention models. However, today there are few purists, meaning those who rigidly stick to one family system model (Nichols & Schwartz, 2001). The three models that follow can be useful for the professional school counselor. However, the brief descriptions that follow give only a general sense of each model. The reference section following this chapter includes works that treat the models in more depth.

### *Strategic Family System Interventions*

Strategic family therapy describes family problems as being maintained by some combination of unsuccessful problem solving, weak leadership or hierarchy, inability to adjust to transitions in the family life cycle, interactive communication patterns that support dysfunctional interactions, or triangular relationships that result in coalitions of family members against each other. Problems are resolved by altering the above factors through techniques strategically applied, which often takes the form of a directive to be practiced outside of the counseling session. For example, the father and mother might be advised when feeling stress while parenting to avoid any anger at the moment. Instead, the two could meet for fourteen minutes in the evening away from the child and each spend seven minutes explaining his or her thoughts and feelings to the other while the other writes them down and gives no nonverbal or verbal responses. When someone is writing down what is said, it lends support to the feeling of being heard.

Haley, in developing strategic family systems, was heavily influenced by a medical doctor and brilliantly creative psychotherapist named Milton Erickson with whom Haley collaborated and about whom Haley wrote (Haley, 1973). Milton Erickson, a hypnotherapist, had an uncanny ability to use language creatively to enlist a client's support in the process of change. One of Erickson's most powerful skills was to use *metaphors and stories* to engage the client and make indirect suggestions, often below the level of consciousness during an intervention. Haley suggested becoming a "metaphor enthusiast." Using metaphors, or recalling an interesting story analogous to the student's own situation, encourages increased engagement of the student in the intervention. The following application of the strategic model demonstrates the application of major strategic techniques in a school setting, including the use of therapeutic metaphor.

*Example 9: Adolescent Who Fights With Peers*

This case involves the family of an adolescent son who had begun to engage in serious fights with peers. A conversation with the family led to the conclusion that since the student had not had this anger problem prior to adolescence, it was possible that something could be happening with the family's adaptation to adolescence. This helped to *normalize* the situation by helping the family move from thinking of the adolescent as being abnormal and their family as dysfunctional to thinking of the family as needing to make a perfectly normal adjustment to a common life cycle event, adolescence. The family set more appropriate limits and response costs and the parents were encouraged to continue to reach out to the son by telling him they were there to help him. The family needed to learn how to avoid getting into *triangular relationships* in which one parent would side with the son against the other when discipline issues at school were reported to the family. They needed support to believe that they still had influence on this young man.

*Example 10: Strategic Use of Metaphor to Support Parents*

The parents in the above example stated that they were worried about making decisions for their son. They said he was always accusing them of disrespecting him by setting all the rules rather than letting him take care of himself. But they said they felt caught in a bind because while they wanted to give him more freedom, they feared the outcome if they did, and they lost power through inaction. The metaphor of a ship at sea in a threatening storm was used to drive home the importance of the parents taking charge in the family. They were told to imagine they were out at sea on an ocean liner and a big storm threatens. They were asked which of the following statements from the captain would make them feel more secure: "Relax, stay inside. We have been through many of these storms before, and we know what to do," or "Look, I'd like to get your opinion on what would be the best course of action." And just imagine one's anxiety if the captain actually offered one control of the ship in such a situation (Lockhart, 1990). The family said they came back to this metaphor over and over again when feeling under duress from their son.

Also, this family had a *repetitive sequence of behavior* which they continued to try even though it failed them. The mother and father, unable to decide what to do about the son's anger at home and school, would sometimes begin to argue with each other over how to respond to their son's behavior. The mother would call for the father's help in disciplining the son. As the father, a rather quiet and analytical man, attempted to reason with his son, the mother would tell the father that he was not being tough enough in supporting her. Soon the parents would be fighting with each other as the son with the anger problem looked on and criticized them. The parents were challenged to communicate in a way that would break this repetitive cycle and be a better model for their son. A metaphor of a real experiment was used in which two rats in a cage receiving electric shock first tried to avoid the shocks by running around, and then, when the shocks continued, turned on each other. The parents said that was exactly how they felt. It was suggested that, when feeling at their wit's end, unlike the rats they could take a break and, when feeling a bit less stressed, return to problem-solving in a better state of mind.

*Structural Family Systems Interventions:*

The professional school counselor using structural family systems interventions looks for maladaptive boundaries, maladaptive hierarchy, or maladaptive reactions to changing developmental or social conditions as factors that can maintain problems. Problems are resolved by creating clear, flexible boundaries and more adaptive and flexible hierarchy responses to changing developmental or social conditions. The sequence of change in the structural model is to 1) join and accommodate to the family, and 2) help the family change its structure.

*Example 11: A Gender Issue in a Stepfamily and at School*

A young man from a blended family was disrespectful to female classmates. The counselor helped the family to focus on the need for the student to learn more appropriate *boundaries*. For example, boundaries between the mother and student were nonexistent, leaving them emotionally fused or *enmeshed.*

The student and mother would talk to each other as friends or equals, and the student would speak to her not as a respected woman, but as a buddy. This made it difficult for the mother to separate herself as the parent. Meanwhile, the boundaries between student and stepfather were closed, resulting in disengagement with little communication. In this situation, the professional school counselor invited the parents in and set an initial goal of *joining* with them. Once joined with the family, the professional school counselor was able to *reframe* the mother's enmeshment in a positive light. This parent behavior of being overly protective of her child, was reframed as, "You just seem to love your child too much." The mother accepted this.

The professional school counselor *highlighted strengths and weaknesses*, such as the need for a discussion and reinforcement of appropriate boundaries for their son with regard to interactions with females. After joining sufficiently to be able to give negative feedback without loss of family respect, the counselor suggested that the stepfather and son spend more time together having fun and discussing, among other things, how to act appropriately with females. This helped by *shifting the family members' relative positions* to interrupt the pattern in which the stepfather and son interacted only for discipline reasons.

## Constructivist Family Systems Interventions

In a constructivist approach, the intervention is conceived as a collaboration in which the counselor and student together construct a more desirable reality. Two examples of constructivist theory are solution-focused interventions and narrative-focused interventions (Hoyt, 1996). The professional school counselor's role in the constructivist approach is to acknowledge, praise and in other ways highlight and punctuate strengths of the family and collaborate with the family to arrive at resources and solutions for facing the family's challenging situation. The constructivist tends to ask questions more about what has gone right rather than what has gone wrong. They tend to collaborate rather than direct or coach. Satir anticipated the constructivist way of viewing the problem when she would refer to a problem as "an accident in the interest of the self" (Hoffman, 2002). The attempt by Satir was to normalize a situation by making it an accident that happened for the best of reasons, the needs of the self.

Constructivist interventions make much use of *looking for exceptions* in which the student and/or family acts competently. The family is then encouraged to do more of their competent-type behavior. Both solution-focused and narrative-focused constructivist approaches make use of the *miracle question* in which the family imagines awaking one morning and finding everything is as it should be. This allows the family to begin building a vision more consistent with their ideal of how they would like to live. Solution-focused interventions are one the most popular of our day because they are cognitive in emphasis, easy to teach, and promise quick solutions (Nichols & Schwartz, 2001). DeShazer has stated that the basic rules of solution-focused interventions are: 1) If it ain't broke, don't fix it. 2) Once you know what works, do more of it. 3) If it doesn't work, don't do it again, do something different (Hoyt, 1996).

In constructivist approaches, the attempt is to help the family construct a sense of hope for the future out of the current situation based on successes in other situations. Both solution-focused and narrative-focused interventions give much attention to the language used to communicate about the situation that is presented. This involves the way in which a family conceives their situation and the language they use will either empower them to find the resources they need to succeed or disempower them. Haley anticipated this concern of the constructivists when he said, "The way one labels a human dilemma can crystallize a problem and make it chronic" (Haley, 1976, p. 3).

*Example 12: A Middle School Student With AD/HD*

A middle school student was not staying on task in class. The family said that the main problem was AD/HD. The student indicated in the session that either she was being unfairly picked on by the teacher or the work was boring and she got fidgety. The parents said that she had told them the main problems were the teacher doesn't like the student, the student can't get any help from the teacher, and the work is either too easy or too difficult. The professional school counselor, using a narrative intervention, asked the whole family for a meeting to discuss the way they would like to see their story proceed. In the narrative approach, the counselor *stayed one down,* on an equal footing or below the power level of the family. The counselor's goal was simply to carry on a conversation to help the family determine how they would like to rewrite their family story so that it fit with their view of how they would like to be a family.

The family preferred a story in which the student would heroically begin to complete homework, stay on task in school doing what she was directed to do, and actively seek help from the teacher when needed. The counselor, using the narrative approach, helped the family to *externalize* the off-task behavior as a monster that would require the family working together to defeat. This *externalization of the problem* is a powerful technique for placing the problem outside the family and removing debilitating blame.

The counselor used *language that suggested a successful ending* by saying to the student and family, "Well, when you are no longer having conflicts with the teacher and you are performing regularly, what kinds of relationships will you then have with your family or teacher? The parents were also asked how they would feel when all of them had succeeded in defeating the monster. They talked of happiness, relief, joy, and a desire to do more interesting and fun things together. The counselor *celebrated small changes* and approximations toward the desired behavior so that successes could begin to be experienced by the student and family. The counselor also worked with the psychiatrist to give feedback on the effects of the medication.

In order to clarify differing opinions, family members used a scaling intervention. Scaling is a technique regularly used in solution-focused interventions to encourage clearer more concrete understandings of how each situation is viewed by family members. Scaling can also be used as a baseline against which to measure change as student, teacher and family report improvement or lack of progress. The student was also helped to *deconstruct a myth* the student had been using to cope with feelings of incompetence. The myth was that it is better to act out than fail, look foolish and take another blow to her self-esteem. This myth made its appearance in statements by the student, such as "What's the use anyway?" The teacher also indicated the student's lack of self-esteem by saying, "When she gets a little help at the start of a new lesson, she does well, but when she doesn't she will just give up after hardly trying." The professional school counselor suggested that learning patience and delaying gratification is a sign of increasing maturity. The parents agreed. The goal of the constructivist approach is that the family will have renewed hope.

## Initial Family Systems Interview for Professional School Counselors

The *initial family interview* is important because it is the first point of meeting the family and attempting to intervene. Following is a four-step initial interview model for professional school counselors using strategic, structural and constructivist techniques and interventions.

*Four Step Initial Family Intervention Model*

*Step one*: *Welcoming, joining, reassuring.* Begin the interview by making sure everyone feels as comfortable as possible, connect with all individuals in a way that helps to establish rapport, and communicate reassurance that the counselor cares about the pain in the family and is here to help all of them. A good reassuring statement to the family by the counselor is, "I am sorry this is happening to you, and I am going to work hard to help you." *Stay one down* and *listen empathetically.*

*Step two*: *Interacting, normalizing & collaborating.* Encourage family interaction and discussion around what has been attempted in the family effort to get unstuck and how the family is succeeding in difficult situations. Often it can help to view the situation as a normal part of the family life cycle or individual development or a bolt from the blue no one could predict which precipitated a crisis. *Highlight family strengths and encourage more of what works.* Discourage continuing what has failed. Treat the family with respect and parents as experts on their child.

*Step three*: *Searching for patterns that connect and planning a new vision.* Listen to the family story of their situation. Whether through directives, coaching or collaboration help them to *frame, reframe, dream or in some way construct a more useful family story* along with concrete goals to make their vision a reality. Metaphors can help make a vision clear. For example, where blame has been a problem, the metaphor "Sounds like you are hoping future sights along the way won't be colored by earlier accidents" could be used. Or one might say, "It is hard to drive a car forward when looking through the rearview mirror."

*Step four*: *Agreeing on a plan of positive action.* This step involves the family planning the necessary action for getting back on the road to a hopeful future. It can be helpful to provide a way to monitor the intervention, perhaps through brief phone calls.

## Summary/Conclusion

"Families don't walk in and hand you the underlying structural patterns that are keeping them stuck. What they bring is the noise - their own confusion and pain" (Minuchin & Nichols, 1998, p. 46). The task of the professional school counselor is to join with the family and look for the patterns that connect. Family members often reveal these patterns in stories that are memories connected to the situation at hand. These stories provide a map of the implicit rules of the family as they attempt to cope with their child's difficulties at school. Many times the family presents the story of their child's school problem as a crisis in their family. Often this crisis of the family involves worrying how to respond to a current demand for changes to their rules and roles. In responding to the family crisis, the professional school counselor must integrate family systems techniques and interventions wisely in a way that empowers the family to help the student cope in school. This is a difficult task. It requires an appreciation of the complexity of family systems. It requires skill to encourage families to alter repetitive patterns of interaction that keep them stuck. Helping families requires the professional school counselor to respect the family's dreams and beliefs while helping them access their own resources to achieve positive change.

## References


Haley, J. (1973). *Uncommon therapy.* New York: W. W. Norton & Company.

Haley, J. (1976). *Problem-solving therapy.* New York: Harper & Row.

Hinkle, J. S. (1992). Family counseling in the schools. *ERIC Digest* [On-line], www.ERIC_Digests/ed347482.html.

Hoffman, L. (2002). *Family therapy: An intimate history.* New York: W. W. Norton & Co.

Hoyt, M. (1996). Solution building and language games. In M. Hoyt (Ed.), *Constructive therapies* (pp. 60-86). New York: The Guilford Press.

Kaplan, H. I., & Sadock, B. J. (1998). Neurological aspects of Human Immunodificiency Virus (HIV) infection and Acquired Immune Deficiency Syndrome (AIDS). *Synopsis of Psychiatry.* Baltimore, MD: Williams & Wilkins.

Keys, S. G., Bemak, F., & Lockhart, E. J. (1998). Transforming school counseling to serve the mental health needs of at risk youth. *Journal of Counseling and Development, 76,* 381-388.

Kraus, I. (1998). A fresh look at school counseling: A family-systems approach. *Professional School Counseling, 1*(4), 12-17.

Lockhart, E. J. (1990). *Communicating with kids: A practical guide to the forgotten language.* Frederick, MD: Undercurrents Press.

Lockhart, E. J., & Keys, S. (1998). The mental health counseling role of school counselors. *Professional School Counseling, 1*(4), 3-6.

Lockhart, E. J. (2002). Students with disabilities. In B. T. Erford (Ed.), *Transforming the school counseling profession,* (pp. 357-410). Columbus, OH: Merrill/Prentice-Hall.

Minuchin, S., & Nichols, M. P. (1998). *Family healing: Strategies for hope and understanding.* New York: The Free Press.

Nichols, M., & Schwartz, R. (2001). *Family therapy: Concepts and methods.* New York: Allyn & Bacon.

Pittman, F. (1987). *Turning points: Treating families in transition and crisis.* New York: W. W. Norton & Company.

# Chapter 18

## Using Multiple Intelligences to Counsel Diverse Students

*David J. Lundberg & Brenda S. Hall*

### Preview

Multiple intelligences theory suggests a broad approach to personal development. Professional school counselors who incorporate elements of multiple intelligences encourage students to view themselves broadly and develop their abilities in wide-ranging areas. Techniques derived from a multiple intelligences framework can encourage less competitive, more productive, team-oriented approaches to life and work.

Much of the effectiveness in counseling and teaching comes from the ability to see human beings from different perspectives and to interact in ways that are appropriate to each person's individuality. Much of the harm that results from stereotyping and prejudice springs from viewing people from narrow perspectives and from losing sight of that individuality.

The benefits of broad, creative approaches to understanding people are enormous, and resulting relationships based on mutual respect and the valuing of diversity are fundamental prerequisites for effective interpersonal interaction. The concept of multiple intelligences offers a refreshing and elevating way of showing respect and empowering diverse students. Just as integrative approaches to counseling have become prominent because of the need to better understand complex human beings, theories of multiple intelligences expand our vision to help people grow and develop.

Theories of multiple intelligences have become more widely utilized in educational classrooms and offer school personnel, including professional school counselors, important considerations for effective practice. The central theme of these theories is that intelligence is more than a single, unitary factor such as intelligence quotient (IQ). Several researchers (Catell, 1987; Guilford, 1982; Thurston, 1938) have attempted to identify different kinds of intelligences. However, the most specific theoretical frameworks have come from the work of Howard Gardner and Robert Sternberg.

*Gardner's Developmental Framework*

A theory of multiple intelligences was first published by Gardner (1993). He suggested that the definition of intelligence using traditional quantitative measures such as the IQ test was far too narrow in scope. Gardner defined intelligence as "the ability to solve problems, or to fashion products, that are valued in one or more culture or community settings" (Oliver, 1997, p. 1). This definition expanded intelligence to include cultural and motivational factors. Gardner rejected the notion that there is only one form of intelligence. He argued that all individuals possess several intelligences although specific types of intelligence are stronger in different persons. He maintained the importance of hereditary factors but insisted that societal values, cultural resources, and individual opportunities are paramount in understanding and recognizing intelligences.

Gardner's perspective is multifaceted and pluralistic. Within his developmental framework are eight independent abilities.

*Linguistic/Verbal.* Focusing on the production and use of words and language, linguistic/verbal intelligence is utilized in listening, speaking, reading, and writing. It is displayed by writers, poets, journalists, politicians, and orators.

*Logical/Mathematical.* Logical/mathematical intelligence pertains to higher order thinking, inductive and deductive reasoning, manipulation of numbers, the capacity to recognize patterns, and the ability to connect logical-mathematical operations. Mathematicians, engineers, and microbiologists generally possess this intelligence.

*Visual/Spatial.* This intelligence utilizes skills involving spatial configurations, such as visualizing an object and creating mental images such as pictures, paintings, diagrams, or maps. It is emphasized in the visual arts, navigation, and architecture. Artists, navigators, designers, and topologists show this intelligence.

*Bodily/Kinesthetic.* Bodily/kinesthetic intelligence addresses skills in using the entire body or parts of the body through physical movement. It involves knowledge of the body, how it moves, and how it can be used to express emotion, solve motor problems, or construct products or displays. Dancers, athletes, actors, and builders typically display bodily/kinesthetic intelligence.

*Musical/Rhythmical.* This intelligence demonstrates itself in tasks related to music such as tonal patterns, rhythm, and beat. It involves recognizing, manipulating, and repeating musical sounds and rhythms. Violinists, singers, and other musical performers manifest this intelligence.

*Interpersonal.* Interpersonal intelligence addresses skills in interactions with others. It involves the ability to get along with others, communication, and sensitivity to the concerns of other people. Counselors, teachers, and salespeople generally possess this intelligence.

*Intrapersonal.* Intrapersonal intelligence centers around knowledge of oneself. Intrapersonal intelligence involves awareness of one's internal aspects and includes access to one's own feelings and emotions as well as an understanding of metacognition (how one thinks about thinking). Individuals who share themselves through literature, art, and speech display this intelligence.

*Naturalist.* This intelligence addresses the ability to recognize and classify living things and features of the natural world (animals, minerals, and plants). Farmers, biologists, and chefs typically use this intelligence.

Gardner's intelligences represent both nature and nurture perspectives. Individuals are born with the capacity to develop all eight intelligences. However, cultural, social, and personal contexts within the child's environment determine to what extent each of the intelligences is manifested. Because each student's experience in the world is different, each child will display a unique range of intellectual strengths and weaknesses. This intellectual profile is a combination of exhibited intelligences and does not provide a definite categorization of one intelligence level. In other words, children should not be categorized as being high or low in an intelligence area, but rather appreciated for the full range of their various intellectual abilities. Gardner proposes that children's intellectual capacities can be strengthened and expanded.

*Sternberg's Triarchic Framework*

Robert Sternberg's early work on intelligence supported the view that traditional intelligence testing was too narrow. He sought to understand the information processing components related to the standard intelligence trait (Spearman's *g*). Sternberg (1985) outlined a theory of intelligence emphasizing three distinct patterns that can be measured and developed. Unlike Gardner, who suggested different types of intelligences, Sternberg posited three facets that make up the construct of intelligence. These abilities are interrelated, but largely distinctive.

*Analytical Intelligence.* Similar to traditionally-valued analytic ability, analytical intelligence involves problem solving, monitoring solutions, and evaluating results. It refers to how individuals process information and relate to the external world.

*Creative Intelligence.* This type of intelligence uses insight and original thought. It reflects how individuals use what they already know and develop new and different ways to complete tasks. Creative intelligence involves using imagination, innovation, and creativity to see the world in different ways.

*Practical Intelligence.* Practical intelligence can be referred to as "street smarts," the ability to take what is learned and apply it to everyday living. This involves the ability to assess a situation and decide how to respond.

In more recent work, Sternberg (1997) outlined a triarchic theory of successful intelligence. In this context, successful intelligence is defined as "that set of mental abilities used to achieve one's goals in life, given a sociocultural context, through adaptation to, selection of, and shaping of environments" (Sternberg, 1998, p.1). Like Gardner, Sternberg emphasizes the cultural, social, and personal influences on intelligence. Sternberg's theory of successful intelligence incorporates universal aspects of cognition as well as sources of group and individual differences.

*Gardner and Sternberg: A Common Ground*

Gardner and Sternberg arrived at their conclusions about intelligence in very different ways. Sternberg worked from a more traditional scientific base and emphasized the empirical foundation for his theory of intelligence. Gardner emphasized the use of data but suggested that his findings are "less a set of hypotheses and predictions than ... an organized framework for configuring an ensemble of data about human cognition in different cultures" (Gardner, 1994, p. 2).

Despite these and other differences, both Gardner and Sternberg proposed that intelligence is much broader than the measurement of a single general intelligence trait. They also share the idea that this broader view of intelligences can be translated into educational practice. Sternberg has formulated specific principles of teaching for developing successful intelligences and reforming education (Sternberg, 1998). Many educators have discussed the applications of Gardner's work to instructional practices in schools and the implementation of multiple intelligences principles has occurred in schools across the country. Common ideas from the work of Sternberg (1997) and Gardner (1993) include the following:

1. All individuals have different minds with unique strengths and weaknesses.
2. People use aspects or types of intelligences based on a multitude of factors (cultural, social, personal) and experiences.
3. Intelligences can be developed and strengthened.
4. Intelligences can be assessed (although a widely accepted single instrument has not been developed).
5. It is important for educators and counselors to recognize different intellectual abilities and to pay attention to individual intelligences.
6. Educators should develop educational strategies and utilize multiple approaches that encourage the use and development of various intelligences or aspects of intelligences.

## Recommended Actions and Strategies

The basic tenets of multiple intelligences theory coincide with current trends in school counseling and can assist professional school counselors in their work with students, teachers, caregivers, and administrators. Multiple intelligences theory is student-centered. The emphasis is on identification of individual capabilities and development of talents. Current counseling theories such as brief counseling also stress the identification and expansion of existing coping mechanisms and strengths. Recognizing the breadth of intelligences, counselors can help students develop and utilize the full range of their abilities.

Multiple intelligences theory requires an understanding of diversity. Individuals differ in the ways they perceive the world, interact with others, make decisions, and solve problems. Using a multiple intelligences framework allows professional school counselors to address diversity in terms of how individuals think and create solutions to problems as well as differences in "looks" and "behaviors."

Multiple intelligences theory promotes action-oriented interventions. Due to the multitude of student problems and issues in the school environment, professional school counselors must be willing to take action and work collaboratively to meet student needs.

Multiple intelligences theory provides a foundation for choosing a variety of activities, strategies, and interventions that speak to specific individuals with particular problems. Professional school counselors can broaden their own practice as well as enhance their function as consultants and team players.

Research linking multiple intelligences and the counseling process is limited. O'Brian and Burnett (2000) reported on the infusion of Gardner's theory into the counseling process. Other researchers (Kerka, 1999; Mantzaris, 1999; Shearer, 1997) discussed multiple intelligences and career development. In general, the use of multiple intelligences theory can enhance the counseling process in three major areas: self-knowledge, possible courses of action, and self-esteem. The following suggestions can improve that process.

*Self Knowledge*

- Find out about the student's culture, including values, resources, and opportunities provided by the environment.
- Pay attention to the specific needs and talents of each child.
- Help students examine their own assumptions about their potential, achievement, environment, thoughts, feelings, behaviors, needs, and concerns.
- Create an environment that exposes individuals to the various intelligences through a variety of activities and a multitude of resources.
- Provide opportunities for students to express themselves through diverse interventions and strategies such as talking, writing, drawing, puppets, role-play, music, poetry, and small group interaction.
- Promote the awareness of individual strengths and weaknesses and the development of hidden talents.
- Involve students in both individual and group interaction so that interpersonal and intrapersonal talents are discovered.

*Possible Courses of Action*

- Encourage students to use self-knowledge and provide opportunities for them to practice new knowledge of self.
- Help students reframe a problem so they can use multiple intelligences to achieve a positive outcome. Once students realize that there is more than one way to resolve an issue or complete a task, they can utilize their self-knowledge, various talents, and resources to successfully address the concern.
- Show students how to synthesize self-knowledge, possible courses of action, and evaluate which talents are most appropriate in specific situations. Synthesizing this information opens eyes to new and different possibilities and allows for new perspectives.

*Self-Esteem*

- Plan activities that allow students to express and apply various types of intelligences that lead students to understand the relationship between their intelligences and their work in school. They can take credit for successes.
- Through interaction in small groups and other intrapersonal activities, individuals build social skills, learn to control their behavior, and enhance their self-esteem with peers. As students gain self-awareness they can appreciate and feel good about themselves as unique individuals. Students, especially low achievers, can build on successes and set goals that allow them to accomplish something meaningful in school.

## Summary/Conclusion

Continual assessment of multiple intelligences in counseling enhances the interaction between student and counselor, creating an environment that allows comfort, expression of the whole person, and maximum growth. Through the counseling process individuals become aware of the types of intelligences, identify their stronger talents, and develop strategies to effectively utilize those skills. Equally important is the opportunity for students to build on prominent intelligences and try new ways of expression, thus using one intelligence area to strengthen another. Professional school counselors who continually evaluate client development within the multiple intelligences framework can promote a fuller spectrum of personal, social, and intellectual capabilities in students. Beyond the school setting, this can lead to less competitive, more productive, team-oriented approaches to life and work.

## References


Catell, R. B. (1987). *Intelligence: Its structure, growth and action.* Amsterdam: North-Holland.

Gardner, H. (1993). *Frames of mind: The theory of multiple intelligences.* New York: Basic Books.

Gardner, H. (1994). Intelligences in theory and practice: A response to Elliot W. Eisner, Robert J. Sternberg, and Henry M. Levin. *Teachers College Record, 95*, 567-583.

Guilford, J. P. (1982). Cognitive psychology's ambiguities: Some suggested remedies. *Psychological Review, 89*, 48-59.

Kerka, S. (1999, January). *Multiple intelligences and career counseling.* Retrieved May 20, 2002 from http://www.ericacue.org/searchinput.asp

Mantzaris, J. (1999, March). Adding a dimension to career counseling. *Focus on Basics, 3*(1), Retrieved May 20, 2002 from http://www.gse.harvard.edu/ncsall/fob/1999/mantzari.htm

O'Brian, P., & Burnett, P. (2000). Counseling children using a multiple intelligence framework. *British Journal of Guidance and Counselling, 28*, 353-372.

Oliver, A. (1997). Plugging into multiple intelligences. *Education Digest, 62*(6), 61-65.

Shearer, C. B. (1997, August). Reliability, validity and utility of a multiple intelligences assessment for career planning. Paper presented at the annual meeting of the American Psychological Association, Chicago, IL. (ED 415 476)

Sternberg, R. J. (1985). *Beyond IQ: A triarchic theory of human intelligence.* New York: Cambridge University Press.

Sternberg, R. J. (1997). *Successful intelligence.* New York: Plume.

Sternberg, R. J. (1998). Principles of teaching for successful intelligence. *Educational Psychologist, 33*(2/3), 65-72.

Thurston, L. L. (1938). Primary mental abilities. *Psychometric Monographs*, 1.

# Chapter 19

## Integrating Learning Styles in Multicultural Counseling

*Brenda S. Hall & David J. Lundberg*

**Preview**

Implementing the concepts of learning styles theory provides professional school counselors with additional tools for working with diverse students. Resultant techniques can provide a practical means to enrich the counseling process and empower individual students by approaching them in readily understandable ways.

Understanding the concept of learning styles opens another avenue for interacting with diverse clients in a way that values each of them as unique individuals. Incorporating various learning style techniques in working with students allows professional school counselors a fresh and different way to expand their approaches to helping.

Trying to understand cultural differences with clients can be an exasperating task, primarily because the factors involved seem almost endless (Lundberg & Kirk, 2003). The concept of learning styles, like that of multiple intelligences, offers a specific framework to interact with diverse students in ways that are harmonious and natural for those clients. These approaches promise not only increased effectiveness for professional school counselors, but also refreshing and stimulating methods to invigorate the counseling process.

*Learning Styles: How They Differ from Multiple Intelligences*

Learning styles theory is concerned with differences in the process of learning. It emphasizes the way individuals think and feel as they absorb, process, and internalize information. An individual learning style is a unique collection of skills and preferences that affect how a person perceives, gathers, and processes information. Learning styles models seek to identify affinities for specific instructional environments, strategies, and resources.

While learning styles and multiple intelligences (MI) are well documented, hold widespread interest in the educational community, and provide important implications for student development, they are very different concepts. Multiple intelligences theory is an effort to understand how culture and experiences shape human potential. MI focuses on the content and products of education, but does not address the individualized process of learning. Gardner (1993) explained that " ... in MI theory, I begin with a human organism that responds (or fails to respond) to different kinds of contents in the world such as language, number, and other human beings... Those who speak of learning styles are searching for approaches that ought to characterize all contents: a person who is deliberate with respect to music as well as to mathematics, a person who sees the 'big picture' whether he is doing physics or painting "(p. 44-45). While both constructs promote a multifaceted approach to learning, their differences can be summarized as follows:

- Multiple intelligences theory focuses on the unique talents and strengths of students. Learning styles theories focus on individual preferences in the learning process.
- Multiple intelligences theory is an outgrowth of cognitive theory related to intelligence testing; learning styles theories have roots in personality theory.

- Multiple intelligences theory addresses what is taught (content); learning styles theories emphasize how it is taught (process).
- Empirical studies relating multiple intelligences and student achievement are limited, while the impact of learning styles on student achievement is well documented statistically.
- Specific instruments for measures of multiple intelligences are being developed and tested. Valid and reliable learning styles assessments already exist.

*Learning Styles Models*

Learning style is broadly defined as the individual difference in the way a learner approaches the task of learning. More specifically, a learning style is the way each person begins to concentrate on, process, internalize, and retain difficult and new information (Dunn, Denig & Lovelace, 2001). One's learning style preferences affect how a person learns, solves problems, and relates to others. Styles of learning tend to change and develop as people grow. Learning styles models recognize the role of cognitive and affective processes, and they bring attention to issues related to motivation and student achievement.

Understanding learning styles can be useful to students and professionals in several ways. Knowing their preferences helps students to plan for learning and to develop personal study strategies. Professionals can utilize individual learning preferences to design and implement effective instructional environments, strategies, and resources. Research supports the idea that when students are taught new and different information through instructional approaches that respond to their learning style preference, they score statistically higher on achievement tests (Dunn et al., 2001).

Assessment tools exist for each of the different learning style paradigms. These archetypes can be either single or dual dimensional and are represented by a few or multiple elements. Kolb (1984) emphasized experiential aspects of learning such as concrete experience (feeling), reflective observation (watching), abstract conceptualization (thinking), and active experimentation (doing). Silver and Strong (1997) outlined four basic styles:

- *Mastery.* The mastery learner approaches learning from a concrete, step-by-step approach. Clarity and practicality are important values.
- *Understanding.* Students who prefer the understanding style enjoy questioning, reasoning, and evaluating using logic and evidence.
- *Self-expressive.* Self-expressive learners use feelings and emotions to handle new ideas and create outcomes. They respond to learning practices that require originality and creativity.
- *Interpersonal.* Individuals who fit the interpersonal learning style see learning as a social activity and a tool to help others.

One of the most widely recognized and researched learning styles models for elementary and secondary school students is the Dunn and Dunn (1992, 1993) framework. It focuses on 21 unique elements that can be classified into five distinct categories:

- *Classroom environment* - Light (bright/soft), sound (sounds/silence), room temperature (cool/warm), and seating (formal/casual) are the environmental elements.
- *Emotionality* - Levels of motivation, persistence, responsibility, conformity, and preferences for structure are elements of emotionality. Some students are persistent in terms of high levels of motivation or focus, and they provide their own structure. Others need direction for task initiation, focus, and structure.
- *Sociological* - Learning alone, with peers, with collegial or authoritative adults, and

the need for variety versus routine are sociological elements.

- *Physiological* - Perceptual elements (auditory, visual, tactile, kinesthetic), time-of-day energy highs and lows, preference for snacks or fluids while learning, and the need for mobility versus passivity are all facets of the physiological category.
- *Psychological* – These elements are methods of processing information. Individuals with strongly analytic preferences approach facts in a step-by-step sequence by first examining specific facts and then gradually integrating them into a whole concept. Global learners first address the overall concept before mastering the specific facts.

*Learning Styles Assessment*

School professionals can assess a few characteristics of learning style preferences through observation, but there are specific instruments designed to examine the multidimensional characteristics of learning. Each learning styles model has its own assessment tool. Dunn, Dunn, and Price (1979) developed the *Learning Style Inventory* (LSI) to correspond with the 21 elements in their model. This questionnaire is the predominant learning preference assessment for school-age children. It was developed using content and factor analysis, and it consists of 104 self-reported questions. The LSI uses a three-point scale for grades 3-4 and a five-point scale for grades 5-12. Completion time is 30-40 minutes. Research supported the LSI as a highly reliable and valid instrument (Dunn & DeBello, 1999). Adaptations of the LSI are *Our Wonderful Learning Styles (OWLS)* for grades 2-5 and *Learning Style: The Clue To You (LS: CY)* for grades 6-8. These tools identify elements associated with processing information from a broad perspective prior to examining the specific facts (global learning). Both assessments utilize various methods such as imagery, humor, fantasy, and imagination (Dunn, 1999).

*Learning Styles and School Counseling*

Current school counseling practices require that professional school counselors actively engage in the on-going development of students. By understanding, assessing, and utilizing learning styles, counselors are better equipped to design and facilitate developmental strategies and interventions that meet the needs of diverse students. Inclusion of learning styles into counseling practice requires an understanding of learning styles models. Conceptualization of specific learning characteristics and preferences provides a framework for addressing individual student differences. With this knowledge, professional school counselors can assess individual learning styles and choose appropriate strategies and interventions.

In consultation with teachers and administrators, counselors can utilize learning styles to develop optimal instructional practices for individual students and assist parents and caregivers in the understanding and accommodation of the child's educational and personal needs. Research in the area of counseling interventions and learning style preferences was limited (Griggs, 1983; Griggs, Price, Kopel & Swaine, 1984), and recent studies tended to focus on learning styles of ethnic and cultural groups (Dunn & Griggs, 1993; Griggs & Dunn, 1995; Griggs & Dunn, 1996; Herring & Meggert, 1994). Griggs (1991) provided a system for matching specific counseling interventions with individual students' learning style preferences. Learning styles models provide counselors with the opportunity to try a multitude of techniques.

## Recommended Actions and Strategies

Griggs (1985) suggested that the learning styles elements of structure, perceptual strength, motivation, the sociological preferences, and the psychological factors are particularly relevant to counseling. The corresponding categories for these characteristics as outlined in the Dunn and Dunn model are emotionality, sociological, physiological, and psychological. The following are examples of possible counseling interventions to accommodate different modes within these areas.

*Emotionality*

With students who exhibit a need for more structure and motivation, professional school counselors may find that behavioral approaches are more suitable. The counselor and student may meet to set specific goals, utilizing structured resources and techniques such as behavioral contracts.

This type of learner tends to expect the professional school counselor to initiate tasks and provide concrete solutions to issues. For students who are not likely to seek additional assistance, it is beneficial for the counselor to actively follow-up on pending issues. Counselors should provide structured exercises as well as expectations for listening and talking for those students engaged in group work. Students preferring less structure may benefit from person-centered approaches, which allow feelings and desires to be expressed freely. Opportunities can be provided by the counselor for the student to initiate new behaviors and solutions.

*Sociological*

Students who prefer learning alone may reject group methods and not respond well to group counseling. Others may respond well in a group setting but have more difficulty with individual modalities. For the group-oriented student, peer groups can be effectively used to promote participation and growth. Group counseling techniques for peer-oriented preferences may include dramatization of past experiences and present situations. Through role-playing and mime, students can safely express emotions, portray various aspects of their personhood, and practice how to handle confrontations.

For the student with a preference for learning on an individual basis, bibliotherapy is an effective strategy. The professional school counselor may choose several types of reading materials with which the counseling theme will be centered, basing the choices on the age, specific concerns, and needs of the individual students. It is important that the counselor be able to discern whether the student is one who prefers the rhythm and routine of regular, predetermined group and individual sessions, or one who is more comfortable "dropping-in" to see the counselor without a scheduled appointment.

*Physiological*

The auditory, visual, tactile, and kinesthetic senses have a great impact on learning. Auditorily perceptive students filter information using their listening skills, preferring to accept data by hearing it. Auditory learners find it easier to repeat words, recall conversations, and recite lines from reading materials. Traditional "talking through" counseling approaches often work best with these individuals.

Visual learners most often think using images and pictures. They translate what is heard into images in their minds. Counseling strategies centered on observation, written materials, and imaging fit the visual preference. It is important for counselors to serve as role models and provide opportunities for observing the behaviors of others, such as peers and family members. Use of videotapes, films, books, and other written texts help individuals in the imagery of desired behaviors and solutions to problems. Once visualized, the behavior is often easily carried out.

Tactile and kinesthetic perceptual styles overlap. Having a tactile learning style means that the person learns best by touching. The kinesthetic style requires that the learner becomes physically involved in the experience for best results. These types of students often prefer to learn through movements that involve gross motor skills. Active learners thrive on "hands on" counseling approaches. The use of puppetry, drawing, painting, dance, and other art therapies provide alternative ways for emotional release and communication. Movement and manipulation of objects throughout the counseling session may assist kinesthetic learners to share their feelings and thoughts.

*Psychological*

Analytic processors think in a step-by-step sequential pattern. They examine the facts, absorb them, and formulate a conceptual framework. Global learners must understand the concept or idea first; then they attend to specifics.

When working with analytic thinkers it is important to be concrete and focus on details. Professional school counselors should be direct and ask pointed questions. Strongly analytic individuals prefer a more formal interaction.

Students who process globally need to gain an understanding of a situation before giving attention to its particular components. Counselors can help these individuals by allowing them to talk in general terms about their concerns before identifying specific aspects they wish to address. The use of illustrations and the sharing of anecdotes are methods counselors can utilize to help clients determine the focus of their counseling experience. Global thinkers feel comfortable in a more casual environment; non-directive strategies work best.

## Summary/Conclusion

Combining learning styles and multiple intelligences can provide holistic models that reflect diversity and individual uniqueness. Attention to both theories provides professional school counselors with multidimensional strategies to fulfill their mission of fostering learning and growth in all children. Multiple intelligences represent individual talents reflected by cultural, social and personal influences. Learning styles define how students acquire, store, and present information. Integration of these theories allows professional school counselors to understand both the broader context of each student's unique personal environment as well as the individualized processes of learning.

## References


Dunn, R. (1999). How do we teach them. *Teaching PreK-8, 29*(7), 50-53.

Dunn, R., & DeBello, T. C. (Eds.). (1999). *Improved test scores, attitudes and behaviors in America's schools: Supervisors' success stories*. Westport, CT: Bergin & Garvy.

Dunn, R., Denig, S., & Lovelace, M. K. (2001). Two sides of the same coin, or different strokes for different folks. *Teacher Librarian, 28*(3), 9-15.

Dunn, R., & Dunn, K. (1992). *Teaching elementary students through their individual learning styles*. Boston, MA: Allyn & Bacon.

Dunn, R., & Dunn, K. (1993). *Teaching secondary students through their individual learning styles*. Boston, MA: Allyn & Bacon.

Dunn, R., Dunn, K., & Price, G.E. (1979). *Learning Style Inventory manual*. Lawrence, KS: Price Systems.

Dunn, R., & Griggs, S. A. (1993). Learning styles of Mexican American and Anglo-American elementary school students. *Journal of Multicultural Counseling & Development, 21*, 237-248.

Gardner, H. (1993). *Multiple intelligences: The theory into practice*. NY: Basic Books.

Griggs, S. A. (1983). Counseling high school students for their individual learning styles. *Clearing House, 56*, 293-296.

Griggs, S. A. (1985). Counseling for individual learning styles. *Journal of Counseling & Development, 64*, 202-206.

Griggs, S. A. (1991). *Learning styles counseling*. Ann Arbor, MI: Educational Resources Information Center for Counseling and Personnel Services.

Griggs, S. A., & Dunn, R. (1995). Hispanic-American students and learning style. *Emergency Librarian, 23*(2), 11-17.

Griggs, S. A., & Dunn, R. (1996). Learning styles of Asian-American adolescents. *Emergency Librarian, 24*(1), 8-14.

Griggs, S. A., Price, G. E., Kopel, S., & Swaine, W. (1984). The effects of group counseling on sixth grade students with different learning styles. *California Journal of Counseling & Development, 5*, 28-35.

Herring, R. D., & Meggert, S. S. (1994). The use of humor as a counselor strategy with Native American Indian children. *Elementary School Guidance & Counseling, 29*(1), 67-77.

Kolb, D. A. (1984). *Experimental learning: Experiences as a source of learning and development*. Englewood Cliffs, NJ: Prentice Hall.

Lundberg, D. J., & Kirk, W. D. (2003). A test user's guide to serving a multicultural community. In J. Wall, & G. R. Walz (Eds.). *Measuring up: Assessment issues for teachers, counselors, and administrators*. Greensboro, NC: ERIC Counseling and Student Services Clearinghouse.

Silver, H., & Strong, R. (1997). Integrating learning styles and multiple intelligences. *Educational Leadership, 55*(1), 22-27.

# Chapter 20

## Group Counseling in Schools

*Gary E. Goodnough & Vivian V. Lee*

**Preview**

This chapter discusses the different kinds of group counseling experiences offered in schools and examines strategies professional school counselors use to form groups and collaborate with other leaders in the school. This chapter also provides a rationale for why professional school counselors need to offer a full menu of groups and information that will help implement group counseling as a central component of a comprehensive developmental school counseling program.

To understand the role of group counseling in schools, professional school counselors must first understand comprehensive school counseling programs. The purpose of comprehensive school counseling programs is to promote academic success by supporting and enhancing the academic, career, and personal/social development needs of all students. These needs are identified through the systematic assessment of all constituencies within the school community. From the identified needs, goals are formulated and competencies are developed. These competencies identify what students should learn as a result of participating in a comprehensive school counseling program. The competencies are delivered to students via the service delivery systems within the structure of comprehensive programs.

The ASCA *National Model for School Counseling Programs* (Bowers & Hatch, 2002; ASCA, 2003) identifies the delivery systems as guidance curriculum, individual student planning, responsive services, and systems support. Within responsive services, group counseling is a means of delivering direct services to K-12 students. In this way group counseling, like other aspects of the comprehensive program, is data driven and linked to the mission of schools. For more details on the school counselor's role within comprehensive programs, see chapter 32.

The professional literature suggests that group counseling is helpful to students (Whiston & Sexton, 1998). First, it is an efficient intervention when compared to individual counseling, as the counselor can see multiple students simultaneously. Second, from a developmental and pedagogical perspective, students often learn best from each other. Group counseling provides an excellent forum to promote such student-to-student learning. Related to this, the power of the peer group can be garnered for positive growth and development under the skillful leadership of the professional school counselor. Finally, groups are a microcosm of society and as such provide real-life settings in which students can work out issues and problems (Brigman & Early, 1991; Gladding, 2003). Group counseling is a major function endorsed by ASCA, and research suggests that professional school counselors spend between eight and twelve percent of their time engaged in it (ASCA, 1999; Partin, 1993).

Group counseling is one of the professional school counselor's most highly specialized skills. As such, it is important for counselors to have a thorough grounding in group counseling theory and practice. In addition, professional school counselors need to know how to take a leadership role and successfully implement group counseling into comprehensive school counseling programs. Therefore, this chapter will examine the different kinds of groups offered in schools, types of group interventions, strategies to use in forming groups, and how to collaborate with other leaders in the school to offer a full menu of group topics that have the potential to benefit all in the school system.

*Group Counseling: Developmental, Remedial and School Climate Groups*

What is group counseling in schools? Group counseling initiatives within a larger comprehensive school counseling program address developmental milestones, provide remediation, and promote a healthy climate within the school. By developmental milestones, we mean that professional school counselors can reasonably expect that most or all students would benefit from participating in groups designed to promote academic, career, or personal/social development. For example, developmental groups that address academic development include study skills, test-taking strategies, and transition to middle or high school. Career development groups include goal setting and decision-making, transitions to post-secondary options, career exploration, and college planning. Personal/social groups include peer relationships, friendship, self-esteem, forming safe/healthy romantic relationships, personal empowerment, and accepting a newborn sibling.

Group counseling is remedial in nature when it addresses topics or issues that impair the learning and development of specific groups of students. Remedial groups help students develop coping skills to assist them in coming to terms with difficult personal and social issues. These groups seek to empower students to regain control over their lives and engage (or reengage) in the learning process. Groups that address remedial issues may include divorce and family separation, sexual identity, substance use (self, family member, or friend), grief and loss, coping with HIV/AIDS in the family, anger management, conflict resolution, and learning to live in a blended family. Some groups are offered around issues that affect a large group of students. For instance, in regions where the military has bases, parents and family members frequently must leave home to serve in the military. Such deployments cause upheaval and uncertainty in a large number of homes and impede the learning process of many students.

Finally, remedial group topics may include issues that affect all students. These issues might be a natural disaster such as a hurricane, a tragic event such as the terror attacks of 9/11/01, a specific incident of school violence, or a student death. Remedial group counseling can help students debrief the trauma they experience in the immediate aftermath of these and other tragedies. The issues that arise from these events, when unresolved, impair personal growth and impede the learning process. By responding to the remedial needs of students through group counseling, professional school counselors deliver an important and highly specialized service.

There is a third category of groups that professional school counselors offer as well. These are groups that address the culture and climate of the school. Some of these groups include issues related to diversity awareness, bias and prejudice reduction, conflict resolution, and respect of self and others. These groups may also address the cultural and institutional barriers to learning of certain groups of students (e.g., students of color; gay, lesbian, bisexual and transgendered youth; lower socioeconomic status students). Professional school counselors need to provide additional support to these and other student groups to help remove individual and systemic barriers and provide for equitable learning conditions and access to the best that school and society offers. (See Table 1 for a brief description of different types of groups presented in the literature.)

In order to form groups in all three categories, professional school counselors need to assess students' needs broadly. The institutional culture and overall climate of the school can limit the access to and equity of group counseling to all student groups. Professional school counselors need to reach out to marginalized groups to encourage them to consider group

**Table 1. Group Counseling Plans: Information from the Literature and Recent Publications.**

| Author(s) | Topic |
|---|---|
| Hines and Fields (in press) | Task management skills, asking for help, and developing academic persistence for ninth grade students |
| Campbell & Bowman (1993) | Academically retained children |
| Nelson, Dykeman, Powell, and Petty (1996) | Disruptive and maladjusted students |
| Stewart & McKay (1995) | Aggressive elementary school students |
| Ripley (in press) | Conflict management |
| LaFountain, Garner, & Eliason (1996) | Heterogeneously-grouped solution-focused group counseling |
| Erford, Moore-Thomas, & Mazzuca (in press) | Understanding learning styles |
| Struder & Allton (1996) | Teenagers from divorced families |
| Riddle, Bergin, and Douzenis (1997) | Lowering the anxiety levels and improving the self-concepts of elementary school children of alcoholics |
| Arman and McNair (2000) | Elementary school-aged children of alcoholics |
| Akos (2000) | A psychoeducational group that helps develop empathy in children |
| Akos (in press) | Transition to middle school |
| Kizner & Kizner (1999) | Adopted children |
| Bradley (2001) | African-American males |
| Bailey & Bradford-Bailey (in press) | African-American males |
| Smith & Chen-Hayes (in press) | Gay, lesbian, bisexual, transgendered, and questioning youth |
| Reeder, Douzenis, and Bergin (1997) | Improving the racial attitudes of primary age children. |
| Zinck & Littrell (2000) | Adolescent at-risk girls |
| Becky & Farren (1997) | Helping high school girls understand and avoid abusive relationships |
| Rosen & Bezold (1996) | High school girls: Preventing dating violence |
| Goodnough & Ripley (1997) | High school seniors transitioning to post-secondary schools and the military |
| Coker (in press) | Substance abuse prevention |
| Brooks (in press) | Stress management |
| Stone (in press) | Perpetrators of sexual harassment |
| Jackson & Grant (in press) | The influence of culture, gender, race and ability on the career development of high school students |
| Sears (in press) | Career development activities for middle and high school students |
| Niles, Trusty, & Mitchell (in press) | Career planning, equity, and access for high schools students |

counseling as a viable means of meeting needs. Previous experiences with societal and institutionalized barriers and biases can diminish trust and cause students to doubt that the school and its representatives have the best interests at heart. In forming relationships with students, it is essential for professional school counselors to validate concerns, earn trust and advocate for needs. This builds the professional school counselor's credibility and assists in creating a sense of inclusion for all students.

*Psychoeducation and Counseling: Group Interventions*

Groups in schools led by professional school counselors exist on a continuum from being primarily didactic and psychoeducational in nature, to being primarily therapeutic counseling experiences. Most groups have some elements of each, and some vary from session to session. Many developmental groups are primarily psychoeducational and focus on providing topic-specific information to small groups of students. The presentation of the information is carefully designed to be directly applicable to students' lives to enhance age-appropriate development and academic success. For example, transitioning students can be taught about the environment they are transitioning into—whether it is middle school, high school or a four-year college.

Psychoeducation also has a place in remedial groups. Students coping with the loss of a loved one need to be taught about the stages of grieving, as such knowledge is helpful to the healing process. In groups dealing with the school climate, information is frequently taught to students. For instance in a group on conflict resolution, students need to be taught about the characteristics of conflict and the different types of conflict (Ripley, in press). Thus, the provision of psychoeducation to students in all types of counseling groups is common in schools, and fits in well with the culture of K-12 education, as the students learn new information.

As stated, psychoeducation can be presented in all three categories of groups. Typically, the provision of psychoeducation leads students to apply information to themselves. As they do this, they often need assistance. Such *processing* leads into the second aspect of group work in schools: counseling. It is in the processing that the professional school counselor's unique skill set is used. When students process information they often reveal confidential information about themselves, thus opening themselves up to psychological risk. Professional school counselors are trained to manage this risk, thereby helping to promote growth and development through risk-taking and sharing.

As students share and process together, the professional school counselor uses counseling skills to promote mutual trust and help members develop a sense of inclusion within the group. Effective group counselors help create an environment where members become known to each other in meaningful ways. In a remedial group for children dealing with family situations in which alcohol or other drugs are being abused, a professional school counselor will not only use psychoeducation (i.e., the professional school counselor might teach about the roles taken in alcoholic families), but will help promote healing by helping all students share their particular situations. By working with all members in this way, the professional school counselor helps students know they are not alone. In sum, professional school counselors provide psychoeducation to students and help them process that information in personally meaningful ways. Further, they harness the power of the group to provide an avenue for growth, remediation, and the improvement of the school climate.

*Two Ways to Form Groups: Homogeneous and Heterogeneous*

The groups described above are homogenous groups in which all students are dealing with similar issues. For several reasons, it is appropriate that membership in some groups should be restricted. First, students who share a common concern are able to identify with each other and help one another in ways that others might not. While group counseling is not about giving others advice, group members do provide their own unique perspectives; within these perspectives may be information and coping strategies that members find helpful. Related to providing support is the concept of *universality*; the knowledge that others share certain experiences and feelings reduces the sense of isolation that many students feel so they know that they are not alone. This process of universality is one of the key group process factors that promote growth and healing (Yalom, 1995). Finally, when groups are homogenously formed, topic-specific psychoeducation can be provided in a manner that is beneficial to all.

While the benefits of homogenously formed groups are evident, there are several reasons why groups might have a heterogeneous composition. In these groups, similarity of presenting concern is not necessary because students learn a method (e.g., solution focused, problem solving, cognitive-behavioral) whereby a variety of problems can be addressed. They also learn that the chosen method can be transferred to other situations with which they might be faced. These types of groups help to de-compartmentalize learning and help empower students as they gain confidence to draw on their new skills to solve problems in a variety of challenging situations.

Another way heterogeneous groups are used is by having one or more group members serve as models for targeted students. For instance, an elementary school social skills group might be less effective if all members have poor social skills. One of the reasons that group counseling works is that students learn from each other. If all students in a group are deficient in social skills, they cannot learn from each other. Because of this, elementary school counselors frequently have behavioral models in social skills groups. These model students are children who have good social skills; the target students can learn from them. As a result, this group is made up of a heterogeneous group of students, not all of whom need remediation in social skills.

*Group Counseling Skills*

To effectively lead groups in schools, professional school counselors need to have skills in the following four dimensions of group counseling in schools: 1) they must be knowledgeable about the interrelationship between developmental theory and counseling theory; 2) they must have knowledge of the topic or content of the group; 3) they must understand group dynamics; and 4) they must understand the contextual factors that influence what their students' behavior means. First, professional school counselors must understand students from multiple *developmental* perspectives (e.g., cognitive, psychosocial, and racial/ethnic identity). From these related perspectives, professional school counselors select group counseling strategies and interventions that are appropriate to the developmental sophistication of students. For example, elementary school counselors may choose to use Adlerian strategies, as many Adlerian concepts are applicable to the developmental needs of young children.

Professional school counselors need to understand theoretical applications well enough to feel confident that selected strategies and techniques are within accepted methods of practice and are robust enough to achieve the objectives of the group. Second, competence in the content or topic to be addressed is essential. While it is not necessary for professional school counselors to be experts in every area of group they offer, they do need specific knowledge—for instance they need to know how the topic tends to manifest in the population with which they are working. For example, to lead a group on bereavement, professional school counselors need not be experts on issues of loss and grieving, but they do need to be quite knowledgeable about it and, particularly, how processing grief and loss is mediated by factors such as the child's cognitive development and religious belief. This relates to the third group counseling skill: understanding the multiple contexts of children's lives.

The multiple contextual factors that impact the lives of students shape the ways in which students process the content and dynamic interactions in groups. For example, factors such as socioeconomic status, race/ethnicity, gender, religious/spiritual beliefs and practices, sexual orientation, institutional barriers to learning, and family composition all become screens through which students filter the content of the group and the process dynamics that exist within the group. These interrelated factors challenge professional school counselors to continually engage in professional development to competently and ethically meet the group counseling needs of students.

Finally, professional school counselors need to keep all of the above in mind as they hypothesize about group members' behaviors, and facilitate the growth of the group. In doing so, professional school counselors are able to encourage group members to participate fully in the group and respect students' varied and diverse styles of meaningful participation. By attending to these dimensions of group counseling, professional school counselors build cohesion and keep the group focused on the task or topic at hand.

*The Context of Public School*

Much has been written about the barriers that prevent effective group work in schools. Some of the obstructive forces described are scheduling problems, teacher resistance, school policies and practices that limit student access, and the overall culture of schools (Dansby, 1996; Ripley & Goodnough, 2001; Schmidt, 2003). In order to overcome these barriers, professional school counselors need to honor and understand the context in which they work. They need to understand that administrators and teachers are held accountable for students' academic performance - often as measured by standardized test scores. Additionally, teacher and administrator pre-service training does not focus heavily on the role and function of comprehensive school counseling programs, methods of service delivery and the appropriate duties of the professional school counselor (Fitch, Newby, Ballestero, & Marshall, 2001; Pérusse & Goodnough, 2002). As a result, many administrators' perceptions of school counseling reflect their own experiences with school counseling, many of which are older, traditional notions of school counseling. When administrators assume leadership positions in schools, they often perpetuate these past practices.

There are three main ways professional school counselors can attend to the legitimate concerns of administrators and help them envision and facilitate the counselor's implementation of group counseling in a contemporary and appropriate manner. The first concerns professional preparation. Prior to initiating a program of group counseling, professional school counselors need to commit themselves and their time to preparing and scheduling group counseling. This requires counselors to design their calendars to allot significant time for group counseling. By building it into their calendars, they give group counseling priority as a service delivery method within a comprehensive school counseling program. Additionally, professional school counselors plan for their groups in the same way teachers plan for an academic unit. For example, math teachers do not create their plans in secret, and neither should school counselors.

Professional school counselors make their group goals, objectives, and supporting materials available to the public as part of the comprehensive school counseling program. In accordance with the ASCA ethical standards, they see the benefits of working with families and seek to team and collaborate with them to assist in student development. As part of the collaborative effort, professional school counselors seek out parent/guardian permission for their child's participation in group counseling. By preparing well for group counseling, they bring professionalism and rigor to this important method of service delivery.

The second way professional school counselors facilitate the implementation of group counseling is by collaborating and teaming with administrators to address, reinterpret, or revise salient school policies. School programs perceived by administrators to be outside the academic mission, such as group counseling, are often denied class time to meet so that students' focus remains on academic tasks. As a result of policies such as this, group counseling is oftentimes only offered during lunch, study hall, or before and after school. A school policy that posits *unconditionally* that instructional time cannot be compromised derails effective group counseling initiatives.

Through leadership and advocacy, professional school counselors need to help teachers and administrators see that exceptions to such an important policy are already granted through other school-sponsored activities. For example, in high schools, athletes in a variety of sports typically miss their last class of the day to travel to away games. This is permitted because participation in interscholastic sports is deemed beneficial for student growth and development—so much so that it supercedes academic time for certain students. It is an accepted belief that athletics offers students benefits that enhance academic achievement by fostering positive peer interactions, learning new skills that foster self-control, and developing a sense of empowerment by accomplishing challenging endeavors.

The task for professional school counselors is to lobby for policy revisions or reinterpretations that allow all students to have the opportunity to gain similar benefits through group counseling if they so desire. To do this, professional school counselors have to remind teachers and administrators that group counseling is part of the larger comprehensive school counseling program and, as such, shares the school's mission for academic success. More specifically, helping students effectively cope with grief and loss so that they can refocus on academic pursuits is as important for some students' personal/social and academic development as wrestling or volleyball is for others'.

Thus when school policy is reviewed, reinterpreted, or revised, professional school counselors collaborate with administrators and teachers to help shift the questions from "When can groups be run?" and "Do they take away from academic time?" to "How can we implement group counseling as a means of improving the quality of students' 'time on task' in math?" Additionally, once policies are reinterpreted or revised, they need to be adhered to by all teachers. This means that teachers' ability to deny students the right to attend groups must be prohibited, and they must not be permitted to count students as absent if they are attending a group meeting. Moreover, students should be given the same amount of time to do makeup work as they would for any other school-sponsored activity (Ripley & Goodnough, 2001).

Finally, professional school counselors and students must honor the privilege that comes with policy revision or reinterpretation. Care must be taken so that neither students nor professional school counselors abuse the system. When applied to attending group counseling during class time this means that group members must arrive to the group session on time, the same as they would for class. It also means that students who abuse or ignore the rules of the school or the group forfeit their participation in group counseling.

Attending carefully to rules such as these and publicizing them broadly creates consistent behavioral expectations for students and reduces the ambiguity of the consequences of failure to follow school policy. Professional school counselors need to navigate dual role issues involved here. In all ways, they must enforce school policies while also being the group leader and embodying the characteristics and skills necessary for effective group leadership. When group counseling is implemented as described in this section, this powerful intervention becomes a valued part of the comprehensive developmental school counseling program.

## Summary/Conclusion

Professional school counselors at all levels who do not lead groups are not adequately performing their jobs. This is because group counseling in schools is a central means of delivering a comprehensive developmental school counseling program. Providing effective group counseling experiences to students requires leadership, specialized knowledge and skills, and the ability to advocate effectively for the inclusion of a program of group counseling within schools.

## References

Akos, P. (in press). Psychoeducation groups to promote the transition from elementary to middle school. *Journal for Specialists in Group Work.*

Akos, P. (2000). Building empathy in elementary school children through group work. *Journal for Specialists in Group Work, 25,* 214-223.

Arman, J. F., & McNair, R. (2000). A small group model for working with elementary school children of alcoholics. *Professional School Counseling, 3,* 290-293.

American School Counselor Association. (1999). Position statement: Group counseling. Retrieved October 15, 2002 at http://www.schoolcounselor.org/content.cfm?L1=100&L2=35.

American School Counselor Association. (2003). *The ASCA national model: A framework for school counseling programs.* Alexandria, VA: Author.

Bailey, D. F., & Bradford-Bailey (in press). Respecting differences: Racial and ethnic groups. In R. Pérusse & G. E. Goodnough (Eds.), *Leadership and advocacy in school counseling.* Pacific Grove, CA: Brooks/Cole.

Becky, D., & Farren, P. H. (1997). Teaching students how to understand and avoid abusive relationships. *The School Counselor, 44,* 303-308.

Bowers, J. L., & Hatch, P. L. (2002). *The ACSA national model for school counseling programs.* Alexandria, VA: ASCA.

Bradley, C. (2001). A counseling group for African-American adolescent males. *Professional School Counseling, 4,* 370-373.

Brigman, G., & Early, B. (1991). *Group counseling for school counselors.* Portland, ME: J. Weston Walch.

Brooks, V. (in press). Stress management: The school counselor's role. In R. Pérusse & G. E. Goodnough (Eds.), *Leadership and advocacy in school counseling.* Pacific Grove, CA: Brooks/Cole.

Campbell, C., & Bowman, R. P. (1993). The "Fresh Start" support club: Small group counseling for academically retained children. *Elementary School Guidance & Counseling, 27,* 172-186.

Coker, K. (in press). Alcohol and other substance abuse: The school counselor's role. In R. Pérusse & G. E. Goodnough (Eds.), *Leadership and advocacy in school counseling.* Pacific Grove, CA: Brooks/Cole.

Dansby, V. (1996). Group work within the school system: Survey of implementation and leadership role issues. *Journal for Specialists in Group Work, 21,* 232-242.

Erford, B. T., Moore-Thomas, C., & Mazzuca, S. (in press). Improving academic achievement through an understanding of learning styles. In R. Pérusse & G. E. Goodnough (Eds.), *Leadership and advocacy in school counseling.* Pacific Grove, CA: Brooks/Cole.

Fitch, T., Newby, E., Ballestero, V., & Marshall, J. L. (2001). Future school administrators' perceptions of the school counselor's role. *Counselor Education & Supervision, 41,* 89-99.

Gladding, S. T. (2003). *Group work: A counseling specialty.* Upper Saddle River, NJ: Merrill/Prentice-Hall.

Goodnough, G. E., & Ripley, V. (1997). Structured groups for high school seniors making the transition to college and to military service. *The School Counselor, 44,* 230-234.

Hines, P. T., & Fields, T. H. (in press). School counseling and academic achievement. In R. Pérusse & G. E. Goodnough (Eds.), *Leadership and advocacy in school counseling.* Pacific Grove, CA: Brooks/Cole.

Jackson, M., & Grant, D. (in press). Equity, access, and career development: Contextual conflicts. In R. Pérusse & G. E. Goodnough (Eds.), *Leadership and advocacy in school counseling.* Pacific Grove, CA: Brooks/Cole.

Kizner, L. R., & Kizner, S. R. (1999). Small group counseling with adopted children. *Professional School Counseling, 2,* 226-229.

LaFountain, R. M., Garner, N. E., & Eliason, G. T. (1996). Solution-focused counseling groups: A key for school counselors. *The School Counselor, 43,* 256-267.

Nelson, J. R., Dykeman, C., Powell, S., & Petty, D. (1996). The effects of a group counseling intervention on students with behavioral adjustment problems. *Elementary School Guidance & Counseling, 31,* 23-33.

Niles, S. G., Trusty, J., & Mitchell, N. (in press). Leading and advocating to foster positive career development in children and adolescents. In R. Pérusse & G. E. Goodnough (Eds.), *Leadership and advocacy in school counseling.* Pacific Grove, CA: Brooks/Cole.

Partin, R. L. (1993). School counselors' time: Where does it go? *The School Counselor, 40,* 274-281.

Pérusse, R., & Goodnough, G. E. (2002, October). *Multiple perspectives: Shaping our future in school counselor education.* Paper presented at the Association of Counselor Education and Supervision Conference, Park City, UT.

Reeder, J., Douzenis, C., & Bergin, J. J. (1997). The effects of small group counseling on the racial attitudes of second grade students. *Professional School Counseling, 1,* 15-18.

Riddle, J., Bergin, J. J., & Douzenis, C. (1997). Effects of group counseling on the self-concept of children of alcoholics. *Elementary Guidance & Counseling, 31,* 192-203.

Ripley, V. V. (in press). Violence prevention and conflict resolution education in the schools. In R. Pérusse & G. E. Goodnough (Eds.), *Leadership and advocacy in school counseling.* Pacific Grove, CA: Brooks/Cole.

Ripley, V. V., & Goodnough, G. E. (2001). Planning and implementing group counseling in a high school. *Professional School Counseling, 5,* 62-65.

Rosen, K. H., & Bezold, A. (1996). Dating violence prevention: A didactic support group for young women. *Journal of Counseling and Development, 74,* 521-525.

Schmidt, J. J. (2003). *Counseling in schools.* Boston: Allyn & Bacon.

Sears, S. (in press). Investigating the world of work. In R. Pérusse & G. E. Goodnough (Eds.), *Leadership and advocacy in school counseling.* Pacific Grove, CA: Brooks/Cole.

Smith, S. D., & Chen-Hayes, S. F. (in press). Leadership and advocacy for lesbian, bisexual, gay, transgendered, and questioning (LBGTQ) students: Academic, career, and interpersonal success strategies. In R. Pérusse & G. E. Goodnough (Eds.), *Leadership and advocacy in school counseling.* Pacific Grove, CA: Brooks/Cole.

Stewart, J., & McKay, R. (1995). Group counselling elementary school children who use aggressive behaviors. *Guidance and Counseling, 11*(4), 33-36.

Stone, C. (in press). School counselors as leaders and advocates in addressing sexual harassment. In R. Pérusse & G. E. Goodnough (Eds.), *Leadership and advocacy in school counseling.* Pacific Grove, CA: Brooks/Cole.

Struder, J. R., & Allton, J. A. (1996). When parents divorce: Assisting teens' adjustment through a group approach. *Guidance & Counseling, 11*(4), 33-36.

Whiston, S., & Sexton, T. (1998). A review of school counseling outcome research: Implications for practice. *Journal of Counseling and Development, 76,* 412-426.

Yalom, I. D. (1995). *The theory and practice of group psychotherapy.* New York: HarperCollins

Zinck, K., & Littrell, J. M. (2000). Action research shows group counseling effective with at-risk adolescent girls. *Professional School Counseling, 4,* 50-59.

# Chapter 21

## Visual Arts and the Professional School Counselor

*Joe Ray Underwood & Nancy B. Underwood*

### Preview

This chapter shows professional school counselors how they may use visual arts as a vehicle to assist students in their self-expression. It was not written as an attempt to encourage the professional school counselor to become an art therapist; rather it was written by a licensed professional counselor and a teacher who utilize visual art as a creative aid to the counseling and educational process. The examples of visual art activities are practical, original, and field tested in the schools. The professional school counselor will find these visual art activities to be effective in both individual and group counseling settings.

### Introduction to the Use of Visual Arts

Art as a means of self-expression has been evident in societies since the advent of the cave art of primitive people. Using art to record events, recall events, and elaborate upon events has become an integral part of our communication system as human beings. Visual art not only is appealing to view, it also can be a means of expressing ideas and relating factual information in a pictorial format. Internationally recognized symbols guide us to destinations and give us a sense of security in an ever-changing world. While visuals symbols provide generality in art, there also is individuality in art evidenced by how people express themselves with art forms. Individual human beings may tell about themselves through artistic expression that is as unique as handwriting. Artistic self-expression is as important as oral communication and written words, and can provide a means for professional school counselors, teachers, and parents to learn more about those students with whom they interact.

People of all ages and abilities, especially K-12 students, can benefit from visual art experiences. Visual art is a "here and now" experience which provides an immediate result, a picture, which is "straightforward" and evokes feelings and emotions (Honore & Allen, 1997, p. 1). Visual art can be spontaneous or planned. Whenever it occurs, visual art represents us, and serves as a biographical record and means of expressing personal information.

Jung actually introduced the use of creative art practices to psychotherapy through active imagination. His work focused on ideas derived from concentration on particular images (McNiff, 1992). Art therapy began as an outgrowth of the clinical application of creative psychologists, such as Jung, Naumburg, and Kramer (Kahn, 1999). McNiff affirmed that art images produced in a counseling situation "expand communication and offer insight outside the scope of the reasoning mind" (1992, p. 3). However, it is the use and explanation of the visual artwork that affirms the uniqueness of individuals and of visual art as a means of self-expression (Keys, 1983).

Campbell (1993) asserted that almost any student could be naturally visually creative. She maintains that visual art can enrich and lead to change in a student's life. Hence, visual art is a valuable tool of self-expression that the professional school counselor may use with students.

Artistic expression can become a neutral outlet for ideas and abstract concepts. It also can become a means of communicating and expressing feelings, with all ages, and can provide a visual record which may be kept confidentially, as would a journal (Kahn, 1999).

## Visual Arts in Counseling

Henderson (1999) has successfully used images of animals as personal metaphors through a guided imagery experience in which participants select an animal as a symbol of self and then define qualities of that animal which relate to themselves. The use of the animal symbols afford the participants a creative means of self-expression.

Many professional counselors and therapists already use visual art in the practice of counseling (France & Edward, 1997; Jordan, 2001; Liebmann,1986). Jacobs (1994) reported frequently using graphs, mirrors, charts, and visual demonstrations with clients to clarify and explore client concerns. Magnusson (as cited in Whitmer, Thompson, & Loesch, 2000) used a spider web as a visual context to discuss friendship and personal support networks. Kottman, Ashby, and DeGraaf (2001) used the image of a large map in an activity to chart and "map" diversity.

Newsome (2003) used the image of a volcano when facilitating anger management training with teens who "blow their top" instead of controlling the release of their emotions. Newsome compared the image of a volcano "exploding" with "blowing your top" when you get angry. Then she assisted her clients in using the same image to develop ways to control their emotions.

Whether visual art is used to explore personal problems, or merely to explore personal creativity, it is a valuable tool for building observable products that represent the personality of the individual. Gladding (1998) addressed the usefulness of visual art activities for the professional school counselor. Professional school counselors should be mindful that the use of visual arts is an evolving process that increases in effectiveness as students become more aware and more comfortable with artistic expression. "Clients who can envision through paints, drawings, and sculpture what they have accomplished over a period of time or what they could be are more likely than not to stay with the process of change until they are satisfied with the process" (Gladding, 1998, p. 65).

Furthermore, visual art experiences enable students to use both visual and verbal skills in learning and communicating what they learn. Students also can be trained to develop left and right brain methods of learning in a creative and comfortable way through art (Edwards, 1989). Therefore, professional school counselors who incorporate the use of visual arts in their interactions with students promote student learning, foster alternative ways of student self-expression, encourage new and exciting ways of viewing student concerns, and affirm the uniqueness of students as individuals (Weiser, 2001).

Although teachers recognize that students have numerous learning styles, teachers typically teach to the visual learner (Haar, Hall, Schoepp, & Smith, 2002). If the visual learning style is the most common student learning style (Griggs, 1985; Silverman & Freed, 1991), the professional school counselor's use of visual arts as a counseling tool, should be welcomed and appreciated by the majority of K-12 students.

## Visual Art Activities To Use With K-12 Students

In the following pages are descriptions and examples of visual arts activities that the professional school counselor may use with students in grades K-12. To protect the privacy of students (Hammond & Gantt, 1998), the authors created the examples which are included in this chapter. These examples are illustrations of concepts. The products produced by the students with whom the professional school counselor uses these activities will vary with the age and talent of the students.

Professional school counselors may align all visual arts activities in this chapter with the National Standards for School Counseling Programs (NSSCP) (Dahir, Sheldon, & Valiga, 2002). Many of the activities may be used to promote positive personal/social development and may be aligned with student competencies from NSSCP Standard B, Personal/Social Development. The counselor may modify the focus of some visual arts activities to address local needs of students. The activities are neither "Jungian" nor "art therapy" based. They are designed only to enhance and motivate students to design visual products that will enhance self-understanding and make students and counselors more comfortable with artistic expression.

When counselors use these activities with students, the process is much more important than the product. Talent and skill levels vary among students. The end product is a means to self-expression. Allow all students to create a visual product that may be used to foster dialogue and communication. The final product is not to be judged by artistic merit. Rather it is to be judged by the quality of self-expression experienced by the students.

### Activity 1. Sandwiched In

*Materials:* Drawing paper, pencils, colored pencils.

*Activity:* Students write about their favorite sandwich by answering the following questions:

1. Why is this particular sandwich your favorite?
2. Do you want it when you are hungry? Sad? Happy? Stressed out? Can't sleep?
3. How often do you eat it?
4. Where do you eat it?

(If they don't have a favorite sandwich, ask for their favorite food or candy.)

Students draw the sandwich with pencil and color it with colored pencils. They create a background for the sandwich with information from the answers they provided. The background is drawn with pencil and not colored. The counselor invites students to discuss the information in their "sandwich drawing." The counselor may present information about healthy ways to handle stress or as an opportunity for students to learn more about eating disorders, weight problems, peer pressure, anger management, ways to seek comfort, etc.

**Figure 1a: Example of Sandwiched In**

**Figure 1b: Example of Sandwiched In**

### Activity 2. Block Letter Autobiography

*Materials:* Writing paper, block letters (for tracing), poster board, colored pencils.

*Activity:* During an individual or group counseling session, the counselor leads a brainstorming session about personal traits and characteristics. Each student generates a 20-word list of traits and characteristics that describe her/him (adjectives or nouns). They next develop pictures and symbols to represent the personal traits and characteristics on their 20-word list. Using letters that are the student's initials, each student traces large block letter patterns on one side of a folded poster board. Students fill the large letters with pictures and words that represent the 20 descriptive traits listed. Students may share meanings of their letter pictures with the counselor or with other students in the group. The counselor may lead a group discussion about the combination of common and unique qualities of the students and affirm the value of each student and talk about ways to achieve balance among the aspects of students' lives that are depicted in the drawings.

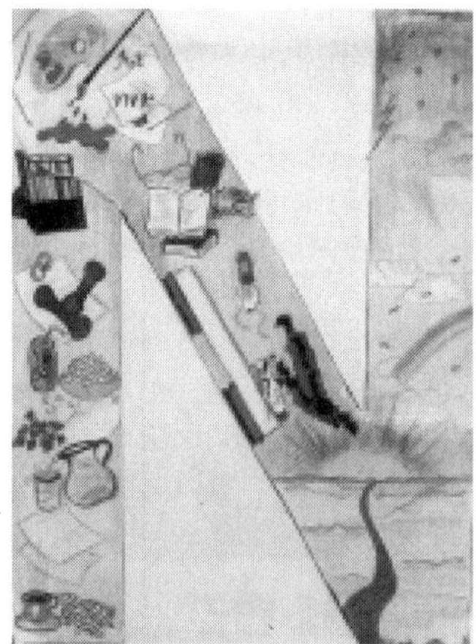

**Figure 2: Examples of Block Letter Autobiography**

## Activity 3. Past, Present, Future Cover Story

*Materials:* Scratch paper, poster board, pencils, rulers, stencils (lettering and picture), Sharpies, colored pencils, markers, dictionaries, thesauruses, and rope (or ribbon).

*Activity:* Using scratch paper, students generate a list of important events in their lives from the past and the present. Students also list future hopes and dreams, such as career plans, travel, family, education, etc. The list should consist of at least six or seven meaningful events or ideas under each of the three time periods. Students draw pictures and symbols to represent the meaningful events/ideas for each of the three time periods of their "cover story" on one side of a folded poster board. (Students may wish to divide the poster board into three equal areas.) Students connect the areas representing the three time periods with a rope, ribbon, road design or some other connecting graphic. Information about each student's "cover story" may be discussed with the counselor. The counselor may encourage students to explore career implications of the cover story, to share common themes, and to affirm individual and group self-expression. Discuss alternative ways of achieving goals and consequences of choices.

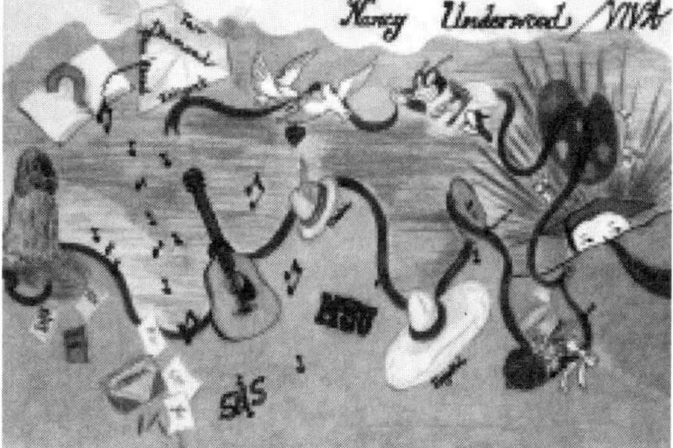

**Figure 3. Examples of Past, Present, Future Cover Story**

## Activity 4. Visual Journals

*Materials:* Black paint (poster or acrylic), heavy art paper, small sponges for blotting (cut into three or four sections), scissors, journal paper, colored pencils, watercolors for elaboration, Sharpies, pens, pencils, brushes.

*Activity:* This is a multiple session activity. Before conducting this activity, the counselor should meet with the students and ask them to provide a personal "scrapbook type notebook" with plain, unlined, white paper pages. Instruct the students to bring this notebook to the "Visual Journal" session. Figures 4a – 4c provide examples of the following activities.

*1st Meeting*. Pour small amounts of black (or dark) paint into bowls. Give each student a piece of art paper. Using the pieces of sponge, students dip the sponge pieces into the paint and dab the sponge on the piece of art-paper top to create a haphazard pattern of blots. Random application to different areas of the paper is best. Younger students may put a glob of paint on the art paper, fold the paper, and press the paper together.
Students remove three different pages from their scrapbook. Students press the painted

art paper onto one side of each of the three blank pages. This transfers an image or images to the blank page. It is OK to use any part of art-paper that is wet with images from the sponges. As students fill their blank pages with images, the counselor can lead a discussion about optical illusions, images in clouds, or the use projective techniques with images such as the ones found in the Rorschach inkblot test. Put the paper aside to dry.

*2nd Meeting*. Students look at their designs and create objects from them. A class or group discussion may follow. Students can be instructed in creative visualization in this way. Next have students cut out their three designs and paste them on three separate sheets of their scrapbook. The remainder of the meeting consists of developing the blots into artwork. A written poem or description can accompany each blot picture. Additional meetings may be necessary to allow time for students to complete their artwork. A single piece of paper could inspire several sessions. This process can be repeated throughout the year to fill the journal.

**Figure 4a. Example of "blots."**

**Figure 4b. Example of a drawing by adding to a "blot."**

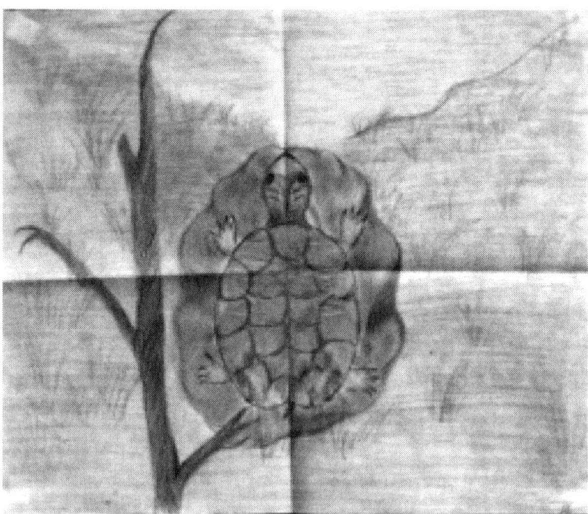

**Figure 4c. Example of Visual Journal drawing (The rock was the blot).**

### Activity 5. Different Strokes for Different Folks

*Materials:* Still-life display, paper, pencils, dictionaries to define perspective in art and in life in general.

*Activity:* Students sit in a circle around a table with a simple still-life display set up on it, e.g., a vase of flowers, hat and ball, teddy bear. Students are instructed to draw what they see.

After 15 minutes, students share their work with the group. Each picture will be different, because they each viewed the display from a different angle. The counselor leads a group discussion about how everyone can view the same situation differently because we view it from different perspectives. Often students react to a situation depending on their perspective. Discuss common problems and how different students coped with the problem as a result of a different perspective. How students manage stress is a function of their perspective on the stress-producing situation. Discuss how students could change their perspective (i.e., reframing, cognitive restructuring) as a means of coping with stress.

Figure 5 provides examples of the Different Strokes for Different Folks activity.

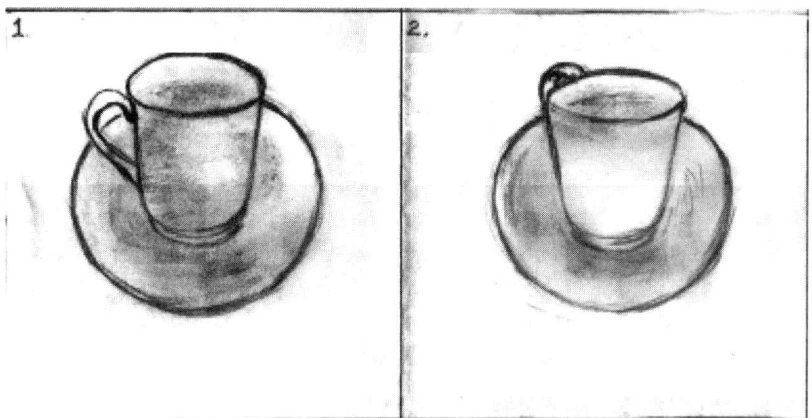


**Figure 5. Example of Different Strokes for Different Folks.**

### Activity 6. Symbol of Self

*Materials:* Paper and pencil for lists, graphic arts books with symbols for items, modeling clay (e.g., Crayola Modelmagic), toothpicks (for shaping), white glue, acrylic paint and inexpensive small art brushes (if students are allowed to paint their symbols of self).

*Activity:* Students brainstorm a list of 20 words that describe them (nouns or adjectives may be used). Students draw pictures and symbols that represent the words. Students pick 12 pictures or words to use to create a clay sculpture. Encourage students to select things they feel they can create with clay. One item will become the base and the other 11 items will be made and glued onto the base. Make the base first and then the items to be mounted on it. You may use colored clay, or paint the items with acrylic paint and then glue them on the base. Let the students' symbol-of-self become the basis for individual/group counseling sessions about student accomplishments. Discuss how to attain balance among those things that are important in the students' lives. Allow students to use the symbol-of-self as paperweights or decorations. Figure 6 provides examples of the Symbol of Self activity.

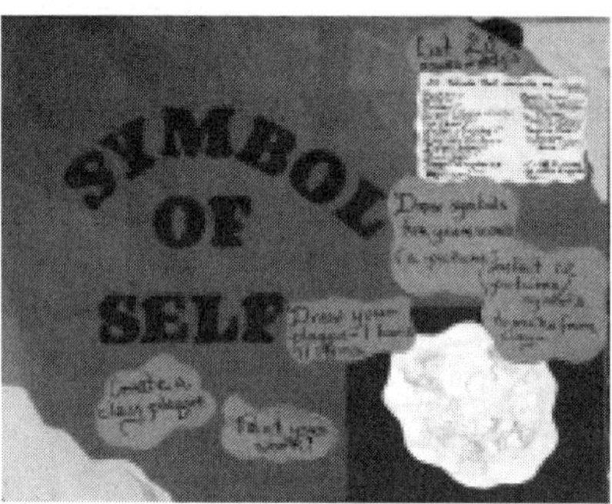


**Figure 6. Examples of Symbol of Self.**

### Activity 7. T-Shirt Design

*Materials:* T-shirt planning sheet, white cotton T-shirt, set of fabric crayons for each student, wax paper, iron.

*Activity:* Students design a personal T-shirt on paper, using the planning sheet provided. Categories may be changed to fit appropriate age groups. Using fabric crayons, recreate the design from the planning sheet onto the T-shirt. When the T-shirt is finished, the counselor may solicit the help of a parent or teacher to "iron" the design into the fabric of the T-shirt. This is best accomplished by placing a piece of wax paper over the colored design areas and ironing on a low setting. The shirt may then be washed in cold water without fading the design. This activity promotes self-discovery, confidence, and independence. (Note: If coloring an actual T-shirt is not appropriate, students may color the T-shirt planning sheet using their own crayons or colored pencils. The colored paper "T-shirt" can be cut out and glued on a notebook to be used by the student.) Figures 7a and 7b provide examples of the T-shirt Design activity.

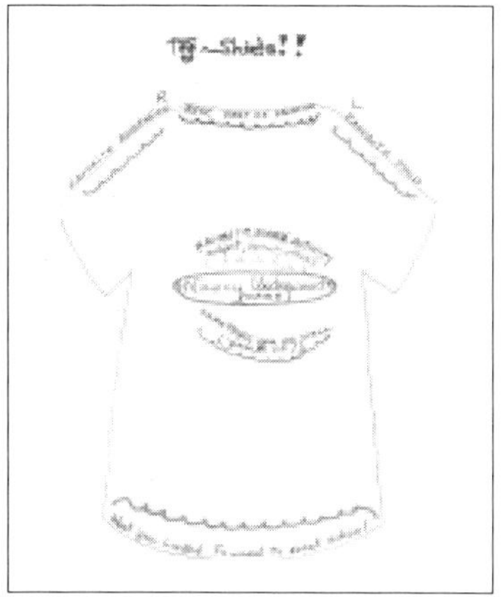

**Figure 7a. T-Shirt planning sheet.** **Figure 7b. Example of T-Shirt designs.**

### Activity 8. Acrostic Self-Poem

*Materials:* Dictionaries, thesauruses, pens, pencils, art or calligraphy paper, calligraphy italic alphabet sheets, lettering stencils.

*Activity:* Students write an acrostic poem about themselves. They may use calligraphy skills, or simply write the words in print or script. The counselor provides a brief explanation of an acrostic before students begin work on the activity. Explain that an acrostic is a word poem in which the student's name is written down the left side of a page. They then write a word or phrase for each of the letters in their name. The counselor should create an acrostic about him/herself to show as an example to the students. The students should brainstorm words and phrases which represent themselves. Using a dictionary and thesaurus, students refine the content of their acrostic. Each student reads her/his acrostic to the group or to the counselor. Be sensitive to negative and degrading content and discuss ways to reframe such comments into positive statements of self. Figures 8a and 8b provide examples of acrostics.

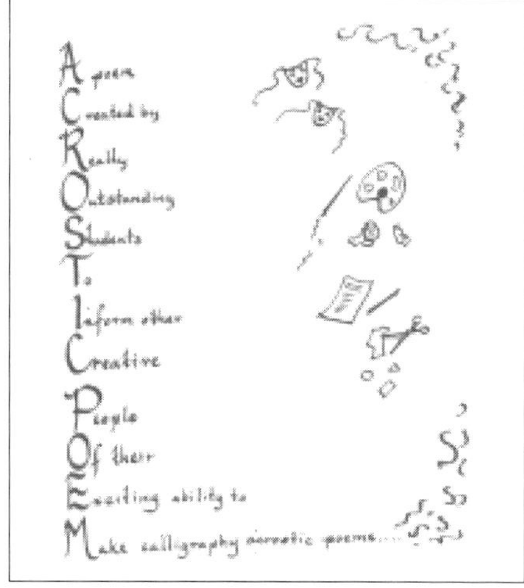

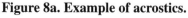

**Figure 8a. Example of acrostics.**

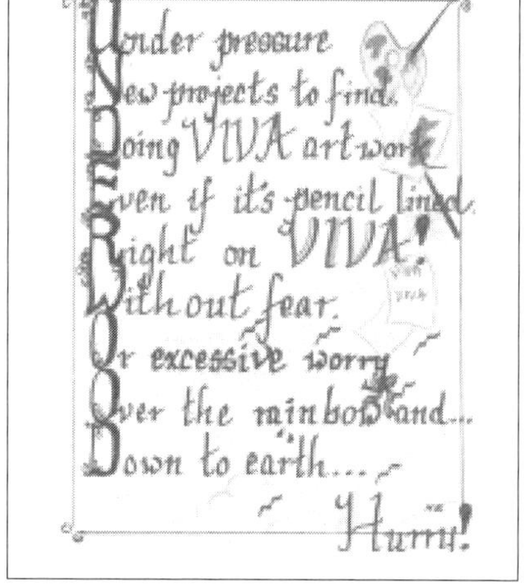


**Figure 8b. Example of an acrostic self-poem.**

## Activity 9. Color Wheel

*Materials:* Art paper, dictionaries, pencils, wheel planner, markers, and watercolor pencils.

*Activity:* Students select their favorite color and create a personal Color Wheel explaining why it is their favorite color. The counselor gives the following directions:

1. Write your favorite color in the circle in the middle of your paper.
2. Describe your favorite color using 12 words which explain why it is your favorite color, e.g., blue – blueberries.
3. Describe the 12 words with an adjective or phrase, e.g., blueberries - blueberry pancakes, sweet and mild in flavor.
4. Students color their Color Wheels with watercolor pencils or markers.
5. The counselor may relate the Color Wheel activity to one of the “color” personality models.

Discussions about personal values represented by the color wheel promote the expression of feeling. Figures 9a and 9b provide examples of the Color Wheel activity.

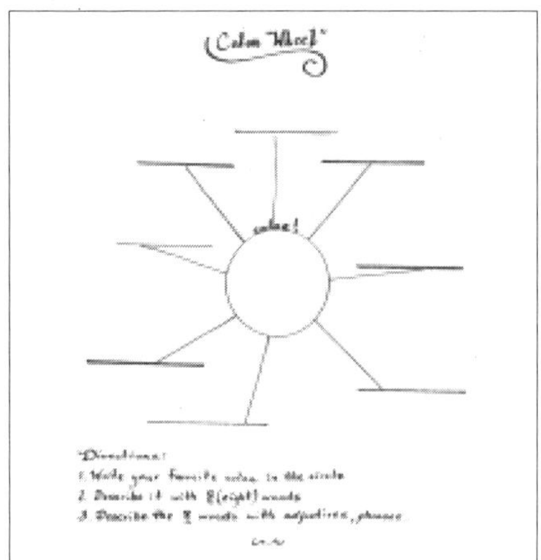


**Figure 9a. Example of instructions for a Color Wheel.**

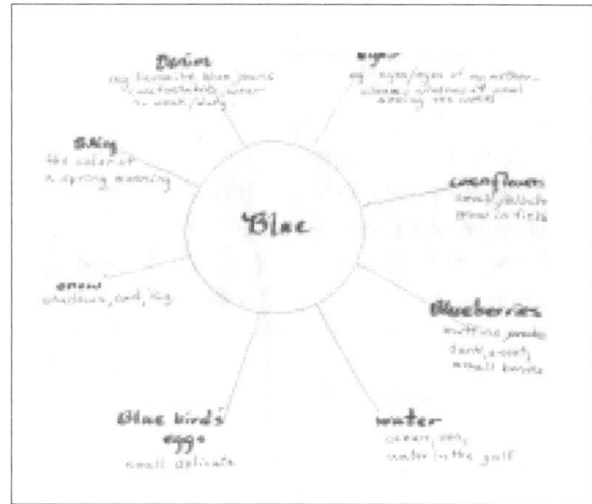


**Figure 9b. An example of a completed Color Wheel.**

## Activity 10. Monochromatic Montage

*Materials:* Art paper, pencils, stencils for picture shapes and letters, rulers, magazines, glue sticks, scissors, watercolor pencils.

*Activity:* Students create a monochromatic (one color) picture using their favorite color as the basis. Students select their favorite color and list on paper 20 things they like that can be the same color. (An explanation of tint, shade, and hue may be used here.) Students draw a picture incorporating images of the 20 things they like, or they may cut illustrations from magazines as well as draw pictures. Students also may include words in their drawing. Each student works independently, but may consult with other students and with the counselor. When pictures are completed, encourage students to explain their final creation, describe what the 20 images represent, and the reason the images were chosen. Figure 10 provides an example of a monochromatic montage.

**Figure 10. An example of a monochromatic montage.**

### Activity 11. A Portfolio/Journal of Visual Art Experiences

*Materials:* Poster board, tape, previously created visual arts.

*Activity:* This portfolio/journal activity may be used with any age group. A poster board may be folded in half and the sides taped together to create a "portfolio like-container" into which visual art creations may be stored. Either of the creations from *Block Letter Autobiography* or *Past, Present, Future Cover Story* could be used as the front of a portfolio. The portfolio could be a repository of visual arts products and other "counseling-related information" that a student maintains. Such a personal portfolio could function as a visual "diary" that describes important aspects of the student's life. Gathering the art works in a journal or portfolio not only affords students and counselors a means for collecting visual arts products, but this activity also provides a means for showing progress in self-expression.

## Summary/Conclusion

Visual arts are an impetus for innovation in self-expression. The activities in this chapter open new windows of opportunity, through written or verbal communication, for students who have difficulty focusing on or defining problem areas. The activities described in this chapter can be used with minimal expenses and with easily obtained materials. They were designed for professional school counselors seeking the outcome of unique self-expression though visual arts.

## References

Campbell, J. (1993). *Creative art in groupwork.* Bicester, Oxon, UK: Winslow Press.

Dahir, C. A., Sheldon, C. B., & Valiga, M. J. (2002). *Vision into action: Implementing the national standards for school counseling programs.* Alexandria, VA: American School Counseling Association.

Edwards, B. (1989). *Drawing on the right side of the brain.* Los Angeles: Jermy P. Tarcher.

France, M. H., & Edward, A. G. (1997). Using art: A Gestalt counseling strategy for working with disruptive clients. *Guidance and Counseling, 12*(4), 24-27.

Gladding, S. (1998). *Counseling as an art: The creative arts in counseling* (2nd ed.). Alexandria, VA: American Counseling Association.

Griggs, S. A. (1985). Counseling for individual learning styles. *Journal of Counseling & Development, 85*, 202-205.

Harr, J., Hall, G., Schoepp, P., & Smith, D. H. (2002). How teachers teach to students with different learning styles. *Clearing House, 75*, 142-145.

Hammond, L. C., & Gantt, L. (1998). Using art in counseling: Ethical considerations. *Journal of Counseling and Development, 76*(3), 271-276.

Henderson, S. J. (1999). The use of animal imagery in counseling. *American Journal of Art Therapy, 38*(1), 20-27.

Honore, F. M., & Edward-Allen, G. (1997). Using art: A Gestalt counseling strategy for working with disruptive clients. *Art Therapy, 12*(3), 24-26.

Jacobs, E. (1994). *Impact therapy*. Odessa, FL: Psychological Assessment Resources.

Jordan, K. (2001). Family art therapy: The joint family holiday drawing. *Family Journal, 9*(1), 52-54.

Kahn, B. B. (1999). Art therapy with adolescents: Making it work for school counselors. *Professional School Counselor, 2*, 291-298.

Keys, M. F. (1983). *Inward journey: Art as therapy*. LaSalle, IL: Open Court.

Kottman, T., Ashby, J. S., & DeGraaf, D. (2001). *Adventures in guidance: How to integrate fun into your guidance program*. Alexandria, VA: American Counseling Association.

Liebmann, M. (1986). *Art therapy for groups: A handbook of themes, games, and experiences*. Cambridge, MA: Brookline.

McNiff, S. (1992). *Art as medicine: Creating a therapy of the imagination*. Boston, MA: Shambhala.

Newsome, D. W. (2003). Counseling interventions using expressive arts. In B. T. Erford (Ed.), *Transforming the school counseling profession* (pp. 231-248).Columbus, OH: Merrill/ Prentice-Hall.

Silverman, L., & Freed, M. A. T. (1991). Strategies for gifted visual-spacial learners. Retrieved on July 11, 2001 from: http://www.gifteddevelopment.com/Present.html.

Weiser, J. (2001). Phototherapy techniques: Using clients' personal snapshots and family photos as counseling and therapy tools. *Afterimage, 29*(1), 3-12.

Whitmer, J., Thompson, D. W., & Loesch, L. C. (2000). *Classroom guidance activities: A sourcebook for elementary school counselors*. Minneapolis, MN: Educational Media.

# Chapter 22

## Mozart to MTV: The Art of Counseling with Music

*James R. (Jamey) Cheek*

### Preview

As part of professional school counseling interventions, music can be easily integrated into the personal/social, academic, and career development that promote and enhance student learning. The activities include music listening, performing, composing, and improvising. No previous musical training or talent is necessary - just enthusiasm and a willingness to allow the creativity and art of music to express itself.

Music has often been characterized as a universal method of communication and expression that encompasses a wide range of emotional, mental, physical, and spiritual responses (Gladding, 1998). As such, adults and children use it, both formally and informally, for their nurturing and healing (Gladding, 1998; Price, Rexroad, & Stephans, 1985). In fact, research indicates that music is a natural developmental extension that can be especially effective in counseling interventions with children and adolescents (Newcomb, 1994; Thomas, 1987).

Although many professional school counselors consistently and effectively integrate music into their counseling repertoire, many others are still hesitant, if not somewhat fearful, of using music as part of their developmental counseling programs. Using music in counseling requires no previous musical training or talent on the part of the professional school counselor. All that is required of the counselor is the willingness to allow the creativity and art of music to express itself, regardless of whether it is Mozart or MTV.

According to Campbell and Dahir (1997), the primary goal of professional school counselors is to promote and enhance student learning through academic, personal/social, and career development. Music can be integrated into each of these developmental areas through both individual/small group counseling and large group/classroom guidance activities. Using counseling in music is not as intense or as prescribed as direct music therapy. Rather, it is the use of components of music such as listening, performing, composing, and improvising that can prove beneficial for the students served by the professional school counselor (Gladding, 1998). The interventions that are suggested below are not meant to be a comprehensive representation of music activities used in professional school counseling; they will hopefully serve as a "creative springboard" for professional school counselors to create their own unique musical interventions as part of their individual school counseling programs.

### Empirical Support for the Positive Effects of Music on Student Development and Performance

There are a plethora of empirical studies involving music with various emotional and educational aspects of children, adolescents, and adults. As part of ongoing research regarding the impact of music on the human brain, Jensen (1998) summarized recent research findings as: (a) the human brain seems to be designed for music and arts; and (b) using music and arts in education activities has measurable, positive, and long-lasting academic and social benefits. Jensen (1998) further suggested that music is an effective tool towards three developmental purposes, as a: (a) means of stimulation, (b) carrier of words; and (c) primer for the brain. First, music is effective in increasing and decreasing the neurotransmitters responsible for attention. In other words, exciting music can be used to "perk up" students for various activities, while softer and quieter music can relax and calm students. Secondly, the melodic nature of music creates memory patterns for the lyrics.

Students will often remember the words to their favorite songs, even if they have cognitive difficulties in other areas. A common example is that many students (and adults) sing or hum the "Alphabet Song" when alphabetizing materials. Finally, music can actually "prime" the neurons of the brain for learning. The well-publicized "Mozart Effect" study (Rauscher, Shaw, Levin, Ky, & Wright, 1993) suggested that listening to classical musical pieces by Mozart temporarily improved spatial temporal reasoning. Other research studies have discovered correlations between music and other specific academic skills including reading and creative thinking (Lamb & Gregory, 1993; Mohanty & Hejmadi, 1992).

In general, music can support and enhance both social and academic proficiencies. Hanshumacher (1980) concluded that music plays a significant role in the overall development of students; it can impact intellectual achievement, facilitate language development, enhance creativity, develop social growth, and foster overall positive attitudes toward school. Furthermore, using music as part of a counseling program enhances students' self-esteem, increases feelings of accomplishment, motivates, and reduces anxiety (Bowman, 1987).

## Recommended Strategies and Interventions

*Personal/Social Development*

One of the most straightforward uses of music is to maximize and support student growth in the area of personal/social development. Counseling using music listening activities is especially effective for this developmental area, and can be easily adjusted for many different issues and age groups (Newsome, 2003). Further, the combination of music with visual images can provide a stimulus for discussing how music represents feelings. Movies, such as Disney's "Fantasia" (1941), could be used with younger students as a catalyst for discussing how feelings can be expressed. The film's use of color and storytelling through music is highly motivational and provides a medium for students to identify and explore the range of human emotions and how they are communicated. An extension for the activity could involve the students creating their own art projects that represent emotions while listening to different types of music. Newcomb (1994) suggested a cooperative non-verbal learning activity involving Vivaldi's piece "Four Seasons." While listening to the music, the students cooperatively created a drawing without speaking. The activity focused on non-verbal communication and collaboration between the students. This activity could be expanded and integrated into a wide variety of counseling situations using a variety of musical selections.

Hendricks, Robinson, Bradley, and Davis (1999) developed a school-based group intervention program using music techniques with depressed adolescents. The intervention involved individual members of the group choosing music that was relevant to them and their current experiences. The music therapy group used the individual selections to process the emotions and experiences that each piece of music evoked. Group members not only discussed the lyrics and their relevance, but also discussed the tone (happy, sad, etc.), the tempo (fast, slow, etc.), and the key (major, minor) as indications of how the music made them feel. Each member of the group had the opportunity to share and process their musical selection. The intervention was shown to be effective in reducing depression.

Besides groups on depression, the use of music can be effective with groups addressing such issues as anger, grief, and divorce. A variation on this technique can use music videos. Often the visual images combined with the music are expressions that the student feels he cannot communicate verbally. The images are often powerful representations of what many adolescents are experiencing, as evidenced by massive popularity of music television networks such as MTV or VH1 (Gladding, 1998). Additionally, this activity can be effective when working with individual students through many of the same techniques.

Since the students are bringing their music and music video recordings to school, limits need to be established regarding explicit lyrics and images that may be presented. Additionally, parents and guardians need to receive communication delineating the professional school counselor's permission and the limitations regarding bringing the music to school. In order to avoid potential problems, it may be helpful to let the students bring their CD and tapes to the counselor's office before the school day starts.

Conflict resolution is another major component of an effective school counseling program. Music can be utilized as an important part of conflict resolution activities. Students can create musical representations of feelings that are involved in conflict through the use of musical instruments including small rhythm instruments such as wood blocks, drums, or tambourines. This activity can also be done with improvisational instruments. Using techniques adapted from the film "Stomp Out Loud" (Yes/No Productions LTD, 1997), which is based on the stage show, students can use any available materials (cards, boxes, pencils, etc.) to create musical instruments. Students then can create a "Feelings Symphony" or "Music Collage" to demonstrate various emotions (Bowman, 1987; Newsome, 2003), especially the feelings involved in the conflict. As part of the conflict resolution activity, the students must communicate with musical instruments before communicating with words. This activity can also be used with two or more individual students who are experiencing a conflict.

Character/civility education programs are becoming increasingly more popular as an important part of effective school climates. The professional school counselor is poised to direct these efforts through classroom guidance activities, and as such, can use music as an important intervention. Educating students about various character words is part of these activities. For example, the character trait of "respect" can be discussed and supported through Aretha Franklin's song "Respect" (1967). Using a recorded background track of the song, the students can create new lyrics to demonstrate the basic concepts of the character trait of respect. As part of the culmination of the activity, students can create a line dance or ribbon movement dance to the song. Most likely, some students will want to assist with the movement activity. Table 1 outlines simple steps to be integrated with the song "Respect" by Aretha Franklin. Adding movement to the composed words further strengthens the cognitive relationship and adds an element of fun, cooperation, and team building to the activity.

Although it sounds complicated, song writing is a fairly simple and effective counseling technique. Newcomb (1994) suggested rewriting lyrics to traditional songs such as "Simple Gifts" and "Happy Birthday" in order to create awareness of personal strengths as well as how to give and receive compliments. One does not have to play a musical instrument in order to implement song writing. Pre-recorded "karaoke" or background accompaniment tracks are readily available in many stores, and provide a fun orchestrated background for new lyrics. Lyrics to popular tunes can be created for a wide variety of counseling uses. Social skills training and other proactive social activities can be supported and rehearsed by creating new lyrics to highly motivational music.

With regard to multiculturalism, the appreciation of ethnic and cultural diversity can be strengthened through classroom guidance where the music and dances of various cultures can be explored. Students of other cultures can present these musical aspects of their cultures for a

**Table 1. Simple Dance Steps to be Used with the Song "Respect"**

1. All students line up shoulder to shoulder.
2. Starting with the right foot, do a "grapevine" step (step right, step behind with the left foot, step right again, and then touch the left foot beside the right foot).
3. Repeat the "grapevine" on the left foot (step left, step behind with the right foot, step left again, and touch the right foot beside the left foot).
4. Three-step turn to the right (take three steps while turning to the right).
5. Three step turn to the left (take three steps while turning to the left).
6. Do a humorous pose to the right ("Cleopatra" pose or "Strong Man" pose).
7. Repeat the pose to the left.
8. "Funky chicken move" (move the legs in and out while flapping the elbows with the hands tucked under the arms).
9. With the right foot, touch heel, then toe, heel, toe, heel, toe.
10. Then turn to the right one-quarter turn so that the lines are now facing the next direction.
11. Repeat the steps.

more diversified view of individual differences. This could also be expanded to a school-wide activity culminating in a "World Party" celebrating the culture, food, history, and musical diversity of various cultures from around the world.

Music has been used for stress reduction in a variety of situations including progressive relaxation techniques (Bowman, 1987; Cheek, Bradley, Reynolds, & Coy, in press; Russell, 1992) and playing instrumental music (Spintge & Droh, 1985). Teachers can be encouraged to use music in their classrooms as a means of stress reduction for their students. The use of music for stress reduction can also impact academic development of students.

*Academic Development*

The developmental school counseling program should implement activities that enable and support students "to experience academic success, maximize learning through commitment, produce high quality work, and be prepared for a full range of options and opportunities after high school" (Campbell & Dahir, 1997, p. 20). Music can play a vital and effective part in activities that support academic development.

Stress in academic situations can directly impact the success and achievement of students. Besides reducing stress, music can also be used to impact specific stress problems, such as test anxiety. As high-stakes testing and standardized examinations become more pervasive, teaching students stress-reducing strategies is an important part of the professional school counselor's responsibilities.

Cheek et al. (in press) suggested a technique called "Stop, Drop and Roll." For students participating in a group addressing test anxiety, instruct students that when they physically feel the "fire" of anxiety and stress, they should "stop" (actually put down their pencils and place their hands on the table while concentrating on the coolness of the surface), "drop" their heads forward, and "roll" them around gently while taking three deep breaths. Have group members practice the relaxation technique as classical music composed by Mozart is played. In this study, students who had participated in the groups taught their classmates the "Stop, Drop, and Roll" techniques with the taped music. Also, during the final days before the test administration, a school-wide motivational assembly was held to motivate all students to practice the "Stop, Drop, and Roll" technique to techno dance music.

Wilson (1986) suggested another musical intervention to assist students with standardized testing. She created a musical theater production using well known tunes in order to promote appropriate test-taking skills. This program could be used with a variety of age ranges, and could be adapted to a variety of testing situations. Table 2 provides an example from "Meeting the Challenge of Standardized Tests."

**Table 2. Musical example from "Meeting the Challenge of Standardized Tests" (Wilson, 1986, p. 340).**

*Verse 1*
[to the tune of "On Top of Old Smoky"]
For standardized testing.
Here's what you must do.
Bring number 2 pencils (hold up pencils)
And scratch paper , too.
(hold up paper)

*Verse 2*
You'll read from a booklet
And mark on the sheet (demonstrate sheet)
Fill in the best answer
And make your marks neat.

*Verse 3*
On a difficult question
You may be in doubt,
But it's better to guess than
To just leave it out.

*Verse 4*
If you finish early
And have time to spare
Check over your answers.
Please take special care.

As with other feelings, students can also demonstrate and process their feelings toward school by bringing selections of music or creating musical collages (Bowman, 1987; Gladding, 1998). By giving students "musical permission" to express their feelings about school, the overall climate of the school can be addressed and positively impacted.

Academically, music can be used for a variety of learning experiences. Through collaboration and cooperation with classroom teachers, the professional school counselor can reinforce academic concepts through music (Crabbs, Crabbs, & Wayman, 1986). The "Schoolhouse Rock" video cartoon series (Newall & Yohe, 2001) addresses content in arithmetic, grammar, social studies, and science. As a professional school counselor, these can be used with certain individuals or prescribed as tutoring for a student who is struggling academically.

Likewise, students with musical intelligence (Gardner, 1999) can use and find success in their abilities that may not be adequately addressed in regular classroom settings. By allowing these students to use their talents and interests, professional school counselors can increase academic and personal self-esteem.

*Career Development*

The professional school counselor's role in career development is to assist students in their transition from school to work, including the development of a positive attitude toward work (Campbell & Dahir, 1997). Although musical interventions for this developmental area are not as apparent as other areas, music can still be effective.

One of the important competencies for career development is awareness of career opportunities. After using the Internet and various other resources to explore career options, groups of students can create "music video commercials" of various career opportunities to share with their classmates. As part of these videos, students should also demonstrate awareness of the training and educational requirements needed to achieve those career opportunities. For example, using music of the students' choice, a group of students can create a commercial for nurses. In the video presentation, both male and female students dress in nursing uniforms and role-play various aspects of nursing care. They include video footage of students studying science and math. When the video projects are presented as part of classroom guidance, then each group can discuss their findings. In addition, this activity is an excellent opportunity for the classroom teacher and the professional school counselor to collaborate in the content areas.

Besides creating video presentations, recorded music and music videos can be used to explore effective job communications. Videos showing both positive and negative representations of communication with supervisors and fellow employees can be shown and discussed. Gender stereotyping can also be addressed by the job roles represented in the selections.

Musical lyrics can be created to support the character traits of responsibility, dependability, punctuality, integrity, and effort in the workplace. By creating a "Worker's Rap for Success," these traits can be defined and explored. Students can create the rap and add the background beats and sounds for the classroom performance. For example:

> Yo, yo whadda ya say...
> Integrity will show the way.
> Say what you mean,
> Do what you say,
> You'll get a job,
> You'll make good pay.

As students get more comfortable with using music as part of their career exploration, they likely will suggest other possible interventions or projects. Once students have been given permission to be creative using music, the possibilities are limitless.

## Summary/Conclusion

In summary, music techniques can be integrated into the areas of personal/social, academic, and career development to promote and enhance student learning. As a part of counseling interventions, music can be incorporated into many components of professional school counseling, including individual, small/large group, and classroom guidance activities. In addition, music is by nature culturally sensitive and naturally leveling. By sharing in students' selection of music, a culture of acceptance and respect for the students' life experiences is created and maintained. Incorporating music does not require extensive musical training or an unlimited financial budget. As stated by Newcomb (1994), using music in counseling "requires minimal musical skill and maximum enthusiasm" (p. 150). The possibilities for counseling interventions are limited only by the professional school counselor's creativity and his or her willingness to let the art of counseling with music enhance and transform the school counseling program.

## References

Bowman, R. P. (1987). Approaches for counseling children through music. *Elementary School Guidance and Counseling, 21*, 284-291.

Campbell, C. A., & Dahir, C. A. (1997). *The national standards for school counseling programs.* Alexandria, VA: American School Counselor Association.

Cheek, J. R., Bradley, L. J., Reynolds, J., & Coy, D. (in press). An intervention for helping elementary students reduce test anxiety. *Professional School Counseling.*

Crabbs, M. A., Crabbs, S. K., & Wayman, J. (1986). Making the most of music: An interview with Joe Wayman. *Elementary School Guidance & Counseling, 20*, 240-245.

Franklin, A. (1967). *Respect* [song title]. New York: Atlantic Records.

Gardner, H. (1999). *The disciplined mind.* New York: Simon & Schuster.

Gladding, S. T. (1998). *Counseling as an art: The creative arts in counseling* (2nd ed.). Alexandria, VA: American Counseling Association.

Hanshumacher, J. (1980). The effects of art education on intellectual and social development: A review of selected research. *Bulletin for the Council for Research in Music Education, 61*(2), 10-28.

Hendricks, C. B., Robinson, B., Bradley, L. J., & Davis, K. (1999). Using music techniques to treat adolescent depression. *Journal of Humanistic Counseling, Education and Development, 38* (1), 39-47.

Jensen, E. (1998). *Teaching with the brain in mind.* Alexandria, VA: Association for Supervision and Curriculum Development.

Lamb, S. J., & Gregory, A. H. (1993). The relationship between music and reading in beginning readers. *Educational Psychology, 13*(2), 19-26.

Mohanty, B., & Hejmadi, A. (1992). Effects of intervention training on some cognitive abilities in preschool children. *Psychological Studies, 37*(1), 31-37.

Newall, G., & Yohe, T.(1995). *Schoolhouse rock: The 30th anniversary edition* [film]. Buena Vista, CA: Walt Disney Company.

Newcomb, N. S. (1994). Music: A powerful resource for the elementary school counselor. *Elementary School Guidance and Counseling, 29*, 150-155.

Newsome, D. W. (2003). Counseling interventions using expressive arts. In B. T. Erford (Ed.), *Transforming the school counseling profession* (p. 231-247). Columbus, OH: Merrill/Prentice-Hall.

Price, R. D., Rexroad, E. F., & Stephans, K. L. (1985). Music and well-being: Viewing philosophies, training models, and operational procedures. In R. R. Pratt (Ed.), *The fourth international symposium on music* (pp. 20-26). Lanham, MD: University Press of America.

Rauscher, F. H., Shaw, G. L., Levine, L. J., Ky, K. N., & Wright, E. L. (1993). Music and spatial task performance. *Nature, 365*, 611.

Russell, L. A. (1992). Comparisons of cognitive, music, and imagery techniques on anxiety reduction with university students. *Journal of College Student Development, 33,* 516-523.

Spintge, F., & Droh, R. (1985). Effects of anxiolytic music on plasma levels of stress hormones in different medical specialties. In R. R. Pratt (Ed.), *The fourth international symposium on music* (pp. 88-100). Lanham, MD: University Press of America.

Thomas, E. (1987). *Stress and schooling: A search for stress profiles of adolescent students.* Paper presented at the International Council of Psychologists Annual Convention, New York. (ERIC Document Reproduction Service No. ED 291 047).

Walt Disney Company (1941). *Fantasia* [film]. Burbank, CA: Buena Vista Home Video.

Wilson, N. S. (1986). Meeting the challenge of standardized tests: A guidance musical. *The School Counselor, 33*, 338-344.

Yes/No Productions Ltd. (1997). *Stomp Out Loud* [film]. New York: HBO Home Video.

# Chapter 23

## Literacy-based Strategies for the Professional School Counselor

*Barbara Thompson & Teesue H. Fields*

### Preview

There are a number of literacy-based strategies that can support comprehensive school counseling services in classroom settings, small groups, and with individuals. These strategies include all of the six language arts: speaking, listening, reading, writing, viewing, and visually representing. While viewing and visually representing are important in a student's development, this chapter will focus on the four traditional language arts - speaking, listening, reading, and writing - and specifically the counseling strategies of journal writing, bibliotherapy, and storytelling.

Literacy-based strategies have a long history in individual and group counseling with K-12 students (Borders & Paisley, 1992). The counselor can ask students to use various writing exercises to illuminate problems and their possible solutions (Riordan, 1996) or can give books to read to provide information or alternate solutions for problems (Gladding & Gladding, 1991). Storytelling has also been used to help students express feelings and handle problems through a neutral vehicle; instead of talking about herself, the student can talk about the story character and lets that fictitious person deal with the problem (Gardner, 1986).

For the professional school counselor, the use of literacy strategies is a natural fit because the students are already engaged in many literacy activities in the classroom. In fact, when a school counselor joins with the already existing academic activities or builds on those activities, the counseling program gains additional leverage and the comprehensive developmental guidance program complements the academic program of the school. As professional school counselors move to align their programs with the academic goals of the school (Fields & Hines, 2000), the use of literacy activities maximizes the professional school counselor's efforts and increases the chance that the school counseling program will be integrated into the school rather than being viewed as an adjunct service. This chapter will highlight some of the literacy activities that might already exist in a school which the professional school counselor can use in classroom guidance and then discuss how some of those same types of activities might be used in individual and small group counseling.

### Writing Activities

*Journaling*

Keeping a daily journal is a cornerstone of many classroom writing programs. Researchers of the writing process have established that professional writers use journals as a place to explore topics prior to their actual writing (Calkins, 1996). Based on this finding, the use of journal writing was introduced into the K-12 writing curriculum.

If the professional school counselor decides to tap into the classroom writing program, it is important to be aware of the way journaling is used in a particular classroom. Many teachers, in a belief that students do not have their own things about which to write, assign students a daily topic. Other teachers, in an effort to hold students accountable, correct and grade journals. Both of these practices tend to be counterproductive to self-expression.

By giving students a daily topic, teachers unintentionally send a message to students that their own ideas, feelings or personal events are not important enough to write about in a journal. While it is true that there are days that students may not have anything they feel is important enough to record in their journals, teachers assume control of the student's writing when supplying a daily topic. As teachers assume control of the journal, students become increasingly less likely to want to write. This begins a cycle in which teachers, believing students don't have anything to write about, assign a topic, and students, not wanting to write about the teacher's topic, won't write or write poorly or uncertainly.

When using writing activities in conjunction with guidance activities, the professional school counselor could alternate open topic days with some assigned topics. However, when assigning topics, it is important to keep the topic broad enough for all students to be able to use. For instance, using the topic "write about your best friend," is constricting, while "write about a friend" is less so. It is important to also honor the wishes of students who choose not to write or who want to write about something else.

While it is unlikely that a professional school counselor would correct a child's journal, it is important to understand that many teachers do grade or correct journal entries and this can affect the responses students have to the guidance journal. By demanding that students write editorially correct prose, a teacher restricts the topics students use in their journals. If a student knows that the teacher is going to correct spelling in a journal, he is unlikely to take risks in topic choice and language. For example, if a second grader has been to his favorite restaurant and wants to write about that experience, he is likely to change the topic because "restaurant" is a difficult word to spell. Knowing that the risk of spelling restaurant incorrectly may result in a red mark in his journal, he may abandon the topic in favor of something easier to spell such as "My Cat" or an "I like" entry. It is important for the school counselor to stress that guidance journals will not be corrected and that taking risks in spelling is acceptable.

*Personal Response Logs*

Another classroom writing activity that professional school counselors might try is the *personal response log* used for reactions to reading assignments. These logs provide students a forum to write about their understandings, questions and comments regarding their readings. These logs also provide students material from which to begin literature discussions with other students (Short, Hartz & Burke, 1996). If the school counselor is using reading materials with students or reading aloud to students, he/she could make use of the personal response logs that are used for other literature activities.

*Writing Notebook*

The writing notebook provides a place for students to collect pieces of their lives (e.g., snippets of writing, scraps of paper, photographs) as a platform from which to launch their own writing (Calkins, 1996). These notebooks could be used by the professional school counselor to launch classroom discussions about life problems or celebrations. For instance, if the counselor is conducting a classroom guidance unit on loss, students could put a variety of things in their writing notebook (e.g., pictures of people who have died, friends who have moved away, reactions to losses, newspaper articles about deaths or disasters, poems). This gives students a way to process different types of loss and share with others in the class some of the losses they have encountered.

While any of these writing activities might be valuable tools for the counseling program, it is also important to be aware of the various writing activities being used by all of the teachers that a student encounters. If a student is asked to keep too many journals or response logs, the student who is already a reluctant writer may resent having to do yet another writing activity. Rather than seeing this reluctance as resistance to the counseling strategy, the professional school counselor could give the reluctant writer an alternate activity.

Journaling, response logs or writing notebooks can also be used in individual and group counseling in ways that are similar to their use in classroom guidance. The primary difference is that because the professional school counselor knows the student better and there is more privacy, more personal topics can be incorporated (Kandt, 1994). Once trust has been established with the individual or within the small group, the professional school counselor can ask the student to select a passage he or she is willing to share and that passage can be the basis for a group or individual discussion. Of course the student must be allowed a "pass" if they do not want to share a passage. To protect the relationship of trust with the school counselor, it is important not to force student sharing.

When using various writing activities in counseling, sometimes a specific topic is assigned and students are free to write about anything they wish within that topic. An example of a specific topic may be an anger journal in which the students record their thoughts, feelings and behavior each time they get angry. The professional school counselor and student then analyze some of those situations to better understand what happened and to problem-solve possible solutions. If the intervention is non-topical journaling, the counselor and student may analyze the entries and notice patterns of depression or anxiety that were previously unrecognized in the counseling sessions.

## Bibliotherapy

Pardeck and Pardeck (1993) defined bibliotherapy as the use of literature to help children cope with changes in their lives. Although most professional school counselors use the term counseling rather than therapy to describe their services, a search of the literature indicates that the term bibliotherapy is still used more often than the alternate term, bibliocounseling.

The classroom guidance program can easily integrate bibliotherapy into the many reading-related activities that are already part of the school curriculum. By joining with the classroom teacher to use techniques common to the school reading program, the professional school counselor can gain more time for the guidance curriculum. There are a number of classroom activities that can broaden the professional school counselor's approach to bibliotherapy.

### *Text Sets*

Text sets (Short et al., 1996) are a collection of books, magazines, videotapes, music, posters, artwork, etc. that are collected around a particular topic. The materials should be chosen to represent a variety of reading difficulties and should depict a range of cultural markers (e.g., race, class, gender, religion). Thus a professional school counselor might assemble a text set on "getting along." This set would include a variety of printed materials depicting various ethnic, class and religious groups, videos, artwork, posters and music.

After assembling the materials, the professional school counselor would introduce the topic of the set and offer the students an opportunity to choose materials they would be interested in exploring. During the exploration time, which might be one class session or several, the counselor serves as a facilitator, helping students choose materials, engaging students in spontaneous discussion, and monitoring the students' responses to the materials. In an ideal setting, the counselor is able to leave the materials with the classroom teacher and the teacher can also facilitate the exploration. This allows students extensive opportunities to use the materials prior to a discussion. Allowing students to choose among a variety of materials instead of having a book assigned to read can enhance the chance of success. Rudman (1995, p. 3) stated, "When a book is assigned as medicine, the chances of its being accepted are slim. Rather if informal strategies are used...the likelihood of success is enhanced."

When students have had ample time to explore a variety of materials, the professional school counselor can let students choose from a variety of ways to respond to the materials including: sharing their favorite piece of the set; creating a word web using the topic as the center focus; brainstorming words the materials evoke; drawing a picture representing their feelings about the materials; writing in their guidance journal about a particular piece. Creating a tangible response to the materials allows students to think through their thoughts and feelings prior to an oral discussion on the topic. Once students have made a tangible response, they can discuss their reaction with partners, in small groups, or with the whole class.

*Literature Discussion Groups*

Literature discussion groups, literature circles (Short, 1997), or grand conversations (Peterson & Eeds, 1990) provide students with opportunities to express their understandings and personal responses to a text. If these already exist in the teacher's curriculum, the professional school counselor can join with the teacher to explore guidance topics. If the classroom teacher does not currently use literature discussion groups, the professional school counselor can introduce the strategy.

It is important to remember that literature discussion groups are not focused on the ability to read material, but rather the personal response to the material at hand. Therefore, it is possible for students to discuss books read to them. This makes discussion groups accessible to students from kindergarten through college. It also makes it possible for less proficient readers to participate in the same group with more proficient readers.

To establish literature discussion groups, the professional school counselor should consider the needs of the students regarding reading ability and, in the case of guidance topics, the students' experience with the topic. For example, if students have been reading books about family relationships, it is a good idea to arrange groups so that a variety of family configurations are represented in each group. Putting students from single parent families in the same group will not produce as rich an experience as having a mixture of family configurations in the same group. The same is true for reading ability. A mixture of abilities provides a mixture of responses and actually strengthens the reading abilities of less proficient readers.

Literature discussion groups can be focused on materials students have read from a text set, a book they are reading during personal reading time, a book the teacher or professional school counselor has read to the entire group, or a book assigned specifically for the discussion experience. In using a book assigned specifically for the discussion, the professional school counselor should make sure that each student has a copy of the book and has had time to read the book prior to discussion time. When using this technique with an entire class, one strategy is to collect five or six titles about the topic and provide four or five copies of each title. The professional school counselor can then assign a book to each student or allow students to choose which book they would like to read based upon a book talk the counselor conducted for the entire class.

Once students have had an opportunity to read their book, they form their discussion group and talk about the book. There are many ways to facilitate the discussion. In her book *Literature as a Way of Knowing,* Short (1997) outlined several strategies for engaging children in discussion. One such strategy is called "Save the Last Word for Me." To begin this strategy, the professional school counselor asks students to write a sentence or two from the book they liked or they thought was important on a note card. When the groups meet, students put the cards in the middle of the group and shuffle them around. One student chooses a card and reads what is on it. Each student then comments on the content of the card, with the writer of the card going last — thus having the last word.

The role of the professional school counselor during the discussion groups can vary. Depending on the students' history with literature discussion, the counselor may actively participate by joining each group for a period of time, or the counselor may just oversee the groups, intervening when she sees that a group needs help moving forward.

It is also important for the teacher and the professional school counselor to remember that the group discussion will not always be about the book. Using the book as a platform from which to launch more personal discussions is part of the technique for the guidance program, and indeed for the reading program as well. Often teachers will feel that if students aren't talking about the book, they are off task. However, part of responding to literature is the opportunity for the students to relate the literature to their lives.

*Reading Aloud*

In conjunction with a text set, or at the beginning of a guidance session, reading aloud to students from a book that contains the topic at hand is a powerful manner in which to engage students in reading (Krashen, 1993). In choosing a book to read aloud, it is important to take into consideration several factors: time frame, developmental level of the students, and quality of the literature.

The first consideration is the timeframe for the read-aloud. If classroom guidance time only allows a brief (20 minute) experience, a picture book might be the best choice. High quality picture books are available for all ages and reading levels. If the guidance session is daily or several times a week, or if the classroom teacher is willing to continue the read-aloud daily when the professional school counselor is not in the classroom, then a chapter book, Hi-Lo reader, or short novel might be an appropriate choice. Suggestions for read-aloud books can be found in *The New Read-Aloud Handbook* (Trelease, 2001).

Another factor to consider in choosing a book is the developmental level of the students. Picture books as a genre are appropriate for all students; however, one needs to consider the students with whom the book is being used. For example, *Smoky Night*, by Eve Bunting, is a book about friendship and tolerance that takes place during a riot. Clearly, this is a picture book that is inappropriate for use with preschool and kindergarten students, but is appropriate for late primary or older students. The same caution applies to chapter books. While some second and third graders can read a book such as *The Giver* by Lois Lowry, it does not mean that the content of the book is appropriate for them developmentally. In a similar way, adolescents are very sensitive to anything that might appear to be too babyish, so they might reject a novel such as *Charlotte's Web,* by E. B. White, based on the age of the protagonist and the focus on talking animals, even though it is a wonderful book about friendship and loss.

Regardless of time or age level, the key to choosing a good read-aloud is that the book be good literature in its own right. In today's children's literature market there are many books published that are issue books which are written to "teach" students a lesson. While some are popular with students and well illustrated, there are an increasingly large number of books that are poorly illustrated and heavily didactic. These books do all the thinking for the student, allowing for no inference or true response on the part of the student. Some books may be so directive that they ask students questions in the context of telling the story. With the plethora of high quality books for students published each year, these didactic books should be avoided. In addition to having dubious value for helping students think about issues, such books do not provide models of good literature that would enhance the academic program.

*Sustained Silent Reading*

The professional school counselor can collaborate with classroom teachers regarding the books students have available for personal reading time (often called Sustained Silent Reading or SSR). Many schools have adopted SSR on a school-wide basis. The professional school counselor can help insure that materials placed in the individual class libraries contain topics that are congruent with the school's counseling program. For example, if the school is focusing in a particular year on maintaining productive friendships, then the professional school counselor can help teachers highlight books in which productive friendships are evident. By having the materials in the classroom and readily available for personal reading, the topic is introduced to students in an unobtrusive manner. Students can then take their personal reading and apply it to the guidance session.

*Book Lists*

Along with helping teachers establish classroom libraries that feature books aligned with the school counseling program the professional school counselor can maintain a list of materials appropriate for guidance in particular areas. These lists may be generated from the counselor's own personal reading or complied from a search of available materials. One technique involves searching websites (e.g., Amazon - www.amazon.com or Barnes and Noble - www.bn.com) for a particular topic. By using "juvenile fiction" or "juvenile non-fiction" and the topic, a list of books is generated. Then, based upon the reviews provided on the same website, the counselor can add the book to the list. Not all reviews are equal, but well respected reviewers such as *Hornbook*, *School Library Journal* and *Kirkus* are cited on these websites. If those reviewers have favorably reviewed the book, the counselor can safely add the book to the list. However, best practice is still for the counselor to read a book before recommending it to students.

There are other sources of booklists to use with students. Perhaps the most used booklist is the one maintained by the American Library Association which can be found on its website (www.ala.org). The American Library Association also publishes *Booklinks,* which contains materials thematically organized for teachers and librarians.

The National Council of Teachers of English (NCTE) and International Reading Association (IRA) also have publications that provide booklists. NCTE publishes a volume entitled *Adventuring with Books,* which is thematically arranged. IRA publishes *The Reading Teacher* and *The Journal of Adolescent and Adult Literacy,* which provide thematically-based reviews of current literature for students and young adults.

## Storytelling

While reading aloud is one way of sharing stories, many classroom teachers also use storytelling as a way to share a myth, book or personal story. Storytelling can allow the teacher or professional school counselor to be creative and involve students in a more dramatic telling of the story. Also, the book is not between the teller and the listener. Although storytelling takes practice and not every professional school counselor may be comfortable telling stories, Mason (1996) reassured the novice storyteller that if the storyteller likes the story and concentrates on the story instead of the performance, then the storyteller's enjoyment will communicate itself to the audience even if the telling isn't perfect. To enhance the story, Mason recommended using different character voices, minimal props, and allowing the students to participate in the story by making sound effects or saying a recurring line.

When selecting a story to tell, the professional school counselor must be sure it is age appropriate and can be adapted to an oral telling. Usually there is also a time issue, so the story must be short enough to allow for reaction and discussion. There are a number of sources that included suggestions for stories that are appropriate for oral sharing (Gallard, 1996; Mason, 1996; Yolen, 1986).

Another approach is to allow students to tell their own stories. Although most writing classes encourage students to compose their own stories in order to encourage self-expression and help students understand the writing process, it is less common for students to make up oral stories within the classroom. This may be due in part to the time involved if each student was allowed to tell an oral story and in part to fears of inappropriate stories or revelations that are too personal for the classroom. Gallard (1996) strongly advocated teaching students to tell their own stories in the classroom. She believed that when students tell their personal stories, whether they are about triumphs or tragedies, they "...strengthen the voices that will allow them to speak their personal truths all through their lives" (p. 18). Telling stories empowers students and allows them some control in situations where they have very little input. Gallard (1996) also addressed the issue of privacy and suggested the teacher and students talk about privacy before teaching students to tell their stories.

If the classroom teacher has taught students to tell their stories, the professional school counselor can join the classroom storytelling with a guidance topic such as dealing with fear, or making friends, or experiencing loss. If the students do not know how to tell stories, the counselor can model storytelling by telling about a personal incident from his or her childhood on the chosen topic and then encouraging students to do the same, either in pairs, small groups or for the whole classroom.

The professional school counselor is probably more familiar with storytelling in the context of individual counseling sessions. Gardner's (1986) mutual storytelling technique directs the counselor to ask the student for a story with a beginning, middle and ending. The counselor then tells his or her own story using the same characters and situation, but might provide some alternative resolutions or frame the feelings of the characters in different ways.

An alternative mutual storytelling approach (Scorzelli & Gold, 1999) has the professional school counselor and student alternate lines in the story. The counselor starts with "Once upon a time..." and the student gives the next line and so forth. The counselor (or student) writes down each line so that both can see the story as it unfolds. As the story is being told, the counselor can emphasize feelings or actions or take the story in a new direction, and so can the student.

Storytelling in individual counseling can be enhanced by a number of props including dolls, puppets or a storytelling board which has a background scene with props and pictures of people that the student can insert as he or she tells the story. The professional school counselor can also make use of new technology and take advantage of computer programs which allow the student to select backgrounds, props and characters on the computer screen to aid in telling the story (Erford, 2001).

## Summary/Conclusion

Literacy-based strategies can be an effective way to support the objectives of a comprehensive developmental school counseling program. By joining with the classroom teacher to adapt activities already in use in the school's literacy program, the professional school counselor can expand opportunities to cover guidance-related goals while enhancing the academic mission of the school. Journaling, bibliotherapy and storytelling can be used in classroom guidance, small group and individual sessions as effective counseling interventions.

## References


Border, S., & Paisley, P. (1992). Children's literature as a resource for classroom guidance. *Elementary School Guidance & Counseling, 27*, 131-139.

Calkins, L. M. (1994). *The art of teaching writing.* Portsmouth, NH: Heinemann.

Erford, B. (2001). *Mutual Storytelling Game: An interactive CD.* Shrewsbury, PA: Counseling Innovations.

Fields, T. H., & Hines, P. L. (2000). School counselor's role in raising student achievement. In G. Duhon & T. Mason (Eds.), *Preparation, collaboration & emphasis on the family in school counseling in the new millennium.* Lewiston, NY: The Edwin Mellin Press.

Gillard, M. (1996). *Storyteller, storyteacher: Discovering the power of storytelling for teaching and living.* York, ME: Stenhouse Publishers.

Gardner, R. (1986). *The psychotherapeutic techniques of Richard A. Gardner.* Cresskill, NJ: Creative Therapeutics.

Gladding, S. T., & Gladding, C. (1991). The ABCs of bibliotherapy for school counselors. *The School Counselor, 40,* 7-13.

Kandt, V. R. (1994). Adolescent bereavement: Turning a fragile time into acceptance and peace. *School Counselor, 41*, 203-212.

Krashen, S. (1993). *The power of reading: Insights from the research.* Englewood, CO: Libraries Unlimited.

Mason, H. (1996). *The power of storytelling.* Thousand Oaks, CA: Corwin Press.

Pardeck, J. T., & Pardeck, J. A. (1993). *Bibliotherapy: A clinical approach for helping children.* New York: Gordon & Breach Science Publishers.

Peterson, R., & Eeds, M. (1990). *Grand conversations: Literature groups in action.* New York: Scholastic.

Riordan, R. J. (1996). Scriptotherapy: Therapeutic writing as a counseling adjunct. *Journal of Counseling and Development, 74*, 263-269.

Rudman, M. K. (1995). *Children's literature: An issues approach* (3rd ed). White Plains, NY: Longman.

Scorzelli, J., & Gold, J. (1999). The mutual storytelling writing game. *Journal of Mental Health Counseling, 21*, 113-124.

Short, K. G. (1997). *Literature as a way of knowing.* York, ME: Stenhouse.

Short, K. G., Harste, J. C., & Burke, C. (1996). *Creating classrooms for authors and inquirers* (2nd ed). Portsmouth, NH: Heinemann.

Trelease, J. (2001). *The read-aloud handbook* (5th ed). New York: Penguin.

Yolen, J. (1986). *Favorite folktales from around the world.* New York: Pantheon.

# Chapter 24

# Professional School Counselors and Reality Therapy

*Robert E. Wubbolding*

## Preview

The WDEP (Wants, Direction or Doing, Evaluation, Plans) system of reality therapy provides a practical useable system for professional school counselors in their many roles. When implementing this system, counselors help students, clients, staff, and parents to conduct inner self-evaluations of their behaviors. Reality therapy also focuses on the overall atmosphere of the classroom and school building through the use of class meetings that have a clearly defined and readily adaptable format.

Most, but not all, human problems are rooted in dysfunctional, disturbed, or out-of-balance relationships. Effective participant interdependence, on the other hand, facilitates and supports the success of most human endeavors. When a school faculty "gets along" with each other, the school is a joyful place and students learn at a higher level (Ludwig & Mentley, 1997). If students believe their teachers care about them, respect their opinions, listen to them, and try to make learning fun, they are more inclined to want to learn and in turn "get along" with each other.

The results of using reality therapy, called lead management in schools, are not perfect, but a total immersion can result in major improvements for individual students and for the entire organization. Chaddock School, a residential school for court-referred students in Quincy, Illinois, reduced behavioral incidents to an insignificant level in just over three years (Wubbolding, 2000). By following the teaching of W. Edwards Deming (1993), institutions and individuals implementing the philosophy of continuous improvement see ongoing progress rather than remaining in a holding pattern emphasizing mere survival. Reality therapy and lead management is an effective vehicle for expediting this journey.

## Professional School Counselor Mission

Clearly the professional school counselor's mission in the context of reality therapy is the enhancement of relationships. This does not imply a blind, cultic uniformity of viewpoints, but rather a healthy give and take based on respect for diverse ways of doing things. A key question professional school counselors ask of students and staff is, "Are our current actions bringing us closer together or are they distancing us from each other?" One of the appealing aspects of reality therapy is its practicality and usefulness with individuals and groups of students, faculty, and parents as well as its organizational applications.

## Implementation

The acronym WDEP summarizes the professional school counselor's use of reality therapy and helps the user remember the concepts. It serves as a pedagogical tool providing all staff members with a common language as well as a structure for intervening in their classrooms and in all their human interactions.

The professional school counselor wears many hats and has a variety of overlapping roles: counselor, consultant, parent educator, in-service trainer, personal growth facilitator, advocate, community leader. The WDEP system of reality therapy applies to each of these roles in that it is based on universal principles applicable to virtually every human interaction.

## The WDEP System

Grounded in choice theory, the WDEP system assists human beings to satisfy five generic human motivators: survival or self-preservation, love or belonging, power or achievement, freedom or independence, and fun or enjoyment. When people interact with their environment, they build an internal collection of specific wants or pictures related to the motivators or needs. In the first step in employing the WDEP system (W – wants), a professional school counselor helps students define and clarify their wants, goals, hopes, and dreams related to belonging, power, freedom, and fun. For example, students define what they want from school, parents, teachers, and friends. In consulting with teachers, counselors assist them to define what they want from students and parents as well as to disclose their own expectations (wants) to their students in direct, firm, but non-punitive ways. When children are obstinate, uncooperative, and resistant, teachers and parents are astounded to see such behaviors diminish or vanish when they ask, "What do you want right now?" or "How hard do you want to work at changing your situation?" Of course, interventions based on this question do not produce a magical, immediate, or total reversal of behavior. Rather, such interventions need to be habitual.

Professional school counselors encourage teachers to teach the five motivators and ask students what they want from themselves, i.e., to define their levels of commitment regarding how hard they want to work at satisfying their needs and getting what they want. If professional school counselors and teachers visibly display the levels of commitment for all to see, they can reinforce their teaching at strategic moments (Wubbolding, 2000).

*Commitment level I. "I don't want to do anything."* This is, in fact, no commitment, but resistant students, parents, and even teachers often manifest little or no commitment to improve. Professional school counselors using the WDEP system see these behaviors as not mere obstacles, but as opportunities to raise their skills to a higher level. Oftentimes, the most negative adults become enthusiastic supporters and users of reality therapy in education.

*Commitment level II. "I'll try." "I might." "I could."* This middle level of commitment is more likely to succeed, but still retains an escape hatch to failure. "Trying" to study, be patient, or develop better interpersonal relationships is not identical with successful follow through. School counselors need to encourage everyone to raise his/her level of commitment. "I know you'll try, but will you do it?" School personnel realize that athletic team members describing their commitment as "we will try to win" appears less confident than the team who yells "We're number one" or "We *will* win."

*Commitment level III. "I will."* Here, the person expresses a genuine desire to move forward, solve a problem, and take effective action. A school faculty might agree to implement the quality school philosophy (Glasser, 1990) and to use the WDEP system to focus on classroom management, absenteeism, raising test scores, or a variety of other objectives.

Consequently, the WDEP system is more than a vague "What do you want?" approach. It can get as intricate and extensive as is necessary for accomplishing the many tasks involved in school improvement.

"What are you doing?" (D) represents a simplified question related to the exploration of four aspects of behavior: physiology – "Does anything hurt?"; feelings - "How do you feel?";

thinking - "What are you telling yourself about your current situation?"; and actions, the most changeable part of this suitcase of behavior – "Tell me what's going on now." "What did she say?" "What happened?" Emphasizing actions in counseling and consultation draws attention to the most easily changed component of the behavioral system. When a person chooses to change his/her actions, the other components are brought along. When a person acts enthusiastic, tagging along behind is a change in feelings. Genuine feelings of enthusiasm are likely to be a consequence of the initial change in actions. Teachers, parents, and others learn that effective change in students' attitudes follow upon a change in students' actions.

Professional school counselors working with children or adults do not ignore feelings; rather they listen empathically to the emotional level. They acknowledge feelings, help clients accept their feelings, and discuss them as openly as is reasonable. Yet, as quickly as possible, they encourage clients to discuss the components of human behavior over which they have most control: actions and, secondarily, thinking. They emphasize that behavior is a choice, especially actions, the most clearly chosen aspect of behavior. Though no one explicitly chooses anger, shame, rage, guilt, loneliness, or depression, still many individuals choose an action that brings pain along with it, as a car brings along a trunk filled with baggage. Thus a student cursing a teacher in anger and rage chooses the action. An inseparable part of the total behavior is the feeling of rage and accompanying self-talk or inner discourse.

Reality therapy lends itself to a discussion of students' thinking as well as actions and feelings. Wubbolding (2000) has identified several negative or less effective self-talk statements concomitant with less effective actions:

A. "I am powerless and have no choices" accompanies depression.
B. "No one can tell me what to do" accompanies anti-social actions.
C. "Even though what I'm currently doing is not effective, still I will choose it again and again" accompanies repeated self-destructive actions.

Professional school counselors using the WDEP system of reality therapy teach this recent addition to students, faculty, parents, and the public. The final and most important self-talk statement is operationalized in many ways: "If I'm frustrating myself by doing something which is ineffective or harmful in order to improve, I will do more of what has not helped me."

Professional school counselors teach more effective cognitive statements to their various groups of consumers. These include:

A. "I have choices and I choose my behaviors."
B. "I am happy when I live within reasonable boundaries."
C. "If my current behavior is not working for me, I'll choose a different action."

Implementing the D (Doing) of the WDEP system means that each component of the behavior is discussed with emphasis on the action element. It is as though the action is the handle of the suitcase of human behavior. When someone chooses to grab the handle and lift, the entire suitcase follows.

Self-Evaluation (E) is the cornerstone of the WDEP delivery system and constitutes the major prerequisite for change. No one changes a behavior or makes a better choice until he/she judges that the current course of action is not helpful. Students not studying, wasting time by hanging out, or yielding to harmful impulses do not change a direction until they formulate a want, look searchingly at their choices, and make a firm judgment about the usefulness of their behavior. Working in groups or individually, professional school counselors help students, faculty or parents describe what they want, and connect their actions to their wants by assisting them to courageously evaluate whether their actions are helping or hurting.

Wubbolding (2000) has enumerated 22 kinds of self-evaluation. Among the most important questions are:

- Is your current behavior bringing you closer or further away from the people around you?

- Is what you're doing getting you what you want?
- Is what you're doing helping or hurting the people around you?
- Is what you're doing against the law, the rules - written or unwritten?
- Is what you want realistic or attainable?
- Is what you want really and truly good for you in the long run not merely in the short run?
- Is your current level of commitment high enough?
- Is your plan for improvement an effective plan?

In any role, the professional school counselor facilitates a discussion of current wants and behaviors, an inner self-evaluation of them, and a plan of action (P). Effective plans need not be grandiose. Useful plans are SAMIC plans:

Simple–not complicated
Attainable–realistically doable
Measurable–answers the question, "When will you do it?"
Immediate–performed sooner rather than later
Controlled by the planner–not dependent on someone else's plans

While asking the question, "What's your plan?" seems clear and direct, there is an underlying meta-communication present. The person asked this simple question and other questions in the WDEP system gains a sense of hope and a belief in personal responsibility through an implicit awakening: "Change is possible and I can make it happen. I cannot blame others for my plight."

### Case Example I: Jamal

Jamal, age 11, says he "hates school." It is evident to all that he has no friends in school, is a discipline problem for teachers, and has poor grades. The professional school counselor helps Jamal define his wants regarding (a) having more friends and getting along with his teachers (belonging), (b) getting better grades and learning school subject matter (power), and (c) making school more enjoyable (fun). Jamal describes his current behavioral choices as the counselor helps him evaluate them with such questions as, "If you tell off the teacher, will you get what you want from her?" and "If you fight with the other students, will you gain any friends?" If Jamal is amenable to the idea, the counselor helps him make a realistic, doable plan perhaps to act appropriately for one hour a day or to attempt to befriend one student. The counselor might tell him, "A journey of a thousand miles is begun with one step." Consequently, this realistic plan is a beginning. If his teachers are learning the WDEP system, they too realize that Jamal will not make an immediate $180^{\circ}$ turn. The philosophy underlying this effort is based on the principle that when Jamal fulfills his needs within the school setting, his failure choices will diminish and he will be on the road of continuous improvement.

### Case Example II: Teacher Group

Seven English teachers in a large high school seek better behavior management skills for their classes. The professional school counselor leads a discussion about the ABC toxic behaviors - behaviors that damage relationships and chill warm friendships. These include: A. arguing, attacking, accusing; B. bossing, blaming, belittling; and C. criticizing, coercing, condemning.

Using the WDEP system the professional school counselor helps the teachers define what they want from the students, what they can settle for and what they're doing to get what they want. In a non-judgmental atmosphere, they evaluate whether and to what degree they are succeeding in achieving their goals. The counselor facilitates plan-making and provides many resources such as the *Phi Delta Kappan* article "Choices for Children: Why and How to Let

Students Decide," by Alfie Kohn (1993). This article provides a review of studies showing that when students are accorded choices in classrooms, their overall performance improves.

## Case Example III: Middle School Teachers

Eight middle school teachers seeking ways to prevent problems and increase students' curiosity for learning meet with the professional school counselor to brainstorm solutions and explore the possibility of coordinated action. They have heard about class meetings as a central component of Glasser's quality school (Glasser, 2001). They ask the professional school counselor to discuss the mechanics and the benefits of implementing this strategy. The counselor, serving as in-service trainer, teaches about class meetings from the outline provided in the following section.

## Class Meetings

*Purpose of Class Meetings*

Class meetings provide a structure for discussion of timely and relevant topics and are designed to help students satisfy one or more of the five human needs or motivators. The teacher helps students gain a sense of belonging, a feeling of inner control (as one student stated, "the teacher respects my opinion"), fun (the reward of learning), and freedom or independence. It should be noted that, while the class meeting leader is most often a teacher, a professional school counselor might also volunteer to conduct class meetings. Thus, the following discussion provides the professional school counselor with knowledge that will help him/her in either a direct intervention role or in his/her role as consultant.

*Topics*

Students begin by discussing intellectual topics, especially if this structure is new to them. Only when they become comfortable with this format should the teacher use the meetings for more emotional topics or problem solving. Consequently, meetings are *not* therapy sessions in which there is confrontation, personal self-disclosure, catharsis, or direct disputation of others' judgments. Selected topics may include: value of homework, need for rules, friendship, respect for property (especially computers), quality of work, and effort. Topics related to curriculum may be: why study math, what is old age, the value of knowing history, and various topics related to science.

*Process*

The teacher plays an unambiguous role as a leader, asking students to express their opinions or to simply "pass" if they don't want to speak aloud. Teachers need to realize that during the class meeting the emphasis is on opinions; therefore, there is no need to correct factual inaccuracies. More direct pedagogy is reserved for the major part of the students' school time outside class meetings. The three-step process, "Define, Personalize, and Challenge," provides a clear, non-threatening format.

- *Define.* Many teachers find a discussion of "effort" useful. This topic could be repeated occasionally when appropriate, e.g., at the start of the school year, after holidays, during the midwinter let down. Questions focus on "What is effort?" "How do you know you are making a good effort to do quality work?" "What is quality?" In a science class a teacher might ask students to define "fire." In one school there had been a fire across from the school making the meeting even more relevant. "What are helpful fires (e.g., the sun) and harmful fires (e.g., a fire in the house)?"

Teacher creativity and ingenuity usually produce many extensions of this component. In another meeting, students defined what old age means to them. Some responded that anyone who is 18 years of age or older is old. Others had grandparents or even great grandparents and saw old age as 70, 80, or older.

- *Personalize.* An effective meeting on "effort" involves questions such as "What motivates you to put forth extra or high quality effort?" "If someone were to see you exerting low, middle, or high quality effort, what would they see?" A skilled teacher, or professional school counselor demonstrating a class meeting, asks such questions as "Have you ever seen a fire?" "What treasures would you take with you if you had to escape from a fire?" "Do you know what to do if we had to leave this building because of fire?" Questions centering on the meeting about old age could include "Do you know anyone who is old?" "What do people who are old do for fun?" "How are they the same or different from anyone else?"
- *Challenge.* In this step teachers push students to reflect on their knowledge, to re-evaluate it, and to further develop it. Three types of questions constitute the challenge phase of the meeting. Keep in mind the focus is on opinions and questions to which there need not be correct answers.
  a) *Why?* Students are challenged to examine the basis of their beliefs. Some "why?" questions are unanswerable, beyond the current intellectual level of students, or require additional thought. "Why do people exert high or low levels of effort?" "Why does fire exist?" "What would we do without fire?" "Why do people grow old?" "If you could drink a potion and live to be 200 years old, would you drink it? Why or why not?" "Would you drink if there were only enough for the members of this class? Why or why not?"
  b) *What if?* Another challenge question revolves around imaginative thinking: "What if people always make the lowest or highest effort possible?" "How would your life be different if everyone made a high-level effort to be your friend, to play the athletic game to the best of their ability, to provide the best service possible?" "What if you could start or stop a fire just by thinking about it?" "What would life be like if the sun became much hotter or cooler?" "What if there were two suns instead of one sun?" "What if no one would grow old?" "What if all diseases were curable?"
  c) *What's the difference?* In "What's the difference between . . .?" questions, students learn to make distinctions in their thinking as a result of class meetings. "What's the difference between low-level effort and high-level effort?" "What's the difference between high-quality and low-quality relationships, toys, bicycles, school work, etc?" "What's the difference between a helpful fire and a harmful fire?" "Could a helpful fire ever become a harmful one?" In one class, students talked about the dangers of sunburn and how to take precautionary steps to avoid it. "What's the difference between maturity and old age?" Does wisdom always come with age?" "Can a young person be wise and an older person not so wise?" "How could people in this class become more wise?"

*Goals*

As a result of stimulating intellectual discussions in which students express a wide range of viewpoints, experiences, and opinions, they learn respect for each other, gain a genuine appreciation of diversity, experience an increase in self-confidence, and develop deeper humanistic values. When students feel a sense of interdependence and connection they grow in knowledge and their behavior improves. Additionally, they develop an appreciation for ideas and for intellectual discussions. This is especially valuable in an age when many kids' discussions and interactions often consist of demeaning and sarcastic humor.

*Types of Meetings*

Professional school counselors understand the value, purpose, and process of class meetings. They provide demonstrations for teachers and coach teachers to conduct three types of meetings: open-ended, educational/diagnostic and problem solving.

*Open-ended meetings.* Meetings described above on the topics of old age and effort/quality are open-ended, opinion-centered, "no-correct answers" meetings. Teachers should conduct these meetings until the students and teachers feel comfortable with such discussions and they come to realize that, regardless of their opinions, they will not be criticized or put down.

*Educational/diagnostic meetings.* Some teachers using educational/diagnostic meetings begin each new study unit with a series of questions related to the topic. In these meetings, teachers conduct an informal verbal assessment of students' prior knowledge of the topic. The meeting centering on fire could be such a meeting, though it could also be an open-ended meeting. A history teacher could begin the school year with a meeting built around such questions as: What is history? Do you have your own personal history? Of what value is history? Why do we study history? What if you didn't know anything that happened prior to today? Science, language, and computer teachers could begin their courses with similar questions. Revisiting these general topics throughout the school year is also useful.

*Problem-solving meetings.* Teachers wishing to solve problems often initiate class meetings focused on antisocial behavior and irresponsible behavior such as class disruption, respect for adults, drug use, homework, or others. These are the most difficult to conduct because of emotional overtones and the tendency for participants to blame individuals.

One teacher, a union leader in a junior high school who taught difficult classes with hard-to-reach students, told the author in October, "I hate to come to this class," when referring to a class of seventh graders. In April, he related that he looked forward to this same class of seventh graders. Describing interventions causing this change, he related that he started with open-ended meetings during which students learned to respect various viewpoints. Then they discussed a school policy regarded as unfair, i.e., punishing all students sitting at a table in the cafeteria when only one acted out. The class agreed to approach the student council, which presented the class consensus to the assistant principal, who agreed to change this ineffective and unfair rule. The teacher related that the students came to believe their judgment was worthy of respect. Their effective choices fulfilled their need for power or achievement in a positive way. They were then less inclined to choose self-defeating actions.

*Guidelines and Cautions*

Experience in implementing class meetings reveals several cautions useful for professional school counselors modeling class meetings or teaching other school staff the art of conducting them.

- Make every attempt to sit in a circle. Ideal and desirable, this rearrangement of chairs might be time-consuming, inconvenient, and even impossible. Students should know that "we're having a meeting" even if adherence to a circled discussion is impractical. Nor should teachers rigidly wed themselves to the large circle structure when variations prove to be useful adjuncts. Some teachers train students to lead the meetings, split the group into two smaller groups, or combine the class meeting with cooperative learning activities (Wubbolding & Brickell, 2001). Buzz words for teachers to consider are flexibility, creativity, reevaluation, outcome focused, and consultation with other professional school counselors and teachers. Meetings can be brief. They need not be lengthy. It is better for students to say, "We need more time" than to say, "Meetings are boring."

- Problem-solving meetings should focus on *conditions, not the behavior of specific students*. Emphasizing the negative behavior of specific students can result in criticism, embarrassment, and even humiliation for scapegoated children. Effective meetings emphasize positive outcomes and specific ways to improve the school atmosphere.
- A helpful first meeting for professional school counselors demonstrating class meetings or coaching teachers is a "meeting on rules" or a "meeting on meetings." Useful questions include: What is a rule? What are rules you find helpful? What is your favorite rule? What's the difference between a rule, a law, and a suggestion? What if we had no rules? How would this class function without rules? How would society function? What rules do we need for our class meetings? Meetings focusing on the nature of a meeting could emphasize questions such as: What is a meeting? Do your parents go to meetings? Why do people have meetings? What if no one ever went to a meeting? What do meetings accomplish? What makes for a good meeting?
- Do not allow meetings to degenerate into gripe sessions. School rules, anti-social behavior, homework, the role of authority, and other topics can easily deteriorate if students and teachers are inexperienced in the art of group meetings. The structured process of "define, personalize, and challenge" combined with the WDEP system provide a viable alternative to such disasters.

## Summary/Conclusion

Professional school counselors interface with virtually every person associated with the school - students, faculty, administrators, parents, community members. The WDEP system provides a practical, research-based structure for counseling and consultation as well as content for in-service training. It also enriches the "define, personalize, and challenge" format for problem-solving class meetings. Asking students, "What do you want?" helps them focus their attention on themselves rather than on everyone else. Asking, "What are you doing?" narrows the discussion by focusing on the most easily controllable component of human behavior - actions. Self-evaluation is the necessary prelude to any change and planning means taking responsibility for the future. Professional school counselors adopting the WDEP system of reality therapy have a comprehensive and programmatic basis for school improvement.

## References

Deming, W. E. (1993). *The new economics*. Cambridge: Massachusetts Institute of Technology.

Glasser, W. (1998). *The quality school: Managing students without coercion.* New York: HarperPerennial.

Glasser, W. (2001). *Every student can succeed.* Chatsworth, CA: William Glasser Inc.

Kohn, A. (1993). Choices for children: Why and how to let students decide. *Phi Delta Kappan. 75*(1), 8-20.

Ludwig, S., & Mentley, K. (1997). *Quality is the key.* Wyoming, MI: KWM Educational Services.

Wubbolding, R. (2000). *Reality therapy for the 21st century.* Philadelphia: Brunner-Routledge.

Wubbolding, R., & Brickell, J. (2001). *A set of directions for putting and keeping yourself together.* Minneapolis, MN: Educational Media Corporation.

# *Section 3*

# Comprehensive School Counseling Services

# Chapter 25

## Introduction to the *National Standards for School Counseling Programs*

*Lawrence E. Tyson*

### Preview

This chapter describes the history and impact of the American School Counselor Association's (ASCA) *National Standards for School Counseling Programs.* The standards and accompanying competencies have been created to provide the direction to help every student acquire attitudes, knowledge, and skills (competencies) in academic, career, and personal-social development. The *Standards* have been incorporated as the foundation for *The ASCA National Model: A Framework for School Counseling Programs* (ASCA, 2003).

The *National Standards for School Counseling Programs* was created in 1997 (Campbell & Dahir, 1997). The American School Counselor Association (ASCA) considers the *National Standards* to be the essential foundation for the content of school counseling programs (Dahir, 2001). They are outcome-based statements of what students should know and be able to do as a result of participating in a comprehensive, developmental school counseling program.

### Discussion

In response to *Goals 2000* and the *Educate America Act* (U.S. Department of Education as cited in Dahir, 2001), ASCA's Governing Board became committed to the development of national standards for America's school counseling programs. The development process incorporated theory and research by completing an exhaustive review of the literature and an examination of more than 35 state school counseling program models. Additionally, extensive field reviews solicited input from more than 4,000 professionals including elementary, middle/junior, and high school counselors, supervisors of school counseling, and counselor educators (Campbell & Dahir, 1997). The intent of this effort was to motivate the school counseling community to identify and implement goals for students that were deemed important by the profession, clarify the relationship of school counseling to the educational system, and address the contributions of school counseling to student success in school (Dahir, 2001).

With the publication of ASCA's *National Standards for School Counseling Programs* (Campbell & Dahir, 1997), professional school counselors across the country gained a significant resource to help restructure and improve their counseling programs and help ensure that all students have access to high quality, comprehensive school counseling programs (Pérusse, Goodnough, & Noel, 2001). The *National Standards* became the foundation for ASCA's design for comprehensive, developmental school counseling programs. As cited by Herr (2001), ASCA, in an executive summary, stated:

> The purpose of a counseling program in a school setting is to promote and enhance the learning process. The goal of the program is to enable all students to achieve success in school and to develop into contributing members of our society. A school counseling program based on national standards provides all the necessary elements for students to achieve success in school. This programmatic approach helps school counselors to continuously assess their students' needs, identify the barriers and obstacles that may be hindering student success, and advocate programmatic efforts to eliminate these barriers. (p. 237)

According to Schmidt and Ciechalski (2001), the primary goal of the *National Standards* is to promote student learning and development while also defining the major components of a comprehensive school counseling program. These include the traditional components of counseling (individual and small group), consultation, coordination, case management, guidance curriculum, program evaluation and development, and program delivery. Additionally, professional school counselors were being encouraged to shift from the delivery of a menu of student services to the development of a more structured and programmatic approach to school counseling to address the needs of all students (Gysbers & Henderson, 2000). This required a change from a position focus to a program focus and, more importantly, involved seeking to impact student achievement and school success through school counseling programs (Dahir, 2001).

The *National Standards* define the vision and goals for 21st century school counseling programs. To support this change in thinking, the nine standards shift the focus from the counselor to the school counseling program.

The standards:

1. Create a framework for a national model for school counseling programs;
2. Establish school counseling as an integral component of the academic mission of the school;
3. Encourage equitable access to school counseling services for all students;
4. Identify the key components of a developmental school counseling program;
5. Identify the attitudes, knowledge and skills that all students should acquire as a result of the K-12 school counseling program; and
6. Ensure that school counseling programs are comprehensive in design and delivered in a systematic fashion for all students (Dahir, Sheldon, & Valiga, 1998).

According to Campbell and Dahir (1997), the *National Standards for School Counseling Programs* facilitate student development in three broad content areas: (a) academic, (b) career, and (c) personal/social development. There are three standards for each content area which provide guidance and direction for individual schools to develop quality and effective school counseling programs. Each of the nine standards is associated with a specific list of student competencies that define the specific attitudes, knowledge, and skills that students should obtain or be able to demonstrate as a result of participating in a school counseling program.

The academic development standards serve as a guide for the professional school counselor to implement strategies and activities to maximize student learning.

The three standards for the academic domain are:

Standard A: Students will acquire the attitudes, knowledge, and skills that contribute to effective learning in school and across the life span.

Standard B: Students will complete school with the academic preparation essential to choose from a wide range of substantial post-secondary options, including college.

Standard C: Students will understand the relationship of academics to the world of work, and to life at home and in the community.

The career development standards serve as a guide for the professional school counselor to provide the foundation for acquiring the skills, attitudes, and knowledge that enable students to make a successful transition from school to the world of work.

The three standards for the career domain are:

Standard A: Students will acquire the skills to investigate the world of work in relation to knowledge of self and to make informed career decisions.

Standard B: Students will employ strategies to achieve future career success and satisfaction.

Standard C: Students will understand the relationship among personal qualities, education and training, and the world of work.

The personal/social standards serve as a guide for the professional school counselor to provide the foundation for personal and social growth that contributes to academic and career success.

The three standards for the personal/social domain are:

Standard A: Students will acquire the attitudes, knowledge, and interpersonal skills to help them understand and respect self and others.

Standard B: Students will make decisions, set goals, and take necessary action to achieve goals.

Standard C: Students will understand safety and survival skills.

According to Herr (2001), the *National Standards* are congruent with results-based approaches (Johnson & Johnson, 1982) to the organization and effects of school-based counseling programs. Today's professional school counselors are challenged to demonstrate the effectiveness of their programs and must collect data supporting and linking the school counseling program to students' academic success (Hatch & Bowers, 2002). Comprehensive, *National Standard*-focused school counseling programs are data-driven. The use of data to effect change within the school system is integral to this type of program, thereby ensuring that every student receives and benefits from the program. Professional school counselors should be able to demonstrate that each activity implemented as part of the school counseling program was developed from a careful analysis of student needs, achievement, and related data.

To create a data-driven school counseling program, professional school counselors must look at a variety of data from several perspectives (Bowers & Hatch, 2002). Types of data to be analyzed by professional school counselors are: achievement data, standards and competency-related data, disaggregated data, program evaluation data, process data, perception data, results data, and, data over time (Bowers & Hatch, 2002).

ASCA's standards and competencies have become the foundation for the ASCA *National Model: A Framework for School Counseling Programs* (Bowers & Hatch, 2002; ASCA, 2003). The model incorporates school counseling standards (ASCA's N*ational Standards*) for every student, focusing the direction for an organized, planned, sequential, school guidance curriculum. Additionally, the model emphasizes an organizational framework and accountability system to determine how well students have met the standards or have achieved intended outcomes.

## Recommended Action

In the process of developing the ASCA National Model, recommendations were developed for professional school counselors and those responsible for implementation of programs. These recommendations, presented in Table 1, are essential for implementation of school counseling programs and for reflection.

**Table 1. Recommendations for the Implementation of School Counseling Programs (Hatch & Bowers, 2002, pp.73-74).**

1. A distinction must be made among the school counseling standards for every student, school counseling standards for the program, and school counseling standards for the professional school counselor.
2. A school counseling program must provide a framework which allows flexibility for states and school districts to create a program based on a district's individual needs and accountability.
3. A school counseling program must be integral to student academic achievement, particularly in facilitating improvement in academic achievement, and must help set higher standards for student achievement.
4. A school counseling program must be data-driven (disaggregated) and result based and should not focus only on methods and techniques.
5. School counseling programs should be developed and implemented district wide, not just at individual schools.
6. Successful development and implementation of a school counseling program relies on school/community collaboration.
7. A school counseling program should provide intentional guidance to specifically address the needs of every student, particularly students of culturally diverse, low socio-economic status and other under served or under performing populations.
8. A school counseling program empowers professional school counselors and teaches them how to work with administrators to reassign non guidance activities, such as master scheduling or testing.
9. The design of a school counseling program model must include accountability tools for measuring results.
10. To facilitate the adoption of a school counseling program model by school districts, ASCA will identify and disseminate best practices for designing, developing, coordinating, implementing, evaluating, and enhancing the program.
11. A school counseling program must include plans for the effective use of counselor time within the delivery system.
12. A school counseling program should be preventative in design and developmental in nature.
13. Professional school counselors play leadership roles in defining and carrying out a school counseling program.
14. Licensed or credentialed professional school counselors must implement a school counseling program.
15. In a school counseling program, professional school counselors work as change agents within the educational system to advocate for student needs and student results.
16. Professional school counselors must use data to advocate for students and a school counseling program.
17. A school counseling program should demonstrate evidence of the utilization of technology to implement the program, to advocate for the program, and to collect, analyze, and interpret data.
18. In a school counseling program, school counselors strive for continued improvement and use results to continually improve the program for students.

## Summary/Conclusion

ASCA's *National Standards for School Counseling Programs* (Campbell & Dahir, 1997) and *The ASCA National Model: A Framework for School Counseling Programs* (Bowers & Hatch, 2002; ASCA, 2003) affect not only the profession of school counseling, but also the training of professional school counselors. Pre-service programs must re-evaluate the focus and content of their training process in order to train professional school counselors for the 21st century. The emphasis placed on counselor education programs to adhere to the CACREP accreditation standards has standardized and strengthened training programs. ASCA's *National Standards* and *National Model* will also strengthen school counseling pre-service programs in counselor education programs across the country.

## References

American School Counselor Association. (2003). *The ASCA national model: A framework for school counseling programs.* Alexandria, VA: Author.

Bowers, J., & Hatch, T. (2002). *The national model for school counseling programs.* Alexandria, VA: American School Counselor Association.

Campbell, C. A., & Dahir, C. A. (1997). *Sharing the vision: The national standards for school counseling programs.* Alexandria, VA: American School Counselor Association.

Dahir, C. A. (2001). The national standards for school counseling programs: Development and implementation. *Professional School Counseling, 4*, 320-327.

Dahir, C. A., Sheldon, C. B., & Valiga, M. J. (1998). *Vision into action: Implementing the national standards for school counseling programs.* Alexandria, VA: American School Counselor Association.

Gysbers, N. C., & Henderson, P. (2000). *Developing and managing your school guidance program* (3rd ed.). Alexandria, VA: American Counseling Association.

Hatch, T., & Bowers, J. (2002). The block to build on. *The ASCA School Counselor, 39*(5), 13-19.

Herr, E. L. (2001). The impact of national policies, economics, and school reform on comprehensive guidance programs. *Professional School Counseling, 4*, 236-245.

Johnson, C. D., & Johnson, S. K. (1982). Competency based training of career development specialists or "let's get off the calfpath." *Vocational Guidance Quarterly, 32,* 327-335.

Perusse, R., Goodnough, G. E., & Noel, C. J. (2001). Use of the National Standards for School Counseling Programs in Preparing School Counselors. *Professional School Counseling, 5,* 49-55.

Schmidt, J. J., & Ciechalski, J. C. (2001). School counseling standards: A summary and comparison with other student services' standards. *Professional School Counseling, 4,* 328-333.

# Chapter 26

## Why Implement a National Standards-Based School Counseling Program?

*Carol A. Dahir*

### Preview

Professional school counselors play a key role in preparing students to meet the complex societal demands that require significantly higher levels of knowledge and skills to succeed in the 21st century. Recent school improvement agendas directed the development of national standards across the academic content areas to improve educational practice and pedagogy, but largely ignored the contributions of school counseling. Counselors in schools face the enormous challenge of preparing students to meet the expectations of these higher academic standards and to become well-educated and contributing members of an ever-changing and complex society. The development of the *National Standards for School Counseling Programs* (Campbell & Dahir, 1997) positioned school counseling to play an increasingly important role in contemporary school improvement.

In this era of increased educational accountability with the spotlight on school improvement, professional school counselors must play a key role in preparing students to meet increasingly complex societal demands that require significantly higher levels of knowledge and skills to succeed in the 21st century. As potential powerful allies in school reform, professional school counselors can document and demonstrate their contribution to student growth and learning, thus contributing to the national goal of improving results for every student.

In order for this to happen, professional school counselors must embrace three important ideological changes to move this agenda forward. By taking a position on important educational issues, professional school counselors advocate for change and continuous improvement (Clark & Stone, 2000). First, it is essential to understand and apply the language of educational reform to school counseling. Current school initiatives have, at their heart and center, standards and competencies to guide student growth, learning and results. School counseling is no different, and the national standards for school counseling programs have established our ability to assess student progress in the areas of academic, career and personal-social development.

The second imperative for school counselors is to shift the focus from position to program with the expressed purpose of ultimately impacting systemic change. The role of the professional school counselor is no longer as important as is the impact of the school counseling program on student achievement and school success. The third imperative for change is the need for professional school counselors to embrace the word "every." No longer is it enough for *some* students to benefit from school counseling services. School counseling programs must benefit and be delivered to every student.

*But Why Change?*

Concerned about the absence of school counseling in *Goals 2000 (*US Department of Education, 1994) and the increasing importance of standards and assessment, the ASCA Governing Board committed to the development of national standards for school counseling programs in July, 1994. ASCA grappled with defining national standards as applied to contemporary school counseling programs. The *National Education Goals Panel* (1994) described program content standards as those that specify what students should know and be able to do. Thus the content standards would define what students should know and be able to do as a result of participating in a school counseling program (Campbell & Dahir, 1997).

ASCA leadership hoped that this effort would motivate the school counseling community to identify and implement goals for students that were deemed important by the profession, clarify the relationship of school counseling to the educational system, and address the contributions of school counseling to student success in school. With accountability driving school reform, there was a critical need to inform stakeholders of the relationship of school counseling programs to student learning and achievement.

As the standards development evolved, extensive field reviews solicited input from thousands of elementary, middle/junior, and high school counselors, supervisors of school counseling, and counselor educators. The input helped to solidify and clarify the balance that was needed to ensure that the standards reflected theory, research and, importantly, the perspective of the professional school counselor who would ultimately be working with students to document achievement of the standards. The result of these efforts are nine national standards, three in each area of academic, career and personal-social development, which are considered to be the essential foundation for the content of school counseling programs (Campbell & Dahir, 1997).

The *National Standards* offer professional school counselors, administrators, teachers, and counselor educators a common language to promote student success through school counseling programs, which is readily understood by colleagues in schools who are involved in school improvement and the implementation of standards across other disciplines. National standards-based school counseling programs have characteristics similar to other educational programs including a scope and sequence, student outcomes or competencies, activities and processes to assist students in achieving these outcomes, professionally credentialed personnel, materials and resources, and accountability methods.

## Making Connections

Over the years, school counseling programs have applied and integrated different paradigms and approaches. For example, developmental school counseling addresses the needs of students that are consistent with the expected stages of growth and learning. The comprehensive model provides a system for delivering and organizing the school counseling program, while the results-based approach offers a methodology for demonstrating outcomes and impact. The national standards complement these established approaches or paradigms and are not a substitute for a comprehensive, developmental and/or results-based program. Rather, the standards provide the content for the school counseling program. The *National Standards* define *what* students should know and be able to do as a result of participating in school counseling programs. A comprehensive, developmental, and results-based program provides direction for *what* and *how* services are delivered. The national standards and the student competencies are not "guidance curriculum" but part of the fabric of every aspect of the work of school counselors with students. These approaches independently and collectively complement each other.

*Comprehensive Model*

The comprehensive school counseling program is a framework for the systemic development, implementation, and evaluation of a school counseling program. The characteristics are similar to other programs in education such as: student outcomes or competencies, activities to achieve the desired outcomes, professional personnel, materials, resources and a delivery system. The process for delivery of the national standards is accomplished by utilizing each of the four components of the comprehensive model: individual student planning, responsive services, system support, and guidance curriculum. The comprehensive model identifies competencies for students and uses varying strategies to deliver the content of the program to every student (National Consortium for State Guidance Leadership, 2000). Most importantly, the comprehensive process links school counseling to the total educational process and involves all school personnel (Stanciak, 1995).

*Developmental Considerations*

Recognizing that all children do not develop in a linear fashion according to a certain timetable, the developmental progression of student growth throughout the pre-K through 12 experience is essential. Developmental school counseling:

> ...is for all students, has an organized and planned curriculum, is sequential and flexible, is an integrated part of the total educational process, involves all school personnel, helps students learn more effectively and efficiently, and includes counselors who provide specialized counseling services and interventions. (Myrick, 1997, p. 48)

Myrick's (1997) developmental approach emphasized programs for all students, the importance of using an integrated approach involving all school personnel in the delivery of "guidance activities," and a guidance curriculum that is sequential, age appropriate, planned and organized. Thus, the school counseling program must include age appropriate and sequential learning experiences to deliver the *National Standards* and competencies to every student.

*Results-Based Considerations*

"Results-based" guidance is also a competency-based approach. Developed by Johnson and Johnson in the 1980's, an emphasis is placed on a total pupil services approach and the student is the primary client (1991). This approach also emphasizes the importance of students acquiring competencies to become successful in school and in the transitions from school to postsecondary education and/or to employment. At the heart and center of the results-based approach is accountability to the student and to the building administrator. Management agreements between the principal and individual counselor are a means of measuring accomplishments.

The competencies delivered at the building and/or district level emphasize early intervention, prevention, and responsive services. The national standards and the competencies selected by the school or district guide the development of the program content for student growth and achievement in the academic, career, and personal-social domains and are an integral part of individual planning, guidance curriculum, responsive services, and system support (Gysbers & Henderson, 2000).

The school counseling program must be organized as an integral and essential part of the broader school mission (Gysbers & Henderson, 2000). The evolution of comprehensive and developmental school counseling and guidance clearly supports the imminent need for school counseling programs to be aligned with and tied to the mission of schools (Gysbers, 2001). School counseling programs promote educational excellence through individual excellence, provide preventative and interventive programs and experiences, create a collaborative model that integrates the expertise of professional school counselors, other pupil services personnel, business and community into the total program, and are current with the needs and expectations of the education agenda and societal issues (Dahir, 2001; Gysbers & Henderson, 2000; Myrick, 1997). Random acts of guidance are no longer acceptable in 21st century schools (Bilzing, 1996).

## Implementing the National Standards

How do we deliver nine standards and student competencies in addition to the numerous services and activities that constitute a school counseling program? We do this by focusing our efforts on student accomplishment of the competencies and standards and by connecting our efforts to student success and school improvement. We do this by engaging others in a school wide effort that supports affective education and student growth in academic, career and personal-social development. We do this by organizing our efforts around the very same delivery methods (individual student planning, responsive services, system support, guidance curriculum) used in the comprehensive, developmental and results-based models.

### *Individual Student Planning*

Students must take ownership and assume responsibility for their academic and affective learning and development. Individual planning provides opportunities for students to plan, monitor and evaluate their progress. Activities also include: goal setting, career planning, understanding, interpreting and applying assessment information in a meaningful way to academic planning. Individual planning is conducted with parental involvement, helps to personalize the educational experience, and helps students to set goals and develop a pathway to realize their dreams. Individual planning also helps to document achievement of specific competencies that will ultimately support every student's attainment of the *National Standards*.

### *Responsive Services*

The tradition of training, both pre-service and in-service for professional school counselors, predominantly focused on interventions for student problems. Counselor education graduate programs provided a strong foundation on mental health interventions and consequently, up until recently, many school personnel believed this was the primary focus and need for counselors in schools. However, responsive services are much broader than interventions needed for at-risk students. We must believe that all students are at risk at some time in their school career. Responsive services consist of individual and group counseling, consultation, referral to community agencies, and crisis intervention and management. The impetus for response and intervention is often dominated by presenting student issues, school building and faculty concerns, parental trepidations and community matters. Responsive services can address issues such as peer pressure, resolving conflict, family relationships, personal identity issues, substance abuse, motivation and achievement concerns. Responsive services can be delivered in a direct (individual and group counseling) or indirect manner (such as consultation or outside referral) and show the achievement of growth and development in academic, career, and personal-social development.

### *Guidance Curriculum*

Counselors developmentally and sequentially provide information, knowledge and skills through academic, career, and personal/social development. This is often delivered through large group meetings that offer the best opportunity to provide guidance to the largest number of students in a school. Counselors should first work with students in large groups whenever appropriate because it is the most efficient use of time. Professional school counselors and teachers in classrooms or advisory groups deliver the guidance and counseling curriculum to students through the use of organized activities. The activities and lessons give attention to particular developmental issues or areas of concern in the school building or district. Professional school counselors often partner with teachers and other members of the school community to deliver part of the guidance and counseling curriculum. The result lies in each student's achievement of specific competencies that will ultimately support attainment of the *National Standards.*

*System Support*

Oftentimes system support is misconstrued as "non-counseling" assignments in schools, such as hall monitoring, class coverage, or bus duty. System support is intended to provide on-going support to the school environment and to organize, deliver, manage, and evaluate the comprehensive school counseling program. Most of the services are considered indirect, that is they are not delivered directly to students. Coordination of services involves planning and connecting activities and services to the *National Standards* and the goals of the counseling program in the school. Hosting an advisory committee helps to inform the direction of the program and provides a sounding board for discussion about what is working, what needs to change, and how the comprehensive school counseling program can better support student success. System support also provides professional school counselors with multiple opportunities as leaders and advocates to facilitate discussions around school improvement, examine data that may be affecting success of some groups of students, and assisting with professional development and in-service activities for the faculty.

For effective service delivery the professional school counselor must possess the attitudes, knowledge and skills to provide both the direct and indirect components of the program. Each of the program components consist of both direct services, which usually target students and typically include individual counseling, small group counseling, and classroom guidance; and indirect services which include the management of resources, consultation, collaboration and teaming, advocacy, and the coordination of services. Indirect services are essential to effect systemic change and support the "new vision" of school counseling (Ripley, Erford, Dahir, & Eshbach, 2003). In all instances, student growth and development is monitored by the achievement of competencies, which ultimately result in the attainment of the nine national standards. And in doing so professional school counselors clearly connect their work to the purpose of school and contribute to student success and achievement.

## Collaborating for Systemic Change

Most professional school counselors agree that their skills, time, and energy should be focused on balancing direct and indirect services to students. School counseling programs and the primary methods of delivery are determined by the extent of the academic, career, and personal–social developmental needs of students. The counselor is in a key position to identify the issues that affect student learning and achievement by becoming involved at the core of school planning, developing programs, and affecting the school climate. This cannot be accomplished unilaterally. The professional school counselor implementing a national standards-based school counseling program uses a collaborative model as a springboard for success. Counselors do not work alone; all educators play a role in creating an environment which promotes the achievement of identified student goals and outcomes. The counselor facilitates communication and establishes linkages for the benefit of students, with teaching staff, administration, families, student service personnel, agencies, businesses, and other members of the community. Student success in school depends upon the cooperation and support of the entire faculty, staff, and student services personnel.

Combining specialized services and competencies helps students learn more effectively and efficiently, and provides opportunities for professional school counselors to assess the impact of these efforts (ASCA, 1994). School counselors coordinate the objectives, strategies, and activities of a comprehensive school counseling program to meet the academic, career, and personal-social needs of all students (ASCA, 1997). Once the school counseling program has an organization and structure like the other disciplines in school, it is no longer perceived as ancillary but as an integral component directly linked to student achievement and school success. When guidance and counseling is conceptualized, organized and implemented as a program, it places professional school counselors at the heart and center of education, making it possible for them to be active and involved (Gysbers, 2001).

Knowledge and skills that students acquire in the areas of academic, career and personal-social development must surpass what are perceived to be predominantly "counseling related" services. Program delivery consists of the many ways that professional school counselors provide services to students including individual and group counseling, large and small group guidance, consultation, management of resources, and through the coordination of services. The professional school counselor utilizes a variety of strategies, activities, delivery methods, and resources to facilitate student growth and development. In order to accomplish this, the professional school counselor must possess a solid knowledge of what he/she needs to know and be able to do to serve as a student advocate, provide direct and indirect services and ascribe to the belief that all children can learn and achieve through one's actions.

## The Motivation and Momentum for Moving Forward

There is consensus among school counseling professionals that the widespread use of the national standards offers consistency in the description of school counseling programs, the content of the program, and how the comprehensive program is delivered. More than 35 state departments of education or state school counselor associations have promoted the implementation of comprehensive school counseling program models (Sink & MacDonald, 1998) and all of the newly revised or designed state models have incorporated the *National Standards* as the content for school counseling state models (Dahir, 1998). Most importantly, collaborative efforts between state departments of education and school counselor associations have increased with additional state models in the development stage that will affect the way programs are designed and delivered across our nation.

Counselor education programs across the nation are using the national standards and the supporting publications as part of their curriculum. The results of a national survey (Pérusse, Goodnough, & Noel, 2000) reported that approximately 69% of counselor education programs were using the *National Standards for School Counseling Programs* to some degree within the curriculum to train the next generation of professional school counselors.

## Renewal and Reform for School Counseling

The national standards movement presented the opportunity to establish the role of school counseling programs in the American educational system. The *National Standards for School Counseling Programs* helped to eliminate the confusion among the public in understanding what school counseling programs accomplish and how school counseling programs benefit students. The most recent school improvement agenda, the *No Child Left Behind Act of 2002* (H.R.1)(U.S. Department of Education, 2001), which intends to close the achievement gap between disadvantaged students and other groups of students, presents yet another opportunity for professional school counselors and school counseling programs to vocalize strategies and create meaningful conversations among school counselors, school administrators, teachers, parents, and representatives of business and community about expectations for students' academic success and the role of counseling programs in supporting and enhancing student learning (Dahir, Sheldon & Valiga, 1998).

National standards-based comprehensive school counseling programs, linked directly to the mission of the school, promote and enhance the learning process (Campbell & Dahir, 1997). The emphasis is on making the school counseling program an integral part of the total school program (Clark & Stone, 2000). Professional school counselors can no longer rely on their reputations and good intentions as dedicated helpers; they must be accountable for their efforts (Johnson, 2000). As part of an educational team, professional school counselors must accept the challenge of preparing students to meet the expectations of higher academic standards and to become productive and contributing members of society. Counselors have been asked to demonstrate positive school outcomes that support the mission of the school (Paisley & McMahon, 2001). Increased accountability practices can meaningfully change the substance and perception of school counseling in the context of today's reform agenda (Johnson, 2000).

## Summary/Conclusion

ASCA has advocated that professional school counselors establish their identity and clearly articulate and define the role that school counseling programs play in promoting student achievement and educational success. Professional school counselors are challenged to demonstrate accountability, document effectiveness, and promote school counseling's contributions to the educational agenda. School counseling programs defined by statements of what students should know and be able to do are seen as accountable, viable, and visible in the eyes of school stakeholders. Comprehensive, developmental, results-based, national standards-based school counseling programs establish our presence and define our future.

## References

American School Counselor Association. (1994). *The school counselor's role in educational reform.* Alexandria, VA: Author.

American School Counselor Association. (1997). *Definition of school counseling.* Alexandria, VA: Author.

American School Counselor Association. (2003). *The ASCA national model: A framework for school counseling programs.* Alexandria, VA: Author.

Bilzing, D. (1996). *School counseling updates.* Paper presented at the meeting of State Department Consultants for Guidance and Counseling, American School Counselor Association, Dallas, TX.

Campbell, C., & Dahir, C. (1997). *Sharing the vision: The national standards for school counseling programs.* Alexandria, VA: American School Counselor Association.

Clark, M., & Stone, C. (2000). The developmental school counselor as educational leader. In J. Wittmer (Ed.), *Managing your school counseling program: K-12 developmental strategies* (2nd ed., pp. 75-81). Minneapolis, MN: Educational Media.

Dahir, C. (1998). Fast facts - The national standards for school counseling programs. *The ASCA Counselor, 36,* 15-16.

Dahir, C. (2001). The national standards for school counseling programs: Development and implementation. *Professional School Counseling, 4,* 320-327.

Dahir, C., Sheldon, C., & Valiga, M. (1998). *Vision into action: Implementing the national standards for school counseling programs.* Alexandria, VA: American School Counselor Association.

Gysbers, N. C. (2001). School guidance and counseling in the 21st century: Remember the past into the future. *Professional School Counseling, 5,* 9-105.

Gysbers, N. C., & Henderson, P. (2000). *Developing and managing your school guidance program* (3rd ed.). Alexandria, VA: American Counseling Association.

Johnson, L. S. (2000). Promoting professional identity in an era of educational reform. *Professional School Counseling, 4,* 31-40.

Johnson, C. D., & Johnson, S. K. (1991). The new guidance: A system approach to pupil personnel programs. *CACD Journal, 11,* 5-14.

Myrick, R. D. (1997). *Developmental guidance and counseling: A practical approach* (3rd edition). Minneapolis, MN: Educational Media Corporation.

National Consortium for State Guidance Leadership. (2000). *A national framework for state programs in guidance and counseling.* Columbus, OH: Author

National Education Goals Panel. (1994). *Building a nation of learners.* Washington, DC: Author.

Pérusse, R., Goodnough, A., & Noel, C. (2001). Use of the national standards for school counseling programs in preparing school counselors. *Professional School Counseling, 5,* 49-55.

Paisley, P. O., & McMahon, J. (2001). School counseling for the 21st century: Challenges and opportunities. *Professional School Counseling, 5,* 106-115.

Ripley, V., Erford, B., Dahir, C., & Eshbach, L. (2003). Planning and implementing a 21st century comprehensive, developmental professional school counseling program. In B. T. Erford, *Transforming the school counseling profession.* Columbus, OH: Merrill/Prentice-Hall.

Sink, C., & MacDonald, G. (1998). The status of comprehensive guidance and counseling in the United States. *Professional School Counseling, 2,* 88-94.

Stanciak, L. (1995). Reforming the high school counselor's role: A look at developmental guidance. *NASSP Journal, 79,* 60-68.

U.S. Department of Education. (1994). *Goals 2000: The Educate America Act.* Washington, DC: Author.

U.S. Department of Education. (2001) *No Child Left Behind Act of 2001 (H.R.1).* Washington, DC: Author.

# Chapter 27

## The ASCA National Model: A Framework for School Counseling Programs, One Vision, One Voice for the Profession

*Trish Hatch*

### Preview

This chapter shares the story of the history behind the need for "One Vision, One Voice" within the profession of school counseling and introduces *The ASCA National Model: A Framework for School Counseling Programs* (ASCA, 2003). The co-author of the document reviews the development of the model, the original criteria agreed upon by summit members, its first public draft release, the final release, and the impact of the document thus far. The article contains a summary version of each component within the model and offers suggestions for the profession's next steps.

The American School Counselor Association (ASCA) created *The ASCA National Model: A Framework for School Counseling Programs* (ASCA, 2003) to connect school counseling with current educational reform movements that emphasize student achievement and success. The ASCA *National Model* provides an organizational framework designed to assist school counselors to develop or redesign their programs to meet current educational needs of students. By utilizing the model to align the school counseling program with the school's mission and school improvement plans, professional school counselors partner as leaders in systemic change, ensure equity and access to a rigorous education, and promote academic, career and personal/ social development for *every* student.

As we head further into the 21st century, school counselors continue to define new directions for the profession. Historically, school counselors have lacked legitimization, have been professionally marginalized, and in many states remain expendable by definition, as there is no education code that requires their services or programs within schools. ASCA's release of *The ASCA National Model: A Framework for School Counseling Programs* (ASCA, 2003) is intended to provide "*One Vision, One Voice*" for the profession, in hopes of addressing this professional need. But before looking to the school counseling profession's future, it's crucial to understand its past.

*Our Past*

At the turn of the 20th century, school counselors didn't exist. Instead, teachers used a few minutes of their time to offer vocational guidance to students preparing for work in a democratic society. The school mission now is not altogether different than in the 1900's. Today, in a world enriched by diversity and technology, school counselors' chief mission is still supporting the academic achievement of all students so they are prepared for life beyond school. However, professional school counselors no longer work in isolation; instead, they align with other educational professionals, integral to the total educational program for student success. This evolution from minutes a day to trained professionals implementing a comprehensive school counseling program did not take place without professional scholars and counselors having the vision, knowledge, and determination to move forward (Gysbers, 2001).

School counselors began as vocational counselors nearly 100 years ago, and the profession has evolved to incorporate the domains of academic, career, and personal/social development (Miller, 1961; Campbell & Dahir, 1997). During this evolution, differing philosophical perspectives developed between and among academic counselors, career counselors, and personal/social or mental health counselors regarding their role and function, purpose, and focus. Lacking clear role definition as a profession, school counseling became a "house divided by controversy" between those who focused on vocational guidance (which later became educational guidance) and those who attended to the personal-social foundational needs of students in education (Aubrey, 1991).

While procedures were similar in counseling, methods varied. Counseling could be either directive or non-directive – two somewhat opposing methods of delivery. In directive counseling, the focus on intellectual interpretation was counselor-directed, while non-directive counseling was client-centered and focused on the release of feelings and the achievement of insight. One approach delivered by the counselor – the other discovered by the student. Most vocational counselors were directive, while social workers, mental hygienists, and child-guidance clinicians were more non-directive (Warters, 1946). In the 1960's the directive approach to counseling was encouraged by the *National Defense Education Act*, in which school counselors identified the "best and the brightest" to herd into math and science majors in college in an effort to win the space race. Meanwhile, Carl Rogers was training counselors in a non-directive, more passive approach.

Counselors trained in programs rooted in psychological and clinical paradigms differed greatly from those rooted in educational paradigms. Post-secondary training programs contained conflicting and varied theoretical perspectives both between and within their programs. Consequently, school counselors' training and perspectives regarding their role and function varied substantially. Not unlike today, professionals within school counseling debated whether counselors are mental health workers within schools or educators with a mental health perspective.

The counseling and guidance movement was also characterized by a proliferation of competing methodologies which focused more attention on the technique of counselors and the process of counseling and less on the content and objectives of the program. This alteration in counseling methodology led to changes in the substance and the priority which guidance programs were given (Aubrey, 1991). "The focus was on a position (counselor) and a process (counseling), not on a program (guidance)" (Gysbers, & Henderson, 1997, p. 1). Consequently, guidance became an ancillary support service and not a program integral to the total educational program of student success. The result was that counselors were (and in some cases still are) more likely to be saddled with administrative tasks and clerical duties (Roeber, Walz & Smith, 1968).

In the 1970's and 1980's, several attempts were made to unify the profession. Emerging from this movement were several theoretical models of comprehensive programs, many of which were based on the expansion of the career guidance model. Norman Gysbers and Patricia Henderson wrote text books and developed and trained districts and states in comprehensive guidance programs models (1997, 1998), C. D. "Curly" and Sharon Johnson (1991) focused their counselor training on designing results-based school counseling programs, and Robert Myrick (2003) wrote his textbook on planned developmental guidance programs. In addition, the ERIC Clearinghouse on Counseling and Student Services published several books and conducted four national conferences that offered training in the development and implementation of comprehensive school guidance programs. Despite the tremendous impact of these forward thinkers, the legitimization of the school counseling program within schools remained quite tenuous.

For decades, the school counseling profession attempted to respond to the question, "*What do counselors do?*" However, that question only served to confuse those within and outside the profession depending on which model one was trained in or loyal to. In addition to listing a myriad of counseling-related duties (e.g., guidance lessons, group counseling, academic planning, individual counseling, consultation, collaboration, etc.), professional school counselors complained about "doing" a variety of quasi-administrative and non-counseling duties. Just as pre-service training varied for school counselors, so too did administrative expectations for school counselors based on administrative pre-service training (or lack of it) with regard to school counseling programs (Olson, 1979).

These changes and varying models confused professional school counselors as well as school administrators, teachers, and parents. "When schools fail to clearly define the counselor's role...School administrators, parents with special interests, teachers or others may feel their agenda ought to be the school counseling program's priority. The results often lead to confusion and criticisms when they are disappointed" (Cunnan & Maddy-Berstein, 1998).

*More Recent Challenges*

In 1992, Phyllis Hart and Marilyn Jacobi wrote *From Gatekeeper to Advocate: Transforming the Role of the School Counselor.* One of the chapters in the book discussed the six problems in school counseling programs. They are summarized here:

1. *Lack of basic philosophy:* Few counselors are guided by a well developed philosophy or belief system, one that indeed drives the entire program and the behaviors of the school counselors within the program. Rather, they tend to work independently and are often reactive.
2. *Poor integration:* School counseling remains ancillary rather than a core component of K-12 education. School counselors must connect with other stakeholders in the school system as an integral partner in the total educational program.
3. *Insufficient student access:* Student-to-counselor ratios are high. Many students don't have the opportunity to see their school counselors. High ratios are only part of the problem. Another problem is some counselors still insist on focusing more on individual counseling rather than ensuring every student receives school counseling services through a school wide guidance curriculum.
4. *Inadequate guidance for some students:* Poor students and students of color are often denied the opportunity to enroll in rigorous academic coursework at the same level as is often afforded other students.
5. *Lack of counselor accountability:* A common understanding does not exist as to what constitutes accountability and in what way counselors are to be held accountable for the results of their program.
6. *Failure to utilize other resources:* School counselors cannot deliver the entire counseling program. Rather, school counselors are encouraged to better utilize school and community resources to create networks, referrals, and meet a variety of needs of students.

*More Recent Trends*

Recent trends in education include the reform and accountability movement, standards-based education, high-stakes testing, achievement gap issues of equity and access, an increase in legislation supporting student retention, the funding of new programs through block grants, the use of technology and data to drive decisions and effect change, school safety issues, and the movement from an educational culture of entitlement to one of performance. No longer can educators focus on how hard they work or how well meaning they are – rather they must answer their stakeholders' questions: *How are students different as a result of your program?*

Current trends in the school counseling field have included the development of the American School Counselor Association's (ASCA) *National Standards* which contain the student content standards used to design competencies for students in the areas of academic, career and personal/social development (Campbell & Dahir, 1997). In 1997, ASCA published *Sharing the Vision: The National Standards for School Counseling Programs* (Campbell & Dahir, 1997) as a conscious effort to participate in the national reform agenda through the development of national standards. This landmark document for the profession, endorsed by national educational and professional organizations, contains student standards for school counseling programs in the areas of academic, career and personal/social development.

*Vision Into Action: Implementing the National Standards for School Counseling Programs* (Dahir, Sheldon & Valiga, 1998) provides professional school counselors tools for selecting student competencies and suggestions for infusing the competencies into the school counseling program. ASCA's *National Standards* have been widely used in designing standards for students in school counseling programs. Other trends include the *Transforming School Counseling Initiative* (Martin & House, 1998; The Education Trust, 2002), which redefines the role of professional school counselors as integral to ensuring equity and access to a rigorous education for every student, particularly students of color and poverty. In addition, state departments, school districts and professional school counselors have developed state and local models; and an increase in legislative activity promoting school counseling for students has emerged. Nonetheless, questions remained unanswered by many school counselors nationwide:

- What is the purpose of your school counseling program?
- What are your desired outcomes?
- What is being done to achieve these results?
- What evidence is there that the objectives have been met?
- Is your program making a difference?

*One Vision, One Voice*

To address these professional concerns, ASCA's Governing Board, at its March 2001 meeting, agreed to develop a national program model. The standards provided content for the foundation of a program; however board members agreed that the next logical step would be the development of a framework to maximize the full potential of the standards documents. This new document would reflect current education reform movements, including the *No Child Left Behind* legislation, which mandates all federally funded programs be accountable for and directly connected to student learning and student improvement. Further, the decision to hold a National Summit to create an ASCA *National Model* was made by ASCA to bring the leaders in the field together and create *One Vision, One Voice* for all professional school counselors. ASCA moved forward to develop the model to address the historical concerns and current challenges and to assist the practicing school counselor in planning for the future of their programs and the profession through one common lens.

*Model Development*

From the first stages of development, ASCA called upon the expertise of national leaders and practicing school counselors. The first *ASCA Summit for School Counseling* was held June 1-3, 2001, in Tucson, Arizona. The purpose of the Summit was to discuss the future of school counseling programs and to develop a framework for a national model for school counseling programs. Participants of the Summit were:

**Dr. Judy Bowers**, ASCA Supervisor/Postsecondary Vice President and Guidance Coordinator, Tucson Unified School District, Arizona
**Dr. Trish Hatch**, ASCA Supervisor/Postsecondary Vice President Elect and Coordinator of Student Services, Moreno Valley School District, California
**Pam Gabbard**, ASCA President Elect and counselor at Ballard County Elementary, Barlow, Kentucky
**Dr. Norm Gysbers**, counselor educator, University of Missouri, Columbia
**Dr. Peggy Hines**, counselor educator, Indiana University, Bloomington
**Dr. Curly (C.D.) Johnson**, consultant, San Juan Capistrano, California
**Dawn Kay**, Utah State Department of Education
**Mark Kuranz**, ASCA President and counselor at Case High School, Racine Wis.
**Dr. Stan Maliszewski**, counselor educator, University of Arizona, Tucson
**Pat Martin**, program director, Education Trust (currently with College Board)
**Susan Mellegard**, counselor educator, Arizona State Department, Phoenix
**Dr. Robert Myrick**, counselor educator,University of Florida, Gainesville
**Dr. Pat Schwallie-Giddis**, counselor educator, George Washington University, Washington, DC
**Richard Wong**, ASCA Executive Director, Alexandria, VA.
(Also invited but unable to attend were: Carol Dahir and Carolyn Sheldon)

*Criteria for the Development of the Model*

For two and a half days, Summit participants brainstormed, collaborated and finally achieved consensus on how the model would be structured. Summit participants agreed to develop a model that would consist of three levels of program implementation: foundation, delivery and management, and accountability. There would be four to five components in each of the three levels. The ASCA *National Standards* would be the foundation upon which the building blocks of the program curriculum would be built.

As a basis for a *National Model*, participants incorporated theories and concepts from programs designed by Dr. Norman Gysbers, Dr. C. D. "Curly" Johnson, Dr. Robert Myrick, The Education Trust, and the ASCA *National Standards*. The document would be written by Trish Hatch and Judy Bowers and incorporate samples of their work with professional school counselors in the Moreno Valley Unified School District in California, and the Tucson Unified School District in Arizona, respectively. State and school counselor association documents of comprehensive programs would also be reviewed and utilized in the development of the document.

In developing the *National Model*, participants agreed on the following assumptions and criteria:

- ASCA's *National Standards* are a framework/foundation for the development of a school counseling program. (Many states also have standards, which align with the ASCA standards.)
- A distinction must be made among the school counseling standards for every student, school counseling standards for the program, and school counseling standards for the professional school counselor.
- A school counseling program must provide a framework that allows flexibility for states and school districts to create a program based on the districts' individual needs and accountability.
- A school counseling program must be integral to student academic achievement, particularly in facilitating improvement in academic achievement, and must help set higher standards for student achievement.
- A school counseling program must be data-driven (disaggregated) and result-based,

and should not focus only on methods and techniques.
- School counseling programs should be developed and implemented district-wide, not just at individual schools.
- Successful development and implementation of a school counseling program relies on school/community collaboration.
- A school counseling program should provide intentional guidance to specifically address the needs of every student, particularly students of culturally diverse, low social-economic status and other underserved or under-performing populations.
- A school counseling program empowers professional school counselors and teaches them how to work with administrators to re-assign non-guidance activities such as master scheduling or testing.
- The design of a school counseling program model must include accountability tools for measuring results.
- To facilitate the adoption of a school counseling program model by school districts, ASCA will identify and disseminate best practices for designing, developing coordinating, implementing, evaluating and enhancing the program.
- A school counseling program must include plans for the effective use of counselor time within the delivery system.
- A school counseling program should be preventive in design and developmental in nature.
- Professional school counselors play leadership roles in defining and carrying out a school counseling program.
- Licensed or credentialed professional school counselors must implement a school counseling program.
- In a school counseling program, professional school counselors work as change agents within the educational system to advocate for student needs and student results.
- Professional school counselors must use data to advocate for students and a school counseling program.
- A school counseling program should demonstrate evidence of the utilization of technology to implement the program, to advocate for the program and to collect, analyze and interpret data.
- In a school counseling program, professional school counselors strive for continued improvement and use results to continually improve the program for students.

A preliminary graphic that included the content of the four major components of the model (foundation, delivery system, management system and accountability system) was developed and approved by the Summit participants. The themes of advocacy, leadership, collaboration and systemic change were woven throughout the model.

*Writing the Model*

Throughout the next many months, Judy Bowers and Trish Hatch set about the task of writing the first draft. They researched dozens of state department and state association school counseling documents. Reading, sorting and sifting through thousands of pages was a daunting task and responsibility. Each document was dissected in light of its possible contribution to the overall agreed-upon framework. The responsibility to effectively represent the requirements of the Summit group and to address each component was taken very seriously. Working with ASCA's graphic artist, several versions of the graphic were reviewed until the final version was agreed upon.

In November 2001, the first rough draft was reviewed by Summit I members and test-driven by professional school counselors in Tucson, Arizona, and at the Moreno Valley School Counselors Academy in California. Counselors and administrators were trained in the model and reviewed the manuscript, providing valuable feedback. The authors made revisions and submitted a new draft in May, 2002, at Summit II, which was held in Washington, DC. Following final revisions, the final draft was released nation-wide to professional school counselors.

*Public Release of the First Draft*

The first public draft version model was unveiled during ASCA's national school counselor conference in Miami in June, 2002. Keynote conference speakers, leaders in the school counseling field who attended the initial model development summit meeting, included: Norman Gysbers; Clarence "Curly" Johnson and Robert Myrick. Several conference sessions were devoted to providing an overview of the model. An intensive, three-hour workshop conducted by Judy Bowers and Trish Hatch (the draft authors) drew over 200 participants. The focus of the workshop was on how counselors could implement the model in their own districts.

ASCA provided an online version of the model and solicited national public comment for the four-month period following the conference. Excitingly, the document received overwhelmingly positive responses. Professional school counselors and counselor educators nationwide provided praise and helpful and constructive criticism and made suggestions for improvement. The authors analyzed the feedback and provided a revised version to the Summit III participants in November, 2002. After a final Christmas vacation re-write, the authors submitted their gift* (a final version) to ASCA for a rushed printing to coincide with National School Counselors Week, 2003.

*The ASCA National Model*

*The ASCA National Model: A Framework for School Counseling Programs* (ASCA, 2003) is written to reflect a comprehensive approach to program foundation, delivery, management, and accountability. It provides a framework for the program components, the professional school counselor's role in implementation, and the underlying philosophies of leadership, advocacy, and systemic change. The model provides the mechanism with which professional school counselors and school counseling teams will design, coordinate, implement, manage and evaluate their programs for students' success.

With the *National Model*, professional school counselors switch their emphasis from service-centered for some of the students to program-centered for every student. The model not only answers the question: "What do professional school counselors do?" but further, it requires us to respond to the question, "How are students *different* as a result of what we do?" School counseling programs based on the *National Model* are designed to ensure that *every* student receives the benefits of the program. Historically, many professional school counselors spent 80 percent of their time responding to the needs of 20 percent of their students, typically the high achieving or high risk. The ASCA *National Model* recommends 80 percent of the professional school counselor's time be spent in direct service to all students so that *every* student receives the program benefits.

The ASCA *National Model* incorporates school counseling content standards and competencies for every student, which serve as the foundation for the program and focus the direction for an organized, planned, sequential and flexible school counseling curriculum. The model uses disaggregated data to drive program and activity development, thus enabling professional school counselors to design interventions to meet the needs of all students and to close the gap between specific groups of students and their peers. The model emphasizes an organizational framework and accountability system to determine how well students have met the standards or have achieved intended outcomes. The school counseling program reduces confusion, aligns goals and objectives with the school's mission, and ultimately leads to student achievement as demonstrated by results data.

The ASCA *National Model* serves as a template for the development of a school counseling program; it is not meant for exact replication. Because attention to local demographic needs and political conditions is necessary for effective school counseling program development, the ASCA *National Model* is meant to integrate with and adapt to the school's current program. There is no one "ideal program" that can or should be used as a cookie cutter approach throughout the nation. Rather, ASCA's goal is to provide professional school counselors with a document that will institutionalize the framework of a comprehensive school counseling program.

Leadership skills are critical to the successful implementation of new or remodeled programs at the school, district, and state levels. Professional school counselors are change agents, collaborators, and advocates. As professional school counselors become proficient in retrieving and analyzing school data to improve student success, they ensure educational equity for every student. Using strong communication, consultation and political skills, professional school counselors collaborate with other professionals in the school building to influence systemic change and advocate for every student.

Learning from the past is critical in developing a new school counseling program. The ASCA *National Model* provides a program audit which, when completed by the school counseling team, assists them in analyzing their current program so that areas of improvement can be identified. Looking at recent and current achievement and achievement-related data in the school will illuminate performance trends. This analysis is imperative as professional school counselors can use this data to recognize if program changes are needed – and they must be prepared to make needed changes no matter how comfortable the *status quo* or how difficult or uncomfortable the change may be.

---

**Elements of the ASCA National Model for School Counseling Programs**
(Advocacy, Leadership and Systemic Change are integrated throughout the model.)

*Foundation*

*Beliefs and Philosophy* – The philosophy is a set of principles (usually a set of "we agree" statements) that guide the development, implementation, and evaluation of the program. Ideally, all stakeholders involved in managing and implementing the program will reach consensus on each belief or guiding principle contained in the philosophy.

*Mission* – A mission statement describes the purpose of the program and provides the vision of what is desired for every student. Ideally, the school counseling program mission statement aligns with and is a subset of the school and district's mission.

*ASCA National Standards/Competencies* – The ASCA *National Standards* and student competencies are the foundation for the school counseling program. Student competencies define the content for knowledge, attitudes, or skills students should obtain or demonstrate as a result of participating in a school counseling program. They are developed and organized into content areas: academic, career, and personal/social development.

*Delivery System*

*Guidance Curriculum* – The guidance curriculum component consists of structured developmental lessons designed to assist students in achieving the competencies. Guidance curriculum is standards-driven and is provided systematically through classroom and group activities K-12. The purpose of the guidance curriculum is to provide every student the knowledge and skills appropriate for their developmental level.

*Individual Planning With Students* – The individual planning component consists of professional school counselors coordinating ongoing systemic activities designed to assist the individual student in establishing personal goals and developing future plans.

*Responsive Services* – The responsive services component consists of activities designed to meet the immediate need of students. Professional school counselors respond by providing counseling, consultation, referral, peer mediation or information.

*Systems Support* – The systems support component consists of the administration and management activities that establish, maintain and enhance the total guidance program.

*Management System*

*Management Agreements* – Professional school counselor/administrator agreements ensure effective implementation of the delivery system to meet students' needs. These agreements, which address how the school counseling program is organized and what will be accomplished, should be negotiated with and approved by designated administrators at the beginning of each school year.

*Advisory Council* – An advisory council is a group of people appointed to review guidance program results and to make recommendations. The group representatives are students, parents, teachers, counselors, administration, and community members.

*Use of Data* – The use of data to effect change within the school system is integral to ensuring that every student receive the benefits of the school counseling program. Professional school counselors use process, perception, and results data to determine areas of need, analyze the effects of their program, and for program improvement.

*Student Monitoring* - Monitoring students' progress ensures each student receives what he or she needs to achieve success in school by monitoring student achievement data, achievement-related data, and standards and competency-related data. Collection, analysis, and interpretation of student achievement data may be systemic by district, or specific to school site, grade, class or individual.

*Closing the Gap* - Closing the Gap (intentional guidance) activities are data-driven. Student needs surface when disaggregated data are analyzed to address attendance, behavior, and achievement gaps. Discrepancies between the desired results and the results currently being achieved are defined as the "Gap." These may be addressed by counseling with students or by working within educational systems to create equitable policies and procedures for all students.

*Action Plans* – There are two types of Action Plans: Guidance Curriculum and Closing the Gap. Guidance curriculum Action Plans are standards-driven and include a scope and sequence for the content of guidance instruction *every* student receives. Closing the Gap (intentional guidance ) Action Plans are data-driven and designed to address the specific data-driven needs of underperforming students in the areas of attendance, behavior, or achievement. (An example of each is included at the end of this chapter).

- Guidance Curriculum Action Plans include the following components: 1) the domain, standard, and competency addressed; 2) a the description of actual activity; 3) curriculum or materials to be used; 4) the time in which the activity is to be completed; 5) the person(s) responsible for the delivery; 6) the means of evaluating student success (i.e., process, perception, and results data); 7) the expected result for student(s); and 8) the implications.
- Closing The Gap (intentional guidance) Action Plans include all of the above, but also provide the specific data which drive the decision to address the attendance, behavior, or achievement gap.

*Use of Time* – ASCA's *National Model* recommends that professional school counselors spend 80 percent of their time in direct service (contact) with students and provides a guide to professional school counselors and administrators for determining the amount of time their program may devote to each of the four components of the delivery system. Resources are limited; therefore, professional school counselors' time must be protected. Professional school counselors' duties must be limited to program delivery and direct counseling services. Non-school counseling activities should be reassigned whenever possible.

*Use of Calendars* – Once professional school counselors determine the amount of time necessary in each area of the delivery system, publishing a master and weekly calendars will assist in keeping students, parents, teachers, and administrators informed. Calendars assist in planning the program and ensuring the implementation of a standards-based guidance curriculum.

*Accountability*

*Results Reports*– Results reports (which include process, perception and results data) ensure that programs are carried out, analyzed for effectiveness, and modified and improved as needed. Sharing these reports with stakeholders serves as an advocacy for the students and the program. Immediate, intermediate, and long-range results are collected and analyzed for program improvement.

*School Counselor Performance Evaluation* – The professional school counselor's performance evaluation contains basic standards of practice expected of school counselors implementing a school counseling program. These performance standards serve as both a basis for counselor evaluation and as a means for counselor self-evaluation.

*Program Audit/Evaluation* – The program audit provides evidence of the program's alignment with the ASCA *National Model.* Completing the program's audit provides initial direction for program development, provides direction for program improvement, and, when completed annually, assesses the program's progress towards full implementation of the ASCA *National Model.*

*Impelementation*

As the school counseling department moves forward with implementation, it will be important to keep administrators engaged early in the process, as they will be partners in program design and development. School boards, staff, and stakeholders must all be informed and involved in the exciting process of the program's transformation and improvement. The school counseling program belongs to the entire school, and as such, it is everyone's responsibility to ensure each student receives the benefit of a school counseling program that is standards-based and aligned, data driven, measures results, and shares successes.

*What's Next?*

The ASCA *National Model* is already becoming the standard of training in counselor education programs on a national level. In less than a year, more than 15,000 copies of the ASCA *National Model* have been sold. Professional school counselors and school districts throughout the nation are already aligning or transforming their programs. Dozens of proposals for the annual ASCA national conference include references to the impact of the ASCA *National Model* on school counseling programs. ASCA also honors schools or districts that meet certain criteria for transforming or aligning their programs and proclaiming them a RAMP (Recognized ASCA Model Program) school or district. ** In addition, the National Board for Professional Teaching Standards (NBPTS) incorporated the concepts of the model into their standards for the new NBPTS school counseling certification.

*Possible Changes?*

To date, the authors have received very few suggestions for changes or improvements to the ASCA *National Model.* Rather, we have been truly overwhelmed by the appreciation counselors and administrators have shown us for our work (and we are very grateful). However, there is always room for improvement and additional clarification. When providing training on the model, I find that counselors appreciate in-depth discussions of the types of data counselors can collect and how they might use this data to determine not only which services to offer, but to measure the results of their program and to provide suggestions for program improvement. After carefully reviewing the differences between process, perception, and results data, counselors are strongly encouraged to start slowly, select carefully what they will measure, and measure only *one thing* first. Counselors are reminded: "You can't measure everything; you'll lose your mind; and we can't have that because we need you!"

Undoubtedly, more support will be needed in this area, and projects are in the works to more clearly demonstrate how counselors can use data to effect not only program, but systems change. In January, 2004, ASCA devoted its entire *School Counselor* magazine to the "Use of Data" issue. One article, "To 'D or not to D', that is the Question" tells the story of professional school counselors who use data to effect a systems change to promote equity and access to a rigorous education (Hatch, Holland & Meyers, 2004). They successfully challenged a curriculum guide with gate-keeping prerequisites for higher-level math courses.

For some, more clarification is need between the two types of action plans: guidance curriculum and closing the gap. It helps to remember that the Action Plan for Guidance Curriculum is standards driven and is designed for every student. The Action Plan for Closing the Gap is data-driven for those students who are identified (when querying the data) as needing more.

More clarification may also be needed to help professional school counselors better understand the relationship between the ASCA *National Model* and the Education Trust's Met Life, *Transforming School Counseling Initiative****. The concepts of advocacy, leadership, systemic change, and collaboration are infused throughout both. However, some confusion remains among professional school counselors with regard to which training to receive: ASCA *National Model* or Met Life *Initiative*. A quick response would be that the ASCA *National Model* is the actual functional organizational system for the school counseling program in place at each site, and Met Life training provides the skills necessary to implement this system in support of every student. They are, therefore, interdependent, intertwined, and interrelated. Professional school counselors who believe strongly in equity, access, and social justice issues are able to utilize the structure of the ASCA *National Model* along with the skills gained in the Met Life training to become leaders and advocates for systems change that benefits every student.

*Final Thoughts*

Writing *The ASCA National Model: A Framework for School Counseling Programs* (ASCA, 2003) has been the highlight of my professional career (so far). The opportunity to collaborate with those involved and to be entrusted (along with Judy) with the challenge to synthesize their work with ours into a single document was an amazing gift. I have learned much and grown incredibly both personally and professionally during this most humbling experience and now move forward to continue working with passionate advocates in the field to promote and preserve the profession of school counseling for the benefit of every student.

The future of school counseling is tenuous. After a hundred years of marginalization and efforts to operationally legitimize a profession – only time will tell if the ASCA *National Model* will move the profession closer to accomplishing this vital and daunting task. While that certainly is my hope, I am well aware that it will take much more than one document. Research supporting the efficacy of model school counseling programs is vital. A recent *National Summit on School*

*Counseling Research* was held to begin these conversations. In addition, the *National Panel for Evidenced-Based School Counseling Practices* is working to design the parameters for research in the field of school counseling by reviewing the research base, determining which practices are evidence-based, and identifying areas where additional research is needed. The goal is to improve the available research within the profession to validate evidenced-based programs and practices. Citing evidenced-based practices is necessary not only for program improvement, but also to advocate at the local, state, and national levels for legislation to support and promote school counseling programs.

These efforts will continue on a national level so that each professional school counselor on the local level can continue at his/her site and district to design, re-design or align current programs, thereby ensuring that *every student* receives the benefit of a school counseling program.

## References


Aubrey, R. F. (1991). A house divided: Guidance and counseling in 20th century America. In D. R. Coy, C. G. Cole, W. G. Huey, & S. J. Sears (Eds.), *Towards the transformation of secondary school counseling*. Ann Arbor, MI: ERIC Counseling and Personnel Services Clearinghouse.

Campbell, C. A., & Dahir, C. A. (1997). *Sharing the vision: The national standards for school counseling programs.* Alexandria, VA: American School Counselor Association.

Cunnan & Maddy-Bernstein. (1998). *Vision into action: Implementing the national standards for school counseling programs. PowerPoint®* presentation.

Dahir, C. A., Sheldon, C., & Valiga, M. (1998). *Vision into action: Implementing the national standards for school counseling programs.* Alexandria, VA: American School Counselor Association.

The Education Trust. (2003). *The Met Life: Transforming school counseling initiative.* Available on-line at www.cdtrust.org.

Gysbers, N. C. (2001). School guidance and counseling in the 21st century: Remember the past into the future. *Professional School Counseling, 5* (2), 96-104.

Gysbers, N. C., & Henderson, P. (1997). *Comprehensive guidance programs that work - II.* Greensboro, NC; ERIC/CASS Publications.

Hart, P. J., & Jacobi, M. (1992). *From gatekeeper to advocate: Transforming the role of the school counselor.* New York, NY: College Entrance Examination Board.

Hatch, T., Holland, L. & Meyers, P. (2004). When it's time to change. *ASCA School Counselor, 41* (3), 18-22.

Henderson, P., & Gysbers, N. C. (1998). *Leading and managing your school guidance program staff.* Alexandria, VA: American Counseling Association.

Martin, P. J., & House, R. M. (1998). Transforming school counseling. In Education Trust, *The transforming school counseling initiative.* Washington, DC: Author.

Miller, F. W. (1961). *Guidance principles and services* (2nd ed.). Columbus, OH: Charles E. Merrill.

Myrick, R. D. (2003). *Developmental guidance and counseling: A practical approach* (4th ed.) Minneapolis: Educational Media Corporation.

Olson, L. (1979). *Lost in the shuffle: A report on the secondary guidance system.* A report on the guidance system in California secondary schools. Santa Barbara, CA: Open Road Issues Research, Citizens Policy Center.

Roeber, E. C., Walz, G. R., & Smith, G. E. (1969). *A strategy for guidance: A point of view and its implications.* Ontario, Canada: The McMillan Company.

Warters, J. (1946). *High school personnel work today.* New York:McGraw Hill.

---

*Trish Hatch, Ph.D., and Judy Bowers, co-authors of the ASCA *National Model, A Framework for School Counseling Programs,* were paid no royalties for their work. They wrote the document as a gift to the profession. ASCA recommended the citing as (ASCA, 2003) to promote "One Vision, One Voice" within the profession.

**For more information on this, contact ASCA at www.schoolcounselor.org

***For more information on the Education Trust Met Life *Transforming School Counseling Initiative* go to www.edtrust.org

# Chapter 28

## The Professional School Counselor's Role in Raising Student Achievement

*Teesue H. Fields & Peggy LaTurno Hines*

### Preview

The Education Reform Movement of the 1990's continues to have a tremendous impact upon schools in the 21st century. Through the *No Child Left Behind Act* of 2001, schools are now held accountable for the academic achievement level of all students. The professional school counselor brings important knowledge and skills to a school's improvement process. This chapter discusses how the professional school counselor can contribute to a school's effort to raise student achievement.

K-12 education in the new millennium has focused upon improving the academic achievement of every student. The U.S. Congress and numerous state legislatures have enacted legislation to hold schools accountable for raising the academic achievement level of all students (Indiana Department of Education, 1999; United States Department of Education, 2002). The belief that schools have the responsibility to teach all students to reach rigorous academic standards is now the norm by which schools are evaluated (Haycock, 2002; Hines & Fields, in press; Reynolds & Hines, 2001b; Tucker & Codding, 1998).

This emphasis on high academic achievement for all students should put professional school counselors at the center of the business of education. Professional school counselors focus on the academic, career and personal/social development of all students and are trained to help students who are having difficulty in those areas. However, education reform models omit professional school counselors from the planning process for achieving educational excellence. For example, professional school counselors are never mentioned in the U. S. Department of Education publication, *School-based Reform: Lessons From a National Study* (Quellmalz, Shield, & Knapp, 1995). When professional school counselors are mentioned in reform models, it is only to include their position on an advisory committee (U. S. Department of Education, 1998). Professional school counselors are seen as peripheral at best, and unnecessary at worst, in the effort to raise student achievement (House & Martin, 1998).

Professional school counselors are the eyes and ears of the school (House, 2002). They know the issues and concerns of students, parents, faculty, administration, and the community. In addition, professional school counselors possess knowledge and skill sets that are unique within the school environment. While both professional school counselors and administrators are trained in leadership and research skills, professional school counselors are the only educators skilled in counseling, group facilitation, collaboration and consultation, and advocacy (Hines & Fields, in press). The uniqueness of the position, coupled with the knowledge and skills, place professional school counselors in a position to contribute significantly to the school's mission of raising student achievement (Fields & Hines, 2000).

The *ASCA National Model: A Framework for School Counseling Programs* (ASCA, 2003: Bowers & Hatch, 2002) stresses the importance of the school counseling program's contribution to student achievement. Professional school counselors play a critical role in efforts to raise student achievement through the implementation of system-centered and student-centered activities. System-centered activities are designed to influence adult behavior or the educational environment. From a system-centered standpoint, professional school counselors join with building administrators to help facilitate school improvement efforts. A critical system-centered professional school counselor activity is facilitating the creation of interventions designed to remove barriers impeding academic achievement. Additional system-centered activities include using data to spur change, task group facilitation, advocacy, collaboration, and conducting research.

Student-centered interventions are activities created to directly affect students. From a student-centered perspective, professional school counselors work to align their counseling program priorities with the school's student achievement goals through the design of a continuum of interventions that help students master the school guidance standards and indicators which will help students be successful in school. Student-centered activities include developmental guidance lessons and small group and individual counseling.

This chapter describes how professional school counselors can use their skills and knowledge to contribute significantly to the academic mission of the school. It will examine system-centered and student-centered ways in which professional school counselors can influence student achievement. Examples will be provided through the lens of South Middle School (SMS), a fictional middle school (grades 6-8) with a student body consisting of 25% African-American students, 3% Asian-American students, 45% Euro-American students, and 27% Hispanic-American students. Forty percent of SMS students receive free or reduced lunch. At SMS, there are three professional school counselors who loop with their grade levels, 6-8. Thus, they work with the same students for three years, and over three years will work closely with all of the teacher teams in the building. The professional school counselors are in a unique position to understand all of the strengths and weaknesses of both the staff and students at SMS as well as the South City community. They are well versed in the educational and community resources available for students and their families.

*System-Centered Activities*

Professional school counselors understand the process of systemic change and are familiar with education reform models. They know that to raise student achievement, the focus must not solely be on helping students gain the knowledge and skills needed to help them achieve. They must also help adults create and implement effective strategies that encourage student achievement. Through the activities of collaboration and teaming, school data analysis, group facilitation, advocacy, and research, professional school counselors can effectively join with building administrators in facilitating the school improvement process.

*Collaboration and teaming.* The creation of an effective school improvement plan requires a tremendous amount of collaboration and teaming. It is important for the school to involve faculty, parents, students, and community stakeholders (Reynolds & Hines, 2001b). Professional school counselors know how to form effective task groups and can use their teaming and collaboration skills to bring teachers, parents, and community members together. Professional school counselors are skilled at utilizing a wide variety of resources and are natural liaisons between the school and community. Professional school counselors can be an invaluable resource for involving the broader community in efforts to raise academic achievement. Collaboration will also be necessary during the strategy implementation process. The counselor can help the various constituent groups stay involved in program and strategy implementation and insure that all groups have an opportunity for continued input.

For example, SMS is beginning a school improvement process. The principal and professional school counselors work together to create a school improvement team (SIT) consisting of faculty, parents, and community representatives. The principal and professional school counselors collaborate on meeting agendas and take turns facilitating various portions of the meetings. At the same time, they also meet with the grade level instructional teams in the building. They actively collaborate to engage the entire faculty in the school improvement effort.

*School data analysis.* Data-driven decision-making is a critical element in successful school improvement efforts (Green, 2001). Professional school counselors are skilled in the collection, analysis, and presentation of student achievement and related data. Their skills can help facilitate the school improvement team's examination of data, such as standardized test scores, grades, teacher assessments, and student management data. They also understand the importance of disaggregating data by variables such as gender, ethnicity, and socio-economic status to discover underlying access and equity issues influencing student achievement. Data analysis is used to drive interventions, programs, and activities designed to raise student achievement.

For example, the SMS counselors may facilitate an in-depth examination of SMS student achievement and related data. The first thing the school improvement team does is to look at the standardized test scores, grade reports and school management data for the current year and for the previous two years. This gives the SIT team an overall report on their student outcomes. All the data are disaggregated by gender, ethnicity, and socio-economic status so that the improvement team can look at gross outcomes as well as the outcomes for subgroups of students. The SMS team discovers that, at all grade levels, female students are well below average in math scores. Girls are also under-represented in pre-algebra and algebra classes. In addition, there is a higher math failure rate for Hispanic girls. The SMS school improvement team shares this information with the entire faculty, who decide to create a goal to improve the math scores of females in general, and Hispanic females in particular.

*Group facilitation.* Small task groups perform much of the work in raising student achievement (Murphy & Lick, 1998). Although a school administrator often leads the school improvement team, other staff members will lead many of the sub-groups and strategy teams. Professional school counselors are logical leaders for these groups due to their task group leadership skills (Fields & Hines, 2000). They understand the stages of group development, the importance of group process, and group facilitation skills. Professional school counselors expect groups to move through the typical stages of forming, storming, norming, performing and adjourning (Tuckman, 1965). Professional school counselors help the group move through these stages in a healthy way so that the group task gets accomplished and the group does not get stuck in any stage.

During early meetings, professional school counselors help the members understand themselves in relation to the task and work to establish a sense of trust, thus enabling the group to proceed more smoothly (Coyne, 1989). As experienced group leaders, professional school counselors recognize that a certain amount of disagreement among members is to be expected (Gladding, 2003) and that their job is to normalize this stage and help the members use the energy to seek better solutions to the task at hand. As the group works to finalize its report and agree on strategies, it is important that conflicts among various viewpoints be resolved. The steps are essentially the same as in conflict resolution, but the leader's issues revolve around the task rather than personal conflicts. Professional school counselors help members examine various perspectives (e.g., whether or not to require a teacher recommendation for algebra enrollment) and then develop strategies that both sides can accept.

For example, Jacinda Brown, the 7th grade SMS professional school counselor is the facilitator of a math curriculum task group. One of the members of the group is Mr. Pi, an experienced math teacher. The group's task is to examine the problem of the low math achievement by female students. The committee is discussing the idea of removing lower level math options for all students as a way of raising the rigor of math. Mr. Pi is adamant that math content not be watered down. He is concerned that any effort to include under-prepared students will affect his ability to teach math in a way that will prepare his students for high school math classes. He believes that not all students can learn math and, therefore, lower level math courses are needed. The other group members have heard this teacher repeat this opinion over the years and they are frustrated with his lack of willingness to try new strategies to reach these students. Ms. Brown carefully facilitates the meeting, making sure that the group hears Mr. Pi. She helps the group begin to brainstorm various strategies, making sure that Mr. Pi's concerns are taken into consideration. Ms. Brown models respect for the opinions of all members and facilitates the resolution of disagreements into the creation of strategies that the group can support.

*Advocacy.* Many forces influence student achievement. These include school policies, teacher quality, attendance and discipline procedures, parent and community involvement, instruction and assessment methods, expectations, and guidance standards (Haycock, 2002; Reynolds & Hines, 2001b). Professional school counselors advocate for programs and experiences needed to lower barriers to learning. They point out inequities and policies that discriminate and use their advocacy skills to gain support with parents and community stakeholders (House & Martin, 1998). Professional school counselors are in a prime position to raise probing questions, be a voice for the students most often left behind, and mobilize allies outside the schools.

For example, at SMS, the 8th grade counselor, Michael Justice, has noticed that a large number of Latina students have limited English proficiency. He is also aware that math is not considered an important skill for girls to learn in many Hispanic-American homes. Mr. Justice approaches the math curriculum committee with his concerns about the influence of limited English proficiency on the Latina student math achievement levels and actively works to find strategies to address this barrier. He also teams with a Hispanic English teacher. They meet with leaders of the local Hispanic community and provide information about the skills needed by Latinas to be successful in the workforce. They collaborate with the leaders to set up tutoring centers in area churches that will work with Hispanic students.

*Action research.* Professional school counselors are trained action researchers. Schools expend many resources on strategies to improve student achievement. It is imperative that the outcomes of these strategies be studied in order to examine their effectiveness. Professional school counselors can help the school plan, collect, and analyze data on school improvement efforts.

For example, as the SMS task groups develop strategies, the professional school counselors collaborate with the groups to develop an evaluation plan. The plan includes the collection of baseline data. The professional school counselors continue to work with the groups through the implementation phase, supporting needed professional development, and working with any resistance.

*Student-Centered Activities*

Professional school counselors are perhaps more familiar with student-centered activities than with system-centered activities. Often student-centered programs and activities are based upon a student needs assessment (Gysbers & Henderson, 2000). However, when professional school counselors are focused upon raising student achievement, student-centered activities are designed from a counseling program that is aligned with the academic goals of the school. Student-centered activities affect student knowledge, skills, and behavior. They contribute to the academic goals of the school by helping all students master those guidance standards that will support goal attainment. In order to ensure that every student masters the standards, it is important that a continuum of interventions be created. Thus, student-centered activities include aligning the school counseling program with the school's academic goals, creating developmental guidance classroom lessons, conducting small group counseling sessions, and counseling individual students.

*Aligning the school counseling program with the school's academic goals.* The ASCA *National Model* (ASCA, 2003; Bowers & Hatch, 2002) emphasizes the importance of aligning the school counseling program with the academic goals of the school. To do this, professional school counselors work with their faculty and advisory council to prioritize the student guidance standards to ensure that the standards with the greatest potential to help students reach the school's academic goals receive the greatest attention (Reynolds & Hines, 2001a). Once the standards are prioritized, the professional school counselor then designs a continuum of interventions designed to make certain that every student masters those standards. While additional interventions are created on a responsive services basis for those students with individual personal/social problems, it is important to note that the focus of student-centered interventions is on contributing to the school's academic goals and, thus, follows a top down, rather than bottom up plan.

For example, SMS's 6th grade team has set a goal to raise math scores on the state standardized test. Ashlyn Glenn is the 6th grade professional school counselor. She works with the faculty and the school counseling program community council to prioritize the student guidance standards and indicators by answering the question, "Which of our school counseling program standards and indicators do you believe are the most important for our 6th grade students to master in order to help them raise their math achievement level?" Ms. Glenn designs the year's guidance curriculum based upon the established priorities. She then works with the faculty to map how the curriculum will be delivered.

*Classroom guidance.* Once the school's counseling program standards are prioritized based upon the school's academic goals, the professional school counselor designs the classroom guidance curriculum. The guidance curriculum may be delivered in many ways. Professional school counselors may come into classrooms, faculty may teach the standards through the regular curriculum or by adapting the curriculum to fit the guidance standards, and appropriate community members may deliver the curriculum (ASCA, 2003; Bowers & Hatch, 2002; Reynolds & Hines, 2001a; 2001b).

For example, Ashlyn Glenn, the 6th grade SMS professional school counselor, goes into each sixth grade classroom the first two weeks of school and conducts lessons on study skills, time management, and asking for help (ASCA Standard A; Campbell & Dahir, 1997). Each teacher follows up on these lessons by giving each student a planner and helping them map out assignments for the first grading period. The teachers also give tips for studying their particular subject and use many study aids for students during the first grading period. Each teacher also uses strategies to encourage students to ask for help, particularly students who are having difficulty. Thus, all students in sixth grade are getting the same study skills instruction. Because SMS has decided to focus on math achievement, the sixth grade counselor and the math teacher present some extra lessons on how to study math and how to deal with math anxiety. These supplemental lessons deal with the specific academic goals of the school to improve math skills.

*Small group counseling.* Professional school counselors often conduct small groups. These groups may be based on a general needs assessment or may be in response to specific problems (Smead, 1995), such as a number of students who have experienced loss of a loved one. While this is one way to establish a small group program, professional school counselors offering a continuum of services aligned with the school's academic goals will use small group counseling as a follow-up to classroom guidance for those students who experience difficulty mastering the guidance standard. Using this model, professional school counselors are able to use group counseling to work on difficulties preventing students from mastering the school counseling program standards.

The small group is an ideal way to work with these types of problems because a level of trust can be established in a small group that is difficult to achieve in the classroom. Professional school counselors can use group counseling leadership skills to establish trust among group members, help the members set individual goals, and provide opportunity for the members to practice new skills (such as asking for help) in the group. Counselors also use basic group work skills in drawing out, connecting, and cutting off to help all members of the group benefit from participation. If personal issues surface in the small group, professional school counselors use evaluation skills to determine the seriousness of such issues and make referrals for individual counseling or other resources as needed.

For example, after the classroom guidance classes on study skills and the additional lessons on math study skills at SMS, there is still a group of girls who teachers identify as being very anxious about learning math. Ms. Glenn, the 6th grade counselor, invites the girls to join a group that will focus on individual ways to deal with math anxiety.

*Individual counseling.* Professional school counselors know that some students need individual counseling to work on issues that are negatively influencing their academic achievement or mastery of the school counseling program standards. Assuming that the system barriers have been removed and that adequate support is now available, it is more likely that each student has an idiosyncratic problem. Individual counseling provides an opportunity for more in-depth help with these issues. This type of counseling is usually short term in nature (ASCA, 2003; Bowers & Hatch, 2002). Professional school counselors are familiar with community resources and refer students and families appropriately.

For example, at SMS, even with the systemic changes, classroom guidance lessons, and small group time, there are still several 8th grade Hispanic girls who are not achieving well in math. At this point, the 8th grade counselor, Michael Justice, sees each girl individually to further analyze the issues. Marisa is a bright Hispanic student who is still making Cs and Ds in pre-algebra, even though she participates in the new group tutoring and homework sessions, and has access to an individual tutor. When Mr. Justice talks with Marisa, he discovers that the family has been under a lot of stress because a family member has a chronic illness. Marisa has had difficulty concentrating on her schoolwork and since math is her most difficult subject, the lack of concentration shows up in pre-algebra the most. Mr. Justice works with Marisa to devise solutions that will relieve some of her anxiety about the family situation while still giving math some of her energy. They go to the math teacher together and explain the situation. All three agree that if there has been a crisis with the sick family member, Marisa can ask to have a test postponed or have an extra day for homework. Just knowing that this is a possibility relieves a lot of Marisa's stress, and her grades start to improve almost immediately.

## Summary/Conclusion

Raising the academic achievement level of all students is the primary goal for K-12 schools. While typically left out of school reform, professional school counselors bring important knowledge and skills to the school improvement process and are valuable and essential resources in raising the academic achievement of all students. Professional school counselors need to be actively engaged in both system-centered and student-centered activities. System-centered activities place professional school counselors in positions that facilitate the school improvement process and advocate for programs, policies, and environments that promote academic growth. Student-centered activities create a school counseling program that is aligned with the academic goals of the school and provide a continuum of strategies designed to help every student master guidance standards that promote learning. The activities of professional school counselors are beneficial to all students and staff as the education community seeks to achieve higher levels of performance.

## References

American School Counselor Association. (2003). *The ASCA national model: A framework for school counseling programs.* Alexandria, VA: Author.

Bowers, J. L., & Hatch, P. A. (2002). *ASCA national model for school counseling programs.* Alexandria, VA: American School Counselor Association.

Campbell, C. A., & Dahir, C. A. (1997). *The national standards for school counseling programs.* Alexandria, VA: American School Counselor Association.

Coyne, R. K. (1989). *How personal growth and task groups work.* Newbury Park, CA: Sage Publications.

Fields, T. H., & Hines, P. L. (2000). School counselor's role in raising student achievement. In G. Duhon & T. Manson (Eds.), *Preparation, collaboration and emphasis on the family in school counseling for the new millennium.* Lewiston, NY: The Edwin Mellen Press.

Gladding, S. T. (2003). *Group work: A counseling specialty.* Upper Saddle River, NJ: Merrill/ Prentice-Hall.

Green, R. S. (2001). Closing the achievement gap: Lessons learned and challenges ahead. *Teaching and Change, 8,* 215-224.

Gysbers, N. C., & Henderson, P. (2000). *Developing and managing your school guidance program* (3rd ed.). Alexandria, VA: American Counseling Association.

Haycock, K. (2002, June). *Dispelling the myth: A role for school counselors.* Paper presented at the annual meeting of the Education Trust on Transforming School Counseling, Chicago, IL.

Hines, P. L., & Fields, T. H. (in press). School counseling and academic achievement. In R. Pérusse & G. E. Goodnough (Eds.), *Leadership and advocacy in school counseling.* Belmont, CA: Brooks/Cole.

House, R. M. (2002, June). *MetLife national school counselor training initiative.* Paper presented at the annual meeting of the Education Trust on Transforming School Counseling, Chicago, IL.

House, R. M., & Martin, P. J. (1998). Advocating for better futures for all students: A new vision for school counselors. *Education, 119,* 284-291.

Indiana Department of Education. (1999). *Standards, assessment, school improvement, and accountability.* Retrieved June 30, 2002 from http://www.doe.state.in.us/pl221/statute.html

Murphy, C. U., & Lick, D. W. (1998). *Whole-faculty study groups: A powerful way to change schools and enhance learning.* Thousand Oaks, CA: Corwin.

Quellmalz, E., Shield, P. M., & Knapp, M. S. (1995). *School-based reform: Lessons from a national study.* Washington, DC: U.S. Department of Education.

Reynolds, S. E., & Hines, P. L. (2001a). *Guiding all kids: Systemic guidance for achievement focused schools* (2nd ed.). Bloomington, IN: American Student Achievement Institute. Retrieved March 3, 2002 from the American Student Achievement Institute Web site: http://asai.indstate.edu

Reynolds, S. E., & Hines, P. L. (2001b). *Vision-to-action: A step-by-step activity guide for systemic educational reform* (6th ed.). Bloomington, IN: American Student Achievement Institute. Retrieved March 3, 2002 from the American Student Achievement Institute Web site: http://asai.indstate.edu

Smead, R. (1995). *Skills and techniques for group work with children and adolescents.* Champaign, IL: Research Press.

Tucker, M. S., & Codding, J. B. (1998). *Standards for our schools: How to set them, measure, them, and reach them.* San Francisco: Jossey Bass.

Tuckman, B. W. (1965). Developmental sequence in small groups. *Psychological Bulletin, 63,* 384-399.

U. S. Department of Education. (1998). *Tools for schools: School reform models.* Washington, DC: Author.

U. S. Department of Education. (2002). *No Child Left Behind Act.* Retrieved June 30, 2002 from http://www.ed.gov/legislation/ESEA02/

# Chapter 29

## Comprehensive Developmental School Counseling Programs

*Cheryl Moore-Thomas*

### Preview

School counseling is an ever-transforming field (Paisley, 2001; Paisley & Peace, 1995). Amidst the change in the field, comprehensive, developmental school counseling programs have remained central to the work of professional school counselors (Green & Keys, 2001; Gysbers, 2001). This chapter discusses the major components of comprehensive, developmental school counseling programs, including developmental approaches, diversity, student competencies, delivery systems, resources, and program evaluation.

Most professional school counselors are familiar with the phrase "comprehensive, developmental school counseling program." Few, however, may be able to clearly define it (Borders & Drury, 1992). Given the variability and flexibility that exist in effective comprehensive, developmental programs, this is understandable. In spite of this variability, effective programs do share some characteristics.

Gysbers and Henderson (2000; Gysbers, 2001) suggested that true comprehensive, developmental school counseling programs are well integrated into a curriculum that supports the mission of the school and district, and complement the existing academic programs. Additionally, comprehensive, developmental school counseling programs provide a full range of services. These include counseling, referral, consultation, information and assessment. Inherent in the provision of a full range of counseling services must be the understanding that professional school counselors are pivotal to, but not the sole service providers of, a school counseling program. Comprehensive, developmental school counseling services are most effectively offered through a team approach. Professional school counselors work in consultation and collaboration with school staff, parents and community stakeholders (Gysbers & Henderson, 2000; House & Martin, 1998).

School counseling programs are developmental in that they provide regular, systematic opportunities for students to achieve competencies focused on their growth and development (Gysbers & Henderson, 2000). Effective school counseling programs result from planned, sequential, flexible curricula which complement the academic curriculum and emphasize the life skills and experiences all students need to become successful in school and adulthood (Myrick, 1997). Further definition of comprehensive, developmental school counseling was offered by Borders and Drury (1992) who suggested that comprehensive, developmental school counseling programs are proactive, preventative and aimed at helping all students acquire the knowledge, skills, self-awareness and attitudes necessary for normal development.

Given these definitions and descriptions, comprehensive, developmental school counseling programs:

- Provide a full range of school counseling services;
- Offer students opportunities to learn the skills, knowledge, and attitudes necessary

for healthy development;
- Embody the school mission and philosophy;
- Complement other school programs; and
- Involve all school staff, parents, and community members.

## Developmental Approach

The research and theoretical base for school counseling programs is largely found in the theory and practice of human development (Green & Keys, 2001). In a basic sense, developmental theory deals with the manner in which individuals change over time (Thomas, 1996). The specific stages, characteristics and considerations of change are described in a variety of human development theories including, but not limited to, psychosocial development, cognitive development, moral development and self-concept development. Gysbers and Henderson (2000) suggested that a human development approach has specific applicability to school counseling. Their conceptualization of life career development is depicted as "... self-development over the lifespan through the integration of roles, settings, and events in a person's life" ( p. 49).

Well planned and executed school counseling programs help students gain the knowledge, skills and attitudes necessary for mastery of normal developmental tasks (Sears & Granello, 2002). Research suggests that students functioning at high levels of development are better able to handle the tasks of living and learning (Borders & Drury, 1995; Paisley & Peace, 1995). These data appear to strongly support developmental school counseling programs. It is prudent, therefore, that professional school counselors and other school counseling program stakeholders appreciate, understand, and utilize the principles of human development theory.

## Developmental Approach and Issues of Diversity

Professional school counselors must make certain that the foundational developmental theories of the comprehensive school counseling program are appropriate for all students. Professional school counselors ensure that school counseling programs meet the needs of students of all racial, ethnic, and socioeconomic backgrounds. Further, comprehensive, developmental school counseling programs serve all students regardless of achievement level, gender, sexual orientation, family structure, language or any other aspect of diversity (Green & Keys, 2001; Gysbers, 2001; House & Martin, 1998; Sears & Granello, 2002). This task is challenging due to the tremendous, rapidly increasing diversity in schools. Today, approximately 38% of the K-12 population is minority (National Center for Education Statistics, 2002). Population projections indicate that by 2020 over 50% of school-age children attending public schools will come from minority (non-white) cultures (Campbell, 1994). Despite the challenge, the relevance, effectiveness, and ethical standing of comprehensive, developmental school counseling programs are dependent upon the critical alignment of culturally sensitive developmental approaches and counseling services. This alignment is imperative. The American School Counselor Association (1999) called professional school counselors to "... take action to ensure students of culturally diverse backgrounds have access to appropriate services and opportunities promoting the individual's maximum development" (p. 1); however, there are data which suggest all students, especially those of color and those from low socioeconomic statuses, are not receiving adequate service (Lapan & Gysbers, 1997). Developmental principles cannot be blindly applied. Effective school counseling programs are built on developmental theoretical models that are applied and interpreted in the context of students and their communities (Green & Keys, 2001).

## Program Benefits

One of the most valuable benefits of a comprehensive, developmental school counseling program is that it provides professional school counselors with a rationale and framework for providing service to all students (Lapan, Gysbers, & Petroski, 2001). Furthermore, comprehensive, developmental programs move the work of professional school counselors from random, ancillary guidance activities that benefit some students to focused, mission driven, research-based school counseling services and programs for all students. The systemic, continuous nature of comprehensive, developmental school counseling programs decreases the likelihood that needy students will go unserved or underserved, while increasing the likelihood that all students will benefit from the school counseling program (Paisley & Peace, 1995). Clearly, students are the greatest benefactors of comprehensive, developmental guidance programs; but the benefits to the entire school community cannot be overlooked. Comprehensive, developmental school counseling programs benefit teachers and other educators, parents, and community stakeholders through the implementation of proactive, collaborative programs that provide continuous data regarding student development.

## Program Competencies

One of the important initial steps in developing a comprehensive, developmental school counseling program is identifying student competencies. Competencies are the skills or abilities students are expected to acquire as a result of participating in the comprehensive, developmental school counseling program. In determining and selecting appropriate competencies for a specific school population, professional school counselors should consult school district goals, needs assessment data, outcome data, professional research literature, and professional organizations' position statements (Gysbers, 2001). Table 1 provides a brief listing of current curricular terminology and definitions. ASCA's *National Standards for School Counseling Programs* (Campbell & Dahir, 1997; Dahir, 2001; Dahir, Sheldon, & Valiga, 1998) propose several student competencies grouped by domains and standards. These resources assist professional school counselors in selecting the complement of competencies that best meets the needs of the students at each developmental level in a particular school community.

Selected student competencies must be further defined by outcomes and indicators. Outcomes and indicators assist the professional school counselor and other stakeholders in assessing student success. Careful consideration and articulation of "what success will look like" (evidence of the achievement of the competencies) goes a long way to support school counseling program accountability.

Selection of an appropriate competency, outcome, and indicator is demonstrated in the following example. The professional school counselor of a large urban elementary school, in consultation with the school counseling advisory committee, reviewed two years of school and district data which seem to suggest that the local suspension rate increases significantly at the fourth grade level. These data were troubling, especially in light of the school and district's mission of success for all students. The professional school counselor, administrator, and school leadership team decided to address this concern through various school programs, including the comprehensive, developmental school counseling program. Knowing that one of the first steps in developing a comprehensive, developmental school counseling program is to select competencies that are aligned with institutional goals, data and standards, and undergirded by sound culturally appropriate developmental principles, the professional school counselor utilized the ASCA *National Standards* (Campbell & Dahir, 1997) as a guide. The counselor incorporated the standards as part of the school counseling plan for the upcoming academic year and highlighted the framework (provided in Table 2) for beginning to address the school's troubling suspension rate.

**Table 1. Terminology**

| *Term* | *Definition* |
|---|---|
| Domain: | Developmental area |
| Goal: | Broad statement of desired student achievement that embodies the mission and purpose of the institution or program |
| Standard: | Statement of what students should know or be able to do indicating a level or *standard* of expected performance |
| Competency: | Skill or ability |
| Indicator: | Specification or delineation of a student outcome |
| Objective: | Measurable evidence of students' skills, knowledge or attitudes |

**Table 2. Framework for addressing suspension rates through a comprehensive, developmental school counseling program.**

| *Program Component* | *Content* |
|---|---|
| School Goal: | Academic success for all students |
| Domain: | Personal/Social |
| Standard: | Students will make decisions, set goals and take necessary action to achieve goals (Campbell & Dahir, 1997) |
| Competency: | Self-knowledge application |
| Indicators: | Students will use a decision-making and problem solving model.<br>Students will understand consequences of decisions and choices.<br>Students will know how to apply conflict resolution skills. |
| Objectives: | 1) After participating in the school-wide classroom guidance unit on conflict resolution skills, 80% of the school's third grade students will be able to apply conflict resolutions skills to a given hypothetical situation with 100% accuracy.<br>2) 80% of the targeted fourth grade students, after having participated in small group counseling on conflict resolution, will be able to identify the three steps of the problem solving model. |

## Program Delivery System

Comprehensive, developmental school counseling programs are delivered to students through many processes. Some of these processes provide direct service to students, others indirect. Guidance curriculum, a direct process, consists of classroom lessons, interdisciplinary curricula, and school-wide activities (Borders & Drury, 1992; Gysbers, 2001). Individual student planning, another direct service, involves small group and individual student appraisal and advisement regarding issues such as test results, career awareness, and course selection. Responsive counseling, the most frequently used delivery system, involves a host of counseling services and activities, including individual and group counseling, consultation, crisis counseling, and referral.

System support activities are indirect services that maintain and enhance the comprehensive, developmental school counseling program and are defined by the delivery of school counseling services through training and professional development, community outreach, advisory boards and councils, and program and total school management.

The professional school counselor and other stakeholders must select the most appropriate delivery process for each aspect of the comprehensive, developmental school counseling program. The primary factor in selection of appropriate delivery processes must be the developmental needs of the students. For example, a group of ninth grade students in one community may be served best by small group counseling services focused on body image and self-esteem, while the developmental needs, regarding the same topic, of a different ninth grade community may most appropriately be met through an interdisciplinary classroom lesson developed and implemented by the professional school counselor and health education teacher.

As illustrated above, program delivery systems clearly suggest that the professional school counselor is central to the comprehensive, developmental school counseling program, but is not the total school counseling program. The success of each delivery system is dependent upon the support of the entire school community.

## Program Resources

Human and financial resources undergird comprehensive, developmental school counseling programs. Human resources for counseling programs include the leadership and service of the professional school counselor working in collaboration with students, teachers, administrators, other school staff, parents and community members (Gysbers & Henderson, 2000). Each has a role and responsibility regarding the development and implementation of effective counseling programs.

Financial resources include district and local dollars and in-kind services provided for school counseling programs. Current budget restraints often prohibit school counseling programs from receiving optimal levels of financial support. This reality demands that all individuals responsible for counseling programs constantly engage in creative problem solving to meet the financial needs of programs. This problem solving could lead to partnerships with community businesses, the seeking of donations from parents and guardians or the facilitation of student-led fund raising activities.

## Program Evaluation

Evaluation of comprehensive school counseling programs is an important, multifaceted process (Gysbers & Henderson, 2000; Lapan, 2001). Terenzini (1989) suggested that program evaluation be framed by two questions: Does the school have a written, comprehensive program that is fully implemented and aligned with district, state, and national standards?; and Does the educational program in fact produce the intended outcomes?

Practical guidelines for conducting program evaluations are important (Atkinson, Furlong & Janoff, 1979; Fairchild, 1986; Krumboltz, 1974). It is practical and highly desirable to connect program concerns to only one or two, well-articulated questions. This practice may help to focus and manage evaluation. It may also work to ensure that the specific program component under evaluation is being fully and appropriately examined.

The school counseling program evaluation process is systematic, ongoing, and cyclical (Lapan, 2001). It starts small and builds upon what the data suggest works. Successful methods and delivery processes are determined and replicated so that, over time, necessary program refinements work to build a comprehensive, developmental school counseling program that meets the school's mission.

Effective evaluation always begins with the school's mission. The mission provides the basis from which meaningful, institution-specific assessment questions arise. These assessment questions lead to the determination of what evidence must be collected. Evidence can provide crucial information about program evaluation and program results.

Evidence can be derived from standardized or informal measures, student performances, or student products. Once evidence has been gathered, it must be interpreted. Then, conclusions and interpretations can be drawn regarding the counseling program's value, strengths, weaknesses and outcomes. Interpretations and conclusions must be used to change the program or parts of the program to improve it. As assessment information is used to prompt programmatic changes, goal setting and the posing of new questions begins again. As is true for other aspects of the comprehensive, developmental guidance program, the professional school counselor alone is not responsible for program evaluation. Meaningful, thorough program evaluation provides professional school counselors opportunities to collaborate with counselor educators, educational accountability experts, consultants, and others with expertise in school counseling program evaluation. Working together they design assessment questions, gather and interpret data, and report results in a way that benefits students.

## Summary/Conclusion

Comprehensive, developmental school counseling programs are vital to the work of today's professional school counselors. Rooted in developmental theory, comprehensive programs utilize well-selected student competencies, delivery systems, resources, and assessment processes to assist students in acquiring the culturally appropriate knowledge, skills and attitudes needed for healthy development. As professional school counselors, administrators, teachers, parents, and others work together to design and implement comprehensive, developmental school counseling programs, continual systematic movement is made toward the healthy development of all students.

## References

American School Counselor Association. (1999). *Position statement: Multicultural counseling.* Alexandria, VA: Author.

Atkinson, D. R., Furlong, M., & Janoff, D. S. (1979). A four-component model for proactive accountability in school counseling. *The School Counselor, 26*, 222-228.

Borders, D. L., & Drury, R. D. (1992). Comprehensive school counseling programs: A review for policy makers and practitioners. *Journal of Counseling and Development, 70*, 487-498.

Campbell, P. (1994). *Population projections for states, by age, race, sex: 1993 to 2020: Current population reports*, 25-111. Washington, DC: U.S. Bureau of the Census.

Campbell, C. A., & Dahir, C. A. (1997). *Sharing the vision: The national standards for school counseling programs.* Alexandra, VA: American School Counselor Association.

Dahir, C. (2001). The national standards for school counseling programs: Development and implementation [Electronic Version]. *Professional School Counseling, 4,* 320-327.

Dahir, C. A., Sheldon, C. B., & Valigia, M. (1998). *Vision into action: Implementing the national standards for school counseling.* Alexandra, VA: American School Counselor Association.

Fairchild, T. N. (1986). Time analysis: Accountability tool for school counselors. *The School Counselor, 34,* 36-43.

Green, A., & Keys, S. (2001). Expanding the developmental school counseling paradigm: Meeting the needs of the 21st century student school [Electronic Version]. *Professional School Counseling, 5,*84-95.

Gysbers, N. (2001). School guidance and counseling in the 21st century: Remember the past into the future [Electronic version]. *Professional School Counseling, 5,* 96-105.

Gysbers, N., & Henderson, P. (2000). *Developing and managing your school guidance program* (3rd ed.). Alexandria, VA: American Counseling Association.

House, R., & Martin, P. (1998). Advocating for better futures for all students: A new vision for school counselors. *Education, 119,* 284-291.

Krumboltz, J. D. (1974). An accountability model for counselors. *Personnel and Guidance Journal, 52,* 639-646.

Lapan, R. T. (2001). Results-based comprehensive guidance and counseling programs: A framework for planning and evaluation [Electronic Version]. *Professional School Counselor, 4,* 289-299.

Lapan, R. T., & Gysbers, N. C. (1997). The impact of more fully impacted guidance programs on the school experiences of high school students: A statewide evaluation study [Electronic Version]. *Journal of Counseling and Development, 75,* 292-302.

Lapan, R. T., Gysbers, N. C., & Petroski, G. F. (2001). Helping seventh graders be safe and successful: A statewide study of the impact of comprehensive guidance and counseling programs [Electronic version]. *Journal of Counseling and Development, 79,* 320-330.

Myrick, R. D. (1997). *Developmental guidance and counseling: A practical approach* (3rd ed.). Minneapolis, MN: Educational Media Corporation.

National Center for Education Statistics. (2002). *State nonfiscal survey of public elementary/ secondary education 1999-2000.* Washington, DC: Author.

Paisley, P. (2001). Maintaining and enhancing the developmental focus in school counseling programs [Electronic version]. *Professional School Counseling, 4,* 271-277.

Paisley, P., & Peace, S. D. (1995). Developmental principles: A framework for school counseling programs [Electronic Version]. *Elementary School Guidance and Counseling, 30,* 85-93.

Sears, S. J., & Granello, D. H. (2002). School counseling now and in the future: A reaction [Electronic version]. *Professional School Counseling, 5,* 164-171.

Terenzini, P. (1989). Assessment with open eyes. *Journal of Higher Education, 60,* 644-664.

Thomas, R. M. (1996). *Comparing theories of child development* (4th ed.). Pacific Grove, CA: Brooks/Cole.

# Chapter 30

## Needs Assessments: The Key to Successful and Meaningful School Counseling Programs

*Jan R. Bartlett*

### Preview

Needs assessments empower professional school counselors through data. By gathering the input of the school's stakeholders, professional school counselors gain the information necessary to create programs that truly reflect the unique needs of their community. This chapter discusses the steps necessary to gain support and cooperation from coworkers, administration, community and the school board to build a strong foundation for conducting a needs assessment.

By bringing together feedback from students, teachers, parents, school board members, administrators, and community leaders, professional school counselors can develop a program which truly reflects the unique needs of the community. *Assessment* and *observable outcomes* are key words frequently heard in education. Increasingly, actions and decisions in our society are guided by findings from collected information, which in turn drive movement and choices; therefore these decisions are based on research. Developing an effective, successful, and meaningful school counseling program is no different. By assessing the specific needs of the community the professional school counselor gathers significant information that emerges from data, enabling the school counseling program to determine a purposeful path of action. This data, aligned with the *National Standards* (Campbell & Dahir, 1997) for school counseling programs, can create a powerful tool for positive change in the school. A comprehensive and developmental school counseling program is based on research and built with the combined efforts of the professional school counselor and stakeholders of the school and community. Needs assessments are about empowering professional school counselors through data.

Approaches to needs assessment vary and there are many surveys available for use in schools. The purpose of the survey may be remedial, preventative, or both. Needs assessments may be purchased commercially, borrowed, or adapted from an existing source; a school district may also decide to create a needs assessment for their own use (Gladding, 2000). Surveys are included in many books that address school counseling program development. Many texts in the field of school counseling include sample needs assessments or address needs assessments in varying detail, including Baker (2000), Cobia and Henderson (2003), Erford (2003), Gladding (2000), Greenberg (2003), Schmidt (2003), and VanZandt and Hayslip (2001). For a reference devoted entirely to the process of developing, administering, and evaluating a needs assessment, Rye and Sparks (1999) is an excellent resource. This resource provides sample needs assessments for all school levels, an example of results, and a plan developed from the sample data provided.

### Needs Assessment Design

Some needs assessment designs promote a comprehensive approach, in which all the elements of goals and topics are addressed that might realistically be components of a comprehensive school counseling program. This may be most suitable for school districts that are establishing a baseline and implementing their initial assessment, with no previously collected data. Other designs consider assessing certain topics or concerns explicitly, so they are targeting issues; this would be helpful when a district or school is updating or altering a program based on an existing needs assessment (Erford, 2003). In all, seven methods have been determined for assessing the needs for a school: questionnaires and inventories, analysis of records, personal interviews, visits to classrooms, contracting an outside consultant, counseling statistics, and systematic evaluation of the existing school counseling program (Stone & Bradley, 1994). Collecting information using any of the sources mentioned is extremely valuable. However, this chapter will focus on the most frequently used tool for needs assessments, the survey. This chapter will also discuss factors that are critical to the successful implementation and utilization of the needs assessment for professional school counselors.

## Getting Started: Build a Strong Foundation

"A school system is no more stable than its base of community support" (Rye & Sparks, 1999, p. 1). The same sentiment may be extended to a school counseling program and its needs assessment efforts. Aim for the highest and most wide-ranging level of support. First, gain the support of the entire counseling staff, either in your building or district; if you succeed in capturing their attention and commitment, the chances for strong involvement and overall success are strengthened. If it is not possible to do a district-wide assessment, then shifting the focus to a specific school may be the best place to start. Second, after gaining the support of professional school counselors, efforts should be directed to gain endorsement and backing of both the administration and the school board. This is accomplished by developing a formal proposal to gain the endorsement for the needs assessment. Not only should the school board and administration be included in the process, but they must also be made aware of the school counseling program's efforts to improve services. Once the proposal is completed, the next step is to request the endorsement of the plan by the school board at a regular meeting. This lends an air of legitimacy to the process, which will hopefully result in supportive principals and central office administrators. Once the needs assessment data has been collected, evaluated, and implemented regarding plans for program development, then the school board should also endorse the final plan. This allows for some sense of permanence and stability for the school counseling program. If changes occur within an administration, then less disruption to the school counseling program may occur.

Another key reason for involving the administration and the school board at the very beginning of the needs assessment process involves efforts to demonstrate accountability for the school counseling program. Data from a needs assessment can be used effectively in establishing priorities for program development (Erford, 2003). Because of the *No Child Left Behind* legislation, it is critical that professional school counselors think of their program in terms of accountability. Purposeful programming based on data collected from the needs assessment which is tied to the personal/social, career, and academic standards and competencies from the *National Standards* developed by Campbell & Dahir (1997) indicates and demonstrates the link to a research base. It is essential that the programming be regularly evaluated to demonstrate measurable outcomes and that this information be presented and shared with the staff, administration, school board, and community. Press releases or articles written by professional school counselors or other committee members regarding the goals and objectives for the needs assessment can further expand support, endorsement, and involvement from students, parents, and the community. Also, the membership and involvement of the advisory board or committee working in conjunction with professional school counselors throughout the entire process should be highlighted.

*Content of Proposal*

The proposal should include at least the following components accompanied with specific and detailed information. First, address the broad aim and purpose for the needs assessment. Discuss general goals for the school counseling program. Topics to touch on might include: creating the highest quality program, continued improvement for the program, identifying and addressing changes in the student body and community (Rye & Sparks, 1999), determining the priorities for services from the stake holders, and matching services with school and community needs. Second, address who will be involved in the process. Introduce the advisory board/ committee and discuss the membership of this group. The advisory board is comprised of representatives of the stakeholders in the school district: administrators, teachers, staff, students, school board members, parents, and a community representative. This is a good time to discuss the organizational needs of the advisory board. A large school district may need a district-wide steering committee as well. Third, how will the needs assessment be organized? Here address in broad terms the responsibilities of the various members, including training, setting goals, conducting needs assessment, planning strategies, and evaluation. Details should be included for implementing the evaluation data and plans for ongoing revisions. Fourth, provide a detailed timeline for the completion of the planning stage for the needs assessment. Emphasize that each planning cycle leads to an evaluation of the data, which is the basis for re-direction and fine-tuning of the existing program (Rye & Sparks, 1999). Fifth, estimate how long it will take. The proposal should include a prediction for when a document will be available for the school board to review and a date for when the plan will be completed. Finally, include a statement regarding the perceived impact of the resulting plan. Remember to stress the importance and benefits of the planning process and not to only emphasize the outcomes.

*Advisory Committee*

The Advisory Committee, sometimes also called the group advisory team or advisory board, is comprised of representatives of the stakeholders in the school. These are individuals in the school and community who are committed to the success of the school and students. It may be wise to identify a list of potential individuals including: students, teachers, administrators, parents, and community leaders (e.g., ministers, business leaders, mental health professionals, law enforcement officers, government officials) (Rye & Sparks, 1999).

The professional school counselors may organize this group or the school board might appoint them. Alternatively, the group could be selected and organized and then appointed by the school board. Along with the professional school counselors, the committee will be involved in planning, implementing, and evaluating the counseling program. Once the group or committee has been identified, work involving essential communication between the members will be necessary to guide the needs assessment forward. This work may be time consuming, but it will provide a solid foundation for future activities and discussion. Each community is unique and the services that are needed from the school counseling program will vary. Because of variables such as the size of the school, socio-economic status of the community, cultural diversity, concentration of learning problems found in the school, educational backgrounds of parents, community's attitude toward the school and education, and leadership of the school and district (Schmidt, 2003), it is essential and advisable that the community be reflected in the advisory committee as closely as possible.

*Building a Program Base*

By bringing together elements of a school and community to design the comprehensive program, the energies are channeled toward a common goal rather than competing or fragmenting the efforts of the needs assessment (Rye & Sparks, 1999). A comprehensive school counseling program is not the sole domain or responsibility of the professional school counselor. It includes many people to expand the base of support (Schmidt, 2003).

Instead of a discussion on the roles and function of professional school counselors, Rye and Sparks (1999) presented fundamental beliefs of a comprehensive school counseling program.

1. Governing values are the foundation of all human endeavors;
2. Education is the top priority for ensuring a positive future for all of us;
3. Comprehensive counseling programs are essential elements of any quality educational process for students;
4. Quality counseling programs must be developed from explicitly stated value bases and have both administrative and community support;
5. Comprehensive services must be systematically planned, implemented, and evaluated over an extended period of time;
6. Program planning is most effective when it is centered in an informed team of school and community representatives;
7. Effective counseling programs are specifically designed to meet identified needs in the school and community populations;
8. Programs of excellence offer services that build self-understanding and a variety of skills in a pattern of increasing levels of difficulty as students move from grade to grade (p. 4).

A decision should be made whether to look at existing models for school counseling programs or to start fresh. One may consult Vanzandt and Hayslip (2001) as a resource that includes information on several models: the Missouri Model, the Multidimensional Model, and the National Model. The professional school counselor should make a basic presentation of the *National Standards For School Counseling Programs* (Campbell & Dahir, 1997) to committee members. The *National Standards* provides detailed student competencies for each of the core domains of personal/social, career, and academic success.

*Core values.* An important beginning point for the committee might be a discussion of the group's understanding of core values. By exploring the committee members' values for the school's counseling program, the chances for success are further enriched. Failure to determine a shared set of values, coupled with lack of a process to resolve value differences, can lead to divisiveness within the committee (Rye & Sparks, 1999). The stated and expressed values from the committee should also be reflected within the larger community and within the cultural context surrounding the school; this is essential to attain and retain credibility.

To explore the respective values held by committee members, examine and discuss mission statements for the school, school counseling program, parent-teacher groups, businesses and any other existing documents. This can help to provide a starting point for processing and clarifying individual values. Are there key words that are prominent in the documents? Is there a common ground? Within the profession there is still some question as to whether there is consensus on core values, but in a school district the professional school counselors should articulate their own values and link them to those of the community (Rye & Sparks, 1999). Is there a common theme that runs through the community committee members? Work in small groups around general questions and then chart the key points on large paper to be shared and organize the discussion. Possible starter questions may be: What elements do members see as essential in a happy and successful student? What are the core values members want to see delivered through a school counseling program?

*Values to vision.* Once the values of the group have been clarified, the next step is to connect them to a shared vision for the future. Several possible questions for exploring the vision for the program might be: How are students different because of the school counseling program? When students move on from this school to another level or graduate what skills do we want them to have? What will be the attributes of this student? One helpful activity might be to ask committee members to close their eyes for a few minutes and reflect on what an exemplary school counseling program would look like and how would it affect students. Then let the group members spend a few moments writing notes based on their reflections. Encourage the members to share their ideas in small groups where ideas are documented and can then be shared with the larger group. Develop a vision or a mission statement for the school counseling program based on what emerges from the group. It should be a vision that all can agree on and support enthusiastically. In larger communities and communities with a wide range of diverse groups in the school district (i.e., cultural, religious, ethnic, racial, or socio-economic status), the professional school counselor might consider conducting focus groups to gather additional information to ensure all voices are included in the vision.

## The Needs Assessment

### *Develop a Time Line*

Rye and Sparks (1999) stated the time commitment for an in depth and thorough needs assessment process will be five to six years, with the first year devoted to:

1. Preparing and organizing the advisory team into a working group;
2. Reviewing and refining the beliefs, vision, and mission of the counseling program;
3. Conducting a needs assessment among students, parents, and school personnel;
4. Identifying high-priority needs;
5. Writing objectives; and
6. Helping the counseling staff develop activities to address identified needs. (p. 34)

The next four years would involve the implementation, monitoring, evaluation, and revision of the plan that was initially developed. In the fifth year another needs assessment could be conducted and a new plan developed and written based on emergent needs.

Within the same time frame is another exciting possibility. An approach using a continuous cycle of assessing program needs, which could be tied to the national standards (Campbell & Dahir, 1997), could allow an assessment of each of the three areas of academic, career, and personal/social to occur on specific years in a six year cycle (Moore-Thomas & Erford, in press). A possible cycle involves a focus in years one and two on assessment of academic needs, years three and four on the needs for career development and educational planning, and years five and six on personal/social issues. Once a program is clearly established, adjustments might be made in a three year improvement cycle (Erford, 2003). If drastic changes occur within the community either because of shifts in demographics or some type of national, state or local crisis of political or natural causes, it may be necessary to respond and adjust in a time frame other than the one planned.

### *Populations To Be Assessed*

All stakeholders in the community will have valuable information and opinions to share regarding the direction for the school counseling program. The groups commonly asked to participate in the needs assessment are students, parents, administrators, and teachers. Critical issues are frequently determined and discovered when surveying these groups (Schmidt, 2003). Information from community organizations and local business leaders can be helpful, but it may be difficult to obtain a large enough response sample. Therefore it may be prudent to gather this data through personal interviews and contacts (Erford, 2003). Additional information may be gleaned from school volunteers, the school nurse, school psychologist, social worker, and professional organizations. Input from these sources can assist in understanding expectations for the services to be provided (Schmidt, 2003) and supplement other feedback.

Return rate is essential for accurate and meaningful needs assessment results. Students should fill out their survey while at school, perhaps at the end of a class period. It is important to share with the students their significant role in the survey. Stress that their opinion and insights are valued and that honest responses are being sought. Teachers and staff generally respond well, especially if the administration is vocally supportive. The challenge is for a high return rate from parents. A "captured audience" can maximize the return rate so consider gatherings at faculty meetings, class or parent meetings for distributing and collecting surveys (Erford, 2003).

Brainstorm ideas with committee members to garner high enthusiasm and participation rates. Free food is always a draw. Consider enlisting the community, students and faculty in a spaghetti dinner or fish fry. The community could donate food and students and school personnel could cook and serve the families of the school. The ticket is a completed parent survey. Send the surveys home with students ahead of time and have plenty of extra copies at the door. This gathering would provide a wonderful opportunity for building connections with parents. It would also be a forum for sharing information on a host of issues at the school and enlisting parent support. Student groups could be asked to participate to encourage further parent involvement.

*The Instrument*

As stated earlier, there are many sample surveys available. The survey can address the same content area even for elementary students with minor adjustments. It is suggested that the questions not use education- and counseling-specific vocabulary (Cobia & Henderson, 2003). Some surveys use a Likert-type scale of rating the severity or importance of the issue or concern from 1 to 5 or 1 to 7, using terms "never" at one end of the spectrum and "always" at the other extreme. Other approaches include answers of "yes," "no," and "sometimes." Another approach has boxes to be checked for "rarely," "sometimes," "frequently," "most of the time," and "almost always." There are many variations, and the committee may decide to alter an existing survey to accommodate perceived needs or create their own. The content for the needs assessment should be topical, such as questions related to social skills, changes within families, substance abuse, or college application procedures (Erford, 2003). The format for the survey may use questions or statements, for example, "How important is it that 'jokes' regarding sexual orientation be eliminated from the school community?" or "Students need to be more tolerant of people whose views, appearances, or actions differ from their own." The committee may also decide to provide a space for collecting qualitative data with an open question. An example might be: Is there anything else you would like to share with the committee? This will allow for information to emerge that may have otherwise been missed or overlooked.

## The Plan & Evaluation

Once the data has been collected and evaluated, the highest priority needs may be determined and utilized to establish program goals (Rye & Sparks, 1999). The committee will need to weigh and rank results from the data and groups surveyed. The students' highest priority may be different from that of the parents. The needs assessment may lead the committee to ask further questions in focus groups and individual interviews to clarify the data. Gathering additional information may be critical to goal setting and sorting the priorities. In the first year after the needs assessment the school counseling program may elect to focus efforts on the top three to five priorities that emerged. These goals should be concentrated on for at least a year before adding additional goals. An exemplary school counseling program evolves over a number of years, not in one year. Remember to seek the school boards' endorsement after the needs assessment is completed and goals and objectives have been determined.

## Summary/Conclusion

After joining and merging the voices from students, teachers, parents, school board members, administrators, community leaders, and professional school counselors, the emerging school counseling program will reflect the unique needs of the community. In turn by focusing on prevention and developmental goals for students, professional school counselors do more than repair wounds and mend fences; they create healthy school climates and enhance human relationships (Schmidt, 2003). Administering a needs assessment is a time-consuming, tedious, and necessary adventure that binds together the school's stakeholders with the professional school counselors in a noble and worthwhile cause: the creation of a meaningful and successful program that makes a real difference in the lives of students, families, and community.

## References

Baker, S. (2000). *School counseling for the twenty-first century.* Upper Saddle River, NJ: Prentice-Hall.

Campbell, C. A., & Dahir, C. A. (1997). *Sharing the vision: The national standards for school counseling programs.* Alexandria, VA: American School Counselor Association.

Cobia, D. C., & Henderson, D. A. (2003). *Handbook of school counseling.* Upper Saddle Creek, NJ: Merrill/Prentice-Hall.

Erford, B. T. (2003). *Transforming the school counseling profession.* Columbus, OH: Merrill/ Prentice-Hall.

Gladding, S. T. (2000). *Counseling: A comprehensive profession.* Upper Saddle Creek, NJ: Prentice-Hall.

Greenberg, K. R. (2003). *Group counseling in K-12 schools: A handbook for school counselors.* Boston, MA: Pearson Education.

Moore-Thomas, C., & Erford, B. (2003). Needs assessment. In J. Walls & G. R. Walz (Eds.), *Measuring up*. Greensboro, NC: ERIC-CAPS.

Rye, D. R., & Sparks, R. (1999). *Strengthening K-12 school counseling programs: A support system.* Philadelphia, PA: Accelerated Development.

Schmidt, J. J. (2003). *Counseling in schools: Essential services and comprehensive programs (3rd ed.).* Needham Heights, MA: Allyn & Bacon.

Stone, L. A., & Bradley, F. O. (1994). *Foundations of elementary and middle school counseling.* White Plains, NY: Longman.

VanZandt, Z., & Hayslip, J. (2001). *Developing your school-counseling program: A handbook for systemic planning.* Belmont, CA: Wadsworth/Thomson Learning.

# Chapter 31

## How to Write Learning Objectives

*Bradley T. Erford & Jennifer A. McKechnie*

### Preview

This chapter helps professional school counselors develop measurable behavioral objectives to guide the activities which comprise developmental guidance programs. Special emphasis is given to aligning behavioral objectives with programmatic standards, competencies and assessment strategies so that evidence can be generated to document that program standards and student learning outcomes are being met.

It has been said that "if you don't know where you're going, you can't get there" (Saphier & Gower, 1997, p. 397). In addition, it doesn't matter in which direction you go. Obviously, such an approach is disastrous in the educational setting because effective instruction is supposed to change behaviors, thoughts and feelings in a desirable direction (Mager, 1997). Yet for years some professional school counselors have entered the classroom to provide developmental guidance activities with wonderfully entertaining materials, interesting activities, or professionally-produced videos, but no clear understanding or statement of what changes in student thoughts, feelings and behaviors were to be accomplished.

The same was true for individual and small group work. Professional school counselors often viewed the provision of these services as ends in themselves, rather than means to an end (Ripley, Erford, Dahir, & Eschbach, 2003). Thus, students of divorce participated in a group or individual counseling experience because these were ways to provide services, but little thought was given as to what the students were to get out of these services (i.e., the outcomes). Often these outcomes simply went unstated, but in many instances there was no guiding plan to move students in a positive developmental direction.

This lack of direction was in part due to the lack of an agreed upon domain of knowledge or behaviors specific to school counseling programs (Herr, 2003). Other academic disciplines (e.g., math, social studies, science) have well-defined and agreed upon domains of knowledge which result in first grade teachers (for example) across the country basically teaching very similar content and skills. While variations in curriculum no doubt occur, particularly as students get into middle and high schools, the fact remains that all academic disciplines plan for learning to occur in a systematic, sequential and developmental manner. Until recently, this domain of knowledge and planfulness have been missing in many school counseling programs.

The ASCA *National Standards* (Campbell & Dahir, 1997) was a very positive step toward conceptualizing and establishing a school counseling domain of knowledge. The *Standards* also provided competencies associated with each standard to further explain what was to be accomplished. In chapters 29 and 32 of this book, the curriculum development sequence is identified as follows: standards, competencies/indicators, objectives, activities, and assessment. Whether one uses the ASCA *National Standards* or state/local standards or goals, good curriculum development starts at the level of standards or goals to ensure the broad domain of knowledge is identified. Competencies (sometimes analogous to the term "indicator") capture in broad terms the actions, skills, or abilities students must develop. Objectives help to further define and explain competencies and must be stated in specific, measurable terms to identify what will be accomplished as a result of the student participating in the planned activities. Lessons or activities then are developed to provide the knowledge or experiences that allow students to accomplish the objectives. Finally, assessment of the objective occurs to determine the extent to which student learning, skills, and abilities developed during the lessons. If the objective is stated correctly, the professional school counselor will be able to assess whether the objective has actually been met.

## The Objective of the Objective

Mager (1997, p. 3) defined an objective as a "collection of words and/or pictures and diagrams intended to let others know what you intend for your students to achieve." In curriculum development, one first must determine where one wants students to end up (the objective) before creating the means to move them there (lessons and activities) and finally evaluating whether they have arrived (assessment). Thus, objectives are focused on outcomes rather than process, measurable and specific rather than broad or general, and student-focused rather than teacher-focused.

### *The Purpose of a Learning Objective*

Learning objectives serve several purposes (Mager, 1997). First, objectives help professional school counselors to develop activities and select procedures, resources and materials. A plumber does not select a tool until he knows what he needs to accomplish. Likewise, a professional school counselor should not select a favored or entertaining activity and make it "fit" into the curriculum. Second, learning objectives help to obtain consistent results. Objectives serve as road maps leading to a reliable and consistent outcome. Finally, learning objectives make instruction more efficient. When a professional school counselor selects appropriate learning objectives, it is assumed that those objectives serve to structure the available time. If activities do not support a learning objective then the activity becomes nonessential. This is not to say that students will not learn important lessons from nonessential activities, just that what they learn might lie outside of the domain of knowledge that should be mastered.

### *Types of "Teacher Thinking"*

According to Mager (1997), there are five basic types of objectives and each is linked to a specific purpose that an instructor may have. A *coverage objective* merely involves a description of what will be covered in a lesson (e.g., students will learn to resolve conflict). An *activity objective* designates the actual activities that students will engage in (e.g., students will read pages 54-59). An *involvement objective* specifies what students will "get into" (e.g., students will react to a poem on the virtues of problem-solving, as opposed to aggression when resolving conflict). *Thinking skills objectives* focus on the thought processes that must be developed in order to achieve mastery objectives (e.g., students will develop the ability to think critically about the causes and solutions to conflict). *Mastery objectives* state in specific, measurable terms what a student will actually be able to do after a lesson (e.g., after observing four role-plays of students in conflict, 90% of students will be able to list at least three nonviolent ways to resolve a conflict). Most educators tend to think in terms of the first four types listed above. However, mastery objectives are essential to the curriculum because they relate to outcomes that result in student change and development, thereby subsuming all the other types of objectives.

*Qualities of Measurable Learning Objectives*

High quality learning objectives effectively communicate what is to be accomplished in specific terms (Mager, 1997). As such, some words commonly used in nonspecific learning objectives (e.g., to know, to understand, to appreciate, to internalize, to believe, to enjoy) leave one wondering how to demonstrate that the student has accomplished what she set out to do. Therefore, words leading to more specific interpretations and which can be demonstrated through student performance should be used (e.g., to write, to compare/contrast, to solve, to construct, to identify, to build).

*Teaching the Elusive Intangibles*

Historically, many professional school counselors have resisted the accountability movement, some out of frustration of trying to describe the complex developmental change processes that students must undergo to become productive citizens. Some particularly recalcitrant professional school counselors take the position that the changes one seeks to make in students are too complex or intangible to measure. After all, how does one measure motivation, self-esteem, and success? This view of school counseling program outcomes as intangible and immeasurable is counterproductive, at best, and self-extinctive, at worst.

Think about it: How long would a math curriculum (or math teacher) survive if the students subjected to it did not improve their math skills? Likewise, now that a domain of knowledge and behavior (standards and competencies) has been established for school counseling programs, how long will school counseling programs (or professional school counselors) survive if the students subjected to it do not improve their academic, career and personal/social development. The issue is no longer can we measure student performance in these three domains, but how will we measure it? The how is made possible through writing specific learning objectives.

"If you are teaching things that cannot be evaluated, you are in the awkward position of being unable to demonstrate that you are teaching anything at all" (Mager, 1997, p. 113). This is a classic dilemma: If one is teaching something that is intangible, it cannot be evaluated; if it cannot be evaluated, one cannot determine that it has been mastered; and if it cannot be mastered, why would one teach it? What value could it possibly have within a curriculum?

The answer to this dilemma, of course, is to teach what can be mastered and write the learning objective in a way that mastery can be determined. At a basic level, this is the difference between process and outcomes. Process has to do with the instructional methodology (e.g., exploring, debating) which is the means and not the end. The *outcome* is the end. The outcome involves the actual learning result that can be demonstrated through assessment of the learning objective. The bottom line is that if one is willing to decide (intuitively) that a student is performing satisfactorily on some intangible process, then with a little more effort, one can understand, describe, and develop criteria to assess the basis for that satisfaction.

## The ABCDs of a Well-Written Learning Objective

A well-written learning objective focuses the lesson on specific student outcomes and accomplishments. While experts generally agree on the essential components of a learning objective, they do not always agree on the components that lead to a determination of mastery. Because the emphasis of this chapter is on helping professional school counselors develop mastery objectives, an integrated approach is used (Goodnough, Perusse, & Erford, 2003; Kellough & Roberts, 1998; Mager, 1997; Saphier & Gower, 1997). The authors of the current chapter offer an ABCD model for writing learning objectives: A) Audience, B) Behavior, C) Conditions, and D) Description of the expected performance criterion.

*Audience*

The first essential component of a well-written learning objective involves the audience for whom the objective is intended. Because the primary recipient of an individual or group counseling session or large-group developmental guidance lesson is the student, almost all applicable objectives will be targeted at the student audience. Thus, many learning objectives begin with phrases such as, "Students will . . . " or "Students will be able to . . . " Less frequently used audiences may include teachers, parents, or an entire class or group of students.

*Behavior*

The second essential component addresses the behavior that one expects the student to engage in or be able to think, solve or do. "These behaviors are typically descriptive verbs that address the . . . outcome around which the lesson is structured" (Goodnough et al., 2003, p. 139). Examples of objectives using these descriptive verbs include, "Students will be able to recognize cooperative group behaviors" or "Students will be able to identify five methods that would help them cope with loss and subsequent grief." The behavioral component of a learning objective deals with cognitive, affective or behavioral outcomes.

*Conditions*

This component describes the conditions under which the behavior is to occur (Mager, 1997). It is essential to identify "when" or "how" measurement of the behavior will occur. Typical conditions are tests, worksheets, observations, role-plays, or after engaging in some structured activity. Examples of the conditions component include, "After completing a worksheet listing ten scenarios of cooperative group behaviors, students will be able to recognize cooperative group behaviors," or "After reading an article on loss, students will be able to identify five methods that would help them cope with loss and subsequent grief." Mager (p. 87) suggested that conditions address three main questions: "What will the learner be expected to use when performing . . . not be allowed to use . . .[and] What will be the real-world conditions under which the performance will be expected to occur."

*Description of the Expected Performance Criterion*

The final component of a well-written learning objective, and the one that is most often left out, is a description of the criterion for expected performance. Generally, this criterion takes the form of the amount of a task the student must perform successfully (e.g., 90% correct on a test) or the percentage of students that successfully display the behavior under the given conditions (e.g., 80% of students). The criterion sets the level of acceptable performance, the level that students are challenged to surpass. Thus, examples of completed objectives using the ABCD model include, "After completing a worksheet listing ten scenarios of cooperative group behaviors, 75% of fifth grade students will be able to recognize one cooperative group behavior in each scenario," or "After reading an article on loss, 80% of students will be able to identify five methods that would help them cope with loss and subsequent grief."

The criterion for mastery is an essential part of a learning objective because, without it, the expectation is for perfection. While it is praiseworthy to strive for perfection, student motivation, preparation, test-taking skills, work habits, instructional strategies and myriad other potential problems often interfere with performance and lead to some degree of nonmastery.

If one sets the criterion too high then the objective is not met. Returning to the earlier discussion of aggregation, if objectives are not met, then no evidence exists that competencies (or indicators) have been met. If competencies have not been met this means that the standards (or goals) have gone unmet. In this case, the professional school counselor has no proof that the school counseling program has had any desirable impact—at all! Thus, it is essential to set a reasonable criterion for each objective so that students are challenged, while at the same time accurate accountability measurement occurs. The criterion can be qualified to include the number of times a student must perform, the length of time of a performance, an accuracy ratio (percent of time), the percentage of students who can perform the task, and the quality of the task (generally scored according to some rubric of quality indicators).

Mager (1997) underscored the importance of the behavioral criterion by pointing out that a criterion provides a standard against which the success of the instruction or intervention can be tested, tells students when they have met or exceeded expectations, and provides a basis for concluding that students can do what an instructor sought to accomplish.

## Avoiding the Pitfalls

While the preceding sections focused on what professional school counselors should do to write effective learning objectives, Mager (1997) pointed out a number of important characteristics of ineffective objectives that should be avoided. First, avoid terms that indicate a *false performance*, or no real performance at all. For example, how would one determine whether a "... thorough understanding of peer mediation ..." ever existed? Second, one should avoid *false givens* (conditions) such as, "Given adequate practice in time management ..." Third, avoid *gibberish* (e.g., "demonstrate a comprehensive understanding of ..."). Finally, avoid identifying *instructor performance*—what the professional school counselor or teacher is supposed to accomplish (e.g., "the professional school counselor will help students to ..."). The emphasis is always on the stakeholder who is to demonstrate mastery. Avoiding the pitfalls will help the professional school counselor construct concise learning objectives that will demonstrate mastery performance and effective school counseling services.

## Summary/Conclusion

A well-written learning objective is an essential starting point for demonstrating the effectiveness of a comprehensive developmental school counseling program. The ABCD model (Audience, Behavior, Conditions, and Description of expected performance criterion) has all the components necessary to craft a well-written mastery-level learning objective. Objectives written in this way provide a built-in process for accountability of school counseling programs, particularly when used to structure and guide individual and group counseling sessions and classroom guidance.

## References

Campbell, C., & Dahir, C. (1997). *National standards for school counseling programs.* Alexandria, VA: American School Counselor Association.

Goodnough, G., Perusse, R., & Erford, B. T. (2003). Developmental classroom guidance. In B. T. Erford (Ed.), *Transforming the school counseling profession* (pp. 121–152). Columbus, OH: Merrill/Prentice-Hall.

Herr, E. (2003). Historical roots and future issues. In B. T. Erford (Ed.), *Transforming the school counseling profession* (pp. 121-152). Columbus, OH: Merrill/Prentice-Hall.

Kellough, R. D., & Roberts, P. L. (1998). *A resource guide for elementary school teaching* (4th ed.). Upper Saddle River, NJ: Merrill.

Mager, R. F. (1997). *Preparing instructional objectives: A critical tool in the development of effective instruction.* Atlanta, GA: The Center For Effective Performance.

Ripley, V., Erford, B. T., Dahir, C., & Eschbach, L. (2003). Planning and implementing a 21st century comprehensive developmental school counseling program. In B. T. Erford (Ed.), *Transforming the school counseling profession* (pp. 121–152). Columbus, OH: Merrill/ Prentice-Hall.

Saphier, J., & Gower, R. (1997). *The skillful teacher.* Carlisle, MA: Research for Better Teaching, Inc.

# Chapter 32

## Designing Developmental Guidance Lessons

*Ann Vernon*

### Preview

This chapter addresses practical considerations to help professional school counselors effectively deliver the developmental and preventive component of a comprehensive school counseling program. Specific topics include how to develop grade level objectives, how to write and adapt lessons using a guidance lesson plan format, and how to determine the scope and sequence of lessons. Sample lessons are provided, as well as a discussion about implementing the school counseling curriculum and the role that teachers and professional school counselors should assume.

In the early years of the counseling profession, guidance was conceptualized as a position, not a program. However, schools must now be more responsive to the increasing complexity and diversity of our society, as well as to changes in personal and social values and social structures. Gysbers (2001) noted that "these changes are creating complex challenges for students as they anticipate the future" (p. 96). Increasing violence, substance abuse, teenage suicide, sexual experimentation, and a rapidly changing work force, among other factors, have a significant impact on student development (Gysbers & Henderson, 2000). According to Gysbers and Henderson, guidance services must be reconceptualized to better address the challenges brought about by these changes.

A significant aspect of the reconceptualization of guidance services has been the gradual evolution from a smorgasbord-of-services approach to a comprehensive program. Green and Keys (2001) pointed out that "a developmental orientation has become a highly desired, core characteristic of school counseling programs" (p. 85). Paisley and Borders (1995) concurred, noting that school counseling programs should be comprehensive and developmental, emphasizing primary prevention and healthy development for all students.

In support of the comprehensive program focus, and in an effort to better prepare students to deal with factors that impact their development, the American School Counselor Association (ASCA) assumed a key leadership role in developing national standards for a comprehensive approach to program delivery, management, and accountability (Hatch & Bowers, 2002). *The National Model for School Counseling Programs* is designed to promote and enhance the learning process by facilitating student development in three domains: academic, career, and personal/social. This model "incorporates school counseling standards and competencies for every student, which serve as the foundation for the program and focus the direction for an organized, planned, sequential and flexible counseling curriculum" (Hatch & Bowers, 2002, p. 15).

As more and more counselors transform their programs to reflect the beliefs and practices of a comprehensive developmental program, it becomes increasingly important that they know how to design, develop, and deliver the developmental and preventive component that forms the core of the comprehensive program. Through the guidance lessons integral to this component, students are taught developmentally appropriate personal/social, academic, and career development concepts to increase their knowledge and skills and help ensure healthy development.

The purpose of this chapter is to describe the process of identifying grade level competencies and how to develop guidance lessons that address specific competencies. A guidance lesson plan format is described, along with information about scope and sequence of lessons and developmental considerations. In addition, the role of the counselor and teacher in implementing guidance lessons as part of the developmental/preventative component of a comprehensive program will be discussed.

## Designing the Developmental Curriculum

Incorporating developmental principles into a comprehensive curriculum is a daunting yet critical task for professional school counselors at all levels. In designing this curriculum, professional school counselors need to assume a leadership role in developing the scope and sequence of the program in accordance with developmental considerations. *The National Standards for School Counseling Programs*, which are based on extensive research and field reviews (Dahir, 2001), provided professional school counselors with the attitudes, knowledge, and skills that students should acquire in the areas of personal/social, academic, and career development and include examples of three broad standards in each of these domains that can serve as a basis for the curriculum. The ASCA standards also identify competencies. These are very general, however, and professional school counselors will need to develop more specific grade-level competencies for each of the standards in each domain.

In designing these competencies, it is important to consider the developmental tasks students must accomplish in grades K-12 and identify specific competencies accordingly. For example, an appropriate interpersonal relationship competency for kindergartners would be to learn to share and cooperate; whereas an appropriate interpersonal relationship competency for 8th graders would be to learn effective ways to deal with peer pressure; and for 11th graders, an appropriate interpersonal relationship competency would be to learn how to deal with dating relationships. It is important to consult sources such as *Developmental Assessment and Intervention with Children and Adolescents* (Vernon, 1993) for information about developmental tasks. In writing the competencies, be very specific and avoid words like "to understand" or "to appreciate" because they are harder to measure. In this era of accountability, words such as "identify," "differentiate," or "describe" allow practitioners to develop ways to measure what students have learned. It is also easier to design a lesson that addresses the competencies when they are very concrete and specific.

It is also necessary to determine the number of competencies per grade level, which is usually based on the number of lessons you intend to deliver throughout the course of a year. Assuming that there will be 30-36 lessons (one per week), you would take the three standards (personal/social, academic, and career development), decide if you want to give equal emphasis to them (12 competencies per standard) or weigh one more heavily than the others, and then identify specific grade-level competencies accordingly. To illustrate, the ASCA standards (Dahir, Sheldon, & Valiga, 1998, p. 16) for personal/social development include:

Standard A—Students will acquire the attitudes, knowledge, and interpersonal skills to help them understand and respect self and others.

Standard B—Students will make decisions, set goals, and take necessary action to achieve goals.

Standard C—Students will understand safety and survival skills.

There are 21 competencies in Standard A, divided into two categories: acquire self-knowledge and acquire interpersonal skills. There are also 12 competencies in Standard B and 11 in Standard C. Professional school counselors should study these competencies to determine if they want to use these as a basis for developing their own grade level competencies, if there are others that should be added, or if there are some that would fit better under one standard than another. For example, "learning to cope with peer pressure," which is listed under personal/social development Standard C (understand safety and survival skills) could also be included under Standard A (acquire the attitudes, knowledge and interpersonal skills to help them understand and respect self and others). Likewise, "demonstrate a respect and appreciation for individual and cultural differences," which is included under Standard B (students will make decisions, set goals, and take necessary action to achieve goals) is perhaps better suited for Standard A since it relates to respecting self and others. As professional school counselors study the competencies, they may also see areas that aren't addressed and should be included. This is the process of *personalizing* the curriculum for individual school districts. Also, remember that while the general focus of a comprehensive program is on development, there may also be some situationally-specific areas that need to be added to the curriculum to address needs in a particular school district. For example, if you live in a high poverty area, you would want to reword the competency that reads "recognize, accept, and appreciate ethnic and cultural diversity" (Dahir et al., 1998, p. 16) to include sensitivity to socioeconomic diversity as well.

After studying the ASCA competencies, you may decide to modify them, not use them at all and write your own, or use them as they are. If you use them verbatim and also incorporate the 43 career development competencies and the 34 academic development competencies, you would have a total of 121 competencies to separate into grade level categories. This would roughly be the equivalent of 10 competencies for each grade 1-12, or 9 competencies grades K-12. Therefore, if you intend to have a year-long curriculum, which would be approximately 30-36 weeks, you would either need to have multiple lessons for each competency or add competencies.

*Grade-Level Competencies*

To illustrate this process, following is part of the personal/social domain with examples of grade-level competencies. The ASCA Standard A under personal/social development has been rewritten as follows: Students will acquire the attitudes, knowledge, and skills to help them understand and respect self and others and identify and effectively express feelings. This standard as reworded includes self-development, emotional development, and social development. Instead of using the ASCA competencies, the following uses specific grade-level competencies/objectives from *The Passport Program: A Journey Through Social, Emotional, Cognitive, and Self-Development* (Vernon, 1998a; 1998b; 1998c). Due to space limitations, Table 1 lists only three competencies per grade level, but there are at least 6 per grade level in this curriculum. Also due to space restrictions, the self-development competencies will be identified only for grades 1-5, emotional development competencies only for grades 6-8, and social development competencies only for grades 9-12, even though there are competencies for each grade in each of these areas. The intent here is to give the reader an idea of the scope and sequence when developing grade-level competencies. Had there been space to reproduce all the objectives, the reader would be able to see the developmental progression from grade level to grade level as well as recognize that most of the ASCA competencies are represented in the more specific grade-level competencies of *The Passport Program*.

When developing a total comprehensive curriculum, a similar process would include grade-level competencies for decision making (ASCA personal/social standard B) and safety and survival skills (ASCA personal/social standard C), as well as competencies for the career and academic development standards.

**Table 1. Selected Competencies From The Passport Program.**

*Self-Development - Grade 1.*

Students will:

- Learn that everyone has strengths and weaknesses.
- Develop an attitude of self-acceptance.
- Identify ways in which they are growing and changing.

*Self-Development - Grade 2*

- Develop awareness of abilities and attributes.
- Learn to accept oneself with these abilities and attributes.
- Recognize that strengths and limitations are part of one's self-definition and to not put themselves down because of limitations.

*Self-Development - Grade 3*

- Learn that how one acts does not determine self-worth.
- Learn that nobody is perfect and to accept themselves as less than perfect.
- Identify characteristics of self, including strengths and weaknesses.

*Self-Development - Grade 4*

- Learn that making mistakes does not make one a bad person.
- Learn that others' approval is not required to be worthwhile.
- Identify individual preferences, characteristics, and abilities.

*Self-Development - Grade 5*

- Identify specific characteristics that are like or unlike oneself.
- Identify feelings associated with varying rates of development.
- Differentiate between making mistakes and being a total failure.

*Emotional Development - Grade 6*

- Learn that feelings can change.
- Learn specific ways to feel happier.
- Understand the connection between feelings and behaviors.

*Emotional-Development - Grade 7*

- Identify what experiences trigger anger and how to effectively control and/or express anger.
- Identify ways to increase positive feelings.
- Identify strategies for dealing with intense negative emotions.

*Emotional-Development - Grade 8*

- Learn effective ways to deal with the ups and downs associated with puberty.
- Learn how thinking affects feeling and how to change feelings by changing thoughts.
- Learn how to distinguish between healthy and unhealthy ways to relieve emotional pain.

*Social Development - Grade 9*

- Develop skills for dealing with interpersonal relationship problems.
- Examine the positive and negative aspects of peer pressure.
- Identify ways to resist peer pressure.

*Social Development - Grade 10*

- Learn how to stop the negative cycle of rumors, gossip, and assumptions that affect relationships.

- Identify feelings and issues involved in the termination of a romantic relationship.
- Identify effective ways to deal with the break up of a relationship.

*Social Development - Grade 11*

- Learn to distinguish between healthy and unhealthy dependence in relationships.
- Learn what one can and cannot control in relationships with others.
- Learn to distinguish between healthy and unhealthy ways to deal with relationship issues.

*Social Development - Grade 12*

- Identify effective strategies for dealing with parent-teen relationships.
- Identify ways to deal with competition in relationships.
- Identify feelings and issues involved in intimate relationships.

---

## Developmental Guidance Lessons

After developing the grade-level competencies for personal/social, academic, and career development, the next step is to identify the objectives and activities to achieve the competency. Again, this may seem like a monumental task, but in reality, the field is replete with emotional education curricula, career development programs, games, workbooks, and bibliotherapy resources. The problem lies in selecting programs or materials that correspond to the specific competencies. Obviously the most effective way to address this problem is to write your own lessons. A sample lesson plan format, developed for *The Passport Program* (Vernon 1998a; 1998b; 1998c) emotional education curriculums, may serve as a helpful guide.

*Lesson Plan Format*

The first step in writing a guidance lesson would be to specify the grade level, the standard (personal/social, academic, or career development), and the grade level competency or competencies (usually no more than two per lesson) and the session objective(s) (also usually no more than two per lesson). The next step is to create a short (15-20 minutes depending on the amount of time allotted) stimulus activity that addresses each competency. The stimulus activity might be a bibliotherapy selection, role play, simulation, game, worksheet, or a music or art activity, among others. Professional school counselors can create their own activities or find activities from commercial sources that match their competencies. In selecting activities from commercial sources, it may be necessary to adapt the activity so that it directly addresses the specific competency. In other words, if the competency is "students will identify various degrees of anger," it would not be appropriate to have a general lesson on feelings. The lesson should specifically relate to anger.

After the activity has been written or selected from commercial resources, the next step is to identify two types of discussion questions to help process the lesson. Although the stimulus activity is an important way to introduce the concepts, the discussion is equally important because it helps students clarify what they learned. This is the part, however, that often gets slighted because the activity takes up too much of the time, so it is critical to allow at least 15 minutes of the allotted lesson time for discussion. The discussion questions developed for this lesson prototype include *content questions* and *personalization questions.* Content questions pertain to the content of the activity (e.g., what happened in the story they read, what occurred during the role play, or what their responses were on the worksheet they completed). Personalization questions help students personalize the information and apply it to their own lives. For example, if they read a story about a boy who was teased, personalization questions might be: Have you ever been teased? If so, how did you handle it? What does it say about you if you are teased? What can you do next time you are teased? The final step in the lesson plan format is the assessment component.

To further illustrate the lesson plan format and the examples of content and personalization questions, the following lesson (Vernon, 1998b, pp. 203-204) is presented. This lesson is for 8th graders. Developmentally, many young adolescents experience discouragement, ambivalence, depression, shame and confusion that often seem unbearable. Many lack the ability to deal constructively with their feelings and adopt unhealthy ways to relieve their pain. A lesson of this nature helps them learn more effective coping strategies.

*Pain Relievers*

*Competency:* To distinguish between healthy and unhealthy ways to relieve emotional pain.

*Objective:* After completing a tag bag poster, all groups of students will be able to identify at least two healthy and unhealthy ways to deal with a painful emotion.

*Materials*: A chalkboard and the following for each group of four students: magazines, scissors, glue, a large sheet of tag board, and markers.

*Procedure/Activities:*

1. Introduce the activity by having students quickly brainstorm examples of painful emotions. As they identify examples, write them on the board. Next, discuss the difference between healthy and unhealthy ways of dealing with painful emotions. For example, anger can be a painful emotion. An unhealthy way to deal with anger would be to get drunk. A healthy way to deal with it would be to talk it out.
2. Divide students into groups of four and distribute the materials. Instruct them to make two columns on the bottom half of the tag board poster and to label one side "Healthy Ways to Deal with Painful Emotions" and the other side "Unhealthy Ways to Deal with Painful Emotions." Ask each group to list several (at least two) painful emotions at the top of the poster. Then have them look through the magazines for pictures representing at least two healthy and two unhealthy ways to deal with these emotions. If they can't find appropriate pictures, have them draw pictures or symbols. In either case students should use words to represent their suggestions.
3. After the posters have been completed, have the small groups share them with the total group.
4. Discuss the content and personalization questions.

*Discussion*

*Content Questions*

1. Which are harder to identify: healthy or unhealthy ways to deal with painful emotions?
2. In general, were the small groups in agreement with each other? Were there some ideas that one group labeled unhealthy that you might have considered healthy, or vice versa? (Ask students to share examples and remember that what students identify as healthy and unhealthy may vary depending on culture.)
3. What makes the unhealthy methods unhealthy? Do you really think they help relieve pain in the long term? Why or why not?

*Personalization Questions*

1. Are your "pain relievers" generally healthy or unhealthy? How do you feel about that?

2. If you have tried unhealthy methods in the past, how has this affected your life? If you had it to do over, what might you do differently, if anything?
3. Did you learn anything from this lesson that will be helpful to you in dealing with painful emotions? Invite sharing.

*Assessment:* The instructor should collect the tag bag posters to verify that each group of students could list at least two healthy and two unhealthy ways to deal with a painful emotion. If all groups are able to do so, the objective for the session has been met.

Using this lesson plan format provides counselors and teachers with a framework that helps organize the lesson and assure greater accountability because the content and personalization questions relate specifically to the identified competency.

### Implementing the Counseling Curriculum

Although the phrase "for all students" is rooted deep within the philosophy of a comprehensive program and has generally been a characteristic of elementary counseling programs since their evolution, this concept necessitates a role change for counselors, particularly at the high school level where functions have been more traditional. Numerous authors (Gysbers, 2001; Gysbers & Henderson, 2000; Paisley & McMahon, 2001; Tollerud & Nejedlo, 1999) support this change because it has the potential to impact so many students and assist them with the mastery of developmental tasks. Tollerud and Nejedlo (1999) stressed that "prevention can be integrated into individual and small group counseling, but for children and adolescents, its primary infusion comes through the counseling and guidance curriculum offered in the classroom" (p. 336).

As counselors transition into the classroom, it is important to remember that classroom developmental guidance needs to be a team effort. As specified in the underlying principles of a comprehensive program, the professional school counselor is *not* the counseling program. Although the intent of a comprehensive program that emphasizes prevention is to reduce the focus on crisis and remedial intervention, it is naïve to assume that we can eliminate all problems through prevention. Because professional school counselors, not teachers, are the ones who are trained to do crisis and remedial intervention, they must continue to assume this role, but it is also unreasonable to think that they can do this on top of all the prevention. For this reason, training teachers to take an active role in delivering developmental classroom guidance lessons is imperative.

According to Tollerud and Nejedlo (1999) professional school counselors can train teachers in the types of lessons as well as the process. They can model teaching of personal/social, academic, and career guidance lessons that ultimately enhance development. In addition, professional school counselors can assist teachers in identifying ways to incorporate personal/social, academic, and career development objectives into their specific subject matter.

Tollerud and Nejedlo (1999) outlined several key principles of a counseling curriculum: that they help students cope with normal developmental issues and problems; that they consider the nature of human development, including the general stages and tasks of normal development; and that they not only encompass a remedial and crisis approach, but a preventative focus as well. Gysbers and Henderson (2001) also stressed that the human development perspective is the foundation for the program and the basis for identifying the competencies that students need to master. Sharing these principles with teachers and administrators will help clarify misconceptions they may have about a guidance curriculum.

## Summary/Conclusion

The purpose of this chapter was to give practitioners suggestions for promoting healthy development in all students by implementing, in conjunction with teachers, the core component of a comprehensive developmental program: the guidance curriculum. Use of the ASCA standards and broad competencies as a basis for developing specific grade-level competencies was described to help professional school counselors move to the next level: identifying or writing developmentally-appropriate guidance activities to achieve the competencies. The lesson plan format that was presented has proven to be a viable format for teachers and professional school counselors to use, and readers are encouraged to use a structure of this nature that emphasizes knowledge and skill acquisition and also helps students personalize the information to their own situations for optimal learning.

## References


Dahir, C. A. (2001). The national standards for school counseling programs: Development and implementation. *Professional School Counseling, 4*, 320–327.

Dahir, C. A., Sheldon, C. B., & Valiga, M. J. (1998). *Vision into action: Implementing the national standards for school counseling programs.* Alexandria, VA: American School Counselor Association.

Green, A., & Keys, S. (2001). Expanding the developmental school counseling paradigm: Meeting the needs of the 21st century student. *Professional School Counseling, 5*, 84–95.

Gysbers, N. C. (2001). School guidance and counseling in the 21st century: Remember the past into the future. *Professional School Counseling, 5*, 96-105.

Gysbers, N. C., & Henderson, P. (2000). *Developing and managing your school guidance program* (3rd ed.). Alexandria, VA: American Counseling Association.

Gysbers, N. C., & Henderson, P. (2001). Comprehensive guidance and counseling programs: A rich history and a bright future. *Professional School Counseling, 4,* 246–256.

Hatch, T., & Bowers, J. (2002). The block to build on. *ASCA School Counselor,* 13–17.

Paisley, P. O., & Borders, L. D. (1995). School counseling: An evolving specialty. *Journal of Counseling and Development, 2,* 179–182.

Paisley, P. O., & McMahon, H. G. (2001). School counseling for the 21st century: Challenges and opportunities. *Professional School Counseling, 5,* 106–115.

Tollerud, T. R., & Nejedlo, R. J. (1999). Designing a developmental counseling curriculum. In A. Vernon (Ed.),*Counseling children and adolescents.* Denver, CO: Love Publishing.

Vernon, A. (1993). *Developmental assessment and intervention with children and adolescents.* Alexandria, VA: American Counseling Association.

Vernon, A. (1998a). *The passport program: A journey through emotional, social, cognitive, and self–development* (grades 1–5). Champaign, IL: Research Press.

Vernon, A. (1998b). *The passport program: A journey through emotional, social, cognitive, and self–development* (grades 6–8). Champaign, IL: Research Press.

Vernon, A. (1998c). *The passport program: A journey through emotional, social, cognitive, and self–development* (grades 9-12). Champaign, IL: Research Press.

# Chapter 33

## Setting up and Managing a Classroom

*Carlen Henington & R. Anthony Doggett*

### Preview

This chapter will provide the professional school counselor with recommendations that school personnel are likely to find helpful in getting the school-year off to a good start and in maintaining an efficient and effective classroom environment throughout the year. This chapter includes information about effective physical arrangement of the classroom, setting up and teaching classroom rules and procedures, and utilizing effective behavior management strategies including differential reinforcement, group contingencies, token economies, behavior contracts, overcorrection, time-out, and response cost procedures. To maximize the recommendations presented in this chapter, it is advised that the professional school counselor assist teachers in developing a comprehensive plan for their classroom at the very beginning of the school year prior to student attendance. However, the information within this chapter can be implemented with minor modifications at anytime during the school year. As such, the professional school counselor may want to consult this chapter throughout the academic year as student and/or classroom referrals are received.

At the end of the first nine weeks Mr. Jones, a new teacher at the school, approached Mrs. Williams, the professional school counselor. He stated that he did not believe he was "cut out" to be a teacher. Mrs. Williams thought, "What had gone wrong?" On his first day of school, Mr. Jones had told her that he was looking forward to having his own classroom, to meeting the children and to making a difference in their lives. He was finally a teacher! As she spoke with Mr. Jones, Mrs. Williams discovered that, like many new teachers, he was having difficulty keeping his students on task. He spent so much of the day trying to redirect them, he was not able to get through the material he had prepared for the class. He asked, "Mrs. Williams, do you have any suggestions?"

The above scenario is not uncommon in schools across the nation. The professional school counselor may be asked to either design a learning environment for students such as a social-skills class for students experiencing peer relation difficulties or to assist a new teacher in getting the new school-year off to a good start. Professional school counselors also need these skills to help facilitate classroom management instructional efficiency in comprehensive developmental school counseling programs. At other times the professional school counselor might be asked to make a presentation to more seasoned teachers so they are more likely to have a smooth running classroom during the school year. Professional school counselors serving as faculty trainers also need to be proficient in classroom management to assist their instruction in a comprehensive developmental school counseling program. For all of these situations, the professional school counselor will find this chapter useful.

Recommendations for classroom management starting before the first day of class and continuing through the school year will be presented. This chapter will include suggestions for:

- physical classroom structure;
- rules, schedules, & procedures;
- managing transitions; and
- enhancing and maintaining student motivation.

Although there are other areas that foster a proficient classroom environment, professional school counselors are frequently asked to address these four areas. In addition, while the following sections focus on suggestions for the classroom teacher, the concepts apply equally to school counselors when conducting developmental classroom guidance.

## Physical Classroom Structure

Organizing a classroom requires planning in a number of areas. The well-prepared professional school counselor will begin these tasks long before the first day of the school year. This preparation includes finding out about the students who will be in the classroom. This foreknowledge allows for anticipation of many of the situations that may cause difficulty later.

*Classroom Arrangement*

Researchers have long established that the physical arrangement of a classroom has a direct effect on student behavior. For example, students with Attention-Deficit/Hyperactivity Disorder are frequently provided with "preferential seating" in which they are placed near the front of the classroom, away from windows, air conditioners and other distracting stimuli, and close to the teacher. When careful consideration is made of these situations, a distractible student has been found to be more productive and less disruptive in the classroom.

Paine, Radicchi, Rosellini, Detchman, and Darch (1983) listed a number of reasons to consider room arrangement including: management of noise level and disruption during activities, facilitation of quality student interactions and deterring inappropriate interactions, effective use of available space, and enhancement of academic productivity. Because large structures such as blackboards and bulletin boards are already in place, furniture placement is usually the primary arrangement consideration in a room.

Before seating arrangements are considered, however, it is important to determine what activities will occur within the classroom. Typically there will be independent work, small group activities, and student-chosen (e.g., free-time) activities. These activities will influence the planning of the classroom arrangement. Additionally, there will need to be a place for storage, a quiet out-of-the-way space for students to retreat when overwhelmed, and a time out or penalty area. There will need to be a place for the teacher's desk and a place to post announcements. Colvin (2002) provided recommendations and considerations for these and other classroom activities and requirements. Table 1 provides information that will assist the professional school counselor and teacher to plan for each of these typical classroom requirements.

*Student Seating*

Once these varying functions and requirements have been considered and the classroom arrangements addressed, it is time to consider the arrangement of the students' desks. A number of strategies for student seating have changed over the years. Historically, teachers have arranged the desks in straight rows with very little flexibility in how the students were assigned to a seat. Current practice shows that a wide variety of arrangements are effective.

Several suggestions have been made in the literature to facilitate classroom management and student learning through student seating. Initially, the teacher should assign seats to the students. However, as the year continues, the teacher may allow the students to participate in selection as well as the arrangement of the desks. Some variations to the straight-row layout include semicircular and cluster arrangements, or a combination of these. Be sure to place students next to someone they have not sat next to in the past. This will increase the opportunity for new friendships to develop. One may vary the seating arrangement dependent upon the unit being taught in a particular subject. Students become aware of this and anticipate the new arrangement when finishing each unit. The teacher can use student selection as a motivator for doing well on the unit exam (this will be discussed further in the motivation section of this chapter).

Classroom arrangement can be an important tool in facilitating student learning, student cooperation, and enjoyment of the classroom. Be sure to consider the functions and activities that will occur in the class. Avoid placing obstacles to traffic flow in high traffic areas. Make sure that all students can see the instructional area and the teacher can see all areas of the

**Table 1. Considerations for classroom space arrangement.**

| *Task/function* | *Considerations and Recommendations* |
|---|---|
| Independent work | *Considerations*: Requires minimal distractions. *Recommendations*: Individual seating, room to spread out, avoid high traffic areas. |
| Small group work | *Considerations*: Requires student attention to teacher and other group members. *Recommendations*: Consider a circle, semi-circle or similar configuration; be sure teacher is placed for monitoring of the entire room. |
| Free-time area | *Considerations*: Usually used when children finish work before others in the class. *Recommendations*: Restrict to an area away from the main classroom to minimize distraction; implement specific rules of use for this area. |
| Storage | *Considerations*: Requires easy access without disrupting the class. *Recommendations*: Keep neat and organized; locate in low traffic area; be sure cabinet does not obstruct view of teacher or students. |
| Quiet area | *Considerations*: Often used for students who require a place to retreat when overwhelmed or stressed; is often used at the student's request rather than the teacher's. *Recommendations*: Place in an isolated area of the classroom to discourage other students from interacting with the child using this area. |
| Time-out area | *Considerations*: This area is used as a consequence for unacceptable behavior. *Recommendations*: This area requires a desk in a corner or other out-of-the-way place, but where the teacher can closely monitor the child. There may need to be more than one time-out area. |
| Teacher's desk | *Considerations*: This area requires confidentiality and security of contents. *Recommendations*: Place out of high traffic area but in a location where the teacher can supervise and monitor all students at the same time; avoid an obstructed view. |
| Bulletin board | *Considerations*: This board has multiple purposes including posting rules and announcements such as news events and special projects. |

classroom when engaged in a variety of tasks and activities. Have frequently used supplies and materials well organized and arranged for easy access.

## Classroom Rules and Procedures

Setting up classroom schedules and teaching students the rules and procedures at the beginning of the school year is extremely important. Often those teachers who are considered to be the most preferred by children and parents are those who imposed structure for classroom behavior and expected adherence to the class rules, procedures, and routines. For those students with special needs such as those with developmental delays, mental deficiencies, behavior disorders (including Attention-Deficit/Hyperactivity Disorder), and learning difficulties, it is important that understanding and strict enforcement of the class rules and routines occur. These behaviors can make the difference between optimal functioning and learning and academic failure.

*Rules.* Much attention has been paid to the importance of rules in the management of a classroom. Rules must be taught by teachers and learned by students. Therefore, one of the first tasks a teacher should undertake is to teach the class rules on the first day of class. The professional school counselor should remind teachers to include the school rules in their lesson. The most effective classroom managers understand that good teaching practice must be applied to teaching of the rules. There are several steps that are necessary in the teaching process and the process may take as much as the first two weeks of school for the students to master all the rules. Colvin (2002) stated that the appropriate behavior of students is dependent upon instruction of the rules and the teacher's expectation for adherence to them.

Rules tell students what to do and what not to do in the school environment. It is generally recommended that teachers have a general idea about which rules will be implemented but include students in the development of the class rules. This increases the likelihood that the students will embrace the rules. Teachers and students should develop around five classroom rules that are proactively stated. Furthermore, rules can address both social and academic behaviors. Common examples include: keep your eyes on the teacher while she is teaching; raise your hand to speak or request permission; keep hands, feet, and objects to self; use appropriate language; walk in the classroom; turn assignments in on-time; and place your homework in the homework tray. Additionally, rules should be placed in a prominent location in the room and should be referred to several times throughout the day when praising students and disciplining them.

*Procedures.* Schools have a plethora of interruptions and breaks imposed on the day. Instructing students about the routines and procedures at the beginning of the school year serves three goals: to increase time for learning, to facilitate access to learning, and to foster self-management skills in students. Obtaining these goals is likely to lead to maintenance of a healthy learning environment with few behavior problems or other unplanned disruptions to distract the teacher and students.

Teachers allocate a specific amount of time for learning; however, time spent actively learning (engaged time or time-on-task) is frequently considerably less than the allocated time. Additionally, time-on-task varies considerably from student to student. An important goal is to have all allocated time spent in learning engagement and to have each student engaged for a similar amount of time. Another consideration is that although students may be on-task, they may not be succeeding at the learning task. When students are really learning and understanding, the time can be termed academic learning time. Researchers have found that, of the over 1000 hours mandated by most states, only 300 to 400 hours are spent in academic learning time (Weinstein & Mignano, 1997).

Researchers have shown that when students work directly with the teacher they have higher rates of engaged time, whereas students who work on their own spend only half the time engaged (Frick, 1990). Thus, when independent seatwork is assigned the teacher should spend more time monitoring the students to increase time-on-task. Two of the most common losses of time during independent seatwork is a lack of understanding by the student about what to do next and a lack of necessary materials at hand. Therefore, a teacher who is aware of everything that is happening in the classroom is more likely to be able to assist students. Several additional skills include supervising several activities at once, keeping several students involved in activities, and keeping the instruction and students as a group moving through assigned tasks at an appropriate pace. One method to accomplishing these multiple tasks is to have set procedures that students understand and can implement with a minimum of close supervision. This fosters students' self-management of their own learning activities.

*Procedures and Rules.* The effective classroom manager communicates to students how activities will be accomplished and expectations for behavior in the classroom. It is important to distinguish between classroom procedures and classroom rules. Effective classroom managers develop clear and simple expectations for classroom behavior that are understood by all the students. According to Weinstein and Mignano (1997), within a typical day in a classroom the following activities occur and can be planned:

1. Administrative routines (e.g., attendance)
2. Student movement (e.g., changing classes, going to lunch)
3. Housekeeping (e.g., putting away instructional materials)
4. Routines for completing lessons (e.g., collecting assignments)
5. Student-teacher interactions (e.g., asking for help)
6. Student-student interactions (e.g., socializing)

Having clear rules and expectations for these six activities will facilitate effective classroom management. Although some of these activities will have their own rules and procedures, a few general rules will often clarify expectations for appropriate behavior and procedures for one activity will generalize to other activities. When teaching the procedures to students be sure to use specific and concrete procedures, model, rehearse, and provide corrective feedback to the students on how well they are following the procedures. Continue to review the procedures for several weeks at the beginning of the school year. It is acceptable to add new procedures if the need arises.

The following are general guidelines for developing and implementing procedures:

1. Determine procedures for housekeeping activities before the first day of class. Teach the procedures to the students and reward compliance during the first several weeks of school. Make sure there is a place for everything and that time is allocated to accomplish housekeeping tasks.
2. Decide how students are to enter and leave the classroom. Teach this procedure to students on the first day. Expect compliance every time students enter or leave the class whether they are in a group or by themselves. When students fail to comply have them come back to enter or leave correctly.
3. Establish a signal for the students to alert them. There may be more than one signal that students learn (e.g., one each for instructional time, recess, walking in the hall).
4. Be sure all students understand the procedures for participation in class. Will the student raise a hand for assistance or to answer questions? How will students know that a choral response is required? What are the procedures for using the different areas of the room?
5. Teach students the procedure for assignment completion. Where will assignments be posted, where are they to be turned in and how will the student know how they did on an assignment?

Now that students understand the procedures for engaging in classroom activities, it is time to develop classroom rules. Researchers have found that having students involved in the development of rules increases their motivation to adhere to the rules. Generally, classroom rules address student-to-student interactions (e.g., hands and feet to self) and personal property (e.g., ask before borrowing). Other rules address teacher expectations for student preparation (e.g., bring all needed materials to class). Finally, rules may be intended to facilitate adherence to more general school rules (e.g., dress codes, forbidden items and activities). When teaching rules, effective classroom managers provide examples and non-examples of the rule to facilitate student understanding. Additionally, it is important for students to understand that they will be held accountable for their behavior in following rules and that rules will have consequences.

*Consequences For Rule Violations.* Generally, it is best to implement a consequence for misbehavior. Alberto and Troutman (1995) outlined the following hierarchy:

1. *Level I*–Differential reinforcement (e.g., reinforcing behavior that is incompatible with problem behavior).
2. *Level II*–Extinction (e.g., withdrawing reinforcement for undesired behavior).
3. Level III–Removal of desirable stimuli (e.g., time-out procedures, response-cost procedures, staying in from recess).
4. *Level IV*–Presentation of aversive stimuli (e.g., corporal punishment, spanking). This is the least desirable form of consequence to use for problem behavior and should be avoided if at all possible.

## Managing Transitions

Changing activities is a common loss of allocated learning time. The average classroom makes 8-10 transitions per day—the equivalent of a full day each week spent in transitions (Rathvon, 1999). Effective classroom managers are successful in limiting the number of transitions in a day and making these transitions smoother with less teaching time lost. Additionally, disruptive behavior is more likely to occur during transition time. Similar to teaching procedures, the effective classroom manager uses direct instruction of the procedures for making a transition and provides guided practice (rehearsal with feedback) to teach students expected behavior. One effective method of decreasing time spent in transition is to use a "beat the clock" game. Another effective method includes peer or self-monitoring with rewards for following procedures and making quick changes between activities. Table 2 includes additional tips for handling misbehavior in the classroom.

## Methods for Motivating Students

*Reinforcement-based Procedures*

One of the most difficult tasks in classroom management is facilitating and maintaining student motivation. However, if students are motivated to do well in the classroom and to follow procedures and rules, the teacher is likely to find that effective classroom management is easier to facilitate. Several methods are available to the teacher for increasing student motivation to follow rules and procedures and engage in academic activities. These include differential reinforcement, the Premack Principle, group contingencies, token economies, behavior contracts and charts, time-out, and overcorrection procedures.

*Differential reinforcement.* One of the most influential management strategies readily available to the teacher throughout the day is the social attention that he or she provides

**Table 2. Tips for Handling Misbehavior in the Classroom.**

1. Always implement a consequence for a broken rule and select an appropriate consequence for the infraction.
2. State the rule and the consequence but nothing else (this prevents arguing and "deal-making").
3. Avoid making an example out of the student in front of his or her peers (this avoids making the student or the teacher feel like they "need to win").
4. Avoid asking questions to which you already know the answer (e.g., "What are you supposed to be doing right now?").
5. Control your anger and try to remember that most rule infractions are not personally directed toward you.
6. Always consider that the preferred outcome is for the student to learn to avoid the infraction in the future.
7. Seek assistance and work with other school professionals in a team format to avoid burnout.

to the students. Unfortunately, teacher attention can be used to reinforce both appropriate behavior and problem behavior so the teacher has to be cognizant of the behaviors for which he or she is providing attention. Differential reinforcement is a procedure whereby the teacher actively ignores or "extinguishes" the display of problem behavior and actively provides social attention for the display of appropriate behavior (Alberto & Troutman, 1995). Using social attention in this manner has been labeled "time-in" or "catching them being good" by Christophersen (1983) and "strategic attention" by Hembree-Kigin and McNeil (1995). Generally, teachers are encouraged to utilize differential reinforcement when teaching students to follow rules and display appropriate behaviors in the classroom.

Hembree-Kigin and McNeil (1995) identified four types of social attention that teachers can use to reinforce rule-following and the performance of appropriate behavior. These include use of descriptions, reflections, imitations, and praise. Descriptions are used to describe the student's actions that are desirable and conducive to active learning. Descriptions acknowledge the performance of behavior without directly providing praise statements. For example, the teacher may say "Timmy, I see that you are looking at the board" while teaching from the front of the room or "Sally, I see that you have completed five math problems" shortly after handing out a math worksheet. Reflections demonstrate to the student that the teacher is attentive and listening while at the same time increasing communication between the teacher and students. For example, after the student has said "Mrs. Jones, look I made a perfect grade on the spelling test," the teacher may say, "Yes, Sarah I do see that you made a 100 on your spelling test." Imitations are used to increase the teacher's involvement with students, improve sharing and turn-taking skills, and increase other students' imitation of appropriate behavior. For example, a teacher may say during an art project "I'm going to draw a tree in my picture like Josie drew in her picture." Finally, praise statements are designed to increase desired behaviors, improve the relationship between the teacher and child, and increase the child's self-esteem. Praise statements can be global and general or very specific. Examples of global praise statements include "great," "good job," or "way to go," whereas specific praise statements include "Thank you, Timmy, for sitting quietly," or "Sarah has a beautiful smile." Teachers can provide praise to students through physical means as well. For example, teachers can increase desirable behaviors by providing hugs, pats on the head or shoulder, high fives or other appropriate forms of physical interaction.

Teacher attention should be contingent upon appropriate behavior and provided regularly and enthusiastically. Social attention follows the "if-then" rule: behaviors that the teacher wants to see repeated should be followed by some positive form of teacher attention. Conversely most minor problem behaviors should receive no attention or very minimal amounts of attention. Appropriate behaviors should receive regular reinforcement. Teachers should provide attention early and often. In fact, researchers have encouraged teachers to follow a minimum 3:1 ratio of providing attention for appropriate behavior versus problem behavior (Sprick & Howard, 1995). Finally, teacher attention should be provided enthusiastically. Teachers should strive to provide attention with expression in their voice and a varied tone as opposed to using a flat, monotone voice. Most students enjoy receiving attention from teachers; however, use of unconvincing or "canned" statements or praise can quickly erode the effectiveness of adult attention.

*Premack Principle.* As discussed previously, appropriately scheduled activities and transitions can effectively prevent the display of many problematic behaviors in the classroom. However, the schedule of activities can also be used to motivate the students. For example, teachers can use "grandma's rule" or the Premack Principle (Premack, 1959) to shape the occurrence of appropriate behavior by students. The Premack Principle involves having the students perform a less preferred activity before being allowed to engage in a more preferred activity. In a sense, this principle is similar to the mealtime rule used by many grandmothers over the generations who have told children that they must eat their vegetables before being allowed to eat any cookies. As such, teachers could schedule more demanding or difficult classes or materials before more socially rewarding activities such as recess, break times, group story times, or individual free time.

This principle also could be used to change seating arrangements in the classroom in the manner previously described in the chapter. The teacher could establish the expectation in the classroom that successful completion of a unit would lead to preferred-seating arrangements decided collectively by the students. With a little creativity, teachers could intersperse preferred and nonpreferred activities or classes throughout the day to both prevent problem behaviors and reinforce the occurrence of appropriate behaviors.

*Group contingency systems.* Another classroom management strategy that has proven successful in managing student behavior and improving academic success involves the use of group contingencies. Litow and Pumroy (1975) identified three group contingency systems. The first system, *dependent group-oriented contingency*, uses reinforcement for the entire class contingent on the performance of a selected student or a particular group of students. For example, if Mark and Sally can improve their vocabulary quiz grade by 10% above their scores on the last quiz, then the whole class will get extra free time after lunch. The second system, *independent group-oriented contingency*, uses reinforcement for each student contingent on their individual performance independent of the group performance or the performance of their peers, e.g., whoever turned their homework in this morning can now go to recess. The third system, *interdependent group-oriented contingency*, provides each member access to reinforcement contingent (or interdependent) upon some group level of performance. For example, "If the class average is 80% or higher on the math quiz today, then we'll have extra free time this afternoon."

One example of an interdependent group-oriented contingency system that has been used with great success in classrooms is the Good Behavior Game (GBG) originally published by Barrish, Saunders, and Wolf (1969). In the GBG, the class is divided into two or more teams. Team names are posted on the board beside a list of target behaviors or classroom rules that have been operationally defined (specifically described with observable and quantifiable behaviors) and discussed with the class. The classroom teacher places a mark under the team name any time a member of the team violates one of the rules. At the end of a predetermined period (academic period, morning, afternoon, end of day), the team or teams scoring below a predetermined criterion wins the game and receives a reward. Although originally developed to increase the performance of prosocial behaviors, replication studies have also found the GBG to effectively increase the performance of academic behaviors. Furthermore, rewards may be varied to include extra free time, special jobs, extra recess, special badges, and other special privileges. Finally, the delivery of rewards may range from several times daily to once per week. For a more thorough review of the GBG, the professional school counselor should read a review by Tingstrom (2002).

*Token economy systems.* Originally utilized in residential settings to improve hygiene, social skills, and work skills of individuals with developmental disabilities (Ayllon & Azrin, 1968), the token economy has also proved to be a beneficial addition to group-contingency systems in school settings. A token economy is a reinforcement system in which conditioned reinforcers called tokens are delivered to students contingent upon the display of appropriate behavior. The tokens are then exchanged for backup reinforcers at a later period in the day.

Token economies can be very effective interventions for managing student behavior in the classroom. However, poor planning in the initial stages of development of the program can often lead to failure of the intervention (Moore, Tingstrom, Doggett, & Carlyon, 2001). As such, Miltenberger (2001) effectively discussed several important issues that the professional school counselor should consider when suggesting the implementation of a token economy in a school setting. First, the professional school counselor and classroom teacher should clearly and concretely define the desired behaviors. These behaviors may include academic skills, social skills, vocational skills, self-help skills, or general compliance with classroom rules.

Second, school personnel should identify developmentally appropriate items for use as tokens. Tokens must be tangible objects that can be delivered immediately upon the display of appropriate behavior. Common examples include poker chips, coins, play money, stamps, stickers, stars, check marks on or hole punches in cards, or puzzle pieces that can be used to complete an entire puzzle.

Third, the professional school counselor and teacher should collaborate to identify effective backup reinforcers. Development of the backup reinforcers should be one of the most important considerations of the system as the tokens obtain their reinforcing value from the backup reinforcers. In other words, if the students do not view the backup reinforcers as valuable then they will not be motivated to engage in appropriate behavior or to exert effort to earn tokens throughout the day. Identifying such reinforcers does not have to be difficult as most students are often motivated by activity reinforcers (e.g., free time, computer time, movie time, special jobs) that can easily be incorporated into the regular classroom routine. Other reinforcers could also be incorporated into the system (e.g., snacks, pencils, erasers, movie rentals, restaurant coupons) to provide variety and to avoid satiation by the students.

Fourth, an appropriate schedule of reinforcement must be decided upon. Initially, the classroom teacher should deliver tokens to the students frequently and liberally throughout each period to "shape up" the display of appropriate behavior. As improvement is observed, the teacher can move from a continuous schedule of reinforcement to a more intermittent schedule to maintain improvement in student behavior.

Fifth, the professional school counselor should help the teacher establish the token exchange rate. School personnel should determine how many tokens students might potentially earn in a day and then set the exchange rate based on this criterion. Smaller items (e.g., pencils, erasers) will typically cost less whereas larger items (e.g., 15 minutes of individual computer time) will require the exchange of more tokens.

Sixth, an appropriate time and place for the exchange of tokens must be decided before implementing the program. Many teachers have created a school store or treasure chest from which students could purchase backup reinforcers at set periods during the day (e.g., morning and/or afternoon break).

Seventh, the professional school counselor assists the teacher with decisions of whether the display of undesirable behaviors compete with the performance of appropriate behaviors in such a manner that a response cost component is warranted. Response cost is defined as the withdrawal of specific amounts of a reinforcer contingent upon the display of problem behavior (Alberto & Troutman, 1995). As such, response cost is often viewed as a system of leveling fines for the display of inappropriate behavior similar to the tickets motorists receive for speeding or parking in a protected parking space. To maximize all parts of the system, the token economy should be implemented for a few weeks before the response cost component is added to ensure that the tokens are truly functioning as conditioned reinforcers. The undersirable behaviors should then be clearly defined and appropriate fine levels should be established. As with the delivery of tokens, fines should be delivered contingent upon the display of problem behavior. It is extremely important to remember that for the entire system to function effectively, the students must earn tokens more frequently than they experience fines.

Overall, school personnel need to examine some practical considerations when implementing a token economy system. For example, the portability and ease of delivery of the actual token should be considered. Additionally, storage of the tokens and the potential of theft must be evaluated. Bartering or trading among students should also be eliminated when setting up a token economy. Finally, the delivery of tokens should always be paired or associated with teacher praise as the system will eventually need to be phased out allowing student behavior to be maintained by natural reinforcers such as teacher praise and attention.

*Behavior contracts and charts.* Up to this point, this chapter has focused primarily on motivating students by applying reinforcement procedures to the entire group of students in the classroom. However, seasoned professional school counselors and classroom teachers know that some students need individual reinforcement systems to assist in managing behavior. One such system involves the use of behavior contracts and/or charts. Specifically, a behavior contract is a written document that specifies a particular target behavior for a student and the consequences that will be delivered contingent upon the occurrence or nonoccurrence of the behavior at the end of a predetermined period of time (Miltenberger, 2001). Generally, these contracts are written in paragraph form with signature lines at the end of the document. In contrast, behavior charts often specify several behaviors that are evaluated at preset periods during the school day, leading to corrective and reinforcing feedback reliably provided throughout the day and at the end of each day. Generally, these are developed as a table with the desired behaviors listed in rows and the evaluation periods grouped in columns next to the behaviors. One example of an empirically-based behavior chart is the school-home note developed by Kelley (1990). Examples of each form are presented in Figures 1 and 2, respectively.

Regardless of which system is used, Miltenberger (2001) identified several important steps that must be considered. First, the target behaviors must be clearly defined in proactive terms. In other words, the form should list the behaviors *to be performed* as opposed to specifying behaviors to be eliminated. Second, all parties must agree on a measurement system for monitoring the behaviors. This can be completed through the evaluation of permanent products (e.g., completion of a worksheet) or through direct observation and documentation of the performance of the behavior (e.g., stayed in seat throughout the reading period).

**Figure 1. Sample Behavior Contract for Homework.**

I, ____________________, agree to complete my homework assignments in __________ with at least __________% accuracy each night from __________ to __________.

For meeting the criterion on __________ out of __________ days, I can earn ____________________ to be delivered on __________ (when) by __________ (person).

____________________ __________
Student Signature Date

____________________ __________
Teacher Signature Date

**Figure 2. Sample School-Home Note.**

STUDENT PROCEDURES

1. Carry the note to school everyday.
2. Have the teacher rate your behavior at the end of each period.
3. Carry the note home each day to be reviewed by your parents.

CLASSROOM PROCEDURES

1. Student behavior is evaluated at the end of each period.
2. Record a A1@ if the behavior was displayed.
3. Record a A0@ if the behavior was not displayed.
4. Provide social praise for behavior that was displayed.
5. Provide a brief explanation and encouragement for behavior that was not displayed.
6. The last teacher of the day should check to see if minimum points were achieved.
7. Consequences at school should be administered based on number of points earned.
8. The note should be sent home at the end of each day to be reviewed by the parent.

HOME PROCEDURES

1. Review the note with your child.
2. Provide praise for behavior that was displayed.
3. Provide the appropriate reward if the criterion was met.
4. Remove the appropriate privileges for lost notes, changed notes, etc.

Note: The minimum number of points currently required is __of a possible ____.

Name: ______________
***Date:___________***

| Behaviors: | Reading | Spelling | Centers | Lunch | Math | Recess |
|---|---|---|---|---|---|---|
| 1.Follows directions 1st time given | | | | | | |
| 2.Keeps Hands & Feet to Self | | | | | | |
| 3. Appropriate Language | | | | | | |
| Total Points | | | | | | |
| Teacher Initials | | | | | | |

Third, the specific times for the performance of the behavior should be clearly stated. Fourth, a reinforcement or punishment contingency must be stated in the form. As with most motivational systems, utilization of positive reinforcement is most desirable with behavioral contracting; however, a response cost component similar to that explained in the token economy section could be used with this system as well. Finally, the behavior contract or chart should identify all parties responsible for providing the contingency or reinforcement or punishment. Doing so will increase the integrity with which the system is implemented. Readers who are interested in further learning about contingency contracting and implementing individual management systems should refer to Jenson, Rhode, & Reavis (1994), Kelley (1990), Miltenberger (2001), and Rhode, Jenson, and Reavis (1992).

*Punishment-based Procedures*

Other methods for managing student behavior involve the use of punishment procedures. By strict definition, punishment is a procedure whereby the presentation or removal of a stimulus or event *decreases* the likelihood that a particular behavior will be performed in the future. Two forms of punishment have been identified. Positive punishment refers to *the presentation of an aversive stimulus* following the occurrence of a behavior that leads to a decrease in the likelihood that the behavior will be performed in the future. Negative punishment refers to the *removal of a preferred stimulus* following the occurrence of a behavior that leads to a decrease in the probability that the behavior will occur at a later time.

Overcorrection is an example of a positive punishment procedure. Originally developed by Foxx and Azrin (1972; 1973) for use with individuals in institutional settings, overcorrection requires a student to engage in a predetermined behavior for an extended period of time contingent upon each occurrence of the problem behavior. Two forms of overcorrection have been identified: positive practice and restitution.

In positive practice, the student is required to engage in the correct form of the appropriate behavior for a specified period of time (e.g., 5-15 minutes) or a specified number of times (e.g., 3 times). For example, a group of students may enter the classroom too loudly. The teacher could have the students go back into the hall and quietly enter the classroom three times. This repetition would provide positive practice of the appropriate behavior. This intervention has application for academic behavior as well. Skinner and colleagues (Skinner, Belfiore, & Pierce, 1992; Skinner, McLaughlin, & Logan, 1997; Skinner, Turco, & Beatty, 1989; Skinner, Shapiro, Turco, & Cole, 1992; Smith, Dittmer, & Skinner, 2002) have utilized positive practice as an effective component of the *Cover, Copy, and Compare* intervention to increase academic accuracy rates for students. In this intervention, the student is required to perform an academic task (e.g., take a spelling test). Upon completion of the test, the student compares her words to a list containing the correct spelling of the words. Upon comparison, the student identifies two words that are misspelled. The student is then required to re-write the misspelled words three times each which provides for positive practice of the correct spelling of each word.

Restitution requires students to not only correct the environmental effects of the problem behavior but to restore the environment to a better condition than before the behavior occurred. For example, two boys were found writing on a wall in a bathroom stall at school. After consultation with the professional school counselor, the teacher decided to have the boys clean the wall on which they wrote words and clean the other walls in the stall as well.

Negative punishment procedures involve the removal of a stimulus or event in order to reduce the probability of the occurrence of problem behavior. One such procedure has already been discussed in the token economy and behavioral contracting sections and involves the use of response cost procedures. Another example of a negative punishment procedure involves the use of time-out. Specifically, time-out is a shortened version of the term "time-out from positive reinforcement" and has been labeled as a Level III management procedure above the use of aversives (Alberto & Troutman, 1995). With the exception of response cost and overcorrection, most of this section has focused on reinforcement procedures for motivating students primarily because such procedures must be in place before a punishment procedure such as time-out is put in place. In other words, the classroom teacher should be discouraged from using time-out until a "time-in" rich environment has been created through the utilization of differential attention, Premack Principle, group oriented reinforcement techniques, and behavioral contracting.

Alberto and Troutman (1995) defined three time-out procedures: seclusionary, non-seclusionary, and exculsionary. In *non-seclusionary time-out*, the teacher denies access to reinforcement, however, the student is not removed from the actual instructional setting (e.g., "Timothy, please place your head on your desk for talking out."). In *exclusionary time-out*, the teacher removes the student from the classroom or activity area (e.g., "Sam, please stand quietly in the hall for pushing Sarah."). In *seclusionary time-out*, the teacher removes the student to a time-out room for a period of time.

Of the three time-out procedures described, non-seclusionary and exclusionary time-out procedures are easier to implement by teachers and are generally favored over the use of seclusionary time-out. In fact, Erford (1999) presented procedures for a particularly effective version of exclusionary time-out, the contingency-delay model. The professional school counselor should be sure to remind the teacher that time-out is a concept involving the removal of all forms of reinforcement (e.g., social attention, food, favorite activities), not simply a location such as a chair, corner of the room, or spot on the floor. It is generally suggested that the teacher have a predetermined location for time-out. However, he or she must remember that if the student still receives access to reinforcement in the form of teacher- or peer-provided stares, comments, smiles, or other types of attention, the time-out procedure may become ineffective. Time-out does not have to last for a long duration of time. In fact, releasing the child after a few seconds of "quiet behavior" can be effective. In most situations, a child should not stay in time-out for longer than 5 minutes after he or she has calmed down and sat quietly in the time-out location. Finally and most importantly, the professional school counselor should remind the teacher to socially reinforce the child for displaying appropriate behavior as quickly as possible after leaving time-out. Doing so will help generate the contrast between receiving reinforcement for appropriate behavior and the loss of reinforcement (i.e., time-out) for problematic behavior. For more assistance with the implementation of time-out in school settings, the professional school counselor is referred to Sterling and Watson (1999).

## Summary/Conclusion

Those who are most likely to motivate students and to be remembered as a special teacher have, according to Alberto and Troutman (1995), personal characteristics such as a sense of humor, warmth and caring manifested as sensitivity and an interest in the personal well-being of the students. One avenue to accomplishing this style as a teacher is to have an effectively managed classroom through the use of well-developed rules, effective instructions, well-managed transitions, proper scheduling, differential attention, group-oriented contingencies, behavioral contracting, response cost, and time-out procedures. As poignantly stated by one effective teacher,

> "A century from now it will not matter what kind of car I drove, what kind of house I lived in, or how much money I had in the bank... But one hundred years from now the world may be a better place, because I was important in the life of a child." (Anonymous, n.d.).

## References


Alberto, P. A., & Troutman, A. C. (1995). *Applied behavior analysis for teachers* (4th ed.). Englewood Cliffs, NJ: Prentice–Hall.

Ayllon, T., & Azrin, N. (1968). *The economy: A motivational system for therapy and rehabilitation.* New York: Appleton–Centur–Cofts.

Anonymous. (n.d.). Retrieved December 20, 2002, from http://www.teacheruniverse.com/news/quotes/

Barrish, H. H., Saunders, M., & Wolf, M. M. (1969). Good Behavior Game: Effects of individual contingencies for group consequences on disruptive behavior in a classroom. *Journal of Applied Behavior Analysis, 2,* 119–124.

Christophersen, E. R. (1983). *Little people.* Kansas City, MO: Westport Publishers.

Colvin, G. (2002). Designing classroom organization and structure. In K. L. Lane, F. M. Gresham & T. E. O'Shaughnessy (Eds.), *Interventions for children with or at risk for emotional and behavioral disorders* (pp. 159–174). Boston: Allyn & Bacon.

Erford, B. T. (1999). The comparative effectiveness of a modified time–out procedure for oppositional and defiant children. *Professional School Counseling, 2,* 205–210.

Foxx, R. M., & Azrin, N. H. (1972). Restitution: A method of eliminating aggressive–disruptive behavior of retarded and brain damaged patients. *Behavior Research and Therapy, 10,* 15–27.

Foxx, R. M., & Azrin, N. H. (1973). The elimination of autistic self–stimulatory behavior by overcorrection. *Journal of Applied Behavior Analysis, 6,* 1–14.

Frick, T. W. (1990). Analysis of patterns in time: A method of recording and quantifying temporal relations in education. *American Educational Research Journal, 27,* 180–204.

Hembree–Kigin, T. L., & McNeil, C. B. (1995). *Parent–child interaction therapy.* New York: Plenum Press.

Jenson, W. R., Rhode, G., & Reavis, H. K. (1994). *The tough kid tool box.* Longmont, CO: Sopris West.

Kelley, M. L. (1990). *School–home notes: Promoting children's classroom success*. New York: Guilford Press.

Litow, L., & Pumroy, D.K. (1975). A brief review of classroom group–oriented contingencies. *Journal of Applied Behavior Analysis, 8*, 341–347.

Miltenberger, R. G. (2001). *Behavior modification: Principles and procedures*. Belmont, CA: Wadsworth/Thomson Learning.

Moore, J. W., Tingstrom, D. H., Doggett, R. A., & Carlyon, W. D. (2001). Restructuring an existing token economy in a psychiatric facility for children. *Child & Family Behavior Therapy, 23*, 53–59.

Paine, S. C., Radicchi, R., Rosellini, L. C., Detchman, L., & Darch, C. B. (1983). *Structuring your classroom for academic success*. Champaign, IL: Research Press Co.

Premack, D. (1959). Toward empirical behavior laws: I. Positive reinforcement. *Psychological Review, 66*, 219–233.

Rathvon, N. (1999). *Effective school interventions*. New York: Guilford Press.

Rhode, G., Jenson, W. R., & Reavis, H. K. (1992). *The tough kid book: Practical classroom management strategies*. Longmont, CO: Sopris West.

Skinner, C. H., Belfiore, P. J., & Pierce, N. (1992). Cover, copy, and compare: Increasing geography accuracy in students with behavior disorders. *School Psychology Review, 21*, 73–81.

Skinner, C. H., McLaughlin, T. F., & Logan, P. (1997). Cover, copy, and compare: A self–managed academic intervention effective across skills, students, and settings. *Journal of Behavioral Education, 7*, 295–306.

Skinner, C. H., Turco, T. L., & Beatty, K. L. (1989). Cover, copy, and compare: A method for increasing multiplication performance. *School Psychology Review, 18*, 412–420.

Skinner, C. H., Shapiro, E. S., Turco, T. L., & Cole, C. L. (1992). A comparison of self– and peer–delivered immediate corrective feedback on multiplication performance. *Journal of School Psychology, 30*, 101–116.

Smith, T. J., Dittmer, K. I., & Skinner, C. H. (2002). Enhancing science performance in students with learning disabilities using cover, copy and compare: A student shows the way. *Psychology in the Schools, 39*, 417–426.

Sprick, R. S., & Howard, L. S. (1995). Compliance and direction following. *The teacher's encyclopedia of behavior management* (pp. 246–254). Longmont, CO: Sopris West.

Sterling, H. E., & Watson, T. S. (1999). An empirically based guide for the use of time–out in the preschool and elementary classroom. *Psychology in the Schools, 36*, 135–148.

Tingstrom, D. H. (2002). The good behavior game. In M. Hersen & W. Sledge (Eds.), *The encyclopedia of psychotherapy* (Vol. 1). New York: Academic Press.

Weinstein, C. S., & Mignano, Jr., A. J. (1997). *Elementary classroom management* (2nd ed.). New York: McGraw–Hill.

# Chapter 34

## Program Assessment and Evaluation

*Bradley T. Erford, Jennifer A. McKechnie, & Cheryl Moore-Thomas*

### Preview

This chapter gives professional school counselors the basic tools needed to design and conduct effective outcomes assessment and program evaluation in order to determine and document the quality of comprehensive developmental school counseling programs.

The increasing push for school reform and educational accountability was driven by the 1983 report *A Nation at Risk* (Angelo & Cross, 1993; Finn & Kanstroom, 2001). The increasing concern regarding quality education across the nation makes outcomes assessment and program evaluation more important than ever. Until recently, however, professional school counselors have provided little evidence that school counseling interventions were achieving intended results; thus, school counseling programs and services lacked substantive accountability.

Historically, the response to this criticism was that school counseling services are so complex that evaluating such services and results is difficult, if not impossible (Ripley, Erford, Dahir, & Eschbach, 2003). Others note that school personnel are so busy meeting the needs of students that they shift time that should be spent in evaluation to instruction and programming. Whatever the reason, the lack of accountability threatens the success of students and the future of school counseling programs. Educators are bound by professional and ethical obligations to ensure that educational programs are of high quality and effective in meeting student needs. Without accountability, the determination of program quality will always be suspect.

The six purposes of evaluation suggested by Stone and Bradley (1994) are to: measure the effectiveness of the total program and its activities; collect data that will help determine what program modifications are needed; determine the level of program acceptance and support from stakeholders; obtain information that can be used to inform the public; collect data that add to staff evaluation; and analyze the program budget and compare expenditures to future program needs. Outcomes assessment and program evaluation allow for documentation and determination of a school counseling program worth and are part of a program of continuous quality improvement (Ripley et al., 2003). Table 1 provides definitions of important terms associated with outcomes assessment and program evaluation (Erford & Moore-Thomas, 2003).

### The Assessment Loop

Two key elements of a comprehensive educational program as described by Gysbers and Henderson (2000) are program evaluation (process) and results (outcomes) evaluation. "Program evaluation is the process of systematically determining the quality of a school program and how the program can be improved" (Sanders, 1992, p. 3). The process of program evaluation is similar to the concept of content validity (Gysbers & Henderson, 2000). Content validity is a systematic examination of a test's content. In the context of school counseling program evaluation, an important, guiding question emerges: Is there a pre-existing, comprehensive written program that is fully implemented and aligned with district, state, and/or national standards? Simply put, program evaluation involves determining whether written documentation exists and whether implementation of the written program is indeed occurring. Schools and school systems should have well-developed standards/goals, competencies/indicators, objectives, and curriculum lessons which guide the implementation of a comprehensive developmental guidance program. School-based programs rely on this curricular information to implement consistent and effective developmental services. Unfortunately, this form of program evaluation, while important, only indicates the existence and adherence to a planned program. It does not indicate the results or outcomes of the implemented program.

**Table 1. Assessment Terminology. (Erford & Moore-Thomas, 2003).**

*Evaluation* is the measurement of worth and indicates that a judgment will be made regarding the effectiveness of a program.

*Evidence* is qualitative or quantitative data that helps make judgments or decisions.

*Formative evaluation* is evaluative feedback that occurs during the implementation of a program and allows for mid-course corrections to occur.

*Summative evaluation* is feedback collected at a specified endpoint in an evaluation process.

A *stakeholder* is anyone involved or interested in or potentially benefiting from a program. Students, parents, teachers, professional school counselors, administrators, community leaders, college faculty and local employers, among others, are potential educational stakeholders.

Outcomes evaluation, on the other hand, answers the question, "Does the program produce the intended outcomes" (Terenzini, 1989)? In order to ensure focused and manageable assessment it is most practical to connect program concerns to only a few clearly defined questions (Atkinson, Furlong, & Janoff, 1979; Fairchild, 1986; Krumboltz, 1974).

A great deal of confusion exists regarding the purpose of program evaluation and outcomes assessments. It is essential to note that assessment of a school counseling program should not focus on the professional school counselor and is not an assault on the school counselor's freedom. Ripley et al. (2003) indicated that program assessment is cyclical and systematic, a way of answering important questions about a program, and a means to a better education for all students through continuous quality improvement.

Because the assessment process is cyclical and systematic, the program evaluation and outcomes assessment processes should start small and build upon successes. Effective methods for individual programs can then be determined and replicated so that, over time, necessary program refinements can be implemented, resulting in a comprehensive developmental school counseling program that meets an institution's mission. The assessment loop presented in Figure 1 helps to visually conceptualize program evaluation and the ways in which outcome studies can be used to improve educational programs. Assessment is often viewed as a component that concludes a process. However, it should be an integrated part of a continuous process to improve the program. The institution's mission drives the program content and, therefore, drives the assessment process. "A school's mission should be evident in its structure, decision-making processes, interpersonal interactions, programmatic regularities, and behavioral regularities [and] provides the basis from which meaningful, institution-specific assessment questions will arise" (Erford & Moore-Thomas, 2003). These questions lead to the determination of the kinds of evidence that must be collected. Evidence provides crucial information about program evaluation and results (outcomes).

**Figure 1. Assessment Loop.**

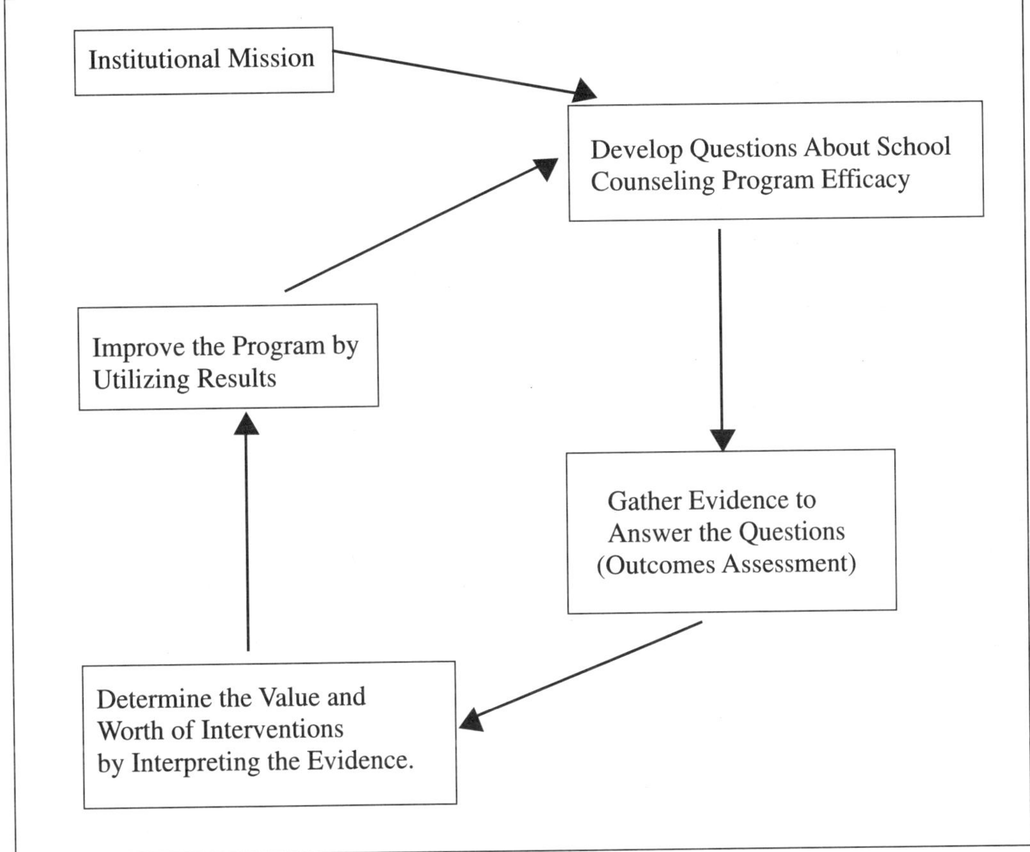


Evidence can come from numerous and varied sources including portfolios, external judges or examiners, observations, local tests, purchased tests, student self-assessments, surveys, interviews, focus groups, standardized or informal measures, student performances, or student products. Importantly, a great deal of evidence is routinely collected in schools. After evidence is collected, interpretation ensues so that conclusions may be reached about the program's value, strengths, weaknesses, and outcomes. As a final step before the process cycles again, interpretations and conclusions are used to adjust to or change program components as needed. Once the changes have been made, new questions can be posed and the cycle begins anew, representing a continuous process of quality improvement.

## Results Evaluation

"Questions of worth and effectiveness are derived from a confluence of values, needs, goals, and mission, and these questions lead to the determination of what evidence must be collected" (Ripley et al., 2003, p. 116). While the types of evidence appropriate in program evaluation were discussed above, the system for how the evidence is collected warrants further discussion—because how one designs evaluation studies will determine the validity of the findings. At least two primary methods for documenting program effectiveness may be useful to professional school counselors: aggregation and outcomes evaluation.

*Aggregation*

Aggregation involves a process of combining many smaller pieces of evidence to document that components of a larger program are indeed effective. A comprehensive developmental school counseling program curriculum is based upon some hierarchical system usually involving standards (or goals), competencies (or indicators), and objectives (or outcomes). Figure 2 provides a simple hierarchical structure demonstrating this typical system. At the most basic level, demonstrating effectiveness through aggregation depends upon well-written learning objectives (see chapter 31).

**Figure 2. Hierarchical Structure of a Typical Curriculum Development System.**

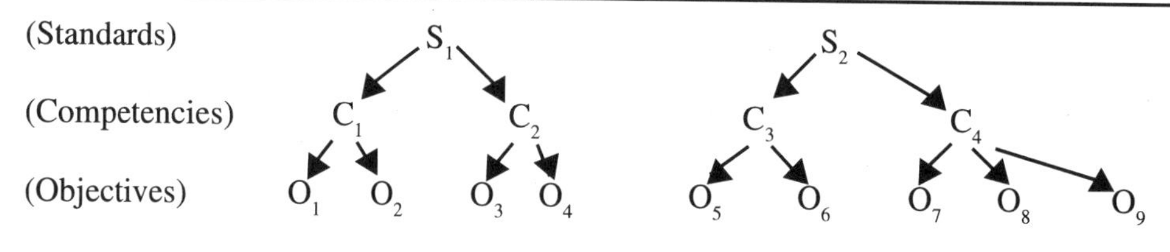


If a learning objective is written in measurable terms with an appropriate expected performance criterion, it can be determined that the objective has actually been met. Demonstrating that an objective has been met provides evidence that a competency has been met. Furthermore, when evidence is provided that competencies (or indicators) have been met, then evidence is also provided that a standard (or goal) has been met. It all starts with measurable learning objectives (see chapter 31)!

Using Figure 2 above, consider an example in which learning objectives $O_1 - O_6$ were met, while learning objectives $O_7$–$O_9$ were not. In such a scenario it is easy to determine that evidence exists that standard 1 ($S_1$) was met because objectives 1–4 ($O_1 - O_4$) were met. The first two objectives ($O_1$ and $O_2$) were met, providing evidence that the first competency ($C_1$) was met. The second two objectives ($O_3$ and $O_4$) were met, providing evidence that the second competency ($C_2$) was met. Because both competencies ($C_1$ and $C_2$) were met, sufficient evidence exists that the first standard ($S_1$) was met.

Now consider the scenario for standard 2 above in which the first two objectives ($O_5$ and $O_6$) were met, thus providing evidence that the first competency ($C_3$) was met. The final three objectives ($O_7$, $O_8$ and $O_9$) were not met, thus failing to provide evidence that the final competency ($C_4$) was met. Because only one of the two competencies ($C_3$ but not $C_4$) was met, sufficient evidence does not exist that the second standard ($S_2$) was met. From this demonstration of the aggregation process, it is easy to conclude that the determination of school counseling program effectiveness begins with learning objectives written in measurable terms, but also relies heavily on setting a challenging, yet attainable, performance criterion (the "D" component of a learning objective discussed in chapter 31).

*Conducting Outcome Studies*

Outcome studies are generally empirical in nature and involve exercising some control over the conditions under which the evidence is collected (e.g., research design). Campbell and Stanley (1963) wrote the classic work on this topic and provide a helpful summary of research designs that professional school counselors can use to show the effectiveness of interventions. Campbell and Stanley conceptualized research designs as pre-experimental, true experimental, and quasi-experimental. Commonly used research designs are presented in Table 2.

In general, true experimental designs are characterized by randomization of participants that controls for all known sources of internal invalidity. This gives true experimental designs the advantage of allowing causative conclusions to be drawn about the effectiveness of the intervention. For example, if a professional school counselor wanted to know the effectiveness of a group counseling experience for students from changing families, she may choose a pretest-posttest control group design (design B from Table 2), randomly assigning the participants to two or more groups and administering an outcome measure (a measure of behaviors, thoughts and feelings that the group counseling intervention was meant to change) to the treatment and

**Table 2. Common Research Designs.**

| Design | | | | | | | | |
|---|---|---|---|---|---|---|---|---|
| *True Experimental Designs* | | | | | | | | |
| A. Posttest-only Control Group Design | | | | | R | T | O | |
| | | | | | R | | O | |
| B. Pretest-Posttest Control Group Design | | | | | R | O | T | O |
| | | | | | R | O | | O |
| *Quasi-experimental Designs* | | | | | | | | |
| C. Time Series | O | O | O | T | O | O | O | |
| D. Nonequivalent Control Group Design | | | | | O | T | O | |
| | | | | | O | | O | |
| E. Separate-Sample Pretest-Posttest Design | | | | | R | O | | |
| | | | | | R | | T | O |
| *Pre-experimental Designs* | | | | | | | | |
| F. One-Group Pretest-Posttest Design | | | | | O | T | O | |
| G. One-shot Case Study | | | | | | T | O | |
| H. Static-Group Comparison | | | | | | T | O | |
| | | | | | | | O | |

Note: R = randomization of participants; O = observation (i.e. data collection procedure); T = treatment (counseling or learning intervention).

control groups before and after treatment. The data can then be analyzed to determine if the participants that received the group counseling intervention changed significantly on the outcome measure (O) as compared to the control group. Of course, if the treatment was effective, the control group should be given the chance to participate in the group counseling intervention.

This example of a group counseling intervention for students from changing families can also be applied to all of the other designs listed in Table 2, randomizing, observing and intervening as specified. Whenever possible, professional school counselors should collect evidence using a true experimental design. Such evidence is conclusive. Pre-experimental and quasi-experimental designs, however, lead to speculative results that can be questioned and explained through alternative means.

## Reporting Assessment Results

It is an excellent and essential practice to report assessment findings to administrators, teachers, staff members, parents, students and other appropriate stakeholders. The school counseling advisory committee and professional school counselor should write and be involved in every step of the reporting process. Generally, a comprehensive report is helpful for program analysis and decision-making, while a one-to-two page executive summary should be released to system administrators and the general school community. As general guidelines for report writing, Heppner, Kivlighan and Wampold (1992) suggested, "(1) be informative, (2) be forthright, (3) do not overstate or exaggerate, (4) be logical and organized, (5) have some style, (6) write and rewrite, and (7) when all else fails, just write!" (p. 376). Perhaps the final guideline was offered in jest, but it is important to note that results must be documented, discussed, and reported for accountability to occur.

## Summary/Conclusion

Program assessment is one of the most important responsibilities of the professional school counselor. It is essential to understand that assessment is a cyclical process that results in continuous quality improvement. The authors advocated for the use of aggregation and outcomes evaluation as strategies for providing documented evidence that the school counseling program is effectively meeting the needs of students and supporting the school's mission.

## References


Angelo, T., & Cross, K. (1993). *Classroom assessment techniques: A handbook for college teachers* (2nd ed.). San Francisco, CA: Jossey–Bass.

Atkinson, D. R., Furlong, M., & Janoff, D. S. (1979). A four–component model for proactive accountability in school counseling. *The School Counselor, 26,* 222–228.

Campbell, D. T., & Stanley, J. C. (1963). *Experimental and quasi–experimental designs for research.* Boston: Houghton Mifflin Company.

Erford, B. T., & Moore–Thomas, C. (2003). Program evaluation and outcomes assessment. In J. Wall, & G. Walz (Eds.), *Measuring up*. Greensboro, NC: ERIC–CAPS.

Fairchild, T. N. (1986). Time analysis: Accountability tool for school counselors. *The School Counselor, 34,* 36–43.

Finn, C., & Kanstroom, M. (2001). State academic standards. *Brookings Papers on Education Policy*, 2001(1), 131–179.

Gysbers, N. C., & Henderson, P. (2000). *Developing and managing your school counseling program.* (3rd ed.). Alexandria, VA: American Counseling Association.

Heppner, P. P., Kivlighan, D. M., Jr., & Wampold, B. E. (1992). *Research design in counseling.* Pacific Grove, CA: Brooks–Cole.

Krumboltz, J. D. (1974). An accountability model for counselors. *Personnel and Guidance Journal, 52,* 639–646.

Ripley, V., Erford, B. T., Dahir, C., & Eschbach, L. (2003). Planning and implementing a 21st century comprehensive developmental school counseling program. In B. T. Erford (Ed.), *Transforming the school counseling profession* (pp. 121–152). Columbus, OH: Merrill/ Prentice–Hall.

Sanders, J. (1992). *Evaluating school programs: An educator's guide.* Newbury Park, CA: Corwin Press, Inc. (ERIC Document Reproduction Services No. ED 423166)

Stone, L. A., & Bradley, F. O. (1994). *Foundations of elementary and middle school counseling.* White Plains, NY: Longman.

Terenzini, P. (1989). Assessment with open eyes. *Journal of Higher Education, 60*(6), 644–664.

# Chapter 35

## Career Development Interventions in the Schools

*Spencer G. Niles & Jerry Trusty*

### Preview

This chapter provides an overview of developmentally appropriate career interventions for students in grades K-12. The *National Standards for School Counseling Programs* (Campbell & Dahir, 1997) provide a general starting point for constructing career interventions; however the National Occupational Information Coordinating Committee (NOICC) developed very specific National Career Development Guidelines to help counselors identify developmentally appropriate career development goals and interventions across the lifespan (NOICC, 1992). The NOICC guidelines are used as a framework for discussing career interventions across educational levels. A primary theme in the chapter is that career development interventions must help students prepare for the tasks they will encounter as adults. Moreover, career development interventions must help students connect current school activities with their futures. This connection is key to increasing school involvement and school success.

*The National Standards for School Counseling Programs* (Campbell & Dahir, 1997) identify career development as an essential element in effective school counseling programs. Specifically, the *Standards* stipulate that, with regard to career development, students will: Standard A—Acquire the skills to investigate the world of work in relation to knowledge of self and to make informed decisions; Standard B—Employ strategies to achieve future career success and satisfaction; and Standard C—Understand the relationship between personal qualities, education and training, and the world of work (Campbell & Dahir, 1997). These standards make sense because school experiences prepare students for subsequent life experiences and work is a central life role for most adults. However, school-based career development interventions have a mixed record of success. Too often, career development programs are not created systematically and too little attention is devoted to devising comprehensive career interventions from early childhood through secondary school. In many cases, counselors do not evaluate the efficacy of career-related interventions, thereby limiting opportunities for improving services and demonstrating the importance of career interventions to school administrators, parents, teachers, students, and other stakeholders in the educational enterprise. Finally, too often career development programs at one level (e.g., middle school) are not coordinated with programs at another level (e.g., high school). Collectively, these limitations present substantial challenges to professional school counselors seeking to implement the *National Standards* in their school counseling programs.

Many of these challenges confronting professional school counselors emanate from individuals who fail to see the value of career interventions. Those questioning the usefulness of career development interventions assume that career-related activities take students away from time spent focusing on core academic subjects. They assume (incorrectly) that career interventions do not connect to academic subjects. Additionally, some career development critics assume that career development programs pressure students to pursue work immediately after high school rather than pursuing a college education. Many people who are unfamiliar with how careers develop do not understand why career development interventions are important at the elementary, middle, and high school levels. Those arguing against career interventions for elementary school students often view career decisions as events that occur at particular points during the course of secondary school education (e.g., when students must select a curriculum of study, when they leave high school). Such perspectives lack an appreciation of the developmental context from which readiness for career decision-making emerges. Thus, to confront these challenges effectively, many professional school counselors must provide career interventions differently. More specifically, career interventions must be systematic, coordinated, comprehensive, and developmentally appropriate.

*Systematic and Coordinated Planning for Career Development Programs in the Schools*

Walz and Benjamin (1984) provided important recommendations that professional school counselors can use to address the challenges confronting them as they design career development programs. These recommendations are also useful for creating systematic, coordinated, and developmentally appropriate career development intervention programs. Specifically, Walz and Benjamin recommended the following when implementing career programs in the schools:

1. Involve a team of knowledgeable professionals, parents, and representatives from the community in all phases of program planning.
2. Use developmentally appropriate interventions.
3. Be sure that the program goals and objectives are clearly communicated to all involved in the program.
4. Make sure the program is based on student needs.
5. Have an evaluation component to determine the degree to which the program goals and objectives have been achieved.
6. Make sure that those involved in program delivery are highly competent.

An implicit theme in these recommendations is that program planners need to be sensitive to the political climate in which they operate. For example, in some locations, not clearly connecting career development interventions to student academic achievement will significantly decrease the chances of program success. Also, not adequately communicating successful program outcomes to educational stakeholders (e.g., school board members, parents, administrators, teachers, etc.) will result in the program resources being vulnerable to funding cuts. If school personnel view the program as an additional burden to their already heavy workloads, then there is little chance that the program will succeed. Thus, the "marketing" of the program to all stakeholders becomes an important aspect of program development and implementation. Clearly defined behavioral objectives that address the specific needs of students will be useful in marketing the program and providing outcome data demonstrating program benefits.

Another theme implicit in these recommendations for planning career development programs is the importance of taking a team approach to service delivery. One person cannot accomplish all the goals and objectives of an effective career development program. Thus, program personnel need to be clear about their roles and responsibilities. Inevitably, there will be some overlap in the functions performed by program personnel. For example, professional school counselors may, at times, provide classroom instruction and teachers may, at times, perform more career counseling-related functions. Although there is no one prescription for how the roles and responsibilities should be defined, it is logical that professional school counselors take the lead role in developing and implementing career development intervention programs. Professional school counselors are often the only professionals in the school system with specific training in career development. Therefore, professional school counselors possess the knowledge of career development theory and practice necessary for formulating appropriate career development program interventions. Moreover, the processes typically used in program delivery relate to counselors' primary areas of expertise. These processes include counseling, assessment, career information services, placement services, consultation procedures, and referrals.

Developing a systematic and coordinated career development program from early childhood through grade 12 (EC-12) requires understanding the developmental tasks confronting students as they progress through school. Understanding the career development tasks confronting students at all levels of schooling prepares school personnel to work collaboratively in program design and implementation. A comprehensive understanding of the career development process also sets the stage for developing program interventions that are sequential and cohesive. Thus, the following sections of this chapter focus on career development tasks, goals, and interventions for elementary, middle/junior high school, and high school students, respectively.

## Constructing Developmentally Appropriate Career Interventions

*Career Development Guidelines for Elementary School Students*

Although the ASCA standards for career development provided general guidelines for career competencies students need to develop, NOICC developed very specific National Career Development Guidelines (1992) to help professional school counselors identify developmentally appropriate career development goals and interventions across the life span. The specific career development competencies identified as appropriate for elementary school children are:

1. Self-knowledge
   a. Knowledge of the importance of self-concept.
   b. Skills to interact with others.
   c. Awareness of the importance of growth and change.
2. Educational and Occupational Exploration
   a. Awareness of the benefits of educational achievement.
   b. Awareness of the relationship between work and learning.
   c. Skills to understand and use career information.
   d. Awareness of the importance of personal responsibility and good work habits.
   e. Awareness of how work relates to the needs and functions of society.
3. Career Planning
   a. Understanding how to make decisions.
   b. Awareness of the interrelationship of life roles.
   c. Awareness of different occupations and changing male/female roles.
   d. Awareness of the career planning process.

*Career Development Interventions in the Elementary School*

These guidelines provide a framework for establishing career development goals and interventions. Before discussing specific interventions, however, it is worth noting that Magnuson and Starr (2000) offered the following thoughts to guide professional school counselors as they plan career development interventions at the elementary school level:

1. Become a constant observer of children:
   - Notice how children approach tasks.
   - Notice the activities in which children choose to participate.
   - Observe and encourage the child's initiative—taking.
   - Notice the thematic patterns emerging in each child's activities.
2. Consider the processing of an activity as important as the activity itself:

- To help children develop a sense of industry rather than inferiority, focus feedback on the specifics of children's efforts.
- Accompany career awareness and career exploration activities with opportunities for students to express their beliefs about themselves in relation to various occupations. (p. 100)

*Self-knowledge.* Because self-awareness provides the foundation for processing career information, career development interventions in the primary grades can focus first on helping students develop more sophisticated self-knowledge. For example, in grades EC-1 students can increase their self-knowledge by describing themselves through drawings, writing sentences describing the things they like and the things that are important to them, and bringing some of their favorite things to school to show to their classmates. Sharing their self-descriptions with others helps students to clarify their self-concepts. Each of these activities can also emphasize the importance of appreciating the similarities and differences that exist among students in the classroom. Activities that encourage students to focus on clarifying their global self-concepts can be emphasized and can be easily infused into the curriculum during the first years of school.

*Educational and occupational exploration.* Activities that help students learn more about themselves can be supplemented with activities that focus on educational and occupational exploration as students progress through the primary and intermediate grades. For example, in the primary grades students can identify the occupations of their family members (e.g., parents, grandparents, aunts, and uncles) as well as the level and type of education each family member attained. As students share this information, the relationship between education and work can be stressed (e.g., some jobs require a college education and others may require a different type of training such as trade school or an apprenticeship). Differences in family members' occupations can be discussed as strengths (e.g., it takes people working in a wide variety of occupations to make our society function effectively). To counteract occupational stereotyping, men and women working in gender non-traditional occupations can be invited to school to discuss their work.

Students in grades K-1 can begin the process of learning about work by focusing on occupations with which they have the most immediate relationship (e.g., occupations of family members, occupations in the school setting, occupations in their neighborhoods and of neighbors). Then, elementary school students can gradually learn about occupations that are more remote (e.g., occupations in the community, occupations in the state, occupations in the nation, and occupations throughout the world) as they progress from grades 2-5. Using a proximity-distance scheme to guide students in the acquisition of occupational information helps students understand the relevance of work in their lives and the ways in which various workers contribute to society. At each level of proximity, the relationship between work and the educational requirements for performing specific occupations can be highlighted. Students can also discuss what is required to perform occupations successfully. Job content skills (the specific skill requirements for each occupation), functional skills (the skills that are transferable across occupations), and self-management skills (e.g., being reliable, getting along with one's co-workers, being trustworthy, completing assignments on time) can be integrated into these discussions as well.

*Career planning.* Activities to help students learn about the career planning and decision-making process could include:

1. Having students read biographies and then discuss the important career decisions people made in the biographies they read. Students can be encouraged to consider what constitutes a "good" rather than "bad" career decision as they discuss the biographies they read.
2. Students can use a timeline to chart the important events that have influenced the decisions that the people they read about made in their lives.
3. Encouraging students to read stories about people working in nontraditional

occupations can contribute to counteracting the effects of occupational sex-stereotyping.

4. Discussions can include the ways in which culture, gender, and social class may have influenced the career development of the person in the biography.

*Parental Involvement*

Parents have substantial influence over the career development of their children, and these influences are strong through elementary school, middle school, high school, and into adulthood (Trusty, 1998; 1999). Young (1994) suggested that the influence parents exert on the career development process is most effective when it is planned, intentional, and goal-oriented. However, many parents possess minimal knowledge regarding career development theory and how environmental factors influence the career development process of children. Thus, it is important that professional school counselors help parents learn ways to contribute positively to the career development of their children. Professional school counselors can begin by providing parents with information about the career development process. Professional school counselors can also explain to parents how the environment impacts options children are willing to consider. For example, the influence of occupational stereotyping within the media and gender role stereotyping can be discussed with parents. Finally, professional school counselors can help parents identify specific strategies they can use to facilitate career development in their children. Herr and Cramer (1996) identify eight ways parents can help children advance in their careers. These strategies included:

1. Parents can encourage children to analyze important self-characteristics (e.g., interests, capacities, and values).
2. When parents are familiar with specific work requirements for jobs, they can communicate these to their children.
3. Parents can discuss the importance of work values in work behavior.
4. Parents can explain the relationship between work, pay, and the economic condition of the family.
5. Parents can connect children with informational resources (e.g., other workers, books, films) for acquiring accurate career information.
6. Parents can be careful to avoid stereotyping occupational alternatives and workers.
7. Parents can provide children with opportunities for work in the home and community.
8. Parents can provide children with opportunities to learn and practice decision-making skills. (p. 364)

There have been several studies supporting the positive effects of parents' involvement on their children's career development, and parental involvement has been quantified in various ways (e.g., parents' school-based involvement, involvement in school policy-making, help with homework). The type of parental involvement that appears to have the strongest positive effects on children's educational and career development is parents' home-based involvement (Trusty, 1999). Home-based involvement is the degree to which parents communicate positively with their children and support children in their educational and career development. Home-based parental involvement does not appear to be domain-specific. That is, through factor analysis using a national sample, Trusty, Watts, and Erdman (1997) found one home-based involvement factor spanning areas of education, vocation, and leisure.

From research on parents and parental involvement (Trusty, 1998; 1999; Trusty, Watts, & Crawford, 1996; Trusty et al., 1997), there are four main reasons that professional school counselors should focus on parents helping their children with their career development:

- There is generally no *generation gap* between parents and children in the area of career development. Children and adolescents want parents' help and parents want

to help their children.
- Work with parents promotes positive communication within the family.
- Work with parents (counselor contact) enhances parents' perceptions of professional school counselors and schools as resources for their children.
- Parents serve as continual resources for their children, whereas professional school counselors' efforts are more temporal.

Professional school counselors helping parents become aware of their own attitudes toward work and occupations, exposing students to work opportunities in the home and community, and providing support to students as they engage in career decision-making tasks are all ways to help students cope effectively with the career development process and lay a solid foundation for coping with the career development tasks of middle/junior high school.

*Career Development Guidelines for Middle/Junior High School Students*

NOICC (1992) guidelines for middle/junior high school students provide information concerning the specific knowledge, skills, and awareness that students need to acquire in the domains of self-knowledge, educational and occupational exploration, and career planning.

1. Self-knowledge
   a. Knowledge of the influence of a positive self-concept.
   b. Skills to interact with others.
   c. Knowledge of the importance of growth and change.
2. Educational and Occupational Exploration
   a. Knowledge of the benefits of educational achievement to career opportunities.
   b. Understanding the relationship between work and learning.
   c. Skills to locate, understand, and use career information.
   d. Knowledge of skills necessary to seek and obtain jobs.
   e. Understanding how work relates to the needs and functions of the economy and society.
3. Career Planning
   a. Skills to make decisions.
   b. Knowledge of the interrelationship of life roles.
   c. Knowledge of different occupations and changing male/female roles.
   d. Understanding the process of career planning.

As with the elementary school guidelines, a variety of career development interventions can be constructed systematically by using the middle/junior high-level guidelines.

*Career Development Interventions in the Middle/Junior High School*

Thematic consideration of middle/junior high school level career development competencies reveals the importance of students acquiring the necessary knowledge, skills, and understanding to advance in their career development.

*Self-knowledge.* It is also important at this developmental level that career interventions continue to stimulate curiosity in students. Students who are curious about their emerging self-concepts (e.g., their avocational and vocational interests, skills, and values) are more likely to engage in exploratory behavior to acquire the information they need for self-concept clarification. Helping students identify and connect with role models can also facilitate a sense of internal control and future time perspective which can, in turn, lead to planful behaviors and the development of effective problem solving skills (Super, 1990).

Providing career assessment activities as described in the career assessment chapter contained in this book are essential to helping students expand their self-knowledge in a systematic fashion. Interest and aptitude assessment are particularly useful at this developmental level. In selecting career assessments, it is important that the reading level, language, and normative samples are appropriate for the school population with which the assessments will be used. Interest inventory results can foster more systematic thinking about the activities in which students enjoy participating. Aptitude tests can also help students acquire accurate estimates of their abilities. Interest and aptitude assessments are often administered to students during the middle/ junior high school grades. Combining interest inventory with aptitude test results provides a useful foundation for the exploration process.

*Educational and occupational exploration.* Students will find it useful to explore occupational areas for which they have high interest and high aptitude. When the results of an interest inventory suggest that a student has no area of above average or high interest, it may be that the student will need exposure to activities across several interest areas to determine if these areas hold any interest for the student. Thus, a key to assessments, especially interest inventories, being useful is that students must have the experiential base to draw upon to respond to assessment items. Students with limited exposure to a variety of activities will be forced to guess at appropriate responses to questions requiring them to identify their likes and dislikes.

When school systems have a systematic career development intervention program in place for all grades, then it is safer to assume that middle/junior high school students have been exposed to activities that have fostered their self and career exploration. When no such programs exist, then counselors must be especially cognizant of the possibility that many students will need more remedial career development interventions prior to being administered career assessments.

Providing middle school students with exposure to work facilitates the acquisition of knowledge, skills, and awareness related to the career development domains of: a) educational and occupational exploration and b) career planning. Teaching students how families of occupations can be clustered according to factors such as skill requirements, interests, and/or training helps students organize the world of work and connect their characteristics to occupational options. For example, Holland's classification system uses six personality types (Realistic, Investigative, Artistic, Social, Enterprising, and Conventional) to organize the world of work. Realistic occupations include skills trades and technical occupations. Investigative occupations include scientific and technical occupations. Artistic occupations include creative occupations in the expressive arts. Social occupations include the helping professions. Enterprising occupations involve managerial and sales occupations. Lastly, Conventional occupations include office and clerical occupations. Occupations are classified according to the degree to which the activities of the occupation draw upon the Holland types. The three most dominant types reflected in the occupation are used to classify each occupation.

Clustering systems such as Holland's can be used to guide career exploration by using the types to organize: career information resources, career fairs, curricula experiences (e.g., students can be assigned the task of writing an essay about occupations that fall within their dominant Holland type), job shadowing experiences, participation in extracurricular activities, avocational pursuits, college exploration, and part-time employment experiences. With accurate self-knowledge and systematic educational and career exploration, students develop readiness to engage in career planning.

*Career planning.* Effective career planning at the middle school/junior high school level requires students to know how to make decisions, understand the interrelationship of life roles, know about different occupations and changing male/female roles and understand the process of career planning. An effective tool for helping middle/junior high school students engage in purposeful planning, exploring, information gathering, decision making, and reality testing related to two prominent life roles (i.e., student and worker) is an educational and career planning portfolio. Educational and career planning portfolios are typically used to help students chart their academic and career decision-making. This charting process can begin in middle/junior high school and continue until the student leaves high school. By making at least annual entries into the portfolio, the student and counselor can track the student's career development progress. They can also make systematic educational and career plans that build upon the growing base of self and occupational knowledge the student is developing. In essence, the portfolio provides a vehicle for the student and counselor to discuss what the student has done and what the student will do next to advance his/her career development.

To help students focus on the interrelationship of life roles, and to engage in planning related to their salient life roles, the educational and career planning portfolio can be expanded to a "life-role portfolio" by addressing students' readiness for life roles beyond those of student and worker. Students can be encouraged to plan, explore, and gather information, etc. for each of the major roles of life. For example, students who anticipate one day being a parent can plan for this role by considering how parenting interacts with other roles. Students can explore different styles of parenting by interviewing parents about their parenting practices and philosophies. Students can also gather information about the skills required for effective parenting (perhaps by taking a parenting class). Through these activities students can learn about the factors that are important to consider in making decisions about parenting. Finally, students can reality test their interest in parenting through participating in childcare activities. Thus, the life-role portfolio serves as a stimulus for counselor and student meetings focused on planning, exploring, information gathering, decision-making, and reality testing vis-à-vis the major life roles. When the portfolio is used over successive years, it also provides developmental documentation of activities and decisions related to major life roles.

*Career Development Guidelines for High School Students*

As students transition from middle/junior high school they focus more directly on the task of identifying occupational preferences and clarifying career/lifestyle choices. According to Super (1957) the tasks of crystallizing, specifying, and implementing tentative career choices occur during early (ages 12-15), middle (ages 16-18), and late (ages 18-24) adolescence, and will be useful to them as they move forward and will help to normalize the transition process.

NOICC guidelines (1992) and the extensive body of literature related to adolescent career development help professional school counselors identify appropriate career development goals and interventions for high school students. The specific career development competencies identified as being appropriate for high school students are:

1. Self-knowledge
   a. Understanding the influence of a positive self-concept.
   b. Skills to interact positively with others.
   c. Understanding the impact of growth and development.
2. Educational and Occupational Exploration
   a. Understanding the relationship between educational achievement and career planning.
   b. Understanding the need for positive attitudes toward work and learning.
   c. Skills to locate, evaluate, and interpret career information.
   d. Skills to prepare to seek, obtain, maintain, and change jobs.
   e. Understanding how societal needs and functions influence the nature and structure of work.
3. Career Planning
   a. Skills to make decisions.
   b. Understanding the interrelationship of life roles.
   c. Understanding the continuous changes in male/female roles.
   d. Skills in career planning.

*Career Development Interventions in High School*

The emphasis on knowledge, skills, and understanding that emerged in the middle/junior high school level competencies is continued in the high school competencies. The high school competencies, however, challenge students to become more focused on making career plans by translating their self and career information into career goals. At the high school level, students' level of sophistication regarding the domains of self-knowledge, educational and occupational exploration, and career planning is such that there is substantial overlap among them. Interventions tend to involve all three domains and this section discusses them collectively.

Savickas (1999) proposed career development interventions that foster the sort of self-knowledge, educational and occupational exploration, and career planning described in the high school competencies. Specifically, these interventions focus on: a) orienting students' comprehension of careers, b) developing students' competence at planning and exploring, c) coaching students to develop effective career management techniques, and d) guiding students in behavioral rehearsals to become prepared for coping with job problems.

To orient ninth grade students to the planning tasks they will encounter as they move through high school, Savickas (1999) recommended using a group guidance format to discuss items on career development inventories such as the *Career Maturity Inventory* (Crites, 1978) or the *Adult Career Concerns Inventory* (ACCI; Super, Thompson, & Lindeman, 1988). Using inventory items to orient students to the tasks they need to address in order to manage their career development effectively helps provide a stimulus for planning and exploring behaviors (Savickas, 1990). For example, the ACCI measures developmental task concern for the career stages of Exploration, Establishment, Maintenance, and Disengagement. Reviewing the career stages and tasks within the ACCI teaches high school students about the general process of career development. Using ACCI items, adolescents can identify those career development tasks they are likely to encounter in the near future. Strategies for coping with current and near future career development tasks can be identified. In this way, high school students' understanding of time perspective or "planfulness" can be enhanced (Savickas, Silling, & Schwartz, 1984).

Results from interest and abilities measures administered at the end of middle school or at the beginning of high school provide direction as to which occupational environments offer the best potential for fruitful exploration. The range of career assessment possibilities that can be used systematically with youth is substantial. To measure interests, professional school counselors can use instruments that provide information related to students' Holland types such as the *Self-Directed Search* (Holland, 1985) and the *Career Assessment Inventory* (Johansson, 1986). Ability measures include the *Differential Aptitude Test* (Bennett, Seashore, & Wesman, 1974), *The Ability Explorer* (Harrington & Harrington, 1996), and assessments of functional skills from school transcripts or educational and career planning portfolios. Areas of high interest and ability can be matched to occupational clusters and students can identify specific occupations for in-depth exploration.

Although interest and ability assessment results provide important data pertaining to career choice content (i.e., relating students' abilities and interests to occupational options), these data fail to address whether students have developed readiness for career decision-making (Super, 1983). Approaches to career assessment must attend to both content and process variables in order to adequately address the needs of youth (Savickas, 1993). Specifically, interests and abilities can be considered as career choice content data that must be viewed in light of career choice process data such as readiness for career decision-making, life-role salience, and values, which can be labeled as moderator variables (Super, Osborne, Brown, Walsh, & Niles, 1992). To be ready to effectively choose and adapt to an occupation it is important for high school students to "see themselves as coping with certain developmental tasks, at a stage in life at which they are expected, and may expect themselves to make certain decisions and acquire certain competencies" (Super, 1983, p. 559). Students who have not successfully accomplished the career development tasks presented to them at previous educational levels will need remedial interventions (e.g., additional opportunities for self-concept clarification, training in acquiring occupational information) prior to focusing on career decision-making.

From this perspective, addressing career choice readiness (Super, 1974) becomes a necessary precursor to the effective use of ability and interest assessment data. According to Super, career choice readiness involves five dimensions: (a) having a planful attitude toward coping with career stages and tasks, (b) gathering information about educational and occupational opportunities, (c) exploring the world of work, (d) knowing how to make good career decisions, and (e) being able to make realistic judgments about potential occupations. These dimensions are important because if an adolescent knows little about the world of work, then interest inventories that use occupational titles or activities may produce misleading scores and poor choices may be made (Super, Savickas, & Super, 1996). Likewise, when adolescents do not engage in appropriate career planning, they often encounter career tasks for which they are not prepared (Herr & Cramer, 1996). Thus, assessing high school students' resources for choosing and adapting to an occupation requires conducting appraisals of career choice content (e.g., abilities, interests, values) and process (e.g., life-role salience, career choice readiness) variables. When a student is lacking in any of the five dimensions comprising career choice readiness, then the professional school counselor should focus interventions to help the student progress in that particular domain prior to focusing on career choice content.

It is important to note that traditional assessment approaches focusing only on career choice content variables assume that all individuals place a high value on work and that all individuals view work as the prime means of values realization. It can be argued that this is a Western middle-class male view of career development and, thus, is a culturally encapsulated view of life-role salience. Different patterns of life-role salience exist and they must be considered in helping high school students clarify and articulate their career goals (Niles & Goodnough, 1996). For example, when salience for the work role is high, youth view work as providing meaningful opportunities for self-expression. In such cases, high school students are often motivated to develop the career maturity necessary (e.g., to be planful, to explore opportunities, to gather information) for making good career decisions. When work-role salience is low, however, adolescents often lack motivation and career maturity. In the latter instances, professional school counselors need to begin the career development intervention process by arousing the individual's sense of importance for the worker role (Super, 1990). Disputing irrational beliefs, exposing young people to effective role models, and providing mentors are examples of activities that foster career arousal (Krumboltz & Worthington, 1999).

To help students further clarify their life-role self-concepts, professional school counselors can encourage high school students to consider life-role salience questions (e.g., How do I spend my time during the course of a typical week? What changes would I like to make in how I spend my time? How important is each life role to me? How important is each life role to my family? What do I like about participating in each life role? What do I hope to accomplish in each life role? What does my family expect me to accomplish in each life role? What life roles do I think will be important to me in the future? What must I do to become more prepared for the life roles that will be important to me in the future?). Discussing these questions helps high school students clarify and articulate their life-role self-concepts. Specifically, by discussing these questions during the first years of high school, adolescents can become clearer as to the values they seek to express in each life role. This information is vital not only for guiding high school students in the selection and pursuit of appropriate educational and occupational options, but also in developing appropriate expectations for values satisfaction within the respective life roles.

These discussion questions also provide opportunities for exploring the individual's level of acculturation, cultural identity, and worldview. For example, high school students can discuss family expectations and other cultural factors influencing their life-role participation. Finally, discussing these questions helps professional school counselors become aware of potential barriers, as well as potential sources of support, for students as they move closer to negotiating the school-to-work or school-to-school transition. These discussions also foster the acquisition of the high school level career development competencies related to understanding the interrelationship of life roles and understanding the changing nature of male/female roles. This information also helps high school students identify those roles in which they spend most of their time, those that they are emotionally committed to, and those that they expect to be important to them in the future. By clarifying information concerning life-role salience (and the cultural factors influencing role salience), high school students establish the foundation for making accurate self-evaluations and developing career choice readiness.

An important task in acquiring adequate self-knowledge for effective educational and occupational exploration is clarifying values. Clarifying values is important because values are indications of the qualities people desire and seek in "the activities in which they engage, in the situations in which they live, and in the objects which they make or acquire" (Super, 1974, p. 4). Because values reflect the individual's goals, they provide a sense of purpose and direction in the career planning process (Super, Savickas, & Super, 1996). However, while many agree that values clarification is critical to choosing an occupation, relatively few put forth the effort to examine their values in a systematic way (Harrington & Harrington, 1996). Values card sorts (e.g., *Career Values Card Sort Kit, Non-sexist Vocational Card Sort*) and instruments such as the *Career Orientation Placement and Evaluation Survey* (COPES) are instruments that are useful in values clarification. Interest inventory results can also be used to identify work-related activities that provide opportunities for values expression.

These interventions represent examples of ways in which high school counselors can help students prepare for a successful school-to-work or school-to-school transition. When professional school counselors at all grade levels work collaboratively to develop systematic career development interventions there is a greater likelihood that students will be prepared for the career development tasks they will encounter as they move through high school.

## Summary/Conclusion

Today, perhaps more than ever, systematic career development interventions are needed to help young people advance in their career development. The nature of work is changing dramatically, requiring new skills sets (e.g., transition skills, stress management, the ability to engage in lifelong learning, personal flexibility, computer skills) that suggest that change, rather than constancy, will be the norm. Workers in the 21st century will experience multiple career changes that will bring associated levels of stress that must be managed effectively. It is naïve to expect parents, many of whom are struggling to manage their own careers effectively, to provide children and adolescents with the competencies they need to advance in their careers in the 21st century. In light of the challenges that young people face, all stakeholders, and especially professional school counselors, parents, and schools, must work together to support students in their career development. Career development interventions must help students prepare for the tasks they will encounter as adults. Moreover, career development interventions must help students connect current school activities with their futures. This connection is key to increasing school involvement and school success.

In many respects, professional school counselors are the human development specialists in the schools. Educating stakeholders about the developmental process students will experience as they move through school helps students, teachers, administrators, and parents develop the awareness to think proactively about the tasks students will encounter. Thus, infusing the curriculum with developmental concepts helps students acquire the awareness that fosters a planful approach to coping with career development tasks.

## References

Bennett, G. K., Seashore, H. G., & Wesman, A. G. (1992). *Technical manual: Differential aptitude tests* (5th ed.). San Antonio, TX: The Psychological Corporation.

Campbell, C. A., & Dahir, C. A. (1997). *The national standards for school counseling programs.* Alexandria,VA: American School Counselor Association.

Crites, J. O. (1978). *Theory and research handbook for the Career Maturity Inventory.* Monterey, CA: CTB, McGraw Hill.

Harrington, T. F., & Harrington, J. C. (1996). *The Ability Explorer.* Itasca, IL: Riverside Publishing.

Herr, E. L., & Cramer, S. H. (1996). *Career guidance and counseling through the lifespan* (5th ed.). New York: Harper Collins.

Holland, J. L. (1985). *Making vocational choices: A theory of vocational personalities and work environments* (2nd ed.). Englewood Cliffs, NJ: Prentice–Hall.

Holland, J. L. (1994). *Self–Directed Search.* Lutz, FL: PAR.

Johanssen, C. B. (1986). *Career Assessment Inventory.* Minneapolis, MN: NCS.

Krumboltz, J. D., & Worthington, R. (1999). The school–to–work transition from a learning theory perspective. *Career Development Quarterly, 47,* 312–325.

Magnuson, C. S., & Starr, M. F. (2000). How early is too early to begin life career planning? The importance of the elementary school years. *Journal of Career Development, 27*, 89–101.

National Occupational Information Coordinating Committee (NOICC). U. S. Department of Labor. (1992). *The national career development guidelines project.* Washington, DC: U. S. Department of Labor.

Niles, S. G., & Goodnough, G. E. (1996). Life–role salience and values: A review of recent research. *The Career Development Quarterly, 45*, 65–86.

Savickas, M. L. (1990). The Career Decision–Making Course: Description and field test. *The Career Development Quarterly, 38*, 275–284.

Savickas, M. L. (1993). Predictive validity criteria for career development measures. *Journal of Career Assessment, 1,* 93–104.

Savickas, M. L. (1999). The transition from school to work: Developmental perspective. *The Career Development Quarterly, 47*, 326– 336.

Savickas, M. L., Stilling, S. M., & Schwartz, S. (1984). Time perspective in vocational maturity and career decision–making. *Journal of Vocational Behavior, 25,* 258–269.

Super, D. E. (1955). Transition: From vocational guidance to counseling psychology. *Journal of Counseling Psychology, 2,* 3–9.

Super, D. E. (1957). *A psychology of careers.* New York: Harper & Row.

Super, D. E. (Ed.). (1974). *Measuring vocational maturity for counseling and evaluation.* Washington, DC: National Vocational Guidance Association.

Super, D. E. (1983). Assessment in career guidance: Toward truly developmental counseling. *Personnel and Guidance Journal, 61,* 555–562.

Super, D. E. (1990). Career and life development. In D. Brown & L. Brooks (Eds.), *Career choice and development: Applying contemporary theories to practice* (2nd ed.) (pp. 197–261). San Francisco: Jossey–Bass.

Super, D. E., Osborne, W. L., Walsh, D. J., Brown, S. D., & Niles, S. G. (1992). Developmental assessment and counseling: The C–DAC model. *Journal of Counseling and Development, 71*, 74–80.

Super, D. E., Savickas, M. L., & Super, C. M. (1996). The life span, life–space approach to careers. In D. Brown & L. Brooks (Eds.), *Career choice and development: Applying contemporary theories to practice* (3rd ed.)(pp. 121–178). San Francisco: Jossey–Bass.

Super, D. E., Thompson, A. S., & Lindeman, R. H. (1988). *Adult Career Concerns Inventory: Manual for research and exploratory use in counseling*. Palo Alto, CA: Consulting Psychologists Press.

Trusty, J. (1998). Family influences on educational expectations of late adolescents. *Journal of Educational Research, 91,* 260–270.

Trusty, J. (1999). Effects of eighth–grade parental involvement on late adolescents' educational expectations. *Journal of Research and Development in Education, 32,* 224–233.

Trusty, J., Watts, R. E., & Crawford, R. (1996). Career information resources for parents of public school seniors: Findings from a national study. *Journal of Career Development, 22,* 227–238.

Trusty, J., Watts, R. E., & Erdman, P. (1997). Predictors of parents' involvement in their teens' career development. *Journal of Career Development, 23,* 189–201.

Walz, G. R., & Benjamin, L. (1984). A systems approach to career guidance. *Vocational Guidance Quarterly, 33*, 26–34.

Young, R. A. (1994). Helping adolescents with career development: The active role of parents. *Career Development Quarterly, 42*, 195–203.

# Chapter 36

## Educational Planning: Helping Students Build Lives By Choice, Not Chance

*Suzanne M. Hobson & Cheryl A. Phillips*

### Preview

Designed for current and future professional school counselors, this chapter provides an overview of educational planning in comprehensive school counseling programs. Educational planning, as addressed in this chapter, is inextricably tied to the career development process and represents an essential component in a school counseling program. The chapter includes step-by-step information to guide professional school counselors through the educational planning process and focuses on the effective use of Educational Development Plans (EDPs) and a variety of delivery methods.

A key component of any successful school counseling program is the educational planning component. Whereas the primary mission of professional counselors in community agencies is to promote mental health, the primary mission of professional school counselors is to promote educational achievement. Ultimately, the hope is that educational achievement will serve as the foundation for the students' career development and productivity as citizens. Toward this end, professional school counselors systematically assist students and parents with the process of educational planning. The goal is to assist students in preparing themselves for careers and fulfilling lives with intentionality. Rather than finishing school and assuming a job, career, or life by chance (whatever option happens to be available and accessible at the time), sound educational planning supports students in exercising choice about their career and life destinations.

Simply put, educational planning can be defined as the process of assisting students and parents in understanding the connection between education and career/life planning, setting goals, making decisions regarding academic course selection and scholastic experiences that will contribute to the achievement of these goals, evaluating progress toward these goals, and modifying educational plans as needed. The purpose of this chapter is to provide an overview of the educational planning process and to offer specific ideas about the integration of educational planning services into an already existing school counseling program.

The process of educational planning may be conceptualized as a role of a professional school counselor (Schmidt, 1999) or as a part of the individual planning component of a comprehensive guidance and counseling program (Gysbers & Henderson, 2000). This latter conceptualization suggests that professional school counselors work within a programmatic framework. According to Gysbers and Henderson (2000), this framework involves the provision of responsive services (e.g., individual and small group counseling), individual planning (which tends to focus on the educational and career planning process), curriculum guidance (in which professional school counselors systematically design and deliver classroom guidance lessons in three broad content areas), and system support (e.g., the managerial aspects of coordinating a program and making fair share contributions to the school as an organization). Although the individual planning component is perhaps most closely related to educational planning, the curriculum guidance component may also be used for this purpose. Consistent with the National Standards put forth by the American School Counselor Association (ASCA) (Campbell & Dahir, 1997), the three content areas targeted by curriculum guidance units are: (1) academic development, (2) career development, and (3) personal/social development. Additionally, Myrick (1997) delineated several aspects of educational planning. These were to: recognize options that are available for planning; illustrate the need to plan ahead; learn a language of educational planning (common terms); learn the sequence of academic courses; identify academic requirements and electives; develop an educational plan for middle or high school; and register for next year's courses (p. 56).

In approaching the topic of educational planning, this chapter is based upon several assumptions. The first assumption is that all students need assistance with educational planning. Regardless of whether they are college-bound or looking toward a career that does not require additional education, all students need and deserve assistance with the educational planning process. Secondly, this chapter is based on an assumption that there is value in all work and that one type of career aspiration is neither better or worse than another. It logically follows, then, that the quality of an educational plan is to be judged not by the highest level of education to be achieved by a student, but rather by the goodness of fit with the student's aspirations. How well an educational plan prepares a student for whatever career and life he/she has chosen is the issue. This second assumption is especially important given that "while only about 30% of new jobs created in the next 10 years will require at least a bachelor's degree, more than 70% of parents seem to believe their child will fill one of these jobs" (Parnell as cited in Hoyt, 2001, p. 6). Finally, the third assumption upon which this chapter is based is that educational planning is necessarily tied to career planning. Indeed, educational plans should be developed to support a student's career aspirations and interests.

## Journeys and Destinations

Before developing an educational plan, therefore, professional school counselors must work with students and parents to develop an understanding of the student's long-term goals. If the educational plan is likened to a road map, the student's career aspirations and interests may be likened to the destination. Certainly, it is difficult to develop a detailed road map without a sense of the destination. Because students need more guidance than "go forward," it becomes essential to begin the career exploration and development process early. It is for this reason that the ASCA recommends career development activities as early as elementary school (Campbell & Dahir, 1997).

Career development experts and professional school counselors are not alone in their perception of the need for educational and career planning. In fact, Libsch and Freedman-Doan (1995) found that 49% of high school seniors indicated that they would prefer more assistance in choosing their courses and 54% expressed a preference for more help in developing educational plans. In addition, 61% reported that they would prefer more attention to career planning and job selection.

As professional school counselors work with students and their parents in looking ahead to post-secondary options, it is important to address: (a) the amount of formal post-secondary education or training a student is willing to attain; (b) the general career pathway (or specific career) in which the student is interested; and (c) the type of education and/or training that is best suited to prepare the student for his/her chosen career pathway. With regard to the amount of formal post-secondary education or training a student is willing to complete, it is helpful to discuss with the students and parents a variety of options rather than erroneously suggesting that a 4-year college degree is the only viable route to a successful career (Hoyt, 2001). When discussing career pathways, professional school counselors will do well to utilize their own state's terminology when labeling the career categories or pathways. Many states, for example, will organize careers into six pathways: (1) arts & communications; (2) business, management, marketing and technology; (3) engineering/manufacturing & industrial technology; (4) health sciences; (5) human services; and (6) natural resources & agri-sciences (terminology from the Michigan Department of Career Development).

Because students are generally unable to identify one specific career goal and better able to identify a cluster of careers in which they are interested and display talent, the use of pathways is becoming the norm in many school counseling programs. Each pathway includes careers that involve a wide range of post-secondary education and training. Some involve four or more years of college whereas others involve on-the-job training and still others require vocational training. In addressing post-secondary options, therefore, professional school counselors will want to work with students and parents to find the length and type of education most likely to assist the student in reaching his or her goals within a given career pathway.

It is essential that the process of discussing post-secondary options begin early—preferably in middle school—in order to develop such an educational plan. As Sears (1995) stated, "students and their parents need to understand... that committing to an educational plan, accidentally or on purpose, has long-range consequences" (p. 37). For example, if a student eventually wants to go to college, his or her ability to do so will depend greatly upon his or her selection of courses as early as middle school. Without appropriate coursework and achievement in middle school math and English, a high school freshman will be positioned poorly to begin college prep coursework in these subjects. Sears reported on a study conducted by the College Board which found that only half of all high school students who intend to go to college were actually enrolled in courses appropriate for this future plan. These students apparently chose their courses without understanding the implications of their selections on their future educational career. Sears suggested that "many parents are also unaware of the significance of these early decisions" (1995, p. 38).

## The Early Decision-Making Process

Clearly, early discussion of career interests and aspirations is inextricably tied to the educational planning process. To assist students and their parents in this early career exploration and educational planning process, professional school counselors will want to proactively guide students and parents through a decision-making process. Ideally, this process will include helping students assess their career-related interests, skills, personality, and values.

With regard to the assessment of interests, professional school counselors may conduct interviews with students on an individual, small group or classroom basis, utilize formal interest inventories, provide informal interest questionnaires, or facilitate the use of computer software programs that include interest assessment components. Standardized interest inventories most commonly used in the K-12 academic setting include the *Self-Directed Search* (SDS) (Holland, Powell & Fritzche, 1994), the *Strong Interest Inventory* (Hansen, Borgen & Hammer, 1994), and the *Career Occupational Preferences System* (COPS)(EdITS, 1995). A number of computer software programs—including DISCOVER (ACT, 1989b), the *Career Explorer Online* (CX Online) (bridges.com, 2002) and *COIN Educational Inventory* (Ryan & Ryan, 1994)—also include components that assess student interests.

The assessment of interest, however, is not sufficient for the career development and educational planning process. Certainly, another important dimension involves skills. Whether these skills are conceptualized as aptitudes, achievement or ability, it is essential that professional school counselors also assist students in considering the relevance of skills to their future. In assessing skills, professional school counselors tend to rely on student self-report during interviews, on academic performance (as evidenced by G.P.A.), and on standardized test scores. Standardized tests commonly used during the career development and educational planning process include the *Differential Aptitude Test* (DAT)(Psychological Corporation, 1992), the *PSAT* (College Board, 1992), *SAT* (College Board, 1991), the *PLAN* (ACT, 1986), *ACT* (ACT, 1989a), and the *Armed Services Vocational Aptitude Battery* (ASVAB) (U.S. Department of Defense, 2002).

Also important to the early decision-making process is the assessment of student personality styles as they relate to career planning. This is based, in part, on Holland's contention that a match between an individual's personality style and the "personality" of a given occupation or career leads to increased job satisfaction and success (Brown & Brooks, 1990). However, formal personality testing is rarely, if ever, conducted by professional school counselors. Instead, professional school counselors tend to use career instruments and/or informal measures in helping students identify career-related personality preferences. For example, the SDS (Holland et al., 1994) helps describe student personalities by identifying a student's three-letter preference. Otherwise known as the "Holland Code," these three letters identify the student's personality preference from six possible styles: realistic, investigative, artistic, social, enterprising, or conventional. Some professional school counselors also use tests such as the *True Colors* program (Imai & Berry, 2001; Kalil & Lowery, 1999) to help students conceptualize aspects of their personality. Still others may use the *Kiersey Temperament Sorter* (Kiersey, 1998) to help students determine the direction of their preference across four domains: (1) extroversion vs. introversion; (2) sensing vs. intuition; (3) thinking vs. feeling; and (4) judging vs. perceiving.

The final aspect of assessment that generally contributes to the early decision-making process involves the exploration of students' education and career-related values. In facilitating this exploration, professional school counselors seek to assist students and their parents in identifying and examining values that should contribute to their educational and career decisions. For example, students may value high salaries, prestige associated with a career, flexibility of scheduling, autonomy, the opportunity to make a difference or contribute to society, adventure, or intellectual stimulation. In helping students identify their values and apply them to the career decision-making and educational planning process, professional school counselors may use formal tests such as the *Minnesota Importance Questionnaire* (Rounds, Henly, Dawis & Lofquist, 1981), informal checklists, interviews, or value card sorts.

Through the process of helping students understand how their interests, skills, personality, and values relate to their educational and career decisions, professional school counselors facilitate the early career decision-making process. Specifically, professional school counselors assist students and their parents in applying this knowledge to select an initial career pathway and to estimate the amount and type of post-secondary education necessary for the student to reach his or her career and life goals.

## The Balancing Act

Helping students make career decisions early enough in their academic career to support the educational planning process for high school course selection requires that professional school counselors successfully negotiate two separate balancing acts. First, because this early decision-making process is ideally completed during the middle school/junior high years, professional school counselors must balance the self-report and autonomy of students (young adolescents) with the influence of others. For example, counselors will want to help students balance their own aspirations, however immature, with the wisdom, caring and, perhaps, dominance of their parents. As another example, it is essential that professional school counselors assist students in ferreting out the influence of their peers when making decisions for themselves. Additionally, professional school counselors will want to proactively assist students in limiting the impact of culturally sanctioned sex-role stereotypes when considering various career options (Campbell & Dahir, 1997; Drummond & Ryan, 1995).

Certainly, the difficulty in achieving this balance and assisting students in deciding how much consideration to give to parental and peer input about their future is considerable during early adolescence, a time in which the students' sense of self and their ability to effectively make decisions that have long-term consequences is limited. Indeed, achieving this balance is difficult even during late adolescence. This balancing act was approached from a constructive developmental perspective by McAuliffe and Strand (1994) when they applied Kegan's (1982) developmental theory to the academic advising process. Although they focused on advising at the college level, the following point would also appear to have salience for the process of assisting young adolescents with making decisions regarding their future educational and career plans:

> Many forces will seem to conspire to maintain Interpersonalism, such as group-think peers or parents who expect adherence to family and cultural norms. Nevertheless, the advisor, from the constructive developmental perspective, must challenge Interpersonally embedded individuals' expectations that others will supply them with decisions. (McAuliffe & Strand, 1994, p. 27)

The second balancing act necessitates an awareness that decisions made by students during middle and even high school may change over time. Whereas a student in middle school may firmly believe that he or she wants to become a physician and seek a medical degree, this same student may alter plans as a result of experiences with college prep coursework. Similarly, another student may initially plan to seek employment immediately following high school graduation but later express an interest in going to college. As students develop their self-awareness (Schmidt, 1999), accumulate real-life experience with academic coursework, and improve their understanding of career possibilities, their educational and career goals may change. Such changes are commonplace and to be expected. Therefore, professional school counselors must balance the process of helping students make enough of a decision to support educational planning with the importance of also allowing room for students to change their plans.

## Match Making

Keeping these balancing acts in mind, the professional school counselor's next task is to assist students and their parents in creating an educational plan designed to facilitate the students' progress toward their post-secondary educational and career goals. Indeed, it is the process of matching educational plans with student goals that constitutes the majority of a professional school counselor's activities within the educational planning domain.

For the majority of students, graduating from high school constitutes a fundamental goal that serves as a foundation for their future plans. In helping students match their educational plans with this goal, professional school counselors typically engage in a myriad of educational planning activities. First, high school counselors educate students about graduation requirements. This process generally begins in the 8th grade year and frequently involves collaboration between the high school and middle school/junior high counselors. In helping students understand graduation requirements, it is necessary to teach them about credits, the curricular requirements necessary for graduation, and the grades needed to achieve credit in any given course. Figure 1 provides a sample handout used to explain graduation requirements. Additionally, Sill (1995) suggested that this early orientation should also address "honors requirements, vocational and

**Figure 1. Sample Handout Explaining Graduation Requirements.**

**GRADUATION REQUIREMENTS**

| | |
|---|---|
| **Credit Rquirements** | 12 Required Credits<br>11 Elective Credits<br>23 Total Credits |
| **Common Learnings** | **3.5 English**<br>1.0 9th Grade English<br>1.0 10th Grade English<br>0.5 Literature<br>0.5 Composition<br>0.5 Speech<br>**2.5 Mathematics**<br>**2.5 Science**<br>**2.5 Social Studies**<br>1.0 U.S. History<br>0.5 Government<br>**0.5 Physical Ed**<br>**0.5 Health**<br>**0.5 Computers Tech** |
| **Electives** | 11 Elective Credits |

| Factors for Admission Consideration |
|---|
| 1. High school diploma from an accredited high school<br>2. Grades in academic subjects<br>3. Grade point average<br>4. Trend of grades<br>5. ACT and/or SAT scores<br>6. Extracurricular activities<br>7. Community service |

**RECOMMEND COLLEGE PREPARATORY PROGRAM**

| Course | Number of Credits | Comments |
|---|---|---|
| English | 4 | Writing emphasis |
| Math | 4 | Algebra 2 and Geometry |
| Science | 3 | Biological and Physical Science |
| Social Studies | 3 | US History and Government |
| Foreign Language | 2 | |

U.S. Government Printing Office.
Educational Planning 1

college prep information, prerequisite information, and other items of interest" (p. 89).

Next, the majority of high schools require the preparation of an Educational Development Plan (EDP) for each student. In addition to ensuring that the EDP includes all graduation requirements, professional school counselors utilize the EDP process to assist students in selecting curricular options that will best meet their post-secondary educational and career plans. The preparation of an EDP may be accomplished through the individual planning or the guidance curriculum components of a comprehensive guidance and counseling program (Gysbers & Henderson, 2000).

However, many professional school counselors mistakenly believe that the individual planning activities must be accomplished through the use of individual sessions with students. Such a use of time is inefficient given the high student-counselor ratios across the country, and the process of assisting with individual planning can also be achieved through the use of classroom and small group meetings (Stanciak, 1995). Professional school counselors interested in quantifying time saved and/or the differential impact of providing individual planning services in classroom or small group settings are referred to the section on impact analysis in Gysbers and Henderson (2000). Professional school counselors using a small group format may wish to group students according to post-secondary plans in order to maximize their efficiency. For example, they may meet with students planning for vocational post-secondary training in one group, with students planning for community college in another group, and with students hoping for admission to Ivy League colleges in yet another.

Regardless of a student's post-secondary plans and regardless of the format in which a professional school counselor chooses to discuss EDP's, the EDP form itself is a primary tool. Figure 2 offers a sample EDP form. This form offers a simple way in which to assist students in: (a) understanding and tracking their progress toward graduation requirements; (b) understanding general university admissions requirements; (c) recording and updating information about educational and career goals; and (d) planning specific coursework for grades 9-12.

Within the section for graduation requirements, students are able to check boxes for each half-credit earned in a given subject. This allows for a quick visual check on progress toward graduation requirements. Within the section on general university admissions requirements, professional school counselors should caution students to verify these requirements with the specific colleges they are considering. The section on educational and career goals should serve as a basis for course selection, and it is the professional school counselor's role to assist students in understanding what courses are best suited to the student's goals. Finally, the section reserved for planning specific coursework will need considerable attention. Each grade level has two columns, one for each semester. In assisting students with coursework planning, professional school counselors will need to be prepared to discuss with students the sequencing of classes; to explain the importance of prerequisites; and to offer insight regarding coursework necessary for a variety of post-secondary educational and career plans.

Figures 3, 4 and 5 present sample EDPs designed to represent varying post-secondary educational and career plans. Figure 3, for example, provides an EDP for Joanie Hansen, a hypothetical student intent on pursuing a doctoral degree in veterinary medicine or pharmacology. Figure 4 provides an EDP for Mike Brady, a fictitious student interested in earning an associates degree in order to become an architectural assistant or a computer-aided designer. Finally, Figure 5 offers an EDP for Elyse Keaton, a fictional student intending to either work in childcare or in her family's business immediately following high school graduation.

In comparing the three completed EDPs (Figures 3, 4 and 5), one will note significant differences in course planning. These differences involve both the level of courses planned and the type of courses selected. With regard to the level of courses planned, for example, Joanie's professional school counselor strongly encouraged her to take high-level math classes throughout high school because she is planning to pursue a doctorate in a medical field. Because Joanie is scheduled to take Accelerated Geometry as a freshman, Joanie will need to have taken prerequisite coursework during middle school. This highlights the importance of early interventions to assist with educational and career planning during middle, and even elementary, school. In comparison to Joanie's math schedule, both Mike and Elyse have planned to take Algebra I during their freshman year.

With regard to the type of courses selected, the professional school counselor has worked with the students to assist them in identifying classes related to their post-secondary educational and career plans. Although the majority of classes are selected for the purpose of meeting graduation requirements and of ensuring a well-rounded education for each student, there invariably exists room for electives. The choice of electives, therefore, can and should allow students to explore more deeply their tentative post-secondary plans. As an illustration, Mike Brady has expressed interest both in architecture and in computer-aided design. In consultation with his professional school counselor, Mike has therefore chosen courses such as manufacturing technology, drafting, and architectural technology as electives. This can be contrasted with Elyse's choice of child development, child care co-op, marketing and personal finance. Each of these electives is intended to assist Elyse in exploring possible careers in child care and in business.

### Turning Vision Into Reality

Once the initial EDP has been developed, students are equipped with a road map to a set of possible post-secondary destinations. As students begin taking courses in accordance with their EDP, they will have an opportunity to reaffirm or question their initial post-secondary plans. Again, their reaction may be to the level of difficulty associated with the courses or to the topics addressed in their courses. Additionally, because students are developing and maturing, it is also possible that their interests may change.

Because of this, it is essential that the educational planning process continue well beyond the completion of the EDP. Professional school counselors will need to periodically meet with students to check on the goodness of fit between the students' EDPs and their developing self-awareness and post-secondary interests and plans. As goals change, of course, it will be appropriate to update the EDP to reflect new post-secondary goals and to identify courses appropriate to the new plans. As the vision changes, a new route must be charted in order to assist the students in turning their vision into reality.

### Continued Career Development

In addition to responding to changes in student goals that develop as a result of coursework and maturation, professional school counselors also proactively work with students to facilitate continued career development. They may do so in a variety of ways: through curriculum guidance units delivered in classroom settings, through a school-based career development center, through after-school seminars offered to students and their parents, through guest speakers, and through job shadowing programs. With regard to curriculum guidance units, ASCA (Campbell & Dahir, 1997) and the National Career Development Association (National Occupational Information Coordinating Committee, 1989) each offered a set of competencies specific to the needs of K-12 students.

School-based career development centers are also common in high schools. Most often, these centers are staffed by a career development specialist or by a professional school counselor. The centers tend to offer a wide variety of career-related resources, including college applications and catalogs, information on scholarships and financial aid, literature about other post-secondary

**Figure 2. Educational development plan (EDP).**

**EDUCATIONAL DEVELOPMENT PLAN**

Name______________________ Student #__________ Professional School Counselor______________ Grade____
(last name, first name)

**Career / Educational Goals from assessment results.**

1. ______________________________

2. ______________________________

**Possible Occupations/Careers from selected pathway.**

1. ______________________________

2. ______________________________

3. ______________________________

Educational/Training Goals

___High school diploma
___Career/Technical Center certificate
___On-the-job training
___Apprenticeship
___Trade & technical certification
___Two-year associate's degree
___Tech Prep (2+2, 2+4)
___Four-year bachelor's degree
___Master's degree
___Doctoral degree
___Military
___Other

| General High School Credit Requirements | General University Admissions |
|---|---|
| 12 Required Units of Credit<br>11 Elective Units of Credit<br>**23 Units of Credit Total for Graduation** | |
| **3.5 English**<br>1.0 9th Grade English<br>1.0 10th Grade English<br>.5 Literature<br>.5 Composition<br>.5 Oral Communications<br><br>**2.5 Mathematics**<br>**2.5 Science**<br>**2.5 Social Studies**<br>1.0 Geography<br>1.0 U.S. History<br>.5 American Government<br><br>**.5 Health**<br>**.5 Personal Fitness** | **Required:**<br>**4.0 English**<br>**3.0 Mathematics**<br>**3.0 Science**<br>**3.0 History/Social Sciences**<br><br>**Recommended**<br>**2.0 Foreign Language**<br>**2.0 Fine & Performing Arts**<br>**1.0 Computer Literacy**<br><br>*Athletes Check NCAA Requirements |

| GRADE 9 | | GRADE 10 | | GRADE 11 | | GRADE 12 | |
|---|---|---|---|---|---|---|---|
| | | | | | | | |
| | | | | | | | |
| | | | | | | | |
| | | | | | | | |
| | | | | | | | |
| Alternate | | | | | | | |

Student Signature______________ Professional School Counselor Signature______________ Parent Signature______________

White - File Yellow - Return with Parent Signature Pink - Student

**Figure 3. EDP for a Student Pursuing an Advanced Medical Degree**

## EDUCATIONAL DEVELOPMENT PLAN

Name__Hansen, Joanie__ Student #__000832__ Professional School Counselor__Phillips__ Grade__9__
(last name, first name)

**Career / Educational Goals from assessment results.**

1. 4 years of college plus graduate school
2. 4 years of college plus pharmacology school

**Possible Occupations/Careers from selected pathway.**

1. Veterinarian
2. Pharmacist
3. ____

**Educational/Training Goals**

___High school diploma
___Career/Technical Center certificate
___On-the-job training
___Apprenticeship
___Trade & technical certification
___Two-year associate's degree
___Tech Prep (2+2, 2+4)
___Four-year bachelor's degree
___Master's degree
_X_Doctoral degree
___Military
___Other

| **General High School Credit Requirements**<br>12 Required Units of Credit<br>11 Elective Units of Credit<br>**23 Units of Credit Total for Graduation** | **General University Admissions** |
|---|---|
| **3.5 English**<br>1.0 9th Grade English<br>1.0 10th Grade English<br>.5 Literature<br>.5 Composition<br>.5 Oral Communications<br><br>**2.5 Mathematics**<br>**2.5 Science** **2.0 Foreign Language**<br>**2.5 Social Studies**<br>1.0 Geography **1.0 Computer Literacy**<br>1.0 U.S. History<br>.5 American Government<br><br>**.5 Health**<br>**.5 Personal Fitness** | **Required:**<br>**4.0 English**<br>**3.0 Mathematics**<br>**3.0 Science**<br>**3.0 History/Social Sciences**<br><br>**Recommended**<br>**2.0 Fine & Performing Arts**<br><br>*Athletes Check NCAA Requirements |

| **GRADE 9** | | **GRADE 10** | | **GRADE 11** | | **GRADE 12** | |
|---|---|---|---|---|---|---|---|
| Acc. English 9 | Acc. English 9 | Acc. English 10 | Acc. English 10 | Acc. English 11 | Acc. English 11 | A P English | A P English |
| World History | World History | A P U. S. History | A P U. S. History | A P Government | A P Government | Indiv. Life Sports | Community Service |
| Molecular Biology | Molecular Biology | Inorganic Chemistry | Inorganic Chemistry | A P Chemistry | A P Chemistry | A P Biology | A P Biology |
| Acc. Geometry | Acc. Geometry | Acc. Algebra 2 | Acc. Algebra 2 | Acc. Analysis | Acc. Analysis | A P Calculus | A P Calculus |
| Physical Education | Information Tech 1 | Health | Zoology | Physics | Physics | A P Physics | A P Physics |
| Spanish 1 | Spanish 1 | Spanish 2 | Spanish 2 | Yearbook | Yearbook | Yearbook | Yearbook |
| Alternate: Chorus | Chorus | Orchestra | Orchestra | Journalism | Info Tech 2 | Career Internship | Career Internship |

Student Signature____ Professional School Counselor Signature ____ Parent Signature____

White - File     Yellow - Return with Parent Signature

**Figure 4. EDP for a Student Pursuing an Associates Degree**

**EDUCATIONAL DEVELOPMENT PLAN**

Name____Brady, Mike______________Student #___000987___ Professional School Counselor______Phillips______ Grade __9_
(last name, first name)

**Career / Educational Goals from assessment results.**

1. Associates Degree ________________

2. Trade & Technical Certification ________________

Possible Occupations/Careers from selected pathway.

1. Architectural Assistant ________________

2. Computer Aided Designer ________________

3. ________________

Educational/Training Goals
___High school diploma
___Career/Technical Center certificate
___On-the-job training
___Apprenticeship
___Trade & technical certification
_X_Two-year associate's degree
___Tech Prep (2+2, 2+4)
___Four-year bachelor's degree
___Master's degree
___Doctoral degree
___Military
___Other

| General High School Credit Requirements<br>12 Required Units of Credit<br>11 Elective Units of Credit<br>**23 Units of Credit Total for Graduation** | **General University Admissions** |
|---|---|
| **3.5 English**<br>1.0 9th Grade English<br>1.0 10th Grade English<br>.5 Literature<br>.5 Composition<br>.5 Oral Communications<br><br>**2.5 Mathematics**<br>**2.5 Science** **2.0 Foreign Language**<br>**2.5 Social Studies**<br>1.0 Geography **1.0 Computer Literacy**<br>1.0 U.S. History<br>.5 American Government<br><br>**.5 Health**<br>**.5 Personal Fitness** | **Required:**<br>**4.0 English**<br>**3.0 Mathematics**<br>**3.0 Science**<br>**3.0 History/Social Sciences**<br><br>**Recommended**<br>**2.0 Fine & Performing Arts**<br><br>*Athletes Check NCAA Requirements |

| GRADE 9 | | GRADE 10 | | GRADE 11 | | GRADE 12 | |
|---|---|---|---|---|---|---|---|
| English 9 | English 9 | English 10 | English 10 | Composition | Mythology | Speech | Research Techniques |
| Geography | Geography | U. S. History | U. S. History | Government | Physical Education | Psychology | Health |
| Physical Science | Physical Science | Biology | Biology | Inorganic Chemistry | Inorganic Chemistry | Physics | Physics |
| Algebra 1 | Algebra 1 | Geometry | Geometry | Algebra 2 | Algebra 2 | Engineering Tech | Engineering Tech |
| Spanish 1 | Spanish 1 | Spanish 2 | Spanish 2 | Architectural Tech | Architectural Tech | Engineering Tech | Engineering Tech |
| Applied Tech | Manufacturing Tech | Drafting 1 | Drafting 1 | Architectural Tech | Architectural Tech | Co-Operative Training | Co-Operative Training |
| Alternate: Drawing 1 | Drawing 2 | Team Sports | Swimming | Photography 1 | Photography 2 | Information Tech | Dual Enrollment |

Student Signature ________________ Professional School Counselor Signature________________ Parent Signature________________

White - File    Yellow - Return with Parent Signature    Pink - Student

**Figure 5. EDP for a Student Pursuing a Career in Child Care or Business**

**EDUCATIONAL DEVELOPMENT PLAN**

Name__Keaton, Elyse__ (last name, first name) Student #_000452_ Professional School Counselor_Phillips_ Grade_9_

**Career / Educational Goals from assessment results.**

1. Employment after high school
2. Trade & Technical Certification

**Possible Occupations/Careers from selected pathway.**

1. Child Care Worker
2. Work in Family Business
3. ________

Educational/Training Goals

_X_High school diploma
___Career/Technical Center certificate
___On-the-job training
___Apprenticeship
___Trade & technical certification
___Two-year associate's degree
___Tech Prep (2+2, 2+4)
___Four-year bachelor's degree
___Master's degree
___Doctoral degree
___Military
___Other

| **General High School Credit Requirements**<br>12 Required Units of Credit<br>11 Elective Units of Credit<br>**23 Units of Credit Total for Graduation** | **General University Admissions** |
|---|---|
| **3.5 English**<br>1.0 9th Grade English<br>1.0 10th Grade English<br>.5 Literature<br>.5 Composition<br>.5 Oral Communications<br><br>**2.5 Mathematics**<br>**2.5 Science**<br>**2.5 Social Studies**<br>1.0 Geography<br>1.0 U.S. History<br>.5 American Government<br><br>**.5 Health**<br>**.5 Personal Fitness** | **Required:**<br>**4.0 English**<br>**3.0 Mathematics**<br>**3.0 Science**<br>**3.0 History/Social Sciences**<br><br>**Recommended**<br>**2.0 Foreign Language**<br>**2.0 Fine & Performing Arts**<br>**1.0 Computer Literacy**<br><br>*Athletes Check NCAA Requirements |

| GRADE 9 | | GRADE 10 | | GRADE 11 | | GRADE 12 | |
|---|---|---|---|---|---|---|---|
| English 9 | English 9 | English 10 | English 10 | Composition | Short Stories | Speech | Creative Writing |
| Geography | Geography | U.S. History | U.S. History | Government | Physical Education | Psychology | Sociology |
| Physical Science | Physical Science | Biology | Biology | Hydrology | Information Tech 1 | Health | Personal Finance |
| Algebra 1 | Algebra 1 | Geometry | Geometry | Cont. Algebra 2 | Algebra 2 | Marketing | Entrepreneur |
| Spanish 1 | Spanish 1 | Spanish 2 | Spanish 2 | Choir | Choir | Choir | Choir |
| Choir | Choir | Child Development | Child Development | Child Care Professional | Child Care Professional | Child Care Cooperative | Child Care Cooperative |
| Alternate: Info Tech 1 | Info Tech 2 | Photography 1 | Photography 2 | Community Service | Office Assistant | Family Living | Life Management |

Student Signature________Professional School Counselor Signature________Parent Signature________

White - File Yellow - Return with Parent Signature Pink - Student

training options, resources about a wide variety of careers, information related to résumé writing and successful interviewing, and employment information. Technological advances have resulted in significant changes in school-based career centers (Refvem, 2000; Sabella, 1999) as centers now also tend to feature computers equipped with career-related software programs and/or access to Internet sites relevant to career exploration and planning. Examples of widely used programs include *SIGI* (Educational Testing Service, 1996), *DISCOVER* (ACT, 1989b) and *CX Online* (Bridges.com, 2002).

After-school seminars may consist of career nights, college nights, and financial aid nights. For each seminar, professional school counselors may serve either as the facilitator/ coordinator or as the actual presenter. Additional topics frequently addressed in after-school and/or in-school seminars involve military educational and career opportunities, vocational training opportunities, and NCAA requirements for Division I eligibility. Finally, professional school counselors frequently coordinate job shadowing programs to facilitate student exploration of possible career options. Each of these career development opportunities assists students in testing their initial aspirations and interests against reality.

## Additional Tips

This chapter was designed to provide current and future professional school counselors with an overview of the educational planning process. In addition to considering the guidelines provided above, a few additional tips may be helpful in improving a school's educational planning component. First, professional school counselors should seek to overeducate the students, their parents, and the school staff. It is essential that education and career planning information be easily accessible. Many schools therefore include education and career planning information in student planners, on hallway bulletin boards, in school newspapers, and in other school literature. A second tip is to make a concerted effort to involve all parents in the educational planning process. Although this is often easier said than accomplished, parents remain an essential resource for students as they begin planning for their post-secondary education and/or career. Third, professional school counselors will want to explore and utilize several delivery methods. As stated earlier, relying solely on individual meetings with students to engage in educational planning is inefficient. Both efficiency and effectiveness may be improved through the use of guidance curriculum lessons, small group meetings, after-school seminars, and school-wide programs. Finally, professional school counselors will also want to use their role to become advocates for student needs. With respect to educational planning, they will want to maintain an awareness of post-secondary plans for students and to advocate for the school's curricular offerings to be responsive to and appropriate for the wide variety of post-secondary plans.

## Summary/Conclusion

To summarize, this chapter provided an overview of the educational planning process and offered specific ideas about the integration of educational planning services into an already existing school counseling program. In doing so, the authors emphasized the inextricable link between career development and educational planning and encouraged professional school counselors to incorporate educational planning into their career exploration, development and planning activities. Toward this end, the authors recommend helping students explore their interests, skills, values, and personality; facilitating student exploration and selection of career pathways; and assisting students with development of an Educational Development Plan (EDP) that is consistent with their preferred career pathway(s). Finally, this chapter emphasized the importance of involving parents in the overall process of career development and educational planning.

## References


American College Testing Program. (1986). *PLAN*. Iowa City, IA: Author.

American College Testing Program. (1989a). *The enhanced ACT assessment*. Iowa City, IA: Author.

American College Testing Program. (1989b). *DISCOVER for colleges and adults* [Computer program]. Hunt Valley, MD: Author.

Bridges.com (2002). *CX Online* [Computer program]. Kelowna, British Columbia: Author.

Brown, D., & Brooks, L. (1990). *Career choice and development: Applying contemporary theories to practice* (2nd ed.). San Francisco, CA: Jossey–Bass Publishers.

Campbell, C. A., & Dahir, C. A. (1997). *The national standards for school counseling programs*. Alexandria, VA: American School Counselor Association.

College Board. (1991). *SAT*. New York: Author.

College Board. (1992). *The new PSAT/NMSQT*. New York: Author.

Drummond, R. J., & Ryan, C. W. (1995). *Career counseling: A developmental approach*. Englewood Cliffs, NJ: Prentice–Hall.

EdITS. (1995). *COPSystem: A career awareness unit*. San Diego, CA: Author.

Educational Testing Service. (1996). *SIGI PLUS* [Computer program]. Princeton, NJ: Author.

Gysbers, N.C., & Henderson, P. (2000). *Developing and managing your school guidance program* (3rd ed.). Alexandria, VA: American Counseling Association.

Harmon, L. W., Hansen, J–I. C., Borgen, F. H., & Hammer, A. L. (1994). *Strong Interest Inventory: Application and technical guide*. Palo Alto, CA: Consulting Psychologists Press.

Holland, J. L., Powell, A. B., & Fritzche, B. A. (1994). *The Self–Directed Search professional user's guide*. Odessa, FL: Psychological Assessment Resources.

Hoyt, K. B. (2001). Helping high school students broaden their knowledge of postsecondary education options. *Professional School Counseling, 5*, 6–12.

Imai, C., & Berry, M. (2001). *Follow your true colors to the work you love: Instructor's guide*. Riverside, CA: True Colors, Inc.

Kalil, C., & Lowery, D. (1999). *Follow your true colors to the work you love: The workbook: A journey in self–discovery & career decision–making*. Riverside, CA: True Colors, Inc.

Kegan, R. (1992). *The evolving self: Problem and process in human development*. Cambridge, MA: Harvard University Press.

Keirsey, D. (1998). *Please understand me II: Temperament, character, intelligence*. Del Mar, CA: Prometheus Nemesis Book Co.

Libsch, M., & Freedman–Doan, P. (1995). Perceptions of high school counseling activities: Response differences according to college plans. *National Association of Secondary School Principals, 79*, 51–59.

McAuliffe, G. J., & Strand, R. F. (1994). Advising from a constructive development perspective. *NACADA Journal, 14*, 25–31.

Myrick, R. D. (1997). *Developmental guidance and counseling: A practical approach* (3rd ed.). Minneapolis, MN: Educational Media Corporation.

National Occupational Information Coordinating Committee. (1989). *National career development guidelines: Local handbook for high schools*. Washington, DC: Author.

Psychological Corporation. (1992). *Differential Aptitude Tests manual* (5th ed.). San Antonio, TX: Author.

Refvem, J. (2000). *Let's go surfing: Use of the Internet for career counseling in the schools*. Greensboro, NC: ERIC–CASS.

Rounds, J. B., Jr., Henly, G. A., Dawis, R. V., & Lofquist, L. H. (1981). *Manual for the Minnesota Importance Questionnaire: A measure of needs and values*. Minneapolis, MN: Vocational Psychology Research, University of Minnesota.

Ryan, J. M., & Ryan, R. M. (1994). *COIN Educational Inventory: An interest assessment for planning post–secondary education.* Toledo, OH: COIN Educational Products.

Sabella, R. A. (1999). *SchoolCounselor.com: A friendly and practical guide to the World Wide Web*. Minneapolis, MN: Educational Media Corporation.

Schmidt, J. J. (1999). *Counseling in schools: Essential services and comprehensive programs* (3rd ed.). Boston, MA: Allyn & Bacon.

Sears, S. J. (1995). Career and educational planning in the middle level school. *National Association of Secondary School Principals, 79*, 36–42.

Sill, A. C. (1995). Fours years at a glance: A simple course work planning sheet. *The School Counselor, 43*, 8–92.

Stanciak, L. A. (1995). Reforming the high school counselor's role: A look at developmental guidance. *National Association of Secondary School Principals, 79*, 60–63.

U.S. Department of Defense. (2002). *Exploring careers: The ASVAB workbook.* Washington, DC: U.S. Government Printing Office.

# *Chapter 37*

# Direct Behavioral Consultation: An Effective Method for Promoting School Collaboration

*T. Steuart Watson, Tonya S. Butler, Adam D. Weaver, & Nancy Foster*

**Preview**

As specified in the American School Counselor Association (ASCA) guidelines, consultation is one of the major roles of professional school counselors. Direct Behavioral Consultation (DBC) is one of the most effective types of consultation and will assist in more efficiently helping the large number of students with diverse concerns.

According to the guidelines of the American School Counselor Association (ASCA), primary roles of the professional school counselor include counseling/therapy, consulting, and coordinating services to help students achieve maximum academic potential (Lum, 2001). Professional school counselors are also required to make referrals to other professionals, serve on interdisciplinary teams, and help ensure school safety (Casey-Cannon, Hayward, & Gowen, 2001). Although ASCA recommends a counselor-to-student ratio of 1:250 (Lum, 2001), actual ratios are typically much higher (Astramovich & Holden, 2002).

Although there are many avenues by which students come to the professional school counselor for services, office referrals are one of the most common. Sugai, Sprague, and Horner (2000), for example, found that the number of daily office referrals increased with the age of students and that almost half of their middle school sample had been referred to the office at least once during the school year. By the time a student is referred from the office to the counselor, the classroom teacher and principal (or another administrator) have spent considerable time addressing the problem. Providing assistance to teachers before they make numerous office referrals would result in less time that teachers and administrators spend "disciplining" or "fixing" the problem and increase the student's amount of academic-engaged time.

Schools are legally mandated to serve the increasing number of students identified as having handicaps. In the academic year 1998-1999, 13% of the school-aged population qualified as having a disability (Wood & Baker, 2002). Students with disabilities are at greater risk of developing academic or behavior problems that are related and unrelated to their particular disability (Rosenberg, Wilson, Maheady, & Sindelar, 1992). Thus, students with a wide range of disabilities may be referred to the professional school counselor for assistance. In some instances, professional school counselors are in charge of coordinating services for students with disabilities (Wood & Baker, 2002).

In addition to providing the services mentioned above, professional school counselors are often obligated to perform many tasks such as clerical, scheduling, disciplining, or other administrative duties that are not part of their professional association job description (Fitch, Newby, Ballestero, & Marshall, 2001). Studies indicated that typical counselors spend approximately 50% of their time devoted to actual guidance and counseling services (Partin, 1993). However, ASCA explicitly stated that professional school counselors should spend 70% of their time providing direct services to students.

As the school counseling profession calls for counselors to have more skills (Herr, 2002) and to work with an increasing number of students, professional school counselors need an efficient method for interacting with teachers that alleviates a problem before an inordinate amount of teacher and administrator time is spent trying to solve the problem. By consulting (i.e., collaborating) with teachers, professional school counselors can assist teachers in improving their overall behavior management and instructional skills and increase their ability to more effectively deal with classroom problems as they occur.

## Discussion

Teachers are faced with a number of challenges in today's classrooms. In addition to meeting the educational needs of their class as a whole, they are often called upon to meet additional and specific academic, behavioral, and emotional needs of students. Many times, however, teacher training programs, in an effort to provide a breadth of training in general educational practices, fail to adequately prepare teachers to meet these additional needs when they arise (Watson, 1994). As a result, there is an increasing need for teachers to collaborate and consult with other professionals including professional school counselors, school psychologists, and school social workers (Dougherty, 2000). Federal and state legislation mandating the inclusion of students with mental, emotional, and physical disabilities have increased interest in consultation and collaboration services as well (Noell & Witt, 1999).

Professional school counselors have long worked with general education teachers to enhance academic and social skills and to prevent special education placement (Gutkin & Curtis, 1999; Noell & Witt, 1999). Generally, the focus has been on academic and behavior challenges (e.g., reading difficulties, inattention, talking out, noncompliance). However, there are many additional areas in which professional school counselors may be asked to assist. These may include mental health concerns (e.g., depression or anxiety) and students adjusting to physical disabilities. In addition, teachers may turn to professional school counselors for assistance in cases when physical or sexual abuse is suspected or when they suspect a student may be involved in unhealthy activities such as substance abuse or promiscuous sex (Lockhart & Keys, 1998).

Referrals such as those listed above will generally take one of two tracks. In some cases, it will be determined that the student's needs would best be met through counseling. In such cases, the professional school counselor provides direct service to the student, either through individual or group counseling, and the teacher shoulders little or no responsibility for intervention. However, in other cases, the determination is made that the student's needs would best be met through a classroom-based intervention. In these cases, the professional school counselor indirectly provides service to the student through consultation or collaboration with that student's teacher.

The primary goal of consulting with teachers is to clarify and resolve the presenting problem (Gutkin & Curtis, 1999; Zins, 1993). When consulting with teachers, it is assumed that there is shared expertise and responsibility for assessment and treatment of the problem. It is important to remember that consultation is an indirect service delivery model in which the consultee (i.e., teacher) is responsible for carrying out the intervention while the consultant (i.e., professional school counselor) provides the expertise and is responsible for the integrity of the process (Gutkin & Curtis, 1999). A secondary, yet very important, goal of consultation is to improve the functioning of the consultee whereby the skills taught during the consultation process will be available in future situations (Dougherty, 2000; Gutkin & Curtis, 1999).

Generally, the professional school counselor's response to student referrals has been to assess the situation through interviews with teacher and student, and occasionally, to augment this information with direct observation of the student in the classroom setting (Fall, 1995; Myers, Shoffner & Briggs, 2002; Sandoval, 2002). Individual counseling with the student has traditionally been seen as the most prominent and important means of benefiting the student (Jackson, 2000; Morse & Russell, 1988). In many cases, individual or group counseling may be an appropriate intervention. However, there are times when the best intervention may be for the teacher to change his or her behavior in response to the problem behaviors of the student (Alberto, & Troutman, 1995; Fall, 1995; Gutkin & Curtis, 1999; Tingstrom & Edwards, 1989).

There are a number of concerns associated with the process of consulting with teachers. First, although consultation is conceptualized as a voluntary activity (Zins, Kratochwill, & Elliott, 1993), this may not be the case in every instance. There are occasions when a teacher may be required by an administrator to work with a professional school counselor. In such cases, there may be significant resistance - either overt or covert - on the part of the teacher to engage in the consultation process. Thus, it is important to be skilled, not only in problem-solving and consultation, but in overcoming teacher resistance as well (Butler, Weaver, Doggett, & Watson, in press).

Second, when the intervention calls for behavior change on the part of the teacher, there is often the belief on the part of consultants that teachers possess the skills required to effectively implement interventions (Noell & Witt, 1999; Watson & Robinson, 1996). However, even the most willing teacher will demonstrate poor treatment integrity if he or she lacks the ability or skills to carry out the intervention.

Finally, without a clearly defined means and method of data collection, it is extremely difficult to gauge and document progress in treating the problem behavior. Thus, assessment and treatment approaches that rely strictly on verbal interaction between the consultant and the teacher or student often make it difficult to evaluate the success of the intervention. Conversely, the success of the treatment or the need to adjust treatment is more easily evaluated if data have been collected throughout the consultation process (Foster, Watson, Meeks, & Young, in press). The following section will outline an empirically supported consultation model and will detail a means of alleviating many of the concerns described above.

## Recommended Actions and Strategies

*Behavioral Consultation*

Behavioral consultation (BC) is the most popular model of consultation used in the schools (Gutkin & Curtis, 1990). In this consultation model, a professional school counselor assists a teacher in changing a student's behavior. The role of the counselor is to teach skills to the teacher that will aid in the problem solving process (Sterling-Turner, Watson, & Moore, 2002; Sterling-Turner, Watson, Wildmon, Watkins, & Little, 2001; Watson & Robinson, 1996).

The interaction between the counselor and teacher is almost completely verbal as the counselor and the teacher discuss the problem behavior and the counselor verbally describes procedures for an intervention. However, teachers often lack the skills or knowledge to effectively carry out an intervention (Sterling-Turner et al., 2001). Research has shown that when teachers were trained with verbal instructions they were not able to identify and analyze problems as accurately as teachers who were trained with modeling and rehearsal methods (Watson & Kramer, 1995). Also, if the teacher is not observed for treatment accuracy and consistency, then it is impossible to determine if treatment failure was due to the intervention or the failure to carry out the treatment properly (Gresham, 1989). Therefore, the role of the professional school counselor should include a more direct role so that teachers can be appropriately trained to address problem behaviors observed in the classroom (Watson & Robinson, 1996).

*Direct Behavioral Consultation (DBC)*

The goal of traditional and direct behavioral consultation (DBC) both include: (1) identifying the problem behavior; and (2) providing teachers with skills that will help in future cases. The difference in the models is evident in the way that the goals are achieved. In traditional BC, the professional school counselor trains the teacher with verbal instructions. In DBC, the professional school counselor models the procedure for the teacher and allows the teacher to rehearse the procedure while receiving positive and corrective feedback (Watson & Robinson, 1996). Findings have indicated that when teachers are trained with the DBC model they are more likely to implement the intervention consistently and accurately than when they are trained with the traditional BC model (Sterling-Turner, et al., 2001; Sterling-Turner, et al., 2002).

DBC includes describing the procedures to the teacher, modeling the procedure with the teacher, and then allowing the teacher to rehearse with the child while receiving corrective and positive feedback (Watson & Robinson, 1996). The four stages used in the DBC model are identical to the stages used in the Behavioral Consultation model: (1) problem identification, (2) problem analysis, (3) plan implementation, and (4) plan evaluation. The differences in the models occur in the role of the counselor at each stage.

*Problem identification.* The professional school counselor begins by interviewing the teacher about the child's behavior so that the target behavior can be selected and defined. To assess the accuracy in the description of the behavior by the teacher, the counselor observes the child in his/her natural setting. This allows the counselor to compare his/her observation of the child's behavior to that reported by the teacher. The counselor can then confirm or disconfirm the teacher's report of the problem behavior.

Direct observation of the child also allows the professional school counselor to collect reliable baseline data and model for the teacher how to accurately record the child's behavior. The data collected also serves as a means for the counselor to form hypotheses on the function of the behavior and plan a functional assessment for the next stage of the consultation process.

*Problem Analysis.* One of the roles of the counselor is to provide a rationale for conducting a functional assessment. This is done by explaining that this procedure aids in the understanding of why the child is engaging in the behavior and in determining the environmental variables and/or skills that need to be modified to change the child's behavior. The counselor is to then model the functional assessment procedures with the teacher. Finally, the teacher practices the procedure while receiving feedback from the counselor.

*Plan Implementation.* The professional school counselor's role in this stage is to ensure that the treatment is understood and carried out correctly by the teacher. There are two primary reasons for failure by the teacher to implement the intervention in this stage: (a) the teacher lacks the needed skills; or (b) the teacher has the skills needed but fails to implement the intervention. The counselor should make no assumptions about the teacher's ability to implement the intervention. The collaboratively derived treatment should always be modeled for the teacher followed by the opportunity to rehearse while receiving feedback from the counselor. The counselor may then fade his/her role once the teacher has demonstrated competence at carrying out the plan.

*Plan Evaluation.* Because the teacher has been trained in data collection, he/she can now collect data during the treatment process. The role of the professional school counselor is to monitor the teacher's data collection periodically for reliability purposes and to aid in the modification of the intervention as needed.

*Case Description Using the DBC Model*

Susan, a third grade teacher, requested that the professional school counselor assist her with Josh, an 8-year-old in her class. During the interview, Susan defined the problem behavior as "aggressive outbursts." The counselor then observed Josh in the classroom and discovered that the "aggressive outbursts" occurred infrequently when compared to his refusal to complete academic tasks. The counselor explained to the teacher that the problem behavior appeared to be Josh's work refusal, which occurred frequently throughout the day and most always preceded the aggressive outbursts. The teacher agreed that it did create problems for the class when he refused to do his work.

The counselor then designed a recording system to collect baseline data (Foster et al., in press), explained the recording system to the teacher, and modeled how to accurately record Josh's work refusal behavior. Following the modeling, the teacher began recording the behavior while receiving feedback from the counselor. Based on the baseline data, the counselor and teacher established a treatment goal for the target behavior.

The counselor then explained that the next step was to conduct a direct descriptive functional assessment to better understand why Josh engages in work refusal and what environmental variables could be changed in the classroom to modify his behavior (Watson & Steege, 2003). Based on their direct behavioral observations and structured interviews, the teacher and counselor hypothesized that escape from the task was maintaining Josh's work refusal. Examination of work samples indicated that Josh had the skills to do the tasks that were being presented to him. The counselor explained the findings to the teacher and modeled the intervention that involved escape extinction (not allowing Josh to escape his work contingent upon his refusal to do tasks) and differential reinforcement (allowing Josh brief breaks and access to more highly preferred activities for brief periods of time when he completed shortened assignments. As he became more proficient at completing assignments without refusing and aggressive behavior, the length of the tasks was gradually increased). The teacher then practiced the intervention with Josh while being coached by the professional school counselor.

The intervention involving extinction and differential reinforcement was sufficiently effective for reducing the frequency of work refusal such that modification of the treatment was not needed. The teacher was also able to use the skills obtained from the consultation process to implement the intervention with other students displaying problem behaviors.

## Summary/Conclusion

As has been discussed, there is a greater need and demand for school-based collaboration than ever before (Gutkin & Curtis, 1999). Because of the abundance and diversity of needs represented in the educational system, and the increasing role of professional school counselors in meeting those needs, it is critical that professional school counselors have at their disposal not only skills in implementing effective interventions, but also the skills necessary to function effectively as collaborators with other school-based personnel. One of the most efficient and effective means of promoting collaboration is through consultation, more specifically Direct Behavioral Consultation.

As discussed earlier, there are a number of potential pitfalls in the consultation process. Specifically, difficulties may arise in the form of consultee resistance and poor treatment integrity and evaluation resulting from skill deficiencies on the part of the consultee in treatment implementation and data collection. The consultant should remain aware and vigilant of these potential difficulties when entering a consultation relationship. The Direct Behavioral Consultation model provides the additional benefit of countering the difficulties listed above. Although more effort-intensive and time-intensive at the outset, this model offers the greatest probability of both treatment integrity and likelihood that consultee skills will generalize to other situations (Watkins-Emonet, Watson, & Shriver, 2002).

The advantages of DBC greatly outweigh the initial time requirement. DBC is easy for the professional school counselor to learn and to implement. In addition, the skills of DBC are applicable to the majority of problems across all ages of children. Even though professional school counselors may initially spend slightly more time using DBC with a referral, the time is made up because teachers can apply their skills obtained during DBC to other situations. As a result, teachers become more reliant on their own classroom management skills and are less dependent on the professional school counselor for daily assistance.

## Suggested Readings

Erchul, W. P., & Martens, B. K. (1997). *School consultation: Conceptual and empirical bases of practice*. New York: Plenum.

Gutkin, T. B., & Curtis, M. J. (1999). School-based consultation theory and practice: The art and science of indirect service delivery. *The handbook of school psychology* (2nd ed.)(pp. 577-611). New York: John Wiley & Sons.

Watson, T. S., & Robinson, S. L. (1996). Direct behavioral consultation: An alternative to traditional behavioral consultation. *School Psychology Quarterly, 11*, 267-278.

## References

Alberto, P. A., & Troutman, A. C. (1995). *Applied behavior analysis for teachers* (4th ed.). Englewood Cliffs, NJ: Prentice-Hall.

Astramovich, R. L., & Holden, J. M. (2002). Attitudes of American School Counselor Association members toward utilizing paraprofessionals in school counseling. *Professional School Counseling, 5*, 203-210.

Butler, T. S., Weaver, A. D., Doggett, R. A., & Watson, T. S. (in press). Countering teacher resistance in behavioral consultation: Recommendations for the school-based consultant. *Behavior Analyst Today.*

Casey-Cannon, S., Hayward, C., & Gowen, K. (2001). Middle-school girls' reports of peer victimization: Concerns, consequences, and implications. *Professional School Counseling, 5*, 138-148.

Dougherty, A. M. (2000). *Psychological consultation and collaboration in school and community settings* (3rd ed.). Belmont, CA: Wadsworth/Thomson Learning.

Fall, M. (1995). Planning for consultation: An aid for the elementary school counselor. *School Counselor, 43,* 151-157.

Fitch, T., Newby, E., Ballestero, V., & Marshall, J. L. (2001). Future school administrators' perceptions of the school counselor's role. *Counselor Education and Supervision, 41*(2), 89-100.

Foster, L. H., Watson, T. S., Meeks, C., & Young, J. S. (2002). Single-subject research design for school counselors: Becoming an applied researcher. *Professional School Counseling, 6,* 146-155.

Gresham, F. M. (1989). Assessment of treatment integrity in school consultation and prereferral intervention. *School Psychology Review, 22,* 254-272.

Gutkin, T. B., & Curtis, M. J. (1990). School-based consultation theory and practice: The art and science of indirect service delivery. In T. B. Gutkin & M. J. Curtis (Eds.), *The handbook of school psychology* (2nd ed.)(pp. 577-611). New York: John Wiley & Sons.

Herr, E. L. (2002). School reform and perspectives on the roles of school counselors: A century of proposals for change. *Professional School Counseling, 5*, 220-235.

Jackson, S. A. (2000). Referrals to the school counselor: A qualitative study. *Professional School Counseling, 3*, 277-286.

Lockhart, E. J., & Keys, S. G. (1998). The mental health counseling role of school counselors. *Professional School Counseling, 1*, 3-6.

Lum, C. (2001). *A guide to state laws and regulations on professional school counselors.* Alexandria, VA: American Counseling Association. (ERIC Document Reproduction Service No. ED 450316.

Morse, C. L., & Russell, T. (1988). How elementary school counselors see their role: An empirical study. *Elementary School Guidance and Counseling, 23*, 54-62.

Myers, J. E., Shoffner, M. F., & Briggs, M. K. (2002). Developmental counseling and therapy: An effective approach to understanding and counseling children. *Professional School Counseling, 5*, 194-202.

Noell, G. H., & Witt, J. C. (1999). When does consultation lead to intervention implementation? *Journal of Special Education, 33,* 29-36.

Partin, R. L. (1993). School counselors' time: Where does it go? *School Counselor, 40*, 274-281.

Rosenberg, M. S., Wilson, R. J., Maheady, L., & Sindelar, P. (1992). *Educating students with behavior disorders*. Boston: Allyn & Bacon.

Sandoval, J. (2002). *Handbook of crisis counseling, intervention, and prevention in the schools* (2nd ed.). Mahwah, NJ: Lawrence Erlbaum Associates.

Sterling-Turner, H. E., Watson, T. S., & Moore, J. W. (2002). The effects of direct training and treatment integrity on treatment outcomes in school consultation. *School Psychology Quarterly, 17*, 47-77.

Sterling-Turner, H. E., Watson, T. S., Wildmon, M., Watkins, C., & Little, E. (2001). Investigating the relationship between training type and treatment integrity. *School Psychology Quarterly, 16*, 56-67.

Sugai, G., Sprague, J. R., & Horner, R. H. (2000). Preventing school violence: The use of discipline referrals to assess and monitor school-wide discipline interventions. *Journal of Emotional and Behavioral Disorders, 8*(2), 94-112.

Tingstrom, D. H., & Edwards, R. (1989). Eliminating common misconceptions about behavioral psychology: One step toward increased academic productivity. *Psychology in the Schools, 26*, 194-202.

Watkins-Emonet, C., Watson, T. S., & Shriver, M. D. *Acquisition and maintenance of teacher skills following direct behavioral consultation*. Unpublished manuscript.

Watson, T. S. (1994). The role of preservice education in training teachers to serve behaviorally disordered children. *Contemporary Education, 65,* 128-131.

Watson, T. S., & Kramer, J. J. (1995). Teaching problem solving skills to teachers-in-training: An analogue experimental analysis of three methods. *Journal of Behavioral Education, 5*, 281-294.

Watson, T. S., & Robinson, S. L. (1996). Direct behavioral consultation: An alternative to traditional behavioral consultation. *School Psychology Quarterly, 11*, 267-278.

Watson, T. S., & Steege, M. W. (2003). *Conducting school-based functional behavior assessment: A practitioner's guide.* New York: Guilford Press.

Wood, D. N., & Baker, S. B. (2002). Readiness to serve students with disabilities: A survey of elementary school counselors. *Professional School Counseling, 5,* 277-285.

Zins, J. E. (1993). Enhancing consultee problem-solving skills in consultative interactions. *Journal of Counseling and Development, 72*, 185-190.

Zins, J. E., Kratochwill, T. R., & Elliott, S. N. (1993). Current status of the field. In J. E. Zins, T. R. Kratochwill, & S. N. Elliott (Eds.), *Handbook of consultation services for children: Applications in educational and clinical settings* (pp. 1-12). San Francisco: Jossey-Bass.

# Chapter 38

# Consulting with Parents and Teachers: The Role of the Professional School Counselor

*Donna M. Gibson*

## Preview

Consultation with parents and teachers is one of the most important roles of the professional school counselor as it bridges the communication gap among adults that can directly affect the life of a child. This chapter focuses on the consultation process and will offer guidelines to professional school counselors in conducting parent and teacher consultation conferences.

The role of the professional school counselor is defined often by the three Cs of school counseling activities: counseling, consulting, and coordination (ASCA, 1999). However, it is the consulting role that is more observable by administrators, parents, and teachers. Thus, it is imperative for professional school counselors to understand the purpose of consulting and how to make these meaningful experiences, especially for parents and teachers.

## The Purpose of Consulting

There can be several purposes for consulting. In general, most consultations are conducted to solve a problem (Dougherty, 1995). However, it is different from counseling in two ways. First, the counseling process involves two parties, the counselor and client. In contrast, consultation involves more than two people. For example, this can be the professional school counselor (consultant), teacher (consultee), and student (client). Second, counseling involves dealing with personal problems. In consultation, the process involves work-related or caretaking-related concerns. In our prior example, the teacher (consultee) would be consulting with the professional school counselor (consultant) about the student's (client) behavior in class. The teacher would be consulting with the professional school counselor about alternative behavior management strategies for dealing with the student in his or her classroom. Therefore, the focus is not on the personal problems of the child as much as the work-related/caretaking concerns of the teacher. Hence, professional school counselors need to monitor their consultation behaviors in order for consulting not to become counseling.

Although the general purpose of consultation may be to solve a problem, professional school counselors need to look at consultation as a systematic process that can be used in a variety of situations. Professional school counselors usually consult with administrators, parents, and teachers. However, holding conferences with parents and teachers provokes the most anxiety for all parties involved. To reduce or eliminate this anxiety, the professional school counselor needs to establish the goal for the consultation.

To establish a consultation goal, the professional school counselor needs to assess the expectations of the consultation with the individual he is meeting (Hall & Lin, 1994). Goals will vary based on the theoretical orientation of the professional school counselor to the stage of the consultation process. For example, if the problem is not clear to the individuals in the consultation, then the goal may be to identify and clarify the problem. Follow-up meetings may focus on the goal of evaluating the progress that has been made in working or caring for the student by the consultee.

In establishing consultation goals, the parent or teacher (consultee) needs to be aware of his role in this process. In this process, the consultee is a collaborator with the consultant (professional school counselor), working in a partnership (Dougherty, 1995). If the professional school counselor is offering information in advisement to help the consultee, the consultee is not obligated to follow that advice. However, the consultee is ultimately responsible for the client. In this case, the parent or teacher is responsible for the welfare of the student.

As the professional school counselor and consultee are working on goals in consultation, they are working on building a relationship with each other (Hall & Lin, 1994). This relationship evolves as consultant and consultee progress through the stages of consultation. Hall and Lin (1994) outline the four stages of consultation: entry, diagnosis, process, and disengagement.

During the entry stage, the primary task of the professional school counselor is to assess the situation. The advantage of the professional school counselor is that she is physically located at the school and is available to teachers and parents. In this assessment process, the professional school counselor needs to determine if he or she is prepared to handle the situation. If necessary, appropriate referrals can be made at this time.

If the situation is appropriate for the professional school counselor, then she can outline expectations to the teacher or parent. This could include meeting with them to identify their concerns and goals for the client. While many students (clients) are not mature enough to understand and contribute to consultation meetings, it may be appropriate to invite mature students to attend early meetings to provide their perception of the problem. Consultants must utilize listening skills, such as empathy, genuineness, and respect, to enlist the consultee's help, lessen anxiety, and avoid resistance to the process (Hall & Lin, 1994).

In the second stage, diagnosis, the purpose of consultation is to define the problem and any relevant factors related to the situation. First, information needs to be gathered about the situation and could include information about the client's behavior, feelings, aptitude, achievement, or social skills. Second, the consultant and consultee need to mutually agree to a definition of the problem. This definition needs to be created in concrete terms in order to formulate interventions and evaluations to address the problem. Third, goals need to be written in specific terms from the definition. Fourth, interventions need to be designed from the goal statements.

The third stage of the consultation process is implementation of the consultation plan. Dougherty (1995) outlines four questions the consultant must ask the consultee to complete this stage. These are: (a) What are we going to do? (b) How are we going to do it? (c) When and where are we going to do it? and (d) How well did we do it? To address the first question, the consultant and consultee can review the interventions planned during the diagnosis stage. Part of planning interventions is to address who will carry them out, when it will occur, and how it will occur. Since consultees have the major responsibility for students, consultees direct most interventions. When professional school counselors meet with parents about their children, parents are responsible for carrying out interventions at home. If necessary, the professional school counselor and parent may have to consult with the child's teacher in order to carry out interventions at school. Of course these interventions should be evaluated for effectiveness as they are carried out and adjusted to meet the consultation goals.

Lastly, the disengagement stage is the ending stage of the consultation process. This stage includes an overall evaluation of the effectiveness of the consultation. This can be a formal or informal process whereby the professional school counselor interviews the consultee about the process or requests that the consultee complete a questionnaire or rating form. It is also during this stage that the consultant and consultee decrease and/or cease their consulting relationship. In the school, it is not necessary to terminate a relationship, but consultation about a student for a specific problem should decrease.

This systematic consultation process can vary in the amount of time allotted for one problem. However, it is necessary to understand the process and utilize the designed activities in order to help the consultee in an effective manner. In the following sections, the role of the professional school counselor in parent and teacher consultations is explained with specific recommendations made to promote effective conferences.

## Consulting with Parents

Professional school counselors have several opportunities to consult with parents. Within the realm of a comprehensive developmental counseling program, counseling activities and programs often induce some form of parent consultation. It may be introduced by either parent or professional school counselor.

Although the majority of professional school counselors do not conduct family counseling within the schools, it is important to understand the functioning of families and family dynamics. Understanding that affecting one family member's behavior will usually have an affect on other family member's behavior will enable the counselor to convey the importance of intervention and will allow the interventions to have a better chance of being supported by the family (Mullis & Edwards, 2001). Professional school counselors can gain the support of faculty and staff when they offer an explanation of the effects of family dynamics on student behavior.

Professional school counselors can serve as primary resources for parents who are trying to sort through various issues, such as divorce, grief, disability, and illness (Mullis & Otwell, 1998). Parents do look to schools for information about these issues, and professional school counselors can provide researched information and resources. In addition, parents look toward schools for both cognitive and emotional support. Consider the following case example:

> Mr. Hampton, the professional school counselor, had an appointment to meet with Jacob's father. Jacob's grades had dropped significantly over the past nine weeks, and he was reported by his teacher to be withdrawn in class. When Mr. Turner, Jacob's father, arrived he appeared upset about the appointment. After Mr. Hampton reviewed the purpose for the meeting, he asked Mr. Turner how things were at home. With some hesitation, Mr. Turner reported that Jacob's mother had moved out of the house. He reported being so preoccupied with his own thoughts and feelings about this change that he assumed Jacob was doing well. After some discussion, Mr. Hampton and Mr. Turner agreed that Jacob may be exhibiting some of these behaviors because of his parent's separation. Mr. Hampton provided some information about the effects of separation and divorce and agreed to see Jacob in counseling. He encouraged Mr. Turner to consult with his wife and possibly seek family counseling.

In this scenario, it took minimal discussion to discover the family dynamics that may have been affecting Jacob's behavior. For the father, this could have been the first opportunity to discuss his separation with his wife and how it has affected his own life. The professional school counselor provided both cognitive and emotional support in this one brief session. However, follow-up consultation will allow the professional school counselor to determine if the simple interventions discussed in the first session have met the desired goal of improved grades and better class participation for Jacob.

Although professional school counselors can be resources for parents, many parents bring anxiety and anger to consultation. This anxiety and anger needs to be evaluated by the professional school counselor to determine the appropriate response to parents. In many cases, anxiety appears as anger or aggression. The majority of parents are worried about their children, and this worry can prevent them from hearing or understanding the purpose of the consultation. Anger can be a natural response for parents who see their children as an extension of themselves and are asking, "What are they saying is wrong with my child (me)?" The following case example illustrates this point:

> Tamara, a 10-year-old girl, was reported by her teacher for bullying a younger girl in the hall at school. After discussing this with her, the professional school counselor decided to contact her parents as per the school policy on bullying. When Tamara's mother arrived, she immediately voiced her annoyance at the school for calling her in because she believes her child needs to take up for herself. Allowing the mother to vocalize her objections, the professional school counselor was able to assess that the mother may have issues of feeling like she needs to defend herself. Instead of revealing her insight, the school counselor reflected the mother's objections and spent some time in establishing rapport with her. After discussion of the details of the bullying incidences, the mother admitted that she had misinterpreted Tamara's disclosure of these incidences. She reported that she had inadvertently supported Tamara's behavior at home. The professional school counselor and Tamara's mother discussed ways that the mother could discuss bullying behaviors with Tamara at home.

When parents appear to take the student's problem on as their own, they may need to vent their frustration and anger initially in the consultation session. Professional school counselors can help diffuse these feelings by engaging in active listening and not becoming defensive. Often the professional school counselor can spend an initial consultation session normalizing behavior or helping parents perceive their children's behaviors, emotions, and attitudes as normal (Mullis & Edwards, 2001).

Parents may see their children in a negative way, so professional school counselors may have to reframe their statements to put a positive light on the problem or situation. Reframing can act as another resource for parents because they may not have been able to see the positiveness of the situation prior to the consultation. It is the encouragement from these reframes that provide parents with the incentive to carry out interventions that will help their children at home and school.

### Consulting with Teachers

Similar to consulting with parents, the professional school counselor's schedule offers several opportunities for teachers to consult with the counselor and vice versa. In fact, professional school counselors strongly rely on teachers for referrals of students (Davis & Garrett, 1998). Therefore, one of the first steps in consulting with teachers occurs prior to the actual consultation. The most important step is establishing strong rapport and mutual understanding between counselor and teacher.

In attempts to establish this relationship, professional school counselors need to make their services known to the faculty of the school. In a study of future school administrators, 100 participants ranked consulting with teachers as the fifth most important duty of professional school counselors (Fitch, Newby, Ballestero, & Marshall, 2001). Enlisting the support of the school administrator in publicizing the duties of the professional school counselor may help endorse these activities for the teachers. Additionally, the professional school counselor can introduce herself at faculty meetings, create and distribute a brochure about the role of the professional school counselor, and visit each teacher on an individual basis to discuss the professional school counselor's role and any concerns of the teacher (Davis & Garrett, 1998).

Professional school counselors are at an advantage because they are based in schools. The majority of consultations are usually about problem academic or social behaviors of students in the school, and their teachers usually have a wealth of knowledge about the students and these behaviors. Although the professional school counselor may be initiating the consultation process, the teacher actually began it when initiating a referral about the student. It is useful to remember that teachers may feel similar to parents when consulting with the professional school counselor. The following case example illustrates this:

> Ms. Allen, the professional school counselor, stopped by Ms. Henry's class during her planning period at an appointed time to discuss Michael's behavior. As they discussed Ms. Henry's observations, Ms. Henry became upset and started to cry. Ms. Allen attempted to understand Ms. Henry's observations and began to reflect her feelings. She reflected that Ms. Henry seemed to be frustrated with Michael's behavior and was afraid that she could not help him learn anything. After Ms. Henry calmed down, Ms. Allen suggested that she, as the professional school counselor, observe Michael. After this observation, they would meet again to plan some interventions for him in Ms. Henry's classroom.

In this example, it became clear that Ms. Henry was placing a lot of responsibility for Michael's behavior on herself. This is not uncommon for teachers, especially in current educational systems where accountability is stressed. Many teachers feel that their self-worth is based on teaching students to learn. When those students are not learning, it can affect the self-worth of those teachers. Hence, we saw and heard Ms. Henry's self-worth being affected by her frustration with Michael's behavior.

Professional school counselors can offer to provide services to teachers in order to help them gain a different perspective on the situation, such as observation. Classroom observation is a way of gathering data and providing additional information to the parties involved in consultation (Davis & Garrett, 1998). In general, teachers do not take issue with the professional school counselor making observations because it indicates the counselor's level of commitment to helping the child and the teacher.

In consulting with teachers, professional school counselors need to be mindful of the teacher's schedule when planning meetings. Additionally, professional school counselors should remember that consultation is a partnership that is based on trust and respect. Therefore, teachers should be made to feel trusted and respected as they are asked for their own expertise in creating, implementing, and evaluating interventions that will help students.

## The Nuts and Bolts of Parent and Teacher Consultation

In helping students achieve success in and out of school, school counselors have the distinction of bridging the communication gap between family and school. Furthermore, communication is often the tool in bridging this gap. Communication between the professional school counselor and faculty is also effective in planning appropriate services for the needs of students in the school.

Table 1 provides a list of suggestions for professional school counselors to review as they plan consultations with parents and teachers. Since many consultations take place in a conference format, logistical recommendations are listed.

**Table 1. Consultation suggestions.**

1. Determine the purpose of the consultation meeting and what needs to be discussed and done during the consultation.
2. Be mindful of parents' or teachers' schedules when planning the consultation meeting. Be flexible in scheduling conferences before or after school hours to meet these needs.
3. When notifying parents or teachers of a needed meeting, explain the purpose and reason for the meeting. This can decrease the anxiety of all individuals involved in the conference.
4. Hold conferences in a comfortable atmosphere with adult-size chairs and a table if needed. In meeting with teachers, their classroom may be the most convenient and comfortable.
5. Greet parents and teachers in a friendly manner. For parents, professional school counselors should introduce themselves immediately and shake the hands of all the individuals attending the meeting. Thank parents and teachers for making the time to meet.
6. Re-explain the purpose and reason for the meeting. Go straight to the point and do not use technical/educational jargon when explaining information. Be honest about the school's concerns.
7. Encourage parents and teachers to provide their perspective of the student's behavior. Use active listening skills, especially when emotions run high. Make sure to have tissues on hand.
8. Provide positive examples when describing the student's behavior. You want to provide another perspective of the student. However, you are emphasizing the behavior that needs to be addressed, which is often not positive.
9. Establish a supportive relationship with parents or teachers in conferences. Do not become defensive and continue active listening in order to collect more information about the student.
10. Create and maintain equal working relationships by encouraging parents or teachers to co-create intervention ideas that can be used at home and/or school. Set-up the plan for implementing and evaluating the interventions.
11. Provide resources for parents and teachers. These may include handouts and books about the specific behavior being exhibited, including a bibliography of references.
12. Thank parents and teachers again at the end of the meeting for investing time into the student's needs.
13. Follow up with parents and teachers to review the child's progress and make needed adjustments to the interventions being implemented.
14. Document all of your contacts with parents and teachers to review when following up or in future consultations about the student.

## Summary/Conclusion

Consulting with parents and teachers is an important part of the role of the professional school counselor. The pivotal role of professional school counselor as consultant can be the catalyst for change in the lives of the families and faculty of students. The change created through consultation can help students become more academically and interpersonally successful.

## References

American School Counselor Association. (1999, June). *The role of the professional school counselor.* Retrieved June 25, 2002, from http://www.schoolcounselor.org/content.cfm

Davis, K. M., & Garrett, M. T. (1998). Bridging the gap between school counselors and teachers: A proactive approach. *Professional School Counseling, 1* (5), 54-55.

Dougherty, A. M. (1995). *Consultation: Practice and perspectives in school and community settings* (2nd ed.). Pacific Grove, CA: Brooks/Cole Publishing Company.

Fitch, T., Newby, E., Ballestero, V., & Marshall, J. L. (2001). Future school administrators' perceptions of the school counselor's role. *Counselor Education & Supervision, 41*, 89-99.

Hall, A. S., & Lin, M. J. (1994). An integrative consultation framework: A practical tool for elementary school counselors. *Elementary School Guidance & Counseling, 29,* 16-27.

Mullis, F., & Edwards, D. (2001). Consulting with parents: Applying family systems concepts and techniques. *Professional School Counseling, 5,* 116-123.

Mullis, F., & Otwell, P. S. (1998). Who gets the kids? Consulting with parents about child custody decisions. *Professional School Counseling, 2,* 103-109.

# Chapter 39

## The Family Resource Center

*Patricia Barton & Gayle Cicero*

### Preview

The Family Resource Center is one approach professional school counselors employ to increase student achievement. Ideally, counselors work collaboratively with a school counseling leadership team, composed of administrators, teachers, pupil services team members, students, parents and community leaders, to develop a Family Resource Center. The team uses a five-phase process that is systematic and results-based to develop an effective center. The ultimate challenge of bringing parents into the center is addressed through continuous evaluation and strategic marketing. A successful Family Resource Center helps professional counselors to work as change agents to increase opportunities for parents to be involved in their children's education.

A Family Resource Center can be an asset to the overall school program. When planning a center, it is important to consider the following:

- How was the decision reached?
- Where will the center be located?
- How will the center be managed?
- Who will be served by the center?
- How will the center continue to grow and serve the needs of the community?

The emphasis through all phases of developing a Family Resource Center is to build collaborative relationships among parents, educators and community representatives. These relationships will sustain and nurture the physical space that is created (*Family Resource Center*, 1997).

Research confirms that students with involved parents perform better at school. "They earn higher grades and test scores than their peers, attend school and complete homework more regularly, are better behaved, and are more likely to graduate from high school and attend college" (Schaeffer, 2002, p. 1). The American School Counselor Association's (ASCA) *National Standards for School Counseling Programs* (Campbell & Dahir, 1997) clearly focus on increasing student achievement and supporting educational equity for all students. Professional school counselors are frequently called upon to develop strategies and programs that will increase academic success for under-achieving students. Providing opportunities to engage parents in the educational process directly supports the national standards.

The Family Resource Center at Willard Model School at Lakewood in Norfolk, VA, is a working example of effective planning and collaboration. A site-based managed school serving 600 students in grades K-5, the Willard Model School serves as "a location for the development of innovative teaching practices and programs to meet the needs of at-risk students" (Raymond,

1996, p. 42). The Family Resource Center at Willard is managed by a parent technician and is the hub of parent involvement initiatives at the school. Parent-centered workshops include a wide range of topics such as budgeting, cooking, sewing, and parenting issues. This ideal center consists of a large, beautiful, comfortable home-like room with couches, tables, a kitchen area, a sewing area and a place to read. The goal of the center was to attract parents into the school and help them to feel more comfortable. To date, the center has expanded its efforts beyond teaching basic skills to sponsoring Family Learning Nights and Weekly Family Computing Nights. The Family Resource Center at Willard has helped to develop a sense of pride and a feeling of community among its families. This and many other examples of successful Family Resource Centers motivate professional school counselors to replicate similar models within their schools and communities.

Joyce Epstein, Director of the Center on School, Family, and Community Partnerships and the National Network of Partnership-2000 Schools at Johns Hopkins University has developed a framework of six major types of parent involvement to help schools develop comprehensive programs of school and family partnerships (Epstein, Coates, Salinas, Sanders, & Simon, 1997). These six types are parenting, communicating, volunteering, learning at home, decision-making, and collaborating with community.

Epstein's research formed the foundation for the National PTA's Standards for Family Involvement to guide program development and provide a means for evaluating program quality. All six types of parent involvement are readily incorporated into the scope of a family resource center. Table 1 provides a list of potential purposes the family resource centers can support (Reaching All Families, 1998).

**Table 1. Purposes of a family resource center.**

- Meeting space for parent groups and workshops.
- Informal location for individual parent-teacher or parent-principal discussions.
- Site for Special Education Team meetings.
- Lounge or "waiting room" for parents in school on other business.
- Recruiting site for tutors and classroom volunteers.
- Central location for information and guidance about higher education opportunities.
- Information source for cultural and community services and agencies that help families with educational, health and social service needs family resource centers may contain.
- Parenting videos and books on a variety of topics such as discipline, learning disabilities, child development, etc.
- A play area equipped with toys and books.
- Educational books and games for parents to use with their children.
- Information about current school-based programs and events.
- A professional library for school staff.
- Telephone service to answer concerns and provide referrals to community resources.
- Brochures/flyers from local agencies and service providers.
- Meeting space for small groups.

### Five Steps In Developing a Family Resource Center.

The Family Resource Center is a mechanism for bringing together resources within the community and focusing these resources on results for children and families (Doktor & Poertner,

1996). Some considerations regarding the establishment of a family resource center are described by The Family Involvement Center (1997).

*Vision Into Action: Implementing the National Standards for School Counseling Programs* (Dahir, Sheldon, & Valiga, 1998) identified five steps for the conception, implementation and evaluation of school counseling programs: discussion, awareness, design, implementation and evaluation. This five-phase process structures the development of the family resource center. Many of the practical suggestions woven into the five steps that follow are taken from The Family Involvement Center (1997).

To develop and sustain a viable family resource center, it is important that the development of the center be a systematic, results-based process. The process and procedures for developing the center will emanate from a team committed to making the vision for the center a reality. The school counseling leadership team (Dahir et al., 1998) can provide the synergy needed to create the family resource center. Because the team consists of major stakeholders (i.e., administrators, teachers, pupil personnel team members, students, parents, professional school counselors and community leaders), it can provide guidance and direction to sustain meaningful development.

*Discussion*

In the *discussion phase*, the members of the team gain the perspective of each of the stakeholders. By combining all points of view with knowledge of the school/community profile, a vision for the center emerges. The vision outlines the ideal expectations and goals for the center. The team will align the goals for the center with the school's strategic plan.

*Awareness*

During the a*wareness phase*, data is collected, analyzed and prioritized. The school/community profile discussed in the first phase is further developed to include the following: standardized test scores, attendance rate, retention/drop-out rate, free/reduced lunch, racial/ethnic data, students with disabilities (percentage and type), mobility rate, discipline statistics, family structure, crime statistics (drug & alcohol, domestic violence, etc.), employment rate and types of employment, educational levels of parents, access to services, and housing.

Though school data is readily available, community information may be gained through census reports, surveys and interviews. Potential survey/interview questions may include: What specific issues and concerns do you have in raising your children? What kind of learning experiences would be most helpful to you (brochures, books, videos, audiotapes, lectures, informal group discussions with other parents, etc.)? What are good/bad times to hold parent events? How can you help us to have the best center possible: volunteer, speaker, business support, marketing, etc.?

Suggestions for getting the best response to a needs survey include: making the survey easy to complete; considering phone surveys, personal interviews and online access; bringing the survey to local events/meetings, service agencies, businesses, churches, etc.; and including all members of the leadership team in collecting the information. As community members are contacted, develop a file for future involvement and solicit resource support, such as brochures, information packets, facilitators for parent information and support sessions, surplus furnishings, and help with meeting expenses. In turn, the school-based family resource center can be offered as a comfortable, familiar location for community workers to meet with families.

When the data is collected, the team will summarize and analyze results. By disaggregating the data, the team will identify the needs of specific populations within the school and community. This procedure will assist the team in linking the goals of the family resource center to achieving the mission.

Measurable results for the center grow out of an understanding of needs. All services provided by the center will focus on identified, measurable results linked to the vision for the center. In alignment with ASCA's *National Standards*, Doktor & Proertner (1996) promoted a focus on results as opposed to services and needs. Doktor and Proertner contended that as long as needs and services are the focal point of discussion, a results orientation seldom occurs.

*Program Design*

During the *program design phase,* the program components are specified. In addition, the nuts and bolts work of securing the ideal location, furnishings and materials are undertaken. Though a spare classroom is an ideal location for the center, other potential sites include a section of the media center, a conference room, a portable classroom, the school foyer or an alcove. What is most valuable in doing the business of the family resource center is phone service with an answering machine. Keeping a confidential phone log is also a helpful organization and evaluation tool.

The design phase involves the following components:

- Objective Setting: What will be accomplished?
- Programming: How will it be accomplished?
- Scheduling: When will activities/services be offered?
- Budgeting: How will financial and time resources be obtained?
- Fixing Accountability: How and when will the objectives be measured?
- Reviewing and Adjusting: How and when will changes be made?

*Implementation*

The fourth phase, *implementation,* initiates the program plan and is best accomplished with a phase-in approach. During this phase the center is open and offering programs and services. Starting with an open house or resource fair will bring people to the center. During the phase-in, consider a short-term plan with several benchmarks toward the long-term goal. Identifying milestones facilitates reporting on the center's systematic development to constituents (School Improvement Team, Board of Education, community associations, local politicians, possible funders, etc.).

The work of the family resource center is divided into operations and management. Management encompasses planning, organizing, staffing, training, directing, coordinating, reporting, budgeting and evaluating. Operations refer to the services provided through the family resource center.

Implementation phase considerations include:

- What is the scope of assistance the staff can provide, (e.g., regular and special education information, school and community sponsored events, referral to school and community services)?
- What level of involvement should staff provide in assisting parents with their problems?
- How will staff ensure that information parents give is accurate?
- Will a "parent to parent" network be established? If so, how will you obtain permission for the use of parents' names and telephone numbers?
- How and to what degree will telephone conversations and personal meetings be documented?
- How will you ensure confidentiality of parents' disclosures?

Ideally, programs and services will be tailored to specific needs of targeted populations. Possible target groups include: parents (whose children have academic challenges, exhibit behavior/self control difficulties, demonstrate poor interpersonal skills, have a history of excessive absences, receive special education services, etc.), economically disadvantaged families, single parents, transient families, ESOL families, stepparents, fathers only, custodial grandparents/ relatives, and foster/adoptive parents.

Strategically marketing programs and services to target groups is essential. A brochure is a simple, inexpensive way to communicate information to the public. Computer resources are easily accessed to assist in the design of a brochure, which that should include the center's name/logo, location, phone number/website/e-mail address, mission and/or objectives, hours of operation, services, and an invitation to participate or volunteer. To use the brochure as an effective marketing tool, it may be mailed out to the community, disseminated at open houses and conference times, given as a resource at Special Education meetings, and displayed at local agencies and businesses.

Another way to market events at the center is through a monthly calendar. The calendar may be attached to the school newsletter, mailed/e-mailed to agencies that work with targeted populations, and posted in local libraries and on the school or school system website. The calendar should be easy to read and should include a phone number and method of registering for events. Consider having the calendar reflect the logo, color, and design of the brochure.

A resource fair also promotes the center and enables the development of collaborative relationships with community agencies and businesses. Offer services that may attract specific populations. For example, blood pressure screening, flu shots, free consultations with mental health providers, inspirational speakers, entertainment for children and refreshments may draw peoples' attention. Families, school staff and community members, including local politicians and Board of Education members, will find a well-planned resource fair of interest. To advertise the fair, inform local newspapers and television stations.

Finally, designing and maintaining a web page is an effective marketing strategy. By linking with an existing school system page, the site will have more hits than a "stand alone" web page. Also, the center will be viewed as part of the existing whole, as it should be.

*Evaluation*

The fifth phase, *evaluating,* is congruent with a results-based approach and guides the center's continued development. Key questions during the evaluation phase include:

- Have timelines established during the design phase been met?
- To what extent have short-term goals been met?
- What data was used to measure results?
- To what degree did the center support the school's strategic plan?
- Were desired results achieved?
    * Was student achievement improved?
    * Was school attendance increased?
    * Was student behavior improved?
    * Did students and families access needed services?

The process of the center's development is documented in the room use log, phone log, and written evaluations from parents, teachers and agency personnel. The process and product (results) evaluations are combined to give a complete picture of the center's success. In addition, the evaluation drives future programming and funding.

Developing and operating a family resource center holds many challenges. Initially, the collaboration process will involve turf and communication issues. Counselors' extensive training in the cycle of change and group dynamics are essential to the effective functioning of the school counseling leadership team.

Budget requirements for the operation of a family resource center can be burdensome. Both financial and time resources need to be considered. Though the time element is often overlooked, it is the people to people contact that transforms the family resource center from a physical space to a functioning, service-providing organization. Financial support may be acquired through school-based organizations and fundraisers, community agencies and businesses, or grants. Data collected during the needs assessment and evaluation phases are critical to developing effective time and financial budgets.

Getting people into the center to use the resources and services is the ultimate challenge. The emphasis on strategic marketing is necessary to sustain the center.

Professional school counselors must remind themselves that their leadership efforts will improve the academic achievement of students (Barton & Cicero, 2003). In particular, they are in a key position to be change agents in increasing opportunities for parents to be involved and supportive of their child's education.

## Summary/Conclusion

A family resource center is a useful tool in breaking down many barriers between home and schools and can create positive outcomes for students. Professional school counselors are positioned to facilitate the development of family resource centers in schools and encourage parent/family involvement in education. The development of a center requires counselors to use their communication and leadership skills to further student achievement. By utilizing the five-phase model, the approach becomes collaborative and includes important stakeholders. Careful planning and evaluation insure the center's sustained presence within the school.

## References

Barton, P., & Cicero, G. (2003). Parental involvement, outreach, and the emerging role of the professional school counselor. In B. T. Erford (Ed.), *Transforming the school counseling profession* (pp.191-207). Upper Saddle River, NJ: Merrill/Prentice-Hall.

Dahir, C. A., Sheldon, C. B., & Valiga, M. J. (1998). *Vision into action: Implementing the national standards for school counseling programs.* Alexandria, VA: American School Counselor Association.

Doktor, J. E., & Poertner, J. (1996). Kentucky's family resource centers: A community-based, school-linked services model. *Remedial and Special Education, 17*, 293-302.

Epstein, J. L., Coates, L., Salinas, K. C., Sanders, M. G.,& Simon, B. S. (1997). *School, family, and community partnerships: Your handbook for action.* Thousand Oaks, CA: Corwin Press.

Family Involvement Center at Oakwood Elementary School. (1997). *Family resource center: An action team approach to getting started.* Glen Burnie, MD: Author.

Raymond, A. (May, 1996). Norfolk's "model" school. *Teaching Pre-K-8*, 42-47.

U.S. Department of Education. (August, 1996). *Reaching all families: Creating family friendly schools.* Washington, DC: Author.

Shaeffer, M. (2002). National standards for family involvement. *Maryland Classroom*, *7*(3), 1 & 3.

# Chapter 40

## Conflict Resolution

**Nadine E. Garner**

### Preview

An overview of conflict resolution programs in the schools, research on their effectiveness, and both immediate and long-range strategies for designing a conflict resolution program are presented. Using a multiple intelligences approach, techniques that professional school counselors can readily integrate into their work with individuals, groups, and guidance experiences are provided.

There is no doubt of the real need for comprehensive conflict resolution programs in the schools. The Centers for Disease Control and Prevention has stated that violence in the nation has reached epidemic proportions and that all students from preschool through twelfth grade should be involved in a conflict resolution program. The summary of the position statement on conflict resolution by the American School Counselor Association (ASCA, 2002, p. 2) declared, "A comprehensive conflict-resolution program promotes a safe school environment that permits optimal personal growth and learning. Through participation in a comprehensive conflict-resolution program, students learn skills that maximize their potential for reaching personal goals and success in school."

Johnson and Johnson (1991, p. 3), after over thirty years of research, stated that "most students simply do not know how to manage their conflicts constructively." They found that students struggled with issues of verbal harassment, verbal arguments, rumors, gossip, and dating or relationship issues.

*Conflict Resolution Programs*

Conflict resolution programs have various names, including Conflict Resolution Education (CRE), Peace Education, Peacemaking, Violence Prevention, or Violence Reduction. Conflict resolution models have common goals because they seek to create opportunities for students and other members of the school community to: recognize that conflict is a natural part of life and that it can be resolved peacefully; develop awareness of their own unique responses to conflict and to understand the diversity with which others respond; learn and practice the principles of conflict resolution and the skills of peaceful problem-solving processes; empower themselves to be individually and cooperatively responsible for resolving conflicts peacefully and to integrate this responsibility in their daily lives.

An authentic conflict resolution program contains two key elements: the **principles** of conflict resolution (separate the people from the problem; focus on interests, not positions; invent options for mutual gain; and use objective criteria as the basis of decision-making) and a **problem-solving process** (negotiation, mediation, or consensus decision-making) (Crawford & Bodine, 1997). (See Chapter 41 of this book for a discussion of the peer mediation process.)

The two key components (conflict resolution **principles** and one or more of the **problem-**

**solving processes**) are common factors in the following four approaches to conflict resolution currently used in the schools:

**Process Curriculum** - a specific time (separate course, distinct curriculum, daily lesson plan) is dedicated to teaching conflict resolution.

**Mediation Program** - adults and/or students who are trained in conflict resolution principles and the problem-solving process of mediation act as neutral third-party facilitators to help disputants reach a resolution.

**Peaceable Classroom** - an integration of conflict resolution into the core curriculum and classroom management. Peaceable classrooms form the foundation for the peaceable school.

**Peaceable School** - all members of the school community (teachers, staff, students, administrators, and parents) receive training in and use conflict resolution (Crawford & Bowdine, 1997).

*The Professional School Counselor's Role*

Nationwide, the number of school-based conflict resolution programs has skyrocketed from about fifty programs in 1984 to over six thousand programs involving over three hundred thousand students in 1995 (Girard & Koch, 1996). Professional school counselors often take a leading role in the implementation of these programs. The specialized expertise of professional school counselors places them in a distinct position to facilitate change in the school culture (Hovland, Peterson, & Smaby, 1996).

ASCA (2002) recommended the professional school counselor assume the leading role in the following components of school-wide, comprehensive conflict-resolution programs: design, implementation, monitoring, and evaluation. Further, ASCA recommended that professional school counselors include the following elements in such programs: prevention services, training, education in recognition of early warning signs, intervention services, crisis response and follow-up, community involvement, peer mediation programs, and evaluation of program effectiveness.

*Indications From the Research*

Research indicates it may take 1-2 years for teachers to feel comfortable integrating the concepts of conflict resolution into classroom activities (Johnson & Johnson, 1991) and other studies show that it may take 3-5 years for it to take hold in the larger school environment. It is not uncommon for programs to be disbanded or be deemed as failures before they are even given a chance.

Lindsay (1998) suggested that the elements of high-quality conflict resolution programs include recognition that school programs alone are no panacea, given the influence of families and communities on students. Programs in the schools should be part of a larger strategy that includes addressing conflict resolution in families and in the community. Sandy (2001) reported that conflict resolution programs can positively affect the school and classroom climate, most strongly when there is an involvement of the total school community.

*Immediate and Long-Range Strategies*

Due to the multidimensional nature of conflict resolution programs, the prospect of implementing a comprehensive conflict resolution program can appear to be an overwhelming task for professional school counselors. A manageable approach to developing a comprehensive conflict resolution program is to plan for its development by using long-range and immediate strategies.

*Long-Range Strategies*

*"It takes a village."* Research indicates that the most successful conflict resolution

programs are ones in which the whole school community is an active partcipant in the process of training, practice, and evaluation and links with mediation agencies to develop training programs for the school community.

*Conflict resolution committee.* Organize a conflict resolution committee to plan and implement the long-range conflict resolution program goals for the school. Membership on this committee builds a foundation of supporters and should include professional school counselors, teachers, students, administrators, parents, and community members. The conflict resolution program should be seen as a shared opportunity. By involving members from all segments of the school community, the professional school counselor is not viewed as the sole proponent of the conflict resolution program.

*Exploration of available curricula.* There are numerous programs that are available and designed specifically for elementary, middle, or high school levels. Many programs offer comprehensive curricula complete with lesson plans, training materials, reproducible handouts, transparency masters, videos, instructor's guides, and evaluation tools.

*Immediate Strategies*

*Small changes lead to larger changes.* Using Milton Erickson's analogy of a hole in a dam, in which only a small hole may lead to changing the structure of the whole dam (Haley, 1973), look for opportunities to integrate concepts that focus on conflict resolution into your existing work with students (see *Sample Techniqes for Immediate Integration).* When consulting with teachers, ask them what small steps they would be willing to take in the present to infuse conflict resolution concepts into their existing curriculum. In so doing, when it is time to implement a comprehensive curriculum, there will already be a core group of people who are taking proactive steps.

*A multiple intelligences approach to conflict resolution.* When selecting conflict resolution activities, use Gardner's (1999) theory of multiple intelligences to draw out students' differing learning styles. The use of multiple intelligences in education is an effective way to teach the most students through a variety of learning pathways. The *Sample Techniques for Immediate Integration* section below describes the intelligences used in each activity.

*Application to real life.* Students are better able to synthesize and retain concepts when they make a personal or real-life connection to the material.

*Sample Techniques for Immediate Integration*

The following four activities are techniques that professional school counselors can readily integrate into their work with individuals, groups, and guidance experiences and can be adapted to suit elementary, middle, and high school settings.

*Glasser's psychological needs.* (Intelligences addressed: logical/mathematical, verbal/ linguistic, intrapersonal, and interpersonal.) Teach students about Glasser's (1984) explanation of psychological needs and their relationship to conflict. We are driven by the needs for *belonging/ love* (belonging, sharing, and cooperating with others); *power* (achieving, accomplishing, being recognized and respected); *freedom* (making choices in our lives); and *fun* (laughing and playing). Conflicts arise, among other reasons, when one does not fulfill one or more of these needs. Teach students about these needs and create the following scenarios to complete in classroom guidance lessons, based on real-life experiences of students. Students can discuss why they choose the answers that they did and whether they can relate this to their own life.

1. Julio does not feel wanted at home. His parents are divorced and have new families now. He does not feel part of either family. He joins a gang where he feels needed and wanted. What psychological need is he filling?
2. Kim likes to be in charge of things. She likes responsibility and needs to have a say

in what goes on at school. She runs for class president. What psychological need is she filling?

3. Takeda has to baby-sit for her three younger siblings while her mom works. She likes being part of a family and enjoys taking care of the kids, but she gets upset when she can't go to the mall with her friends because of her responsibilities to her family. What psychological need is she ***not*** having fulfilled? What psychological need ***is*** she filling?

*Needs circle.* (Intelligences addressed: visual/spatial, intrapersonal, interpersonal, and verbal/linguistic.) Students draw a large circle on a sheet of paper and divide the circle into four quadrants. Each quadrant is then labeled with one of Glasser's psychological needs. Students write in each quadrant how they get this particular need filled in their life. Students share with a partner or small group the elements of their needs circle. This activity can be used in individual, group, or classroom guidance experiences. This is an especially useful activity for a student who has moved or experienced a recent life change. The student can complete two circles: one before the change and one that represents the present time.

*Draw a picture of conflict.* (Intelligences addressed: visual/spatial, intrapersonal, and interpersonal.) Students draw a picture of what conflict looks like to them. They share the pictures and try to understand others' meaning of conflict. Younger students are often better able to synthesize their understanding of conflict by creating pictures first and then explaining them.

*Folding paper cranes for peace.* (Intelligences addressed: bodily/kinesthetic, verbal/linguistic, logical/mathematical, visual/spatial, interpersonal, and intrapersonal.) For more information on this activity, visit www.sadako.com (Informed Democracy, 2002). This activity borrows from the true story of Sadako Sasaki, a girl who developed leukemia in 1955 from the effects of radiation caused by the bombing of Hiroshima. There is an ancient Japanese legend that says that by folding one thousand paper cranes, your wish will come true. Sadako began folding a thousand cranes while hospitalized, wishing for world peace and personal health, but she died before the project was completed. To this day, people all over the world are still folding cranes and sending them to Hiroshima's Peace Park.

Schools often use this activity to unite the school community with a common theme around peace. One recent example is from Millersville University, in which the Department of Housing and Residential Programs coordinated a project to enlist the campus in making 3,022 cranes, each representing a life lost in the World Trade Center tragedy of September 11, 2001. The cranes were fashioned into large mobiles and displayed in the Multipurpose Room on September 11, 2002 during a "Remembrance Ceremony." This activity is easily integrated into the curriculum, as students learn about history and multicultural issues and need to use math and cooperation skills.

## Summary/Conclusion

Conflict resolution programs encourage the development of useful skills for resolving conflict peacefully that can be applied across the lifespan. When implemented comprehensively, such programs promote a positive school climate. There are a variety of approaches from which to choose. The most effective program is a comprehensive one that strives to train and support all members of the school community. A conflict resolution program is not an instant solution – it is a long-term commitment requiring patience, training, support at all levels of the school community, and ongoing evaluation to tailor the program to the needs of the school. Resources for further consideration include:

- American School Counselor Association: www.schoolcounselor.org
- Baker, S. (Ed.)(1996a). Conflict resolution: Part I [Special issue]. *The School*

*Counselor, 43*(5).
- Baker, S. (Ed.)(1996b). Conflict resolution: Part II [Special issue]. *The School Counselor, 44*(1).
- Teaching Tolerance, www.teachingtolerance.org: a free magazine for educators focusing on reducing conflict and promoting multicultural awareness. Free video and text kits are also available. It is published by the Southern Poverty Law Center, a nonprofit legal and educational foundation.

The author would like to acknowledge Jon Rovers, graduate assistant in the school counseling program at Millersville University, for his research assistance.

**References**

American School Counselor Association. (2002). *Position statement:Conflict resolution.* Retrieved June 28, 2002, from http://www.schoolcounselor.org/content.

Crawford, D., & Bodine, R. (1997). *Conflict resolution education: A guide to implementing programs in schools, youth-serving organizations, and community and juvenile justice settings*. Washington, DC: U.S. Department of Justice.

Gardner, H. (1999). *Intelligence reframed: Multiple intelligences for the 21st century.* New York: Basic Books.

Girard, K., & Koch, S. J. (1996). *Conflict resolution in the schools: A manual for educators.* San Francisco: Jossey-Bass.

Glasser, W. (1984). *Control theory.* New York: Harper & Row.

Haley, J. (1973). *Uncommon therapy: The psychiatric techniques of Milton H. Erickson, M.D.* New York:Norton.

Hovland, J., Peterson, T., & Smaby, M. (1996). School counselors as conflict resolution consultants: Practicing what we teach. *The School Counselor, 44*(1),71-79.

Informed Democracy. (2002). *The Sadako Project.* Retrieved June 28, 2002 from http://www.sadako.com.

Johnson, D. W., & Johnson, R. T. (1991). *Teaching students to be peacemakers.* Edina, MN: Interaction Book Co.

Lindsay, P. (1998). Conflict resolution and peer mediation in public schools: What works? *Mediation Quarterly, 16*(1), 85-99.

Sandy, S. V. (2001). Conflict resolution education in the schools: "Getting there." *Conflict Resolution Quarterly, 19*, 237-250.

# Chapter 41

## The Evolution and Application of Peer Mediation in Schools

*Shelly F. Sheperis, Adam Weaver, & Carl J. Sheperis*

### Preview

Peer mediation is a popular and frequently endorsed form of conflict resolution for today's schools. In fact, over 10,000 peer mediation programs are currently in existence across the United States (Ripley, 2003). Although authors have detailed the fundamental aspects of mediation programs, few have reported the effects those programs have on school climate, discipline referrals or on the mediators themselves. This chapter provides an overview of the structure of peer mediation programs and evidence related to the efficacy of mediation as a tool for conflict resolution.

School violence is a topic of concern for many professional school counselors. School shootings, such as those at Colombine High School in Colorado and Pearl High School in Mississippi, have been heralded in the media, placing a focus on shootings or guns at school. However, school violence also includes behaviors such as teasing, bullying, and fighting or arguing at recess or between classes. Although these interpersonal conflicts receive less attention in the media, they represent the majority of conflicts occurring in school settings on a daily basis.

The traditional method of addressing interpersonal conflicts in schools has been "punishment based" (e.g., parent conferences, detentions, suspension, or expulsion)(Johnson & Johnson, 1995a). However, there is little evidence to support the efficacy of these methods in reducing interpersonal conflict in schools. Further, researchers usually have concluded that punishments do not resolve interpersonal problems among students or produce the desired result of increased positive behavior. Therefore, education professionals still seek new methods to address aggressive behavior and conflict among and by students. One popular and frequently endorsed potential solution for today's schools is peer mediation (D'Andrea & Daniels, 1996).

Peer mediation is a form of conflict resolution often used in school settings that involves use of a third-party, presumably an impartial person, to assist in resolving a dispute between two or more people. This voluntary negotiation helps to define and clarify issues and needs, create solutions, and reach mutually satisfactory agreements (Roush & Hall, 1993). Peer mediation is a form of facilitated interpersonal communication that requires the application of problem-solving methods to achieve agreement between or among disputants (Sweeney & Carruthers, 1996). Peer mediation differs from other peer led programs such as peer counseling or peer helpers, because it involves a well-defined, structured process with distinct roles for each participant (Smith & Daunic, 2002).

School districts within the United States have increasingly adopted peer mediation programs over the last decade with over 10,000 programs in existence today (Ripley, 2003). Many authors have detailed the fundamental aspects of mediation programs (e.g., Ripley, 2003; Schrumpf,

Crawford, & Usadel, 1991; Schrumpf, Crawford, & Bodine, 1997; Smith & Daunic, 2002), but few have reported the effects those programs have on school climate, discipline referrals or on the mediators themselves. This chapter will provide professional school counselors with an overview of the structure of peer mediation programs and report on evidence related to the efficacy of mediation as a tool for conflict resolution. The authors have given specific attention to several areas, including (a) the evolution of conflict resolution, (b) models of peer mediation, and (c) the efficacy of mediation programs. With regard to the efficacy of programs, this chapter explores the impact of these mediation programs on school climate, mediators, and reduction in number of discipline referrals. The material presented will assist professional school counselors in the selection of mediation programs and provide appropriate rationale for school administration.

## Conflict Resolution

Before engaging in a discourse about peer mediation, it is important for professional school counselors to recognize that conflict is a naturally occurring phenomenon. Maurer (1991) defined conflict as "disagreement resulting from incompatible demands between or among two or more parties" (p. 1). Throughout history, conflict has been resolved through a continuum that ranges from the most destructive form, warfare, to instances of cooperative and other constructive resolutions (Sweeney & Carruthers, 1996). In fact, conflict is often associated with negativity when actually it can be positive if it provides insight and personal growth as well as social change (Cowan, Palomares, & Schilling, 1992; Deutsch, 1994; Johnson & Johnson, 1991; Ripley, 2003). Every conflict has a consequence and if seen as a process, it will lead to an eventual conclusion. Since conflict is dynamic, change begins the very moment conflict arises and continues until the conflict is resolved. The quality of change due to conflict is dependent upon the skill in which the conflict is managed and resolved (Cowan et al., 1992; Johnson & Johnson, 1991).

Research conducted by DeCecco & Richards (1974) revealed that 90 percent of conflicts reported by students were either unresolved or resolved in destructive ways. Negotiation of conflicts was almost nonexistent. In order for students to manage their conflicts constructively, there must be a shared understanding of appropriate procedures (Johnson & Johnson, 1991). Constructive conflict management becomes more pressing with the knowledge that conflicts with destructive outcomes among students in the United States are climbing at an alarming rate. Arrest rates for aggravated assault by youth were 70 percent higher in 1999 as compared to 1983 (U.S. Department of Health and Human Services, 2000). It is also estimated that over 25,000 handguns enter schools daily and a quarter of all high school seniors have reported threats of violence (U.S. Department of Health and Human Services, 2000).

### *Peer Involvement*

Myrick and Erney (1985) emphasized that one of the most important conflict-related educational concepts to emerge has been that of students helping students. The modern view on student discipline moves the emphasis away from punitive measures as an outcome of conflict to more self-discipline and student controlled methods of conflict resolution (i.e., negotiation and mediation). Programs that depend solely on adult decision-making fail to teach students appropriate resolution skills to use in the absence of adult supervision (Roush & Hall, 1993). Maxwell (1989) stated that self-regulation can be fostered in students when they are given the opportunity to participate in decisions relating to their own lives.

### *Elements of Conflict Resolution Programs*

The use of conflict resolution techniques in schools has grown rapidly. For example, the

National Association for Mediation in Education (NAME) estimated that the number of school-based conflict resolution programs has grown from 50 in 1984 to well over 8,500 today (Cornell, 1999). The Responding to Conflict Creatively Program (RCCP), one of the earliest CR programs, now operates in approximately 300 schools nationwide. Other programs have increased and expanded similarly. For example, the New Mexico Center for Dispute Resolution has conducted a statewide school mediation program for ten years and its programs currently involve over 30,000 students. Similarly, through the Community Board Program, a majority of San Francisco's schools have peer conflict managers (National Institute for Dispute Resolution, 1993).

Conflict resolution programs typically include a curriculum designed to provide basic knowledge to students about individual differences, changing win-lose situations to win-win solutions and using negotiation to resolve conflicts effectively (Smith & Daunic, 2002). These programs often focus on social skills such as empathy training, effective communication, and stress and anger management; attitudes about conflict; bias awareness; and/or negotiation and large group problems solving (Cowan et al., 1992; Johnson & Johnson, 1991). Teachers or other school professionals help students learn a process for handling interpersonal conflict by focusing on skill development within a general conceptual framework rather than on how to solve an immediate, specific problem (Smith & Daunic, 2002).

Through a variety of learning experiences and focus on student empowerment, conflict resolution curricula can (a) facilitate the understanding of conflict and its determinants, (b) teach students effective communication, problem solving, and negotiation, (c) provide a foundation for education about peace and nonviolence, and (d) transfer students' responsibility for choosing which strategy to use in response to actual conflict situations (Cowan et al., 1992; Johnson & Johnson, 1991; Smith & Daunic, 2002).

## Peer Mediation as Conflict Resolution

Peer mediation is both the most typical and most recommended form of conflict resolution in today's schools (Johnson & Johnson, 1995a; Ripley, 2003). Typically, there are three stages in the implementation of a school-based peer mediation program. The introductory stage involves (a) making operational decisions, (b) introducing the program to the school staff, and (c) gaining support for its implementation from a variety of interested parties. This process is followed by the training stage which involves selecting and training the peer mediators. The final operational stage involves (a) operating the program, (b) evaluating its effectiveness, and (c) planning for its future (Lupton-Smith & Carruthers, 1996).

Johnson and Johnson (1995b) claimed that peer mediation programs can be implemented in either total school or cadre approaches. The cadre approach, which has two models (elective course or student club), involves training a small number of students to serve as peer mediators and is based on the assumption that a few specially trained students can defuse and constructively resolve interpersonal conflicts among students. This type of training usually occurs in an intensive workshop or semester-long course.

Although the approaches and models of peer mediation implementation maintain theoretical distinctions, they can overlap in practice. For example, some schools have established both club and elective course models simultaneously, while other schools have a total school program that has evolved from a cadre approach (Lupton-Smith & Carruthers, 1996; Ripley, 2003).

### *Club Model*

The student club model of peer mediation involves selecting students from the entire student body and bringing them together at a time and place outside of their regular curriculum. Training times may occur while school is in session (e.g., club periods, study halls, specific class period) or outside of school hours (e.g., weekends, before/after school, or summer). An advantage to this model is the ability of the coordinator to select mediators from the school population who will represent the total student body, ensuring diverse perspectives and representation among mediators. Some disadvantages to this model include: (a) less depth in training, (b) decreased access to support systems as compared to the elective course model, and (c) difficulty with supervision for mediations (Lupton-Smith & Carruthers, 1996; Ripley, 2003).

*Elective Course Model*

Graham and Cline (1989) suggested that an elective course model, dedicated to conflict resolution and specifically peer mediation training, can be implemented either as a general elective or as a part of a social studies curriculum. This model provides more consistency with regard to training conditions (e.g., training, supervision, debriefing, and further leadership development) and flexibility for scheduling mediations. However, a considerable weakness in this model is that selection of mediators is limited to only those students enrolled in the course. Thus, diversity within the mediator pool is limited by nature of the model. Within this model, the pool of mediators is further limited by restrictions to class size (Lupton-Smith & Carruthers, 1996; Ripley, 2003).

*Total School Model*

Johnson & Johnson (1994) have advocated for the total school approach in which all students are taught the principles and practices of conflict resolution and peer mediation and are encouraged to serve as mediators. This approach can be easily infused into a language arts or social studies curriculum (Ripley, 2003). The total school approach ensures that the entire student body is exposed to conflict resolution concepts resulting in a developmental learning opportunity within each student's educational experience. However, this approach requires a considerable amount of time and commitment from the school staff and administration. In addition, this approach may be more applicable in an elementary school format where teachers retain the same students for most of the school day (Lupton-Smith & Carruthers, 1996).

Although there are several models of mediation, all tend to follow the same general process where mediators (a) provide a non-threatening environment in which disputants can tell their side of the story, (b) focus disputants on mutually identified problems and identify any common ground, (c) help disputants develop a list of possible solutions and rationale for each solution, (d) assist disputants to take each other's perspective accurately and fully, and (e) guide disputants to mutually agreed upon resolutions and formalize each agreement (Johnson & Johnson, 1991; Smith & Daunic, 2002).

## Efficacy of Peer Mediation Programs

When examining the literature to determine the effectiveness of peer mediation programs, two things become apparent. One is that despite the widespread popularity and use of peer mediation programs, there is as of yet a relatively small amount of literature on the evaluation of such programs (Webster, 1993). What also quickly becomes apparent is the lack of consistency in available research results. This may be due to a number of factors, including (a) methodological shortcomings, (b) the number of different models of peer mediation programs in existence (i.e., total school model versus cadre model), and (c) the fact that many programs are used in conjunction with other types of conflict resolution programs (Carruthers & Sweeney, 1996). It is important to remember that because such programs are in place in schools, they will naturally lack the research safeguards that are in place in the laboratory setting. Thus, it is difficult to control for internal as well as external variables in school-based research.

It is also important to remember that adequate evaluation of mediation programs requires specific parameters and criteria. For instance, a given program may be said to improve the social standing and negotiation abilities of peer mediators and yet have little impact on the number of disputes referred to teachers from the student body. Without standard criteria to gauge the success of such a program, the door is open for disagreement among teachers, parents, and the public at large on whether or not the program has been successful.

One potential causative factor in the lack of available parameters for evaluating mediation programs is the lack of applicability of quantitative evaluation methods. More specifically, the characteristics of mediation programs (e.g., lack of consistency in design and implementation) violate the rules of many statistical analyses. For instance, proponents of mediation may decide that a specific peer mediation program will be considered successful if it improves the school climate in those schools in which it has been implemented. In such a case, evaluation is difficult because school climate is based on perception. The questions then become "Whose perception —students? teachers? administrators? parents?" and "How are these perceptions measured?"

Because of the amount of resources necessary to establish and effectively operate a peer mediation program, it is critical that such expenditures of time and energy be justified on a continual basis. For this reason alone, despite all the difficulties involved in conducting research in school settings, it is crucial that such evaluation does take place. At present, many school officials base their justification on several claims that have been made regarding the efficacy of school peer mediation programs. Proponents of mediation as an effective method of conflict resolution have claimed that such programs may improve school climate, may improve certain skills and functioning of the mediators, and may reduce the number of disputes reported to teachers (Lam, 1989; Tolson, McDonald, & Moriarty, 1992). Following is a review of the literature related to each.

*Impact on School Climate*

A number of studies on the nature and pervasiveness of school conflict have followed the seminal efforts of DeCecco and Richards (1974). Although there are varied reports on the most common types of school conflict (Johnson, Johnson, & Dudley, 1992; Johnson, Johnson, Dudley, Ward, & Magnuson, 1995), researchers have painted a picture of widespread conflict and daily disputes in the lives of most students. Many researchers and practitioners have thus begun to focus on ways to improve students' skills in dealing with conflict (Johnson, Johnson, & Dudley, 1994). It was hoped that by improving these skills in students, a more positive school climate could be achieved.

Claims of improved school climate are typically based on the perception of a group of people familiar with the school both before and after implementation of the program. The vast majority of studies reviewed included some type of assessment of the attitudes of students, teachers, administrators, or parents toward the program and its impact (e.g., Johnson et al., 1994; Lindsay, 1998; Roush & Hall, 1993). Generally, these attitudes have been very positive, and it is common for teachers and parents to report an improvement in school environment, morale and safety. S. M. Thompson (1996) found that 92% of surveyed teachers reported the belief that a peer mediation program at a middle school in Georgia had effectively improved school morale. It is also not uncommon for mediators themselves to report an improved attitude toward school and school activities (Araki, 1990). However, because peer mediation programs reviewed in the literature were often used as a part of larger conflict management programs, it is impossible to state affirmatively that improvements in school climate were due only to the peer mediation portion of conflict resolution programs.

*Impact on Peer Mediators*

A number of studies have looked at changes in the abilities and social status of student mediators following implementation of a peer mediation program. The reported findings have been quite interesting though far from consistent. Generally, there have been positive findings in the areas of mediator skills and abilities. Roush and Hall (1993) found that following implementation of a peer mediation program, teachers reported positive changes in peer mediators in areas of listening and problem-solving skills. Lane-Garon (1998) demonstrated that mediation training may benefit mediators by increasing cognitive and affective perspective taking. Some researchers have also suggested that mediation training may have a positive effect on academic performance (Araki, 1990; Johnson & Johnson, 1994).

There is also evidence that the conflict resolution skills derived from training at school may generalize to other settings (Johnson et al., 1992). Gentry and Benenson (1992) reported that following participation in peer mediation, mediators perceived a decrease in the frequency and intensity of conflicts with their siblings at home. Parents of these mediators also reported a decrease in conflicts between their children. Despite the evidence on generalization, there is less evidence on how well these skills are maintained over time. Studies have shown that mediators retain conflict resolution skills after training (Johnson et al.,1992), but no studies have demonstrated maintenance over a longer period of time.

In the area of mediator social status, there has been far less agreement. One might expect that there would be some positive changes in how peer mediators are perceived by other students. Looking at students' methods of dealing with conflict and social status apart from any type of mediation program, Bryant (1992) found a correlation between the two variables. Students who were generally regarded more favorably by peers were viewed as more likely to use a calm approach to conflict resolution. Thus, it should not be surprising that most mediators report enjoying being mediators (Humphries, 1999; Schrumpf et al., 1991).

However, many mediators also reported some drawbacks to the experience. Humphries (1999) interviewed peer mediators at an elementary school program. Although every mediator stated that they enjoyed being a peer mediator and a large majority viewed the process as favorable overall, many also reported negative aspects. Problems mentioned included being antagonized by non-peer mediators and having a negative popularity status. Though it is impossible to empirically establish a causal relationship between participation as a peer mediator and such negative experiences, these reports rightfully raised concerns among professional school counselors. Self-concept is another area that has yet to be fully understood. Roush and Hall (1993) found a significant increase in the self-concept of junior high students enrolled in a conflict resolution course, but no increase in the self-concept of elementary school peer mediators.

*Impact on Reduction of Discipline Referrals*

One of the most common findings in research literature on peer mediation is the high percentage of disputants who reach agreement after having their conflict mediated by a peer. Most evaluations (Johnson & Johnson, 1994; Johnson et al., 1992, 1994; Schrumpf et al., 1991) have reported agreement rates of over 80%. Using this factor, among others, as criteria for success, Daunic, Smith, Robinson, Landry, and Miller (2000) and Smith and Daunic (2002) reported positive results in three middle schools. Over the course of several years, over 95% of mediated conflicts resulted in a solution acceptable to both parties. However, in each of the three schools, peer mediation was used in conjunction with a school-wide conflict resolution program (Pitts et al., 1996), thus it is impossible to measure the effects of peer mediation alone. Lupton-Smith and Curruthers (1996) discussed three peer mediation programs used in an elementary school, a middle school, and a high school. Although each program was different, the authors reported that each of the three programs resulted in at least 95% of mediated disputes resolved peacefully. However, they cautioned that program evaluation should be based on additional factors beyond the number of disputes peacefully mediated.

In addition, some reports have claimed that peer mediation programs have helped to reduce the number of discipline events or discipline referrals at school. For example, S.M. Thompson (1996), reporting on the effectiveness of one peer mediation program, found that over the course of two years, student suspensions were reduced by 50%. While this claim is one of the most powerful arguments for implementing peer mediation programs, there is a lack of strong empirical evidence for such claims. Carruthers and Sweeney (1996) noted that reductions in discipline referrals may simply be the result of different classifications for incidents that go to mediation as opposed to incidents that are referred to administration. As evidence, Tolson, McDonald, and Moriarty (1992) reported that a peer mediation program in a suburban high school showed a significant reduction in the number of discipline referrals for interpersonal problems; however, there was no change in the total number of discipline referrals.

## Summary/Conclusion

As more research is produced, a clearer picture regarding the impact of peer mediation on schools, mediators, and disputants will emerge. At present, it appears that peer mediation can be a positive and significant resource for professional school counselors. Although a number of authors have questioned the effectiveness and/or the utilization of peer mediation programs for adolescents (Gerber, 1999; Webster, 1993), others have described successful high school programs (e.g., Lupton-Smith & Carruthers, 1996). The claims related to benefits of peer mediation are numerous, including that peer mediation programs foster a cooperative and comfortable atmosphere in which students can learn more efficiently and teachers can spend more time teaching. In addition, there is some evidence that students involved in peer mediation programs develop feelings of empowerment, learn to take responsibility, and develop constructive solutions for interpersonal problems (Maxwell, 1989). Evidence also exists that peer mediation programs offer potential reductions in violence, vandalism, chronic school absence, and student suspensions in schools (Araki, 1990; Koch, 1988; McCormick, 1988). Finally, some authors have asserted that peer mediation reduces the time teachers spend involved in resolving conflicts in their classrooms, thus focusing more time on student learning (Johnson & Johnson, 1994). Although more research needs to be conducted in order to further substantiate these claims, it appears that peer mediation programs have an overall positive impact on school systems, mediators, and disputants.

## References

Araki, C. (1990). Dispute management in the schools. *Mediation Quarterly, 8*(1), 51-62.

Bryant, B. K. (1992). Conflict resolution strategies in relation to children's peer relations. *Journal of Applied Developmental Psychology, 13*, 35–50.

Carruthers, W. L., & Sweeney, B. (1996). Conflict resolution: An examination of the research literature and a model for program evaluation. *School Counselor, 44*(1), 5–19.

Cornell, D. G., Loper, A. B., Atkinson, A. J., & Sheras, P. L. (1999). What works in youth violence prevention. In P. Sheras (Ed.), *Youth violence prevention in Virginia: A needs assessment*. ERIC document # ED440172.

Cowan, D., Palomares, S., & Schilling, D. (1992). *Teaching the skills of conflict resolution: Activities and strategies for counselors and teachers.* Spring Valley, CA: Innerchoice Publishing.

D'Andrea, M., & Daniels, J. (1996). Promoting peace in our schools: Developmental, preventive, and multicultural considerations. *School Counselor, 44*, 55–65.

Daunic, A., Smith, S. W., Rowand, R. T., Landry, K. L., & Miller, M. D. (2000). School–wide conflict resolution and peer mediation programs: Experiences in three middle schools. *Intervention in School & Clinic, 36*(2), 94–101.

DeCecco, J., & Richards, A. (1974). *Growing pains: Uses of school conflict.* New York: Aberdeen Press.

Deutsch, M. (1994). Constructive conflict resolution: Principles, training, and research. *Journal of Social Issues, 50*(1), 13–32.

Gentry, D. B., & Beneson, W. A. (1992). School–age peer mediators in the home setting. *Mediation Quarterly, 10*(1), 101–109.

Gerber, S. (1999). Does peer mediation really work? *Professional School Counseling, 2*, 169–172.

Graham, T., & Cline, P. C. (1989). Mediation: An alternative approach to school discipline. *The High School Journal, 72*(2), 73–76.

Humphries, T. L. (1999). Improving peer mediation programs: Student experiences and suggestions. *Professional School Counseling, 3*, 13–21.

Johnson, D. W., & Johnson, R. T. (1991). *Teaching students to be peacemakers*. Edina, MN: Interaction Book Company.

Johnson, D. W., & Johnson, R. T. (1994). *Teaching students to be peacemakers: Results of five years of research.* Minneapolis: University of Minnesota.

Johnson, D. W., & Johnson, R. T. (1995a). Conflict resolution. In D. W. Johnson, & R. T. Johnson (Eds.), *Reducing school violence through conflict resolution* (pp. 19–23). Alexandria VA: Association for Supervision and Curriculum Development.

Johnson, D. W., & Johnson, R. T. (1995b). Training elementary school students to manage conflict. *Journal of Social Psychology, 135*, 673–687.

Johnson, D. W., Johnson, R. T., & Dudley, B. (1992). Effects of peer mediation training on elementary school students. *Mediation Quarterly, 10*, 89–99.

Johnson, D. W., Johnson, R. T., & Dudley, B. (1994). Effects of conflict resolution training on elementary school students. *Journal of Social Psychology, 134*, 803–818.

Johnson, D. W., Johnson, R. T., Dudley, B., Ward, M., & Magnuson, D. (1995). The impact of peer mediation training on the management of school and home conflicts. *American Educational Research Journal, 32*, 829–844.

Koch, M. S. (1988). Resolving disputes: Students can do it better. *National Association of Secondary School Principals Bulletin, 72*(504), 16–18.

Lam, J. (1989). *The impact of conflict resolution programs on schools: A review and synthesis of the evidence* (2nd ed.). Amherst, MA: National Association for Mediation in Education.

Lane–Garon, P. S. (1998). Developmental considerations: Encouraging perspective taking in student mediators. *Mediation Quarterly, 16*, 201–217.

Lindsay, P. (1998). Conflict resolution and peer mediation in public schools: What works? *Mediation Quarterly, 16*, 85–99.

Lupton–Smith, H. S., & Carruthers, W. L. (1996). Conflict resolution as peer mediation: Programs for elementary, middle, and high school students. *School Counselor, 43*, 374–392.

Maurer, R. E. (1991). *Managing conflict: Tactics for school administrators*. Boston: Allyn & Bacon.

Maxwell, J. P. (1989). Mediation in the schools: Self regulation, self-esteem, and self-discipline. *Mediation Quarterly, 7*(2), 149–155.

McCormick, M. (1988). *Mediation in the schools: An evaluation of the Wakefield Pilot Peer Mediation Program in Tucson, Arizona*. Washington, DC: American Bar Association.

Myrick, R. D., & Erney, T. (1985). *Youth helping youth: A handbook for training peer facilitators.* Minneapolis: Educational Media Corporation.

National Institute for Dispute Resolution. (1993). *Facts and information: 1992-1993.* Washington, DC: Author.

Pitts, J. H., Smith, S., Miller, D., Sheperis, C. J., Austin, G., & Robinson, R. (1996). *The conflict resolution curriculum manual.* Gainesville, FL: The Conflict Resolution/Peer Mediation Project.

Ripley, V. R. (2003). Conflict resolution and peer mediation in schools. In B. T. Erford (Ed.), *Transforming the school counseling profession.* Columbus, OH: Merrill/Prentice Hall.

Roush, G., & Hall, E. (1993). Teaching peaceful conflict resolution. *Mediation Quarterly, 11,* 185–191.

Schrumpf, F., Crawford, D., & Usadel, H. (1991). *Peer mediation: Conflict resolution in the schools program guide.* Champaign, IL: Research Press.

Schrumpf, F., Crawford, D. K., & Bodine, R. J. (1997). *Peer mediation: Conflict resolution in schools.* Champaign, IL: Research Press.

Smith, S. W., & Daunic, A. (2002). Using conflict resolution and peer mediation to support positive behavior. In P. Kay (Ed.), *Preventing problem behaviors: A handbook of successful prevention strategies* (pp. 142–161). Thousand Oaks, CA: Corwin Press.

Sweeney, B., & Carruthers, W. L. (1996). Conflict resolution: History, philosophy, theory, and educational applications. *School Counselor, 43,* 326–345.

Thompson, R. (1996). *Counseling techniques: Improving relationships with others, ourselves, our families and our environment.* Washington, DC: Accelerated Development.

Thompson, S. M. (1996). Peer mediation: A peaceful solution. *School Counselor, 44,* 151–155.

Tolson, E. R., McDonald, S., & Moriarty, A. R. (1992). Peer mediation among high school students: A test of effectiveness. *Social Work in Education, 14*(2), 86–93.

U.S. Department of Health and Human Services. (2000). *Surgeon general's report on youth violence.* Retrieved December 10, 2001, from http://www.surgeongeneral.gov/library/youthviolence/sgsummary/summary.htm

Webster, D. (1993). The unconvincing case for school-based conflict resolution programs for adolescents. *Health Affairs, 12*(1), 126–141.

# Chapter 42

## Organization Development in Schools

*Joyce A. DeVoss*

### Preview

Organization development is an ongoing effort to create and maintain a model, structure, and environment that produce the highest possible effectiveness. This chapter describes organization development in schools, some models for K-12 school reform, potential benefits, and limitations. Recommendations for professional school counselor involvement in the school improvement process are provided.

School districts across the country are trying to improve instruction. The extent to which reform efforts affect individual schools or whole districts varies, as do the methods used including new curricula, extensive professional development programs, and comprehensive school reform.

The federal government created the Comprehensive School Reform Demonstration (CSRD) Act in 1998, earmarking $145 million for incentives to schools utilizing one or more comprehensive improvement plans or developing their own. The interventions used are departures from current practice, requiring all members of school communities to learn new knowledge, skills and practices. Often, these interventions require organizational changes and incorporate collective learning. The more ambitious and unconventional the interventions, the more learning is necessary; and the more comprehensive the approach, the greater the need for organization development.

Comprehensive school reform focuses on reorganizing and revitalizing entire schools, rather than implementing isolated reforms. It is a systemic approach to school reform that uses well-researched models for change supported by expert trainers and facilitators. Most comprehensive school reform models include high academic standards, relevant professional development and community involvement.

Schools undergoing reform typically engage in some degree of organization development, which refers to "an ongoing effort to create and maintain a model, structure, and environment that produce the highest possible effectiveness" (Cull, 1994 p. 47). Successful organization development is ongoing, organization-wide, and supported by school stakeholders, with the overall goal being to improve student academic achievement.

The professional development component of organization development is critical to comprehensive school reform. Hixson and Tinzmann (1990) identified three challenges for professional development in 21st century schools: meeting the needs of diversity in the student population, adopting appropriate goals for schooling, and implementing organizational structures to promote shared responsibility, collaboration and a community of continual learning.

In light of these challenges, Hixson and Tinzmann (1990) identified new priorities for professional development: a focus on systemic change, or change in the "culture" of the school; continuing focus of change at the school level and focus of professional development on developing "learning communities;" learning that is continuous for students, teachers, [counselors] and administrators; and responsibility that falls on all educational staff to continue their professional development.

## Models for K-12 School Improvement

Numerous reform models have been developed and evaluated. This section reviews a few of the many models available to schools and their approaches to organization development.

*North Central Regional Educational Laboratory (NCREL)*

Hassell, Raack, Burkhardt, Chapko and Blaser (2000) developed a guide for NCREL with five components: strategizing through goal and standard setting; building support from stakeholders; facilitating informed choice with each school developing their own strategy to meet their school's needs; forging a new compact with schools whereby they receive greater authority for reform strategies along with accountability for results; and building capacity for strengthening teaching, learning and leadership. Capacity refers to readiness to accept change.

Each component has related action steps. Examples for the first component are: identifying the district's key priorities; determining how comprehensive school reform supports the district's mission, vision and goals; identifying the district's assets; determining method and schedule of implementation; identifying financial resources for comprehensive school reform efforts; and determining evaluation strategies.

This guide was developed to help districts make comprehensive school reform an integral part of strategies for improving student achievement. When identifying the district's assets, the following should be considered: leadership, media relationship, dedication level of personnel, support of constituents, commitment level of teachers and staff, local business support, funding through grants and other sources, partnerships, and collaboration.

*Vision-based Leadership and the Learning School*

Wallace, Engel, and Mooney (1997) stressed leading with vision as critical to school success. They defined vision-based educational leadership and proposed a model of a learning school in which everyone is a learner. Their model demonstrated how theory and research influence educational vision. They incorporated concepts from Senge (1990) in their discussion of the role of leadership in the learning school.

For Senge (1990), dialogue is critical among all levels of the organization. He identifies five disciplinary elements that are key for the learning organization: personal mastery, mental models, shared vision, team learning, and systems thinking.

In his analysis of leadership, Sergiovanni (1992) stated that discussion about attitudes and values inform the role of the leader. His version of moral leadership based on the learning community is related to and compliment Senge's (1990) concept of a learning organization. He contributed the concept of the moral dimension. Sergiovanni spoke of shared leadership with emphasis on the content of education. He provided a moral basis for educational leadership through the leader's perceived obligations and duties from shared values, ideas and ideals. The model for the learning school included four integrated elements: shared vision, authentic teaching and learning, supportive school organization, and assessment.

Wallace at al. (1997) explained how to achieve shared governance and how leaders can engage others to achieve a shared vision. They discussed how to engage the broader community in the learning community model, borrowing their underlying message from the Bible, "Where there is no vision, people perish" (Proverbs 29:18). Wallace et al. believed that the sharing of a mission should be systemic, and that the values, sentiments and beliefs of communities connect people in a common cause. Communities give us norms to structure what we do and give us reason why we do what we do.

*New Designs for Learning*

New Designs for the learning process (Copa, 1999) is one in which staff, students, community and a team of school designers work together to discover new ways to design a school's learning experiences and environment. Goals include:

- representing the leading edge of a new breed of schools,
- promising the idea of a common set of learner outcomes for all,
- relating learner expectations to challenges and opportunities in work, family and community and personal life,
- operating the school as a learning community,
- more closely aligning learner expectations with learning process organization and environment,
- drawing more attention to learning versus teaching,
- providing a positive special school character with more focus, coherence and spirit to learning, and
- wanting schools that do not cost any more to build or operate.

Twelve learning elements are important in this model: context, audience, signature, expectations, process, organization, partnerships, staff and staff development, environment, celebration, finance, and accountability. At the inception of the comprehensive school reform process, school leadership carefully chooses a team devoted to the design of the school's learning process and environment. Design group members come from inside and outside the school. They think comprehensively and long-term. The model seeks to reawaken learners' potential, as well as that of staff and community, and fosters a special spirit giving meaning to all dimensions of learning. This model gives students multiple pathways to learn, thus leveling the playing field for all learners.

The learning community's attention to learning organization concepts influences organization of time, learners, staff, process, decision-making technology and settings. Emphasis is given to the learning staff and staff development focused on current and future needs. Consideration is also given regarding who can best provide staff training. Design group members act as role models for others, relying on more than one way of doing things, bringing the rest of the learning community along with reform efforts, and thinking comprehensively and long-term.

*The Coalition of Essential Schools (CES)*

Theodore R. Sizer founded CES while at Brown University in 1984. The initial focus was on high schools, but was then expanded to lower grades. CES reform came from the grassroots, included the local community, and held the belief that no two good schools are the same.

CES reform used ten principles, highlighting school climate and advocating eight organizational principles to govern behavior and beliefs of member schools and the national organization. The beliefs include the importance of documenting change, valuing local wisdom and responding flexibly to local contexts. CES values collaboration and stresses changes to school structures to accommodate the ten principles. The changes stressed include: student as worker, smaller class sizes, personalization, professional sharing among teachers, and collaborative conceptions of curriculum, instruction and assessment.

*Success for All (SFA) and Roots and Wings*

Success for All (SFA) is a comprehensive school-wide reform model developed by Robert

Slavin and colleagues at Johns Hopkins University (Lockwood, 1998) for elementary schools focused on reading and students at-risk of academic failure. The program stresses that reform efforts must deal with instruction, curriculum and school organization in order to be successful over time and not regress to the old system.

SFA believes that all children must read at grade level by third grade. They use tutors to insure that students do not fall behind. Furthermore, they administer assessments at eight-week intervals to regularly monitor progress. This model has the advantage of also being available in Spanish.

Roots and Wings (Slavin, Madden, & Wasik, 1996; Slavin & Madden, 2000) is a comprehensive school reform model that incorporates all elements of Success for All. It also includes MathWings, based on National Council of Teachers of Mathematics standards, and WorldLab, which utilizes simulations and group learning projects for social studies and science. Schools implementing Roots and Wings generally do so over a 3-year period, starting with the SFA components in the first year, MathWings in the second year, and WorldLab in the third year.

SFA and Roots and Wings are structured models that provide complete sets of student materials, teacher's manuals and other support. Furthermore, Roots and Wings utilize a Family Support Team in each school made up of concerned school personnel focused on attendance, school-based intervention, parent involvement and connections with community service providers.

*The Paideia Program*

The Paideia Program (Lockwood, 1998) was based on the writings and ideas of American educator and philosopher Mortimer Adler and now supported by the National Paideia Center (NPC), founded in 1988 and housed at UNC at Chapel Hill. It provides training and technical assistance in Paideia methods, researches the results of the methods and acts as a clearinghouse for schools establishing the Paideia program.

The basic belief of this model is that a democratic society needs to provide excellent education to all students. The program provides a rigorous liberal arts education in K-12 that fosters critical thinking and skills necessary for full participation in a democratic society.

There are many other promising whole-school reform programs including the Comer Model, Schoolwide Projects and eight designs representing diverse approaches within the New American Schools programs (NAS). Information on these programs can be found in the ERIC Digest entitled *Whole School Reform* (McChesney, 1998).

## Limitations of School Reform Efforts

Cohen and Loewenberg Ball (2001) reported that the history of instructional intervention is one of very limited success. They noted that interventions tend to be surface level, do not last long, are affected by rapid staff turnover and subject to poorly integrated accumulation of past interventions. They offer three plausible explanations for these observations. First, while no intervention can be totally comprehensive, most have been partial. Second, many interventions provide principles and directions but leave a lot of specifics to be filled in by teachers and schools. Finally, those who initiate the interventions rarely provide the training needed for school personnel, parents and students. These observations and explanations offer support for whole-school, systemic approaches to school reform.

Schwartz (2001) reported that school efforts to close the achievement gap between ethnic and racial minorities and white students have generally been unsuccessful to date. However, there is optimism with the knowledge-based strategies recently developed for school improvement.

Rose (2001) also contended that policy makers need to listen to the public and improve the public schools that currently exist, to provide all children with education in safe buildings conducive to quality education. However, it may be difficult for policy makers to remain focused on the public school with the charter school and voucher systems on their agenda.

Goertz (2001) observed that while state and federal policies gave strong signals about goals of standards-based reform, they offered limited direction as to its substance. This has led to teacher and district complaints about standards that are too general, leaving the task of developing appropriate curriculum and instruction up to teachers. Teachers do not have the time to develop new curriculum to fit under the new standards. Simply setting goals for standards-based reform is not enough to guarantee adequate success in America's schools. Policy makers must consider the benefits of providing more specific standards while allowing enough flexibility in local school improvement efforts.

In past school reform movements, schools were often focused on as the primary unit of change, frequently overlooking the role of the school district. Under these circumstances, states intervene directly in low performing school operations, ignoring district responsibilities for school performance. With the focus on school instead of district accountability, the consequences for individual schools can be more serious than in the past, and can include substantial bonuses or school closure and reconstitution. Under the recent *No Child Left Behind* legislation, the emphasis is shifting back to school district accountability.

Hatch (2002) identified a paradox in improvement programs. He emphasized that schools are frequently faced with the task of putting more than one improvement program in place at one time. He observed that this can create too much demand on the school's resources, teachers, and administrators. School personnel in this predicament often experience high levels of frustration and anger. Schools often face competing and even conflicting demands from a variety of sources. Hatch recommended that in order to embrace improvement programs which were likely to be successful, school leaders needed to select appropriate programs based on sufficient knowledge, plan for adequate resources to be devoted to the programs chosen, and figure out how to integrate school improvement interventions into the school.

## The Role of the Professional School Counselor in School Improvement and Organization Development

There are many opportunities for professional school counselors to participate in comprehensive school reform and organization development. First and foremost, they can and should be represented on the school leadership team. In that role, the professional school counselor can assure that comprehensive school guidance programming with the trifold focus on academic, career and personal/social student needs is integrated into the school improvement plan.

Because of their personal connections with and knowledge of the school community, professional school counselors can help foster support for comprehensive school reform from teachers and parents, identify some of the district's key resources and help craft "homegrown comprehensive school reform models" (Hassel et al., 2000). Counselors can help implement the action steps and promote school-wide support for the comprehensive school reform.

ASCA (Hatch & Bowers, 2002) has developed a *National Model for School Counseling Programs.* The model emphasizes a direct connection between the comprehensive school counseling program and the mission of the school. In addition, the model stressed an organizational framework and accountability systems. This national model positions counselors to integrate school counseling programs with comprehensive school reform.

Johnson (1997) noted that with increasing decentralization of power in school districts, educators have begun to use data not only to assess student performance, but also to make changes at a systems level, "to help them make better choices and uncover better ways of serving students and the community" (p. 1). Educators, including professional school counselors, can create databases used to make program changes, to share with other educators and to adjust teaching styles based on what is learned. These databases hold keys to identifying target areas for school change at a systems level. Johnson suggested making better use of existing data on attendance, grades, referrals, retentions and standardized test results to make comparisons with other, similar schools.

Schools can begin to make better use of the existing data by first analyzing what the data can reveal as to patterns not previously seen and opportunities for continuous data-driven improvement. The data can be broken down (i.e., disaggregated) by such categories as gender, race, socioeconomic status, etc. Other data can be collected such as test results and numbers of books read. Counselors and teachers, individually and collaboratively, are in an excellent position to do small-scale relevant research, called action research because the educator typically takes action based on the results of the findings.

By virtue of their unique training and expertise, professional school counselors can be excellent resources for providing staff development and facilitation of teams. Such functions are generally important in comprehensive school reform and organization development activities. Professional school counselors' knowledge of systems theory and group dynamics are necessary qualifications for roles as trainers and facilitators. Professional school counselors have historically been left out of the school reform movement. Recently, the profession has strongly emphasized the importance of aligning the school counseling program with the mission of the school. Furthermore, emphasis has been placed on the role of the professional school counselor as leader, collaborator, change agent and advocate for quality education for all students. The potential contributions of professional school counselors to school leadership teams and comprehensive school reform are numerous. School leaders can reap benefits for their schools by utilizing the previously untapped resource of professional school counselors as they plan for school reform and organization development.

For school districts interested in further development of professional school counselors as resources for leadership teams, the Education Trust offers specific workshops to professional school counselors and administrators focusing on transforming the work of professional school counselors. The goal is to develop professional school counselors who aggressively support quality education for all students, creating a school climate where access and support for rigorous preparation is expected. The trainers are a cadre of Metlife Fellows who were trained in February, 2002, to become workshop presenters and consultants to school systems. The workshops for the school districts address four themes: working as members of the school leadership team, teaming and collaboration to increase access and equity for all students, serving as advocates for success of all students, and designing and delivery of data-driven counseling programs. To set up training for a school district, contact Reese House at the Education Trust, at rhouse@edtrust.org.

## Summary /Conclusions

This chapter defined and described organization development in the context of school reform efforts, provided a brief examination of some models of school improvement, looked at the limitations of reform attempts and explored the potential for professional school counselors' involvement in school improvement efforts and organization development in schools. In addition, the valuable contributions professional school counselors can make to school reform were identified and described.

Successful school improvement takes an investment of limited time, effort and money which need to be allocated where they will make a difference in quality of education and academic results. Professional school counselors are an untapped resource for school leadership teams. Their professional organization (ASCA) and the Education Trust support their roles as leaders, advocates and collaborators in school improvement. They can contribute their valuable knowledge base and skills to a partnership in comprehensive school reform.

## References


Brandt, B. (1992). On rethinking leadership: A conversation with Tom Sergiovanni. *Educational Leadership, 49* (5), 46-49.

Cohen, D. K., & Loewenberg Ball, D. (2001). Making change: Instruction and its improvement. *Phi Delta Kappan, 83,* 73-78.

Coll, J. H. (1994). Organizational models and structures. In J. J. Hampton (Ed.), *AMA management handbook* (p. 47). New York: American Management Association.

Copa, G. H. (1999). *New designs for learning: K-12 schools.* Berkeley, CA: National Center for Research in Vocational Education.

Goertz, M. E. (2001). Redefining government roles in an era of standards-based reform. *Phi Delta Kappan, 83,* 62-66.

Hassell, B., Raack, L., Burkhardt, G., Chapko, M., & Blaser S. (2000). *Making good choices: Districts take the lead.* Oak Brook, IL: North Central Regional Educational Laboratory.

Hatch, T. (2002). When improvement programs collide. *Phi Delta Kappan, 83,* 626-634.

Hatch, T., & Bowers, J. (2002). The block to build on. *ASCA School Counselor, 39*(5), 13-17.

Hixson, J., & Tinzmann, M. B. (1990). *What changes are generating new needs for professional development?* Retrieved April 16, 2002 from the North Central Regional Educational Laboratory Web site: www.ncrel.org/sdrs/areas/rpl-esys/profdev.htm.

Johnson, J. H. (1997). Data-driven school improvement. *ERIC Digest, 109,* 2-3.

Lockwood, A. T. (1998). *Comprehensive reform: A guide for school leaders.* Oak Brook, IL: North Central Regional Educational Lab.

McChesney, J. (1998). *Whole school reform.* (ERIC Document Reproduction Service No. ED427388)

Rose, L. C. (2001). Grades for schools reach all-time high. *Phi Delta Kappan, 83,* 2.

Schwartz, W. (2001). *Closing the achievement gap: Principles for improving the educational success of all students.* (ERIC Document Reproduction Service No. ED460191)

Senge, P. M. (1990). *The fifth discipline: The art and practice of the learning organization.* New York: Doubleday/Currency.

Slavin, R. E., & Madden, N. A. Roots and wings: Effects of whole-school reform on student achievement. *Journal for Students Placed at Risk, 5*(1/2), 109.

Slavin, R. E., Madden, N. A., & Wasik, B. A. (1996). Roots & wings. In S. Stringfield, S. Ross, & L. Smith (Eds.), *Bold Plans for school restructuring: The new American schools design* (pp. 207-232). Hillsdale, NJ: Lawrence Erlbaum & Associates.

Wallace, R. C., Jr., Engel, D. E., & Mooney, J. E. (1997). *The learning school: A guide to vision-based leadership.* Thousand Oaks, CA: Corwin Press, Inc.

# *Chapter 43*

## Assessing and Changing School Culture

*Mei Tang*

### Preview

School culture is important for professional school counselors because the mission and goals of education cannot be fulfilled if the context in the school setting is not supportive. Professional school counselors, with their special training, are capable of taking a leadership role to make the school culture more accommodating for teacher and staff development and students' growth and learning. This chapter will discuss the importance of assessing and changing school culture and strategies professional school counselors can implement to improve the school climate for quality education.

*Definition of School Culture (Structure, Teacher, Student Process and Product)*

The definition of school culture is varied because different people have different understandings of what constitutes culture. In the literature, a similar concept, school climate, is often used as well. The study of school culture was derived from anthropology and organizational cultural studies, with an aim to improve the school environment by understanding various dimensions of school life. In this sense, school culture is a multifaceted concept that makes a difference in the effectiveness of schooling (Maehr & Midgley, 1996). Each school has distinguishable characteristics and a kind of social psychological life of its own. These characteristics might be the shared set of organizing principles (Erickson, 1991); beliefs and values (Cunningham & Cresso, 1993); or accustomed ways of thinking and acting (Sarason, 1995). A school culture is "a system of ordinary, taken-for-granted meanings and symbols with both implicit and explicit content [i.e., norms, values, beliefs, assumptions] that is, deliberately and non-deliberately, learned and shared among members" (Erickson, 1987, p. 1).

From an organizational perspective, school culture includes three levels (Schein, as cited in Shaw & Reyes, 1992): observable behaviors (visible but often not decipherable, such as artifacts), shared values (may or may not be visible, requiring greater awareness, members' sense what ought to be); and organizational assumptions about reality (invisible and preconscious, such as teachers' orientations and outlooks). The specific nature of school personnel's shared norms, values, beliefs and assumptions defines the content of a school's culture (Leithwood, 2002).

Importantly, school culture is shaped by its members, including teachers, staff, students, parents, and the community (Cunningham & Cresso, 1993). Schools are not separable from social context; therefore, the development of school culture is embedded in the school organization, policies, resources, ethos, school district and state policies, local communities, educational professional environment, occupational systems, and societal cultures (Talbert & McLaughlin, 1999).

## Importance of School Culture

The most significant factors in shaping minds are the cultural settings where learning takes place, activities participants engage in, and discussion among participants (Wells & Claxton, 2002). School culture has been found to have impacts on teacher and staff development and empowerment (Hamilton & Richardson, 1995; Short & Rinehart, 1993), teacher collaboration (Andringa & Fustin, 1991), students' academic and social behavior and performance (McEvoy & Welker, 2000), students' aspiration (Plucker, 1991), and professional school counselors' self-efficacy and outcome expectancy (Sutton, Jr. & Fall, 1995). School culture is equally important for reform and improvement in schools because success is not possible if there is no supportive environment or climate to nourish the change.

Maehr and Midgley (1996) argued that the cultures of school directly relate to the purpose of schooling, i.e., motivation and learning. In other words, students' investment in learning - whether they involved themselves in the school activities and how much effort they put forth - is related to what school stresses and rewards. Students might be turned off if schools emphasize ability demonstration and achievement (outcomes) versus task approach and growth (process).

The perceived family and school environment has a significant impact on students' academic achievement. According to Marchant, Paulson & Rothlisberg (2001), school context (teacher responsiveness, school responsiveness and a supportive social environment) and family context (parental values) have been found to be significantly related to students' motivation, school competence and academic achievement. Similarly, a school environment promoting academic achievement promotes higher aspirations of students (Plucker, 1998). The conditions for the positive school environment included positive relationships with adults, valuing a positive outlook in life, and respecting diversity.

After all, how members in the schools perceive and feel about their interaction with the environment matters. It is the culture that makes the difference in teacher, student, and staff lives in schools. "Greatness does not grow out of a focus on structure and process, but is found in the culture of the organization and the spirit and purposefulness of the lives of people who belong to that organization" (Cunningham & Cresso, 1993, p. 25).

### *Characteristics of Effective Schools*

Research indicates that effective schools are characterized by a culture that focuses on collaboration among all shareholders, open communication, and continuous improvement (Cunningham & Cresso, 1993; Johnson, Snyder, Anderson, & Johnson, 1997; Smith & Scott, 1990). Specifically, the characteristics presented in Table 1 are considered to define and sustain educational excellence.

### *Unfavorable Factors for Effective Schools*

DeWit et al. (2000) found that low teacher and classmate support, student conflict, unfair school rules and disciplinary practice, and low student autonomy in decision making were associated with low attachment to learning, behavior problems, attendance and substance abuse. A similar finding by Plucker (1998) also showed that the lack of support for curiosity, respect for independent thinkers, and care from adults tended to lower students' aspirations for learning.

## Assessing School Culture

### *Purpose of Assessing School Culture*

"The secret for successful change in a school is to identify an existing school culture and reshape it" (Bulach, 2001, p. 8). Before implementing any change, it is necessary to understand

**Table 1. Characteristics of effective schools.**

1. Key members work together to develop a collective vision of what school should be like, focusing on a vision, not deficiencies.
2. Foster individual identities of group members and build a collegial relationship among members.
3. Trust, support and mutual understanding of each other within the organization.
4. Access to quality information for all members.
5. Open and fluid communication.
6. Promoting lifelong professional development and personal growth.
7. Empowerment of individuals to take risks and make a difference.
8. Collaboration between administrators, teachers, parents, community partners, and students to make a decision.
9. Face to face involvement of appropriate stakeholders.
10. Shared values, interests and vision of an ideal school.
11. Strategic planning by groups within the organization.
12. Continuous improvement that is incremental and systematic.
13. Valuing students' growth and improvement rather than mere achievement.
14. Every student is important and has equal rights to adequate opportunities.
15. Accountability and constant feedback on results.
16. Sustainable changes

what is going on in the school and to have a complete picture of the practice and perceptions of all shareholders. It is important to know what works and what does not work. Otherwise, the change loses its direction.

The other purposes of assessing school culture include: providing baseline data for future evaluation, a need for accountability (Milstein, 1993), identifying positive features and areas for improvement, and providing necessary information for strategic planning. It is important to note that assessment is an integral part of restructuring the school for better results, and not cause for anxiety.

*Methods of Assessing School Culture*

Since the concept of school culture is complex and multifaceted, no single source or method of assessment can answer all the questions. Variety of information as well as multiple ways of collecting the information should be used to obtain a comprehensive understanding of the numerous aspects of school culture. Culture is a product as well as a process, therefore, the strategies for assessing school culture should incorporate process into the assessment plan.

*Where to look for data.* Records and documents such as handbooks, mission statements, announcements, newsletters, students' newsletters, school calendars, year books, and annual reports can be the source of information for understanding the symbolic aspects of school environment (Wren, 1999). School rules, ceremonies, rituals and routines can also provide valuable information about school culture. So do the school policies regarding behaviors and performance (i.e., how they reward and discipline students' conduct in non-academic and academic domains).

Other sources of data come from the subjective measures of the members in the school setting. These members' perceptions and observations of the school operation are essential because they construct the "culture." The members may include, but are not limited to, teachers, administrators, staff, paraprofessionals, students, parents, community partners, custodians, bus drivers, and volunteers.

Interactive data are comprised of information about interaction among members and practices in various school settings, e.g., interactions among administrators, staff and teachers in meetings, teacher and student interactions in classrooms, how school personnel interact with parents, or how students interact with each other in classrooms, on playgrounds, and on the bus.

*How to gather the data.* The data collection methods vary depending on the data needed and the purpose of assessment. The advantages of formal measurement and use of standardized instruments are the reliability and validity associated with these methods, but the disadvantages are the costs and time consumed. The following suggestions are easy-to-use and low-cost ways of collecting data:

- Design a chart to collect pertinent information from records and documents about the nature, frequency, intensity, and scope of the event.
- Interview the members within the organization regarding their perceptions and insights about the schools or the specific aspects of school life.
- Develop a questionnaire to solicit participants' input about different aspects of school culture. The content and format of the questionnaire need to be consistent with the purpose of the inquiry as well as the target participants. For instance, the questionnaire about resource allocation might mean different things to teachers and students.
- Observation is most useful when interactive data is needed. Professional school counselors can go to classrooms, faculty meetings, student-oriented activities, etc. to make an observation as a participant or as only an observer. The field notes and audio or video equipment could be utilized for documenting the observation.
- Informal, cost-effective index card (Bulach, 2001) methods can be used to understand teachers' and students' expectations about the school environment and leadership styles of administrators. This method can also be used to collect information on how a particular change is perceived by the stakeholders in the school. Writing responses to one question on one index card makes it easier and less labor-intensive to analyze.

Figure 1 provides an informal "School Culture Assessment Grid" helpful in assessing school culture.

*Standardized Instruments*

Among the instruments for measuring school climate and environment, the most popular is the Charles F. Kettering Ltd. (CFK) School Climate Profile (Johnson & Johnson, 1995). The CFK School Climate Profile has four sections—General Climate Factors, Program Determinants, Process Determinants and Material Determinants—for a total of 120 questions. The section of General Climate Factors is most frequently used in research and has 8 subscales: respect, trust, high morale, opportunity for input, continuous academic and social growth, cohesiveness, school renewal and caring. Several studies (Dixon & Johnson, 1991; Johnson & Johnson, 1992a; 1995) found the scale to be valid for the intended purpose, but had different subscales that might not correspond with the original design. "What works" and "what doesn't work" seem to be the two new structures underlying the subscales. Table 2 includes other measures used for assessing school climate and environment.

## Strategies to Change School Culture

"Culture building requires that school leaders give attention to the informal, subtle and symbolic aspects of school life which shape the beliefs and actions of each employee within the system" (Cunningham & Cresso, 1993, p. 25). The discussion about school culture is found more often in the educational administration literature, however, it does not mean the leadership role can only be taken by principals. In fact, professional school counselors should and can take the leadership roles to transform the culture of schools (Littrell & Peterson, 2001). Professional school counselors also possess the skills to bridge the school administration rules and the purposes of schooling for students (Kaplan, 1995).

A shared sense of purpose is essential. Professional school counselors are in the position to help the school community develop a shared mission and goal. Working with principals and other members, professional school counselors could help create a safe, orderly and clean environment, maintain order, regularity, and predictability, specify clear expectations and norms, and sustain the changes (Maehr & Midgley, 1996). Professional school counselors' training addresses the affective dimensions of school culture. They should work with teachers to incorporate the following goals into curriculum: treating each student with dignity and as an individual who can learn and be successful in school; changing the thinking from "own students in an isolated classroom" to "our students in teams and families" (Burrello & Reitzug, 1993, p. 672); making opportunities for students to identify meaning and relevance in their school experiences and future lives (Kaplan & Geoffroy, 1990); promoting teacher and student ownership and investment in their own growth; developing open and effective communication skills; solving the problems with a solution rather than focusing on victims; and presenting meaningful and interesting lessons and units of study (Ediger, 1997).

Professional school counselors, being in a unique position by interacting with every member in the school, have great potential to be change agents for school culture (Kaplan & Geoffroy, 1990). The following activities summarize what professional school counselors can do to promote school culture change:

- Identify the need for change by conducting assessment and evaluation of school culture.
- Advocate for changes to address the unmet needs of teachers and students and other members of the schools. Every player needs to be healthy and happy to make the system work.
- Collaborate with administrators to develop clearly defined and fair school policies and rules for discipline and performance.
- Provide in-service training for teachers and staff to help them interact more effectively with all students regardless of their backgrounds.
- Coordinate with every member in the school system to find meaning in common experiences and a sense of belonging and community.
- Take the initiative in developing strategic plans that are proactive and focused on continuous improvement.
- Facilitate member involvement in school reform and improvement.
- Make changes incremental, systematic, and sustainable.

## Summary/Conclusion

School culture explicitly or implicitly tells the individuals within the school system what is important, expected and valued. School culture defines a school, so it is essential for professional school counselors to be cognizant of the various dimensions of school culture and make the necessary changes to provide a healthy, safe, and supportive environment for learning and growth. Professional school counselors should take the leadership role in constructing a school environment in which every member feels safe, valued, respected, and a sense of belonging; a context where individuals can find personal and professional development and growth; and an experience that every member finds meaningful and purposeful.

**Figure 1. School culture assessment grid.**

| Area | What is now | What should be | Strategies to Change |
|---|---|---|---|
| Vision/ Mission | To what extent has the school attained goals in the "what should be" list? | Every student is important and deserves quality education.The school promotes lifelong professional development and personal growth.All members of the school and community are involved in the educational process. The reward system should be fair and focus on improvement/ growth rather than merely academic achievement. | What can be done to change the school culture in this area? |
| Communication | | There are open channels for everyone to voice his/her opinion. There is a system for all shareholders to exchange information and ideas.All members have equal access to information.The school's mission and policies are clearly communicated to all shareholders via multiple methods. | |
| Relationships | | There is a trust and mutual understanding of each other within the organization.Administrators support teachers' work and vica versa.Teachers and students keep a trusting relationship. | |
| Shared Values | | Members within the organization share the values, interests and vision of an ideal school.Strategic planning should be shared by all members.All members believe in the mission of the school. | |
| Collaboration | | Any decision is made with collaboration between administrators, teachers, parents, community partners, and students.All shareholders do strategic planning collaboratively. | |
| Structure | | The organization should be accountable for its mission.Organizational structures are effectively designed and aimed at achieving excellence. Every member within the organization is accountable for his/her responsibility. | |
| Physical Environment | | The school building should be clean and safe.The school environment should be inviting and friendly for students and parents.The classroom should have basic facilities for learning. | |

**Table 2. Other assessment instruments for assessing school climate and environment.**

| *Assessment* | *Description* |
|---|---|
| 1. The Litwin and Stringer Climate Questionnaire | 50 items assessing 8 dimensions: structure, responsibility, reward, risk, support, standards, conflict and identity. |
| 2. Halpin's and Croft's Organizational Climate Description Questionnaire (Halpin, 1966) | 64 items measuring the degree of satisfaction with teacher-principal interaction. |
| 3. The Likert Profile of a School Questionnaire | 100 items measuring goal commitment, decision-making processes and team cooperation. |
| 4. The High School Characteristics Index (Stern & Richman, 1964) | 300 items assessing teacher perceptions of climate and students' attitudes and feelings about their school's environment, curriculum, staff, student activities and interests. |
| 5. The Brookover Elementary School Social Climate Questionnaire (Brookover, 1978) | 115 items assessing relative contribution of composition and climate variables (pertaining to teacher, students and principal) to differences in school achievement (Johnson & Johnson, 1992a). |
| 6. Quality of School Life Scale (Epstein & McPartland, 1976; Johnson & Johnson, 1992b) | 27 items measuring students' general reaction to school, levels of students' interests in school work, and nature of student-teacher relationships. |
| 7. School Administrator Assessment Survey (Braskamp & Maehr, 1985) | 19 scales assessing school administrators' perception of the culture of the school district, and their perceptions of job opportunities, individual improvement and personal development, and the culture or climate of the work setting. |

## References

Andringa, J. W., & Fustin, M. (1991). Learning to plan for and implement change: School building faculty responds. *Journal of Educational Research, 84*, 233-238.

Braskamp, L. A., & Maehr, M. L. (1985). *School Administrator Assessment Survey.* Retrieved from http://testcollection.ets.org/cgi/swebmnu.exe?act=3&ini=TestColl

Brookover, W. B. (1978). Elementary school social climate and school achievement. *American Educational Research Journal, 15,* 301-318.

Bulach, C. R. (2001). Reshaping school culture to impower its partners. *Education Digest, 67,* 8-11.

Burrello, L. C., & Reitzug, U. C. (1993). Transforming context and developing culture in schools. *Journal of Counseling & Development, 71*, 669-677.

Cunningham, W. G., & Cresso, D. W. (1993). *Cultural leadership: The culture of excellence in education.* Boston, MA: Allyn & Bacon.

DeWit, D. J., Offord, D. R., Sanford, M., Rye, B. J., Shain, M., & Wright, R. (2000). The effect of school culture on adolescent behavioural problems: Self-esteem, attachment to learning, and peer approval of deviance as mediating mechanisms. *Canadian Journal of School Psychology, 16*, 15-38.

Dixon, P. N., & Johnson, W. L. (1991). Revising the Charles F. Kettering, Ltd. School Climate Profile: Further analysis of the subscale structure. *Educational & Psychological Measurement, 51,* 135-141.

Ediger, M. (1997). Improving school culture. *Education, 118,* 36-41.

Epstein, J. L., & McPartland, J. M. (1976). *Quality of School Life Scale.* Chicago, IL: Riverside Publishing Co.

Erickson, L. (1987). Conceptions of school culture. *Educational Administration Quarterly, 23,* 11-24.

Erickson, F. (1991). Conceptions of school culture: An overview. In N. B. Wyner (Ed.), *Current perspectives on the culture of schools* (pp. 1-12). Cambridge, MA: Brookline Books.

Halpin, A. W. (1966). *Organizational Climate Description Questionaire.* Available: Dr. Andrew E. Hayes; Department of Educational Design and Management, UNC-Wilmington, 601 S. College Rd., Wilmington, NC 28403-3297.

Hamilton, M. L., & Richardson, V. (1995). Effects of the culture in two schools on the process and outcomes of staff development. *Elementary School Journal, 95,* 367-385.

Johnson, W. L., & Johnson, A. M. (1992a). A study on the Kettering School Climate Scale. *Education, 112,* 635-642.

Johnson, W. L., & Johnson, A. M. (1992b). Validity of the Quality of School Life Scale: A primary and second order factor analysis. *Educational & Psychological Measurement, 53,* 145-153.

Johnson, W. L., & Johnson, A. M. (1995). A Rasch analysis of factors derived from the Charles F. Kettering Ltd. School Climate Profile. *Educational & Psychological Measurement, 55,* 456-467.

Johnson, W. L., Snyder, K. J., Anderson, R. H., & Johnson, A. M. (1997). Assessing school work culture. *Research in the Schools, 4*, 35-43.

Kaplan, L. S., & Geoffroy, K. E. (1990). Enhancing the school climate: New opportunities for the counselor. *School Counselor, 38*, 7-12.

Kaplan, L. S. (1995). Principals versus counselors: Resolving tensions from different practice models. *School Counselor, 42*, 261-266.

Leithwood, K. (2002). Organizational conditions to support teaching and learning. In W. D. Hawley & D. L. Rollie (Eds.), *The keys to effective schools: Educational reforms as continuous improvement* (pp. 97-110). Thousand Oaks, CA: Corwin Press.

Littrell, J. M., & Peterson, J. S. (2001). Transforming the school culture: A model based on an exemplary counselor. *Professional School Counseling, 4,* 310-319.

Maehr, M. L., & Midgley, G. (1996). *Transforming school cultures.* Boulder, CO: Westview Press.

Marchant, G. J., Paulson, S. E., & Rothlisberg, B. A. (2001). Relations of middle school students' perceptions of family and school contexts with academic achievement. *Psychology in the School, 38,* 505-519.

McEvoy, A., & Welker, R. (2000). Antisocial behavior, academic failure, and school climate: A critical review. *Journal of Emotional and Behavioral Disorders, 8,* 130-140.

Milstein, M. M. (1993). *Restructuring schools: Doing it right.* Newbury Park, CA: Corwin Press.

Plucker, J. A. (1998). The relationship between school climate conditions and student aspirations. *Journal of Educational Research, 91,* 240-246.

Sarason, S. B. (1995). *School change: The personal development of a point of view.* New York: Teachers College Press.

Shaw, J., & Reyes, P. (1992). School cultures: Organizational value orientation and commitment. *Journal of Educational Research, 85,* 295-302.

Short, P. M., & Rinehart, J. S. (1993). Teacher empowerment and school climate. *Education, 113,* 592-595.

Smith, S. C., & Scott, J. J. (1990). *The collaborative school: A work environment for effective instruction.* Eugene, OR: ERIC Clearinghouse on Educational Management.

Stern, G. G. (1975). *Organizational Climate Index, Short Form.* Skaneateles, NY: Instructional Resources Corporation

Stern, G. G., & Richman, J. (1964). *High School Characteristics Index.* Available: Dr. Joel L. Richman, 770 James Street Suite 215, Syracuse, NY 13203.

Sutton, J. M., Jr., & Fall, M. (1995). The relationship of school climate factors to counselor self-efficacy. *Journal of Counseling & Development, 73,* 331-336.

Talbert, J. E., & McLaughlin, M. W. (1999). Assessing the school environment: Embedded context and bottom-up research strategies. In S. L. Friedman & T. D. Wachs (Eds.), *Measuring environment across lifespan: Emerging methods and concepts* (pp. 197-227). Washington, DC: American Psychological Association.

Wells, G., & Claxton, G. (2002). *Learning for life in the 21st century: Sociocultural perspectives on the future of education.* Malden, MA: Blackwell Publishers.

Wren, D. J. (1999). School culture: Exploring the hidden curriculum. *Adolescence, 34,* 593-596.

# *Section 4*

# Assessment in School Counseling

# Chapter 44

## What Assessment Competencies Are Needed by Professional School Counselors?

*Patricia B. Elmore & Ruth B. Ekstrom*

### Preview

The assessment competencies used and needed by today's professional school counselors have been identified through research conducted by a joint committee of the American School Counselor Association (ASCA) and the Association for Assessment in Counseling (AAC).

Assessment is an important part of counseling. The professional school counselor's historic role in assessment and appraisal has been described by Baker, "Without basic knowledge of measurement principles, test users are navigating without compasses" (2000, p. 278). Work behaviors related to assessment are fundamental to the general practice of counseling (Sampson, Vacc, & Loesch, 1998).

The American School Counselor Association (ASCA) Role Statement (1990) includes assessment as part of the coordination role of the professional school counselor, citing activities such as collecting data from a student needs assessment or disseminating information to help students interpret standardized tests. Although assessment is not specifically mentioned in the school counseling models of Myrick (1993) or Gysbers and Henderson (2000), a survey showed that assessment was one of five major activities of professional school counselors (Burnham & Jackson, 2000). These authors found that 90% of the professional school counselors in their sample interpreted tests individually for students, parents and teachers and that 81% conducted in-service training with school faculty about assessment instruments and procedures. Professional school counselors are often asked to serve in these roles because they have a better understanding of assessment information than do teachers or secondary school principals, especially as assessment involves test selection, validity, communication of test results, and ethical practices (Impara & Plake, 1995). Elmore, Ekstrom, Diamond, and Whittaker (1993) found that 67% of a group of 423 ASCA members considered assessment and testing to be an important or very important part of their work.

What are the assessment competencies needed by today's professional school counselors? This was the question put to a joint committee of the American School Counselor Association (ASCA) and the Association for Assessment in Counseling (AAC). These two professional organizations appointed a joint committee to develop a statement, in collaboration with practicing school counselors, about the assessment competencies needed to work as a professional school counselor.

The committee began by finding out what others have said about the role of the professional school counselor and the assessment competencies needed in this role. Organizations and groups concerned with the preparation and certification of professional school counselors have given considerable attention to the assessment competencies needed by counselors. In the 2001

Standards, the Council for Accreditation of Counseling and Related Educational Programs (CACREP) listed assessment as one of the eight common core areas in which all counseling students are expected to have curricular experiences and demonstrated knowledge. According to the standards, counseling students should have an understanding of individual and group approaches to assessment and evaluation including: (1) historical perspectives about assessment; (2) basic concepts of standardized and nonstandardized testing and other assessment techniques; (3) statistical concepts; (4) reliability; (5) validity; (6) how age, gender, sexual orientation, ethnicity, language, disability, culture, spirituality, and other factors are related to the assessment and evaluation; (7) strategies for selecting, administering and interpreting assessment and evaluation instruments; and, (8) ethical and legal considerations in assessment.

In addition, it is also expected that all professional school counselors will know about research and program evaluation, two areas that are closely related to assessment. The CACREP Standards include a section about what professional school counselors are expected to know regarding the development, implementation, and evaluation of school counseling programs; counseling and guidance; and consultation. The development and evaluation of counseling programs requires that professional school counselors use data from standardized testing and needs assessments to improve student outcomes.

The complete CACREP statement about the skills expected of all counselors, and specifically professional school counselors, can be found at http://www.counseling.org/cacrep/2001/standards. The joint ASCA/AAC committee also reviewed the National Association of State Directors of Teacher Education and Certification standards for the approval of school counseling programs (NASDTEC, 1991) and each state's requirements for the certification of professional school counselors. The state requirements can be viewed at http://schoolcounselor.org in the section on careers and roles. As you read the CACREP Standards and the certification requirements for your state, think about your own counseling skills. Are there areas in which you might benefit from additional training?

A list of 39 assessment-related activities that professional school counselors are often expected to do was developed. This list was based on the CACREP Standards and state certification requirements. All of the 39 activities appear in one or more state descriptions of professional school counselor work, although they may not always be *typical* of the work of professional school counselors. These assessment-related activities became the basis of a questionnaire that was administered to a random sample of counselor educators and professional school counselors selected from the ASCA membership list. Both the counselor educators and the professional school counselors were asked to indicate how important it is for professional school counselors to be able to carry out each activity (using the scale 3 = essential, 2 = desirable, and 1 = not necessary). Responses were received from 179 school counselors and from 63 counselor educators.

Ten skills and abilities to carry out certain activities were rated as essential by 65% or more of both the counselor educators and professional school counselors. These essential skills and abilities are:

- Referring students to other professionals, when appropriate, for additional assessment/appraisal.
- Communicating and interpreting test/assessment information to students and helping them use it for educational and career planning.
- Making decisions about the type(s) of assessments to use in counseling groups or individual students.
- Interpreting scores from tests/assessments and using the information in counseling.
- Reading about and being aware of ethical issues in assessment.
- Communicating and interpreting test/assessment information to parents.

- Communicating and interpreting test/assessment information to teachers, school administrators, and other professionals.
- Making decisions about the type(s) of assessments to use in planning and evaluating counseling programs.
- Reading about and being aware of current issues involving multicultural assessment, the assessment of students with disabilities and other special needs, and the assessment of language minorities.
- Synthesizing and integrating testing and nontesting data to make decisions about individuals.

In addition, the counselor educators rated eight other skills and abilities as essential, including several related to counseling program planning and evaluation.

- Selecting, administering, and interpreting instruments for use in career counseling.
- Reading or referring to test use standards such as "Responsibilities of Users of Standardized Tests" or the "Code of Fair Testing Practices in Education."
- Selecting assessment instruments to use with counseling groups and individual students.
- Interpreting data from needs assessments and other counseling program planning assessments.
- Selecting assessment instruments to use in planning and evaluating counseling programs.
- Adapting or designing surveys or other instruments to use in needs assessment for counseling program planning and/or in counseling program evaluation.
- Designing and implementing plans to collect data for use in counseling program planning and evaluation.

Many of the skills rated as essential by both professional school counselors and counselor educators are similar in content to parts of the ASCA Role Statement (1990) and the ASCA Ethical Standards (1998). One can read the Role Statement and Ethical Standards at the ASCA web site (http://www.schoolcounselor.org) in the careers and roles section and in the ethics section, respectively.

Survey results show that the counselor educators felt it was essential for professional school counselors to have the skills needed to develop and evaluate school counseling programs. They also felt it was essential for professional school counselors to be familiar with test standards such as the Code of Fair Testing Practices in Education (Joint Committee on Testing Practices, 1988), Responsibilities of Users of Standardized Tests (AACD/AMECD, 1989), and other key testing documents. You can find these documents at http://aac.ncat.edu/resources.html.

The results of this survey were used by the ASCA/AAC Joint Committee to develop a statement of Competencies in Assessment and Evaluation for School Counselors published in *Assessment Issues and Challenges for the Millennium* (Joint Committee of ASCA and AAC, 2001). This statement of competencies was approved by both ASCA and AAC in 1998 and can be found in Figure 1 below, and at http://aac.ncat.edu/documents/atsc_cmptny.htm.

This statement is intended to help professional school counselors review and evaluate their own skills in the areas of assessment and evaluation. By reviewing these competencies, professional school counselors will be able to determine their own professional development and continuing education needs in the area of assessment and evaluation. After you have read the competencies ask yourself how your assessment skills measure up to these standards and take steps to improve your own assessment skills.

## COMPETENCIES IN ASSESSMENT AND EVALUATION FOR SCHOOL COUNSELORS

Approved by the American School Counselor Association on September 21, 1998, and by the Association for Assessment in Counseling on September 10, 1998[1]

The purpose of these competencies is to provide a description of the knowledge and skills that school counselors need in the areas of assessment and evaluation. Because effectiveness in assessment and evaluation is critical to effective counseling, these competencies are important for school counselor education and practice. Although consistent with existing Council for Accreditation of Counseling and Related Educational Programs (CACREP) and National Association of State Directors of Teacher Education and Certification (NASDTEC) standards for preparing counselors, they focus on competencies of individual counselors rather than content of counselor education programs.

The competencies can be used by counselor and assessment educators as a guide in the development and evaluation of school counselor preparation programs, workshops, inservice, and other continuing education opportunities. They may also be used by school counselors to evaluate their own professional development and continuing education needs.

---

School counselors should meet each of the nine numbered competencies and have the specific skills listed under each competency.

**Competency 1. School counselors are skilled in choosing assessment strategies.**

a. They can describe the nature and use of different types of formal and informal assessments, including questionnaires, checklists, interviews, inventories, tests, observations, surveys, and performance assessments, and work with individuals skilled in clinical assessment.

b. They can specify the types of information most readily obtained from different assessment approaches.

c. They are familiar with resources for critically evaluating each type of assessment and can use them in choosing appropriate assessment strategies.

d. They are able to advise and assist others (e.g., a school district) in choosing appropriate assessment strategies.

**Competency 2. School counselors can identify, access, and evaluate the most commonly used assessment instruments.**

a. They know which assessment instruments are most commonly used in school settings to assess intelligence, aptitude, achievement, personality, work values, and interests, including computer-assisted versions and other alternate formats.

b. They know the dimensions along which assessment instruments should be evaluated, including purpose, validity, utility, norms, reliability and measurement error, score reporting method, and consequences of use.

c. They can obtain and evaluate information about the quality of those assessment instruments.

**Competency 3. School counselors are skilled in the techniques of administration and methods of scoring assessment instruments.**

a. They can implement appropriate administration procedures, including administration using computers.
b. They can standardize administration of assessments when interpretation is in relation to external norms.
c. They can modify administration of assessments to accommodate individual differences consistent with publisher recommendations and current statements of professional practice.
d. They can provide consultation, information, and training to others who assist with administration and scoring.
e. They know when it is necessary to obtain informed consent from parents or guardians before administering an assessment.

**Competency 4. School counselors are skilled in interpreting and reporting assessment results.**

a. They can explain scores that are commonly reported, such as percentile ranks, standard scores, and grade equivalents. They can interpret a confidence interval for an individual score based on a standard error of measurement.
b. They can evaluate the appropriateness of a norm group when interpreting the scores of an individual or a group.
c. They are skilled in communicating assessment information to others, including teachers, administrators, students, parents, and the community. They are aware of the rights students and parents have to know assessment results and decisions made as a consequence of any assessment.
d. They can evaluate their own strengths and limitations in the use of assessment instruments and in assessing students with disabilities or linguistic or cultural differences. They know how to identify professionals with appropriate training and experience for consultation.
e. They know the legal and ethical principles about confidentiality and disclosure of assessment information and recognize the need to abide by district policy on retention and use of assessment information.

**Competency 5. School counselors are skilled in using assessment results in decision-making.**

a. They recognize the limitations of using a single score in making an educational decision and know how to obtain multiple sources of information to improve such decisions.
b. They can evaluate their own expertise for making decisions based on assessment results. They also can evaluate the limitations of conclusions provided by others, including the reliability and validity of computer-assisted assessment interpretations.
c. They can evaluate whether the available evidence is adequate to support the intended use of an assessment result for decision-making, particularly when that use has not been recommended by the developer of the assessment instrument.

d. They can evaluate the rationale underlying the use of qualifying scores for placement in educational programs or courses of study.
e. They can evaluate the consequences of assessment-related decisions and avoid actions that would have unintended negative consequences.

**Competency 6. School counselors are skilled in producing, interpreting, and presenting statistical information about assessment results.**

a. They can describe data (e.g., test scores, grades, demographic information) by forming frequency distributions, preparing tables, drawing graphs, and calculating descriptive indices of central tendency, variability, and relationship.
b. They can compare a score from an assessment instrument with an existing distribution, describe the placement of a score within a normal distribution, and draw appropriate inferences.
c. They can interpret statistics used to describe characteristics of assessment instruments, including difficulty and discrimination indices, reliability and validity coefficients, and standard errors of measurement.
d. They can identify and interpret inferential statistics when comparing groups, making predictions, and drawing conclusions needed for educational planning and decisions.
e. They can use computers for data management, statistical analysis, and production of tables and graphs for reporting and interpreting results.

**Competency 7. School counselors are skilled in conducting and interpreting evaluations of school counseling programs and counseling-related interventions.**

a. They understand and appreciate the role that evaluation plays in the program development process throughout the life of a program.
b. They can describe the purposes of an evaluation and the types of decisions to be based on evaluation information.
c. They can evaluate the degree to which information can justify conclusions and decisions about a program.
d. They can evaluate the extent to which student outcome measures match program goals.
e. They can identify and evaluate possibilities for unintended outcomes and possible impacts of one program on other programs.
f. They can recognize potential conflicts of interest and other factors that may bias the results of evaluations.

**Competency 8. School counselors are skilled in adapting and using questionnaires, surveys, and other assessments to meet local needs.**

a. They can write specifications and questions for local assessments.
b. They can assemble an assessment into a usable format and provide directions for its use.
c. They can design and implement scoring processes and procedures for information feedback.

**Competency 9. School counselors know how to engage in professionally responsible assessment and evaluation practices.**

a. They understand how to act in accordance with ACA's *Code of Ethics and*

*Standards of Practice* and ASCA's *Ethical Standards for School Counselors.*

b. They can use professional codes and standards, including the *Code of Fair Testing Practices in Education, Code of Professional Responsibilities in Educational Measurement, Responsibilities of Users of Standardized Tests,* and *Standards for Educational and Psychological Testing*, to evaluate counseling practices using assessments.
c. They understand test fairness and can avoid the selection of biased assessment instruments and biased uses of assessment instruments. They can evaluate the potential for unfairness when tests are used incorrectly and for possible bias in the interpretation of assessment results.
d. They understand the legal and ethical principles and practices regarding test security, copying copyrighted materials, and unsupervised use of assessment instruments that are not intended for self-administration.
e. They can obtain and maintain available credentialing that demonstrates their skills in assessment and evaluation.
f. They know how to identify and participate in educational and training opportunities to maintain competence and acquire new skills in assessment and evaluation.

**Definitions of Terms**

***Competencies*** describe skills or understandings that a school counselor should possess to perform assessment and evaluation activities effectively.

***Assessment*** is the gathering of information for decision making about individuals, groups, programs, or processes. Assessment targets include abilities, achievements, personality variables, aptitudes, attitudes, preferences, interests, values, demographics, and other characteristics. Assessment procedures include but are not limited to standardized and unstandardized tests, questionnaires, inventories, checklists, observations, portfolios, performance assessments, rating scales, surveys, interviews, and other clinical measures.

***Evaluation*** is the collection and interpretation of information to make judgments about individuals, programs, or processes that lead to decisions and future actions.

## Improving Assessment Skills

Here are some suggestions to improve assessment competencies. First, check with ASCA at both the state and national levels to see what in-service training programs may be available. Check also with colleges to see if courses in assessment skills for professional school counselors are offered. Second, explore the Association for Assessment in Counseling web site (http://aac.ncat.edu). Look for links to helpful topics.

## Summary/Conclusion

This chapter identified the assessment competencies needed by professional school counselors. Professional school counselors are encouraged to engage in self-evaluation to determine if they have these competencies and use the identified resources to improve assessment skills.

## References


American Association for Counseling and Development/Association for Measurement and Evaluation in Counseling and Development. (1989). *Responsibilities of users of standardized tests*. Alexandria, VA: Author.

American School Counselor Association. (1990). *Role statement*. Alexandria, VA: Author.

American School Counselor Association. (1998). *Ethical standards*. Alexandria, VA: Author.

Baker, S. B. (2000). *School counseling for the twenty-first century* (3rd ed.). New York: Prentice-Hall.

Burnham, J. J., & Jackson, C. M. (2000). School counselors' roles: Discrepancies between actual practices and existing models. *Professional School Counseling, 4*, 41–49.

Council for Accreditation of Counseling and Related Educational Programs. (2001). *CACREP accreditation standards and procedures manual*. Alexandria, VA: Author.

Elmore, P. B., Ekstrom, R. B., Diamond, E. E., & Whittaker, S. (1993). School counselors' test use patterns and practices. *The School Counselor, 41*, 73–80.

Gysbers, N. C., & Henderson, P. (2000). *Developing and managing your school guidance program* (3rd ed.). Alexandria, VA: American Association for Counseling and Development.

Impara, J. C., & Plake, B. S. (1995). Comparing counselors', school administrators', and teachers' knowledge in student assessment. *Measurement and Evaluation in Counseling and Development, 28*, 78–87.

Joint Committee of the American School Counselor Association and Association for Assessment in Counseling. (2001). Competencies in assessment and evaluation for school counselors. In G. R. Walz & J. C. Bleuer (Eds.), *Assessment Issues and Challenges for the Millennium* (pp. 95–100). Greensboro, NC: ERIC Counseling and Student Services Clearinghouse.

Joint Committee on Testing Practices. (1988). *Code of fair testing practices in education*. Washington, DC: Author. (Available from NCME, 1230 17th St., NW, Washington, DC 20036-3078. Single copies free.)

Myrick, R. D. (1993). *Developmental guidance and counseling: A practical approach* (2nd ed.). Minneapolis: Educational Media.

National Association of State Directors of Teacher Education. (1991). *Manual on certification and preparation of educational personnel in the United States*. Dubuque, IA: Kendall/Hunt Publishing Company.

Sampson, J. P., Jr., Vacc, N. A., & Loesch, L. C. (1998). The practices of career counseling by specialists and counselors in general practice. *The Career Development Quarterly, 46*, 404–415.


[1] A joint committee of the American School Counselor Association (ASCA) and the Association for Assessment in Counseling (AAC) was appointed by the respective presidents in 1993 with the charge to draft a statement about school counselor preparation in assessment and evaluation. Committee members were Ruth Ekstrom (AAC), Patricia Elmore (AAC, Chair, 1997-1999), Daren Hutchinson (ASCA), Marjorie Mastie (AAC), Kathy O'Rourke (ASCA), William Schafer (AAC, Chair, 1993-1997), Thomas Trotter (ASCA), and Barbara Webster (ASCA).

# Chapter 45

## High-Stakes Testing: What Counselors Need to Know

*Patricia Jo McDivitt*

### Preview

The scores on many of the tests administered in the classrooms today are often tied to accountability systems where the results might be used to have an impact upon the life chances of students. This chapter serves to summarize what counselors need to know about high-stakes testing, including understanding the purpose and the link to the standards-based educational reform movement.

In today's educational setting, a heavy focus is placed upon the use of high-stakes testing in order to determine what students should know and be able to do. The scores on today's tests are now tied to accountability systems where the results might have an impact on teaching and learning. The changing purpose and use of tests over the past few years serve to underscore how important it is for professional school counselors and all assessment professionals to understand the role that high-stakes testing plays in today's classroom, including its link to curriculum standards, teaching, and learning.

As a result of today's high-stakes testing, professional school counselors and other assessment professionals are challenged not only to be actively engaged in understanding the use of high-stakes tests and the interpretation of the results, but also learn more about what these tests actually measure and whether or not students have had the opportunity to learn what the test questions are asking. This chapter serves to summarize what professional school counselors need to know about high-stakes testing, including understanding the purpose and the link to the standards-based educational reform movement.

### Defining the Purpose of Accountability

It is important for professional school counselors and assessment professionals to understand the definition of high-stakes testing and its purpose in today's educational settings. In the broadest sense, the purpose of any test is to gather data to facilitate decision-making. However, there are many kinds of decisions, as well as many kinds of information that help make such decisions (Mehrens, 2000). In the past, the results of tests given to students were often used to determine students' academic strengths and weaknesses so that teachers could plan instruction. Other tests were used so that the results might help students understand their aptitudes and interests in order to explore possible career options and/or future educational plans. However, in today's educational setting a great deal of the testing involves the use of tests that are directly tied to school accountability systems where the results are used to make major decisions about an individual, decisions that might have a direct impact on the individual's future life opportunities.

A test is defined as "high stakes" if it carries with it serious consequences for students and/or others in the educational community, including teachers and administrators. For example, the results of high-stakes tests are sometimes used, along with other requirements, to determine whether or not a student is promoted to the next grade in school or whether or not a student graduates from high school. In addition, school-wide average student scores on a high-stakes test may also be used to judge an entire school's academic performance. For example, high scores on a given high-stakes test might receive praise and financial awards from the community at large; low scores on the same test might bring heavy sanctions.

High-stakes testing applications such as those outlined above often put pressure on students, parents, teachers, and others in the educational community. For example, professional school counselors are now becoming more aware of the added pressure and impact that high-stakes tests are beginning to have on opportunities for students. In fact, while many students today are becoming desensitized to the entire testing process, once they become aware of what is really at stake the pressure to pass the test can be overwhelming.

Parents and guardians today are also experiencing new pressures. The results of school-wide high-stakes tests may provide them with the opportunity to make important decisions concerning what might be the best educational opportunities for their children. For example, parents and guardians of students in low-performing schools might be faced with the decision as to whether or not to enroll their children in a different school or a charter school, or they might also be given the opportunity to use federal or state funds to provide their children with additional special training. These decisions may well have a direct impact on a student's future opportunity.

Teachers also face significant added pressure as they are now more than ever challenged to help all students achieve the level of performance expected by administrators, parents, and the community at large. "There is a tremendous push to expand national and state testing — including testing students with disabilities and those with limited English proficiency – many of whom have not been included in those assessment systems in the past" (NCEO, 2002, p. 2).

As a result, according to Herr, today's tests have

> become a high-stakes mechanism affecting the life chances of many young people and substantially defining the curriculum to which teachers will teach in order to have their students perform as well as possible in state assessments to which they are exposed. (Herr, 2001, p.7)

## High-Stakes Test: Raising Academic Achievement for All Students

High-stakes testing is also the key component of today's educational reform movement. In 2001, President George W. Bush signed into law the *No Child Left Behind Act of 2001* (NCLBA) (Public Law 107-110). NCLBA significantly strengthens the federal government's role in both elementary and secondary education and includes a plan for educational reform that places a key focus upon accountability and the use of high-stakes test results to help raise the academic achievement for all students. NCLBA outlines the requirements that all states are to implement reading and mathematics tests in grades 3-8 and once again during grades 10-12. Science tests are also to be administered to all students at least once in the elementary, middle, and high school years. In addition, NCLBA requires that high-stakes tests be aligned with state content curriculum standards and designed to provide results concerning each student's progression toward mastery of the defined standards. Schools are also to be held accountable for making sure that all students are making adequate yearly progress in learning. Because schools today are being asked to prove that their students are attaining the desired knowledge and skills that will enable them to be contributing members of society, professional school counselors and everyone involved in the process of educating students are now more than ever being asked to assume some responsibility for the outcome (Ardovino, Hollingworth, & Ybarra, 2000).

## Curriculum Content Standards: What Students Should Know and Be Able to Do

The use of high-stakes tests in the educational setting today has its roots within the larger movement of the educational standards-based reform. The reform movement that emerged in the 1990s called for high standards for all students centering around challenging subject matter, acquisition of higher-order thinking skills, and the application of abstract knowledge when solving real-world problems (Swanson & Stevenson, 2002). Basically, the reform movement is based upon the following premise:

> All students must learn at high levels, regardless of such factors as race, ethnicity, socioeconomic status, native language or gender. Too often, disparities in achievement among urban, rural, and suburban schools, or between schools in rich and poor neighborhoods, or even between schools from seemingly similar communities are accepted as inevitable. Expectations from some students are often lower than for others, frequently leading to a narrowly defined curriculum for those students. Defining what students need to know and be able to do is intended to facilitate holding all students accountable for the same high learning, no matter what their background or particular school. (Woodward, 1999, p. 19)

In 1993 a Technical Planning Group for the National Education Goals Panel published *Promises to Keep: Creating High Standards for American Students*. The publication served to outline the establishment of curriculum content standards. Curriculum content standards specify what students should know and be able to do (McMillan, 1997). In most educational settings today, the term "standard," much like the term "objective," entails a process of coming to an agreement about what should be taught. Traditionally, the content curriculum standards or learning targets would parallel educational goals, teaching objectives, and outcomes. However, the term "standard" in today's educational setting, has an implication of higher levels of expectation and monitoring that were not commonly connected to the widely used educational objectives in the past (Solomon, 2002). Therefore, the goal of the educational reform movement in the 1990s has been to encourage the development of new and rigorous academic expectations that all students should meet as the nation enters the increasingly complex information age of the 21st century (Woodward, 1999).

In response to the national standards-based reform movement that took place in the early 1990s, many states adopted their own state specific curriculum content standards. "What is common to standards initiatives is the aim to 'raise the bar' of learning for all students and to replace the minimum competency model sometimes relied on in the past" (Woodward, 1999, p. 20).

Many states also developed their own high-stakes tests designed specifically to measure students' mastery of these state-specific content curriculum standards. These high-stakes tests are called criterion-referenced tests or standards-based assessments. Traditional norm-referenced tests are used to compare performance and determine relative strengths and weaknesses of students based upon the generalized set of objectives common across the country for a given content area. Standards-based assessments are used to determine what students can do and what they know, not how they are compared to other students who took the same test at a given grade level. "Standards-based assessments are the tools used to measure whether or not students have met a particular set of standards and to what level of proficiency" (Woodward, 1999, p. 23). In other words, standards-based assessments report how well students are doing relative to a predetermined performance level on the specified set of educational goals, skills, or outcomes included in the specific school, district, or state curriculum.

In order to understand high-stakes testing and its impact upon teaching and learning, professional school counselors and all assessment professionals need to become familiar with the content curriculum standards upon which the high-stakes test questions are based. The analysis of the content curriculum standards will provide the professional school counselor with the opportunity to gain a full understanding of the fundamental principles underlying what is to be taught. When examining a state's content curriculum standards, professional school counselors might want to follow the guidelines outlined in the report on the review of education standards from the goals 3 and 4 technical planning group to the National Education Goals Panel (1993). A summary of the guidelines is provided in Table 1.

**Table 1. Guidelines for review of standards.**

*Are the content standards:*

- challenging or do they simply hold students accountable to minimum acceptance levels of competency?
- useful for helping students to attain career or educational goals, including becoming productive citizens and lifelong learners?
- accurate and do they reflect sound instructional practices?
- clear and usable so that students, teachers, and parents can easily understand what the standards mean and what they require?
- assessable for all students and specific so that the attainment of the standards can be measured?
- adaptable and able to be implemented in a number of ways depending upon the needs of the students?
- developmentally appropriate?

## Performance Standards: Understanding Levels of Performance

The National Education Goals Panel's (1993) publication, *Promises to Keep: Creating High Standards for American Students*, also served to outline the establishment of performance standards. A performance standard is a statement that articulates the expectation about what standard all students are expected to meet for a given criterion. It describes an action of the student or a quality of his final product (Zmuda & Tomaino, 2001). Performance standards serve to indicate the degree to which the student has mastered the curriculum content standards. In other words, "performance criteria help define the standards by specifying what one would look for as evidence that the standards have been achieved" (Arter & McTigue, 2001).

In terms of high-stakes testing, performance standards are also translated into scoring guidelines or performance-level descriptors. Performance level descriptors are typically written to provide clear guidelines for what should constitute the different levels of performance on the high-stakes test. They form the foundation for determining what and how much students are expected to know and be able to do in a given domain of content for a particular subject area.

Performance standards can be defined in a number of ways. For example, in a physical education class a performance-level descriptor or standard might be defined by whether or not a student can perform a set of physical activities to perfection. These activities might include running in place for several minutes, walking on a balance beam without falling, and jumping rope for a specified number of minutes. If the student is able to perform all of these physical activities to perfection, he/she would be deemed as having mastery of the standard. In this example, not every student may have successfully completed each activity; however, the standard is obvious and easy to understand.

Developing good performance level descriptors involves a careful analysis of the curriculum content standards in order to summarize dimensions of performance. McMillan (1997) outlined six steps to follow when summarizing the dimensions of performance used to assign student work to a given level. These steps are outlined in Table 2.

**Table 2. Steps for summarizing dimensions of performance (McMillan, 1997, p. 36).**

1. Identify dimensions of excellence.
2. Categorize and prioritize dimensions.
3. Clearly define each dimension.
4. Identify examples.
5. Describe performance continuums.
6. Try out and refine the continuums.

It is important to know that both curriculum content standards and performance standards have been articulated at a national level in documents published by national organizations, including the National Council of Teachers of Mathematics, the National Council of Teachers of English, the National Council of Teachers of Social Studies, the American Association for the Advancement of Science, and the National Science Teachers Association. For example, the *National Council of Teachers of Mathematics Curriculum and Evaluation Standards for School Mathematics* outlines a set of content standards for a reformed mathematics curriculum. The content standards are designed to build students' mathematical power which involves higher order thinking skills such as problem solving, mathematical reasoning, communicating ideas, and the understanding of mathematics as it relates to real-life situations (NCTM, 1989).

In addition to understanding the performance standards or what is to be expected, professional school counselors also need to have some knowledge of how the standards for performance or the "cut scores" for those who pass or fail are established. Establishing "cut scores" is directly tied to the purpose of the test. According to a recent American Educational & Research Association (AERA, 2002, p. 5) policy statement,

> There is often confusion among minimum competency levels (traditionally required for grade-to-grade promotion), grade level (traditionally defined as a range of scores around the national average on standardized tests), and 'world-class' standards (set at the top of the distribution, anywhere from the 70th to the 99th percentile. Once the purpose is clearly established, sound and appropriate procedures must be followed in setting passing scores or proficiency levels.

With high-stakes testing, standards are typically set by a group of educators during a standard-setting process. Professional school counselors need to verify that the process by which the cut scores are determined is clearly documented and defensible. The purpose and meaning of the scores or performance standards needs to be clearly stated, and validity evidence must be gathered and reported, consistent with the test's stated purpose.

## Recommended Actions and Strategies: Technical Quality and What Counselors Need to Know

High-stakes tests need to be fair and all students should be given the opportunity to learn the material covered in the test. In other words, a fair test is one that provides all students with an equal opportunity to demonstrate achievement. Fair tests are not biased against particular groups. In high-stakes testing fairness also refers to students having the right to an opportunity to learn the material that will be on the test. For example, students must be told in advance what they need to do to show mastery of the standards, earn a diploma, or what behaviors are expected in school. The notice will give them the opportunity to prepare to meet the requirements (Freedman, 2001).

In addition to the need for high-stakes tests to be fair, they must also be valid. "Test validity means that the test measures what its producer intends it to measure – that is, what it purports to measure" (Freedman, 2001, p. 12) It is important for professional school counselors to know that whether or not a high-stakes test does in fact measure what it is intended to measure depends upon its clearly defined purpose and the domains of content which serve as the foundation for guiding the entire test development process. McMillan (1997) provides the following questions to help professional school counselors and other assessment professionals determine whether or not a test is valid: 1) What is the extent to which the test matches what is taught and what is assessed? 2) How closely does the test correspond to what has been covered in class and in assignments? and 3) Have students had the opportunity to learn what has been assessed?

In the development of any high-stakes test, therefore, professional school counselors need to understand that the development process must begin with a clear vision of what it means to succeed within a given context. At various times during the schooling process, students are expected to know and understand specific subject content, some of which they must know outright and some of which they must be able to retrieve using references when needed (Stiggins, 1999). Knowing what is to be asked of students and what students will be taught is important because different achievement targets require the application of different assessment methods. The nature of learning is also qualitatively and quantitatively different for certain disciplines. For example, teaching and learning in the subject area of mathematics is often tied to a specified instructional sequence. Therefore, what students should know and be able to do is usually tied directly to the level and quality of the instruction in the classroom. However, when developing a high-stakes test to assess third grade English/language arts standards, the learning targets might be more generalized and not tied to a specified instructional sequence.

In addition to being fair and valid, high-stakes tests must follow all relevant professional standards as outlined in *The Standards for Educational and Psychological Testing* (AERA/APA/NCME, 1999). The *Standards* covers major aspects of assessment including validity, reliability, standard setting, item development, bias, and fairness review.

The AERA (2002) has also issued guidelines on high-stakes testing. Table 3 provides a summary of these guidelines, with a special focus on those most applicable to the work of the professional school counselor. Additional information that serves to describe how a given guideline might apply to the professional school counselor as a test user and assessment leader in the educational and counseling setting is also provided.

## Summary/Conclusion

The standards-based educational reform movement and the more recent *No Child Left Behind Act of 2001* (Public Law 107-110) with its major focus on high-stakes testing and accountability, have had and will continue to have a major impact on many professional school counselors and assessment professionals. In summary, professional school counselors need to make sure that the high-stakes test is fair and students have the opportunity to learn the material to be covered by the test questions; is valid and measures what it is intended to measure; includes the purpose and meaning of the scores or the performance standards are clearly stated; and follows all relevant professional standards as outlined in the *Standards* (AERA/APA/NCME, 1999).

**Table 3. Guidelines for high-stakes testing (AERA, 2002).**

1. *Protection against high-stakes decisions based on a single test.* Decisions that affect individual student's life chances or educational opportunities should not be made on the basis of a single test score or test scores alone.
2. *Adequate resources and opportunity to learn.* When curriculum content standards are introduced as a component of educational reform and to improve teaching and learning in the educational setting, students must have adequate resources and the opportunity to learn.
3. *Alignment between the test and the curriculum.* If a high-stakes test is going to be used to measure students' mastery of curriculum content standards, the test questions must validly measure the content standard as required by the test blueprint.
4. *Validity of passing scores and achievement levels.* When high-stakes tests use specific scores to determine whether or not a student passes, the purpose and meaning of the passing scores must be clearly stated. The validity of the scores must also be established.
5. *Opportunities for meaningful remediation for examinees who fail high-stakes tests.* Students who do not pass a high-stakes test should be given opportunities for remediation. Remediation should focus upon the knowledge and skills the high-stakes test is intended to measure, not just the performance itself.
6. *Sufficient reliability for each intended use.* Scores must be reliable. "Reliability is concerned with the consistency, stability, and dependability of the results. In other words, a reliable result is one that shows similar performance at different times or under different conditions" (McMillan, 1997 p. 60).
7. *Ongoing evaluation of intended and unintended effects of high-stakes testing.* Ongoing evaluation is necessary. Professional school counselors need to be aware of both the positive and negative effects of high-stakes tests.

## References

American Educational Research Association. (2002). *AERA position statement concerning high-stakes testing in pre K-12 education.* Washington, DC: Author.

American Educational Research Association, American Psychological Association, & National Council on Measurement in Education. (1999). *Standards for educational and psychological testing.* Washington, DC: APA.

Ardovino, J., Hollingsworth, J., & Ybarra, S. (2000). *Multiple measures: Accurate ways to assess student achievement,* Thousand Oaks, CA: Corwin Press.

Arter, J., & McTighe, J. (2001). *Scoring rubrics in the classroom: Using performance criteria for assessing and improving student performance.* Thousand Oaks, CA: Corwin Press.

Freedman, M. K. (2001). *Testing students and the law.* Boston, MA: Miriam Kurtzig Freedman.

Herr, E. (2001). Contemporary assessment: A hotbed of issues and challenges. In G. R. Walz & J. C. Bleuer (Eds.) *Assessment issues and challenges for the millennium.* Greensboro, NC: CAPS Publications.

McMillan, J. H. (1997). *Classroom assessment: Principles and practice for effective instruction.* Needham Heights, MA: Allyn & Bacon.

Mehrens, W. A. (2000). Selecting a career assessment instrument. In J. T. Kapes & E. A. Whitfield (Eds.) *A counselor's guide to career assessment instruments* (4th ed.), Alexandria, VA: National Career Development Association.

National Center on Educational Outcomes. (2002). *Universal design applied to large scale assessments*. NCEO synthesis report 44.

National Council of Teachers of Mathematics. (1989). *Curriculum and evaluation standards for school mathematics*. Reston, VA: Author.

National Education Goals Panel. (1993). *Promises to keep: Creating high standards for American students*. Washington, DC: Author

Solomon, P. G. (2002). *The assessment bridge: Positive ways to link tests to learning standards and curriculum improvement.* Thousand Oaks, CA: Corwin Press.

Stiggins, R. (1999). Are you assessment literate? *The High School Magazine*, *6*, 2-6.

Swanson, C. B., & Stevenson, D. L. (2002). Standards-based reform in practice: Evidence on state policy and classroom instruction from the NAEP state assessments. *Educational Evaluation and Policy Analysis*, *24*(1), 1-27.

Woodward, K. S. (1999). *Alignment of national and state standards: A report by the GED testing service.* Washington, DC: American Council on Education & GED Testing Service.

Zmuda, A., & Tomaino, M. (2001). *The competent classroom: Aligning high school, curriculum, standards, and assessment – a creative teaching guide*. New York: Teachers College Press & NEA.

# Chapter 46

# Parents' Questions about Testing in Schools and Some Answers

*Mary Ann Clark & Larry C. Loesch*

## Preview

Testing in schools is both extensive and complex, and consequently, parents have many questions about testing and their child's part in it. This chapter presents some of the questions most frequently asked by parents about testing and some effective responses to those questions that can be used by professional school counselors.

Testing, or "assessment," plays a vital role in education today and is used for a multitude of purposes. For example, assessment results may be used to monitor student performance, assess student potential, improve teaching and learning activities, evaluate programs and schools, and serve as the basis upon which to make school policy decisions. Test results also are often a major criterion underlying public perception about the quality of schools. Thus testing is a fundamental activity in every school and a vital component for setting educational standards and monitoring progress toward them (CTB-McGraw Hill, 2002).

## Why do we have testing in the schools?

Tests yield individual and group student data that can be helpful in educational decision-making and planning. Of course each student is unique and varies in his/her range of abilities, talents, and achievements. For example, some are good at reading while others excel in math and some achieve at their current grade level while others function above or below their current grade level. Because of the individuality and associated range of possibilities, school teachers, counselors, administrators, and parents need as much information as possible about students in order to provide the best teaching and learning environments and activities for each student and classroom group. Testing is an effective and efficient way to obtain useful information about students. Some more specific reasons for testing include the following.

*To increase learning for each student.* Education is most effective when it is tailored to the greatest extent possible to the specific needs and abilities of each student. Test data can help to pinpoint each student's strengths and areas in need of improvement, and to identify the best ways for each student to be taught and to learn.

*To compare students with others and with themselves.* Educators and others responsible for making decisions that affect a child's education need comparative information. That is, it is important to know how each student is performing in specific learning and skill areas relative to other students in his or her grade as well as how the student is performing over time. Decisions to be made include which principles and competencies are to be taught, which activities and materials are to be used, which curriculum is to be followed, and how students should be organized in a classroom or school. Assessment data can provide decision makers such comparative information. Of course, the information also is helpful as feedback for each student and his/her parents.

*To facilitate appropriate educational placement.* Test scores are one type of information (among others, such as grades and teacher and parent observations) that helps to place each student in the most appropriate educational situation. For example, although standardized test data may not be used as the sole criterion to enroll a student in a specific educational placement, they may be used for initial screening for further, more comprehensive evaluations as well as subsequently to determine the effectiveness of the placement.

*To improve instruction.* Test results are perhaps the most common way to determine if learning objectives are being met, including learning objectives developed at the local, state, or national levels. Examination of total test and individual item results can help educators adjust teaching methods to achieve the highest possible learning benefits for all students. Also, grade- and school-wide test scores may be used to assist in planning school improvements and curriculum modifications.

*To inform parents.* Parents have both a right and desire to know how their child is performing in school, particularly in regard to level of mastery of specific learning and performance objectives in relation to his/her grade level and/or peers locally, statewide, or nationally. Standardized test results are an objective way to provide such information to parents.

*To inform community members.* Test data help all members of a school community be informed about the performance of students in the community's schools in both absolute (i.e., how much knowledge and how many skills are actually being learned) and relative (i.e., compared to similar students at the state or national level) contexts. With this information, areas of both strength and concern at a classroom, school, and district levels can be readily identified.

### What kinds of tests are given, at what grade levels, and when?

A wide variety of tests are administered in schools and for an equally wide variety of reasons. In general, tests may be administered in schools to assess a student's general cognitive ability (i.e., intelligence), academic and other aptitudes, level of achievement in various academic areas, career and leisure interests, and personal characteristics. All but one of these types of tests usually are only administered by student services specialists, such as professional school counselors or school psychologists, in response to the unique needs and circumstances of individual students (e.g., for identification of learning problems and/or placement in specialized instructional circumstances, assistance with career planning, or application for post-secondary education). The notable exception is achievement testing, which is by far the most common type of testing done in schools. Achievement tests typically are either nationally standardized tests purchased from commercial testing companies by the local school system or statewide (and mandated) tests created and distributed by the state educational agency and administered in all public schools in the state.

Frequently, representatives of the local school system determine whether or which and at what grade levels nationally standardized tests will be administered in the local schools. The tests selected usually have been chosen because they closely reflect the learning objectives of the school system at the various grade levels in which the tests are administered. Most school systems administer nationally standardized achievement tests because local-area learning objectives are usually more numerous (i.e., comprehensive) than those stipulated at the state level, and therefore national standardized tests usually give more specific information than statewide tests. For example, nationally standardized tests are used frequently to measure learning in areas such as reading comprehension and mathematics, social studies, and language arts skills.

All states have their own, state-specific testing programs and there are both similarities and differences from one state to another. Typically, the states administer their own (i.e., statewide) tests to measure the mastery of student competencies deemed necessary at particular grade levels. In the vast majority of states, mastery at minimum criterion levels also is required for high school graduation. Frequently, students are given multiple opportunities to pass the tests.

Nationally standardized tests are administered at various times throughout the school year at the discretion of the local school district. However, statewide achievement tests typically are administered in the spring of the academic year.

## What are all these different types of test scores?

In general, there are two major categories of achievement tests. The most common type is known as "norm-referenced" tests. Norm-referenced tests yield scores that compare a child's performance to that of a much larger group of other children at the same grade (and/or ability) level who took the same test at approximately the same point in the school year. This larger group is called the norm group. A student's test scores are often reported in percentile ranks, which tell where the student's score is in relation to the larger group. Percentile ranks range from a low of 1 to a high of 99, with 50 representing the middle (and average) score. For example, if a student has a percentile rank of 75, it means that 75% of the norm group members achieved a score lower than the student's score and 25% of the norm group members achieved a score higher than the student's score. Of course, the greater the similarity between the student and the norm group members, the more valid the comparison.

Students do not "pass" or "fail" a norm-referenced test. Scores from norm-referenced tests are intended to give educators and parents an objective picture of how a particular student at a specific grade level is progressing in a specific subject or in school in general. Typically, norm-referenced scores can show whether a student is doing better in some academic areas than others improving in specific subject matter or skill areas over time.

Sometimes percentiles may be reported for several norm groups. For example, a student's score(s) may be compared to national, state, and/or local-area norm groups. Although a student's actual (known as a "raw") score is the same on a particular test, the percentile corresponding to that score may vary depending on the norm group to which it is compared.

The results of a norm-referenced test are sometimes reported as stanines instead of as percentile ranks. Stanine is an abbreviation for "standard nine" because the range of percentiles is divided into nine groups of percentile ranks. Thus, a stanine is actually a grouping of percentiles. Stanines vary from a low of 1 to a high of 9. The *approximate* "percentile rank bands" represented by stanines (1-9) are 4, 8, 12, 16, 20, 16, 12, 8, and 4, respectively. For example, a student performing in the 1$^{st}$ stanine may have a percentile rank of 1,2,3, or 4. A student in the 9$^{th}$ stanine may have a percentile rank of 97, 98, 99 or higher. A student whose score is reported as the 5$^{th}$ stanine has achieved a score that is between the 40$^{th}$ and 60$^{th}$ percentile. Stanines provide much less specific information than percentiles because each student's score lies within a band of percentiles.

Another frequently reported type of score is the grade equivalent, which shows the grade level of students for whom a score is considered average or typical. For example, a grade equivalent of 4.5 means that the student's score is the same as what the average score of students in the fifth month of the fourth grade would have been if those students had taken the same test.

Grade equivalent scores should not be compared across test takers because the same grade equivalent score may not always stand for the same amount of learning for the students compared.

The other major category of achievement tests is criterion-referenced tests. The "criteria" to which the title refers are statements of specific skills or competencies for particular curricular areas, such as mathematics, science, or language arts. Although the scores from criterion-referenced tests may be reported in different ways, all of them basically reflect the numbers of skills or competencies the student has mastered in a particular educational area (i.e., subject). These scores are most often reported as percentage of correct answers achieved on a particular criterion-referenced test. Each score thus represents an individual level of achievement rather than a comparison to a norm group.

Many statewide testing programs use criterion-referenced tests and have a specific score that must be equaled or exceeded (often called a "cut" score) for the student to "pass" the test. A student's score for these tests also may be reported as a percentile rank to show how the student scored compared to a statewide norm group.

Both norm-referenced and criterion-referenced tests provide information about each individual student's level of performance and that of the student's peer group. Although one type is not necessarily better than the other, it is important to know which type of test is used in order to be able to interpret the resulting scores correctly.

**How are achievement tests different from college admissions tests?**

Achievement tests are used for a variety of educational purposes in schools and are administered at various grade levels. On the other hand, college admissions tests are intended to predict success in college and therefore have a very specific purpose: to assist in determining who is to be admitted to a college or university and who is not. They are administered to high school students, usually juniors or seniors, seeking admission to an institution of higher education. The students' test results are usually submitted with their college or university applications.

The Scholastic Assessment Test (SAT) I: Reasoning, administered by the College Board, a commercial testing company, yields two main scores: verbal (i.e., language usage) and quantitative (i.e., mathematics). The College Board also administers the SAT II, a set of achievement tests in subject areas such as history, mathematics, foreign languages, and science. Students usually have a choice in regard to which tests in the SAT II they take, although the tests taken may be specified and/or required by the college or university to which admission or advanced placement is sought. Scores on each form of the SAT are reported using a scale between 200 and 800, with an intended mean of 500. A percentile rank also is given on the student's score report, with the norm group being college applicants. More information about the SAT and issues related to it can be found at http://www.collegeboard.com.

The ACT, produced and administered by the American College Testing Program, another commercial testing company, is a curriculum-based achievement test having four sections: mathematics, reading, English, and science reasoning. Each section yields a score on a scale between 1 and 36. A composite score, which is the average of the four sections, also is reported. Corresponding percentile ranks are reported for college bound seniors. For 2001 college-bound high school seniors, the average ACT Composite score was 21.9. More information about the ACT and issues related to it can be found at http://www.act.org.

Colleges and universities often give applicants the choice of taking either the SAT or the ACT. However, some colleges do not require either for admission and some require it only for placement purposes once the student has been admitted and enrolled. SAT and/or ACT scores also are often used for academic advising and scholarship or loan applications prior to or soon after admission to a college or university.

The Preliminary Scholastic Aptitude Test (PSAT)/National Merit Scholarship Qualifying Test (NMSQT) is administered each October to high school sophomores and/or juniors. It is designed to give students practice for the SAT I and the SAT II Subject Test in Writing. However, the scores also are frequently used as criteria for students to qualify for scholarship and recognition programs. The scores range between 20 and 80 for each section, with 50 being the intended average score.

### What other types of assessment are used in the schools?

One type of assessment becoming more widely used in schools is writing samples, and in fact many statewide testing programs now require students to write narrative answers to questions. Another approach to assessment used more frequently is a portfolio of student work. With a focus on the outcomes of educational experiences, students display samples of their work in various subject matter areas and are evaluated in regard to the "final product(s)" of their efforts. Many educators believe it important to look at the "whole" student, and work samples provide for such an approach to evaluation of student performance.

### Are testing accommodations made for children who have a disability?

In accord with the Americans with Disabilities Act (as well as other applicable laws), any student who has a physical, emotional, or cognitive (e.g., learning) disability *may* be given special accommodation(s) during testing. Evidence of the disability must be presented to the school system (or other agency administering the test) before a test is administered; accommodation (*vis-á-vis* scoring) is not required for evidence of a disability presented "after the fact." Typically, a student who has a disability that would qualify him or her for a testing accommodation will also have an Individualized Education Plan (IEP) on file at the school. Therefore, the planning team that worked with the parents, teachers, and child to develop the IEP will have given consideration to accommodation(s) for the student's involvement in any testing situation. The college testing programs described previously also provide accommodation(s) for students with documented disabilities.

The testing accommodation(s) provided to a student is determined on an individual basis depending on the nature of the individual student's disability. Some typical accommodations for students with disabilities include extending the testing time period, administering the test in an isolated (i.e., distraction free) environment, using a large print version of the test, having a "reader" present the items to the student orally, and allowing responding on a computer instead of paper-and-pencil form of the test. Testing companies or agencies are aware of when a student is given a testing accommodation in order to be able to score the test properly. However, test accommodation information may or may not be disclosed to test score recipients.

### What can parents do to help their child do well on tests?

One of the best things parents can do in this regard is to become informed about the testing done in their child's school. Parents should talk with professional school counselors, teachers, and administrators to learn which tests will be administered to their child, when, and most importantly, for what purposes. Parents who are knowledgeable about the testing done in schools are the best possible test preparation and performance resources for their child.

Another important thing parents can do is to help their child adopt an appropriate attitude about participation in the testing process. Children do best on tests when they have a clear sense of why it is important to perform well and the appropriate motivation to do so. Parents can help their child achieve this perspective by talking with him/her about the testing process, its purposes, and how the results will, and will not, be used. In the ideal situation, the child will have a *little* anxiety about participating in the examination (because a *little* anxiety represents motivation to do well), but not be so anxious so as to inhibit performance on the examination.

Children will do best on national or state tests when they are well prepared in regard to the material and/or skills being assessed. Therefore, parents can help children perform well on tests by helping them to keep up with their schoolwork on a regular basis. There is a strong, positive relationship between how well children do in school and how they perform on tests. In general, good students are good test-takers.

Parents also can help children do well on tests by helping them review what is to be covered on the tests. For example, parents can help children review what they have learned in their classes at school, help them organize class notes and study aids, and develop a schedule for preparation. In other words, parents can help children develop good study habits, which are similar in many ways to good test preparation habits. Many schools currently send home a booklet prior to test taking for parents to review with their child that contains sample test instructions and questions. Going over such materials can help familiarize a child with the format and sample content of tests they will be taking. It also can help parents become more familiar with what to expect with regard to the testing program.

Human performance of any kind has the greatest chance for success when the human body is well prepared to function. Test taking is no exception. Therefore, parents can help children do better on tests by insuring that they are well rested prior to and well fed at the beginning of the testing period. Sufficient sleep and appropriate nourishment are essential for maximized mental performance, and parents can have a direct influence on these conditions for their child as the testing time approaches. For example, eating fresh fruits and vegetables and drinking "natural" fruit juices can help to reduce stress and enhance mental functioning, while eating processed (so-called "junk") foods such as burgers and fries and drinking carbonated drinks may increase stress and inhibit mental functioning.

Parents also can advise their child about good test-taking practices. For example, they can advise their child to arrive at an appropriate time before the test, have the appropriate test-taking materials ready, and to listen to or read the test directions carefully. They can help their child with a time management plan for taking the test, such as helping the child to determine the average time for response to each item while allowing some time at the end for review of responses. Parents also can advise their child to find a sitting position of good posture and to shift sitting positions as necessary during the testing. They can discuss with their child whether guessing at answer choices is appropriate for the test, based on information that can be obtained from the test administrator before the testing. And finally, parents can talk to their child about reading each item and response choice carefully before making or selecting an answer.

### What are some other good sources of help about tests and test preparation for parents?

Get on the Net! The Internet provides a wealth of information that is current and useful. A good tactic is to do a keyword search using any of the major Internet search engines. Search using phrases such as "educational testing," "test taking," "test preparation," "study skills," or "learning skills." In addition, most states have a website for their department/division of education, and information about state testing programs is usually found at a link from it. Also, many local school systems have their own websites and information and test dates concerning local testing programs is described in them. However, it should be remembered that there are no "quality controls" on what is placed on the Internet, so caution must be exercised in interpreting what is found.

## References

American College Testing Program. (2002). *2001 ACT national and state scores.* Retrieved May 23, 2002, from http://www.act.org/news/data/01/index.html

College Board. (2002). *Most frequently asked questions and answers about the SAT program.* Retrieved May 1, 2002, from http://www.collegeboard.com/sat/html/students/mofaqtxt.html

CTB-McGraw-Hill. (2002). *A guide to effective assessment.* Retrieved April 15, 2002, from http://www.ctb.com/

# Chapter 47

## What Professional School Counselors Need to Know about Intelligence Tests

*Jose Arley Villalba & Peg Byrer*

### Preview

Professional school counselors need to understand the basic concepts behind intelligence testing. This chapter presents general information on intelligence tests and types of intelligence tests, characteristics of certain intelligence tests, ethical guidelines, multicultural aspects, and the responsibilities of professional school counselors with regard to these types of tests.

Cognitive and general ability instruments, or intelligence tests (IQ tests), form the basis for most educationally oriented psychological reports (Esters, Ittenbach, & Han, 1997). For this reason, it is imperative that school personnel, specifically professional school counselors, have some background knowledge regarding cognitive assessment measures and how they impact children in the schools. Although most educators have received some type of basic instruction regarding appraisal, as well as instrument development, professional school counselors with a master's degree tend to have advanced coursework in assessment (Esters & Ittenbach, 1999).

While school psychologists are responsible for administering and interpreting most intelligence tests, they tend to be assigned to several schools and only visit one particular school once or twice per week. This usually means that, at most schools, the professional school counselor is the most knowledgeable on-site staff member when it comes to intelligence tests. Consequently, professional school counselors become the person most colleagues and parents regularly turn to when a concern arises on the subject of intelligence testing.

Cognizant of the fact that most professional school counselors have already had one or more college-level course in assessment, this chapter will focus on basic characteristics of the more widely used intelligence instruments, understanding test results, how to use test results to develop an appropriate educational plan for a particular child, how to assist parents and colleagues with attaining a clearer idea of what tests actually measure, what test scores mean, and how to use these tests to make important decisions about children. Furthermore, ethical and multicultural issues will be discussed, specifically with regard to what professional school counselors are and are not responsible for when dealing with intelligence and ability tests.

### Basic Characteristics of Intelligence and General Ability Tests

Before the subject of common characteristics can be addressed, the types of intelligence tests must taken into account. Basically, there are two types of intelligence tests: brief tests which are frequently used for screening purposes, and comprehensive tests which are commonly used for educational placement and the cornerstone of most psychological evaluations and psycho-educational reports. Many professional school counselors, who have completed a master's degree and have taken a course in assessment, may administer a brief test, such as a Kaufman-Brief

Intelligence Test (K-BIT) or a Slosson Intelligence Test-Revised (SIT-R) (Whiston, 2000). Comprehensive tests, such as the Standford-Binet V (SB-V), the Weschler Intelligence Scale for Children-IV (WISC-IV) and the Weschler Adult Intelligence Scale-III (WAIS-III), the Kaufman Assessment Battery for Children (K-ABC) and the Woodcock-Johnson Tests of Cognitive Ability (WJ-III COG) must be administered and interpreted by certified or licensed school psychologists or other licensed professionals. The SB-V, WISC-IV, K-ABC, and WJ-III COG are mentioned here because they are the most frequently used intelligence tests for assessing children (Whiston, 2000).

Whether an IQ test falls under the category of brief or comprehensive, the instrument is used to assess the cognitive ability of individuals (Cohen & Swerdlik, 2002). Perhaps a better way of interpreting the previous statement is that IQ tests are used to gauge someone's "current ability" – the combined effect of potential and experiences. Most of the instruments used to assess intelligence are indirectly or directly based on theories of intelligence. However, regardless of what particular theory an instrument is based on, most tests of cognitive ability share a few common characteristics.

Intelligence tests, whether they are administered to an individual or a group, rely on normative data and statistical analysis to determine their usefulness and appropriateness for measuring intelligence. From this data, test administrators are able to determine if a test is valid and reliable and, therefore, applicable for administration to children, adolescents and adults. For example, the WISC-IV was piloted or "normed" using 2200 children before it was published and made available for use by professionals (Wechsler, 2003).

Most cognitive ability measures provide a global, thorough, overall IQ score, as well as scores for specific dimensions, or categorical components of intelligence. Many test developers divide an overall IQ score into factors or areas. For example, the K-ABC derives an IQ score from how a person performs on the sequential processing facets and simultaneous processing facets of the test (Kaufman & Kaufman, 1983). For the WISC-IV, the overall IQ score is based on how a person performs on both the verbal comprehension, perception reasoning, working memory, and processing speed indexes (Wechsler, 2003). In another example, the SB-V derives an overall IQ score from four different areas (if all four areas are assessed)(Riverside Publishing, 2004).

Regardless of the comprehensive intelligence test used to determine a student's ability, professional school counselors should recognize that IQ scores are not derived from one area or type of intelligence. Rather, efforts are made to test a child's full range of abilities (i.e., verbal reasoning, short-term memory, auditory processing, mathematical ability). More so, professional school counselors need to understand how these test results can be used in establishing a child's educational plan.

## Understanding Test Results

Professional school counselors are responsible for familiarizing themselves with the more frequently used intelligence tests for children, even if they are not administering them to children (Whiston, 2000). The more comfortable a professional school counselor becomes with the different components of intelligence tests, background information on how tests were developed, what population the tests are intended for, and the significance of the results, the more effective they will become at understanding intelligence tests, as well as helping others understand the results on a particular test.

The calculation of IQ scores depends on two parts: the chronological age of the person taking the test, and her raw score on the instrument she was administered. These two parts are used to determine the person's IQ score, or standard score (Cohen & Swerdlik, 2002).

A person's chronological age, basically, is how old he/she is in years and months. In addition, a person's raw score is simply how many questions he or she correctly answered. Using these two pieces of information, the test administrator compares a test-taker's raw score to other people in the same age range, as established by the test's developer. Age ranges and corresponding scores are determined by test developers, based on how the normative sample performed on the test. This information, usually presented as a series of tables, is provided in the administrator's manual as part of the instrument kits available to counselors, such as the K-BIT and SIT-R, and to school psychologists, such as the WISC-IV and K-ABC. Once standard scores have been established, it is possible for the test administrator to interpret the score. In essence, it becomes fundamental that professional school counselors understand what these standard scores mean before they can interpret them or help others, like colleagues and parents, understand the significance of the scores.

In order to understand the significance of a child's standard score, or IQ score, a counselor must comprehend three things: the mean of the test in use, the standard deviation of the test in use, and the bell-shaped normal curve (see figure 1). In order for an IQ score to signify something, it must be compared to the mean score on that test. The mean standard score for the WISC-IV and WAIS-III, K-ABC, SB-V, SIT-R, WJ-III COG, and K-BIT is 100. In addition, a test administrator must also know the standard deviation of these tests. With the case of the aforementioned instruments, the standard deviation is 15 points, with the exception of the SIT-R, which has a standard deviation of 16 points. Without getting too mired in statistical jargon, these two components, the mean and standard deviation of a particular intelligence test, allow the test administrator to determine if a test-taker's score is above or below the average and by how much. Finally, where a particular IQ score falls on the normal curve distribution can help determine if a child is of "average intelligence" or "below average." It may also help determine, for the purposes of special education, if the child is functioning in the gifted or mentally handicapped range. Intelligence test scores are also instrumental in diagnosing specific learning disabilities. However, eligibility for those programs also depends on administering academic achievement measures and processing instruments, among other instruments.

### How Intelligence Test Results Impact Educational Plans

As has been mentioned in this chapter, IQ tests form the foundation for most psychological assessments and psycho-educational reports (Esters et al., 1997). In some instances, brief IQ tests are administered as screening measures, prior to referring a child for a full battery of psycho-educational tests to determine  if additional comprehensive testing is warranted. How a child performs on an IQ test can affect his formal or informal educational program.

An individual's results on an intelligence test administered by a certified or licensed school psychologist, like the K-ABC or the WISC-IV, are used as one of the principle determinants for placement in some special education programs (Whiston, 2000). If a student scores high enough, usually two standard deviations beyond the mean of a particular test, then he could be eligible for gifted and talented services in some public school settings. If a student scores two standard deviations below the mean of a particular test, then he could be eligible for mild mentally disabled, or educable mentally handicapped services in most public schools. Placement in these types of programs requires that an individualized educational plan be established for these students.

Although placement in a specific learning disability (SLD) program requires the administration of an achievement test in addition to an intelligence test, again it is the individual's intelligence test results that are of the utmost importance (Whiston, 2000). Since a person's IQ score represents her current cognitive ability, a person's acquired knowledge, (i.e., what is measured by an achievement test) must be tested to establish if she is attaining her potential.

**Figure 1. Normal Distribution (Bell-Shaped Curve)**
**Mean = 100, Standard Deviation = 15.**

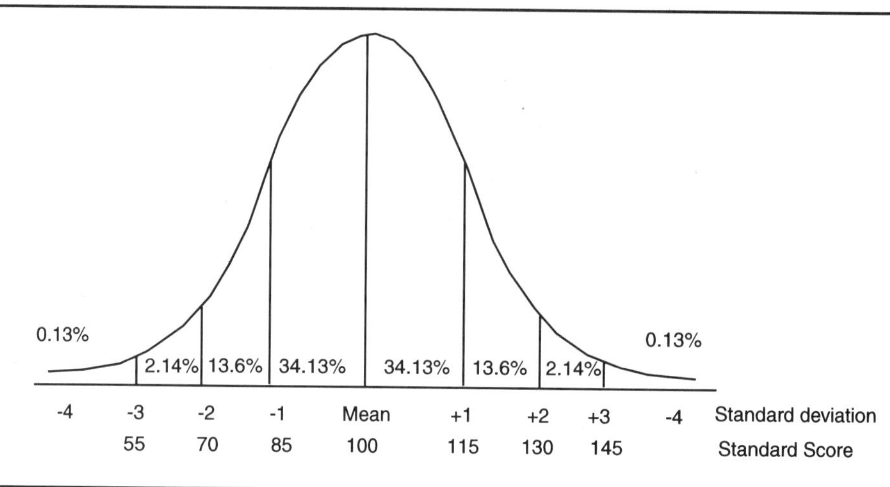


If it is determined that a student's acquired knowledge in math, reading or language is significantly lower (one to two standard deviation, depending on the age of the student and the state regulations) than her potential, then she may be eligible for placement in an SLD program. Again, an individualized educational program is established to better meet the needs of these students.

Results on IQ tests and other psycho-educational tests can also assist professional school counselors and other educators in determining the most effective way to teach a particular student, even if he/she does not qualify for specific special education services. The information gained from professional school counselor-administered tests, as well as those administered by a school psychologist, provide a wide array of information on how a student learns best, what may be strengths and weaknesses, and perhaps how proficient he is at grasping, retaining, and retrieving new information. All of this data may be used by the professional school counselor to advocate for children, whether or not they qualify for special services (Bowen & Glenn, 1998).

## Helping Others Understand Intelligence Tests

The mere fact that intelligence tests are based on statistical principles and use professional jargon is enough to confuse most teachers and parents, not to mention cause them to become disinterested or disengaged. Professional school counselors must use their communication skills to determine the point at which a parent or teacher becomes lost when discussing the results of a student's IQ tests, and then intervene to ensure that all parties are well and correctly informed. In other words, professional school counselors must have the skills to communicate test results in meaningful terms.

Although it typically is not the job of a professional school counselor to interpret the results of a comprehensive intelligence test to parents and colleagues, it is important that, if necessary, the school counselor use terms or analogies that may help parents and teachers understand what the results mean for a particular student. Most parents want to know if their children are fine, if their future is going be difficult, and, sometimes, parents may think they did something wrong to cause their child to have a lower-than-average intelligence test score (Bowen & Glenn, 1998).

With regard to teachers, professional school counselors should make themselves available to answer questions regarding intelligence tests. Professional school counselors must be supportive and non-threatening when responding to questions about cognitive ability tests. Not only can school counselors be instrumental in explaining the subtests, sample procedures and administration issues, school counselors can also help teachers understand how to best use the test results so as to augment their teaching strategy towards a particular student (Bowen & Glenn, 1998).

Some examples of how professional school counselors can communicate with parents and teachers in order to help them better understand intelligence tests include:

- Explaining the idea of "intellectual ability" (standard IQ scores) as "potential," perhaps by comparing it to how many ounces of liquid a container can potentially hold (capacity), or how fast a car is capable of driving (velocity).
- Often times, parents or teachers may be confused by the phrase "your child's IQ is in the 75th percentile" and left wondering, "Is that good or bad?" When explaining percentile ranks, it is helpful to look at the "unmentioned number" by subtracting the percentile from 100 and stating that new number along with the percentile rank. In the case of an IQ standard score in the 75th percentile, saying "in other words, your child's score is in the top 25% when compared to other children his age" may be easier to comprehend.
- Using common, interpretative labels to categorize IQ standard scores, such as "average" for scores around 100, "above average" for scores between a 115 and 129, "superior" for scores above a 130, or "below average" for scores below an 85, is helpful when discussing a child's particular IQ.
- Although individual achievement tests such as the Kaufman Test of Educational Achievement (K-TEA) and Wechsler Individual Achievement Test (WIAT) are not discussed in this chapter, it may be necessary for parents and teachers to understand more clearly how achievement tests and ability tests are related. If a child has an IQ standard score of 109 and a reading achievement score of 79, then the professional school counselor may help the parent and teacher understand the discrepancy by saying,

> The closer your child's reading score is to his potential, the IQ score, the more certain we can be that he is working to his potential. The 30 point difference between these two scores tells us we need to help your child read closer to his potential.

- Finally, parents and teachers should understand that IQ scores are neither "good" or "bad." In other words, it is not fair to attach a letter grade of "A" to a score above a 130 of a grade of "F" to something below 70, considering how few people score in those areas. Professional school counselors can help parents and teachers attain more realistic expectations by using what percentage of the population actually scores in certain ranges (i.e. only 2% of the population is in the "superior" intellectual range; most children (68%) score in the "average" range of intelligence), instead of referring to a particular score as "really good" or "not so great."

### Professional School Counselors and Ethical Issues Regarding Intelligence Tests

Professional school counselors are responsible for proper use and interpretation of assessment instruments (Whiston, 2000). Furthermore, it is up to the professional school counselor to gauge his or her own limits (ACA, 1995). For these reasons, professional school counselors must determine for themselves what tests they are comfortable using and have the ethical right to use. In addition, professional school counselors must be knowledgeable of when they cannot administer or interpret a particular instrument.

According to Whiston (2000), most brief intelligence tests, such as the K-BIT and SIT-R, fall under the category of Level B tests. A Level B test can be administered and interpreted by individuals with a master's degree in education or psychology that have also had graduate level coursework in psychological appraisal. Therefore, professional school counselors with the proper education should be capable of using these tests. However, Level C tests (comprehensive intelligence tests such as the WISC-IV or SB-V), those tests requiring specific coursework related to particular instruments as well as advanced knowledge in psychometrics, should only be administered and interpreted by appropriately trained professionals, such as school psychologist or licensed psychologist (Whiston, 2000). Professional school counselors should know their limits when it comes to Level C tests and should let colleagues and parents know about these ethical limits. Letting others know the ethical guidelines of the professional school counselor, with regard to cognitive ability instruments, should assist in clarifying to others what professional school counselors are and are not responsible for.

## Intelligence Tests and Multicultural Populations

Developers of current editions of the more commonly used intelligence tests have accounted for increased numbers of minority children in the schools. Test developers of the K-BIT, WISC-IV and SIT-R have made strides to include significant numbers of African American, Hispanic American and Asian American children in the normative samples for these tests (Whiston, 2000). However, that does not signify that these intelligence tests are completely applicable for use with minority populations.

Although most current editions of intelligence tests contain statistical information specific to most major ethnic groups, Cohen and Swerdlik (2002) believed these tests still show bias against some ethnic groups, such as African American and Hispanic American children, and children from families who classify as being lower social-economic status. These are some of the reasons intelligence tests are multidimensional (contain various subtests), as well as contributing to the rationale that placement in special education programs cannot be based on IQ scores alone.

Even though most of the items on intelligence tests have been designed to be culture-fair, i.e., without showing a positive or negative slant to a particular culture, none are culture-free (Whiston, 2000). Tests that are culture-free, i.e., not impacted by the culture of the person completing the test, are very difficult to find. For this reason, professional school counselors must try to find those brief tests that are as culture-fair as possible.

In addition, when possible, professional school counselors must make sure that a minority child's ethnicity or race does not negatively impact his scores on a comprehensive intelligence test, such as a K-ABC or a WISC-IV. Again, it is the responsibility of professional school counselors to familiarize themselves with the more popular IQ tests, even if they are not responsible for their administration, in order to best advocate for children, particularly children from diverse background, and their families.

## Summary/Conclusion

Professional school counselors are responsible for many aspects of a child's educational development. Being knowledgeable of intelligence tests is part of this responsibility. Professional school counselors must be familiar with IQ tests and how they impact children and families within their school. They also must be aware of the expectations their colleagues may have with regard to cognitive testing.

The only way that professional school counselors can begin to meet this aspect of their career-related duties is to acquire the knowledge and skills necessary to effectively use data from intelligence tests. In addition, professional school counselors also must be cognizant of where their responsibilities stop and where other professionals' responsibilities start. Together with the appropriate school personnel, professional school counselors can ensure that intelligence test data is used to help students, parents and teachers, in order to assist in providing the very best educational plan.

## References

American Counseling Association. (1995). *Code of ethics and standards of practice.* Alexandria, VA: Author.

Bowen, M. L., & Glenn, E. E. (1998). Counseling interventions for students who have mild disabilities. *Professional School Counseling, 2*, 16-25.

Cohen, R. J., & Swerdlik, M. E. (2002). *Psychological testing and assessment: An introduction to tests and measurement* (5th ed.). Boston: McGraw-Hill.

Esters, I. G., & Ittenbach, R. F. (1999). Contemporary theories and assessments of intelligence: A primer. *Professional School Counseling, 2*, 373-376.

Esters, I. G., Ittenbach, R. F., & Han, K. (1997). Today's IQ tests: Are they really better than their historical predecessors? *School Psychology Review, 26*, 211-224.

Kaufman, A. S., & Kaufman, N. L. (1983). *Kaufman Assessment Battery for Children: Interpretive manual.* Circle Pines, MN: American Guidance Service.

Riverside Publishing (2004). *The Stanford-Binet Intelligence Scale: 5th edition, technical manual.* Chicago: Riverside.

Wechsler, D. (2003). *Wechsler Intelligence Scale for Children - 4th Edition.* San Antonio, TX: The Psychological Corporation.

Whiston, S. (2000). *Principles and applications of assessment in counseling.* Stamford, CT: Wadsworth.

# Chapter 48

## A Practical Approach to Career Assessment in Schools

*Jerry Trusty & Spencer G. Niles*

### Preview

In this chapter, a practical framework for career assessment in schools is presented. The authors take a comprehensive, developmental perspective on career assessment. Various areas of career assessment are discussed, and priority areas for assessment at various developmental levels are presented. Formal and informal career assessments are included, and the use of career development portfolios is described. The authors take a particular focus on using existing student-data and employing assessment methods that are inexpensive and practical in terms of professional school counselors' budgets and time.

According to the American School Counselor Association (ASCA, 2002), the average ratio of professional school counselors to students in U.S. schools in 1999-2000 was 1 to 490. Traditional, individual-based career assessment for every student is not practical for most counselors. Professional school counselors' time and budgets are likely limited, and assessment materials can be expensive. Thus, in this chapter we offer effective methods of career assessment that are inexpensive in terms of time and money; and we offer a practical and flexible framework for assessment.

*Assessment* can be defined as the use of any formal or informal technique or instrument to collect data about a student (Niles & Harris-Bowlsbey, 2002). There are four basic reasons for using assessment to help students advance in their career development:

- Counselors can learn more about the needs of students.
- Counselors can learn more about the characteristics of students (e.g., interests, abilities, skills, values).
- Counselors can measure the progress of students in their career development.
- Students can learn more about themselves and increase their understanding of the career development process.

Career assessment is something that professional school counselors definitely need to do. The *National Standards for School Counseling Programs* and the related student competencies (Campbell & Dahir, 1997) speak directly to career assessment. When needs assessments are administered to students in schools, students generally indicate a high degree of need in career development areas. In fact, in the authors' experiences, career-related needs are consistently the highest priority for students as a whole.

Career assessments can be formal or informal. Formal assessments have psychometric evidence such as reliability and validity data and normative data appropriate for the group with which the measure will be used. Because formal assessments often have a standard way for interpreting scores, the results can be reviewed, at least initially, with a large group of students. Examples of formal career assessments include the *Strong Interest Inventory*, the *Differential*

*Aptitude Test Battery*, and the *Career Maturity Inventory*. Although data from informal assessments are more subjective, they can be informative—but in ways different from formal assessments. The results of informal assessments should not be used for comparisons of students, and informal assessments often have no standard way for interpreting the results. The results of informal assessments are often reviewed in a collaborative way between the counselor and an individual student or small group of students, and thus they are flexible. Examples of informal assessments include checklists, games, career fantasies, interviews, and card sorts (Niles & Harris-Bowlsbey, 2002). Both informal and formal career assessments provide important and useful information to the counselor and student, and informal and formal assessments often compliment one another.

The authors' career assessment framework stresses the use of ***career development portfolios*** for students. These portfolios—including collections of formal and informal assessment results, products resulting from guidance activities, samples of academic performance, and so forth—would follow students through elementary, middle, and high schools. At first thought, this might seem burdensome for professional school counselors. But these data are easy to collect; they are valuable data for students, parents, teachers, and counselors; they provide information across transitions from school to school; and these data can help counselors develop and evaluate their programs across students' early-childhood-through-twelfth-grade (EC-12) development.

Although career development and career assessment become more focused as students progress to middle and high school, an EC-12 approach to career development and assessment is needed (Starr, 1996). That is, professional school counselors need to take a longitudinal view on career development and career assessment. Experiences and assessments of elementary school students should articulate well with their middle and high school experiences and assessments. In reality, all career assessments are formative evaluations, and none of the assessment data we use should be conceptualized as static outcomes, including assessments in the twelfth grade.

Career development and career assessment should also be comprehensive. Although counselors use the categories of students' (a) academic development, (b) career development, and (c) personal-social development, all areas are conceptualized as career development because all are naturally related. To illustrate, Stone and Bradley (1994), in their school counseling text, noted that practically everything that elementary counselors do for students is for students' career development. For example, when elementary counselors deliver classroom guidance targeting study strategies or group counseling focused on social competency, these activities provide students with skills needed for their career development. Other authors and practitioners (e.g., Gysbers & Henderson, 2000; McDaniels & Gysbers, 1992) take a similar holistic and comprehensive view on career development across the lifespan.

In this chapter, a practical, flexible, developmental, and comprehensive approach to career assessment for elementary-school, middle-school, and high-school students is presented. Readers who are counselors may be tempted to only devote attention to sections below that pertain to the students they serve directly. The authors, however, assume and encourage an EC-12 perspective. Actually, the perspective is more a lifespan perspective. In the last section of this chapter, the authors present a qualitative, flexible method for career assessment at the middle-school and high-school levels.

## Career Assessment Areas

The Career Assessment Priority Matrix is presented below in Figure 1. This matrix does not include all possible areas of career assessment. However, it is fairly comprehensive, covering skills and abilities, self-perceptions, perceptions of the world of work, self-awareness, decision-making, goal-setting, and environments and perceptions of environments. In the columns on the right, the priority of the assessment area at the particular grade level is indicated (low, moderate, high). If the assessment area is not appropriate at the particular grade level, no priority level is indicated.

**Figure 1. Career assessment priority matrix.**

| Assessment Areas | Priority/Appropriateness at Grade Levels | | |
|---|---|---|---|
| | Elementary | Middle School | High School |
| academic achievement | high | high | high |
| career exploration behavior | high | moderate | moderate |
| perceptions of careers | high | high | moderate |
| self-perceptions | moderate | high | high |
| interpersonal skills | high | high | high |
| environments (e.g., families) | high | moderate | moderate |
| perceptions of environments (e.g., barriers, opportunities) | low | high | high |
| self-awareness: | | | |
| strengths and obstacles | low | high | high |
| interests | | high | high |
| values | | moderate | high |
| career awareness | | moderate | high |
| decision-making | | moderate | high |
| goal setting | | moderate | high |
| ability self-estimates | | moderate | high |

*Academic Achievement*

Of the above areas in the matrix, the first, academic achievement, is very important from the elementary level onward. Researchers have found that early academic achievement has long-lasting effects on students' career development. For example, school grades, even in the early elementary school years, are strongly related to whether students complete high school or not (Barrington & Hendricks, 1989); and achievement test scores in middle school strongly predict what postsecondary majors students choose (Trusty, Robinson, Plata, & Ng, 2000) and how much postsecondary education they pursue (Trusty, in press). Achievement in middle school is clearly the result of what students learned in elementary school.

Professional school counselors generally have access to achievement data at the elementary, middle, and secondary levels. The criterion-referenced, basic-skills mastery tests now required in several states supply limited information because of their nature. Information from these instruments will be less useful for students who are achieving at moderate or high levels. Group-administered, formal ability assessments are used in many schools to determine which students should be tested further for gifted or enrichment programs (e.g., *Otis-Lennon School Abilities Test, Cognitive Abilities Test*), and these supply some information. However, the best sources of achievement information are generally (a) scores on some national, standardized, norm-referenced comprehensive achievement instrument (e.g., *Iowa Test of Basic Skills, Stanford Achievement Test*); and (b) school grades and other in-school performance criteria. Score reports on standardized achievement instruments generally identify degrees of competence and obstacles in several specific academic areas. School grades are often inconsistent across schools and across teachers, but they may hold valuable information for identifying students' strengths and obstacles. Local performance criteria and students' performance products might become part of the career development portfolio that follows students through schools. When counselors, teachers, parents, and students have access to comprehensive data regarding students' achievement, all people involved in students' education are better prepared to make decisions (e.g., special programs, appropriate courses).

In high school, an important gauge of achievement is the academic rigor of courses completed by students. In a large national study, Adelman (1999) reported that U.S. college students who completed more academically intensive coursework in high school were much more likely to graduate from college. The positive effects of rigorous high-school coursework on degree completion were evident for all major U.S. racial-ethnic groups. With regard to particular courses, completing advanced high-school math courses had a particularly strong influence on college success. Students' grades in these rigorous courses mattered little. Academic achievement is also related to most other aspects of career development and career assessment. For example, environments, and especially parents, have a strong influence on achievement.

*Career Exploration Behavior*

The elementary school years should be a time of open exploration of careers. Career-related fantasy should be encouraged. As Herr and Cramer (1996) maintained, the elementary-school years are not a time in which children are encouraged to narrow their career options, but a time when they are encouraged to broaden their perspectives. Across the elementary grades, the range of careers familiar to students should grow exponentially. Assessment of exploratory behavior might be reflected in students' knowledge of various careers and career areas, their fantasy or enthusiasm reflected in products they create, or in the career-related stories they tell or understand. At the middle- and high-school levels, career exploration may be needed for specific students, but as students develop they generally become more focused on particular careers or career areas.

*Perceptions of Careers*

Students' exploratory behavior and perceptions of careers are closely related. Students often form perceptions of careers early. For example, students often form ideas about occupational prestige and gender roles when they are in elementary school. At the elementary level, students should begin learning various educational opportunities, and in a general way, begin connecting educational tasks to careers. Students should also begin connecting occupations and educational and training requirements. In middle and high school, and even into college, students are susceptible to over-generalized or otherwise faulty perceptions of careers. At the more advanced educational levels, perceptions of careers are generally conceptualized as *career awareness*, an area discussed later in this chapter.

One critical area is students' perceptions based on gender roles. Students develop ideas about the association between genders and careers very early (Helwig, 1998). Additionally, gender seems to be a primal basis for eliminating and choosing careers (Gottfredson, 1981); and students may limit their ranges of desired occupations very early in their lives. Therefore, assessments and activities focused on gender stereotyping of careers are appropriate at the elementary level and onward. And efforts should focus on both girls and boys. Over the last several years, girls and women have become less gender-stereotypical in their career aspirations and postsecondary educational choices, whereas boys and men have remained relatively gender-traditional in their aspirations and choices (Helwig, 1998; Trusty et al., 2000). The issue of traditional versus non-traditional gender roles is often political and controversial, and likely cultural. However, a system that functions best for individuals and society as a whole is one that utilizes all its talent and potential effectively. It seems that if this perspective is taken by professional school counselors, their work with students on gender roles would be less controversial for parents, teachers, school administrators, and communities. Professional school counselors should always consider the caveat that in traditional cultures, gender roles may be highly delineated.

Students' perceptions of careers and occupations can be assessed readily simply by having them indicate if they perceive particular careers or occupations positively, negatively, or neutrally. Also, having students relate the positive, negative, and neutral specific aspects of careers would provide more data on their perceptions. Students' ability to connect occupations, tasks, and education/training requirements is also easily assessed in classroom guidance format.

*Self-Perceptions*

A fairly high level of cognitive development is required for young people to reflect on themselves, reflect on the world of work, and match self and work. This requires abstract, second-order thinking, which is associated with the *formal operations* level of cognitive development, a level that is generally reached in adolescence (Muus, 1996). However, children do develop self-perceptions and self-awareness—at a more concrete level—through the elementary years (Herr & Cramer, 1996). In the elementary grades, students begin to make concrete connections between their performance and their self-perceptions, and these early self-perceptions are the foundation for later, more complex and specific self-perceptions, career-related values, and ability self-estimates, which in turn are the bases for choices.

In recent years, counselors and researchers have come to focus on students' self-competence and self-confidence in their academic skills and other career-related areas of performance. Social self-perceptions are also important to young people's learning and functioning. There are various instruments that measure either general self-perceptions (e.g., self-concept, self-esteem) or specific self-perceptions (e.g., self-efficacy for specific tasks, domain-specific self-esteem or self-competence). Self-perceptions could also be assessed in a less formal manner. For example, a counselor might ask an eighth-grader, "On a scale of 1 to 10, with 10 being the best, how are you at making things with your hands?" Special types of self-perceptions (career self-awareness, interests, values, ability self-estimates) become more important in middle and high school, and are discussed later in this chapter.

*Interpersonal Skills*

Children learn and refine cooperation and teamwork skills in elementary school, and according to the ASCA student competencies (Campbell & Dahir, 1997), these are career development skills. In fact, it is usually advantageous for professional school counselors to categorize interpersonal skills as career development skills. In the first authors' experience as a professional school counselor in a middle school, a teacher once stated, "These kids don't need interpersonal skills, they need academic skills." Obviously, the teacher was not making the connections between interpersonal skills and education and work, and perhaps the teacher would have been more cooperative himself if he had. The message of this interchange was that interpersonal-skills and social-skills activities should be labeled as *career skills activities*.

Cooperative skills and teamwork skills can be assessed best through observations by teachers and counselors. A brief rating of students' strengths and obstacles would provide important data in students' career-development portfolios. Often, teamwork and interpersonal skills receive more attention in elementary and middle schools. The authors' contention is that interpersonal skills for high school students are often ignored, and that interpersonal skills are necessary for advanced levels of career development. For example, interpersonal skills are actually the major part of job-interviewing or college-interviewing; and interpersonal skills are often the major contributor to occupational advancement.

*Environments*

Students' environments have powerful influences on their career development. Students in communities of lower socioeconomic status are likely limited in career-related resources. For example, youth clubs and organizations may not be available in particular communities; rural or otherwise isolated areas may be limited in career options; parents may not have access to professionals or extended family with knowledge of particular careers; mentors may not be available for children; or schools may not have budgets sufficient for extracurricular activities.

The most influential environmental force is students' parents. The educational goal transmission process in families is very strong (Trusty & Pirtle, 1998). That is, the educational goals that parents hold for their children correspond highly to the goals that children hold for themselves. Parents want to help their children, and children rely on parents for career development help. In addition to parents' expectations for their children, parents' involvement in their children's education also carries strong influence. Parents' school-based involvement (e.g., involvement in parent-teacher organizations) carries some positive influence, but the major influence is from parents' home-based involvement. Home-based involvement includes (a) parents' regular communication with children regarding school and career, and (b) parents' support of their children's educational and career development. The influences of parental involvement carry into adulthood (Trusty, 1998).

Data on environments can be assessed relatively easily. Teachers and professional school counselors, after working with students for a few months, will have a good idea of the resources, supports, and difficulties in elementary school children's environments. Some environmental characteristics are obvious, whereas others are not obvious. For example, if a child is not receiving adequate physical care, problems are easily recognized. However, the emotional climate in families is not often readily recognized. Data on students' environments would identify opportunities and barriers to career development, and should provide professional school counselors with important contextual information.

*Perceptions of Environments*

At the middle-school level and beyond, young people begin to have some comparative gauge of the positive and negative influences from their environments. In fact, middle-school students' perceptions of parents' home-based involvement are more reliable than parents' reports of their involvement. Parents tend to positively bias reports of their own involvement (Trusty, 1996). Perceptions of environments have often been conceptualized as barriers and opportunities. Barriers are frequently described as *real barriers* and *perceived barriers*. If barriers to career development are perceived by a student as real, then barriers are real for that student; and barriers function to block the student's development, although other people may not perceive the barrier to be an actual barrier. Students' perceived barriers and opportunities can easily be assessed. Needs assessments administered to high school students often reveal perceived barriers. Also, the classroom guidance session is an appropriate format for assessing barriers and opportunities, although students may want to keep private their perceptions of some environmental barriers. Counselors should be aware that lack of information (e.g., financial aid information for postsecondary education or training) causes students to perceive barriers.

*Self-Awareness: Strengths and Obstacles, Interests, Values*

In middle school, students are forced to make decisions about the high school program they will pursue. These decisions are coming earlier and earlier in middle schools. High schools are requiring more and more credits for graduation; more students are taking high-school credit courses in middle school; and decisions are pushed deeper into the middle school years. For example, in many school systems, students and parents must decide during the sixth-grade if students will take pre-algebra in the seventh-grade so they can take high-school Algebra I in the eighth-grade so they can take Calculus in the twelfth-grade. In the context of increased credits for graduation and an increasingly prescriptive high-school curriculum required by colleges and universities, there is little flexibility once students have begun a particular high-school program track. Add to this mixture the cognitive developmental level of middle school students (concrete operations) and the psychosocial developmental crisis of students (identity vs. role confusion—if prior development was optimal), and it is clear that students are not ready for these decisions. However, this is the current reality in most schools.

Students' awareness of their own strengths and obstacles, interests and preferences, and values is necessary for effective decision-making and goal-setting. The correspondence of skills and abilities, interests, and values is salient for decision-making and goals. It is important to remember that students and assessments of students are not static. For example, a student may lack skill and interest in mechanics because the student has not had learning experiences associated with mechanics. The interest inventory score and mechanical aptitude score are low because of lack of learning opportunity. Therefore, scores should be a starting point for new learning experiences, and not a static judgment of the young person's characteristics.

Aptitudes, interests, and values can be measured fairly quickly with a battery like the COPS System (the COPS-interests, CAPS-abilities, and COPES-values), CDM System, or with other instruments. Many commercial vendors of instruments are offering aptitude, interests, and values assessments in an online format, and sometimes the online versions are less expensive than the printed versions. Computer Assisted Career Guidance Systems (e.g., DISCOVER, SIGI+, CHOICES) also include assessments of interests and values, and may incorporate aptitude scores from other instruments. Some commercial instruments and computer programs have versions specific to middle-school students. With regard to interest inventories, the *Self-Directed Search* and the *Vocational Preference Inventory* are relatively inexpensive.

However, the school or counseling program may not have budgets to cover commercial instruments or computer programs. There are alternatives. For example, *card sorts* are inexpensive and can be used in a group format for prioritizing career-related interests and values. The *Guide for Occupational Exploration* (GOE), published by the U.S. Department of Labor, is fairly inexpensive. Work values exercises, along with other activities, are included in the book, and these may be copied and used in a classroom guidance format with middle-school or high-school students. There are additional resources that are free on the Internet, through U.S. government websites, state sites, and university sites (e.g., http://stats.bls.gov/oco/home.htm, http://online.onetcenter.org/). Professional school counselors are encouraged to search the Internet for usable resources. Some instruments available through the Internet may not have the psychometric strength of some published, commercially available instruments; but several non-commercial instruments would likely be very useful for professional school counselors and their students. Counselors could access the website http://www.freeteachingaids.com/. The *Educators Guide to Free Guidance Materials*, among several other guides to free resources, may be accessed at this site.

*Career Awareness*

If students have access to the Internet, there are many resources that can be used for occupational, educational, and leisure information. For example, the *Occupational Outlook Handbook* is accessible through the Internet, along with many other government materials. Various national associations and societies representing numerous fields also have useful websites. Commercial materials (e.g., occupational card files, books) are available from vendors. However, printed materials on occupations become out-of-date quickly, and are often a substantial investment.

Professional school counselors' assessments of students' career awareness might be connected to guidance activities aimed at career awareness; or degrees of awareness might be evidenced through products students produce. Assessments might be as simple as recording students' frequencies of accessing materials. Assessment may also include assignments connected to regular classes. For example, students in mathematics classes could be required to research surveyors' use of global positioning system (GPS) technology.

*Decision-Making*

It is fortunate that most decisions required of middle-school students are not highly specific (an exception might be decisions on what foreign language to take). However, several general educational decisions do come in middle school, and more specific decisions (e.g., part-time work, postsecondary education or work) are rapidly approaching. What is important for students in middle school and high school is that they learn decision-making models and apply models to the decision-making process (McDaniels & Gysbers, 1992). Students then have a template for decision-making throughout their career development. It is difficult for professional school counselors to assess the wisdom of students' decisions. However, counselors can and should assess if students have learned and applied decision-making models. These data might simply be represented by a check on a checklist (e.g., student applied the decision-making model to the decision process). Similar to other data, these data are included in students' career development portfolios.

*Goal-Setting*

Decision-making and goal-setting are closely related. When students make decisions, they are often deciding on goals. Setting goals comes easy for some students, but is difficult for others. Some students experience high levels of ambiguity and discomfort when engaging in goal-setting tasks. For some, there is a real fear to decide. Assessing if students have goals is relatively easy. An assessment of the clarity, consistency, and detail in long-term, intermediate, and short-term goals is straightforward. Assessing how realistic and appropriate those goals are is more difficult, and requires counselors to make judgments regarding the consistency among students' goals, potential, previous behavior, personality, and so forth.

*Ability Self-Estimates*

Ability self-estimates are a special type of self-perception. They relate strongly to students' learning experiences, achievement, and choices. In fact, ability self-estimates are generally a better predictor of career choices than scores on aptitude instruments (Prediger, 1999). This is good news for professional school counselors because ability self-estimates are easy to assess quickly. Also, ability self-estimates can target work-relevant abilities that are not generally assessed in aptitude or achievement tests. The typical format for ability self-estimates is having students rate, on a scale of 5 or 10 degrees, their abilities in 10 or 15 areas. For example, professional school counselors could easily construct assessments with which students estimate their abilities in some of the following areas:

| | | |
|---|---|---|
| Mathematics | Writing | Reading |
| Organization | Teamwork | Selling things |
| Cooking | Carpentry | Growing things |
| Mechanics | Sewing | Electronics |

Generally, each listed area is accompanied by a two- or three-sentence description of the tasks associated with the area. This list is by no means exhaustive, and students could supply ability self-estimates not included in a list but deemed important to them. Professional school counselors could easily tailor assessments to students in their schools. Ability self-estimates will be most accurate for students at more advanced levels (e.g., later high school grades and beyond), and should be relied upon more at these higher levels. ACT has an *Inventory of Work-Relevant Abilities* (IWRA) available commercially.

Another format for ability self-estimates is to have students do comparisons of their abilities. For example, students are asked their level of agreement with statements like, "Math is one of my best subjects." Using a national sample of high school students, Trusty and Ng (2000) found that tenth-graders' comparative perceptions of math and English as best subjects were highly predictive of types of college majors chosen after high school. These intra-individual, comparative self-perceptions seem to guide young people's choices, and they are included in the qualitative career assessment structure presented below.

## Qualitative, Group-Format Career Assessment

The *Life Career Assessment* (LCA) (McDaniels & Gysbers, 1992) is a qualitative form of career assessment based on Adlerian theory. It is generally used in an individual-counseling setting. Because of high student-to-counselor ratios in schools, we adapted the LCA to a classroom guidance format. The authors have found adaptations of the LCA to be very effective, providing rich data on adolescents' career development. It is effective for middle-school students, but more useful for high-school students. The data provide professional school counselors with a deeper understanding of students, and provide students with a deeper understanding of themselves. The LCA is a sequence of items for assessing students' experiences and perceptions. In individual counseling, these questions are intermixed with counselors' reflections and empathy responses. In a classroom guidance format, these questions are presented to students on paper, and students write their responses. Students' responses then go into students' career development portfolios. When professional school counselors meet with students for individual counseling or individual planning, professional school counselors use the data to facilitate students in self-awareness and career awareness, career planning, decision making, goal setting, and so forth. An outline for the Group-Format LCA is presented below in Table 1.

## Summary/Conclusion

A flexible, general, EC-12 framework for career assessment by professional school counselors has been presented here. Professional school counselors are encouraged to use information in this chapter to tailor assessment plans and methods to meet the needs of students in their particular schools. When using any type of assessment, professional school counselors must be sure that they have taken the necessary steps to use assessments in an ethical way. The *Code of Fair Testing Practices* lists six specific ways in which professional school counselors need to prepare for using assessment instruments. Specifically, professional school counselors must:

1. Have a good base of general knowledge about assessment and psychometrics.
2. Have detailed knowledge about the specific instruments they use.
3. Know how to prepare students for taking assessments.
4. Administer instruments properly and under the appropriate conditions.
5. Interpret assessment results properly.
6. Follow through with students appropriately after the assessment has been conducted.

**Table 1. Outline for Group-Format Life Career Assessment**

- I. Educational Experiences
  - A. General appraisal of your educational experiences
    1. dislikes
    2. likes
  - B. Particular subjects/classes
    1. dislikes
    2. likes
    3. your best subject(s)
  - C. Teacher characteristics
    1. dislikes
    2. likes
    3. your favorite teacher
  - D. Learning setting preferences
    1. independent versus collaborative learning
    2. experiential versus didactic learning
    3. study style
    4. memorable learning experiences within and outside school

- II. Work Experiences
  - A. Last job
    1. dislikes
    2. likes
  - B. Job supervisor/supervision style
    1. dislikes
    2. likes
  - C. Repeat for previous jobs

- III. Leisure
  - A. Describe weekend, week-day, evening activities
  - B. Fun and relaxation
  - C. Friends and social life

- IV. Strengths and Obstacles
  - A. Three main obstacles
  - B. Three main personal (intrinsic) strengths
  - C. People who are resources for you

---

Effective assessment does not necessarily require a large budget, but it does require careful and systematic planning and organization. Systematic counseling program development involves assessing students' needs, developing measurable objectives/competencies for students, and designing programs around objectives for meeting the needs of all students. If professional school counselors are engaged in effective program development, assessment and evaluation of students' career development comes naturally and easily, and use of career assessment portfolios for students comes naturally and easily.

## References

Adelman, C. (1999). *Answers in the tool box: Academic intensity, attendance patterns, and bachelor's degree attainment.* U.S. Department of Education, Office of Educational Research and Improvement. Retrieved June 8, 2002, from http://www.ed.gov/pubs/Toolbox/Title.html

American School Counselor Association. (2002). *State-by-state student-to-counselor ratio (1999-2000).* Retrieved June 4, 2002, from http://www.schoolcounselor.org/library/ratio.jpg

Barrington, B. L., & Hendricks, B. H. (1989). Differentiating characteristics of high school graduates, dropouts, and nongraduates. *Journal of Educational Research, 82,* 309-319.

Campbell, C. A., & Dahir, C. A. (1997). *The national standards for school counseling programs.* Alexandria, VA: American School Counselor Association.

Gottfredson, L. S. (1981). Circumscription and compromise: A developmental theory of occupational aspirations. *Journal of Counseling Psychology, 28,* 545-579.

Gysbers, N. C., & Henderson, P. (2000). *Developing and managing your school guidance program* (3rd ed.). Alexandria, VA: American Counseling Association.

Helwig, A. A. (1998). Gender-role stereotyping: Testing theory with a longitudinal sample. *Sex Roles, 38,* 403-423.

Herr, E. L., & Cramer, S. H. (1996). *Career guidance and counseling through the life span: Systematic approaches* (5th ed.). New York: Harper Collins.

McDaniels, C., & Gysbers, N. C. (1992). *Counseling for career development: Theories, resources, and practice.* San Francisco: Jossey-Bass.

Muuss, R. E. (1996). *Theories of adolescence* (6th ed.). New York: McGraw-Hill.

Niles, S. G., & Harris-Bowlsbey, J. (2002). *Career development interventions in the 21st century.* Columbus, OH: Merrill/ Prentice-Hall.

Prediger, D. J. (1999). Basic structure of work-relevant abilities. *Journal of Counseling Psychology, 46,* 173-184.

Starr, M. F. (1996). Comprehensive guidance and systematic educational and career planning: Why a K-12 approach? *Journal of Career Development, 23,* 9-22.

Stone, L. A., & Bradley, F. O. (1994). *Foundations of elementary and middle school counseling.* White Plains, NY: Longman.

Trusty, J. (1996). Relationship of parental involvement in teens' career development to teens' attitudes, perceptions, and behavior. *Journal of Research and Development in Education, 30,* 317-323.

Trusty, J. (1998). Family influences on educational expectations of late adolescents. *Journal of Educational Research, 91,* 260-270.

Trusty, J. (in press). African Americans' educational expectations: Longitudinal causal models for women and men. *Journal of Counseling & Development.*

Trusty, J., & Ng, K. (2000). Longitudinal effects of achievement perceptions on choice of post-secondary major. *Journal of Vocational Behavior, 57,* 123-135.

Trusty, J., & Pirtle, T. (1998). Parents' transmission of educational goals to their adolescent children. *Journal of Research and Development in Education, 32,* 53-65.

Trusty, J., Robinson, C., Plata, M., & Ng, K. (2000). Effects of gender, SES, and early academic performance on post-secondary educational choice. *Journal of Counseling & Development, 76,* 463-472.

# Chapter 49

## A Selective Overview of Personality and Its Assessment

*Ralph L. Piedmont*

### Preview

This chapter presents an overview of what personality is and summarizes this concept from the perspective of the psychoanalytic and trait schools. Strengths and weaknesses of the two schools are outlined and relevant measurement issues are discussed. The practical value of personality theory for counselors is highlighted.

Perhaps one of the most important concepts we have for understanding people is that of "personality." However, as a term with widespread colloquial use, it has lost some of its professional precision. The purpose of this chapter is to provide some clarity as to how this term is used in the social sciences. This will include a basic definition of what personality is as well as providing a synopsis of two major schools of thought in the area. Also, this chapter will discuss some of the measurement issues that coincide with these different theoretical schools. It is hoped that this chapter will give readers a general sense of the term's value as well as a framework for thinking critically about people: who they are, how they got here, and where they seem to be going.

*Personality: A Definition*

The term "personality" is certainly applied often. Pets are frequently said to have personality. Some people seem to lack this important characteristic, while others just seem to "ooze" personality. Personality is often thought of as the ultimate definition of who each of us is as a person, but many believe that it is always changing. Such varied connotations underscore just how diffuse our understanding of the term really is. We all know personality when we see it, but it may be hard to put our fingers on what exactly we mean by "it." As such, a basic definition is in order.

Personality can be defined as the intrinsic, adaptive organization of the individual that is stable over time and consistent across situations (Piedmont, 1998). There are four important points to this definition. First, personality represents some structured system by which individuals organize themselves and orient to the world around them. This system is clearly located *within* the person and is not imposed by the environment. Second, personality is an adaptive structure, which means that it enables us to manage effectively the many competing, often conflicting, demands we encounter from both within ourselves and from the environment. As such, we should not think about personality as being "good" or "bad." It is what it is - a systematic way of optimizing our ability to survive and thrive in the world in which we live. Rather, the question we need to ask occurs when people wish to change their environments, will their personalities work as well in the new context as they did in the original? Third, personality is stable over time. This means that there is something about who we are and what we are that remains consistent throughout our lives. There is more to say about personality change, but for now we can say that despite all the "change" we may have experienced over our lifetimes, there is some thread that seems to tie together all our developmental experiences around consistent themes. There is something about who we were as children or adolescents that lingers with us today. Finally, personality is consistent from one situation to another. Although specific behaviors may change from one context to another, our view of the world and the personal goals we are pursuing remain essentially unchanged.

This definition should not be interpreted as saying that the environment does not have anything to do with how our personality develops. Culture, context, and situation all have an influence on our development and how we may express our personality. But there does lie within us some kind of psychological "stuff" that provides our basic needs, shapes how we perceive and interpret our external world, and selects the goals we ultimately pursue in our lives. Nor should this definition be construed as arguing that personality is a static quality. To the contrary, personality is a dynamic structure. It is always responding to the demands that develop from both within us and from the world around us. Adaptation is an active process in which we continually contour ourselves to the changing features of our environment. Further, there is a developmental aspect to personality. Just as we are not born physically mature, so, too, personality is something that begins in a simple form and becomes progressively more sophisticated as we age. These changes do follow an orderly and lawful path, so that when one looks back over life, there can be seen patterns in behavior that lend a sense of continuity to one's life.

With this basic definition in mind, it should be evident that "personality" is a scientific construct that helps to organize the many diverse, and sometimes conflicting, behaviors and feelings of people into a more organized system that both promotes understanding and increases predictiveness. We now turn to a brief overview of two major schools of thought concerning how personality is defined and understood. These major schools are the Psychoanalytic and Trait perspectives. Of course there are many other theoretical orientations, but these two were selected for three reasons: 1) these two approaches represent popular perspectives on personality and assessment; 2) they are perhaps maximally different from each other; and 3) they are particularly relevant to counseling professionals, who are most likely to encounter both of these perspectives in their own work. For those interested in learning more about personality theories from other perspectives as well as to learn more details about the theories presented here, the reader is referred to more specific texts on the topic (e.g., Cloninger, 2000; Monte, 1998).

## The Psychoanalytic Perspective

The first person to provide a comprehensive, scientific description of personality was Sigmund Freud (1916; 1923; 1924). Freud is perhaps the best known of all the personality theorists. Although originally formulated over a century ago, Freud's ideas continue to have an impact on how we think about people today. Freud's theory was revolutionary for his time, and made three great contributions to our understanding of people. First was his notion of the *unconscious*. The unconscious represents a region of our psychological world that is outside of our immediate sense of awareness and control. Despite its absence from our daily sense of experiencing, the unconscious has a direct and powerful impact on our behavior. For Freud, all of our motivations for life come from the unconscious regions of our mind. Freud likened the human personality to an iceberg. Just as most of the ice in the berg is located under water, most of the important aspects of who we are reside in the unconscious. Thus, for Freud, it is not what our conscious minds say that is important, rather it is what emerges from the dark recesses of our unconscious that is valuable.

The second great insight that Freud provided was the notion of *childhood sexuality*. For centuries, children were seen as just miniature adults, but without the same passions and motivations that characterize adult life. There was very little recognition that children had their own psychological needs. Freud pointed out that children are very sensual creatures. Having a limited cognitive capacity, children rely more on their feelings and emotions to guide them through their interactions with the world. The most important instinct is the one defined by the pleasure/pain continuum. Children always seek to find gratification for their pleasure needs (e.g., to be fed, held, relieved, comforted) and to reduce the tensions associated with unfulfilled desires. Whether or not these needs to avoid pain and to obtain pleasure are gratified has important implications for how the child's personality will develop.

The third contribution that Freud made was the idea of *psychic determinism*. This is the belief that there is a reason for every action a person performs. Just as in nature there is a reason for everything, so, too, in our inner minds there is a logic and consistency to what we do. That logic, especially of the unconscious mind, may not always appear as rational, but there are essential patterns and meanings to things in the inner world that once known, can unlock our understanding of the person. These three ideas were revolutionary for their time and helped to significantly stretch our understandings of how the mind works. These concepts also define how Freud looked at people, as organic machines following an innate set of commands in an effort to find security and comfort. To understand psychoanalysis, there are two basic ideas to grasp: the structure of the mind and the processes by which it operates.

*The Structure and Process of Psychoanalysis*

*Psychoanalytic model of the mind.* Every personality theory posits an underlying structure to personality. For psychoanalysis, there is a tripartite structure that describes our inner world. The first structure is called the *id*. This is the basic element of personality and is the source of all our psychic energies and motivations (which Freud referred to as instincts). The id contains the basic impulses that drive our behavior. There is no logic or sense of order to the id. It runs on what Freud termed *primary process energy*. This is our basic, instinctual need to attain pleasure and to avoid pain. The second structure is the *ego*. The ego represents our more conscious processes, it embodies the logic and order of conscious thought and operates on what is termed *secondary process energy*. The function of the ego is to gratify the needs of our psychic system in ways that are appropriate and respectful of environmental realities. Two qualities of a healthy ego are its abilities to tolerate tension (go without meeting or satisfying our needs) and synthesize diverse needs into a more unified set of goal strivings. The third structure is termed the *superego*. The superego contains our moral values or conscience. The superego, like the id, is very demanding and requires an individual to provide immediate gratification of its needs. In the case of the superego, it demands that the person live up to very high levels of virtuous behavior.

*The process of personality*. What is of central interest to psychoanalysts is the dynamic way each of these three structures relate to one another. Each part of the mind has its own needs and drives. Both the id and the superego are very demanding and require instant gratification. The ego has the arduous task of working hard to gratify those needs, along with its own, in the context of specific environmental demands. There is no doubt that this system generates much conflict and tension. However, it is in the process of successfully resolving these tensions/conflicts that one's personality develops and creatively engages the external world. For example, the id always wants to have immediate sensual satisfaction, in this case let us say that it wants to eat. You are shopping at the supermarket and the id is demanding food *NOW*. The ego must provide it because not satisfying an instinctual need only makes it grow stronger. To satisfy the id, the ego could just reach out and take that bag of potato chips sitting on the supermarket shelf and start eating. However, the superego realizes that stealing is morally wrong—someone has to pay for those potato chips first. The superego chastises severely, creating more demands on the ego. The environment poses its own challenges: the security guard will arrest you if you do not pay for the chips. So, the id has to wait (which it does not like to do), and the longer it has to wait, the more demanding it becomes. The ego has to devise clever and effective strategies for managing all these conflicting desires. This is where *defense mechanisms* come in.

Defense mechanisms are ego-based methods individuals use to help gratify the basic instinctual desires of the id. Defense mechanisms allow the ego to gratify needs either directly (through consuming some object that provides satisfaction) or indirectly (through the use of imagery, ideas, or other substitutes to "fool" the id or superego into thinking that we have gratified the need). For example, say we are back walking through the supermarket and the hunger demands begin. You know this is not the time or place for eating. What does the ego do? Well, it reaches into the pocket and pulls out a piece of gum to chew on. It is not food that fills the belly, but it could help the id believe that it is eating something, thus partially gratifying the instinct. This takes some pressure off the ego. Also, it is not morally wrong to eat gum, so the superego remains contented, and more tension is reduced (keep in mind that reducing tension is very pleasurable). If there is no gum, perhaps putting a pencil in the mouth, or maybe drinking a glass of water will work. All of these behaviors are substitute actions that help defend the ego against the ranting id's need for food. Then, once we have bought the chips and are outside in the car, we reach in and take a big handful of those salty, tasty taters; ultimate satisfaction is attained! In each instance, the ego has worked to reduce the conflicting needs of the psychic world in ways that are appropriate and effective.

In understanding a person, a psychoanalyst wishes to know how the individual copes with the stresses and conflicts associated with instinct gratification. What types of defense mechanisms are used? There are all different kinds, ranging from very simple or childish (e.g., *repression*, where you just unconsciously deny the existence of something), to more sophisticated techniques, like *sublimation*. With sublimation, a basic primitive impulse is transformed into a more mature, sophisticated impulse that is socially accepted and valued. For example, a sadistic need to cut and destroy animals gets turned into a desire to become a surgeon. The former, something scorned and infantile, gets changed into a noble urge to want to help others in pain. For Freud there is not much difference between the little boy who likes to pull the wings off of flies and the surgeon who operates on people in order to manipulate various body parts. Sublimation helps us to live effectively in social groupings by transforming baser instincts into urges that promote a greater social interest. Other defense mechanisms include displacement, projection, reaction formation, isolation, and rationalization.

*Measuring the Psychoanalytic Personality*

How does one go about measuring these levels of conflict and types of defense mechanisms? How does one gain access to a person's unconscious? To accomplish this, psychoanalysts use *projective testing*. A projective test is based on the principle of psychic determinism; that everything we do bears our characteristic stamp. If we put a person in an unstructured situation and ask that she make sense of this chaos, anything that the person creates will be an expression of her own internal, unconscious view of the world.

Perhaps the most well known projective test is the *Rorschach Inkblot Test*. Here, individuals are presented with essentially meaningless inkblots. The designs are basically random but respondents are asked to create a meaningful picture. The only way for them to make sense of this nonsense stimulus is to project some of their own inner organization onto it; respondents provide their own frame of reference for the interpretation. Therefore, when we look at the response, it tells us something about how the respondents structure their psychological worlds. People are not aware that they are projecting something of themselves onto the inkblot. But to the skilled interpreter, the Rorshach is like an x-ray of the personality revealing the details of the unconscious domain. However, to interpret those responses requires an extensive amount of training and experience. The language of the mind, from the psychoanalytic perspective, is quite sophisticated and complex. It is a world of symbols and disguised meanings that do not always conform to the rules of logic adhered to in our conscious reality.

There are a number of different projective tests, and what characterizes most of them is their unstructured, fluid format. Most of these tests allow an individual to make as many or few responses as he or she wishes. There are also no right or wrong answers, and respondents are free to give any response they feel. The aim of this class of measures is to make plain the many hidden wishes residing in the unconscious. Another popular projective test is the *Thematic Apperception Test* (TAT). Here individuals are given a picture of some event and asked to relate what led up to the situation pictured, what is happening now, and what the outcome will be. Again, responses are evaluated for emotional conflicts and how they are handled by the person. *The House-Tree-Person Test* (HTP) is another commonly used projective technique. Here, a person (usually a child) is asked to draw a picture of a person, a house, and a tree. The drawing is evaluated for the size of the respective elements, their location on the page, and the details that are present (or absent; e.g., the person has no hands, the house has no door). These details are sometimes referred to as emotional indicators. Whether or not they are present says much about the emotional world of the artist (e.g., figures that do not have hands may indicate the presence of depression). Again, it requires much training and experience to interpret this test. Nonetheless, any situation that is unstructured and allows a person to create something can be considered a projective test. Interpreting what is created is believed to reveal important aspects of a person's unconscious world.

*Strengths and Weaknesses of Psychoanalytic Personality Theory*

The value of psychoanalysis is that it is a quite comprehensive theory that explains virtually everything about people. It offers insights that link together in meaningful ways behaviors and actions that on the surface may appear contradictory and counterproductive. The theory can highlight the clever and creative ways individuals find to cope with the worlds they live in. However, the theory is quite complex and requires much study to master.

That the psychoanalytic orientation is mostly clinically oriented is both a strength and a weakness. Its focus on conflict and primitive instincts provides a rich fabric for weaving an understanding of a person's adaptive struggles with reality. This provides a clear point of departure for developing and implementing interventions. However, these interpretations usually stress personal weaknesses and inadequacies of the individual. Truly mature and healthy functioning is experienced by only a lucky few. Thus, the theory is lacking in its ability to document true strengths.

It also makes some assumptions about men and women that may be considered objectionable today. In fact, some see the theory as being a product of late Victorian Age thinking. The plain fact of the matter is that the entire theory developed out of the observations of one man, and usually in response to experiences with only a single patient. Although important and insightful, it is not clear whether all of these insights are valid and generalizable to today. Few aspects of psychoanalysis are amenable to true scientific testing, and therefore there are few data available to speak about the ultimate utility of the theory. Yet despite very little supporting empirical data, psychoanalysis is still one of the dominant scientific theories in the field today.

## The Trait Approach

The Trait Approach to personality takes a very different perspective to understanding the individual. Unlike psychoanalytic constructs, traits are empirically developed variables. Using sophisticated statistical analyses, trait researchers identify behaviors, attitudes, and beliefs that appear to covary with one another. In other words, seemingly diverse behaviors are identified that are observed to occur together frequently. A trait is then developed to explain or define why these various behaviors and attitudes cluster together. For example, we may notice that people who are very talkative also tend to be outgoing and sociable, like going to parties and being the center of attention. They also seem to be very "perky" and energetic, and they can also be very welcoming and approachable. In order to understand why these different behaviors go together, we may develop the trait of *extraversion*. Extraversion is a psychological construct that refers to an innate tendency of people to orient themselves to the actions and activities of the outer world of people and events. Behaviors such as time spent talking on the telephone, enjoying the presence of other people, feeling upbeat and positive can all be linked together because they all reflect this underlying characteristic of extraversion.

Costa and McCrae (1990, p. 23) have defined traits as "dimensions of individual differences in tendencies to show consistent patterns of thoughts, feelings, and actions." There are two points of interest in this definition. First, traits are dimensions, empirically constructed labels that help us organize human behavior along meaningful lines. Second, traits are referred to as individual differences, qualities that describe people and upon which people vary in terms of how much they possess. Thus, when people talk about extraversion, it is recognized that not everyone has the same desire to talk on the phone and spend time in the company of others. Some people may, in fact, avoid doing those types of activities. These individuals would be considered "low" on extraversion (i.e., they are introverted). Traits are frequently bipolar in nature, in that the two ends of the dimension represent opposite qualities (e.g., organized versus sloppy).

One major characteristic of trait psychology is its emphasis on measuring people on specific traits, and then determining how much of the trait the person has by comparing his/her score to the scores of some group (known as a normative sample). A person is considered "high" on the trait if he scores higher than many of the people in the normative sample, and is considered "low" if he does not. Most people usually fall in the middle of this distribution and are said to be *ambiverts* (this term refers to someone who can exhibit both aspects of the trait depending upon the context). For example, an ambivert on the extraversion trait would be someone who, at times, may like going out and meeting others but can also, at times, have a desire for privacy and solitude.

But traits are more than just descriptive labels for organizing clusters of behaviors. They provide information about people that enable us to predict accurately outcomes in other aspects of the psychosocial world. In short, traits have been shown to carry impressive *surplus meaning*. Given the scientific basis to traits, much research has been done examining their predictive utility. We know that one's tendency to talk on the phone and desire to be with other people (i.e., one's level of extraversion) is linked to levels of happiness a person will experience in mid to later adulthood; it will predict levels of job success in certain types of jobs as well as predict specific types of occupational aspirations. Other traits (e.g., neuroticism and conscientiousness, defined below) have been shown to be powerful predictors of competitive performance outcomes in the academic, athletic, and occupational areas.

Traits have been linked to one's genetic makeup. It appears that about one-half of the variance observed in traits is inherited genetically from our parents. Traits also have been shown to generalize cross-culturally, so the same patterns in behaviors, attitudes, and actions we see in Western culture are also found to occur in other cultural contexts as well, such as in Asia and Africa. Thus, traits seem to be human universals for understanding human behavior. Perhaps the most intriguing aspect of research on traits has been the discovery that one's trait profile does *not* change in adulthood. After age 30, all things being equal (e.g., no psychotherapy or religious conversions), personality seems to be pretty much set; our trait dispositions will remain stable over our adult lives. The value of this finding is that it tells us that once we know someone's trait standing, we can make accurate predictions about behavior well into the future. However, until age 30, our personality is still in flux and capable of modification. But after 30, we have created for ourselves an adaptive orientation to the world that will lead us in very specific directions in order to pursue personal goals that are the most satisfying to our needs (e.g., the achievement-oriented person will seek out competitive situations, the extravert will seek out the company of others).

There are literally thousands of personality trait variables available today in hundreds of different inventories and scales. Such a cornucopia of constructs can easily lead to confusion when deciding which traits to use. Fortunately, recent research has discovered that the majority of these traits cluster themselves around five, broader dimensions know as the *Big Five Personality Domains*. These "Big Five" factors are: *Neuroticism*, the tendency to experience negative affect; *Extraversion*, which reflects the quantity and intensity of one's interpersonal interactions; *Openness to Experience*, the proactive seeking and appreciation of new experiences; *Agreeableness,* the quality of one's interpersonal interactions along a continuum from compassion to antagonism; and *Conscientiousness*, the persistence, organization, and motivation exhibited in goal-directed behaviors (Costa & McCrae, 1992). Research has shown that these five dimensions do provide a useful language for talking about trait variables and that these factors do predict a wide range of important psychosocial outcomes, including mental and physical health, occupational, academic, and intrapersonal criteria [see Piedmont (1998) for an overview].

*Measuring Traits*

Trait-based measures are perhaps the most common type of tests used today. They are frequently referred to as *objective tests*. Unlike the projective tests discussed previously, objective instruments provide the test-taker with very specific questions to which a response is made on a provided response format (e.g., from strongly agree to strongly disagree). There is no room for individualized responses on these types of tests. Scores are presented numerically, usually in the form of a *T-score*. A T-score is a standardized score which has a mean of 50 and a standard deviation of 10. Scores between 45 and 55 are considered normative (these are people who are in the middle of the distribution and are considered ambiverts). Scores above 55 are considered "high" (the individual scores higher than most in the normative sample), while scores below 45 are "low." Only scores in the high or low ranges are seen as interpretable and defining of the person.

Perhaps one of the most widely used objective-type measures is the *Minnesota Multiphasic Personality Inventory* (MMPI). This scale is widely used to assess "pathological functioning," although scores on the instrument are also used to assess normal levels of functioning as well. It is important when looking at a trait scale to determine what level of functioning is being assessed, normal versus clinical. The former refers to characteristics that define everyday traits in people not suffering from a mental disorder. Clinical traits represent aspects of psychological functioning that characterize more dysfunctional patterns of behaving. Although the two types of traits are related to one another (pathological traits are usually just more extreme versions of nonclinical traits), they do capture very different dynamics of the person. One should generally not use a clinical index to make hypotheses about nonclinical qualities. The MMPI is most adept at capturing these more dysfunctional elements of personality. There are 10 clinical scales that capture broad aspects of psychopathology (e.g., depression, psychosis) as well as hundreds of smaller scales aimed at more specific traits (e.g., masculinity, somatic complaints). The instrument is used routinely by psychologists and psychiatrists in making psychological diagnoses. It also provides insights into one's psychological capacities and soundness.

The *Revised NEO Personality Inventory* (NEO PI-R; Costa & McCrae, 1992) is the only commercially available instrument designed to capture the Big Five Personality dimensions. This instrument contains 240 items that measure each of the broad personality domains as well as more specific traits that underlie each of these five broad domains. Each domain has six subfacet scales. For example, the Conscientiousness domain is broken down into the facet scales of Competence, Order, Dutifulness, Achievement Striving, Self-Discipline, and Deliberation. These smaller scales can provide specific information on traits that may be directly relevant to specific counseling outcomes (e.g., academic success, interpersonal skills, self-esteem). McCrae and Costa (1991) have outlined the value of the NEO PI-R for counselors in diverse contexts.

*Strengths and Weaknesses of the Trait Approach*

The relative omnipresence of self-report trait measures is testimony to the popularity and utility of this approach to understanding personality. The value of trait measures is that they are empirically derived constructs, so that they do represent something that does exist in nature. Further, trait measures provide an efficient method for collecting systematic information about people. Easy to administer and score, these scales can provide a wide range of information that has significant implications for predicting future behavior. Scores from trait scales are readily interpreted by comparison to normative samples, and information obtained from one respondent can be readily compared to another respondent, thus facilitating comparative assessments.

However, trait theory does not have the same interpretive depth as psychoanalysis. The psychoanalytic perspective provides detailed insights into the inner world of the person. Issues surrounding emotional conflicts and maturity are central to psychoanalytic interpretations. Trait theory is still in its infancy and needs to generate more insights into how traits are acquired, both from genetic and environmental sources. Many questions still remain to be answered, including how traits develop over time, and identifying the factors that influence how and when they become expressed.

Because traits reflect self-reported regularities in people's perceptions of their own behaviors, attitudes, and actions, there is no consideration of the unconscious. From the psychoanalytic perspective, self-report measures only tell you about superficial aspects of functioning. The more important, latent aspects of personality are not touched upon. If the unconscious is important to your understanding of a client, then trait measures may have limited utility. However, trait measures do have empirically documented predictive validity. Even if traits only capture more superficial aspects of personality, research shows that these dimensions can explain significant amounts of the variance in a wide range of outcomes. Projective tests, on the other hand, are hard to quantify and do not show as high levels of predictiveness as traits. Trait advocates still need to see some empirical support for the notion of an unconscious as well as some empirical justification for the interpretations that are generated by projective tests.

Another value of traits is their focus on mostly nonclinical characteristics. Traits provide useful summary descriptions of normal functioning. Although traits do have implications for clinical issues (e.g., differential diagnosis, treatment selection, and response to treatment), they also help us to understand a student's strengths. Projective testing frequently results in interpretations that are problem-focused, highlighting the weaknesses and vulnerabilities of the student. Even "normal" individuals can appear pathological on a projective report. Trait measures allow for a more circumspect examination of both the liabilities and assets of a student. However, unlike the psychoanalytic approach, trait theory does not have built into it a methodology for making clinical interventions. Although traits can describe what a student is like and the types of treatments that may be helpful, there are no current techniques for changing actual trait levels.

## Implications for the Professional School Counselor

The value of personality theory and measurement for professional school counselors cannot be understated. A personality theory provides a framework for systematically integrating the multidimensional nature of an individual into a form that promotes a sophisticated understanding of the developmental/adaptive journey of the student, and provides a platform for intervening purposefully and effectively in the student's life. There are three benefits to using personality theories. First, professional school counselors can develop an appreciation for both the emotional weaknesses of a student as well as the psychological resources the student has available to draw upon. All too often, difficult students are seen only in terms of what they lack or what limitations they have. Personality theories cast an eye towards the possibilities for growth and development, and thus promote a more holistic, integrative understanding of the individual.

Second, personality theory provides an explanation for behavior that speaks to the fundamental motivations of the student. Understanding what needs a student is trying to have gratified in the school environment can enable the professional school counselor to anticipate the kinds of problems a student may encounter. Personality theory can outline the typical ways which a student will cope with stress or react to pressured situations. It can also outline the types of instructional climates that may be most conducive for optimizing a student's learning.

Finally, personality theories can enable a professional school counselor to identify strategies for engaging students in meaningful dialogues, and for selecting appropriate intervention strategies that will be more readily accepted by the student. By understanding how personality develops and influences behavior, professional school counselors can develop a realistic appreciation for which aspects of personality are changeable and which are not. Using personality theories as a way to understand how and why students struggle to adapt to their worlds, professional school counselors can provide the "intra-psychic lubricant" needed to smooth out problems and to enable healthy adjustment and personal growth.

## Summary/Conclusion

This necessarily brief overview of these two major schools of thought only scratches the surface of what each approach has to offer in terms of understanding our inner adaptive worlds. There is much more to know about each of them. These two theoretical models are only a limited sampling of the larger number of such theories that exist in the field of personality. The Humanistic, Psychosocial, Cognitive, Behavioral, and Biological, to name a few, provide rich insights into who we are that do not overlap with those contained in the Psychoanalytic and Trait perspectives reviewed here. There is much to be learned from studying personality theories. Although no one theory may have all the "answers," learning about personality teaches the right questions to ask.

Professional school counselors should be strongly encouraged to learn a variety of personality theories and models of the mind. Learning and applying personality theories can greatly enhance the quality of counseling services. A personality theory provides a framework for systematically integrating the multidimensional nature of an individual into a form that promotes a sophisticated understanding of the developmental/adaptive journey of the student, and provides a platform for intervening purposefully and effectively in the student's life. Further, many personality theories also have associated measurement models and scales that help one to collect and collate relevant information about an individual. There are seven advantages to using personality measures in counseling practice.

First, measures of personality help promote an understanding of the student in terms of both strengths and weaknesses. Personality assessment can provide a holistic evaluation of the student in terms that are clinically relevant. Second, such an understanding can breed increased empathy and rapport with the student. A better understanding of the student's conflicts, struggles, and aspirations helps to present a more nuanced portrait of the issues that surround his seeking treatment. Such information highlights multiple ways of engaging a student. Third, the results of personality assessment can be used to provide the student with feedback and insight into her life patterns. Using a particular measurement model can provide both the student and the professional school counselor with a common language for describing and discussing the conflicts, problems, and issues the student is experiencing. This language can be used by the professional school counselor for making interventions and providing insights. Fourth, data from personality assessments can also aid in differential diagnosis. Test scores provide an independent source of information about a student's behaviors and attitudes that is relevant for nosological classification. The information contained in such scores can help clarify underlying issues that may not be evident upon initial examination. Fifth, test information can be used to anticipate the course of treatment for a student. Knowing the personality styles of the student can help the professional school counselor anticipate potential problems and conflicts that may emerge in the therapeutic relationship (e.g., a person low in Agreeableness may frequently challenge the professional school counselor because such a person tends to hold a skeptical and suspicious outlook towards others). Professional school counselors can then either move to head off such potential disruptions or at least prepare for their emergence. Sixth, the results of personality assessment can also be used to match students to treatments from which they are most likely to benefit. For example, individuals high on Extraversion, who are sociable and talkative, will find interventions that require interpersonal interactions more helpful than do introverts, who may prefer and benefit from individual-based approaches.

Perhaps the most important benefit of personality assessment is what it affords our field as a whole. Using personality assessments enables professional school counselors to obtain objective, scientifically-based information on students that can allow us to empirically document the value of our services. Regardless of what type of professional context one is in, the pressure is always on for counselors to do more and more in shorter and shorter periods of time. Through it all, both the providers and the consumers of our services are continuously exhorting us to demonstrate the impact of our interventions. How effective are our counseling services? In what ways do we impact our students? How much do we impact them? These are important, empirical questions that need to be answered. Personality measurements are one way of addressing these concerns. Working from a conceptual model that is consistent with the professional philosophy of the professional school counselor, personality measures provide systematic, verifiable data that can document the extent of our impact and the practical value of our services.

## References

Cloninger, S. C. (2000). *Theories of personality: Understanding persons* (3rd ed.). New York: Prentice Hall.

Costa, P. T., Jr., & McCrae, R. R. (1992). *The Revised NEO Personality Inventory, manual.* Odessa, FL: Psychological Assessment Resources.

Freud, S. (1916). *Introductory lectures on psychoanalysis.* Volumes XV and XVI of the Standard Edition. London: Hogarth.

Freud, S. (1923). *The ego and the id.* In Vol XIX of the Standard Edition. London: Hogarth.

Freud, S. (1924). *A short account of psychoanalysis.* In Vol. XIX of the Standard Edition. London: Hogarth.

McCrae, R. R., & Costa, P. T., Jr. (1990). *Personality in adulthood.* New York: Guilford.

McCrae, R. R., & Costa, P. T., Jr. (1991). The *NEO Personality Inventory*: Using the five-factor model in counseling. *Journal of Counseling and Development, 69,* 367-372.

Monte, C. F. (1998). *Beneath the mask: An introduction to theories of personality* (6th ed). New York: John Wiley & Sons.

Piedmont, R. L. (1998). *The Revised NEO Personality Inventory: Clinical and research applications.* New York: Plenum.

# *Chapter 50*

## Behavior Assessment

*Carlen Henington*

### Preview

The use of behavior assessment has been the focus of many school personnel in education due to recognition of the recent focus on behavioral problems in the educational environment. Although in the past, personality characteristics have been an important consideration of problematic behavior for many professional school counselors, current emphasis has been on directly and accurately assessing the behavior and associated characteristics (Ollendick & Hersen, 1984; Shapiro & Krotchwill, 2000). To increase the accuracy of behavior assessment, procedures must be systematic, objective, and multidimensional.

### Models of Behavior Assessment

One of the first tasks in behavior assessment is selection of an assessment model and the assessment techniques. To accomplish this task, it is important to consider the nature (e.g., on-going versus a one-time assessment) and the goal (e.g., screening, diagnosis, prognosis, treatment design, evaluation of an intervention) of the assessment. Although it is important to remember that there is no "perfect" assessment system or method, the information (or data) provided by the assessment must be reliable, valid, and useful. In part, the difficulty of evaluating behavior is that there are broad ranges of behavior and a variety of classification systems used to describe problematic behavior. Furthermore, there is often no clear distinction between normal and abnormal behavior; nor is there always a clear agreement between respondents and interviewees. One person may label a behavior as "difficult" and another may indicate it as "acceptable."

There are two broad models that can be used to evaluate a student's behavior. The first, the medical model, assumes sharp distinctions between normal and abnormal behavior with the cause of the difficult behavior within the child. This model is best characterized through the *Diagnostic and Statistical Manual* (DSM). The other model, known as the multivariate model, uses statistical or psychometric properties to compare behavior of an individual to the general population and emphasizes quantitative differences between normal and abnormal behavior. Most experts in assessment of behavior use a combination of these two models and then design the assessment process, or system, with the goal of interpreting the assessment results from a specific theoretical perspective.

Although a number of theories are available from which to choose, behavior theory is particularly useful for assessing behavior. The information obtained through behavioral techniques can be used in a variety of ways and a broad range of useful information can be gathered. Multiple informants can be used, providing a broad picture of the behavior in question. The results lead directly to intervention and the same assessment techniques can be used to evaluate intervention effectiveness.

## Methods of Assessment

It is important to note that each method of behavior assessment provides different and important information. Therefore, each of the methods described within this chapter offer information that will be useful in determining the behavior and are likely to be valuable in designing an intervention for the behavior. Generally, a preferred method is to directly assess the behavior as it occurs. An example of direct assessment would involve coming to the classroom to observe a child with behavior difficulties, whereas an indirect assessment would involve asking the teacher to describe the child's problematic behavior. It is also preferable to assess the behavior in the natural environment. There are times, however, that this direct assessment is not possible (e.g., too difficult or too dangerous).

This chapter will briefly present four common direct and indirect behavior assessment methods: direct observation, self-monitoring, self-report and informant report. These methods will be presented in sequence starting with the most direct and ending with the most indirect. When several variations of a particular method are presented, those that can be considered more direct will be presented first followed by the indirect methods. For each method, a brief description will be provided, followed by an example typical to the school environment. Although some instructions for the methods will be provided, this is beyond the scope of this chapter. Therefore, interested professional school counselors are directed to the annotated bibliography at the end of this chapter (Table 1), which provides additional resources to assist in learning more about each method.

## Direct Observation

Direct observation involves assessment of behavior at the time it occurs and is the most direct of the behavior assessment methods or procedures. There are two forms of direct observation: observation in the setting where it naturally occurs and observation conducted in a contrived or analogue setting. Direct observation in a natural setting is the most direct of all methods or procedures of assessment. In this method, the behavior is observed by a trained individual (this may be a professional school counselor, teacher, teacher aide, etc.) who observes the child in a natural environment (e.g., classroom, playground, lunchroom). This procedure is time intensive, but allows the greatest flexibility in collection of a wide variety of valuable data related to problematic behaviors. Direct observation is particularly useful for determining the precise problematic behavior with information regarding its pattern, level, and likelihood of occurrence. Observation is also useful to determine levels of the behavior prior to, during, and following intervention to determine treatment effectiveness (Skinner, Rhymer, & McDaniel, 2000).

*Case example.* Although there are a number of observation procedures that are commonly used in the schools, the following example uses a momentary time sampling procedure to directly observe disruptive behavior in the lunchroom. The disruptive behavior is described as "standing up and yelling to others across the room." The professional school counselor, asked to conduct a behavior assessment, would observe the child on several days in the lunchroom. At 5-minute intervals, the school counselor observes the child and determines whether the behavior is occurring at that precise time. Because a clipboard with an observation sheet would be too noticeable in the lunchroom, another method of tallying the behavior is necessary. One simple strategy would be to move a paperclip from one pocket to another if the behavior is occurring. At the end of lunchtime, the number of paperclips in the "observed" pocket are counted and noted. The same procedure is followed on at least one more day. This procedure provides a direct, empirical method for assessing the number of times disruptive behavior occurs in the lunchroom.

*Alternative observation methods*. Another procedure is to observe the problem behavior using a narrative recording procedure. This is a less direct method, potentially offering rich information, but requires further assessment of the behavior. This method requires the professional school counselor to use a clipboard to write down as much information about the disruptive behavior as possible. This includes what happens before, during, and after the child yells across the room. This information is also known as the antecedent, behavior, and consequence(s). For example, the professional school counselor may notice that frequently when the student yells across the room the teacher has left the room and the teacher's aide is in charge. This is the antecedent to the behavior. In directly observing the behavior, the professional school counselor may notice that when the student yells there are a number of behaviors that also occur. For example, when the student yells out in the classroom he looks around at the other students to see if they are watching. This information provides a hint that the student is yelling to obtain peer attention and an appropriate intervention may be to encourage other students to ignore this student when he yells in the classroom. Finally, it is important for the professional school counselor to note what happens after the student yells. For example, if the teacher sends the student out of the room and to the principal's office it may be that the student is allowed to avoid school work when he yells out and therefore yelling serves the function to escape from the classroom and the required class work. Thus, from this information the professional school counselor can determine what might need to change in the environment to assist the student in changing the disruptive behavior.

Not all behaviors can be easily assessed using this method. For example, internal conditions such as fear cannot be observed. However, there are indicators of fear and these can be directly observed (e.g., changes in breathing, heart-rate). Another behavior that cannot be readily observed is an individual's thought process or behaviors that occur outside the typical school environment (e.g., nighttime sleep-patterns of a student who falls asleep in the classroom). A possible alternative less direct than observation in the natural environment is assessment of the behavior in a contrived situation that is engineered to simulate the natural setting. However, any departure from direct observation of behavior in the natural environment requires inference about the behavior. In this situation, additional data about the behavior must be collected to reduce the likelihood of error and to support the inferences (Cone, 1988). For example, using the student who yells out in the classroom to illustrate, it may not be possible to observe the student in the classroom, or when the observer is in the classroom the behavior may not occur. Then a contrived situation may be constructed. For example, based on the information provided by the teacher, the professional school counselor suspects that the student is able to avoid or escape school work when he is disruptive. To test this the professional school counselor may be required to provide the student with an academic task to be completed. Because the situation does not directly reflect actual occurrences in the classroom, the professional school counselor may have to collect additional data. An example of such data might be to determine the amount/difficulty/type of academic work that the student is likely to avoid.

## Self-Monitoring

Self-monitoring is a procedure that uses the individual to observe, record, and report behavior. Researchers have shown that a variety of populations can effectively use self-monitoring to assess behavior (e.g., individuals with developmental delays, learning disabilities, emotional/behavioral disorders). Self-monitoring has also been shown to be effective in assessing academic and nonacademic behavior. Nearly any behavior that occurs in a school setting can be assessed using self-monitoring (Cole, Marder, & McCann, 2000). Unlike direct observation, self-monitoring requires very little of professional school counselor's resources. This procedure can be used either as a behavior assessment tool or as an intervention. One key asset is that self-monitoring can be used when direct observation is not possible (e.g., an adult is not present; the behavior is non-observable, such as anger).

When using self-monitoring to assess behavior it is important to provide the child with instruction about the procedures. The first step is to describe self-monitoring and when it might be useful. This allows the child to understand that he/she is going to be working on the problem "situation." Next, be sure that the child understands what the behavior is that will be monitored. Then explain that when it is time to monitor the behavior, the student, using an internal dialogue, will ask himself if the behavior was occurring. If so, he is to record the behavior. Generally, it is helpful to problem-solve with the student how the behavior will be recorded (e.g., an observation form, or the "paperclip" method previously described). Once the child understands the self-monitoring procedure, it will be necessary to practice. Initially, the professional school counselor may find it helpful to model self-monitoring using example and non-example behaviors. Then have the student practice the procedure in as natural a setting as possible, with the professional school counselor providing feedback. This step is very important because it increases the likelihood of accurate monitoring. However, if the student understands and accuracy is still a concern due to compliance of the student, or even truthfulness, then the professional school counselor may want to add a systematic check that another individual conducts. For example, every so often when the time to monitor occurs, the professional school counselor also records his or her observation and a comparison is made between the two observers.

When a student uses self-monitoring it may be helpful to implement a reminder (a cue or prompt) to remind the student when to observe the behavior. This can be done with a verbal or nonverbal signal from another individual or through self-prompting (the child checks his/her behavior on his/her own). The observation can be done using a schedule (e.g., momentary time sampling described in direct observation, a less formal system).

*Case example.* The following example is about a 6-year-old boy who often forgets to turn off the water in the boys' bathroom after he washes his hands. The female professional school counselor cannot accompany him into the bathroom to observe his behavior. Therefore, self-monitoring is an appropriate assessment technique. The professional school counselor discusses the problem with the child early in the morning or after school when others are not present. She describes self-monitoring. Then the counselor models self-monitoring by enacting a scenario were she uses the bathroom to wash her hands. The boy stands outside the bathroom. When the professional school counselor leaves the bathroom, she asks herself if she has remembered to turn off the water. If she has, she says "Good" and makes a note of it by marking on a card taped to her desk. Then the student enacts the same scenario, following all the steps. If he forgets, the professional school counselor reminds him. If he does it correctly, the professional school counselor praises him and rewards him with a star on top of his tally mark.

*Alternatives to self-monitoring.* A common variation of self-monitoring is peer-monitoring (Henington & Skinner, 1998). The predominant difference between the two is that in peer-monitoring a peer observes and records the data, whereas in self-monitoring the student implements the procedures. It is important to remember that the more complex or difficult the behavior being assessed, the more training time will be needed. In some cases, the behavior may not be appropriate for self-monitoring.

## Self-Report Measures of Behavior

There are two broad methods of obtaining information from the individual with the problematic behavior: individual interviews and self-report rating scales. It is generally believed that the individual may be a better reporter of their non-observable and non-disruptive (internalized) behaviors such as fears, anxiety, and depression. Conversely, it is also generally believed that individuals with observable and more disruptive (externalized) behaviors such as oppositional defiance, attention deficit disorder, and conduct disorders are less reliable in their reports of their own behavior. Although at times self-report data may be questionable in its validity, when the other methods of behavior assessment are also used, self-report can add information that will be helpful.

*Individual interview.* This method assesses the individual's perceptions of the behavior in question. Interviews can be viewed as lying on a continuum, with structured interviews at one end and unstructured interviews at the other end. Structured interviews provide a set of questions that the professional school counselor asks. The interview generally starts with broad information about the individual and progresses to information about the problematic behavior. The information about the individual assists in building an understanding of events, characteristics, and other relevant issues that may assist in assessing the behavior. Information obtained about the behavior may include a description of the setting and/or circumstances surrounding the behavior, including the response of the individual and others to the behavior; the onset, duration, frequency, and severity of the behavior; and the history of the behavior and presence of the behavior in other family members (Lane, Gresham, & O'Shaughnessy, 2002). Structured interviews can be completed independently by the individual using a written form or a computer program. Another common method of conducting the interview is in a more traditional counseling model with the professional school counselor asking questions while writing the responses of the individual on a form.

In unstructured interviews the professional school counselor might begin with broad questions and then follow up the response with additional questions to provide detailed information. The same information that is obtained in the structured interview can be collected, but the professional school counselor allows the individual to provide the information with less direction. Most professional school counselors provide a combination of the structured and unstructured interview. In this case, the interview might be considered semi-structured. The professional school counselor follows a form and/or a general outline for obtaining information, but pauses to ask follow-up questions as needed.

*Self-report measures.* Self-report measures, also called self-report ratings, provide information regarding an individual's perceptions of his/her behavior. Self-report measures, similar to interviews, provide qualitative information, but quantitative data is often also available. There are as many types of self-report measures as there are types of behavior disorders and concerns. Some measures only assess one aspect of behavior, for example depression, anxiety, or self-esteem. These measures are considered narrow-band measures. Conversely, some self-report measures assess a broad spectrum of behaviors. These measures are commonly called broad-band or omnibus measures and are generally used as screening mechanisms, often followed by the more specific measures to closely assess a specific diagnosis.

Self-report measures can be based on a theoretical perspective (using a specific theory about behavior to evaluate the behavior) or psychometric (using a statistical analysis to evaluate the behavior). When the measure is based on theory, often the questions or statements on which the individual rates him/herself is taken directly from the diagnostic criteria for the disorder or problem. For example, a question related to depression would state "I am often sad." The individual rates how valid this response is for him/her. For young children, a forced choice is often used (e.g., true or false). For older individuals, the choices are more expansive (e.g., very true, somewhat true, neutral, not usually true, never true). In both cases, a number value is assigned to the response. For example, 'very true' would be assigned a 5-point value, whereas 'somewhat true' would be assigned a 4-point value, and so on to 'never true" with a 1-point value. The number of items within the measure often depends on the criteria and the desired amount of specificity, information, and reliability of the measure. Each item will have a response, therefore a number value can be determined for each item dependent upon the individual's response. A total of the number values is then calculated. Once this is done, the total is usually compared to a set of reference scores that indicate whether the reported behavior/perceptions are noteworthy.

The psychometric procedure often uses the same rating format and varies very little in appearance from the theoretically-based measures, and often the questions are constructed from a theoretical perspective. However, the set of reference scores is empirically derived. In general terms, the measure is administered to a large number of individuals who are considered to exhibit a broad range of possible behaviors and responses, typical and atypical. Then the data from all of these individuals, called the norm sample, are statistically examined in two ways.

Without going into great detail, the purpose of these analyses will be described. The first analysis, a factor analysis, determines what questions are related to each other in some way. Using this information the questions are usually refined and those that are related are considered to assess a specific behavior or characteristic determined by an examination of the items themselves. The second analysis determines what is a typical score and what might be considered a score that is not typical. Using these numbers, a derived score, usually a T score, can be assigned. The T score has a mean of 50 and a standard deviation of 10. These scores are also often expressed as a cut score (similar to the theoretically derived scales) to indicate noteworthy response patterns. Often a percentile score is also provided. It is important to note that because self-report measures usually compare an individual to a pre-selected group or norm sample, the norm sample should be as much like the individual as possible. For example, a child from a rural southern state should not be compared to children from a large urban setting. Likewise, it would not be appropriate for a young child to be compared to adolescents.

*Case example.* The following example illustrates a combination of an individual interview, an omnibus self-report assessment measure, and a follow-up narrow-band measure. The professional school counselor has received a referral for a preadolescent girl for whom her teacher has concerns about withdrawal and social isolation.

Once proper consent and assent has been obtained, the professional school counselor meets with the student and conducts a semi-structured interview. In the interview, the professional school counselor obtains information that leads her to believe that the student may be depressed. After collecting information about the child's perception of her behavior, the professional school counselor then asks the child to complete a broad-based screening measure used by the school district to evaluate children. The professional school counselor scores the broad measure and learns that there are a number of concerns uncovered by the screener including depression. The professional school counselor then follows the screener with a measure that specifically measures depression in children. The professional school counselor then scores the narrow-band measure. If the scores are consistent with those of children the same age in the norm sample who have been diagnosed with depression, the professional school counselor can be reasonably assured that the child is experiencing distress similar to that of children with depression. The professional school counselor can then determine an appropriate intervention to assist the student with reasonable certainty that the intervention is targeting the correct behavior.

## Other-Report Measures of Behavior

The other-report method of assessing behavior, especially behavior of children, is the most frequently used method. One of the reasons for this popularity is that, by their nature, report measures are a relatively brief method of obtaining information across a broad range of behaviors from multiple informants. This method is flexible enough to be applied to nearly any type of behavior without losing the integrity of the assessment process.

Other-report measures, also known as informant-report, are similar to self-report measures. Interviews are conducted with others to determine their perceptions of the behavior and other informants can also complete rating forms. Those most likely to provide appropriate information include parents, caretakers, and teachers. Generally, informant-report measures are conducted with adults only, however peers can also be asked to evaluate behavior. When peers are used, special care must be taken to protect the relationship of the child and their peers. Only in rare circumstances is the information provided by peers of sufficient importance that risk to the child is outweighed by the need for the additional information. Similar to self-report measures, there are two broad types of informant report measures: informant interviews and informant report rating scales.

*Informant-report interviews*. According to Sattler and Mash (1998), the goal of assessment is to "obtain relevant, reliable, and valid information about the interviewees and their problems" (p. 3). The focus of the interview is determined by the nature of the behavior. Great diversity exists within interview techniques and, frequently, the form and structure of the interview is based on the theoretical training of the professional school counselor. Similar to student interviews, informant interviews can be structured, semi-structured, or unstructured. When the professional school counselor is unsure of the problem behavior or questions the proposed referral question, he/she is likely to use a structured interview to gather a broad range of information. This increases the possibility of determining other hypotheses about the behavior and allows a more flexible approach to problem-solving in behavior assessment. A professional school counselor who uses an unstructured interview method is more likely to focus on obtaining information directly related to a specific behavior or problem.

Generally, key informants of a student's behavior are those who are most likely to be in a position to observe the behavior: parents and teachers. Information obtained in a parent interview should include the following: family and developmental history of the child and a history of the behavior (e.g., symptom description, onset, duration, intensity or severity, past interventions). Teacher interviews are more likely to be behavior-specific, narrow in scope, and focus on obtaining detailed information about the behavior (Busse & Beaver, 2000). Information obtained in a behavior-specific interview should include: an exact definition of the behavior, a history of the problem behavior (e.g., setting(s), surrounding events—antecedents and consequences), past interventions and their effectiveness, the goal of the assessment/intervention, potential incentives to use during intervention, and other available resources.

When conducting an interview with the parents, it is usually desirable to have both parents present to obtain the perspectives of the mother and father. Some professional school counselors may also want the child present for a part of the interview to allow direct observation of the parent/child interaction. Another variation is to have the entire family present. This allows observation of family interaction. Another alternative is to conduct a conjoint interview with the parents and the teacher. Sheridan, Kratochwill, and Bergan (1996) described a procedure for conjoint meetings.

*Informant-report rating scales.* Although informant-report rating scales are considered to be the least direct form of behavior assessment, they are one of the most used assessment methods because they have strong psychometric properties and are relatively objective. Merrell (2000) described these strengths, stating that rating forms have been shown to have same rater consistency across time, items, and situations (i.e., reliability). He also stated that rating scales provide consistent information across respondents (i.e., validity). Additionally, they can be used for comparison across individuals and behaviors (i.e., norm referenced) and can be applied in meaningful ways (i.e., used to develop treatment and interventions). Other researchers have also discussed the strengths of the rating scale method (Schaffer, Fisher, & Lucas, 1999). Relatively little training is required to administer and score rating measures. Additionally, rating measures can provide information about behaviors that are difficult to assess more directly (e.g., low occurrence behaviors, behaviors that the child may not accurately report). Rating scales often provide information about behavior that has been observed across long periods of time. This allows the professional school counselor to determine the presence of the behavior at other times in the child's development.

Potential problems with rating scales are predominately related to the vulnerability of rater bias. These biases include: halo effect (a tendency to view a child in a more positive way than would typically occur) and leniency or severity effect (a tendency to be too easy or too difficult in evaluation of the behavior). It is important that the professional school counselor remember that ratings are perceptions and therefore, as stated previously, must be compared for consistency with other data collected about the behavior and the child.

*Case example.* In this example, a third grade teacher has approached the school's male professional school counselor about classroom management. The school counselor uses a brief behavior-specific interview, obtaining the teacher's perceptions of the behavior of her class. He discovers that the teacher has concerns about only one child in her class and that she has spoken with the parents about the child's behavior. The teacher reports that the parents have similar concerns. This behavior assessment potentially will require a formal assessment and intervention with the child. The professional school counselor then contacts the parents to obtain permission for a formal assessment. He sends some broad-based parent report measures to the parents and asks them to complete and bring them in when they come for an interview. The professional school counselor then asks the teacher to complete similar broad-based report measures. During the parent interview, the school counselor asks that the teacher be present for part of the interview so that more comprehensive information can be collected about the behavior. The parents and the teacher agree and the school counselor uses the rating scale responses of the parents and teacher to conduct a behavior-specific interview.

The professional school counselor has now built a "team of problem-solvers" to address the behavior. The team determines that a comprehensive assessment should be conducted. The professional school counselor makes arrangements to observe the child in the classroom and to interview the child. When the team completes their conjoint meeting they leave with a belief that the behavior will be properly assessed and will lead to an effective intervention that will improve the child's behavior.

## Summary/Conclusion

As can be seen from this last example, a comprehensive behavior assessment is likely to include most, if not all four, components of behavior assessment: direct observation, self-monitoring, self-report measures, and informant-report measures. The more comprehensive the behavior assessment, the more likely important information will be collected and used to correctly identify the problem; and based on this information, the more likely an appropriate intervention will be developed to address the problem behavior. That is the ultimate goal of a behavior assessment - to address the behavior and alleviate distress that may either be a symptom or a cause of the behavior. Table 1 includes annotated bibliographies of several excellent sources for further information on behavior assessment. Table 2 provides annotated bibliographies of commonly used behavior assessments.

**Table 1. Annotated bibliography.**

Salvia, J., & Ysselkyke, J. E. (2004). *Assessment* (9th ed.). Boston, MA: Houghton Mifflin Co.
Provides a comprehensive examination of a variety of assessment techniques and procedures, including traditional standardized, norm-referenced measures and non-traditional measures.

Sattler, J. M. (1998).*Clinical and forensic interviewing of children and families: Guidelines for the mental, education, pediatric, and child maltreatment fields.* San Diego: Author.
Provides a detailed set of guidelines for a variety of interviewing tasks completed with children and their families.

Shapiro, E. S., & Kratochwill, T. R. (2000). *Conducting school-based assessments of child and adolescent behavior.* New York: Guilford Press.
This edited book compiles useful, detailed information for the professional school counselor in the four areas briefly described in this chapter.

**Table 2. Assessment instruments.**

*Self-Report Inventories*

*Behavior Assessment System for Children – Self-Report of Personality* - (BASC-SRP; Reynolds & Kamphaus, 1992).
Assesses student's perceptions and feelings about school, parents, peers, and his/her own behavior problems. Two forms: ages 8 - 11 (SRP-C) and ages 12 - 18 (SRP-A). Includes 14 subscales (10 clinical and 4 adaptive). Yields T scores from 152 to 186 items using norms for the general population, males, females, and a clinical population. Strength is the ability to assess response sets or validity indices (e.g., "fake good," "fake bad") and use as a multi-informant instrument. Publisher: American Guidance Service.

*Children's Depression Inventory* - (CDI; Kovacs, 1991).
A 27-item scale appropriate for individuals ages 6-17. Assesses a number of depressive symptoms. Strength is ease of administration and scoring and use as either a screener or diagnostic tool. Uses cut scores rather than derived scores. Publisher: Multi-Health Systems.

*Reynolds Adolescent Depression Scale* - (RADS; Reynolds, 1986).
A 30-item instrument appropriate for ages 13 - 18. Uses a 4-point rating scale to assess depressive symptomology. Strength is ease of administration and scoring. Publisher: Psychological Assessment Resources.

*Revised Children's Manifest Anxiety Scale* - (RCMAS; Reynolds & Richmond, 1985).
Assesses state and trait symptoms of anxiety. Appropriate for ages 6-19 using 37 items to yield T scores on four subscales including a validity scale and a total score. Strengths

include broad number of anxiety symptoms assessed, ease of administration and scoring, and the validity scale. Publisher: Western Psychological Services.

*Informant Inventories*

*Behavior Assessment System for Children - Parent Rating Scale* (BASC-PRS) and *Behavior Assessment System for Children - Teacher Rating Scale* (BASC-TRS; Reynolds & Kamphaus, 1992).

Published concurrently with the BASC-SRF, these two versions of the BASC are intended to assess a child's clinical and adaptive behavior in the home and community (Parent Rating Scale) and school environment (Teacher Rating Scale). The BASC-PRS has three forms: ages 4-5, 6-11, and 12-18. Requires approximately 20 minutes to complete. Yields T scores using norms for the general population, males, females, and a clinical population. Strength is the variety of scales for differential diagnosis, validity indices, strong psychometric properties, and use as a multi-informant instrument. Publisher: American Guidance Service.

*Child Behavior Checklist - Parent Report Form* (CBCL-PRF) and *Child Behavior Checklist - Teacher Report Form* (CBCL-TRF; Achenbach, 1991).

For use with children ages 4-18 years. Yields T scores to reflect internalizing and externalizing behaviors, as well as competencies. Strengths include large research base to support validity of the instrument and wide familiarity to a number of professions in the mental health fields. Publisher: Author.

*Devereux Scales of Mental Disorders* -(DSMD; Naglieri, LeBuffe, & Pfeiffer, 1994).

New version of the *Devereux Scales* (School Form) with two forms: 111-item scale for ages 5-12 and 110-item scale for ages 13-18. Either parents or teachers can complete this new version that provides T scores on 6 clinical scales, Attention (ages 5-12 only) and Delinquency (ages 13-18 only). Strengths include ratings that can be compared across raters and good discrimination between emotionally disturbed and non-disturbed children. Publisher: The Psychological Corporation.

*Functional Assessment Informant Record for Teachers* - (FAIR-T; Doggett, Mueller, & Moore, 2002; Edwards, 2002).

Uses teacher provided information to assist in developing hypotheses about the function of students' behavior in the school environment including additional information about the problem behavior, antecedent events (task information, preceding activity), maintaining functions (persons present/absent), consequences of behavior and other actions, and past interventions. Strengths include ease of administration, direct link to behavior that either will supplement direct observation or allow hypotheses generation when observation is not an option. Publisher: Author.

*Specialty or Narrow-band Informant Rating Scales*

*Attention Deficit Disorders Evaluation Scale - School and Home Versions* (ADDES; McCarney, 1989a; 1989b).

This rating scale has two versions: Home (46 items) and School (60 items); and yields three subscale scores: Inattention, Impulsivity, and Hyperactivity. Although lacking in construct validity for the three subscales, internal consistency tends to be high. Strengths include support materials for interventions, large nationwide normative base. Publisher: Hawthorne Educational Services.

*Social Skills Rating System* - (SSRS; Gresham & Elliot, 1990).

This instrument includes self-, parent-, and teacher-rating forms to assess children's social behaviors. Useful for screening purposes for social difficulties, but behavioral and emotional problem scales may be less useful and valid than other instruments. Strength: multi-informant measure. Publisher: American Guidance Service.

*Sutter-Eyberg Student Behavior Inventory* - (SESBI; Sutter & Eyberg, 1984).
Designed to be the companion to the *Eyberg Child Behavior Inventory* (Eyberg & Robinson, 1982), the SESBI focuses specifically on 36 behavior problems using a 7-point rating scale and yes-no problem identification system. Strength of this measure is that its use facilitates identification of problematic behavior for direct intervention. Publisher: Author.

*Formal Behavior Observation Systems*

*Behavior Assessment System for Children - Student Observation System* (BASC-BOS; Reynolds & Kamphaus, 1992).
Brief observation system that allows for examination of 65 specific target behaviors (4 categories of positive/adaptive behaviors and 9 categories of problematic behaviors). Uses a momentary-time sampling procedure, narrative procedure, and a checklist of behaviors. Strengths include ease of use, time efficiency, and direct observation of children and adolescents. Publisher: American Guidance Services.

*Behavior Observation of Students in Schools* - (BOSS; Shapiro, 1996).
Assesses key components of a student's academic behavior including three types of off-task behavior (verbal, motor, passive) as well as active and passive on-task behavior. Uses a time-sampling procedure. Teacher's direct behavior toward the target students is also tracked. A comparison peer is also observed. Strengths include distinction between active and passive behavior, focus on academic behavior. Publisher: Guilford Press.

*State-Event Classroom Observation System* - (SECOS; Saudargas, 1992).
Observational coding procedure with a long history that uses a brief observation using a time sampling procedure. Provides for assessment of instructional situations, categories of student behavior (states and events), and teacher behavior. Strengths include the ability to assess a wide range of classroom occurrences, including peer and teacher behavior. Publisher: Author.

---

## References

Achenbach, T. M. (1991). *Integrative guide for the 1991 CBCL/4-18, YSR, and TRF profiles.* Burlington, VT: University of Vermont, Department of Psychiatry.

Busse, R. T., & Beaver, B. R. (2000). Informant report: Parent and teacher interviews. In E. S. Shapiro & T. R. Kratochwill (Eds.), *Conducting school-based assessments of child and adolescent behavior* (pp. 235-273). New York: Guilford Press.

Cole, C. L., Marder, T., & McCann, L. (2000). Self-monitoring. In E. S. Shapiro & T. R. Kratochwill (Eds.), *Conducting school-based assessments of child and adolescent behavior.* (pp. 121-149). New York: Guilford Press.

Cone, J. D. (1988). Psychometric considerations and the multiple models of behavioral assessment. In A. Bellack & M. Hersen (Eds.), *Behavioral assessment: A practical handbook* (pp. 42-66). New York: Pergamon Press.

Doggett, R. A., Mueller, M. M., & Moore, J. W. (2002). *Functional Assessment Informant Record for Teachers:* Creation, evaluation and future research. *Proven Practice, 4,* 25-30.

Edwards, R. P. (2002). A tutorial for using the *Functional Assessment Informant Record for Teachers (FAIR-T). Proven Practice, 4,* 31-38.

Eyberg, S. M., & Robinson, E. A. (1982). Conduct problem behavior: Standardization of a behavioral rating scale with adolescents. *Journal of Clinical Child Psychology, 12*, 347-354.

Gresham, F. M., & Elliot, S. G. (1990). *Social Skills Rating System.* Circle Pines, MN. American Guidance Services.

Henington, C., & Skinner, C. H. (1998). Peer monitoring. In K. Toping & S. Ehly (Eds.), *Peer-assisted learning* (pp. 237-253). Mahwah, NJ: Lawrence Erlbaum Associates.

Kovacs, M. (1991). *The Children's Depression Inventory (CDI).* North Tonawanda, NY: Multi-Health Systems.

Lane, K. L., Gresham, F. M., & O'Shaughnessy, T. E. (2002). *Interventions for children with or at risk for emotional and behavioral disorders.* Boston: Allyn & Bacon.

McCarney, S. B. (1989a). *Attention Deficit Disorders Evaluation Scale - Home Version technical manual.* Columbia, MO: Hawthorne Educational Services.

McCarney, S. B. (1989b). *Attention Deficit Disorders Evaluation Scale - School Version technical manual.* Columbia, MO: Hawthorne Educational Services.

Merrell, K. W. (2000). Informant report: Rating scale measures. In E. S. Shapiro & T. R. Kratochwill (Eds.), *Conducting school-based assessments of child and adolescent behavior* (pp. 203-234). New York: Guilford Press.

Naglieri, J. A., LeBuffe, P. A., & Pfeiffer, S. I. (1994). *Devereux Scales of Mental Disorders.* New York: The Psychological Corporation.

Ollendick, T. H., & Hersen, M. (1984). An overview of child behavioral assessment. In T. H. Ollendick & M. Hersen (Eds.) *Child behavioral assessment: Principles and procedures* (pp. 3-19). New York: Pergamon Press.

Reynolds, C. R., & Kamphaus, R. W. (1992). *Behavior Assessment System for Children (BASC).* Circle Pines, MN: American Guidance Services.

Reynolds, C. R., & Richmond, B. O. (1985). *Revised Children's Manifest Anxiety Scale (RCMAS).* Los Angeles: Western Psychological Services.

Reynolds, W. M. (1986). *Reynolds Child Depression Scale.* Odessa, FL: Psychological Assessment Resources.

Sattler, J. M., & Mash, E. J. (1998). Introduction to clinical interviewing. In J. M. Sattler (Ed.), *Clinical and forensic interviewing of children and families: Guidelines for the mental, education, pediatric, and child maltreatment fields* (pp. 2-44). San Diego: Author.

Saudargas, R. A. (1992). *State-Event Classroom Observation System* (SECOS). Knoxville, TN: Department of Psychology, University of Tennessee

Schaffer, D., Fisher, P. W., & Lucas, C. (1999). Respondent-based interviews. In D. Schaffer, C. P. Lucas, & J. E. Richters (Eds.), *Diagnostic assessment in child and adolescent psychopathology* (pp. 3-33). New York: Guilford Press.

Shapiro, E. S. (1996). *Academic skills problems workbook.* New York: Guilford Press.

Shapiro, E. S., & Kratochwill, T. R. (2000). Introduction: Conducting a multidimensional behavioral assessment. In E. S. Shapiro & T. R. Kratochwill (Eds.), *Conducting school-based assessments of child and adolescent behavior* (pp. 1-20). New York: Guilford Press.

Sheridan, S. M., Kratochwill, T. R., & Bergan, J. R. (1996). *Conjoint behavioral consultation: A procedural manual.* New York: Plenum Press.

Skinner, C. H., Rhymer, K. N., & McDaniel, C. E. (2000). Naturalistic direct observation in educational settings. In E. S. Shapiro & T. R. Kratochwill (Eds.), *Conducting school-based assessments of child and adolescent behavior* (pp. 21-54). New York: Guilford Press.

Sutter, J., & Eyberg, S. M. (1984). *Sutter-Eyberg Student Behavior Inventory.* Gainesville, FL: University of Florida.

# Chapter 51

## Conducting a Structured Observation

*Cyrus Marcellus Ellis*

### Preview

Effective structured observations begin with proper planning and the involvement of teachers, parents and students. Professional school counselors, in order to increase the effectiveness of the learning environment for teachers and students, need to develop a systematic process to properly categorize problematic behaviors and conditions affecting the learning environment.

The new millennium presents professional school counselors with myriad issues related to accurately determining and meeting the educational, career and interpersonal needs of students (Paisley & McMahon, 2001). As students, teachers and administrators interact, there will undoubtedly be misunderstandings and problems. Professional school counselors work together with all members of the school community to recognize, evaluate and determine intervention strategies to improve interpersonal behavior and academic performance. Of the many job related duties professional school counselors perform, conducting interviews and observations directly relates to the role of ensuring that all programs foster student success (ASCA, 2000). In this role, professional school counselors may be asked to conduct structured observations to critically determine environmental forces influencing student behavior and learning.

Conducting a structured observation allows professional school counselors to assess student behavior, classroom environment, school climate, instructor behavior and the impact of physical and psychological disabilities of students in the school (Asmus, Vollmer & Borrero, 2002; Drummond, 2000; Ellis & Magee, 1999; Freiberg, 1998; Hagborg, 1998; Webb, Baxter & Thompson, 1997).

*Planning the Structured Observation*

While there are various methods for observing students in academic settings, direct observation methods tend to offer the highest degree of credible data (Gordon, Meadows, & Dyal, 1995; Shapiro & Skinner, 1990). Direct observation provides the best possible chance for obtaining salient information and the individuals being observed can become reactive during the observation. "If the client knows he is being observed, his behavior may be quite different from when he is unaware of it" (Drummond, 2000). A structured observation, then, requires a systematic approach requiring the observer to attend to a series of factors shown to provide the greatest opportunity for credible results. Figure 1 shows the initial planning considerations for a structured observation.

Professional school counselors need to pay particular attention to whether their active participation will inhibit data collection. If the planning phase determines the professional school counselor should be removed from the observation, the substitute observer (i.e., paraprofessionals or support personnel) need to engage in every dimension of the planning process, as well as receive training in observation methods, data collection and construct identification.

**Figure 1. Instruction sheet for Pre-Observation Checklist.**

## Pre-Observation Checklist Instructions

| | |
|---|---|
| **Institution** | Write in host school's name. |
| **Planned Observer** | Write in the name of the individual planned to conduct the observation. |
| **Planned Location of Observation** | Write in the location where the observation is planned to be conducted. |
| **Planned Observation Date, Start & End Time** | Write in the information concerning the date of the observation, when it will begin and when it will end. |
| **Student to be Observed** | Identify the student to be observed (ensure confidentiality of student by assigning case number or some other means). |
| **Description of Questionable Behavior** | Through meeting with all concerned members of the educational team, be sure to clearly write down the behavior being exhibited by the child in question. Make sure that you document as precisely as possible what the student is doing and what makes it disruptive or suspect behavior. |
| **Acceptable Behavior Is:** | Be clear, from interviews with the educational team, on what acceptable behaviors are permitted. |
| **Unacceptable Behavior Is:** | State clearly what behaviors are unacceptable to the learning environment. |
| **Possible Distractions Occurring During Observation** | List the possible distractions to an observer's observation. Be sure to include social desirability issues as well as other school functions that may impede the observation. |
| **Procedures for Addressing Social Desirability** | Provide a plan of action to consider the impact of the observer on the data collection. |

Professional school counselors, as well as support personnel, need to be involved in gathering background information from teachers, teaching assistants and students to ensure that the targeted issue to be observed is clearly stated and understood *before* the observation is to commence (ASCA, 2000). Drummond (2000) echoed these concerns by identifying four areas that must be addressed when conducting observations which include (a) an observable behavior understood by the observer, (b) an easy method of recording observations, (c) eliminating observer distractions and (d) treating the observed with respect. Figure 2 provides a pre-observation checklist to address the concerns raised by Drummond.

**Figure 2. Example of Pre-Observation Checklist.**

**Pre-Observation Checklist**

Institution____________________ Planned Observer________________________

Planned Location of Observation ______________________________________________

Planned Observation Date and Start Time__________________ End Time____________

Student to be Observed________________________________________________________

---

Description of Questionable Behavior

Acceptable Behavior

Unacceptable Behavior

Possible Distractions to Observation

Procedures for addressing social desirability

Ellis and Magee's (1999) work in determining the impact of the school environment on unsettling student behavior in the classroom provides a systematic approach to critically observe behavior. In their examination of student's disruptive behavior, Ellis and Magee reviewed the student's background information, clearly identified the student's negative behavior (e.g., daily emotional outbursts, impulsive yelling, aggression towards other members of the school community, etc.) and evaluated the response of the school community to the student's exhibited behavior. Social desirability on the part of the observed and a lack of preparation of professionals are two factors that contributed to awkward observation approaches yielding inaccurate conclusions. Using Ellis and Magee's work can assist in providing professional school counselors insight into describing unacceptable behavior.

*Behavioral Observations*

Professional school counselors may be called upon to observe student behavior within or outside of the classroom (Ellis & Magee, 1999; Shapiro & Skinner, 1990; Webb, Baxter & Thompson, 1997). Through direct observation methods, observers document the unconcealed actions of students as well as the environmental forces acting upon a student or a group of students (Shapiro & Skinner, 1990). Observing student behavior requires professional school counselors to correctly identify and define the behaviors that are problematic for student and teacher. Identifying problematic behaviors that disrupt student learning is a combined effort between the professional school counselor, other school personnel, students, and parents. As stated in the previous section, conducting a structured observation is a systematic process.

Asmus et al.'s (2002) work in developing a functional behavioral assessment model mirrors the work of Ellis and Magee (1999) by incorporating a process for behavior identification as a part of their model. Asmus et al. described the basis for their functional behavioral analyses as including "both a descriptive assessment of natural conditions and a functional analysis using analog conditions" (p. 70). While their functional analysis approach involves the process of experimentation, descriptive assessment involves a clear statement of the environment, behaviors to observe, and the method of collecting information. Ellis and Magee (1999), as well as Asmus et al. (2002), recognized the importance of targeting observable behaviors. Additionally, each recognized the need for pre-observation interviews, direct observation techniques, clear data collection methods, multiple periods of observation and observation congruence between all observers.

*Methods of Data Collection*

Zirpoli and Melloy (1997) underscored the necessity of employing a systematic approach to behavioral assessment by stating four points that reflect the benefits of such an approach. Zirpoli and Melloy stated that a systematic approach to behavioral measurement assists school personnel in classifying a range of behavior problems, evaluating criteria concerning the efficacy of programs, targeting program modifications, and communicating needs with parents as well as all members of the school community. Asmus et al. (2002) confirmed this latter point by promoting the use of the assessment devices for guiding conversations with parents and teachers.

Reviewing the work of Zirpoli and Melloy (1997) provides professional school counselors with a variety of systematic approaches for conducting a structured observation. Table 1 lists two methods of observation, data collection practices and the benefits of their use. The techniques utilized in the methods section of Table 1 are consistent with Shapiro and Skinner (1990), as well as Drummond (2000), as the best approaches for conducting observations. Figures 3 and 4 provide examples of forms for anecdotal and frequency of behavior observations, respectively. As human beings are the individuals conducting the structured observation, professional school counselors need to pay strict attention to additional variables to ensure the observation is free of confounding variables. In addition to the process of determining observation needs, professional school counselors involved in structured observation need to (a) ensure the objectivity of the observers, (b) remain inconspicuous, (c) address the behaviors specified in the planning phase, and (d) rehearse observations to ensure proper documentation. Proper planning and efficient design promote the best possible chances for an observation to yield credible results.

**Table 1. Direct Observational Methods.**

| Observational Method | Method of Collection | Benefits |
|---|---|---|
| Anecdotal Observation: ABC analysis | Counselor prepares an observation form divided in three sections to record antecedent events, observed behaviors and consequent events. | • Easy organization.<br>• Recognizes events supporting inappropriate behavior.<br>• Recognizes environmental conditions that assist or inhibit positive behaviors. |
| Frequency of Behavior: Tallying/Frequency/ Timed Observations/ Period Observation | Checklists, Rating Scales, professional school counselor generated forms. | • Can focus on occurrence of behavior as well as duration.<br>• Can establish an overlapping observation cycle.<br>• Provides flexibility in the planning phase of the observation. |

## Summary/Conclusion

Conducting a structured observation is important for teachers and educators to understand the nature of the academic environment. Initiating a structured observation involves more than watching students. It encompasses the blending of teacher, parent, student, and administrator views toward the clear identification of problematic conditions needing modification. Properly planned observations provide credible results that work to isolate and remedy problem behaviors ensuring the academic success of each student.

**Figure 3. Example of Anecdotal Observation Report using ABC analysis.**

**OBSERVATION RECORD**

Institution______________________ Observer______________________
Observation participant_________________ Location of observation_______________
Observation period
Start Time: _____________
End Time: ______________

---

**Antecedent Events**
*State time and briefly describe events*

Ex. 1) 1020hrs student running in hallway

---

**Observed Behavior**
*State time and briefly describe events*

Ex. 1) student collides with teacher's aid

---

**Consequent Behavior**
*State time and briefly describe events*

Ex. 1) teacher's aid drops books, turns and makes the student stand against the wall

**Figure 4. Frequency and Duration Observational Record.**

**Frequency Observation Record**

Child's Name ______________________ Date of Observation ___________

Observer_______________________ Identified Behavior_________________

| Date/Time | Frequency of behavior / | Duration of observation ——— | Duration of behavior |
|---|---|---|---|
| Example | | | |
| 2-22/1430hrs | 10X | 25 Minutes | 0.4 per min. |

## References

American School Counselor Association. (2000). *Position statement: Noncredentialed personnel.* Retrieved June 26, 2002, from http://www.schoolcounselor.org content.cfm? L1=1000&L2=27.

Asmus, J. M., Vollmer, T. R., & Borrero, J. C. (2002). Functional behavioral assessment: A school based model [Electronic version]. *Education and Treatment of Children, 25,* 67-90.

Drummond, R. J. (2000). *Appraisal procedures for counselors and helping professionals* (4th ed.). Saddle River, NJ: Merrill.

Ellis, J., & Magee, S. K. (1999). Determination of environmental correlates of disruptive classroom behavior: Integration of functional analysis into public school assessment process [Electronic version]. *Education and Treatment of Children, 22,* 291-316.

Freiberg, H. J. (1998). Measuring school climate: Let me count the ways [Electronic version]. *Educational Leadership, 56,*22-27.

Gordon, B. G., Meadows, R. B., & Dyal, A. B. (1995). School principals' perceptions: The use of formal observation of classroom teaching to improve instruction [Electronic version]. *Education, 116,* 9-16.

Hagborg, W. J. (1998). An investigation of a brief measure of school membership [Electronic Version]. *Adolescence, 33,* 461-499.

Paisley, P. O., & McMahon, G. (2001). School counseling for the 21st century: Challenges and opportunities [Electronic version]. *Professional School Counseling, 5,* 106-115.

Shapiro, E. S., & Skinner, C. H. (1990). Best practices in observation and ecological assessment. In A. Thomas & J. Grimes (Eds.), *Best practices in school psychology* (pp. 507-518). Washington, DC: The National Association of School Psychologists.

Webb, N. M., Baxter, G. P., & Thompson, L. (1997). Teachers' grouping practices in fifth-grade science classrooms [Electronic version]. *The Elementary School Journal, 98,* 91-114.

Zirpoli, T. J., & Melloy, K. J. (1997). *Behavior management: Application for teachers and parents* (2nd ed.). Upper Saddle River, NJ: Merrill.

# Chapter 52

## Students, Technology, and Testing: Why Counselors Must Care

*Janet E. Wall*

### Preview

In the future, technology and assessment as aids to professional school counselors will change dramatically. It is almost a certainty that: testing will become more efficient; testing will take on more interesting, creative, and relevant forms; testing and instruction will be more closely aligned; many more tests will be given online; and students will expect and even demand greater use of computers and the Internet. This chapter addresses these issues and provides online resources that professional school counselors need to stay in tune with how their assessment responsibilities are evolving.

### Testing Will Become More Efficient

With the introduction of computers and the Internet into the educational systems, various measurement approaches have blossomed. The most popular is a set of procedures and processes that fall into the category of computer adaptive testing. This approach to testing uses the rapid calculation capabilities of the computer to select items tailored to a person's particular level of achievement or ability. Sireci (2003) provided a good overview of the intricacies of computer adaptive testing, but a somewhat simplistic description follows. Consider a student who is taking a mathematics test via computer. The computer selects an item of average difficulty and presents it to the student. The student answers the question correctly (or incorrectly). The computer then selects a more difficult (or easier) item to see how the student answers the question. If the student still answers the question correctly (or incorrectly) the computer then selects and even more difficult (or easier) item. The process continues until the computer, programmed by rules created by educational testing specialists, has honed in on the actual achievement level of the student in question.

Such a process would be enormously cumbersome, if not impossible, to use in a paper/pencil testing environment. However, the computer is able to determine a student's level of achievement faster, with fewer items, and more accurately. This obviously creates efficiency useful to school personnel both in time and money.

### Testing Will Take on More Interesting, Creative, and Relevant Forms

Bennett (2002) suggested going beyond the limitations of multiple-choice tests and use available technology to develop assessments that support learning and instruction in ways that paper/pencil assessment cannot.

Consider how technology can make assessment more interesting, performance-oriented, realistic, and authentic. The introduction of audio, video, interactivity, graphics, and the ability to access multiple resources has allowed test developers to create, and test users to access, assessment items that move well beyond familiar repeat and recall items.

Technology-based assessment in the area of science can pose a situation in which the student has to create a hypothesis, collect and analyze data, test the hypothesis, render conclusions, and predict further action. This can be accomplished through items that offer the student the opportunity to select the tools of the experiment, collect the data, create graphs that display the data, change the variables, and draw conclusions. The computer can then judge how well, efficiently, and accurately the student was able to handle the necessary problem-solving and experimental requirements.

A language teacher can provide the opportunity for students to link up audio and video with native language speakers to assist students in perfecting their pronunciation, dialect, and general competence in the language they are trying to learn. Consider further how valuable it could be for a student to understand better the culture and politics of the country whose language he is trying to master through interaction with citizens of that country.

Think about performance tests in areas such as nursing, architecture, physician assistant, realty, driver's education, history, social studies, etc., that present the student with a scenario to analyze. The computer allows the student to select the tools to be used in handling the problem posed, to seek and select the information that might be needed, to sort and categorize the information, and propose the best solution to solve the problem through a written composition that is analyzed by computer, not human scorers. Further, the technology can allow for a comprehensive evaluation of how well the scenario was analyzed, all in a matter of moments, rather than days (or months).

Ponder the possibility of the counselor educator who needs to monitor and evaluate his interns at a school or agency. Technology such as video-teleconferencing can be used to assess and critique students through real-time observations of how they interact and assist students/clients, or to observe the intern as he/she interprets assessment results with a student or client.

Recognize the benefits associated with the possibilities of administering and scoring written essays and passages by computer, as opposed to waiting for a team of readers to make a determination of the quality of the writing. Further, appreciate the speed and consistency with which computers can operate in scoring these essays.

Technologies such as instant messaging, electronic chats, audio/video, video-teleconferencing, web cams, and artificial intelligence can augment and facilitate the previous examples, and many more, to improve assessment in areas of responsibility for teachers and professional school counselors. The professional's creativity is the limiting factor, not the technology.

## Tests Will Be More Closely Aligned With Instruction

There are multiple pressure points forcing school personnel to provide testing that is more closely aligned with instruction, and instruction more closely aligned with agreed upon standards. The first pressure point is the issue of fairness. If a student is judged by a test to be competent or not, pass a class or be promoted, then the test questions that help make that judgment must relate to the instructional program provided to the student. There are many ethical and legal ramifications to situations in which important decisions are made from assessments that do not reflect the curriculum that is provided to the student. The second major pressure point is the recent passage of the No Child Left Behind legislation that mandates alignment of tests to state standards. Finally, technology will facilitate the matching of assessment to instruction, and then standards. Items can be stored electronically and coded to instructional objectives and standards so that large-scale assessments can focus on the particular standards of interest to state policy-makers and school personnel. Another benefit of this approach is that both teachers and professional school counselors would be able to access student information in near real time so that interventions can be implemented just as soon as the test results are known.

## Many More Tests Will Be Given Online

Figure 1 indicates a number of states are implementing or planning to implement statewide assessments over the Internet (Education Week, 2002).

**Figure 1. States using or planning large-scale assessments over the Internet.**

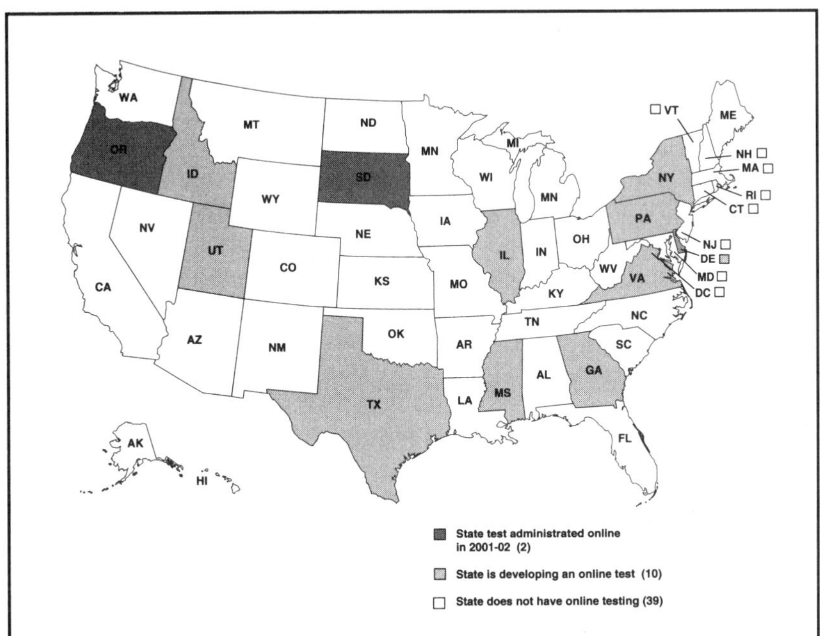


Online testing and assessment offers the capability of obtaining achievement information from many students with rapid data retrieval in time for policy makers to identify the curricular strengths and weaknesses that require specific attention. It offers the chance for classroom teachers and professional school counselors to access achievement information on individual students at the level of instructional objectives at a time when instructional interventions can actually make a difference, not months later. Since most schools have the capability to make information available to parents directly through e-mail or websites (Kleiner & Ferris, 2002), test results can be transmitted to parents for their edification and action.

The examples cited above are some positive ways that computers and the Internet can expedite testing. The other side of the coin involves easy access to tests and assessments that are lacking in technical evidence and documentation or developed by individuals without appropriate expertise. Pick your favorite search engine and enter the term "educational testing." If you use http://www.google.com, be ready to view 1.6 million websites or links that claim to have related information. Try http://www. altavista.com; the site reports that it has found over 20 million websites coded to that term. Many online tests, assessments, and inventories can be downloaded or taken online.

Wall (2003) provided a summary of how a professional school counselor should think about the advantages and disadvantages of technology-delivered assessments. Professional school counselors will need to be able to discern the differences between credible and not credible instruments that are available via a few clicks on an Internet browser. Some guidelines for sorting tests that are credible from those that are not have been identified. These guidelines include statements of best practice in test administration, test quality, credibility of the developer, test interpretation, and access to professionals (Wall, 2000).

Despite the availability of both good and bad assessments over the Internet, pertinent information on tests and testing in general can be found on the Internet. Clearly, it is impossible to keep track of those millions of websites related to educational testing. The websites listed in Table 1 are a few that offer excellent, credible and updated information on assessment issues in counseling and education.

**Table 1. Suggested assessment-related websites.**

1. *American Educational Research Association (AERA)*: This organization is concerned with the educational process through scholarly inquiry and information dissemination. Many publications, newsletters, and reports are available via its website [http://www.aera.net]. AERA is a member of the Joint Committee on Testing Practices (JCTP).
2. *American Psychological Association (APA) – Science Directorate*: The Science Directorate of APA focuses its efforts on providing information for American Psychological Association's scientific and academic members. APA is a member of the JCTP, and the Committee's website is housed on APA's website [http://www.apa.org/science/].
3. *Association for Assessment in Counseling (AAC)*: AAC is an organization of counselors, counselor educators, and other professionals that was created to advance the counseling profession by providing leadership, training, and research in the creation, development, production, and use of assessment and diagnostic techniques. Information on assessment issues, test reviews and other important information can be found on this website [http://aac.ncat.edu]. This site has a comprehensive set of links that direct the user to standards, guidelines, policies, and associations related to testing.
4. *Association of Test Publishers (ATP)*: ATP is a non-profit organization representing providers of tests and assessment tools and services related to assessment, selection, screening, certification, licensing, and educational or clinical uses of tests. The organization has many publications and information on assessment available on its site [http://www.testpublishers.org/].
5. *Board on Testing and Assessment (BOTA)*: BOTA advises the federal government on a wide range of issues concerning the science and policies of testing and assessment in education, employment, and the military. Issues addressed by BOTA include the role of assessment in standards-based reform of education, the effects of high-stakes testing, the development of professional testing standards and policies to ensure appropriate test use, and the uses of assessment as tools of program evaluation and accountability [http://www4.nationalacademies.org/dbasse/bota.nsf].
6. *Buros Institute of Mental Measurements*: This site represents the well-known Buros products and services including test reviews and searches. The reviews of tests can be very useful to individuals searching for an instrument with a particular purpose and set of characteristics [http://www.unl.edu/buros/].

7. *Joint Committee on Testing Practices (JCTP)*: This site provides information on the activities of the JCTP. Available for downloading from this site are several of the products produced by working groups of this organization [http://www.apa.org/science/jctpweb.html].
8. *National Association of School Psychologists (NASP)*: NASP's prime goal is to promote educationally and psychologically healthy environments for all children and youth. Many policy statements, position papers, and responses to frequently asked questions can be found on its site. NASP is a member of the JCTP [http://www.nasponline.org].
9. *National Association of Test Directors (NATD):* NATD is an association of professionals with responsibilities for administering assessment programs in K-12 public educational settings. Various publications, legislative information, and useful links can be found on this site. NATD is a member of the JCTP [http://www.natd.org].
10. *National Center for Educational Statistics (NCES):* This government office oversees the creation and implementation of the nation's large-scale assessment program called the National Assessment of Education Progress (NAEP). It is responsible for implementing the assessment plan, analyzing the results, and reporting the results to the general public and policy makers. It is perhaps best known for its product, The Nation's Report Card. NCES also collects, analyzes, and reports on various other data about schools and education. [http://nces.ed.gov].
11. *National Council on Measurement in Education (NCME)*: This organization is devoted to educational assessment issues. NCME is a member of the JCTP [http://www.ncme.org].
12. *Office of Educational Research and Improvement (OERI):* OERI is part of the U.S. Department of Education [http://www.ed.gov/offices/OERI]. It provides national leadership for educational research and statistics. Many of its efforts involve evaluation and assessment. This office supports many of the research labs that investigate and disseminate information on educational progress, including assessment.

---

In addition to keeping in touch with the information provided on the websites listed above, professional school counselors need to keep in mind the various professional association testing standards in order to differentiate what is credible from what is not on the Internet. These testing standards apply to tests in paper/pencil format, but also those available on-line or via computer. Professional school counselors need to be familiar with professional codes, standards and policies such as the *Standards of Educational and Psychological Testing* (AERA, APA & NCME, 1999), *Code of Fair Testing Standards in Education* (JCTP, 2002), the *Responsibilities of Users of Standardized Tests* (AAC, 2003), *Qualifications of Test Users* (ACA, 2003), and *Rights and Responsibilities of Test Takers: Guidelines and Expectations* (JCTP, 2000). The guidance provided in these standards go a long way in assisting professional school counselors to identify, select, administer, score, and interpret test information.

### Students Will Expect and Even Demand Greater Use of Computers and the Internet

The U.S. Department of Commerce (2002) claimed that 90% of 5-17 year-old students use computers, many of those obtaining information over the Internet. A recent study by the Pew Foundation (Levin & Arafeh, 2002) indicated that students rely, even depend, on information obtainable over the Web. The report suggested that students state that they use the Internet: to help them do their school work; to perform most learning functions and activities, such as school papers; as a virtual textbook and reference library; for tutoring, study and study groups; for guidance and counseling when making decisions about academics, careers, and future plans; and as a backpack, virtual locker, and notebook. In other words, students consider the computer and Internet access as common as the radio, television, telephone, or microwave. It is not a novelty, but rather a normal, natural, and expected part of their world.

This same report identified a critical disconnect between school personnel and students with regard to technology capability. This is particularly disconcerting because more students use computers at school than at home (Newberger, 2001). Some of the conclusions listed in the report included:

- School administrators and teachers have not yet recognized or responded to the new ways in which students communicate and obtain information over the Internet.
- Administrators and teachers set the tone and provide leadership for the way the Internet is used in schools.
- Teachers do not use the Internet in an inspiring and engaging way.

As gently as this study couches its findings, the bottom line is that school personnel have not kept pace with the capabilities of the students.

The message is clear. Professional school counselors and other educational personnel need to upgrade their own capabilities to deal successfully with the competencies of their school clientele. They should learn about Internet Service Providers (ISPs), understand search engines, interact with colleagues via e-mail, find information on the Internet, join a listserv, follow information provided on assessment and counseling that can be found on the Web, and take courses to upgrade knowledge and skills.

## Summary/Conclusion

Access to current and new technologies will only increase over time. As such, professional school counselors need to harness the power of the Internet in performing their job functions. In doing so, professional school counselors can expand their influence and assist students in dealing with academic, career, and personal/social needs and issues.

## References

American Counseling Association. (2003). *Qualifications of test users.* Alexandria, VA: Author.

American Educational Research Association, American Psychological Association, & National Council on Measurement in Education. (1999). *Standards for educational and psychological testing.* Washington, DC: American Psychological Association.

Association for Assessment in Counseling. (2003). *Responsibilities of users of standardized tests.* Alexandria, VA: Author.

Bennett, R. E. (2002). Inexorable and inevitable: The continuing story of technology and assessment. *Journal of Technology, Learning, and Assessment, 1,* 1-23.

Education Week. (2002). *Technology counts 2002: E-defining education.* Bethesda, MD: Author.

Joint Committee on Testing Practices. (2000). *Rights and responsibilities of test takers: Guidelines and expectations.* Washington, DC: American Psychological Association.

Joint Committee on Testing Practices. (2002). *Code of fair testing practices in education.* Washington, DC: American Psychological Association.

Kleiner, A., & Farris, E. (2002). National Center for Education Statistics. *Internet access in U.S. public schools and classrooms: 1994-2001,* NCES 2002-018. Washington, DC: U.S. Department of Education.

Levin, D., & Arafeh, S. (August, 2002). *The digital disconnect: The widening gap between Internet savvy students and their schools*. Washington, DC: Pew Internet & American Life Project.

Newberger, E. (2001). *Home computers and Internet use the United States: August 2000*. Washington, DC: US Census Bureau.

Sireci, S. (2003). Computer adaptive testing: An introduction. In J. Wall & G. Walz (Eds.), *Measuring up: Assessment issues for counselors, teachers, and administrators*. Greensboro, NC: ERIC-CAPS.

U.S. Department of Commerce. (2002). *A nation online: How Americans are expanding their use of the Internet*. Washington, DC: Author.

Wall, J. E. (2000). Technology-delivered assessment: Power, problems and promise. In J. Bloom & G. Walz (Eds.), *Cybercounseling and cyberlearning: Strategies and resources for the millennium* (pp.237-251). Alexandria, VA: American Counseling Association.

Wall, J. E. (2003). Harnessing technology for assessment. In J. Wall & G. Walz (Eds.), *Measuring up: Assessment issues for counselors, teachers, and administrators*. Greensboro, NC: ERIC/CAPS.

# *Section 5*

# Clinical Issues in School Counseling

# Chapter 53

## Helping Students with Attention-Deficit/Hyperactivity Disorder (AD/HD)

*David J. Carter, Bradley T. Erford, & Ralph Orsi*

### Preview

This chapter provides awareness, knowledge and skills to address the specific needs of the student with Attention-Deficit/Hyperactivity Disorder (AD/HD) through a team approach. In most cases, students affected by this complex disorder are disadvantaged in the school, home and social settings. This chapter provides facts and strategies to dispel the myths and provide user- friendly strategies and support for addressing the needs of the student with AD/HD.

Attention-Deficit/Hyperactivity Disorder (AD/HD) is a complex medical condition affecting about 3 million school-aged children (about 3-5% of school-aged population) and is so multifaceted that one student with AD/HD may have very different symptoms than another student. The purpose of this chapter is to increase the awareness, knowledge and skills of the professional school counselor regarding AD/HD to better help students with this condition.

Over the years the terms used to describe AD/HD have changed (Barkley, 1990). During the first half of the 20th century these children were described as brain-injured or brain-damaged. During the 1950's and 1960's the terms minimal brain dysfunction (MBD), hyperactive child syndrome and hyperkinetic reaction of childhood were introduced into the literature. In 1980, the *DSM-III* introduced the term Attention Deficit Disorder (ADD). ADD with Hyperactivity was used to describe students with characteristic distractibility, impulsivity and overactivity. ADD without hyperactivity described the distractible and impulsive children who lacked significant hyperactivity. In 1987, the *DSM-III-R* introduced the term Attention Deficit Hyperactivity Disorder (ADHD) and listed 14 criteria. This conceptualization did not distinguish subtypes based on activity levels and reflected the thinking of that time that distractibility in and of itself was not characteristic of a mental disorder. Finally, in 1994 with the release of the *DSM-IV*, the current term Attention-Deficit/Hyperactivity Disorder (AD/HD) was introduced.

AD/HD is currently divided into three subtypes. Certain students, referred to as Predominantly Inattentive Type, have little or no problem sitting still but may have difficulty with organizational skills or staying focused on a task or activity. Others, referred to as Predominately Hyperactive-Impulsive Type, may be able to pay attention to a task, but have significant difficulty controlling their impulses and motor activity. The most commonly diagnosed form of AD/HD is the Combined Type; these students have significant symptoms of both Inattentive and Hyperactive-Impulsive Types.

Not all professionals distinguish between types of AD/HD in the same way; therefore a team approach will provide the best support for students affected by this disorder. Professional school counselors, school psychologists, teachers, school administrators and parents are all key members of the team who observe and report on the student's progress. Professional school counselors have the responsibility of selecting and monitoring the students' treatment, making referrals, and linking parents to community resources. When parents know their role on the team, they are empowered to seek the best support for the student.

AD/HD applies not only to children but also adults who consistently display characteristic behaviors such as distractibility, impulsivity, or hyperactivity for an extended period of time. The focus of this chapter will be on elementary, middle and high schools students with AD/HD.

*Common Myths Surrounding AD/HD*

*AD/HD is an "imitation disorder" and is not a real or recognized condition.* AD/HD has been recognized as a debilitating disorder and disability by all major professional medical, psychiatric, psychological, legal and educational associations (Booth et al., 2002).

*Stimulant medications cure AD/HD.* Research has repeatedly shown that children and adolescents diagnosed with AD/HD benefit from therapeutic treatment with stimulant medications, which have been used safely and studied for more than 50 years. However, medication only reduces symptoms during treatment. "Skills, not pills," create lasting changes in the lives of students with AD/HD.

*Individual Educational Plans (IEP) will always be provided for students with AD/HD.* In most school districts, unless a diagnosis of AD/HD has been provided by a physician or by a mental health professional after a psychological assessment, an IEP will not be initiated. In these cases the professional school counselor can recommend intervention strategies to the teacher or advocate for appropriate referral and treatment. Students with AD/HD are often given accommodations through section 504 of the US Rehabilitation Act of 1973 or, when eligible, special education services through IDEA, usually with a handicapping condition of other health impaired (OHI) or learning disability (LD).

*Students with AD/HD are learning to make excuses, rather than take responsibility for their actions.* Counselors, educators, and physicians routinely teach students and parents that AD/HD is a challenge, not an excuse. Medication may address an underlying chemical imbalance, but coping skills give them a fair chance of facing the challenges of growing up to become productive citizens.

*ADHD is the parent's fault and due to bad parenting and lack of discipline. All that students with AD/HD need is old-fashioned discipline.* Faraone and Biederman (1998) demonstrated that while AD/HD may be an inherited condition, not all children in a family will develop AD/HD. Simply providing more discipline without any other interventions generally worsens rather than improves the behavior of students with AD/HD.

*Teachers and professional school counselors around the country routinely advocate for medication for students who are even a little inattentive or overactive.* When teachers and professional school counselors see students who are struggling to pay attention, concentrate, or are fidgety and disruptive, it is their responsibility to bring this behavior to parents' attention so parents can make an informed decision and take appropriate action. The majority of professional school counselors and teachers do not simply promote medication; they provide information so that parents can seek out appropriate diagnostic and treatment services. While professional school counselors do not ordinarily diagnose students with AD/HD, being on the front lines with children, they collect information, raise the possibility of AD/HD, and bring the information to the attention of parents who then need to have psychological and medical evaluations conducted, either privately or in cooperation with school personnel.

*Children will eventually outgrow AD/HD*. AD/HD may not disappear as a student grows older. While 70% of students with AD/HD will continue to manifest the full clinical syndrome in adolescence, only 15-50% will continue to manifest the full clinical syndrome in adulthood (Barkley, 1990). Generally, hyperactive symptoms are likely to decline in adulthood while symptoms of distractibility and disorganization remain.

*Sugar, dyes and additives will increase AD/HD activity.* Sugar causes a burst of energy (in anyone, not just students with AD/HD). Restricting sugar intake will not reduce AD/HD symptoms. Food dyes and additives should be eliminated from everyone's diet, but this is becoming more difficult due to current food processing methods. Studies (Barkley, 1990) have shown that some students (perhaps 20%) have allergic reactions to these substances. However, food dyes and additives do not cause hyperactive symptoms in the vast majority of students with AD/HD.

*It is not possible to accurately diagnose AD/HD in children.* Although scientists have not yet developed a single medical test for diagnosing AD/HD, diagnostic criteria have been developed, researched, and refined over several decades. The current generally accepted diagnostic criteria for AD/HD are listed in the *DSM-IV-TR* (APA, 2000). Using these criteria and multiple methods to collect comprehensive information from multiple informants, AD/HD can be reliably and accurately diagnosed in students.

## Diagnosis

When diagnosing AD/HD, professional school counselors can help uncover evidence of clinically significant impairment in social or academic functioning as well as document that the symptoms were evident prior to seven years of age and occur in more than one setting. Symptoms of AD/HD must persist for at least six months and to a degree that is maladaptive and inconsistent with the student's developmental level. Table 1 contains the *DSM-IV-TR* (APA, 2000) diagnostic criteria for AD/HD Predominately Inattentive Type. Table 2 contains the diagnostic criteria for Predominately Hyperactive-Impulsive Type (APA, 2000).

It is widely believed that many students are misdiagnosed with AD/HD because they have medical or psychological conditions that mask or mimic the symptoms of AD/HD. While it is always possible that a student with AD/HD can have an additional diagnosable condition (comorbid), it is essential that conditions which mimic AD/HD be ruled out to increase confidence that the student truly has AD/HD. Following are medical and psychological conditions which often cause students to behave in a distractible or overactive manner: Oppositional Defiant Disorder, Conduct Disorder, Generalized Anxiety Disorder, Dysthymic Disorder, BipolarDisorder, Posttraumatic Stress Disorder, Major Depressive Disorder, Manic Episode, Schizoid Personality Disorder (and Schizophrenia, Schizotypal, and Schizo-affective Disorders), physical or sexual abuse, grand mal seizures, petite mal seizures, substance use or abuse, asthma (actually the use of the inhalator causes overactivity in some), lead poisoning, hyperactive thyroid, anemia, allergies, Pervasive Developmental Disorder, auditory processing disorder, visual processing disorder, Motor Coordination Disorder, and others. When diagnosing AD/HD, each of the above conditions should be ruled out (or determined to be comorbid) during clinical interviewing.

**Table 1. The *DSM-IV-TR* criteria for AD/HD – Predominantly Inattentive Type (APA, 2000, pp. 83-84).**

Six or more symptoms must be evident to a significant degree:

- often fails to give close attention to details or makes careless mistakes in schoolwork, work or other activities
- often has difficulty sustaining attention in tasks or play activities
- often does not seem to listen when spoken to directly
- often does not follow through on instructions and fails to finish schoolwork, chores, or duties in the workplace (not due to oppositional behavior or failure to understand instructions)
- often has difficulty organizing tasks and activities
- often avoids, dislikes, or is reluctant to engage in tasks that require sustained mental effort (such as schoolwork or homework)
- often loses things necessary for tasks or activities (e.g., toys, school assignments, pencils, books or tools)
- is often easily distracted by extraneous stimuli
- is often forgetful in daily activities

**Table 2. The *DSM-IV-TR* criteria for AD/HD – Predominately Hyperactive/Impulsive Type (APA, 2000, p. 84).**

Six or more of the following symptoms must be evident to a significant degree:

- often fidgets with hands or feet or squirms in seat
- often leaves seat in classroom or in other situations in which remaining seated is expected
- often runs about or climbs excessively in situations in which it is inappropriate (in adolescents or adults, may be limited to subjective feelings of restlessness)
- often has difficulty playing or engaging in leisure activities quietly
- is often "on the go" or often acts as if "driven by a motor"
- often talks excessively
- often blurts out answers before questions have been completed
- often has difficulty awaiting turn
- often interrupts or intrudes on others (butts into conversations or games)

## How Parents and Educators Can Help Students with AD/HD

Teachers, parents, administrators and professional school counselors can enact numerous strategies to help students with AD/HD experience academic and behavioral success at school and home. These strategies are typically aimed at reducing inappropriate symptoms of distractibility/ disorganization and impulsiveness/hyperactivity. Table 3 presents strategies that may be used to help students with AD/HD. Parents play a key role in the academic and personal success of their child. Professional school counselors can reassure parents that AD/HD is not their fault and that it can be treated effectively through parent training and family education, regular monitoring, behavior management and medication, when appropriate. Parents can compliment the team process and provide continuity between the school and home.

**Table 3. Helpful strategies for educators and parents of students with AD/HD.**

1. Set time limits for chores/tasks to help the student develop a sense of time management. Maintain a consistent schedule to promote the student's mental organization.
2. Use behavior management techniques such as token economy, positive reinforcement, behavior contracts, behavior charts, Premack Principle, time-out, response cost and overcorrection (see chapter 33, "Setting Up and Managing a Classroom").
3. Use positive attention. Praise behaviors you want to see more often. Acknowledge good behavior immediately and be specific and genuine in your praise.
4. Establish a routine, rules and procedures. Students with AD/HD generally do better in a structured environment. Stay on a schedule and alternate between low and high interest activities.
5. Involve peers in the learning process. Encourage the use of peer tutors and study buddies for students with AD/HD to help develop better organizational skills. It is important that the peer not become involved in administering punishment to the student with AD/HD.
6. Create tools to help students improve organizational skills. Write descriptions of daily and long-term goals. Color-coding, assignment folders and creating checklists are helpful ways to promote good organizational skills.
7. Try incentives and rewards. Use privileges and activities as rewards and have students pick their own rewards. Have students set realistic goals, monitor and evaluate their own behavior.
8. Give just one warning. Catch problem behavior as soon as it begins, be brief and matter of fact, and give feedback privately.
9. Involve parents. When the student does not act appropriately, contact the parent/guardian and try to establish a sense of collaboration between the student, parent and teacher. Make everyone's expectations explicit.
10. Match academic assignments to the student's level of ability and attention span.
11. Give only one task at a time.
12. Provide frequent feedback. Maintain close proximity to the child. Give adequate "getting started" instructions.
13. Monitor the student's progress frequently and with a supportive attitude.
14. Allow the student to seek assistance from others if needed.
15. Make sure to test knowledge and not attention span.
16. Increase supervision at transition times, e.g., lunch, recess, specials.
17. If the student with AD/HD has slow processing and writing speed, he will benefit from extra time given to complete standardized tests. Extra time should also be given on in-school tests so that his grades will reflect mastery of content, rather than time constraints.
18. Use the word processor to compose written work whenever possible. Improve keyboarding skills by completing either a tutorial or software-based keyboarding learning system immediately and use these skills to complete writing assignments and homework. This will help counterbalance the frustration accompanying slow writing speed, as well as that stemming from rewriting handwritten compositions in the future.
19. Cut back on repetitive homework assignments beyond the point of mastery.
20. Allow preferential seating near the primary area of instruction with the student's back facing any distracting students or stimuli.

21. Surround the student with focused role-models who will neither distract the student or allow the student to distract them.
22. Have the student check with you after completing the first item, then again at the half-way point and upon concluding the entire task. Compliment the student when proceeding correctly and redirect his performance when off track.
23. Insist the student follow through and finish each task correctly before moving onto a more desired activity. This is called the Premack Principle - high frequency behaviors must follow low frequency behaviors. For example, have the student finish language homework BEFORE engaging in a play activity.
24. When testing, the student may perform better in a study carrel in another area of the classroom where distractions can be minimized.
25. Have the student divide long-term assignments into sections, setting a due date for each section, and complying with each due date.
26. Have the student rework all errors on tests and assignments to reinforce mastery and stress careful initial work habits.
27. Have the student redo a messy or incorrect assignment to understand that carefulness and accuracy are more important work habits than quickness.
28. If the student has difficulty with multi-step tasks, she can be helped to better understand task directions when she, and her teachers and parents, break down multi-step directions into a sequence of ordered steps.
    a. Write down and number the steps so the student can complete the steps one at a time.
    b. Have the student check with an adult after completing each step and before moving on to the next step.
    c. Have an adult check progress at each step before moving on.
    d. When beginning the assignment, check to be sure the student is on the right track.
    e. Give an example of what the student is to do.
    f. Check progress frequently.
    g. Have the student rephrase the directions in his own words to be sure he understands.
    h. Have a well-organized student help transition the student with AD/HD from step to step.
    i. Have the student do 2-3 examples under supervision of a teacher, parent, or student helper to be sure she understands the process before beginning to complete items independently.
    j. Make sure multi-step directions are written down, whether on the paper, chalkboard, or an index card.
29. Require a daily assignment notebook that allows daily or at least weekly communication between the parent and teachers. This notebook should be signed by teachers and parents.
30. Use behavioral contracts which identify specific academic and behavioral goals.
31. Use a timer to break assignments into smaller time units of more intense focus. For a child with a short attention span, timed units should not generally exceed 10-15 minutes; for adolescents, 15-30 minutes. After a short break with plenty of performance feedback and encouragement, as well as some physical movement of exercise, the next timed task can ensue.
32. Set up appropriate home and school study spaces, with set times, no distraction, and a recognized routine.

33. Increase structure and routine by:
    a. being consistent in behavioral programs
    b. giving multiple choice tests as opposed to fill-in-the–blank or essay tests to benefit these contextual learners
    c. providing visual-tactile and multi-sensory approaches to instruction
    d. marking off worksheets into blocks and number columns
    e. having a review session at the end of the day for homework assignments, key points, etc.
34. Arrange student seating to lower distractions:
    a. front of classroom
    b. face the area of greatest instructional relevance
    c. study office (carrel) for independent work
    d. away from doors, windows, and other distracting students
    e. keep materials in cabinets rather than on display when not in use
    f. use earphones (white noise, soft instrumental music) to keep down distractions.
35. Facilitate rule internalization by:
    a. creating posters with rules for various work periods
    b. asking the student to re-state rules from time-to-time
    c. teaching the student to use self-instruction during work
    d. having the student recite rules to another student before beginning an assignment
    e. using tape-recorded cues or reminders
    f. developing nonverbal cues as a reminder
    g. defining clear and reasonable limits
    h. giving the student specific times when it is appropriate to get up out of his seat
    i. timing the student for getting started (e.g., "10 seconds to get your name on the paper").
36. Teach and reinforce problem-solving strategies.
37. Allow access to rewards at multiple points during the day.
38. Use response cost behavioral monitoring, such as a leaf or apple from the tree or three wooden sticks before a privilege is lost.
39. Set time limits for work completion.
40. Use timers.
41. Use tape-recorded time prompts. When the tone beeps have the students self-monitor and self-reward to determine if he/she was on task.
42. Develop a system for coordinating home and school consequences including: daily home-school token economy; daily report from teacher; daily home-school journal (the move to weekly or monthly monitoring is the goal and should be accomplished gradually).
43. Recommend parent support group association meetings.
44. Providing more spacing on paper gives the feeling of accomplishment and increases visual organization.
45. Initially establish lower accuracy expectations that increase over time with the students' success.
46. Have the student do a shortened version of a class project.
47. Realize that the student will be more inattentive just before lunch and late in the afternoon. Plan instruction accordingly.
48. For young students, allow the use of math manipulatives or other visual tactile techniques.
49. Divide and shorten assignments with rewards in between, avoid heavy doses of

desk work and provide opportunities for purposeful movement.

50. Establish a nonverbal cue (touch or signal to let the student know when she is inattentive or behaving improperly).
51. For young students, tape record the homework and schoolwork instructions for moderate to complex assignments so the student can go back to listen to them later in class or at home.
52. The student may need to be tested orally rather than through traditional written techniques.
53. Brightly colored instructional materials, having a clear and specific instructional purpose, may be effectively used to engage the student's attention.
54. Occasional voluntary activity (e.g., "getting the wiggles out") can interrupt the uncontrolled movement and gradually allow more voluntary control. The exercise must be viewed as helpful and not as punishment.
55. Role-play action scenes which emphasize patient, deliberate activities.
56. Provide many opportunities for activity during instruction.
57. Change activities and posture frequently. If possible, alternate between desk, floor, standing, group and movement activities.
58. Give the student sanctioned times out of his seat to let off energy.
59. Use a behavioral contract system in which the student actively participates.

---

## Medication

Medication is effective for treating impulsivity, inattention, and hyperactivity. Approximately 75 percent of students with AD/HD respond positively to psychostimulants or tricyclic antidepressants (Barkley, 1990; Kaplan & Sadock, 1996). According to Hartmann (1997) medications are often prescribed by child psychiatrists for three to twelve months in order to develop new patterns of behavior and then the dosage is reduced or discontinued depending on the needs of the student. However, in some students medication may be required well into adolescence, while others show a continued need for medication into adulthood. The reader is directed to chapter 71, "Medication Issues in Schools," contained in this book for further information.

## Case Vignettes

The following vignettes are typical of the types of behavior students with AD/HD will exhibit in the classroom. It is important to recognize that although these behaviors are typical of a student with AD/HD, not all students who exhibit these behaviors have AD/HD.

*Case 1: Mark*

Mark has more energy than most boys his age. But then, he's always been overly active. Starting at age three, he was a human tornado, dashing around and disrupting everything in his path. At home, he went from one activity to the next, leaving a trail of toys behind him. At meals, he upset dishes and chattered nonstop. He was reckless and impulsive, even running into the street with oncoming cars no matter how many times his mother explained the danger or scolded him.

On the playground, he seemed no wilder than the other kids. But his tendency to overreact, like hitting playmates simply for bumping into him, had already gotten him into trouble several times. His parents didn't know what to do. Mark's caring grandparents reassured them, "Boys will be boys, he'll grow out of it," but he didn't. In third grade, Mark's teacher threw up her hands and said, *"Enough!"* In one morning, Mark had jumped out of his seat to sharpen his pencil six times, each time accidentally knocking into other children's desks and toppling books and papers. He was finally sent to the principal's office when he began kicking a desk he had overturned. In sheer frustration, his teacher called a meeting with his parents and the professional school counselor. But even after they developed a plan for managing Mark's behavior in class, Mark showed little improvement. Finally, after an extensive assessment, they found that Mark had AD/HD - Combined Type. He was put on medication to control the hyperactivity during school hours. With the professional school counselor's help, Mark's parents learned to reward desirable behaviors and send Mark to "time out" when he refused to follow parental directions (Erford, 1999). Soon Mark was able to sit still and focus on learning. Today, at age 14, Mark is doing much better in school. He channels his energy into sports and is a star player on the football team.

Although Mark still gets into scuffles now and then, the professional school counselor is helping him learn to control his tantrums and frustration, and he is able to make and keep friends.

*Case 2: Lisa*

At age 17, Lisa still struggles to pay attention and act appropriately; but this has always been hard for her. She still gets embarrassed thinking about that night her parents took her to a restaurant to celebrate her 10th birthday. She had gotten so distracted by the waitress's bright red hair that her father called her name three times before she remembered to order. Then before she could stop herself, she blurted, "Your hair dye looks awful!" In elementary and middle school, Lisa was quiet and cooperative but often seemed to be daydreaming. She was smart, yet couldn't improve her grades no matter how hard she tried. On numerous occasions, she failed exams. Even though she knew most of the answers, she couldn't keep her mind on the test. Her parents responded to her low grades by taking away privileges and scolding, "You're just lazy. You could get better grades if you only tried." One day, after Lisa had failed yet another exam, the teacher found her sobbing and wondered what was wrong with her. Because Lisa wasn't disruptive in class, it took a long time for teachers to notice her problem.

Lisa was first referred to the school's child study team when her teacher realized that she was a bright girl with poor to failing grades. The team ruled out a learning disability but determined she had AD/HD - Predominately Inattentive Type. The professional school counselor recognized that Lisa was also dealing with depression. Lisa's teachers and the professional school counselor developed a treatment plan that included participation in a program to increase her attention span and develop her social skills. They also recommended that Lisa receive counseling to help her recognize her strengths and overcome her depression. Lisa is about to graduate from high school. She's better able to focus her attention and concentrate on her work, and this has led to an improvement in her grades.

Overcoming her depression and learning to accept herself has also given Lisa more confidence to develop friendships and try new things. Lately, she has been working with the school counselor to identify the right kind of job to look for after graduation. She hopes to find a career that minimizes the impact of her attentional problems and makes the best use of her assets and skills. She is now more alert and focused and is considering trying college in a year or two. Her school counselor reminds her that she's certainly smart enough.

## Summary/Conclusion

AD/HD is a chronic behavior disorder of uncertain etiology that always begins in childhood. AD/HD is most commonly diagnosed in boys and the disorder often continues into adulthood. The central aspects include inattention/ disorganization and hyperactivity/impulsiveness and the student can exhibit one or both of these difficulties.

The three most typically used interventions for AD/HD include specifically designed school services such as a structured classroom for children with behavior disorders, behavior management techniques, and medications. Classroom and home techniques include securing attention before directions, checking for comprehension, reducing environmental distractions, shortening assignments, and assigning work that is interesting.

Finally, a collaborative team approach provides educators, family members, and the student with AD/HD with a mechanism for new possibilities. Working together will enable each member to grow through the team process toward a common purpose – to enhance the life of the student affected by AD/HD, and prepare for the challenges of the future.

## References


American Psychiatric Association. (2000). *Diagnostic and stastical manual of mental disorders* (4th ed., text revision). Washington, DC: Author.

Barkley, R. A. (1990). *Attention-Deficit Hyperactivity Disorder: A handbook for diagnosis and treatment.* New York: Guilford Press.

Booth, B., Fellman, W., Greenbaum, J., Matlen, T., Markel, G., Morris, H., Robin, A. L., & Tzelepis, A. (2002). *Myths about ADD/ADHD.* Retrieved on June 25, 2002 from http://www.edd.org.

Erford, B. T. (1999). The comparative effectiveness of a modified time-out procedure for oppositional and defiant children. *The Professional School Counselor, 2,* 205-210.

Faraone, S., & Biederman, J. (1998). Neurobiology of Attention-Deficit/Hyperactivity Disorder. *Biological Psychiatry, 44,* 122-131.

Hartmann, T. (1997). *Attention Deficit Disorder, a different perspective.* Grass Valley, CA: Under Wood Books.

Kaplan, H., & Sadock, B. (1996). *Pocket handbook of clinical psychiatry.* Baltimore, MD: Williams & Wilkins.

# Chapter 54

## Helping Students with Alcohol and Other Drug (AOD) Problems: Cognitive-Behavioral Interventions for School Counselors

*Gerald A. Juhnke*

### Preview

Alcohol and Other Drug (AOD) abuse continues to be a major problem for high school and middle school students. The more routinely correlated negative effects of such abuse by students are well documented within existing literature (e.g., poor academic performance, student retention). However, more severe and sensational negative effects often reported via the news media are also correlated with AOD abuse among this population (e.g., suicide, aggravated assault). The cognitive-behavioral and adjunctive interventions described in this chapter provide school counselors practical and effective treatment options that can be readily implemented with students who abuse alcohol and other drugs.

Existing literature clearly supports many professional school counselors' perceptions and beliefs that high school and middle school students are: (a) abusing alcohol and other drugs (AODs) more frequently than ever before, (b) beginning AOD abuse at earlier ages, and (c) ignoring the inherent dangers associated with AOD abuse (Hogan, 2000; Johnston, O'Malley, & Bachman, 2000). An example of research reflecting such student AOD abuse and attitudinal deterioration is a University of Michigan Institute for Social Research longitudinal study. The research began in 1975 and is funded by the National Institute on Drug Abuse (NIDA). This research surveys nationally representative samples of 8$^{th}$, 10$^{th}$, and 12$^{th}$ grade classes and annually includes nearly 50,000 students from more than 400 public and private secondary schools. Survey results indicated: (a) 54% of the participants had used an illicit drug by the time they reached their senior year in high school, (b) the annual use of any illicit drug among seniors increased from 27% in 1992 to 42% in 1997, and (c) the percentage of seniors who had used an illicit drug within 30 days prior to survey participation increased from 14% in 1992 to 26% in 1997 (NIDA, 1997).

Some of the most recent available data provided by the Substance Abuse and Mental Health Services Administration [SAMHSA] (1996; 1999) reported that: (a) 38% of girls between the ages of 12 and 17 have used alcohol, (b) 19% of adolescent girls reported alcohol use within the previous 30 days, (c) students are using alcohol earlier in their lives, thus placing them at greater risk for future substance dependence, suicide, and other health-related problems, (d) nearly 7% of girls aged 12 to 17 report binge drinking, and (e) by the early 1990's 31% of new female alcohol users were between the ages of 10 and 14. Regretfully, alcohol is not the only substance abused by students.

Inhalant use is fast becoming one of the first substances abused by preadolescent and younger students (Hogan, 2000). Inhalant use is also prominent among adolescent students

(Johnston et al., 2000). Concomitantly, hallucinogenics are also used with increased frequency among adolescent students. However, among adolescent students, marijuana still accounts for 75% of all illicit drug abuse (Hogan, 2000). This data clearly demonstrates the need for professonal school counselors to be able to effectively intervene with AOD abusing students.

## Cognitive-Behavioral Counseling Interventions

Cognitive-behavioral counseling interventions have significant utility for professional school counselors due to their emphasis upon brief, time-limited interventions directed toward immediate student concerns. Three primary cognitive-behavioral counseling goals exist for school counselors helping AOD abusing students (Nystul, 1999). First, professional school counselors help students understand how the students' thoughts, feelings, and behaviors engender AOD abuse. In other words, school counselors help students better understand what students say to themselves (e.g., "If I do drugs, others will think I'm cool and like me"), feel (e.g., anxiety, depression, anger), or do (e.g., argue, fight, withdraw) immediately before they AOD abuse. Second, school counselors promote understanding of how the students' AOD abuse is connected to negative consequences (e.g., failing grades, arguments with peers) and positive consequences (e.g., interactions with peers, feelings of confidence). Finally, professional school counselors help students explore new, healthier ways of thinking and acting which reduce the probability of continued AOD abuse.

*Understanding The AOD Abuse Sequence*

*Recognizing triggers.* Professional school counselors treating AOD abusing students first need to help students recognize the triggers (e.g., thoughts, feelings, behaviors, situations), which occur immediately prior to the students' AOD abuse (see Table 1).

**TABLE 1. Alcohol and other drug trigger and nonuse sequence-outcome list.**

| Thought Triggers | Feeling Triggers | Behavior Triggers | Situation Triggers | Positive Outcome | Negative Outcome |
|---|---|---|---|---|---|
| | | | | | |
| | | | | | |
| | | | | | |
| Nonuse Thoughts | Nonuse Feelings | Nonuse Behaviors | Nonuse Situations | Positive Outcome | Negative Outcome |
| | | | | | |
| | | | | | |
| | | | | | |

Commonly, AOD abusing students will be able to describe the internal dialogue they have with themselves or the physical or psychological signals which foretell of their upcoming AOD abuse. For example, a student might indicate that her internal dialogue just before abusing goes something like this: "I'm stressed. There is no way I can get through the rest of this math class without taking a hit to calm myself down." Additionally, she may describe physical feelings like an inability to relax or concentrate, and physical behaviors like involuntary muscle contractions or psychomotor agitation (e.g., tapping her fingers, bouncing her leg). Psychological signals might include remembering how calming it was when she smoked marijuana the previous day or describing the depressed symptomatology experienced most days when she is AOD abstinent.

Furthermore, she might be able to identify specific situations or circumstances which increase the probability of her AOD abuse (e.g., the class prior to each Friday's math quiz, the nights before her math tests, the days in which she receives her math quiz scores).

Once triggers are recognized by students, trigger lists are made. Students rank order the triggers on the lists, indicating which triggers are the most powerful and which are most frequently encountered. Thus, students first rank the strength of the individual triggers from "0" ("When I experience this, I will not use drugs at all.") to "10" ("When I experience this, I am inevitably going to use drugs.") and rank the trigger frequency from "0" ("I never experience this trigger.") to "10" ("This trigger occurs constantly throughout my awake hours"). Priority is then given to triggers identified by students as being the most powerful and occurring most often. In other words, triggers which students identify as indicating both inevitable AOD use and which constantly occur are the triggers which warrant the most attention at the onset of the counseling process.

*Establishing trigger baselines.* Concomitantly, the self-described severity and frequency of triggers presented by students serve as baselines which can be used to measure progress. In other words, these baselines allow both students and professional school counselors to track treatment efficacy. Should students report a decrease in severity and frequency of triggers, progress is likely occurring and the interventions being used should be continued. However, should the severity and frequency of triggers be increasing, treatment and interventions warrant revision.

*Nonuse lists.* In addition to the trigger list, professional school counselors may wish to help students construct a "Nonuse List." Here, the emphasis is on identifying thoughts, feelings, behaviors, and situations occurring when students don't abuse. The purpose of this list is to help students identify different ways of positively experiencing life without the need to abuse.

Many professional school counselors with whom this author has spoken have noted significant portions of their frequently AOD abusing students will be AOD abstinent when: (a) they are interacting with respected and admired peers who do not use, (b) students are participating in activities in which they are invested and find interesting (e.g., athletics, engine repair class, choir), and (c) they do not experience overwhelming anxiety related to future performance (e.g., upcoming examinations, athletic events). This list provides students ideas on how they might better cope with experiences which commonly lead to AOD abuse by describing how they think, feel, and behave when they are not driven by the urge to use.

*Positive consequences.* Unfortunately, positive consequences resulting from student AOD abuse are often ignored or inappropriately minimized by helping professionals. This is a significant treatment error which dilutes counseling efficacy and disinvests student participation.

Students frequently experience multiple positive consequences as a result of their AOD abuse. These positive consequences can vary greatly depending upon the individual student. Perceived peer support provided by other AOD abusing students, escape from pressing concerns, and pure enjoyment of being under the influence are key reasons students AOD abuse. Honest discussion regarding the potential loss of these perceived positive consequences is necessary before students can begin the abstinence process. Therefore, statements such as, "Tell me about the positive things you experience when you use" or "Help me understand what it is like drinking with your peers" are helpful.

The intent of these queries is not to have students romantically portray AOD abuse. Instead, professional school counselors are learning "why" AOD abuse and AOD experiences are important to the individual student. Once the "why" is answered, professional school counselors can begin working to appropriately address the void which will inevitably be created should students eliminate their AOD abusing behaviors.

For example, should a 13-year-old male indicate that drinking with other teens provides him friendships, the professional school counselor and the student may need to identify other ways the student can secure friendships without AOD abuse. Given the importance students place upon their acceptance by peers and their desire to fit in, this is a daunting challenge. However, failing to address this student's need for new, nonAOD-abusing friends, at best, destines the counseling process to limited success.

*Negative consequences.* When reviewing negative consequences resulting from student AOD abuse, it is helpful to first ask about the presenting circumstances which brought students to counseling and then link these to academic, family, peer, psychological, or legal problems resulting from or "potentially linked" to their AOD abuse. A vignette is provided below.

*PSC:* "Shondra, I know that Vice Principal Myers referred you to my office. As I understand the situation, you had consumed alcohol and then had gotten sick at last Saturday night's homecoming game. Help me understand what that was like for you?"

*Shondra:* "It was awful. I was trying to be cool and instead, I got drunk. When I got to the game everything started spinning, and I threw up in the stands. I was so embarrassed. Now my parents know I was drinking and I'm grounded, and the people I was trying to impress laugh at me."

*PSC:* "That sounds rough."

*Shondra:* "Yeah . . .it is."

*PSC:* "What have you learned from all of this?"

*Shondra:* "Well, I've learned that I don't want to drink anymore before games."

*PSC:* "Tell me about other times you had some bad things happen when you drank beer or used drugs."

*Shondra:* "I can't think of any."

*PSC:* "Sometimes people tell me that they perform badly on tests or get bad grades, because they were under the influence of alcohol when they took their tests or because they missed a lot of school due to their drinking. Has anything like that ever happened to you?"

*Shondra:* "Naw, nothing like that."

*PSC:* "At other times students tell me that when they drink they get into arguments with their parents or family members."

*Shondra:* "Well, a couple weeks ago, when my friends and I had been out drinking, I ran my mom's car into a ditch. I had to call my dad to get the car out. He was really upset. He said I'd have to pay the $480 to get the car fixed."

*PSC:* "So, your drinking got you into trouble with your dad and caused you to pay the expenses for repairing your mom's car?"

*Shondra:* "Yeah, I guess I'm learning that drinking costs me a lot."

Within this vignette, the professional school counselor first attempts to help Shondra begin understanding the link between her drinking behaviors and other potential negative consequences. The professional school counselor describes the primary reason Shondra came for counseling, the Vice Principal's referral. Shondra reports two specific problems resulting from this incident (e.g., embarrassment, parental punishment [grounding]). The counselor then investigates potential negative consequences of alcohol consumption related to Shondra's school experience. This is denied. Therefore, the professional school counselor continues asking about other potential negative consequences of alcohol consumption occurring within Shondra's relationship with her parents. Toward the end of this session the school counselor would likely summarize the problems reported by the student as linked to her alcohol use and ask the student to clarify how continued alcohol consumption is helpful.

*PSC:* "Shondra, help me understand. You say that you were terminated from Wal-Mart, because you've been too drunk to work your scheduled shift. You've said that you've gotten in trouble with the police for drinking and driving and had to pay over $400 to get your mom's car repaired. And, you've told me that you get real anxious when you buy beer, because your mom and dad would kick you out of the house if they knew you were continuing to drink. How is it helpful to you to continue drinking alcohol?"

*Shondra:* "I guess it's not."

*PSC:* "Based upon your trigger list, you've basically said you consume alcohol when you get bored. So, what will you do differently when you get bored in the future?"

*Shondra:* "Well, I guess I'm not going to drink."

*PSC:* "O.K., what will you do instead when you find yourself becoming bored or thinking that you may become bored."

*Shondra:* "I don't know."

*PSC:* "Well, on your Nonuse List, you said when you are with Stacey, you don't use alcohol, because she is fun and she doesn't like beer. I'm wondering if you would be willing to call Stacey if you begin to feel bored."

*Shondra:* "Yeah, I could do that."

*PSC:* "What else could you do?"

*Shondra:* "I guess I could do some of the other things I said in my nonuse list, like take my dog for a walk or practice my clarinet."

At the conclusion of this vignette the professional school counselor gently confronts Shondra by asking how continued drinking is helpful. Instead of dropping the discussion when Shondra reports her alcohol consumption is not helpful, the counselor uses the client's trigger list to help Shondra recognize one of the primary reasons she reportedly consumes alcohol (e.g., to escape boredom). Therefore, the professional school counselor is therapeutically using both the student's trigger list and nonuse list to help provide appropriate interventions.

Sometimes students either lack knowledge regarding potential negative consequences of their AOD abuse or purposely deny any negative consequences. Under these circumstances, professional school counselors may wish to use circular questioning. Here, the intent is to learn how students believe they are perceived by valued and respected significant others. Thus, school counselors might ask a question like, "Shondra, who is the most important person in your life?" Once students identify their most important significant others, professional school counselors can ask, "Based upon what you've told me, your mother is very important to you. Tell me, what would she say were the negative consequences of your drinking and drug behaviors?"

*Assorted Adjunctive Interventions*

Using cognitive-behavioral interventions to help students more thoroughly understand their AOD abuse sequence (i.e., triggers, nontriggers, positive consequences, and negative consequences) is helpful. However, two other adjunctive interventions warrant discussion when counseling AOD abusing students.

*Contingency contracting.* Many professional school counselors use contingency contracting when counseling AOD abusing students. Contingency contracts are clearly worded contracts which describe acceptable and unacceptable student behaviors. Jointly, professional school counselors and students develop an outline indicating that AOD abuse will not be tolerated. Sanctions are stated (e.g., expulsion from school, specialized placement) as well as rewards for contract compliance (e.g., the student can attend shop class at no cost for materials, the student can participate in athletics).

Sobriety contracts can be one form of contingency contract. For example, a professional school counselor may have a student who is prescribed both Ritalin for Attention- Deficit/ Hyperactivity Disorder and Antabuse for his alcohol abuse. The school counselor and the student can identify a time at the beginning of each school day when they can meet for approximately 10 minutes or longer if necessary. During the scheduled meetings, the student verbally commits to remaining alcohol free and learning so he may graduate from school. Thus, the student may say something like, "OK, I'm going to stay drug free today and promise to do my very best at learning so I may graduate and attend college." The professional school counselor then voices any specific concerns she might have about upcoming events that day which may trigger an alcohol use relapse. Here, Ms. Penn might say, "Charlie, I know you want to stay alcohol free and are committed to graduating, but I also know that today begins midterm exams. I am concerned you might feel overwhelmed or anxious and begin using alcohol to cope." The student then responds to how he anticipates handling the noted concern, "Oh, Ms. Penn, if I feel anxious or overwhelmed because of the midterms, I promise to speak with you first. I know I can handle it." Once the student indicates how he will respond the professional school counselor is not allowed to ask further questions that day. The student then takes his medications in front of the professional school counselor and places an "X" on the Sobriety Contract Calendar for that specific day. At the conclusion of each week the school counselor and the student identify the progress made and discuss any changes warranted for the following week. The intent of this experience, then, is to ritualize this daily experience and encourage students to direct their own recovery.

*12-step support groups.* One final intervention which warrants discussion is the use of support groups. Twelve-step support groups such as Alateen and Teen Rational Recovery provide members peer support. Alateen, like Alcoholics Anonymous, is founded upon a 12-step philosophy and requires students only to have a desire to discontinue drinking. Rational Recovery is founded upon Rational Emotive Therapy and encourages members to combat irrational thoughts related to their personal recovery. Students often find these support groups helpful in their recovery.

## Summary/Conclusion

This chapter described literature indicating the prominence of AOD abuse among middle and high school students. Practical cognitive-behavioral interventions were described. Specifically, readers learned about the AOD abuse sequence and gained intervention ideas on how to help students: (a) recognize AOD triggers, (b) recognize nonuse triggers, (c) discuss perceived positive AOD abuse consequences and cope with the potential loss of these positive consequences, and (d) link AOD abuse to negative consequences. Concomitantly, two adjunctive intervention techniques were described. These included both contingency contracting and 12-step programming. Although counseling AOD abusing students is a challenging charge for professional school counselors, the above interventions clearly provide a fundamental approach which can be helpful.

## References

Hogan, M. J. (2000). Diagnosis and treatment of teen drug use. *Medical Clinics of North America, 84*, 927-966.

Johnston, L. D., O'Malley, P. M., & Bachman, J. G. (2000). *National survey results on drug use from the Monitoring the Future study, 1975-1999*. Rockville, MD: U.S. Department of Health and Human Services.

National Institute on Drug Abuse. (1997). *High school and youth trends: Monitoring the Future study*. [On-line].

Nystul, M. S. (1999). *Introduction to counseling: An art and science perspective*. Boston, MA: Allyn & Bacon.

Substance Abuse and Mental Health Services Administration. (1996). *National Household Survey on Drug Abuse, Substance Abuse among Women in the U.S.* Rockville, MD: U.S. Department of Health and Human Services.

Substance Abuse and Mental Health Services Administration. (1999). *Summary of findings from the 1998 National Household Survey on Drug Abuse.* Rockville, MD: U.S. Department of Health and Human Services.

# Chapter 55

## Helping Students with Eating Disorders

*Dana Heller Levitt*

### Preview

Eating disorders and their less clinical forms of disordered eating and body image preoccupation continue to be on the rise. Professional school counselors are likely to see students presenting with such issues from elementary through high school. This chapter provides a brief overview of the symptoms and behaviors of eating disorders followed by discussion of counseling and prevention strategies. Attention to developmental differences is provided, including manifestations and interventions. A final section provides resources for counselors as well as students, teachers, and parents.

Clinical eating disorders (e.g., Anorexia Nervosa, Bulimia Nervosa, and Binge Eating Disorders) can be found in about 5% of the general population. A greater number of people are included when the definition is expanded to include those with sub-clinical manifestations, such as disordered eating and disturbances in body image. Disorders that do not meet diagnostic criteria can affect 4 to 16% of the general population, with such cases being two to five times more common among adolescent girls (Musell, Binford, & Fulkerson, 2000). Clinical eating disorders may be conceived on one end of a continuum and healthy eating attitudes and body image on the other end, with differing values of each lying in between. Students who are dissatisfied with their bodies, dieting, or even at the healthiest point all have the potential to develop more serious problems.

The most common forms of clinical eating disorders are Anorexia Nervosa, Bulimia Nervosa, and Binge Eating Disorder. Anorexia is marked by intense desires to lose weight, misperceptions about one's actual weight, refusal to gain weight, and a body weight that is at least 15% less than it should be (for example, a student who should, according to height and body composition, weigh 100 pounds currently weighs no more than 85). Students with anorexia may intentionally fast and avoid food and may or may not engage in compensatory activities, such as excessive exercise or self-induced vomiting after periods of feeling that they have eaten too much. Such acts of purging are a defining point of Bulimia Nervosa, a cycle of binge eating and purging. A binge is defined as eating an excessive amount of food in a discrete period of time, such as 2,000 calories in a 2-hour period. This should be differentiated from normative binges such as snacking with friends or eating a lot of food at a social event. Purging, such as self-induced vomiting, use of laxatives or diuretics, or excessive exercise, is used as a means of compensating for the binge or may simply be a way to alleviate feelings of guilt, stress, anxiety, or another feeling that is released through this activity following a binge. Similarly, Binge Eating Disorder is characterized by binge episodes as described above, absent of the purging cycle (American Psychiatric Association, 2000).

Disordered eating (dieting or in some other way modifying food intake to lose weight) affects students of all ages to eating disorders (Gabel & Kearney, 1998; Phelps, Sapia, Nathanson,

& Nelson, 2000). Other factors must also be considered, including the evaluation of body size and negative attitudes towards the body (Pesa, Syre, & Jones, 2000). Body image dissatisfaction has been reported as the strongest predictor of eating disorders (Phelps et al., 2000). Eating disorders or their sub-clinical manifestations may have little or nothing to do with eating or body image. Sometimes they are responses to traumatic events or feelings of loss of control, and manipulation of eating may be one means of establishing a sense of identity or personal power. There is a direct link between self-esteem and body perceptions (Brook & Tepper, 1997; Franko & Omori, 1999; Israel & Ivanova, 2002; Loewy, 1998; Pesa et al., 2000; Phelps et al., 2000), and, as a result, little argument that eating disorders need attention in schools.

## Identification of At-Risk Students

Eating disorders and related issues still predominantly affect females, with gender differences emerging at around ages eight to ten (Ricciardelli & McCabe, 2001). Male body image ideals and values have more recently spurred development of such concerns among boys and young men. The primary concern for boys is about being underdeveloped or not muscular enough, while girls are drawn toward thinness (Cohane & Pope, 2001). Eating pathology and appearance preoccupation are associated with depression and dysfunctional thinking, both of which affect students' overall self-esteem and well-being (Franko & Omori, 1999). There are numerous warning signs of eating disorders (see Table 1) on any point along the continuum beyond dieting, such as weight concerns, drives for thinness, feeling inadequate, and negative self-evaluation. If a student presents with any of these warning signs (particularly the physical and behavioral symptoms) it is important for the professional school counselor to ensure the student consults a health care professional.

**Table 1. Physical, behavioral, and psychological warning signs of eating disorders.**

| *Physical* | *Behavioral* | *Psychological* |
|---|---|---|
| *weight loss | *frequent trips to the bathroom | *low self-esteem |
| *hair loss | *avoiding snack foods | *external locus of control |
| *edema (swelling) | *frequent weighing | *helplessness |
| *skin abnormalities | *substance abuse | *depression |
| *discolored teeth | *social avoidance | *anxiety |
| *scarring on the backs of hands | *isolation | *anger |
| *abnormal eating habits | *perfectionism | |

## Counseling and Prevention Strategies

The most widely used treatments for eating disorders in the schools are individual and group counseling, involvement of family members, and classroom guidance programs. Professional school counselors can also implement school-based changes to create a more safe and accepting environment around the issues of eating disorders, weightism, and physical and overall self-esteem.

Prevention efforts generally centered on body satisfaction and education may be conceived at primary (curb dieting behaviors, address concerns about weight/shape), secondary (reduce the duration of eating disorders), and tertiary levels (address & reduce impairment of established disorders)(Gabel & Kearney, 1998).

Activities should address all of the systems at play in the development of eating disturbances:

family, sociocultural, self-deficits, body image concerns, self-esteem, and peer and parental involvement (O'Dea, 2000). Attempts should address the negative consequences of unhealthy weight control as well as encourage healthy eating and exercise (Mussell et al., 2000).

Professional school counselors and other personnel must first examine their own beliefs and feelings about weight, shape, appearance, and self-esteem. Regardless of the form of intervention or age group to which it applies, professional school counselors' work should foremost focus on promoting body satisfaction. Counselors may then help students enhance self-esteem and personal efficacy by recognizing positive aspects of their physical appearance (Phelps, et al., 2000).

Some approaches, particularly peer-led, can have negative effects. Programs that provide information about eating disorders, led by recovered peers, increases students' knowledge of eating disorders, but also increases their symptoms (O'Dea, 2000). Students introduced to beliefs, attitudes, and behaviors preceding eating disorders may hear suggestions to lose weight and the means of doing so. For younger children, frequent coverage of eating disorders in this manner can normalize the problem and thereby create longer-term difficulties.

A positive approach providing information on body image can be more beneficial. Addressing what makes them satisfied and dissatisfied with their bodies and introducing activities that desensitize them to the events eliciting body image dissatisfaction and eating disorders are useful tools (Gore, VanderWal, & Thelen, 2001). Helpful activities may include guided imagery and relaxation, envisioning oneself as brave and strong, and encouraging pleasurable body-related riding, getting a haircut, or wearing favorite clothes.

*Individual Counseling*

The professional school counselor must be mindful of his or her limits, and be prepared to refer students who have severe impairments to counselors in the community who can offer more constant and intensive care. In addition to therapists, professional school counselors should become familiar with other helping professionals who can assist with eating disorders, such as nutritionists, dieticians, physicians, exercise physiologists, and psychiatrists.

Counseling the eating disordered student can be tricky. Education about nutrition, exercise, self-acceptance, and the physical dangers associated with eating disorders are essential. At the same time, the student's emotional distress and academic performance need to be addressed, as well as development of identity and appropriate coping mechanisms (Gabel & Kearney, 1998; Garner, Garfinkel, & Irvine, 1986; Levine & Smolak, 2001). Many students with eating disorders may be defensive and resistant to help because they believe their behavior has been effective in getting what they want (attention from peers, parental affection, a socially acceptable body size). Other times, students will refer themselves because their eating disorder has gotten out of control. In these cases, the student's willingness to deal with the eating disorder and other problems in the student's life, and to seek help in doing so, should be acknowledged and praised (Omizo & Omizo, 1992).

Garner et al. (1986), pioneers in eating disorder treatment, suggested that there are two tracks. The first track involves issues of weight, starvation, erratic eating, bingeing, vomiting, strenuous exercise, or whatever the student's physical manifestation of the eating disorder may be. Cognitive-behavioral approaches might include restructuring thoughts, assistance with meal planning, and challenging distorted attitudes about weight and shape. The second track is the emotional context that may involve underlying developmental issues, personality, and family and peer themes. A psychodynamic approach might include a developmental understanding of eating disorders as a type of fear, family separation issues, parental inattention to the student's needs, and a lack of self-regulation. Garner et al. suggested that eating disorders can be dealt with initially from either track, as each communicates to the student a desire to help and commitment to ensuring that both physical and emotional health is restored. Cognitive- behavioral and psychodynamic approaches are the most widely used with individuals with eating disorders; the affective level should be particularly attended to among pre-adult populations.

Counseling should match student developmental levels. The use of journals can be particularly helpful in tracking feelings and behaviors. For younger students with less cognitive capacity, simply keeping a 'food-mood' diary may be enough. Professional school counselors working with older students in middle and high school may be successful in eliciting more complex processing by examining what was happening during periods of wanting to binge, purge, abstain from eating, and so forth. Engaging students in the process of analyzing, identifying, and transforming their environments is empowering at any developmental level (Levine & Smolak, 2001).

*Group Counseling*

Groups that focus on body image and the factors that lead to eating disorders are more likely to occur within the school setting. These groups provide students with opportunities to engage in activities and practice new behaviors with peers at a time when they are vulnerable to peer influences (Levine & Smolak, 2001). Students in body image awareness groups build support systems and facilitate connections with one another. It is important for counselors leading groups to ensure that they are being positive role models by addressing their own issues on the subject.

Structured group counseling gives students a focused means of talking about ways to promote positive body image. Several approaches incorporate education, insight, and action. Groups can focus on realistic goal setting, healthy body image, assertiveness, and perfectionism over 8 to 10 sessions (Rhyne-Winkler & Hubbard, 1994). Games, role-plays, and activities that encourage putting into perspective sociocultural and media messages about the importance of appearance empower students to feel good about themselves while contributing to the self-esteem of their peers. Activities may include identifying characteristics of admired people or collecting advertisements that teach students that fat is bad. Group sessions often include: information on dieting and exercising, developing a food log, healthy exercise, eating behaviors, emotions associated with eating, self-esteem and autonomy, body image and goal setting, and developing coping skills. In all likelihood this information will be most effective when working with students in elementary and middle school.

In this way students learn about advocacy and the forces that influence their feelings about their bodies, while learning how to cope with everyday interactions with others and teasing about their bodies. These protective factors and the immediate feedback from peers in groups enables students to be more proactive in preventing their own and peers' eating disorder risks.

There are dangers in running groups of this nature, as they can at times be explosive, heavily emotionally laden, or difficult to get students to share openly about their often private feelings. The professional school counselor should therefore exercise caution and patience and have appropriate supports in place for students in these groups.

*Involving Family Members*

Few individual or group interventions are effective without the support of parents and family members. Parents and other family members have a significant impact on students' self-image and self-esteem. Family members may contribute to unhealthy attitudes and behaviors about the body through modeling dieting and disordered eating, as well as comments about students' and others' appearances, and criticism of their students' changing bodies (Gore et al., 2001; Loewy, 1998; Maine, 2000; Mussell et al., 2000). Family dynamics have also been implicated in the development of eating disorders. Girls who report high levels of eating problems live in families marked by less cohesion, organization, and expressiveness. Families of students with eating disorders are also more conflictual, lacking in secure attachments and warmth (Byely, Archibald, Graber, & Brooks-Gunn, 2000). In any circumstances parents must be involved in treatment. Consult ACA and ASCA codes of ethics and local school policies for guidance on informed consent.

Because of the nature of eating disorders, family therapy is often highly recommended to explore the child's expression of anger, conflict, depression, anxiety, and any host of other feelings that may be influenced by the home and family environment (Garner et al., 1986). This is further cause for professional school counselors to know community resources and make referrals for needed services. Professional school counselors will also need to work collaboratively with the students, therapists, and medical doctors when applicable. Caution: Recognize your limits and make referrals as necessary. Table 2 includes activities professional school counselors can engage in to help families cope with eating issues. Within the school setting, professional school counselors can take on a number of roles to prevent, identify, and provide services for students with eating disorders.

**Table 2. How to help families cope with eating disorders.**

1. Educate families about eating disorders.
2. Send written correspondence home.
3. Facilitate family discussions about weight and health.
4. Alert families to how they might send harmful messages.
5. Set limits and openly discuss issues.
6. Ascertain eating habits and foster family relationships by spending mealtimes together.
7. Facilitate an examination of family members' own feelings and prejudices about weight.
8. Make appropriate referrals to community medical and mental health professionals.
9. Emphasize that spending time with children can foster cohesive, warm relationships, protecting students from eating disorders.
10. Plan programs through parent-teacher association meetings.
11. Educate families about normal puberty and developmental changes.

*Developmental Guidance Programs*

Eating disorders can be covered as a topic within several elective courses as well as the health and physical education curricula. Professional school counselors can encourage teachers to combine issues of nutrition, exercise, and self-acceptance into appropriate classes such that children learn positively about healthy and active lifestyles (Gabel & Kearney, 1998). Students can also be educated about the negative effects of starvation, erratic eating, and bingeing, including: depression, anxiety, irritability, feelings of inadequacy, fatigue, preoccupation with food, poor concentration, and social withdrawal (Garner et al., 1986). Other content to address with students in classrooms includes body-esteem and self-esteem, locus of control, approval-seeking behavior, body image and nutrition, excessive exercise, and perfectionism (Rhyne-Winkler & Hubbard, 1994).

Classroom guidance programs addressing these topics create an environment in which students examine knowledge and attitudes about food and eating, develop positive and realistic attitudes towards their bodies, and gain accurate information (Rhyne-Winkler & Hubbard, 1994). Given the influence of peers, training students to provide peer-led programs might be a useful means of disseminating such information effectively. Students will be more likely to listen to one another on most issues. A select group of students to teach others about eating disorders and positive body image can be empowering for both leaders and recipients. Such opportunities can serve as protective factors, much in the same way as peer mentoring programs on other issues, such as substance abuse, violence and transition to new schools. In one such program, the Ophelia Project (www.opheliaproject.org), high school girls are mentors to middle school students in order to prevent and process relational aggression. Program coordinators found that increasing self-esteem in another realm creates more positive body image among participants. Students involved with the program also had significant influences on the school environment as a whole.

*Systemic School-based Changes*

Professional school counselors should become knowledgeable about eating disorders and provide information and consultation to personnel, parents, and students (Mussel et al., 2000). Discussions about biases and views can take place with teachers, coaches, and administrators who address weight reduction (Gabel & Kearney, 1998). Teachers may also be trained to infuse eating disorders into curricula and to listen actively, provide feedback non-judgmentally, and to teach without lecturing such that they are more likely to identify students at risk and refer them for help.

A safe school environment can begin with the professional school counselor. Training for awareness of signs and symptoms of eating disorders is just the beginning. Table 3 addresses continuing initiatives that will prompt systemic changes, and reduce the prevalence of eating disorders (Ryhne-Winkler & Hubbard, 1994).

## Developmental Considerations

*Elementary School*

Starting to appropriately teach students early about eating disorders and body and self-esteem maximizes impact and decreases the likelihood of issues later in childhood and adolescence (Ohring et al. 2002). Because young children respond well by doing, experiential components such as poetry, humor, and games in prevention curricula and interventions has proven successful (Mussell et al., 2000).

Young children have likely not had experiences with failed or chronic dieting and may not understand the concept of bingeing (Ricciardelli & McCabe, 2001). For those who show early signs of disordered eating, gradual exposure to feared foods with relaxation training, role playing to address social and familial problems, and developing alternative ways of thinking about problems are helpful elements (Gore et al., 2001).

*Middle School*

Perhaps most important at this level is the normalization of physical changes that take place in puberty (Ohring et al., 2002). Bodily changes, especially for students who mature earlier, are unfamiliar and create differences. Peer support is vital in middle school, particularly relative to eating disorders. Peer-led programs, whether groups, prevention workshops, or merely

**Table 3. Initiatives to enhance systemic change.**

1. Promote activities that foster healthy attitudes about weight, shape, growth, and nutrition.

2. Monitor how health and physical activity requirements are communicated to students and families.

3. Create an atmosphere in which students confront negative body talk.

4. Advocate for nutritional food and snack offerings.

5. Enforce purchase of library and classroom materials with positive images about self-esteem and body image.

6. Encourage use of the term 'fat' as neutral and non-derogatory.

7. Create a wellness program.
   a. Focus on prevention and early intervention.
   b. Involve teachers and administrators.
   c. Promote healthy attitudes and habits towards eating.
   d. Encourage self-control.
   e. Focus on improving self-esteem and autonomy.
   f. Provide appropriate materials in the hallways.
   g. Foster discussions among the whole school community.
   h. Continually focus on the overall well-being of students.

facilitated small group discussions, allow students to promote sensitivity and positive body talk while learning that they may seek one another (Mussell et al., 2000). As peers are so influential during middle school, encouraging students to talk sensitively and providing training for peer mentoring and facilitation to teach others about these issues can be empowering and a positive use of peer influence.

O'Dea and Abraham (2000) described a 9-week program based solely on self-esteem that was effective in improving body image and offsetting dieting, weight loss, and eating disordered behavior among female middle school participants. Based on the principle of student-centered learning, students worked in groups and incorporated teamwork, games, play, and drama in this content-free curriculum. The program itself was intended to foster a positive sense of self, positive and safe student environment, vicarious learning, feedback exchange, and a positive and supportive environment in which these girls felt that they could not fail. The success of this program in modifying body image without directly addressing the topic demonstrates the benefits of self-esteem based programming.

*High School*

It may be important to target girls with low self-esteem as well as other early signs of eating disorders. Small groups are particularly useful in facilitating intimate discussions among high school peers about this issue (Mussell et al., 2000). Peers help to debunk myths about appearance and offer alternative ways of handling difficult problems.

It is also useful to incorporate activities that have an activist twist, enabling students to work productively towards a solution to eating disorders, the pressures to be thin, and the negative attributions placed on fat people by society. A program developed by the National Eating Disorders Association, GO GIRLS! (Giving Our Girls Inspiration and Resources for Lasting Self-esteem), teaches high schoolers about media awareness, activism, and advocacy and simultaneously increases self-esteem and prevents eating disorders (see www.nationaleatingdisorders.org). GO GIRLS! and other weekly groups discuss social pressures from media, peers, and parents before moving into subsequent sessions focusing on increasing physical self-esteem, building personal competence and developing an internal locus of control, reducing body dissatisfaction, and exploring appropriate weight control measures.

Culminating sessions with young adults who have recovered from eating disorders might also be included (Phelps et al., 2000), but should be done so with caution and supervision since students are particularly vulnerable at this time when hearing others' experiences with eating disorders. This is especially true as students have access to other attitudes about eating disorders. For example, "proanorexic" and "probulimic" websites are extremely dangerous places where people with active eating disorders attempt to convince others that these are positive and adaptive ways of coping and promote the ultra-thin, sickly, emaciated appearance of anorexia. Students have greater access to these sites with increased unsupervised time on the Internet, and the popularity of the chat sessions within them is high. Professional school counselors should be aware that such propaganda exists and that students are readily able to find, access, and be subject to the dangerous content therein.

Most counseling interventions are designed for work with adults. Adolescents who have the ability to think abstractly are likely to respond well to such approaches. The professional school counselor should be mindful of the developmental level and pressures that the student faces. Challenging students to think about the connection between their thoughts, problems, fears, or pressures and their eating disordered behaviors must be accompanied by the generation of alternatives that can be directly applied.

The developmental level of students is an important consideration in determining the course of action for the professional school counselor. Table 4 describes differences regarding weight and appearance for students at different points of development.

## Resources for Students, Parents, and Other Personnel

Professional school counselors have a tremendous impact on students and the school community by being intentional about helping students with eating disorders and related image concerns. Interventions at individual, group, familial, classroom, and school-wide levels can be challenging and require appropriate resources. The references that follow may be shared with students, parents, and school personnel. Professional school counselors should consult these and other resources in their efforts to treat eating disorders:

Bodywise - www.4woman.gov - 1-800-628-3812;
Eating Disorders Coalition for Research, Policy & Action-
www.eatingdisorderscoalition.com;
Maine, M. (2000) - *Body wars: Making peace with women's bodies.*Carlsbad, CA: Gurze Books;
National Eating Disorders Association - www.nationaleatingdisorders.org, Seattle, WA 206-382-3587;
The Ophelia Project: www.opheliaproject.org, Erie, PA; and
Pipher, M. (1994). *Reviving Ophelia: Saving the selves of adolescent girls.* New York: Ballantine Books.

**Table 4. Development of differences related to eating and appearance.**

*Elementary School*

At an age when the focus should be on making friends and growth, boys and girls today worry about appearance and fitting in.

- Students as young as age 5 express concerns about body image and becoming fat (Maine, 2000; Shapiro, Newcomb, & Loeb, 1997).
- By age 6 students use adult cultural criteria to judge physical attractiveness (Gabel & Kearney, 1998).
- Students tease, shame, and avoid friendships with peers who are fat or not conventionally attractive peers.
- Students imitate actions and attitudes of parents and adults; what messages are adults sending about dieting and appearance?

*Middle School*

During middle school, dissatisfaction with body shape and size worsens:

- Body image dissatisfaction increases from 40% in third grade to 79% in sixth grade (Ricciardelli & McCabe, 2001).
- Self-esteem is directly linked to body satisfaction; students with low self-esteem in other realms may be at high risk.
- The #1 wish for 11 to 17 year old girls: lose weight (Maine, 2000).

*High School*

High school students have the increased burden of beginning to make adult decisions, added to the stress of trying to fit in both socially and physically.

- Discontent about their bodies and feeling fat has become normative, particularly for girls (Maine, 2000).
- 67% of females and 82% of males believe appearance influences romantic appeal; 72% and 68%, respectively, attribute happiness to appearance (O'Dea & Abraham, 1999).
- High school students have lower physical self-esteem and more unhealthy weight control behaviors than younger students (Cohane & Pope, 2001; Israel & Ivanova, 2002; McCabe & Ricciardelli, 2001; Nylander, 1971).

## Summary/Conclusion

Eating disorders and their sub-clinical manifestations do not appear to be going away in our society. Professional school counselors are on the front line to intervene and prevent the development of eating disorders among students. At all developmental levels, students need attention and education about eating disorders, which can be addressed through classroom guidance, individual counseling, and group counseling. Parents can be educated about eating disorders, how to detect them in their students, and how home can be a safe haven or contribute to these disorders.

As agents of change, professional school counselors are likewise encouraged to educate teachers and other administrative personnel about eating disorders, for example, how to detect and approach students about whom they have concerns, and ways to make the school a safe environment accepting of all body shapes. It is incumbent upon professional school counselors to attend to the reality of eating disorders in their schools, whether they are overt or more subtle manifestations among their students. Through prevention, education, and intervention, professional school counselors play an integral role for students, their families, the school, and the greater community to appropriately and effectively address this dangerous phenomenon.

## References

American Psychiatric Association. (2000). *Diagnostic and statistical manual for mental disorders* (4th ed., text revision) (DSM-IV-TR). Washington, DC: Author.

Brook, U., & Tepper, I. (1997). High school students' attitudes and knowledge of food consumption and body image: Implications for school based education. *Patient Education and Counseling, 30,* 283-288.

Byely, L., Archibald, B., Graber, J., & Brooks-Gunn, J. (2000). A prospective study of familial and social influences on girls' body image and dieting. *International Journal of Eating Disorders, 28,* 155-164.

Cohane, G. H., & Pope, H. G. (2001). Body image in boys: A review of the literature. *International Journal of Eating Disorders, 29*, 373-379.

Franko, D. L., & Omori, M. (1999). Subclinical eating disorders in adolescent women: A test of the continuity hypothesis and its psychological correlates. *Journal of Adolescence, 22,* 389-396.

Gabel, K. A., & Kearney, K. (1998). Promoting reasonable perspectives of body weight: Issues for school counselors. *Professional School Counseling, 1,* 32-35.

Garner, D. M., Garfinkel, P. E., & Irvine, M. J. (1986). Integration and sequencing of treatment approaches for eating disorders. *Psychotherapy and Psychosomatics, 46*, 67-75.

Gore, S. A., Vander Wal, J. S., & Thelen, M. H. (2001). Treatment of eating disorders in children and adolescents. In J. K. Thompson & L. Smolak (Eds.), *Body image, eating disorders, and obesity in youth: Assessment, prevention, and treatment* (pp. 293-311). Washington, DC: American Psychological Association.

Israel, A. C., & Ivanova, M. Y. (2002). Global and dimensional self-esteem in preadolescent and early adolescent children who are overweight: Age and gender differences. *International Journal of Eating Disorders, 31,* 424-429.

Levine, M. P., & Smolak, L. (2001). Primary prevention of body image disturbances and disordered eating in childhood and early adolescence. In J. K. Thompson & L. Smolak (Eds.), *Body image, eating disorders, and obesity in youth: Assessment, prevention, and treatment* (pp. 237-260). Washington, DC: American Psychological Association.

Loewy, M. I. (1998). Suggestions for working with fat children in the schools. *Professional School Counseling, 1,*18-22.

Maine, M. (2000). *Body wars: Making peace with women's bodies.* Carlsbad, CA: Gurze Books.

McCabe, M. P., & Ricciardelli, L. A. (2001). Parent, peer, and media influences on body image and strategies to both increase and decrease body size among adolescent boys and girls. *Adolescence, 36*, 225-240.

Mussell, M. P., Binford, R. B., & Fulkerson, J. A. (2000). Eating disorders: Summary of risk factors, prevention programming, and prevention research. *The Counseling Psychologist, 28*, 764-796.

Nylander, I. (1971). The feeling of being fat and dieting in a school population: An epidemiologic interview investigation. *Acta Socio-medica Scandinavica, 1,* 17-26.

O'Dea, J. (2000). School-based interventions to prevent eating problems: First do no harm. *Eating Disorders, 8,* 123-130.

O'Dea, J. A., & Abraham, S. (1999). Onset of disordered eating attitudes and behaviors in early adolescence: Interplay of pubertal status, gender, weight, and age. *Adolescence, 34,* 671-679.

O'Dea, J. A., & Abraham, S. (2000). Improving body image, eating attitudes, and behaviors of young male and female adolescents: A new educational approach that focuses on self-esteem. *International Journal of Eating Disorders, 28,* 43-57.

Ohring, R., Graber, J. A., & Brooks-Gunn, J. (2002). Girls' recurrent and concurrent body dissatisfaction: Correlates and consequences over 8 years. *International Journal of Eating Disorders, 31,* 404-415.

Omizo, S. A., & Omizo, M. M. (1992). Eating disorders: The school counselor's role. *The School Counselor, 39,* 217-224.

Pesa, J. A., Syre, T. R., & Jones, E. (2000). Psychosocial differences associated with body weight among female adolescents: The importance of body image. *Journal of Adolescent Health, 26,* 330-337.

Phelps, L., Sapia, J., Nathanson, D., & Nelson, L. (2000). An empirically supported eating disorder prevention program. *Psychology in the Schools, 37,* 443-452.

Rhyne-Winkler, M. C., & Hubbard, G. T. (1994). Eating attitudes and behavior: A school counseling program. *The School Counselor, 41,* 195-198.

Ricciardelli, L. A., & McCabe, M. P. (2001). Children's body image concerns and eating disturbance: A review of the literature. *Clinical Psychology Review, 21,* 325-344.

Shapiro, S., Newcomb, M., & Loeb, T. B. (1997). Fear of fat, disregulated-restrained eating, and body-esteem: Prevalence and gender differences among eight- to ten-year-old children. *Journal of Clinical Child Psychology, 26,* 358-365.

# Chapter 56

## Helping Students with Depression

*Debbie W. Newsome*

### Preview

Depression in youth has been the focus of increased concern during the past three decades. Whereas it used to be considered a disorder of adulthood, current researchers and mental health professionals are aware that many children and adolescents also deal with depression, a disorder that can be serious, complex, and, most important, treated (Merrell, 2001). Indeed, feeling depressed is one of the most common emotional responses experienced during adolescence (Yarcheski & Mahon, 2000). Young adolescents, in particular, are susceptible to depression due to the intense biological, social, and psychological changes that occur from late childhood to early adulthood.

Professional school counselors are in a unique position to initiate activities and services designed to help prevent, identify, and coordinate the treatment of depression in youth (Rice & Leffert, 1997). In this chapter, facts about depression are presented, including information regarding types of depression, signs and symptoms of the disorder, factors influencing its onset, and associated risks. Suggestions for interventions that are based on outcome studies and research are described, including a list of resources to help professional school counselors with preventive and remedial activities.

---

*I'm normal, sort of. I take honors and Advance Placement courses. I was in the marching band, I played varsity soccer for two years—but I have a distinct quality that separates me from the masses—I am sad most of the time. I don't sulk around or constantly plot ways to end my life; instead, I withdraw from regular activities a lot and spend a good deal of time thinking about my life and my purpose here. Somewhere down the line, amidst all the action and continuous responsibility, I lost track of myself. I felt trapped in all my relationships and virtually had no time to myself. I discontinued communication with my best friends, and my goal every week was to survive to the weekend, where I could relax and put everything on hold. I viewed myself as capable, but also as always fallible. By November of my junior year, I was a wreck. Still, I refused to acknowledge my feelings as depression. I didn't think it could happen to me.*

17-year-old high school student who was treated for depression

---

*Depression Defined*

According to the National Institute of Mental Health (NIMH, 2001; 2002), depression is a condition that can affect thoughts, feelings, behaviors, and overall health. It can impact sleeping and appetite, the way one feels about oneself, and the manner in which one thinks about things. In addition to affecting a student's current quality of life, depressive symptoms and disorders that begin during childhood or adolescence predict recurring or ongoing depression in adulthood. Unless the disorder is treated, early onset of the disorder can predict more severe and negative symptoms later in life.

Depression is an internalizing disorder, as are anxiety disorders, social withdrawal, and somatic problems (Merrell, 2001). Internalizing disorders are characterized by overcontrol, which implies that individuals may overregulate or inappropriately control their emotions. In the case of internalizing disorders, the problems are maintained *within* the individual, in contrast to externalizing disorders, such as Oppositional Defiant Disorder and Attention-Deficit/ Hyperactivity Disorder (AD/HD), which are characterized by acting out (Merrell). The defining characteristic of the internalizing problem of depression is mood disturbance. Depressed youth experience difficulty regulating negative emotions effectively once they are experienced (Stark, Sander, Yancy, Bronik, & Hoke, 2000).

Whereas much of the research on depression refers to clinical depressive disorders, other manifestations of depression, while not severe enough to merit a clinical diagnosis, can cause distress in young people and call for the attention of school counselors. Petersen, Compas, and Brooks-Gunn (1992) described three types of depression: depressed mood, depressive syndrome, and clinical depression. Depressed mood is characterized by negative emotions, especially sadness and anxiety. Other emotions associated with depressed mood include guilt, disgust, anger, and fear. Students may experience depressed mood for a short or extended period of time. Depressed mood is one of the key symptoms of clinical depression; however, a child can experience depressed mood without being clinically depressed. Approximately one-third of adolescents experience depressed mood (Petersen et al.) and may benefit from prevention or intervention activities initiated by the professional school counselor.

Depressive syndrome refers to a collection of common symptoms associated with depression. The individual is in distress of some form, but does not necessarily have a diagnosable problem (Merrell, 2001). Symptoms can include anxiety, sadness, loneliness, fearfulness, guilt, self-consciousness, and worry. The person may feel unloved and unlovable or a need to be perfect. Depressive syndrome, which is usually identified through the use of questionnaires, affects approximately 15% of adolescents (Petersen et al., 1992). Group counseling may be especially helpful for students struggling with depressive syndrome.

For depression to be considered a clinical disorder, a collection of symptoms must be evidenced that meet specific diagnostic criteria according to standardized classification systems, such as the *Diagnostic and Statistical Manual of Mental Disorders* (*DSM-IV-TR*, American Psychiatric Association, 2000). Diagnosis is based on the intensity and duration of a set of symptoms that are serious enough to interfere with one's level of functioning. Examples of depressive disorders include Major Depressive Disorder and Dysthymic Disorder (see Tables 2 and 3). Adjustment Disorder with depressed mood (or mixed anxiety and depressed mood) also is marked by depressive symptoms, as are Bipolar Disorders, Cyclothymic Disorder, and Mood Disorder due to medical condition or substance abuse (see Table 4). In this chapter, specific recommendations for helping students with bipolar, cyclothymic, or substance abuse-related disorders will *not* be addressed; instead, the focus is on helping students who struggle with depressive symptoms, Major Depressive Disorder, Dysthymic Disorder, or Adjustment Disorder with depressed mood.

It is likely that professional school counselors will encounter students dealing with depressed mood, depressive syndrome, and depressive disorders. Therefore, it is important to be knowledgeable of the diagnostic criteria for depression and other mood disorders so that appropriate interventions and/or referrals can be made (Kaffenberger & Seligman, 2003).

## Signs and Symptoms of Depression

Identifying depression in young people may be challenging because symptoms are often masked. Although the diagnostic criteria and key defining features of major depressive disorder are the same for youths as for adults, it may be difficult for them to identify or describe their feelings (NIMH, 2000). Instead, depressed students may appear irritable, act out, or withdraw from family and friends. Also, anxiety symptoms and somatic complaints are more common in depressed children and adolescents than in adults (Surgeon General, 2002). A list of common signs and symptoms of depression evidenced in young people is presented in Table 1 (NIMH, 2000; Rice & Leffert, 1997).

**Table 1. Signs and symptoms of depression in children and adolescents.**

- Feeling sad, empty, or hopeless
- Increased emotional sensitivity
- Lack of interest or ability to engage in pleasurable activities
- Decreased energy level
- Physical complaints (headaches, stomachaches, tiredness)
- Frequent absences from school (or poor performance)
- Outbursts (shouting, complaining, crying)
- Boredom
- Substance abuse
- Fear of death
- Suicide ideation
- Sleep/appetite disturbances
- Reduced ability to think clearly and make decisions
- Increased irritability, anger, or restlessness
- Failure to make expected weight gains
- Reckless behavior
- Difficulty with relationships

The diagnostic criteria for Major Depressive Episode and Dysthymic Disorder are outlined in Tables 2 and 3. However, as noted earlier, students may exhibit signs of depression without meeting the full diagnostic criteria. These students, as well as students who are clinically depressed, are likely to benefit from early intervention by professional school counselors.

Depression in children and adolescents often is accompanied by other problems, some of which are clinically diagnosable. Examples of disorders that frequently co-occur with depression in youth are Anxiety Disorders, Conduct Disorder, Eating Disorders, Personality Disorders, and Substance Abuse Disorders (Petersen et al., 1992; Rice & Leffert, 1997). Particularly high rates of comorbidity exist between depression and anxiety disorders, with reported co-occurrence rates ranging from 30 to 70 percent (Kovacs, 1990). Also, depression may accompany medical conditions such as diabetes or other illnesses. Given the high rate of co-occurrence, professional school counselors will want to be sensitive to the possibility that the depressed student may also be struggling with one or more other conditions and plan interventions accordingly.

**Table 2. DSM-IV-TR Criteria for Major Depressive Episode (APA, 2000, p 356).**

A. Five (or more) of the following symptoms have been present during the same 2-week period and represent a change from previous functioning; at least one of the symptoms is either (1) depressed mood or (2) loss of interest or pleasure.

**Note:** Do not include symptoms that are clearly due to a general medical condition, or mood-incongruent delusions or hallucinations.

1) depressed mood most of the day, nearly every day, as indicated by either subjective report (e.g., feels sad or empty) or observation made by others (e.g., appears tearful). **Note:** In children and adolescents, can be irritable mood.
2) markedly diminished interest or pleasure in all, or almost all, activities most of the day, nearly every day (as indicated by either subjective account or observation made by others)
3) significant weight loss when not dieting or weight gain (e.g., a change of more than 5% of body weight in a month), or decrease or increase in appetite nearly every day. **Note:** In children, consider failure to make expected weight gains.
4) insomnia or hypersomnia nearly every day
5) psychomotor agitation or retardation nearly every day (observable by others, not merely subjective feelings of restlessness or being slowed down)
6) fatigue or loss of energy nearly every day
7) feelings of worthlessness or excessive or inappropriate guilt (which may be delusional) nearly every day (not merely self-reproach or guilt about being sick)
8) diminished ability to think or concentrate, or indecisiveness, nearly every day (either by subjective account or as observed by others)
9) recurrent thoughts of death (not just fear of dying), recurrent suicidal ideation without a specific plan, or a suicide attempt or a specific plan for committing suicide

B. The symptoms do not meet criteria for a Mixed Episode.

C. The symptoms cause clinically significant distress or impairment in social, occupational, or other important areas of functioning.

D. The symptoms are not due to the direct physiological effects of a substance (e.g., a drug of abuse, a medication) or a general medical condition (e.g., hypothyroidism).

E. The symptoms are not better accounted for by Bereavement, i.e., after the loss of a loved one, the symptoms persist for longer than 2 months or are characterized by marked functional impairment, morbid preoccupation with worthlessness, suicidal ideation, psychotic symptoms, or psychomotor retardation.

**Table 3. DSM-IV-TR Criteria for Dysthymic Disorder (APA, 2000, pp 380-381).**

A. Depressed mood for most of the day, for more days than not, as indicated either by subjective account or observation by others, for at least 2 years. **Note:** In children and adolescents, mood can be irritable and duration must be at least 1 year.

B. Presence, while depressed, of two (or more) of the following:
   1) poor appetite or overeating
   2) insomnia or hypersomnia
   3) low energy or fatigue
   4) low self-esteem
   5) poor concentration or difficulty making decisions
   6) feelings of hopelessness

C. During the 2-year period (1 year for children or adolescents) of the disturbance, the person has never been without the symptoms in criteria A and B for more than 2 months at a time.

D. No Major Depressive Episode has been present during the first 2 years of the disturbance (1 year for children and adolescents); i.e., the disturbance is not better accounted for by chronic Major Depressive Disorder, or Major Depressive Disorder, in Partial Remission. **Note:** There may have been a previous Major Depressive Episode provided there was a full remission (no significant signs or symptoms for 2 months) before development of the Dysthymic Disorder. In addition, after the intial 2 years (1 year in children or adolescents) of Dysthymic Disorder, there may be superimposed episoders of Major Depressive Disorder, in which case both diagnoses may be given when the criteria are met for a Major Depressive Episode.

E. There has never been a Manic Episode, a Mixed Episode, or a Hypomanic Episode, and criteria have never been met for Cyclothymic Disorder.

F. The disturbance does not occur exclusively during the course of a chronic Psychotic Disorder, such as Schizophrenia or Delusional Disorder.

G. The symptoms are not due to the direct physiological effects of a substance (e.g., a drug of abuse, a medication) or a general medical condition (e.g., hypothyroidism).

H. The symptoms cause clinically significant distress or impairment in social, occupational, or other important areas of functioning.

*Specify* if:
**Early Onset:** If onset is before age 21 years
**Late Onset:** If onset is age 21 or older

*Specify* (for most recent 2 years of Dysthymic Disorder):
**With Atypical Features**

**Table 4. Other disorders that have depressed mood as a symptom.**

| *Type of Disorder* | *Characteristics* |
|---|---|
| Bipolar Disorder | Rare in young children but can appear in children and adolescents. Involves unusual shifts in mood, energy, and functioning. May begin with manic, depressive, or mixed manic and depressive symptoms. When the onset is before or soon after puberty, it may be characterized by a continuous, rapid-cycling, irritable, mixed symptom state and may co-occur with Attention-Deficit/Hyperactivity Disorder or Conduct Disorder (NIMH, 2000). |
| Cyclothymic Disorder | Onset typically is early adulthood, but the disorder can occur at younger ages. Characterized by chronic, fluctuating mood disturbance with many periods of hypomanic symptoms and many periods of depressive symptoms. During the initial one-year period (for children and adolescents), any symptom-free periods do not last longer than two months (APA, 2000). |
| Adjustment Disorder with Depressed Mood | An Adjustment Disorder is a psychological response to an identified stressor that results in the development of emotional or psychological symptoms that are distressing to the individual. The symptoms must develop within three months after the stressor occurs and should resolve within six months after the stressor or its consequences have ended, unless the stressor is chronic. The predominant characteristics of Adjustment Disorder with Depressed Mood are tearfulness, feelings of hopelessness, and depressed mood (APA, 2000). |

*Prevalence*

It is difficult to estimate rates of depression in children and adolescents with certainty (Merrell, 2001). A conservative estimate of 5-8% of adolescents struggle with either clinical depression or depressive syndrome (NIMH, 2001; Rice & Leffert, 1997). According to a recent NIMH report (2001), approximately 2.5% of children and between 3-5% of adolescents experience clinical depression each year. Ten to forty percent of youth report depressed or unhappy mood, with the rates increasing throughout adolescence (Rice & Leffert). The onset of depressive disorders appears to be occurring earlier in life than in previous decades. Early diagnosis and treatment can help offset difficulties that are associated with untreated depression when children reach adulthood (NIMH, 2001).

Prior to age thirteen, the rates of depression for boys and girls are similar. However, gender differences emerge between the ages of thirteen and fourteen, with girls twice as likely to become depressed as boys (Merrill, 2001). One hypothesis for this difference is that girls tend to experience more challenges and stressors in early adolescence than boys. They are more likely to go through puberty during the transition from elementary to secondary school, and the pressure to be popular and attractive can be greater, especially for early maturing girls (Petersen et al., 1992). Furthermore, early maturing girls may feel pressure to engage in sexual activity before they are emotionally ready to do so, which can contribute to depressed mood. Regardless of the reasons for the differences, the increased rate of depression in girls may make it more likely that professional school counselors will work with girls struggling with depressive symptoms.

*Factors Associated with Depression*

Several models of depression have been proposed, many of which have reciprocal components. Recognizing that interaction among causal factors is likely and that research on the etiology of depression is ongoing, current research on biological and psychosocial factors associated with depression in youth is presented next.

*Biological factors.* Much of the research about biological influences on depression has been conducted with adults rather than youth. Consequently, it is important to keep in mind, when reading this section, that generalizations about biological influences on depression may not be completely applicable to young people. Specific biological factors associated with the development of depression include abnormalities in the functioning of neurotransmitters and/or the endocrine system. In many cases, individuals may have a genetic predisposition to such abnormalities (Merrell, 2001).

Certain brain chemicals, including serotonin and norepinephrine, affect mood and have been linked with mood disorders (Merrell, 2001). When there are abnormalities in the neurotransmission of these and other chemicals (in other words, in the sending and receiving of neurotransmitters), mood disorders can develop. Antidepressant medications developed within the past two decades, such as fluoxetine (Prozac), fluvoxamine (Luvox), sertraline (Zoloft), and paroxetine (Paxil) block the reuptake of serotonin, thereby increasing its availability to brain cells. Other medications, such as venlafaxine (Effexor) and nefazodone (Serzone) affect the transmission of both serotonin and norepinephrine and can bring about relief from depressive symptoms (Stark et al., 2000).

Also associated with depression is abnormal functioning of the endocrine system, which releases hormones into the bloodstream. Various abnormalities in the functioning of the pituitary gland, thyroid gland, adrenal gland, and glands that release sex hormones have been linked with mood disturbances in youth and adults (Merrell, 2001; NIMH, 2001). In particular, hormonal changes during puberty may be associated with depressive symptoms (Stark et al., 2000).

Genetics play an important role in a person's vulnerability to depression and other mental disorders. It is theorized that multiple gene variants, rather than a single gene, act in conjunction with environmental factors and developmental events, thus making a person more likely to experience depressive symptoms (NIMH, 2001).

*Cognitive and behavioral factors.* Cognitive theory describes a strong link between an individual's cognitions, emotions, and behaviors. According to cognitive theory, people's interpretations of events, rather than the events themselves, trigger emotional upsets and mood disturbances (e.g., Beck, 1976). Such interpretations affect one's view of self, the world, and the future. Inaccurate interpretations, or faulty information processing, can lead to depressive symptoms in youth and adults (Asarnow, Jaycox, & Tompson, 2000; Beck, 1976; Kendall, 2000). Examples of faulty information processing include negative attributions and cognitive distortions.

Children with negative attributional styles may believe that they are helpless to influence events in their lives. They may also believe that they are responsible for any failures and problems that are experienced, but not for successful, positive events (Merrell, 2001). For example, a student may believe that she is responsible for her parents' divorce and thus continually blame herself for the break-up of their marriage. Or when something positive happens, like winning an award for achievement, the student attributes the event to luck.

Cognitive dysfunctions refer to negative, inaccurate biases that can result in unhealthy misperceptions of events. To illustrate, in a study comparing depressed youth to nondepressed youth, the depressed students viewed themselves as less capable than their classmates, even though their teachers did not (Kendall, Stark, & Adam, 1990). Cognitive theorists have identified several types of cognitive dysfunctions, including exaggerating the negative, minimizing the positive, overgeneralizing, catastrophizing, and personalizing. Cognitive distortions also are evidenced when young people engage in all or nothing thinking or selective abstraction, such as when taking a detail out of context and using it to negate an entire experience. Such distortions can result in negative automatic thoughts, which then affect emotions and mood states. Teaching students ways to correct faulty information processing is one way to effectively help young people who are depressed (Kendall, 2000).

Behaviors associated with negative cognitions and feelings can both contribute to and maintain depressive symptoms in children and adolescents. In particular, withdrawing from peers and family members can exacerbate feelings of depression and loneliness through the resulting lack of social reinforcement (Merrell, 2001). Related to social withdrawal is the tendency of depressed individuals to quit engaging in activities that formerly were pleasurable, such as athletics or hobbies, thereby creating a cycle that makes it difficult to alleviate depressive symptoms. To break the cycle, professional school counselors can help children identify activities they consider pleasurable and make commitments to participate in those activities between sessions (Stark & Kendall, 1996).

*Challenges and stressors.* Youth who experience numerous stressors may be more likely to experience depression than those who do not. Indeed, one model of adolescent depression developed by Petersen et al. (1992) and Peterson et al. (1993) proposed that the number and timing of changes and challenges in early adolescence affect mental health, with negative consequences being moderated by parental and peer support and coping skills. Challenges can be categorized as normative life events (expected changes, such as school entry and puberty), non-normative events (e.g., divorce, abuse, moving away), and daily hassles (e.g., conflict with friends, excessive schoolwork). In a study of adolescents between the ages of 12-14, stress was found to have a strong causal effect on depression as well as a negative effect on self-esteem (Yarcheski & Mahon, 2000). The manner in which stress is experienced varies greatly from one student to another. Recognizing the potential detrimental effects of stress, professional school counselors can conduct classroom guidance lessons and group sessions to teach students ways to manage stress effectively (see chapter 82, "Helping Students Manage Stress," for specific examples).

*Family and peer influences.* A number of family-related factors are associated with depression, including extensive conflict, poor communication patterns, low family cohesion, and the emotional unavailability of parents (Merrell, 2001; Petersen et al., 1992). Having a parent with a mood disorder increases a young person's risk of experiencing depression, due in part to heredity and in part to the family interactions that occur if the parent's condition is not being treated successfully. In community settings, family counseling is often recommended when a member of the family is depressed; however, this option may not be available in the school setting. If not, professional school counselors can be instrumental in helping families become aware of opportunities for family counseling in the community.

Poor relationships with peers, not having a close friend, and being considered unpopular or "different" also can lead to depressive symptoms in students (Petersen et al., 1992). Certain populations, including gay, lesbian, and bisexual youth, may experience a greater degree of peer rejection and isolation, thus increasing their vulnerability to depression (Rice & Leffert, 1997). A critical role of the professional school counselor is to serve as an advocate for all students. Tolerance and acceptance can be demonstrated and taught in multiple ways, including parent and teacher training programs, class guidance lessons, and small group sessions. See Table 5 for a list of risk factors for depression (NIMH, 2000).

**Table 5. Risk factors for depression.**

- Family history of mood disorders
- Gender (adolescent girls twice as likely as boys to develop depression)
- Stress
- Loss of parent or loved one
- Break-up of a romantic relationship
- AD/HD, conduct disorder, or learning disorder
- Cigarette smoking
- Chronic illness (e.g., diabetes)
- Abuse or neglect
- Other trauma, including natural disasters

*Consequences of Depression*

A wide range of intrapersonal and interpersonal problems can arise when depression goes undiagnosed and untreated in young people. A diminished sense of self-worth, lack of confidence, and a general tendency to view oneself negatively often go hand-in-hand with depression (Merrell, 2001). For some students, the depression and ensuing fatigue can result in difficulties in concentration, motivation, and academic performance. As stated earlier, impaired relationships with peers and family members can both lead to and be a consequence of depression. Interpersonal difficulties associated with acute stages of depression have been found to continue after recovery, sometimes persisting into adulthood (Mufson, Moreau, Weissman, & Klerman, 1993). In addition, youth with untreated depression are at an increased risk for physical illness, substance abuse, recurrent episodes of depression, and suicidal behavior (NIMH, 2000; 2001). Consequently, there is a strong need to identify depressive symptoms early and make it possible for youth struggling with depression to get the help they need.

*Suicide risk.* The most severe problem associated with depression is the risk of suicide. Although most people who are depressed do not commit suicide, depressed youth, especially those dealing with what they perceive as a crisis, are at a greater risk for suicidal behaviors. The strongest risk factors for attempted suicide in young people are depression, substance abuse, and aggressive or disruptive behaviors (NIMH, 2002a). The suicide rate among youth has increased dramatically during the past three decades, with suicide reported as the third leading cause of death among 15- to 24-year-olds (NIMH, 2002b). More girls attempt suicide than boys; however, boys are four times as likely to actually kill themselves and tend to use more lethal means (Surgeon General, 2002). In 1997, 21 percent of high school students nationwide reported that they had seriously considered attempting suicide within the past year, and 8 percent had actually attempted suicide (Center for Disease Control, 2002).

Suicide attempts are often preceded by signals, warnings, or actual threats. Some of the signs to watch for include verbal messages (e.g., "I wish I were dead," "There's only one way out," or "I won't be around much longer"), a preoccupation with death, changes in sleeping and eating patterns, decline in school performance, or giving away possessions. Suicidal behaviors and threats represent a cry for help and must be taken seriously. Professional school counselors typically have been trained in suicide assessment, and most schools have policies and procedures related to crisis intervention. When a professional school counselor has reason to believe that a student is contemplating suicide, the counselor will want to assess the nature and intensity of the student's thoughts and follow up with a response that will keep the student safe. Merrell (2001) lists six basic steps that can be followed in responding to potentially suicidal youth [Note: Be sure these steps are consistent with your school system policy before implementing them]:

1. *Thinking about suicide.* If there is plausible reason to believe that a student is considering suicide, ask the student about it directly. Keeping the wording developmentally appropriate, the counselor can ask, "Have you been thinking about hurting yourself?" or "Have you been thinking about wanting to be dead?"
2. *Suicide plan.* If there is any indication of suicidal ideation, the next step is to determine whether the student has made an actual plan. Ask questions such as "Have you thought about how you might do it?" or "How would you do it?" Generally, more specific, thought-out plans indicate a greater risk of an attempt, although with impulsive youth, this is not necessarily the case.
3. *Method.* If the student has a plan, determine what has been already put in place to carry out the plan. What methods are being considered and how available are they? Determine the exact location of any lethal means (e.g., firearms, drugs).
4. *Intended place or setting.* Where does the student intend to commit the suicide act? Has he or she written a note, and if so, what does it say?
5. *Immediate protective action.* If there is reason to believe that the student is seriously considering suicide, immediate protective action should be taken. If there is a risk of imminent danger, notify parents and whoever else needs to be notified, depending on the circumstances, school policy, and local laws. Do not leave a suicidal student alone, even briefly.
6. *Suicide contract and follow-up planning.* If there is no evidence of imminent danger but the professional school counselor is still concerned about the possibility of suicide, help the student complete a written contract in which he or she promises to (a) not engage in any self-destructive behavior, and (b) call an appropriate person or agency if he or she is considering self-harm. Make sure the student has names and phone numbers of people to contact. Plan for ongoing counseling, be mindful of confidentiality issues, consult with others, and meet with the student's parents if the situation warrants doing so. (p. 30)

*Interventions*

Professional school counselors have opportunities to intervene at multiple levels to help children and adolescents deal with depressive symptoms. Intervention can take the form of prevention, which is designed to reduce incidences of depression before problems begin, or direct counseling services for at-risk groups and individuals. Interventions at all levels need to be developmentally informed, with an overarching goal of enhancing or modifying students' internal and external resources that are amenable to change (Rice & Leffert, 1997).

A number of factors, including school policy and size, may dictate the nature and type of interventions in which the professional school counselor is involved. Professional school counselors are responsible for a wide range of services and work with a large number of students, teachers and parents. If too much time is spent with only a few students, the larger proportion of the student body may be shortchanged (Ripley, Erford, Dahir, & Eschbach, 2003). Recognizing the challenge of balancing multiple responsibilities, professional school counselors play crucial roles in assessing, coordinating referrals, and, when needed, providing direct treatment or follow-up services for depressed students (Rice & Leffert, 1997). They also are key leaders in planning and implementing prevention programs for students, parents, and teachers.

*Assessment and Evaluation*

Accurately assessing depression in children and adolescents can be a challenging task. Often, the symptoms cannot be observed directly and therefore may go unrecognized. By being aware of the signs, symptoms, and co-occurring conditions associated with child and adolescent depression, professional school counselors can help identify students who may be in need of services. The purpose of assessment is to inform treatment, which may involve direct counseling services at the school or elsewhere.

Typically, multiple sources of information are used to guide decision-making and treatment planning. It helps to gather information from the child, parents, and teachers. Self-report instruments, structured or semi-structured interviews, and behavior rating scales are some of the methods that can be used in assessment. Professional school counselors who have been trained in appraisal procedures may choose to use assessment instruments designed for depression screening, such as the *Children's Depression Inventory (CDI)*, the *Beck Depression Inventory (BDI)*, and the *Center for Epidemiologic Studies Depression (CES-D) Scale* (see NIMH, 2000). If a professional school counselor has not been trained to use a particular instrument, he or she should get supervision to ensure that the instrument is administered and interpreted properly. If the screening evaluation indicates the student has depressive symptoms and possibly a depressive disorder, the professional school counselor will want to provide referral information to parents so that a more comprehensive diagnostic evaluation can be conducted. In such cases, the professional school counselor can serve as a liaison between the referral agency and the family (Rice & Leffert, 1997).

*Direct Counseling Services*

*Individual counseling.* For some students, short-term individual counseling or group counseling in the school may be warranted. Research has demonstrated the efficacy of certain types of counseling, especially cognitive-behavioral therapy (CBT), in alleviating depressive symptoms in young people (NIMH, 2001). The goal of CBT is to help children and adolescents develop cognitive structures that will positively influence their future experiences (Kendall, 2000). The cognitive component of CBT helps individuals identify and change negative, pessimistic thinking, biases, and attributions. The behavioral component, also important to the process, focuses on increasing positive behavior patterns and improving social skills (Asarnow et al., 2001).

Another type of counseling, interpersonal therapy for adolescents (IPT-A), was adapted from IPT for adults. Although it has not been researched as extensively as CBT with young people, studies have shown it to be effective in treating depression in adults (e.g., Mufson et al., 1993). The two primary goals of IPT are to reduce depressive symptoms and to improve disturbed personal relationships that may contribute to depression. Both CBT and IPT were developed to treat depression but differ in theory and practice. Both approaches require training to be used effectively with students.

In conducting individual counseling with students who have depressive symptoms, Rice and Leffert (1997) recommended a cognitive-behavioral approach that focuses on developing internal and external resources that are amenable to change. The first step is to build a working alliance with the student, thereby fostering the development of an external resource. Next, other strategies can be implemented such as the ones described below:

> Coping or problem-solving strategies could be explored and improved. Students can learn how to match appropriate coping strategies to the type of problem situations they encounter. For example, active problem-solving in which an adolescent sets a goal, brainstorms possible solutions, anticipates consequences, and implements a plan of action, generally works for events or circumstances that are under an adolescent's control. Emotion-focused strategies (e.g., relaxation) may be used when circumstances are not under the adolescent's control but are nevertheless upsetting. Cognitive interventions could be implemented to challenge and revise inaccurate perceptions of self and others. Social skills (e.g., assertiveness training) could be

> addressed and practiced in order to increase the quantity and quality of relationships with peers and family members. (p. 26)

Professional school counselors who work individually with depressed students will want to collaborate with family members and teachers so that they can support the work that is being done with the child. By consulting with parents and teachers, professional school counselors can help significant others in the student's environment learn how to encourage the student's use of new skills (Stark et al., 2000).

*Referral.* At times, professional school counselors will work with students whose problems are severe and chronic. When this occurs, the appropriate response may be to make referrals to mental health professionals in the community. In particular, if the required interventions cannot be implemented in the school, if medication is a possibility, or if the student appears to be in danger of harming anyone, making a referral may be the preferred course of action. In such cases, the professional school counselor will want to meet with the parents of the student to discuss concerns and determine their willingness to pursue outside help. If they are willing to consider outside help, a letter written by the professional school counselor to the referral source can facilitate treatment and collaboration (Merrell, 2001).

*Group counseling.* Group counseling provides another mode by which students with depressive symptoms can be helped. Several outcome studies have demonstrated the efficacy of implementing comprehensive intervention programs that emphasize cognitive behavioral techniques (see Kaslow & Thompson, 1998, for a review of outcome studies of interventions with depressed children and adolescents). The intervention programs implemented in these studies followed a treatment-manual format, thereby providing a replicable scope and sequence of interventions. Three of the programs that have been used successfully with young people are: (1) the *Adolescent Coping with Depression Course* (CWD-A; Clarke, Lewinsohn, & Hops, 1990), the *Taking ACTION Program* (ACTION; Stark & Kendall, 1996), and *Interpersonal Psychotherapy for Adolescents with Depression* (IPT-A; Mufson et al., 1993). Sources for these programs, including a brief description of each, are listed in Table 6.

Three of the intervention programs described in Table 6 range from a minimum of 12 sessions to as many as 30 sessions; consequently, in some schools it will not be feasible to implement them as designed. Merrell (2001) suggested devising a modified comprehensive group program, incorporating key elements that the programs have in common, which include:

> (a) developing a therapeutic relationship based on trust and respect;
> (b) education regarding depression;
> (c) activity scheduling (monitoring, increasing participation in pleasant events);
> (d) emotional education (identifying and labeling emotions, identifying situations in which emotions are likely to occur, recognizing the link between thoughts and feelings);
> (e) cognitive change strategies (challenging negative or irrational thoughts, practicing appropriate attributions, increasing the focus on positive thoughts and events);
> (f) problem-solving, negotiation, and conflict resolution;
> (g) relaxation training;
> (h) social skills and communication skills; and
> (i) goal setting and relapse prevention. (p. 76)

**Table 6. Resources and intervention programs for helping students with depression.**

| Title | Description | Publishing Information |
|---|---|---|
| *Helping Students Overcome Depression and Anxiety: A Practical Guide* (Merrell, 2001) | Provides comprehensive information about child and adolescent depression and other internalizing disorders.Offers practical guidelines for assessment and intervention. Describes over 40 psychoeducational and psychosocial intervention techniques that can be adapted for youth at different developmental levels. Provides reproducible worksheets for use with students. | The Guilford Press<br>72 Spring Street<br>NewYork,NY<br>10012<br>800-3657006<br>www.guilford.com |
| *Taking ACTION Program* (Stark & Kendall, 1996) | A comprehensive intervention program designed for youth between the ages of 9 and 13, although activities can be adapted for younger or older students. Provides guidelines for 30 group counseling sessions that focus on affective education, problem-solving skills, social skills, coping skills, and cognitive interventions. | Workbook Publishing<br>298 Llanfair Road<br>Ardmore, PA 19003<br>610-896-9797 |
| *Adolescent Coping with Depression Course* (Clarke et al., 1990) | A comprehensive cognitive-behavioral intervention program designed for small group work with adolescents ages 14-18 (although it may be adapted for younger students).Provides directions for 16 two-hour psychoeducational sessions. Activities are highly structured. Length of sessions may be problematic in a school setting. | Castalia Publishing Co.<br>P.O. Box 1587<br>Eugene, OR 97440<br>541-343-4433 |
| *Interpersonal Therapy for Adolescents with Depression* (Mufson et al., 1993) | Provides an overview of interpersonal therapy and depression, an in-depth description of applications of IPT for depressed adolescents, and a discussion of special issues related to working with youth. May be more appropriate for mature, insightful adolescents. Due to its clinical focus, it may be less applicable in a school setting. | Guilford Publications<br>72 Spring Street<br>New York, NY 10012<br>800-365-7006<br>www.guilford.com |

When conducting groups for students who are depressed or who are at risk for depression, professional school counselors will want to adapt activities so that they are developmentally appropriate and so that students' real-life concerns are integrated into the format (Stark & Kendall, 1996). Including homework assignments between sessions, involving parents, and adding booster sessions that occur after the program has been completed are ways to increase the efficacy of the experience. Attention should be given to age range, gender composition, and group size, with four to ten students in a group being ideal (Merrell, 2001).

Whereas individual and/or group counseling may be beneficial and needed for some students, a way to reach even more students is through school-based prevention programs, which are discussed next.

*School-based Prevention Programs*

*Student-oriented programs.* Professional school counselors can be instrumental in coordinating and leading life skills training programs to promote positive mental health in young people. Because all youth are exposed to sources of stress and many youth are at risk for experiencing depressive symptoms of some type, it is important for professional school counselors to enhance students' ability to respond adaptively and cope well (Petersen et al., 1992). The goal of prevention programs is to help an entire population of students develop internal and external resources to help prevent the onset of depression or to lessen its intensity should it occur (Rice & Leffert, 1997). Prevention programs can be designed as classroom guidance, which is geared toward students, or as training programs, which are geared toward parents and/or school personnel. Topics for student-oriented prevention can include many of the elements that were described in the section on group counseling: emotional awareness, recognizing the link between thoughts and feelings, coping skills, problem-solving skills, interpersonal skills, conflict resolution, and relaxation training.

An example of a student-oriented prevention program—the Penn State Adolescent Study—was developed by Petersen et al. (1992) and Peterson et al. (1993) to promote mental health and increase coping skills among sixth-grade students. This 16-session psychoeducational program helped students develop positive emotional, cognitive, and behavioral responses to stressors and challenges. Each session emphasized a particular social skill, coping method, or challenge, and began with an activity that demonstrated the topic. Students were given opportunities to practice new problem-solving skills for issues such as peer pressure, making friends, and family conflict. Each session ended with a summary and discussion of major points that were then linked to upcoming sessions. Evaluation indicated that students' coping skills and problem-solving abilities improved after participating in the program, but the effects were not observable one year later, leading to the suggestion of following up with booster sessions throughout the school year to enhance the program's long-term effectiveness.

*Parent and teacher training programs.* In addition to planning student-oriented prevention programs, professional school counselors can initiate training programs for teachers and parents. Teachers and parents typically have more interaction with youth than any other adults. Training programs that facilitate the development of skills in communication, coping, and behavior management can be instrumental in promoting healthy interactions, thus helping prevent the development of depressive symptoms in young people. Also, programs designed to raise parent and teacher awareness about depression can help improve access to needed mental health care for children whose depression might otherwise go undetected. Many parents and teachers may feel reluctant or unprepared to relate children's academic or social difficulties with poor emotional health (Kirchner, Yoder, Kramer, Lindsey, & Thrush, 2000). Professional school counselors can collaborate with mental health providers in the community to lead workshops designed to disseminate information about depression, possible interventions, and community resources.

Kirchner et. al. (2000) developed a pilot program, *Depression in the Classroom*, for K-12 teachers to educate participants about depression and suicidality among children and adolescents. Program goals were to provide: (a) information about the biological and psychosocial basis of depression, and (b) tools to increase educators' ability to detect depressive disorders, educate others about depression, and make referrals within the community. The program, led by mental health specialists from an academic medical center, combined didactic instruction with experiential activities (e.g., responding to video vignettes) and represented a collaborative effort between a medical academic center and school systems. Outcome results indicated that participants not only increased their own knowledge about depression but also shared their knowledge with colleagues and students. Also, the majority of the participants applied the skills learned in the course when interacting with depressed students in their classroom.

The program described in the above paragraph represented a large collaborative effort between an academic medical center and several school systems. Similar programs, perhaps on a smaller scale, could be designed through the collaborative efforts of professional school counselors and community mental heath practitioners.

## Summary/Conclusion

Child and adolescent depression is a serious but treatable condition that has received considerable attention during the past three decades. Many youth will experience depressed mood and other depressive symptoms, even though they may not be clinically depressed. Depression and depressive symptoms can interfere with learning, psychosocial development, and interpersonal relationships. If untreated, depressive symptoms can lead to mood disorders that continue into adulthood. On the other hand, early identification and treatment of symptoms can help put young people on a healthy developmental trajectory.

Professional school counselors have the knowledge and skills needed to enhance the psychological development and well-being of youth (Rice & Leffert, 1997). By understanding the signs, symptoms, and etiology of depression, professional school counselors can play crucial roles in identifying students who may be struggling with these disorders. They can intervene on multiple levels, both from a preventive and a remedial perspective. Prevention activities directed toward students can facilitate the development of positive coping and interaction skills. Programmatic efforts directed toward parents and teachers can increase knowledge about depression and skill in adult-child interaction. Individual and group counseling can help students address dysfunctional cognitive processes, learn strategies for dealing with interpersonal concerns, and develop skills for coping with stress and negative emotions. Through such efforts, professional school counselors can be instrumental in helping students meet the challenges of development in ways that promote mental health.

## References

American Psychiatric Association. (2000). *Diagnostic and statistical manual of mental disorders* (4th ed., text revision). Washington, DC: Author.

Asarnow, J. R., Jaycox, L. H., & Tompson, M. C. (2001). Depression in youth: Psychosocial interventions. *Journal of Clinical Child Psychology, 30,* 33-45.

Beck, A. T. (1976). *Cognitive therapy and the emotional disorders.* New York: International Universities.

Centers for Disease Control. (2002). *Preventing Suicide.* Retrieved May 25, 2002, from http://www.cdc.gov/safeusa/suicide.htm

Clarke, G., Lewinsohn, P., & Hops, H. (1990). *Coping with adolescent depression course: Leader's manual for adolescent groups.* Eugene, OR: Castalia.

Kaffenberger, C. J., & Seligman, L. (2003). Helping students with mental and emotional disorders. In B. T. Erford (Ed.), *Transforming the school counseling profession* (pp. 249-283). Columbus, OH: Merrill/ Prentice-Hall.

Kaslow, N. J., & Thompson, M. P. (1998). Applying the criteria for empirically supported treatments to studies of psychosocial interventions for child and adolescent depression. *Journal of Clinical Child Psychology, 27,* 146-155.

Kendall, P. C. (2000). Guiding theory for therapy with children and adolescents. In P. C. Kendall (Ed.), *Child and adolescent therapy: Cognitive-behavioral procedures* (2nd ed., pp. 3-27). New York: Guilford.

Kendall, P. C., Stark, K., & Adam, T. (1990). Cognitive deficit or cognitive distortion in childhood depression. *Journal of Abnormal Child Psychology, 18,* 267-283.

Kirchner, J. E., Yoder, M. C., Kramer, T. L., Lindsey, M. S., & Thrush, C. R. (2000). Development of an educational program to increase school personnel's awareness about child and adolescent depression. *Education, 121,* 235-246.

Kovacs, M. (1990). Comorbid anxiety disorders in childhood-onset depressions. In J. D. Maser & C. R. Cloniger (Eds.), *Comorbidity of mood and anxiety disorders* (pp. 272-281). Washington, DC: American Psychiatric Press.

Merrell, K. W. (2001). *Helping students overcome depression and anxiety: A practical guide.* New York: Guilford.

Mufson, L., Moreau, D., Weissman, M. M., & Klerman, G. L. (1993). *Interpersonal psychotherapy for depressed adolescents.* New York: Guilford.

National Institute of Mental Health. (2000). *Depression in children and adolescents: A fact sheet for physicians.* Retrieved May 28, 2002, from http://www.nimh.nih.gov/publicat/depchildresfact.cfm

National Institute of Mental Health. (2001). *Depression research at the National Institute of Mental Health.* Retrieved May 30, 2002, from http://www.nimh.nih.gov/publicat/depresfact.cfm

National Institute of Mental Health. (2002a). *Let's talk about depression.* Retrieved May 28, 2002, from http://www.nimh.nih.gov/publicat/letstalk.cfm

National Institute of Mental Health. (2002b). *Suicide facts.* Retrieved June 20, 2002 from http://www.nimh.gov/research/suifact.cfm

Petersen, A. C., Compas, B. E., & Brooks-Gunn, J. (1992). *Depression in adolescence: Current knowledge, research directions, and implications for programs and policy.* New York: Carnegie Corporation. (ERIC Document Reproduction Service No. ED358384)

Petersen, A. C., Compas, B. E., Brooks-Gunn, J., Stemmler, M., Ey, S., & Grant, K. E. (1993). Depression in adolescence. *American Psychologist, 48,* 155-168.

Rice, K. G., & Leffert, N. (1997). Depression in adolescence: Implications for school counselors. *Canadian Journal of Counselling, 31,* 18-34.

Ripley, V., Erford, B. T., Dahir, C., & Eschbach, L. (2003). Planning and implementing a 21st-century comprehensive developmental school counseling program. In B. T. Erford (Ed.), *Transforming the school counseling profession* (pp. 63-119). Columbus, OH: Merrill/ Prentice-Hall.

Stark, K. D., & Kendall, P. C. (1996). *Treating depressed children: Therapist manual for ACTION.* Ardmore, PA: Workbook Publishing.

Stark, K. D., Sander, J. B., Yoncy, M. G., Bronik, M. D., & Hoke, J. A. (2000). Treatment of depression in childhood and adolescence: Cognitive-behavioral procedures for the individual and family. In P. C. Kendall (Ed.), *Child and adolescent therapy: Cognitive-behavioral procedures* (2nd ed.)(pp. 173-234). New York: Guilford.

Surgeon General. (2002). *Depression and suicide in children and adolescents.* Retrieved February 28, 2002, from http://www.surgeongeneral.gov/library/mentalhealth/chapter3/sec5.html

Yarcheski, A., & Mahon, N. E. (2000). A causal model of depression in early adolescents. *Western Journal of Nursing Research, 22,* 879-894.

# Chapter 57

# Helping Students Deal with Obsessive Compulsive Disorder

*Gail Mears*

## Preview

Obsessive-Compulsive Disorder (OCD), a neurobiological disorder once thought to be rare in children, affects one out of every 200 children. Professional school counselors knowledgeable about the signs of OCD, can help ensure early detection of OCD, referral for appropriate services, and effective in-school interventions.

Obsessive Compulsive Disorder (OCD), previously thought to be uncommon in students, affects approximately 1 out of 200 students. There are likely to be several students struggling with the debilitating effects of this disorder in most schools at any one time (March & Mulle, 1998). Children with OCD are consumed by intrusive, repetitive, distressing thoughts and accompanying repetitive rituals. These symptoms can significantly interfere with academic, psychological, and social functioning.

Unfortunately, OCD in school-aged children often goes undetected or is misdiagnosed. Even when detected, the treatments that students receive are often inappropriate (March & Mulle, 1998). This leaves students and their families confused and hopeless. However, with the right psychological, behavioral, medical, social, and academic interventions, students with OCD and their families can find relief from the debilitating effects of this condition.

Professional school counselors are in a key position to ensure that students with OCD are identified and effective resources located. The purpose of this chapter is to aide professional school counselors in their efforts to help students with OCD, their families, and school personnel identify and better manage this condition.

## What Is OCD?

OCD is a neurobiological disorder characterized by obsessions and compulsions. These may occur alone or in combination with each other. An obsession is a persistent irrational thought, image or impulse that causes distress for the student. The student generally recognizes that these thoughts are irrational but is not able to stop these thoughts, images, or impulses from intruding. Obsessions cause the student significant anxiety and the student seeks to manage this anxiety through the use of compulsions. These are behavioral or thinking rituals that reduce the anxiety caused by the student's obsession. However, the relief is temporary and the student feels obliged to continue the use of rituals to manage the resulting anxiety (Adams & Torchia, 1998; APA, 2000; Chansky, 2000; March & Mulle, 1998).

OCD is a chronic disorder with symptoms that worsen over time if left untreated. This disorder has many ups and downs. During periods of stress, students with OCD may notice a significant increase in symptoms. The symptoms of OCD are similar for children, adolescents, and adults; however, unlike adults and adolescents, young children may not view their obsessions as irrational (Adams & Torchia, 1998).

Most young students engage in some form of ritualized behavior. These behaviors are not typically symptoms of OCD. Childhood rituals usually are in the service of helping children gain more mastery over their environment and they ultimately lead to a sense of competence. There is no excessive distress associated with these behaviors and these behaviors do not interfere with social and academic functioning (Chansky, 2000; Thomsen, 1998). Children who insist on a particular bedtime ritual, carry a special object, or want favored stories read over and over again are not suffering from OCD; rather they are engaging in normal childhood behaviors. The adolescent who takes a long time to get ready for a date or who spends major blocks of time practicing a sport or instrument is also not suffering from OCD. These behaviors, while sometimes vexing to adults, do not interfere with the child's academic, social, and psychological development. However, the student who needs to touch every object in their bedroom ten times before leaving for school is showing definite symptoms of OCD. The symptoms of OCD cause distress to students, are time-consuming, and likely interfere with social, emotional and academic functioning. The following are examples of students with OCD.

- Mary, age 13, finds school harder and harder to attend. For the past two years she has been increasingly plagued by sexual images that she finds offensive, and worries that she is crazy. She recites prayers to deal with the anxiety these images cause. It is becoming harder for Mary to pay attention to her class work. She is often preoccupied by the need to pray. Additionally, the proximity of the males in her classes seems to trigger these sexual images. Her grades are dropping and her school attendance is erratic. She no longer likes to spend time with her friends, is irritable at home, and is feeling more and more despondent.
- Sammy, age 10, is in fourth grade. He worries constantly about germs and getting sick. He is particularly worried about getting AIDS. He is careful not to touch anything that he considers dirty, such as doorknobs, faucets, trash, and toilets. He also does not like to touch things that other students have handled. He is often late for school, as he needs to wash and rewash his hands many times during the course of getting ready in the morning. During the school day he repeatedly asks to go to the bathroom in order to wash his hands after touching objects handled by other students. His hands are red and raw and Sammy seems to be anxious most of the time. He does not play with the other children anymore.
- Jimmy, age 9, feels the need for things to be "just right." He spends hours arranging objects in his room at home in order to feel comfortable. In school he is having increasing difficulty with his written work and with reading. His papers are full of erasure marks and he generally is unable to finish assignments. When reading, Jimmy needs to reread each word making sure that he pronounces each correctly. Jimmy has frequent anger outbursts in the classroom.

### What Types of Obsessions Do Children Have?

Obsessions may take many forms. It is the intrusive, irrational, and distressing nature of these thoughts, images, or impulses that mark them as obsessions (APA, 2000). Obsessions commonly reported by children include fear of contamination (worry about germs, getting sick, dying), fear of hurting oneself or others, obscene imagery or thoughts of inappropriate sexual behavior, fear of sinning, need for symmetry or the need to have objects arranged in certain ways, doubting (did I really lock the door?), or the need to repeat actions a certain number of times (Chansky, 2000; Thomsen, 1998; Waltz, 2000). Fear of dirt and germs is the most common obsession experienced by students and is reported by about 40% of students with OCD (Thomsen, 1998).

### What Type of Compulsions Do Children Have?

Compulsions are behavioral or thinking rituals that the student feels compelled to perform in order to reduce the anxiety caused by the obsessions. In order to meet criteria for a compulsion, the behavior or mental ritual must cause marked distress to the student, consume more than an hour a day, or interfere significantly with daily functioning (APA, 2000). Rarely, students experience compulsions without accompanying obsessions. Common forms that compulsions take in students include washing, checking, repeating behaviors, counting, hoarding, praying, and arranging things symmetrically. Washing rituals are the most frequent compulsions displayed by children and boys are more likely than girls to engage in counting rituals (Adams & Torchia, 1998; Chansky, 2000; Thomsen, 1998).

### What Causes OCD?

Historically, OCD was thought to be a disorder that resulted from poor parenting, or some other form of environmental stress. Currently, OCD is understood to be a neurobiological disorder. OCD is associated with over-activity and structural abnormalities in multiple regions of the brain (Adams & Torchia, 1998; Osborne, 1998; Waltz, 2000). Students with OCD often have other neurological irregularities, such as tics and non-verbal learning problems (Adams & Torchia, 1998; March & Mulle, 1998). Serotonin, a neurotransmitter, is the brain chemical most likely involved in OCD (Adams & Torchia, 1998; Chansky, 2000). While it is not known if disregulation of serotonin is the main causative factor in OCD, all medications effective in relieving OCD symptoms effect serotonin pathways (Thomsen, 1998).

Stress can precipitate or exacerbate symptoms of OCD, but students with OCD are in the grip of a brain malfunction. Chansky (2000) referred to the symptoms of OCD as a brain hiccup. The obsessions and compulsions are involuntary and intrusive and students with OCD do not feel as if they have the ability to stop the intrusive obsessions or to not engage the resulting compulsions. Students with OCD are literally stuck in their respective obsessions and resulting behavioral or mental rituals. This information is very important for parents who often feel responsible (and may have been actually blamed!) for producing this condition in their children.

Heredity is a likely factor in the development of OCD. Students may inherit a vulnerability to OCD, but heredity alone does not explain the actual expression of the disorder (Thomsen, 1998). Higher rates of OCD have been observed in students who have family members diagnosed with OCD, depression, anxiety disorders, or Tourette's Disorder (Adams & Torchia, 1998).

Research from the National Institute of Mental Health indicated that there is a group of students who develop an acute and severe onset or exacerbation of OCD symptoms that is associated with a strep infection. This is called Pediatric Autoimmune Neuropsychiatric Disorder Associated with Strep (PANDAS) (Swedo, Leonard, et al. as cited in Chansky, 2000). When a child presents with a sudden onset or increase in OCD symptoms, a referral should be made to a pediatrician to rule out PANDAS.

### Who Gets OCD?

It is estimated that one in 200 students can be diagnosed with OCD at any one time. This is likely an underestimate of the prevalence rate of OCD because students are often secretive about their symptoms and family members and professionals often don't understand that the troubling behaviors displayed by the student may be a result of OCD (March & Mulle, 1998). The *DSM-IV-TR* (APA, 2000) sets a lifetime prevalence rate of OCD in children at 1-2.3% and notes that the prevalence rate of OCD in students is consistent across cultures. Students diagnosed with OCD may also have other diagnosed disorders including ADHD, Tourette's Disorder, developmental disabilities, non-verbal learning disabilities, anxiety disorders, and depressive disorders (Adams & Torchia, 1998). Ten to 30% of students diagnosed with ADHD and 40-60% of children diagnosed with Tourette's Disorder also qualify for a diagnosis of OCD (Comings, as cited in Dornbush & Pruitt, 1995).

Males and females are diagnosed with OCD in equal numbers. However, OCD tends to occur at an earlier age in boys than in girls. The average age of onset for males is between ages six and 15 and the average age of onset for females is between the ages of 20-29 (APA, 2000). Clinically, OCD is similar for boys and girls. There is some indication that there is an increased likelihood that boys have family members with OCD and boys seem to have higher rates of tic disorders than do girls (Thomsen, 1998).

### What Are the Signs That a Student May Have OCD?

Children's obsessions and compulsions are not always apparent to an observer. Young children are more open about their compulsions, but older children and adolescents often hide these symptoms. Whether visible or not, the symptoms of OCD weigh heavily on students. The stress of dealing with their symptoms may lead to other behavioral problems. Sometimes students are able to control their compulsions in school but not at home. Parents' reports of OCD symptoms should be taken seriously even if the student does not demonstrate the same behaviors in school (Chansky, 2000).

During school time there are multiple signs that might indicate a student is struggling with the symptoms of OCD. According to specialists (Adams & Torchia, 1998; Chansky, 2000; Chansky & Grayson, n.d.; Dornbush & Pruitt; 1995; Johnston & Fruehling, 2002), school personnel should be attentive to a number of common signs (see Table 1).

### How Is OCD Diagnosed?

A professional qualified to diagnose and assess mental disorders should always make the diagnosis of OCD. This professional will want to gather information from the student, parents, and relevant school professionals. Standardized questionnaires are often used to help in the diagnosis and evaluate the extent to which OCD is interfering with the child's social, emotional, and academic functioning. The diagnosis of OCD is often complicated by the presence of other comorbid conditions such as anxiety disorders, Oppositional Defiant Disorder, depression, eating disorders, AD/HD, developmental disabilities, Tourette's Syndrome, or non-verbal language disorders (Adams & Torchia, 1998; Adams, Wass, March, & Smith, 1994; March & Mulle, 1998; Thomsen, 1998). It is important to know experienced diagnosticians in your community who are equipped to evaluate students showing symptoms of OCD.

### How Is OCD Treated?

Cognitive behavior therapy (CBT) and behavior therapy (terms often used to indicate similar treatment formats) are considered the most effective treatment for students with OCD (Johnston & Fruehling, 2002; March & Mulle, 1998; Thomsen, 1998). Cognitive and behavioral

**Table 1. Common signs of OCD.**

1. *Repeated requests to go to the bathroom.* The child seeks to engage in washing rituals to manage the anxiety caused by contamination fears that get triggered in the normal course of the school day.
2. *Repeated reassurance-seeking from teachers and other adult authorities.* This goes well beyond the typical questioning that might be expected from any school child.
3. *The appearance of daydreaming or disinterest in schoolwork.* Students with OCD are preoccupied with their frightening obsessions and compensating ritual. When so much attention is focused internally, it is difficult to stay engaged with the classroom activity.
4. *Bouts of anger of anxiety.* This can be the result of being exposed to situations that trigger obsessions. A student with contamination fears may get quite upset when expected to share materials with another student. Anxiety and irritability may result when students are frustrated in their attempts to engage in compulsions. Therefore, the student whose request to go to the bathroom is denied may become quite agitated.
5. *The need to do things in "just the right way."* This can dramatically interfere with schoolwork. These types of obsessions can prevent students from finishing tasks in a timely way. Students may suffer from reading or writing compulsions. OCD may prevent the students from finishing written or reading assignments as they struggle with the need to write or read perfectly, resulting in erasures and undone work. Students with OCD may resist writing or reading in an effort to avoid the associated obsessions and compulsions. As school becomes more and more burdensome, students may try and avoid school altogether.
6. *Frequent tardiness for school or classes.* Obsessions and resulting compulsions can make getting ready for school or the transition between classes very time consuming. A student who needs to repeat behaviors over and over again, or arrange and rearrange objects, or repetitively wash his/her hands may be frequently tardy for school and classes.
7. *Social isolation.* The time students spend managing their OCD symptoms can greatly interfere with the time they have available for friends. Being with other students may reduce their ability to engage in compulsions or may risk triggering obsessions and compulsions (such as fear of hurting another). These students worry that their inability to control their compulsions will lead to being ridiculed by their peers. Social isolation is a way of managing these fears.
8. *Depression and low self-esteem.* The ongoing battle with obsessions and compulsions that students with OCD face is extremely discouraging, potentially leaving the student demoralized and hopeless.

strategies are designed to help students delay and reduce compulsive rituals when exposed to situations that trigger obsessions. They are also designed to empower students by providing information regarding the neurobiological roots of OCD, and by helping students develop cognitive strategies that empower them to feel in control of, rather than controlled by, OCD symptoms (March & Mulle, 1998). Medication should be considered for students when symptoms are so severe that CBT is too anxiety provoking or when there is little or no response to CBT alone. Treatment in these cases should be a combination of CBT and medication. Medication alone does not help students develop the behavioral and cognitive strategies so useful in minimizing the impact of OCD symptoms (Johnston & Fruehling, 2002).

The medications most commonly prescribed for childhood OCD include Clomipramine (Anafranil®), Fluoxetine (Prozac®), Fluvoxamine (Luvox®), Paroxetine (Paxil®), and Sertraline (Zoloft®). Clomipramine, Fluvoxamine, and Sertraline have FDA approval for use with students diagnosed with OCD. All of these medications affect serotonin levels in the brain. All but Clomipramine are in the family of drugs known as Selective Serotonin Reuptake Inhibitors (SSRIs) (Johnston & Fruehling, 2002).

Parents need to be involved in their child's treatment. Having a child with OCD is extremely stressful and parents as well as children need support, information, and coping strategies. Sometimes, in an attempt to deal with their child's distress, parents become involved in their child's rituals. An example of this would be a parent that agrees to repeatedly wash the same article of clothing before the child agrees to wear it. Parents are important partners in their child's effort to learn strategies to better manage OCD (Chansky, 2000; March & Mulle, 1998).

### How Can School Counselors Help?

Professional school counselors are key school resources for students struggling with the symptoms of OCD. According to experts (Adams & Torchia, 1998; Chansky, 2000), the following are important actions that can help minimize the impact of OCD on students while at school.

1. Professional school counselors can educate school personnel about the signs of OCD. Statistics suggest that there are likely multiple children in any school with OCD. Educating teachers, principals, and parents about the signs of OCD will increase the likelihood that students will get the help that they need and avoid the academic, psychological, and social consequences of untreated OCD.
2. Professional school counselors can consult with parents, teachers, the school psychologist and outside mental health providers to ensure that students diagnosed with OCD receive appropriate in-school interventions. Some students with mild OCD will need no accommodations from the school. In fact, the school may not even be aware of the diagnosis. However, students with moderate to severe OCD may need professional school counselors and teachers to help manage programs designed to delay or reduce compulsive rituals.
3. Professional school counselors can provide a place where students with OCD get a reprieve from the stress of the classroom and the stress of delaying rituals. The treatment of OCD involves helping students develop a plan to delay participating in compulsive rituals. The goal is a reduction in these rituals, not necessarily the elimination of these rituals. Part of that plan will likely include a "safe place" where students can go to recover from the stress of dealing with OCD.
4. Professional school counselors can be alert to both the positive and negative changes that result from medication. Negative effects may include, but are not limited to, dry mouth, increased irritability, upset stomach, drowsiness, insomnia, and headaches.
5. Professional school counselors can help parents find the educational, psychological, and medical resources that they will need to help their child manage OCD. Understanding that OCD is a neurobiological disorder and not the result of bad parenting can be an enormous source of support for parents.
6. Professional school counselors can advocate that students with OCD get appropriate in-school accommodations. Students with OCD may be eligible for special educational services under section 504 of the Rehabilitation Act of 1973 or, if educational functioning is severely compromised, under the Individuals with Disabilities Education Act.
7. Professional school counselors can help create a positive classroom environment

with peers. In more severe cases, it may be helpful to educate the student's classmates about OCD. In most cases, however, a more general classroom curriculum is recommended. Chansky (2000) suggested units on health issues that affect the body from head to toe. Most students will know someone struggling with a disabling condition and this identification may increase their ability to empathize with the student struggling with OCD in the classroom. Consent from the student and parent(s) should always be secured before talking with classmates about an individual child's condition.

### What Are Some Classroom Strategies That Will Help Children With OCD?

Students should not be punished for symptoms of OCD over which they have no control. Taking away recess or giving detentions may only worsen the behaviors these punishments are designed to eliminate (Adams & Torchia, 1998). Some of the helpful classroom strategies identified by Adams & Torchia and Chansky & Grayson (n.d.) include:

- Find ways to accommodate the student's symptoms. Examples of supportive classroom accommodations include: 1) Allow students with writing compulsion to take tests orally, 2) grade students on the content, not the neatness, of their papers, 3) provide resources for a student with reading compulsions to listen to books on tape, 4) give extra time on tests, 5) develop signals and phrases with students to cue them when they appear stuck in OCD rituals that you are willing to help.
- Support students with OCD by identifying areas of strength. OCD is a demoralizing illness and students need to be reminded of what they do well.
- Help students with OCD manage social interactions. Set up opportunities for students to work collaboratively with peers. Avoid putting these students in situations where they are likely to be ignored or left out.

For more specific ideas about classroom interventions, the reader is referred to *Teaching the TIGER: A Handbook for Individuals Involved in the Education of Students With Attention Deficit Disorders, Tourette Syndrome or Obsessive-Compulsive Disorder* (Dornbush & Pruitt, 1995).

### Summary/Conclusion

Students today can expect significant help with the debilitating symptoms of OCD. Though considered a chronic illness, with appropriate treatment and school and home support, students with OCD will likely experience a significant reduction in the distress and subsequent functional impairments associated with this condition. Unfortunately, educators and mental health practitioners are often misinformed about the cause of OCD and effective intervention strategies. Professional school counselors are in a key position to ensure that teachers and other school personnel are informed and alert to the signs and symptoms of OCD. Through partnerships with teachers, school nurses, school psychologists, and qualified mental health professionals in the community, professional school counselors can promote in-school strategies that will support students with OCD in their academic, social and emotional development. Professional school counselors play an important role in making school a satisfying experience that is not overshadowed by symptoms associated with OCD for students living with this disorder. (See Table 2 for additional resources for helping students with OCD.)

**Table 2. Additional resources.**

*Organizations*

Obsessive-Compulsive Foundation (OCF), 337 Notch Hill Road, North Branford, CT 0697, http://www.ocfoundation.org

Obsessive Compulsive Information Center (OCIC), Madison Institute of Medicine, 7617 Mineral Point Road, Suite 300, Madison, WI 53717, http://www.helathtechsys.com/mim.html

NIMH, Building 10, Room 4N 208, Bethesda, MD 20892-1255, http://www.intramural.nimh.nih.gov/pds/web.htm

National Alliance for the Mentally Ill, Child and Adolescent Network (NAMI-CAN), 200 North Glebe Road, Suite 1015, Arlington, VA 22203-3754

*Books*

Adams, G. B., & Torchia, M. (1994). *School personnel: A critical link in the identification, treatment and management of OCD in children and adolescents* (3rd ed.). Milford, CT: OC Foundation, Inc.

Chanksy, T. E. (2000). *Freeing your child from Obsessive-Compulsive Disorder: A powerful practical guide for parents of children and adolescents.* New York: Three Rivers Press.

Dornbush, M. P., & Pruitt, S. K. (1995). *Teaching the tiger: A handbook for individuals involved in the education of students with attention deficit disorders, Tourette Syndrome or Obsessive-Compulsive Disorder.* Duarte, CA: Hope Press.

Johnston, H. F., & Fruehling, J. J. (2002). *Obsessive Compulsive Disorder in children & adolescents: A guide.* Madison, WI: Child Psychopharmacology Information Center, University of Wisconsin.

March, S., & Mulle, K. (1998). *OCD in children and adolescents: A cognitive behavioral treatment manual.* New York: Guilford Publishers.

Rapoport, J. (1991). *The boy who couldn't stop washing.* New York: Penguin Books.

Thomsen, P. H. (1999). *From thoughts to obsessions: Obsessive Compulsive Disorder in children and adolescents.* Philadelphia: Jessica Kingsley Publishers.

Waltz, M. (2000). *Obsessive-Compulsive Disorder: Help for children and adolescents.* Cambridge: O'Reilly.

*Video*

*How to recognize and respond to obsessive-compulsive disorder in school age children: An awareness and training educational module for teacher sponsored by the Obsessive-Compulsive Foundation.* Available though the Obsessive-Compulsive Foundation: http://www.ocdfoundation.org.

## References

Adams, G. B., & Torchia, M. (1998). *School personnel: A critical link in the identification, treatment and management of OCD in children and adolescents* (3rd ed.). Milford, CT: OC Foundation, Inc.

Adams, G. B., Wass, G. A., March, J. S., & Smith, M. C. (1994). Obsessive Compulsive Disorder in children and adolescents: The role of the school psychologist in identification, assessment and treatment. *School Psychology Quarterly, 9*, 274-294.

American Psychiatric Association. (2000). *Diagnostic and statistical manual of mental disorders-4th ed., text revision (DSM-IV-TR).* Washington, DC: Author.

Chanksy, T. E. (2000). *Freeing your child from Obsessive-Compulsive Disorder: A powerful practical guide for parents of children and adolescents.* New York: Three Rivers Press.

Chansky, T., & Grayson, J. (n.d.). *Teacher's guidelines for helping children with Obsessive-Compulsive Disorder in the classroom.* Milford, CT: The Obsessive-Compulsive Foundation, Inc.

Dornbush, M. P., & Pruitt, S. K. (1995). *Teaching the tiger: A handbook for individuals involved in the education of students with attention deficit disorders, Tourette Syndrome or Obsessive-Compulsive Disorder.* Duarte, CA: Hope Press.

Johnston, H. F., & Fruehling, J. J. (2002). *Obsessive Compulsive Disorder in children & adolescents: A guide.* Madison, WI: Child Psychopharmacology Information Center, University of Wisconsin.

March, S., & Mulle, K. (1998). *OCD in children and adolescents: A cognitive behavioral treatment manual.* New York: Guilford.

Osborn, I. (1998). *Tormenting thoughts and secret rituals.* New York: Random House Inc.

Thomsen, P. H. (1998). Obsessive-Compulsive Disorder in children and adolescents. Clinical guidelines. *European Child and Adolescent Psychiatry*, *7*(1), 1-11.

Waltz, M. (2000). *Obsessive Compulsive Disorder: Help for children and adolescents.* Cambridge: O'Reilly.

# Chapter 58

# Separation Anxiety Disorder in the Schools

*Henry L. Harris*

## Preview

Separation anxiety is a common emotional reaction that many students experience daily. However, it becomes problematic when the emotional reactions negatively affect normal academic or social activities. For some students, separation anxiety is the cause of school refusal and other disruptive behaviors. This chapter discusses characteristics of students with Separation Anxiety Disorder as well as interventions that could be helpful during the remediation process.

Anxiety is an emotional response experienced on a daily basis. It is considered an important part of social development and a helpful reaction in a variety of situations. Even so, anxiety is often negatively perceived and misunderstood (Huberty, 1990). For example, some parents and teachers perceive students with anxiety disorders to be readily recognizable and not having serious problems. However, when asked to actually identify students with anxiety, parents and teachers seem to have a difficult time doing so. When descriptions are provided about the behaviors of anxious students, their ability to identify those students significantly increases (Walkup & Ginsberg, 2002). Many students with anxiety:

- have trouble leaving the car and entering the school in the mornings;
- have trouble learning and sharing in group or social activities;
- regularly visit the school nurse with physical complaints;
- have difficulty demonstrating their knowledge on tests or through classroom participation and are considered underachievers;
- have high rates of absences (Walkup & Ginsberg, 2002, p. 85).

Given such negative consequences it is imperative that professional school counselors be proactive when addressing this serious issue.

## Anxiety Disorders

The *Diagnostic and Statistical Manual of Mental Disorders–4th Edition - Text Revision* (DSM-IV-TR; American Psychiatric Association, 2000) lists the following anxiety disorders specific to children: Separation Anxiety Disorder, Simple Phobia, Social Phobia, and Generalized Anxiety Disorders. Much information is known about Separation Anxiety Disorder because it is one of the more frequent clinical anxiety disorders presenting in children (Berstein & Borchardt, 1991). Separation anxiety is initially seen in small children when they are 9-18 months old. Some become apprehensive in the presence of strangers and when placed in unfamiliar surroundings, experience general distress, cry, become withdrawn, or cling to parents, especially when parents attempt to leave (Huberty & Eaken, 1994).

For most children, normal separation anxiety intensifies during early childhood and then gradually decreases between 3 - 5 years of age (Masi, Mucci, & Millepiedi, 2001). Separation anxiety becomes an issue of concern for professional school counselors when: the normal functioning of the student is hampered by the intensity, length, and frequency of behavior; the demonstrated behavior is inappropriate for the current situation; the student lacks the ability to make the behaviorally appropriate transition; and the behavior significantly impacts how the student functions in society (Huberty, 1990; Huberty & Eaken, 1994).

### Separation Anxiety Disorder

Separation Anxiety is a childhood condition (see Table 1) that occurs in approximately 4% of young children and adolescents (APA, 2000); median age for onset is approximately 7.5 years of age (Last, Perrin, & Hensen, 1992). Separation Anxiety Disorder is characterized by excessive anxiety and worry about being separated from home or a major attachment figure and students with this disorder often believe that something tragic will happen to them or their parents (APA, 2000). Sometimes when students are asked what they are afraid of they may communicate a fear of being displaced and never finding their parents again (Sarason & Sarason, 1987). They may also be preoccupied with dreadful images of crooks, monsters, or other dangerous animals that could possibly harm them or their parents. Students suffering with Separation Anxiety Disorder have often been described from one extreme as individuals who are intrusive, demanding, and in need of constant attention, to being very conscientious and constantly desiring to please others (APA, 2000).

**Table 1. Diagnostic criteria for Separation Anxiety Disorder (APA, 2000, p. 113).**

A. Excessive anxiety concerning separation from home or major attachment figure, as evidenced by three (or more) of the following:
   1) excessive levels of stress when separation from home or major attachment figures occurs or is anticipated
   2) constant and excessive worry about something bad happening to a major attachment figures
   3) constant and excessive worry that some unfortunate event will lead to separation from a major attachment figure (e.g. getting lost or being kidnapped)
   4) constant unwillingness or refusal to go to school or other places because of fear of separation.
   5) excessive fear or reluctance of being alone or without major attachment figures at home
   6) constant unwillingness or refusal to go to sleep without being near a major attachment figure or to sleep away from home
   7) reoccurring nightmares involving separation
   8) reoccurring complaints of physical symptoms (such as headaches, stomachaches, nausea, vomiting) when separation from major attachment figure.

B. The disturbance must last a minimum of 4 weeks.

C. The onset began before 18 years of age.

D. The disturbance causes clinically significant distress or impairment in social, academic (occupational), or other important areas.

E. The disturbance does not occur exclusively during the course of other psychotic disorders.

Specify if disorder began before age 6 .

Sleep could also be an issue for some students with Separation Anxiety Disorder because they are afraid to stay in a room by themselves and may insist someone stay with them until they fall asleep. They may have repeated nightmares and report occurrences of seeing people in their room or peering eyes staring at them. Sometimes during the night when they awake, they seek comfort in their parent's bedroom. When this is not possible, they will either sleep next to their parent's bedroom door or seek the companionship of a sibling or family pet (Tongue, 1994). Even during the day some students may refuse to let the major attachment figure out of their sight and at times become hysterical when that figure is physically in another room (APA, 2000). Similar reactions may occur when separation is anticipated, as when students are getting dressed and ready in the morning. They will cry, become angry, and even try to physically strike the individual who is causing the separation (APA, 2000).

Some students with Separation Anxiety Disorder experience excessive worry only when they are away from their home surroundings. If they participate in a camp of some sort, attend school, or visit relatives or friends, these students have a strong desire to return home. When this is not possible, they may feel sad, lose their ability to concentrate, become contentious, or experience social withdrawal (Tongue, 1994).

It is important to realize that older students with Separation Anxiety Disorder have fewer symptoms than younger children and may report feeling faint or dizzy (ACA, 2000). More often, unrealistic worry about major attachment figures and school refusal are behaviors reported by students from 5-8 years of age. Extreme worry and distress at the time of separation is more common in students ranging from age 9–12. Adolescents most often report somatic complaints and school refusal (Masi et al., 2001).

*School Refusal*

Approximately 75% of students with Separation Anxiety Disorder present with school refusal (Masi et al., 2001). School refusal is not about the student's fear of school but rather the student's fear of the separation from their parent. Jongsma, Peterson, & McInnis (1996) offered the following behavioral definitions for school refusal:

- Constant hesitancy or refusal to attend school because of the desire to stay at home with the parent. Some are preoccupied with thoughts that, if separated, something terrifying will happen to them or their parents.
- Shows emotional strains and complaints such as crying, temper outbursts or begging the parents not to take them to school (when expecting separation from home to attend school or following arrival at school).
- Commonly expressed complaints of headaches, stomach pains, or feeling nauseated prior to attending school or following arrival.
- When departing home or arriving at school, the student may stay excessively close to the parent.
- Fear of the separation from the parents is accompanied by low levels of self-esteem and self-confidence.
- Students communicate and express a fear of failure and anxiety along with the refusal to attend school.

When students with Separation Anxiety Disorder refuse to attend school it could lead to academic problems and social isolation. Even when attending school, their excessive demands "often become a source of teacher and peer frustration, resulting in resentment, ridicule, and conflict within the classroom" (Deluty & Devitis, 1996, p. 108).

## Interventions

There are a number of interventions professional school counselors can use to help students and families cope with Separation Anxiety Disorder. The interventions designed and selected should ideally reflect a team effort involving the professional school counselor, parents, teachers, administrators, the school psychologist, and school nurse. Professional school counselors should first have adequate knowledge about separation anxiety and the behavioral characteristics associated with this condition. Professional school counselors must be aware of their personal feelings and biases toward students and parents who may be experiencing separation anxiety. One way this can be accomplished is by exploring the following questions: (1) How do I honestly feel about students with Separation Anxiety Disorder?; (2) Am I able to accurately identify students with Separation Anxiety Disorder?; (3) Do I believe the parents are solely responsible for their children's behavior?; (4) Do I feel more discipline would solve the problem?; (5) Is this child a "cry baby" and simply trying to gain attention?; (6) Do I perceive this child's behavior as disruptive and caused by overprotective parents?; (7) Am I displaying too much sympathy towards this child?; and (8) Do I have the time, skills, or available resources needed to help these students and their families? The intervention team should also explore the same questions.

Once the questions have been thoroughly explored, the next phase should involve professional school counselors consulting with parents and teachers to provide information on students suspected of having anxiety-related issues, such as excessive worry, frequent absences, or somatic complaints (Scott, Culley, & Weissberg, 1995). During the consultation process professional school counselors should make sure that parents and teachers are knowledgeable about various aspects of Separation Anxiety Disorder and how it potentially impacts the academic and social development of students. For teachers and administrators, in-service training focusing on separation anxiety issues would be helpful (Huberty, 1990).

The school psychologist can be a valuable resource for the professional school counselor. The role played by the school psychologist will depend largely upon a variety of factors, including: the severity of the problem; level of parent involvement; and school policy (some school systems may require outside help). The school nurse may contribute by conducting a preliminary physical on students experiencing somatic complaints. They are also in a position to recommend to parents that the student undergo a thorough physical examination. Elimination of physical ailments as causes of the pain and discomfort experienced by the student (Scott et al., 1995) allows the association to be made between anxiety and somatic issues. The process of creating a mental health or developmental plan can begin to help the student develop more effective coping skills.

*Consulting With Parents*

When discussing Separation Anxiety Disorder with parents, professional school counselors should gather as much information as possible about the child and the family. It would be helpful to explore with parents: (1) any recent sudden or negative life events or stressors; (2) their perspective on the student's personality and behavior; (3) the length of time the student has been experiencing separation anxiety; (4) whether or not other family members have previously encountered this problem; (5) if the student's siblings have been affected by the behavior; and (6) their role in helping design and implement selected interventions.

Professional school counselors can also assist parents during consultation by helping them recognize their own feelings about Separation Anxiety Disorder, because some feelings could reveal personal, subconscious levels of anxiety and discomfort regarding the student. Professional school counselors should encourage parents to be aware of their child's personality and convey relevant information to school personnel. Furthermore, professional school counselors may assist parents by:

- teaching parents appropriate ways to prepare the student before the separation occurs;
- making parents aware of appropriate transitional objects to use with the student, such as a picture or a small toy;
- encouraging parents to never make fun of their child or say things like "big boys and girls don't cry," or "other kids are going to tease you if you cry" (Hewitt, 1995);
- encouraging parents to leave school when it is time to leave, because sometimes the situation becomes more chaotic when the parents stays longer than normal;
- encouraging parents to never sneak away from their child, always say goodbye, and return at the expected time (Unknown author, 1999).

*Systematic Desensitization*

Systematic desensitization is a behavioral modification intervention designed by Wolpe (1958) to eliminate fear and anxiety by exposing the individual to the feared stimulus in a carefully graduated manner (Carson, Butcher & Coleman, 1988). The first step in this process consists of relaxation training. Children with Separation Anxiety Disorder could be taught simple relaxation techniques such as learning how to breathe, or tightening and relaxing different muscles in the body (progressive muscle relaxation training). Some students may be too young to fully understand this concept; therefore the professional school counselor should modify this technique according to the student's developmental level. The student is then instructed to practice relaxation skills daily, ranging from 10-20 minutes while listening to a tape of relaxation instructions.

The next step includes developing a hierarchy of fears with situations producing the highest level of anxiety placed at the top followed by the next least anxiety-provoking situation until the situations causing little or no anxiety appear at the bottom. (See Table 2 for a sample hierarchy.)

The student should be in a relaxed mood when each session begins. The professional school counselor asks the student to imagine the lowest anxiety-provoking situation on the hierarchy and signal by raising a finger if they experience anxiety. If no anxiety is experienced, this format is followed until the student reaches the highest situation on the hierarchy without experiencing any anxiety (Huberty, 1990; Lee & Miltenberger, 1996). This approach may be more applicable for use with older children or adolescents.

*In vivo Desensitization*

*In vivo desensitization* is an alternate form of systematic desensitization and may be more practical for professional school counselors to use in the school setting, especially for students who refuse to attend school. This approach requires the student and parent to be active participants (Huberty & Eaken, 1994).

**Table 2. Sample hierarchy.**

| | |
|---|---|
| Step 11. | Child is in the classroom with activities occurring around him/her |
| Step 10. | Child is alone in the classroom |
| Step 09. | Child is alone in the classroom with the teacher |
| Step 08. | Child enters the classroom alone |
| Step 07. | Child enters the classroom with a parent |
| Step 06. | Child walks to the classroom alone |
| Step 05. | Child walks to the classroom with the parent |
| Step 04. | Child enters the school building alone |
| Step 03. | Child enters the school building with the parent |
| Step 02. | Child gets into the car with the parent |
| Step 01. | Child gets dressed and prepares to go to school |

Note: From Huberty, 1990, pp. 272-2

The professional school counselor, parents, teachers, school nurse, and the school psychologist cooperate in varying degrees to establish a hierarchy of tasks specifically designed to bring the child closer to the class or school environment where the most anxiety occurs. The professional school counselor is responsible, along with the help of the parent, for gradually exposing the student to each step in the hierarchy. When anxiety is reported, that particular step is repeated until the anxiety no longer exists. The process requires patience and continues until the student has completed all steps in the hierarchy without experiencing anxiety (Huberty & Eaken, 1994). A sample hierarchy developed by Huberty (1990) is provided in Table 2.

This technique can also be taught to parents for them to use with children outside of school. For example, the hierarchy could include items for the anxious child such as playing outside in the backyard with the parent inside, playing alone in a room for 5 minutes, sleeping in their own room one night a week, or staying at home with a sitter (Phelps, Cox, & Bajorek, 1992).

*Token Economies and Positive Reinforcement*

The token economy is a type of positive reinforcement system. This intervention rewards students with tokens or points only when a level of desired behavior is reached. Parents should be involved in designing the reward system, which could range from using actual tokens for use at the local arcade or exchanging points for prizes. In some situations, this intervention could be paired with *in vivo* desensitization and tokens/points awarded when one of the steps in the hierarchy is completed.

*Play Therapy*

Play therapy is another form of counseling that professional school counselors should consider using when helping students with Separation Anxiety Disorder. During the play sessions students are provided the opportunity to express their emotions through what they do best, play. According to Landreth (1993) and Guerney (1979), play is the student's symbolic language of self-expression and during the process of play therapy students have the opportunity to fully experience all parts of the self because the play is self-directed and safe. Students with Separation Anxiety Disorder are ideal candidates for this form of counseling because one of the major goals of play therapy is to help reduce anxiety and stress levels in the emotional mind of a vulnerable child (Landreth, 1993).

*Other Interventions*

Professional school counselors should also consider conducting classroom guidance activities focusing on separation anxiety. Reading animated books about characters confronting this sensitive issue could prove beneficial (see Table 3 for a list of resources). Other appropriate cognitive behavioral interventions could include modeling, cognitive restructuring, shaping, and flooding. Group counseling is another option professional school counselors should take into consideration for students, along with filial therapy training for parents (Guerney, 1997; Johnson, 1995). Ultimately, the type of counseling approach used will vary and depend on a number of different factors including the severity of the problem, available school resources, professional school counselor's training experience, and the level of parent involvement.

**Table 3. Books on separation anxiety PreK-6th grade level.**

Brown, M. W. (1991). *The runaway bunny*. New York: Harper Collins Children's Books.
Brandt, A. (2000). *Benjamin comes back/Benjamin regresa*. New York: Harper Collins.
Chorao, K. (1997). *Lester's overnight*. New York: Dutton/Plume.
Cole, J. (2001). *When mommy and daddy go to work*. New York: Harper Collins.
Corey, D. (1999). *You go away*. Chicago, IL: Albert Whitman Publisher.
Crarey, E. (1996). *Mommy don't go*. Seattle, WA: Parenting Press.
Crarey, E. (1996). *I'm scared (Dealing with feelings)*. Seattle,WA: Parenting Press.
Edwards, B. (2002). *My first day at nursery school*. New York:Bloomsbury-USA Publishers.
Howe, J. (1999). *Pinky & Rex go to camp*. New York: Simon & Schuster.
Henkes, K. (2000). *Wemberly worried*. New York: Harper Collins.
Kandoian, E. (1990). *Maybe she forgot*. New York: Cobblehill/Dutton.
Marcus, P. (2001). *Into the great forest: A story for children away from parents for the first time*. Washington, DC:American Psychological Association.
Newton, S. (1991). *Where are you when I need you?* New York: Penguin Putnam Books for Young Readers.
Pappas, D. (2001). *Mommy, daddy, come back soon*. Washington, DC: American Psychological Association.
Penn, A. (1995). *The kissing hand*. Child Welfare League of America.
Selway, M. (1994). *Don't forget to write*. Nashville, TN: Ideal Children's Books.
Steele, D. (1992). *Freddie's first night away*. New York: Dell Publishing.
Viorst, J. (1992). *The good bye book*. New York: Simon & Schuster.
Weeks, S. (2002). *My somebody special*. New York: Harcourt.

## Summary/Conclusion

Separation anxiety is an emotional reaction that is normal for many children and should only become a concern for professional school counselors when the anxiety begins to negatively impact the individual academically, emotionally, and socially. Professional school counselors must have accurate knowledge about the characteristics associated with Separation Anxiety Disorder, including appropriate assessment tools and appropriate interventions. Professional school counselors make the effort to work collaboratively with parents, teachers, administrators, school nurses, and school psychologists to formulate a plan to help families and students with Separation Anxiety Disorder, always striving to convey patience, empathy, understanding, and a sense of hope.

## References

American Psychiatric Association. (2000). *Diagnostic and statistical manual of mental disorders* (4th ed., text revision). Washington, DC: Author.

Berstein, G. A., Borchardt, C. M. (1991). Anxiety disorders of childhood and adolescence: A critical review. *Journal of American Academy of Child and Adolescent Psychiatry, 30*, 519-532.

Carson, R. C., Butcher, J. N., & Coleman, J. C. (1988). *Abnormal psychology and modern life* (8th ed). Glenview, IL: Scott, Foresman, & Company.

Deluty, R. H., & DeVitis, J. L. (1996). Fears in the classroom: Psychological issues and pedagogical implications. *Educational Horizons, 2,* 108-113.

Guerney, L. F. (1979). Play therapy with learning disabled children. *Journal of Clinical Child Psychiatry, 3,* 242-244.

Guerney, L. F. (1997). Filial therapy. In K. O'Conner & M. L. Braverman (Eds.), *Play therapy theory and practice: A comparative presentation* (pp. 131-159). New York: Wiley & Sons.

Hewitt, D. (1995). *So this is normal too?* Beltsville, MD: Redleaf Press

Huberty, T. J. (1990). Reducing academic related anxiety. *Special Services in the Schools, 5,* 261-276.

Huberty, T. J., & Eaken, G. J. (1994). Interventions for children's anxiety disorders. *Special Services in the Schools, 9,* 97-117.

Johnson, L. (1995). Filial therapy: A bridge between individual child therapy and family therapy. *Journal of Family Psychotherapy, 6,* 55-70.

Jongsma, A., Peterson, M. L., & McInnis, W. P. (1996). *The child and adolescent psychotherapy.* New York: John Wiley & Sons.

Landreth, G. L. (1993). Child-centered play therapy. *Elementary School Guidance and Counseling, 28,* 17-29.

Last, C. G., Perrin, S., & Hersen, M. (1992). *DSM-III-R* anxiety disorders in children: Sociodemographic and clinical characteristics. *Journal of the American Academy of Child and Adolescent Psychiatry, 31,* 1070-1076.

Lee, M., & Miltenberger, R. G. (1996). School refusal behavior: Classification, assessment, and treatment issues. *Education and Treatment of Children, 19,* 474-483.

Masi, G., Mucci, M., & Millepiedi, S. (2001). Separation anxiety disorders in children and adolescents. *CNS Drugs, 15,* 93-104.

Phelps, L., Cox, D., & Bajorek, E. (1992). School phobia and separation anxiety: Diagnostic and treatment comparisons. *Psychology in the Schools, 29,* 384-394.

Sarason, I. G., & Sarason, B. R. (1987*). Abnormal psychology: The problem of maladaptive behavior* (5th ed). Englewood Cliffs, NJ: Prentice-Hall.

Scott, J., Culley, M., & Weissberg, E. (1995). Helping the separation anxious school refuser. *Elementary School Guidance & Counseling, 29,* 289-296.

Tongue, B. (1994). Separation Anxiety Disorder. In T. H. Ollendick, N. J. King, & W. Yule (Eds.*), International handbook of phobic and anxiety disorders in children and adolescents* (pp. 145-168). New York: Plenum Press.

Unknown Author. (1999). Saying goodbye: Making hard transitions easier. *Texas Childcare, 23,* 8-11.

Walkup, J. T., & Ginsberg, G. S. (2002). Anxiety disorders in children and adolescents. *International Review of Psychiatry, 14,* 85-86.

Wolpe, J. (1958). *Psychotherapy by reciprocal inhibition.* Stanford, CA: Stanford University Press.

# Chapter 59

# Test Anxiety

*Vickie Brooks*

## Preview

The importance of test scores continues to be a focal point for grade promotion. Anxiety can develop when a student feels pressure to perform. Professional school counselors who understand the physiological and psychological responses to anxiety can facilitate student development of positive coping strategies. Included in this chapter are suggestions for parents, teachers, and students to reduce test anxiety and increase test performance.

Stress, fear and anxiety are terms which are often used interchangeably. The anticipation of a happy up-coming event (e.g., dance or award) is an example of *eustress* or good stress (Seaward, 2002). Acute *distress* is instantaneous (e.g., being scared by a clap of thunder) while chronic stress or anxiety occurs slowly over time and results in a continued state of heightened anxiety. An example of chronic stress or anxiety would be the expectation of performing near superior levels on tasks both at home and school.

Professional school counselors can often be helpful in determining if the cause for concern is due to anxiety or a phobia. *Phobia* (e.g., fear of heights) is defined as an irrational fear specific to an identified source and extends beyond the normal fears associated with child and adolescent development (Terry, 1998). Extreme measures are often used to avoid the source of fear (e.g., repeatedly ill on testing days; emotional outbursts when testing occurs). Certainly, students can develop test phobias and in such instances, professional school counselors need to suggest outside resources for consultation, evaluation and intervention.

In the current educational context, standardized tests continue to be a focal point for progress monitoring and grade promotion. When a student feels pressure to perform at exceptionally high levels, anxiety can develop. Basic human fears (Seaward, 2002) can be translated into test anxiety as follows:

1. Fear of the unknown: What is the test about?
2. Fear of failure: What if I don't pass?
3. Fear of rejection: Will my family love me if I fail?
4. Fear of isolation: What if I am the only one who fails?
5. Fear of loss of self-control: What if I am so scared during the test that I can't think?

A basic understanding of physiological responses to anxiety can assist professional school counselors in developing appropriate intervention strategies. Two categories of anxiety are evidenced in the literature: state (e.g., specific moment in time; result of an event) and trait (e.g., over time; personality characteristics)(Landers & Arent, 2001). Anxiety affects all domains of the individual: spiritual, emotional, social, intellectual and physical. Under stress/anxiety, the body responds physiologically by initiating the flight or fight syndrome (See Figure 1). When the stress is continued over time, the body's systems begin to weaken. Visible external symptoms (e.g. sleeplessness, irritability) can appear.

Sport performance research has identified the relationship between arousal and performance (see Figure 2) (Landers & Arent, 2001). Simply put, as arousal increases from a minimal state (waking up) to a fully conscious and alert state, performance increases. However, if arousal continues and creates a heightened anxious state, performance begins to decline.

**Figure 1. The body's response to stress.**

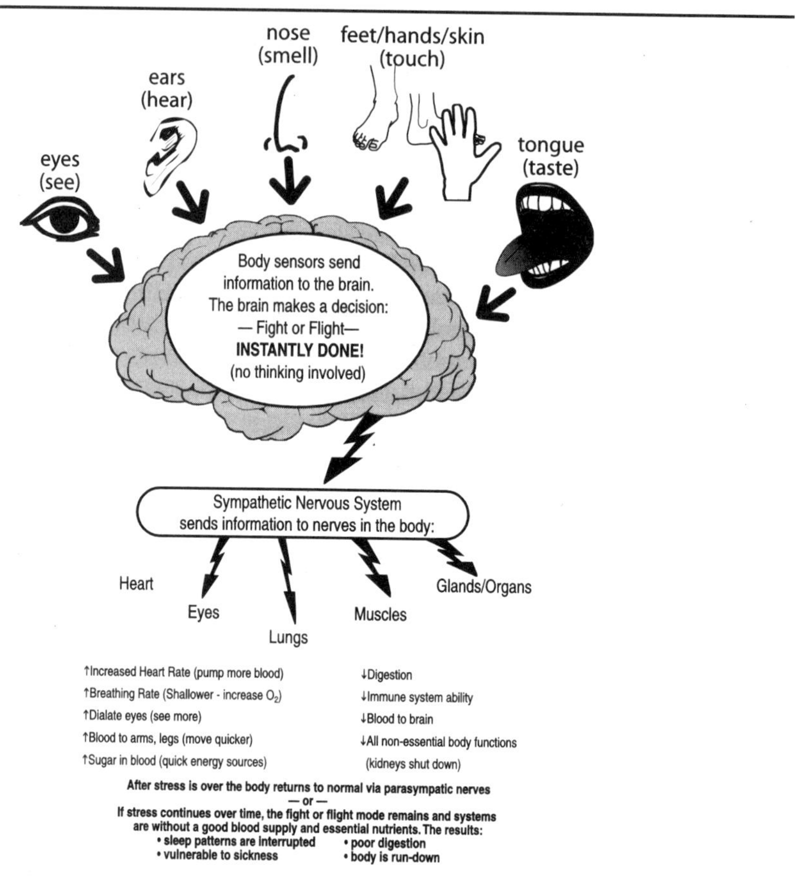


**Note.** Illustration by Michael T. McNamara. Stress management.
From *Leadership, Advocacy, and Direct Service Strategies for Professional School Counselors* 1st edition by PERUSSE/GOODNOUGH. © 2004. Reprinted with permission of Wadworth, a division of Thomson Learning: www.thomsonrights.com. FAX 800 730-2215.

The optimal state of performance is called eustress (Seaward, 2002). Further anxiety creates distress and a decline in performance occurs (Landers & Arent, 2001; Seaward, 2002).

Anxiety can create psychological roadblocks to learning (Slavin, 2000). Among the major student stressors are peer acceptance and classroom performance, including test results (Brooks, in press). Tables 1-4 provide numerous tips for various stakeholders to help reduce test anxiety.

**Figure 2.**

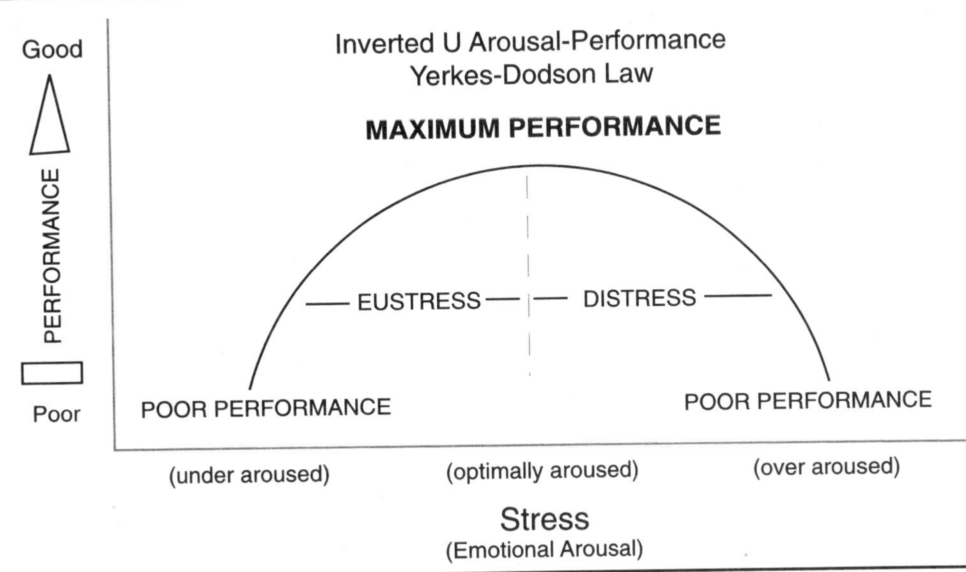


**Note.** Illustration by Michael T. McNamara. From Seaward, B. L. (2002). *Managing stress: Principles and strategies for health and well being.* Sudbury, MA: Jones & Bartlett. Reprinted with permission.

**Table 1. Suggestions for parents/guardians to help students reduce test anxiety (adapted from Squires & Jacobs, 2001).**

1. Keep reactions and personal feelings about the test to a minimum (whether positive or negative).
2. Focus on the range of scores rather than specific scores.
3. Reframe negative reactions (e.g., I'm a failure) to one of hope (e.g., *We* can work together to do better).
4. Check-ins can include discussion of feelings about the upcoming test.
5. Understand fears associated with testing. Allow time for discussion of "what-ifs."
6. Instill acceptance of the student BEFORE the test; regardless of the results, the student is NOT the test.
7. Keep YOUR fears to yourself.
8. Avoid negative words (e.g., scared) when talking about the test.
9. Understand the test, ask questions about it, and become familiar with it.
10. Ask the student to create a practice test or together create a mini-version of the test.
11. Carefully regulate the addition of extra homework. It can be interpreted as overkill.
12. Know when to ask for professional outside help (e.g., Is this student exhibiting trait anxiety? Is this a phobia?).
13. Teach positive coping strategies (see Chapter 80, "Helping Students Acquire Time Management Skills").
14. Help identify assets (e.g., learning style).

**Table 2. Suggestions for teachers to help students reduce test anxiety (adapted from Slavin, 2000).**

1. Create a classroom environment that is welcoming, encouraging and accepts repeated trials to attain success.
2. Engage students in planning how and what will be learned. This team approach can help reduce subject matter anxiety.
3. Make sure subject matter matches test content.
4. Give practice tests containing similar content and format as the standardized or final test.
5. In testing situations:
    a. Give clear and simple instructions.
    b. Break down directions and/or the test into segments.
    c. Avoid time constraints (or if timed tests are necessary, conduct dress rehearsals with time factors).
    d. Teach students to check their work.
    e. Begin each test with the least difficult and work up to most difficult.
    f. Provide an easy to follow format for selecting answers.

## Relaxation Techniques

Relaxation techniques vary greatly and are subject to one's preferred style of learning, cognitive and affective abilities. Students with acute visualization and imagery capabilities are essentially unlimited with regard to relaxation and visualization development.

Research conducted over the last four decades documented the positive effects of visualization, relaxation and imagery in overall psychological and physiological function and performance. The study of psychoneuroimmunology (mind, nerve and immune system) provides exciting data supporting the interconnectedness of the body (Seaward, 2002).

Professional school counselors may want to inform or, if necessary, obtain consent from parents before sharing with the student visualization, imagery and relaxation information or materials. Familial religious and personal preferences might preclude the professional school counselor from using relaxation, visualization or imagery as coping strategies for reducing test anxiety. Tables 5-7 present sample relaxation exercises.

## Decreasing Test Anxiety Via Systematic Desensitization

Systematic desensitization requires the individual to be in a relaxed state while introducing small doses of the anxiety producing event (e.g., test). During daily relaxation practice, additional test anxiety factors can be introduced (e.g., smells and noises in the room, the teacher's voice, pencil in hand, reading the directions, taking the test). A minimum of four weeks should be allowed for the practice of systematic desensitization. The gestalt of the entire test day can be replicated visually in the mind while consciously practicing the mastered relaxation exercise (Seaward, 2002).

A practice test could be given while the student is in a relaxed state and continues reinforcement of the learned skills (e.g., deep breathing, cloud breathing). A support person may need to assist the student on the first several attempts to verbally encourage relaxation and deep breathing. Verbal instructions may need to be given to the student (e.g., put the pencil down, close your eyes and complete 5-10 cycles of deep breathing before picking your pencil up and continuing with the test).

**Table 3. Tips for students.**

1. Study at a regular time and place. Identify a location for study.
2. Plan study sessions with a group of successful students.
3. Study as soon after the class as possible. Make study checklists for each class.
4. Use odd hours during the day to study (one hour intervals are excellent).
5. Limit blocks of time for studying to no more than 30-45 minutes on one course. Take a 3-5 minute break before moving to another subject.
6. Eat complex carbohydrates or protein on breaks, not high sugar foods (e.g., candy, cola).
7. Keep organized notes from class. Match and file assignments with each chapter.
8. Review your notes daily and weekly.
9. Do not re-write notes. Use a highlighter for identifying important points. Review highlighted material for tests.
10. Write key words/phrases in margins; use these for last minute review.
11. Study the most difficult or boring subjects first.
12. Identify when you learn the best (morning or evening).
13. Block this time for intensive study.
14. Sit in the front of the class.
15. If the teacher talks fast, learn to work with another student to share notes.
16. If the teacher is organized, take notes in outline form or use information from the board or overheads.
17. If the teacher is disorganized, take notes by leaving space between notes to fill in later.
18. If the class is mostly discussion, take bulleted notes and write key ideas or statements below the bullets.
19. If the class has a lab with it, make sure you have a lab notebook for recording all materials (e.g., drawings).
20. Try to incorporate all learning styles: auditory, visual and kinesthetic. Hear the lecture (auditory), write the notes (kinesthetic) and review the notes/materials by reading (visual) and sharing with a study group (auditory).
21. Study by self-testing with note cards; divide pages length-wise (e.g., left side for questions and right side for answers); use a cover sheet to cover answers when studying from the book or notes.
22. Learn relaxation and visualization skills (see Table 5).
23. Know how to develop short and long term goals (see Chapter 80).
24. Vocabulary is important on all standardized tests; read recreationally as well as academically.

**Note**. Adapted from Athletic Counseling Center materials, University of Wyoming.

**Table 4. Suggestions for increasing academic performance.**

1. Continually monitor academic progress in each class.
2. Meet with teachers (months ahead of time, if necessary) to identify material being taught and regularly covered.
3. Consult the school learning specialist for additional suggestions.
4. Hire a tutor to enhance skills.
5. Learn test-taking tips.
6. Know the test scoring criteria. If there are no penalties for guessing, always supply an answer. If there is a penalty for guessing, only guess when answers can be narrowed to two choices.
7. Read all answers before selecting a choice; sometimes when several choices are possibly correct, a best answer exists.
8. Use the entire allocated time (e.g., bring a watch to place on the desk to self-monitor time). Check work if finished early (e.g., mark on worksheet questions to review if time permits).
9. Answer the easiest and shortest questions first.
10. Answer questions in this order: multiple choice, true/false, fill-in-the-blank and short answer/essay last.
11. Look for answers in other test questions. Make notes in the margin or on scratch paper.
12. When taking an essay test:
    a. Quickly jot down information prior to writing your response.
    b. Read all questions and develop a plan/outline before beginning.
    c. Highlight words in the question that guide the answer (e.g., *compare* = similarities and differences; *describe* = details; *prove* = evidence).
    d. Begin writing by re-phrasing the question, stating the answer, providing details to support the answer and summarizing main points for the conclusion.
    e. Essay questions often require a synthesis of class discussions.
13. When taking multiple choice tests:
    a. Read the directions carefully.
    b. The first time through the test, answer only the questions with known answers; mark others to come back to.
    c. Watch for grammatically correct answers (e.g., matching the question).
14. Predict test questions from class and written notes.
15. Save all tests, lab handouts, and class materials. Keep materials organized by chapter/lecture/lab.
16. The night before the test, get enough sleep and eat well.
17. The day of the test, get up early, have a healthy breakfast, relax, and arrive at the test site early.
18. Take water to drink (if allowed). During breaks, eat a protein bar (not candy or high sugar foods).

**Note**. Adapted from Slavin (2000); Squires & Jacobs (2001).

**Table 5. Progressive muscle relaxation.**

Ideally, the individual should be lying on their back with the arms comfortably at the sides. After initial familiarity with the process, relaxation can be accomplished in a variety of positions, although not necessarily with the same results.

- Begin by contracting the toes (curling) and holding the contraction for a count of five, then relaxing the toes while taking one cycle of breathing (see breathing example below).
- Continue moving up the legs, torso, shoulders and head. Individual muscle group contractions should be held for five seconds followed by relaxing the muscle(s) and completing a breathing cycle before moving to the next set of muscles. Suggested order of progression: feet, calves, thighs, buttocks, stomach, chest, back (press to floor), hands, arms (press to floor), neck (press back of head to floor), and face (wrinkle/scrunch).
- Practice contracting and relaxing individual muscle groups in a progressive order. Focus on identifying muscle groups potentially holding the tension or anxiety. This can be used for future identification of anxiety and early application of interventions.
- Upon initial mastery of individual muscle group relaxation, combining muscle groups (e.g., feet, legs and buttocks) can reduce time allocation.

**Note**. Adapted from Seaward (2002).

**Table 6. Breathing.**

*General breathing:*

- Assume a comfortable position (preferably lying down)
- Close the eyes
- Inhale through the nose to the count of five
- Hold the air for a count of three
- Exhale slowly through the mouth to a count of five
- Before inhaling pause (1-2 count), then repeat

*Breathing with visualization:*

- Assume a comfortable position
- If the position is sitting up, rest the hands on the thighs
- Close the eyes
- Visualize a cloud and inhale the cloud through the nose for a count of five
- Hold the cloud in the lungs giving it a "hug" with the lungs
- Slowly exhale the cloud out through the mouth to a count of five
- Make sure all of the cloud is out of the lungs
- Pause before repeating

**Note**. Adapted from Seaward (2002).

**Table 7. Sailing Your Ship (also called *Your Special Room*).**

This activity combines all five senses (olfactory, auditory, visual, affective and kinesthetic). Beginning level muscle relaxation and breathing exercises will need to be mastered prior to this exercise. Initially an outside person may need to talk the student through the exercise. The voice should remain soft, slow and calm. Elapsed time in early attempts will be 10-20 minutes. Upon visual mastery, the entire mental exercise can be completed with positive results in 3-5 minutes. Another option is to move directly to the *special* room without the pre-*special*-room activities.

Assume a comfortable position (preferably lying on the back) with the eyes closed. Take several slow and deep breaths (using the counting or cloud method). When ready, begin with the following thoughts or commands (allowing several seconds between each to inhale through the nose and exhale through the mouth):

- Picture a large, white, sandy ocean beach, feel the wind blowing gently through your hair.
- Smell the fragrance of the sea. Feel the warmth of the sand beneath your feet as you walk toward the dock.
- The sun's rays warm your skin. The smell of the sea is familiar and comforting.
- At the dock, observe the *special* boat, noting its colors, the magnificent woodwork and all the details that make it such a *special* boat.
- Slowly walk along the dock, feeling the sun, smelling the sea.
- Arriving at the boat, step onto the deck.
- Gently untie the boat and begin to slowly sail out to sea and feel the gentle rocking of the waves.
- The warmth of the sun feels relaxing and the sea smells fresh.
- Walk down the steps in the middle of the boat to the cabin. Upon reaching the bottom of the stairs, the *special* door to the *special* room is visible.
- Reach into your pocket and pull the key out to open the door to the *special* room.
- Unlock the door and enter the room; look around and feel comfortable and relaxed with all the beauty in the *special* room.
- Lie down and enjoy this *special* place while feeling the gentle rocking of the boat and the fresh smell of the sea.

Continue by allowing time to lapse while in the *special* room. Then, reverse the order: sit up, walk to the door, open/shut the door, lock the door, walk up the stairs, stand on the deck, sail back to shore, tie up the boat, walk along the dock to the sand and walk along the beach. All the while, continue to reinforce the warmth of the sun and sand and fresh smell of the ocean.

When learning relaxation skills, consideration should be given to several key components: a safe and peaceful space is essential, the mind must be quiet, and a comfortable position should be obtained before beginning the relaxation exercise.

**Note**. Adapted from Seaward (2002).

**Table 8. Ideas for applying systematic desensitization (Seaward, 2002).**

- Include the student when developing the practice test and brainstorming the scenarios.
- Allow the student to take a shortened test to explore the possibilities for incorporating relaxation and imagery during the test.
- Allow the student to verbalize "what ifs" and encourage dialogue of successful coping strategies (e.g., breathing).
- Mantras can also be successfully employed prior to or during the test (e.g., calm; I know I'm good).

## Summary/Conclusion

The pressure for students to achieve academically can lead to increased anxiety and fear. By first understanding the physiology of the fight or flight response (See Figures 1 and 2) and then applying successful strategies and interventions (See Tables 1-8), all stakeholders can begin to feel a sense of control over the requirements and standards for academic success in today's schools. Various websites (see Table 9) can also provide timely and updated information on testing tips, managing stress and learning strategies.

**Table 9. Additional resources.**

*Testing Information Websites*

www.ed.gov/databases/ERIC_Digests/ed429987.html - Lists common mistakes made during tests and offers tips.

http://familyeducation.com/article/0,1120,2-21889,00.html - Offers test tips, interactive tutorials and information on specific state standards.

http://nces.ed.gov/nationsreportcard - Compares test results by state and includes exam questions.

www.edtrust.org - Gives individual state results.

www.fairtest.org - Advocacy group working to reduce flaws in standardized tests and equity for all students.

www.educate.com - Sylvan Learning Centers can help pinpoint weak academic areas. Has fees/costs attached.

www.escore.com - Can help identify weak academic areas. Has fees/costs attached.

*Stress Management and Emotional Wellness Links*

www.imt.net/~randolfi/StressLinks.html - Excellent resource links (e.g., relaxation techniques, humor, time management, social support, kids/stress).

www.stresstoughness.com

www.aboutlearning.com - Website for books, classroom ideas, self assessments, lesson plans, 4MAT Learning/Teaching. (800-822-4628).

## References

Brooks, V. (2003). Personal and social development: Standard C: Stress management. In R. Perusse & G. E. Goodnough (Eds.), *Leadership and advocacy in school counseling.* Belmont CA: Brooks/Cole.

Landers, D. M., & Arent, S. M. (2001). Arousal-performance relationships. In J. M. Williams (Ed.), *Applied sport psychology: Personal growth to peak performance* (pp. 206-228). Mountain View, CA: Mayfield.

Seaward, B. L. (2002). *Managing stress: Principles and strategies for health and well being.* Sudbury, MA: Jones & Bartlett.

Slavin, R. E. (2000). *Educational psychology: Theory and practice.* Needham Heights, MA: Allyn & Bacon.

Squires, S., & Jacobs, K. (2001, November). Guiding your student through testing mania. *Family Life*, 60-65.

Terry, P. M. (1998). Do schools make students fearful and phobic? *Journal for a Just and Caring Education, 4*, 193-212.

# Chapter 60

# Helping Students with Posttraumatic Stress Disorder

*Kelly M. Murray*

## Preview

Students are increasingly exposed to traumatic events and diagnosed with Posttraumatic Stress Disorder (PTSD). PTSD is characterized as a reexperiencing of the trauma, avoiding the trauma, and persistent physiological arousal. Familiarity of symptoms, how to conduct an assessment, and common treatment modalities are of paramount importance to the professional school counselor.

Current research suggests that students are increasingly exposed to traumatic events and consequently diagnosed with Posttraumatic Stress Disorder (PTSD). There is substantial research suggesting that students may suffer significant psychological, social, and biological distress in relation to exposure to a traumatic event (Perrin, Smith, & Yule, 2000; Stallard, Velleman, & Baldwin, 1999). A number of studies have investigated the sequelae of symptoms evident when students are exposed to major traumas, such as violence in the home or community, exposure to war, natural disasters, man-made disasters, serious medical illness, accidents, and sexual abuse. These studies also indicated that symptoms of PTSD, although similar in many respects to those observed in adults, are sometimes manifested differently by students. Therefore, assessment and treatment modalities must be shifted accordingly. Professional school counselors may see students present with exposure to any number of traumatic events. Familiarity with the types of symptoms likely to be seen, how to conduct an assessment and the most common types of treatment modalities is important in helping students work through trauma.

## History

PTSD was formally recognized as a disorder for the time in 1980. Prior to that it was brought to public awareness during World War I when named *combat neurosis*. In World War II the symptoms of PTSD were defined as *traumatic neurosis* and manifested by consciously reliving and resolving traumatic memories associated with war experiences (Kardiner, 1941; Kardiner & Spiegel, 1947). The first large scale study of PTSD occurred as a result of the Vietnam War (Egendorf, Kadushin, Laufer, Rothbart, & Sloan, 1981; Yager, 1976). It was also at this time that studies were conducted to document the prevalence of PTSD in the general population as a result of other traumatic stresses such as rape, domestic violence, and childhood sexual abuse (Frank, Turner, & Steuwart, 1980; Kilpatrick, Veronen, & Best, 1985; Russell, 1983). *The Diagnostic and Statistical Manual of Mental Disorders* – Third Edition (*DSM-III*) (American Psychiatric Association, 1980) first recognized the constellation of posttraumatic symptoms as a disorder in 1980. However, there was initial skepticism about the diagnosis of PTSD being used for children (American Academy of Child and Adolescent Psychiatry, 1998). Since that time there has been considerable research on how trauma impacts children, how symptoms of

PTSD are manifested in children, and how assessment and treatment may differ for children compared to adults.

## Clinical Presentation

According to the *DSM-IV-TR* (American Psychiatric Association, 2000), in order for a person (child, adolescent, or adult) to meet the criteria for PTSD, symptoms must follow exposure to an extreme traumatic stressor. The person must have experienced, witnessed, or been confronted with an event that involved actual or threatened death or serious injury, or a threat to the physical integrity of self or others. The person's response must have involved fear, helplessness or horror and this may have been expressed by disorganized or agitated behavior. Table 1 includes diagnostic criteria for PTSD from the DSM-IV-TR (APA, 2000). The way that a student re-experiences the trauma and manifests distress is likely to change with age and maturity, becoming more adult-like and closer to the *DSM-IV-TR* description of the disorder.

Students will often exhibit irritability, anger and aggression, or may be quite verbal about the trauma and their ensuing feelings, while others do not wish to discuss the incident or how they are feeling. Very young children who have experienced trauma may present with few symptoms listed in the *DSM-IV-TR*. This may be in part because they do not have the necessary verbal or cognitive skills to communicate their symptoms. Therefore, infants, toddlers, and preschoolers may present with anxiety symptoms such as fears of monsters, animals, separation anxiety, and fear of strangers. These children may avoid situations or circumstances that may or may not have a link with the trauma, have sleep disturbances, and have preoccupations with symbols or words that may or may not have a certain link with the traumatic event (Drell, Siegel & Gaensbauer, 1993; Scheeringa, Zeanah, Drell, & Larriey, 1995). The student (like an adult) must express his/her symptoms for longer than one month to meet the criteria for PTSD. The disturbance must also cause clinically significant distress or impairment in social or academic functioning.

## Epidemiology

The student's subjective appraisal of the situation appears to be an important factor in explaining why some are significantly affected by a traumatic event while others are not (Joseph, Williams, & Yule, 1997). A review of 25 studies indicated that three factors have consistently been found in the development of PTSD in students: 1) the severity of the trauma exposure; 2) trauma-related parental distress; and 3) temporal proximity to the traumatic event (Foy, Maduiq, Pynoos, & Camilleri, 1996). Prevalence rates varied from 3% - 100% depending on the assessor, assessment measures used, type and degree of exposure to the traumatic event, and gender.

Parental reaction to the traumatic event is another factor that has been found to influence the student's PTSD symptomology. Numerous studies have reported the impact of familial support and parental emotional reaction to the trauma on the student's PTSD symptoms. These studies indicated that familial support across a broad range of different traumas mitigated the development of PTSD in students. Parental distress about the trauma and/or the presence of parental psychiatric disorders also predicted higher levels of PTSD in the student. A study of Holocaust survivors and their offspring found that the offspring were more likely to respond to trauma with PTSD if their parents had PTSD (Yehuda, Schmeidler, Giller, Siever, Binder-Brynes, 1998). Lyons (1987) postulated that the best predictor of outcome for students was the ability of parents and other significant adults to cope with the trauma. Another predictor for positive outcome was intelligence (IQ); higher IQ appears to protect people from developing PTSD and is a strong predictor of resiliency (Silva et al., 2000).

**Table 1. Diagnostic criteria for PTSD (APA, 2000).**

The traumatic event is persistently reexperienced in one or more of the following ways:

1. recurrent and intrusive distressing recollections of the event (in young children repetitive play may occur)
2. recurrent distressing dreams of the event (in children there may be frightening dreams without recognizable content)
3. acting or feeling as if the traumatic event were recurring (in young children, trauma specific reenactment may occur; there is often vivid reenactment of the trauma in drawings, stories and play)
4. intense psychological distress at exposure to internal or external cues that remind the person of the traumatic event
5. physiological reactivity on exposure to internal or external cues that remind the person of the event

The person persistently avoids stimuli associated with the trauma and there is often a numbing of general responsiveness, as indicated by three (or more) of the following:

1. efforts to avoid thoughts, feelings, or conversations associated with the trauma
2. efforts to avoid activities, places, or people that remind them of the trauma
3. inability to remember some aspects of the trauma
4. diminished interest or participation in significant activities
5. feelings of detachment or estrangement from others
6. restricted range of emotions
7. sense of foreshortened future

A person who has PTSD will also have symptoms of increased arousal as indicated by two (or more) of the following:

1. difficulty staying or falling asleep (fears of the dark, bad dreams, nightmares and wakening are common in young children)
2. irritability or outbursts of anger
3. difficulty concentrating (especially relating to school work for children and adolescents)
4. hypervigilence (children may become alert to danger in their environment and become anxious about other related traumatic events)
5. exaggerated startle response

The literature has differed on gender differences in the development of PTSD. Some researchers have found no gender differences in the development of PTSD. Others have indicated that girls develop more severe and long-lasting PTSD symptoms when exposed to traumatic events, but boys are more likely to be exposed to such events (Helzer, Robins, & McEvoy, 1987). Some studies have found age of the student at the time of exposure to significantly mediate the development of PTSD symptoms. These findings have not been consistent and are more likely a reflection of developmental differences in clinical manifestations of PTSD rather than age mediated differences in prevalence (AACAP, 1998). Many studies have evaluated students of diverse ethnic backgrounds and have documented that PTSD occurs across numerous cultural and ethnic groups.

Traumatized students often exhibit symptoms of co-occurring disorders in addition to PTSD. It is not always easy to diagnose PTSD as both the students and parents may minimize symptoms. For young children who do not have the cognitive or verbal skills to accurately self-report their symptoms it is often difficult to get a clear diagnostic picture. Relying on parental report can also be problematic as parents may be dealing with their own trauma as well as trying to support their child. Parents may also not be aware of the existence or severity of their child's symptoms.

Students who present with PTSD may also exhibit symptoms of depression. Brent et al. (1995) reported a large overlap in symptom criteria between PTSD and Major Depressive Disorder (MDD). MDD sometimes precedes and predisposes students to the onset of PTSD. The comorbidity of students with PTSD and other anxiety disorders is also not uncommon. Given the many manifestations of traumatization, it is not surprising that rates of comorbidity with PTSD are high. Many students develop fears associated with specific aspects of the trauma, which can eventually become phobic in nature. Others find themselves extremely anxious much of the time and have difficulty controlling their worries. Panic disorder is not uncommon as children react to their own internal state of anxiety with physical symptoms. Some children experience "survivor guilt" and ruminate over cognitions that they should have done more to help others. Increased alcohol use by adolescents exposed to a traumatic event has been documented as has comorbidity to a host of other psychiatric disorders.

## Assessment

PTSD is often a difficult disorder to diagnose. While the professional school counselor may not be directly involved in the diagnosis of PTSD, the following assessment procedures are helpful in understanding the diagnostic process. According to the *DSM-IV-TR* (APA, 2000), symptoms usually begin within 3 months after the trauma, although there may be a delay of months, or even years, before symptoms appear. The symptoms of the disorder and the relative predominance or re-experiencing, avoidance, and hyperarousal symptoms may vary with time. Duration of the symptoms varies, with complete recovery occurring within 3 months in approximately 50% of cases, with many others having persisting symptoms for longer than 12 months after the trauma. In some cases, the course is characterized by a waxing and waning of symptoms. Symptom reactivation may occur in response to reminders of the original trauma, life stressors, or new traumatic events.

A thorough and proper assessment requires a face-to-face interview with the student in which she is directly asked questions about the traumatic symptoms experienced. It is important to also interview the parents so as to gather as much information as possible. The use of empathy, establishment of rapport, and a safe environment where the student can discuss painful and angry feelings are very important to acquiring accurate information. Particular attention should be given to using developmentally appropriate language when assessing the student.

Both the parents and the student should be asked directly about the traumatic event and about PTSD symptoms in detail. Specific questions related to re-experiencing, avoidant, and hyperarousal symptoms as described in *DSM-IV-TR* should be asked. Other symptoms that often present comorbidly with PTSD should be assessed, such as symptoms of depression, anxiety, substance abuse, and acting out behaviors. Obtain reports of any preceding, concurrent, or more recent stressors in the student's life as well. Some examples of stressors may be child abuse, significant conflict within the family, frequent moves, death in the family, and exposure to community violence (AACAP, 1998).

The professional school counselor should be aware of developmental variations in the presentation of PTSD symptoms, especially with young children. For an accurate assessment ask about developmentally specific symptoms when interviewing young children. AACAP (1989) reports there are a few published semi-structured assessments available such as the *Structured Clinical Interview for DSM-III-R*, and the *Diagnostic Interview Schedule Clinician-Administered PTSD Scale for Children and Adolescents*. AACAP also reported that the following child/parent rating forms may be clinically useful for following the course of PTSD symptoms in children: (1) *PTSD Reaction Index;* (2) *Trauma Symptom Checklist for Children;* (3) *Checklist of Child Distress Symptoms-Child and Parent Report Versions;* (4) *Children's Impact of Traumatic Events Schedule;* (5) *Child PTSD Symptom Scale;* and (6) *Impact of Events Scale*. However, there is no single instrument that is considered optimal. Using a single instrument limits the type of information needed to make a PTSD diagnosis, as a student must have a certain number of symptoms from each of three different categories to meet *DSM-IV-TR* criteria. It is difficult for any single instrument to assess for all of these criteria. Therefore, there is no good substitute for a good, thorough and direct interview with both the student and parents. It is also sometimes useful to speak with the student's teacher(s) to get a history of symptomology manifested at school with a particular emphasis on changes in school behavior, interaction with peers, concentration, activity level, and academic performance since the traumatic stressor.

In addition, it is a good idea to initially meet with the parents separately from the student. When interviewing parents, the goal is to gather as much information as possible so that an understanding of the parents' perspective on the trauma and relationship with the child can be determined. It is also important to assess information on: (1) family psychiatric and medical history; (2) marital conflict, separation, divorce, abuse; (3) developmental history, including the student's temperament and mood; (4) academic history and performance in school prior to and after the trauma; (5) student's current functioning; (6) impact of the trauma on the family and parent(s); (7) presence of parental PTSD symptoms; and (8) the perception of how much support is available to the child from the family (Perrin, Smith, & Yule, 2000).

When interviewing the student, have the student recall as much of the trauma as possible. After the student has told her story, go back and clarify or prompt with additional questions. Tracking the time line of the trauma and subsequent symptoms is useful in making a diagnosis of PTSD. If unsure about the sequence of events or a particular symptom, ask about it directly. As much as possible try to obtain the student's report of trauma-related attributions and perceptions. Query beliefs about the event, how the student feels subsequent to being exposed to the stressor, level of responsibility, and perception of family support (AACAP, 1998). The student's feelings, thoughts, and behaviors related to the event should be queried, as well as their thoughts and feelings about the future. With very young children who find it difficult to developmentally discuss the trauma and their thoughts, feelings, and behaviors related to it, it is often useful to use other methods of gathering information. According to Perrin et al. (2000), giving the student pencil and paper and encouraging him to draw something about which he can tell a story is useful in gathering information and helps the student feel comfortable enough to disclose. Encourage the student to elaborate on his story and then try to link the story with some part of the traumatic event in order to facilitate emotional release. After the student has become more comfortable, ask him to draw the traumatic event. Discuss the picture with the student and ask him to describe the sensory components, feelings, thoughts, and coping strategies used during and since the trauma. It is also important to help normalize the student's reactions to the traumatic event as well as positively reinforce the student for having courage to draw about and discuss the traumatic event.

While the professional school counselor is assessing the student for PTSD symptoms and the associated sequelae symptoms, she should also be asking the student about, and noting, other symptoms often associated with PTSD such as depressive symptoms, suicidal ideations, anxiety symptoms, substance abuse, and conduct disorder behavior.

## Treatment

To date there is limited empirical outcome research on the treatment of students with

PTSD. Direct exploration of the event is likely to be more efficacious the older and more mature the student is. For younger children, more indirect methods of addressing traumatic issues, such as art and play therapy (use of drawings, puppets, dolls, etc.) may be indicated. The use of multiple informant assessment, especially with young children, is likely to elicit more information about the traumatic event and the manifestation of symptoms. For this reason, information collected from young children should be supplemented by parent reports.

A treatment plan should be based on the clinical presentation of the child and should address PTSD symptoms as well as other emotional/behavioral symptoms the student may be experiencing. Each student's course of PTSD and associated symptoms will be variable and may be extremely idiosyncratic in the nature, intensity and length of symptoms. Therefore, different treatment modalities may be needed depending on the student and the nature of the presenting symptoms and problems. Some will require short-term, long-term or intermittent treatment. Others may require different levels of care, e.g., outpatient care, partial hospitalization, or inpatient hospitalization. The professional school counselor may also need to decide which treatment modality will be the most efficacious for the student – individual, family, or group therapy (AACAP, 1998).

There are quite a few authors who advocate for psychoeducation for parents, teachers, and family members in order to help normalize PTSD symptoms and enlist their help in treating the student who has PTSD (Gallant & Foa, 1986; Molta, 1995). Education about the traumatic experience and subsequent symptoms may also be helpful to the student who has been exposed to a stressor. The student often has perceptions, feelings, and symptoms about the stressor that can be normalized in order to help increase self-efficacy and, thereby, decrease anxiety.

Individual therapy is another modality that can be extremely helpful to students who have been exposed to a stressor. There are many different theoretical orientations that are used by professional school counselors in order to help students with PTSD. Psychoanalytic/psychodynamic approaches are sometimes used and often help expose defense mechanisms that are being utilized and also help to redefine current significant relationships in the student's life. Play and art therapy are also often used to accommodate students who are developmentally incapable of benefiting from a direct verbal exchange with a professional school counselor. These indirect methods of addressing traumatic issues may be helpful to students so as not to retraumatize them as they think about and talk about the traumatic event.

There is also significant empirical support for cognitive-behavioral therapy (CBT) in the present literature for the treatment for PTSD. The goals of CBT treatment are the reduction of PTSD symptoms, the development of positive coping skills, and an increase in the individual's sense of well-being. It is helpful to provide both the parents and student with education and information on PTSD and its effects on all levels of functioning. Normalizing the student's, parents', and family's feelings and responses also may help to lessen anxiety and alleviate the severity of symptoms. This form of psychotherapy also focuses on the teaching of progressive muscle relaxation, thought-stopping, positive imagery, and deep breathing prior to having the student discuss the traumatic event. Mastering these skills gives the student a sense of control over thoughts and feelings rather than being overwhelmed by them, and will help the student approach the discussion of the traumatic event with confidence, thereby reducing uncontrollable re-experiencing of fears and symptoms. At the center of CBT is also the use of imaginal or *in vivo* exposure to help the emotional processing of traumatic memories. This process is done in such a way as to help the child process his or her emotional reactions to the event in a safe and trusting way to master and lessen feelings about the traumatic event.

Pynoos and Nader (1988) described a "psychological first aid" approach for students exposed to community violence which may be offered in schools as well as traditional treatment settings. This model emphasized clarifying the facts about the traumatic event, normalizing student's PTSD reactions, encouraging expression of feelings, teaching problem-solving techniques, and referring the most symptomatic children for ongoing treatment.

Family therapy is a way to integrate the whole family into the student's treatment. Parental support and reaction to the child/adolescent are likely to affect the child/adolescent's symptomology. Most experts assert that inclusion of the parents and/or supportive others in treatment is important for resolution of PTSD symptoms for children and adolescents. Including parents in treatment helps them monitor their child's progress and symptomology and also helps the parents resolve their emotional distress related to the trauma (AACAP, 1998; Cohen, Berliner, & March, 2000).

Trauma-focused groups for children/adolescents, as well as parents, can lead to beneficial and encouraging open discussions of perceptions, attributions, and feelings about the traumatic event. Group therapy is often used after major traumas and disasters as a way to help debrief and normalize the event for the child/adolescent. School-based group crisis intervention may be particularly useful after trauma and disaster situations.

## Summary/Conclusion

As students are increasingly exposed to traumatic stressors and events it is likely that the professional school counselor will be called upon to assess and intervene with a student with PTSD or PTSD-like symptoms. Familiarity and knowledge of *DSM-IV-TR* criteria for PTSD is essential for the professional school counselor to understand the complexity of this disorder. With a comprehensive assessment and proper treatment most students will typically improve within three to six months, while others may need longer term treatment.

## References


American Academy of Child and Adolescent Psychiatry (AACAP). (1989). Practice parameters for the assessment and treatment of children and adolescents with Posttraumatic Stress Disorder. *Journal of American Child and Adolescent Psychiatry, 737:10 Supplement,* 4S-26S.

American Psychiatric Association. (1980). *Diagnostic and statistical manual of mental disorders, 3rd edition (DSM-III).* Washington, DC: Author.

American Psychiatric Association. (2000). *Diagnostic and statistical manual of mental disorders, 4th edition- text review (DSM-IV-TR).* Washington, DC: Author.

Brent, D. A., Perper, J. A., Moritz, G., Liotus, L., Richardson, D., Cannobio, R., Schweers, J, & Roth, C. (1995). Posttraumatic Stress Disorder in peers of adolescent suicide victims. *Journal of American Academy of Child and Adolescent Psychiatry, 34,* 209-215.

Cohen, J. A., Berliner, L., & March, J. S. (2000). Treatment of adolescents and children. In E. B. Foa, T. M. Keane, & M. J. Friedman (Eds.), *Effective treatments for PTSD* (pp. 106-138). New York: Guilford Press.

Drell, M. J., Siegel, C. H., & Gaensbauer, T. J. (1993). Posttraumatic Stress Disorder. In C. H. Zeanah (Ed.), *Handbook of infant mental health.* New York: Guilford Press.

Egendorf A., Kadushin, C., Laufer, R. S., Rothbart, G., & Sloan, L. (1981). *Legacies of Vietnam: Comparative adjustment of veterans and their peers, Vols I-IV.* Washington, DC: US Government Accounting Office.

Foy, D. W., Madvig, B. T., Pynoos, R. S., & Camilleri, A. J. (1996). Etiologic factors in the development of Posttraumatic Stress Disorder in children and adolescents. *Journal of School Psychology, 34,* 133-145.

Galante, R., & Foa, D. (1986). An empirical study of psychic trauma and treatment effectiveness for children after a natural disaster. *Journal of American Academy of Child and Adolescent Psychiatry, 25,* 357-363.

Frank, E., Turner, S. M., & Steuwart, B. D. (1980). Initial response to rape: The impact of stressors within the rape situation. *Journal of Behavioral Assessment, 2,* 39-53.

Helzer, J. E., Robins, L. N., & McEvoy, L. (1987). Posttraumatic Stress Disorder in the general population. *New England Journal of Medicine, 317,* 1630-1634.

Joseph, S., Williams, R., & Yule, W. (1997). *Understanding posttraumatic stress: A psychological perspective on PTSD and treatment.* Chichester, U.K.: John Wiley.

Kardiner, A. (1941). *The traumatic neuroses of war.* New York: Hoeber.

Kardiner, A., & Spiegel, H. (1947). *War, stress and neurotic illness.* New York: Hoeber.

Kilpatrick, D. G., Veronen, L. J., & Best, C. L. (1985). Factors predicting psychological distress among rape victims. In C. R. Figley (Ed.), *Trauma and its wake, Vol I: The study and treatment of Posttraumatic Stress Disorder* (pp. 113-141). New York: Brunner/Mazel.

Lyons, J. A. (1987). Posttraumatic Stress Disorder in children and adolescents: A review of literature. *Journal of Developmental and Behavioral Pediatrics, 8,* 349-356.

Molta, R. W. (1995). Childhood Posttraumatic Stress Disorder and the schools. *Canadian Journal of School Psychology, 11,* 65-78.

Perrin, S., Smith, P., & Yule, W. (2000). Review: The assessment and treatment of Post-Traumatic Stress Disorder in children and adolescents. *Journal of Child Psychology and Psychiatry, 41,* 277-289.

Pynoos, R. S., & Nader, K. (1988). Psychological first aid and treatment approaches for children and adolescents. In J. Wilson & B. Raphael (Eds.), *International handbook of traumatic stress syndromes* (pp. 535-549). New York:Plenum Press.

Russell, D. (1983). The incidence and prevalence of intrafamilial and extrafamilial sexual abuse of female children. *Child Abuse and Neglect, 7,* 133-146.

Scheeringa, M. S., Zeanah, C. H., Drell, M. J., & Larrieu, J. A. (1995). Two approaches to diagnosing Post-Traumatic Stress Disorder in infancy and early childhood. *Journal of the American Academy of Child and Adolescent Psychiatry, 34,* 191-200.

Silva, R., Alpert, M., Munoz, D., Singh, S., Matzner, F., & Dummit, S. (2000). Stress and vulnerability to Posttraumatic Stress Disorder in children and adolescents. *American Journal of Psychiatry, 157,* 1229-1235.

Stallard, P., Velleman, R., & Baldwin, S. (1999). Psychological screening of children for Posttraumatic Stress Disorder. *Journal of Child Psychology and Psychiatry, 40,* 1075-1082.

Yager, J. (1976). Postcombat violent behavior in psychiatrically maladjusted soldiers. *Archives of General Psychiatry, 33,* 1332-1335.

Yehuda, R., Schmeidler, J., Giller, E. L., Jr., Siever, L. J., & Binder-Brynes, K. (1998). Relationship between Posttraumatic Stress Disorder characteristics of Holocaust survivors. *American Journal of Psychiatry, 155,* 841-843.

# Chapter 61

## Habits and Tics: A Behavioral Approach to Assessment and Treatment

*T. Steuart Watson & Brad A. Dufrene*

### Preview

The purpose of this chapter is to provide a guide for identifying, assessing, and treating habits and tics. Information related to the etiology and epidemiology of habits and tics will also be provided.

### Tics

Tics are sudden, brief, repetitive, rapid stereotyped motor movements or vocalizations that are non-rhythmic and generally believed to be involuntary. Tics can be exacerbated by fatigue, stress, and medical conditions and may also be triggered by specific environmental events. Motor tics involve the singular or recurrent contraction of one or more of the body's muscle groups (e.g., eye blinking, head jerking, shoulder shrugging). Vocal tics involve singular or recurrent vocal sounds, words, and/or phrases (e.g., throat clearing).

Tics may be categorized as being either simple or complex. Simple tics are those that are limited to individual muscle groups (e.g., eye blinking, facial grimacing) or utterances (e.g., sniffing, snorting). Complex motor tics are those that involve recurrent coordinated patterns of motor movement such as retracing one's steps or twirling when walking. Complex vocal tics are those that involve recurrent repetition of words, phrases, or complete sentences. Tics often emerge as simple and over time may develop into more complex patterns.

The average age of onset for tic disorders is approximately 7 years of age. However, the onset of tic disorders has been observed in individuals as young as one year of age and as old as 18 years of age (Burd & Kerbershian, 1987). Most often, motor tics appear before vocal tics. Typically, tics take a cephalo-caudal trajectory (head-downward) in that they begin in the face and gradually move downward to affect the neck, shoulders, and trunk.

*Diagnosis of Tic Disorder*

An accurate diagnosis of tic disorders depends upon the length of time that tics have been present as well as the concurrent or independent presence of motor and/or vocal tics. Three classifications of tic disorders that occur across a continuum of severity are listed in the *Diagnostic and Statistical Manual of Mental Disorders, 4th Edition - Text Revision* (*DSM-IV-TR*; American Psychiatric Association, 2000). *Transient tics* are singular or recurrent episodes of motor or vocal tics that are present for at least four weeks but not longer than 12 months. *Chronic tics* are motor or vocal tics that are present for more than one year. *Tourette's Disorder* (TS) is characterized by the presence of multiple motor and one or more vocal tics that have been present for more than one year. However, a diagnosis of TS does not require that motor and vocal tics occur concurrently.

*Etiology and Epidemiology of Tic Disorders*

Although tic disorders have been studied since the early 20th century, their exact etiology is unknown. Currently, the areas that are receiving the greatest attention are genetic and neurobiological influences, although some researchers have approached the etiology of tic spectrum disorders from a learning perspective.

*Genetics and neurobiology*

Results of family and twin studies indicate that genetic factors may play an important role in the transmission and expression of tic disorders. Family genetic studies have found that the recurrence of tic disorders in affected families is higher than the expected rate (Pauls, Raymond, Leckman, & Stevenson, 1991). In studies of monozygotic twins, the concordance rate for TS and tic spectrum disorders has been found to range from 50% to 90% (Hyde, Aaronson, Randolph, Rickler, & Weinberger, 1992; Price, 1985; Price, Kidd, Cohen, Pauls, & Leckman, 1985; Walkup et al., 1988). Studies using dizygotic twins have found concordance rates for TS and tic disorders that range from 8% to 23% (Price, 1985). Although these studies suggest that genetics may be responsible for tic spectrum disorders, to date no genetic markers have been identified.

While evidence of genetic contributions to tic spectrum disorders is mounting, a body of research exists that implicates neurobiological factors. Neurochemical systems that have been implicated in tic disorders are the dopaminergic, serotonergic, noradrenergic, opiod, cholinergic, GABAergic, cAMP, arginine, vasopressin, and oxytocin systems (Haber, Kowall, Vonsattel, Bird, & Richardson, 1986; Leckman et al., 1988; Peterson, Leckman, & Cohen, 1995; Sallee, Stiller, & Perel, 1992). Neurochemical explanations of tic disorders are based on EEGs and other brain-imaging techniques as well as the effect of specific drugs for treating tics.

Although tic spectrum disorders may be more common in students than previously thought, prevalence data suggested that TS remains a relatively rare disorder. TS affects between 3.1 and 105 out of 100,000 school age children (Apter et al., 1993; Caine et al., 1988). Boys are five times more likely to be diagnosed with TS (Burd, Kerbeshian, Wikenheiser, & Fisher, 1986) while Caucasians are more likely than African Americans and Hispanics to develop TS. Prevalence rates for Transient Tic Disorder in children have been reported between 12% and 16% (LaPouse & Monk, 1964; Torup, 1972). According to Peterson, Campose & Azrin (1994), the prevalence rate for Chronic Tic Disorder was unknown; however it was believed to be somewhere between the rates for transient tic disorder and TS.

*Environmental variables*

Some researchers have approached the etiology of tic spectrum disorders from a learning perspective (Watson, Dufrene, Weaver, Butler, & Meeks, in press; Watson & Sterling, 1998). These researchers have argued that tic behaviors are normal movements or vocalizations that, due to a variety of consequences, increase in frequency over time and assume varied and unusual forms as a result of shaping and response generalization (Houlihan, Hofschulte, & Patten, 1993; Pray, Kramer, & Lindskog, 1986).

In addition to explaining the origin of tics, a body of literature is emerging in which specific environmental stimuli that alter the rate of tic behaviors (Malatesta, 1990; Watson, Dufrene, Weaver, Butler, & Meeks, in press; Watson & Sterling, 1998; Woods, Watson, Wolfe, Twohig, & Friman, 2001) are being identified. Identifying such variables may allow practitioners to quickly develop effective and individually tailored interventions (Watson et al., in press).

## Habits

Habits are learned, benign, persistent, stereotyped behaviors that appear to serve no meaningful purpose for the individual. Habits may be maintained by positive reinforcement (attention), negative reinforcement (escape from a particular task), or automatic (sensory stimulation) reinforcement and elicited by many discriminative stimuli (e.g., transitional objects). Most individuals will engage in some habit behavior (e.g., foot tapping, thumb sucking, hair twirling) over the course of their lives. Because most habits are benign and often transient, most go untreated. However, some habits may result in substantial negative physical, social, academic, occupational, and psychological discomfort for the individual who exhibits them. For instance, habits may result in negative interactions with parents, teachers, or peers. The student who sucks her thumb may be teased by peers, scolded by parents, and suffer physical damage (e.g., malocclusions). Because habits may result in substantial negative consequences, they are an important concern for parents, professionals (e.g., physicians, psychologists, professional school counselors), and the student who engages in the habit. The most common habits seen in clinical settings are trichotillomania (hair pulling), bruxism (teeth grinding or clenching), nail biting, and thumb sucking.

*Etiology and Epidemiology of Habit Disorders*

Current research indicates that habits are learned behaviors that are not indicative of underlying psychopathology. Children who engage in habits do not significantly differ from children who do not on measures such as the *Child Behavior Checklist* (*CBCL*; Achenbach, 1991) or *Eyeberg Child Behavior Inventory* (Friman, Larzeler, & Finney, 1994). It has been suggested that habits are caused by states of anxiety or tension (Hadley, 1984) fostering the idea that individuals who exhibit habits are "nervous" and the anxiety or tension they feel causes them to exhibit these "nervous" habits. Support for the theory that individuals who exhibit habits experience significantly more anxiety and tension than others has been mixed (Glaros & Melamed, 1992; Klatte & Deardorff, 1981; Woods, Miltenberger, & Flach, 1996).

From a behavioral perspective, it is likely that some habits are directly reinforced while others become conditioned reinforcers (i.e., they are paired with either an unconditioned reinforcer like food or with another conditioned reinforcer like playing in the tub), and as a result, are maintained for long periods of time. For instance, a student who normally receives little social attention from parents may be reprimanded when he sucks his thumb. Social attention provided contingent upon thumb sucking might serve to increase the future likelihood of thumb sucking. Thumb sucking may also provide tactile and kinesthetic stimulation of the oral tissue during times of minimal stimulation which may also maintain the behavior (i.e., automatic reinforcement).

Because habit disorders cover such a wide range of topographically different behaviors, it is extremely difficult to obtain overall prevalence estimates. However, rough estimates for specific habits have been reported. Peterson et al. (1994) reported prevalence data for habits most commonly seen in clinics. Bruxism is estimated to occur in 7% to 88% of the population. The wide range in prevalence rates is due to the varied definitions used by researchers who study bruxism. Estimates for the prevalence of trichotillomania are only available for adults, for whom it is estimated that 10% exhibit. Trichotillomania is more common in females, except for during the preschool years when it is more common in males. Prevalence rates for nail biting increase from preschool to adolescence where they peak at roughly 45%, but then steadily decline to a rate of 4.5% in adults. Nail biting is most common in females. Thumb sucking occurs in 30%-40% of preschool children and 10%-20% of children six years and older.

## Identification of Habits and Tics

Identifying, assessing, and treating habits and tics focuses on operationally defined, observable behaviors and employs a multimethod and a multi-informant approach for collecting data (Haynes, 1998). Methods for accurately and operationally identifying habit and tic behaviors include interviews, direct observation, and permanent product measures (e.g., nails, hairs) where possible.

*Interviews*

Interviews should be conducted with parents, teachers, and the student (when appropriate). The purpose of the interview is to first gain general information related to the student's developmental, medical, social, and academic histories. During the medical portion of the interview (with parents), information related to current and past medications as well as physician evaluations should be gathered in order to determine if there are possible organic causes for the habit or tic.

After developmental, medical, social and academic histories have been gathered, specific information regarding the habit or tic should be obtained. Questions related to when the behavior was first noticed, what the behavior looks like (having the student or parent perform the behavior may be appropriate), previous treatment attempts, and other areas of concern are important at this point. Following this, questions related to the times when the behavior is most frequently exhibited, events that precede the behavior (both physiological and environmental) and events that typically follow the behavior (e.g., social attention, removal of unpleasant physiological stimulation) should be asked. Information gathered from such questions can facilitate the development of hypotheses regarding possible functions of the behavior (e.g., escape from difficult tasks, social attention). The function of behavior can generally be regarded as the "why" of behavior.

Any student may exhibit a particular behavior for a number of reasons. Research indicates that there are four general classes of reasons (consequences) that account for the maintenance of problem behaviors (tangible reinforcement, social attention, negative reinforcement, and automatic reinforcement) (Iwata, Dorsey, Slifey, Bauman, & Richman, 1982/1994). However, social attention, negative reinforcement (escape or avoidance of an unpleasant activity or physiological state), and automatic reinforcement (sensory stimulation) appear to be the most common consequences that maintain habits or tics. In the function based treatments of this chapter, it will become apparent that determining the "why" of behavior (identifying maintaining consequences) can be extremely useful for developing treatment.

*Direct Observation*

Following interviews with parents, teachers, and the student, direct observations of the student should be conducted. Direct observations can be used to verify information gathered during interviews as well as to obtain additional information related to the presenting problem. Observation times may be selected based on information gathered during interviews that indicates when the habit or tic is most likely to occur. Ideally, direct observations should be conducted across a number of occasions and settings (again based upon information gathered during interviews). During direct observations, the practitioner should record the presenting problem on dimensions including frequency and duration. Such information can be useful in developing a baseline for which to evaluate treatment success (Foster, Watson, Meeks, & Young, in press). In addition, close attention should be paid to those events that precede (antecedents) and follow (consequences) the presenting problem. Such information can be useful for developing and verifying hypotheses regarding the potential functions for a particular behavior. A number of published observation forms are available to aid practitioners in recording antecedents, behaviors, and consequences (Watson & Steege, in press).

*Permanent Products*

In some cases it may not be possible to directly observe habits. For instance, if the student engages in hair pulling only in private, then it would be impossible to observe such behavior. Additionally, some students may react to observation such that the behavior may not be exhibited at this time. Permanent products can serve as one means to overcome such hurdles. Permanent products refer to those relatively enduring "remnants" of behavior. With trichotillomania, it may be possible to measure bald spots on the scalp to determine if hair is being pulled from a particular region. The student may also be instructed to save pulled hairs in order to obtain an accurate count of the number of hairs pulled during a day. In the case of nail biting, the length of the nails on each hand can be measured. Permanent product measures provide information that can be used to verify behaviors reported by parents, teachers, or the student. Permanent product measures are not amenable to the measurement of all habits (e.g., thumb sucking, hair twirling) or tics because tics do not leave enduring, measurable "remnants."

## Function Based Treatments

*Antecedent Interventions*

Information gathered during interviews and direct observation may identify specific antecedent events that consistently precede the habit or tic. If a reliable antecedent is identified, then the following procedure may be implemented. First, identify similar antecedents that have not elicited the habit or tic in the past. Next, arrange the environment such that there are numerous opportunities for the non-eliciting antecedent to occur and heavily reinforce all appropriate behaviors other than the habit or tic (differential reinforcement of other behavior). Finally, the event that elicited the habit or tic may be gradually reintroduced. For example, if assessment data indicated that a vocal tic is most often exhibited when a student is assigned difficult multiplication problems (e.g., double digit multiplication with regrouping), then the student can be provided with simpler math problems (e.g., single digit multiplication problems) and then provided positive social attention contingent upon the absence of the vocal tic (e.g., "I really like the way you are quietly working on your math worksheet."). Difficult multiplication problems can be gradually reintroduced while continuing to provide positive social attention contingent upon the absence of the vocal tic.

*Social Attention*

If interview and direct observation data indicate that social attention is maintaining the occurrence of a habit or tic, the primary intervention is to withhold attention when the habit or tic is exhibited (extinction) and to provide social attention when appropriate behaviors other than the habit or tic are exhibited (differential reinforcement). Watson and Sterling (1998) identified social attention as the maintaining variable for a vocal tic exhibited by a 4-year old girl during meal times. Treatment consisted of withholding social attention following the vocal tic (extinction) and providing verbal statements (social attention) contingent upon not exhibiting the vocal tic (differential reinforcement).

*Negative Reinforcement*

If interview and direct observation data indicate that escape from an unpleasant activity (negative reinforcement) is maintaining a habit or tic, then the practitioner must develop an intervention in which the student cannot escape the unpleasant activity. In one case of a student who exhibited a vocal and motor tic primarily in the classroom setting, it was determined (from interview and observation data) that the student was able to escape academic demands following the exhibition of the vocal and motor tics by being directed by the teacher to go to the back of the class to "calm down." Thus, vocal and motor tics allowed the student to escape academic demands that were present in the classroom. After discovering why the student exhibited vocal and motor tics, it was rather easy to develop treatment based on this information. First, the student was no longer allowed to escape academic tasks following the vocal and motor tics (extinction). Next, the student was allowed to take breaks (escape academic tasks) following completion of gradually increasing work requirements (differential reinforcement and shaping).

*Automatic Reinforcement*

Quite often, habit and tic behaviors are maintained by automatic reinforcement (sensory stimulation). In such cases, the practitioner must develop an intervention that either blocks sensory stimulation or punishes the behavior. For instance, Watson and Allen (1993) attached a post to the child's thumb, thus preventing the child from receiving tactile/kinesthetic stimulation provided by thumb sucking (extinction). Sometimes, however, it may not be possible to simply prevent access to sensory stimulation gained by the habit or tic. In such cases, it may be necessary to punish the habit or tic. A very effective treatment for eliminating thumb sucking is to place an unpleasant tasting substance on the thumb (e.g., Stopzit, Thumbz, Ambisol) after the child is observed sucking his/her thumb (punishment) and rewarding behaviors other than thumb sucking (differential reinforcement). It is important to note that whenever punishment procedures are implemented, some sort of reward should be provided for the nonoccurrence of the problem behavior (differential reinforcement).

## General Treatment Procedures

*Habit Reversal*

Some treatment approaches are effective despite the fact that they are not based on the function of the behavior. Habit reversal (HR) procedures represent one such approach. HR techniques are one of the most effective nonpharmacological treatments for habits and tics. The original habit reversal procedure (Azrin & Nunn, 1973) contained 13 steps. Follow-up research indicated that all 13 steps were not necessary. Three of the original 13 components are now considered sufficient for effective treatment: (a) awareness training, (b) competing response training, and (c) social support training. This approach to habit reversal has been labeled as simplified habit reversal (SHR).

The first step in SHR is *awareness training*. Awareness training involves the student becoming aware of his/her habit or tic and the sensations that precede it. Awareness is accomplished by having the student describe his habit or tic, describe the sensations that precede the habit or tic, acknowledge therapist demonstrations of the habit or tic, and acknowledge his own habit or tic.

*Competing response training* follows awareness training and involves the student and practitioner selecting a competing response, the practitioner demonstrating the competing response, and finally the client practicing the competing response. Typically, the behavior chosen as the competing response is physically incompatible with the target response (e.g., hands in pockets for trichotillomania). The student is trained to engage in the competing response for one-minute contingent upon the occurrence of the habit or tic. The final component of SHR is *social support training*. The purpose of social support training is to provide the student with an aid who will help implement the habit reversal procedure. Social support training involves three components. First, recruiting an aid for the student. Second, training the aid to praise accurate implementation of the competing response procedure by the student. And third, training aides to prompt students to complete the competing response procedure. For a more detailed account of SHR, readers should refer to *Tic Disorders, Trichotillomania, and Other Repetitive Behavior Disorders: Behavioral Approaches to Analysis and Treatment* (Woods & Miltenberger, 2001).

*Pharmacological Treatments*

Pharmacological agents traditionally have been the treatment of choice for tic spectrum disorders. Neuroleptics are the most commonly used pharmacological agents and work by blocking the reuptake of the neurotransmitter dopamine. Neuroleptics are categorized into two types: typical and atypical. Typical neuroleptics include haloperidol (Haldol®) and pimozide (Orap®). Haloperidol and pimozide are equally effective in treating tic spectrum disorder, with each reducing the frequency of tics by roughly 70%-80% (Kurlan, 1997; Leckman, Peterson, Pauls, & Cohen, 1997). Although typical neuroleptics are effective in significantly reducing tic frequency, they possess a long list of possible side effects including those that range from mild (e.g., dry mouth, constipation, weight gain) to severe (e.g., extra-pyramidal symptoms [EPS], tardive dyskinesia [TD], and seizures) (Arana, 2000).

Atypical neuroleptics are becoming increasingly popular and include olanzapine (Zyprexa®), clozapine (Clozaril®), and risperidone (Risperdal®). The atypical neuroleptics are often as effective as the typical neuroleptics but carry less of a risk for serious side effects such as EPS and TD. The atypical neuroleptics may, however, cause less serious side effects (e.g., dry mouth, constipation, weight gain, restlessness, and incontinence) (Blin, 1999).

## Self-Mutilation

Self-mutilation (SM) has been defined as the deliberate, direct destruction or alteration of body tissue without the presence of suicidal intent (Favazza, 1998; Miller & DeZolt, in press). The *DSM-IV-TR* (2000) does not classify SM as a specific disorder. The most widely accepted classification system for SM was developed by Favazza (1996). In this classification, SM is divided into three categories: (1) major, which refers to infrequent but highly destructive behaviors such as enucleation, castration, and limb amputation, (2) stereotypic, which refers to behaviors such as head banging and self-biting, and (3) superficial/moderate, which refers to behaviors such as trichotillomania, scratching, skin cutting, and burning. Superficial/moderate SM is the most common form of SM. Superficial/moderate SM behaviors overlap considerably with behaviors that are often classified as habits (e.g., trichotillomania, nail biting). The remainder of this discussion will focus on skin cutting since it has recently become an important topic for school personnel.

Skin cutting may be the most common form of episodic superficial/moderate self-mutilation (Favazza, 1998). Skin cutting is most often a symptom, or an associated feature, of Borderline, Histrionic and Antisocial Personality Disorders, Posttraumatic Stress Disorder, dissociative disorders, eating disorders, and depression (Favazza, 1998). Research indicates that cutting behaviors appear most often during adolescence, may be more prevalent in girls, may sometimes, but not always, be precipitated by incidents of sexual and/or physical abuse, and have an underestimated prevalence (Favazza, 1998; Ross & Heath, 2002).

Because individuals who engage in skin cutting are often secretive and reluctant to contact mental health services, identification, assessment, and treatment are often difficult. Furthermore, the lack of standardized instruments for assessing SM is problematic. A comprehensive assessment of skin cutting should include direct observations and interviews with the student suspected of cutting, caregivers, and other adults who frequently observe the individual (e.g., school personnel). Direct observations should include checking for cuts and the presence of heavy clothing that may serve to hide damage. When the student is interviewed, she should be asked directly whether or not she is engaging in skin cutting. If the student is engaging in skin cutting, then a suicide risk assessment should be immediately conducted.

Functional assessment techniques may also be employed in the assessment of skin cutting. While few empirically-based assessment instruments are available for skin cutting, functional assessment techniques may be appropriate because skin cutting is topographically similar to other superficial/moderate SM behaviors (e.g., trichotillomania, nail-biting) which are amenable to functional assessment procedures. During the assessment stage, information related to antecedents (e.g., anxiety invoking events, depression), specific behaviors (e.g., jagged lacerations to the thigh) and consequences (e.g., social attention, relief of internal physiological states such as depression, anxiety, and distress) of skin cutting should be gathered. Precise definitions and reliable antecedents and consequences of skin cutting may be useful during the treatment stage. For example, one individual may frequently engage in skin cutting in response to anxiety evoking events and may be maintained or negatively reinforced by anxiety reduction. Treatment for such an individual may involve teaching the individual to engage in diaphragmatic breathing and progressive muscle relaxation in the face of anxiety-evoking situations because such behaviors could produce similar consequences (i.e., anxiety reduction).

The empirical literature contains scant data regarding effective treatments for skin cutting for children and adolescents. Pharmacological treatment (e.g., SSRIs) may be effective for treating conditions (e.g., anxiety, depression) that are associated with skin cutting thereby reducing the occurrence of cutting (Favazza, 1998). Additionally, behavioral techniques such as simplified habit reversal may be effective because skin cutting is topographically similar to other habit behaviors (e.g., trichotillomania, nail-biting) that are effectively treated by simplified habit reversal. Finally, function based treatments (e.g., modification of antecedent events, programming alternative responses, manipulating consequences) may prove effective for treating skin cutting. It is important to note that the discussion of SM provided here is cursory at best. Interested readers should refer to Favazza (1998; 1999) for a more detailed discussion of assessment and treatment for SM.

## Summary/Conclusion

Although habits and tics appear to be benign disorders, there exists the possibility for significant social, educational/occupational, psychological, and physical damage. From a learning perspective, habits and tics represent learned behaviors that are affected by specific environmental events. The research literature supports the use of behavioral procedures for the assessment and treatment of habits and tics. Those procedures appear to offer relatively quick and effective means for treating habit and tic disorders.

## References

Achenbach, T. M. (1991). *Manual for the Child Behavior Checklist/4-18 and 1991 profile.* Burlington, VT: University of Vermont, Department of Psychiatry.

American Psychiatric Association. (2000). *Diagnostic and statistical manual of mental disorders (4th ed. - text revision).* Washington, DC: Author.

Apter, A. et al. (1993). An epidemiologic study of Gilles de la Tourette's Syndrome in Israel. *Archives of General Psychiatry, 50,* 734-738.

Arana, G. W. (2000). An overview of side effects caused by typical antispsychotics. *Journal of Clinical Psychiatry, 61,* 5-11.

Azrin, N. H., & Nunn, R. G. (1973). Habit reversal: A method of eliminating nervous habits and tics. *Behavior Research and Therapy, 11,* 619-628.

Blin, O. (1999). A comparative review of new antipsychotics.*Canadian Journal of Psychiatry, 44,* 235-244.

Burd, L., & Kerbeshian, J. (1987). Onset of Gilles de la Tourette's Syndrome before 1 year of age. *American Journal of Psychiatry, 26,* 706-710.

Burd, L., Kerbesian, J., Wikenheiser, M., & Fisher, W. (1986). A prevalence study of Gilles de la Tourette syndrome in North Dakota school-age children. *Journal of the American Academy of Child Psychiatry, 25,* 552-553.

Caine, E. O., McBride, M. C., Chiverton, P., Bamford, K. A., Rediess, S., & Shapiro, J. (1988). Tourette's Syndrome in Monroe County school children. *Neurology, 38,* 472-475.

Favazza, A. R. (1996). *Bodies under siege: Self-mutilation and body modification in culture and psychiatry.* Baltimore: Johns Hopkins University Press.

Favazza, A. R. (1998). The coming of age of self-mutilation. *The Journal of Nervous and Mental Disease, 186,* 259-268.

Favazza, A. R. (1999). Self-mutilation. In D. G. Jacobs (Ed.), *The Harvard Medical School guide to suicide assessment and interventions* (pp. 125-145). San Francisco: Jossey-Bass.

Friman, P. C., Larzelere, R., & Finney, J. W. (1994). Exploring the relationship between thumb-sucking and finger sucking. *Journal of Pediatric Psychology, 19,* 431-441.

Foster, L., Watson, T. S., Meeks, C., & Young, J. S. (in press). Single subject research design for school counselors: Why and how to become an applied researcher. *Professional School Counselor.*

Glaros, A. G., & Melamed, G. G. (1992). Bruxism in children: Etiology and treatment. *Applied and Preventive Psychology, 1,* 191-199.

Haber, S. N., Kowall, N. W., Vonsattel, J. P., Bird, E. D., & Richardson, E. P. (1986). Gilles de la Tourette's Syndrome: A postmortem neuropathological and immunohistochemical study. *Journal of Neurological Sciences, 75,* 225-241.

Hadley, N. H. (1984). *Nail biting.* New York: Spectrum.

Haynes, S. N. (1998). The changing nature of behavioral assessment. In A. S. Bellack & M. Hersen (Eds.), *Behavioral assessment: A practical handbook* (4th ed.). Needham Heights, MA: Allyn & Bacon.

Houlihan, D., Hofschulte, L., & Patten, C. (1993). Behavioral conceptualizations and treatments of Tourette's Syndrome: A review and overview. *Behavioral Residential Treatment, 8,* 111-131.

Hyde, T. M., Aaronson, B. A., Randolph, C., Rickler, K. C., & Weinberger, D. R. (1992). Relationship of birth weight to the phenotypic expression of Gilles de la Tourette's Syndrome in monozygotic twins. *Neurology, 42,* 652-658.

Iwata, B., Dorsey, M. F., Slifer, K. J., Bauman, K. E., & Richman, G. S. (1982/1994). Toward a functional analysis of self-injury. *Analysis and Intervention in Developmental Disabilities, 2,* 3-20. Reprinted in *Journal of Applied Behavior Analysis, 27,* 197-209.

Klatte, K. M., & Deardorff, P. A. (1981). Nail-biting and manifest anxiety in adults. *Psychological Reports, 48,* 82.

Kurlan, R. (1997). Treatment of tics. *Neurologic Clinics, 15,* 403-409.

LaPouse, R., & Monk, M. A. (1964). Behavior deviations in a representative sample of children: Variations by sex, age, race, social class, and family size. *American Journal of Orthopsychiatry, 34,* 436-446.

Leckman, J. F., Peterson, B. S., Pauls, D. L., & Cohen, D. J. (1997). Tic disorders. *Psychiatric Clinics of North American, 20,* 839-861.

Leckman, J. F., et al. (1988). Elevated CSF dynorphin A[1-8] in Tourette's Syndrome. *Life Sciences, 43,* 2015-2023.

Malatesta, V. J. (1990). Behavioral case formulation: An experimental assessment study of Transient Tic Disorder. *Journal of Psychopathology and Behavioral Assessment, 12,* 219-232.

Miller, D. N., & DeZolt, D. M. (in press). Self-mutilation. In T. S. Watson & C. H. Skinner (Eds.), *Comprehensive encyclopedia of school psychology.* New York: Kluwer Press.

Pauls, D. L., Raymond, C. L., Leckman, J. F., & Stevenson, J. M. (1991). A family study of Tourette's Syndrome. *American Journal of Human Genetics, 48,* 154-163.

Peterson, A. L., Campose, R. L., & Azrin, N. H. (1994). Behavioral and pharmacological treatments for tic and habit disorders: A review. *Journal of Developmental and Behavioral Pediatrics, 15,* 430-441.

Peterson, B. S., Leckman, J. L., & Cohen, D. J. (1995). Tourette's Syndrome: A genetically predisposed and environmentally specified developmental psychopathology. In D. Cicchette & D. J. Cohen (Eds.), *Manual of developmental psychopathology* (pp. 213-242). New York: Wiley.

Pray, B., Kramer, J. J., & Lindskog, R. (1986). Assessment and treatment of tic behavior: A review and case study. *School Psychology Review, 15,* 418-429.

Price, R. A. (1985). Gilles de la Tourette Syndrome. *Neurology and Neurosurgery, 8,* 1-8.

Price, R. A., Kidd, K. K., Cohen, D. J., Pauls, D. L., & Leckman, J. E. (1993). Human basal ganglia volume asymmetrics in magnetic resonance images. *Magnetic Resonance Imaging, 11,* 493-498.

Ross, S., & Heath, N. (2002). A study of the frequency of self-mutilation in a community sample of adolescents. *Journal of Youth and Adolescence, 31,* 67-77.

Sallee, F. R., Stiller, R. L., & Perel, J. M. (1992). Pharmacodynamics of pemoline in Attention Deficit Disorder with Hyperactivity. *Journal of the American Academy of Child and Adolescent Psychiatry, 31,* 244-251.

Torup, E. (1972). A follow-up study of children with tics. *Acta Paediatrica, 51,* 261-268.

Walkup, J. T., Leckman, J. F., Price, A. R., Hardin, M. T., Ort, S. I., & Cohen, D. J. (1988). The relationship between Obsessive Compulsive Disorder and Tourette's Syndrome: A twin study. *Psychopharmacology Bulletin, 24,* 375-379.

Watson, T. S., & Allen, K. D. (1993). Elimination of thumb-sucking as a treatment for severe trichotillomania. *Journal of the American Academy of Child and Adolescent Psychiatry, 32,* 830-834.

Watson, T. S., Dufrene, B. A., Weaver, A. D., Butler, T. S., & Meeks, C. (in press). Brief antecedent assessment and treatment of tics in the general education classroom: A preliminary investigation. *Behavior Modification.*

Watson, T. S., & Steege, M. (in press). *A practitioner's guide to school-based functional assessment.* New York: Guilford.

Watson, T. S., & Sterling, H. E. (1998). Brief functional analysis and treatment of a vocal tic. *Journal of Applied Behavior Analysis, 31,* 471-474.

Woods, D. W., & Miltenberger, R. G. (Eds.). (2001). *Tic Disorders, Trichotillomania, and other repetitive behavior disorders: Behavioral approaches to analysis and treatment.* Boston: Kluwer.

Woods, D. W., Miltenberger, R. G., & Flach, A. D. (1996). Habits, tics, and stuttering: Prevalence and relation to anxiety and somatic awareness. *Behavior Modification, 20,* 216-225.

Woods, D. W., Watson, T. S., Wolfe, E., Twohig, M. P., & Friman, P. C. (2001). Analyzing the influence of tic-related talk on vocal and motor tics in children with Tourette's Syndrome. *Journal of Applied Behavior Analysis, 34,* 353-356.

# Chapter 62

# Reactive Attachment Disorder in Schools: Recommendations for Professional School Counselors

*Carl J. Sheperis, R. Anthony Doggett, & Nicholas E. Hoda*

## Preview

Children who experience pathogenic care prior to age five can develop Reactive Attachment Disorder (RAD). This disorder, which manifests in a host of behavioral problems, is of growing concern to professional school counselors. This chapter discusses the characteristics of RAD, diagnostic criteria, issues related to the school system, and recommendations for professional school counselors.

When students transfer in and out of school systems, professional school counselors face a host of difficult administrative issues (e.g., maintaining student records, gathering accurate evaluations of progress, and establishing relationships with families). No school population is more transitory than foster care children. Some children in foster care experience as many as 50 or 60 placements in several different school districts (Sheperis, Renfro-Michel, & Doggett, in press). Many of these children also have mental health issues related to abuse or neglect that eventuated their foster care placement, thus creating more concerns for professional school counselors. In fact, some evidence suggests that children in foster care are more likely to receive behavioral health care services than any other group of Medicaid-eligible children ("Children in foster care," 2001, April ). Often these health care services are related to a disruption of healthy attachment patterns resulting in Reactive Attachment Disorder (RAD).

A commonly misunderstood and under-diagnosed disorder, RAD is becoming a growing concern for professional school counselors (Parker & Forrest, 1993). This disorder, which begins in early childhood and affects various domains (e.g., academic, behavioral, cognitive, affective, social, physical, and spiritual/moral development) (Doane & Diamond, 1994; Leick & Davidsen-Neilson, 1990; Levy & Orlans, 1998), can be positively treated through a professional school counselor's intervention (Hayes, 1997). Professional school counselors are in a unique position, by nature of their prolonged interactions with these students, to recognize symptoms of serious underlying problems and to make appropriate referrals (Hayes, 1997). This chapter presents professional school counselors with information about Reactive Attachment Disorder, its development, some methods of treatment, and guidelines for intervention in a school system. However, before expounding upon the nature of RAD, it is important to explain the process of attachment and its function in a student's life.

## Attachment

Attachment is a process common to humans and many animal species. Disruptions in the process affect us throughout our lives and can negatively impact our ability to form healthy relationships. Bowlby (1969) saw attachment as an instinctual, evolutionary process occurring in four-stages. He believed that the process of attachment functions as a drive toward survival of the species. The process begins with an infant's communication of needs for proximity and physical contact through vocal and behavioral cues (e.g., crying, latching on, & grasping). Acknowledgement and fulfillment of these needs by a caregiver begin to positively shape the infant's behavior. Infants begin the second stage of attachment between 8 and 12 weeks of age by establishing indicators of caregiver preference through behavioral cues such as reaching and scooting. The third stage of attachment, according to Bowlby, occurs from 12 weeks of age through the second birthday. This is the stage that Ainsworth, Blehar, Waters, and Wall (1978) believed to be the true process of attachment. In this stage, infants and toddlers begin to anticipate caregiver actions and adjust their own behavior in accordance with these anticipated events. Thus, primary caregiver consistency in the display of affection and attention to needs of the child are critical components in the formation of healthy adjustments on the part of the child. An understanding of caregiver independence and the development of reciprocity in the infant/caregiver relationship characterize Bowlby's fourth stage of attachment development, thus moving into a more sophisticated aspect of the process. The key facet across all of these stages is consistency in the provision of behavioral reinforcement to infant and toddler basic emotional and physical needs. This reinforcement is, in essence, a method of conditioning the child to utilize human relationships as a sense of security and comfort (Wilson, 2001).

When the provision of infant and toddler basic needs is not conducted in a consistent fashion, attachment becomes disrupted resulting in insecure attachment patterns and adverse reactions toward human relationships. In research, disrupted attachment has been linked to psychiatric syndromes, criminal behavior, and drug use (Allen, Hauser & Borman-Spurrell, 1996; Rosenstein & Horowitz, 1996). Chronic inconsistency in meeting infant and toddler needs as well as the introduction of early childhood trauma (i.e., abuse or neglect) may result in the formation of RAD.

## Reactive Attachment Disorder

A personal difficulty that professional school counselors may face with regard to RAD is a lack of ability to prevent the development of the disorder. RAD develops from a lack of appropriate bonding between infant and primary care giver. Thus, the goal for professional school counselors is identification of problem behaviors and acquisition of appropriate resources (Hayes, 1997). The *DSM-IV-TR* (American Psychiatric Association, 2000) criteria for RAD include: (a) "evidence of a clearly disturbed and developmentally inappropriate social relatedness in most contexts, beginning before age five" (p. 130), (b) evidence of pathogenic care, and (c) a presumption that the pathogenic care is responsible for the disturbed behavior. There are two types of RAD, Inhibited and Disinhibited, that relate to the presentation of behavioral problems.

## Identification of RAD

Childhood psychological disorders often impact various areas of functioning (e.g., behavior, cognition, academic progress, and developmental processes)(Achenbach, 1995). Many disorders also share similar symptoms. These commonalities make it difficult to differentiate RAD from disorders such as Attention-Deficit/Hyperactivity Disorder (AD/HD), mental retardation, depression, Oppositional Defiant Disorder (ODD), Conduct Disorder, Autism and other Pervasive Developmental Disorders, learning disabilities, and Expressive and Mixed Receptive-Expressive Language Disorders (Sheperis et al., in press). In order to effectively coordinate academic services, it is necessary for professional school counselors to understand how to differentiate between a student with RAD and a student exhibiting behaviors characteristic of other disorders. Thus, an understanding of diagnostic criteria for the disorder is warranted.

The principle factor in accurate identification is the presence of an abusive and neglectful environment (i.e., pathogenic care) prior to age five (APA, 2000). However, this factor alone is not solely indicative of RAD (Sheperis et al., in press). Students with RAD often have poor interpersonal skills and have difficulty establishing appropriate relationships with peers and adults (Levy & Orlans, 1998). These boundary issues manifest in an inability to interact with either familiar people (i.e., inhibited type) or in an "indiscriminant sociability" (i.e., disinhibited type) (APA, 2000). For example, students with an inhibited type may be very introverted and, similar to autism, may not respond to familiar people or caregivers (Sheperis et al., in press). These students may also respond to cordial interactions in an aggressive manner. Their general pattern of response is unpredictable and vacillates between avoidant and approaching behaviors (Levy & Orlans, 1998). On the opposite end of the spectrum, students with a disinhibited type of RAD often attempt to become overly acquainted with strangers or attempt to connect with people unselectively (Levy & Orlans, 1998). This behavior can establish a pattern of further victimization through interactions with predatory individuals. In order to accurately diagnose either type of RAD, the disturbed pattern of interaction must have begun prior to age five (APA, 2000).

## Similarities To Other Disorders

When psychological disorders share similar characteristics, a process of differential diagnosis is warranted. Differential diagnosis requires attention to exclusionary criteria of disorders with similar characteristics. For example, a student with RAD may appear very similar to a student with Attention-Deficit/Hyperactivity Disorder (AD/HD). Specifically, both may exhibit little connection between cause and effect thinking and may behave impulsively and hyperactively. However, unlike students with RAD, students with AD/HD will have formed relationships with caregivers and other supportive persons (APA, 2000). Also, the impulsive/hyperactive behavior of students with AD/HD differs somewhat from disinhibited behavior exhibited by students with RAD. In particular, the student with RAD displays inappropriate boundaries and may act as if a relationship exists with a complete stranger rather than being uninhibited and curious (APA, 2000).

Students with RAD may also display behaviors and characteristics similar to mental retardation (MR). However, if criteria are met for mental retardation, the student cannot be diagnosed with RAD. Accurate assessment of a student's behavior requires a working knowledge of human developmental levels (e.g., cognitive functioning and age-appropriate behaviors). Accurate diagnosis of RAD requires that disruptive behavior must be a result of pathogenic care rather than mental retardation or other cognitive deficits (APA, 2000). However, RAD may occur in conjunction with cognitive deficits and developmental delays. More specifically, although both RAD and MR may result in a student's inability to form meaningful, healthy relationships with significant persons such as caregivers, failed relationships for a student with RAD result from pathogenic care rather than developmental issues (APA, 2000).

Some behaviors exhibited by students diagnosed with RAD can also be characteristic of childhood depression. With either disorder, a sense of depression can be manifested in isolation and a lack of pleasure from customary activities. The attitude of children with RAD is often pouty, sulky, and sullen (Sheperis et al., in press). To further exacerbate depressive characteristics, students with RAD typically have a wide range of cognitive distortions and lack belief in fairness and good in the world. Considering the deprivation of basic needs that students diagnosed with RAD often suffer due to pathogenic care during infancy and early childhood, these distortions can be understood to some degree; however, they should not be accepted. This distorted belief system may result in a lack of belief about being able to influence the path their life will take (Sheperis et al., in press). Such an extreme external locus of control in students with RAD may increase inhibition and decrease self-modulation related to more serious behavior (e.g., suicide, reactive and predatory behaviors, and juvenile delinquency). A student with RAD may often exhibit behaviors similar to students with either Oppositional Defiant Disorder (ODD) or Conduct Disorder (CD) (APA, 2000).

Characteristic of either CD or ODD, a student with RAD may be both overtly and passively aggressive. Also characteristic of either disorder, students with RAD may be deceitful or lie to manipulate others (Sheperis et al., in press). According to Levy and Orlans (1998), RAD also manifests in chronic lying and generalized delinquent behavior (e.g., stealing and fighting). Because the behaviors characteristic of RAD, CD, and ODD are so similar in nature, it is difficult to differentiate the disorders without an appropriate psycho-social history. The main differentiating criteria is the presence of pathogenic care prior to age five that is thought to be responsible for the behaviors.

Students with RAD may also share similarities with students who are autistic or have other Pervasive Developmental Disorders (APA, 2000). Both fail to make appropriate attachments to caregivers. The primary difference is that behaviors related to RAD must have developed within the framework of an abusive or detrimental environment while a student with autism or a Pervasive Developmental Disorder may have been raised in a supportive and caring environment. The *DSM-IV-TR* (APA, 2000) stated that students with autism or a Pervasive Developmental Disorder will also present impairment in the quality of communication and will display patterned behavior consisting of restricted, repetitive, and stereotyped movements (e.g., overly preoccupied with a stereotyped and restricted pattern of abnormally intense or abnormally focused interest, need to perform a routine or ritual which has no apparent purpose, hand-flapping or wringing, and obsession with parts of objects).

## Academic Issues Related to RAD

Repeated changes in foster care and school settings often lead to academic skills or performance deficits for students with RAD (Zirkie & Peterson, 2001). Professional school counselors can help establish effective learning environments in which teachers can recognize individual learning preferences and realize when a student needs assistance in learning a particular skill. A skill deficit can occur when a student has not met the mastery criteria of a curriculum but advances to the next grade (e.g., social promotion). This promotion becomes a problem because the student is expected to complete tasks at a more advanced level than his ability. An example of an academic performance deficit occurs when behavior problems impact academic performance (e.g., a student with RAD who is unwilling to complete assignments because of a general dislike and mistrust of adults). Unlike students with reading and math disorders or expressive and mixed receptive-expressive language disorders, the academic difficulties of students with RAD may stem from a lack of stability and continuity of care rather than from a cognitive or neurological deficit. Professional school counselors can affect positive outcomes for these students through the acquisition and coordination of quality services (Zirkie & Peterson, 2001). The primary step in this process for a student exhibiting symptoms of RAD, particularly a foster child or an adopted child, is to review the student's academic record to examine the frequency of school transfers and the length of stability in each school. The professional school counselor should also examine academic records for patterns of problems, both in academic behavior (e.g., previous grade retentions or advancements) and in social behavior (e.g., numerous suspensions, refusal to complete tasks or assignments, lying, and/or impulsive or aggressive behavior). One potential method of achieving this task is to conduct regularly scheduled meetings with the student (Parker

& Forrest, 1993). Although a professional school counselor's schedule is demanding, the results of inattention to the student with RAD provide clear impetus for preventive measures. Because professional school counselors are often asked to perform different functions within a school system, it should be cautioned that the counselor should avoid performing the dual role of support person and disciplinarian.

RAD is most amenable to mental health intervention during early childhood (Zeanah, 1996). Thus, early identification of problem behaviors and appropriate referral are key tasks for professional school counselors (Pfaller & Kiselica, 1996). Although early intervention programs such as *Headstart* are often warranted, appropriate academic services may not be identified until the student is of school age. Once in the schools, these students are in need of structure and order in a caring and supportive environment to succeed academically (Parker & Forrest, 1993). Professional school counselors, by virtue of their knowledge of the school system, can identify and advocate assignment to appropriate teachers who could provide such an environment for these students.

Because of the multitude of school-related problems identified, students diagnosed with RAD are at-risk for academic failure. Professional school counselors may also establish dropout prevention services for these students. However, the efficacy of such programs with this population is yet to be tested. Early identification of academic difficulties is preferred to dropout prevention. If academic problems are identified early, professional school counselors can advocate for intervention in academic areas as needed. The professional school counselor may refer the student to be tested for special education services.

When individualized education plan (IEP) meetings are held for the student, the professional school counselor and special education coordinator should ensure that the appropriate personnel are present (e.g., legal guardian of the student, special education representative, administration representative, juvenile justice officer and, most importantly, an expert on RAD such as a school psychologist or mental health professional). The professional school counselor may also act as a liaison ensuring that appropriate services are provided for the student. This role would provide added success to IEP meetings, because the professional school counselor would have ongoing contact with mental health counseling agencies and other psychological service providers, juvenile justice officials, child welfare agencies and other parties providing services to the student and family. The professional school counselor is in a good position to establish open communication with the student's guardian(s), ensuring that they are informed about the services being provided. Serving as a liaison also provides the family with a contact person for questions about the process.

## Legal Issues

Students who are in foster care or who have been adopted often have complex custodial issues and professional school counselors are in a unique position to ensure that the school is a safe and secure environment (Zirkie & Peterson, 2001). School officials must be aware of the custodial rights of each student and limit access to and disclosure of information to appropriate sources as dictated by the Family Educational Rights and Privacy Act (FERPA) of 1974 and the amendments to the Individuals with Disabilities Act (IDEA) of 1997. For example, school officials must obtain appropriate consent for individualized assessment procedures, special education services or any special treatment that is not provided to all students. Also, school officials must ensure that students are only released from school to those with custodial power. Custodial rights and the power to consent may be legally granted to a biological parent, adoptive parent, foster parent, guardian *ad litum*, or human services agency. Professional school counselors can ensure appropriate care in these matters through review of academic records and appropriate dissemination of information to school officials.

## Recommendations for Professional School Counselors

Following are recommendations for best practice in working with students with RAD.

1. If a student is suspected of having reactive attachment disorder, he or she should be referred for appropriate assessment by a mental health professional.
2. Establish a supportive relationship with the student.
3. Obtain accurate academic records from all previous school districts.
4. Examine academic records for evidence of patterns of problem behavior.
5. Obtain behavioral observation data.
6. Consult the school psychologist.
7. Establish an Individualized Educational Plan (IEP) and include all key players in the formation of the plan (i.e., foster parents, guardians *ad-litum*, human services professionals, and mental health counselors).
8. Identify appropriate services for the student.
9. Coordinate efforts with teachers and IEP team members.
10. Maintain continued contact with classroom teachers.
11. Conduct regularly scheduled parent meetings.
12. Maintain phone contact with parents or caregivers.

## Summary/Conclusion

Attachment is an instinctual process that occurs between a student and his primary caregiver. When that process is disrupted, students have difficulty with self-regulation and forming healthy relationships. This disruption, under chronic abuse or neglect conditions (e.g., pathogenic care), can develop into Reactive Attachment Disorder (RAD). RAD affects many areas of a student's life, including school. Professional school counselors are in a unique position to help stabilize several domains through advocacy and targeted interventions. Because disrupted attachment has been linked to psychiatric syndromes, criminal behavior, and drug use (Allen et al., 1996; Rosenstein & Horowitz, 1996), it is important to intervene early and to work toward stabilization. Professional school counselors can help students and their families to access appropriate resources and can ensure that appropriate academic interventions are in place.

## References

Achenbach, T. M. (1995). Behavior problems in 5- to 11-year-old children from low-income families. *Journal of the American Academy of Child & Adolescent Psychiatry, 34,* 536-537.

Ainsworth, M. D., Blehar, M. C., Walters, E., & Wall, S. (1978). *Patterns of attachment.* Hillsdale, NJ: Lawrence Erlbaum Associates.

Allen, J.P., Hauser, S. T., & Borman-Spurrell, E. (1996). Attachment theory as a framework for understanding sequelae of severe adolescent psychopathology: An 11-year follow-up study. *Journal of Consulting and Clinical Psychology, 64,* 254-263.

American Psychiatric Association. (2000). *Diagnostic and statistical manual of mental disorders: Text revision* (4th ed.). Washington, DC: Author.

Bowlby, J. (1969). *Attachment and loss* (Vol. 1). New York: Basic Books.

Children in foster care have more SA/MH needs. (2001, April 2). *Alcoholism & Drug Abuse Weekly, 13,* 5.

Doane, J. A., & Diamond, D. (1994). *Affect and attachment in the family: A family based treatment of major psychiatric disorder*. New York: Basic Books.

Hayes, S. H. (1997). Reactive Attachment Disorder: Recommendations for school counselors. *School Counselor, 44*, 353-361.

Leick, N., & Davidsen-Neilson, M. (1990). *Healing pain: Attachment, loss and grief therapy.* New York: Routledge, Chapman, & Hall.

Levy, T. M., & Orlans, M. (1998). *Attachment, trauma, and healing: Understanding and treating attachment disorder in children and families*. Washington, DC: Child Welfare League of America.

Parker, K. C., & Forrest, D. (1993). Attachment disorder: An emerging concern for school counselors. *Elementary School Guidance & Counseling, 27*, 209-215.

Pfaller, J. E., & Kiselica, M. S. ( 1996). Implications of attachment theory for the role of school counselors. *School Counselor, 43*, 208-217.

Rosenstein, D. S., & Horowitz, H. A. (1996). Adolescent attachment and psychopathology. *Journal of Consulting and Clinical Psychology, 64,* 244-253.

Sheperis, C. J., Renfro-Michel, E., & Doggett, R. A. (in press). In home treatment of reactive attachment disorder in a therapeutic foster care system: A case example. *Journal of Mental Health Counseling.*

Wilson, S. L. (2001). Attachment disorder in children. *Journal of Psychology, 135*(1), 37-51.

Zeanah, C. H. (1996). Beyond insecurity: A reconceptualization of attachment disorders of infancy. *Journal of Consulting and Clinical Psychology, 64*(1), 42-52.

Zirkie, D. S., & Peterson, T. L. (2001). The school counselor's role in academic and social adjustment of late adopted children. *Professional School Counseling, 4*, 366-369.

# Chapter 63

## Helping Students with Mental Retardation

*Amy J. Newmeyer & Mark D. Newmeyer*

### Preview

The professional school counselor can play an important role in advocating for students with mental retardation. The following chapter reviews the current definition of mental retardation and educational implications from existing federal education laws. Issues surrounding sexuality, vocational training, and comborbidity are also addressed.

### Definition of Mental Retardation

In 2002, The American Association of Mental Retardation (AAMR) published a revision of the 1992 definition and classification system for mental retardation. The AAMR definition is generally considered the "gold standard" for the diagnosis of mental retardation. However, it is important to keep in mind that individual state laws may have alternative definitions/cutoffs when determining eligibility for services, and it is therefore of great importance for professional school counselors to be aware of their local laws regarding eligibility. For further information, please refer to the AAMR website (http://www.AAMR.org).

The 2002 AAMR definition of mental retardation is as follows:

> Mental retardation is a disability characterized by significant limitations both in intellectual functioning and in adaptive behavior, as expressed in conceptual, social, and practical adaptive skills. This disability originates before age 18. (p. 8)

In the 2002 revision, five dimensions for classification and diagnosis have been defined (see Table 1).

The goal of defining these dimensions for any individual is to determine needed supports that will improve the individual's overall functioning in the environment.

Once descriptions of each dimension have been made, they should be incorporated into a profile of support needs. Support needs can change during different periods of an individual's life (childhood vs. adulthood). Supports are defined as: "resources and strategies that aim to promote the development, education, interests, and personal well-being of a person and that enhance individual functioning"(AAMR, 2002, p. 15). Support functions are: "teaching, befriending, financial planning, employee assistance, behavioral support, in-home living assistance, community access and use, and health assistance" (AAMR, 2002, p. 152). There should be an understanding that support needs and intensity of supports will change over the lifespan of an individual, and should be reassessed on a regular basis.

*Educational Implications*

There are several current laws that affect student placement and special education services

**Table 1. Five dimensions for classification and diagnosis of mental retardation.**

- Dimension I - Intellectual Abilities
  - * The person's intellectual functioning is approximately two standard deviations or more below the mean on standard psychometric tests (typically the Stanford-Binet IV or Weschler intelligence test appropriate for the age of student).
  - * Standard error of the mean should be considered when interpreting the results of any test.
- Dimension II - Adaptive Behavior (conceptual, social, and practical skills)
  - * Three basic factor clusters exist
    - cognitive, communication, and academic skills
    - social competence skills
    - independent living skills
  - *Adaptive skills should be interpreted in light of the following:
    - Weaknesses in certain adaptive skills may coexist with strengths in other adaptive skills.
    - Strengths and weaknesses should be interpreted in light of community and cultural environments of the individual.
- Dimension III - Participation, Interactions, and Social Roles
  - * Constitutes the environments that are typical of their chronological age peers and are consistent with the cultural diversity of the individual.
- Dimension IV - Health (physical health, mental health, and etiologic factors)
  - * Can be described by using ICD-10 diagnoses for physical health, and DSM-IV criteria for mental health.
  - * It should be understood that these factors may affect outcomes of intellectual and adaptive measures.
- Dimension V - Context (Environment and Culture)
  - * The 2002 definition uses an ecological approach, involving consideration of three levels:
    - immediate setting (person, family, and advocates)
    - neighborhood, community, and organizations providing support
    - patterns of culture, country, and sociopolitical influences
  - * Factors should be identified which provide opportunities and foster well-being.

in the school setting. IDEA (Individuals with Disabilities Education Act of 1975; Amendments in 1997) indicates that individuals with mental retardation may receive services through their local school district through age 21. Additionally, starting at 14 years of age, and updated annually, a statement of transition needs (Individualized Transition Program) should be added to the Individualized Education Plan (IEP). By 16 years of age, a statement of transition services for the individual must be in place, including a statement of interagency linkages as appropriate. Meanwhile, the student's school program must be in the Least Restrictive Environment (LRE) that allows optimal functioning.

The Rehabilitation Act of 1973 and Amendments, commonly called section 504, prevents discrimination against individuals with disabilities in any institution receiving federal financial assistance. This includes the local school district.

The professional school counselor has a vital role in several of the above processes. The professional school counselor should be part of the team meeting to develop the IEP. Several types of assessment are routinely used in assisting with development of the IEP and the

Individualized Transition Plan (ITP), which have implications for counselors in the school setting.

Assessment of student activity needs and skills in relevant domains for development of the IEP can involve an ecological inventory and observations in various community settings. This is relevant to students of all ages and should be completed every 3 years. Planning for school-to-work transition, and development of the ITP involves a vocational and transitional assessment by interview and observation in various settings. The professional school counselor may also serve as a link to appropriate community agencies that can offer job assistance and community assistance following graduation from high school. This assessment should be updated annually from age 14 through matriculation.

Evaluation of behavioral problems that may affect school and community functioning may involve functional analysis, interview, observation, and referral to appropriate community resources. This may occur on a daily or weekly basis until the behavioral problems have stabilized. Evaluation of IEP objectives by observation in the school setting as well as interview of parents may occur on a more frequent basis as needed. Determination of student and family satisfaction with services provided may be by interview, questionnaire, or observation. This should be performed at least annually or more often if needed.

*Support Services for Families*

The professional school counselor may also be involved in provision of other services to families of students with mental retardation. Many families will adapt to having a child who has been diagnosed with mental retardation. However, other families may require ongoing counseling and intervention in their adaptation to the special needs of their child. Various factors found to be associated with adaptation include stability of the marriage, age of parents, parental self-esteem, number of siblings, socio-economic status, degree of disability, parental expectations, support of extended family, availability of community programs and respite services. Professional school counselors may play a vital role in identifying families at risk and assisting families with accessing available resources and respite services within the community setting (Shapiro & Batshaw, 1999).

*Sexuality Issues*

The professional school counselor can play an important role in assuring that sexuality issues are addressed for students with mental retardation. Traditionally, issues of sexuality have been largely avoided in this population. However, this lack of communication can lead to risk for exploitation and misunderstanding. In 1996, the American Academy of Pediatrics (AAP) Committee on Children with Disabilities released a policy statement regarding sexuality education of children and adolescents with developmental disabilities. In this statement, summarized in Table 2, they emphasized major objectives to sexuality education for this group of students.

Families of children with mental retardation may also raise questions regarding sterilization. Sterilization is greatly discouraged, unless there is a medical reason for doing the procedure.

Alternative methods of birth control should be discussed with the student and the student's physician. Laws regarding sterilization do vary locally, and the family should be referred to the physician for a detailed discussion of options (AAP, 1999).

*Social Skills Training*

Many students with mental retardation may have difficulty with social skills in the school setting, often because their developmental level lags behind that of same-age peers. The professional school counselor may be able to assist these children with social skills by providing counseling and training regarding appropriate behavior in certain settings, such as how to have a conversation with another peer. Learning these skills may greatly enhance a student's ability to function in an inclusive setting.

**Table 2. Major objectives of sexuality education for students with mental retardation.**

- Information should be tailored to the level of understanding of the particular student.
- Teaching students to express physical affection in an appropriate manner.
- Discouraging inappropriate public displays of affection in the community, e.g., hugging strangers.
- Expressing expectations that behavior conforms to family and community standards for privacy and modesty.
- Teaching students about appropriate behaviors in a public setting and private setting.
- Teaching students their right to refuse to be touched at any time, and the importance of telling a parent or caregiver if they have been touched inappropriately.
- Discussing pleasure and affection when teaching students about sex (AAP, 1996).

*Comorbid Issues*

Students with mental retardation often have comorbid behavioral and mental health conditions such as depression, anxiety, or aggressive behavior that will impact their functioning in a school or community environment. It is important that these issues be addressed appropriately to ensure maximum functioning of the individual. The professional school counselor can play a role in identifying these conditions, providing counseling services, and referring the student and his/her family for interventions including medication management or psychological services when appropriate.

## Summary/Conclusion

The professional school counselor can play an important role in advocating for students with mental retardation. This role may include being part of the IEP team as an advocate for the child to receive appropriate services at school. The professional school counselor may be involved in obtaining information regarding the student's functioning in the school and home settings that will assist with forming appropriate IEP goals, as well as an effective Individualized Transition Program (ITP) to maximize the student's community functioning upon graduating high school. Issues of sexuality and social skills may be effectively addressed by interventions offered by the professional school counselor.

## References

American Academy of Pediatrics. (1996). Sexuality education of children and adolescents with developmental disabilities. *Pediatrics*, *97*, 275-277.

American Academy of Pediatrics. (1999). Sterilization of minors with developmental disabilities. *Pediatrics*,*104*, 337-340.

American Association of Mental Retardation. (2002). *Mental retardation: Definition, classification, and systems of support* (10th ed.). Washington, DC: Author.

Shapiro, B. K. & Batshaw, M. L. (1999). Mental retardation. In F. D. Burg, J. Inglefinger, E. Wald, & R. A. Polin (Eds.), *Current pediatric therapy* (16th ed.) (pp. 417-420). Philadelphia: W. B. Saunders.

# Chapter 64

## Students with Learning Disabilities: Counseling Issues and Strategies

*Adriana G. McEachern*

### Preview

Approximately 51% of students in exceptional education classes have been diagnosed with learning disabilities (LDs). Professional school counselors can help these students be successful academically and cope with personal and social issues imposed by their disability. This chapter will discuss LD issues relevant to professional school counselors and counseling strategies that can be used to help these students.

Learning disabilities (LDs), intriguing and puzzling disorders, are of concern to educators, parents, researchers, professional school counselors, and the students themselves (Coplin & Morgan, 1988; Kirk, Gallagher, & Anastasiow, 2000). The intriguing aspects of LD are that there is no one specific cause, there are multiple types, and even students with the same type of LD may have different sets of deficiencies. Learning disabilities are puzzling because these students may have normal or gifted intelligence, yet they are not always successful in schools. Researchers have been studying LD since the 1800's, and the term *learning disabilities* was first proposed by parents and Samuel Kirk in 1963 to describe the condition (Kirk et al., 2000).

### Definitions and Prevalence

Learning disabilities (LDs) are disorders that affect the understanding or use of language, written or spoken, that manifest themselves in difficulties with listening, thinking, reading, writing, spelling, and mathematical calculations (U.S. Office of Education, as cited in Smith & Luckasson, 1995). These disorders affect students' ability to either interpret what they see and hear, or link information from different parts of the brain (National Institute of Mental Health [NIMH], 2002). Others have defined LD as a discrepancy between academic achievement and the capacity to learn (Brody & Mills, 1997; Marsh & Wolfe, 1999). One or more standard deviations below the mean on achievement tests can indicate a learning disability (Mendaglio, 1993). Students with learning disabilities may fall into one of three intellectual ability categories: gifted, average, or severe with cognitive deficits (Skinner & Schenck, 1992).

LD can manifest itself in several ways, such as specific difficulties with spoken and written language, coordination, self-control, or attention (NIMH, 2002). Students with LD may experience problems with learning tasks, memory, and paired-associate learning (Bender, 2001). Many researchers indicate that these impairments are due to central nervous system dysfunction causing the brain and the perceptual systems of the brain to work differently from the way they function in students without LD (Kirk et al, 2000; Obrzut & Hynd, 1983; Rourke, 1994). Nutritional factors, such as food allergies, have been suggested as another possible cause for LD, and recent evidence has linked prevalence of LD with heredity (Thompson & Rudolph, 2000).

It is estimated that 15% of the U.S. population (Cramer & Ellis, 1996) and between 51 – 54% of the children receiving special education services have a specific learning disability (Kirk et al., 2000; Thompson & Rudolph, 2000). The U. S. Department of Education (1996) reported that approximately 39% of these children are served in regular classrooms, 60% in special classes or resource rooms, and a small number (1%) in separate facilities. These students experience academic difficulties, often fall behind, and are at more risk of failure and dropping out of school than peers (Lombana, 1992). All students with LD can benefit from the specialized services provided by professional school counselors.

## Characteristics and Identification of Students with LD

Characteristics of students with LD will differ among individuals who may exhibit deficits in the cognitive, motor, or social domains (Cartwright, Cartwright, & Ward, 1995). Those with cognitive difficulties will experience problems in reading, arithmetic, or thinking; some have problems with gross or perceptual-motor skills; still others may have social deficiencies. Reading deficiencies are the most common among students with LD, and the term *dyslexia* has become synonymous with a reading disability. Many students with LD may also have poor spelling and handwriting, and difficulty with grammar and punctuation. A student with language deficits may experience problems understanding what is said and in expressing himself/herself verbally.

Most students with LD are achieving academically below the expected level in one or more academic areas in spite of IQs in the normal or higher range of intelligence (Thompson & Rudolph, 2000). Other characteristics of these students can include disorganization, inattentiveness, inability to stay on task for prolonged periods, lack of motivation, and poor problem-solving skills (Smith & Luckasson, 1995). Some children may also experience hyperactivity and impulsivity and are distracted easily (Ariel, 1992). Toro, Weissberg, Guare, and Liebenstein (1990) found that students with LD were not able to generate as many alternative solutions to problem-solving situations when compared to students without LD. The students with LD also tended to be more disruptive in class, had more classroom behavior problems, and showed less tolerance for frustration. In addition, they were more prone than their non-LD peers to have family-related problems such as financial difficulties and lack of educational stimulation.

Studies have shown that LD students have lower academic self-concepts than their normal achieving peers (Hagborg, 1996), and exhibit deficits in social problem solving skills when compared to non-LD students (Thompson & Rudolph, 2000; Toro et al., 1990). They often experience difficulty making and keeping friends and may demonstrate inappropriate social behavior (Cartwright et al., 1995; Thompson & Rudolph, 2000). One study that asked individuals with LD to rank order areas in which they felt deficient showed that they listed social relationships and skills, developing self-esteem and confidence, and overcoming dependence as the top three areas (Chelser, 1982, cited in Skinner & Schenck, 1992).

The federal government outlines specific procedures for identifying students with LD and a process that must be followed in evaluating these students under the Education for All Handicapped Children Act of 1975 (PL 94-142) and the Individuals with Disabilities Education Act (IDEA) of 1997 (PL 105-107) (Cartwright et al., 1995; Kirk et al., 2000). Failure to follow this process can result in civil court actions, state and federal sanctions, and loss of funding for the school district. A multidisciplinary team (e.g., teachers, school psychologist, social worker, professional school counselor, behavioral specialist) must conduct the evaluation, and the child's parents must be involved. Professional school counselors often participate in the multi-disciplinary team (Parette & Holder-Brown, 1992). Assessment instruments must be administered in the child's native language and more than one criterion (e.g., verbal or written expression, listening comprehension, reading, mathematics reasoning and calculations) must be evident for the diagnosis. The learning disability cannot be due to another disabling impairment (e.g., visual, hearing, mental retardation, emotional disturbance), or to environmental, cultural, or economic disadvantages (Thompson & Rudolph, 2000).

An Individualized Education Program (IEP) is developed based on the unique needs of the student (Ariel, 1992). The IEP specifies the educational and related services (e.g., counseling) that will be provided and acts as a monitoring device to assure the student is in fact receiving them as agreed by the parents and school personnel. The IEP must include (a) an assessment (e.g., medical, personal-social, behavioral functioning, current educational performance, academic achievement, cognitive and motor functioning), (b) goals and short and long-term objectives; (c) educational services to be provided, name of individuals who will provide such services, and specific timelines, and (d) annual evaluation procedures.

## Personal, Social, and Educational Needs

Students with LD experience frustration in completing day-to-day tasks and assignments. They may display fear of failure, fear of learning, and approach tasks with reticence. One may often hear them say, "I can't do this," "I don't know how," or "I'll never learn this." In addition, these students may demonstrate low frustration tolerance and be prone to exhibit temper tantrums and disruptive behavior when confronted with learning situations (Ariel, 1992). Feelings of failure, worthlessness, and low self-esteem can further compound learning problems; therefore, students with LD often need individualized counseling to help them cope with their feelings and adjust to their disability (Thompson & Rudolph, 2000; Vernon, 1993). They will need encouragement and support from parents, teachers, professional school counselors, and other significant adults in their lives. They will also need to develop academic strategies that will help them cope with the specific deficiencies imposed by the LD.

Students who have difficulty forming interpersonal relationships, or who may act socially inappropriately, will benefit from group counseling and social skills training. Those with behavior problems can be helped with behavior modification and contingency contracting strategies implemented by the counselor as well as teachers in the classroom. High school age students will need help in developing career goals and plans (Skinner & Schenck, 1992). Students with LD also need professional school counselors to act as advocates for them to assure they receive the services identified in the IEP.

## Counseling Strategies

The use of brief solution-focused counseling has been recommended and proven effective for use with middle and high school students with LD (Amatea, 1989; Littrell, Malia, & Vanderwood, 1995). This approach can be implemented in both individual and group counseling interventions. Thompson and Littrell (1998) used a four-step, brief counseling model with a small sample of high school students with LD who were experiencing personal problems. The four steps included (1) identifying and defining the problem, (2) discussing previous attempted solutions and outcomes, (3) using the Miracle Question (i.e., "Suppose that one night, while you were asleep, there was a miracle and this problem was solved. How would you know? What would be different? How will parents, friends, and teachers know without your saying a word about it?"; de Shazer, 1988, p. 4), and (4) having students generate a task or activity to accomplish their desired goal(s). The researchers reported that all students participating in the study made progress toward their goals, with all but one reaching their desired goals. Positive changes in cognition and affect were also reported.

Play techniques, art, music, and expressive writings can be used with elementary school students in individual counseling to elicit and express feelings toward the disability, school-related experiences, peer conflicts, and family difficulties (Lockhart, 2003; Newsome, 2003). These interventions provide a non-threatening and creative outlet for students that can be adapted to their developmental levels, needs, and unique concerns (Newsome, 2003). Journal writing and timed writing exercises can encourage self-exploration and reflection (Bradley & Gould, 1999; Gladding, 1998).

Some contend that group activities may be more effective than individual counseling in helping students with LD address social, personal, and self-esteem problems because of the nature of the interaction with others (Elbaum & Vaughn, 2001; Lombana, 1992). For example, group counseling has been proven to be successful with students with LD to increase self-esteem, increase social skills and competence, and improve behavior (Omizo & Omizo, 1988). Small group activities that include the use of role play and puppets with elementary age LD children have improved school attendance and reduced suspensions (Schmidt & Biles, 1985). Educational groups at all grade levels can help students with LD identify and use learning strategies and techniques to help them compensate for academic deficiencies (Baum, 1990). Some of these strategies include checking for spelling errors before submitting assignments, using a calculator to assure accuracy, writing down all homework assignments, and finding alternative ways of learning (e.g, films, visitations, hands-on activities, use of technology). Bibliotherapy and audiovisual resources with elementary age children with LD can also be used to demonstrate appropriate behavior in certain situations (Vernon, 1993). Students who have difficulty remembering can be taught mnemonic strategies (memory devices and strategies); those created by students themselves are most effective (Hunt Reigel, Mayle, & McCarthy-Henkel, 1988). Academic interventions with an emphasis on peer collaborative work and feedback have proven successful with middle school students in enhancing academic abilities and self-esteem (Elbaum & Vaughn, 2001).

*Cognitive-Behavioral Approaches*

Cognitive-behavioral counseling techniques can be applied in individual and group counseling to teach skills and coping strategies. These techniques can be especially useful for students with LD who demonstrate inattentiveness, impulsivity, and hyperactivity (Williams & Mennuti, 1997); however, it can also be used with students who exhibit fear of learning and low self-concept. Designed for older elementary and adolescent students, cognitive-behavioral approaches can be most effective when combined with concurrent consultation and training for parents and teachers. The professional school counselor links the school and home components thus providing an integrative, multi-modal, holistic, collaborative approach to address the student's needs. Group sessions and parent and teacher training can occur simultaneously, and the professional school counselor may want to provide these opportunities. The objectives of this approach should include (a) increasing knowledge of, and adjustment to, LD, (b) teaching the cognitive-behavioral approach so faulty beliefs and distorted thoughts can be disputed and new thoughts, feelings, and behavior can be generated, (c) changing self-defeating, self-deprecating, absolutist language, and (d) changing behaviors and feelings associated with negative thinking patterns. Behavioral self-management should be included along with contingency contracting and weekly cognitive/behavioral homework assignments to monitor students' motivation throughout the intervention process (Corey, 2001; Williams & Mennuti, 1997).

Omizo and Omizo (1987) successfully used a group counseling approach with students to eliminate self-defeating behavior and increase self-esteem and internal locus of control of middle school students with LD. The intervention consisted of seven one-and-one-half hour weekly sessions that focused on helping students identify self-defeating behaviors, the feelings and consequences associated with these behaviors, and the choices needed to eliminate them. A visual imagery activity was used in which group members visualized barriers preventing them from eliminating self-defeating behaviors and ways of surmounting these barriers.

*Stress Reduction, Imagery, and Relaxation Training*

In the same way Omizo and Omizo (1987) incorporated guided visual imagery into their group counseling intervention, professional school counselors can use visual imagery, relaxation, and stress reduction techniques in individual and group counseling sessions (Romas & Sharma, 2000; Vernon, 1993). Visual imagery is a powerful technique that can be used to help students visualize beforehand situations that may be potentially threatening or stressful (e.g., speaking in front of the class, taking an exam, asking a peer to a social event). Regular practice of visual imagery has been shown to improve competitive performance (Romas & Sharma, 2000). Autosuggestion or talking with oneself can also help these students build self-confidence and self-esteem (Romas & Sharma, 2000). Students can couple self-talk with other relaxation methods such as progressive muscle relaxation or meditation. Some examples of self-talk are, "I can behave calmly in stressful situations," "I can perform to the best of my abilities," and "I am a happy and competent person." Students can make up their own self-affirmations and repeat them periodically throughout the day.

*Career Counseling*

In comparison to their non-LD peers, students with LD tend to lack skills in identifying and attaining career choices and have been described as being less mature in work-related attitudes (Biller, 1985; Rojewski, 1993). Consequently, providing career counseling services to adolescents with LD is critical. An important factor for professional school counselors to understand when providing career services is the effect of the disability on specific job requirements of chosen careers; these need to be presented realistically to students (Lockhart, 2003). Referral to a rehabilitation services agency may be appropriate to help students with LD develop transition plans and obtain training or employment upon graduation from high school. IDEA requires that the multidisciplinary team prepare a transition plan for students with disabilities when he or she reaches 14 years of age.

College-bound students will need help identifying post-secondary institutions that fit and can accommodate their special needs. Consequently, professional school counselors should familiarize themselves with admissions policies, support services, and academic requirements of institutions in the surrounding area (Skinner & Schenck, 1992). College admissions' recruiters can be contacted to set up school-based appointments to speak individually to students with LD about programs available for them such as tutors, academic support, readers, books-on-tape, psycho-educational assessment, disability services, and counseling. Students with LD should be advised that special testing accommodations can be made to take admissions examinations (i.e., ACT and SAT) through the American College Testing (ACT) and Educational Testing Services.

Computer assisted career guidance systems such as DISCOVER (American College Testing Program, 1984) and the System of Interactive Guidance and Information (SIGI and SIGI Plus) (Katz, 1975) and Internet resources can help high school students become more involved in the career awareness and exploration process (Zunker, 2002). Students can work individually on computers and receive immediate feedback. Access to large databases at the local, state, and national levels can provide students with college admissions, financial aid, vocational-technical training, internships, and scholarship information. Professional school counselors can help students interpret and discuss the results of their searches along with helping them with résumé preparation, employment interviewing, conducting job searches, and learning other career related skills by using computer-assisted guidance programs and the Internet. Counselors may want to purchase the book entitled, *The Internet: A Tool for Career Planning* (Harris-Bowlsbey, Dikel, & Sampson, 1998) published by the National Career Development Association, by calling (888) 326-1750.

*Peer Facilitation Programs*

Peer helpers can be used to work with students with LD to help them adjust to school situations, to provide tutoring, and to act as special friends (Myrick, 1997; Vernon, 1993). Professional school counselors can pair trained peer helpers based on special needs and interests of students with LD. These helpers act as role models, can help to diffuse or mediate conflict, and provide advice and guidance in helping students with LD to navigate successfully in the school environment. The professional school counselor can monitor interactions and provide supervisory feedback during peer helper classes and meetings.

## Teacher and Parent Consultation

Some have suggested that teachers and parents tend to have more negative feelings about students with LD than they do of other children (Rothman & Cosden, 1995). Further, some teachers feel under-prepared to work with students with disabilities in their classrooms (Smith & Luckasson, 1995). They report needing assistance with teaching and classroom management strategies. Professional school counselors can consult with teachers individually or in groups to assist in building skills and developing effective academic interventions. Professional school counselors can help teachers learn more about the effect of LD on students' learning and classroom behavior by conducting workshops and in-service training during faculty meetings. Some classroom strategies that have worked with students with LD include:

- assigning work in smaller amounts (e.g., 8 math problems instead of 20)
- providing demonstrations of expected tasks and giving explanations in brief, clear steps
- organizing materials in color-coded folders
- moving around the room more often to check on students' progress
- having students write instructions down and using felt tip pens to highlight information
- repeating important points
- tape recording directions
- using written checklists
- using individualized cues and prompts
- presenting material in a variety of ways (visually, orally, kinesthetically)
- rewarding students for demonstrating appropriate behaviors (Hunt Riegel et al., 1988).

Similarly, groups can be conducted for parents to help them strategize ways they can help their students be successful. One study showed that students of parents who participated in a nine-week parent effectiveness workshop improved their self-concept in comparison to students whose parents did not participate (Elbarum & Vaughn, 1999). In addition to parent effectiveness workshops, professional school counselors can also help parents by teaching them (a) behavior management techniques; (b) how to help their children with school assignments; (c) how to structure the home and study environment; and (d) how to communicate more effectively with their children and teachers (Lombana, 1992). Many parents will need help in understanding their children's behavioral reactions to their disability and the challenges it presents for them.

Support groups can be developed to help parents share successful strategies and to increase awareness that others share similar frustrations and challenges (Lombana, 1992; Thompson & Rudolph, 2000).

## Advocacy and Collaboration

Advocacy begins by helping to ensure that students with LD are appropriately identified so that educational and counseling services can be provided to facilitate school success. Professional school counselors can facilitate the identification process by educating teachers, parents, and other school staff on the characteristics and needs of these students. Advocacy entails continuous, collaborative consultation with multi-disciplinary team members to effectively pool resources, identify and resolve problems, and share decision-making and responsibilities for the implementation of educational strategies (VanTassel-Baska, 1991). It is also critical that professional school counselors serve as members of their school improvement and strategic planning committees as other avenues for advocacy.

Professional school counselors can help parents become effective advocates for their children by helping them to learn as much as possible about LD, the needs of their children, public policy and laws related to LD, and special educational programs (Maker & Udall, 1985). Parents will need assistance in navigating through the educational system as they attempt to help their children and participate in the IEP process (Lockhart, 2003). Professional school counselors must become knowledgeable of community resources and appropriate specialists that can help students with LD and their families outside the school setting (Lockhart, 2003). In addition, professional school counselors need to demonstrate sensitivity and understanding with parents from different cultures who may not be fluent in English or knowledgeable about the expectations of the school or of their child's disability (Lockhart, 2003). Finally, students with LD need to be taught to be their own advocates. Self-advocacy skills can help these students become more involved in decision-making that affects their academic and career goals. Advocacy skills can be taught and practiced by students in small group and large group guidance interventions (Bailey, Getch, & Chen-Hayes, 2003).

## Summary/Conclusion

Learning disabilities affect the understanding or use of language and can manifest in various ways, differently in each student. These may include cognitive deficiencies in writing, spelling, reading, arithmetic, and thinking; gross or perceptual-motor skills may also be affected. Problems with hyperactivity, impulsivity, distractibility, problem-solving, and social skills may be evident. Students coping with LD may experience low self-esteem, feelings of failure, frustration, and difficulty making and keeping friends.

Counseling strategies implemented through individual and group counseling can help students with LD at all levels to develop effective problem-solving, social, and academic skills that will help them be successful in school. Some of these include brief-solution focused counseling, play techniques, expressive arts and writings, role-play, puppets (elementary age), bibliotherapy, cognitive-behavioral techniques, stress reduction, relaxation, guided visual imagery, and career exploration. To help these students compensate for academic difficulties, educational focused groups can be conducted to teach them specific techniques such as mnemonic strategies, organizing school materials, using calculators and computers to check for math and spelling errors, and the use of audiovisual and other instructional aids.

The federal government has delineated specific procedures in the Education for All Handicapped Children Act (PL 94-142) and IDEA (PL 105-107) that involve a multidisplinary approach to identify and place students with LD in appropriate learning environments. An individual educational plan is developed for each student that outlines the educational, social, and counseling services that will be provided.

Professional school counselors can also conduct workshops with teachers and parents to assist them in dealing more effectively with the needs of these students in the classroom and at home. Support groups can help parents connect with others who share similar concerns. Advocacy and collaboration with school staff and community personnel is critical to ensure the needs and rights of students with LD are being met. Teaching students with LD self-advocacy skills can also help them become more self-sufficient in making academic and career choices.

## References

Amatea, E. S. (1989). *Brief strategic intervention for school problems.* San Francisco: Jossey-Bass.

American College Testing Program. (1984). *DISCOVER: A computer-based career development and counselor support system.* Iowa City, IA: Author.

Ariel, A. (1992). *Education of children and adolescents with learning disabilities.* New York: Macmillan.

Bailey, D. F., Getch, Y. G., & Chen-Hayes, S. (2003). Professional school counselors as social and academic advocates. In B. T. Erford (Ed.), *Transforming the school counseling profession* (pp. 411-433). Columbus, OH: Merrill/ Prentice-Hall.

Baum, S. (1990). The gifted/learning disabled: A paradox for teachers. *Education Digest, 8,* 54-57.

Bender, W. N. (2001). *Learning disabilities: Characteristics, identification and teaching strategies.* Needham Heights, MA: Allyn & Bacon.

Biller, E. F. (1988). Career decision-making attitudes of college students with learning disabilities. *Journal of Postsecondary Education and Disability, 6,*14-20.

Bradley, L. J., & Gould, L. J. (1999). Individual counseling: Creative interventions. In A. Vernon (Ed.), *Counseling children and adolescents* (2nd ed.)(pp. 65-95). Denver, CO: Love.

Brody, L. E., & Mills, C. J. (1997). Gifted children with learning disabilities: A review of the issues. *Journal of Learning Disabilities, 30,* 282-296.

Cartwright, G. P., Cartwright, C. A., & Ward, M. E. (1995). *Educating special learners.* Belmont, CA: Wadsworth.

Coplin, J. W., & Morgan, S. B. (1988). Learning disabilities: A multidimensional perspective. *Journal of Learning Disabilities, 21,* 614-642.

Corey, G. (2001). *Theory and practice of counseling and psychotherapy* (6th ed.). Belmont, CA: Brooks/Cole.

Cramer, S., & Ellis, W. (1996). *Learning disabilities.*Baltimore: Paul H. Brooks.

de Shazer, S. (1988). *Clues: Investigating solutions in brief therapy.* New York: Norton.

Elbaum, B., & Vaughn, S. (2001). School-based interventions to enhance the self-concept of students with learning disabilities? A meta-analysis. *Elementary School Journal, 101,* 303-329.

Gladding, S. T. (1998). *Counseling as an art: The creative arts in counseling* (2nd ed.). Alexandria, VA: American Counseling Association.

Hagborg, W. J. (1996). Self-concept and middle school students with learning disabilities: A comparison of scholastic competence subgroups. *Learning Disability Quarterly, 19,* 117-126.

Harris-Bowlsbey, J., Dikel, M. R., & Sampson, J. P. (1998). *The Internet: A tool for career planning.* Columbus, OH: National Career Development Association.

Hunt Riegel, R., Mayle, J. A., & McCarthy-Henkel, J. (1988). *Beyond maladies and remedies: Suggestions and guidelines for adapting materials for students with special needs in the regular class.* Novi, MI: RHR Consultation Services.

Katz, M. R. (1975). *SIGI: A computer-based system of interactive guidance and information.* Princeton, NJ: Educational Testing Service.

Kirk, S. A., Gallagher, J. J., & Anastasiow, N. J. (2000). *Educating exceptional children* (9th ed.). Boston: Houghton Mifflin.

Littrell, J. M., Malia, J. A., & Vanderwood, M. (1995). Single-session brief counseling in a high school. *Journal of Counseling and Development, 73,* 451-458.

Lockhart, E. (2003). Students with disabilities. In B. T. Erford (Ed.), *Transforming the school counseling profession* (pp. 357-409). Columbus, OH: Merrill/ Prentice-Hall.

Lombana, J. H. (1992). Learning disabled students and their families: Implications and strategies for counselors. *Journal of Humanistic Education and Development, 31,* 33-40.

Maker, J., & Udall, A. J. (1985). *Giftedness and learning disabilities.* Retrieved January 9, 2001 from the World Wide Web: http: //ericec.org/digests/c427.htm/

Marsh, E. J., & Wolfe, D. (1999). *Abnormal child psychology.* Belmont, CA: Wadsworth.

Mendaglio, S. (1993). Counseling gifted learning disabled individuals and group counseling techniques. In L. K. Silverman (Ed.), *Counseling the gifted and talented* (pp. 131-149). Denver, CO: Love.

Myrick, R. D. (1997). *Developmental guidance and counseling: A practical approach* (3rd ed.). Minneapolis, MN: Educational Media Corporation.

National Institute of Mental Health. (2002). [On-Line]. Available: http://www.nimh.nih.gov/ publicat/learndis. htm#learn3

Newsome, D. W. (2003). Counseling interventions using expressive arts. In B. T. Erford (Ed.), *Transforming the school counseling profession* (pp. 231-247). Columbus, OH: Merrill/ Prentice-Hall.

Obrzut, J. E., & Hynd, G. W. (1983). The neurobiological and neuropsychological foundations of learning disabilities. *Journal of Learning Disabilities, 16,* 515-519.

Omizo, M. M., & Omizo, S. A. (1987). The effects of eliminating self-defeating behavior of LD children through group counseling. *School Counselor, 34,* 282-288.

Omizo, M. M., & Omizo, S. A. (1988). Group counseling's effect on self-concept and social behaviors among children with learning disabilities. *Journal of Humanistic Education and Development, 25,* 109-117.

Parette, H., & Holder-Brown, L. (1992). The role of the school counselor in providing services to medically fragile children. *Elementary School Guidance and Counseling, 27,* 47-55.

Romas, J. A., & Sharma, M. (2000). *Practical stress management: A comprehensive workbook for managing change and promoting health* (2nd ed.). Needham Heights, MA: Allyn & Bacon.

Rothman, H. R., & Cosden, M. (1995). The relationship between self-perception of a learning disability and achievement, self-concept, and social support. *Learning Disability Quarterly, 18,* 203-212.

Rourke, B. P. (1994). Neuropsychological assessment of children with learning disabilities. In G. Lyon (Ed.), *Frames of reference for the assessment of learning disabilities* (pp. 475-514). Baltimore: Paul H. Brookes.

Schidmt, J. J., & Biles, J. W. (1985). Puppetry as a group counseling technique with middle school students. *Elementary School Guidance and Counseling, 20,* 67-73.

Skinner, M. E., & Schenck, S. J. (1992). Counseling the college-bound student with a learning disability. *The School Counselor, 39,* 369-378.

Smith, D., & Luckasson, R. (1995). *Introduction to special education: Teaching in an age of challenge.* Needham Heights, MA: Allyn & Bacon.

Rojewski, J. W. (1992). Key components of model transition services for students with learning disabilities. *Learning Disability Quarterly, 15,* 135-150.

Thompson, C. L., & Rudolph, L. B. (Eds.). (2000). *Counseling children* (5th ed.). Belmont, CA: Brooks/Cole.

Thompson, R., & Littrell, J. M. (1998). Brief counseling for students with learning disabilities. *Professional* School *Counseling, 2,* 60-67.

Toro, P. A., Wessberg, R. P., Guare, J., & Liebensteing, N. L. (1990). A comparison of children with and without learning disabilities on social problem-solving skill, school behavior, and family background. *Journal of Learning Disabilities, 23,* 115-120.

U.S. Department of Education. (1996). *Eighteenth annual report to Congress on the implementation of the Individuals with Disabilities Education Act.* Washington, DC: Author

VanTassel-Baska, J. (1991). Serving the disabled gifted through educational collaboration. *Journal for the Education of the Gifted, 14,* 246-266.

Vernon, A. (1993). *Counseling children and adolescents.* Denver, CO: Love.

Williams, B. B., & Mennuti, R. B. (1997). Cognitive-behavioral group therapy for children with Attention-Deficit/ Hyperactivity Disorder, their parents, and teachers. In D. L. Smallwood (Ed.), *Attention disorder in children: Resources for school psychologists* (pp. 181-188). Bethesda, MD: National Association of School Psychologists.

Zunker, V. G. (2002). *Career counseling: Applied concepts of life planning* (6th ed.). Pacific Grove, CA: Brooks/Cole.

# Chapter 65

## Developmental Solutions for Students with Severe Behavioral Problems

*Gregory R. Janson*

### Preview

Professional school counselors are often called on to provide support, crisis resolution, and treatment and prevention strategies for students with severe behavioral problems. Effective interventions that offer the most promising approach to helping students are systemic, with the professional school counselors serving as both counselor and facilitator, bringing together students, teachers, parents, administrators, and staff. In this chapter, strategies are presented for working with all these groups within the context of the extended community.

When the subject of classroom behavior arises, the comment most often heard is: "Times have changed." Teachers and administrators polled just fifty or sixty years ago reported their most significant behavioral challenges were gum chewing, cutting in line, running in hallways, talking out of turn or making noise, and violating the school's dress code. Just the kind of developmentally appropriate infractions one would expect of a student with an excess of energy, exuberance, and enthusiasm.

In the 1990s, a similar poll demonstrated that these minor offenses have been replaced by robbery, assault, drug abuse, pregnancy, and suicide (Toch, 1993). Sexually transmitted infections are rampant among adolescents and the age of experimentation with alcohol, drugs, smoking, and reckless behaviors has dropped into early adolescence and even middle childhood. This trend, combined with the increasing severity and frequency of crimes committed by and against young persons, has created a public health crisis (Schwartz & Perry, 1994).

Professional school counselors today are not only expected to help deal with classroom behaviors that are severely disruptive and potentially dangerous, but with equally severe, self-injurious behaviors, from cutting (self-mutilation) and eating disorders to suicide (Pipher, 1994). All of these actions represent severe behaviors whose symptoms play out in the classroom. Limiting our understanding of severe classroom behaviors to disruptive behaviors ignores damaging and dangerous behaviors that are expressed in different ways. Female students may be at greatest risk since they have been traditionally less prone to violent acting-out than males. Their sadness and anger may be inwardly directed, making them less likely to receive aid and support. A newly emerging concern is the growing degree of physical violence among female students, which tends to be discounted and ignored.

Mounting school violence, as seen in school shootings such as in Littleton, CO, and Conyers, GA, have led to "frenzied debates" on student behavior, causes of school violence, and how to prevent future occurrences. Good intentions and a desire to ensure safety have led to creating disciplinary systems that are more punitive, harsher, and tougher, an approach that models power as the solution to interpersonal problems. Identity tags, metal detectors and security officers provide reassurance for some, but also serve as visible reminders that danger may be just out of that officer's line of sight. Over-reliance on rules and authority, like over-reliance on punishment, tends to raise the stakes, creating greater isolation, less effective communication, and an increase in negative symptoms both in communities and in families (Miller & Prinz, 1990). Worse, this approach may create a siege mentality and rigidity of response that impede progress and reform (Gutscher, 1993). Rules may reassure adults, but they do not make the dangerous realities of school hallways any safer or the prospect of attending school any more palatable.

## School and Community Climate

School climate often reflects community climate (Menacker, Weldon, & Hurwitz, 1990). Levels of violence have risen at frightening rates in American schools (Boothe, Bradley, Flick, Keough, & Kirk, 1993; Evans & Evans, 1985; Ordovensky, 1993; Singer, Anglin, Song, & Lunghofer, 1994) reflecting the reality that violence has become a chronic stressor in urban America (Osofsky, Wewers, Hann, & Fick, 1993). A reciprocal cycle has emerged in which acts of school violence create fear and uncertainty in students, teachers, parents, and administrators, and national traumas, such as the destruction of the World Trade Towers in September of 2001, in turn, make even the safest schools feel unsafe. Times have changed.

As Columbine demonstrated, living in a less urban setting is no protection against the increasing level, intensity, and frequency of violent acts. In a large suburban Ohio high school 75% of the students saw other students threatened or assaulted (punched or slapped) during the school year (Singer et al., 1994). Students commented:

> In today's world, you don't know how long you will survive. It stays on your mind when you go out. You don't know who will hurt you . . . it's no fair to feel unsafe . . . I hold in so much rage that if it ever came down to it, I could kill someone with no remorse. (p. iii)

Even students living in small communities, where there is a presumption of cohesion and safety, are not immune to victimization. Three out of four students from small-town schools reported being bullied (Hazler, Hoover, & Oliver, 1991), and 90% of these students also stated that they experienced problems as a result (Hazler, Hoover, & Oliver, 1992). Other research has suggested that bystanders—students who observe these events without participating—suffer psychological and physiological risks that are serious, and similar to those experienced by direct victims (Hazler, 1996b; Janson, 2000).

Living on edge, in environments that feel dangerous, even if they may not be life-threatening, makes students physically and psychologically reactive. These students reported a full range of short-term trauma symptoms and shared beliefs that included the inescapability of violence, hopelessness about the future, fear of dying, and concern with shootings, gangs, drugs, sexual abuse, and racism. In this climate, it may be difficult to discriminate between severe behavior problems and behaviors associated with stress reactions. Some students become the "identified patient," while the factors that create or contribute to maintaining and exacerbating the behaviors are environmental, familial, or contextual. Even when this is not the case, there is a tendency to pathologize the difficult student, and to view medication, punishment, suspension, and expulsion as the most effective responses. In this context, professional school counselors are expected to do more, with fewer resources.

Professional school counselors do not have the resources to deal with all these challenges, but they are the professionals in the system with the skills, training, and potential mandate to affect change on a broad, systemic basis. The best place to start is by developing a sense of self-awareness gained through an assessment of your school's climate.

## Conducting a School Climate Assessment

The first step toward dealing with severe or disruptive behavior problems is to consider your school and the community context in which it is set. Is the neighborhood safe? Is the community safe? Is your school a safe place where students can learn without looking over their shoulder or worrying about being bullied in the restrooms or playing field? Are there places within your school students avoid out of fear? Some studies have reported that one out of five high school students will not use the restrooms in their school out of fear for their own safety (Learning Publications Inc., 1988). Most important, do students feel as though they are coming to a safe environment every morning? Do they feel like stakeholders or prisoners? What looks like anger or depression in a classroom might well be an appropriate reaction to the stress of living in a potentially dangerous environment.

Twenty years ago, the president of Yale University described American schools as being in danger of becoming "warehouses for the angry," places more like prisons where students felt disconnected, bored, and unsafe. One survey conducted in the Houston school system found only 29% of 63,997 students surveyed reported that they enjoyed school (Rogers & Freiburg, 1994). Students felt that they were acquiring useless facts, while being treated as though their feelings, opinions, and ideas were of no value. Ask these questions: Do students like coming to school? Are they enthusiastic about learning? Are students passive or active? Do they seem bored and disinterested? Involved or discounted? Is there a balanced emphasis on grades and individual growth? Or is weight given to acquiring facts to meet the demands of proficiency testing rather than acquiring the skills and enthusiasm needed to self-direct lifelong learning, a virtual necessity in the future?

Do administrators feel helpless? Do teachers describe themselves as isolated and unsupported? When parents call school, is it to express anger and frustration? Do they feel as though the experts do not know what to do? A professional school counselor attuned to the heartbeat of the school may already know the answers to these questions. Even so, it may be necessary to create and conduct surveys, focus groups, or questionnaires to raise the awareness of other groups in the system.

Connection and systemic interventions that are inclusive of all of the groups in the community is the antidote to disconnection, isolation, and disaffection. For change to occur each group must have a part in deciding what kind of school and community they want. A systemic approach may be slow and often frustrating to implement, considering the logistics involved, but the changes accomplished will be more permanent and accepted by more people than changes established by fiat.

## What Is Severe Behavior?

A school climate assessment helps to put student behaviors in context and discriminate between acceptable reactions to difficult circumstances and more individual pathology. On a secondary level, severe behavior can be distinguished from irritating, frustrating, exasperating behavior, which may be developmentally appropriate and predictable, by its frequency, intensity, and duration. There is a pattern that develops with severe behavioral problems that goes beyond one or two incidents, and spans multiple environments.

Severe behavior problems are seldom limited to classrooms, affecting students at home and in social settings, and may be expressed in maladaptive ways during the after-school hours when students are most likely to be unsupervised by parents. Problems can include substance abuse, expressions of anger through vandalism or violence, depression, anxiety, suicidality, sexual activity, an unexpected pregnancy, or self-injurious behaviors such as cutting oneself (Pipher,

1994). Helping students with severe behavioral problems goes far beyond teaching anger management techniques, though that may be a necessary first step.

*The Continuum of Anger Disorders and Disruptive Behaviors.*

Clinically, disorders that are characterized by disruptive, aggressive, oppositional and defiant behaviors can be thought of as existing on a continuum. At the lower, less severe end is behavior that is more oppositional and defiant: spite, temper tantrums, defiance, irritability, and an uncanny knack for annoying others. The next level is more serious and may involve fighting, bringing a weapon to school, habitual lying, cheating, and bullying. In this middle level, if there is sufficient anger present, it may be directed at animals or be seen in vandalism and firesetting. The third level is characterized by severe physical assaults, running away, stealing and habitual truancy.

Often, these symptoms follow a history of trauma, abuse, and neglect. In the absence of these disruptive, aggressive symptoms, there may be symptoms of anxiety, dissociation, or depression related to disorders of attachment (James, 1989; 1994; Stosny, 1995). It can be challenging to discriminate developmental from pathological issues when trauma is involved.

Defining severe behavior is also dependent on whose definition is being used. Smoking marijuana on school grounds and threatening another student with a knife both earn suspension or expulsion, but they are radically different acts. Dying one's hair black is not the same as bringing a gun to school. Fidgeting and a refusal to follow instructions due to the anxiety of being homeless or because of familial stress may lead to the same behaviors in class as a student suffering from Attention Deficit/Hyperactivity Disorder, but the interventions will need to be radically different. Careful assessment is needed to place these behaviors in context and view them with a perspective that focuses consequences that contribute to the student's growth and learning, rather than punishment.

*Assessing Behaviors*

Assessment must be broad-based, longitudinal, and consider all the systems in which the student functions. Developmental issues, trauma, and family stressors often cloud the process of assessment. Know what you are really looking at. The same stressor could cause one student to lash out verbally at a teacher, and another to withdraw into isolation.

Imagine that a student has been referred to you during his first month in school. He has been biting and punching his classmates without provocation. His mother reports that he displays violent and aggressive behavior at home. However, his grandmother says, "Well, when he's here, he's such a good boy. He always does what I ask him." One might have good cause to wonder what is happening in the student's home. Is there a divorce or separation in his family? A new partner living in? A birth? Is there an underlying learning disability that is obscured by the behavior? Can the student see and hear? Read? Understand? Does the student possess adequate language skills? Social skills?

Good assessment is an ongoing process that involves regular consultation with teachers, who are often in the best position to identify students whose behavior or pattern of behaviors have changed. School records are easily accessible and worth reviewing; however, could a teacher from a previous grade shed light on a student's behavior? Ask the student's parents to come in for a talk, not just when there is a crisis. Search out all possible problems so you can formulate a treatment plan that addresses each challenge and identifies necessary referrals.

*Medications.* Adjusting to medications and coping with side effects may be a major concern in working with students at every age and grade level. Medications may cause students to fall asleep during class, suffer from reduced impulse-control, or constantly feel irritated and angry.

Prescription drugs used to treat asthma, allergies, epilepsy, depression, anxiety and other disorders of childhood and adolescence typically have side effects that include dry mouth, gastric complaints, headaches, stomachaches, bowel complaints, dizziness, sedation, irritability, and confusion (Willens, Spencer, Frazier, & Biederman, 1998). Something as simple as sucking on a sugar-free lozenge can go a long way towards alleviating the discomfort of a student with dry mouth from a medication.

Does a student need medication? If a student displays psychological and/or physical symptoms associated with enuresis or encopresis, is there adequate information available to the family on how to treat these common developmental disorders? Access to a physician? Funds for medication? If a student is suffering from severe acne, does the family have access to the resources needed to obtain needed medication? The other side of the medication issue is what to look for if a student stops taking medication that has been prescribed. Could that be a contributing factor to current behavioral problems?

*Culture and language.* When families immigrate to the United States, students who are taught English are seldom taught feeling words. This makes it possible for a teacher to misinterpret a student's reaction as angry when the real emotion is frustration. Students who learn English faster than their parents may become mediators between the family and the outside world, a position of power and control that may create problems in relating to adults and authority figures at school. Part of an intervention might involve helping a student's parents access the resources to master a new language, which can do a great deal to reduce stress at home and stabilize the family.

## Counseling Interventions

An effective systemic approach requires building relationships with everyone in the system —students, parents, teachers, staff, and administrators—and facilitating relationship-building between these groups. This is a challenging task under the best of circumstances and not always compatible with the minutiae of your everyday professional responsibilities. It means leaving your office for the uncertainty of the hallways, cafeteria, and other areas of the school where you can interact with people in genuine, personal ways that build interpersonal relationships outside the confines of "the school counselor's office," where relationships are more formally and strictly defined (Hazler, 1998).

Counseling techniques for building relationships can be taught to anyone willing to learn, and can be highly effective when used by teachers. There is a personal incentive involved, as well. Many teachers who learn and use these skills in the classrooms and hallways report their own relationships, self-confidence, and self-image have improved (Kottler & Kottler, 2000). That is a significant payoff!

Hazler (1998) has provided a model filled with practical suggestions for enhancing relationships using spontaneous interactions and chance encounters in hallways, cafeterias, the playground, playing fields and other areas outside the classroom or office. Administrators who know students by name, teachers who blend feelings and ideas in their teaching (Rogers, 1974), school staff who like and respond to students, and parents who participate in the life of the school, not just when there is a crisis, are elements that make schools strong, democratic institutions that are exciting to attend. Though the following interventions are addressed to discrete groups within the system, the guidelines for professional school counselors apply equally well to teachers or administrators.

### *Counseling Interventions with Students: They Notice, You Notice*

*Accentuate the positive and personal.* Notice positive points about students with behavior problems and comment on them! Can't find a positive point? Search until you do. Students may not respond to you and may seem irritatingly indifferent, but they will notice you noticed!

Keep tabs on students so you can identify positive behavioral changes, encourage them, and communicate these successes to parents as well as students when confidentiality permits.

*Make your enthusiasm and optimism contagious.* Human beings are connected to each other to a far greater extent than most of us realize. People are affected daily by the behavior and emotions of others. Spending time with friends who are anxious and depressed can leave us feeling the same way. Being with people who are friendly, cooperative, and optimistic can often improve our own moods. A ready smile and unexpected word of encouragement make students feel acknowledged and valued.

*Be prepared to drive on one-way streets.* Professional school counselors are trained to give students unconditional positive regard, and to be genuine and empathetic. This is more difficult for other educational professionals. It might never occur to a teacher to say to a student referred for an outburst in class: "It must be tough to have people telling you what to do all the time." With some students, even the most skilled professional school counselors may be left with one-way relationships. Attachments take time to form, especially with isolated students who have few reasons to trust others.

*Have faith in students and communicate that faith.* No one can predict future behavior and to try to do so with a troubled student only reinforces a negative expectation that can become a self-fulfilling prophecy. You may or may not see positive results from your actions, but it is not unusual for many professional school counselors (and teachers) to hear from students long after they leave school. What they often hear is: "You were the only person who believed in me...," not "You really knew a lot about physics." Faith and encouragement counter discouragement and disaffection; at least one affirmative, predicable relationship with an adult is necessary for positive growth and development (Hamburg, 1986).

*Use what students are interested in to build relationships.* What do they care about? Are they wearing a university sweatshirt or team colors? Are they wearing a shirt with the logo of a band that you or your own children may like? Find small starting places to build relationships.

*Risk sharing yourself and who you are.* This makes one real to young people who pay far more attention to how an adult acts rather than what an adult says. Professional school counselors receive extensive training in self-disclosure and are able to practice these skills under supervision, but teachers, staff, and administrators may feel awkward, uncomfortable or vulnerable making self-disclosures. Help others gain a degree of comfort and practice talking about themselves with difficult students. Good topics include revealing what they like, what they succeeded at, what they are not good at. What teams do they root for? What foods do they like? How about music, bands, cars, movies? These tidbits need not be major disclosures, but each interaction forms another strand of potential relationship, another possible connection that starts the process of reducing a student's isolation and loneliness.

*Accept discomfort, frustration, anger, and even fear as appropriate reactions for you to feel.* Students with behavioral problems can be frustrating, aggravating, difficult to work with, and hard to like. Daunting to engage, they can also be intimidating, menacing or scary to peers and teachers alike. Accepting one's own discomfort and validating teachers' discomfort is a solid starting point. Many of these students are unaware of the impact they have on others, and when their behavior alienates others, it contributes to more isolation, anger, sadness, and withdrawal. Guilt and worry are common reactions: Have we done the right thing? Helped enough in ways that were helpful? Interactions with students who are depressed, despondent, or whom they suspect as having an eating disorder can leave professional school counselors feeling inadequate, unsure, and concerned about the possibility of self-injury or suicide.

*Provide encouragement and positive reinforcement.* Separate students from behaviors. Be the person who says: "I know that you have what you need to accomplish what you need to accomplish, and when you are ready, you will do it" or "I may not approve of the direction you are taking, but I will wait for you as long as it takes." There are a number of excellent resources that provide the specific language and techniques of encouragement you can share with teachers and administrators (Dreikurs, 1972, 1990; Sweeney, 1989).

*Be concrete.* Put things in writing and help teachers to understand how important predictability is to students who display severe behaviors. Make up calendars for these students with events and requirements clearly written out. Have students repeat back to you what you have said to them to make certain they understand. If you find yourself getting frustrated, stop and ask what the student is hearing. What they tell you may have little to do with what you were trying to say.

*Touch carefully, and then only in the context of affirmation.* Share your knowledge about appropriate touch. Be careful about touching students without having built a solid relationship first. An affirming pat on the back or light touch on the forearm may be rejected; grabbing a student's arm, as a teacher may do with a younger child or even with an adolescent, may earn them a punch. Students who have been traumatized, sexually, physically, and emotionally abused, or placed in foster care may react violently to physical contact. Within the context of their experiences, this reaction may be appropriate.

*Do not reinvent the wheel!* Make connections with professionals in the community to supplement your efforts. Bring in educators from local colleges or universities to talk about suicide, sexuality, and violence. Make use of undergraduates from academic programs in family studies, sociology, social work, and psychology who are looking for service learning opportunities. See if graduate programs may be willing to place practicum and internship students in the school. Use online resources, and share them directly with teachers.

*Make use of available resources.* Make certain students have full access to services they may be entitled to, including an appropriate educational plan and access to special services related to speech, language, and hearing. Have a list of qualified referral sources to use when needed.

*Hunger and homelessness.* These are chronic stressors for growing numbers of students and families. Concentrating in math class may be impossible when you are hungry. Accepting a verbal reprimand from a teacher without lashing out may be hard if you are homeless. Many school districts need to develop contingency plans to help manage the emotional trauma of being homeless while at the same time helping with shelter, food, clothing, and hygiene. Loss of school and attendance records is a major challenge for homeless families.

*Get parents, teachers, staff, and administrators on board.* This is where your interpersonal and relationship skills as a professional school counselor can pay the greatest dividends for the least investment of time. Behavioral change starts at home; let parents do their share, and show them how to get the job done. School principals know how much students appreciate positive recognition; even such a small thing as knowing a name tells a student "this person knows me and is interested in who I am." Help administrators be the ones who lead by example. Help teachers model the behaviors they want to see; the degree of kindness, concern, empathy, cooperation, and negotiation needed to reach most difficult children are learned skills. Help students focus on choices instead of confrontations. Students with severe behavioral problems may not see a future for themselves, and without a vision of a positive future, there is not much cause to listen to you or follow the rules. Help them create that vision.

*Special Emphasis: The Psychology of Anger and Stress Management Techniques*

Students who display aggressive and disruptive behaviors make it easy to forget that it takes two to fight; angry people need another person to fight with (Sweeney, 1989). When we get angry, we know there are physiological changes that occur in our bodies that fuel our anger, yet it is hard to meet another's anger with calmness when one's fight/flight reflexes kick in and one wants to stand up toe to toe with the other person. However, we also know that it is not possible to be relaxed and angry at the same time. Educating others about anger, anger management, and relaxation techniques is a vital role for professional school counselors (Kassinove, 1995).

*Attend to the physiological aspects of severe behavior, yours and theirs.* It is no simple matter to remain calm during another's emotional outburst. Defensiveness, fear, anger, and the activation of our fight/flight reflex can leave one breathing faster, dry-mouthed, and sweaty-palmed. One's stomach feels tied in knots, jaws clench hard enough to make the muscles bulge so that little veins that run up the forehead and suddenly stand out in stark relief. An angry reaction can be seen by everyone, and can raise the level of potential danger. Exercise self-awareness of your bodily reactions as you evaluate the potential threat. If you can sit, then sit. Sitting interrupts and decreases the force directed against you when the student suddenly has to look down at you instead of stepping up to you. Lower your voice so the other person must be silent to hear it. Breathe slowly, talk quietly and calmly, and offer choices. Acknowledge the student's emotion, communicate your understanding, and identify an acceptable alternative course of action (Landreth, 2002).

*Use relaxation and meditation to readjust emotional thermostats.* Students with behavioral problems have difficulties with impulse-control and regulating their "emotional thermostats." Teach them how to identify emotional triggers, develop an awareness of bodily responses, and learn techniques to help counter these reactions with deep breathing, disengagement, and progressive muscle relaxation. These are practical skills needed to prevent crises or reduce the frequency and intensity of crises.

All students can be taught progressive muscle relaxation, relaxation techniques, deep, cleansing breathing, and emotional self-regulation (Fink, 1979). Keep a comfortable chair in your office with a set of headphones and a quilt. Have older students put the headphones on and listen to an album like Enya's *Watermark* or any soothing music with a slow beat. Cover the student with the quilt, which provides warmth to counter the shocking effects of stress and gives a sense of comfort and security. Make your office a safe haven. You will find that for most students, just 10-15 minutes is all that is required for a crisis to pass and their bodies and minds to settle down.

*Special Emphasis: Elementary School Children*

Play therapy techniques are highly effective with younger students who are angry, upset, distressed, anxious or just need a timeout. Play therapy techniques can be adapted for use by teachers in the classroom and by parents at home. The benefits of play therapy can be woven into and across an entire curriculum (Van Hoorn, Scales, Nourot, & Alward, 1999), and there are a number of books filled with techniques and ideas for working with children who seem unreachable (Axline, 1964, 1969; Kottman, 1995; Webb, 1991).

Every elementary school should have a playroom or special area where students can retreat to play through stressful experiences and difficult feelings. Time alone in a playroom or with a professional school counselor teaches students the helpfulness of disengagement. It teaches responsibility and pride in the ability to self-regulate emotions. The power of play with angry students, especially water play, is remarkably soothing, and play therapy is a practical method for dealing with the entire range of children's problems (Landreth, Homeyer, Glover, & Sweeney, 1996; Webb, 1991). If it is not possible to make use of a play therapy area, a short timeout that does not involve shaming the child is a viable alternative. Five minutes in a timeout is just as effective in calming a child as twenty minutes (McGuffin, 1991).

*Special Emphasis: Middle School Children*

The transition from the relative safety of an elementary school to a middle school, a different building in new surroundings with new teachers and unfamiliar faces, can be a harrowing process filled with excitement, fear, adventure and anxiety. This alone can generate significant stress. Bullying is a major factor in middle schools, as children begin to experiment with and flex their physical and psychological power. Grades six through nine tend to be the worst, during which many students are not physically and emotionally intimidated just once or twice, but repeatedly over time (Hazler et al., 1991). Isolation and withdrawal are common responses, exacerbated by student beliefs that teachers and administrators either do not care if students are victimized, do not notice, or, at best, are ineffectual in dealing with the problem (Hazler et al., 1992). Bullying is widespread, and for many students who are victimized, the impact spans the social, emotional, and academic spectrum. Bystanders may also be at-risk (Hazler, 1996b). Victims and bystanders often share experiences that are characterized by a full range of traumatic psychological and physiological reactions that follow many of them into later life (Janson, 2000). Bullies, like their victims, are also more likely to experience future relationship problems. Bullies tend to maintain their aggressive behaviors during the time they are in school (Olweus, 1996), and a past history of bullying is associated with later criminal behavior (Huesmann, 1994). Counseling interventions that address all three groups - bullies, victims, and bystanders - in a manner that stresses community and cooperation, are those most likely to minimize the negative consequences of aggression and violence (Hazler, 1996a).

*Special Emphasis: High School Students*

*Different developmental pathways.* Adolescence is a time of dramatic physical, cognitive, emotional and social growth. However, these areas of development seldom occur concurrently, creating significant challenges for many students. When one area outpaces another, confusion, awkwardness, and isolation can result. These developmental changes can create emotional reactions that sometimes make it hard to tell when behavior is appropriate, severe, or improved. Fights may be the result of horseplay that went too far, and not indicative of deeper problems. During this time, students gain size and weight, making them potentially physically intimidating to teachers and administrators as well as school counselors. Traumatic experiences from childhood may emerge symptomatically, and students may compensate with drugs and alcohol, as well as disruptive behavior.

*Social skills.* Adolescence includes a developmental shift to more time spent with same-sex peers, learning to relate to sexual identity and feelings, opposite-sex feelings and activities, hormonal changes, and increased expectations for responsibility (Petersen & Hamburg, 1986). Acquiring well-developed social skills and competencies becomes critical. However, when social skills are poorly developed, isolation, loneliness, self-injurious behaviors, aggression, and other severe behaviors may emerge. Social skills deficits can be assessed using teacher ratings and checklists, and treated with standard training in communications, assertiveness, problem-solving, anxiety management, anger management and interventions that are based on group, peer-mediation, self-training (Hansen, Giacoletti, & Nangle, 1995). These interventions can go a long way towards reducing severe behaviors.

*Counseling Interventions with Teachers*

*Make time to build relationships.* When teachers believe in a student, against the odds, the possibility of changing that student's behavior improves considerably. Without positive relationships with teachers, students tend to respond instead to negative expectations. Help teachers find ways to build relationships with difficult students both in and out of the classroom. With disruptive behavior, returning to a classroom lecture may be an effective way of calming down a group of students after an incident. However, when problems arise, teachers must decide whether to ignore the issues, address the student privately, or devote class time to processing the issues; severe behaviors impact the learning of everyone in the room. Class time taken away from learning content material may be worrisome to many teachers, however, the most effective learning includes affective as well as cognitive material (Palmer, 1998; Rogers, 1974; Rogers & Freiburg, 1994). Discussion time about why Shawn reacts the way he does when other students look at his girlfriend, or why Tawanda seems so angry all the time may be time well spent. How should students handle excluding others or being excluded, mocking others or being bullied? These types of learning have a place in classroom life.

*Use the same hallway techniques as professional school counselors.* Most of the teachers who are popular with students, who seem to have the least trouble managing lunch period in the cafeteria, or who give the least number of detentions, are most often the teachers who have taken the time to form relationships with students outside the bounds of the classroom. Facts and curricula can constrict classroom relationships, but in the hallways, there is freedom to interact more freely as people (Hazler, 1998).

*Help teachers teach as they are.* It takes courage for teachers to stand up in front of a classroom and be themselves. It takes genuineness, openness and a willingness to be vulnerable as a person that many understandably fear (Palmer, 1998). Addressing our defensiveness, our inadequacies, and our avoidance can make it easier to form positive relationships with difficult students, once they realize that adults, too, are far from perfect. Developing a clear teaching philosophy that embraces imperfection as well as achievement can also help us achieve our own potential, personally and professionally. Help teachers support each other by setting time aside to develop these beliefs more formally. A clear teaching philosophy should also include beliefs and biases about severe behavior and how to respond to students.

*Provide support for a beleaguered teacher's frustration, anger, fear, and feelings of being overwhelmed.* It is not uncommon for teachers to have more than one student in a class with severe behaviors of different types. Teachers dealing with these students often feel overwhelmed and unsupported. Your encouragement, professional expertise, and helpful techniques can turn a hopeless morning into a day with possibilities. Sometimes, placing a college student interested in service learning in the classroom can provide a needed extra boost.

*Help teachers support each other.* Help teachers schedule regular in-services or gatherings that connect them with each other in ways that enhance their professional growth and development. These informal gatherings can provide opportunities to debrief, brainstorm, share ideas and techniques, and keep tabs on difficult students and their progress. An informal brown bag lunch or even dinner out every couple of weeks can pay large dividends in terms of building a sense of collegiality and decreasing feelings of isolation. These gatherings should be used for personal and professional support; avoid using these occasions for administrative tasks and agendas. Conduct or arrange in-service trainings to give teachers opportunities to learn and practice crisis resolution skills, debriefing, behavioral assessment for less obvious forms of severe behavior, peer-mediation, and alternative ways of resolving interpersonal differences. Some of these in-services may qualify for continuing education credits making the time invested serve a dual purpose.

*The payoff for forming closer relationships with difficult students may not be academic.* Teachers who build positive relationships with difficult students may not see improvement in classroom work, though behavior might improve. What the relationship can achieve is to improve the student's quality of life, self-esteem, and sense of inclusion, all of which may have solid future payoffs. Teachers may say, "I'm a teacher, not a counselor," but teaching is one of the most ancient helping professions. Students with behavioral problems may often strain a teacher's limits as a person. Empathy and unconditional positive regard may not be foremost in a teacher's mind when a student has been threatening, disruptive, or indifferent. Teachers do not have to become professional school counselors, but can easily learn counseling techniques that help them become more effective helpers and teachers (Kottler & Kottler, 2000).

*Be content with less than perfection.* Behavioral change is a painstakingly slow process for most of us. This will be particularly true for a student with behavior problems, who has had a long history of negative reinforcement and a failure identity or "bad guy" reputation (which to him is better than no identity!). Look for small improvements in attitude, interactions with peers, and the way he or she relates to you. The goal is to watch for a decrease in intensity, frequency, and duration of behavior. A student who is able to sit in class, rather than disrupt it, has achieved an enormous success, whether or not she earns an A or F. A student who looks at you and other students as they speak instead of staring down at his hands for an hour's class represents solid progress. Academics come later.

*Avoid reviewing past failures.* Past failures burn in our hearts and minds; we do not forget them. Students do not need reminders of where they have gone wrong. They know. When not feeling defensive, most troubled students pronounce harsher judgments on themselves than do adults. They focus on negatives. Reminding students of past successes is an effective counter-strategy. Every angry or disheartened student ready to give up and drop out in junior year has successfully completed ten grades. That is a lot more success than failure.

*Enlist teachers' aid in identifying at-risk students and students in need of help.* Aside from reporting obviously disruptive behaviors, there are numerous rating scales and checklists to help teachers identify students with severe behaviors that may not be immediately apparent, or that can help you identify patterns and symptoms.

*Negotiating contracts.* Is a teacher willing to negotiate varying timelines, passing scores, places to take exams or special treatment for students with behavior problems? Teachers sometimes worry about explaining to other students the appearance of special treatment for those students who "do not deserve it." These issues only apply if students are in competition with each other. In a school that encourages every student to do his or her personal best, providing extra consideration for those who need it is a community responsibility. Some students need little support from a teacher to work hard and excel. Others need more help and support to hang on. Providing what students need to thrive models caring, consideration, and kindness and helps develop students' skills in negotiating (versus "lawyering") to obtain what they need.

*Impact of assignments.* Raise awareness that certain assignments that involve talking or writing about family and family experiences can be triggers for severe behavior. Students in foster care who have been abused or traumatized at home may be ashamed and may react by withdrawing or acting out. Assignments relating to personal experiences should be carefully considered for their impact on these students.

*Attend to practical logistics.* Where should students sit? Will a student need a break before class ends? This can often be quietly accomplished by asking a student to run an errand. Where can students go if they need to calm down?

*Meet the student wherever he or she is.* Reassure teachers that not liking a difficult student and being afraid of that student are normal reactions. These are often the hardest students to reach. They may be violent and aggressive, anxious and isolated, or indifferent, withdrawn and depressed. Help make a realistic appraisal of any threat; safety comes first. Help teachers understand a student's context and put the student's behavior in perspective. Coming back to school from a suspension can create major problems for both teacher and student; these events are seldom well-planned or structured by the system. Professional school counselors are trained to anticipate these bumps in the road. They are also in a unique position to advocate for students and support teachers at the same time.

*Become a Windtalker.* During World War II, Native Americans who spoke Navajo played a key role in transmitting coded information by communicating in their unique language. Help teachers become Windtalkers by developing their own special language or code to communicate with difficult students. The code can be used to communicate to the student when to get back on task and used by the student to tell the teacher when a time-out is needed. Signals can be discrete messages expressed in words or nonverbally that are unique and private to the two individuals. Just having such a code helps build a positive relationship.

*Identify hot buttons.* Some teachers seem to be able to tolerate and manage behaviors that others cannot. All of us have hot buttons. When friends, family, students and others push those buttons, we react. Some students, particularly those with severe behaviors, have a marvelous ability to ferret out and push our hot buttons. Swearing or abusive language sends some teachers spiraling; others will have little or no reaction, leaving them freer to offer the student a choice: amend the behavior or deal with the consequences. Identifying and managing areas of a personal reactivity adds a measure of control and response options for teachers.

*Counseling Interventions with Administrators and Staff*

It is common to hear administrators report that they are powerless to act. "I'm sorry, but my hands are tied," accompanied by a rueful expression is a statement often heard from administrators, and often discounted by those who hear it. Many administrators find that their exercise of power is severely limited since they must answer to different groups with varying agendas that are far from compatible. However, we also know that an involved and committed principal who is willing to lead by example can be the single most powerful and effective means of moving a school community from disconnection and disaffection to involvement and connection. Building a solid relationship with your school's administrators can gain you a strong ally in your efforts to improve your school's climate.

*Explain and promote a systemic approach.* Solicit ideas and opinions from administrators before making recommendations. Then, make certain administrators and staff clearly understand what is being proposed and why. Develop a written plan that outlines a general approach, and the roles administrators and staff might play. As the plan is implemented, it should also have a means for gauging outcomes. Setting goals and objectives, with reasonable means to accomplish them, creates a sense of hope and optimism for the future that can also become a self-fulfilling prophecy.

*Administrators can facilitate a culture of recognition and appreciation.* Schools characterized by cheerful cooperation, appreciation, and mutual respect are schools that students look forward to attending. They are also places where teachers, staff, and administrators look forward to coming to work. They are the schools where principals know students by name, and set policies that foster pride, inclusion, and cooperation. Help administrators develop programs that provide recognition and mutual appreciation (teacher of the week, most improved student or class, most friendly). Time invested in creating a culture of appreciation pays off in better grades, enthusiastic students, better behavior, and less vandalism. Less money is spent on repairs and disciplinary efforts like detentions and Saturday schools. Higher attendance rates can mean increased funding. Relationships initiate these changes and make them stick, not rules, regulations, and punishment.

*Recognize administrators as conduits to the school board and community-at-large.* Community resources are not always well coordinated with school resources. Administrators are ideally positioned to promote opportunities and make outside connections that help students to learn new skills and competencies, use their creativity, and enhance their physical well being, particularly after school, when many students are on their own until their parents get home.

*Include staff in your interventions.* Secretaries, office managers, support staff, cafeteria workers, and custodial staff are all part of students' and parents' line of contact with the school.

They can play important roles in helping students and parents feel welcome and included, or like outsiders looking in. Involve these essential members of the school community in your trainings and activities to help them react to severe behaviors in positive ways that provide understanding and avoid punishment. Inclusion and increased job satisfaction help make the school day more productive and enjoyable.

*Disciplinary codes.* Corporal punishment is not effective with students who have severe behavior problems, though some school districts in America still use paddling. Suspension and expulsion often serve as negative reinforcements for students. Sometimes, a suspension can help break a student's cycle of behaviors. However, more often than not, suspension serves to separate students from the school community and further isolate them, or be welcomed by students as sanctioned truancy.

Developing a discipline plan for your school that is educational rather than punitive and relies on consequences rather than punishment should top your agenda (Sweeney, 1989). In-school consequences are always preferable to out-of-school consequences. Most often, this means amending an existing plan. Educational discipline should have a focus on how to help students learn, be reasonable, and have consequences that are logically connected to the offense (Dreikurs, 1972; 1990; Sweeney, 1989). An effective plan should involve everyone in the system. That makes students stakeholders in the system, just like teachers, parents, and administrators.

*Dealing with resistance.* Resistance will be encountered. Teachers will say, "Don't waste your breath. Things around here never change." Administrators may respond, "Sorry, there's nothing I can do." Students will look skeptical: "Yeah, right. When pigs fly." Be prepared! Like students with severe behaviors, others in the system may not have hope and optimism that the future can be better. Forge relationships in non-crisis times. Model qualities you want others to model for students: patience, understanding, openness, affirmation, a group ethic, and willingness to cooperate and negotiate.

When necessary, view your ethical code as a formidable force for change: aspirational ethical practice requires proactive intervention on your part. Use research to back up what you are proposing. Demonstrate the clear advantages of what you propose, including economic advantages, if you can identify them. In practical terms, a school with students who look forward to attending school is a school with a high attendance rate, yielding fiscal benefits in most systems.

*Corporal punishment.* You may have to address beliefs about discipline and corporal punishment with administrators and teachers before bringing parents on board. As previously stated, corporal punishment and harsh discipline is not effective in managing severe behaviors (Wenning, 1996). However, the belief in corporal punishment is so ingrained in Western culture that some studies have found that 40–75% of teachers and administrators believe corporal punishment is an effective way to manage student behavior (Brown, 1988; Holland, Mize, & White, 1991; Richardson & Evans, 1994). One researcher who conducted a national poll of principals found that the majority supported the use of corporal punishment with students with learning disabilities and mentally disabled students (Rose, 1989), putting disabled students at greater risk for physical discipline than their non-disabled peers (Zirpoli, 1990). Be ready to offer creative alternatives to corporal punishment, especially to parents.

*Counseling Interventions with Parents and Caregivers*

*Environmental factors.* When you form a relationship with a student's parents or caregiver, you gain an opportunity to glimpse the contextual fabric of the student's life. Who is the student's primary caregiver(s)? Biological parent(s)? Step-parent(s)? Grandparent(s)? Foster parent(s)? Each of these circumstances brings with it distinct advantages and unique stressors. Who else lives in the home? Does the student get adequate rest and nutrition? Live in a secure setting? Is there a place to study? A recent birth, divorce or separation in the family? Acute or chronic illness? Joblessness? Homelessness? Each of these circumstances carries a specific set of potential stressors that must be addressed if change is to occur.

*Help parents and caregivers understand what causes severe behaviors.* Community and school violence, heredity, temperament, family stress, home environment, and poor communication styles all contribute to creating difficult behaviors. The good news is what we know from social learning theory: young people learn most of their behaviors, which in turn can be changed with the use of appropriate consequences, positive reinforcement, and encouragement (Bandura, 1977).

*Stress calm, consistent responses to difficult behavior.* It is hard for parents to ignore negative behaviors and use creative consequences rather than punishment. Good behavior is ignored, or not rewarded, and consistency seems elusive when parents are exhausted from work and dealing with their children and each other. Sometimes it is just easier to ignore behaviors that are inappropriate, dangerous, or aggressive. Then punishment tends to become arbitrary. Inconsistent parenting styles, or parenting styles that are overindulgent or extremely authoritarian create chaos in children. Patterns of communication that are based on screaming, yelling, nagging and threats foster oppositional and defiant behavior. Corporal punishment often simply aggravates the severity and frequency of negative behaviors. The primary cause of treatment failure with these students is that parents abandon the treatment plan too soon and do not stay the course of treatment (Wenning, 1996).

*Help parents and caregivers model the behaviors they want to see.* If the adults in the household are separated or divorced, or have ended a relationship, advise them not to criticize their ex-partner in front of the children. They should avoid fighting in front of their children, and practice offering choices with well thought out consequences for negative behaviors. As a professional school counselor, make sure that parents of students with behavior problems hear from you personally when things go right, not just when there is a crisis.

*Who is in control? Get parents on the same page.* Parents often forget that they are the adults in a household. Students' behaviors at home often lead to fights between parents, or between parents and teachers and the school. The child who is "out of control" at home is all too often the one who is really running the show. Tip parents off that if they find themselves fighting over a child's behavior, they should stop and consider what is really happening. Once parents and teachers start arguing, the focus shifts off the student, who is often then "in the clear."

*Be clear in communications and expectations.* Help parents avoid sarcasm and state what they expect directly and calmly. If there are rules to be followed and chores to be done, the list should be posted in writing in a prominent place.

*Strive to be nonviolent, praise-oriented, and non-punitive* (Wenning, 1996). Help parents ignore bad behavior and model kindness, cooperation, and patience in the face of rudeness, defiance, and disobedience. Unless parents can stick with the treatment approach long enough for change to occur, home life is liable to worsen rather than improve. With younger students who are having problems with aggressive behavior, only non-violent videos, games and television programs should be permitted.

*Let the past stay in the past.* Keep the focus in the present and future. Students are all too well aware of their failures and shortcomings, especially students with behavioral problems. When parents focus on failure, students become discouraged. When parents are not optimistic about a child's future, children are likely to meet that negative expectation.

*Help parents create reasonable consequences that are logical, respectful and connected to the behavior* (Sweeney, 1989). With many students, a poor grade is a motivator to do better. Parental supports such as assigned study times and mild restrictions can be effective in improving behavior and school performance. However, with children who suffer from severe behaviors, both behaviors that are directed towards others and those directed inwardly, multiple consequences can create a cycle of increasing opposition or withdrawal and isolation.

Consequences should be well understood by students in advance, and should not be piggybacked. For students with chronic history of behavioral problems, an "F" in English should not be compounded by adding social restrictions, grounding, removal of privileges, and other, harsher punishments. When too many consequences pile up, they lead to discouragement and make behavioral improvement virtually impossible. Most parents underestimate the tremendous emotional and social pressure on any child with multiple academic deficits and a failure identity at school, which extends well beyond a poor grade.

*Create opportunities for success.* Help parents brainstorm how they can create situations in which their children can experience success, two or three times a day, and how they can express appreciation for each others' actions. A simple task properly executed - getting home on time, knowing the difference between one tool and another when helping with a project — each tiny success contributes to building self-esteem and reducing severe behavior. Do family members know how to express appreciation for each other? Do parents reward good behavior? Checklists and specific instructions about how to express appreciation and give encouragement are essential tools that are readily available in most counseling texts (Sweeney, 1989).

*Give interventions that create immediate symptom relief at home.* The stress of dealing with a student at home can be overwhelming for a parent who works full-time and has other children and challenges as well. Single parents may be doubly stressed. Rigid patterns of interaction among family members often develop, maintaining severe behaviors. Suggest adults "do the unexpected" (Dreikurs, 1990). When an isolated, withdrawn student comes home with a failing grade, take that child out for a favored excursion that provides empathy and support. When there has been an outburst or aggressive incident at school and the adolescent arrives home ready to do battle again, do not argue with an angry adolescent; disengage from him, as hard as that may be. Let him go to his room and "stew" over the predicament (which is his, not yours). Give choices and avoid ultimatums that only serve to escalate the level of tension. Whatever your pattern of behavior might be, change it and things will most likely improve (Sweeney, 1989, p. 23). When parents break their pattern of interaction by acting positively and unexpectedly, students are often astonished and must change their own behavior to adjust to an unanticipated change of events for which they are not prepared. Behavioral change is based on modest beginnings that best begin at home.

## Summary/Conclusion

The professional school counselor is an invaluable resource to the school with a professional mandate to change the school and the lives within it. Exercise that mandate by avoiding responsibilities that put one in dual roles (e.g., counselor and substitute teacher or proficiency test administrator) and by clearly defining the role as a professional school counselor to all those in the system. This may not prove a simple task. The profession of school counseling is in the process of redefining itself, with practitioners moving from a model of guidance and education to one more orientated towards counseling and mental health intervention (Keys, Bemak, & Lockhart, 1998). One may find that administrators are resisting this shift, which would require them to obtain additional assistance to perform clerical and administrative tasks that have been delegated to the professional school counselors in the past. Teachers may not view the professional school counselor as an effective resource for helping with severe classroom behaviors (Peterson & Maddux, 1988), since many professional school counselors in the past have not been adequately trained or supervised to work with at-risk students who have mental health issues (Paisley & Borders, 1995; Roberts & Borders, 1994). Parents may view efforts as intrusive or contrary to their own beliefs (Kaplan, 1996). All of these concerns are legitimate, and responding to them should be an anticipated first step towards creating systemic prevention and interventions.

Even as one cares for others and struggles to create systemic change for students, families, the school, and community, make certain that personal needs are met, including adequate peer supervision and support, good nutrition, exercise, and adequate rest. The best example one can set for students with severe behavioral problems is the example of a satisfying and productive life, lived in close connection with caring people.

## References

Axline, V. (1964). *Dibs in search of self.* New York: Ballantine.

Axline, V. (1969). *Play therapy.* New York: Ballantine.

Bandura, A. (1977). *Social learning theory*. Engelwood Cliffs, NJ: Prentice- Hall.

Boothe, J. W., Bradley, L. H., Flick, T. M., Keough, K. E., & Kirk, S. P. (1993). The violence at your door. *The Executive Educator, 15*(1) 16-22.

Brown, W. E. (1988). Policies/practice in public school discipline. *Academic Therapy, 23,* 297-301.

Dreikurs, R. (1972). *Coping with children's misbehavior.* New York: Hawthorn Books.

Dreikurs, R. (1990). *Children: The challenge.* New York: Plume.

Evans, W. H., & Evans, S. S. (1985). The assessment of school violence. *The Pointer, 29*(2), 18-21.

Fink, B. (1979). *Relaxation techniques for children.* Cincinnati, OH: Finlar & Kats.

Gutscher, C. (1993, Fall). Violence in schools: Death threat for reform? *America's Agenda,* 10.

Hamburg, D. A. (1986). *Preparing for life: The critical transition of adolescence* (Annual Report). New York: The Carnegie Corporation of New York.

Hansen, D. J., Giacoletti, A. M., & Nangle, D. W. (1995). Social interaction and adjustment. In V. B. Van Hasselt & M. Hersen (Eds.), *Handbook of adolescent psychopathology: A guide to diagnosis and treatment* (pp. 102-129). New York: Lexington Books.

Hazler, R. J. (1996a). *Breaking the cycle of violence.* Washington, DC: Accelerated Development.

Hazler, R. J. (1996b). Bystanders: An overlooked factor in peer on peer abuse. *The Journal for the Professional Counselor, 11*(2), 11-21.

Hazler, R. J. (1998). *Helping in the hallways: Advanced strategies for enhancing school relationships.* Thousand Oaks, CA: Corwin.

Hazler, R. J., Hoover, J., & Oliver, R. (1991). Student perceptions of victimization in schools. *Journal of Humanistic Education and Development, 29*(4), 143-150.

Hazler, R. J., Hoover, J., & Oliver, R. (1992). What kids say about bullying. *The Executive Educator, 14*(11), 20-22.

Holland, G., Mize, T., & White, R. (1991). *Teachers' perceptions of the use of corporal punishment in the public schools.* (Paper Presentation). Lexington, KY: Mid-South Educational Research Association.

Huesmann, L. R. (Ed.). (1994). *Aggressive behavior: Current perspectives.* New York: Plenum Press.

James, B. (1989). *Treating traumatized children.* New York: The Free Press.

James, B. (1994). *Handbook for treatment of attachment-trauma problems in children.* New York: Lexington Books.

Janson, G. R. (2000). *Exposure to repetitive abuse: Psychological distress and physiological reactivity in bystanders as compared to victims.* Unpublished Dissertation, Ohio University, Athens, OH.

Kaplan, L. (1996). Outrageous or legitimate concerns: What some parents are saying about school counseling. *The School Counselor, 44,* 255-263.

Kassinove, H. (Ed.). (1995). *Anger disorders: Definition, diagnosis, and treatment.* Washington, DC: Taylor & Francis.

Keys, S., Bemak, F., & Lockhart, E. J. (1998). Transforming school counseling to serve the mental health needs of at-risk youth. *Journal of Counseling & Development, 76*(4), 381-388.

Kottler, J. A., & Kottler, E. (2000). *Counseling skills for teachers.* Thousand Oaks, CA: Corwin Press.

Kottman, T. (1995). *Partners in play: An Adlerian approach to play therapy.* Alexandria, VA: American Counseling Association.

Landreth, G. L. (2002). *Play therapy: The art of the relationship* (2nd ed.). New York: Brunner-Routledge.

Landreth, G. L., Homeyer, L. E., Glover, G., & Sweeney, D. S. (1996). *Play therapy interventions with children's problems.* Northvale, NJ: Jason Aronson.

Learning Publications Inc. (1988). Shocking violence in schools. *School Intervention Report, 7*(1), 1-2.

McGuffin, P. (1991). The effect of timeout duration on frequency of aggression in hospitalized children with conduct disorders. *Behavioral Residential Treatment, 6,* 279-299.

Menacker, J., Weldon, W., & Hurwitz, E. (1990). Community influences on school crime and violence. *Urban Education, 25*(1), 68-80.

Miller, G. E., & Prinz, R. J. (1990). Enhancement of social learning family interventions for childhood conduct disorders. *Psychological Bulletin, 108*(2), 291-307.

Olweus, D. (1996). *Bullying at school: What we know and what we can do.* Cambridge, MA: Blackwell Publishers.

Ordovensky, P. (1993). Facing up to violence. *The Executive Educator, 15*(1), 22-24.

Osofsky, J. D., Wewers, S., Hann, D. M., & Fick, A. C. (1993). Chronic community violence: What is happening to our children? *Psychiatry, 56,* 36-45.

Paisley, P. O., & Borders, L. D. (1995). School counseling: An evolving speciality. *Journal of Counseling & Development, 74,* 150-153.

Palmer, P. (1998). *The courage to teach: Exploring the inner landscape of a teacher's life.* San Francisco: Jossey-Bass.

Petersen, A. C., & Hamburg, B. A. (1986). Adolescence: A developmental approach to problems and psychopathology. *Behavior Therapy, 17,* 480-499.

Peterson, D., & Maddux, D. C. (1988). Rural regular and special education teachers' perceptions of teaching hyperactive students. *Rural Special Education Quarterly, 9*(2), 10-15.

Pipher, M. (1994). *Reviving Ophelia: Saving the selves of adolescent girls.* New York: Ballantine Books.

Richardson, R. C., & Evans, E. T. (1994). Keep on paddling: A study on corporal punishment in Louisiana's public schools. *Louisiana Education Research Journal, 19*(2), 97-106.

Roberts, E., & Borders, L. D. (1994). Supervision of school counselors: Administrative, program, and counseling. *The School Counselor, 41,* 149-157.

Rogers, C. (1974). Can learning encompass both ideas and feelings? *Education, 95*(2), 103-114.

Rogers, C., & Freiburg, H. J. (1994). *Freedom to learn.* New York: MacMillan College Publishing.

Rose, T. L. (1989). A survey of corporal punishment of mildly handicapped students: Five years later. *Remedial and Special Education, 10*(1), 43-52.

Schwartz, E. D., & Perry, B. D. (1994). The post-traumatic response in children and adolescents. *Psychiatric Clinics of North America, 17*(2), 311-326.

Singer, M. I., Anglin, T. M., Song, L. Y., & Lunghofer, L. (1994). *The mental health consequences of adolescents' exposure to violence: Final report.* Cleveland, OH: Center for Practice Innovations, Mandel School of Applied Social Sciences, Case Western Reserve University.

Stosny, S. (1995). *Treating attachment abuse.* New York: Springer Publishing Company.

Sweeney, T. (1989). *Adlerian counseling: A practical approach for a new decade.* Muncie, IN: Accelerated Development.

Toch, T. (1993, November 8). Violence in the schools. *U.S. News & World Report,* 31-37.

Van Hoorn, J., Scales, B., Nourot, P., & Alward, K. (1999). *Play at the center of the curriculum* (2nd ed.). Upper Saddle River, NJ: Merrill.

Webb, N. B. (Ed.). (1991). *Play therapy with children in crisis.* New York: Guilford Publications.

Wenning, K. (1996). *Winning cooperation from your child.* Northvale, NJ: Jason Aronson.

Willens, T. E., Spencer, T. J., Frazier, J., & Biederman, J. (1998). Child and adolescent psychopharmacology. In T. H. Ollendick & M. Hersen (Eds.), *Handbook of child psychopathology* (3rd ed., pp. 603-636). New York: Plenum Press.

Zirpoli, T. (1990). *Physical abuse: Are children with disabilities at greater risk? Intervention, 26*(1), 6-11.

# Chapter 66

## Helping Students with Enuresis and Encopresis

*Gregory R. Janson*

### Preview

Elimination disorders are common in school-aged students, carrying a severe social stigma that can negatively impact relationships with peers and adults, academic achievement, and personality development. Emotional, social, cognitive, and physical growth and well-being may also be threatened. Rarely associated with psychopathology, these disorders are highly treatable using simple behavioral methods that are well within the professional school counselor's scope of practice.

### Scope and Nature of the Problem

Enuresis (the voiding of urine in clothes or the bed) and encopresis (fecal soiling in clothes or other inappropriate places) are developmental disorders commonly found in school-aged children (Goin, 1998; Mikkelsen, 2001). Nearly seven million American students awaken to a wet bed (Du Mars, 1999) and encopresis affects 1% to 1.5% of students between the ages of 5 and 12 (American Psychiatric Association, 2000). Kelleher (1997, p. 73) suggested there is still "widespread misunderstanding among parents, teachers, and primary care providers on the causes and management options for these children."

In large part, this misunderstanding can be attributed to the cultural prudishness that still exists regarding bodily functions. Social taboos, shame, embarrassment and discomfort continue to inhibit open discussion of bowel movements and urination—even among helping professionals. A quick referral tends to be the first choice of most helping professionals (Schaefer, 1996). Those few parents who seek a physician's aid are usually told the issue is one of immaturity that the child will outgrow; frequently no treatment is prescribed or recommended (Vogel, Young, & Primack, 1996). No formal medical standard of care even exists for evaluating encopresis (Houts & Abramson, 1990).

There is a clear call in the literature for counselors, psychologists, and physicians to work more closely to treat enuresis and encopresis. There is also recognition that professionals are not educated or emotionally prepared to deal with elimination disorders, though they are easily and safely treatable (Houts & Abramson, 1990; Ondersma & Walker, 1998).

This lack of support frequently leaves parents on their own, with few options. It leaves children feeling isolated and hopeless that continence can ever be achieved, living in a vacuum of desperation and misery. Professional school counselors, with their professional training and understanding of children, families, and the school environment, are in an ideal position to help.

### Impact of Enuresis and Encopresis

The impact of enuresis and encopresis is significant, and can affect every aspect of child and adolescent growth and development. The presence of an elimination disorder beyond the ages of 4 and 5, the respective ages at which fecal and urinary continence are usually achieved, makes students a target for scorn and humiliation. This creates a host of immediate social difficulties with peers, parents, and teachers, as well as longer term developmental challenges that can affect personality, identity formation, self-esteem, academic achievement, relationship development, and daily functioning. Secondary emotional consequences can include depression, anxiety, hopelessness, shame, anger, and loneliness. Physical symptoms can include lethargy, headaches, stomachaches, upper respiratory problems, and pain (Murphy & Carr, 2000).

The social disgrace attached to encopresis is extremely damaging. Nighttime bedwetting, by far the most common form of elimination disorder, can remain a secret outside the home. However, encopretic events at school instantly stigmatize students. Serious deficits in self-esteem and self-image, isolation and withdrawal are common developmental risks for these children. In addition, physical pain can accompany chronic constipation, from which most encopretic children suffer (Ondersma & Walker, 1998).

These students are doubly at risk; most parents are poorly informed and ill-equipped to deal with elimination disorders, preferring secrecy and silence, or punishment and folk remedies (Schaefer, 1996). The risks are not just psychological. After crying, elimination disorders have been identified as the leading cause of child abuse (Kempe & Helfer, 1980).

## Attitudes of Parents and Family Environment

Parental attitudes and the degree of family difficulties are the most significant factors in predicting the length of time needed to achieve continence, deal with relapse and maintain long term continence. Most parents do not seek help for a child who is suffering from an elimination disorder. Parents commonly believe that their child has control over wetting or soiling but will not exercise it, or is lazy, careless, or defiant (Schaefer, 1996).

It is common for parents to blame and punish enuretic children, creating situations that pose a threat to the emotional, psychological, and physical safety of the child (Walker, Kenning, & Faust-Capanille, 1989). Enuretic children from dysfunctional families may be at the greatest emotional and physical risk (Warzak, 1993). Bedwetting can create tremendous strain within a family, and professional school counselors can anticipate the need for stress-management strategies. Broken sleep, cleanup and remaking the bed in the middle of the night, the seemingly endless piles of laundry to be washed the next day, and the social stigma of being a "bed-wetter" or the parent of one, all contribute to a shared sense of futility, hopelessness, shame, and failure in both children and parents (Foxman, Valdez, & Brook, 1986). Even with parents who are emotionally supportive and non-punitive, enuretic children often feel shamed, embarrassed, isolated and alone, avoiding social events such as sleepovers, attending camp, or overnight trips (Ondersma & Walker, 1998).

One argument made by parents who ignore bed-wetting is that their children appear fine, are remarkably well-adjusted emotionally, and possess a positive self-image, though most of their children reported wanting to stop wetting (Wagner & Geffken, 1986). A problem with this type of self-esteem measurement is that parents and children often give conflicting reports. Parents state their children are not suffering deficits in self-esteem due to enuresis, yet their children report the opposite is true (Wagner, Smith, & Norris, 1988). Although some positive links have been made between moderate sibling teasing and good treatment response (Butler, Brewin, & Forsythe, 1988), children faced with multiple negatives from parents, siblings, peers, and others are still at greater risk for threats to their sense of self-worth and development (Warzak, 1993).

Children with encopresis are at particular risk since most encopretic events occur when the child is fully awake, leading others to believe that soiling is an intentional act. Parents, teachers, and other students do not realize that soiling is most often caused by constipation, when liquid seeps around a bowel blockage. It is hard to imagine how these children deal with the anger, disgust, frustration, hopelessness, and abuse expressed by their own families, as well as that of peers and teachers.

Some parents may choose to ignore or tolerate an elimination disorder while supporting the child or adolescent emotionally, in the hope that their child will simply outgrow the behavior (Mikkelsen, 2001). There is some truth to this belief. Encopresis after age 16 is unusual, and the rate of spontaneous remission for enuresis after age 5 ranges from 5% to 10% per year. However, what this means is that a child who is enuretic and not treated at age 5 only has a 50% chance of achieving dryness by age ten. Ignoring an elimination disorder means needlessly subjecting a child to potentially severe social, emotional, and relational consequences, which are only likely to become more problematic as a child grows older.

In most cases, parents simply do not know that treatments are inexpensive and effective within time frames that vary from a few days or weeks to a few months. The sense of hopelessness and discouragement that accompanies a history of failed attempts at continence means they are less likely to help their child follow through with a treatment plan and more likely to prematurely terminate treatment once it starts (Kelleher, 1997).

Against this backdrop, professional school counselors are ideally positioned to anticipate the potential problems these disorders may create. No professional is better situated to engage in proactive education for teachers, parents, and students, place enuresis and encopresis in an appropriate, affirmative developmental context, and provide support, observation, and ongoing encouragement.

## The Role of Professional School Counselors

Professional school counselors do not typically receive much training or supervised experience regarding elimination disorders (personal communication, Catherine Ziff, September 15, 2002). In practice, professional school counselors may only see cases of elimination disorders in younger students who are referred by teachers or administrators because of a classroom or playground incident of wetting or soiling, or from a special behavioral classroom where children and adolescents might have severe co-morbid behavioral disorders. Either way, many professional school counselors feel overwhelmed and uncertain of how to help. Often unsure of their ethical obligations regarding intervention and scope of practice, professional school counselors frequently decide that referral is the best solution, even though 95% of these disorders are not associated with comorbid psychopathology or medical conditions (Murphy & Carr, 2000).

To put this in perspective, we know that in any given classroom of seven-year-olds, 7% to 15% of the students are likely to be enuretic, yet only 5% of wetting is associated with psychopathology. This suggests that elimination disorders are an invisible developmental threat to many students; the only visible indicators may be secondary emotional symptoms. It also suggests that treatment of these disorders is well within the professional school counselor's developmental scope of practice.

Most professional school counselors already possess the interpersonal skills, assessment training, and counseling experience needed to treat elimination disorders. The investment of time and energy needed to acquire the additional skills and knowledge necessary to help most students achieve continence is relatively minimal.

## What Professional School Counselors Need to Know About Elimination Disorders

A basic understanding of how elimination disorders are defined can be helpful in educating parents, children, and teachers about enuresis and encopresis. Key points to communicate include: (1) elimination disorders are common among elementary students and can affect students in middle school and beyond; (2) symptoms and course appear in different ways in individual students; (3) simple behavioral treatments are very effective, requiring minimal involvement by the professional school counselor; and (4) enuresis and encopresis cannot be due to a medical condition or use of a substance (e.g., a prescription diuretic or laxative) and is described as either primary (continence never achieved) or secondary (continence achieved for a uninterrupted period of six months or more).

*What Causes an Elimination Disorder?*

Little is known about the causes of elimination disorders. Genetics seem to play a role, but no specific genetic links have yet been identified (Mikkelsen, 2001). Only 15% of students with enuresis come from families in which the biological parents reported no history of enuresis. About 75% of enuretic students have a first-degree biological relative with a history of enuresis. In 85% to 98% of cases of encopresis there is no underlying medical condition; yet some research has shown that these students may have had far fewer bowel movements as infants (Pettei & Davidson, 1991). Identical twins are six times more likely to develop constipation problems than fraternal twins (Bakwin & Davidson, 1971). This suggests the possibility of a genetic factor in encopresis, but this factor has not been identified.

*What Professional School Counselors Need to Know About Enuresis*

Enuresis can be intentional or involuntary, and must occur at least twice a week for three months. Enuresis can occur just at night (nocturnal), just during the day (diurnal) or both. Males with nocturnal enuresis outnumber females by 2:1. Diurnal enuresis is more common in females, but seldom seen in children over nine (de Jonge, 1973). Children with diurnal enuresis are the most likely to have an underlying medical condition, but whether they do or not, daytime wetting is so stressful that drug treatment is almost always recommended (Reiner, 1995). Females tend to achieve dryness quicker than males, in whom enuresis is so much more prevalent and enduring that some researchers suggest that boys have different criteria for diagnosis, raising the age limit to eight (Verhulst & al, 1985).

Enuresis can be due to a sudden urge to urinate and loss of control, the intentional delay of urination due to anxiety or over-involvement in activities, or more rarely, in conjunction with behavioral disorders. Professional school counselors are likely to receive a referral for daytime wetting, since these events tend to take place on school days early in the afternoon and are extremely distressing to the child. Understandably, these children report lower levels of self-esteem than children with nocturnal enuresis (Wagner et al., 1988).

*What happens when continence is lost?* The distinction between primary and secondary enuresis does not bear heavily on treatment strategies (Mikkelsen, 2001). Secondary enuresis usually occurs between ages 5 and 8 and is associated with disturbing or traumatic events. These may include divorce, separation, a sibling's birth, having a new partner move in, or a family life in which chaos, abuse, neglect, punishment, or overprotection are the norm.

*What School Counselors Need to Know About Encopresis*

Encopresis can be intentional or unintentional and must occur at least once a month for three months. Most common is Encopresis With Constipation and Overflow Incontinence (retentive encopresis with seepage due to constipation). Encopresis Without Constipation and

Overflow Incontinence is intentional soiling, rare, and usually associated with trauma and behavioral disorders. For encopresis, the male to female ratio is nearly 5:1 at every age level (Rutter, Tizard, & Whitmore, 1970).

Encopresis can be retentive (caused by constipation and resulting overflow incontinence), stress-related (diarrhetic in nature and caused by trauma, stress, or anxiety) or manipulative (intentional soiling in clothes or the intentional depositing of feces in specific locations, without constipation) (Walker, 1978). Implementing an effective treatment plan means careful charting and observation over time to discriminate between these subtypes. The professional school counselor is the one person outside the family in a position to monitor behavior and gather critical assessment information that can then be dovetailed with information gleaned from parents, teachers, and the student.

*Counseling Strategies with Students and Families*

The same basic counseling strategies apply to enuresis and encopresis, starting with preventative education for students, teachers and parents. When a child with an elimination disorder is identified, or parents request help, information can be given, treatment options described, and assessment begun. Appropriate referrals and broad-based behavioral treatment strategies that are holistic in approach produce success rates in the 80% to 85% range for both disorders (Mikkelsen, 1991, 2001; Murphy & Carr, 2000; Ondersma & Walker, 1998). Behavioral conditioning, as it is used in the treatment of elimination disorders, does not appear to have any adverse emotional consequences (Sacks, de Leon, & Blackman, 1974).

Professional school counselors can play a crucial role by supporting and observing a student from initial assessment through the treatment period. This process allows for fine-tuning and encouragement. It is critical to success, especially during the three months after treatment starts, yet this role is nearly always omitted for logistical reasons (Ciminero & Doleys, 1976; Dittman & Wolter, 1996). The most important first step is crisis resolution if an enuretic or encopretic event occurs at school.

*Take positive action when an enuretic or encopretic event has occurred: Be prepared!* Provide reassurance to the student and other students. Make certain that teachers are aware of how to react and are ready to follow established procedures that ensure good hygiene. This might involve having a parent pick the child up from school to wash and change, then return. However, this approach could become negative and increase the level of anger and frustration experienced by parents. If possible, a more effective process might call for a gentle reprimand, and instructions to the child to wash out his or her clothing, followed by a shower or wash. Afterwards, the child would change into fresh clothing kept at the school for just this purpose (Schaefer, 1996). Important questions might be: who will supervise the child during this process, and how will the teacher address the incident with the rest of the class? A school may be prepared for occasional "accidents" that occur with young children. However, an older student with a chronic encopretic condition represents an ongoing challenge that many schools are not well prepared to meet.

*Meet with parents to provide information, reassurance, and a treatment strategy.* Maintain a resource library containing resources and pamphlets you can obtain online or from a counseling resource center. Create simple fact sheets to convey essential information. Normalize the prevalence of elimination disorders. Reassure students and caregivers that treatment outcomes are very positive. Build a therapeutic relationship that gives hope and creates optimism. Stress that information alone is almost never enough to achieve continence and always extend an invitation to talk (Houts, Whelan, & Peterson, 1987).

*Make a referral to a physician.* Ruling out a possible organic or medical cause comes first. Develop a referral list of professionals, including clinicians, physicians, and family counselors who are skilled in the treatment of elimination disorders. Following the referral process and the physician's report, parents may then decide to ask you to remain involved and help design a treatment plan. Make certain you have the proper releases from all the parties before starting.

*Check access to services.* Is immigration status or homelessness a barrier to applying for aid? Consider the possibility that many families may not have medical insurance or be able to pay for counseling services or medications. Can they afford to consult a pediatrician or purchase a bell and pad urine alarm system? Many parents, when they discover the cost, choose to live with an elimination disorder rather than treat it. Are alternative medications available if cost is an issue?

*Make broad-based assessments conducted from a systems perspective.* Standard assessment formats are appropriate, and should include questions regarding traumatic events. Specific attention should be given to the attitudes of both child and caregivers to episodes of enuresis or encopresis, feelings about past failed attempts to achieve continence, and beliefs about achieving future success. There is an excellent scale available to measure these attitudes (Morgan & Young, 1975).

*Consider co-morbidity.* Be aware that there seems to be a 30% higher co-morbidity rate of Attention-deficit/Hyperactivity Disorder and enuresis than expected by chance alone, requiring simultaneous treatment of both disorders (Biederman, Santangelo, Faraone, Kiely, et al., 1995; Boon, 1992). Most students with enuresis do not suffer from psychiatric disorders, however, there is a strong chance that enuresis is only one of several hurdles faced by children, whether those obstacles are cause or symptom (Swadi, 1996). Levels of depression, anxiety, and loneliness that do not meet diagnostic thresholds are common, as are higher rates of behavioral and emotional problems, night terrors, sleep disturbances, and delays in speech, learning, and the development of motor skills (more so with older children).

*Make parents or caregivers your co-counselors as part of your treatment plan, if at all possible* (Van Londen, Van Londen-Barentsen, Van Son, & Mulder, 1993). A good relationship with the student's mother in particular can improve a home environment, and help maintain parental commitment to treatment long enough to achieve continence. Training parents in effective ways to give positive reinforcement is a critical success element.

*Make the child or adolescent an active member of the treatment team.* Active participation means lower relapse rates, and improvements in self-esteem and self-efficacy. With younger children, play therapy may be the best method of communicating with, involving, and supporting the student (Landreth, 2002; Landreth, Homeyer, Glover, & Sweeney, 1996). Encopretic children tend to have personalities characterized by shyness, passivity, obedience, and stubbornness. Stoic and depressive, they can seem irritatingly indifferent and oblivious to peers and adults (Schaefer, 1996). Outside the professional school counselor, few within the school may have the patience or communication skills necessary to effectively gain the trust and cooperation of these students.

*Create perspective, reasonable expectations, and a safe environment.* Students and parents who have experienced multiple failures are discouraged and lack hope that continence is achievable. Prepare them for the time commitment needed to attain continence, and teach parents to remain calm and non-punitive; corporal punishment is not effective with elimination disorders (Schaefer, 1996). Bedwetting does not cease overnight. With encopresis, ongoing incidents of soiling should be expected during treatment and prior provisions made for following a process that everyone, including the student, has agreed is reasonable. Teach educators, parents and other students to respond to soiling incidents quietly and calmly. Adults should avoid recriminations, ridicule, or shaming. Use your counseling skills to reframe failures and setbacks as steps to success.

*Identify potential barriers to success.* Pessimistic parental attitudes, failure to follow a treatment plan long enough, familial distress, and psychiatric disturbance in the student are the most serious threats to achieving continence. With encopresis, the treatment plan must be followed without deviation to succeed. Other barriers include lack of motivation on the student's part, unrealistic expectations, previous failures, and harsh and punitive parenting styles.

*Consider cultural factors.* There is evidence in the literature that African Americans tend to distrust White medical personnel. More specific research suggests that Afro-Caribbean families are less likely than Whites to seek the help of a physician in dealing with enuresis (Rona, Li, & Chinn, 1997). Degree of acculturation, ethnicity, immigration status, and access to services should be a vital part of your assessment.

*Is counseling effective with elimination disorders?* Individual and family counseling are not effective treatments for enuresis (Houts, Berman, & Abramson, 1994) or encopresis (Achenbach & Lewis, 1971; Wells & Hinkle, 1990), except for those situations in which issues arise that are related to traumatic events, stress, anxiety, or difficulties in family communication (Protinsky & Dillard, 1983; Protinsky & Kersey, 1983; Stein, 1998). Psychological factors tend to be more significant issues for older children (Rutter, 1989). In complicated family situations, in which there may be domestic violence, chemical dependency, and abuse, referral to a community mental health agency or a family counselor may be the most helpful course of action.

## What School Counselors and Parents Need to Know About Treatment

### *Treating Enuresis*

Behavioral treatments using a urine alarm in combination with other behavioral approaches are the most effective therapy for enuresis, achieving improvement in 85% of cases (Ondersma & Walker, 1998). A urine alarm system alone is not as successful in treating enuresis as combining an alarm with psychological interventions, especially those that involve parents as co-counselors (Houts et al., 1994). Initial interventions can be as simple as creating a chart with stickers rewarding dry nights.

The use of medications can be helpful, but potential side-effects and high relapse rates make behavioral treatments the first choice in most instances (Friman & Vollmer, 1995; Friman & Warzak, 1990). In those cases when a motivated child is not able to achieve dryness using the methods described above, a combination of desmopressin (DDAVP; a synthetic anti-diuretic hormone), a urine alarm, and a mix of other behavioral interventions combined with supportive family counseling has produced 100% success rates (Mellon & McGrath, 2000).

*Bell and pad/urine alarms.* Urine alarms work on a simple principle: when urination begins, it completes an electrical circuit, setting off a loud buzzer or bell. Children either wake up or contract their pelvic floor muscles to refrain from urination. Modern versions offer sealed pads, strips worn inside pajamas or clothing, body-worn alarms, and even miniature ultrasound monitors worn around the waist that measure bladder capacity and ring at a preset point. All yield results similar to the traditional bell and pad (Pretlow, 1999).

A urine alarm alone is an effective means to achieve complete dryness for nearly two-thirds of enuretic children over a five to twelve week period (Houts et al., 1994). Relapse is common, particularly in students with secondary enuresis. However, reconditioning using the bell and pad is successful with more than two-thirds of those who relapse (Doleys, 1977; 1979).

*Arousal training.* If cost is an issue (bell and pad kits range from $60 or $70 to $130), similar success can be achieved by anticipating when bladder capacity might be reached (2-3 hours after falling asleep) and using an alarm clock to wake the child (El-Anany, Mahraby, Shaker, & Abdel-Moneim, 1999).

*Dry-bed training (DBT).* DBT seems to be the single most effective treatment for enuresis, combining a urine alarm with other behavioral and psychological interventions (Azrin, Sneed, & Foxx, 1974; Azrin, Thienes Hontos, & Besalel-Azrin, 1979; Scott, Barclay, & Houts, 1992). These include retention control; over-learning; rapid awakening; hygiene; hourly awakening of the child by the parents; positive rewards for staying dry and urinating in the bathroom; and gentle reprimands for wetness. Rehearsal is also a component of the DBT program, with the child practicing getting out of bed and physically going to the bathroom.

DBT is one of the least used approaches, employed by just 5% of families and seldom recommended by physicians, possibly due to the time and effort required to achieve dryness. For professional school counselors, developing the competence to teach this method to children and parents is relatively simple since the techniques are clearly and simply described in the literature.

*Over-learning.* Over-learning involves having children increase liquid intake by small amounts each evening until they can drink a large volume before bed. Dryness takes longer to achieve using this method, which adds effectiveness to a urine alarm and lowers relapse rates (Houts, Peterson, & Whelan, 1986).

*Retention control training.* Retention control training gives positive rewards for drinking and retaining large fluid amounts (Butler, 1998). Practicing stream interruption can help to improve functional bladder control (Friman & Warzak, 1990). These methods alone can help some children achieve dryness, but are far more effective when used in conjunction with a urine alarm (Walker, 1995).

*Full spectrum home training.* Full spectrum home training combines retention control, over-learning, bed-changing, hygiene, and charting dry and wet nights with a basic urine alarm. Students are also rewarded for retention control (holding urine) during the day. This approach is of particular interest to professional school counselors since it has a success rate of about 80% with only one session with a counselor (Houts & Liebert, 1984; Houts, Liebert, & Padre, 1983).

*Drug treatment.* Drugs can produce dramatic results within two weeks. However, relapse rates of 95% are common when drugs are discontinued (Monda & Husmann, 1995). The two most commonly used drugs are imipramine (Tofranil) and desmopressin (DDAVP). Imipramine is an inexpensive tricyclic antidepressant that seems to act on renal systems (Vogel et al., 1996). Common side effects include exhaustion, disturbed sleep, and gastric discomfort. Higher doses can affect cardiac function; overdoses can be fatal.

DDAVP is a synthetic anti-diuretic hormone that comes as a nasal spray and concentrates urine, reducing urinary output. It is the present drug of choice for treating enuresis and reported to be most successful when a family history of enuresis exists (Butler, Holland, Devitt et al., 1998; Hogg & Hussman, 1993). Headaches and stomachaches are common side effects of DDAVP, which is considered a safe drug with minimal negative effects.

### *Treating Encopresis*

The vast majority of encopretic students (85% or more) suffer from retentive encopresis, a condition characterized by chronic constipation with overflow incontinence that occurs when liquid seeps around a bowel impaction. Short term behavioral interventions combined with medical management have produced 85% success rates with children suffering from encopresis within a six month timeframe (Fireman & Koplewicz, 1992). Step one is always a medical examination to rule out physiological pathology, which is rare. The next step is to evaluate for constipation and the presence of bowel distention (psychogenic megacolon) caused by chronic constipation. The physician will then outline a medical management strategy for the parents to follow. This includes the use of laxatives and a dietary plan high in fiber and liquids, which forms the foundation for behavioral interventions (e.g., toileting routines, mild consequences for soiling, such as washing one's own clothing, biofeedback for anal sphincter training, positive rewards and avoidance of negative reinforcement, and a plan for dealing with encopretic events that occur in a school setting).

*Soiling events.* Most soiling occurs during the daytime, at a frequency that can vary from once a month to multiple episodes in a single day, creating one of the most severe psychosocial stressors a child can experience. Episodes tend to take place later in the afternoon or immediately following the end of the academic school day during play. Elementary school teachers, school counselors, or the school nurse are most frequently the people outside the family who must deal with an encopretic event. These professionals should have procedures in place that ensure good hygiene, minimize the impact of the event on the child, and help teachers manage the reactions of other students.

*Attitudes of parents and children.* Most parents blame their children for soiling and are too embarrassed to seek help from counselors and physicians, often concealing the behaviors unless directly questioned (Walker, 1995). Students with encopresis may seem indifferent to their episodes of soiling, which is perhaps their most effective psychological defense against scorn, ridicule and anxiety; however, most also report that they are eager to become continent (Landman, Rappaport, Fenton, & Levine, 1986). These children suffer deficits in self-esteem, present with emotional and behavioral problems, and like their parents, report feelings of shame, frustration, hopelessness, and distress.

*Forming the treatment team.* Successful treatment requires a multi-disciplinary, co-operative approach that includes coordinating the efforts of parents, professional school counselors, teachers, physicians, dieticians, and the school nurse. Families need a broad range of support services, starting with a thorough education on the importance of diet and nutrition. Critical elements of treatment also include emotional support, the encouragement to weather predictable setbacks, and the understanding that less than 100% compliance can sabotage the program due to physiological factors involved in restoring bowel control lost due to chronic constipation.

*Assessment.* As with enuresis, standard assessment formats are appropriate for professional school counselors to use, as long as there is a focus on encopresis. Questions asked of both parents and students should be direct and explicit (Schaefer, 1996): Was continence ever achieved? How often does soiling occur? Do you know when you need to go to the bathroom? How often do you have a bowel movement? Is moving your bowels painful for you? Were coercive methods used in toilet training? Was training commenced prior to age 15 months? Are there specific patterns related to soiling events? Is there a family history of bowel difficulties? Have there been other gastric complaints, psychological problems other than encopresis, or traumatic experiences or events? Are you afraid to use the bathrooms here at school? Bullying often takes place in school bathrooms and many children avoid restrooms for fear of being victimized (Hazler, Hoover, & Oliver, 1991; Hazler, 1996). As with enuresis, the most effective way to elicit information from younger children may be through parent interviews or with play therapy, dolls, puppets, sand tray play, or drawings. All of these have the dual benefit of building a relationship and providing affirmation and empathy. When possible, information should be shared by physicians and professional school counselors.

*Charting progress, encopretic events, and diet and fluid intake.* Charting is an essential task for parents, students and teachers. Most students soil themselves without realizing it; others hide their feces or dispose of their underwear out of shame. Some may intentionally deposit feces in bureau drawers, under furniture, or in other more obvious places. Careful diaries of toileting behaviors and soiling episodes can help determine if encopresis is retentive, related to trauma or anxiety, or manipulative in nature. Establishing these patterns will have a central bearing on treatment and referral decisions. These diaries also provide a record that can be reviewed, enabling professional school counselors to assess progress (and demonstrate that progress to the student!), reframe soiling behaviors and beliefs about continence, and re-tailor the plan to accommodate each individual student and family (Goldstein & Book, 1983).

*Look for a decrease in frequency and signs of hope that continence can be achieved.* The average course of untreated encopresis tends to be two to three years with a spontaneous annual remission rate of approximately 28%. Encopresis is extremely rare after age 16, but it does exist. With treatment, improvement can occur in a matter of weeks and continence achieved within two to three months. As a group, these children tend to be first born, male, and exhibit symptoms and a course that suggests the disorder may be psychological in origins but physiologically self-perpetuating once constipation is established and becomes chronic (Schaefer, 1996). As the bowel trauma caused by chronic constipation begins to heal and more sensitivity and stable bowel control is gained, fewer incidents of soiling will occur. Look for and encourage small changes in the child's attitude and movement from isolation to one of greater connection with others.

*Medical management, laxative administration, and diet.* The treatment of retentive encopresis begins with the treatment of chronic constipation. While professional school counselors and teachers may not be directly involved in medical management, a working knowledge of what a child's morning is like prior to school is important to understanding and supporting the healing process. Medical management almost always includes the use of laxatives to establish a predictable toileting schedule. With students suffering from retentive encopresis, laxative treatment success rates average 70% (Nolan, Debelle, Oberklaid, & Coffey, 1991). It can take a year for an enlarged bowel to heal, yet students do not seem to develop dependence on laxatives after treatment (Houts & Abramson, 1990; Murray, 1994). A well-planned diet high in bulk fiber and liquid intake, if followed, can be as effective as laxative treatments (Houts & Peterson, 1986).

Parents administer laxatives under medical supervision and on a rigid schedule, usually daily to start. To establish a predictable toileting routine and restore normal colon shape and tone, parents encourage children to defecate when they get up every morning. If they cannot, parents then administer a glycerin suppository. Following breakfast, if the child is still unable to defecate, a Fleet enema is given, insuring a bowel movement at a regular time each day. When soiling ceases and bowel movements occur regularly, the use of suppositories can be slowly discontinued. One suppository-free day is chosen by the child for the first week following cessation of soiling, then one suppository-free day is added to each successive week as long as soiling does not occur, until suppositories are completely discontinued. If soiling occurs, the process begins anew until two weeks without suppositories or soiling is achieved. Continence is generally achieved within four or five months using this method (Wright, 1973).

*Understanding the physiology of encopresis and effects of constipation.* Nearly all encopretic episodes are associated with constipation and overflow incontinence, not with oppositional and defiant or conduct disordered behavior (Murphy & Carr, 2000). Constipation in children is common and can be due to dehydration, a diet low in fiber, or hereditary factors. Other factors include the intentional avoidance of defecation due to anxiety, stress, fear of an unfamiliar environment, unwillingness to stop an activity, or intentional manipulation. Constipation easily becomes chronic, stretching the bowel walls and weakening colon muscles. This causes a decrease in the physiological cues that indicate the need to defecate, and leaves the child in a state of lethargy and pain (Christophersen & Edwards, 1992). A condition known as psychogenic megacolon can then arise, in which stools become hard and dry, forming an impaction. These stools block and distend the colon, enlarging and thinning out walls of the bowels.

Overflow incontinence occurs when liquid collects above the impaction (which has become rock-like and impervious to liquid) and drains around it, leaking from the anal sphincter, which has lost tone and sensitivity. Soiling then occurs without the child's awareness; odor is the first cue that something is wrong. The seepage is often yellow in color, may have a pasty consistency, and has an extremely noxious odor. This condition is common and dangerous in encopretic children, requiring immediate medical attention (Walker, 1978). Sometimes, the damaged section of thinned bowel must be removed surgically.

Education is a critical part of the professional school counselor's mandate, since teachers and parents are seldom aware that overflow incontinence can take place without a student's awareness, or that soiling can be associated with severe constipation. Providing facts about encopresis can help insure that a student with a potentially dangerous condition is quickly identified and receives the appropriate medical referral. It can also help adults and peers become more sensitive and supportive, relieving the intense psychological pressure on the student.

As easier, more regular bowel movements occur, avoidance of defecation due to the fear of painful movements is reduced (Walker, 1995). Teachers can help make certain that daily liquid intake meets therapeutic levels and that a toilet routine is followed without singling out a student for ridicule. Once constipation is resolved and normal toileting established, colon and bowels will regain tone and sensitivity (Murray, 1994).

*Prevention.* Opportunities for prevention are significant and can be easily identified by the professional school counselor since insufficient intake of fiber and liquids are principle contributing factors to constipation and encopresis. Referral to the school nurse or dietician or a nutritionist can help parents and school personnel create a balanced diet, high in dietary fiber and fluid intake. Fiber from vegetables may be preferable to fiber from fruits. Water is the preferred liquid. Beverages that contain caffeine should be avoided. Prune juice, prunes, prune bread, and prune cookies may be palatable and effective treats to help students adjust their diet and food preferences.

*Behavior and biofeedback therapy.* Behavior therapy consists of a system of positive rewards and reinforcement for proper toileting routines, checking clothing for soiling, gentle reprimands for soiling incidents, and good hygiene (cleanliness and having the student wash out his laundry). Combining behavioral techniques increases effectiveness. Adding biofeedback training can be helpful since encopretic children tend to tighten their anal sphincters rather than relax them when attempting to defecate, anticipating that the bowel movement will be painful (Loening-Baucke & Cruikshank, 1986).

*Responding to incidents of soiling: Creative consequences and positive and negative reinforcers.* Parents, teachers, and most helping professionals are usually unsure how to respond to incidents of soiling. Professional school counselors can help parents develop an effective repertory of consequences and rewards to help reduce soiling and attain continence. A thorough review of the literature shows that the single most important factor in treating all types of encopresis or enuresis is positive reinforcement (Houts & Abramson, 1990). The use of desired rewards provides powerful incentives for students and should be given for each bowel movement made on the toilet and for each day of continence. The reward most prized by children is one-on-one time with parents engaged in an activity of the child's choice (Wright, 1973).

Secondary positive reinforcements consist of typical token rewards for toys, candy, movies, games, or a trip to a water park or video arcade. Negative reinforcement, administered after each soiling incident, should be limited to a mild reprimand, having the child wash soiled clothing, 5 to 15 minute time-outs, extended periods of time in the tub or shower (15 to 30 minutes), and loss of play or television time. Some researchers suggest simply using only mild reprimands. All recommend having the child wash her own clothing. Professional school counselors can help educate others that encopretic children suffer enough punishments; what is most needed is encouragement, hope, and affirmation.

*Intentional or manipulative soiling.* As part of a pattern of oppositional and defiant behavior or conduct disorder, intentional soiling is uncommon; however, coping with this type of behavior is a challenge most adults find impossibly difficult (Walker, 1995). Trauma, neglect, abuse and abandonment are almost always a part of the clinical picture with these disturbed children and adolescents. Treating them and their families may well require referral to a clinician. What professional school counselors can do is educate teachers, administrators, and students, help students recognize secondary behavioral gains, and identify better ways to communicate or gain significance (Walker, Milling, & Bonner, 1988). Of all students, these are perhaps the ones most in need of unconditional positive regard if change is to be possible.

## Summary/Conclusion

Students afflicted with enuresis, and to a lesser extent, encopresis, will be found in every professional school counselors' setting. The vast majority of these students do not suffer from any form of psychopathology, yet the overwhelming prospect of dealing with an elimination disorder and the social taboos against discussing bowel and bladder functions often leaves these students isolated and hopeless. If their problem becomes publicly known, they are ostracized and humiliated, shamed by adults, blamed by parents, and ridiculed by peers. The tendency of helping professionals is to ignore these disorders, or "medicalize" them, when they are in fact developmental in nature and highly treatable.

A professional school counselor is the one person who is ideally situated to educate, coordinate treatment, observe progress, fine-tune strategies over time, and work with a student and his family to achieve continence. Most physicians are minimally involved with treatment, if at all. Most mental health counselors or play therapists have contact with their clients once a week, assuming clients even have the resources to utilize these professionals. These professionals, like parents, are often not aware of a student's day-to-day life, but professional school counselors and teachers do. As a summary, Table 1 contains helpful information to consider when helping students with enuresis and encopresis.

**Table 1. How to help students with elimination disorders.**

1. *Conduct a self-inventory.* Consider your feelings and personal experiences with elimination disorders as a student, or with a student you know. Are you comfortable talking to students, parents, and teachers about bodily functions? Are you revolted by the prospect of dealing with an encopretic incident? Talk with colleagues and examine your biases and fears.
2. *Self-educate.* Get the training and supervision you need to develop competency and self-confidence. Learn the step-by-step treatment plans and interventions described in the literature.
3. *Educate others* through brief in-service trainings for teachers, administrators, and staff. Send literature to all parents and invite them to a training and discussion group. Be prepared to deal with the biases of others as part of your everyday scope of practice.
4. *Expand comfort zones* by practicing directness and modeling open discussion about bodily functions with teachers, parents, and students. Validate the discomfort of others as these are not easy topics to discuss. Incorporate these topics into your overall psycho-educational curriculum.
5. *Dispel myths* that elimination disorders are shameful, should be ignored, and are the child's fault, or that treating these disorders requires extensive training and expertise.
6. *Raise awareness.* Help others understand the prevalence and "invisibility" of elimination disorders, particularly nocturnal enuresis. Alert teachers to secondary

symptoms: academic deficits, lethargy, depression, anxiety, and somatic complaints.

7. *Curricula.* If you serve on a college or university advisory board, suggest programmatic changes that give school counseling students firmer grounding in treating elimination disorders.
8. *Teach positive reinforcement techniques* that are highly effective, and do not consist just of praise and encouragement, but include more concrete rewards that a student might very much want. Children's number one choice of a reward is one-on-one time with a parent doing an activity that the child chooses.
9. *Promote flexibility and patience,* which are the hallmarks of any successful treatment for an elimination disorder. Every child is unique and comparisons with other children should be avoided. The one constant with the course and presentation of enuresis and encopresis is that cases are vastly heterogeneous.
10. *Decide what services you are willing to offer.* Can you provide general education for all teachers, students, and parents? Direct services? Treatment planning? Charting? Trainings? Perhaps a single session of Full Spectrum Home Training for individuals or groups? Instructions on how to use a urine alarm? Dry Bed Training or supportive counseling for students and families? What services you can provide depends on your education, training and experience.
11. *Publish and circulate a formal standard of care for your school* that anticipates the needs of students with elimination disorders. This should include specific plans and procedures. Conduct in-service trainings for teachers and administrators to reduce the impact of episodes that occur at school. Network with others such as the school nurse and dietician to provide services. Develop an in-school plan and referral plan for students with multiple challenges and intentional wetting and soiling. Consider acting as the point person on a treatment team.
12. *Remember,* helping a student with an elimination disorder may be one of the most challenging undertakings you accept as a professional school counselor. However, these students have few advocates and little hope. No other professional is better placed or better qualified to ensure a continuity of care and create hope for the student's future.

---

## References


Achenbach, T. M., & Lewis, M. (1971). A proposed model for clinical research and its application for encopresis and enuresis. *Journal of the American Academy of Child Psychiatry, 10,* 535-554.

American Psychiatric Association. (2000). *Diagnostic and statistical manual of mental disorders* (4th edition, text revision) (DSM-IV-TR). Washington, DC: Author.

Azrin, N. H., Sneed, T. J., & Foxx, R. M. (1974). Dry-bed training: Rapid elimination of childhood enuresis. *Behaviour Research & Therapy, 12,* 147-156.

Azrin, N. H., Thienes Hontos, P., & Besalel-Azrin, V. (1979). Elimination of enuresis without a conditioning apparatus:An extension by office instruction of the child and parents. *Behavior Therapy, 10*(1), 14-19.

Bakwin, H., & Davidson, M. (1971). Constipation in twins. *American Journal of Diseases of Children, 121,* 179-181.

Biederman, J., Santangelo, S. L., Faraone, S. V., Kiely, K., et al. (1995). Clinical correlates of enuresis in ADHD and non-ADHD children. *Journal of Child Psychology & Psychiatry & Allied Disciplines, 36,* 865-877.

Boon, F. (1992). "Comorbidity of attention deficit hyperactivity disorder with conduct, depressive, anxiety, and other disorders": Comment. *American Journal of Psychiatry, 149*(1), 148.

Butler, A., Holland, P., Devitt, H., Hiley, E., Roberts, G., & Redfern, E. J. (1998). The effectiveness of desmopressin in the treatment of childhood noctural enuresis: Predicting response using pretreatment variables. *British Journal of Urology, 81,* 29-36.

Butler, R. J. (1998). Annotation: Night wetting in children: Psychological aspects. *Journal of Child Psychology & Psychiatry & Allied Disciplines, 39,*453-463.

Butler, R. J., Brewin, C. R., & Forsythe, W. I. (1988). A comparison of two approaches to the treatment of nocturnal enuresis and the prediction of effectiveness using pre-treatment variables. *Journal of Child Psychology &Psychiatry & Allied Disciplines, 29,* 501-509.

Christophersen, E. R., & Edwards, K. J. (1992). Treatment of elimination disorders: State of the art 1991. *Applied & Preventive Psychology, 1*(1), 15-22.

Ciminero, A. R., & Doleys, D. M. (1976). Childhood enuresis: Considerations in assessment. *Journal of Pediatric Psychology, 4*(1), 17-20.

de Jonge, G. A. (1973). Epidemiology of enuresis: A survey of the literature. In I. Kolvin, R. C. Mac Keith & S. R. Meadow (Eds.), *Bladder control and enuresis* (pp. 39-46). Philadelphia: Lippincott.

Dittman, R. W., & Wolter, S. (1996). Primary nocturnal enuresis and desmopressin treatment: Do psychosocial factors affect outcome? *European Child & Adolescent Psychiatry, 5*(2), 101-109.

Doleys, D. M. (1977). Behavioral treatments for nocturnal enuresis in children: A review of the recent literature. *Psychological Bulletin, 84*(1), 30-54.

Doleys, D. M. (1979). Assessment and treatment of childhood encopresis. In A. J. Finch & P. C. Kendall (Eds.), *Treatment and research in child psychopathology* (pp. 185-205). New York: Spectrum.

Du Mars, R. C. (1999). Treating primary nocturnal enuresis: The counselor's role. *College Student Journal, 33*(2), 211-216.

El-Anany, F. G., Mahraby, H. A., Shaker, S. E., & Abdel-Moneim, A. M. (1999). Primary nocturnal enuresis: A new approach to conditioning treatment. *Urology, 53,* 405-408.

Fireman, G., & Koplewicz, H. S. (1992). Short-term treatment of children with encopresis. *Journal of Psychotherapy Practice & Research, 1*(1), 64-71.

Foxman, B., Valdez, R. B., & Brook, R. H. (1986). Childhood enuresis: Prevalence, perceived impact, and prescribed treatments. *Pediatrics, 77,* 482-487.

Friman, P. C., & Vollmer, D. (1995). Successful use of the nocturnal urine alarm for diurnal enuresis. *Journal of Applied Behavior Analysis, 28*(1), 89-90.

Friman, P. C., & Warzak, W. J. (1990). Nocturnal enuresis: A prevalent, persistent, yet curable parasomnia. *Pediatrician, 17*(1), 38-45.

Goin, R. P. (1998). Nocturnal enuresis in children. *Child: Care, Health & Development, 24,* 277-288.

Goldstein, S., & Book, R. (1983). A functional model for the treatment of primary enuresis. *School Psychology Review, 12*(1), 97-101.

Hazler, R., Hoover, R., & Oliver, R. (1991). Student perceptions of victimization by bullies in school. *Journal of Humanistic Education and Development, 29,* 143-150.

Hazler, R. J. (1996). *Breaking the cycle of violence: Interventions for bullying and victimization.* Washington, DC: Accelerated Development.

Hogg, R. J., & Hussman, D. (1993). The role of family history in predicting response to desmopressin in nocturnal enuresis. *Journal of Urology, 150,* 444-445.

Houts, A. C., & Abramson, H. (1990). Assessment and treatment for functional childhood enuresis and encopresis: Toward a partnership between health psychologists and physicians. In S. B. Morgan & T. M. Okwumabua (Eds.), *Child and adolescent disorders: Developmental and health psychology perspectives* (pp. 47-103). Hillsdale, NJ: Lawrence Erlbaum Associates.

Houts, A. C., Berman, J. S., & Abramson, H. (1994). Effectiveness of psychological and pharmacological treatments for nocturnal enuresis. *Journal of Consulting & Clinical Psychology, 62,* 737-745.

Houts, A. C., & Liebert, R. M. (1984). *Bedwetting: A guide for parents and children.* Springfield, IL: Thomas.

Houts, A. C., Liebert, R. M., & Padre, W. (1983). A delivery system for the treatment of primary enuresis. *Journal of Abnormal Child Psychology, 11,* 513-519.

Houts, A. C., & Peterson, J. K. (1986). Treatment of a retentive encopretic child using contingency management and diet modification with stimulus control. *Journal of Pediatric Psychology, 11,* 375-383.

Houts, A. C., Peterson, J. K., & Whelan, J. P. (1986). Prevention of relapse in full-spectrum home training for primary enuresis: A components analysis. *Behavior Therapy,17,* 462-469.

Houts, A. C., Whelan, J. P., & Peterson, J. K. (1987). Filmed versus live delivery of full-spectrum home training for primary enuresis: Presenting the information is not enough. *Journal of Consulting & Clinical Psychology, 55,* 902-906.

Kelleher, R. E. (1997). Daytime and nighttime wetting in children: A review of management. *Journal of the Society of Pediatric Nurses, 2*(2), 73-82.

Kempe, C. H., & Helfer, R. E. (1980). *The battered child.* Chicago: University of Chicago Press.

Landman, G. B., Rappaport, L., Fenton, T., & Levine, M. D. (1986). Locus of control and self-esteem in children with encopresis. *Journal of Developmental & Behavioral Pediatrics, 7,* 111-113.

Landreth, G. L. (2002). *Play therapy: The art of the relationship* (2nd ed.). New York, Brunner-Routledge.

Landreth, G. L., Homeyer, L. E., Glover, G., & Sweeney, D. S. (1996). *Play therapy interventions with children's problems.* Northvale, NJ: Jason Aronson.

Loening-Baucke, V., & Cruikshank, B. M. (1986). Abnormal defecation in chronically constipated children with encopresis. *Journal of Pediatrics, 108,* 562-566.

Mellon, M. W., & McGrath, M. L. (2000). Empirically supported treatments in pediatric psychology: Nocturnal enuresis. *Journal of Pediatric Psychology, 25*(4), 193-214.

Mikkelsen, E. J. (1991). Modern approaches to enuresis and encopresis. In M. Lewis (Ed.),*Child and adolescent psychiatry: A comprehensive textbook* (pp. 583-591). Baltimore: Williams & Wilkins Co.

Mikkelsen, E. J. (2001). Enuresis and encopresis: Ten years of progress. *Journal of the American Academy of Child & Adolescent Psychiatry, 40,* 1146-1158.

Monda, J. M., & Husmann, D. A. (1995). Primary nocturnal enuresis: A comparison among observation, imipramine, desmopressin acetate and bed-wetting alarm systems. *Journal of Urology, 154,* 745-748.

Morgan, R. T., & Young, G. C. (1975). Case histories and shorter communications. *Behaviour Research and Therapy, 13*, 197-199.

Murphy, E., & Carr, A. (2000). Enuresis and encopresis. In A. Carr (Ed.), *What works with children and adolescents? A critical review of psychological interventions with children, adolescents and their families* (pp. 49-64). Florence, KY: Taylor & Francis.

Murray, R. D. (1994). Elimination disorders: Medical issues. In R. A. Olson, L. L. Mullins, J. B. Gillman & J. M. Chaney (Eds.), *The sourcebook of pediatric psychology* (pp. 42-45). Boston: Allyn & Bacon.

Nolan, T., Debelle, G., Oberklaid, F., & Coffey, C. (1991). Randomised trial of laxatives in treatment of childhood encopresis. *Lancet, 338,* 523-527.

Ondersma, S. J., & Walker, C. E. (1998). Elimination disorders. In M. Hersen (Ed.), *Handbook of child psychopathology* (3rd ed.)(pp. 355-378). New York: Plenum Press.

Pettei, M. J., & Davidson, M. (1991). Idiopathic constipation. In W. A. Walker & J. B. Watkins (Eds.), *Pediatric gastrointestinal disease: Volume 1. Pathophysiology, diagnosis, management* (pp. 818-829). Philadelphia: B.C. Decker.

Pretlow, R. A. (1999). Treatment of nocturnal enuresis with an ultrasound bladder volume controlled alarm device. *Journal of Urology, 162,* 1224-1228.

Protinsky, H., & Dillard, C. (1983). Enuresis: A family therapy model. *Psychotherapy: Theory, Research & Practice, 20*(1),81-89.

Protinsky, H., & Kersey, B. (1983). Psychogenic encopresis: A family therapy approach. *Journal of Clinical Child Psychology, 12*(2), 192-197.

Reiner, W. G. (1995). Enuresis in child psychiatric practice. *Child & Adolescent Psychiatric Clinics of North America, 4,* 453-460.

Rona, R. J., Li, L., & Chinn, S. (1997). Determinants of nocturnal enuresis in England and Scotland in the '90s. *Developmental Medicine & Child Neurology, 39,* 677-681.

Rutter, M. (1989). Isle of Wight revisited: Twenty-five years of child psychiatric epidemiology. *Journal of the American Academy of Child & Adolescent Psychiatry, 28,* 633-653.

Rutter, M., Tizard, J., & Whitmore, K. (1970). *Education, health, and behaviour.* London: Longmans & Green.

Sacks, S., de Leon, G., & Blackman, S. (1974). Psychological changes associated with conditioning functional enuresis. *Journal of Clinical Psychology, 30*(3), 271-276.

Schaefer, C. E. (1996). *Childhood encopresis & enuresis.* Northvale, NJ: Jason Aronson.

Scott, M. A., Barclay, D. R., & Houts, A. C. (1992). Childhood enuresis: Etiology, assessment, and current behavioral treatment. In M. Hersen, R. M. Eisler & P. M. Miller (Eds.), *Progress in behavior modification* (Vol. 28) (pp. 83-117). Sycamore, IL: Sycamore Publishing Company.

Stein, S. M. (1998). Enuresis, early attachment and intimacy. *British Journal of Psychotherapy, 15*(2), 167-176.

Swadi, H. (1996). Nocturnal enuresis and psychopathology: Associations in a community sample. *Arab Journal of Psychiatry, 7*(2), 111-118.

Van Londen, A., Van Londen-Barentsen, M. W., Van Son, M. J., & Mulder, G. A. (1993). Arousal training for children suffering from nocturnal enuresis: A 2.5 year followup. *Behaviour Research & Therapy, 31,* 613-615.

Verhulst, F. C., et al. (1985). The prevalence of nocturnal enuresis: Do *DSM III* criteria need to be changed? A brief research report. *Journal of Child Psychology & Psychiatry & Allied Disciplines, 26,* 989-993.

Vogel, W., Young, M., & Primack, W. (1996). A survey of physician use of treatment methods for functional enuresis. *Journal of Developmental & Behavioral Pediatrics, 17*(2), 90-93.

Wagner, W. G., & Geffken, G. (1986). Enuretic children: How they view their wetting behavior. *Child Study Journal, 16*(1), 13-18.

Wagner, W. G., Smith, D., & Norris, W. R. (1988). The psychological adjustment of enuretic children: A comparison of two types. *Journal of Pediatric Psychology, 13*(1), 33-38.

Walker, C. E. (1978). Toilet training, enuresis, and encopresis. In P. Magrab (Ed.), *Psychological management of pediatric problems* (Vol. I) (pp. 129-189). Baltimore, MD: University Park Press.
Walker, C. E. (1995). Elimination disorders: Enuresis and encopresis. In M. C. Roberts (Ed.), *Handbook of pediatric psychology* (2nd ed.) (pp. 537-557). New York: Guilford Press.
Walker, C. E., Kenning, M., & Faust-Capanille, J. (1989). Enuresis and encopresis. In E. J. Mash & R. A. Barkley (Eds.), *Treatment of childhood disorders* (pp. 423-448). New York: Guilford Press.
Walker, C. E., Milling, L. S., & Bonner, B. L. (1988). Incontinence disorders: Enuresis and encopresis. In D. K. Routh (Ed.), *Handbook of pediatric psychology* (pp. 363-397). New York: Guilford Press.
Warzak, W. J. (1993). Psychosocial implications of nocturnal enuresis. *Special edition: Treatment of childhood enuresis,* 38-40.
Wells, M. E., & Hinkle, J. S. (1990). Elimination of childhood encopresis: A family systems approach. *Journal of Mental Health Counseling, 12,* 520-526.
Wright, L. (1973). Handling the encopretic child. *Professional Psychology: Research & Practice, 4,* 137-144.

# *Section 6*

# Serving Special Populations

# Chapter 67

# Multicultural Counseling Competence in School Counseling

*Cheryl Moore-Thomas*

## Preview

The rapidly changing demographics of the nation's student population demand that professional school counselors work effectively with all students. Multicultural counseling competence, therefore, is imperative. This chapter explores key definitions and elements of multicultural counseling competence for the professional school counselor. General strategies and considerations regarding the role of the multiculturally competent professional school counselor are identified. The chapter concludes with sample counseling interventions appropriate for the elementary, middle, and high school levels.

Public and private school enrollments have increased 14 percent over the previous decade. This record enrollment, totaling over 46 million in 2000, is expected to continue to increase, setting new records the next three years (National Center for Education Statistics, 2001).

Closer examination of these demographics indicate substantial increases in the minority student population. In 2000, public and private school minority enrollment was approximately 38% of the total K-12 enrollment. This represents a gain of 16 percentage points in minority enrollment over the past twenty years (National Center for Education Statistics, 2001). Projections indicate that by 2020 most school-age children attending public schools will come from minority (non-white) cultures (Campbell, 1994).

These changing demographics demand that professional school counselors be able to effectively work with students from various cultures (Constantine, 2001; Lee, 2001). The American School Counselor Association (ASCA) (1999) position statement on multicultural counseling calls on professional school counselors to " . . . take action to ensure students of culturally diverse backgrounds have access to appropriate services and opportunities promoting the individual's maximum development" (p. 1). Professional school counselors must understand diversity in order to be effective (Herring, 1997). Multicultural counseling competence, therefore, is an issue of great consequence for the professional school counselor.

## Definitions

*Multicultural counseling* is "a helping process that places the emphases for counseling theory and practice equally on the cultural impressions of both the counselor and the client" (Lee & Richardson, 1991, p. 3). More simply, multicultural counseling is the "... facilitation of human development through the understanding and appreciation of cultural diversity" (ASCA, 1999, p. 1). Multicultural counseling demands that professional school counselors work with students within appropriate cultural contexts. In order to do this, professional school counselors must fully consider the language, values, beliefs, social class, level of acculturation, race, and ethnicity of their students, and only use counseling interventions and techniques that are consistent with those cultural values.

The ramifications of multicultural counseling may initially appear overwhelming. It is important, however, that multicultural counseling not be reduced to an "add-on," or a list of stereotyped preferences. Multicultural counseling is a process (Spindler & Spindler, 1994; Sue, Ivey, & Pedersen, 1996). For the professional school counselor, the multicultural counseling process involves a shift in paradigm, which leads to true acceptance and respect of the student in relation to self, others, and the environment.

Within discussions of multicultural counseling the terms culture, race, and ethnicity are often used interchangeably. These terms include important distinctions. *Culture* is the set of "values, beliefs, expectations, worldviews, symbols, and appropriate behaviors of a group that provide its members with norms, plans, and rules for social living" (Gladding, 2001, p. 34). As the definition suggests, culture is complex, multidimensional, and integrated. Professional school counselors may recognize several cultures and subcultures within their student population. Although this adds to the complexity of the construct, understanding and appreciating culture and its multidimensionality gives professional school counselors valuable insight regarding their students' sense of self, language and communication patterns, dress, values, beliefs, use of time and space, relationships with family and significant others, food, play, work, and use of knowledge (Whitefield, McGrath & Coleman, 1992).

*Race*, often referenced in conjunction with culture, is a separate construct that has little if any relevance to the understanding of culture. Race is an anthropological concept based on the classification of physiological characteristics (Gladding, 2001). There exists, however, a strong argument that race is a political and socioeconomic construct, which is correlated with artificially categorical differences in physical appearance (Brace, 1995; Yee, Fairchild, Weizmann, & Wyatt, 1993). This understanding is crucial for the professional school counselor. Understanding this concept enables the professional school counselor to more appropriately address students' concerns that on the surface may appear to involve race, but on closer examination involve issues that are political, psychological, social or economic in nature. This consideration also enables professional school counselors to examine the effects of students' *racial identity development*, a race-related adjustment process rooted in sociopolitical and cultural constructs, on academic, career, and personal/social development (Dahir, Sheldon,& Valigia, 1998; Helms, 1995).

*Ethnicity* refers to the "group classification in which members believe they share a common origin and a unique social and cultural heritage such as language or religious belief" (Gladding, 2001, p. 45). Ethnicity describes a shared social and cultural heritage that is often passed from generation to generation. Ethnic classifications may help to shape students' sense of identity, appropriate behavior, and opportunity (Blum, 1998). Ethnic classifications include African American, Asian American, European American, Latino, and Native American. In an attempt to be inclusive, institutions such as educational systems have adopted the use of many categories of ethnicity. This growth in awareness and sensitivity is to be commended. In the midst of this growing and ever changing terminology, the professional school counselor must remember that sensitivity to students' needs is paramount. When it is necessary to identify ethnicity it is essential to use the term most preferred by the student and the student's family. It is equally important to remember not to rely on any single term to define students.

*Diversity* simply means differences. The professional school counselor appreciates and understands diversity in a number of areas including race, ethnicity, gender, age, exceptionality, language, sexual orientation and socioeconomic status. The professional school counselor works to ensure that students of diverse backgrounds have access to needed services and opportunities (ASCA, 1999).

## Role of the Multiculturally Competent Professional School Counselor

The professional school counselor uses the helping processes of counseling, consulting and coordination to assist students, parents, teachers, and administrators (Campbell & Dahir, 1997). These processes must become manifest in comprehensive developmental counseling programs that are appropriate for students of culturally diverse backgrounds. Working to design such a counseling program, professional school counselors should consider utilizing the following:

- Strategies that increase sensitivity and awareness of the school population to cultural diversity, culturally diverse persons and populations, and enhance the school and community climate;
- Consultation skills that identify factors in attitudes and policies which hinder the learning process of culturally diverse students;
- Approaches that ensure all students' rights are respected and all students' needs are met; and
- Counseling interventions that maximize students' potential (ASCA, 1999).

Additionally, the professional school counselor must continually work toward multicultural counseling competence by:

- Increasing awareness of one's own culture and the culture of others through articles, books, conversations, activities, reflection, and experiences;
- Becoming aware of and working to eliminate personal and school-wide barriers to effective multicultural counseling;
- Refraining from utilizing a cookbook, stereotypical approach to counseling students from specific racial or cultural groups;
- Demonstrating mastery of a variety of individual and group counseling approaches and techniques that when evaluated based on the students' needs prove appropriate for individual culturally and ethnically diverse students;
- Respecting the indigenous support and healing systems of all students;
- Understanding possible stressors for students of diverse cultures. These may include issues of acculturation, identity development, self-esteem, worldview, values, social isolation, prejudice, oppression, opportunity, and discrimination;
- Understanding the specific ways race, ethnicity and culture may affect students' academic, career and personal/social development;
- Assuming multiple helping roles based on the needs of students. These may include advisor, advocate, facilitator of indigenous support systems, facilitator of indigenous healing systems, consultant, and change agent (Atkinson, Thompson, & Grant, 1993);
- Providing student resources that are reflective of a diverse population; and
- Promoting school-wide programs and staff development opportunities that are inclusive of the school community and reflective of a diverse population.

## Multicultural Counseling Competence in Practice

The following sample lessons illustrate the use of many of the multicultural counseling strategies listed above. The samples integrate strategies in multiculturally competent school counseling interventions appropriate for the elementary, middle, and high school levels. These samples, aligned with the *National Standards for School Counseling Programs,* Personal/Social Development: Standard A (Campbell & Dahir, 1997), demonstrate just a few of the many effective ways professional school counselors may work with students from diverse cultural and racial backgrounds.

**Figure 1. Elementary level lessons.**

---

*Standard:* Personal/Social Development: Standard A. Students will acquire the knowledge, attitudes, and interpersonal skills to help them understand and respect self and others.

*Competency:* Students will identify and recognize changing family roles.

*Objective:* After participating in the developmental guidance lesson on families in the community, 80% of the students will be able to identify two ways families differ.

*Materials*: One "Families" Worksheet for each student (See Appendix A).

*Activity*: Primary grade level developmental guidance lesson conducted in classroom settings. The professional school counselor works in collaboration with teachers to introduce primary students to various family structures and family roles. The professional school counselor ensures that ethnically and racially diverse families are represented through visual and audiovisual materials. Students discuss characteristics of families (members, customs, practices, etc.). The professional school counselor ensures that students understand that families are different in membership, member roles, practices, etc. The term diverse is introduced. Students complete the "Families Worksheet" (Appendix A). Students are given an opportunity to share their worksheets. In closing, the professional school counselor emphasizes the value of all families not being the same.

*Evaluation:* The professional school counselor collects and evaluates the students' worksheets. If 80% of the students completed the worksheet identifying at least two ways families are different, the goal was met.

---

**Figure 2: Middle school level lessons.**

---

*Standard*: Personal/Social Development: Standard A. Students will acquire the knowledge, attitudes, and interpersonal skills to help them understand and respect self and others.

*Competency:* Students will develop a positive attitude toward self as a unique and worthy person.

*Objective:* After participating in the counseling group on self-esteem, 90% of the participants will complete the "Self-Esteem Questionnaire" (See Appendix B) reporting positive characteristics and statements about themselves.

*Materials:* One "Self–esteem Questionnaire" for each student (See Appendix B); popular magazines and books designed for young female audiences

*Activity:* Girls Counseling Group on Self-Esteem.

*Session 1.* The professional school counselor discusses the purpose of the group. The group works to establish ground rules. The members interview and introduce each other to the entire group. The group concludes with similarities to create universality, while noting differences to promote acceptance and tolerance.

*Session 2.* Participants review the ground rules and what occurred last session. Students use a go-around technique to respond to the following: "I feel good about myself when . . . " The professional school counselor links commonalities and similarities to create universality, while noting differences to promote acceptance and tolerance.

*Session 3.* Students summarize what happened last session. The professional school counselor facilitates the group's processing of factors that get in the way of positive self-esteem. Media images are considered. Specifically, the messages given to girls of diverse racial, cultural, and ethnic backgrounds are explored. Multiethnic magazines, video clips, and books should be provided as resources. Responses and feelings in reference to those images are processed.

*Session 4.* The group members summarize content and feelings explored last session. The professional school counselor works with the students to process strategies that can be used to combat factors and emotions that hinder positive self-esteem development. Group members should be encouraged to share, but not to advise. The professional school counselor models acceptance and appreciation of each member's participation. Attention is given to the diverse ways and the context within which group participants foster self-esteem development. Issues of self in relation to self, others, and the environment are explored.

*Session 5.* Students use a go-around technique to respond to the following: "Share one thing you learned about yourself and others in the group. Share one thing you value about yourself and others in the group." The professional school counselor summarizes the group sharing/learning. Appreciation of diversity and other emergent diversity themes are emphasized.

*Session 6.* Members conclude the group experience by responding to the prompt: "I feel good about myself when . . . " The professional school counselor links commonalities and similarities to create universality, while noting differences to promote acceptance and tolerance. Group members are encouraged to share and celebrate positive changes in each other's responses. Growth in depth and quality of the responses is noted. Group members complete the Self-Esteem Questionnaire (Appendix B) to culminate the group experience. The professional school counselor collects the questionnaires to review and evaluate them. The questionnaires are returned to group members in individual follow-up/feedback sessions.

**Figure 3. High school level.**

*Standard:* Personal/Social Development: Standard A. Students will acquire the knowledge, attitudes, and interpersonal skills to help them understand and respect self and others.

*Competency:* Students will identify and discuss changing personal and social roles.

*Objective:* After completing the junior counseling session, 80% of the students will be able to identify two implications of their impending role change from high school student to high school graduate.

*Activity:* Individual counseling sessions with high school juniors. The professional school counselor conducts an individual counseling session with each junior. In addition to discussing senior year course selections and graduation requirements, the counselor engages the student in a consideration of changing roles, expectations, and feelings. The professional school counselor's knowledge of cultural and racial identity development and other issues of diversity allows conceptualization of the student's needs and responses that is appropriate, culturally sensitive, and facilitates the beginning of the successful transition from the role of high school student to graduate. The professional school counselor uses multiculturally competent counseling skills to help the student identify effective strategies for effectively addressing any noted expectations, feelings, and implications within the appropriate cultural context. Specifically, the professional school counselor asks each student to identify at least two implications of the role change from high school student to graduate. An action plan is discussed and implemented as appropriate.

*Evaluation:* If 80% of the students were able to identify two implications of their impending role change from high school student to prospective graduate, the objective was met.

## Summary/Conclusion

Student populations are undoubtedly becoming more diverse. As the professional school counselor looks toward the future, professional integrity and competence must include the ability to effectively meet the needs of all students. The rapid growth of diversity in public and private school populations may make the task of meeting all student needs appear, at times, quite awesome. However awesome, the professional school counselor must certainly meet the challenge. The professional school counselor's commitment to students' uniqueness and maximum development of potential demands no less.

## References

American School Counselor Association. (1999). *Position statement: Multicultural counseling.* Alexandria, VA: Author.

Atkinson, D., Thompson, C., & Grant, S. (1993). A three-dimensional model for counseling racial/ethnic minorities. *The Counseling Psychologist, 21,* 257-277.

Blum, D. (1998). *The school counselor's book of lists.* West Nyack, NY: The Center for Applied Research.

Brace, C. (1995). Race and political correctness. *American Psychologist, 50,* 725-726.

Campbell, P. (1994). *Population projections for states, by age, race, sex: 1993 to 2020: Current population reports*, P25-111. Washington, DC: U.S. Bureau of the Census.

Campbell, C., & Dahir, C. (1997). *Sharing the vision: The national standards for school counseling programs.* Alexandria, VA: American School Counselor Association.

Constantine, M. (2001). Theoretical orientation, empathy, and multicultural counseling competence in school counselor trainees. *Professional School Counseling, 4,* 342-348.

Dahir, C., Sheldon, C., & Vaglia, M. (1998). *Visions into action: Implementing the national standards for school counseling programs.* Alexandria, VA: American School Counselor Association.

Gladding, S. (2001). *The counseling dictionary: Concise definitions of frequently used terms.* Upper Saddle River, NJ: Prentice-Hall.

Helms, J. (1995). An update of Helms' white and people of color racial identity models. In J. Ponterotto, J. Casas, L. Suzuki & C. Alexander (Eds.), *Handbook of multicultural counseling* (pp.181-198). Thousand Oaks, CA: Sage.

Herring, R. (1997). *Multicultural counseling in schools: A synergetic approach.* Alexandria, VA: American Counseling Association.

Lee, C.(2001). Culturally responsive school counselors and programs: Addressing the needs of all students. *Professional School Counseling, 4,* 257-261.

Lee, C., & Richardson, B. (Eds.). (1991). *Multicultural issues in counseling: New approaches to diversity.* Alexandria, VA: American Association for Counseling and Development.

National Center for Education Statistics. (2002). *State nonfiscal survey of public elementary/ secondary education 1999-2000.* Washington, DC: Author.

Spindler, G., & Spindler, L. (1994). *Pathways to cultural awareness: Cultural therapy with teachers and students.* Thousand Oaks, CA: Corwin.

Sue, D., Ivey, A., & Pedersen, P. (1996). *A theory of multicultural counseling and therapy.* Pacific Grove, CA: Brooks/Cole.

Whitefield, W., McGrath, P., & Coleman, V. (1992, October). *Increasing multicultural sensitivity and awareness.* Paper presented at the annual conference of the National Organization for Human Services Education, Alexandria, VA.

Yee, A., Fairchild, H., Weizmann, F., & Wyatt, G. (1993). Addressing psychology's problems with race. *American Psychologist, 48,* 1132-1142.

## Appendix A

### Families

Name______________________________
Directions: Draw a picture of your family in the box. Complete the sentences below. You may use the word bank to help you.

| My Family |
|---|
| |

Families are ______________________________.
All families are not the ______________________________.
My family______________________________,but some families______________________________.
Some families__________________but my family__________________
______________________________.
It is good that families are different!
That means each family is ______________________________.

Word Bank:

| Diverse | Unique |
|---|---|
| Special | Same |

---

## Appendix B

# Self Esteem Questionnaire

Name__________________________
Date __________________________

Directions: Complete each of the following sentences.

1. I feel good that I ______________________________.
2. My best quality is ______________________________.
3. Group members appreciated that I
______________________________.
4. I am proud that I ______________________________.
5. When I don't feel good about myself, I know that I can
______________________________.

# Chapter 68

# Understanding Special Education Policies and Procedures

*Tracy Leinbaugh*

## Preview

Professional school counselors are often members of multidisciplinary teams charged with determining student eligibility for special education and related services. In addition, students with disabilities are served within the framework of a comprehensive developmental counseling program. A summary of special education policies and procedures is presented for the professional school counselor.

As the role of the professional school counselor has evolved and expanded over the past 50 years (Baker, 2000), so have the challenges, including the challenge of providing services to students with disabilities. Results of a survey of professional school counselors indicated that professional school counselors provide many services to students with disabilities, but that they only felt "somewhat prepared" (Milson, 2002). It is reasonable to expect the number of students with disabilities to increase, since enrollments of these students have risen yearly since data began to be collected in 1976-1977 (Parrish, 1999). To effectively meet this challenge, it is the professional school counselor's responsibility to acquire a basic knowledge of the disabilities which qualify students for special education and related services under the Individuals with Disabilities Act (IDEA) and the policies and procedures followed by schools to ensure that students with disabilities receive a free and appropriate public education (Schmidt, 1999).

## A Brief History and Description of Special Education Law

The Education for All Handicapped Children Act (P.L. 94-142) was enacted by Congress in 1975 in order to meet the needs of students with disabilities. The federal regulations implementing the law were put in place in 1977. The 1990 Amendments to the Education of All Handicapped Children Act (P.L. 101-476) changed the name of the act to the Individuals With Disabilities Education Act and added "people first" language (e.g., student with a disability, child with a specific disability) throughout (Yell, 1998). The act was again amended in 1991 (P.L.102-119), reauthorizing Part H, the section providing funding for the planning and implementation of early intervention programs and naming the section The Early Intervention Program for Infants and Toddlers with Disabilities (Murdick, Gartin, & Crabtree, 2002). In 1997, the Amendments to IDEA (P.L. 105-17) included clarifications to the law and extended and restructured the original nine subchapters into four subchapters, or parts (Yell, 1998).

The first subchapter of IDEA is Part A, which provides the definitions, or general provisions, of the law. Part B provides detailed information regarding the grant program that requires every state receiving federal assistance under IDEA to ensure that a free and appropriate public education (FAPE) is provided to all qualified children and youth with disabilities within the state. Procedural safeguards protecting the interests of students with disabilities are also included here.

Parts C and D are discretionary support programs. Part C, originally Part H of the Education of the Handicapped Act Amendments of 1986 (P.L. 99-457), extends the protections in Part B to infants and toddlers with disabilities (birth to age three).

Part B has been permanently reauthorized, but Parts C and D are discretionary and support programs which are authorized on a limited basis and must be reauthorized approximately every five years. All 50 states are participants in federal funding and have developed policies and procedures to implement a free and appropriate education to all children and youth with disabilities.

## Principles and Provisions of IDEA

It is important for professional school counselors to know that not all students with disabilities are included in the categories served by the IDEA. Only those whose disability adversely impacts their education and who require special education and related services to achieve are covered. IDEA specifies the following categories of disabling conditions (Turnbull, Turnbull, Shank, Smith, & Leal, 2002; Yell, 1998): specific learning disabilities, speech or language impairments, mental retardation, emotional disturbance, other health impairments, multiple disabilities, deafness, hearing impairments, orthopedic impairments, autism, visual impairments (including blindness), traumatic brain injury, development delay, and deaf-blindness.

These categories are the minimum which states are required to serve. States do not have to adopt every category exactly as specified. They may combine categories, divide categories, use different terminology, or expand the definitions, but all students with disabilities who fall within the categories and meet the appropriate criteria as specified by IDEA must be served for states to receive the federal funding provided by the law.

In addition, states must identify and evaluate all children and youth with disabilities from birth through the age of 21. If a state does not require that students without disabilities receive an education between the ages of 3 - 5 and 18 - 22, they are not required to provide an education for those with disabilities.

IDEA contains provisions to ensure that all students with disabilities who qualify for special education and related services receive a FAPE and that procedural protections are granted to the students and their parents or guardians (Yell, 1998), including:

1. zero reject
2. free and appropriate education (FAPE)
3. least restrictive environment (LRE)
4. identification and evaluation
5. confidentiality of information
6. procedural safeguards
7. technology-related assistance
8. personnel development
9. placement in private schools.

Following is a closer examination of each of these provisions and what each means.

### *Zero Reject*

The zero reject principle means that all students who are eligible for special education and related services under the IDEA are entitled to a FAPE. This entitlement is unconditional and without exception, and extends to students attending private schools. The local public school district is responsible for identifying, assessing, evaluating, and providing services for all eligible students in private schools within the district's boundaries. Parents do not have to request that a school district do this. Each school district is legally responsible for locating all children and youth with disabilities. States generally meet this mandate through the establishment of "child find" programs.

*Free and Appropriate Public Education (FAPE)*

IDEA requires each state to have policies that ensure all students with disabilities a free and appropriate public education. Each state may establish its own special education standards to meet this mandate, but they must, at a minimum, meet those specified by IDEA. State standards may exceed those set by IDEA. Local school districts must meet their state's standards regardless of whether they meet or exceed IDEA's. To ensure that a FAPE is provided to each student with a disability receiving special services, an Individualized Education Program (IEP) must be developed.

*Least Restrictive Environment (LRE)*

The provision of least restrictive environment mandates that all students with disabilities are to be educated with their peers without disabilities to the maximum extent *appropriate* for each individual student. This is determined by the multidisciplinary team, which includes the parents, professionals, and the student when possible, during the development of the IEP.

*Identification and Evaluation*

IDEA mandates a nondiscriminatory (fair and unbiased) evaluation that serves two purposes: 1) to determine whether a student has a disability and, 2) if it is determined that a disability exists and the student is eligible, to decide the nature of the special education and related services the student needs to ensure that a free and appropriate public education is provided. This evaluation must be full and formal, consisting of many different procedures which are specified by IDEA. All procedures must conform to certain standards and are administered and interpreted by trained personnel. Protection is guaranteed in evaluation procedures by the following:

- Tests must be administered in the native language or mode of communication of the child.
- Standardized tests must be validated for the intended purpose and must be administered by trained personnel following the publisher's instructions.
- The evaluation must assess the child's specific areas of educational need. Useful information provided by the parents is included in the evaluation.
- Technically sound instruments must be used to assess multiple areas: cognitive, behavioral, physical, and developmental.
- No single test or procedure may serve as the sole criterion for determination of disability, programming, or placement.
- The evaluation team is multidisciplinary and includes at least one member who has knowledge in the suspected area of disability.
- All areas related to the suspected disability must be assessed.

*Confidentiality*

The privacy rights specified by IDEA are similar to those in the Family Educational Rights and Privacy Act (FERPA), often referred to as the Buckley Amendment. IDEA extends protection to four areas: 1) the right of parental access to records, 2) the right of the parent or guardian to amend their child's records, 3) the right of protection from disclosure of information to others without permission from the parent or guardian (or the student if he or she has reached the age of majority), and 4) the destruction of records.

*Procedural Safeguards*

IDEA includes procedural safeguards to protect the interests of students with disabilities. Included are general safeguards, the right to an independent educational evaluation, the right to the appointment of surrogate parents if needed, and dispute resolution.

General safeguards of particular importance to the professional school counselor are the requirement of notification and consent and the stay-put provision. Schools must notify parents of any change in placement or program and must obtain consent from the parents before the initial evaluation and placement in special education. All parties on the multidisciplinary team must agree to any change in program.

*Technology-related Assistance*

The IDEA mandates that assistive technology devices and services must be provided and included in the IEP if necessary to provide a FAPE as special education or a related service or to maintain the student with a disability in the LRE.

*Personnel Development*

Personnel providing services to students with disabilities must be trained and licensed in their specific fields, and in-service training must be provided to all education personnel working with students with disabilities, including general education teachers. Professional school counselors should participate in opportunities to increase their knowledge and skills in order to effectively serve students with disabilities.

*Private School Placement*

When the local education agency is unable to provide a FAPE and places a student with a disability in a nonpublic school, the local education agency retains responsibility for seeing that the IEP is implemented, a FAPE is provided, and that all education expenses are provided. The parents or guardians of the student are not financially responsible for the costs of the placement.

## Implementation of IDEA

Although states develop their own procedures for implementing IDEA, the basic process of identification of students with disabilities and provision of special education and related services is similar for each. As a member of the school based team, the professional school counselor should be familiar with the basic procedures. The specific policies and provisions for each state are outlined in a manual with sample forms which can be obtained from the special education directors of each school district or from the state's department of education. Following are the steps generally followed when implementing the provisions of the IDEA.

*Screening*

Screening, although not required, is considered good practice. It helps identify which students might need further testing to determine whether they qualify for special education. Screening often is done through the administration of group tests.

*Prereferral*

Schools are prohibited from placing students into special education who have experienced lack of instruction or who have limited English proficiency and who, because of those educational needs, do not perform well in general education. Many schools have teams of teachers and other education specialists, including professional school counselors, for the purpose of providing immediate and necessary help to teachers experiencing challenges with students and to guard against misidentifying students as having disabilities, as this practice can have serious consequences. Accurate records of all interventions and the results are kept, often by professional school counselors, to document the need for a full evaluation, should the team decide that the next step is needed.

*Referral*

The prereferral intervention team may decide to submit to the child study team a formal, written request for a student to receive a full and formal nondiscriminatory evaluation. The form for this request usually asks for specific and comprehensive information regarding basic screening results, areas of education concerns that prompted the referral, the nature of prereferral interventions and results, and any concerns expressed by the student or the family.

*Nondiscriminatory Evaluation*

This requirement of IDEA is for the purpose of finding the answers to two questions: 1) does the student have a disability and 2) if so, what is the nature of the specifically designed instruction and related services that the student needs? Parental consent is required for the evaluation to proceed. The evaluation consists of many different procedures that measure the student's cognitive, behavioral, physical, and developmental functional levels and must conform to certain standards and involve specified individuals. All areas related to the suspected disability must be assessed, including health, vision, hearing, social/emotional functioning, intelligence, academic performance, communicative ability, and motor ability.

Procedures used in the evaluation must be nondiscriminatory on a racial or cultural basis, must be valid for the purpose used, and must accurately reflect the student's aptitude and achievement level. All existing data on the student are reviewed, including school records, observations, work products, and information from the parents. The whole child is evaluated and a broad view is taken of the student's needs and strengths.

*Evaluation Team*

The multidisciplinary evaluation team includes, at a minimum, the student's parents, at least one of the student's general education teachers, at least one special education teacher, a representative of the school district qualified to provide or supervise instruction to meet the unique needs of students with disabilities and who has knowledge of the general education curricula and of the availability of local education resources, someone who can interpret the instructional implications of the evaluation results, related services personnel, and the student when appropriate. The professional school counselor, who possesses many of the skills required by IDEA, may be an important member of this team.

Each professional who administers a test compiles a written report of the instrument used and the findings and presents it at a team meeting. If the student is found to not have a disability and is ineligible for special education, the parents must be given a notice on ineligibility and the student remains in general education without special education and related services. If the student has a disability and qualifies, the team determines specifically what kind of specially designed instruction and related services the student needs, keeping in mind that the school has a duty to provide an appropriate education and access to the general education curricula to the maximum extent appropriate (Reddy, 1999). The school must provide a continuum of placements, from least to most restrictive, which can include regular class placement, special education resource services, a self-contained classroom, a special school, home instruction, or hospital or institution placement (Little & Little, 1999).

*Developing the IFSP and IEP*

Infants and toddlers with disabilities require an Individualized Family Services Plan (IFSP) which takes into consideration the strengths and needs of the family as well as the child. Schools which include preschool programs for children with disabilities may stipulate that the professional school counselor provide many of the services required by the family, including case management. Professional school counselors may also provide case management for elementary and secondary special education students (Dunn & Baker, 2002; Shepard-Tew & Creamer, 1998). Students with disabilities ages 3 through 21 require an Individualized Education Plan (IEP) based on the student's development and needs and specifying outcomes for the student.

The IEP assures that the student will benefit from special education and have the opportunity for an equal education, independent living, economic self-sufficiency, and full participation and is often developed by the same team as that which conducted the evaluation. In the development of the IEP, the team must consider the student's strengths, the parents' concerns, the results of the evaluation, and any special factors, including:

- appropriate strategies to address behavior for students whose behavior impedes the learning of self or others;
- language needs as related to the IEP for the student with English as a second language;
- the use of Braille or other appropriate reading and writing media for the student who is blind or has a visual impairment;
- language and communication needs and opportunities to communicate with peers and professionals in their language and mode for students who are deaf or have hearing impairments; and
- assistive technology devices and services as appropriate (Turner et al., 2002).

The IEP must contain the following:

- the student's level of performance;
- how the disability affects the student's involvement in the general education curriculum;
- measurable annual goals (short-term objectives);
- special education and related services provided to the student, modifications to the program, and supports provided;
- amount of participation in both academic and nonacademic activities with peers without disabilities;
- individual modifications in the administration of state and/or district wide assessments of achievement given to all students;
- dates for beginning services and anticipated frequency, location, and duration of services;
- transition plans, including: 1) beginning at the age of 14, a statement of needs related to transition services, 2) beginning at the age of 16, a statement of needed transition services, and 3) one year before the student reaches the age of majority, a statement that the student has been informed of his rights under IDEA; and
- how progress toward annual goals will be measured and how the parents will be informed of the student's progress.

Movement in school must be promoted by the IEP related to seven adult outcomes: postsecondary education, vocational training, employment with others without disabilities, continuing and adult education, adult services, independent living, and community participation (Turnbull et al., 2002).

IEP team meetings must be scheduled at times that will facilitate parent attendance. If the parents do not participate, the team must develop the IEP to serve the student. Parent consent is not required to implement the IEP, but the parents may challenge it at any point. The IEP must be in effect at the beginning of the school year. In cases where students are determined eligible for services at some time during the school year, the team may not wait until the beginning of the next school year to begin the development of the IEP.

The IEP must be reviewed at least annually and the team must review and revise it to address five matters:

1. any lack of expected progress;
2. the result of a reevaluation (required every three years);
3. information about the student provided to or by the parents;
4. anticipated needs; and
5. other matters related to the student's education.

The professional school counselor may write annual goals for the student with a disability related to social/personal development. Goals may address helping the student and the parents understand the nature of the student's disability and the possible effects on learning, socialization, and personal development and helping the student adjust to school and socialize with peers. Methods of achieving these goals may include parent education, parent support groups, individual counseling with the parents, and individual counseling, group counseling and support groups, and classroom guidance activities involving the student. Among others, such student services may address issues such as personal adjustment, loss and grieving, social skills, family and peer relationships, conflict resolution, decision-making and problem-solving, goal-setting, study skills, career planning, and self esteem (Allen & Laturre, 1998).

## Summary/Conclusion

Students with disabilities are increasingly receiving special education in general education classrooms with their peers without disabilities. Professional school counselors are highly trained educational specialists who provide services to all students, including students with disabilities. These services may require serving as a member of a prereferral intervention team or a multidisciplinary team. The professional school counselor may write annual goals for the IEPs of students with disabilities and be responsible for the implementation of those goals. When implementing a developmental, comprehensive guidance and counseling program, students with disabilities are recipients of responsive services, classroom guidance, and individual planning, just as students without disabilities are. A basic understanding of the federal laws, provisions and procedures relating to special education are beneficial for the professional school counselor to understand and to ensure that each and every student may benefit from his or her education.

## References

Allen, J. M., & LaTorre, E. (1998). What a school administrator needs to know about the school counselor's role with special education. In J. M. Allen (Ed.), *School counseling: New perspectives and practices* (pp. 99-104). Greensboro, NC: ERIC/CASS.

Baker, S. B. (2000). *School counseling for the twenty-first century* (3rd ed.). Upper Saddle River, NJ: Merrill.

Dunn, N. A., & Baker, S. B. (2002). Readiness to serve students with disabilities: A survey of elementary school counselors. *Professional School Counseling, 5,* 277-284.

Little, S. G., & Little K. A. A. (1999). Legal and ethical issues of inclusion. *Special Services in the Schools, 15*(1/2), 125-144.

Milson, A. S. (2002). Students with disabilities: School counselor involvement and preparation. *Professional School Counseling, 5,* 331-338.

Murdick, N., Gartin, B., & Crabtree, T. (2002). *Special education law.* Upper Saddle River, NJ: Merrill.

Parrish, T. B. (1999). *Special education at what cost to general education?* Palo Alto, CA: Center for Special Education Finance, American Institutes for Research.

Reddy, L. A. (1999). Inclusion of disabled children and school reform: A historical perspective. *Special Services in the Schools, 15*(1/2), 3–24.

Schmidt, J. J. (1999). *Counseling in the schools: Essential services and comprehensive programs* (3rd ed.). Needham Heights, MA: Allyn & Bacon.

Shepard-Tew, D., & Creamer, D. A. (1998). Elementary school integrated services teams: Applying case-management techniques. *Professional School Counseling, 2*(2), 141-145.

Turnbull, R., Turnbull, A., Shank, M., Smith, S., & Leal, D. (2002). *Exceptional lives: Special education in today's schools* (3rd ed.). Upper Saddle River, NJ: Merrill.

Yell, M. L. (1998). *The law and special education.* Upper Saddle River, NJ: Merrill.

# Chapter 69

## Understanding Section 504 Policies and Procedures

*Amy J. Newmeyer & Mark Newmeyer*

### Preview

Section 504 of The Rehabilitation Act of 1973 can be used to provide school accommodations for a variety of disabilities not covered under the Individuals with Disabilities Education Act (IDEA) guidelines. It is important that professional school counselors have an understanding of this law and how it can be utilized to best serve students who need various accommodations in the school setting. This chapter reviews Section 504 policies, discusses differences between policies and procedures for the IDEA and Section 504, and concludes with two case examples.

Section 504 of The Rehabilitation Act of 1973 is a law that prohibits discrimination on the basis of disability in any program or activity that receives federal financial assistance. Thus all public school systems are covered under the scope of this law. The U.S. Department of Education, Office for Civil Rights, is responsible for enforcing this law in different areas: employment practices; program accessibility; and preschool, elementary, secondary, and post-secondary education. In a school setting, this means that students with disabilities should be able to access the same services as students without disabilities. Section 504 defines eligible students as those who have a physical or mental impairment, have a record of such an impairment, or are perceived as having such an impairment (Schulzinger, 1999).

There are several important differences between IDEA and Section 504:

- Section 504 applies to elementary, secondary, postsecondary, and work settings, while IDEA only applies to elementary and secondary school settings (Betz, 2001).
- Section 504 does not list specific groups of eligible students; rather, it defines eligible students as those who have a physical or mental impairment which substantially limits one or more major life activities, including caring for self, performing manual tasks, walking, seeing, hearing, speaking, breathing, learning, and working.
- Section 504 describes "appropriate education" as those services that meet the needs of the student with a disability as adequately as those students without a disability.
- Section 504 does not require that a diagnostic evaluation be performed to determine eligibility.
- Section 504 does not provide funds to the school system to provide services.
- Section 504 requires that the school district designate an employee that will ensure compliance with the law and handle any grievances.
- Section 504 requires the school district to ensure that tests and other evaluation measures are given in a way that reflects the student's skills and are not affected by impairment.
- Students eligible for section 504 accommodations remain in a general education classroom because 504 guarantees access, not services or specialized instruction (Schulzinger, 1999).

Examples of students who may qualify for Section 504 accommodations:

- Students who have a chronic medical condition that causes them to miss extended periods of time at school due to appointments for health care and therapies or symptoms of pain and fatigue.
- Students who have side-effects from prescribed medications.
- Students who need an assistive communication device to participate in the classroom.
- Students who are evaluated for IDEA but may be ineligible. These conditions may include learning disabilities or Attention-Deficit/Hyperactivity Disorder.
- Students who cannot take written or oral tests due to impaired writing or communication skills (Schulzinger, 1999).

Reasonable accommodations for eligible students may include the following areas: physical rearrangement of the classroom, lesson presentation, assignments, test-taking, organizational skills, behaviors, or medication administration. Some examples include:

- changing the volume of homework while maintaining the same educational standards;
- allowing rest periods for children who are easily fatigued, or rearranging the classroom schedule to allow for a shortened academic day;
- providing an extra set of materials for the student to use at home;
- providing access to health care during field-trip and off-campus activities;
- seating the student near the teacher to minimize distractions;
- asking the teacher to repeat instructions or write them down for the student;
- breaking assignments into smaller segments (Schulzinger, 1999).

Section 504 states that the decision regarding placement and services should be made by a group of professionals, rather than an individual. The referral for a section 504 plan may come from a professional, parent, or the student. The school must have a designated 504 coordinator who is responsible for coordinating services and assembling the team (Belz, 2001). However, the law does not state which school personnel must be present as members of the team. The professional school counselor can play a vital role in assisting this team with determining appropriate services and advocating for students with special needs. Other personnel who should be present include the student's teachers, parents, school nurse, and other related service providers. Although the law does not require a written document, it is generally encouraged to ensure that everyone involved is aware of the accommodations and plan for services. Many experts recommend the 504 plan follow the same format as an IEP.

*The Role of the Professional School Counselor*

The professional school counselor is in a position to advocate for a student who may benefit from a 504 plan. The school counselor can initiate a referral for a 504 plan by contacting the school's 504 coordinator. Additionally, by providing a linkage between the family, classroom, school, 504 coordinator and other support systems, the school counselor often greatly facilitates the collaborative process. The school counselor also plays a vital role by informing and educating principle individuals regarding the benefits of utilizing 504 accommodations. That is to say, educators and families may not fully understand the importance that 504 accommodations may have in a student's educational development.

*Case Study #1*

A 9-year-old female student in a third grade classroom has recently been diagnosed with Attention-Deficit/Hyperactivity Disorder, Predominantly Inattentive Type. She has normal intelligence and does not have any evidence of learning disabilities or a language disorder. She does not have any significant behavioral problems in the classroom setting. However, she is inattentive and distractible, and frequently forgets to write down assignments or turn them in, significantly impacting the grades that she receives. This student may qualify for accommodations under Section 504. Possible accommodations include:

- Changing her classroom seat so that she is close to the teacher and distractions from other students are minimized.
- Establishing an assignment book that is checked by her teacher at the end of the day to ensure that she has written down all assignments. Her parents can be responsible for checking the assignment book to ensure that assignments are completed and returned to school.
- Repeating directions if necessary to ensure that she has heard them correctly.
- Giving extra test-taking time, if needed.
- If medications are administered, excusing her from the classroom at the appropriate time to receive the medication.

*Case Study #2*

A 13-year-old male has recently been diagnosed with cancer. He has always been a good student, and has no known behavioral or academic problems. However, he has missed several weeks of school for hospitalization, and now is on a medication regimen at home that also requires medications during the day at school. Although he wants to attend school, his teachers are noticing that he seems exhausted by the end of the school day and often falls asleep in class. Possible accommodations for this child include:

- Rearranging his class schedule so that all academic courses are attended in the morning, so that he is excused for the afternoon if fatigued.
- Providing an extra set of books for use at home or in the hospital to be able to keep up on homework.
- Allowing for more than the maximum number of days to be missed if he is able to complete the missed work on time.
- Allowing for a note-taking buddy in his classes to send him notes when he is absent.
- Excusing him from class when necessary to administer medications.
- Allowing for use of a wheelchair for off-campus field trips if his participation is limited due to exhaustion.

## Summary/Conclusion

Section 504 of The Rehabilitation Act of 1973 is a law ensuring that students with medical or psychological conditions have equal access to services in facilities and programs receiving federal financial assistance. However, many school and medical professionals are not fully aware of the regulations set forth in Section 504. This often results in confusion regarding the use of a 504 plan, and thus available services and accommodation may be overlooked (American Academy of Pediatrics, 2000). The professional school counselor should be aware of the presence of the 504 statute, as it can be used to provide certain accommodations to students with disabilities who do not qualify for services under the IDEA regulations. Additionally, the professional school counselor is frequently called upon to be the 504 case manager for students and can also act as an advocate for the student with a disability by initiating the process of forming a 504 plan and serving as a member of the 504 team.

## References

American Academy of Pediatrics. (2000). Provision of educationally-related services for children and adolescents with chronic diseases and disabling conditions: Committee on children with disabilities. *Pediatrics, 105*, 448-451.

Betz, C. (2001). Use of 504 plans for children and youth with disabilities: Nursing application. *Pediatric Nursing, 27*, 347-352.

Schulzinger, R. (1999). *Understanding the 504 statute: The role of state Title V programs and health care providers*. An occasional policy brief of the Institute for Child Health Policy, Gainesville, FL.

# Chapter 70

## Helping Students with Disabilities Through Multidisciplinary Teams

*Amy S. Milsom*

### Preview

Multidisciplinary teams are widely used in school districts to assess the needs of students with disabilities and to develop interventions for those students. Bringing specialized skills and knowledge, professional school counselors are often integral members of those teams, which can include school personnel, community agency personnel, parents, and students. By identifying specific roles, this chapter outlines ways that professional school counselors can help students with disabilities via multidisciplinary teams through the various stages of the special education process (i.e., referral, assessment, IEP development, implementation, and evaluation). Advantages and disadvantages of three different team models (multidisciplinary, interdisciplinary, transdisciplinary) are also discussed.

It is estimated that 10-12% of school age students have disabilities (Glenn, 1998). The Individuals with Disabilities Education Act (IDEA) Amendments of 1997 (P.L. 105-17) defined the term "students with disabilities" as students who meet the criteria for one or more of the following: autism, emotional disturbance, hearing impairment, specific learning disability, mental retardation, orthopedic impairment, speech or language impairment, traumatic brain injury, visual impairment, or some other health impairment (e.g., Attention Deficit/Hyperactivity Disorder, asthma) that adversely affects educational performance.

Since 1975, federal disability legislation (i.e., P.L. 94-142, the Education for All Handicapped Children Act) has mandated that school districts identify and provide special education and related services to students with disabilities. As a result, these students are now being educated in public schools and, to the greatest extent possible, in regular education classrooms. In addition, as part of their ethical responsibility to provide comprehensive counseling and guidance services to all students, professional school counselors perform a variety of activities for students with disabilities.

In order to receive federal funding, school districts must adhere to guidelines outlined in P.L. 94-142 (renamed IDEA in 1990). Although some guidelines have changed over time, the specific requirements for the assessment and evaluation of students with disabilities have remained fairly consistent. IDEA mandates the use of multidisciplinary teams (MDTs) for the assessment of students with disabilities and for determining placement in, and types of, special education services to be provided. Many students with disabilities also receive special services under Section 504 of the Rehabilitation Act of 1973 (Section 504). Even though Section 504 does not specifically require the use of MDTs, these teams are frequently used during the implementation of services under this legislation.

## Multidisciplinary Teams

MDTs are known by many names including child study teams, staffing teams, and assessment teams, to list but a few. Based on the belief that input from a variety of individuals will be less biased than input from only one individual (Kaiser & Woodman, 1985), the main purpose of using MDTs is to provide an unbiased evaluation of a student.

MDTs can be used for a variety of purposes in schools, however they are probably most commonly associated with initial assessments of students to determine eligibility for special education services, for Individualized Education Program (IEP) development and implementation decisions, and for reviewing special education placement decisions on an informal basis (Pfeiffer & Heffernan, 1984).

Logically, an MDT consists of a group of individuals from a variety of disciplines. Team composition will vary depending on the purpose of the team. For example, IDEA requires that an MDT used for the initial assessment of a student must include an individual with knowledge or understanding of the particular disability. Overton (1996) indicated that these types of MDTs often consist of a special education teacher, school psychologist, and school administrator. Other members of an assessment team might include a parent, a regular education teacher, and a professional school counselor or other support staff member, such as a speech clinician or rehabilitation counselor.

Yell, Rogers, and Rogers (1998) indicated that an MDT used for assessment of a student and an MDT formed for the purpose of generating an IEP do not necessarily consist of the same individuals, although they could. In addition, team composition will vary depending on the needs of the student. The 1997 IDEA Amendments stated that the IEP team must contain a special education teacher, regular education teacher, parent, local education agency (LEA) representative (typically a school administrator), the student (when appropriate), and other support personnel such as a professional school counselor or speech clinician. Table 1 provides examples of how team composition might vary depending on the purpose of the team and the individual needs of the student.

## Professional School Counselors and MDTs

The American School Counselor Association (ASCA) supports professional school counselor involvement with students with disabilities and created a position statement to guide practitioners in determining appropriate roles and responsibilities related to those students (ASCA, 1999). ASCA indicated that while participating on and providing feedback to MDTs are important responsibilities, professional school counselors should not participate on MDTs as representatives of the administrative staff (i.e., replacing a school administrator as an LEA) or on teams for students who are not normally part of their caseloads. In addition, ASCA encouraged professional school counselors to engage in collaboration with school staff, parents, and community members or agencies, involvement with the development of transition and behavior modification plans, implementation of counseling and guidance services (individual, small group, and classroom), and advocacy for students with disabilities in the school and community.

Although they are not required to participate on MDTs, professional school counselors are often integral members of those teams. In fact, in a national survey of professional school counselors, 100% indicated that they provide services to students with disabilities and 80% indicated that they participated on MDTs for those students (Milsom, 2002). Fairchild (1985) indicated that because MDT members often tend to focus mainly on the academic needs of students with disabilities, professional school counselors can help bring focus to students' holistic needs. In addition to academic concerns, self-esteem, behavior, interpersonal skills, and

**Table 1. MDT variation.**

| Student | Purpose | Team Members |
|---|---|---|
| 15 years old with a learning disability | Initial assessment | School psychologist<br>Special education teacher<br>Parent<br>Professional school counselor |
| | IEP development | Special education teacher<br>Regular education teacher<br>Administrator (LEA)<br>Parent<br>Student<br>Professional school counselor |
| 6 years old with severe mental retardation | Initial assessment | School psychologist<br>Special education teacher |
| | IEP development | Parent<br>School psychologist<br>Special ed. teacher<br>Regular ed. teacher<br>Administrator (LEA)<br>Parent<br>Speech clinician<br>Physical therapist<br>Professional school counselor |

career development are areas that professional school counselors can contribute knowledge and expertise.

Professional school counselors can become involved with MDTs in a variety of ways, and it is likely that their involvement will vary not only from school district to school district, but also from building to building within the same district. Through MDT involvement, professional school counselors provide services to students with disabilities during the initial referral process, assessment, IEP development, IEP implementation and evaluation. Professional school counselors can help students with disabilities in a variety of ways during these different stages.

*Referral Stage*

Professional school counselors are often the first individuals in the school to be contacted when a student is having academic difficulties or when some other need becomes apparent. Parents or teachers might contact the professional school counselor to find out what options are available to students with suspected disabilities. In those instances, professional school counselors might choose to initiate a team meeting. They might be responsible for making initial contact with family members, sharing information with a school psychologist or special education coordinator, and possibly scheduling the initial team meeting.

*Assessment Stage*

Professional school counselors might be responsible for collecting data related to the student's academic history and current academic status, interpersonal functioning, or classroom behavior. In addition to summarizing academic records and looking for patterns, professional school counselors might use a variety of checklists to evaluate social skills or to monitor behavior in an attempt to identify strengths and weaknesses in those areas. Classroom observations can also be used to gather data for the assessment team.

*IEP Development Stage*

The role of the professional school counselor on the IEP team will vary. For students who are age 14 or older, professional school counselors can be valuable contributors to the development of the transition plan that is required by IDEA. They can identify skill or knowledge deficits as well as appropriate resources and interventions to help a student prepare for the transition to work, postsecondary school, or supported living environments after high school. Professional school counselors can also collaborate with special education teachers to develop appropriate transition interventions.

In addition, if the team determines that a student would benefit from counseling services, the professional school counselor would design a counseling intervention plan. Many students with disabilities could benefit from counseling interventions targeting issues such as self-esteem, social skills, or anger management, and professional school counselors possess the knowledge and skills needed to develop interventions in these areas. In addition, professional school counselors are familiar with counseling approaches (e.g., behavioral techniques, play techniques, group work) that have been shown to be effective with students with disabilities.

In addition to developing transition programs and counseling interventions, professional school counselors might also be involved with the development of a behavior management plan. With knowledge of issues such as human development, motivation, and reinforcement, professional school counselors can help teachers to develop behavior management plans that will be developmentally appropriate, manageable, and effective. They may also consult with family members to help establish consistent expectations between home and school.

Finally, professional school counselors often perform what some might describe to be administrative tasks during this stage. For example, if team decisions result in the need for a revised student schedule, the professional school counselor could be responsible for creating an appropriate course schedule. Also, if the main needs of the student fall into the expertise of the professional school counselor (e.g., while a student is receiving academic accommodations under Section 504 related to severe burns, he is mainly having difficulty coping with and accepting his new appearance), it may be appropriate for the professional school counselor to chair the IEP meeting. In those instances, professional school counselors will have opportunities to practice group facilitation skills and model effective leadership characteristics (Lockhart, 2003).

*Implementation Stage*

During this stage professional school counselors can implement the programs and interventions designed during the IEP meeting. Interventions might include one-on-one counseling, small group work, or classroom guidance lessons related to academic, career, or personal/social areas. As mentioned previously, target areas might include transition planning, interpersonal needs, and behavior management.

Collaboration and consultation with team members is also important during this stage. Professional school counselors are frequently the liaisons between the school and community agencies that might be involved in providing services to a student. Professional school counselors might also be responsible for coordinating communication with families. Finally, continued consultation and collaboration with teachers and other team members can help ensure the successful implementation of services along with effective team functioning.

*Evaluation Stage*

Evaluation of student progress can involve independent as well as collaborative data collection. For example, professional school counselors can attempt to individually evaluate the effectiveness of the social skills interventions they have implemented, or they can also obtain feedback from other team members regarding student progress in relation to that goal area. In addition, professional school counselors might be responsible for collecting and summarizing data related to specific IEP goal areas (e.g., academics, social skills, behavior).

## Team Functioning

Professional school counselor involvement also requires an understanding of team dynamics. Hardman, Drew, Egan, and Wolf (1993) indicated that MDTs help to facilitate collaboration among professionals; however, researchers argue that collaboration and communication among MDT members is often minimal (Carpenter, King-Sears, & Keys, 1998; Heubner & Gould, 1991; Ogletree, Bull, Drew, & Lunnen, 2001). A discussion of three team models (multidisciplinary, interdisciplinary, and transdisciplinary) will help to clarify this potential problem.

*Multidisciplinary Teams*

MDTs involve team members functioning independently of one another. MDT members independently assess students and share findings with the team. For example, a special education teacher might collect data related to reading comprehension and a professional school counselor might conduct an observation to assess interpersonal needs. This information would be brought to the team, but a team leader (perhaps a school psychologist) is then responsible for moving the team toward final decisions regarding placement and type of services to provide. Team members proceed to independently provide services specific to their areas of expertise. While they might have an awareness of what services other team members are providing, they are not influenced by those activities (Carpenter et al., 1998). Ultimately, there is little teamwork involved in MDTs. In addition, families are typically excluded from the decision-making process and team members independently initiate family involvement to monitor progress or provide feedback (Ogletree et al., 2001).

Although professional school counselors have training in group process and dynamics, MDTs provide them little opportunity to use these skills. In addition, while they could certainly initiate consultative or collaborative relationships with team members, the team philosophy might encourage team member resistance to these types of relationships. As a result, professional school counselor involvement on MDTs likely would include independent assessment and implementation of services with minimal interaction with other members outside of the team meeting. Finally, with family contact being inconsistent across team members, professional school counselors might find contact with families to be awkward. Also, with minimal awareness of the services that other team members are providing, they may struggle to respond to family questions regarding non-counseling related services.

*Interdisciplinary Teams*

Interdisciplinary teams (IDTs) are characterized by interdependence rather than independence (Ogletree et al., 2001). IDT members assess students within the realm of their own disciplines, but assessment activities are coordinated with those of other team members

(Carpenter et al., 1998). Decisions regarding types of services to provide are jointly determined and members occasionally work together to provide services (Ogletree et al.). A case manager, rather than a team leader, helps to facilitate communication among team members and often acts as a family liaison (Carpenter et al.).

IDTs allow professional school counselors to perform some of the roles ASCA (1999) recommended in relation to students with disabilities. First, IDTs support and encourage professional school counselor collaboration with other team members, particularly during the IEP development stage. They also allow opportunities to provide direct services to students. In addition, IDTs provide greater opportunities for professional school counselors to influence group process. Finally, consultation and collaboration with families is expected.

*Transdisciplinary Teams*

The third team model, transdisciplinary teams (TDTs), is often believed to be the most effective approach for the assessment and evaluation of students with disabilities. TDTs involve a coordination of services, cooperation and collaboration among team members, and active parent involvement throughout the process (Carpenter et al., 1998). A case coordinator works with the family to determine assessment needs. Then, with the consultation of other team members, only a few team members conduct the assessment. Service delivery decisions are collaboratively determined. In addition, services are provided by a few team members with input from the rest of the team. The result is a well-coordinated effort (Ogletree et al., 2001).

Carpenter et al. (1998) indicated that professional school counselors perform many roles on TDTs, with one of the main roles being that of a collaborative consultant working jointly with team members during the assessment, IEP development, implementation, and evaluation stages. Professional school counselors can also act as family and community liaisons, case managers, and providers of direct services. Also, TDTs provide professional school counselors ample opportunities to facilitate group process.

Although TDTs are often believed to be the most effective means of providing comprehensive, coordinated services to students with disabilities, each team model has advantages and disadvantages (see Table 2). These advantages and disadvantages must be weighed before deciding how to approach the provision of special education services. Ogletree et al. (2001) believed "teams must be satisfied and confident in their adopted model" (p. 142). In an attempt to create a model that matches the needs of the school district and the team members, it is not uncommon for teams to combine various aspects of the three models discussed previously. With their understanding of group processes and the importance of collaboration, professional school counselors can help school districts decide how they want to approach the formation of MDTs and determine which components of the three different models (MDT, IDT, TDT) should be adopted.

## Summary/Conclusion

MDT involvement supports the provision of comprehensive school counseling services to all students. Table 3 shows how helping students with disabilities through MDTs encourages professional school counselors to integrate the components of a comprehensive school counseling program into their work with students with disabilities.

Although their services are not mandated by disability legislation, it is apparent that professional school counselors can bring specialized skills and knowledge to MDTs. In addition, MDTs support a proactive approach, collaboration, and the comprehensive provision of services to students, all of which are consistent with national school counseling program models. MDTs

**Table 2. Advantages and disadvantages of team models.**

| | MDT | IDT | TDT |
|---|---|---|---|
| **Advantages** | Convenient<br>Efficient | Equality among team members<br><br>Complementary services<br><br>Efficient | Collaboration<br><br>Empowers families<br><br>Holistic services |
| **Disadvantages** | Exclusion of family<br><br>Lack of collaboration<br><br>Fragmented services | Minimal family involvement<br><br>Time-consuming | Team member resistance<br><br>Time-consuming |

also allow professional school counselors to collaborate with others in targeting the academic, career, and personal/social needs of students with disabilities. Thus, in order to most effectively help students with disabilities, professional school counselors should initiate and advocate their involvement on these teams. Having a basic understanding of disability legislation, team models, and the roles they can assume during different stages of the special education process is important if professional school counselors want to contribute to the team process.

**Table 3. MDT roles related to comprehensive school counseling program components.**

| Comprehensive School Counseling Program Component | Professional School Counselor's Role on the MULTIDISCIPLINARY TEAM |
|---|---|
| **Counseling** | Individual counseling<br>Small group counseling<br>Group facilitation |
| **Consultation & Collaboration** | MDT member – consult and collaborate with teachers, parents, community agencies, etc. |
| **Coordination** | Schedule initial meeting; Generate revised course schedule |
| **Case Management** | Chair MDT meeting; Plan counseling intervention |
| **Guidance Curriculum** | Implement guidance curriculum |
| **Assessment**<br>**Leadership & Advocacy** | Data collection and analysis<br>Referral; Chair meeting<br>Group facilitation |

## References

American School Counselor Association. (1999). *The professional school counselor and the special needs student.* Retrieved February 25, 2002, from http://www.schoolcounselor.org/content.cfm?L1=1000&L2=32.

Carpenter, S. L., King-Sears, M. E., & Keys, S. G. (1998). Counselors + educators + families as a transdisciplinary team = more effective inclusion for students with disabilities. *Professional School Counseling, 2,* 1-9.

Education for All Handicapped Children Act of 1975, 20 U.S.C. 1400 *et seq.*

Fairchild, T. N. (1985). The school counselor's role as a team member: Participating in the development of IEPs. *The School Counselor, 32,* 364-370.

Glenn, E. E. (Ed.). (1998). Counseling children and adolescents with disabilities [Special Issue]. *Professional School Counseling, 2*(1).

Hardman, M. L., Drew, C. J., Egan, M. W., & Wolf, B. (1993). *Human exceptionality: Society, school, and family* (4th ed.). Boston, MA: Allyn & Bacon.

Huebner, E. S., & Gould, K. (1991). Multidisciplinary teams revisited: Current perceptions of school psychologists regarding team functioning. *School Psychology Review, 20,* 428-434.

Individuals with Disabilities Education Act Amendments of 1997.20 U.S.C. 1400 *et seq.* (West 1998).

Kaiser, S. M., & Woodman, R. W. (1985). Multidisciplinary teams and group decision-making techniques: Possible solutions to decision-making problems. *School Psychology Review, 14,* 457-470.

Lockhart, E. (2003). Student with disabilities. In B. T. Erford (Ed.), *Transforming the school counseling profession* (pp.357-410). Columbus, OH: Merrill/Prentice-Hall.

Milsom, A. S. (2002). *Students with disabilities: School counselor involvement and preparation. Professional School Counseling, 5,* 331-338.

Ogletree, B. T., Bull, J., Drew, R., & Lunnen, K. Y. (2001). Team-based service delivery for students with disabilities: Practice options and guidelines for success. *Intervention in School and Clinic, 36,* 138-145.

Overton, T. (1996). *Assessment in special education: An applied approach* (2nd ed.). Englewood Cliffs, NJ: Prentice Hall.

Pfeiffer, S., & Heffernan, L. (1984). Improving multidisciplinary team functions. In C. A. Maher, R. J. Illback, & J. E. Zins (Eds.), *Organizational psychology in the schools: A handbook for professionals* (pp. 283-301). Springfield, IL: Charles C. Thomas.

Section 504 of the Rehabilitation Act of 1973, 29 U.S.C. Section 794 *et seq.*

# Chapter 71

## Medication Issues in Schools

*Mark D. Newmeyer & Amy J. Newmeyer*

### Preview

The professional school counselor can serve an important role regarding medication management in the school setting by facilitating communication between the student, family, school and physician, thereby maximizing therapeutic benefit. This type of multimodal approach has been shown to result in the best benefit to the student. The professional school counselor can be actively involved in providing many of these ancillary services, including personal counseling, social skills training, and management of behavior in the classroom setting. Although the focus of this chapter is on psychotropic medications, the principles discussed are generally applicable to medication management in other chronic conditions.

A considerable number of students are diagnosed with chronic conditions requiring treatment regimens that are complex, time consuming, and require ongoing management over the course of a lifetime (Newacheck & Taylor, 1992). The quality of life for this population and their families is frequently influenced by their capacity to successfully manage the conditions and integrate treatments into daily functioning. Student and family non-adherence with treatment regimens for pediatric chronic illnesses has been recognized as an important clinical problem that may contribute to unnecessary hospitalizations and increase risk for illness-related complications, psychosocial maladjustments, and increased medical costs (Riekert & Drotar, 2000).

Changes in health care and how services are delivered, such as briefer duration of hospital stays, limited reimbursements, and limited time a practitioner may spend with patients, have created a responsibility shift. Families are much more responsible for assuming treatment services that were typically delivered in clinical settings, e.g., administration of medicines to childhood cancer patients (Tebbi, Richards, Cummings, Zevon, & Mallon, 1988). Riekert and Drotar (2000) observed that families may not be prepared or capable of assuming such treatment-related duties. Additionally, trends in scientific investigation that have emphasized a biological base for mental health disorders have contributed to various new classes of pharmacological interventions (Ingersoll, 2000).

Since students spend a major portion of the day in a school setting, it is important that school personnel are mindful of the students' medical management. Professional school counselors and school nurses are in an important position to facilitate student adherence to medication management.

## Laws, School Policies and Recommendations

The professional school counselor should be aware of individual state laws and local school policies regarding medication administration in the school setting, because these vary regionally. In some schools, non-medical personnel can administer medication. Some students may be required to self-report for medications each day without any reminder by school personnel. The following is a review of American Academy of Pediatrics (AAP)(1993) committee on school health recommendations for administration of medication in the schools.

- Each school or school district should develop a defined policy regarding medication administration in the schools.
- The school should require a written statement from the physician that provides the name of medication, dose, time of administration, and physician's phone number. Diagnosis should be provided unless there is a reason that this information is confidential.
- The physician should alert the school of any serious side effects of medication.
- If there is a risk of severe reaction, the appropriate emergency response plan should be outlined by the physician.
- The physician should state whether the child is capable of self-administering the medication. (This may not be possible in some states.)
- The parent or guardian should provide written permission for medication administration at the school.
- The school should develop a policy regarding self-administration of over-the-counter medications. (This may not be possible in some states.)
- Secure storage should be available for all medications.

Many longer-acting medications are now available that allow the student to take dosages only at home, eliminating the necessity of school administration. The professional school counselor and school nurse should be aware of what medications the student is taking at home and whether infrequent home administration may be contributing to non-response in the school setting, although there is no legal basis for requiring parents to inform school personnel. Appropriate intervention with the student and family may prevent serious health issues associated with non-administration of medications.

## Basic Classifications of Drugs, Names and Properties

Many different medications are available to address behavioral and psychiatric issues in children and adolescents. Rapid development of new medications in the last few years has resulted in a dramatic increase in the number of available medications. Because students often receive these medications at school and spend a significant portion of their day at school, it is important for the professional school counselor to be familiar with these medications and their uses and side effects. Any noted side effects should be reported to the student's parent and the prescribing physician, if consent has been obtained from the parent. The following review will be limited to psychotropic medications, as these are the most common types of medications used in the school setting. However, this list is not exhaustive. Review of the current edition of the *Physician's Desk Reference* (PDR) is recommended for extensive information about any medication.

### *Anti-Depressant Medications*

Selective serotonin reuptake inhibitors (SSRI's) are used to address symptoms of anxiety and depression. Commonly used medications in this class include Prozac® (fluoxetine), Zoloft® (sertraline), Paxil® (paroxetine), Celexa® (citolopram), and Luvox® (fluvoxamine). These medications are most commonly administered once daily in the morning or evening. Common side effects include nausea, weight loss, insomnia, excessive sweating, and sedation.

Tricyclic antidepressants may also be used to address anxiety, depression, or inattention and hyperactivity. Commonly used medications include Tofranil® (imipramine), Pamelor® (nortriptyline), and Elavil® (amitriptyline). Side effects include fatigue, constipation, dry mouth, blurred vision, and drowsiness. These medications may have effects on the electrical pattern of the heart.

Wellbutrin® (buproprion) may also be used for anxiety, depression, or inattention and hyperactivity. Side effects are similar to those of tricyclic antidepressants. Wellbutrin® may increase a student's risk of seizures.

Eskalith® (lithum) may also be used to address mania and/or depression. Common side effects include fine tremors, increased thirst, nausea, headache, weight gain, and increased urinary frequency (Kline, Silver & Russell, 2001).

Remuron® (mirtazapine) is a newer antidepressant not related to the above medications. Side effects include drowsiness and nausea (Physician's Desk Reference, 2002).

*Stimulant Medications*

Stimulant medications are commonly used to address inattention, hyperactivity, and impulsivity often associated with Attention-Deficit/Hyperactivity Disorder (AD/HD). Commonly used medications include Ritalin®, Metadate®, Methylin®, and Concerta® (methylphenidate), Dexedrine® (dextroamphetamine), and Adderall® (dextro and levo-amphetamine). These medications are available in short-acting formulations lasting up to 4 hours per dose, and long-acting formulations lasting up to 12 hours per dose. This information may be relevant when determining medication effects in the classroom setting. Common side effects include loss of appetite, headaches, stomachaches, and motor tics (Kline et al, 2001).

*Antipsychotic Medications*

Antipsychotic medications are used to address aggression and psychosis. Traditional or "typical" antipsychotic medications include Haldol® (haloperidol), Thorazine® (chlorpromazine), and Mellaril® (thioridazine). Common side effects include sedation, dystonia (increase in muscle tone and spasms of neck, mouth, and tongue), and tardive dyskinesia (involuntary movements of extremities, trunk, or facial muscles). New medications in this class are called "atypical" antipsychotics. These include Risperdal® (risperidone), Zyprexa® (olanzapine), Seroquel® (quetiapine), and Geodon® (ziprasidone). These medications have lower risk of muscular side effects, but may cause hyperglycemia and weight gain. Any muscular side effects should be reported immediately to the prescribing physician (Kline et al., 2001; Physician's Desk Reference, 2002).

*Antiepileptics*

Although these medications are most commonly used to control seizures, they may also be used for symptoms of aggression. Commonly used medications include Depakote® and Depakene® (valproic acid), and Tegretol® (carbamezapine). Side effects may include nausea, vomiting, sedation and easy bruising. Monitoring of liver and blood functioning should occur while individuals are taking this medication (Kline et al., 2001). New antineuroleptics , including Lamictal® (lamotrigine), Topomax® (topirimate) and Neurontin® (gabapentin), have fewer side effects and do not require extensive monitoring with blood tests (PDR, 2002).

## Comorbid Factors: Learning Disabilities, Language Disorder, and Other Psychiatric Issues

Many students with psychiatric conditions have co-morbid conditions that are often overlooked when focusing on the behavioral issues in the classroom. For instance, many children with AD/HD may also have learning disabilities, language disorders, and other psychiatric conditions such as depression or anxiety (Blondis, 1996). These co-morbid conditions should also be addressed in order to maximize the student's functioning at school. Co-morbid factors that are not addressed may limit response to medical treatment of the target condition. For example, a student being treated for AD/HD who has a reading disability may continue to demonstrate AD/HD-like behavior despite medication management if the reading disability is not addressed.

## Linkage Between the Family, School, Classroom and Medical Community

The professional school counselor is in a distinct and important position to advocate for a student requiring medication management. The professional school counselor and school nurse may serve as a link between the family, the classroom, the school, and even the medical community, not merely in providing support, but also valued information.

While families may adapt well to having a student requiring medication on an ongoing basis, some do not. Various research studies examining effective parental roles in managing their child's asthma indicated an alarmingly high non-adherence rate in spite of potential adverse risks to the child (Milgrom et al, 1996). Results are not that dissimilar across a variety of other student conditions requiring medications. Professional school counselors can influence the families' adaptation by providing these families with information on the student's functioning in the school setting, encouraging a collaborative relationship with the medical community, making referrals for additional family support, and serving as a link between the school, classroom, student, and family.

A crucial component of medication management is feedback given to the physician regarding medication efficacy. Particularly in the area of psychotropics, school performance and behavior are often part of the target symptoms of medication use. The communication between the physician and the school is often substandard, due to lack of understanding of what information needs to be conveyed, and in what manner. A recent study surveyed pediatricians regarding what information they would find crucial in helping to manage AD/HD medications (Hailemariam, Bradley-Johnson & Johnson, 2002). The results indicated that pediatricians found the following information most useful, listed in descending order of preference: rating scales, informal observation, summary of 1 to 3 paragraphs, school achievement, side effects checklist for medication, and classroom direct observation.

The professional school counselor can play a vital role in obtaining this information and conveying it to the physician in a timely manner.

## Summary/Conclusion

In conclusion, the professional school counselor can serve an important role regarding medication management in the school setting by facilitating communication between the student, family, school and physician, thereby maximizing therapeutic benefit. This type of multimodal approach has been shown to result in the best benefit to the student (Pelham, 2000). The professional school counselor can be actively involved in providing many of these ancillary services, including personal counseling, social skills training, and management of behavior in the classroom setting. Although the focus of this chapter has been on psychotropic medications, these principles are generally applicable to medication management in other chronic conditions.

## References

American Academy of Pediatrics. (1993). Guidelines for the administration of medication in school: Committee on school health. *Pediatrics*, *92*, 499-500.

Blondis, T. A. (1996). Attention-Deficit Disorders and hyperactivity. In A. J. Capute & P. J. Accardo (Eds.), *Developmental disabilities in infancy and childhood: Vol. II. The spectrum of developmental disabilities* (2nd ed.)(pp. 417-451). Baltimore: Brookes.

Hailemariam, A., Bradley-Johnson, S., & Johnson, C. M. (2002). Pediatricians' preferences for ADHD information from schools. *School Psychology Review*, *31*, 94-105.

Ingersoll, R. E. (2000). Teaching a course in psychopharmacology to counselors: Justification, structure, and methods. *Counselor Education and Supervision*, *40*, 58-69.

Kline, F. M., Silver, L. B., & Russell, S. C. (Eds.). (2001). *The educator's guide to medical issues in the classroom*. Baltimore: Brookes.

Medical Economics Company. (2002). *Physician's desk reference.* Montuale, NJ: Author.

Milgrom, H., Bender, B., Ackerson, L., Bowry, P., Smith, B., & Rand, C. (1996). Non-compliance and treatment failure in children with asthma. *Journal of Allergy and Clinical Immunology*, *98*, 1051-1057.

Newacheck, P. W., & Taylor, W. R. (1992). Childhood chronic illness: Prevalence, severity, and impact. *American Journal of Public Health, 82*, 364-371.

Pelham, W. E. (2000). Implications on the MTA study for behavioral and combined treatments. *The ADHD Report, 8*(4), 9–13, 16.

Riekert, K. A., & Drotar, D. (2000). Adherence to medical treatment in pediatric chronic illness: Critical issues and answered questions. In D. Drotar (Ed.), *Promoting adherence to medical treatment in chronic childhood illness: Concepts, methods, and interventions* (pp. 2–32). Mahwah, NJ: Lawerence Erlbaum Associates.

Tebbi, C. K., Richardson, M. D., Cummings, K. M., Zevon, M. A., & Mallon, J. C. (1988). The role of parent-adolescent concordance in compliance with cancer chemotherapy. *Adolescence*, *23*, 599-611.

# Chapter 72

# Helping Students with HIV and Other Health Problems

*Cyrus Marcellus Ellis*

## Preview

Helping students with HIV and other health problems is an immense undertaking by professional school counselors. Professional school counselors developing programs to intervene in students' health concerns need to be cognizant of their professional stance while building a credible program that addresses the needs of the student and the community.

Students in America's schools are faced with multiple risk factors that have the potential to damage their emotional well being, academic success, and family interaction (Landgraf, Rich, & Rappaport, 2002; Zweig, Lindberg, & McGinley, 2001). In addition to factors such as school violence, substance abuse, and poor performance, there exist additional risk factors that involve students' health status concerning sexually transmitted diseases (STD's), poor physical health following illicit drug use, chronic illness, Human Immunodeficiency Virus (HIV), and Acquired Immunodeficiency Syndrome (AIDS) (Sweeny, Lindegren, Buehler, Onorato & Janssen, 1995; Zweig et al., 2001). Students affected by the aforementioned issues need qualified and competent professionals to attend to the physical and emotional needs across the various developmental stages of their lives. Professional school counselors possess the education and training and are poised to intervene at various points of student growth, especially for students who are in need of specific health-related services (ASCA, 2001).

Professional school counselors attempting to intervene with students' various health problems need to be aware of the etiology and course of various diseases, as well as the co-occurring physical and environmental factors influencing the affected student. Regarding adolescent HIV status, the Centers for Disease Control (CDC) (2002b) reports HIV infection among adolescents in 2000 (aged 13 to 19) to be 39% male and 61% female ($n$ = 879). In addition, students possess other health problems such as diabetes, tuberculosis, and anorexia, and frequently engage in risky activities that cause health problems such as smoking, excessive drinking, and steroid use (CDC, 2002a; Zweig et al., 2001). A comprehensive intervention for students affected by HIV/AIDS and other health problems requires: (a) establishing a professional stance on HIV and other health problems, (b) understanding the prevalence of HIV and other health-related problems for children and adolescents, (c) recognizing the physical and psychological factors associated with students affected by HIV and other health problems, and (d) developing a comprehensive counseling program encompassing psychosocial support, education and coping strategies.

## Establishing a Professional Stance

Professional school counselors addressing HIV/AIDS and other health-related issues may experience a variety of thoughts and emotions concerning the disease, the individuals affected, and the manner in which individuals become infected. It is important that professional school counselors are clear on their professional orientation towards HIV, as well as their conduct while working with infected persons. With regard to HIV/AIDS, the American School Counselors Association (ASCA) stated that HIV and AIDS are diseases and not issues of morality. "The professional school counselor promotes prevention, health and education, while providing a vital link to the well being of students, staff, parents and the community" (ASCA, 2001). As it is the responsibility of professional school counselors to encourage a safe learning environment while safeguarding the rights of all persons associated with the school community, school counseling professionals should establish their professional stance by incorporating the laws and ethics governing their profession and state. Every counselor is a professional governed by codes of behavior (Pate, 2000). Central to a professional school counselor's ethical stance is the need to recognize the student's and parent's choice in disclosing HIV information. A student's HIV status is confidential and the student and/or parent are not required to disclose this information. Professional school counselors who are clear on their professional stance are able to communicate this view to the public thereby ensuring professional accountability and establishing the basis for trust between parents, teachers, administrators and students. Figure 1 summarizes ASCA's (2001) position statement concerning HIV/AIDS and the role of the professional school counselor. This information is critical for the formation of a sound professional stance when beginning to address HIV/AIDS and other health problems.

**Figure 1. Professional school counselor stance relating to HIV/AIDS.**

**American School Counseling Association Position Statement**
**HIV/AIDS**

- HIV and AIDS is a disease
- Professional school counselors promote prevention, health, and education
- Professional school counselors are the link to student well being, school staff, parents, and the community

**The Professional School Counselor's Role**

Provide:
- Counseling
- Support
- Collaboration between school health personnel to facilitate education programs for all members of the school community
- Clear and accurate information
- Active involvement in professional associations supporting professional codes of conduct

Collecting Necessary Reference Material:
- The school policy concerning enrollment of students with HIV and AIDS
- Community resources that promote healthy living, education, subject matter experts, and outreach programs
- The identification of medical facilities providing medication, medication education, and support groups

Professional school counselors are encouraged to sit down with school personnel and communicate the importance of a sound counseling program addressing student health issues and HIV/AIDS. Professional school counselors, when communicating their professional stance to school administrators, must understand local school policy and eliminate potential conflicts to ensure the establishment of effective counseling interventions (Shoffner & Williamson, 2000).

## The Prevalence of HIV/AIDS and Other Health Problems

To effectively address students' needs concerning HIV/AIDS and other health problems, the professional school counselor needs to understand the nature of the disease and its impact in our society. The CDC (2002a) reported that males comprised 39% and females 61% of HIV infection rates for 2000 ($n$ = 879) for students aged 13-19 years. In addition, males constituted 49% and females 45% of all reported AIDS cases during the same time period ($n$ = 1,608) for youth aged 18-24 years. CDC exposure rates to AIDS through June 2001 indicated the vast majority of youth are exposed through a mother with HIV ($n$ = 8,207), while fewer are exposed through blood transfusions and hemophilia/coagulations ($n$ = 382 & 237, respectively). For HIV/AIDS and other health related information, contact the CDC (www.cdc.gov). The CDC offers a wide variety of informational documents that can aid the professional school counselor in understanding the nature of these and other health risks for students. The CDC has additional information professional school counselors can use to assist in establishing a comprehensive educational program for parents, students, and staff. In order to focus on the depth of the multiple health problems facing students, Table 1 lists the types of risky behaviors experienced by students that play a role in causing intentional and unintentional injuries as compiled by the Youth Risk Behavior Surveillance System (YRBSS) (Kann et al., 2000). This surveillance report provides a summary of national data covering thirty-three states and is used by health and education officials at all levels to assist educators in creating programs to reduce these risk behaviors. The depth of this report is beyond the scope of this chapter; however, obtaining this report can provide the professional school counselor significant insight into the leading health risks facing students.

**Table 1. Student health risk behaviors.**

| Health Risk Behaviors | |
|---|---|
| **Actions causing unintended injuries** | **Actions causing intended injuries** |
| Seat belt use in cars | Carrying a weapon |
| Helmet use on bikes and motorcycles | Fighting |
| Injury during physical activity | Date violence |
| Riding with individuals under the influence | Forced sexual intercourse |
| Drinking and driving | School violence |
| | Suicide |
| | Tobacco/alcohol use |
| | Illicit drug use |

In addition to health risk behaviors, students encounter physiological problems better known as chronic medical conditions (Thies, 1999). "More than 200 chronic physical conditions affect youth under age 18 . . ." (p. 392). Students frequently contend with asthma, diabetes, leukemia and gastrointestinal illnesses. The impact of these illnesses hampers the educational attainment of students and creates strain within the family. Thies's work details the impact chronic physical conditions have on the cognitive capacity of youth and can help in coordinating appropriate academic interventions and health services between school health officials and community health and human service professionals.

### Recognizing Physical and Psychological Factors Associated with HIV and Other Health Problems

Students suffering from HIV and other health problems possess a multitude of physical and psychological problems associated with their illnesses. Professional school counselors working with affected students need to be aware of student physical and psychological needs when developing an intervention program. The ability to concentrate, visually focus, and sustain energy may all be manifested as physical and psychological side effects of an infected student (Thies, 1999). Additionally, students suffering with HIV and other health problems often experience non-compliance with medication regimens, and depression and anxiety resulting from a variety of negative life events that reduce the student's emotional well-being and the family's inability to function (Elliott, 2001).

Professional school counselors need to work closely with teachers, school health personnel and families to gain information concerning a student's health status as it relates to the course of the illness and the impact of the medications treating the illness. Students experiencing constant illness are at risk for academic difficulty. "Forty-five percent (45%) of students with chronic illness report falling behind in their school work, leading them to dislike school. At the high school level, 35% of students identified as 'other health impaired' report failing grades." (Thies, 1999, p. 392). The next step for the professional school counselor in constructing a comprehensive intervention addressing health issues is to develop a list of behavioral and emotive symptoms that are associated with students affected by HIV and other health problems. This list of symptoms needs to be inclusive of identifying the illness, the medications treating the illness and their side effects, and the emotive responses of affected students.

### Developing a Comprehensive School Counseling Intervention

At this point, professional school counselors are prepared to construct a comprehensive intervention addressing HIV and other health problems in students. By incorporating the previous sections involving establishing a professional stance concerning HIV and other health related problems, understanding the prevalence of HIV and health problems in children and adolescents and the recognition of the physical and psychological factors associated by various illnesses and HIV, the professional school counselor can operate a program from a sound foundation.

It is important to understand that the core of a program addressing HIV and other health related illnesses revolves around the reduction of negative risk behaviors of the people receiving the intervention or assistance. Therefore, the successful intervention implemented in schools needs to be based on behavioral practices designed to reduce risky behaviors in students that can lead to exposure or exacerbation of HIV and other illnesses (Holtgrave et al., 1995).

Holtgrave et al. (1995) provided a classic review of literature detailing the characteristics of successful HIV prevention programs in the community and schools. According to Holtgrave et al., a successful intervention addressing HIV and other health problems requires the professional school counselor to incorporate at least three ideological positions: community relevance, cultural competence and sustaining effective practices guiding interventions. Additionally, successful interventions encompass counseling and support that address negative life events that are barriers for positive health practices. In order to conceptualize Holtgrave et al.'s work, brief descriptions of their concepts are illuminated below.

*Community Relevance*

As stated previously, the prevalence of HIV and AIDS is growing and affecting students. Interventions need to be clear and aligned with the requirements of the community being served; otherwise the program will be seen as inattentive, nonessential and a burden on school personnel and district assets (Holtgrave et al., 1995). Professional school counselors need to understand the reality of the students they serve while incorporating the desires of the community. Working closely with health and human service professionals, community hospitals and local social workers begins the process of determining the relevance for the community and individuals.

*Cultural Competence*

The demographics of school systems are changing rapidly. Interventions addressing HIV and other health problems need to address all students from various perspectives. As professional school counselors develop programs, it is important to develop a culturally responsive program that sends a message that involves all levels of culture involving race, demographics, gender, ethnicity, social mores and familial value sets. Professional school counselors responsible for various educational levels need to ensure that their program is reflective of the developmental nature of their audience. Professional school counselors need to develop the proper message for elementary, middle/junior high, and high school students. For schools where language may present barriers to clear communication, working with community members who can provide insight into how the message of the program will be received by its respective audience is also important.

*Effective Practices*

Table 2 displays Holtgrave et al.'s (1995) six empirically validated dimensions for effective practices when designing school-based HIV programs. The following characteristics of effective school-based programs are determined effective in part due to the program's ability to provide educational information, self-empowerment of involved individuals, and the teaching of positive behavioral practices.

Lohrmann, Blake, Collins, Windsor and Parillo (2001) offer additional points of effective school-based HIV programs, finding that parents need to be involved in the review of the curricular materials to determine if their children will take part in the educational program. Indeed, most school systems require parent involvement in this process. It is important that all members of the educational team review local LEA policies to ensure compliance with policies that govern health-related programs. In many cases this information is located on the web for districts, school boards or state departments of education. Additionally, effective practices for school-based HIV programs include policy revision and development. Professional development training emerged as a necessary requirement for teachers in the following areas: HIV prevention, violence prevention, suicide, sexual behavior, the influence of drugs and alcohol, and sexually transmitted infections prevention activities. Lohrmann et al. also indicated that significant amounts of time (four or more class periods) must be dedicated to the topics of HIV instruction and prevention. Professional school counselors undertaking this endeavor need to be aware of all the building blocks of effective HIV intervention and prevention programs.

**Table 2. Six empirically validated best practices for school-based HIV programs.**

1. The use of social learning theory in program development.
2. Reducing sexual risk-taking in adolescents to prevent undesired health risks.
3. Accurate dissemination of HIV, AIDS and other health information.
4. Addressing media influences on sexual behavior.
5. Addressing personal and group mores regarding the use of protection when engaging in sexual behavior.
6. The use of role playing to demonstrate appropriate communication.

## Other Health Problems

Comprehensive interventions for other health problems follow the same process as for HIV programs. Referring to Thies' (1999) work with chronic illness in children, Thies addressed the need to identify the condition and become familiar with the impact that condition has on the affected student. One may refer to the CDC website (CDC, 2002b) for additional information concerning a variety of health conditions and effects on students.

In order to gain insight into the concepts presented in this chapter, Figure 2 provides the conceptual framework for organizing, implementing and evaluating a comprehensive intervention for HIV and other health problems. This cycle indicates the need to develop a firm professional stance while constantly re-evaluating the merits of the intervention.

## Summary/Conclusion

Professional school counselors developing programs to assist students with HIV and other health problems face a variety of challenges. Effective in-school health programs require professional school counselors to be knowledgeable of their ethical and professional stance concerning HIV and other health issues. The development of a sound intervention requires the professional school counselor to establish a credible health education program, become knowledgeable concerning the prevalence of various illnesses in the student's community and understand the impact that physical and psychological factors have on learning. An efficient and successful program is constantly reviewing its practices to ensure students and parents are receiving credible information, learning appropriate decision-making skills and developing the ability to recognize risky behaviors that are destructive to student health.

**Figure 2. The organizational cycle of a comprehensive intervention for HIV and other health problems.**

The professional school counselor develops a professional stance

**Determine needs based on population**
- Determine prevention education or intervention education
- Identification of the illness
- Identification of medications treating the illness and side effects
- Physiological and psychological stressors of affected students
- The impact of the illness, medication and psychological factors on learning

**Determine personnel support and logistics**
- School resources
- Community resources
- Professional development for teachers and health support personnel
- Parental involvement
- Meeting space
- Number of hours devoted to HIV and health education

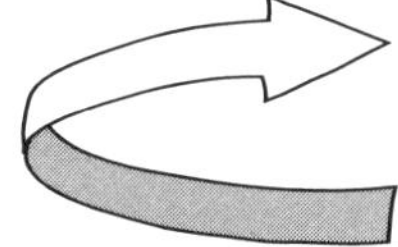

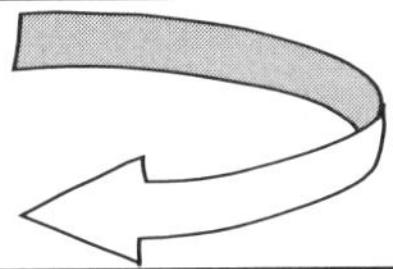

**Program review**
- Review program goals to determine success
- Review feedback from parents, community members, and school personnel and make improvements where necessary
- Evaluate curricular materials for efficiency and usefulness
- Evaluate professional development training
- Review school policy and include any revisions into the education plan

**Program development**
- Inclusion of social learning theory
- Culturally appropriate
- HIV and health policy inclusion
- Community and parent review of educational curriculum
- Age appropriate
- Developmentally appropriate
- Addressing explicit and implied community needs

## References


American School Counselor Association. (2001). *Position statement: HIV/AIDS.* Retrieved April 11, 2002, from http://www.schoolcounselor.org/content.cfm?L1=1000&L2=22.

Centers for Disease Control. (2002a). *Young people at risk: HIV/AIDS among America's youth.* Retrieved May 15, 2002, from http://www.cdc.gov/hiv/pubs/facts/youth.htm.

Centers for Disease Control (2002b). *National center for health statistics.*Retrieved June 20, 2002, from http://www.cdc.gov/nchs/fastats/Default.htm.

Elliott, V. S. (2001). Teens with HIV aren't taking their meds [Electronic version]. *American Medical News, 44,* 36.

Holtgrave, D. R., Qualls, N. L., Curran, J. W., Valdiserri, R. O., Guinan, M. E., & Parra, W. C. (1995). An overview of the effectiveness and efficiency of HIV prevention programs [Electronic version]. *Public Health Reports, 110,* 134-145.

Kann, L., Kinchen, S. A., Williams, B. L., Ross, J. G., Lowry, R., Gunbaum, J., & Kolbe, L. J. (2000). Youth risk behavior surveillance-United States, 1999. *Journal of School Health, 70,* 271.

Landgraf, J. M., Rich, M., & Rappaport, L. (2002). Measuring quality of life in children with Attention-Deficit/Hyperactivity Disorder and their families: Development and evaluation of a new tool [Electronic version]. *Archives of Pediatrics & Adolescent Medicine, 156,* 384-392.

Lohrman, D. K., Blake, S., Collins, T., Windsor, R., & Parillo, A. V. (2001). Evaluation of school-based HIV prevention education programs in New Jersey [Electronic version]. *Journal of School Health, 71,* 207-212.

Pate, R. H. (2000). Ethics and counseling practice. In H. Hackney (Ed.), *Practice issues for the beginning counselor* (pp. 102-118). Needham Heights, MA: Allyn & Bacon.

Shoffner, M. F. & Williamson, R. D. (2000). Engaging preservice school counselors and principals in dialogue and collaboration [Electronic version]. *Counselor Education and Supervision, 40,* 128-140.

Sweeney, P., Lindegren, M. L., Buehler, J. W., Onorato, I. M., & Janssen, R. S. (1995). Teenagers at risk of Human Immunodeficiency Virus type 1 infection: Results from seroprevalence surveys in the United States [Electronic version]. *Archives of Pediatrics & Adolescent Medicine, 149,* 521-529.

Thies, K. M. (1999). Identifying the educational implications of chronic illness in school children [Electronic version]. *Journal of School Health, 69,* 392-397.

Zwieg, J. M., Lindberg, L. D., & McGinley, K. A. (2001). Adolescent health risk profiles: The co-occurrence of health risks among females and males [Electronic version]. *Journal of Youth and Adolescence, 30,* 707-728.

# Chapter 73

## School Reentry for Students with Chronic Illness

*Carol J. Kaffenberger*

### Preview

Information concerning ways in which a professional school counselor can facilitate school reintegration for children with chronic illnesses will be presented. Barriers faced by children with chronic illness will be reviewed. A model for supporting children with chronic illness will be presented and strategies and resources for supporting children with chronic illness will be offered.

It is estimated that 21% of all students have a chronic illness, and 10% of this population suffer severe enough consequences of their disease to interfere with school performance (Thompson, & Gustafson, 1996). A chronic illness is one that has no cure but is not necessarily terminal (Huegel, 1998). Chronic illnesses require medical interventions and often result in debilitating consequences (Thompson, & Gustafson, 1996). Cancer, asthma, congenital heart defects, lupus, bowel disorders, cystic fibrosis, diabetes, hemophilia, juvenile rheumatoid arthritis, mental illness, and HIV/AIDS are among the most common chronic illnesses affecting students (Phelps, 1998).

Students with chronic illness are absent from school more frequently, experience psychosocial consequences including depression, difficulties with social and peer interaction, and have a higher incidence of cognitive disabilities as a result of their illness or its treatment (Armstrong & Horn, 1995; Fasciano, 1996; Sexson & Madan-Swain, 1993; Thompson & Gustafson, 1996). Among the population of students with chronic illness, a significant number of students are out of school for extended periods of time. The process of supporting these students at home and in hospitals, and as they make the transition back to school, is called school reentry or *school reintegration.*

For the child with a chronic illness, being in school represents a return to normalcy; school is what students "do." Making a successful transition back to school is associated with more positive long-term outcomes for students (Boekaerts & Roder, 1999; Houlahan, 1991; Prevatt, Heffer, & Lowe, 2000; Sexson & Madan-Swain, 1993). Therefore, it should be the goal of schools to facilitate a smooth and successful school reentry for students with chronic illness.

School reintegration is a complex process because schools are not always able to accommodate the special needs of chronically ill children. School reentry must be tailored to the individual needs of the student and the family as well as the specific characteristics of the student's illness. School attendance and grading policies and homebound instruction regulations are often inflexible and serve as a barrier to successful school reentry (Fasciano, 1996; Gaynon, 1993; Prevatt et al., 2000). School personnel often feel unprepared to meet the individual needs of these students, and lack information and resources concerning the disease or an understanding of the individual needs of the students and their families (Gaynon, 1993; Prevatt et al., 2000).

*Models for Successful School Reintegration*

A considerable amount of research has been conducted, and literature published, concerning recommended strategies for helping students make the transition back to school. Model programs have been described in the literature (Fasciano, 1996; Houlahan, 1991; Katz, Varni, Rubenstein, Blew & Hubert, 1992; Prevatt et al., 2000; Sachs, 1980; Shields, Heron, Rubenstein, & Katz, 1995). According to Prevatt et al. (2000), "there are many more articles that suggest components of school reintegration programs than there are actual programs" (pp. 447-448). Model comprehensive school reentry programs have six features in common (Armstrong & Horn, 1995; Fasciano, 1996; Prevatt et al., 2000). Model programs identify a coordinator of services, provide direct services to the student, consult with the family, educate school personnel, provide information to classmates, and involve the medical team.

*Coordination component of school reentry programs.* The success of model programs described in the literature depends upon the identification of a liaison who takes responsibility for coordinating the school reentry process (Shields et al., 1995). The liaison oversees the first phases of the process by conducting individual interviews or assessments with the family and the student. It is important for the liaison to have access to the family, the student, the medical team, and the school.

The liaison meets with the parents to determine the student's continuing needs, how they want information transmitted to teachers and the student's peers, to assess resources and available family support, and to obtain necessary parent permission to communicate with others about the student. The liaison begins the school reentry process by providing information to the family about school services available, the importance of involving the school from the time of diagnosis, and the school reentry process. With permission of the parents, the liaison communicates with the hospital team, gaining information about the diagnosis and treatment, and any handicapping conditions or constraints placed on the student.

Next the liaison meets with the student to assess his understanding of the disease and treatment process, and to talk about how the student wants peers to find out about the illness. The liaison determines how much involvement and communication with peers and the school the student wants.

The liaison works with the school to educate and inform school personnel. A workshop for teachers and administrators is recommended as the best vehicle for sensitizing school personnel to the unique needs of a student, and how to handle the classroom responses to the sick student (Baskin et al., 1983). The liaison is also called in to work directly with classrooms and peers (Benner & Marlow, 1991). Finally the liaison keeps the lines of communication open, passing along updated information, and planning for school reentry.

*Challenges to implementing model programs.* While the benefits of a comprehensive school reentry program cannot be denied, the reality is that such programs are not available to serve most chronically ill students (Prevatt et al., 2000). While there is agreement that a comprehensive school reintegration program is ideal, staffing issues, funding, and lack of supporting research data about the effectiveness of existing programs limits the number of programs being implemented.

The critical factor determining the success of the comprehensive school reentry program is the identification of a liaison to coordinate services. As Prevatt et al. (2000) recognized in their review of school reintegration programs, how the liaison is staffed and funded is one of the most significant barriers to the successful implementation of programs. While the literature underscores the importance of the liaison role, guidance about who is best suited to play this role is not offered.

*A role for professional school counselors in the school reentry process.* Typically the transition process is put together in a piecemeal fashion. Families are unsure of what their child's future holds and what their student will need, and struggle to understand the school regulations and how to access services. Frequently the school's response is slow. Schools scramble to educate themselves about the diagnosis, the needs of the student and family, and available resources. Well-meaning school personnel, lacking clarity about their role, knowledge about the illness and available resources, feel unprepared to meet the needs of these children and their families. Professional school counselors, however, by virtue of their training, skills, and leadership role in the school, are ideally suited to facilitate the school reentry for children with chronic illnesses and support the sick student's siblings and family.

*Strategies for Working with Children with Chronic Illness*

The following strategies are offered to professional school counselors as steps to be taken to coordinate school reentry for students with chronic illness.

1. *Make early contact with the family* (See Figure 1). As soon as you learn of the diagnosis of an illness contact the parents. Recognize that the family is struggling to respond to the medical needs of the student and may postpone contact with the school. Early contact with the family provides a sense of hope as well as additional resources. No matter how long the student is expected to be out of school, planning for school reentry should begin.

**Figure 1. Questions to consider in your early contact with the family.**

> Parents at the time of the crisis often postpone contact with the school. When the professional school counselor takes the initiative and makes early contact with the family, you give the family and child a sense of hope, provide resources outside the family circle, establish your role as advocate for the sick child and the siblings, and help to facilitate successful school reentry.

- Tell me more about your child's diagnosis, treatment process and how you expect it to impact him/her.
- Would you be willing to come to school for a meeting to share information, to hear about school resources available to help your child, and to plan for school reentry?
- How will school performance/attendance be affected?
- How much does your child know and understand about the illness?
- What do you want school staff, your child's teacher, the school community and other children to know about the illness?
- Who do you want to tell them about it?
- Is there someone on the medical team we can contact for information and to coordinate services?
- How will we get updates? Who can we contact? Who will contact us?
- What contact would you like with/from the school? Cards? Homework? Video of class? Calls? Visits?
- Are you aware of resources/information/support groups dealing with this illness?
- Have you used the Internet to access information and materials? Are you willing to share what you learn with the school? Would you like me to help you find information?
- Who is helping *you* through this?
- What can the school do to help you and your family?
- How are the sick child's siblings doing? How can the school support the siblings?

2. *Form a school reintegration team composed of stakeholders* (See Figure 2). The purpose of a school reintegration team is to coordinate services and implement the

**Figure 2. Suggested checklist for school reintegration team.**

- Convene school reintegration team meeting
- Contact parent(s) of ill student
- Gather information from the parent and other resources
- Arrange for parent conference:
    - * Educate parents about school resources
    - * Refer student to Child Study Team
    - * Consider a 504 plan
    - * Negotiate a plan for school involvement
    - * Gain permission to discuss the student's illness with faculty, students and medical professionals caring for the student
- Conduct infomation workshop for faculty
- Provide direct and indirect support of the ill student and/or consult with his/her teachers
- Provide direct and indirect support of the sibling(s) and/or consult with their teachers
- Conduct classroom guidance sessions with student's peers
- Consult with homebound teacher
- Consult with student's doctor, psychiatrist, or other medical personnel

school reentry plan. The school reintegration team may include the professional school counselor, public health or school nurse, social worker, teacher, and administrator. The school reintegration team should consist of three to four individuals who will assume responsibility for providing and coordinating services to the student and family. Members of this team should be determined by school district organization and staffing and by the unique situation of each student and family. The school reintegration team should identify a liaison that will assume primary responsibility for contact with the family and the health care professionals. The liaison may be the school nurse, professional school counselor, social worker, teacher, or other school staff members. Consider documenting roles, responsibilities and activities of the school reintegration team (See Figure 3).

**Figure 3. School reintegration team planning.**

| *Suggested Intervention* | *Team Member* | *Date* | *Comments* |
|---|---|---|---|
| Contact family | | | |
| Convene school reintegration team | | | |
| Identify team leader | | | |
| Facilitate parent conferences | | | |
| Develop school reentry plan | | | |
| Conduct faculty workshop | | | |
| Conduct classroom guidance | | | |
| Consult medical personnel | | | |
| Support ill child | | | |
| Support for siblings & peers | | | |
| Follow-up | | | |

3. *Hold a school reintegration meeting with the parents as soon as possible.* Determine who should attend this meeting based on the individual needs of the student and family. This meeting could include the school reintegration team members, the student's teacher, school nurse, a special education teacher (if appropriate), 504 coordinator, and an administrator, or it could just be a meeting between the parents and the professional school counselor. The purpose of this meeting is to coordinate the school reentry process and negotiate the way the school can support the student and family. Discuss the following with the parents:
   - Learn all you can from the parents about the illness, the expected course of treatment, and the psychological impact the experience is having on the student with the chronic illness and the student's parents and siblings.
   - Provide the parents with resources (See Figure 4) and information about the services the school can provide, such as special education and Section 504 modifications, homebound instruction, and ways in which the student's peers can continue to have contact with the student. Provide information about the impact the illness may have on the siblings.

**Figure 4. Resources.**

***Recommended Reading***

Blitzer, A., Kutscher, A. H., Klagsbrun, S. C., DeBellis, R., Selder, F. E., Seeland, I. B., & Carney, K. L. (1999). *What is cancer anyway? Explaining cancer to children of all ages.* Wethersfield, CT: Dragonfly Publishing Co.

Deasy-Spinetta, P., & Irwin, E. (1993). *Educating the child with cancer.* The Candlelighters Foundation.™

Heugel, K., & Verdick, E.(Ed.). (1998). *Young people and chronic illness: True stories, help and hope.* Minneapolis, MN: Free Spirit Publications.

*Illness, Crises & Loss* (journal). Philadelphia: The Charles Press. (See Special Issue on Cancer Survivorship, 5(1), 1995.)

Keene, N., Hobbie, W., & Ruccione, K. (2000). Childhood cancer survivors: *A practical guide to your future.* Sebastopol, CA: O'Reilly & Associates.

Meyer, D. J., Vadasy, P. F., & Pillo, C. (1994). *Sibshops: Workshops for siblings of children with special needs.* Paul Brookes Publ. Inc.

Singer, A. T. (1999). *Coping with your child's chronic illness.* San Francisco: Robert D. Reed Publishers.

*Toward inclusive classrooms.* Teacher-to-Teacher Series. NEA Professional Library. (Order from NEA #2903-8-KT 1-8—229-4200).

***Recommended Reading for Children and Adolescents***

Meyer, D. (1997). *View from our shoes: Growing up with a brother or sister with special needs.* Bethesda, MD: Woodbine House. (ISBN 0-295-97547-4)

Mills, J. C. (1992). *Little tree: A story for children with serious medical problems.* New York: Brunner/Mazel, Inc.

Vadasy, P., & Meyer, D. J. (1996). *Living with a brother or sister with special needs: A book for siblings.* Seattle, WA: University of Washington Press.

***Online Resources for Information and Support***

American Cancer Society – 1-800-ACS-2345 http://www.cancer.org.
American Diabetes Association – 1-800-232-3472 http://www.diabetes.org
American Heart Association – 1-800-AHA-USA1
http://americanheart.org/Health/Lifestyle/Youth/index.html (Youth section of AHA Web Site)
American Juvenile Arthritis Organization - (404) 872-7100 http://www.arthritis.org/ajao
Association of Online Cancer Resources - Provides listservs regarding childhood oncology. They provide access to 99 mailing lists, a variety of online support groups and related websites. http://www.acor.org
Band-Aids and Blackboards - This website was created by a nurse educator to help kids and teens cope with chronic illness and returning to school. http://funrsc.fairfield.edu/~jfleitas/contents.html
Brave Kids – Online resources for children with chronic and life-threatening illnesses. http://www.bravekids.org
Candlelighters Childhood Cancer Foundation - Provides support for children and families. http://www.candlelighters.org
The Childhood Brain Tumor Foundation - http://www.chilhoodbraintumor.org
Children's Health Information Network - http://www.tchin.org
Children With Diabetes – For families of children affected http://www.childrenwithdiabetes.com/index_cwd.htm
Crohn's and Colitis Foundation of America - 1-800-932-2423 http://www.ccfa.org
Cystic Fybrosis Foundation - (301) 951-4422 http://www.cff.org
Depression and Related Affected Disorders Association (DRADA) – Provides resources for teenagers and opportunities to buy depression related material.http: www.hopkinsmedicine.org/drada/
Epilepsy Foundation of America -1-800-EFA-1000 (Information and referral line) http://www.efa.org
Health Care Information Resources – Illness – Health care information for patients, families, friends, and health care workers http://www-hsl.mcmaster.ca/tomflem/ill.html
How to Handle Living with Cystic Fibrosis – From a patient with CF, it gives helpful hints for living with CF http://www.geocities.com/HotSprings/Villa/4210/
Juvenile Diabetes Foundation – 1-800-223-1138 http://www.jdfcure.com
Kids With Heart National Association for Children's Heart Disorders – 1-800-538-5390 http://www.execpc.com/~kdswhrt/kwhhome
Leukemia Society of America 1-800-995-4LSA. http://www.leukemia.org
Lupus.Org – Educational site provided by the Lupus Foundation of America http://www.lupus.org
National Childhood Cancer Foundation – The NCCF provides resources for infants, children and adolescents with cancer. NCCF supports a network of childhood cancer treatment and research institutions throughout North America. http://nccf.org

---

- Help the parents understand the needs of the siblings and offer assistance.
- Gain the parents' permission to discuss the student's illness with staff, peers, and the medical team treating the student.
- Develop a school reentry plan.

4. *Components of a school reentry plan.* Recognize that each student and family will require individualized services. Consider the following issues:

- Identify a liaison who will be the point of contact between the school and family, and the school and medical professionals.
- Obtain the parent's permission to allow the liaison or designated school personnel to coordinate services and have access to medical information or a member of the student's medical team.
- Decide how the staff will hear about the student's illness, who on the staff will be told, and how they will be told. Decide how they will receive updated information.
- Decide how the student's class and peers will hear about the illness, who will tell them and what will they be told. Decide how they will receive updated information.
- Decide what steps should be taken to continue the student's education. If the student will receive homebound services, provide the parents with the necessary information for gaining those services. If the student's attendance is expected to be irregular, decide how the student will receive schoolwork and who will supervise its completion.
- Decide whether the student should be referred to the Child Study committee for consideration of special education or 504 modifications.
- Decide how peers and classmates will stay in contact with the student.
- Decide how the siblings will be supported.
- Discuss the student's return to school. Determine what medical and educational modifications will be required.

5. *Coordinate support services.* While the professional school counselor is not responsible for providing all of the services the student with a chronic illness might require, the professional school counselor can coordinate and facilitate those services. Support services could include the following:
    - Provide a workshop for the faculty and staff (See Figure 5). The purpose of the workshop is to help the faculty and staff understand the medical and

**Figure 5. School reintegration for children with chronic illness: Presentation guidelines.**

**Purpose**: The purpose of a staff workshop or class presentation is to provide accurate information to the staff and the classmates of the student with the chronic illness, and to allay the fears of staff and classmates. It is believed that school reintegration will be more successful when staff, peers, and classmates are informed about the illness and have had a chance to voice their concerns.
**Who should facilitate:** The workshop or classroom presentation could be conducted by school personnel (public health nurse, professional school counselor, social worker, teacher or administrator); a member of the child/adolescent's medical team (social worker, psychologist, nurse practitioner, physician, child life specialist); or by the parent of the student. The facilitator should be knowledgeable about the specifics of the disease, and able to provide age appropriate information to the students.
**Before conducting the session:** Obtain permission of the family and student before conducting the workshop or presentation. Plan with the parents and the student concerning what is to be shared.
**Who should participate in the staff workshop:** At a small elementary school the workshop could involve the entire faculty and staff. At a large elementary school or a middle school the student's team, those faculty and staff members

who have contact with the student, should participate. At the high school level it is suggested that the workshop be conducted with the members of the faculty and staff who have contact with the adolescent.

**Who should participate in the classroom presentation:** At the elementary level the lesson should involve the student's classroom and peers. At the middle school level the student's team should participate. At the high school level it is suggested that the lesson be conducted in the science class to discuss the medical aspects of the disease and in the homeroom to discuss the social and personal impact of the disease.

**What to expect from the faculty, staff, and students:** A discussion of serious medical issues will prompt memories of people in their lives who have been sick or died. The facilitator should expect to hear personal stories and questions. Faculty and staff will want to hear about how to treat the student, the ongoing medical concerns and responsibilities of the school, and what will be expected of the school staff. Students will have many questions about what it is like to have disease and how they should treat the sick student. At the high school level expect existential questions about life and death.

## Faculty/Staff Workshop Outline

*Suggested Procedures (30 to 45 minutes):*

**Opening:**

1. Introduce the presenters, especially if they are unknown to the staff.
2. Begin with an explanation about the purpose of the presentation:
    - To learn about the disease that ________ has
    - To understand why he/she is out of school
    - To learn what we can expect when he/she comes back to school
    - To talk about what we can do to help the student
    - Ask the staff what they know about the disease

**Information about the disease:**

1. Provide information about the disease.
    - Definition of the disease, including types, prevalence among children/adolescents, general prognosis, medical treatment and side effects
2. Provide information about the particular medical needs of the student

**Describe the school reintegration plan:**

1. Provide information about when the student will be back in school.
2. Describe feelings and concerns of the students and parents.
3. Present homebound instruction plan and/or 504 plan if needed.
4. Discuss the responsibilities of faculty and staff for educational, medical and psychological support of the student.
5. Identify a liaison, the point of contact, for updated information about the student and the student's medical/educational needs.

**Discuss faculty responsibilities to help the sick student:**

1. Brainstorm ideas of how to help the sick student. How will contact with school be continued when at home/hospital (including cards, emails, visits, phone calls, etc.)?
2. Discuss ways to keep the student involved in school activities.
3. Discuss issue of siblings of the sick student and ways to support them.
4. Discuss faculty questions and concerns.

### Presentation to Classmates Lesson Plan

*Suggested Procedures (30 – 45 minutes):*

**Opening:**

1. Introduce the presenters, especially if they are unknown to the students.
2. Begin with an explanation about the purpose of the lesson:
   - To learn about (the disease) that (name of the student) has
   - To understand why he/she is out of school
   - To learn what we can expect when he/she comes back to school
   - To talk about what we can do to help the student
   - Ask the children what they know about <u>(name of the disease)</u>

**Information about the disease:**

1. Provide age-appropriate information about the disease.
   - Definition of the disease, including types, prevalence among children/ adolescents, general prognosis, medical treatment, and side effects
   - Visuals including videos, overheads, worksheets may be used to reinforce the goals of the lesson.
2. Address the following typical concerns of classmates:
   - Can I catch this disease? How did ____ get this disease?
   - Will ____ get better? Will ____ die? How does ___ feel? Is it painful?

**Discuss what to expect when the student is back at school:**

1. Provide information about when the student will be back in school.
2. Describe the sick student's feelings and concerns about returning to school.

**Discuss what classmates can do to help the sick student**:

1. Brainstorm how to help the sick child. Talk about what is helpful and unhelpful.

---

psychological needs of the student. Helping the school staff understand the needs of the student will increase the chances of a successful school reentry (Peckham, 1993). A member of the student's medical team, the public health or school nurse assigned to the student's school, the parents of the student, or the professional school counselor might provide the workshop.

- Conduct classroom presentation (See Figure 5). The purpose of the classroom presentation is to increase the peers' understanding of the medical and social needs of the student (Benner & Marlow, 1991; Treiber & Schramm, 1986). It is suggested that at the high school level a group session for peers close to the adolescent be held. The focus of this session is to help the peers gain accurate information about the illness, and sensitize them to the social needs of the chronically ill adolescent. The information could also be provided in a science class focusing on a scientific understanding of the illness. A teacher, a member of the student's medical team, the public health or school nurse assigned to the student's school, the parents of the student, or the professional school counselor might provide the classroom presentation.

6. *Provide support for the siblings.* Often the siblings' needs are overlooked (Johnson, 1997). Well-meaning teachers, not knowing how to address the issue with the healthy siblings, ignore the opportunity to provide direct support. The professional school counselor can provide both direct and indirect help to the siblings by helping the staff and the siblings' peers understand the needs of the siblings. If the siblings

attend a different school, it is also important to contact the professional school counselor at the siblings' school.

7. *Coordinate support to the chronically ill student.* Support for the sick student may include providing direct services, individual or small group counseling concerning adjustment to illness, coping strategies, school reentry preparation, and peer or academic issues. The professional school counselor can maintain contact with the student while out of school and encourage peers and teachers to maintain contact. By helping the school community to be aware of the ongoing needs of the student with chronic illness, the professional school counselor is providing necessary services. The professional school counselor might facilitate communication between the homebound teacher and school.

## Summary/Conclusion

The professional school counselor can play an important role in the school reentry process for students with chronic illnesses. By making early contact with the family, forming a school reintegration team, negotiating a role for the school, providing information and resources, developing a school reentry plan, supporting the siblings of chronically ill students, providing a classroom presentation to the student's peers, and helping the school community to understand the needs of these students and families, professional school counselors can facilitate successful school reintegration for students with chronic illnesses.

## References


Armstrong, F. D., & Horn, M. (1995). Educational issues in childhood cancer. *School Psychology Quarterly, 10*, 292-304.

Baskin, C. H., Saylor, C. F., Furey, W. M., Finch, A. J., Jr., & Carek, D. J. (1983). Helping teachers help children with cancer: A workshop for school personnel. *Children's Health Care, 12,* 78-83.

Benner, A. E., & Marlow, L. S. (1991). The effect of a workshop on childhood cancer on students' knowledge, concerns, and desire to interact with a classmate with cancer. *Children's Health Care, 20*, 101-107.

Boekaerts, M., & Roder, I. (1999). Stress, coping, and adjustment in children with a chronic illness: A review of the literature. *Disability and Rehabilitation, 21*, 311-337.

Fasciano, K. M. (1996). *A model of school consultation for children with cancer.* Massachusetts School of Professional Psychology. UMI Microform 9629997. DAI 57, No. 05B, (1996): 3408.

Gaynon, S. S. (1993). T*he school's contribution to the quality of life of long term cancer survivors.* (University of Wisconsin). Dissertation.

Houlahan, K. E. (1991). School reentry program. *Association of Pediatric Oncology Nurses Conference Proceedings*, pp. 70-71. Boston, MA: Children's Hospital.

Huegel, K. (1998). *Young people and chronic illness.* Minneapolis, MN: Free Spirit Publishing.

Johnson, L. S. (1997). Developmental strategies for counseling the child whose parent or sibling has cancer. *Journal of Counseling & Development, 75*, 417-427.

Katz, E. R., Varni, J. W., Rubenstein, C. L., Blew, A., & Hubert, N. (1992). Teacher, parent, and child evaluative ratings of a school reintegration intervention for children with newly diagnosed cancer. *Children's Health Care, 21*, 69-75.

Peckham, V. C. (1993). Children with cancer in the classroom. *Teaching the Exceptional Child, 26,* 27-32.

Phelps, L. (Ed.). (1998). *Health-related disorders in children and adolescents: A guidebook for understanding and educating.* Alexandria, VA: American Psychological Association.

Prevatt, F. F., Heffer, R. W., & Lowe, P. A. (2000). A review of school reintegration programs for children with cancer. *Journal of School Psychology, 38*, 447-467.

Sachs, M. B. (1980). Helping the child with cancer go back to school. *The Journal of School Health, 50*, 328-331.

Sexson, S. B., & Madan-Swain, A. (1993). School reentry for the child with chronic illness. *Journal of Learning Disabilities, 26*, 115-126.

Shields, J. D., Heron, T. E., Rubenstein, C. L., & Katz, E. R. (1995). The eco-triad model of educational consultation for students with cancer. *Education and Treatment of Children, 18*, 184-200.

Thompson, R. J., & Gustafson, K. E. (1996). *Adaptation to chronic childhood illness.* Washington, DC: American Psychological Association.

Treiber, F. A., Schramm, L., & Mabe, P. A. (1986). Children's knowledge and concern toward a peer with cancer: A workshop intervention approach. *Child Psychiatry and Human Development, 16*, 249-260.

# Chapter 74

## Helping Students Who Have Been Physically/Sexually Abused

*David J. Carter*

### Preview

This chapter discusses causes, symptoms and treatment strategies regarding the physical and/or sexual abuse of students. The legal responsibility and consequences are briefly discussed and the recognition, intervention and reporting of student physical and sexual abuse are explored. The material in this chapter is especially important for the professional school counselor who works closely with the student and serves as advocate and first line of defense against abuse. Misperceptions about the experience, including those about self, the abuser, and the behavior or act that was forced upon the student must be understood in order to address the abuse cycle.

Any professional school counselor who has reason to believe that a student's physical or mental health and welfare has been or may be affected by physical or sexual abuse has a professional and legal responsibility to report the case immediately to a law enforcement agency and/or to the state's department of child protection services. This is especially important for the professional school counselor who works closely with the student, to serve as the first line of defense. This chapter will look at the recognition, intervention and reporting of student physical and sexual abuse.

Child abuse is defined as "any recent act or failure to act resulting in imminent risk of serious harm, death, serious physical or emotional harm, sexual abuse, or exploitation of a child (minor age as described by state statutes) by a parent or caretaker (including out-of-home care providers) who are responsible for the child's welfare" (Child Abuse Prevention & Treatment Act [CAPTA], 1996, p. 29).

CAPTA (1996) defined sexual abuse as "employment, use, persuasion, inducement, enticement or coercion of any child to engage in, or assist any other person to engage in, any sexually explicit conduct or any simulation of such conduct for the purpose of producing any visual depiction of such conduct; or rape, and in cases of caretaker or inter-familial relationship, statutory rape, molestation, prostitution, or other form of sexual exploitation of children or incest with children."

Even though legislation regarding child abuse combines physical and sexual abuse, their individual effects on children and professional counselors are very specific. Professional school counselors working with abused students must be familiar with the complex dynamics that arise when abuse is experienced. One of the most critical components of rapport building with any child is to comprehend his or her internal frame of reference. Often, particularly in cases of sexual abuse, this is difficult to do. An abused child is often more confused about the issue than what is apparent to those involved.

A student exposed to abuse will harbor many emotional concerns arising from the abuse. Misperceptions about the experience, including those about self, the abuser, and the behavior or act that was forced upon the child, lingers throughout life and can be debilitating to the abused child. In many instances, total recovery from the emotional trauma may not occur; rather, the abusee develops coping skills/defense mechanisms to help him or her through the highly stressful recall of memories or ensuing flashbacks that may occur.

An abused student struggles to cope with abusive experiences while accomplishing developmental tasks common to all students. After the abuse, the student may expend a significant amount of mental energy attempting to cope with the abuse, rather than being free to fulfill developmental tasks, such as acquiring social skills, developing a sense of self, and learning to achieve. Although professionals have noted that a "loss of innocence" occurs when a student is abused, another loss may also occur, that of lost opportunities.

Rather than being free of mind to pursue playful, healthy, ego-strengthening activities, an abused student may struggle to survive emotionally, and sometimes physically. In cases where familial abuse occurs repeatedly over many years, an abused student must develop self-reliance (Daro, 1988; Reyes, 1996; Smith & Carlson, 1997) and inner strength as a means of survival; however, not all children are able to achieve this, especially when sexual abuse is involved.

How we come to regard abuse and sexuality is a result of what we have learned in our relationships with others. Our fundamental sexual feelings and attitudes are based on early life experiences. There is nothing particularly new in this concept; professional school counselors enter the academic arena understanding that they may have to deal with students' physical and sexual abuse problems.

Childhood experiences based on trust and safe physical boundaries set the stage for healthy coping skills. When trust is violated students develop defenses against being hurt. Defenses (i.e., attitudes of excessive self-sufficiency, self-love, self-hate, blame-taking, or blame-giving) come together to form our personality. It is the professional school counselor's responsibility to differentiate between student demonstrated defense mechanisms and coping strategies and act accordingly.

## Signs and Symptoms

Professional school counselors should have regular contact with the students and be able to recognize indicators of abuse in order to make educated observations and opinions. Watch for mood swings, withdrawal, and atypical acting out. Physical signs include scratches, burns, welts, broken teeth, cuts, and bruises not associated with sports, skate boarding, etc.

Pay attention to students who don't want to sit down or who sit carefully, as if injured. Young students may exhibit precocious sex play with classmates or objects, may ask more questions than normal, or know sexual terminology inappropriate for their age group. Others may refuse to undress for physical education or not be allowed to spend the night at a friend's house or vice versa.

Abused students can be habitually late to school or exhibit prolonged absences because the parent wants to keep an injured child at home until the evidence of abuse disappears. In some cases students frequently arrive early at school and remain after classes rather than return home.

They may be inappropriately dressed for the weather; students who wear long sleeve shirts and sweaters on hot days may be covering up bruises, burns, or other marks of abuse. The student may be wary of physical contact, especially from adults and peers. Students may also try desperately to get attention from adult figures such as teachers and the professional school counselor.

As a professional school counselor, keep in mind that abuse of students can be facilitated by other students as well. For these reasons, become an expert at unmasking sexual con games that take place between students. The goal of any perpetrator is to successfully increase the trust and secrecy between himself/herself and the victim (Herron & Sorensen, 1997). Be on the look out for students who violate boundaries, such as by wearing revealing clothing, standing too close to others, saying too much about themselves too soon, making sexual comments about other students' body parts, asking very personal questions, touching another students' legs or other parts of the body, or saying or doing things that are offensive or vulgar.

Also watch for victim boundaries that may be too closed, such as students who have few friends, rarely share feelings with others, rarely ask for help, isolate themself, or are cautious regarding letting trustworthy adults appropriately touch them (i.e., hand shakes, pats on the back, etc.). With the professional school counselors help, students who have been abused can learn to set appropriate boundaries and identify and avoid students who look out only for their own interests. Table 1 provides a developmental listing of symptoms and strategies for helping students who have been abused.

## Helpful Strategies

Disclosure of the abuse may be accidental or purposeful. Accidental disclosure occurs in cases where the abuse is observed by others, when the student is injured, or when the student acts out sexually. Purposeful disclosure occurs when the student desires to end the abusive relationship. Whatever the circumstances of the disclosure don't assume that the student will be anxious to talk openly about the abuse. Assuming that the student is verbal, it is essential to evaluate the student's level of trust, emotional stability, memory skills, cognitive ability, social maturity, accuracy of recall of past events, and ability to verbalize accurately.

The purpose of the initial meeting with the student is to determine the type of abuse that has occurred and to ensure that the student is protected. The meeting should be conducted in a safe place and the student should be comfortable in the setting. If the student gives any indication of experiencing high stress levels or retraumatization, alternative strategies and arrangements should be made to avoid revictimization of the student (Thompson & Rudolph, 2000). In general:

- Set boundaries while giving the student a safe space for self-expression. The primary goal is to help the student merge self-expression with self-discovery, leading to an emotional catharsis.
- In an effort to stay neutral and objective, the professional school counselor may be perceived as cold and uncaring. It is permissible for the professional school counselor to self-disclose and show empathy in a warm and caring manner when appropriate and accurate to the situation. Express caring in a nonsexual manner. Remember that unconditional positive regard is a therapeutic process.
- Address the abusive issues in a straightforward manner and explore with the student his/her feelings and thoughts in a firm, but warm and fair manner. Examination involves helping the student get in touch with the irrational beliefs that affect his/her self-esteem and confidence. Explore the student's behavior therapeutically as a result of the abusive situation.
- Do not attempt to intervene by contacting parents regarding suspected abuse. This may alert the parent or perpetrator and give him/her an opportunity to cover his/her actions and/or be covert in their abuse.
- Refer the student for counseling outside the school setting when it is critical to the mental health of the student. Professional school counselors must get in touch with their own questions prior to working with students; "Have I been adequately trained in this area of counseling?" "Should the student be seen by a school social worker, school psychologist or professional counselor outside the school system?" "Can I

be objective about this case?" "Will I become too emotional about these issues?"

- Collaborate with the student to develop a contract specifying the conditions under which counseling will proceed and the goals to pursue.
- Good team collaboration is an essential component of counseling in order to foster effective and responsible interaction with students with abusive life situations.
- Conduct classroom guidance and lessons to specifically orientate students in effective ways of responding to abuse so that the abuse will be brought to a close (e.g., harassment).

**Table 1. Symptoms and strategies for working with abused students.**

| SYMPTOM | STRATEGIES |
|---|---|
| **ELEMENTARY SCHOOL** | |
| • Withdrawn, cries easily<br>• Avoids eye contact, sinks down in chair<br>• Squirms in seat, painful to sit<br>• Suspicious or frequent bruises, welts, cuts, etc.<br>• Violent or sexual drawings or stories<br>• Advanced sexual vocabulary<br>• Imitating sexual or violent behavior alone or with other children during play, with toys<br>• Restroom accidents<br>• Not allowed to spend the night at a friend's house | • As a prevention, provide "good touch, bad touch" education<br>• With intervention, stay calm, sit down with the student and use active listening<br>• Remember perpetrators rely on trust and secrecy to victimize, so be patient<br>• Let the child know that you believe him/her<br>• Help the child feel powerful by sharing that he/she has options available to him/her<br>• Place the blame on the offender<br>• Report the abuse, contact the protective service worker/police to come to the school for a written report |
| **MIDDLE SCHOOL** | |
| • Vandalism, destruction of property<br>• Self-mutilation<br>• Bullying, using force or intimidation of smaller children<br>• Angry or violent outbursts<br>• Withdrawal from physical contact from teachers or other students<br>• Physical complaints of headaches, dizziness, muscle cramps<br>• Few, if any, friends<br>• Severe drop in grades<br>• Precocious sex play<br>• Won't undress for gym<br>• Vacillates between being ultra-adult and ultra-immature | • Affirm the child's feelings and reassure him/her that he/she took an important step in talking with you<br>• Provide students with an orientation on sexual harassment and the professional school counselor as a professional resource<br>• Provide a friendly, warm, genuine, and empathic approach with the child<br>• Report the abuse, contact the professional service worker/police to come to the school for a written report |
| **HIGH SCHOOL** | |
| • Self destructive behavior (drugs, alcohol)<br>• Extreme moodiness<br>• Depression – suicidal thoughts<br>• Pseudomature behaviors<br>• Withdrawal from friends and family<br>• School truancy/poor school performance<br>• Sexually vulgar conversations and behavior with opposite sex | • Invite the school resource officer to educate students on sexual con games throughout the school year<br>• Don't make unrealistic promises and remember that reporting alone does not always stop abuse<br>• Report the abuse, contact the protective service worker/police to come to the school for a written report |

- When you find a strategy that is appropriate, be sure that you implement it with an extra bit of care and compassion given the student's troubled situation.
- Increase all students' awareness, knowledge and skills regarding abuse and its intervention.
- Become sensitive to and educate students regarding sexual con games that take place between students.

In a majority of the cases the professional school counselor becomes the first person that the student talks to about his/her abuse and so the counselor becomes the "outcry witness." Because the counseling relationship is addressing such sensitive issues with legal consequences, professional school counselors must be well apprised of the legal and policy protocols within their state and school district.

## Counselor/Organizational Liability

All states now have laws requiring professional school counselors who suspect that a student has been abused to report it to the designated authorities. When counseling is conducted following disclosures or accusations of abuse from others, rigid guidelines must be followed. When engaging in counseling it is imperative to adhere to ACA and ASCA ethical standards and the legal guidelines of your school system and respective district. If you are not sure what the protocol is in your school, immediately check with your building administrator. One professional school counselor had this to say, "I learned from a veteran counselor in my school that if I suspect abuse I am to immediately notify the principal. Not the assistant principal. Not the school psychologist. The principal." Other school districts require the professional school counselor to notify the law enforcement officer as the initial contact.

Consistent, effective reporting of abuse is dependent upon understanding the dynamics of abuse and the reporting procedures. Cooperation among the professional school counselor, staff, administration, law enforcement and child protective services is essential.

## Summary/Conclusion

Students who are physically and sexually abused are robbed of more than innocence, they are robbed of emotional stability, rational thinking, and interactions built on trust and well-being. The ability to form and maintain protective and appropriate boundaries is exhausted. Emotional desires that need to be explored and fulfilled are stunted and go unattended or are repressed and can lead to depression or anger.

A student's physical and mental welfare is a top priority in school and the professional school counselor must serve as the student's safety advocate. With every interaction the school counselor can help the student take new steps toward an enhanced quality of life. In turn, through the student's taking control of his/her issues, both the professional school counselor and the student become empowered survivors.

## References

Child Abuse Prevention and Treatment Act. (1996) Available:http://www.acf.hhs.gov/programs/cb/laws/.

Daro, D. (1988). *Confronting child abuse: Research for effective program design.* New York: Free Press.

Francis, A., First, M., & Pincus, H. (1995). *DSM-IV guidebook.* Washington, DC: American Psychological Press.

Hampton, R., Gullotta, T., Adams, G., Potter III, E., & Weissberg, R. (1993). *Family violence: Prevention and treatment.* London: Sage Publications.

Herron, R., & Sorensen, K. (1997). *Unmasking sexual con games, student guide.* Boys Town, NE: Boys Town Press.

Kagan, S. (1991). *United we stand, collaboration for child care and early education services.* New York: Teachers College Press.

Reyes, C., Kokotovic, A., & Cosden, M. (1996). Sexually abused children's perception: How they may change treatment focus. *Professional Psychology: Research & Practice, 27,* 588-591.

Schwartz, M., & Cohn, L. (1996). *Sexual abuse and eating disorders.* New York: Brunner/Mazel Publishers.

Smith, C., & Carlson, B. (1997). Stress, coping and resilience in children and youth. *Social Service Review, 71*, 231-257.

# Chapter 75

## Counseling Sexual Minority Students in the Schools

*Mark Pope, Lela Kosteck Bunch, Dawn M. Szymanski,*
*& Michael Rankins*

### Preview

This chapter addresses the issues that are important for professional school counselors who are counseling sexual minority students, including gay, lesbian, bisexual, transgender, intersex, queer, and questioning (GLBTIQQ) youth. The issues that are addressed include developing a context in which to discuss these issues; "coming out" or the developmental aspects of sexual identity development; the extent of the problems that sexual minority youth face in the schools and society; the effects of negative attitudes and violence toward these youth; and ethical and legal issues in dealing with sexual minority youth in the schools. In addition, school-based interventions are discussed that focus on the role of the parents and schools, separation (e.g., separate schools for sexual minority youth) or culture change, deliberate psycho-affective education, valuing differences, and the power of subtle symbols.

"Fag." "Dyke." "Geek." "Wuss." "Dweeb." "Queer." "Lezzie." These are some of the words that sexual minority youth often hear as they progress through elementary and secondary schools in the United States. Whether it is directed at them because they look and act different or it is said about others who look and act different, the point has been made. "You are different and that is bad." "You're different and not a member of our group." These statements occur at a time when sexual minority youth so desperately want and need to belong.

> This is the lexicon of adolescence in America. This verbal and physical harassment is designed to elicit conformity from those so targeted and security for the deliverer, 'no matter how bad my life is, at least I'm not one of THEM.' To be a boy or girl who is 'different' from your peers' notions of what a male or female is supposed to do or be is to become the object of derisive comments challenging your sexual orientation. In the USA if you are a sensitive boy who cries at movies, or an athletic girl who wears jeans and no makeup, you are subject to whispers or catcalls from your peers. To be different during a time when conformity to your peer group is the norm is to be a target for verbal and physical harassment from that same group, especially about sexuality. (Pope, 2000, p. 285)

Professional school counselors are confronted regularly with elementary, middle, and secondary school students who are gay, lesbian, bisexual, transgender, intersex, queer, or simply questioning (GLBTIQQ) if they are different. Fontaine (1998) surveyed professional school counselors and found that more than half (51%) of both middle and high school counselors had worked with at least one student who was questioning their sexual orientation and 42% had worked with at least one self-identified lesbian or gay student. Twenty-one percent (21%) of elementary school counselors also reported that they were aware of students in their schools who were identifying as gay or lesbian, or were questioning their sexual orientation. School counselors need to know what to do when that young person walks into the school counseling office and says, "I think I might be a lesbian."

Unfortunately, there are no easy answers. This chapter, however, does provide some guidelines to aid the professional school counselor in helping these courageous young people. Young people who are different face physical and verbal harassment because they are different or just perceived as being different from peers.

In this chapter the following issues will be addressed: developing a context in which to discuss sexual minority student issues; "coming out" or the developmental aspects of sexual identity development; the extent of the problems that sexual minority youth face in the schools and society; the effects of negative attitudes and violence toward these youth; and ethical and legal issues in dealing with sexual minority youth in the schools. In addition, school-based interventions are discussed that focus on the roles of parents and schools, separation (e.g., separate schools for sexual minority youth) or culture change, deliberate psycho-affective education, valuing differences, and the power of subtle symbols.

*Developing a Context in Which to Discuss These Issues*

This chapter will discuss sex — sexuality, sexual orientation, and other related issues. Sex and sexuality in American society are taboo subjects. We know that we are supposed to know about it, we are excited about it, we talk about it in indirect ways, we sometimes even talk about it in direct ways, but that is generally considered unseemly. Perhaps our parents talked to us (rarely with us) about it. Our schools have had to fight hard to get an opportunity to teach about it. Socially, we are just not very comfortable with sex (LeVay & Valente, 2002).

Here, we will use the general term "sexual minority" to include a variety of young people who are in various stages of their psychosocial, gender, sexual, and cultural identity development processes. The term "sexual minority" includes gays (males who identify with a same-sex sexual or affectional orientation), lesbians (females who identify with a same-sex sexual or affectional orientation), bisexuals (males or females who identify with both a same-sex and opposite sex sexual or affectional orientation), transgender (individuals who are physiologically one gender but who are psychologically the opposite gender), intersex (individuals who have biological characteristics of both males and females), queer (individuals who identify as "different" sexually than the majority culture), and questioning (individuals who are unsure of their sexual or affectional orientation or gender identity). This sometimes will be abbreviated as GLBTIQQ or even GLBT in this chapter.

Further, there are a number of well written articles and books on the etiology of sexual orientation (LeVay, 1991, 1999; LeVay & Valente, 2002). The topic of sexual orientation can be expected to be complex, evocative, and confusing. To date, it remains unclear exactly how sexual orientation is determined. Moreover, because conservative religious and political groups tend to view homosexuality as a moral issue, while others see it as a civil rights issue, it cannot be separated easily from either context: a person's sexual orientation has both political and religious implications. Finally, given the lack of definitive answers from scientific research, confusion and uncertainty tend to underlie the often-intense discussions about the sexual behavior and mental health needs of sexual minorities in our society (Barret & Logan, 2001; Barret & Robinson, 2000; Pope & Barret, 2002b). Rarely does anyone agree on anything, yet it appears that there is a growing research consensus about the roots of sexual orientation. It is imperative that this type of information be readily available to both parents and students. This chapter makes the assumption that the causes of sexual orientation are not known definitively, but that sexual orientation is not mutable.

Social attitudes toward homosexuality have also undergone many changes. From the acceptance and integration of same-sex persons into the Native American tribes of North America (Roscoe, 1989), to the acceptance of same-sex unions by the Christian church in the middle ages (Boswell, 1980; 1995), to the persecution of homosexually-oriented persons under the Victorians (Rowse, 1977), to the enlightened approaches of pre-Nazi Germany (Hirschfeld, 1935), pre-Stalinist Russia (Thorstad, 1974), and imperial China (Ruan, 1991), and finally to the removal of homosexuality from the psychiatric manual of mental disorders (Bayer, 1981), history has seen an ebb and flow in the social acceptance of same-sex orientations (Pope & Barret, 2002b).

In the past, sexual minority adults had to cope with active anger, religious hatred, psychiatric labels, and occupational discrimination. Pope and Barrett (2002a) described how aspects of this discrimination were reflected in the workplace:

> If they did not live in large cities such as New York, San Francisco, and Boston where vital lesbian and gay culture thrives, gay men and lesbians generally kept their sexual orientation a closely guarded secret .... Many of them fabricated social lives that included dates with persons of the opposite sex and rarely would share their vacation photographs with their co-workers. If there were a social event with co-workers, many would bring opposite sex "dates" that had been secured to help "cover" their secret. Some even chose careers on the basis of its "safety" in the event they did decide to come out. For example, it was not unusual to hear young gay men or lesbians speak of avoiding careers that involved working with children or commenting on "conservative" corporations that would not deal with their sexual orientation easily. Others carefully guarded their sexual orientation for fear that the promotions would be denied them if they were more "out." Fortunately today, for many lesbian and gay clients, much of this is changing, as it is not unusual to hear casual conversations about the social and relationship aspects of gay and lesbian co-workers in the workplace. (p. 215)

For today's sexual minority youth, there are many positive sexual minority role models available. GLBTIQQ individuals appear in virtually every aspect of daily life. They are more "out" to their families and co-workers, visible in their neighborhoods, assertive in demanding equal rights, and have moved beyond the fear and shame that used to keep most of them invisible. This change can be seen in all aspects of the media, gay-positive-statements from national and local political candidates, and in the debates within virtually all Christian denominations about the role of gay men and lesbians within the church (Barret & Logan, 2001).

*"Coming Out" or the Developmental Aspects of Sexual Identity Development*

"Coming out to self," or accepting one's own same-sex feelings, attraction, and orientation, is an important and necessary developmental task for anyone who is gay or lesbian, but is especially important for the gay or lesbian adolescent (Pope, 1995). Males tend to define themselves as gay in the context of same-sex erotic contact, but females experience lesbian feelings in situations of romantic love and emotional attachment (Troiden, 1979). Coleman, Butcher, and Carson (1984) provided a good explanation of general developmental stages and the tasks associated with each stage:

> If developmental tasks are not mastered at the appropriate stage, the individual suffers from immaturities and incompetencies and is placed at a serious disadvantage in adjusting at later developmental levels — that is, the individual becomes increasingly vulnerable through accumulated failures to master psychosocial requirements. . . . Some developmental tasks are set by the individual's own needs, some by the physical and social environment. Members of different socioeconomic and sociocultural groups face somewhat different developmental tasks. (p. 111)

Pope (1995) stated that this developmental task of discovery and acceptance of who one is and how one functions sexually plays an important role, especially in adolescence. This is, however, also the time for many gay males and lesbians when there exists the greatest denial of differences from their peer group. Unfortunately, if the developmental tasks of sexual orientation identification are not accomplished during this critical time and are denied and delayed, then other tasks, such as relationship formation, are also delayed, causing a developmental "chain reaction." It is very common to hear that gay men who came out when they were substantially past adolescence have all the problems associated with those of teenagers who have just begun dating. It is important to note that once the critical period has passed in the developmental task, it may be very difficult or impossible to correct the resulting psychological difficulties.

Adolescence is not an easy time in anyone's life because of the required psychosexual identity development. This tumultuous time is only made more difficult, however, when homophobic slurs and insults are hurled at young persons who may have already begun to realize that their sexual orientation may be different from their heterosexual peers. Both verbal and physical harassment are designed to elicit conformity from those so targeted along with security for the deliverer, "no matter how bad my life is, at least I'm not one of THEM." A large study of Minnesota junior and senior high school students found that about 11% were still unsure about their sexual orientation (Remafedi, Resnick, Blum, & Harris, 1992). Twenty percent of self-identified gay and bisexual men surveyed on college campuses knew about their sexual orientation in high school and another 17% knew as far back as grade school they were gay. The figures are 6% and 11% respectively for lesbians (Elliott & Brantley, 1997).

Coming to terms with one's sexual differences during the teen years make forming a sexual identity a greater challenge (D'Augelli, 1992). This is because youth are socialized in the home and school, in the media, and throughout most of life to appreciate falling in love with members of the other gender (Rotheram-Borus & Fernandez, 1995). Though there is wide variation in sexual identity formation in adolescence, some common themes emerge for many gay teens: feeling different, experiencing confusion, and finally expressing acceptance (Mannino, 1999). Chung and Katayama (1998) reported that the formation of sexual identity is a developmental process with these stages: awareness of same-sex feelings, feeling confused because one's assumed sexual orientation differs from one's perceived orientation, tolerance and acceptance of a lesbian or gay identity, and integration of a sexual identity with other aspects of one's life.

Gay men and lesbians often report feeling different from others during childhood. Many of these differences are in gender nonconformity, that is, play and sport interests are more congruent with the other gender (Mondimore, 1996). Boys may find they are quieter, less active, and more sensitive than other boys, while girls may find that they are more physically active, assertive, and more "tom-boyish" than their peers. Marinoble (1998) described the difficulties experienced by many such sexual minority youth: including identity conflict, feelings of isolation and stigmatization, peer relationship problems, and family disruptions. Omizo, Omizo, and Okamoto (1998) found that common sentiments among young sexual minority persons include confusion, fear of not being understood, fear of negative or violent reactions from others, concerns about what kind of a future they might have, poor self-esteem, and internalized feelings of self-hatred. Within especially conservative cultures or families, such as those of some Asian American youth, there are few if any positive role models with whom sexual minority youth may identify (Chung & Katayama, 1998). For such youth, it is likely that feelings of isolation and confusion are magnified.

Somc gay youth copc with their confusion by concretizing their gay identity very quickly. This is sometimes initiated by puberty, where feeling different takes on a clearer, more precise feeling of sexual attraction. Herdt and Boxer (1996), in a study of 200 ethnically diverse lesbian, gay, and bisexual youth, found that awareness of same-sex attraction occurred between ages 11 and 12 on average. Other gay teens try to deny their same-sex feelings and become super-heterosexual in an effort to retrain themselves, and still others become bewildered, guilt ridden, and lonely, escaping into substance abuse, depression, and suicidal ideation.

Not all gay and lesbian teenagers accept themselves, which is understandable given the constant battering they receive from some cultures and religions, as well as from their peers, family, and society (Mannino, 1999). Eventually, however, the majority of gay youth who do accept their sexuality begin to feel a need to disclose their sexual orientation to others. There are many strategies to such disclosure, but close friends are usually told first, with parents being told later. The fear of rejection and isolation, along with parental sanctions, tend to be ever present; therefore, some sexual minority youth decide not to disclose at all, especially if they are still in high school or living with their parents or other family members (Newman & Muzzonigro, 1993). When young people do decide to reveal their sexual orientation to their parents, having some idea of a "format" for such a coming out process is often helpful. Savin-Williams (1990) reported in a study of gay and lesbian youth that most of those who had successfully come out to self could be described as: a) being politically and socially involved with other gays and lesbians, having numerous same-sex sexual encounters, regularly frequenting bars, and describing an early onset of same-sex sexual feelings that were beyond their control; b) feeling accepted by family members and friends and feeling that they had more friends; c) feeling they were accomplished and self-sufficient, but not feeling competitive and forceful or affectionate and compassionate; d) being generally older and well-educated, coming from wealthy urban families; e) measuring their self-esteem and sense of well being by their relationships with friends and by their career and academic achievements rather than by their possessions and good looks; and f) being politically liberal and supportive of the feminist movement.

*Extent of the Problems that Sexual Minority Youth Face in the Schools and Society*

Although a number of social and environmental difficulties which sexual minority youth may encounter have previously been discussed, a more intensive focus on education and socialization issues is warranted because the schools are the workplace for young people. Owens (1998) captured the experience of sexual minority students in the schools:

> Schools are social molds where rigid expectations of conduct and behavior are reinforced. Conformity is tyrannical. The wrong clothes or the wrong comment can result in ostracism. Sexual conformity is enforced most rigidly. Those that do not conform are open to the physical, verbal, and mental bullying of the majority. Reports from lesbian and gay teens range from put-downs and "rude comments and jokes" through "profanities written on my locker" and threats to actual violence and physical abuse. The overall result is loneliness, fear, and self-loathing. (p. 95-96)

Sexual minority youth face stigmatization and a significant number of stressors in the school environment, including ostracism, physical violence, and verbal harassment (Allport, 1958; Gustavsson & MacEachron, 1998; Jordan, Vaughan, & Woodworth, 1997; Pope, 2000). The search for one's sexual identity (male or female) is an important part of adolescence (SIECUS, 1995), but when that search is intertwined with minority status, that is, either race or sexual orientation, it is even more complex (Chung & Katayama, 1998).

There is great fear and loathing of gay and lesbian people in general in the USA. Ilnytzky (1999) reports that all anti-gay attacks in the entire United States dropped 4% in 1998, but the assaults which did occur were more violent and led to more hospitalizations. The number of attacks dropped from 2,665 in 1997 to 2,552 in 1998; however, the number of victims requiring inpatient hospitalization more than doubled, from 53 in 1997 to 110 in 1998. There also was a 71% rise in assaults and attempted assaults with guns. Incidents in which bats, clubs and other blunt objects were used increased by 47%.

There is great fear and loathing of gay and lesbian adolescents in particular. In fact gay and lesbian high school students face greater prejudice in school than African American teen students according to a CBS News poll that surveyed the attitudes of the high school senior class of the year 2000. The findings included the following: a) one-third of students know that gay or lesbian students were made fun of, verbally or physically abused, and threatened; b) 28% of students polled have made anti-gay remarks themselves; c) nearly a third of those polled have a family member or close friend who is gay or lesbian; d) among those making anti-gay remarks, boys are more than twice as likely than girls to have done so; and e) those who report their parents make anti-gay remarks are more than twice as likely to do so themselves (CBS News Poll, 1999). A survey conducted in 14 American cities found over 46% of gay youth who disclosed their same-sex sexual orientation ("came out") to friends lost at least one of them as a friend (Ryan & Futterman, 1997). Marsiglio (1993), in a national survey of young people who were 15 to 19 years of age, found only 12% would feel "comfortable" having a lesbian or gay male friend. Male youth in particular were more likely to hold negative stereotypes regarding lesbian and gay youth, as 89% of the male adolescents in this study reported that they felt sex between two men was "disgusting." Malinsky (1997), in a study of 27 self-identified lesbians and bisexual girls between the ages of 15-21, found that 25 (93%) of the study participants reported direct, first hand knowledge of harassment based on actual or perceived sexual orientation. It is important to note that such harassment was sometimes directed at those who simply associated with these young lesbian or bisexual women.

GLSEN rated 42 of the nation's largest public school districts on their policies and programs designed to serve sexual minority students and school workers. Only four districts got an "A" — Los Angeles, San Diego, Philadelphia, and Dade County, Florida. Twenty major school districts received a grade of "D." According to spokesperson Kate Frankfurt, "that means nearly 2 million students go to school in districts that fail" in basic gay human rights (Herscher, 1998, p. A20).

These negative feelings toward sexual minority youth are being reinforced by the indifference of school workers to these issues. Derogatory remarks by fellow students directed to sexual minority students often go unchallenged by teachers, administrators, or professional school counselors, whereas a similar racist statement would more likely prompt a reprimand (Krivascka, Savin-Williams, & Slater, 1992; O'Conor, 1994; Pope, 2000). The dynamics are complicated when sexual minority school employees are trying to hide their sexual orientation and to distance themselves from sexual minority youth (Jordan et al., 1997). Reluctant or unable to support sexual minority youth, these sexual minority teachers, professional school counselors, administrators, or other school staff fail to provide the role modeling or safety that other cultural minority school workers (e.g., African American, Asian American, Native American, or Hispanic American) provide for students from their own specific culture.

Fontaine (1998) found that those who were the perpetrators of harassment and intimidation of sexual minority students were aided by the indifference of school workers:

> Homophobic and intolerant educational environments can only exist with the implicit and/or explicit cooperation of schools' officials and personnel. Evidence suggests that teachers, counselors, and administrators exhibit distressingly high levels of homophobic attitudes and feelings. (p. 8)

Rofes (1989) wrote eloquently about the violence against sexual minority youth and pointed out its effects:

> Many young people — especially those who were cross-dressers, or young men who were effeminate, or young women who were "too butch" (tough, independent, and "masculine") — found their peers hostile, often to the point of violence. For gay youth who could "pass" and remain undetected in the school system, advocates found the hiding process robbed students of much of their energy and vitality. Whether lesbian and gay youth were open about their identities or were closeted, societal prejudice took its toll; young gay people were often anti-social, alcohol- and drug-abusing, and/or depressed to the point of suicide. (p. 449)

Anthony Gomez, a 14 year old student at Hayward, California, describes his own experience in the following manner:

> A lot of people pick on me at school and pick fights with me. At school, I've had fag spray-painted on my locker, gay porn pinned to my locker, and death threats on my locker too. I had three boys suspended the other day for harassing me, saying they're trying to pick fights with me, calling me a faggot, a queer, and all that stuff (Gray, 1999, p. 81).

Finally, The Associated Press (1999) reported that two college preparatory school students in Greenwood, MA at the Northfield Mount Hermon School — one with an appointment to the Naval Academy — were convicted of assault and battery for carving an anti-gay slur into another student's back because he liked to listen to the British rock band Queen. Jonathan Shapiro, 18, and Matthew Rogers, 20, used a pocket knife to cut "HOMO" into the back of a 17-year-old student at the school. "There was apparently a disagreement over the style of music he liked," said Police Chief David Hastings. "Rogers called it a gay band." Hastings described the wounds as "deep enough to draw blood. When I saw them, they were three days old and they were still very visible. The letters were 4- to 5-inches high and ran all the way across his back." The victim, a junior, did not require hospitalization, and initially kept quiet about the incident. He left school and returned to his family. Shapiro, of Keene, NH, and Rogers, of Franklin, TN, were placed on probation for three years for this crime. Rogers had accepted an appointment to the U.S. Naval Academy, but Rogers' appointment to the U.S. Naval Academy was withdrawn, because of the incident. Concerned Students of Des Moines reported that the average high school student hears approximately 25 anti-gay remarks in a typical school day (The Advocate, 1997).

*Effects of Negative Attitudes and Violence toward These Youth*

Adolescents who are different face a variety of barriers to healthy psychological development, most created and delivered by their peers, family, culture, and society (Pope, 2000). Besner and Spungin (1995) reported a variety of consequences for the lesbian and gay adolescent such as: a high incidence of acting out in school; rebelling against authority; abusing alcohol and other substances; feeling depressed, isolated, and confused; engaging in prostitution; and attempting suicide, many times succeeding. Jordan et al. (1997), in a study of 34 lesbian and gay high school students, reported a clear relationship between derogatory language directed against sexual minority students by their peers and adults in the school setting and self-harmful behavior, such as suicidal ideation, attempted suicide, running away, poor academic performance, and truancy. Considering the stress of adolescence and the additional "cultural minority stress" of being a sexual minority youth, it is particularly disheartening to discover that a survey found less than one in five lesbian and gay adolescent students could identify someone who was very supportive of them (Telljohann & Price, 1993).

Remafedi (1987) found, through a series of studies of self-identified gay male adolescents, that they were at high risk for physical and psychosocial dysfunction as a result of experiencing strong negative attitudes from parents and peers. In a followup to those studies, Remafedi, Farrow, and Deisher (1991), in a study of 137 gay and bisexual male youths, found that 30% had attempted suicide once and 13% had made multiple attempts. The mean age of those attempting suicide was 15.5 years. Three quarters (75%) of first attempts came after the teenagers had labeled themselves as bisexual or gay. (Risk factors that increase the potential for suicide in sexual minority youth are posted at www.umsl.edu/~pope.)

According to Gibson (1989), suicide is the leading cause of death among gay youth. They are from three to five times more likely to attempt suicide than their heterosexual peers (Bailey & Phariss, 1996; Brown, 1991; Gibson, 1989; Hafen & Frandsen, 1986; Mondimore, 1996). Gibson (1989) also found that gay male adolescents are six times more likely to attempt suicide than their heterosexual counterparts.

Currently, there is much discussion among researchers about these statistics based on the skewed demographics of the populations sampled (Muerher, 1995; Saulnier, 1998). The results of many of these studies have been criticized for the retrospective nature of the reports, the involvement of many of the youths in social service systems, and the recruitment of study participants from bars, which might inflate the actual numbers. It is quite difficult to gather generalizable data on this population because of the difficulty of operationalizing sexual orientation and the previously cited issues.

*Ethical and Legal Issues in Dealing with Sexual Minority Youth in the Schools*

The question of what is the ethical and legal role of the professional school counselor when counseling sexual minority students is an important practical one. Ethically, the role is clear. Professional school counselors are there to assist students in discovering who they truly and honestly are and to help them develop a strong and positive personal and cultural identity.

Research conducted by Nicolosi (1991) described an approach called "reparative therapy" (RT) that claims to change sexual orientation (always from gay to straight, rather than the opposite). RT parallels another "treatment," "conversion therapy" (CT), hailed by conservative Christian groups as proof that prayer and meditation can "drive the sin out" and bring the "sick homosexual" back to health. Both RT and CT have received abundant attention and both have been soundly condemned by the American Counseling Association, the American Psychiatric Association, the American Psychological Association, the National Association of Social Workers, the National Association of School Psychologists, the American School Health Association, the American Federation of Teachers, the National Education Association, and the American Academy of Pediatrics. Mental health workers are warned that research indicates both of these "treatments" are more likely to be harmful than helpful. Many believe it is unethical for mental health professionals to practice CT or RT (Barret, 1999; Just the Facts Coalition, 2000).

As to queries regarding whether sexual orientation is open to change, Money (1990) stated:

> The concept of voluntary choice is as much in error (as applied to sexual orientation) as in its application to handedness or to native language. You do not choose your native language as a preference, even though you are born without it. You assimilate it into a brain pre-natally made ready to receive a native language from those who constitute your primate troop and who speak that language to you and listen to you when you speak it. Once assimilated through the ears into the brain, a native language becomes securely locked in — as securely as if it has been phylogenetically preordained to be locked in pre-natally by a process of genetic pre-determinism or by the determinism of fetal hormonal or other brain chemistries. So also with sexual status or orientation, which, whatever its genesis, also may become assimilated and locked into the brain as mono sexually homosexual or heterosexual or as bisexually a mixture of both. (p. 43-44)

Further, according to Coleman (1982):

> It is unethical and morally questionable to offer a 'cure' to homosexuals who request a change in their sexual orientation. While there have been reports that changes in behavior have occurred for individuals seeking treatment, it is questionable whether it is beneficial to change their behavior to something that is incongruent with their sexual orientation. (p. 87)

Legally, the role of the professional school counselor is limited by school district policies as well as by state laws and regulations that govern the credentialing of professional school counselors in their state. Also, if the school counselor is licensed as a professional counselor or other mental health professional, the person must operate within the bounds of confidentiality as outlined in the state laws and judicial cases which govern the specialty. Some school districts may require parental disclosure and consent; others may not. School counselors, therefore, must be knowledgeable of the specific policies, laws, and regulations that govern their conduct. It is, however, of the utmost importance to sexual minority students that school counselors be seen as their ally and their protector in the school.

Clearly, the shift toward the protection of sexual minority students in the schools is gaining momentum. In 1993, Massachusetts became the first state to ban anti-gay discrimination in its schools and create a statewide "safe schools" program. The U.S. Department of Education issued guidelines in March of 1997 stating that gay and lesbian students are covered by federal prohibitions against sexual harassment.

In 1996, a jury in a federal appellate court in Nabozny v. Podlensy, 92 F.3d 446 (Nabozny v. Podlensy, 1996) deliberated for only two days and found Ashland, WI public school officials liable for not protecting Jamie Nabozny, a student who had suffered years of relentless physical, sexual, and verbal harassment for being gay. He had been beaten to the point of requiring surgery, urinated on, called anti-gay epithets, and made to suffer repeated assaults and indignities. In a landmark settlement reached after that verdict, he was awarded over $900,000 in damages. In its decision, the federal appellate court decision spelled out the constitutional obligation of public schools everywhere to treat abuse of lesbian and gay students as seriously as any other abuse.

In 1998 a jury in Louisville, KY awarded $220,000 to a 17-year-old girl because the school she attended acted with "deliberate indifference" by permitting other students to call her "lezzie," assault her, and attempt to rape her. Other lawsuits are working their ways through the courts including a 12-year-old boy who is suing his Pacifica, CA school district for refusing to intervene in his years of harassment, and a gay teen brutally attacked by eight other students who secured the American Civil Liberties Union to aid his lawsuit against the Kent, WA school district, as well as lawsuits filed by the American Civil Liberties Union in Kentucky and Texas on school board's prohibiting the gay and lesbian school clubs from meeting.

## School-Based Interventions

In order to protect sexual minority students, schools must take an active role in eliminating anti-gay harassment and creating a positive environment for these students. In this section, the role of parents and school workers will be explored along with specific issues dealing with separation (e.g., separate schools for sexual minority youth) or culture change, deliberate psycho-affective education, valuing differences, and the power of subtle signs.

### *Role of Parents and School Workers*

Parents and school workers often teach homophobic attitudes in quite subtle, and sometimes not so subtle, ways (Besner & Spungin, 1995; Fontaine, 1997). Some adults do this very consciously because they believe that this is the best way to eliminate such behavior in young people, that it will somehow persuade the student — through their disapproval — not to be gay or lesbian. For other adults it is not a conscious process, only one that is ingrained and reinforced through others in their environment. Many never contemplate that they are, in fact, emotionally victimizing the sexual minority student.

Through persistent derogatory jokes, behavioral admonitions ("don't be a sissy" or "don't hold your hand that way, that's too gay" or "girls don't sit like that"), and overheard homophobic conversations, gay and lesbian students absorb these negative attitudes regarding sexual minorities becoming victims of the adults they trust and who profess love for them. How do these gay and lesbian children deal with this incongruity?

> Some respond by denying their sexual orientation and dating and engaging in sexual activities with members of the opposite sex, trying to pass as heterosexual. Others respond by developing a strong contempt for those gays and lesbians who are more open and obvious. They may take out their own sexual frustrations through varying degrees of aggression toward gay and lesbian members of the community. Other gay and lesbian teenagers respond by withdrawing from society and becoming shy and isolated. They are reluctant to join in social activities with friends and family and live in a world all their own. Some of these teenagers are so filled with self-hatred they cannot find anything acceptable or positive to say about themselves. Some seek out groups that believe their homosexual orientation can be changed. These individuals will go to great extremes and will be highly motivated to do whatever it takes to be straight. (Besner & Spungin, 1995, p. 47)

In Savin-Williams' (1990) study predicting self-esteem among lesbian and gay youth, the teenagers with the highest levels of self-esteem felt accepted by their mothers, male and female friends, and their academic advisors. Lesbian youth who had positive parental relationships felt comfortable with their sexual orientation. Satisfying parental relationships, maternal knowledge of their homosexuality, and having relatively little contact with fathers predicted positive self-esteem for gay men. Mothers are important for self-esteem for both gay men and lesbians and are viewed as considerably more supportive, warm, and compassionate than fathers. Early parent-child interactions, physical affection, childhood rearing practices, and family religious teachings are considered good predictors of the state of comfort students have with their sexual orientation.

Pope (2000) and Pope and Englar-Carlson (2001) reported that messages that parents give to their children are important in the child's developing self-esteem. Phrases such as "be who you are and never be afraid to express your feelings" or "I love you for you" or "it's okay to talk about anything with me, even if I do not like what you have to say, I will always love you" convey a message of unconditional positive acceptance no matter what the situation is. Unfortunately, parental words spoken in haste and anger can destroy years of positive communication. The best parents weigh the impact of their words before speaking them to children, never saying to children "you are so stupid" or similar phrases, even in jest, as these negative phrases are powerful, rarely being forgotten.

When a student discloses their sexual minority status ("comes out") to school personnel, this is a major event in his/her life and deserves to be treated in a sensitive and caring way by the school worker. (Some guidelines to help school personnel respond to students when they disclose their sexual minority status are posted at http://www.umsl.edu/~pope.)

*Separation or Culture Change*

During the 1980s and 1990s, between the political far-right's attempts to take control of school boards and the unionization of school workers, the schools became the battleground on which many of the tough political questions of the day were played. During this time, the issue of what to do with sexual minority students also came to the top of the school agenda.

Responses to these issues varied considerably among schools. In the New York City schools, the Harvey Milk School was established in 1985 for gay and lesbian students who were not succeeding. In Dallas, TX, a private school for lesbian and gay youth opened in 1997 (Williams, 1997). In the Los Angeles Unified School District, Dr. Virginia Uribe established "Project 10," a dropout prevention program offering emotional support, information, and resources to young people who identify themselves as lesbian, gay, or bisexual or who wish to obtain information about sexual orientation (Uribe & Harbeck, 1992). Shortly thereafter, the San Francisco Unified School District, under the leadership of Kevin Gogin, began a similar program called Project 21 (Gustavsson & MacEachron, 1998). Most other school districts have established programs like Project 10 and have not chosen to go with the separate school that isolates sexual minority students from the mainstream.

Changing the school culture is imperative in this process of stopping school violence against sexual minority youth (Pope, 2000). Each stakeholder in the school system has a vital role in solving this problem, including: school board members, administrators, teachers, professional school counselors, school nurses, school social workers, school psychologists, and cafeteria, maintenance, and transportation workers. School stakeholders need tools to combat this violence that will enable them to at least promote an environment of tolerance, and ideally to foster the creation of an environment in which sexual minority youth, like all other youth, are appreciated and valued. Merely being a sympathetic teacher is insufficient; teachers need more training themselves. Sears (1992) in a study of 258 teachers-in-training, found that fully 75% of the sample expressed interest in attending a school sponsored workshop on strategies in working with sexual minority students. Such a workshop would be expected to provide up-to-date information along with more knowledge and skills regarding sexual orientation, sexual identity, and gender identity.

Schremp (1999) reported in the *St. Louis Post-Dispatch*:

> A school newspaper survey in the Kirkwood Call last year showed 61% of the students who had answered said they insult people every day using such words as "gay." (Kirkwood, Missouri High School Principal Franklin) McCallie equated his student's use of "gay" or "fag" as a putdown to a racial or ethnic slur. ... In November, his teachers took a "Teaching Respect for All" workshop (created by the Gay, Lesbian, Straight Educators Network and Parents and Friends of Lesbians and Gays). ... 'I just felt that it is so obvious that a principal and a staff of a high school ought to be on the side of safety for all students, that it really shouldn't be a monumental step whatsoever,' he said. 'I'm not telling you that everyone agrees on the subject of homosexuality. I think that we are in agreement that everyone be safe in the schools.' (p. B4)

The "Teaching Respect for All" workshop was created by the Gay, Lesbian, Straight Educators Network (GLSEN) and Parents, Family, and Friends of Lesbians and Gays (PFFLAG) and is an important resource in combating violence against sexual minority students and transforming the school culture that tolerates such violence. Bauman and Sachs-Kapp (1998) outlined a "Hate Hurts" campaign to raise awareness of sexual minority youth issues among school stakeholders. As Principal McCallie said in the newspaper article, "you do not have to accept homosexuality as equal to heterosexuality, but you do have to accept that everyone should be safe in the schools" (p. B4). Professional school counselors must be in the forefront of such programs.

*Deliberate Psycho-affective Education*

What connects the recent shootings in the schools with anti-gay violence is reported in the May 3, 1999 article and cover story in U.S. News and World Report:

> "Surely it is a rare and complicated convergence of factors. Still, experts see some common threads in the spate of shootings: These adolescent boys can't manage their emotions. They feel rejected, enraged, jealous." They were boys who never learned how to identify, accept, and cope with their feelings (p. 19).

In American culture, boys are not taught how to handle feelings, not by their fathers, nor by the schools (Pollack, 1998; Pope & Englar-Carlson, 2001). Pope (1998, 2000) stated that elementary and secondary schools in the U.S. do an acceptable job of cognitive education, excellent on information, and okay on critical thinking, but most schools fail when it comes to "affective" education. This is not what is being termed "moral education," or "character education;" it is *affective education, psychological education, or psycho-affective education.* Teaching these important affective skills, such as interpersonal, social, and psychological skills, is rarely included in any school curriculum even though such pioneers as Sprinthall (1984) have written about "deliberate psychological education" for many years.

The deliberate psycho-affective education of our children must become a priority or we will continue to see even more school killings by young people who feel they have no hope, no place to turn, no one to talk with, no one who listens, and who have no perspective on life (Pope, 1998, 2000; Pope & Englar-Carlson, 2001). These students feel that any personal rejection or emotional hurt they experience is a tragedy from which they can "never" recover. Because they are only in touch with feelings of hurt and emotional pain and have no other interpersonal skills to cope with these overwhelming feelings, they blast away, taking out some who they feel have caused them that pain and others who are innocent bystanders, but it is directed at the institution they know best. Their parents take their rage to their workplace as that is their primary institutional focus; their children take their rage to schools.

For example, in the Jonesboro, Arkansas massacre of 10 students and a teacher by an 11-year-old boy and a 13-year-old boy with semi-automatic weapons, shooting their victims as they exited school during a fire alarm, many of their classmates now tell how the boys had talked about doing this for awhile. What caused this? According to news reports, one of the boys was "enraged" over having been "dumped by his girlfriend."

Pope (1998, 2000) reported that many people in U.S. society and school systems undervalue psycho-affective education. Although the schools cannot cure all the ills of our society, education is more than information and even more than critical thinking. It is also about who we are and who we love during a time in our lives (school age) when we have many questions about those issues. Not enough attention to these issues is given in our schools. We must educate the whole child not just the cognitive part. What we are seeing is the effect of that omission.

Professional school counselors are important to the total care and education of our students, from elementary school through high school (Pope, 1998, 2000). The following three types of professional school counselor activities are examples of deliberate psycho-affective education in the school: mental health counseling, career counseling, and providing a safe place to openly discuss sex (Morrow, 1997; Pope & Barret, 2002a; Pope, Prince, & Mitchell, 2000). The more that homosexuality and sexuality in general is treated as a taboo subject and not discussed openly, the greater the risk of homophobia and misinformation, and the greater the risk of violence to sexual minority youth. Many of these issues are addressed in the Personal/Social domain of the American School Counselor Association's new standards for school counseling programs (www.schoolcounselor.org).

*Valuing Differences*

Respect, appreciation, and valuing of differences is essential to stopping the violence against sexual minority students (Pope, 2000). "Teachers, counselors, administrators, and parents need to be more outspoken in their desire to teach their children about developing positive self-esteem and greater acceptance of differences. Although most individuals would agree with this on a case-by-case basis, everyone seems to have his or her area of difficulty in the acceptance of diversity" (Besner & Spungin, 1995, p. 36).

As a result of such difficulty, inclusive diversity training workshops have been developed. *Inclusive* is used here to mean that "diversity" is inclusive of ethnic and racial minorities as well as sexual minorities (Pope, 1995). An excellent tool in teaching individuals to appreciate and value human differences is the Myers-Briggs Type Indicator (MBTI), a Jungian personality inventory. One of the most important outcomes of using the MBTI is to teach the importance of the individual's opposite personality traits. For example, although your personality preference may be for extraversion and others for introversion, there is no inherent hierarchy in which one is better than the other; in fact, both are required for successful functioning in the world (Myers & McCaulley, 1985).

Other tools are available for teaching multicultural and diversity lessons, including GLSEN's "Teaching Respect for All" and Besner and Spungin's (1995) model workshop for educators on homophobia in their Appendix B. The National Coalition Building Institute, B'nai B'rith, and the American Friends Service Committee all offer excellent workshops on these topics and more (Owens, 1998; Pope, 2000).

In terms of the school curriculum, it is important to integrate and infuse gay and lesbian examples into all courses where appropriate (Pope, 1995; 2002). For example, when discussing U.S. history and the role of Native Americans, it would be appropriate to mention the revered position of "winktes" and "berdaches" (Native American terms for sexual minority persons) in the spiritual life of American Indians as the shaman or medicine person of the tribe as well as the many examples of female warriors (Katz, 1976). After reading "The Picnic," a short story by James Baldwin, a world famous African American author, teachers can discuss Baldwin's gay orientation and the results of having a double oppression (gay and African American).

Finally, school workers who are sexual minorities themselves should be encouraged to disclose their sexual orientation or gender identity and be offered support and employment protection. One openly gay or lesbian teacher can affect the atmosphere of the entire school in a positive way. The importance of sexual minority role models cannot be overstressed and open sexual minority school workers challenge the myths and stereotypes for all students, not just the GLBTIQQ ones (Owens, 1998).

*The Power of Subtle Signs*

There are also many ways of letting sexual minority students know that professional school counselors, teachers, administrators, and other school workers, are supportive of their struggle. If, because of your school district, you are unable to be as overtly supportive as you would like to be, there remains a number of other ways in which you can still relay to sexual minority students a message of your support.

Here are a few of the more obvious ones:

1) Have a "safe zone" sticker at the entrance to your office or classroom (available from the Bridges Project of the National Youth Advocacy Coalition or at www.glsen.org).
2) Have available in your school guidance office and library literature on sexual minority youth concerns (see www.umsl.edu/~pope for a

bibliography).

3) Post online resources for sexual minority students such as: International Lesbian and Gay Youth Association (www.ilgya.org); Parents, Family, and Friends of Lesbians and Gays (www.pfflag); Gay, Lesbian, and Straight Educators Network (www.glsen.org); Gay and Lesbian Teen Pen Pals (www.chanton.com/gayteens.html); National Resources for GLBT Youth (www.yale.edu/glb/youth.html); Oasis (teen magazine) (www.oasismag.com); Outright (www.outright.com); Out Proud, National Coaltion for GLBT Youth (www.cybrespaces.com/outproud); The Cool Page for Queer Teens (www.pe.net/~bidstrup/cool.html); and National Gay and Lesbian Task Force (www.ngltf.org).
4) Offer free family counseling services on campus to deal with the issues of homosexuality.
5) Use gay and lesbian positive examples in your teaching or counseling.
6) Use inclusive, stigma-free language in the classroom and in all communication, such as "partners" instead of "husbands and wives."
7) Post pictures of famous sexual minority people (see list at www.umsl.edu~pope).

By demonstrating an accepting attitude, school workers can send a strong message to students and create a tolerant environment within the entire school. The issues of tolerance, acceptance, and value can all be explored under the umbrella of diversity.

## Some Final Thoughts

The role of the professional school counselor in working with sexual minority students is clear. Professional school counselors are there to assist students in discovering who they truly and honestly are and then to help them develop a strong and positive personal and cultural identity so that they can live happy, successful, and productive lives in our society.

Further, the professional school counselor is expected to take a leadership role in protecting and advocating for sexual minority students as well as developing and implementing school policies that eliminate the verbal and physical harassment of all students, including sexual minority students. This is especially important because research indicates that sexual minority students are more likely to disclose their sexual minority status to their professional school counselors than to any other school worker (Harris & Bliss, 1997). Professional school counselors must, therefore, be prepared for their sexual minority students when they do present themselves for counseling (Brown, 1991; Pope, 2000).

Further, the relationship is clear between derogatory language/harassment directed against sexual minority students by their peers and adults in the school setting and self-harmful behavior, such as attempted suicide, suicidal ideation, running away, poor academic performance, and truancy (Jordan et al., 1997). Professional school counselors must not allow such language or physical harassment for any student.

Clearly the momentum is turning toward the protection of sexual minority students in the schools. In 1993, Massachusetts became the first state to ban anti-gay discrimination in its schools and create a statewide "safe schools" program. The U.S. Department of Education issued guidelines in March, 1997, stating explicitly that lesbian and gay students are covered by federal prohibitions against sexual harassment.

Indeed changes are occurring for sexual minority students. Sam Hanser, a 16-year-old high school student in Newtown, Massachusetts, has spoken on national television of assaults at the hands of his classmates: "A lot of people called me faggot and spat on me and did a lot of annoying things," said Hansen. Massachusetts, however, was the first state to pass a law making harassment of lesbian and gay students a crime. As a result of this, Sam has been empowered and taken on a role of leadership. He runs a hotline for lesbian, gay, bisexual, transgender, and questioning youth, and speaks publicly about sexual minority youth issues. "I think that seeing diversity starts the whole process of being comfortable and acceptance of different people" (CBS Morning News, January 21, 1999).

Attitudes on sexuality and sexual orientation are indeed changing, and this should bode well for sexual minority students. Although the message is not as strong as many of us would like, it is becoming clear that people can have their own private hatreds; however, when this becomes public as physical or verbal harassment or written into policy, it will not be allowed. The harassment of sexual minority students and teachers should not be tolerated in America or in any society.

Heterosexism, which according to Audre Lorde (1984) is defined as a "belief in the inherent superiority of one pattern of loving and thereby its right to dominance" (p. 45), and homophobia, which is the fear of being gay and hatred of gays and lesbians (Herr, 1997), must be exposed just as racism and sexism have been.

The Massachusetts Governor's Commission on Lesbian and Gay Youth issued a report in 1993 that summarized succinctly a blueprint for ending violence in the schools against gay and lesbian youth. The recommendations included: 1) promulgating school policies which protect gay and lesbian students through: a) anti-discrimination policies which explicitly include sexual orientation for students and teachers, including teacher contracts; b) policies which guarantee equal access to education and school activities; c) anti-harassment policies and guidelines which deal with handling incidents of anti-gay language, harassment, or violence; and d) multicultural and diversity policies which are inclusive of lesbian and gay culture (Pope, 1995; 2002); 2) training teachers in multicultural issues (which are inclusive of lesbian and gay culture) and suicide and violence prevention as well as changing teacher certification requirements and school accreditation to include this training (Pope, 1995; 2002); 3) school-based support groups for gay and straight students; 4) curriculum that includes gay and lesbian issues; and 5) information in school libraries for gay and lesbian adolescents. As a consequence of this report, the Massachusetts Board of Education unanimously adopted the nation's first state educational policy prohibiting discrimination against lesbian and gay elementary and secondary students and teachers (Besner & Spungin, 1995). Many cities in the U.S. have adopted similar policies in their schools.

## Summary/Conclusions

This chapter presented the issues that are important for professional school counselors who are counseling sexual minority students, including gay, lesbian, bisexual, transgender, intersex, queer, and questioning youth. The issues that are addressed include developing a context in which to discuss these issues; "coming out" or the developmental aspects of sexual identity development; the extent of the problems that sexual minority youth face in the schools and society; the effects of negative attitudes and violence toward these youth; and ethical and legal issues in dealing with sexual minority youth in the schools. In addition, school-based interventions were discussed that focus on the role of the parents and schools, separation (e.g., separate schools for sexual minority youth) or culture change, deliberate psycho-affective education, valuing differences, and the power of subtle symbols.

The lives of sexual minority students in the schools are getting better and the sad picture painted by many may not apply to all sexual minority youth. It is important, however, not to minimize the detrimental effects of verbal and physical violence and harassment on sexual minority students' academic performance and social development. What professional school counselors must focus on are the recommendations in this chapter for improving the school environment and the quality of the life for sexual minority students. It just makes it better for all students.

## References


The Advocate (1997, April 15). *Agenda.*

Allport, G. W. (1958). *The nature of prejudice.* Garden City, NY: Doubleday Anchor Books.

The Associated Press (1999, June 2). *Anti-gay slur carved on student.*

Bailey, N. J., & Phariss, T. (1996). Breaking through the wall of silence: Gay, lesbian, and bisexual issues for middle level educators. *Middle School Journal, 27*, 38-46. Washington, DC: National Middle School Association.

Barret, B. (1999, March). Conversion therapy. *Counseling Today,* 12.

Barret, B., & Logan, C. (2001). *Counseling gay men and lesbians: A practice primer.* Belmont CA: Brooks/Cole.

Barret, R. L., & Robinson, B. E. (2000). *Gay fathers.* San Francisco: Jossey-Bass.

Bauman, S., & Sachs-Kapp, P. (1998). A school takes a stand: Promotion of sexual orientation workshops by counselors.*Professional School Counseling, 1*(3), 42-45.

Bayer, R. (1981). *Homosexuality and American psychiatry: The politics of diagnosis.* New York: Basic Books.

Besner, H. F., & Spungin, C. I. (1995). *Gay & lesbian students: Understanding their needs.* Washington, DC: Taylor & Francis.

Boswell, J. (1980). *Christianity, social tolerance, and homosexuality.* Chicago: University of Chicago Press.

Boswell, J. (1995). *Same-sex unions in premodern Europe.* New York:Vintage Books.

Brown, S. (1991).*Counseling victims of violence.* Alexandria, VA:American Counseling Association.

CBS News (1999, January 21). *CBS poll: Gay intolerance.* New York:CBS News. Retrieved on February 3, 1999 from www.cbs.com.

Chung, Y. B., & Katayama, M. (1998). Ethnic and sexual identity development of Asian-American lesbian and gay adolescents. *Professional School Counseling, 1*(3), 21-25.

Coleman, E. (1982). Changing approaches to the treatment of homosexuality: A review. In W. Paul, J. D. Weinrich, J. C. Gonsiorek, & M.E. Hotvedt (Eds.), *Homosexuality: Social, psychological, and biological issues* (pp. 81-88). Beverly Hills, CA: Sage.

Coleman, J. C., Butcher, J. N., & Carson, R. C. (1984). *Abnormal psychology and modern life* (7th ed.). Glenview, IL: Scott, Foresman and Company.

D'Augelli, A. R. (1992). Teaching lesbian/gay development: From oppression to exceptionality. In K. Harbeck (Ed.), *Coming out of the classroom closet* (pp. 213-227). New York:Harrington Park Press.

Elliott, L., & Brantley, C. (1997). *Sex on campus: The naked truth about the real sex lives of college students.* NewYork: Random House.

Fontaine, J. H. (1997). The sound of silence: Public school response to the needs of gay and lesbian youth. In M. B. Harris (Ed.), *School experiences of gay and lesbian youth* (pp. 101-109). New York: Harrington Park Press.

Fontaine, J. H. (1998). Evidencing a need: School counselors' experiences with gay and lesbian students. *Professional School Counseling, 1*(3), 8-14.

Gibson, P. (1989). Gay male and lesbian youth suicide. In M. R. Feinleib (Ed.), *Report of the Secretary's task force on youth suicide. Volume 3: Preventions and interventions in youth suicide* (pp. 110-142). (U.S. Department of Health and Human Services Pub. No. ADM 89-1623). Washington, DC: U.S.Government Printing Office.

Gray, M. L. (Ed.) (1999). *In your face: Stories from the lives of queer youth.* New York: Harrington Park Press.

Gustavsson, N. S., & MacEachron, A. E. (1998). Violence and lesbian and gay youth. In L. M. Sloan & N. S. Gustavsson (Eds.), *Violence and social injustice against lebian, gay and bisexual people* (pp. 41-50). New York: Harrington Park Press.

Hafen, B. Q., & Frandsen, K. J. (1986). *Youth suicide: Depression and loneliness.* Evergreen, CO: Cordilerra Press.

Harris, M. B., & Bliss, G. K. (1997). Coming out in a school setting: Former students' experiences and opinions about disclosure. In M. B. Harris (Ed.), *School experiences of gay and lesbian youth* (pp. 85-100). New York: Harrington Park Press.

Herdt, G., & Boxer, A. (1996). *Children of horizons: How gay and lesbian teens are leading a new way out of the closet* (2nd ed.). New York: Beacon Press.

Herr, K. (1997). Learning lessons from school: Homophobia, heterosexism, and the construction of failure. In M. B. Harris (Ed.), *School experiences of gay and lesbian youth* (pp. 51-64). New York: Harrington Park Press.

Herscher, E. (1998, September 10). S.F. schools get A, from gay group- but Oakland gets C, in safety rating. *San Francisco Chronicle,* p. A20.

Hirschfeld, M. (1935). *Men and women: The world journey of a sexologist.* New York: Putnam.

Ilnytzky, U. (1999, April 7). *Anti-gay attacks said more violent.* The Associated Press.

Jordan, K. M., Vaughan, J. S., & Woodworth, K. J. (1997). I will survive: Lesbian, gay, and bisexual youths' experience of high school. In M. B. Harris (Ed.), *School experiences of gay and lesbian youth* (pp. 17-34). New York: Harrington Park Press.

Just the Facts Coalition. (2000). *Just the facts about sexual orientation & youth: A primer for principals, educators & school personnel.* Washington, DC: Author.

Katz, J. (1976). *Gay American history.* New York: Thomas Y. Crowell Company.

Krivascka, J. J., Savin-Williams, R. C., & Slater, B. R. (1992). *Background paper for the resolution on lesbian, gay, and bisexual youths in schools.* The American Psychological Association Council of Representatives Agenda, February 26-28, 1993, 454-489. (Available from the American Psychological Association, 750 First Street, N. E., Washington, DC 20002).

LeVay, S. (1991). A difference in hypothalamic structure between heterosexual and homosexual men. *Science, 253,* 1034-1037.

LeVay, S. (1999). *Queer science.* New York: McGraw-Hill.

LeVay, S., & Valente, S. M. (2002). *Human sexuality.* Sunderland, MA: Sinauer Associates.

Lorde, A. (1984). *Sister outsider.* Freedom, CA: The Crossing Press.

Malinsky, K. P. (1997). Learning to be invisible: Female sexual minority students in America's public high schools. In M. B. Harris (Ed.), *School experiences of gay and lesbian youth* (pp. 35-50). New York: Harrington Park Press.

Mannino, J. D. (1999). *Sexual themes and variations: The new millennium.* New York: McGraw-Hill.

Marinoble, R. M. (1998). Homosexuality: A blind spot in the school mirror. *Professional School Counseling, 1*(3), 4-7.

Marsiglio, W. (1993). Attitudes toward homosexual activity and gays as friends: A national survey of heterosexual 15- to 19-year-old males. *Journal of Sex Research, 30,* 12.

Mondimore, F. M. (1996). *A natural history of homosexuality.* Baltimore: Johns Hopkins University Press.

Money, J. (1990). Agenda and credenda of the Kinsey scale. In D. P. McWhirter, S. A. Sanders, & J. M. Reinisch (Eds.), *Homosexuality/heterosexuality: Concepts of sexual orientation* (pp. 41-60). New York: Oxford University Press.

Morrow, S. (1997). Career development of lesbian and gay youth: Effects of sexual orientation, coming out, and homophobia. In M. B. Harris (Ed.), *School experiences of gay and lesbian youth* (pp. 1-15). New York: Harrington Park Press.

Muerher, P. (1995). Suicide and sexual orientation: A critical summary of recent research and directions for future research. *Suicide and Life Threatening Behavior, 25* (supplement), 72-81.

Myers, I. B., & McCaulley, M. (1985). *Manual to the development of the Myer-Briggs Type Indicator.* Palo Alto, CA: Consulting Psychologists Press.

Nabozny v. Podlensy, 92 F.3d 446 (7th US Circuit Court, 1996).

Newman, B. S., & Muzzonigro, P. G. (1993). The effects of traditional family values on the coming out process of gay male adolescents. *Adolescence, 28,* 213-226.

Nicolosi, J. (1991). *Reparative therapy of male homosexuals.* Northvale, NJ: Aronson.

O'Conor, A. (1994). Who gets called queer in school? Lesbian, gay and bisexual teenagers, homophobia, and high school. *The High School Journal, 77,* 7-12.

Omizo, M. M., Omizo, S. A., & Okamoto, C. M. (1998). Gay and lesbian adolescents: A phenomenological study. *Professional School Counseling, 1*(3), 35-37.

Owens, R. E. (1998). *Queer kids: The challenges and promise for lesbian, gay, and bisexual youth.* New York: Harrington Park Press.

Pollack, W. (1998). *Real boys: Rescuing our sons from the myths of boyhood.* New York: Random House.

Pope, M. (1995). The "salad bowl" is big enough for us all: An argument for the inclusion of lesbians and gays in any definition of multiculturalism. *Journal of Counseling & Development, 73,* 301-304.

Pope, M. (1998, March 25). School counselors and whole person education. *The Education Forum,* an online electronic mailing list.

Pope, M. (2000). Preventing school violence aimed at gay, lesbian, bisexual, and transgender youth. In D. S. Sandhu & C. B. Aspy (Eds.), *Violence in American schools: A practical guide for counselors* (pp. 285-304). Alexandria, VA: American Counseling Association.

Pope, M. (2002). Incorporating gay and lesbian culture into multicultural counseling. In J. Trusty, E. J. Looby, & D. S. Sandhu (Eds.), *Multicultural counseling: Context, theory and practice, and competence* (pp. 203-218). Hauppauge, NY: Nova Science Publishers.

Pope, M., & Barret, B. (2002a). Providing career counseling services to gay and lesbian clients. In S. G. Niles (Ed.), *Adult career development: Concepts, issues, and practices* (3rd ed.), (pp. 215-232). Tulsa, OK: National Career Development Association.

Pope, M., & Barret, B. (2002b). Counseling gay men toward an integrated sexuality. In L. D. Burlew & D. Capuzzi (Eds.), *Sexuality counseling* (pp. 149-176). Hauppauge, NY: Nova Science Publishers.

Pope, M., & Englar-Carlson, M. (2001). Fathers and sons: The relationship between violence and masculinity. *The Family Journal, 9,* 367-374.

Pope, M., Prince, J. P., & Mitchell, K. (2000). Responsible career counseling with lesbian and gay students. In D. A. Luzzo (Ed.), *Career counseling of college students: An empirical guide to strategies that work* (pp. 267-284). Washington, DC: American Psychological Association.

Remafedi, G. J. (1987). Adolescent homosexuality: Psychosocial and medical implications. *Pediatrics, 79,* 331-337.

Remafedi, G. J., Farrow, J., & Deisher, R. (1991). Risk factors for attempted suicide in gay and bisexual youth. *Pediatrics, 87*, 869-875.

Remafedi, G. J., Resnick, M., Blum, R., & Harris, L. (1992). Demography of sexual orientation in adolescents. *Pediatrics, 89*, 714-721.

Rofes, E. (1989). Opening up the classroom closet: Responding to the educational needs of gay and lesbian youth. *Harvard Educational Review, 59*, 443-453.

Roscoe, W. (1989). Strange country this: Images of berdaches and warrior women. In W. Roscoe (Ed.), *Living the spirit: A gay American Indian anthology* (pp. 48-76). New York: St. Martin's Press.

Rotheram-Borus, M. J., & Fernandez, I. (1995). Sexual orientation and developmental challenges experienced by gay and lesbian youths. *Suicide & Life Threatening Behavior, 25*, 26-34.

Rowse, A. L. (1977). *Homosexuals in history: A study in ambivalence in society, literature and the arts.* New York: Carroll & Graf Publishers.

Ruan, F. F. (1991). *Sex in China: Studies in sexology in Chinese culture.* New York: Plenum.

Ryan, C., & Futterman, D. (1997). Lesbian and gay youth: Care and counseling. *Adolescent Medicine—State of the Art Reviews, 8*, 221.

Saulnier, C. F. (1998). Prevalence of suicide attempts and suicidal ideation among lesbian and gay youth. In L. M. Sloan & N. S. Gustavsson (Eds.), *Violence and social* injustice *against lesbian, gay and bisexual people* (pp. 51-68). New York: Harrington Park Press.

Savin-Williams, R. C. (1990). *Gay and lesbian youth: Expressions of identity.* New York: Hemisphere.

Schremp, V. (1999, February 10). Kirkwood High fosters a culture of openness. *St. Louis Post-Dispatch*, p. B4.

Sears, J. T. (1992). Educators, homosexuality, and homosexual students: Are personal feelings related to professional beliefs? In K. Harbeck (Ed.), *Coming out of the classroom closet* (pp. 29-79). New York: Harrington Park Press.

SIECUS (Sexuality Information and Education Council of the United States). (1995). *Facts about sexual health for America's adolescents.* New York: Author.

Sprinthall, N. A. (1984). Primary prevention: A road paved with a plethora of promises and procrastinations. *Personnel & Guidance Journal, 62*, 491-495.

Telljohann, S. K., & Price, J. H. (1993). A qualitative examination of adolescent homosexuals' life experiences: Ramifications for secondary school personnel. *Journal of Homosexuality, 26*,48.

Thorstad, D. (1974). *The Bolsheviks and the early homosexual rights movement.* New York: Times Change Press.

Troiden, R. R. (1979). The formation of homosexual identities. *Journal of Homosexuality, 17*, 362-373.

U.S. News & World Report. (1999, May 3). *Why? There were plenty of warnings, but no one stopped two twisted teens.* p. 19.

Uribe, V., & Harbeck, K. (1992). Addressing the needs of lesbian, gay, and bisexual youth: The origins of Project 10 and school-based intervention. In K. Harbeck (Ed.), *Coming out of the classroom closet* (pp. 9-28). New York: Harrington Park Press.

Williams, M. (1997, September 21). Nations' first private school for gays opens in Dallas education facility is run by two teachers as a haven from the harassment that occurs on traditional campuses. So far, enrollment totals seven. *The Los Angeles Times,* p. 35.

# Chapter 76

## Helping Students from Changing Families

*Estes J. Lockhart*

### Preview

This chapter provides interventions for professional school counselors who must address the needs of students from families with diverse living arrangements such as stepparents, single parents and interracial parents, in this chapter referred to as the surface structure. This chapter provides general guidelines, assessment procedures, and actual case histories with interventions.

*"But my family also carried strengths into the fray, these strengths let almost all of us survive the descent of the Furies"* (Pat Conroy, 1986, p. 10).

To be a professional school counselor is to be sensitive to the changing nature of families. Day in and day out, professional school counselors witness the transformations of families in diverse forms of living arrangements, which in this chapter will be referred to as the *surface structure* of families. (McCubbin, McCubbin, Thompson, Han, & Allen,1997), Dean of the School of Human Ecology and Director of the Institute for the Study of Resiliency in Families at University of Wisconsin-Madison, stated, "The 21st century will be characterized as the era of family transformation and stress. Diverse family forms such as single-parent households, blended family units, interracial marriages and what demographers refer to as the new 'stepfamily systems' created by cohabitation already have changed the family landscape." Professional school counselors are called upon to provide interventions for the challenges that family transformations and stress present in an atmosphere of rising levels of poverty, substance abuse, homelessness and violence (Erford, House & Martin, 2003; Keys, Bemak, & Lockhart, 1998; Lockhart, 2003; Lockhart & Keys, 1998; Weist, 1997).

The task of helping students and their families in often-stressful transformations through a landscape filled with mountains of substance abuse, poverty and violence can be seen as dismal. It can also be seen as a great opportunity to take part in the creation of a new chapter in the history of human resiliency. This chapter provides specific examples and guidelines for helping students from families in transition (such as single parent and stepparent, and those students from nontraditional families such as gay lesbian, interracial and homeless) in the interest of assisting professional school counselors determined to promote competency and resiliency in the face of these challenges.

### Single Parenting, Stepparenting and Cohabitating Surface Structures

How much are the surface structures of students and their families changing today? Recent demographic data from the Population Resource Center provides strong evidence that the American family is experiencing vast change (Sado & Bayer, 2001). For example, in terms of surface structure, in the year 2000 one-quarter of U.S. households (23%) were made up of nuclear families, a married man and woman and their children, which significantly differed from the 1960's when the nuclear family made up nearly one half of households (45%).

Cohabitation, unmarried individuals living together as couples, doubled in the 1990's going from 3.2 million in 1990 to 5.5 million in 2000. Cohabitation is becoming a significant trend, with one third of cohabitants parenting children. In 1990, 9% percent of children under age 18 lived in single-parent families, but by 1999 27% of children under 18 resided in single parent homes. One of the reasons for many of the single-family homes was out-of-wedlock birth, which reached its highest rate in 1999 when 33% of all births in the U.S. were out-of-wedlock. However, one must not be quick to assume that single parenting or any other surface structure provides a simple cause and effect relationship with a student experiencing difficulty at school. For example, while children of divorce have a higher rate of emotional and substance abuse problems, these effects are "caused not by divorce alone but by other frequently coexisting yet analytically separate factors" (Coontz, 1997, p. 29). Research from a Rand study, titled "Student Performance and the Changing American Family," implied no negative effects on academic performance based on changed family surface structure alone; however the Rand study pointed out that predictions for youth in single parent families show a negative effect academically because these families tend to have increased poverty and lower educational attainment by mothers (Grissmer, Kirby, Berends & Williamson, 1994).

While a professional school counselor can't directly alter the economic well being or educational attainment of a single parent, they can provide resources for single parents, referring them to agencies and groups in the community that can provide economic support, educational opportunities, and/or mental health and physical health services. Professional school counselors can also assist single parents with parenting skills either through direct consultation or referral to parenting programs. Professional school counselors can also help students find the strength to rise above troubled backgrounds, in part by running loss groups in which students from families in transition can find needed support. Perhaps one of the most important things a professional school counselor can do is to be a person who the student knows cares for him. In that role of trusted, caring significant other, the professional school counselor can help the student understand that the challenges facing his family were not caused by him, nor are they his responsibility to correct. However, the student can learn to cope and have a successful, meaningful life.

*Trauma in Changing Families*

As the trend toward diverse surface structures in families grows, some of the patterns that are currently thought of as nontraditional will become the tradition. For example, increasingly families are living in metropolitan areas. In 1970, two out of three households were in metropolitan areas, while by 1995 four out of five households were in metropolitan areas (Bryson, 2001). In urban schools, from 30% to 60% of students lived with caregivers other than their biological parents (Hampton, Rak, & Mumford, 1997). These caregivers may be foster parents, grandparents, stepparents, or adoptive parents. Many of the families in caregiving arrangements will require more services, because the students suffer from the effects of traumatic early life experiences (Schwartz, 1999).

Professional school counselors can support families suffering trauma by helping them find social support and therapy in the community, by listening to the student and family in a caring way, and by helping the student and caregiver to maintain a supportive relationship with each other. Professional school counselors can also inform teachers and administration, with parent permission, of the situation and seek their support of the student, particularly in helping the student feel a sense of belonging and identification. Professional school counselors can help students experiencing trauma to use individual strengths and resources. Some crucial aspects of a recovery environment (resiliency) for students from traumatic family situations are: parental distress, parental psychopathology, individual strengths and resources of the child, social and system resources and intelligence, communication skills, sense of self-efficacy, coping abilities, talents, and feelings of bonding (Meichenbaum, 2002).

## Homeless, Interracial and Gay and Lesbian Surface Structures

Increasingly, professional school counselors help students from homeless families, interracial marriages and gay and lesbian couples. An increase in interracial marriages has led to a surge in interracial babies, increasing from less than 2% in 1960 to 5% by 1997 (Sado & Bayer, 2001). Families with children constitute 40% of people who become homeless in cities and this percentage is higher in rural areas (Shinn & Weitzman, 1996). The main service most students from homeless, gay and lesbian and interracial families will require is help with acceptance and full inclusion.

*Homelessness*

Homeless students present with a specific set of difficulties. These include frequent relocation, lack of a permanent address, lack of a place to study, lack of a place to store personal items including school items, difficulty attending or participating in school events, and the stress of living in shelters with no private space and strangers - many of whom have mental problems. A homeless student may carry in her backpack all that is important to her. Help the student find a safe place to keep a few personal items. It can be helpful to assist the student to find a place to study or arrange for the student to have a study period at school for completing homework that otherwise will be very difficult to complete and thus lead to the student falling behind. Embarrassment about living arrangements is prevalent and helping the students to know how to speak about it with other students is valuable. Often the homeless have difficulty accessing special education programs. Professional school counselors can be advocates for special education services where needed.

Perhaps most significant are the problems the homeless families experience on the street and in the shelters that the student may need to discuss with the professional school counselor. It is important to know that the student may be hesitant to discuss his/her family situation. Joining with the student so that the student will risk sharing his secrets is a key to providing help. Additional information on homelessness may he found at the U.S. Department of Housing and Urban Development (www.hud.gov/homeless).

*Gay or Lesbian Families*

Students from gay or lesbian families most often need help coping with the issues of anger and embarrassment. They may be angry with one or both of their parents. It can be helpful for the student who is angry to take part in family therapy with a mental health counselor. To the extent that the professional school counselor will deal with this anger at school, it can often be addressed as anger would be in counseling a student for loss. The embarrassment can be addressed through the cognitive technique of challenging assumptions. The student's belief that his peers will label him on the basis of his gay or lesbian parents needs to be challenged. Existing data on students of lesbian mothers suggests that students may fare better when the mothers are in good psychological health and living with a lesbian partner with whom childcare is shared (Patterson, 2002). It is helpful for the student to normalize his/her situation as much as possible. It is supportive for children in lesbian and gay families to be able to interact with peers in similar situations. Additional information on gay and lesbian families can be found on the American Psychological Association web site (www.apa.org/pi/parent.html).

*Interracial Families*

Many interracial families share close, caring relationships and strong parenting skills, which will be strengths to draw upon when intervening to help these students find acceptance and full inclusion. The professional school counselor is encouraged to search for strengths in the culture and race of students who present with a need for acceptance and inclusion. Professional school counselors need to be aware of different approaches families from diverse cultures and races may take in relation to issues such as parenting, spirituality, or the anger they may express toward outside agencies, or even the practitioner (Boyd-Franklin & Bry, 2002). For example, a family member who has experienced racism or who feels alienated by outside agencies may go to school meetings with a "chip on her shoulder." The professional school counselor can join with this parent prior to the school meeting and gain that parent's respect or at least the beginning of trust, and can therefore make the parent feel she has an advocate within the system and feel more secure in the meeting.

The remainder of this chapter provides basic information a professional school counselor must consider when helping students from families with diverse surface structures, particularly those in transition. It provides specific examples of the kind of issues presented to professional school counselors by America's changing families in a landscape of high stress and suggests interventions for students and families that can be helpful. These interventions not only focus on assessing needs and surface structures, but also strengths, resources, and resiliency. For example, numerous studies have concluded that when interventions in which a student comes to feel someone in or outside the family truly cares, it promotes resiliency in the face of substantial risk factors (Boyd-Franklin & Bry, 2000; Werner, 1989).

## Basic Considerations When Counseling Students from Changing Families

*Note Differences in Families with Similar Surface Structure*

The first thing one learns when helping families, including those in transition, is that there are nearly infinite ways to be a family. Therefore, while the considerations offered in this chapter for intervening with families based on their surface structure can be helpful, interventions must always be used wisely in the context of the actual family the professional school counselor is attempting to help. For example, the popular image of the single parent may be the mother on welfare, but one-seventh of single parent households are headed by fathers, and two thirds earn enough to be above the poverty line (Sugarman, 1998).

A family that has become a single-parent family due to the separation of very supportive and caring yet incompatible parents has different needs than a single-parent family in which the parents are very angry with each other, poorly educated, and, prior to the divorce, were attempting to cope with alcoholism. Single-parent families often result from the death of a loved parent and spouse. In the first family, the focus will be on ensuring that the students understand that they were neither the cause nor cure for the troubles between two very loving and supportive parents. In the second family the focus likely will need to be on the possible traumatic effects resulting from living in a family filled with anger and alcoholism and making sure that the angry parents don't put the student in the middle of their anger. In the third family the focus will be on loss. Professional school counselors who help single parent families will have to be able to shift flexibly from one set of intervention skills to another.

*Assess Comorbidity and Premorbidity in the Family*

Attempting to cope with one stressor is very different from being forced to cope with a series of unexpected short-term traumas or a sustained series of traumatic events including a prolonged trauma (Meichenbaum, 2002). Clinicians refer to having more than one serious need as *comorbidity,* and a significant need prior to the problem at hand as *premorbidity.*

Comorbidity and premorbidity are important factors to consider when addressing the needs of a student from a family that is undergoing a challenging transition. For example, children who witnessed domestic abuse exhibit more control problems and more hostile cognitions about women (Geffner, Jaffe, & Sugarman as cited in Meichenbaum, 2001). Thus, a professional school counselor helping a student from a family transitioning through a difficult divorce where there has been domestic abuse should be sensitive to the need for intervention or referral for additional clinical services in order to address a serious condition premorbid to the stress of the divorce. There may be a need to help the student through group work with social skills and control problems at school, but concurrently the family should seek clinical counseling to address the trauma of victimization and negative thoughts associated with women.

*Stay Positive No Matter How Stressful the Family Challange*

It is essential to stay positive. Stressful life events can also have long-term positive effects (Updegraff & Taylor, 1999). The author recently spoke with a young man who, 20 years earlier, had been a student in an alternative school founded by the author. The young man said he remembered a counseling session in which the author had asked him to think about what he could take that was positive from his current situation to carry with him in life. He said prior to his mother's separation from his father he had experienced physical abuse and watched his mother be physically abused. He said, looking back it was easy to see why he'd become aggressive enough to end up in the alternative school. He said that he had decided back then in response to the directive in the counseling session to always remind himself when tough situations faced him in life that he had already made it through worse than he would ever face. He told this writer that when he was feeling upset about his recent employment situation, he said to himself, "I've been through much worse and handled it, so I know I'll make it through this fine." Thus, it is useful for professional school counselors helping families undergoing difficult transitions to remember the folk wisdom that says, "What doesn't kill me will make me stronger." It is important to communicate to students and families going through tough or even traumatic experiences that their ability to endure and continue to attempt to cope is impressive.

*Stay Aware of General Factors Fostering Family Resilience*

Child-focused studies have pointed to the importance of ten general factors in the family system in fostering resilience (McCubbin et al., 1997). These include: family problem-solving communication, equality, spirituality, flexibility, truthfulness, hope, family time and routine, social support, health, and family hardiness (in which the family steels itself and views itself as having a sense of control and influence over the outcome). Meichenbaum (2002) cited a list of studies that suggested protective factors characteristic of resilient children and adolescents, including: close relationships to a caring parent figure, supportive extended kin, a sense of belonging and identification, warmth, structure and high expectations in parenting, cohesive families, socioeconomic advantages, and extended family networks. The effective professional school counselor helps students develop these resiliency characteristics through work with students and families.

*Assess Basic Family Strengths and Needs*

It is helpful when assessing family strengths and needs to collapse the family resiliency factors mentioned by McCubbin and the protective factors of resilient children and adolescents mentioned by Meichenbaum into five main categories: 1) Parenting; 2) Legal-Economic; 3) Structural-Social; 4) Beliefs; and 5) Health. *Parenting* includes decisions regarding schooling, academics, and discipline, as well as warmth, structure, and high expectations. *Legal and*

*Economic* refers to the custody, school records and alimony issues, as well as financial well-being of the family. *Structural-Social* refers to all the structural relationship issues in a family such as hierarchy, leadership, alliances, coalitions, cohesion, boundaries, differentiation, extended kinship, social network support, family time, family hardiness, sense of belonging and identification and communication style (see Chapter 17 in this book, "Using Family Systems Interventions in Schools" ). *Beliefs* include values, sense of equality, spiritual issues, sense of hope, and truthfulness. *Health* refers to mental and physical health issues.

Often when intervening with high stress families in transition, the professional school counselor will have to assist the family in parenting issues around academics and will have to encourage teacher support for the student during times of crisis. After all, the bottom line for educators is academic performance.

*Provide for the Direct or Indirect Delivery of Support*

Most professional school counselor direct services will be in the parenting, academic support and social support areas. The professional school counselor will often become a case manager or consultant for the family in the area of mental and physical health and economic support, providing referrals and liaison services to other professionals. The area of belief systems is a difficult one for the professional school counselor. Issues of truth, hope, trust and spirituality, when they are conceived as a search for meaning, are the stock and trade of a professional school counselor's work, and yet when applied to families in crisis, based on the family's view of these issues, the professional school counselor may choose to refer out for these services. However, even this decision is made complex by the work setting of the professional school counselor. A professional counselor working in a public school would generally stay away from spirituality, specifically in terms of religion, when it is approached by the family, while a professional counselor working in a parochial school might find the issue of religion appropriate and even central. The examples given throughout the remainder of this chapter come back to these general factors of resiliency and protection, giving specific guidelines in areas that are central to the surface structure of families.

## Intervention Examples by Surface Structures

*Single Parent Family: Basic Guidelines*

1. *Parenting.* Being a single parent can lead to work overload with accompanying high stress. Along with the health and safety of the children is the need to provide and maintain a home environment that encourages learning and good behavior in school. This educational dimension of parenting can be very demanding for single parents because of time that quality collaboration and coordination between home and school often requires.
2. *Legal-economic.* Single parents frequently must raise children with fewer financial resources. Custody battles, child-support payments, and alimony payments may cause financial, social and other stresses. Also, there may be issues between custodial and noncustodial parents over visits and access to school meetings and records. The law is that noncustodial parents have the same access to school records as custodial parents unless a judge has ruled otherwise and that ruling with the judge's signature is in the student's record.
3. *Structural-social.* A parent and child may become enmeshed or emotionally fused, thereby feeding each other's emotional problems. A child may assume the role of a spousal child taking the place emotionally of the absent parent. Either of these situations can lead to conditions of anxiety or depression. Hierarchy issues can result

in fights over who is in control and coalitions of the child and one parent against the other parent may occur. At the same time close relationships between parent and child in times of crisis can be helpful, and a child taking on an appropriate supportive role such as helping the parent with monitoring siblings for a limited period of time can be a growth experience for the student. With divorce it is important to help parents avoid putting the child in the middle of spousal disagreements or emotional upset. Professional school counselors should not witness angry couples fighting whether the child is there or not. The message should always be that no matter what your interactions in other places, in the professional school counselor's office everyone can feel safe and emotionally protected. This can be particularly important in gaining the respect of the parents. It can be helpful for the parents to see that for a brief period of time they are able to interact appropriately and when the child is present the child can observe them being able to interact in a way that is appropriate, not hurtful.

4. *Belief systems.* The return of a single parent to the courtship stage by dating can bring new individuals into the home and cause a host of difficulties, including the children feeling that the parent cares more for a new friend than for them. Children may also worry that someone they don't know will be making decisions for them. This can also lead to conflicts around trust and loyalty. Where the single parent family came into being through separation or divorce, the parent may believe she is guilty for not preventing the divorce. Children may worry that in some way they helped to cause a separation or should be responsible for fixing it. Children may even imagine that their parents will reunite. In such cases the use of the "*Three C's Maxim*" can be helpful. The parent or parents need to tell the child that he didn't *cause* the separation and can't *correct* the situation, but can learn to *cope* with the situation.
5. *Mental-emotional and physical health issues.* Parents and children may experience feelings of loss. Financial weakness may result in family members not having proper health services. Lack of appropriate dental, vision, and medical services can seriously affect education. Community health services, service clubs and helpful medical providers often can address the most serious of these problems.

*Example One: Single Parent with a Middle School Student*

Tom was a student who grew up in a home with an abusive father and found it hard to understand why his mother continued to live with his father. When he stated these feelings to his mother she always responded that she loved his father and hoped he would change. Tom's father frequently did inform his mother and the children that he would change because he cared too much for them to go on hurting them. However, he was an alcoholic and became very angry when drunk. The final straw for Tom's mother came when Tom was a middle school student and his father sexually abused Tom's sister. Tom's mother reported her husband to social services and criminal charges were filed.

At school Tom evidenced much social anxiety. He missed school frequently, particularly on stressful occasions such as test days. He hung out with antisocial peers who verbally abused other students and teachers. One-on-one, Tom was very pleasant with adults but was frequently referred to the office for joining in verbal attacks on others.

*Assessment.* The professional school counselor began to work with Tom and witnessed the school avoidance, verbal threats and taunts, academic failure, and social anxiety. She decided to invite Tom's mother to the school for a brief family session. In the session she learned about the stressful family abuse Tom had witnessed. The mother said she barely could get by financially, as she was a clerk in a local department store and made just above minimum wage. Now with her husband in jail, the home was the most pleasant it had been in many years, but financially she was slipping and having to work an extra half job which didn't give her the time to help Tom or his sister with their school work. Parenting was stressful for Tom's mother, as she didn't have the time or energy to provide the high structure or academic help Tom needed. She and Tom had become close allies when his father was in drunken rages.

The professional school counselor determined that Tom and his mother had an *enmeshed relationship*, meaning they were fused emotionally and were feeding into each other's anxiety. The professional school counselor figured that the enmeshment had much to do with Tom's social isolation and school avoidance. At the same time the professional school counselor was aware that during the trauma suffered by the family it was normal for Tom and his mother to have become extremely protective of each other as well as becoming the eyes and ears for each other's pain. The professional school counselor learned from Tom and his mother that Tom had very low self-esteem. He expected to be treated poorly and figured he got what he deserved. On the positive side, Tom felt his mother and sister loved him. Even his father, while treating him horribly, nonetheless maintained that he cared for Tom. Tom had on-grade-level academic skills and loved to read. Also, in one-on-one interactions he was very sociable and pleasant. Tom possessed some strengths and it is essential for the professional school counselor to help him recognize and build on these strengths.

*Intervention.* To address parenting concerns about supervision, the professional school counselor suggested to the mom that she ask social services to help arrange and pay for a slot in a YMCA afternoon program where Tom would be supervised and also get help with his homework. The professional school counselor, after receiving appropriate releases of information, called social services and followed up with a short memo requesting the YMCA afternoon program for Tom. To address the possible trauma, enmeshment, and parenting skills, she also asked about the possibility of social services paying for mental health counseling. In the process the professional school counselor learned that in criminal cases such as that of Tom's father, the court provided money for therapy for children through a state fund, and that social services would recommend and pay for mental health counseling. The professional school counselor assured the social services case worker that she would encourage the mother to make an appointment for Tom and herself for mental health counseling. The professional school counselor, after receiving appropriate releases of information from Tom's mother, was able to inform the family therapist of the need for boundaries in the enmeshed relationship between Tom and his mother.

To address issues of self-esteem and personal trauma, the professional school counselor also let Tom know that she understood the pain he had suffered and wanted him to drop in for short meetings to get things off his chest, as needed. During these meetings the professional school counselor learned that Tom had been traumatized by his father's behavior and made to feel worthless. Following suggestions by Meichenbaum (2002) for child focused intervention in cases of trauma, the professional school counselor provided Tom an opportunity to talk about his experiences in an appropriate way. She nurtured Tom's coping skills and worked on stress-related symptom reduction. She helped Tom to find meaning in his experiences that he could take with him in life and value himself. She helped him combat his sense of isolation and encouraged him to have hope. The professional school counselor gave Tom's mother a ten-minute telephone check-in every two weeks to see how things were going and to reassure her that she was available to the mother, when needed.

*Stepparent Surface Structure: Basic Guidelines*

*1. Parenting.* Parenting issues are often the focus of difficulty in step-families. Both parents may have had different parenting experiences in previous marriages. The ex-spouses of the two remarried parents may have been more supportive or less supportive. Children often expect to continue in a comfortable and habitual pattern. This can be a set-up for the stepparent who then ends up in a battle with the child resulting in stress for the entire family. Being a member of two different households, the child may have difficulty handling the parenting differences when he goes from one biological parent's home to the other.

2. *Legal-economic.* In some stepfamilies, resentment over payments to the ex-spouse can become an issue. Also, finances can become an issue in the stepfamily when parent and stepparent have differing opinions over how money for a stepchild is to be managed, such as for buying clothes, autos, trips, and education. As with single parents, access to children from another marriage or to the school records might become an issue for the non-custodial parent.
3. *Structural-support.* Remarriage may increase or decrease the support networks that were in place prior to the remarriage. If one stepparent is older and didn't expect to parent a young child the other spouse brings to the marriage, different expectations as to duties with children can lead to stress. Where children feel they are members of two different households, stressful relationships can result. It is important for parents to realize that bonding with a stepparent is not necessarily easy and will take time.
4. *Beliefs.* Beliefs about issues such as religion, discipline, academics, dress, curfews, dating, and extracurricular activities can lead to stress for the family and children.
5. *Mental and physical health.* In stepfamilies, a major issue is often the emergence of feelings of loss. The child may suffer the loss of a close relationship with a biological parent. The children may still be hoping that somehow their biological parents can come back together.

*Example Two: Stepparent with High School Student*

Linda was a high school student who had lived with her father for ten years after her parents' separation and divorce. Her father remarried a woman who felt very strongly that children should be parented using an authoritarian model. She had a daughter who was in college that she pointed to as an example of high success with authoritarian parenting. The father on the other hand believed in a much looser, hands off approach. He and his new wife were both intellectuals who constantly battled over authoritarian parenting versus what the father defined as humanitarian parenting. While the daughter in college and the one in high school didn't engage in sibling rivalry, the parents of the two fought over the differences in the two children. Linda, who had a good relationship with her stepmother when her father and her stepmother were dating, began to express extreme anger toward her stepmother when her stepmother began to discipline her.

Many of their battles were over issues such as fifteen and thirty-minute late curfew violations which her father felt should be ignored or merely mentioned and forgotten, while her stepmother demanded punishment. Other issues such as drunkenness after dates worried both parents. However even in this area, the father argued that these kinds of events only happened occasionally, and should be punished mildly, while the stepmother felt the girl should be seriously monitored and sent for therapy. Additionally, Linda and her father both indicated a feeling of loss of the close relationship they had prior to the father's remarriage. The stepmother on the other hand felt that Linda and her father still had a close relationship, and that she, the new wife, was less important to her new husband than his daughter. The father stated that while he didn't want his new family to function this way, if he had to choose one over the other, it would have to be his child, "his blood."

Decline of Linda's academic performance brought on additional battles between stepmother and father. The stepmother, as one might expect, wanted the father to set tight limits and monitor his daughter's work. The father said that his work prevented rigorous monitoring as he frequently had to go to meetings at night. The stepmother said she could provide the necessary monitoring with the father's support. When the father agreed, Linda began a war with her stepmother and accused her father of abandoning her. Linda demanded to spend more time with her biological mother who didn't have the wherewithal or desire to take on additional parenting duties. The non-custodial biological parent refused to level with Linda and instead led her to believe that maybe Linda would at some time in the future be able to live with her.

*Assessment.* Much of Linda's decline in academic performance at school was directly related to structural issues in the family that interfered with the parents' ability to parent her. A battle raged constantly over the hierarchy and leadership of the family. The stepmother wanted a very conservative and authoritarian leadership style and expected to be at the top of the hierarchy. She had grown up in a family in which her father was very troubled mentally and her mother took charge and provided what little order existed. She had vowed to herself that in her life there would not be the frustrations, anxiety, and embarrassment born of the chaos brought on by her father. Her role model had been a strong woman leading the family and protecting the family from a weak man. The father had grown up in a very liberal family where any behavior was acceptable and he became highly responsible because he chose to. His belief was that being a family was essentially a task in democracy in which all the family members, parents and children, had equal votes and voices.

In this situation the daughter constantly used her alliance (and almost spousal relationship) with her father prior to the coming of her stepmother to build a coalition against her stepmother. The daughter constantly complained to the father that her evil stepmother was victimizing her. The wife complained that Linda was in charge of the family and would send both Linda and the family in a tailspin if not stopped. The father felt caught in the middle of powerful forces, between his own beliefs about being a family, his loyalty to his daughter, his desire to succeed in his marriage, and his hope for his daughter to succeed academically.

When school teachers or the professional school counselor attempted to intervene with the family, the educators would experience the frustration of a family who meant well but could not agree on a plan for getting the daughter back in line academically. Also it was clear that the family was not going to carry out a plan consistently even if it was ever agreed upon.

*Intervention.* The main issues here were parenting and academics, beliefs, and family structure. These issues all were intricately wound together keeping the family stuck and the child in trouble. The initial approach in this situation involves determining whether there are any serious family problems such as alcoholism or mental illness, and to address structural issues that keep the family from being able to make decisions or follow through on them. If there are serious problems (ruled out in this case), the professional school counselor should provide referral information. Clearly in this family the structural issue is the daughter's coalition with the father that kept the stepmother feeling in a one-down position and left feeling that her husband was not supportive. This is a very difficult situation usually requiring couples therapy, as it is usually accompanied by bitterness of a spouse who feels the expectations of the marriage are not being met. In this case the stepmother also has differentiation issues from her family of origin, meaning she becomes very emotionally upset in the face of what she sees as the same loose, undependable, democratic leadership that wrecked her family. She is unable to stay in a cognitive problem-solving mode with her husband or anyone else who she feels represents this type of thinking— even a professional school counselor or family therapist.

The key for the professional school counselor is not to suggest couples therapy, as this will alienate the couple (although if the couple brings it up, the professional school counselor should commend them on their wisdom and give them several good referrals). What can be done is to ask the parents if they would be willing to shelve their personal beliefs about parenting and academics in the interest of arriving at a compromise plan that all could carry out successfully. Getting that agreement, the professional school counselor would suggest that they simply list what is necessary for a young person to succeed in school. The list needs to include proper study time in the evening, monitoring by a parent to ensure that homework and test reviews are being done appropriately, and communication between home and teachers to check on results and performance in class. The father and stepmother can agree to those things. The structured nature of the plan will appeal to the stepmother. The father can be told that he can still have close discussions with his daughter, but at the end of the day, he must require that the very simple plan be followed. He can talk with his daughter about her feelings but not about blaming anyone for anything.

The issue here is to get around the whole host of serious structural and belief issues that will require much commitment and therapy to address while going for a simple plan that will enable the daughter to perform in school. If the couple should ask how the professional school counselor feels about their beliefs, it is important to say that there are many ways to parent a child successfully, but all successful plans require consistency, commitment and support. Do not try to resolve the stepmother and daughter issues. Do use the father and daughter relationship as a way to reward the girl for success, and suggest that the parents make certain to find individual time for themselves to have fun while enduring the stress of parenting a young adolescent in a stepfamily arrangement. Commend the parents on coming for help and caring enough to do the right thing.

*Interracial Parent Surface Structure: Basic Guidelines*

1. *Parenting.* Different cultures frequently have different beliefs about parenting. For example, Latinos typically place a high value on respect for parents from children. Adolescent rebellion or disrespect to parents can be horrifying to a Latino parent while fully acceptable as a stage of development to Western Europeans (Boyd-Franklin & Bry, 2000).
2. *Legal-economic.* Different cultures have differing beliefs about who should and should not work and under what conditions.
3. *Structural-social.* The child with parents of different heritage may experience her identity as multiracial. Many of the positive or negative feelings that can be generated around this multiracial identity, especially as the young person enters adolescence, is influenced by parental attitudes about classifications of race and societal attitudes. Where the child with a multiracial identity encounters strong racist attitudes toward her, the child's identity can be influenced in very negative ways. The child can become socially isolated in a community that lacks appreciation of diversity. Extended family problems between the grandparents and parents regarding racial issues also can bring tension to the home of the multiracial child.
4. *Beliefs.* Issues with the school system around classification can arise. It is important for the school system to honor the family's belief about how their child is to be identified.
5. *Health.* Where racial victimization or bullying exists, the professional school counselor will want to intervene to prevent future trauma. Schools can affirm students' feelings, take their concerns seriously and enforce regulations against hate-bullying toward students. There are also programs for sensitizing the student body, staff, and parents about the effects of bullying and how to address it.

Consider the case of a male high school student whose identity was multiracial. He lived in a town where he encountered strong racism on an almost daily basis both among school classmates and from town's people while simply walking down the street. The essential intervention was to help him build a couple of close relationships with kids in the town. He was to ignore taunting on the streets from adults and discuss it at school with his professional school counselor and at home with his parents, but not to retaliate. Several important student body leaders were invited and responded positively to coming to his defense at school when any bullying started.

*Foster Parent, Adoptive Parent, and Grandparent Surface Structure: Basic Guidelines*

1. *Parenting.* Foster children may have seen many parenting styles and may need help adapting to yet another one. In the case of grandparents, they may be a little behind on the parenting issues of the day and need help updating their parenting skills. Also, grandparents and others who adopt or serve as foster parents may be doing so in the interest of friends, relatives, or their own children who may be divorcing or have died. In this case the foster, grand-, or adoptive parents will themselves be grieving while trying to take on the new task of parenting. Where a foster family takes on numerous children their attention may be divided. The neediest children tend to get most of the attention. Where the child has moved from school to school, academic performance may be affected, students may lack good learning and study skills, or students may focus more on meeting basic survival needs than education needs.
2. *Legal-economic.* Legal issues are similar to single parenting and stepparenting.
3. *Structural-social.* Finding after-school programs for students so that guardians can rest may be helpful. The child may have trouble bonding with new parents and this may result in conflict at home and worry on the part of the foster, grand- or adoptive parent.
4. *Beliefs.* Particularly if they have lived in several foster homes, children might not believe that they are really able to stay with their adoptive parents. Foster and adoptive children may believe they will not be staying at the school they are attending and therefore not have a strong commitment to the school or teachers. These children may have guilty beliefs about why they do not have a stable home life and parents.
5. *Health.* Other children who learn of the foster or adoptive child's status may ridicule him. Also these children might have suffered trauma, neglect, or serious emotional stress in previous settings and be in need of psychotherapy.

*Example Three: Interracial Parent with Adopted Elementary Student*

Terrence was a second grade child who was adopted by an interracial couple. The woman was Caucasian and the father was African American. They were both professionals but decided that the woman would stay home with the child. The woman was happy with this because she felt her husband could provide better economically and she felt more competent to parent a young child than her husband. He agreed. The wife also looked forward to taking some classes during the day at a local college.

At school the child was very active. When informed of this the parents questioned if they should have the child assessed for AD/HD. Teachers reported the child was difficult to keep on task and had trouble gaining acceptance from the other children because of his over-active behavior. Though very active, Terrence did not hurt anyone.

At home the family reported no trouble getting Terrence to bond with them. Yet he spoke as though he would be leaving the home and that nothing in the house, including things in his room, belonged to him.

*Assessment.* Terrence had lived in many foster homes and was having trouble understanding that adoption meant he would stay forever with these parents. Also, Terrence had learned to bond quickly as a survival mechanism. He wanted the love and caring immediately and for as long as he could with the parents with whom he was placed. Terrence placed little value on the schoolwork or students because he believed that he would have to leave any friendships, school projects or work fairly soon. He lost many friendships, teachers, and parents and had developed a survival mechanism to protect himself. He never committed completely to friends and schoolwork. He felt much anxiety because he never knew what would happen to him next, and he knew he could not perform in school as well as many of the other students.

*Intervention.* The main intervention was for the parents to convince him that he would be with them forever. His adoptive father and mother informed him that the furniture in his room was his forever, and that he would never be leaving their home. At school the professional school counselor and teachers reinforced the stability of his placement. They said they expected him to stay with them, and they wanted to help him do well. Terrence's mother began helping him get on track academically. The professional school counselor suggested that the parents wait and see how Terrence did at the school before considering an evaluation for AD/HD. The school counselor said it was natural for Terrence to be a little anxious given his situation and perhaps he was just a very active boy. The plan was to provide him with structure in the class to help him learn to follow class rules, and as he adjusted to parents and school, hopefully he would find friends and begin to replace his old survival skills with some new ones. The professional school counselor set up some times for the adoptive mother to visit the classroom and even become a parent volunteer to help Terrence make the adjustment. In addition, the professional school counselor made an appointment to meet with the family in a month and review how Terrence was adapting.

## Summary/Conclusion

A key to helping changing families is to not get lost in their differences. It helps to be aware of issues that frequently arise with a particular type of family, and at the same time stay open and sensitive to the individual nature of the family. There are many ways to be a family, and a particular family, no matter how they may be typed in terms of surface structure, may not evidence the issues typically associated with that type of living arrangement. For example, there are gay and lesbian relationships in which children feel embarrassed and there are those in which they do not. Some interracial families receive tremendous support from their extended families and others do not. Some single, step and cohabiting families have educational attainment, economic well-being and social support which makes coping with family transitions much easier for them than for those families lacking in any of these three factors. Many individuals will experience traumatic events, about 61% of men and 51% of women, but Post Traumatic Stress Disorder (PTSD) is quite low, in general 5% among men and 10% among women (Meichenbaum, 2002). Individuals and the families in which they grow up may respond very differently to similar events and circumstances. It is important when working with families in transition to keep a very open mind. Professional school counselors need to approach all changing families according to both their strengths and needs.

## References


Boyd-Franklin, N., & Bry, B. (2000). *Reaching out in family therapy: Home-based, and community interventions.* New York: Guilford Press.

Bryson, K. (2001). *Family Composition Changing, Census Report.* United States Department of Commerce News. Source: U.S. Census Bureau, Public Information Office (301) 763-3030. [On-line] pio@census.gov.

Conroy, P. (1986). *Prince of tides.* New York: Bantam Books.

Coontz, S. (1997). *The way we really are: Coming to terms with America's changing family.* New York: Basic Books.

Erford, B. T., House, R., & Martin, P. (2003). Transforming the school counseling profession. In B. T. Erford (Ed.), *Transforming the school counseling profession.* Columbus OH: Merrill/Prentice-Hall.

Geffner, R., Jaffe, P., & Sudermann, M. (Eds.) (2002). Children exposed to domestic violence. *Journal of Aggression, Maltreatment and Trauma, 3*(1).

Grissmer, D., Kirby, S., Berends, M., & Williamson, S. (1994). *Student achievement and the changing American family* [On-line]. Available Rand Distribution Services, Hostname: order@rand.org.Rand.

Hampton, F. M., Rak, C., & Mumford, D. A. (1997). Children's literature reflecting diverse family structures: Social and academic benefits for early reading programs. *ERS Spectrum, 15*(4), 10-15.

Keys, S. G., Bemak, F., & Lockhart, E. J. (1998). Transforming school counseling to serve the mental health needs of at-risk youth. *Journal of Counseling and Development, 76,* 381-388.

Lockhart, E. (2003). Students with disabilities. In B. T. Erford (Ed.), *Transforming the school counseling profession.* Columbus OH: Merrill/Prentice-Hall.

Lockhart, E. J., & Keys, S. G. (1998). The mental health counseling role of school counselors. *Professional School Counseling, 1,* 3-6.

McCubbin, H., McCubbin, M., Thompson, A., Han, S., & Allen, C. (1997). *Families under stress.* Based on the 1997 American Association of Family and Consumer Sciences Commemorative Lecture delivered by Hamilton I. McCubbin on June 22, 1997, in Washington, D.C. Retrieved on November 15, 2002 from www.cyfernet.extension.umn.edu/research/resilient.html.

Meichenbaum, D. (2001). *Treatment of individuals with anger-control problems and aggressive behaviors: A clinical handbook.* Clearwater, FL: Institute Press.

Meichenbaum, D. (2002). *PTSD: Treating adult victims, children, adolescents and their families.* Workshop on November 7 & 8, 2002, Lancaster, PA.

Patterson, C. J. (2002). *Research summary on lesbian and gay parenting.* Retrieved November 7, 2002 from http:/apa.org/pi/parent.html

Sado, S. & Bayer, A. (2001). *Executive summary: The changing family.* From Population Resource Center: Providing the Demographic Dimensions of Public Policy. Retrieved November 15, 2002 from www.prcd.org/summaries/family/family.html.

Schwartz, W. (1999). Family diversity in urban schools. *Eric Digest.* Eric Clearinghouse on Urban Education, Institute on Urban and Minority Education, 148, Retrieved on September 15, 2002 from http://eric-web.tc.columbia.edu/dig148.asp.

Shin, M., & Weitzman, B. (1996). Homeless families are different. In J. Baumont (Ed.), *Homelessness in America.* Washington, DC: Oryx Press.

Sugarman, S. (1998). Single parent families. In M. A. Mason, A. Skolnick, & S. Sugarman (Eds.), *All our families: New policies for a new century.* New York: Oxford University Press.

Updegraff, J., & Taylor. S. (1999). From vulnerability to growth: Positive and negative effects of stressful life events. In J. H. Harvey & E. D. Miller (Eds.), *Handbook of loss and trauma.* New York: Brunner/Mazel.

Weist, M. (1997). Expanded school mental health services: A national movement in progress. In T. Ollendick & R. Prinz (Eds.), *Advances in clinical child psychology* (Vol. 19) (pp. 319-352). New York: Plenum Press.

Werner, E. (1989). Children of the Garden Island. *Scientific American, 260*(4), 106-111.

# Chapter 77

# Helping At-Risk Students

*Jill Holmes-Robinson*

## Preview

This chapter addresses the professional school counselor's role in assisting students "at-risk." This chapter provides pragmatic strategies, such as Rational Emotive Behavior Therapy (REBT) and other cognitive-behavioral approaches centered in brief modified formats for use with elementary and secondary students. These therapeutic techniques will assist the professional school counselor in providing effective counseling to help students identified as at-risk.

In accordance with the American School Counselor Association (ASCA), the primary goal of the professional school counselor is to "assist in the growth and development of each individual [student]" (ASCA, 1998, p. 1). This includes contributing to the mental health as well as the "academic, career and personal/social success of 'at-risk' students" (ASCA, 1998, p.1). The following chapter will address the needs of at-risk students and will provide pragmatic strategies centered in brief cognitive-behavioral approaches modified for use with elementary and secondary students. These therapeutic techniques will assist the professional school counselor in providing effective counseling for helping students deemed "at-risk."

## The Student At-Risk

There are probably as many definitions of students at-risk as there are school districts (ASCA, 1998). Students may be considered "at-risk" if they have a greater potential for performing poorly academically, dropping out of school, becoming truant, or engaging in behaviors that are harmful to self or others. For the purpose of this chapter, at-risk students are defined as students who exhibit one or more of these problems.

It is the charge of the professional school counselor to use his or her "specialized skills" in working with the counselee in developing integrated and effective counseling plans that are consistent with the abilities and circumstances of the counselee (ASCA, 1998, p. 1). With this charge in mind, it is imperative that professional school counselors view students at-risk with an appreciation and clear perspective for the student's background, life circumstances and likely reasons for at-risk behaviors.

The Research Network on Successful Adolescent Development among Youth in High-Risk Settings (as cited in Jessor, 1993) suggested that knowledge of the development of youth growing up in social contexts that place them at risk (e.g., poverty, limited access to opportunity, racial/ethnic marginality) is essential for individuals working with students at-risk. In addition, the professional school counselor must understand the underlying reasons for "at-risk" behavior, such as the student trying to deal with personal and social issues (e.g., low self-esteem, family problems, unresolved grief, neglect or abuse).

## Issues Affecting the At-Risk Student

During the latter part of the twentieth century, nearly one in every five adolescents (which equates to about 4 million youth living in America) aged 13 to 18 was a member of a family living below the poverty level (Jessor, 1993). When this figure was examined by race/ ethnicity, the percentage was 11% White, 37% Hispanic, and 44% African-American. The majority of these youths were living and attending schools in urban and rural settings. The majority of low-income urban youth tend to be living within metropolitan areas and are of minority (African-American and Hispanic) ethnic backgrounds. In contrast, rural youth grow up in poor (often farming) communities and are a part of the majority (White/Caucasian) ethnic population. Of course ethnic minority youth (African-Americans, Hispanics and Native Americans) often live in rural settings, such as Indian Reservations and other rural poverty stricken communities throughout the South and Western U.S. Understandably, there are a number of issues that arise regarding the mental health and wellness of low income students growing up in urban and rural communities that place these students at-risk. Professional school counselors must provide comprehensive school counseling services to this growing population.

In addition to poverty, personal issues such as smoking, binge drinking, and lifetime use of marijuana, cocaine and inhalants can place one at-risk.

## The Goal in Helping At-Risk Students

When counseling students at-risk, the primary goal of the professional school counselor is to identify characteristics and maladaptive behaviors and intervene before these students establish a pattern of self-destructive behavior (ASCA, 1998). According to ASCA ethical guidelines, when providing services to students at-risk, the professional school counselor is primarily responsible for "provid[ing] responsive programming, including short-term individual, group, family and crisis counseling . . . programs to strengthen personal/interpersonal skills (choice, self-acceptance, feelings, beliefs and behaviors, problem-solving, decision-making)" (p. 2).

## Cognitive-Behavioral Approaches for Use with Students At-Risk

Various psychotherapeutic interventions, such as modified forms of cognitive-behavioral therapies (CBT) for students, consist of a variety of techniques in which the student/counselee is taught to use cognitive mediational strategies to guide his/her behavior and thus improve his/her adjustment (Durlak, Fuhrman & Lampman, 1991; Glasser, 1998). Cognitive-behavioral approaches are based on the assumption that a reorganization of one's self-statements will result in a corresponding reorganization of one's behaviors.

Many researchers and seasoned mental health professionals have concluded that various cognitive-behavioral strategies are effective for use with students with dysfunctional behaviors (DiGiuseppe & Barnard, 1990; Durlak et al., 1991; Barnard, 1990; Zionts & Zionts, 1997). When using CBT with school-aged children, CBT seems best suited for preadolescents (ages 11 to 13). This age group has been shown to exhibit substantial gains from treatment regardless of presenting difficulties (Durlak et al., 1991). Although younger children (ages 5 to 11) have been shown to benefit from CBT, their treatment gains reflect only half as much change as preadolescents (Durlak et al., 1991). Therefore, modified versions of various forms of CBT approaches are likely required for serving younger elementary age counselees. The remainder of this chapter will focus on practical CBT interventions that have been modified for use by the professional school counselors when providing services to elementary and secondary students at-risk.

## Rational Emotive Behavior Therapy for Use with Students At-Risk

Rational Emotive Behavior Therapy (REBT) is a theory and strategy based on the works of Albert Ellis. REBT can be used to help students manage behaviors and emotions that are preventing them from succeeding in school and developing appropriate personal and social behaviors (DiGiuseppe & Barnard, 1990; Zionts & Zionts, 1997). The goal of REBT is to teach students who exhibit emotions (e.g., high anxiety, depression, extreme anger, hate, low frustration tolerance, social isolation) to handle these emotions in more productive ways. By counseling students and teaching them a modified form of REBT conducive to the student's age and cognitive abilities, REBT can serve to reduce levels of maladaptive thoughts and provide the at-risk student with more appropriate, less self-destructive behaviors.

Empirical studies have shown REBT to be effective when used by school psychologists or professional school counselors with school-aged children (DiGiuseppe & Bernard, 1990), with the greatest effects on behavior change, reduction of anxiety, and on students' adjustment and personality (DiGiuseppe & Bernard, 1990; Hajzler & Bernard, 1989). Additionally, REBT has been cited as effective in reducing self-defeating emotions, poor self-esteem, anger, and conduct disorders.

Integral to REBT is the philosophy that the majority of an individual's maladaptive behaviors are the result of how the person thinks and feels about a situation. The basic assumption is that thinking, evaluating, analyzing, questioning, doing, practicing, and re-deciding are at the base of behavior change. Emotional problems are viewed as a result of one's irrational beliefs that need to be challenged. Zionts and Zionts (1997) gave examples of three types of irrational beliefs that can lead to disturbed thinking:

> 1. I **must** do well and win approval, or else I rate as a rotten person.
> 2. Others **must** treat me considerately and kindly in precisely the way I want them to treat me; if they don't, society and the universe should severely blame . . . and punish them for their inconsiderateness.
> 3. Conditions under which I live **must** be arranged so that I get practically all that I want comfortably, quickly, and easily and get virtually nothing that I don't want. (p. 104)

When counseling students, it is clearly apparent how unproductive irrational beliefs can be in the lives of the developing youth. The core irrational belief is that of "absolutizing," which involves exaggerated or grandiose thinking suggesting that the individual's world should be "absolutely" the way that they believe it to be (Zionts & Zionts, 1997). Because REBT implores the need to teach students how to recognize, dispute and replace irrational beliefs with rational ones, professional school counselors must apply a didactic approach to counseling when using REBT because therapy is a process of "reeducating" the student.

Professional school counselors can use REBT on an individual or group basis. Group counseling is deemed effective and efficient because more than one student will benefit from the process. Additionally, group counseling allows students to see that others have similar problems, and it allows students to assist each other in identifying irrational beliefs and substitute more rational, productive ways of thinking and behaving.

### *REBT for Use with At-Risk Elementary School Children*

When planning to use REBT with elementary students, professional school counselors must take into consideration the age and cognitive ability of the student, and modify the technique accordingly. Students under the age of seven should be taught "rational self-talk" (Zionts & Zionts, 1997). The professional school counselor must keep in mind that REBT is designed to teach students to handle feelings that prevent them from meeting their individual goals, to promote less static, self-defeating behaviors, and produce more flexible and self-empowering behaviors. The goal is to minimize harmful emotions (Zionts & Zionts, 1997). The following are examples of REBT therapeutic activities that professional school counselors can use when counseling elementary aged students:

1. In a group setting the professional school counselor can have "flash cards" depicting various scenes or words in which extreme emotions are displayed (such as anger, rage, hate, etc.). A child saying "I feel angry" can be taught to use the words "I feel disappointed, annoyed or upset." The professional school counselor can facilitate an age appropriate discussion regarding the difference between "anger" (which can illicit self-destructive or self-defeating behavior or depression) and "disappointment" or being "upset" or "annoyed" (which are more "rational" less self-defeating words and emotions).
2. Likewise, the professional school counselor can teach children the distinctions between: (a) "regret" as opposed to "guilt" and (b) feeling "sad" as opposed to feeling "depressed."

When implementing these techniques, keep in mind that REBT is *not* designed to solve practical problems (e.g., "Eric took my crayon"). When children have deep emotional problems, resolving situations using temporary solutions does little to change the child's emotional state (Zionts & Zionts, 1997). The professional school counselor using REBT is trying to help students learn to explore self-defeating, maladaptive or extreme emotions/feelings and deal with their feelings in a more productive manner, cognitively and behaviorally.

Students aged seven to 11 can be taught how to dispute irrational concepts such as "shame," which can occur when children are overwhelmingly concerned about how they are perceived by others (e.g., "I don't want to try because everyone will laugh at me"). Students older than 11 can be taught how to dispute irrational beliefs. Irrational beliefs can be explored and disputed with this age group and beyond because these students are at a more mature cognitive level. Their thoughts become more static and can be negatively influenced by society at large (e.g., students encounter the negative stereotyping of ethnic, gender, religious, and socio-economic status which can contribute to irrational beliefs such as: (1) "Girls can't play sports as well as boys," (2) "Black kids are not as smart as White kids," or (3) "Smoking marijuana wont hurt you, everyone does it.") At this age and beyond young people begin to express their irrational beliefs in personally distinctive terms containing the static belief structures of "musts." Dryden and DiGiuseppe (1990) suggested these irrational beliefs illicit the following demands:

1. Demands about self: "I must be approved of by significant others [such as family or peers]; if I'm not, then it's too awful and I won't be able to stand it." Beliefs based on this often lead to anxiety, depression, shame, or guilt [or maladaptive behaviors such as aggression].
2. Demands about others: "You must treat me well or justly [fairly within the context of my definition]." Beliefs based on this "must" are associated with feelings of anger and rage, as well as with passive-aggressiveness and acts of violence.
3. Demands about the world/life conditions: "Life conditions [or the way I want things] must absolutely be how I want them to be, and if not I can't stand it, poor me." Such beliefs are associated with feelings of self-pity and hurt, as well as problems of self-discipline (e.g., procrastination or addictive behavior).

*Teaching REBT Steps to Middle School Students Using The ABC Model*

REBT is based on the A-B-C theory of personality. The various components of this model are explained below (see Dryden & DiGiuseppe, 1990). The *Activating Event (A)* is the student's problem, the actual event, or the student's inferences or interpretations about the activating event. Regardless of the **A**'s factual basis, the professional school counselor must understand that the student believes it to be true.

The *Beliefs (**B**)* are evaluative thoughts or constructed views of the world that are either rigid (irrational) or flexible (rational). Irrational beliefs are rigid or static beliefs that take the form of words and concepts such as: (absolute) musts; (absolute) shoulds; and have to's. Irrational beliefs can be explained to elementary and middle school students as the difference between fact and opinion (Zionts & Zionts, 1997). It is best to teach fact and opinion concepts independent of one another before asking students to discriminate between them, defining terms in simple language that are age appropriate. For example, a "fact" can be defined as something that is true or can be proven; an "opinion" is how we think and feel about a fact. The term "not-fact" is suggested as a substitute for an opinion for beginning learners. Students should master the concepts of fact and opinion before REBT is fully implemented.

A simple way to access the student's **B** (belief structure) is to ask the student what he/she is or was thinking or saying to himself/herself when the Activating Event (the **A**) occurred. Take notice if the student is using statements that include musts, shoulds, or have to's (which suggest irrational beliefs). Do not ask questions that reinforce the assumption that the Activating Event caused/made the student behave inappropriately (such as "How did the situation make you feel?"). You want the student to "own" his/her actions by asking "What were *you* thinking or saying to yourself when the event occurred?"

The next step is the consequence (Dryden & DeGiuseppe, 1990). The *Consequence (**C**)* is the behavioral action or consequence that occurs as a result of the way the student perceives the activating event. They are the maladaptive and/or self-defeating behaviors that are a result of irrational beliefs turned into actions.

If the professional school counselor is providing preventative didactic counseling to a group, the **A-B-C** steps are followed and explained in sequence. However, if the professional school counselor is providing individual counseling to an at-risk student who has already engaged in maladaptive behaviors (e.g., student punched another student and is coming to counseling after having returned from suspension), the professional school counselor should follow the steps in order of **C-A-B**. In the case of the aforementioned example, the **(C)**onsequence was hitting the student and being suspended from school, the **(A)**ctivating Event involved the other student calling the counselee a bad name, and the **(B)**elief was the counselee's thoughts, "I was angry and thinking that everyone will think that I'm a punk if I let her call me a name" or "I was thinking, she shouldn't have done that, I'm going to kill her."

The last two steps in REBT are those of challenging (disputing) irrational beliefs and developing new productive behaviors (Dryden & DeGiuseppe, 1990). The *Dispute (**D**)* occurs when the student's irrational belief (the **B**) is challenged (disputed). The professional school counselor (in individual counseling) or the group participants along with the professional school counselor assists the student in disputing his irrational belief.

Prior to the step of disputing irrational beliefs, the professional school counselor will have to explain to the student or the group members the connection between **B** and **C** (the **B**elief about the **A**ctivating event and the **C**onsequence). It is important for students to understand how they choose to think about an event (their internal self-talk) which will illicit how they choose to react to an event. The professional school counselor can have students role-play the activating event (**A**) and act out the various consequences (**C**) that can occur due to the belief (**B**) about the activating event or issue (as expressed in the previous example). Students can act out both non-productive and productive consequences.

**D**isputing can be achieved by engaging in activities, seeking factual information, using humor, or through traditional use of questioning. Questions posed to the student may include:

(a) Is your belief about the situation or event really awful?, (b) How do you know this is true?, (c) Was that really an unbearable situation?, or (d) Was everyone really laughing at you or at what you did?

An important caveat regarding disputing irrational beliefs is for the professional school counselor to be aware of the student's cultural and life circumstances. The school counselor should be careful not to label a belief as irrational which in the context of the student's world/life is factual and thus rational. An example of this may involve a student who expresses that he believes that he will be killed while walking home from school. The counselor may think this belief extreme but must get further information from the student before labeling his belief as irrational. Upon questioning, the counselor finds that the student lives in a gang infested environment that is not in the immediate vicinity of the school, and there is a real potential of being accidentally shot. What initially sounded irrational is thus rational. The professional school counselor should not dispute the belief, but she can help the student identify appropriate feelings of concern rather than debilitating feelings of fear/anxiety. Also, the professional school counselor can help the student develop a plan to get to and from school safely by suggesting another route or suggesting that he walk with a group.

The final step in the REBT process (Dryden & DeGiuseppe, 1990) is the Effect (**E**), which encompasses assisting the student in developing a new and/or healthier way of looking and thinking about the event. Healthy negative emotions include feelings such as: disappointment (as opposed to anger), concern (as opposed to anxiety), or annoyance (as opposed to sadness).

After identifying more positive belief structures, and thus new reactions to negative events, the student should make a behavioral contract with the professional school counselor to commit to change. Reinforcement of the **A**-**B**-**C** theory and careful monitoring of the student's progress are crucial to positive therapeutic outcome. Additionally, when teaching REBT to students who are at-risk, the professional school counselor must keep in mind that the process may take longer as students will need to establish a trusting relationship with the counselor or comfort level with the group.

## Cognitive Behavioral Brief Therapy: An Integrative Approach for Counseling Middle and High School Students At-Risk

Cognitive-behavioral approaches tend to be more successful as students mature in age and as their cognitive abilities become more concrete. For the at-risk middle and high school students, it is most productive to provide them with brief therapeutic forms of CBT coupled with reality-based therapies that are conducive to their short teenaged attention span. It is also beneficial for the professional school counselor who serves as a counselor and administrator and thus who also has time constraints.

Holmes (1999) developed an integrative approach to counseling that merges two philosophies and CBT approaches with an intrusive counseling style couched in a brief therapeutic format. Intrusive counseling can be defined as probing and direct information-seeking counseling. This style of counseling can assist the counselor in expediting case conceptualization, thus helping the professional school counselor to develop a quick and clear understanding of the student's issues. The approach merges philosophical views of Choice Theory (William Glasser's Reality Therapy) and REBT (Albert Ellis' Rational Emotive Behavior Therapy, as previously discussed) implemented in a brief therapeutic format.

Choice Theory maintains that our behavior is internally motivated and chosen. The theory supports the belief that the only behavior we can control is our own (Glasser, 1998). Reality Therapy is the intervention and promotes counseling that helps students deal with personal problems by creating more realistic quality worlds (what they want) and/or figuring out better choices (Glasser, 1998). Reality Therapy differs from most psychotherapies because it focuses on the present and helps people understand that they can choose a better future.

REBT maintains that beliefs contribute to or cause one's emotional reactions; how you think about a situation reflects how you will react and feel. REBT contends emotional problems are the result of one's beliefs, which need to be challenged.

The philosophical views of both Choice Theory and REBT can be utilized in assisting at-risk students in a cognitive-behavioral brief therapeutic format. The concept of brief therapy may be familiar to most practitioners, however there is little consensus in the defining features of brief therapy (Steenbarger,1992). Conceptually planned, brief counseling is typified by the intentional consideration of time limits throughout the change process. Brief cognitive-behavioral approaches focus on the following: (a) coping skills, teaching students ways of dealing with potential stressors, and (b) restructuring therapy emphasizing the learning of new beliefs and thought patterns. Perhaps a comprehensive explanation of brief counseling would be an intentional acceleration of those change ingredients found in all therapies. By actively bonding with students and, when appropriate, having an intrusive counseling approach, brief therapists serve as developmental catalysts, initiating change that could otherwise take months or years. The brief counseling model views students' concerns as ongoing problems maintained within a particular context. The professional school counselor and student focus on attainable goals and successes to empower the student to take responsibility and control. There are four components emphasized for therapeutic change in planned, brief counseling: (a) strong working alliance; (b) acknowledgment and use of student's strengths and resources; (c) active involvement and connection between counselor and student; and (d) identification of clear, concrete goals (Steenbarger, 1992).

## The Effectiveness of Brief Counseling

Students who benefit most from brief therapy are those who have a recent onset of problems, and who primarily require focused symptom relief as opposed to a broad personality change. This certainly describes the at-risk secondary school-aged student who is dealing with issues of peer pressure, and a host of other developmental issues. Brief therapy also may be more conducive to at-risk minority students who, according to the literature, are often seeking direct, clear and immediate coping skills for their problems and prefer active rather than passive approaches to counseling (Sue, 1990). Students unsuitable for brief counseling include those who have underlying patterns of chronic maladaptive behavior that may require long term counseling and referrals for outpatient treatment. Brief therapy has been effective in a variety of practice settings, including preference of use by professional school counselors and in college counseling centers. Studies incorporating long-term follow-up in their design reported that changes produced in brief counseling were positively sustained. This was particularly shown in individuals counseled for depression who maintained symptom relief for periods of a year or longer (Steenbarger, 1992).

## Holmes Model of Brief Counseling – An Option for Professional School Counselors for Use with At-Risk Youth

Holmes (1999) suggested an integrative model of brief therapy that incorporates four phases: (a) contact, (b) challenge, (c) conversion, and (d) empowerment. The first phase, contact, involves the active fostering of a positive alliance with the student, information gathering using an intrusive style, assessing the student's patterns, and determining the student's appropriateness for brief work. The intrusive counseling style is displayed in the form of asking pertinent, factual questions in an assertive manner such as, “Tell me what happened?” or “How long has this occurred and what have you done to try to deal with the situation?” In the contact phase emphasis is placed on understanding the student’s issue and worldview.

The second phase, challenge, uses the relationship of an established working alliance to challenge non-productive, maladaptive patterns of behavior. This phase incorporates the use of various cognitive-behavioral techniques to facilitate the student’s thinking about his/her non-productive behavior. Questions can be asked such as, “How did you contribute to the situation?” or “Tell me how you are thinking about the situation, what thoughts are going through your mind?” This phase ends with helping the student establish a plan for change via brainstorming and offering suggestions.

In the third phase, conversion, the professional school counselor serves as a support to the student, encouraging his/her ability to change. The professional school counselor again assists the student in identifying more productive behaviors and/or actions and offers the student the opportunity to commit to a goal, plan of action or new behavior, and to test, apply, and rehearse newly developed insights and skills. The professional school counselor does this while offering feedback on performance and reinforcement of goals. This process of recognizing negative or ineffective behaviors or thought patterns and developing more productive behaviors (the process of rehearsing these steps each time the student encounters problems) proceeds to the final stage of empowerment.

During the empowerment stage, the student, while working in conjunction with the professional school counselor, achieves symptom relief and learns an effective process of self-help. In brief counseling, both the professional school counselor and student take responsibility for the flow of work involved in the counseling process. However, in the Holmes model the professional school counselor serves as a facilitator allowing the student to think, process her actions, and actively work on establishing better goals and more effective behaviors. The professional school counselor avoids pitying, enabling, or taking responsibility for the student’s actions (or inaction) by requiring the student to help in identifying new behavioral goals/actions. It is also important that the professional school counselor get a commitment from the student that the student wants to and is willing to try the new agreed upon behavior.

Figure 1 displays the Holmes model of brief therapy. This model was specifically designed for use with students who seek assistance from professional school counselors, although other-referred students can benefit as well. The model should be read as an inverted triangle. The professional school counselor can quickly move though the model or utilize it progressively depending on the amount of contact and time with the student. The model can be utilized to facilitate student thinking, problem solving and development.

## Summary/Conclusion

The professional school counselor providing services for at-risk youth has a substantial challenge. Given the population’s unique circumstances it is imperative for the professional school counselor to have a comprehensive appreciation for at-risk students’ backgrounds and be able to use a variety of counseling techniques that are both effective and efficient. Cognitive-behavioral therapies such as REBT, and integrative approaches such as the Holmes model, can assist the professional school counselor in providing students with symptom relief in a pragmatic format that is beneficial for the student and easily applied by the professional school counselor.

**Figure 1. Holmes model of brief counseling.**

***Empowerment***
Achieve Symptom Relief
*(Continue to work through steps with the stated problems/issues the student presents, allowing the student to learn the processes of facilitating empowerment, symptom relief, and self-help)*
CONVERSION
Get Commitment from the Student for Change
*(Offer the student an opportunity to test, rehearse, apply new behaviors or plan, then return to the counselor with feedback on progress)*
*Use of Relationship to Support Student Change*
*(Counselor provides feedback and encouragement)*
CHALLENGE
Establish a Plan
*(Facilitate student's brainstorming about various productive behaviors, helping with suggestions)*
Challenge Non-Productive Patterns
Use of Cognitive-Behavioral Interventions
*(e.g., Use of REBT and Choice Theories)*
CONTACT
Determine Appropriateness for Brief Work; Assess Student Patterns; Use Intrusive Counseling Style for Information Gathering; Actively Foster a Positive Working Relationship/Alliance

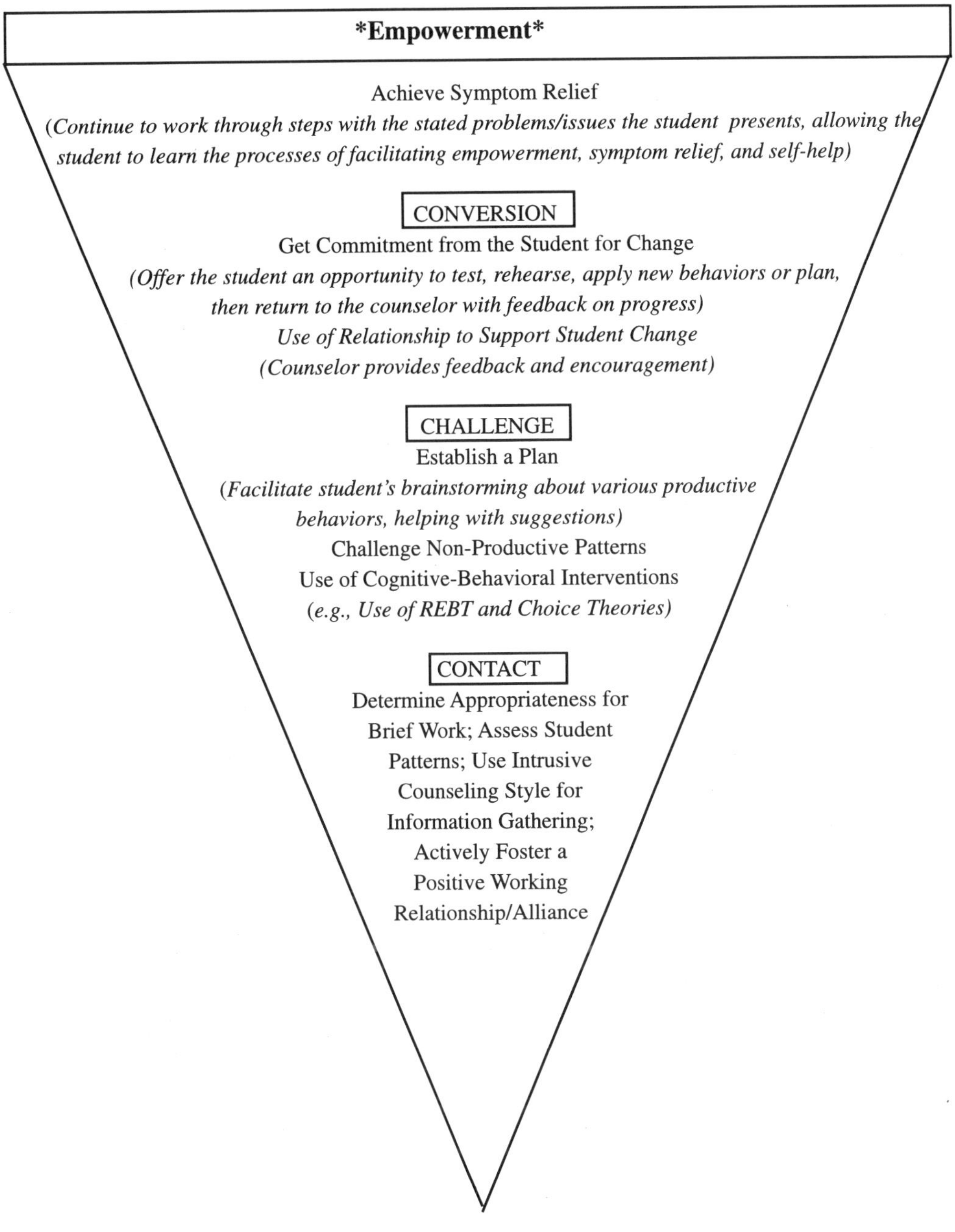

*Note:* This model should be read as an inverted triangle, starting first with contact ("actively fostering . . .") and proceeding upward to student empowerment.

## References

American School Counselor Association. (1998). *About ASCA and ethics: Ethical standards for school counselors.* Retrieved on November 15, 2002 from http:/ www.schoolcounselor.org.

American School Counselor Association. (1999). *About ASCA and position statement: At-risk students.* Retrieved on November 15, 2002 from http://www.schoolcounselor.org.

Barnard, M. (1990). Rational-emotive therapy with children and adolescents: Treatment strategies. *School Psychology Review, 19,* 294-304.

DiGiuseppe, R., & Bernard, M. (1990). The application of rational-emotive theory and therapy to school-aged children. *School Psychology Review, 19,* 268-291.

Dryden, W., & DiGiuseppe, R. (1990). *A primer on rational-emotive therapy.* Champaign, IL: Research Press.

Durlak, J., Fuhrman, T., & Lampman, C. (1991). Effectiveness of cognitive-behavior therapy for maladapting children. *Psychological Bulletin, 110,* 204-214.

Glasser, W. (1998). *Choice theory: A new psychology of personal freedom.* New York: Harper Collins Publishers.

Hajzler, D., & Barnard, M. (1989). *A review of rational-emotive education outcome studies.* Unpublished manuscript.

Holmes, J. (1999). *Counseling in student affairs: Utilizing brief therapy to bridge the gap between theory and practice.* Unpublished manuscript, University of Virginia, Charlottesville, VA.

Jessor, R. (1993). Successful adolescent development among youth in high-risk settings. *American Psychologist, 48,* 117-126.

Steenbarger, N. B. (1992). Toward science-practice integration in brief counseling and therapy. *The Counseling Psychologist, 20,* 403-450.

Sue, D. W. (1990). Culture-specific strategies in counseling: A conceptual framework. *Professional Psychology: Research and Practice, 21,* 424-433.

Zionts, P., & Zionts, L., (1997). Rational emotive behavior therapy with troubled students. *Reclaiming Children and Youth, 6,* 103-108.

# Chapter 78

# The Professional School Counselor in the Rural Setting: Strategies for Meeting Challenges and Maximizing Rewards

*Deborah Drew & Dorothy Breen*

## Preview

The rural setting presents challenges and rewards to the professional school counselor. This article offers strategies to assist professional school counselors in creating and delivering programs, which truly meet the needs of the one quarter of United States students attending rural schools.

The practice of school counseling in a rural setting is both rewarding and uniquely challenging. There is a sense of close community, caring, and trust and appreciation of skills and services offered. Circumstances unique to the rural setting, such as isolation, cultural issues, and limited resources, present challenges to the professional living and working in those settings.

Sutton and Pearson (2002) provided statistics from the 1998 U.S. Department of Education's National Center for Education Statistics stating that "rural and small town schools comprise 37.8% of the total number of schools and serve 25.4% of the total number of enrolled students … more than a quarter of U.S. public school students receive their education in rural and small town schools." (p. 226).

Professional school counselors play a critical role in students' lives (Kuranz, 2002), especially in rural settings. To be most effective, professional school counselors must recognize the challenges and thrive on the rewards of the rural setting. This chapter will discuss four prominent challenges presented in the literature: rural isolation, rural culture, limited resources, and ethical dilemmas. Strategies will be offered for meeting these challenges and maximizing the counseling benefits to the rural school setting. Admittedly, the research was sparse regarding these strategies and will be supplemented with findings from ongoing research by the authors.

*Isolation*

In rural settings, the professional school counselor may be the only counselor in the school, school district, and community. There is often a lack of contact with other school counselors (Breen & Drew, 2001). Consequently, peer support and access to professional colleagues for collaboration, supervision, or consultation may not be available nearby. There are few opportunities for professional development and those that are available may require the professional school counselor to drive long distances. The need for socialization, especially for young, unmarried professional school counselors, is difficult to meet. As one counselor stated, "Isolation is difficult - it's very difficult being a single person in this community" (Sutton & Pearson, 2002, p. 272). According to Helge (as cited in Sutton & Pearson, 2002), the impact of isolation has been identified as a contributor to high turnover rates among education specialists in rural schools.

*The Rural Culture*

"Unique" is a term used in the literature when describing the rural culture and the rural school environment (Apostal & Bilden, 1991; McIntire, Marion, & Quaglia, 1990; Sutton & Southworth, 1990). The rural community offers close personal relationships, personal recognition, caring, involvement, traditional values, and independence. However, it takes time to get to know the people and become established. Other challenges include limited resources, distrust of the unfamiliar, and lack of privacy and anonymity (Breen & Drew, 2001).

Rural schools also have unique characteristics. They tend to be smaller, more personal centers of community identity (McIntire et al., 1990). By their very definition, rural schools are usually "geographically isolated, located in less densely populated areas. These conditions limit opportunities of rural youth for adequate health services, social and recreational activities, relevant educational experiences and exposure to vocational life styles which could be a means of changing their future" (Sweeney, 1971, p. 6).

*Limited Resources*

Lack of resources is one of the chief complaints that professional school counselors have about the rural setting. Financial resources are limited and counseling resources may not be readily available. The professional school counselor may perceive that he or she is expected to "wear many hats" and "be all things to all people" (Breen & Drew, 2001). The professional school counselor might take on the role of "generalist." "In the small, understaffed school, the realities of limited resources demand that the counselor, or few counselors, take responsibility for the total range of student needs" (Sutton & Pearson, 2002, p. 276).

The National Institute of Mental Health in September, 2000, stated that "the nearly 60 million Americans living in rural and frontier areas have the same kinds of mental health problems and needs for services as individuals who live in urban and suburban areas. Yet, rural areas have unique characteristics that present barriers to mental health care" (National Institute of Mental Health, 2000, p. 1). "For many students and families the school counselor is the first mental health provider they see" (Paisley & McMahon, as cited in Kuranz, 2002, p. 173) and "may be the only mental health provider they ever see" (Kuranz, 2002, p. 173).

The unique circumstances of the rural setting affect career development. "Reduced accessibility to higher education, narrow rural school curricula, limited exposure to the world of occupations and few role models have been major limitations" (Apostal & Bilden, 1991, p. 153).

*Ethical Dilemmas*

The unique characteristics of the rural setting also present dilemmas to the professional school counselor trying to maintain good ethical standards. Maintaining boundaries is especially difficult for counselors who may face expectations to "be all things to all people" (Breen & Drew, 2001). Both the ACA Code of Ethics (1995) and the ASCA Ethical Standards (1998) require counselors to practice within the bounds of individual professional competence. Though ethical standards require referral, resources for referral may be remote.

"The professional school counselor keeps information confidential . . ." (ASCA Ethical Standards, 1998, A.2.b.). Small school expectations of "knowing" about students may challenge adherence to this standard. Teachers, administrators, and parents in rural settings are accustomed to "knowing" and "knowing about" students. In fact these people may know much more about the student than the professional school counselor does because of their involvement in the rural community. School policies may not adhere to this ethical standard and counselors may be caught between school policy and the Code of Ethics.

The ACA Code of Ethics (1995) and the ASCA Ethical Standards (1998) advise that counselors avoid multiple relationships when possible. Multiple relationships provide both the counselor and the client and families with a sense of closeness, familiarity, and community, but they also can present ethical dilemmas. Meeting clients in a variety of roles and settings – at school, the store, church, the gym, the doctor's office, the bank, and so on - challenge basic ethical principles of confidentiality and the mandate to avoid multiple relationships when possible. The rural setting makes avoiding multiple relationships virtually impossible. A professional school counselor who has worked or lived in the same community for several years may be familiar with siblings, cousins, aunts, uncles, parents and grandparents of current students. It is possible that too much familiarity can compromise objectivity and challenge sound practice. High visibility, while at times a benefit, makes the analogy of "living in a fishbowl" quite applicable to the rural professional school counselor (Miller, 1994). "Particularly in small towns and rural communities it is difficult for school counselors to avoid overlap between their personal and professional lives" (Herlihy & Corey, 1997, p. 145).

The "counselor everywhere you go" (Breen & Drew, 2001) phenomenon can create an ethical dilemma by leading to stress and burnout, thus compromising good practice. The ACA Code of Ethics calls for counselors to "refrain from offering professional services … when their physical, mental, emotional problems are likely to cause harm to clients or others" (1995, C.2.g.). But, who takes over when the professional school counselor is sick?

## Strategies for Working in Rural Communities

There are many strategies available to address the needs of the rural professional school counselor. The following are designed to help deal with the isolation of working in a rural setting, understand the rural culture, enhance the limited available resources, and resolve ethical dilemmas.

### *Coping with Isolation*

*Lead the way!* The rural professional school counselor may avoid the sense of working in isolation by becoming a leader and taking responsibility for meeting the needs created by the isolation of the rural community. Worzbt and Zook (1992) suggested that professional school counselors take a leadership role, rather than a service provider role. Build networks and partnerships in your community. The proverb "it takes a village to raise a child" resonates with truth (Bunch & Gibson, 2002, p. 16). Look for opportunities *within* the rural setting to meet the needs created by the setting. Invite professionals from the community, county, state, and university or college faculty and graduate students to provide training, consultation, and services. Request that your state department of education hire counselors to work as consultants, supervisors and mentors for rural professional school counselors.

*Develop support networks.* Network with neighboring school districts. Engage in consultation and supervision. Use structured group and peer supervision models. Ask your administration to provide time and funding for supervision, mentoring and professional development. Become involved in state and regional professional counseling associations. Together, advocate for the needs of rural professional school counselors (Allen & James, 1990; Breen & Drew, 2001; McIntyre, et al., 1990; Sutton & Southworth, 1990).

### *Understanding the Rural Culture*

The rural community is unique. Getting to know and appreciate the unique aspects of rural culture will contribute to the effectiveness of the professional school counselor (Allen & James, 1990; Braucht & Weime, 1990; Breen & Drew, 2001; McIntire, et al., 1990; Sutton & Pearson, 2002; Sutton & Southworth, 1990; Worzbyt & Zook, 1992). Become involved in the community in order to learn the cultural roles, norms, biases, and issues. Volunteer in the community. Spend time talking with individuals and families in an effort to respect rural lifestyle and values. Take time to carefully plan the school counseling program for the rural setting. Administer a needs assessment to determine specific areas to address.

*Enhancing Limited Resources*

Use resources that are available in the school, local community, surrounding communities, and nearest cities (Allen & James, 1990; Braucht & Weime, 1990; Breen & Drew, 2001; Sutton & Southworth, 1990).

Think of school counseling services as a program, not a person. "Look at your school in a new light. It's an employer filled with highly qualified professionals in teaching, health services, administration and support services, transportation, and food services" (Bunch & Gibson, 2002, p. 14).

Encourage these professionals, staff, and community members to collaborate in the school counseling program. For example, enlist the help of administrators, teachers, nurses, custodians, cooks, secretaries, bus drivers, parents, grandparents, and students as peer counselors, mentors and tutors. Work with teachers to integrate developmental counseling services into the classroom curriculum.

*Use technology.* Search websites for resources. Table 1 lists several websites, some with links to other helpful programs and information.

**Table 1.**

| |
|---|
| www.counselor.org |
| www.schoolcounselor.org |
| www.apa.org |
| www.nami.org |
| www.narmh.org |
| www.nrharural.org |
| www.collegeboard.com |
| www.princetonreview.com |
| www.fafsa.ee.gov |

*Involve parents in the process.* Help parents to understand opportunities, deadlines, and expectations of career and college planning. Remember that people in rural areas are accustomed to solving their own problems – enlist their help.

*Use regional programs.* Help plan regional programs with other professional school counselors to offer greater exposure to information on health issues, careers, and colleges. Engage students in extracurricular activities that provide opportunities to interact with students from larger cities. Promote job shadowing.

*Make appropriate referrals.* Stay within your role as a professional school counselor and refer. Kuranz (2002) stated: ... the context of the school mission ... is to support academic achievement" (p. 173). Form relationships with community agencies and mental health agencies and health professionals.

In the rural community professional school counselors need to think broadly when looking for mental health referrals and support services. There is a list of ideas in Table 2.

**Table 2. Referrals and support services.**

- Physicians, physicians' assistants, nurse practitioners, community health nurses
- State and county agencies and local town offices
- Clergy and church programs
- Police and fire departments
- Funeral directors – for bereavement
- United Way programs
- Regional and county assistance programs
- School to work programs
- State and national career resource centers
- Upward Bound and Talent Search programs
- Job service offices and offices for training and development
- State offices of substance abuse prevention and intervention
- State department of behavioral health services
- Vocational rehabilitation
- Local or regional domestic violence programs and child abuse prevention programs
- Local transportation services

*Resolving Rural Ethical Dilemmas*

Keep ethical thinking in the forefront at all times. Be aware of ethical dilemmas presented by the rural setting. Provide school officials with a copy of the Codes of Ethics and educate them (Dansby-Giles, 2002).

*Clarify, define, publicize and communicate the professional school counselor role* (Herlihy & Corey, 1997). Develop and use a disclosure statement. Update job descriptions (Dansby-Giles, 2002). Educate administrators and school board members about the boundaries of competence, time and the need for ongoing training and supervision. Follow, but influence, school policies.

*Discuss multiple relationships and confidentiality.* Talk with students and their families about familiarity in the rural setting and how to handle dilemmas such as confidentiality and multiple relationships.

*Set clear boundaries.* Set limits on your work. Stay within the bounds of your competence, time, and job description. Refer! Keep the welfare of your students and their families in the forefront of your thinking, but recognize that you cannot and should not "be all things to all people."

*Follow an ethical decision-making model.* A variety of practice-based models for ethical decision-making are available. Cottone and Claus (2000) summarized and compared nine models. Table 3 is an example of an easy to use model from the work of Herlihy and Corey (1996).

*Consult and seek supervision.* Engage in regular consultation with other professionals. Use the telephone to overcome distances. Discuss ethical issues in ongoing supervision.

*Engage in professional development.* Stretch the boundaries of your competence through regular professional development. Attend workshops on ethics and ethical decision-making to stay current. Codes are revised about every five years. Use online resources for information and questions (www.counseling.org, www.schoolcounselor.org).

*Practice personal stress management.* Take care of yourself. Use your support system and do not practice when impaired.

*Purchase malpractice insurance.* Even the best professional school counselors can be accused of ethical or legal violations. Help yourself by obtaining professional liability insurance. Your professional organization offers insurance for professional school counselors. Don't assume your school liability insurance will cover you (Remley & Herlihy, 2001).

**Table 3. Ethical decision making model.**

1. Identify the problem.
2. Apply the ACA Code of Ethics.
3. Determine the nature and dimensions of the dilemma.
4. Generate potential courses of action.
5. Consider the potential consequences of all options and determine a course of action.
6. Evaluate the selected course of action.
7. Implement the course of action. (Herlihy & Corey, 1996, p.15)

## Summary/Conclusion

Unique circumstances of the rural setting present both challenges and rewards to the professional school counselor. The rewards of close relationships, a sense of community, and appreciation of what the professional has to offer contrast with challenges that come from isolation, cultural issues, limited resources, and ethical dilemmas. More than one quarter of United States public school students attend rural and small town schools. Professional school counselors play a critical role in the lives of these students. Employing effective strategies to maximize the benefits of the rural setting can help professional school counselors create school programs which truly meet the needs of rural students. Taking a leadership role, building networks, learning to value the rural culture, using the resources of the community, using technology, and practicing ethically are some of the ways that rural professional school counselors can meet the challenges and maximize the rewards.

## References

Allen, S., & James, R. (1990). A developmental guidance program for the rural schoolhouse. *The School Counselor, 37*, 184-191.

American Counseling Association. (1995). *Code of ethics and standards of practice*. Alexandria, VA: Author.

American School Counselor Association. (1998). *Ethical standards for school counselors.* Alexandria, VA: Author.

Apostal, R., & Bilden, J. (1991). Educational and occupational aspirations of rural high school students. *Journal of Career Development, 18*, 153-160.

Braucht, S., & Weime, B. (1990). Establishing a rural school counseling agenda: A multi-agency needs-assessment model. *The School Counselor, 37*, 179-183.

Breen, D., & Drew, D. (2001, September). *Interviews with rural school counselors.* Paper presented at the meeting of the North Atlantic Association for Counselor Education and Supervision, Amherst, MA.

Bunch, C., & Gibson, M. J. (2002). School-to-career models: Some assembly (and assistance) required. *ASCA School Counselor, 39*(4), 12-17.

Cottone, R. R., & Claus, R. E. (2000). Ethical decision-making models: A review of the literature. *Journal of Counseling and Development, 78*, 275-283.

Dansby-Giles, G. (2002). Ethics: Handling requests for confidential information is not always as simple as black and white. *ASCA School Counselor, 39*(3), 22-25.

Herlihy, B., & Corey, G. (1996). *Ethical standards casebook* (5th ed.). Alexandria, VA: American Counseling Association.

Herlihy, B., & Corey, G. (1997). *Boundary issues in counseling. Multiple roles and responsibilities.* Alexandria, VA: American Counseling Association.

Kuranz, M. (2002). Cultivating student potential. *Professional School Counseling, 5*, 172-179.

McIntire, W. G., Marion, S. F., & Quaglia, R. (1990). Rural school counselors: Their communities and schools. *The School Counselor, 37*, 166-172.

Miller, P. J. (1994). Dual relationships in rural practice: A dilemma of ethics and culture. *Human Services in the Rural Environment, 18*(2), 4-7.

National Institute of Mental Health (2000). *Rural mental health research fact sheet.* Bethesda, MD. NIH Publication No. 00-4741.

Remley, T. P., & Herlihy, B. (2001). *Ethical, legal, and professional issues in counseling.* Upper Saddle River, NJ: Prentice-Hall.

Sutton, J. M., & Pearson, R. (2002). The practice of school counseling in rural and small town schools. *Professional School Counseling, 5*, 266-276.

Sutton, J. M., & Southworth, R. S. (1990). The effect of the rural setting on school counselors. *The School Counselor, 37*, 173-178.

Sweeney, T. J. (1971). Rural poor students and guidance. *Guidance Monograph Series, Series VI: Minority Groups and Guidance.* Boston, MA: Houghton Mifflin.

Worzbyt, J. C., & Zook, T. (1992). Counselors who make a difference: Small schools and rural settings. *The School Counselor, 39*, 344-350.

# *Section 7*

# Special Issues in School Counseling

# Chapter 79

# Why School Counselors Need to Understand the Magnitude of the Problem of "Unfocused Kids"

*Suzy Mygatt Wakefield*

## Preview

This chapter offers insight into the magnitude of the issue of "unfocused kids." These are students who demonstrate an unwillingness or inability to focus on school and understand how their progress and choices while in school contribute to their options after high school. Many influences distract high school students from achieving their potential: distracting peer influence and excessive socializing, long working hours, and/or over-involvement in non-academic activities. These "unfocused kids" seem to be an American phenomenon, and often, without adequate support, are allowed to follow "the path of least resistance."

## What Is Going on Behind the Scenes to Produce So Many "Unfocused Kids"?

> Two decades ago, a teacher in an average high school in this country could expect to have three or four 'difficult' students in a class of thirty. Today, teachers in these same schools are expected to teach to classrooms in which nearly half of the students are uninterested. (Steinberg, 1996, p. 184)

Fundamentally, "unfocused kids" are students who appear to have done very little purposeful thinking about why they are in school (except to socialize and "get by" with minimum effort). They also appear to have put little thought into what they want to do with their lives, as far as planning ahead. They tend to go through high school without a clear sense of educational focus or purpose. Most do at least the minimum to stay on track toward graduation, although dropout statistics tell us that many do not even do that (Bylsma & Ireland, 2002; Greene, 2002; Mortenson, 2001). They do not appear to connect what they are learning in school with what really matters to them—their lives outside of school. Many have apparently lost hope in school's value for them (Snyder, Feldman, Shorey & Rand, 2002). If they do not see value in what they are learning in terms of their personal goals, they appear to expend minimum effort, becoming academic underachievers. Brophy (1998) describes student motivation as "the degree to which students invest attention and effort in various pursuits, which may or may not be the ones desired by their teachers" (p. 3). Not only do unfocused, unmotivated students appear to invest little effort in pursuits having to do with their formal schooling, but they may also show little interest in career guidance activities, as they do not see their relevance.

There may be other reasons that students do not focus on their plans after high school or make little connection to their future. They may come from homes where preoccupied parents or guardians spend little time helping them think through their future plans, let alone take an interest in their grades, their friends, and their activities. These teens may not feel that anyone really cares; the adults around them may appear to be so busy that they do not take time to sit down with their teens and help them think through their options. Adults often counter that it's the "school's responsibility" to provide career guidance. As Schneider and Stevenson (1999) point out, parents believe that " . . . the major responsibility for helping adolescents select a career path and take the appropriate steps to get there rests with the school" (p. 165). On the other hand, teens may be resistant or just indifferent to any efforts adults do offer to help them think about their futures. They themselves may be so busy, with going to school, socializing with their friends, involvement in after-school activities, and work responsibilities that they simply have little time left over to sit down and think about their plans, let alone talk them over with someone else. They may not even think their thoughts about their future are worthy of someone else's time so they are reluctant to discuss them. If there is no comprehensive career exploration and planning program at their school for all students, the problem is compounded.

One wonders, when looking in on a typical American classroom, why some students appear focused and purposefully occupied with the teacher and classroom activities, while others seem so unfocused and preoccupied. They may pass notes to their friends, or stare into space, or simply sleep at their desks. *In this country of remarkable opportunity, what is going on? How is it that we have so many adolescents in high school who appear so disengaged and unfocused?* Even educators with many years of experience appear to be puzzled about this strange reality.

Laurence Steinberg, in his book *Beyond the Classroom—Why School Reform Has Failed and What Parents Need to Do* (1996), has provided considerable insight as to what is going on behind the scenes. His fundamental premise is that we cannot reform public school education in this country by simply analyzing and revitalizing how teachers teach and what curriculum is taught. Steinberg (1996, p. 184) suggests that it is student motivation and attitude that has changed.

> The achievement problem we face in the country is due not to a drop in the intelligence or basic intellectual capability of our children, but to a widespread decline in children's interest in education and in their motivation to achieve in the classroom; it is a problem of attitude and effort, not ability . . . Our findings suggest that the sorry state of American student achievement is due more to the conditions of students' lives outside of school than it is to what takes place within school walls.

He suggests that the forces on students *outside of school* must be considered; they usually are not. Based on extensive research involving Temple University, Stanford, and the University of Wisconsin, with two years of planning and pilot testing, four years of data collection and another four years of data analysis, a team of researchers (including psychologists, sociologists, psychiatrists, and educational researchers), studied more than 20,000 teenagers and their families in nine very different but reasonably typical school districts (none were extreme or atypical) in two states (California and Wisconsin) during 1987-88, 1988-89, and 1989-90. The students were not necessarily high risk or exceptional in any way. They were typical of American teens everywhere. (The entire research project took ten years to complete.)

The results of this comprehensive study of outside-of-school variables indicated that many forces may be at play simultaneously in the lives of teens. These include: the effect of *parenting styles* (i.e., authoritarian, permissive, authoritative, and disengaged or "checked out"); *students' own healthy and unhealthy achievement attributional styles* (that is, some students may see their achievements as a result of hard work and consistent effort, which is a healthy attributional style—incorporating variables under their control, while others may see their occasional good grades as a result of luck, a favorable teacher, an easy assignment, or their native intelligence—that is, an unhealthy attributional style based on variables not under their control); the *positive and negative impact of peer cultures; the adverse impact of working more than 20 hours per week*; and *the constant pressure on American adolescents to be involved in many activities at the same time*, besides keeping up and/or excelling in their classes. In all, it is suggested that these variables combine to make our students far less competitive in the global marketplace than their Asian and European counterparts, who, in the aggregate, must prioritize school, take a much longer school day, (including attending school on Saturdays), take more difficult academic subjects, spend more time studying, work very few hours outside of school, and limit their socializing. Many American teens would undoubtedly find these expectations and limitations unpleasant, if not downright intolerable. To be sure, there are also many teens who work very hard in school, taking highly demanding courses, planning their curriculum pathways carefully, putting in long hours of homework night after night, limiting work hours to week-end down time, and achieving to their potential, but this chapter is about the other students—who are not so inclined.

Regarding the number of hours American high school students work, the Education Trust (2001) reports that:

> The amount of time students spend at work, particularly in the senior year, is a uniquely American phenomenon. More than half of US twelfth graders (55 percent) report working three or more hours daily at a paid job, three times the international average. No other advanced country expects students to work, or permits them to work long hours at low-skill jobs just to earn spending money. (p. 6)

Clearly, working long hours is a detriment to most students' ability to excel in their class work in school. Steinberg (p. 19) reports that "More than one-third of students who work say they take easier classes so that their job won't hurt their grades." Students in other industrialized nations seem to have more restricted work hours, and put in considerably more time on their homework (four hours a *day*, instead of four hours a week), which would contribute substantially to their being able to focus much more on academic achievement.

Steinberg (1996) discusses the construct of "engagement," which is:

> the degree to which students are psychologically 'connected' to what is going on in their classes ... .When highly engaged students are in class, they are there emotionally as well as physically. They concentrate on the task at hand, they strive to do their best when tested or called upon, and when they are given homework or other outside assignments, they do them on time and in good faith. They participate actively in class discussions, think about the material covered in their course, and genuinely care about the quality of their work. (p. 15)

Disengaged students present quite a different picture, as many public educators in America can tell you. Disengaged students do what they need to do to stay out of trouble and to get by, exerting minimum effort in class and doing little homework. According to Steinberg (1996):

> They have a jaded, often cavalier attitude toward education and its importance to their future success or personal development. When disengaged students are in school, they are clearly just going through the motions. When they are not in school, school is the last thing on their mind. (p. 15)

Steinberg (1996) further suggests that about 40 percent of students are just going through the motions of going to school: "According to their own reports, between one-third and 40 percent of students say that when they are in class, they are neither trying very hard nor paying attention" (p. 67).

## The Importance of Parents on Student Achievement

The contrast between engaged and disengaged students is stark. One wonders how we have spawned an entire population of disengaged students in many of our public high schools. What forces could be operating on these adolescents? To summarize, Steinberg's major findings are that: a high proportion of students do not take school seriously; considerable time is spent on socializing with peers; time is spent on out-of-school activities that do not reinforce what is being learned in school; Black and Hispanic adolescent peer cultures tends to devalue achievement in school as it is tantamount to selling out to white middle class values (Steinberg, 1996, p. 158) with the exception of the Asian peer culture that helps peers to succeed in school; and many American parents are just as disengaged from school as are their teens.

This last finding is particularly insightful as Steinberg (1996) details four parenting styles: *authoritarian* (rigid, strict, and controlling); *permissive* (accepting, indulgent, and lenient); *authoritative* (accepting, firm, and supportive of developing a child's independence); and *disengaged* (emotionally aloof, and uninvolved with their teen's progress in school, their spare time activities, or their friends). Steinberg speculates that 25-30 percent of parents are in this last category, which results in so many students being absent from school and eventually dropping out. To determine parenting attitudes, the researchers asked probing questions to assess how involved parents were in various aspects of their child's life—their spare time activities, their friends, and so forth. It is an interesting coincidence that some researchers suggest that our high school dropout rate is about 30 percent (Greene, 2002; Mortenson, 2001), reflecting almost exactly the percentage of disengaged parents determined by Steinberg. As high school counselors, teachers, or administrators, it is easy for us to assume that *most* parents are involved with their teens as so many seem to contact the school. In fact, some parents never do! Steinberg tells us that "only about one-fifth of parents consistently attend school programs. More than 40 percent *never* do" (p. 20). Steinberg also shares that research shows over and over, if parents are involved with their teens, their students do better in school. A key reason is that:

> acceptance seems to matter most for children's overall adjustment and sense of self-worth; because they feel loved, they feel lovable. As a result, children who feel valued and supported by their parents have higher self-esteem, more positive self-conceptions, and a happier, more enthusiastic outlook on life. Not surprisingly, they are more sociable and more socially skilled. (p. 109)

When parents are involved, their teens feel accepted and valued. Quattrociocchi (2000) frequently emphasizes this point in her writing and presentations to educators and parents by pointing out that "research shows that parental involvement is the single greatest factor in determining student success. Teens with highly involved families are three times more likely than their peers to earn a bachelor's degree or to complete other post-secondary programs" (p. 2).

## Other Influences on Achievement: Peer Groups, Work Hours, and Multiple Activities

> Nearly 20 percent of all students say they do not try as hard as they can in high school because they are worried about what their friends might think. (Steinberg, 1996, p. 19)

As remarkable as this finding may appear, many educators and parents are aware of this negative peer influence on American students. Steinberg (1996) found that peer groups could have both a positive and a negative effect on student achievement, and that teens are particularly vulnerable to peer influence between the ages of 12-16. When looking at peer influence in all four predominant peer groups (Asian, White, Black and Hispanic), Steinberg found that:

> Specifically, Asian students' friends have higher performance standards (that is, they hold tougher standards for what grades are acceptable), spend more time on homework, are more committed to education, and earn considerably higher grades in school. Black and Hispanic students' friends earn lower grades, spend less time on their studies, and have substantially lower performance standards. White students' friends fall somewhere between these two extremes on these various indicators. (p. 157)

Steinberg (1996) has further found that in Asian peer groups, students frequently turn to each other for academic support and consultation in their classes while this is rarely done in white, Black, or Hispanic peer groups. In fact, the opposite appears to be true for Black and Latino students, "who are far more likely than other students to find themselves in peer groups that actually devalue academic accomplishment" (p. 158). The reason is that scholastic success is equated with "selling out" one's ethnic and cultural identity to White, middle class values.

Working long hours may be detrimental to school achievement, particularly if students work more than 20 hours per week, according to Steinberg (1996). Students who work long hours often do not have the energy left over to focus on their classes and class assignments, as educators are acutely aware. Most students do not, in fact, work to save for college but tend to spend the money on their personal expenses. Worse, most students are not engaged in jobs that will help them explore a potential career interest. Steinberg makes the distinction that it is not working that is detrimental to academic achievement but the number of hours worked (p. 169):

> It has become clear from our research, as well as a host of other studies, that the key issue is not whether a student works, but how much time he or she devotes to a job. Working for more than 20 hours per week is likely to be harmful, but working for less than 10 hours per week does not seem to take a consistent toll on school performance.

Further, very few jobs offer training that will be transferable to adult jobs as most teens work in restaurants, supermarkets, and retail stores. Steinberg gives a grim picture of employers' stranglehold on teenage workers, indicating that some major employers of teenagers lobby assiduously to keep child labor laws flexible; they also wage a public relations campaign "designed to convince American parents and students that adolescents somehow reap characterological, if not moral, benefits from spending their afternoons and evenings flipping hamburgers, stuffing burritos, and operating cash registers" (p. 167). Teens may receive little support from employers when asked to work longer hours than is beneficial for their progress in school, although a number of American employers may be sensitive to students' academic demands and limit their job responsibilities accordingly.

State laws may serve to restrict students' working hours somewhat. Normally a 16- or 17-year old cannot work more than 20 hours per week, without a signed variance (by a parent, a school official, and the employer), but variances for working 40 or more hours a week are granted. According to the Department of Labor and Industries in Washington State:

> For 16- and 17-year old students who want or need to work more than four hours a day and 20 hours per week, there is a special variance. The variance requires approval by the student's employer, parent, and school. The maximum is 28 hours a week, 6-hour shift lengths and limited to 16- and 17-year-olds during the school year in non-agriculture employment . . . Additional variances may be granted by Labor and Industries. The request for a standard variance

> is originated by the employer. The variances can be granted up to and beyond 40 hours a week, 8-hour shift lengths and start and finish times during school and non-school weeks. (Department of Labor and Industries Brochure—*Teen Workers*)

Another powerful force on teens is the pressure to participate in multiple activities. Some teens are involved in so many activities, particularly athletic activities, that their schoolwork suffers. Practice before and after school not only uses valuable study time but may leave a student exhausted and unable to concentrate on difficult academic material. Students and their coaches need to be honest about what makes up a reasonable amount of participation, although some coaches highly encourage and expect strong academic achievement, and students may be given team awards for their collective outstanding academic achievement by their local and state athletic associations. In Washington State, the Washington Interscholastic Activities Association (W.I.A.A.) makes these team awards possible. Teams with the highest cumulative grade point averages are honored by the state association. Coaches are encouraged to send in their team members' grades; the cumulative grade point averages of winning teams are made known to the public, thus encouraging academic achievement throughout the sports programs (*WIAA 2002-2003 Handbook).*

American high school students are known for spending a lot of time socializing with their friends, in addition to being involved in multiple activities and/or working long hours. It adds up. The national average for time spent on homework, according to Steinberg (1996) is less than five hours per week, hardly competitive with European and Asian adolescents. Recently in Seattle, Nathan Hale High School administrators decided to start school one hour later, from 7:45 AM to 8:45 AM, so that students could get an extra hour of sleep. However, the change ran into resistance as many were concerned that "team sports, such as baseball and fast-pitch softball, will not have enough daylight to finish their games, or that they will conflict with classes" (Jensen, 2003). Many students choose to play a sport each season. Many teams require a minimum grade point average or a passing grade in four or more classes for students to qualify to stay on the team through the season, but sports, like other activities, may take away from needed study time. It's all a matter of priorities. Further, many students feel pressured to list multiple activities on their résumés to be competitive as candidates for selective college admission. Some American high school students seem to want to do it all (sports and/or other school activities, and part-time work) at the expense of excelling in their academic classes.

## Lack of Planned, Sequential Career Development Programs

Further, at school, there may not be planned, comprehensive career development programs, integrated at each grade level, to help students think about, identify, and articulate their strengths, interests, and values and to explore the many occupational options in the world of work. Or students may find that the career guidance programs are so few and far between that it is difficult to maintain a sense of continuity between one career presentation and the next. Students may be further discouraged as they may have no mechanism, such as an education and career plan, or a career planning portfolio, in which to keep their assignments, papers, and notes. The career guidance program may appear disorganized in many high schools, with no clear guidelines or activities expected of all students. Gysbers (2001) addresses this concern with his vision:

> My vision for guidance and counseling in the 21st century is fully implemented comprehensive guidance and counseling programs in every school district in the United States, serving all students and their parents, staffed by active, involved school counselors. When guidance and counseling is conceptualized, organized, and implemented as a program, it places school

> counselors conceptually and structurally in the center of education and makes it possible for them to be active and involved. As a result, guidance and counseling becomes an integral and transformative program, not a marginal and supplemental activity. It provides school counselors with the structure, time, and resources to fully use their expertise. (p. 103)

Kuranz (2002) reports that according to ASCA (the American School Counselor Association) "the average U.S. student-to-counselor ratio is 551:1." With ratios that high, it is virtually impossible for school counselors alone, without the help of other appropriate educators, to provide substantive, systematic, and sequential career guidance activities for all students. The high student-counselor ratios demonstrate the obvious need for sharing this responsibility with appropriate others. National leaders in the American School Counselor Association (Campbell & Dahir, 1997; Dahir, Sheldon & Valiga, 1998) have developed the *ASCA National Standards*, student content standards for school counseling programs in the areas of academic, career, and personal/social development. The ASCA National Standards in career development are:

A) Students will acquire the skills to investigate the world of work in relation to knowledge of self and to make informed career decisions.
B) Students will employ strategies to achieve future career success and satisfaction.
C) Students will understand the relationship among personal qualities, education and training, and the world of work. (Campbell & Dahir, 1997, p. 17)

ASCA has developed the *ASCA National Model: A Framework for School Counseling Programs* (ASCA, 2003), which incorporates a delivery system (for guidance curriculum) with integrated management and accountability systems. According to Bowers and Hatch (2002),

> Historically, many school counselors spent much of their time responding to the needs of a small percentage of their students, typically the high achieving or high risk. The *National Model for School Counseling Programs* recommends the majority of the school counselor's time be spent in direct service to all students so that every student receives the program benefits.

It is hoped that, in schools in which these standards and model are put into place, that all students will be provided with age-appropriate, sequential, and meaningful career development activities. These carefully planned activities, based on the assessed needs of students, should help them with their career exploration, educational planning and goal-setting, and their academic and technical preparation—for their postsecondary education and workplace endeavors.

### The "Academic Middle" and High School and College Dropout Rates

In high schools across the country, many students may receive little in the way of career guidance and educational planning. Sadly, a testimony to this lack of career guidance programming is our alleged public high school dropout rate of approximately one in three students (Greene, 2002; Mortenson, 2001), or one in four (Isaacson & Brown, 2000, p. 269), depending on the source. Using the cohort group of students in grades 9-12, a dropout rate of one in three means that for every three ninth graders, only two will graduate from high school four years later. The national college dropout rate is about the same: in the aggregate, one in three freshmen does not return for their sophomore year (ACT, 2002). For university level students, the dropout rate is about one in four. The dropout rate in public community and technical colleges after one year is almost one in two (ACT, 2002)! These are disturbing figures, indicating that even many of our college-bound young people do not spend enough time thinking about and planning carefully for their futures, both educationally and financially.

A further testimonial to this issue is the number of students who need to take remedial courses when they get to college—up to 40 percent. "In a district-sponsored follow-up study of the class of 2002, 35 percent of respondents said they had taken a remedial reading class in college and 38 percent said they took one in math" (Solomon, 2003). The colleges and universities must then compensate (with remedial programs) for students' weak academic preparation in reading and math as demonstrated on freshmen placement tests.

Weak academic preparation for college is corroborated by Gray and Herr (1995), who suggest that many students from the "academic middle" are encouraged to enter college when they do not really have the strength of academic preparation needed, despite the fact that they have taken "honors" or college-preparatory classes. It seems that students in the academic middle are enrolled in honors classes that do not really prepare them for the rigors of college level work. These researchers attribute our high college dropout rate to the "the right to try/the right to fail" phenomenon that, in turn, creates a sort of massive social inefficiency.

In most countries, the idea of supporting the attendance of large numbers of youth in college who do not have the academic ability and/or preparation to be successful would be unimaginable, and dropout rates of 50% would be intolerable. But this belief is not shared in the United States, at least not yet. Why? First, until recently, the United States was perhaps the only nation that could afford these social inefficiencies. Second, this situation is tolerated because of a basic value that career development specialist Ken Hoyt (1994) calls "the right to try" and the "right to fail." That '1 in 100' individual who "battles the odds" and succeeds despite a poor high school record seems always to be in the back of the minds of Americans.

Gray and Herr (1995) further share that "Because of open admissions, getting into college is relatively easy, whereas graduating is not. Only about half who matriculate ever graduate in 6 years" (p.109). The other half leave college, often in debt, to look for something else. Krumboltz and Worthington (1999) offer the notion that "floundering" (when students drop out) is not necessarily bad. "Much valuable learning occurs in the trial-and-error work experiences that occur during this interval. However, the learning is haphazard and sometimes results in the learning of self-defeating attitudes and habits" (p. 314). Some students drop out of college when they run out of financial support (often with a loan obligation) and/or realize they have merely acquiesced to the wishes of others. They may realize that they need to think for themselves and make their own way, which may be to work full-time or go into the military, fundamentally to get a chance to mature and to re-evaluate their goals. These students, who have had time to align their ambitions, may return some years later with a much stronger sense of their own commitment and purpose.

### Having Aligned, Misaligned or No Clear Ambitions at All

At some level, however, all of our young people do grapple with what they want to do with their lives. They do give some thought about what they want to become—what skills they would like to develop, how they want to earn money, and what sort of lifestyle and friends they would like to have. Some, who have put in a lot of time thinking about their futures, have well-defined goals and realistic plans involving the amount of education and training needed to reach their goals. Schneider and Stevenson (1999) have coined the useful term "aligned ambitions." They would describe these students as having aligned ambitions as they know what goals they want to pursue and have a realistic understanding of the educational pathways required to attain them. Others have well-defined goals but have unrealistic plans about how to achieve them. These students would be described as having "misaligned ambitions." They have articulated goals but erroneous information about how to achieve them. For example, a student who wants to become an attorney might assume that a Master's Degree is required and not understand the requirement of three years of law school, culminating with passing the state bar exam.

Still other young people have very unclear goals; some teens appear to have almost no goals or ambitions that they can articulate. From casual observation, it appears that left unattended, without guidance, this last group of young people will tend to take the "path of least resistance." They will do what makes the most sense to them in their perception of how the world works, from the way they see things. This, of course, may not be the way the world really works, but their unique (and possibly distorted) perceptions will dictate their behavior.

## Limited Choice Repertoire

Capuzzi and Gross (1989) suggest that young people who make poor decisions about their lives make choices from their "limited choice repertoire." They report that it is "their selected way of coping with the myriad challenges placed in their path that differentiates at-risk individuals from their peers" (p. 11). Capuzzi and Gross add that their personal circumstances, over which they have little or no control, may impinge greatly on their ability to complete school. These circumstances might include: a dysfunctional, destructive and/or abusive family environment; low family income forcing the student to work; and/or marginal academic ability. These at-risk young people tend to choose what gives them an immediate solution, instead of considering a range of alternatives or soliciting different advice from different people. That is, they demonstrate limited decision-making ability, a lack of significant persons they can go to for help and advice, and/or limited ability to model successful coping strategies demonstrated by others. Their limited choice repertoire is partly due to a lack of information; they are unaware of the range of choices they have and do not take adequate time to research their options.

Another term for a dysfunctional decision-making style is that of foreclosure—making choices too soon without considering enough appropriate alternatives. A purpose of career development in elementary grades, as well as in the secondary grades, is to help students "avoid premature foreclosure of choices based on inaccurate, incomplete, or biased information and stereotypes" (Herr, 1997). When disengaged, unfocused teens come to high school (which is increasingly more academically difficult for them than were the lower grades) and find that there is really nothing there for them, in terms of their own interests or goals, many choose to leave the public school system, as it is the path of least resistance. It is often reported that many students drop out in their senior year, as is true in the state of Washington, given that only 71.9 percent of seniors at the beginning of the school year in September, 2000, graduated in the spring of 2001. Bylsma & Ireland (2002) confirmed that "grade 12 experienced the largest annual dropout rate."

Reasons given for dropping out, reported in *Graduation and Dropout Statistics for Washington's Counties, Districts, and Schools Final Report, School Year 2001- 2002*, include the following: "expelled or suspended, poor grades, school not for me/stayed home, married and needed to support family, pregnant or had a baby, offered training, chose to work, or other" (Bylsma & Ireland, 2002, p. 9). By far, the greatest number of students who dropped out in their senior year reported "attended 4 years, did not continue." One can speculate why this occurs. As students realize that they have fallen too far behind in credits to graduate with their friends, they opt to leave school before embarrassing themselves with this eventuality. At least, they can get a job, earn money, and do some of the things they want to do. Hoyt (2001) reports that approximately 22 million of the anticipated 50 million new jobs between the years 1996-2006 will only require 2 to 3 weeks of short-term, on-the-job training, so low-skilled, low wage, dead end jobs abound in the American economy. The downside for young people leaving school for these jobs, if that is what they are leaving for, is that these jobs do not usually provide a living wage; students must pursue further education and training if they wish to qualify for higher paying jobs. One's level of education is closely related to a lifetime salary, as the National

Dropout Prevention Center Network points out. Dropouts earn substantially less than those with some college or further training, as the following shows:

> Education is important to employees and employers. Workers without a high school diploma earn approximately $852,000 over a 40-year career. This is $672,000 less than those with an associate degree. A bachelor's degree can increase earning more than $1.9 million over a 40-year period, and a doctorate or professional degree can add more that $2.8 million. (Dolin, 2001, as cited on the National Dropout Prevention Center/Network)

## The Path of Least Resistance

Fritz (1984) gives us a conceptual framework for the path of least resistance. His insights are particularly helpful when working with these young, unfocused students. Fritz uses the metaphor of the river and suggests that, "You are like a river. You go through life taking the path of least resistance." He indicates that it is the layout of a riverbed across a terrain that determines the flow of the river.

> If a riverbed remains unchanged, the water will continue to flow along the path it always has, since that is the most natural route for it to take. If the underlying structures of your life remain unchanged, the greatest tendency is for you to follow the same direction your life has always taken... (p. 5)

This metaphor applies to unfocused young people, who tend to follow the path of least resistance unless there is some sort of intervention that changes the "underlying structure" of their lives. As engineers might excavate a new riverbed to redirect the flow of a river, so educators (and parents) need to support and redirect disengaged young people to help them take charge of the direction of their lives in more productive and positive ways.

## The Relationship Between an Inadequate Education and Poverty

School is academically challenging, and for many (given their state of readiness to learn), too challenging. Adelman and Taylor (2002) report disturbing findings across the country when they surveyed teachers with the question, "Most days, how many of your students come to class motivationally ready and able to learn?" Their results indicated that,

> In urban and rural schools serving economically disadvantaged families, teachers tell us they are lucky if 10 percent to 15 percent of their students fall into this group. In surburbia, teachers usually say 75 percent fit that profile. It is not surprising, therefore, that teachers are continuously asking for help in dealing with problems. (p. 235)

These are disturbing findings, showing the basis of why so many students may ultimately drop out of school, if there are no safety nets (i.e., remedial courses, small classes, alternative programs, adult mentors, tutoring) in place to help keep them in school. Adelman and Taylor (2002) further report that,

> The litany of barriers is all too familiar to anyone who lives or works in communities where families struggle with low income. In such neighborhoods, school and community resources often are insufficient for providing the basic opportunities (never mind enrichment activities) found in higher income communities. (p. 236)

Dropout rates are about the same for males and females but are higher for students from different ethnic groups and for students from disadvantaged backgrounds (U.S Dept. of Education/ *Consumer Guide*, 1996). According to the National Center for Educational Statistics (NCES, 2001),

> In 1999, young adults living in families with incomes in the lowest 20 percent of all family incomes were five times as likely as their peers from families in the top 20 percent of the income distribution to drop out of high school.

Put another way, according to NCES (1996):

> The annual event dropout rates for students with family incomes in the lowest 20 percent of the family income distribution range from 4.5 to 11 times the dropout rates recorded for students with family incomes in the top 20 percent of the family income distribution.

These are concerning data from NCES, clearly demonstrating the relationship between income and schooling. Those in the higher income brackets have a far better chance of completing their high school education. From this information, one can infer that income is a greater predictor of high school completion than is ethnicity.

## The Working Poor

*The New York Times* (Pear, 2002) ran a headline recently declaring "Number of People Living in Poverty Increases in U.S." According to the Census Bureau, "Of the 32.9 million poor people in the United States last year, 11.7 million were under 18, and 3.4 million were 65 or older." According to this source, poor people, or the working poor, are defined in this way:

> A family of four was classified as poor if it had cash income less than $18,104 last year. The official poverty levels, updated each year to reflect changes in the Consumer Price Index, were $14,128 for a family of three, $11,569 for a married couple, and $9,039 for an individual.

It is important to make the connection between the number of students who drop out of school who then may become part of the working poor, thus contributing to the poverty rates in this country. We are presumably losing one out of three students from our public school system from grades 9 through 12 (Mortenson, 2001; Greene, 2002), although some believe that we are losing only one in four (Isaacson & Brown, 2000, p. 269), as was true about 20 years ago. Either way, we are losing *far too many* students from the public education system.

Herbert (2002), a New York Times writer, reflected on Barbara Ehrenreich's book *Nickel and Dimed: On (Not) Getting by in America,* which captures the frustration of adults who cannot earn above the minimum wage (or poverty) level.

> The poor are pretty well hidden from everyone except each other in the United States. You won't find them in the same neighborhoods or the same schools as the well-to-do. They're not on television, except for the local crime-casts. . . Hiding the poor has been quite a trick, because there are still millions upon millions of them out here . . . (p. 7)

As is widely recognized, adults and their children living at the poverty level may not have enough food, even with food stamps, or be able to get needed medical care. They may be evicted from their housing, and their utilities may be disconnected. Many adults, locked in at minimum wages due to their low skills, must work two or three jobs, on evenings and week-ends, to try to make ends meet. This is reality for millions of adult Americans.

## Boomerang Effect—"Adultolescents"

We have a relatively new phenomenon in this country—the phenomenon of "adultolescents." These are young people who choose (and are allowed) to remain with their parents or guardians, after most of their peers have chosen to be on their own. Many parents and guardians believe that if their graduating seniors "go off to college," or a postsecondary training program (assuming that they even graduate from high school), that their futures will be somewhat secure. Some parents then experience a sort of "boomerang effect"—their youngsters leave home to attend college only to return after a year or so to live at home again, while they are sorting out their priorities. Adultolescents—young adults still living at home—were featured recently in *Newsweek* (Tyre, 2002), which reports that there are four million young adults, ages 25-34, living with their parents:

> Whether it's reconverting the guest room back into a bedroom, paying for graduate school, writing a blizzard of small checks to cover rent and health-insurance premiums or acting as career counselors, parents across the country are trying to provide their twenty-somethings with the tools they'll need to be self-sufficient—someday. In the process, they have created a whole new breed of child—the adultolescent" . . . Relying on your folks to light the shadowy path to the future has become so accepted that even the ultimate loser move—returning home to live with your parents—has lost its stigma. (p. 39)

## Conclusion

*A Call for Action—What Needs to Be Done?*

*Acknowledgment of problem of "Unfocused Kids."* Professional school counselors need to be aware of the *magnitude* of the problem of "unfocused kids." Usually, in any public school, many students are "unfocused:" they do not see the connection between what they are doing in school and how they are preparing a foundation for their lives after high school. Students who do not develop a plan for their education and goals tend to apply minimum effort and just get by. Many even drop out—as many as one out of three! The phenomenon of "unfocused kids" is not isolated; it is commonplace. Students who skip school report that "their number one reason why they skipped school was that they were discouraged about being behind" (Houtz & Shaw, 2003). The reason many students drop out of school is that they are discouraged about being behind—in credits toward graduation. The highest dropout rate occurs in the senior year of high school (Bylsma & Ireland, 2002). School counselors need to understand the impact of this phenomenon; discouraged students leave school not only unprepared academically and vocationally, but also they leave without a plan to continue their training and further develop their goals. For high school dropouts, this is a double loss. No diploma. No plan.

*Why is this particularly a problem with American students?* Laurence Steinberg, in his book *Beyond the Classroom, Why School Reform Has Failed and What Parents Need to Do* (1996), has brought to light a number of factors contributing to low achievement: disengaged parents (which he estimates to be as high as thirty percent of parents); time spent on socializing; negative peer influence—particularly among Black and Hispanic groups, if they tend to devalue academic accomplishment as being tantamount to "selling out" to white, middle class values; long work hours; and involvement in multiple, non-academic activities. Steinberg (p. 182) reports that "to European and Asian parents, school is the defining activity of both childhood and adolescence. Everything else comes second." And worse, Steinberg (p. 19) reports that "the average American high school student spends about four hours per week on homework outside of school. In other industrialized countries, the average is about four hours per *day*." This is an astonishing contrast! No wonder our students struggle so much in competing with their international counterparts. Zuckerman, editor-in-chief of *U.S. News and World Report,* shares the following news about international competition for jobs:

> What's going on here? Well, clearly international competition and outsourcing have hit some sectors hard. In the past decade, China became the world's workshop. In this decade, India is becoming the world's back office. Cheap bandwidth and the Internet permit companies to tap into a huge supply of English-speaking workers, happy to take knowledge-based jobs for 10 to 20 percent of what American employees receive. 'Offshoring' is moving up the food chain of services to include professions like engineering, design, accounting, legal work, actuarial and insurance work, medical services, and financial analysis. (2004, p. 68)

So, where does this leave our students? It leaves them with a more competitive marketplace than ever, and a more urgent need than ever before to develop an education and career plan, take courses judiciously, do as well as they can, and prepare for the next step in their educational program. Otherwise, they will default to entry-level, unskilled work with low pay.

Unfocused, disengaged students need extra support in developing their future plans—from professional school counselors, teachers, and their parents/guardians. As suggested, some may end up as young adults ("adultolescents"), living at home long after most of their peers have moved out on their own. Unfocused young people need adults who care about them and who will take the needed time to guide them, one-on-one. (This is the most effective form of help.) While they are in school, they may need help with placing limitations on their work hours and participation in non-academic activities. They may need help with study skills and understanding that they are in control of their academic achievement. That is, their achievement level is not dependent on luck but is related to factors under their control—the amount of time they are willing to study and do their assignments, and the willingness to get help when they need it, instead of just ignoring the problem. (Unfocused students need to be *encouraged* to get help when they feel they need it, as they tend to "sweep their learning difficulties under the rug," as the saying goes.) They also need to understand that they will have the opportunity to work for wages for many years; high school, by contrast, is fleeting. For students who do not see the value of high school, they need to be encouraged to see the connections between what they want to do and the training/education needed to do it.

*Interventions that can help students to become more focused.* Students need to be encouraged to consider technical training, as the world of work is filled with technical jobs, often requiring two years of technical training or less. Hoyt (2001) shares that there are more than 100,000-300,000 college graduates a year than there are jobs requiring a college degree! Gray and Herr (1995) report that, "technical workers are the fastest-growing and economically most promising segment in the labor force," and "the largest number and fastest growing group of jobs among technical workers can be trained for at the 2-year associate degree level" (p. 109). Students can learn at home, if they have the self-discipline to sit in front of a computer for long periods of time, as on-line "distance learning" technical training programs are available.

*Ideas generated by Authors in the Book, "Unfocused Kids: Helping Students to Focus on their Education and Career Plans."*

Many useful approaches are thoughtfully presented in this book to help educators (and parents) help young people with their educational and career planning (Wakefield, 2004). Topics covered include:

- Societal Trends and Workplace Issues;
- Comprehensive School Counseling Programs;
- Project-Based Career Guidance Models;
- Innovative Approaches to Workplace Training;
- Games, Models and Activities;
- Innovative Career Development Practices for Special Populations;
- Internet Delivery Systems in Career Guidance.

Essentially, this book has something for everyone, including specific ideas in working with parents, how the ASCA Standards can be implemented using the template of the ASCA *National Model*, changes in the workplace from the old pyramid to the new diamond-shape (which does not utilize any unskilled workers), newly developed O*NET and electronic portfolios, the value of teaching employability skills and how districts are combining many ideas in their new comprehensive career guidance programs. This book is virtually encyclopedic in its coverage, so readers are encouraged to look at chapters of their own particular interest. The information is current, and, hopefully, interesting and useful to you.

*Why School-Wide Systemic Change Is Needed in Our Career Guidance Programs for Teens*

Many students are leaving (either through graduation or dropping out) our public education system without much career guidance training and support. This writer suggests that we need some *systemic* changes, including:

- **an education and career plan**, required of all students beginning in the 8th grade (partly because we lose so many students in the ninth grade—the high school dropout phenomenon begins as students reach high school, often because state laws don't require them to be in school; there are no legal reprisals if they leave);
- **a career planning portfolio**, required of all students beginning in the 9th grade, so that students have some systematic way of keeping track and storing the information they pick up through career guidance units, classroom presentations, field trips, shadow experiences, essays, interest tests, ability tests, and other portfolio items; and
- **a culminating project**, required of all students in the senior year, which may focus on a career interest. These projects usually have a prescribed time period for completion, and certain content requirements, often with a presentation to a panel.

If students could just complete these three items, they would be far more equipped with skills and tools with which to navigate both their educational endeavors and their work experiences after high school. The Franklin-Pierce School District in Tacoma, Washington provides an excellent example of a program already in place that incorporates these three components. (See www.fp.k12.wa.us)

The really difficult issue in designing a program with these three components is that of *monitoring student progress*, and that issue must be carefully discussed with administrators, teachers, school counselors, career specialists, and district curriculum specialists, so that the workload does not become a difficult, if not unpleasant, battle. All appropriate personnel need to play a role, as monitoring a thousand or more students through a given high school, with each student completing three different program components, can be a tracking nightmare. So this workload issue must be discussed and carefully worked out before the program is put in place. Otherwise, there are sure to be very difficult disagreements about who is to do what. With careful coordination, and often the use of computer monitoring as students complete the various competencies of the three components (plan, portfolio, and project), the comprehensive career guidance program can run smoothly, and be of great benefit to students who complete it.

*Professional School Counselors Need to Make Others Aware of the Issue of "Unfocused Kids"*

As professional school counselors work with other educators (administrators, teachers, career specialists, district curriculum coordinators, and superintendents), they need to help others understand the uncomfortable situation, if not crisis, that so many young people find themselves in when they are ready to graduate (if they haven't already dropped out) and don't really understand how to proceed with their plans. Maybe the initial plans sounds simple enough, like *going to college*, but young people need to quickly learn the value of back-up plans, financial aid strategies, support groups for studying, and strategies for keeping their stress level under control as they move through their educational programs and workplace experiences. Otherwise, they may give up or quit. Many do. The college dropout rate (after the first year) for universities is about one in four, and for community college about one in two. The monetary as well as psychological cost to our young people for making poor or unsupported choices is staggering. Professional school counselors can do much to help parents and other educators understand the big picture. In a recent article in the *Seattle Times*, Solomon reports that:

> One in four freshmen at four-year colleges don't [sic] return for their sophomore year, according to Education Trust, a nonprofit group that promotes high academic achievement. One in two freshmen at two-year colleges does not return. 'I think people are catching on and beginning to recognize that this is one of the most serious issues confronting America,' said Peter Negroni, senior vice president of K-12 education at the College Board, which develops the SAT, the PSAT and the AP program. 'To me, it is the issue of our time.' (2003)

And indeed it is, professional school counselors. Indeed it is.

## References


*ACT National Dropout Rates, 1983 to 2002*. Retrieved on August 22, 2002 from http://www.postsecondary.org/ archives/Reports/Spreadsheets/ACTDropout.htm

Adelman, H. S., & Taylor, L. (April, 2002). School counselors and school reform: New directions. *Professional School Counseling*, *5*(5), 235-248.

American School Counselor Association. (2003). The *National model: A framework for school counseling programs*. Alexandria, VA: Author.

Bowers, J. L., & Hatch, P. A. (2002). *Draft: The national model for school counseling programs.* Alexandria, VA: The American School Counselor Association. Retrieved on August 8, 2002 from http://www.schoolcounselor.org

Brophy, J. (1998). *Motivating students to learn.* Boston: McGraw Hill Publishers.

Bylsma, P., & Ireland, L. (2002). *Graduation and dropout statistics for Washington's counties, districts, and schools. Final report, school year 2000-01.* Olympia, WA: Office of the Superintendent of Public Instruction.

Capuzzi, D., & Gross, D. R. (1989). *Youth at risk: A resource for counselors, teachers and parents.* Alexandria, VA: American Association for Counseling and Development.

Campbell, C. A., & Dahir, C. A. (1997). *American School Counselor Association—Sharing the Vision. The national standards for school counseling programs.* Alexandria, VA: American School Counselor Association.

Dahir, C. A., Sheldon, C. B., & Valiga, M. J. (1998). *Vision into action: Implementing the national standards for school counseling programs.* Alexandria, VA: American School Counselor Association.

Department of Labor of Industries (Washington State). (n.d.) *Teen workers have two jobs.* [Brochure] Olympia, WA: Author.

Education Trust. (2001). *The lost opportunity of the senior year: Finding a better way. Summary of findings*. Retrieved April 30,2004, from http://www.woodrow.org/CommissionOnTheSeniorYear/Report/CommissionSummary2.pdf

Fritz, R. (1984). *The path of least resistance*. New York: Fawcett Columbine.

Gray, C. G., & Herr, E. L. (1995). *Other ways to win: creating alternatives for high school graduates.* Thousand Oaks, CA: Corwin Press Inc.

Greene, J. P. (2002). *Graduation rates in Washington state*. New York: Manhattan Institute for Policy Research. Retrieved December 19, 2002, from http://www.manhattan-institute.org/html/cr_27.htm

Gysbers, N. C. (2001). School guidance and counseling in the 21st century: Remember the past into the future. *Professional School Counseling*, *5*(2), 103.

Herbert, R. (2002, July). Unmasking the poor. *Encore Magazine*, *6*(4), 7.

Herr, E. L. (1997). *Career development and work-bound youth.* Greensboro, NC: ERIC/CASS. (ERIC Document Reproduction Service No. ED051199).

High Tech Learning Centers. (n.d.). *Overview of High Tech Learning Centers Program.* Retrieved February 11, 2003, from http://www.hightechlearning.org./overview/advisory_board.html

Houtz, J. & Shaw, L. (2003, December 7). One in four high-school students here fails to graduate on time. *Seattle Times*, 3.

Hoyt, K. B. (2001). Helping high school students broaden their knowledge of postsecondary options. *Professional School Counseling*, *5*(1), 6-12.

Isaacson, L. E., & Brown, D. (2000). *Career information, career counseling, and career development.* Boston: Allyn and Bacon.

Jensen, J. J. (2003, January 29). Seattle high school to let pupils sleep in. *Seattle Times.*

Krumboltz, J. D., & Worthington, R. L. (1999). The school-to-work transition from a learning theory perspective. *The Career Development Quarterly, 47*(4), 312-325.

Kuranz, M. (2002). Cultivating student potential. *Professional School Counseling, 5*(3),172-179.

Mortenson, T. G. (2001). High school graduation trends and patterns 1981-2000. *Postsecondary Education Opportunity*, *108*, 2.

National Center for Educational Statistics. (1996). *Dropout rates in the United States, 1996: Event, status, and cohort dropout rates.* Washington, DC: U. S. Department of Education.

National Center for Educational Statistics. (2001). *Dropout rates in the United States, 1999. Executive Summary.* Washington, DC: U. S. Department of Education.

National Dropout Prevention Center/Network. *Career Education/Workforce Readiness Overview (Dolin, 2001).* Retrieved on April 30, 2004 from:http://www.dropoutprevention.org/effstrat/career/career_over.htm

Pear, R. (2002, September 25). Number of people living in poverty increases in U. S. *New York Times.* Retrieved September 25, 2002, from http://www.nytimes.com/2002/09/25/national/

Quattrociocchi, S. M. (2000). *Help! A family's guide to high school and beyond.* Olympia, WA: Washington State Workforce Training and Education Coordinating Board.

Schneider, B., & Stevenson, D. (1999). *The ambitious generation—America's teenagers: Motivated but directionless.* New Haven: Yale University Press.

Snyder, C. R., Feldman, D. B., Shorey, H. S., & Rand, K. L. (2002). Hopeful choices: A school counselor's guide to hope theory. *Professional School Counseling, 5*, 298-307.

Solomon, C. (2003, December 8). College-prep expectations don't mesh with realities. *Seattle Times.*

Steinberg, L. (1996). *Beyond the classroom: Why school reform has failed and what parents need to do*. New York: Touchstone.

Tyre, P. (2002, March 25). Bringing up adultolescents. *Newsweek,* 39-40.

U. S. Dept. of Education. (1996, March). *Consumer Guide (No.16): National Institute on the Education of At-risk students: High school dropout rates*. Washington, DC: Author. Retrieved April 30, 2002 from http://www.ed.gov/pubs/OR/ ConsumerGuides/dropout.html

Wakefield, S. M. (Ed.) (2004) *Unfocused kids: Helping students to focus on their education and career plans.* Greensboro, NC: CAPS Press.

Washington Interscholastic Activities Association (WIAA). *2002-2003 Handbook.* Renton, WA: Author.

Zuckerman, M. B. (2004, February 9). The case of the missing jobs. *U.S. News and World Report*, 68.

# Chapter 80

## Helping Students Acquire Time Management Skills

*Vicki Brooks*

### Preview

Developing and applying time management strategies can help reduce frustration and missed deadlines. This chapter provides examples of positive strategies, including goal setting, prioritization, development of timelines and action plans, as well as worksheets for accomplishing these strategies.

Time management falls under a larger construct called social engineering. Simply defined, social engineering is the ability to reduce obstacles (without avoiding them) in order to achieve the desired goal with minimal effort (Seaward, 2002). To perform this strategy efficiently and effectively is the essence of time management.

Symptoms of poor time management can include rushing, vacillation, missed deadlines, and feeling overwhelmed. In time, poor time management can lead to burn out. Burn out occurs when the individual cannot effectively maintain normal routines or behaviors (Henschen, 2001). Psychological symptoms include apathy, anxiousness, confusion, and incomplete task completion. Increased heart rate, sleep patterns changes, and increased blood pressure are physiological symptoms of burn out (Henschen, 2001; Seaward, 2002) (see chapters 59 and 93 in this book).

Applying successful problem solving strategies (e.g., goal setting) can help reduce time management issues. For example, maintaining an overall 3.0 GPA can only be met by setting short and long-term goals for each subject. For math, the short-term goal might be to obtain 80% or higher on tests. Short-term steps are needed to achieve the ultimate 80% goal and can include meeting with a study group three times per week, or regularly reviewing homework with a checklist for completion. The time management strategy of prioritization could assist in short-term goal achievement.

Professional school counselors' tasks include asking open-ended questions leading to the identification of both short- and long-term goals. After goal identification, the development of an action plan can begin. Progress checks and identifying available assets (e.g., parent or other adults) can increase the likelihood of goal achievement. Although the pace of everyday life has increased, the tested methods of time management remain the same (Roesch, 1998) and the worksheets included in this chapter are applicable across nearly all age groups with minor modifications.

Time management can be a learned familial or cultural trait (e.g., acceptance of late arrivals). Certainly, some behavior characteristics get in the way of effective time management (e.g., perfectionism and procrastination) (Seaward, 2002).

Effective management of time is a learned skill. Key to overall success is planning and organization. An excellent beginning would be the purchase of a daily/weekly/monthly planner and parents and teachers should be included in the student's efforts to utilize the planner.

## Control of Time

Managing daily activities can be made easier by following simple guidelines involving setting goals and getting organized. The guidelines have a built in assumption: success is the end goal. Success here refers to all aspects of life (e.g., school, home and friends).

### *Set Goals*

One must set goals specific to each task or accomplishment desired. Short-term goals are essential for reaching the stated long-term goal. Both short and long-term goals should be clearly defined with a plan of action and measurable outcomes. In other words: What do I want (goal)? How I am going to get there (action plan)? How will I know when I get there (measurable outcome)?

The goal setting worksheet (see Figure 1) assists individuals in identifying the long-term goal (LTG)(e.g., 3.0 GPA) while establishing short-term goals (STG) with specified action plans (P). Each STG has a measurable outcome (MO) indicating what a successful result is for specific goals. Finally, the summation of each STG's MO leads to LTG successful completion (e.g., attaining a 3.0 GPA).

### *Getting Organized*

Attaining goals involves planning and organizing time. Organizational tips include:

1. *Keep a daily/weekly planner*; write homework assignments and tasks down immediately upon receiving them; transfer information to a monthly/semester calendar.
2. *Prioritize tasks using the prioritization worksheet* (see Figure 2). This worksheet can be used for daily, weekly, monthly or semester prioritization. In the top section, no order or ranking should occur when listing tasks. Ranking occurs in the ABC Section. Utilizing information from the ABC section, prioritize tasks as follows: high urgency with high importance (I); low urgency with high importance (II); high urgency with low importance (III); and, low urgency with low importance (IV). The last section provides a list with (I) having the highest priority for immediate completion and (IV) the lowest priority for completion. Prioritization errors often occur when enjoyable tasks are ranked as urgent-important (e.g., calling my friend).
3. *Monitor one's use of time for one week* (see Figure 3). Figure 3 provides a means for recording time spent on individual activities. The right hand column summarizes the total hours/week for each activity while the bottom row summarizes daily totals. Time should only be recorded in half-hour increments. After tallying time use over a week, a schedule of time can be created to assist with urgent-important task completion.
4. *Schedule time for task completion* (see Figure 4). After completing the goal setting (Figure 1), prioritization (Figure 2) and time allocation (Figure 3) worksheets, development of a schedule can begin. Several methods can be employed (e.g., boxing and time mapping). Table 1 provides additional time management tips.

**Figure 1. Goal setting worksheet.**

## Goal Setting

Long-term Goal (LTG):

To get to the long-term goal (LTG), I must:

Short-term Goals (STG):

1. ______________________________
2. ______________________________
3. ______________________________
4. ______________________________

My plan (P) for each short-term (STG) to be accomplished:

| STG #1 (P) | STG #2 (P) | STG #3 (P) | STG #4 (P) |
|---|---|---|---|
| | | | |
| | | | |
| | | | |
| | | | |
| | | | |
| | | | |
| | | | |

I will know when I have achieved each STG by this measurable outcome (MO)

STG # 1 ______________________________

STG # 2 ______________________________

STG # 3 ______________________________

STG #4 ______________________________

**STG #1MO +STG #2 MO + STG #3 MO + STG #4 MO = LTG = SUCCESS**

*Note.* Illustration by Michael T. McNamara.

## Figure 2. Prioritization worksheet.

Write down all tasks needing to be completed. Do not worry about order or rank.

| | |
|---|---|
| 1. | 6. |
| 2. | 7. |
| 3. | 8. |
| 4. | 9. |
| 5. | 10. |

### ABC Rank Order

Under **Column A** write the items that ***MUST*** be done. Under **Column C** write the items that you would ***LIKE*** to get done but are not essential (can wait). Under **Column B** write all others.

| Column A | Column B | Column C |
|---|---|---|
| ______________ | ______________ | ______________ |
| ______________ | ______________ | ______________ |
| ______________ | ______________ | ______________ |
| ______________ | ______________ | ______________ |
| ______________ | ______________ | ______________ |

Now organize the list in the important versus urgent matrix.

| URGENT | | IMPORTANT | |
|---|---|---|---|
| | | High Importance | Low Importance |
| | High Urgency | A.<br>B. I.<br>C. | A.<br>B. III.<br>C. |
| | Low Urgency | A.<br>B. II.<br>C. | A.<br>B. IV.<br>C. |

Then, begin to work on these tasks in the following order:

| | |
|---|---|
| **I.** (A)<br>(B)<br>(C) | **III.** (A)<br>(B)<br>(C) |
| **II.** (A)<br>(B)<br>(C) | **IV.** (A)<br>(B)<br>(C) |

*Note.* Adapted from Seaward (2002).

**Figure 3. Activities time sheet.**

**My time: hours per day**

| | Mon | Tue | Wed | Thurs | Fri | Sat | Sun | Total |
|---|---|---|---|---|---|---|---|---|
| Sleep: | | | | | | | | |
| School: | | | | | | | | |
| Classes | | | | | | | | |
| Lunch | | | | | | | | |
| Clubs | | | | | | | | |
| Sports | | | | | | | | |
| Friends | | | | | | | | |
| Free | | | | | | | | |
| Dressing: | | | | | | | | |
| School | | | | | | | | |
| Date | | | | | | | | |
| Other | | | | | | | | |
| Study: | | | | | | | | |
| Math | | | | | | | | |
| English | | | | | | | | |
| History | | | | | | | | |
| Science | | | | | | | | |
| Other | | | | | | | | |
| Other: | | | | | | | | |
| Total = 24 hours | | | | | | | | |

**Figure 4. Scheduling time.**

**Boxing Example** (effective for weekends):

| | | |
|---|---|---|
| 8:00-12:00 | = | work on term paper (research) |
| 12:00-1:00 | = | lunch/exercise |
| 1:00-5:00 | = | 2 hrs draft writing; other classes 2 hrs |
| 5:00-7:00 | = | time with family/dinner |
| 7:00-9:00 | = | movies |
| 9:00-10:00 | = | relax/bed |

**Time Mapping Schedule** (Saturday example):

| | | |
|---|---|---|
| 9:00-9:30 | = | eat breakfast; gather research materials |
| 9:30-10:00 | = | travel to library |
| 10:00-10:30 | = | determine how to locate needed reference using the librarian for assistance |
| 10:30-11:00 | = | gather first section of paper's research |
| 11:00-11:30 | = | take notes; write up outlines/narratives |
| 11:30-12:00 | = | organize for next section of research |
| 12:00-12:30 | = | gather second section references |
| 12:30-1:00 | = | take notes; write up outlines/narratives |
| 1:00-1:30 | = | travel home |
| 1:30-2:00 | = | lunch |
| 2:00-2:30 | = | reward for hard morning in library |
| 2:30-3:00 | = | review English |
| 3:00-3:30 | = | review science |
| 3:30-4:00 | = | math |
| 4:00- | = | relax; dinner; fun with family or friends |

**Boxing & Time Mapping Schedule** (weekday example for study time):

| | | |
|---|---|---|
| 7:30-3:00 | = | classes (if free hour: library research) |
| 3:00-6:00 | = | sports/clubs |
| 6:00-7:00 | = | dinner |
| 7:00-7:45 | = | math homework (most difficult subject) |
| 7:45-8:30 | = | English homework |
| 8:30-9:15 | = | science homework |
| 9:15-10:00 | = | history homework (easiest) |

*Note.* Adapted from Seaward (2002) with permission.

## Summary/ Conclusion

Effective use and management of time can create opportunities for engaging in pleasurable and fun activities. Through development of positive habits (e.g., using a daily planner) organization can become a reality. Once essential tasks are identified and goals established, the process for attainment becomes a roadmap for success. Clearly, success can occur as a result of careful thought, planning, organization and effective time management. Table 2 provides a listing of websites and additional information for aid in time management.

**Table 1. Additional tips for managing and scheduling time.**

1. Calculate time needed per assignment.
2. Record the time it takes to read 5 pages of the textbook. Use this time as a measure for blocking out time needs by class.
3. Identify the best time of day for learning (e.g., early morning or early evening).
4. During each study session, review previous lecture notes or materials. Re-read the notes highlighting the important word(s) or ideas. Review the highlighted material for the test.
5. Take breaks during study time (e.g., every 30 minutes take a 5-minute break).
6. Pre-determine a stop time for studying. Hold to it. This will provide a short-term goal with a reward at the end.
7. Break large tasks down into smaller tasks (see the Figure 4 example of Time Mapping).
8. Identify the time of day in which you are most productive (see Figure 3). Utilize this time for completing urgent and important tasks (see Figure 2).
9. Let go of attempting low priority items. Do not stop a high priority task for a less ranked task (see Figure 2).
10. Each day review the daily/weekly/monthly/semester planner. Re-assess and re-direct if necessary.
11. Learn to speak up. Share with others (especially family) urgent and important tasks and goals with assigned timelines. By knowing these, others can support you in achieving your goals.

*Note:* Adapted from study handout materials used in the Athletic Counseling Center, University of Wyoming.

**Table 2. Web-sites and additional references.**

www.mtsu.edu Links titled: Strategies for Success and Links to Other Useful Sites are excellent resources. The Useful Site category has a large link page for additional tips from colleges and universities.

www.co.broward.fl.us/agriculture/english/consfam/he795.htm - Teaching and working with younger children on time management issues. Contains tips for parents.

www.familyeducation.com/article/0,1120,59-16518-0-4,00.html - Time management strategies for gifted children of all ages.

http://teacher.scholastic.com/professional/futureteachers/time_management.htm - Tips for managing and creating effective teaching time.

www.wannalearn.com/Academic_Subjects/Study_Skills/ - Links to study skills information, videos, books (by age groups) for helping students learn to study.

http://dmoz.org/Reference/Education/How_To_Study/ - Links to study guides, creating good study habits, academic tips.

www.education.com/ourfamilyspace/homeworkplanner/ - Links for teachers, administrators, adults, and children of all ages for study tips (includes a homework planner); free membership with log in; free newsletter. (Note: Sylvan Learning Center logo is at the top).

http://cuip.uchicago.edu/www4teach/98/teams/Peerpals/timemanage.htm - Links for time management, note taking, homework, test taking, reading strategies and time use charts.

http://www.ucc.vt.edu/stdysk/htimesug.html - Time scheduling suggestions from Virginia Tech.

www.adm.uwaterloo.ca/infocs.study - Tips/links for study skills, time management, note taking.

Davis, M., & Eshelman, E. R. (2000). *The relaxation and stress reduction workbook.* Oakland, CA: New Harbinger.

Gore, M. C., & Dowd, J. F. (1999). *Taming the time stealers: Tricks of the trade from organized teachers.* Thousand Oaks, CA: Corwin Press.

## References

Henschen, K. P. (2001). Athletic staleness and burnout: Diagnosis, prevention and treatment. In J. M. Williams (Ed.) *Applied sport psychology: Personal growth to peak performance* (pp. 445-455). Mountain View, CA: Mayfield.

Roesch, R. (1998). *Time management for busy people.* New York: McGraw Hill.

Seaward, B. L. (2002). *Managing stress: Principles and strategies for health and wellbeing.* Sudbury, MA: Jones & Bartlett.

# Chapter 81

## Helping Students Improve Their Learning and Study Skills

*Susan Jones Sears, James Moore, III, & Anita Young*

### Preview

This chapter addresses what professional school counselors can do to help students acquire study and learning skills. Professional school counselors are shown how to teach students a self-regulatory cycle of task analysis, strategy selection and use, and self-monitoring so students can take responsibility for their own learning. A small group counseling plan shows professional school counselors how they can help students apply the self-regulatory cycle to five basic study skills: planning and using study time more effectively, understanding and summarizing text material better, improving methods of note-taking, anticipating and preparing better for exams, and writing more effectively.

With the national emphasis on standards-based educational reform, professional school counselors have been encouraged to demonstrate how they can contribute to increased student achievement and remove barriers to student learning. In addition, professional school counselors have been urged to help close the achievement gap and advocate for rigorous preparation of all students including low-income and minority youth (Education Trust, 1997). Reflecting the national interest in educational reform and closing the achievement gap, the American School Counselor Association (ASCA) developed the *National Standards for School Counseling Programs* (Campbell & Dahir, 1997). The *National Standards* address three domains: personal/ social development, career development, and academic development. One of the student standards under the academic development domain reads: "Students will acquire the attitudes, knowledge, and skills that contribute to effective learning in school and across the life span" (Dahir, Sheldon, & Valiga, 1998, p. 7).

The ASCA standards are designed to influence what professional school counselors do and what students learn as a result of participating in school counseling programs. The standard cited above, as well as the other eight, attempt to connect professional school counselors and school counseling programs to current educational reform efforts and to the mission of educational institutions – the improvement of student learning.

Some researchers have encouraged professional school counselors to help students acquire study and learning skills to improve achievement (Carns & Carns, 1991). Professional school counselors could either train teachers to add learning strategies to subject matter courses or assist in teaching study and learning strategies to students. For example, professional school counselors could assist the sixth (middle school) or ninth grade (high school) English teachers in delivering a five- or six-week unit on study and learning strategies. Ideally, all teachers would be motivated to include learning strategies in their classes so these skills could be reinforced throughout the curriculum. However, that ideal may not be achievable in many schools for various reasons, e.g., teacher or principal resistance, lack of training.

Other researchers, in support of the same general goal of improved student achievement, have suggested that professional school counselors teach study skills courses focusing on when, where, how, and why to study (Anderson & Anderson, 1992). In their view, a five or six week course for all sixth or ninth graders can be a valuable use of student and professional school counselor time. Regardless of whether school counselors train teachers to teach study skills or teach study and learning strategies in small group counseling or classroom guidance venues, professional school counselors can help students acquire the skills needed to take more control of their own learning.

*New Discoveries About Learning*

During the last three decades, there have been many exciting new discoveries about the nature of learning and about how students regulate their own learning processes (Zimmerman & Schunk, 2001). Research on metacognition (awareness of and knowledge about one's own thinking) and social cognition has resulted in new perspectives about students' individual differences in learning. For example, some researchers attribute individual differences in learning to students' lack of self-regulation. They claim that students need to learn how to manage their limitations during their efforts to learn and thus learn to exert more control over their own learning processes (Zimmerman & Schunk, 2001). The remainder of this chapter draws upon new perspectives on how students learn to learn and concludes with an activity designed to help professional school counselors put these new perspectives into practice.

## Developing Self-Regulated Learners

> Tanya, a ninth grade student, checks her academic planner (all students receive a planner at the beginning of the ninth grade). She is upset to find that her science project is due on Friday and she hasn't even been to the library to begin her research. She also is reminded that her history report is due that afternoon. Since it is only half done, Tanya has to try to think of an excuse that the teacher might accept and give her until tomorrow to finish it. Oh no, she also sees that she has a poem due in English class tomorrow. The poem is supposed to use metaphors but she can't even remember what a metaphor is. She begins to panic. She can't possibly get all of this work done.

Tanya is not alone. Many students do not regulate their academic studying well (Butler, 2002). They do not set goals for themselves or use specific learning strategies for condensing and memorizing important material. Many also do not plan their study time well and usually cannot evaluate their academic preparation accurately. Students often attribute their learning difficulties to vague generalities such as "I'm poor in math" or "I just don't test well." They may not ask for help from others because they don't want to "sound dumb" and they have little confidence they can succeed. Educators and researchers are interested in helping students develop the key processes of: goal setting, time management, selection of appropriate learning strategies, ability to evaluate oneself accurately, help seeking, and self-motivational beliefs.

One reason many students simply are ineffective learners by the time they have reached middle or high school is that they have not been taught how to learn (Kiewra, 2002). Instruction in learning strategies was not incorporated into schools' curricula. Educators almost always teach content, but appear not to be teaching students how to learn.

*Self-Regulated Learners*

Students who take control of their own learning are often referred to as self-regulated learners. Academic self-regulation refers to self-generated thoughts, feelings, and actions intended to attain specific educational goals, such as analyzing a reading assignment, preparing to take a test, or writing a paper (Zimmerman, Bonner, & Kovach, 1996).

Self-regulated learners engage in a cycle of cognitive activities as they progress through a given task or assignment (Butler & Winne, 1995). First, they analyze task demands. For example, in our vignette above, Tanya had a history report to do. To begin, she would review the teachers' written or verbal instructions regarding the assignment to make sure she understood the topic, the required products or outcomes, and the criteria upon which the teacher was going to evaluate the report. As she engaged in this first step, she also would draw upon her prior knowledge of what contributes to a good report (metacognitive knowledge about the task). Thus, she might remember that her history teacher wants the report to be clearly written, include appropriate references, and be at least five pages long. This first step of task analysis is very important because it sets the stage for further learning. Students' subsequent decisions about what learning strategies to use are based on their perception of the task demands (Butler, 2002).

Based on their task analysis, self-regulated learners then select, adapt, and may even invent strategic approaches to achieve the objectives related to the task or assignment facing them. Self-regulated learners draw upon their prior knowledge and experience to make decisions about what learning strategies to choose. For example, when trying to select learning strategies to apply to their current task, they try to remember approaches that worked for them in past situations with similar requirements or expectations.

When self-regulated learners have chosen and implemented specific learning strategies (examples of learning strategies are provided in the next section of the chapter) they must monitor the outcomes associated with strategy use. Students need to know if the learning strategy or strategies they selected are helping them progress toward completing their tasks or assignments. Smart learners engage in self-evaluation by comparing their progress against criteria for successful completion of the task to generate judgments about how they are progressing. If students see gaps between their desired and actual performance, then they must adjust their learning strategies or activities. In addition, smart learners pay attention to external feedback such as scores and comments on tests and teacher or peer comments on written assignments so they can self-evaluate their performance. They use this feedback to diagnose their difficulties and find possible solutions. Thus, monitoring the outcomes of their learning activities is another very important step because students generate judgments about their progress and then make decisions about subsequent learning activities.

*What Professional School Counselors Can Do*

To promote or encourage self-regulation in students, professional school counselors, with the help of teachers, must assist students to engage flexibly and adaptively in a cycle of task analysis, strategy selection and use, and self-monitoring (Butler, 2002). Some researchers (Zimmerman et al., 1996) suggested applying cyclic self-regulatory methods to five basic study skills: (1) planning and using study time more effectively; (2) understanding and summarizing text material better; (3) improving methods of note-taking; (4) test anticipating and preparing better for exams; and (5) writing more effectively.

These researchers noted that most students have not developed these five skills and yet each skill is essential for effective academic learning. All five essential academic skills, and selected strategies for implementing each appear in Figures 1-5, respectively.

**Figure 1. Planning and using study time more effectively: Selected strategies.**

1. Set regular study periods each day. By setting aside regular times each day, students discover that studying becomes more of a habit.
2. Set realistic goals. Many students tend to underestimate the amount of time needed to complete homework and assignments and thus need to overestimate the time needed until their estimates are more realistic.
3. Use a regular study area. Students are more time efficient when they study in a study area that is well-lighted and free from distractions or noise. For some students, libraries may be effective places to study while others can create study areas at home.
4. Prioritize tasks. Students need to prioritize those activities that need to be completed first. Because one's attention is usually better at the outset, it is better to study difficult subjects before studying easy ones.
5. Learn to say no to distractions. Students must be willing to say no to their friends and others who want to talk or skip studying altogether.
6. Self-reward success. Students can improve their attention by making desirable activities contingent on completion of studying. This can include incentives such as food treats, watching television, or talking to friends on the phone. (Zimmerman et al., 1996)

**Figure 2. Understanding and summarizing text material better: Selected strategies.**

1. Clarify and confront difficulties encountered. For example, students can slow down to read more carefully and reread if the text meaning is unclear.
2. Engage in self-questioning. Students can ask themselves questions such as "Why is that true?" or "What does that mean?" to understand the material at a deeper level.
3. Predicting what will come next. Stopping to anticipate what the author will say before reading a text passage can help students develop greater understanding.
4. Finding the main idea. Analyzing passages in a paragraph and identifying the main idea that is being discussed increases understanding.
5. Summarizing. Students can summarize by paring down passages to their core meaning, focusing on the most important information, and substituting super-ordinate terms for lists of items.
6. Relating text to prior knowledge. Students can relate new ideas in their text to previously stored information and can do so by developing analogies, examples, and comparisons. (Zimmerman et al., 1996)

**Figure 3. Improving methods of note-taking: Selected strategies.**

1. Use recording strategies. Students need to be selective about what to include in their notes. Write down only main ideas and supporting facts. Listen for summary statements and write them down. Also, listen for signal words or phrases such as, "There are four main ideas in this article." Writing everything down burdens students and they often fall behind the teacher's comments.
2. Use linear outlines. Make a list of the topics and subtopics in traditional outline form and leave room in between for additional note-taking.
3. Try mapping outlines. Students can use a revision strategy involving the use of graphic representations to relate information visually using techniques such as tree diagrams, flow charts, concept webs and matrices. For example, a lecture comparing and contrasting religions might be depicted in a two dimensional matrix.
4. Use the Cornell system. In this system, a page is divided vertically with one column for recording and another for revising notes after the class is finished and using one of the note-taking methods above. (Zimmerman et al., 1996)

**Figure 4. Anticipating and preparing better for examination: Selected strategies.**

1. Revise lecture and text notes first. Trying to memorize all oral and textual matter is not going to work for most students. Instead, students should concentrate on organizing only the most important information using one of the revision (note taking) strategies discussed above.
2. Use elaborative interrogation. Students should ask themselves questions intended to produce elaborations of the test material, for example, Why is this fact true? This strategy helps integrate new material with information already known.
3. Use representational imagery. By forming a vivid image of the word and its definition, students can remember lists of words or even concepts.
4. Use first-letter mnemonics. This entails remembering the first letter for each of a list of key words. For example, the names of the Great Lakes could be encoded in the form of the word HOMES (Huron, Ontario, Michigan, Erie, and Superior). Another example uses the word FACE to describe the spaces on the treble clef of the music staff. Students can learn to devise their own mnemonics.
5. Use mnemonic sentences. Students can remember a series of facts by constructing a sentence starting with the same letters: "my very eccentric mother just served us nine pizzas" for the planets in the solar system: Mercury, Venus, Earth, Mars, Jupiter, Saturn, Uranus, Neptune, and Pluto. (Zimmerman et al., 1996)

**Figure 5. Writing more effectively: Selected strategies.**

1. Goal setting. Students should use a planning strategy for deciding the goals of the paper (e.g., to compare, to analyze, and to describe) and the sub-goals (e.g., what things to compare, analyze, and describe).
2. Idea generating questions. Students can ask questions to generate prose (e.g., what the object is, what the sequence of events is, what the facts on the object are, what the arguments or opinions are, and who the key players are).
3. Mapping or webbing. Students can use strategies for establishing relations between ideas or events with visual concept maps or webs (e.g., linking generals to the wars they were in, the battles they fought, and the battles they won and lost.
4. Varying sentence structure. Students should make sure paragraphs vary in sentence structure from simple to compound and complex.
5. Locating a peer editor. Students can identify an appropriate classmate to read and give feedback about various aspects of the draft and do the same for the student helping them.
6. Become a self-editor. Students can learn to examine their draft by using a series of questions (e.g., Is there an introduction and conclusion? Did I achieve my main goal? Are any parts unclear or not supported? Did I give examples to illustrate the important points?). (Zimmerman et al., 1996)

These five essential academic skills can be taught successfully to elementary through high school students as long as the students understand they need to engage in task analysis before selecting the appropriate learning strategy or strategies and then self-monitor to determine the effectiveness of the chosen strategy, adapting whenever necessary.

## Practical Applications of the Self-Regulatory Cycle and Essential Academic Skills

When students begin to learn unfamiliar material, frequently they cannot break down or analyze the task or assignment into components. They fail to set specific goals, develop effective learning strategies, or monitor progress. With instruction or training in the self-regulatory cycle, students can learn to analyze tasks, set effective goals, choose appropriate learning strategies, and monitor progress toward task completion. Learning the steps involved in a self-regulatory cycle not only enhances students' learning skills but also increases students' perceptions of control over their learning process.

To help professional school counselors apply the information in this chapter, Table 1 contains a small group counseling plan for either middle or high school. The outline used to describe the activity includes: a) the ASCA Standard it illustrates; b) student competencies identified in the activity; c) background notes to school counselors to help them prepare for the group; d) activities and procedures to be followed in each session; and e) suggestions for student handouts.

**Table 1. Small group counseling plan for high school or middle school students.**

*ASCA Standard A. Academic Development*: Students will demonstrate the attitudes, knowledge, and skills that contribute to effective learning in school and across the life span (Campbell & Dahir, 1997).

*Student Competencies/Benchmarks:*

1. Students can identify skills and behaviors that lead to successful learning; and
2. Students can demonstrate time management and task management skills to improve student learning.

*Note to Counselor:* Ask teachers to help you identify students who can benefit from instruction in learning strategies. Include students who are struggling and students who are "B" students, but with help, might become better students. This mix of group members provides balance for your group. Form small groups of 4-6 students. If possible, work with students who are taking the same subject that will allow you to use their subject matter to help them apply the skills you are introducing. Describe what you are doing to the students and teacher(s) so they can reinforce your efforts.

*Suggestions for Student Handouts*: Consider making a one-page handout of each of the five essential academic skills and selected strategies that are discussed in this chapter and distribute them to members of the group when discussed.

*Activities/Procedures for Each Session*

*Session One:* Follow these steps:

1. Conduct a warm-up activity to help the students get to know each other.
2. Explain the purpose of the group to the students and generate, with the members, a set of ground rules to guide the group process, e.g., listen to others, don't interrupt, respect the views of others.
3. Give students a copy of the handout in which you have reproduced the vignette of "Tanya" and ask them if they have ever been in a similar situation. Ask the students to describe the situations they experienced and the outcomes of those situations. Many will report negative rather than positive outcomes. Ask students if they would like to learn ways to avoid being in those situations again. This discussion should increase their interest in the group.
4. Using the information provided about self-regulated and "smart" learners in this chapter, describe how effective learners approach studying. In your discussion, stress that students must engage flexibly and adaptively in a cycle of task analysis, strategy selection and use, and self-monitoring.
5. Ask each student to choose one subject in which to improve his or her grade. Tell students you would like them to apply the self-regulatory cycle (task analysis, strategy selection and use, and self-monitoring) in that subject to see if they can improve their learning. Explain to students that you are going to teach them some learning strategies that they can select and use in their studying.
6. Ask each student to describe a current assignment. Use one of the student's assignments and show him how to engage in task analysis. Ask the other students to listen carefully. After you have completed your demonstration, answer students' questions about the process of task analysis. Give students some examples of learning strategies described in this chapter.

*Session Two:*

1. Briefly review the self-regulatory cycle explained in session one. Ask the students to describe how they have tried to apply what they learned in the previous session.
2. Distribute "Figure 1. Planning and Using Study Time More Effectively" and lead a discussion of each strategy. As a general rule for each of the sessions, ask students which of the strategies they now use and how effective the strategy is for them. Ask the students to choose a strategy to work on after each session. Give them homework (using one of the strategies or more) each session during the last five minutes of the group.

*Session Three:*

1. Distribute "Figure 2. Understanding and Summarizing Text Material Better." Proceed in the same way as session two. Show students how to engage in self-questioning and summarizing. Use information from a text students are currently using so they can see you apply the skill.

*Session Four:*

1. Distribute "Figure 3. Improving Your Methods of Note-Taking." Review what has been learned so far. Introduce note-taking. The leader may need to demonstrate some of the note-taking strategies such as mapping or linear outlining. Perhaps one of the students can help. Brief the student before the session so she can explain various strategies to the others.

*Session Five:*

1. Distribute "Figure 4. Anticipating and Preparing Better for Examinations." Show students how to use first letter mnemonics and mnemonic sentences to remember a series of words or facts. Using their own texts and assignments, help them see how they can use mnemonics to improve their recollection of facts for tests.

*Session Six:*

1. Distribute "Figure 5. Writing More Effectively." Show students how to set goals for their written work. If they have assignments due, use something of theirs to show how they can set written goals to help them think how they will approach the paper or assignment they are expected to complete.

Depending on how the sessions have gone, you may need to plan for a follow-up session to review all of the strategies and have students discuss which strategies have worked effectively for them.

*Evaluation:* Keep careful records of the students' grades on tests and homework at the beginning, during, and five weeks after the group has terminated. You can use this information to determine if the students have made any improvement in their grades. Also, you may wish to interview the students to see if they feel more in control of their own learning.

---

## Summary/Conclusion

This chapter focused on what professional school counselors can do to help students acquire study and learning skills. Self-regulated learners were described and a self-regulatory cycle of task analysis, strategy selection and use, and self-monitoring was discussed. A small group counseling plan was presented to encourage professional school counselors to apply the self-regulatory methods to five basic study skills: planning and using study time more effectively, understanding and summarizing text material better, improving methods of note-taking, test anticipating and preparing better for exams, and writing more effectively.

## References

Anderson, S. G., & Anderson, C. E. (1992). Study skills made easy. *The School Counselor, 39,* 382-384.

Butler, D. L. (2002). Individualizing instruction in self-regulated learning. *Theory Into Practice, 41,* 81-92.

Butler, D. L., & Winne, P. H. (1995). Feedback and self-regulated learning: A theoretical synthesis. *Review of Educational Research, 65,* 245-281.

Campbell, C. A., & Dahir, C. A. (1997). *The national standards for school counseling programs.* Alexandria, VA: American School Counselor Association.

Carns, A. W., & Carns, M. R. (1991). Teaching study skills, cognitive strategies, and metacognitive skills through self-diagnosed learning styles. *The School Counselor, 38,* 341-346.

Dahir, C. A., Sheldon, C. B., & Valiga, M. J. (1998). *Vision into action: Implementing the national standards for school counseling programs.* Alexandria, VA: American School Counselor Association.

Education Trust. (1997). *The national guidance and counseling reform program.* Washington, DC: Author.

Kiewra, K. A. (2002). How classroom teachers can help students learn and teach them how to learn. *Theory Into Practice, 41,* 71-80.

Zimmerman, B., Bonner, S., & Kovach, R. (1996). *Developing self-regulated learners: Beyond achievement to self-regulation.* Washington, DC: American Psychological Association.

Zimmerman, B. J., & Schunk, D. H. (Eds). (2002). *Self-regulated learning and academic achievement: Theoretical perspectives* (2nd ed.). Mahwah, NJ: Erlbaum.

# Chapter 82

## Helping Students Manage Stress

*Debbie W. Newsome & Nancy H. Whitlatch*

### Preview

Stress is a pervasive problem that affects students at all grade levels. Within recent decades, youth have exhibited more stress-related difficulties than in years past. Pressures that accompany living in an increasingly more complex society, accompanied by declining coping skills and social support, contribute to the increase in numbers of students facing stress-related health issues. This chapter addresses sources of stress, outcomes associated with stress, and resources that help students cope more effectively with stressful events and provides prevention suggestions professional school counselors can initiate in classrooms and intervention strategies for group and individual counseling.

"I don't know how I'm going to get it all done," lamented Abby, a 14-year-old high school freshman. "I have two big projects, three tests, and a ton of math homework. Mrs. Cook is going insane; I think she's mad at all of us. And soccer tryouts are tomorrow after school. Tiffany is acting all moody again and won't talk to me. Nobody understands—it's just too much."

Abby's concerns reflect what many young people experience on a regular basis. Time demands, relationships, and developmental transitions are just a few of the many stressors that are an ongoing part of students' lives. Do youth today feel more stressed than in previous generations? What exactly is stress, and how does it affect students' mental and physical well-being? Why is it that some individuals seemingly handle pressure and change with ease, while others suffer deleterious effects? What can professional school counselors do to help young people develop strategies to manage stress effectively? In this chapter, stress, its effects on young people, and examples of prevention and intervention activities that can be implemented by professional school counselors are described.

### Stress

The number of youth experiencing stress-related disorders, including depression, eating disorders, anxiety, social dysfunction, and substance abuse, has increased in recent years (McNamara, 2000). An estimated 35% of young people in the United States experience stress-related health problems (Lau, 2002). According to Heaven (1996), "teenagers and even children face stressful events that have the potential to severely disrupt their lives and negatively affect their psychological adjustment and health" (p. 44). Increased pressures faced by youth, coupled with declining coping skills and decreased social support, represent a challenge to professional school counselors and others who work with children and adolescents.

*What is Stress?*

Stress can be defined in multiple ways. Lazarus and Folkman (1984) defined stress as "a particular relationship between the person and the environment that is appraised by the person as taxing or exceeding his or her resources and endangering his or her well-being" (p. 19). Stress can refer to an internal state, an external event, or the interaction between a person and the environment (McNamara, 2000). Perceptions of what is stressful vary widely among individuals. Indeed, something perceived as stressful by one person may be seen as trivial or even positive by another (Lau, 2002).

Stress can be viewed as a relationship between the events that happen to us and our physical, cognitive, emotional, and behavioral responses to them (McNamara, 2000). Several models describing the stress process have been proposed. Psychological models of stress focus on the reciprocal interactions between an individual and the environment. An example of such a model is presented in Figure 1. Adapted from work conducted by Lazarus (1966), McNamara (2000), and others, the model is comprised of the following components: environmental stressors, an individual's subjective perceptions of the stressors, short-term responses, and long-term effects. Frequency, intensity, and timing of stressors can affect mental health, with outcomes being moderated by parental and peer support, individual psychological traits, and coping skills. Coping with stress is the process by which a person handles stressful situations and the emotions they generate.

**Figure 1. The Stress Process**

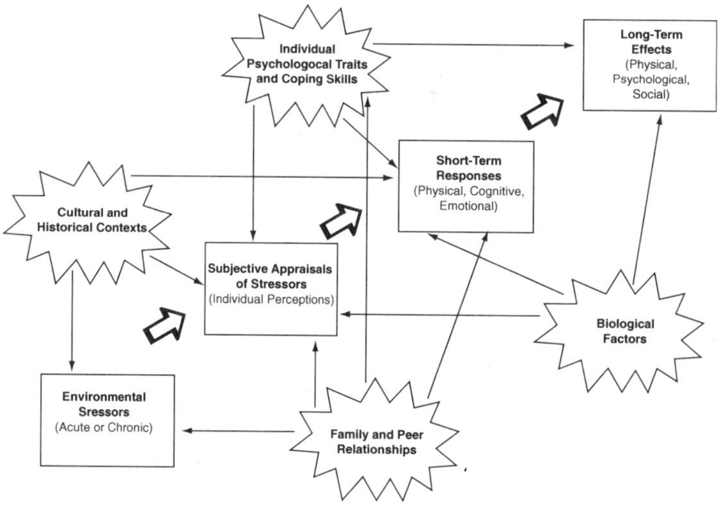

*Types of Stressors*

Childhood and adolescence may be marked by extremely stressful events and transitions as well as daily aggravations that require responses (Lau, 2002). Chronic demands or stressors are enduring aspects of the environment that involve deprivation or hardship and create ongoing challenges for an individual. Poverty, physical disability, and family dysfunction are examples of chronic stressors. In contrast, acute stressors, sometimes referred to as life events, involve changes or disruptions in existing conditions (Compas, 1987). Chronic and acute stressors can be further classified as normative life events, non-normative events, and daily hassles (McNamara, 2000).

- *Normative life events*: generic developmental challenges that everyone encounters. Normative events include physical changes, school transitions, emerging sexuality, changing peer and family relationships, and changes in cognitive levels.

- *Non-normative life events*: unexpected, demanding events that may challenge the transitional experience. Examples include catastrophic phenomena (sudden, powerful events requiring major adaptive responses from the groups sharing the experience, including natural disasters, accidents, and terrorism) and unexpected changes such as parental divorce, injury, unemployment, or a family member's death or major illness.
- *Daily hassles*: stable, repetitive stressors that tend to be irritating or annoying. Examples include parent-child conflict, academic demands, peer pressure, interpersonal concerns, and financial concerns. Ongoing hassles, in some ways, are more predictive of psychological symptoms than acute, episodic stressors and are associated with depression, anxiety, and conduct problems.

Normative, non-normative, and daily stressors can occur in multiple contexts, including school, home, and neighborhood.

*School.* Normative educational transitions, such as entering school for the first time, changing schools, or moving from one level to another (e.g., elementary school to middle school) can be significant sources of stress for young people. School-related factors that are unrelated to such transitions also can be stressful. Concerns about grades, teachers, homework, exams, extracurricular activities, and fitting in with peers are ongoing challenges that can be potentially taxing. Specific stressors in the school environment include impatient teachers, fear of failure, unclear assignments, work overload, expectations to achieve, and peer pressure, to name just a few. In an ongoing research study, middle school and high school students cited poor facilities, unfair grading policies, uncommitted teachers, and negative school reputations as factors that impeded learning, thus serving as significant sources of stress (Shoffner & Newsome, in press).

One area that has particular relevance for students and school personnel is the emphasis placed on student and school performance, especially as it relates to high-stakes testing. Test anxiety has become more prevalent in young people, possibly due to the increasing frequency of testing and the importance placed on results (McDonald, 2001). Although low levels of stress can serve to motivate some students, high levels of stress can lead to test anxiety, which can be detrimental to performance. Being pressured to perform and then not meeting expectations can have upsetting, long-lasting effects (Lau, 2002). There are several things professional school counselors can do to help with test-related stress, including conducting workshops for parents and teachers, teaching psychoeducational lessons to classes about managing stressful feelings, and counseling small groups and individual students who struggle with test anxiety.

*Family and peers.* Relationships with parents, siblings, and other family members can be both a source of support and a source of stress for young people. Conflict and/or change in any of these relationships can be particularly stressful. Children and adolescents who are undergoing developmental transitions such as puberty may be especially vulnerable to strained family relationships or dysfunctional family systems. Parental divorce or remarriage, siblings leaving home, birth of a new family member, or parental unemployment are life events that can be quite stressful for children and adolescents. Distress arising from family relationships has been associated with several mental health problems, including depression, anxiety, and eating disorders (McNamara, 2000).

As in the case of family interactions, relationships with peers can be supportive, stressful, or both. As children grow older, peers become increasingly more important and influential. Cliques, prejudice, and bullying can create difficult demands on young people, as can conflicts in values, increased intimacy, and issues related to sexuality. Professional school counselors are skilled at helping students with interpersonal issues, and preventive and remedial efforts targeted toward peer relationships can benefit students of all ages.

*Other sources of stress.* Anything perceived as a source of threat, harm, loss, or challenge has the potential to be stressful for children and adolescents. Personal health, health of friends and family members, and planning for the future are among the many additional sources of stress that are commonly dealt with. Chronic poverty, when children and parents struggle with the ongoing difficulty of trying to make ends meet, can serve as a chronic stressor (Hains, 1994), as can minority group status and prejudice. The timing of puberty and its accompanying physiological changes can be quite stressful, especially for girls. When numerous stressors are experienced simultaneously, or when the timing of events departs significantly from the norm, youth are more likely to experience distress. Indeed, students who perceive combinations of school, family, peer group, and other life situations as stressful are likely to display symptoms of emotional and physical distress (McNamara, 2000).

Unfortunately, catastrophic events are a part of our world and all too often must be dealt with by people of all ages. Following the September 11th, 2001, terrorist attacks on New York City and Washington, D.C., the American sense of safety and security was shaken to the core. Emotional distress associated with those attacks and other tragic events, including natural disasters and accidents, is expected. All youth should be watched for signs of emotional distress in the wake of exposure to any type of catastrophe. Helping young people cope with their distress is one of the most important challenges a mental health professional can face (National Institute of Mental Health, 2002).

*Stress-Related Outcomes*

Exposure to stress triggers several physical, emotional, and cognitive changes in the body. Immediate, short-term reactions to stress potentially can motivate people toward action; however, long-term exposure can lead to physical and psychosocial difficulties (Sharrer & Ryan-Wenger, 2002). Of critical interest to mental health professionals is the manner in which stress is appraised because subjective appraisals affect the nature and intensity of stress-related responses.

*Physiological responses.* When someone perceives an event as acutely stressful (i.e., harmful, threatening, or challenging), several automatic physiological responses are activated. Blood pressure, heart rate, respiration rate, and perspiration increase, helping mobilize the body's resources for action (McNamara, 2000). The chemical messengers dopamine and norepinephrine are released in the sympathetic nervous system. The adrenal hormones cortisol and epinephrine, responding to signals passed from the hypothalamus, begin to circulate. Muscles tense and blood sugar increases as the body prepares for an anticipated emergency (Disaster and Trauma, 2002).

As short-term responses, these physiological reactions to stress are not harmful and, indeed, may be helpful in cases of actual emergency. However, when exposure to stress is chronic and the stress response is overactivated, several health-related problems may be experienced. Gastrointestinal, circulatory, respiratory, and musculoskeletal disorders have been linked to stress, as have migraine, heartburn, diabetes, certain cancers, and rheumatoid arthritis (McNamara, 2000). Chronic stress can alter the immune system and hypothalamic-pituitary-adrenal (HPA) axis activity, leaving individuals more susceptible to physical illness and mental health disorders such as depression, alcoholism, and certain anxiety disorders.

Most of the research on physiological responses to stress has been conducted with adults, although children's responses are thought to be comparable. However, children may not describe or interpret their physical symptoms in the same way as adults. In a recent study focusing on children's responses, second through sixth grade students were asked to describe the way their bodies felt during a past stressful event (Sharrer & Ryan-Wenger, 2002). The five most common physiological symptoms listed were headache, stomachache, getting sweaty, heart beating fast or feeling "funny," and feeling sick. Children also mentioned having tight muscles, being shaky, and tingling. Because people experience symptoms in different ways, professional school counselors will want to give students opportunities to describe the physiological responses they have to stressful situations. Physiological symptoms can serve as signals to let youth know that they are dealing with something stressful that may require them to take some type of action (active problem-solving, relaxation exercises, etc.).

*Cognitive and emotional responses.* Just as people respond physiologically to perceived stress, they also respond cognitively and emotionally. These responses, which are dependent upon the individual's appraisal of the situation, are directly related to the process of coping, which is discussed in the next section. Immediate, short-term cognitive responses to stress include increased arousal and alertness and increased cognition and vigilance (McNamara, 2000). Initial emotional responses can include anger, fear, nervousness, and anxiety. In the study cited previously (Sharrer & Ryan-Wenger, 2002), children described feeling mad, worried, sad, nervous, and afraid when they were in stressful situations, with "mad" being the most common response. In instances of extreme stress (e.g., trauma), emotionally significant memories may be triggered (Disaster and Trauma, 2002).

As in the case of physiological stress responses, short-term cognitive and emotional reactions to stress typically serve a purpose and are not, in and of themselves, harmful. However, exposure to long-term stress can have negative effects on psychological well-being. Some of the cognitive problems associated with too much stress include concentration difficulties, distractibility, and disorganization. For adolescents, the most common psychological outcome associated with stress overload is depression (Frydenberg, 1997). Other mental health conditions that are linked to stress include post-traumatic stress disorder (PTSD), obsessive-compulsive disorder, panic disorder, other anxiety disorders, substance abuse, and eating disorders (McNamara, 2000). Symptoms associated with these conditions can interfere severely with students' self-esteem, interpersonal relationships, and academic functioning.

*Coping with Stress*

Lazarus and Folkman (1984) defined coping as cognitive and behavioral efforts directed toward managing any demands that are appraised as taxing or exceeding one's available resources. Personality and situational factors influence the ways in which people cope with these demands (McNamara, 2000). There is evidence that the manner in which young people cope with stress is more important to their psychological and physical development and well-being than is the stressful impact itself (Olbrich, 1990). A person's subjective appraisal of a situation affects the selection of coping strategies, which differ depending on the situation.

One way researchers categorized coping responses is based on whether the response is *problem-focused* or *emotion-focused* (see McNamara, 2000). Problem-focused coping strategies attempt to alter the source of stress, whereas emotion-focused coping strategies attempt to reduce the emotional distress associated with the situation. Generally, problem-focused strategies are associated with adaptive coping, reduced depression, and other positive outcomes, whereas relying exclusively on emotion-focused strategies can lead to maladaptive functioning (McNamara). With problem-focused coping, individuals take active steps to deal with the situation, thus enhancing one's sense of control over the environment. Emotion-focused coping, in contrast, may involve avoidance, which provides temporary symptom relief but, over time, is a less effective coping tool. Professional school counselors can implement stress management interventions that are tailored toward helping students use active, problem-focused coping strategies. Examples of stress management interventions are described later in this chapter.

Many types of coping strategies are used by children and adolescents. Typically, young people use a combination of problem-focused and emotion-focused strategies to cope with stressful situations, some of which are listed in the chart below. Coping strategies used by youth form the foundation for coping strategies used in adulthood (Plunkett, Radmacher, & Moll-Pharana, 2000).

Young people differ in their use of coping styles based on a number of factors (see Table 1), including age and gender (McNamara, 2000). Girls tend to use a wider range of coping styles and are more likely to seek social support. They also are more likely to vent feelings, seek spiritual support, positively reframe situations, and engage in wishful thinking. Boys, on the other hand, show a stronger preference for using humor, engaging in sports, and seeking other diversions, both positive and negative. Males may come across as more stable and difficult to irritate, whereas girls may ruminate and self-evaluate more. By being aware of these potential differences in coping style, professional school counselors can be better prepared to help all students develop and practice strategies that will facilitate adaptive adjustment.

**Table 1. Coping strategies used by young people.**

- *Accessing Support* (staying connected with family, friends, school personnel, church)
- *Enhancing Self-Reliance* (making decisions, problem solving, reframing)
- *Ventilating Feelings* (may be appropriate or inappropriate ventilation)
- *Seeking Diversions* (relaxing, engaging in activities or exercise)
- *Avoidance* (escaping, denying, or avoiding issues and/or people; substance use)

(Plunkett et al., 2000)

*Protective Resources*

What factors help students cope effectively with stressful situations, thereby avoiding the negative psychological and physical effects of stress? Research on resilience in young people indicates that protective resources, including social support and personal attributes or dispositions, seem to help people cope with stress more constructively, even in adverse circumstances (D'Imperio & Dubow, 2000; McNamara, 2000).

*Social support.* Supportive relationships with family members, peers, and other significant people play an important role in helping students cope with negative events. Supportive relationships can have a buffering effect on stress by: preventing stressful events and hassles from occurring in the first place; making individuals feel less vulnerable when they do occur; reducing the impact and intensity of stress-related symptoms; and providing help, advice, and support to remove the stressor (McNamara, 2000).

Supportive families characterized by warmth, high levels of communication, involvement, and appropriate structure help promote positive adjustment and self-efficacy in children (Herman-Stahl & Petersen, 1996). Professional school counselors have the unique opportunity to help parents understand the connection between a child's life at home and life at school. Toward this end, professional school counselors can lead workshops designed to teach effective parenting practices and healthy family interaction patterns.

Similarly, positive relationships with peers can help buffer negative effects of stress. Class guidance lessons and small group sessions focusing on peer relationships can provide children with the skills needed to develop and maintain necessary friendships. Beyond this, professional school counselors can facilitate the development of a positive, supportive school climate by leading in-service workshops and providing consultation for teachers and other school personnel who work with students.

*Personal attributes.* Several personal characteristics can serve as protective factors against stressful events, including self-esteem, self-competence, optimism, and a sense of control, (Herman-Stahl & Petersen, 1996; McNamara, 2000). Young people who view themselves as worthy and competent are less vulnerable to stress-related problems. Likewise, youth who approach life with expectations of favorable outcomes tend to cope more competently with stress (Herman-Stahl & Petersen, 1996). An internal locus of control, characterized by beliefs that outcomes are contingent upon personal effort, also appears to have a buffering effect against stressors (McNamara). Students who believe that their efforts can influence the outcome in a given situation are more likely to engage in proactive coping strategies when faced with difficulties. When internalized control is taken to the extreme, however, uncontrollable events may evoke maladaptive coping efforts rather than buffer against stress.

By overseeing the delivery of comprehensive developmental guidance programs, professional school counselors address the personal attributes of self-esteem, positive outlook, and sense of control. By ensuring that all students receive systematic, developmentally appropriate instruction in these domains, professional school counselors can facilitate the bolstering of student resiliency.

## Interventions in Schools

If we are going to help young people cope in our increasingly demanding world, it is crucial to invest in primary prevention methods (McNamara, 2000), the goal of which is to help all children develop the psychosocial skills needed for meeting life's challenges. For those students who have been exposed to trauma or excessive stress, and for other students who may not be coping well, additional interventions in the form of group counseling, individual counseling, parent or teacher consultation, and/or referral to outside resources may be warranted. In this section, preventive measures that can be initiated by professional school counselors are described. Attention also is given to ways professional school counselors can help vulnerable students through group and individual counseling.

### *Psychoeducational Interventions for Students*

Professional school counselors can influence the largest number of students through classroom psychoeducational activities. Depending on school size, school policy, and the professional school counselor's role in the school, the professional school counselor may teach the lessons herself/himself or may train classroom teachers to do so. Initiating preventive measures *before* stress becomes a problem prepares students to deal with demanding situations more effectively. Equipping students with generalizable coping strategies can help curtail many of the problems associated with stress overload (McNamara, 2000).

Stress management programs for children and adolescents, which can be a part of a comprehensive developmental guidance program, typically focus on (a) identifying sources of stress, (b) recognizing the physical and emotional consequences of stress, and (c) learning and implementing adaptive coping responses. Recommended components for preventive programs include (McNamara, 2000): education about the causes and consequences of stress; training in methods to reduce psychological and physical arousal; general problem-solving and decision-making skills; general cognitive skills (including cognitive restructuring); physical ways of coping with stress; study skills and time management; skills for increasing self-control and self-esteem; and social skills, including effective communication, conflict resolution, and assertiveness training. Numerous resources for professional school counselors describe developmentally appropriate activities for each of these topics, and several of the components (i.e., social skills, self-esteem, problem-solving) are already part of the scope and sequence that comprise comprehensive guidance programs. In this section, general suggestions related to the components that have particular relevance to stress management are provided. These suggestions are broad, and professional school counselors will want to ensure that activities related to those suggestions take into account students' developmental levels.

*Education about the stress process.* It is important for students to be able to identify what they consider stressful and recognize their own personal physical and emotional responses to stress. McNamara (2000) offered some "starting questions" that can help students recognize their own responses to stress (see Table 2).

To help students develop self-awareness, it may be helpful to ask them to keep a stress awareness diary in which they record stress-triggering events as well as their symptoms and reactions. When the stress diaries are discussed, encourage students to describe their personal appraisals of the events.

**Table 2. Recognizing stress.**

- How does it feel when you are stressed?
- How can you know that you are stressed?
- What sorts of thoughts do you have?
- How do you feel in your body?
- How does stress affect your behavior?
- How do you act toward other people when you are stressed? How do they act toward you?
- How can you tell when other people are stressed?
- Who do you know that is stressed?

**Table 3. Stink'in think'in (4 steps in reducing negative thoughts).**

**STOP:** Stop before you react.

**BREATHE:** Belly breathe to keep from getting tense. It is impossible to be tense and relaxed at the same time.

**REFLECT:** Examine the situation. What is the concern? Am I threatened? What thoughts and feelings am I having? What's the worst that could happen? Can I handle it? Am I jumping to conclusions? Is there another way to look at the situation?

**CHOOSE:** What do I want to happen? What can I do? What coping behaviors will work? Do I have the time, skills, and desire to achieve a solution? Am I avoiding? DECIDE!

(Adapted from materials used by the Learning Assistance Center at Wake Forest University, 2000)

The discussion can provide an opportunity to teach ways to restructure negative thoughts (see Table 3).

*Physical ways to manage stress.* Nutrition, physical activity, and sleep quality all impact people's mental health (McNamara, 2000). Professional school counselors can share information about the relationship between good health and coping with stressors. Unfortunately, many students do not eat nutritionally-balanced meals at home or at school. Also, insufficient sleep and exercise contribute to feelings of fatigue and irritability. Studies have shown that physical activity, in addition to strengthening muscles, bones, the cardiovascular system, and the respiratory system, helps decrease fatigue and moodiness (Lau, 2002). Regular physical exercise can boost self-confidence, increase resilience, and make students better able to handle frustration. Similarly, sleeping well "is central to coping with life, managing stress, and having positive feelings of well-being" (McNamara, 2000, p. 152). Children and adolescents, as well as adults, often spend far fewer hours than necessary getting quality sleep (Lau, 2002). Helping young people determine how much sleep they need and encouraging them to make commitments toward meeting that need can facilitate the stress management process.

Learning how to relax is another important stress management tool. Relaxation helps prevent some of the damaging physiological effects of stress and also helps prepare people to cope with stress more effectively. Being relaxed can refer to both an outlook on life (i.e., calm, laid back) and a skill that can be learned. Developing relaxation techniques can help replace depleted energy resources and prevent the build-up of tension. People have many different ways to relax, including listening to music, taking a hot bath, drawing or painting, working in the yard, and participating in imagery exercises. Help students explore ways of relaxing that are helpful to them and encourage them to participate in at least one relaxation activity daily. Abdominal breathing (or "belly breathing"), progressive relaxation, and imagery are relaxation techniques that are easily taught and can be used by students in virtually any surrounding. It may be helpful to tell students that some people feel silly when trying out these relaxation skills, especially at the beginning. With time and practice, the techniques become more comfortable and can be employed easily to help reduce tension (see Table 4).

**Table 4. Abdominal breathing.**

Abdominal breathing can be done in a sitting or standing position. Speaking slowly and quietly, ask students to close their eyes and do the following:

*Take a deep breath through your nose, very slowly. Pull the breath deeply into the bottom of your stomach (count 1-2-3-4). Then breathe out slowly through your mouth to the count of 8. (Repeat the breathing cycle) Place your hand on your stomach. You should be able to feel it move as you breathe. You will notice that as you continue breathing like this, you become very relaxed. (Repeat the breathing cycle) Now open your eyes. Notice the feelings you have in your body.*

Guided imagery or visualization can be used in conjunction with deep breathing to enhance the relaxation experience. Imagery can be used with classes, small groups, or individuals. To normalize the process and ensure that students do not confuse it with hypnosis, the professional school counselor may want to explain that commercials use visualization to sell products and that athletes use visualization to improve performance. There are many examples of imagery exercises in resource books. Typically, the professional school counselor will begin with abdominal breathing. Below is a short example (see Table 5) of an imagery exercise that can be read aloud after students have closed their eyes and started the breathing activity. After the students have completed the visualization exercise, tell them that when they feel stress in their bodies or have disturbing thoughts, to imagine this safe place again and to practice breathing deeply. Depending on the age of the students, the professional school counselor may encourage them to draw what they visualized, talk about their pictures, and/or discuss when they might imagine this safe place again.

**Table 5. Guided imagery.**

---

*First help the students move to a relaxed state through abdominal breathing. The counselor continues to speak slowly and quietly:*

Your whole body feels more relaxed. I am going to ask you to picture something in your mind's eye. If at any time you feel uncomfortable, open your eyes. Now, picture a place where you feel safe and cared for. *(Wait several seconds.)* Look around this safe, safe place. *(Wait several seconds.)* What is around you? *(Wait several seconds.)* Is this place inside or outside? *(Wait several seconds.)* Are there people or pets around you? *(Wait several seconds.)* What do you hear? *(Wait.)* Do you smell anything? *(Wait.)* Now stay in this safe place for a few minutes. *(Wait a few minutes.)* When you are ready, take a deep, deep breath and open your eyes.

---

*Study skills and time management.* Assignments, tests, and the pressure to succeed can all be sources of stress for students of all ages. Developing good study skills and time management skills are essential to academic success and stress reduction. Students can be taught to handle academic tasks in ways that are efficient and effective. Some suggestions that promote effective use of study time include:

- Practice active studying.
  - * Read the summary at the end of the chapter first. This will help you know what the author considers important.
  - * Read the questions at the end of the passage and all picture captions in advance. Try to answer the questions as you read.
  - * If you encounter a section that doesn't make sense, keep reading. Many times, questionable areas become clear with further reading.
  - * Review what you have read.
  - * Use mnemonics to help remember important facts. (Adults will need to teach children how to use this tool.)
- Find an ideal study environment.
  - * Establish a regular place to study. This can help with structure and motivation. Keep it attractive and organized.
  - * Control internal and external distractions.
  - * Be aware of your own body clock. Choose times to study when your energy level is high.
  - * Take breaks.
- Use time management tools.
  - * Clarify your goals. What is most important and why?
  - * Avoid procrastination. Establish a routine and reward yourself for completing tasks on time (e.g., invite a friend over, participate in a favorite activity).
  - * Keep a calendar or day-timer. Write down assignments, due dates, and other scheduled events.
  - * Break down large tasks into manageable units and plan for their completion.
  - * Keep a daily and weekly "to do" list to help prioritize activities and assignments. Check off completed tasks.
  - * Recognize the need for balance and flexibility.
  - * Keep things in perspective. Worry saps time and energy and is nonproductive. If you find yourself getting anxious about schoolwork, take time to relax and practice deep breathing. By simply breathing deeply, anxiety decreases.

*Working with Parents and Teachers*

*Parent workshops.* Involving a child's primary caregivers in stress management instruction can benefit students in numerous ways. Parents (or adults responsible for the student's care) are the experts on their children and interact with them on a daily basis. By offering parent education workshops, which might be titled, "Helping Your Student Deal with Stress," parents can be given tools to help children manage stress more effectively and learn ways to reduce stress in the home environment. Any of the topics listed in the section on *Psychoeducational Interventions for Students* can be included in a parent workshop. Additional things professional school counselors may want to share with parents include the following:

- Teach parents deep breathing techniques to use themselves when they feel stressed and so that they can reinforce the practice with their children.
- Television, movies, and computer viewing of virtual violence can create stress.
- Sharing adult worries with children can contribute to children's stress.
- Overly high expectations can be stressful. Many times, parents are not aware of the expectations their children perceive. Although parents may not require straight A's, children hear what is not said. A parent who expects perfection in himself/herself delivers a strong message that perfection is expected from each member of the family.
- Encourage parents to establish routines. Routines provide structure, eliminate uncertainty, and reduce chaos, which creates stress (Lau, 2002).
- Parents can be sensitive to overload on their families or their children and take steps to remove stressors. Parents have the responsibility of intervening on their children's behalf when necessary.
- Parents can be reminded of the importance of nutrition, exercise, and quality sleep to combat stress.
- Parents are essential in helping children at all levels with the study skills and time management skills described in the previous section.
- Parents can help children appraise stressful situations constructively and then implement appropriate coping strategies.
- Many parents need to hear and realize that THEY must be in control of the family. Parents, with the best of intentions, are increasingly allowing children to make adult decisions. Children who are asked to make these decisions before they are developmentally able suffer stress. The mantra, "Our family is a benign and loving monarchy," allows children to know that they are being cared for, loved, and protected.

*Working with teachers.* In addition to working with parents, professional school counselors will want to consult with teachers and offer in-service training on topics related to stress management. Teachers need information that will help them identify students who are suffering from stress. Behaviors that may indicate problems with stress in students include nail biting, fidgeting, separation anxiety, school phobia, bullying, violent and/or disruptive behavior, obsessive-compulsive behaviors, social problems, crying, and excessive worry. Helping teachers understand the link between thoughts, feelings, and behaviors promotes understanding, if not acceptance, of students' behaviors and can pave the way for making necessary interventions. Conceivably, teachers need to be reminded that the professional school counselor is available for individual and small group counseling, as well as whole class guidance, to help students cope with stress more effectively.

In-service workshops for teachers on stress management can focus on the same topics that are listed as psychoeducational topics for students. In particular, professional school counselors will want to provide information to school personnel about the stress process, stress symptoms, and associated consequences. It may be helpful to engage the group in deep breathing or progressive relaxation exercises as tools to use themselves and with their students.

Numerous stressors exist in schools, some that are unavoidable and others that are not. Professional school counselors can work with school personnel to identify stressors that are part of the school environment and find ways to eliminate or ameliorate those stressors that are amenable to change. For example, high stakes testing, which has become more and more prevalent over the past decade, has added stress to the school environment. Anxiety and stress surrounding educational evaluation is considerable (McDonald, 2001). Teachers sometimes unknowingly add to this pressure by reminding students throughout the year, "This will be on the final exam." During in-service workshops, it might be beneficial to have teachers brainstorm other wordings that might be less anxiety-provoking. Most teachers want students to understand the importance of tests but unwittingly add to student anxiety and stress by focusing too strongly on that importance. Test anxiety can impair performance and impact test results negatively.

*Group and Individual Counseling*

*Group counseling.* Students who have been exposed to trauma, non-normative changes, or failure are vulnerable to adverse stress reactions and may benefit from small group counseling (Robinson & Rotter, 1991). Professional school counselors can help these students explore self in relation to the life events that have affected them. Also, therapeutic stress reduction skills and coping strategies can be shared in counseling groups that deal with family changes, relationships, anger management, inappropriate behaviors, anxiety, and depression. When planning for group counseling, professional school counselors can use the following procedures:

- School policy sometimes requires that students have parental permission to participate in counseling groups. Other policies require that parents be notified about the group and the types of activities that will occur. Check with the head administrator before initiating any group.
- Survey the teachers to identify students who might benefit from stress management groups. Frequently this is done by putting a note in all the teachers' mailboxes explaining the nature of the group and requesting names of students who might benefit.
- After receiving these names, interview students to determine whether the student is an appropriate candidate for group participation and whether the student wants to participate.
- Notify or seek permission from parents. If a note is sent home, state the type of group, length and number of sessions, and activities that will take place in the group. Include a phone number where the professional school counselor can be reached if there are questions.
- Plan for the group, including time, place, and number of sessions. Include the activities that will take place in each session. Students' developmental levels need to be considered as activities are planned.
- Proceed with group sessions. During the first session, include an explanation of confidentiality and its limits in age-appropriate terms and describe the purpose of the group.
- Provide information about stress, its causes, and typical responses. Ask students to think of a situation that stresses them, then ask, "Where in your body do you feel that worry or stress?" and "What are your thoughts when you have those feelings?"
- Teach students relaxation techniques, including deep breathing, progressive relaxation, and visualization.

- In subsequent sessions, focus on learning and implementing coping strategies (mental strategies, physical ways of coping, interpersonal skills, problem solving, etc.). Provide students with opportunities to "rehearse" (through role play or other methods) their responses to anticipated stressful experiences.
- Encourage students to use their new skills and to teach them to family members.
- At the conclusion of the group, give students an opportunity to evaluate their experience.

*Individual counseling.* When stress seems to be a significant problem for a particular student, individual counseling may be warranted. Students may self-refer or be referred by teachers or parents. In many schools, long-term individual counseling is discouraged, and it may be necessary to make an outside referral so that the student gets the necessary help.

When working with any student individually, professional school counselors will want to explain confidentiality and its limits. Take time to build a therapeutic relationship and give the student an opportunity to tell his or her story. This will help the professional school counselor assess the severity of the problem and make decisions about next steps. Is the stress fear-based, and if so, is the fear specific or generalized? What is the students' sense of control, security, and self-worth? Some of the recommended interventions for helping individuals deal with stress include cognitive restructuring, cognitive self-control, systematic desensitization, and relaxation training, with combined approaches being most effective (Robinson & Rotter, 1991). In particular, professional school counselors will want to give students the opportunity to talk about what is stressful, identify their reactions to the stressful situation, explore effective coping strategies, and implement those strategies. If the student continues to manifest symptoms of distress or if the counselor suspects a more chronic condition (e.g., anxiety, PTSD, depression, abuse), it would be appropriate to suggest individual or family counseling in the community.

## Summary/Conclusions

Stress is a pervasive problem that affects students at all grade levels. Within recent decades, it appears that youth are experiencing more adverse reactions to stress than in the past. Stressors can come in many forms, including developmental transitions, life events, catastrophic events, and daily hassles. Indeed, change of any type can be stressful. When students experience stress, several different physical, cognitive, and emotional responses are likely. Chronic, long-term exposure to stress can be detrimental to physical and emotional health and well-being.

People cope with stress in numerous ways, with some coping strategies being more adaptive than others. Active, problem-focused coping tends to yield better outcomes than emotion-focused coping, particularly when the coping style is characterized by avoidance. In addition to individual coping styles, protective factors such as family and peer support, self-confidence, and an internal sense of control appear to affect the manner in which young people manage stress.

Professional school counselors can intervene on multiple levels to help students manage stress more effectively. Primary prevention methods include classroom guidance lessons, parent workshops, and teacher training sessions and consultation on topics related to stress management. In cases where students are at risk for stress-related problems or have evidenced poor coping skills, professional school counselors can offer group and individual counseling as well as coordinate services for those students who need outside professional help. Professional school counselors play instrumental roles in helping create safe, supportive schools and in teaching students and their caregivers life skills that will help them cope effectively with present and future stressors.

## References


Compas, B. E. (1987). Stress and life events during childhood and adolescence. *Clinical Psychology Review, 7*, 275-302.

D'Imperio, R. L., & Dubow, E. F. (2000). Resilient and stress-affected adolescents in an urban setting. *Journal of Clinical Child Psychology, 29,* 129-142.

Disaster and Trauma. (2002, January). *Harvard Mental Health Letter, 18*, 1-5.

Frydenberg, E. (1997). *Adolescent coping: Theoretical and research perspectives*. London: Routledge.

Hains, A. A. (1994). The effectiveness of a school-based cognitive-behavioral stress management program with adolescents. *School Counselor, 42*, 114-125.

Heaven, P. C. L. (1996). *Adolescent health: The role of individual differences*. London: Routledge.

Herman-Stahl, M. A., & Petersen, A. C. (1996). The protective role of coping and social resources for depressive symptoms among young adolescents. *Journal of Youth and Adolescence, 25,* 733-753.

Lau, B. W. K. (2002). Stress in children: Can nurses help? *Pediatric Nursing, 28*, 13-19.

Lazarus, R. S. (1966). *Stress and the coping process.* London: McGraw-Hill.

Lazarus, R. S., & Folkman, S. (1984). *Stress, appraisal and coping*. New York: Springer.

McDonald, A. S. (2001). The prevalence and effects of test anxiety in school children. *Educational Psychology, 21*, 89-92.

McNamara, S. (2000). *Stress in young people: What's new and what can we do?* New York: Continuum.

National Institute of Mental Health. (2001). *Helping children and adolescents cope with violence and disasters.* Retrieved July 1, 2002, from http://www.nimh.nih.gov/publicat/depchildresfact.cfm

Olbrich, E. (1990). Coping and development. In H. Bosma and S. Jackson (Eds.), *Coping and self concept in adolescence* (pp. 35-47). London: Springer-Verlag.

Plunkett, S. W., Radmacher, K. A., & Moll-Pharana, D. (2000). Adolescent life events, stress, and coping: A comparison of communities and genders. *Professional School Counseling, 3,* 356-367.

Robinson, E. H., & Rotter, J. C. (1991). *Coping with fears and stress.* (Report No. EDO-CG-91-3). Washington, DC: Office of Educational Research and Improvement. (ERIC Document Reproduction Service No. ED341888)

Sharrer, V. W., & Ryan-Wenger, N. A. (2002). School-age children's self-reported stress symptoms. *Pediatric Nursing, 28,* 21-27.

Shoffner, M. F., & Newsome, D. W. (2002). Using focus groups to examine adolescents' career-related interests in science, math, and technology. Manuscript submitted for publication.

# Chapter 83

## Helping Students Manage Anger

*Jack Charlesworth*

### Preview

The purpose of this chapter is to provide an introduction to anger management interventions, with specific focus on applications and techniques that professional school counselors can use in providing individual and group counseling to students with anger-related problems. Classroom guidance topics and activities for educating students about anger and effective anger management are also discussed.

The *Dictionary of Psychology* (2nd ed.)(Chaplin, 1985) defines anger as "an acute emotional reaction elicited by any of a number of stimulating situations, including threat, overt aggression, restraint, verbal attack, disappointment, or frustration" (p. 27). Although mental health practitioners and researchers have discussed the lack of conceptual clarity of anger and its related processes (Smith, Larson, DeBaryshe & Salzman, 2000), it is commonly accepted that anger is a normal human emotion that can be viewed at three levels: 1) *physical symptoms* of feelings of anger may include increased heart rate, muscular tension, and adrenaline flow; 2) *cognitive experiences* of anger frequently include distorted negative perceptions and interpretations of others' behaviors; and 3) *behavioral indications* of anger may include a variety of physical and verbal outbursts such as yelling, screaming, kicking, and fighting. These reactions to anger can be directed towards others or self.

Anger is generally perceived negatively because, unmanaged, it can lead to aggression and violence. But anger can also serve an adaptive, positive function. Anger can stimulate us to take action when we or loved ones are under the threat of attack, and can serve as an impetus for us to take appropriate actions to bring about needed changes, such as better or more equitable rules or laws (Bowers, 1994).

Because anger is an emotion that can have adverse consequences for both self and others, it is important that the problem be addressed early. Childre & Rozman (2003) noted that the problem is not anger, but that individuals frequently do not know how to manage anger. Nowhere has the problem of anger management been more evident than with school-age students.

Professional school counselors are in a unique position to be able to help individuals in our society understand and effectively cope with feelings of anger. Professional school counselors provide students with needed classroom guidance and individual and group counseling anger management programs and services, beginning with their entrance into elementary schools.

The purpose of this chapter is to provide an introduction to anger management interventions, with specific emphasis on practical applications and techniques that professional school counselors can use in working with students in individual and small group counseling. In addition, instruction and activities that can be incorporated into guidance classroom lessons that educate students about anger and anger awareness and methods for reducing the development of anger related problems will also be discussed.

*Cognitive-Behavioral Interventions*

The most frequently used individual and group treatment approaches for anger, and those considered to be most effective, have a basis in cognitive-behavioral therapy (Beck & Fernandez, 1998; Childre & Rozman, 2003). Smith et al. (2000) conducted a comprehensive review of anger management programs for students covering school-based programs and a variety of other treatment centers, including clinical and residential settings. The review provided professional school counselors with an understanding of the types and content of anger management programs contained in the professional literature. Of the 37 articles included in the review, the vast majority (29 out of 37, or 78%) of the studies incorporated two or more treatment approaches, and the use of cognitive-behavioral interventions in these studies was almost universal.

The two most recognized cognitive-behavioral theoretical approaches to anger management are Beck's (1976; 2000) Cognitive-Behavioral Therapy (CBT), and Ellis' (Ellis, 1977; Ellis & Harper, 1975) Rational Emotive Behavior Therapy (REBT). Although each of these approaches has distinctive features, both have much in common. Both approaches require students to identify the situations/events in which they experience anger. Emphasis is then placed on helping students to identify the thoughts/cognitions that precede anger. The major intervention common to both approaches is to help students determine whether these cognitions (thoughts) are rational or irrational (Ellis, 1977; Ellis & Harper, 1975), correct or false, distorted or inaccurate (Beck, 1976; 2000) and to replace irrational/inaccurate thoughts with more rational or accurate ones.

Ellis and Harper (1975) believed that students' unhealthy emotions are due to their adherence to ten basic false philosophical beliefs or irrational thoughts. From his approach, Ellis attempts to change students' false assumptions by confronting their irrational thoughts, demonstrating how illogical the thoughts are, and teaching how to replace the thoughts with more rational thoughts that can result in students changing basic philosophical assumptions and values.

In contrast to Ellis' REBT, which is often highly directive, persuasive, confrontive and didactically oriented, Beck's (CBT) places more emphasis upon the importance of the student/counselor relationship, and primarily utilizes open-ended Socratic questioning to help students reflect upon and discover the inaccuracies of their own thinking. Both approaches value homework assignments including reading assignments, have students engage in behaviors designed to test the validity of cognitions, and frequently draw upon a wide range of behavioral techniques.

The following brief scenario illustrates some examples of the irrational/inaccurate thoughts that both Ellis and Beck believed frequently lead to inappropriate feelings of anger, and how a counselor might intervene:

> Tom asked his best friend and classmate, Jason, to wait for him so they could walk home together after school. When Tom discovered that Jason wasn't waiting for him after school, Tom had the following thoughts that created feelings of anger for him:
>
> - "Jason *should have* waited for me."
> - "It is *terrible* and *awful* that Jason didn't wait," and
> - "You can *never* count on Jason for anything."

Given this scenario, both Ellis and Beck would help Tom see that his thoughts are irrational/inaccurate and help him to replace them with more rational/accurate thoughts. Ellis would be more likely to didactically teach Tom that his thoughts are irrational by confronting and telling him something like the following: "Although it would have been nice if Jason had waited for you, there is no law that says that he *must, has to, or should have* waited for you," "Although Jason didn't meet you, it isn't terrible or awful, your world isn't collapsing, but this is a minor annoyance because he didn't do what you wanted," and finally "Jason has done many things for you, and that not doing one thing doesn't mean you can't count on him for other things."

In contrast to Ellis' intervention in the scenario, Beck would be more likely to achieve the same ends by using Socratic questions, such as "Other than that you wanted Jason to wait for you, is there any reason why he *should have* waited for you? Was Jason's not waiting for you terrible or awful, or merely disappointing or annoying for you?" And, "Does Jason's not waiting for you in this one instance mean that you can never count on him, or does it just mean that he didn't wait this one time?"

Donald Meichenbaum's (1977) cognitive behavior modification (CBM) is another major cognitive-behavioral therapy that has been successfully used in treating anger. Like REBT and CBT, CBM shares the assumption that distressing emotions are typically due to maladaptive thoughts. CBM focuses more on making students more aware of their self talk, and training them to develop more effective self talk that will enable them to cope more effectively in problematic situations.

Stress inoculation training (SIT) (Meichenbaum, 1985) is a particular coping skills program developed by Meichenbaum to aid in stress reduction, and has been demonstrated to be effective with a number of problems, including anger (Corey, 2000). SIT appears to be particularly beneficial when the student experiences anger in relatively specific situations. In addition to helping the student learn helpful behavioral techniques, the student is taught a number of relatively specific coping thoughts to assist them in working through the anger provoking situation.

*Behavioral Interventions*

Cognitive-behavior approaches differentially incorporate a wide variety of behavioral techniques in treating anger problems. These include:

- *Relaxation training.* Students can be taught to relax using a variety of modalities including progressive relaxation (learning to systematically tighten and then relaxing the muscle groups of the body), yoga exercises, or meditation.
- *Homework assignments.* Students may be assigned to engage in self-monitoring of their thoughts and/or behaviors, keep an anger log, practice engaging in new behaviors, or participate in bibliotherapy.
- *Assertiveness training.* Before students are taught behavioral assertiveness skills, students are frequently taught the difference between non-assertive, assertive, and aggressive behavior. In addition, any cognitive distortions or irrational thoughts impeding assertive behavior are replaced (Lange & Jakubowski, 1976). Students can then learn assertiveness skills, through modeling, role-playing, and graded task assignments in real life situations.
- *Distraction techniques.* After learning to identify cognitive and/or bodily cues that are precursors of anger, students can be taught a variety of distraction techniques, including counting to 10, removing themselves from the environment, or using humor (seeing an aggressor in their underwear or wearing a clown's costume).
- *Imagery.* Imagery can be used in helping students learn relaxation and as another distraction technique by envisioning themselves in calm, peaceful scenes. Professional school counselors can also use imagery to help students see themselves effectively using their learned cognitive and behavioral skills in what previously were anger provoking situations.
- *Problem solving skills.* Students can be taught a "general problem solving model" to assist in identifying a wider repertoire of methods for coping with anger provoking situations.
- *Social skills training.* Students can be taught a wide range of social skills, such as smiling and providing eye contact, to assist in developing interpersonal skills.
- *Communication skills.* Students can be taught how to actively listen and how to produce "I messages."

Phillips-Hershey & Kanagy (1996) provided practical suggestions on how to teach middle and high school students communication skills as a proactive way to deal with anger in a positive way. They specifically emphasized the need to teach students how to effectively use "I-Messages" and provided a number of methods they believed could be effectively used in classroom guidance or small group counseling sessions. First, students are directed to identify all the things they feel angry about, what they do when they feel angry, the consequences of their actions, and whether the consequences experienced are what they wanted. The students are then informed that anger is OK, but that frequently the way people express anger makes a conflict situation worse. Secondly, a professional school counselor orally gives the students a "You-Message" and then asks that they discuss the impact of the message upon them. The students are then given the same content in an "I-Message" format and again asked the impact of the message upon them. After discussing the difference between their reactions to the "You-Messages" and the "I-Messages" students are directed to role-play two skits, each involving one of the messages, and then again asked to compare the different impact of the two messages. Next, students are given brief written scenarios and asked to write appropriate "I-Messages" for each. Finally, students are asked to role-play giving "I-messages" to someone they feel anger towards. Phillip-Hershey and Kanagy (1996) also provided a method for evaluating the program for both the students and professional school counselor.

Professional school counselors who come from more of a pure behavioral counseling approach also use many of the behavioral techniques just described. As opposed to cognitive-behaviorally-oriented counselors who see the main benefit of the behavioral techniques as producing changes in cognition, traditional behaviorists see the main benefit of these techniques as producing changes in behavior. Traditional behaviorists are also more likely to use positive reinforcement for students engaging in appropriate behavior, and extinction or punishment when needed to help eliminate aggressive behavior.

*Play Therapy*

Another viable method for reducing anger problems is individual play therapy (Fischetti, 2001). Rather than accepting that one standardized play therapy approach is the most effective for all clients and situations, Fischetti (2001) preferred a prescriptive approach that enabled a professional school counselor to choose one they believe will be most effective.

Fischetti (2001) identified three approaches useful for planning treatment for students with anger management problems. *Client-centered play therapy* is a nondirective approach that is a viable choice when the clinician can provide the student time to pursue their issues and personal growth. *Release play therapy* is a structured approach to assist clients in reenacting a stressful event and working through the pain and anger associated with it. Finally, *cognitive-behavioral play therapy* enables the clinician to utilize a wide range of behavioral techniques, such as, antecedents, reinforcers, contingencies, modeling, relaxation training, systematic desensitization, and cognitive interventions, such as learning to identify and replace dysfunctional thoughts, to best meet the treatment goals jointly developed with the student. A frequent component of cognitive-behavioral play therapy is student homework.

In addition to describing play-therapy approaches, Fischetti (2001) provided a number of case examples intended to demonstrate their treatment effectiveness. Kaduson and Shaefer (1997, 2001) and Jones (1998) provided a variety of individual and group play therapy techniques and activities that can be incorporated into appropriate play therapy approaches to assist students in working through anger management issues. Examples of such techniques and activities are:

- *The Mad Game* (Davidson, 1997, pp. 224-225) is used to help clients (ages 3 – 13 years) in individual or group play therapy learn how to express anger appropriately both verbally and kinesthetically. Participants in the game are asked to take turns stacking cardboard bricks or plastic blocks one on top of the other as they make statements about what angers them. Once all bricks or blocks are stacked the identified student is asked to express something he/she really feels angry about and then knocks down the bricks using any manner they choose.

- *Computer Storytelling* (Brewer, 1997, pp. 32-34) is used in individual play therapy to help students develop alternative feelings, thoughts, and methods for resolving a current struggle. The student is asked to develop an original story with a beginning, middle and end. The student may choose to type the story, dictate and have the therapist type the story, or alternate typing paragraphs with the therapist. While the student is developing the story the therapist looks for the character representing the student and any themes or patterns that relate to problem solving or relationship issues, and may ask the student questions about them. Aggressive students enjoy a sense of mastery and control over the computer, while learning to abide by the rules and procedures required to use it effectively.
- *Relaxation Training: Bubble Breaths* (Cabe, 2001, p. 346) is used in play therapy to help students learn relaxation training that can be used to reduce feelings of anxiety and anger, and the accompanying physical reactions.

  > Children fill the room with bubbles and "pop" them as they fall. Children are then invited to "pop" the bubbles one at a time which is more challenging but can be done with practice. Attention is then directed toward the deep breathing and controlled exhaling involved. The therapist follows this with instruction on how to breathe from the tummy. Students are taught how they can use a series of three bubble breaths to relax when they begin to feel anxious or angry. This approach has been used successfully with all age ranges and with individuals as well as large groups.

- *Out of Control* (Jones, 1998) is a group play therapy activity for 4 to 15 students who experience anger and frustration when things don't go the way they want. Some small prize items (a few more than the number in the group) and a pair of dice are placed on a table in front of the group members. There are two rounds to the game. In the first round, each participant rolls the dice in turn. Those who roll a double dice select a prize and open it; participants not rolling a double dice cannot choose a prize. The dice is passed until all the prizes are gone. One participant may end of up with several prizes while others may end up with none. Before beginning the second round, students are told that this round is timed (5 minutes for smaller groups, 10 minutes, for larger ones), and that double rolls are now used to select prizes from other members. The game continues until the allotted time elapses. Again, some participants may have several prizes while others may have none. At the end of the game the participants are given numerous questions to discuss, including: What do you do when things don't go your way? How do you handle things when life doesn't seem fair or is out of control? What can you do when life seems out of control? Did anyone feel angry during the game, and, if so, how did you handle it?

*Classroom Guidance*

There are many ways that professional school counselors can incorporate anger, anger prevention, and anger management into their classroom guidance and psychoeducational efforts. A combination of age-appropriate direct instruction, activities, and exercises can be used to help students learn:

- what anger is;
- the physiological cues associated with angry feelings;
- the relationship between thoughts and feelings;
- the difference between thoughts, feelings, and behavior;
- cognitive and behavioral strategies for reducing arousal;
- "healthy versus unhealthy anger";
- consequences of anger;
- general problem solving and coping skills.

## Summary/Conclusion

Anger is a normal human emotion that can stimulate people to engage in constructive acts, or lead to destructive behaviors. Frequently anger problems first become apparent during a student's school years. Professional school counselors, particularly elementary counselors, are in a unique position to proactively help students better understand anger and learn effective anger management through classroom guidance classes. In addition, with knowledge and skill using cognitive-behavioral, behavioral or play therapy interventions, professional school counselors can provide students with anger problems effective, age-appropriate individual and group counseling services.

## References

Beck, A. T. (1976). *Cognitive therapy and emotional disorders.* New York: International Universities Press.

Beck, A. T. (2000). *Prisoners of hate: The cognitive basis of anger, hostility, and violence.* New York: Perennial.

Beck, R., & Fernandez, E. (1998). Cognitive-behavioral therapy in the treatment of anger: A meta-analysis. *Cognitive Therapy & Research, 22,* 63-74.

Bowers, R. (1994). Children and anger. In A. Thomas & J. Grimes (Eds.), *Children's needs: Psychological perspectives* (pp. 31-37). Silver Springs, MD: National Association of School Psychologists.

Brewer, N. E. (1997). Computer storytelling. In H. G. Kaduson & C. E. Schaefer (Eds.), *101 favorite play therapy techniques* (pp. 32-34). Northvale, NJ: J. Aronson.

Cabe, N. (2001). Relaxation training: Bubble breaths. In H. G. Kaduson & C. E. Schaefer (Eds.), *101 more favorite play therapy techniques* (pp. 346-349). Northvale, NJ: J. Aronson.

Chaplin, J. P. (1985). *Dictionary of psychology* (2nd ed.). New York: Dell Publishing.

Childre, D., & Rozman, D. (2003). *Transforming anger: The HeartMath solution for letting go of rage, frustration, and irritation.* Oakland, CA: New Harbinger Publications.

Corey, G. (2000). *Theory and practice of counseling and psychotherapy* (6th ed.). Pacific Grove, CA: Brooks/Cole.

Davidson, P. (1997). The mad game. In H. G. Kaduson & C. E. Schaefer (Eds.), *101 favorite play therapy techniques* (pp. 224-225). Northvale, NJ: J. Aronson.

Ellis, A. (1977). *Anger: How to live with and without it.* Secaucus, NJ: Citadel Press.

Ellis, A., & Harper, R. (1975). *A new guide to rational living* (rev. ed.). Hollywood, CA: Wilshire Books.

Fischetti, B. (2001). Use of play therapy for anger management in the school setting. In A. A. Drewes, C. E. Schaefer, & L. Carey (Eds.), *School-based play therapy* (pp. 238-255). New York: Wiley.

Jones, A. (1998). *104 Activities that build: Self-esteem, teamwork, communication, anger management, self-discovery, coping skills.* Richland, WA: RecRoom Publishing.

Kaduson, H., & Schaefer, J. (1997). *101 favorite play therapy techniques.* Northvale, NJ: J. Aronson.

Kaduson, H., & Schaefer, J. (2001). *101 more favorite play therapy techniques.* Northvale, NJ: J. Aronson.

Lange, A., & Jakubowski, P. (1976). *Responsible assertive behavior: Cognitive/behavioral procedures for trainers.* Champaign, IL: Research Press.

Meichenbaum, D. (1977). *Cognitive behavior modification: An integrative approach.* New York: Plenum.

Meichenbaum, D. (1985). *Stress inoculation training.* New York: Pergamon Press.

Phillips-Hershey, E., & Kanagy, B. (1996). Teaching students to manage personal anger constructively. *Elementary School Guidance & Counseling, 30,* 229-235.

Smith, D., Larson, J., DeBaryshe, B., & Salzman, M. (2000). Anger management for youths: What works and for whom? In D. S. Sandhu & C. B. Aspy (Eds.), *Violence in American schools: A practical guide for counselors* (pp. 217-230). Alexandria, VA: American Counseling Association.

# Chapter 84

## Bereavement in Schools: How to Respond

*Susan Norris Huss & Antoinette Banks*

### Preview

This chapter will describe how the professional school counselor can take a leadership role in making his/her school "grief friendly." An overview of children's perceptions of death and typical grief reactions of different age groups is provided, followed by a brief description of the stages of grief and how these stages are experienced as age driven and individual specific. While a major focus of the chapter involves individual and group techniques, brief attention will be given to preventive programs which can be included in a comprehensive developmental counseling program.

Bereavement is present in many forms in every school. Grief occurs any time a student experiences a loss. One out of every 20 American students under the age of 15 loses at least one parent to death (Steen, 1998). It is also estimated that in a secondary school of 800 students, 24 students will experience the death of a family member (Selekman et al., 2001). There are no estimates of how many children experience the death of a grandparent, sibling, close friend or even a pet (Myers, 1999). Grief also occurs through non-death-related losses (e.g., not making the football team, losing a homework assignment, moving to a new building, or anytime there is a major change in one's life). This prevalence of bereavement dictates that professional school counselors must understand bereavement and its manifestations in students, as well as be able to provide the security, continuity, and support that bereaved students need.

Students from preschool to late adolescence experience grief when a loss occurs. This is a relatively new belief. At one time it was believed that children did not have the capacity to grieve (Freud, 1957, Miller, 1971). Through the work of Piaget (Wadsworth, 1984) and Erickson (Bowlby, 1980; Eggan & Kauchak, 1992), this belief has changed. Bereavement and grief is very much a part of students' school experience and, thus, becomes important for professional school counselors to be able to assist students and school personnel in the bereavement process.

The goal should be to create a "grief friendly" school environment (McGlauflin, 2002). McGlauflin described this environment as one that not only responds in a healthy way to a crisis, but is also sensitive to the numerous and various losses students experience throughout a school year. Table 1 provides several characteristics of McGlauflin's "grief-friendly" school.

**Table 1. McGlauflin's (2002) "grief-friendly" school characteristics.**

- Supportive crisis action team
- Knowledgeable about grief
- Recognition of the uniqueness of every crisis, death, and loss in the school
- Open and honest communication with students about any loss
- Respect for all feelings
- Acceptance of the consciousness of grief
- Acknowledgment and respect of all the good-byes in the school throughout the year
- Remembering that education is the mission of the school
- Maintenance of standards in compassionate manner
- Collective support for each other

## Beliefs About Death

Age is a major contributing factor to how a student perceives death. Although past experience and cognitive ability also impact these beliefs for each individual, there are some general perceptions about and general reactions to death for different age groups (see Table 2). It is important for professional school counselors to understand these differences in order to provide appropriate interventions for the student.

**Table 2. General age-related perceptions of death.**

| Ages 3-5 | Ages 6-9 | Ages 10-13 | Ages 14-18 |
|---|---|---|---|
| Reversible | Permanence is understood | Overwhelmed | Accepts that death is universal |
| Temporary | Universality belief begins | Wants facts | Intense feelings of adolescence carries over to grief |
| Magical | Personifies death | Believes may have caused the death | Turns to friends for support more so than adults |
| Sense of security is threatened | Wider social network | Begins to understand finality of death | May be suicidal |
| May regress in behavior | Model adult reactions | Begins to realize they may die | May feel pressure to assume more adult roles |
| May cry and become clingy | Curious about rituals | May have psychosomatic symptoms | |
| | Very concrete questions | Grieves more like adults and "want to get on with life" | |

Note: Compiled from Christ, 2000; Selekman et al. 2001; Worden, 2001

When working with bereaved students it is essential to understand the developmental nature of the grieving process. As students develop cognitively, their level of understanding of a death experience changes. With this new understanding comes a new set of questions related to the death as well as the possibility that they will grieve again for the death of a loved one. It is not only important to remember that anniversaries (death, birthdays) and significant events (graduation, prom, parents' night) may cause a reoccurrence of some grieving, but also that simply a new level of understanding can bring about the same reoccurrence of grief.

The generally accepted concept of "stages of grief" takes on a new meaning when working with children. Those stages are generally shock and denial, anger, bargaining, depression, and acceptance (Kubler-Ross, 1969). Generally one thinks of moving through one stage and then another. However, it can also be seen as a roller coaster because it goes up and down in intensity. Other students' experiences may be more like a coil with them grieving again and again in a spiral manner as their understanding increases. The major implications of this spiraling effect is to be aware that interventions such as loss support groups should not be limited to only recently bereaved students; just as one should not be surprised at the repetitive nature of student questions. The resolution of grief often requires cyclical processing as students grow up.

Although each person grieves in his/her own unique way, there are some general reactions that could be considered "normal" grieving processes (Perry, 2001). These may include (but are not limited to): denial; emotional numbing; anger, irritability, episodic rage; fear and characteristic rushes of anxiety; confusion; difficulty sleeping; regressive behaviors; physical complaints such as stomachaches or headaches; changes in appetite. All stakeholders need to acquire an understanding of common student bereavement characteristics.

## Proactive Programming

A "grief friendly" school provides opportunities (workshops, seminars, in-services) for all stakeholders in the school (teachers, staff, parents) to be informed about the common characteristics of grief in students as well as what is considered to be normal grief reactions. There should also be an updated, functioning crisis response plan in place for those crisis situations that create losses in schools. There is not space in this chapter to detail these two preventive programs but a professional school counselor can play an instrumental role in insuring that these aspects are in place.

The comprehensive developmental school counseling program should include classroom guidance activities related to bereavement and the grieving process. Since this form of "death education" may be questioned, it can be positively marketed as helping students to develop loss coping skills since there are so many losses commonly experienced in schools. The information learned by students in these sessions provides the basis for student belief that the school is "grief-friendly." Learning loss coping skills can provide all students with the skills needed to cope with these daily losses and provide a resource of learned behavior for the major losses such as the death of a parent.

## Interventions

When a student has suffered a loss it is important that interventions be designed to: provide opportunities to share feelings and memories; assist in identifying support systems; assist in the development of coping mechanisms to help them process as they go through the grieving experience; normalize their feelings; provide a safe environment to do all the above (Huss, 1997).

*Group Counseling*

One recommended way of providing the interventions listed above is through group work (Jacobs, Harvill & Masson, 1994; Johnson-Schroetlin, 2000; Sharpnack 2000; Yalom, 1985). Group work is efficient because more than one student is being served at a time, there are more resources and viewpoints within the group than within a single individual and groups provide the needed sense of universality and commonality for the bereaved child. Detailed group program plans are available from several sources (Haasl, 2000; Lehmann, 2001a; Lehmann, 2001b; Webb, 2002).

Expressing, acknowledging, and owning one's feelings is extremely important when working with a bereaved student. Students are often confused by conflicting feelings (e.g., relief and sadness if the death was after a prolonged illness). Having never experienced a feeling before may be frightening and they need to understand that any feeling is OK and normal for someone experiencing grief. Most of the interventions discussed here can be used to assist in the understanding of feelings, expression of feelings, and understanding of the universality and commonality of feelings. This understanding of the universality and commonality allows bereaved students to move through the grieving process. In addition, the interventions described in the rest of this chapter can be used in group settings as well as when working with individuals.

*Artistic activities.* Art in many forms (e.g., music, drawing, sculpture) can be an effective means of expressing feelings about a loss. Students can draw pictures of how they feel or pictures of the loved one who has died (or the loss), and share pictures and stories with the group. Students can express how they felt about the activity, whether or not it helped them to talk about the loss, what the picture means to them, or how it relates to the way they feel. Modeling clay and play dough can also be used to give the student the experience of creating images that express feelings. Another good activity is to have students draw a picture of their family before and after the loss. This provides a basis for discussion about family differences and similarities after the loss. It also provides an opportunity to discuss the student's remaining support system.

*Bibliotherapy.* Books provide a wide variety of opportunities for intervention with bereaved students. Books can be read to the student, with the student, or by the student and then discussed at a later session. A book about death can also be read to a class that is anxious about a classmate who has experienced death and preparing a list of recommended books can provide support for families as they strive to assist in the bereavement process. The professional school counselor should develop a resource library, preferably in the media center. Reading or creating poetry that expresses feelings or grief concerning the loss can also help the student during the grieving process.

*Playing.* Toys and playing with young students may be helpful as a means of expressing feelings that are hard to express and hard to understand. Dolls, aggressive toys, animals (stuffed or plastic), and other toys and games can be used by the student in playing out anxieties and emotions involved with issues related to grief or loss. Puppets are especially helpful for reluctant participants.

*Storytelling.* Students from pre-school through middle school may benefit from storytelling. Students can be given sentence starters that they can use to either tell or write a story. Examples of sentence starters are: Someday I would like to. . . . ; I wish I would have . . . .; If I could . . . .; Whenever I see . . . . ; and When I think about . . . . Sentence starters can be created to meet the specific circumstances of the student's loss.

*Letter writing.* Writing a letter to the person who died can be a powerful tool for saying good-bye or to share something that was left unsaid because of the death. A letter written to someone with whom the student desires to share feelings concerning the loss can be the beginning of communication. Families often send unintentional messages that it is not OK to talk about a loss. Writing a letter can begin the much needed communication process.

*Journaling.* Students can be encouraged to keep a journal of the feelings they are experiencing as well as questions they may have. Journal entries can be used to facilitate discussion with students to assist them during this transitional time in life. Keeping a journal allows students to express feelings and can be a record of their bereavement journey. They can reflect about feelings and see that feelings change during their journey in intensity, type, and duration.

*Celebrating life through memory work.* Memory work is also a way of both expressing feelings and normalizing what has happened. It also provides a means of keeping the deceased in the student's life in an appropriate manner. Group or individual collages can be made from pictures of the deceased loved one. Show-and-tell type activities can be effective. Students can bring items belonging to the deceased person and share something about the relevance of the item or the memory of the person to whom the item belongs. Memory books can be made either individually or as a group. Pictures, drawings, and letters are samples of what can be included in memory books. Memory books provide a way to keep the person who died in the student's life in an appropriate manner. By creating a memory book, the student is honoring the deceased without obsessing, thereby providing a mechanism for moving forward through the grieving process.

*Closure.* It is very important in working with bereaved students to plan events to provide closure when the student is ready. This does not mean that the deceased is forgotten. It means the child is ready to move forward. Balloons and bubbles can be used in concluding activities when presented as methods of releasing or letting go. This could include letting go of someone, a feeling, an attitude or other emotions connected to loss.

## Special Circumstances

A great many students will experience the death of a close family member. The professional school counselor is often confused about the appropriate role to play. Some specific suggestions follow.

*Death of a Family Member.*

When a member of a student's family dies, the professional school counselor, if at all possible, should make contact with the family. Depending on the religion/culture of the family, the professional school counselor should participate in an appropriate manner. An example would be to visit the mortuary and talk with the student. That discussion could include:

- An expression of sympathy.
- Informing the student the professional school counselor will be visiting his classroom(s), asking for input into what he would like to be said, and telling the student exactly what will be shared. This eases the mind of the student and gives direction to the professional school counselor.
- What kind of support the professional school counselor will provide once the student returns to school (e.g., opportunities to talk, providing a quiet place when needed, talking with other students).

The professional school counselor should then visit the classroom(s) of the bereaved student and talk about how to be a good friend to a bereaved student. This visit should include:

- Setting the record straight. This is particularly needed if it is a violent death since there may be many rumors.
- Helping the class decide how they will express their sympathy to the bereaved family (e.g., flowers, cards, visit to the funeral home or funeral).
- A discussion of how the student wishes to be treated when she returns to school. This often assures the students that the bereaved student is doing OK since the professional school counselor has talked with her.
- A general discussion of grief and bereavement.
- A discussion about the feelings students are experiencing and why (e.g., fear that their parent may die, reoccurring feelings from a loss they have experienced in the past). It may be helpful to encourage students to tell their families that a friend has experienced this loss or, with younger students, to send a note home. This gives the families the opportunity to be alert to any needs that may arise from this experience.
- Awareness that this is a "teachable moment." It is an opportunity to either reinforce what was taught in a developmental guidance unit presented before the loss occurred or, if that hasn't happened, to teach those concepts now.

Of concern for many professional school counselors when a family death occurs is the religious or spiritual questions that are often asked by the bereaved student (e.g., Do you believe that when someone dies, they go to heaven?). These questions should be redirected to what the student and student's family believes. The same is true of certain rituals associated with the funeral. These kinds of questions may also be asked during the classroom visit.

*Suicide Situations*

Educators may be unsure how to talk with students about suicide. Goodman (2002) suggested ways to talk about suicide with students.

1. Define suicide as when "someone chooses to make their body stop working."
2. Give age appropriate facts and explanations.
3. Dispel myths about suicide.
4. Retell good memories.
5. Model feelings and thoughts for students.
6. Emphasize suicide is a mistake because there "is always another way out."

It is important to get the message to all students that suicide is not a good choice and to provide other choices so there is less chance of a "copycat suicide."

*Complicated Grief*

Determining when a referral needs to be made is difficult because of the developmental nature of student bereavement, but generally if the symptom persists for an extended period of time or does not lessen in intensity it could be cause for alarm. Some possible serious problems related to grief (which may indicate the presence of complicated grief) include: extended loss of interest in activities; prolonged inability to sleep or sleeping all the time; persistent loss of appetite; fear of being alone; long-term regression; imitating the dead person; statements of wanting to join the deceased; withdrawal from friends; school phobia. Cases involving complicated grief should be immediately referred to mental health professionals specializing in the treatment of such cases.

## Summary/Conclusion

This has been a brief description of some of the more important aspects of working with bereaved children in a "grief friendly" school. The school may be and should be the most stable place in a student's life during the time immediately following the death of the loved one. This stability is supported by remembering the educational mission of the school and maintaining the usual discipline, expectations, and academic standards. At the same time, it is important to create an environment that respects the needs of the bereaved child whether the loss involves a low grade, a lost friendship, or the death of a parent. It should also be the place that understands the developmental nature of childhood bereavement and thus provides ongoing support for the bereaved student. The professional school counselor needs to work continuously to keep informed of resources available to use in the school as well as resources available outside the school not only for the bereaved students, but for those within the school.

The "grief friendly" school has both proactive and reactive programming in place to assist all stakeholders in the bereavement process. This may be one of the most challenging aspects of the school counseling program, but since there is such a prevalence of grief in the school it is also one of the most important.

## References


Bowlby, J. (1980). *Attachment and loss: Volume III. Loss: Sadness and depression.* New York: Basic.

Christ, G. H. (2000). Impact of development on children's mourning. *Cancer Practice, 8,* 72-81.

Eggan, P. D., & Kauchak, D. (1992). *Educational psychology: Classroom connections.* New York: Merrill.

Freud, F. (1957). *On narcissism. The complete psychological works of Sigmund Freud.* New Haven, CT: Yale University.

Goodman, R. F. (2002). Art as a component of grief work with children. In N. B. Webb (Ed.), *Helping bereaved children: A handbook for practitioners* (2nd. ed., pp. 297-322). New York: Guilford Press.

Haasl, B. (2000). *Bereavement support group program for children: Participant workbook.* (2nd ed.). Philadelphia: Accelerated Development.

Huss, S. N. (1997). The effect of peer bereavement support groups on the self-esteem, depression, and problem behavior of parentally bereaved children. *Dissertation Abstracts International* (UMI No. 9729145).

Jacobs, E. E., Harvill, R. L., & Masson, R. L. (1994). *Group counseling: Strategies and skills.* Pacific Grove, CA: Brooks/Cole.

Johnson-Schroetlin, C. A. (2000). Childhood grief: Are bereavement support groups beneficial for latency age children? *Dissertation Abstracts International, 61*, 2764.

Kubler-Ross, E. (1969). *On death and dying.* New York: MacMillan.

Lehmann, L. (2001a). *Mourning child grief support group curriculum: Middle childhood edition: Grades 3-6.* New York: Brunner-Routledge.

Lehmann, L. (2001b). *Mourning child grief support group curriculum: Early childhood edition: Kindergarten-grade 2.* New York: Brunner-Routledge.

McGlauflin, H. (2002). *Encouraging your school to be grief friendly.* Retrieved on December 5, 2002 from http://www.cgemaine.org/schoolart/htm.

Miller, J. B. (1971). Children's reactions to the death of a parent: A review of the psychoanalytic literature. *Journal of American Psychoanalytic Association, 19*, 697-719.

Myers, T. W. (1999). Childhood grief: A teacher's perceptions and role. *Dissertation Abstracts International, 60*, 656.

Perry, B. D. (2001). Death & loss: Helping children manage their grief. *Early Childhood Today, 15,* 22-23.

Selekman, J., Busch, T., & Kimble, C. (2001). Grieving children: Are we meeting the challenge? *Pediatric Nursing, 27,* 414-419.

Sharpneck, J. D. (2000). The efficacy of group bereavement interventions: An integrative review of the research literature. *Dissertation Abstracts International, 61*, 6721.

Steen, K. F. (1998). A comprehensive approach to bereavement. *The Nurse Practitioner, 23,* 54-62

Wadsworth, B. J. (1984). *Piaget's theory of cognitive and affective development* (3rd ed.). New York: Longman.

Webb, N. B. (2002). *Helping bereaved children: A handbook for practitioners* (2nd ed.). New York: Guilford.

Worden, J. W. (2001). Grief counseling and grief therapy: *A handbook for the mental health professional.* New York: Springer.

Yalom, D. G. (1991). Groups for grief and survivorship after bereavement: A review. *Journal for Specialists in Group Work, 16,* 46-55.

# Chapter 85

## School Violence

*Doris Rhea Coy, Henry L. Harris, & Joel Muro*

### Preview

This chapter addresses recent events that have focused the nation's attention on violence in U.S. public schools. While there is a growing perception that not all public schools are safe, statistics verify that one of the safest places for students is the school. Suggestions for addressing issues surrounding a safe school are provided for professional school counselors, teachers, and parents.

School violence impedes learning and student achievement. The well-being of students, school staff, and communities is threatened by violence in and around schools. Violence is a broad term, encompassing both physical assault and social-emotional attacks. Both types can be detrimental to the student.

Physical school violence includes: theft, bullying, fighting/assault, carrying weapons, using weapons, rape/sexual assault, and group or gang attacks. In comparison, social emotional attacks are levied through such manners as threats, vandalism, hate crimes, and extortion. School violence can occur inside the school building, on the school grounds, and on the way to or from school.

> No matter where you are, parents want their students to be safe and secure . . . that might even precede a quality education . . . With drugs, gangs, and guns on the rise in many communities the threat of violence weighs heavily on most principals' minds these days . . . Anyone who thinks they are not vulnerable is really naïve. (Granat, 1997, p. 13)

The United States government, at the time of this writing, was aware of the palpable threats that have surfaced throughout the nation. Therefore, as part of the "No Child Left Behind" dictum, there are ways to ensure safety at educational institutions. The "Unsafe School Choice Option" stated that children must be offered a choice to attend a safe school if they are victims of a violent criminal offense, or if they attend a school that has been deemed "persistently dangerous."

State criminal laws address crimes of violence in differing ways because the state must decide what is a criminal offense. Although we have offered some ideas of what violence in the school may entail, some states would differ from that list. For example, the state of Maryland delineates crimes of violence as: abduction, arson, assault in the first or second degree, kidnapping, rape, maiming, and murder.

As part of the "No Child Left Behind" movement, unsafe schools have been identified by using the following standards: (1) identifying categories of suspensions ten days or more for violent acts; (2) 2.5% of the school population must be suspended for these offenses over a period of three years; (3) after two years, a school is designated dangerous and is required to create a corrective action plan; (4) if after three years the symptoms of violence persist, transfer options for students begin; and (5) excludes schools with special education and alternative education.

## Statistics on Violence

For youth ages 15-19 the firearm homicide rates increased 155% between 1987-1994 (Centers for Disease Control and Prevention/National Center for Injury Prevention and Control, 1996). For youth ages 14-17, homicide arrest rates increased 41% between 1989 and 1994 (Fox, 1996). Increasing the shocking value of that statistic, it has also been reported that ten percent of the 23,000 annual homicides in the United States are committed by persons under the age of 18 (Garbarino, 1999).

According to the U.S. Department of Education, National Center for Educational Statistics (1998), more than 1/2 of U.S. public schools reported experiencing at least one crime incident in school year 1996-97, and 1 in 10 schools reported at least one serious violent crime during that school year. Serious violent crimes were defined as murder, rape or another type of sexual battery, suicide, physical attack or fight with a weapon, or robbery. The crime in public schools that led the list was physical attacks or fights without a weapon. Crime and violence were more of a problem in middle and high schools than in elementary schools. Middle schools and high schools were more likely to report experiencing one or more incidents of any crime and one of more incidents of serious violent crime than elementary schools. Schools that reported serious discipline problems were more likely to have experienced serious violent crime than those with less serious discipline problems.

## School Factors That Contribute to Violence

The following school factors contribute to violence and should be addressed when consideration is given to developing a safe school. Schools that are more violent are typically larger and have a principal who appears to be ineffective or invisible to students. Less violent schools have clear rules of conduct enforced by the principal, fair discipline practices (as reported by students), small class sizes, student perception of control of their lives, principals that provide opportunities for teachers and students to be participatory members of decision-making, and cohesiveness among teachers and principals (Batsche & Moore, 1992).

## How to Prevent School Violence

Glasser (2000) said unhappiness, in conjunction with the vehement belief that others should be punished for how the perpetrator feels, are motivating factors as to why someone launches an attack on others. He hypothesized that by diminishing the number of unhappy students; the logical consequence would be reduction of the number of problems in a school, including violence. Glasser advocated that such a program is not expensive to implement or difficult to explain and can be implemented in every school.

Sandhu (2000) offered the following counseling strategies and suggestions for reducing school violence:

- *Become proactive.* School personnel often become reactive when problems related to violence occur. Professional school counselors need to be proactive and reach out to all students to maximize students' development.
- *Develop sensitivities.* The characteristics of troubled students need to be recognized by teachers and other educators. Trainings could be conducted to help them recognize these characteristics. After learning the characteristics, the educator can develop

sensitivities to those students and learn how to help them. Collaboration between the professional school counselor and teacher in developing a procedure for referring students for counseling will benefit all concerned.

- *Develop comprehensive approaches.* Professional school counselors need to involve parents, guardians, teachers, administrative staff, mental health professionals, and possibly their peers when attempting to help the student.
- *Develop counseling/therapeutic relationships.* Because these students lack trust in others and may resist sharing confidential information, developing this relationship is vital but may be difficult.
- *Organize individual counseling.* Catharsis and anger management will be addressed by the professional school counselor and may take a considerable amount of time. By exploring emotional pain, the professional school counselor will help the student alleviate the pain. Through individual counseling, the counselor will help the student develop resiliency and a sense of empowerment.
- *Organize group counseling.* Students should participate in group counseling to experience the power of the group, the sharing of similar experiences, and feelings of catharsis.
- *Make referrals.* Can the student benefit from additional counseling services? If long-term therapy appears to be appropriate, referrals to licensed professional counselors, psychologists, social workers, and/or psychiatrists might be considered. However, before discussing this with the student, the professional school counselor should address this with the student's parents or guardians, as well as attain their written permission before implementing any counseling or therapeutic arrangement.

Adequate assessment is vital to the counseling process and critical to the establishment of pertinent treatment goals and objectives. According to Dwyer, Osher and Warger (1998), this is especially true when counseling violent and potentially violent students.

## Measures Schools Are Taking to Deal with Crime and Violence

Most school systems have zero tolerance policies toward serious student offenses. School or district policy mandates predetermined consequences for various student offenses. In addition, low levels of security measures to prevent violence have been employed by most schools. Stringent security measures were in place by 2% of the schools, including a full-time guard and daily or random metal detector checks. Moderate security measures such as a full-time or part-time guard, restricted access to the school, or metal detectors were in place in 11% of schools. Low level security-restricted access to schools without guards or metal detectors were in place in 84% of schools. Of the items listed in the survey, 3% reported that none of the listed security measures were in place.

Formal school violence prevention programs were in place in most schools. Some type of formal violence-prevention or violence-reduction program or effort was reported in 78% of the schools. Nearly 50% of schools had a violence-prevention program for almost all students.

In those schools that did not develop a violence prevention program or are considering such a program, Coy & Allen (2003) suggested that schools can: assess needs in the school and community; develop a safe and supportive school climate; develop and implement a bully or violence prevention program; adopt a school-wide respect policy; insure that there is parent involvement and community participation in formulating prevention programs; provide informational meetings for parents; provide classroom guidance sessions as part of bullying or violence prevention programs; hold staff training sessions.

## What Professional School Counselors Can Do

A publication by the Idaho School Counselor Association (1999) suggested that professional school counselors provide the following services for teachers and the school district: assist teachers and all staff with training needs in student behavior and discipline; coordinate a school-wide program that promotes no tolerance for fighting, bullying, harassing, discriminating, or other unsafe, inequitable behavior; team with other pupil services staff to develop an effective system of referral and assessment for students exhibiting troublesome behaviors; serve on the school and district crisis response teams.

Riley (2000) cited the Idaho School Counselor Association's approach to school violence prevention (p. 121), listing four things that professional school counselors should do:

1. Provide group and individual counseling dealing with academic, career, personal, and social needs.
2. Coordinate mentor programs available to all students to assist with academic and peer concerns.
3. Facilitate programs (e.g., conflict resolution, peer mediation, and anger management) that train students how to handle their anger and peer problems.
4. Conduct regular discussion groups on the school district's code of student behavior and discipline.

## Preventing Violence: What Parents Can Do

The development and use of essential social skills during the elementary and middle school years by students is extremely important. Aggression and being rejected by others are related. It is unknown whether aggressive behavior prevents the development of friendships, or whether rejection by peers makes a student feel hostile and aggressive. The cycle of rejection and hostility is likely to continue unless the student learns how to make and keep good friends. Violent behavior or becoming a victim of violence can result from this cycle (Patten & Robertson, 2002). Parents and other family members play a critical role as children learn appropriate ways to handle conflict without becoming aggressive. Children learn from role models they observe. Table 1 presents a number of suggestions by Coy & Allen (2003) and Patten and Robertson (2002) for parents to help students cope with violence and aggression. Table 2 provides suggestions by Coy & Allen (2003) and the Idaho School Counselor's Association (1999) for how professional school counselors can help prevent violence and aggression in the school setting.

## Office Discipline Referrals as an Intervention

Sugai, Sprague, Horner, and Walker (2000) explained how office discipline referrals may be used as an information source to give an indicator of the prevalence of school-wide discipline and enhance the accuracy with which schools monitor, manage, and modify interventions for all students, in addition to the students with the most severe problem behaviors. Since school personnel already collect office discipline referrals, looking at these referrals may be of great value as they try to plan for prevention of violence in the school. Sugai, et al. suggested that administrators and faculty examine: "(a) the total number of office discipline referrals for a school year, (b) the number of students enrolled during the school year, (c) the number of school days in the year, and (d) the allocation of office discipline referrals by student, location, and date" (p. 2). This information can be utilized to decide whether to concentrate school discipline reform efforts on targeted, individualized interventions, selected interventions, and/or universal interventions. Several years of information should be compared to gain the most from the data.

**Table 1. Suggestions for parents to help children deal with aggression.**

| Action Taken | Reason |
|---|---|
| Listen to your child | Active listening helps children communicate personal needs |
| Negotiation and compromise | Gives decision making power to both parties |
| Give reasons for rules | So children can understand boundaries |
| Refrain from physical discipline | Giving spankings may cause acting out behavior at school |
| Communicate directly | Receive direct answers from children |
| Look for signs of school violence (torn clothes, etc.) | May tell why the child fears school |
| Open communication with school personnel | Planning for intervention |
| Become active in the school | Implement planning for different anti-violence ideas (e.g., anti-bullying programs) |
| Ask for referrals | Outside help with experts |
| Reduce child's media consumption | Less exposure to violent acts |
| Zero tolerance policy for your child's violent acts | Unacceptable violent behavior will not be tolerated |
| Consistent discipline | Children need structure |
| Spend more time with your children | Allows child to feel valued by most important support group |
| Model conflict management | Reduces children acting out violent behavior |
| Promote empathy | Reduces violent acts |
| Document violent incidents that happen to or are done by your child | Legal purposes |
| Role play | Preparation for children |
| Encourage safety in numbers | Protection from bullying and other violent acts |
| Assure child's safety | Allows child to know you will help |

**Table 2. Suggestions for how professional school counselors can help students deal with violence and aggression.**

| Action | Reason |
|---|---|
| Provide discipline resources | Assist in working with strong willed, violent children |
| Have a referral system | Sources for parents seeking help with a violent child |
| Facilitate faculty discussion | Open communication to target students who may be a problem and develop a contingency plan |
| Act as a change agent for the school | Help to adopt a respect policy, promote safety |
| Research anti-bullying programs | To be better informed about the causes and treatments of the behavior |
| Individual counseling with students | Assist students' understanding of feelings |
| Meet with parent groups | Disseminate information regarding school violence and bullying |
| Teach guidance lessons | Assist in helping students' understanding about violence and bullying |
| Work with faculty and staff about bullying and violence | Greater understanding of the positive learning environment created by the end of threats of violence |
| Provide leadership | Promoting a safe environment for students' matriculation |
| Advocate for students' rights | Address systemic barriers |

## A Violence-Suicide Reduction Model

Speaker and Petersen (2000) developed a violence-suicide reduction model which addressed and integrated the five factors that significantly contributed to school violence: family violence, violence in the media, collapse in moral/ethical education of youth, lack of school resources or ability to deal with violence, and a decline in the family structure. The model included the following components:

*Family Inclusion*

A comprehensive restructuring of the current school structure needs to occur. The family needs to be included within the educational structure. The school should support, include, and engage the whole family in the educational setting and provide an assortment of needed services.

*Evolution of Teacher/Administrator Roles*

Schools should staff their facilities with personnel trained in comprehensive values education. The role of professional school counselors should be essential to the whole process of violence prevention and intervention. All school employees should be part of executing an ethical and social skills curriculum and expanding an integrated and complete school environment involving the everyday modeling of these skills by school employees for students.

*Student Success*

Help students create a "success identity" through individual responsibility. Students develop positive self-esteem and a sense of identity when they learn effective ways to fulfill basic needs enthusiastically, and effectively deal with life's difficulties.

*Conflict Mediation*

The curriculum of every classroom should include teaching empirically field-tested conflict mediation, constructive resolution skills, and negotiation procedures. Cooperative leadership between administrators and teachers should occur to permit these different groups to get together, talk about, collect, analyze, and make decisions concerning resolution of conflict at all levels.

*Media Intervention*

Students need to be taught to assess critically the violence they see in television, movies, and arcades. This teaches students they are in control of their viewing options and can evaluate the impact of those options on their lives.

## Recreational Strategies for Reducing Violence

Recreational strategies were recommended to prevent violence in the schools (Wilson-Brewer & Spivak, 1994). The authors believed that sports could offset delinquency by offering an outlet for anger, stress, and tension, as well as presenting a constructive use of free time. Coben, Weiss Mulvey, and Dearwater (1994) suggested after-school programs, evening sport leagues, clubs and camps.

Zivin et al. (2001) addressed the effectiveness of traditional martial arts in preventing violence and delinquency in middle school. The students attended 30 classes, three per week, for 45 minutes each class. The martial arts program appeared effective in reducing violent behavior and psychological traits that are associated with violence and delinquency.

## Summary/Conclusion

This chapter described many suggestions on ways to decrease violence in the schools. An implication for schools and professional school counselors is to become involved with the students and collaborate with other organizations and helping professionals. There is a need to redefine the roles of school personnel in a way that will lead to all-inclusive school-based prevention programs that are an incorporated part of efforts within the greater community (Keys, 2000).

## References


Batsche, G., & Moore, B. (1992). *Helping children grow up in the 90s: A resource book for parents and teachers*. Bethesda, MD: National Association of School Psychologists.

Centers for Disease Control and Prevention/National Center for Injury Prevention and Control. (1996). *National summary of injury mortality data, 1987-1994*. Atlanta, GA: Author.

Coben, J. H., Weiss, H. B., Mulvey, E. P., & Dearwater, S. R. (1994). A primer on school violence prevention. *Journal of School Health, 64*, 309-313.

Coy, D. (2001). *Bullying*. Greensboro, NC: ERIC/CASS. (ERIC Document Reproduction Service No. ED459405)

Coy, D., & Allen, J. (2003). *Bullying: A resource & activity book for parents, teachers and school counselors*. Carson, CA: Jalomar Press & Innerchoice Publishing.

Dwyer, K., Osher, D., & Warger, C. (1998). *Early warning, timely response: A guide for safe schools*. Bethesda, MD: National Association of School Psychologists. (ERIC Document Reproduction Service No. ED418372)

Fox, J. A. (1996). *Trends in juvenile violence: A report to the United States Attorney General on current and future rates of juvenile offending*. Washington, DC: Department of Justice, Bureau of Justice Statistics.

Garbarino, J. (1999). *Lost boys: Why our sons turn violent and how we can save them*. New York: The Free Press.

Glasser, W. (2000). School violence from the perspective of William Glasser. *Professional School Counseling, 4*(2), 77-80.

Granat, D. (1997, September). Hello, Mr. Durso. *Washington Magazine,* 13-15.

Idaho School Counselor Association. (1999). Newsletter.

Patten, P., & Robertson, A. (2002). *The violence prevention resource guide for parents*. Champaign, IL: ERIC/EECE.

Riley, P. L. (2000). School violence prevention, intervention, and crisis response. *Professional School Counseling, 4*, 120-125.

Sandhu, D. S. (2000). Alienated students: Counseling strategies to curb school violence. *Professional School Counseling, 4*, 81-85.

Sugai, G., Sprague, J. R., Horner, R. H., & Walker, H. M. (2000). Preventing school violence: The use of office discipline referrals to assess and monitor school-wide discipline interventions. *Journal of Emotional & Behaviors Disorders, 8*, 94-101.

U. S. Department of Education, National Center for Education Statistics. (1998). *Violence and Discipline Problems in U.S. Public Schools: 1996-97* (NCES 98-030). Washington, DC: Author.

Wilson-Brewer, R., & Spivak, H. (1994). Violence prevention in schools and other community settings: The pediatrician as initiator, educator, collaborator, and advocate. *Pediatrics, 94,* 623-630.

Zivin, G., Hassan, N. R., DePaula, G. G., Monti, D. A., Harlan, C., Hossain, K. D., & Patterson, K. (2001). An effective approach to violence prevention: Traditional martial arts in middle school. *Adolescence, 36*(143), 443-459.

# Chapter 86

## Crisis Intervention with Individuals in the Schools

*Fran Steigerwald*

### Preview

Crisis work with individuals in the schools is becoming more common. Professional school counselors need to gain knowledge about the various physical, cognitive, emotional, and behavioral manifestations of crises in children so that they can recognize, assess, and intervene with students. Development of positive characteristics and skills along with an understanding and practice of some intervention and assessment models provide the needed resources for a crisis worker to plan the appropriate course of intervention with the individual student in crisis.

In this millennium, some have called crises in children's lives not only a reality, but an epidemic. Pressures of violence and abuse, bullying, terrorism, family discord, economic depression, loss, disease, and addiction bombard our children who are either victims or witnesses. Gratuitous violence in the media makes our children regular bystanders to crisis. The effects of this exposure impact children's school life, where they are expected to learn and grow in a structured academic setting. Knowledge of support and intervention with coping strategies in crisis situations may not have kept pace with what is required to truly help students in crisis. This chapter is an overview of the work needed within the life of an individual student in crisis in a school setting. The following chapter deals with the systemic crisis work that is needed when an entire school ecology is impacted by crisis.

This chapter begins with a definition of crisis and then explores some pivotal crisis concepts, including the physical, mental, emotional, and behavioral components to crisis, in general and specific reactions of students. Next, this chapter examines the training, characteristics, and qualities of effective crisis professionals. This is followed by appropriate intervention and assessment models that have been shown effective in the school setting. A special emphasis on understanding suicidal ideation, behavior, and intervention is stressed because of the destructive risks involved. The chapter ends with a summary of effective guidelines for working with school children in crisis.

### A Look at Crisis

*Definition of Crisis*

There are many definitions of crisis. James and Gilliland (2001) worked these definitions into a consolidated idea that encompassed the major points and was easy to understand: "Crisis is a perception or experiencing of an event or situation as an intolerable difficulty that exceeds the person's current resources and coping mechanisms" (p. 3). Key in this definition is the importance of the "perception" of the crisis, the response of the person exposed to it. This concept is emphasized in the Chinese word for crisis that is composed of two symbols, one representing "danger" and the other "opportunity." How a person is helped to perceive the crisis will provide much information as to whether he or she will cope well and grow from it, be overwhelmed and immobilized by it, or survive by protecting and blocking but have negative after-effects.

A crisis event is defined as "an event which produces a temporary state of psychological disequilibrium and a subsequent state of emotional turmoil" (Mitchell & Everly, 1993, p. 5). This disequilibrium or turmoil has been commonly referred to as stress, a phenomenon identified by Selye (1956) as a mind-body reaction that causes "wear and tear" upon the person. Stress has been defined as "a response characterized by physical and psychological arousal arising as a direct result of an exposure to any demand or pressure on a living organism" (Mitchell & Everly, 1993, p. 5).

### *Concepts of Crisis*

Crisis can be developmental, situational, or existential in nature (James & Gilliland, 2001). Whatever the nature of the crisis, stress is always a major component. This stress is deeply personal and its corresponding impairment is dependent upon the perception the person has of the crisis situation. Crisis stress is often observed as a combination of symptoms that are cognitive, emotional, physical, and behavioral. Researchers have worked to synthesize the many signs and symptoms of crises and stress. Tables 1-4 list general physical, mental or cognitive, emotional, and behavioral symptomology information gathered from the research of Girdano, Everly, & Dusek (1993), Mitchell & Everly (1993), and Myer (2001). Additional information from the New York Office of Mental Health (2002) and Greenstone & Leviton (2002) has been added pertaining to age-related reactions of students to stress and crises. The level of symptomology needs to be individually considered on a continuum from no impairment to severe impairment in each area.

A crisis in a person's life usually exists for a maximum of six to eight weeks (Hendricks & McKean, 1995; Janosik, 1984). After that amount of time, the symptoms usually diminish along with the obvious discomforts that have been felt. What is done to help the student during this time is of great importance in determining whether the student is able to resume the normalcy of life, or whether there are resulting residual complications and long-term effects from the crisis. "Unless the person obtains relief, the crisis has the potential to cause severe affective, behavioral, and cognitive malfunctioning" (James & Gilliland, 2001, p. 3).

## Post-Traumatic Stress Disorder (PTSD)

Not all effects of crisis and stress are relieved over a relatively short time. It has become clear that trauma of any kind can produce persistent symptoms that were not there before the trauma, causing a diagnosable condition of stress and anxiety called Post-Traumatic Stress Disorder (PTSD). PTSD is a complex disorder that is often comorbid and requires specialized help, and new crises can exacerbate and complicate PTSD. It is important for crisis workers to understand this disorder to make appropriate referrals.

PTSD was added to the DSM-III in 1980. The reader is referred to chapter 60, "Helping Students with Posttraumatic Stress Disorder," in this book for further information on this topic.

## Understanding and Structuring Crisis Work

Corsini (1981) stated that counseling and crisis intervention are elementally different. Crisis intervention or management work requires quick and immediate action with the student in crisis to provide the support and direction that the student in crisis cannot provide for him or

**Table 1. Physical symptoms of crisis and stress.**

The body strongly reacts to crisis and stress. Repeated or prolonged stress can cause exhaustion, decreased immunity, and psychosomatic illness across a lifespan. Common symptoms include:

- secreted stress hormones (cortisol, aldosterone, epinephrine)
- increased neural excitability (rapid breathing, dizziness)
- increased cardiovascular activity (heart rate, blood pressure, stroke volume, cardiac output)
- increased metabolic activity (gluconeogenesis, protein mobilization, muscle wasting, decreased antibody production, fat mobilization)
- increased sodium retention and neurological sweating
- change in salivation and in gastrointestinal system tonus and motility.

Symptoms common in preschool children (1-5 years)

- loss of bladder or bowel control, constipation
- speech difficulties, such as stammering
- loss of or increase in appetite

Symptoms common in school age students (5-11 years)

- headaches or other physical complaints as stated above

Symptoms common in preadolescent students (11-14 years)

- appetite disturbances
- physical pain, such as headaches, vague pain, bowel problems, psychosomatic complaints
- skin eruptions

Symptoms common in adolescent students (14-18 years)

- physical complaints such as headaches, psychosomatic symptoms, bowel problems, rashes, asthma
- appetite and sleep disturbances
- hypochondriasis
- amenorrhea or dysmenorrhea
- loss of sexual interest
- agitation or decrease in energy levels.

---

herself. Crisis counseling may be appropriate once a person has been stabilized from the initial crisis.

Lindemann (1944; 1956) first offered a theory of crisis work helping professionals and paraprofessionals to understand the needs of clients in crisis. He clearly provided a new framework for normalizing, not pathologizing, behaviors specific to people suffering from loss and trauma who felt unbalance or disequilibrium. Lindemann's proposed process took the clients through their disrupted state with brief intervention and grief work, to problem-solving or working through the loss, and finally to a return to equilibrium. Lindemann's model is presented in Figure 1.

**Figure 1. Lindemann's crisis intervention process.**

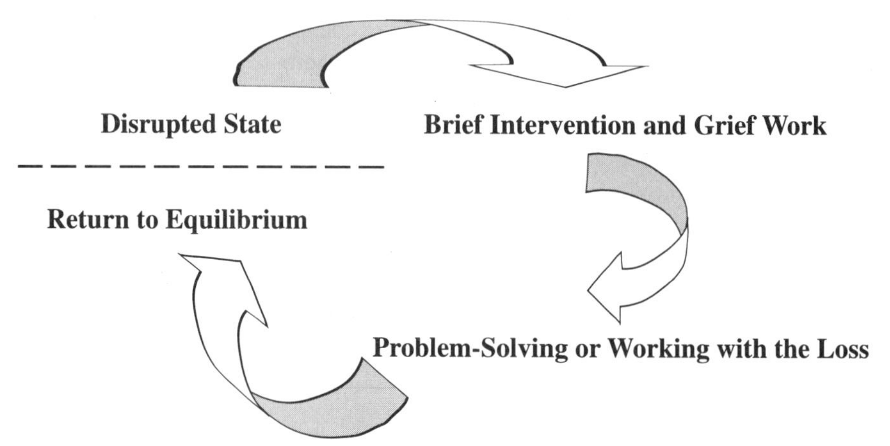


Today, brief solution-focused therapy follows much the same format. While not working on any ongoing problems as brief therapy would, crisis work focuses on facilitating an understanding of the crisis and its manifestations. Cournoyer (1996) stated that brief treatment approaches are in the forefront of intervention models and that the research has shown effective outcomes. It is important to remember that crisis intervention is not a long-term counseling approach. It is short-term problem or solution-focused work to get the client back to a state of balance (Myer, 2001). Regardless of the approach, it is clear that crisis intervention involves an established procedure. "Every action and intervention must be thoughtful, measured, and purposeful" (Greenstone & Leviton, 2002, p.7).

## A Look at Crisis Professionals

Since crisis intervention and management is time-limited, the ability to quickly establish rapport and an environment of trust and caring is essential. Rogers (1957) established the core conditions for successful counseling: empathic understanding, unconditional positive regard, and congruence. These basic conditions are necessary in crisis work to gain an understanding of the client's perception of the crisis. However, the crisis worker needs to be able to quickly exhibit these principles to the student while being supportive and often directive and in control of the crisis event. In crisis intervention the crisis worker is extremely active in working through the set phases, and it is this needed structure that helps the student in crisis proceed to balance (Cournoyer, 1996).

Effective communication skills are essential, including listening, clarifying, understanding non-verbal cues, asking questions to obtain accurate information, legitimizing feelings, and responding well to the client's feelings and perceptions. These skills, along with withholding judgment, shame, and advice-giving, are skills that develop rapport and begin to help manage the student's crisis (Greenstone & Levitan, 2002).

Training in crisis theory, symptomology, intervention, and assessment are necessary for a competent crisis worker. It is also vital to understand the referral process, state and local law, legal implications of working with minors, parental notification, and commitment or hospitalization procedures. In addition to previously discussed qualities of crisis counselors, Myer & Hanna (1996) have included: quick thinking, tolerance of medical trauma, sense of reconciliation with death, and sense of humor.

**Table 2. Mental or cognitive symptoms of crisis and stress.**

There are always beliefs, attitudes, perceptions, and cognitions that go along with crisis. The negativity and intensity of these cognitions help determine the psychological interpretation of the crisis and the subsequent level of the stress response and/or impairment. These cognitive impairments reduce coping ability:

- thought overload
- confused thinking
- difficulty making decisions
- lowered concentration
- memory dysfunction
- intrusive thoughts
- nightmares
- reduced problem-solving
- lowering of all higher cognitive functions.

Symptoms common in preschoolers (1-5 years)

- night terrors
- confusion

Symptoms common in school age students (5-11 years)

- night terrors, nightmares, fear of darkness
- poor concentration
- lost of interest in school

Symptoms common in preadolescent students (11-14 years)

- loss of interest in peer activity
- denial

Symptoms common in adolescent students (14-18 years)

- confusion
- poor concentration
- tendency to blame

---

Awareness of multicultural perspectives, culturally biased assumptions of crisis, and the client's worldview of the events are necessary for correct assessment and intervention. Misinterpretation because of lack of sensitivity to cultural values, social or political backgrounds, and cultural behaviors in crisis can unfairly label clients and result in inappropriate interventions (Pederson, 1987).

> Almost everyone can be taught the techniques. . . and with practice can employ them with some degree of skill. However, the crisis worker who can take intervention to the performance art level is more than the sum of techniques read about and skills mastered. A master of this art is going to have some combination of the two and a good deal of. . . life experiences. . . professional skills. . . poise. . . creativity and flexibility. . . energy. . . quick mental reflexes... [and] attributes that crisis interventionists have found of utmost importance to themselves and their clients. These attributes are tenacity, the ability to delay gratification, courage, optimism, a reality orientation, calmness under duress, objectivity, a strong and positive self-concept, and abiding faith that human beings are strong, resilient, and capable of overcoming insurmountable odds. (James & Guilland, 2001, pp. 17-20)

**Table 3. Emotional symptoms of crisis and stress.**

"Emotion is an energy complex. . . Our emotions form an immediate experience. When we are experiencing our emotions, we are in direct contact with our physical reality" (Girdano et al., 1993, p. 62). Emotions are immediate triggers in crisis. Expression of emotions in a crisis is healthy and should be encouraged. In crisis situations, it is normal for emotions to rise to uncomfortable levels as:

- emotional shock
- fear
- anger
- grief or sadness
- depression
- feeling overwhelmed (helpless or hopeless)
- emotional flattening or denial
- moodiness and irritability
- decompensation
- depersonalizing

Symptoms common in preschoolers (1-5 years)

- fears of darkness, animals, strangers, or abandonment

Symptoms common in school age students (5-11 years)

- generalized anxiety
- irritability
- withdrawal from peers
- fears about weather, safety, harm, loss or abandonment
- depression

Symptoms common in preadolescent students (11-14 years)

- depression
- loss of interest in peers and social activities
- anger
- fear of loss of family, friends, home, or personal harm

Symptoms common in adolescent students (14-18 years)

- depression
- indifference or apathy
- anger at perceived unfairness of crisis
- fear of loss
- guilt

## A Look at What Works

*Planning Ahead*

For professional school counselors, it is important to realize that crisis work will be part of the routine. Planning ahead through knowledge of crisis and stress, training in handling these events, and on-going self-preparation is essential. In the moment of the crisis there is no time to sit down, refer to a manual, nor look up a step-by-step process in the files. Determine your state

**Table 4. Behavioral symptoms of crisis and stress.**

Emotional energy prepares for action and in times of crisis behaviors may be the first things seen and attended to. Behaviors are purposeful. They are often manifestations of the intent of working out the discomfort caused by the crisis, no matter how misdirected it may seem to the observer. Such behaviors include:

- changes in ordinary behavior patterns or regression
- inability to perform daily functions
- changes in eating, drinking, or sleeping habits
- self-harming behaviors
- changes in personal hygiene
- hyperarousal
- withdrawal, prolonged silences
- rebellion, fighting

Symptoms common in preschoolers (1-5 years)

- bed-wetting
- clinging to parents
- thumb-sucking
- cries or screams for help
- immobility with trembling and frightening expressions
- running either toward an adult or in aimless motion

Symptoms common in school age students (5-11 years)

- thumb-sucking
- whining
- clinging
- aggressive behaviors
- competition with siblings for parental attention
- school avoidance
- regressive behaviors

Symptoms common in preadolescent students (11-14 years)

- sleeplessness or too much sleeping
- fighting
- attention-seeking behaviors
- withdrawing behaviors
- refusal to do chores

Symptoms common in adolescent students (14-18 years)

- poor or reduced performance
- aggressive behaviors
- withdrawing or isolating behaviors
- changes in peer group or friends
- irresponsibility
- delinquent behaviors
- rebellion
- refusal to do chores
- attention-seeking behaviors
- decline in struggling with parents

law and school policy for parental notification, minor clients, and confidentiality. Make clear your ethical practice on involving family and guardians in crisis situations. Your plans need to be known, practiced, handy, and visible. Several models are clear, well-established, and proven effective. Two models of intervention and one model for assessment are outlined and discussed below with the emphasis on working with students. It is important to decide which model of intervention will be employed and make the necessary preparation. All three of these models offer practical interventions that can be implemented by a professional school counselor when an individual crisis erupts in a child's day.

*Models*

Roberts (1996) (see Table 5) outlined a seven-stage crisis intervention model that "can facilitate early identification of crisis, problem-solving, and effective crisis resolution" (p. 26). It is important to maintain close contact and provide the student and family with resource information and community assistance as needed.

**Table 5. Roberts' seven stage crisis model.**

Beginning with a thorough assessment,
**Stage 1 - ASSESS LETHALITY**, examines how dangerous the student is to self and others, or looks at the immediate psychosocial needs.

**Stage 2 – ESTABLISH RAPPORT,** stresses the need to rapidly bond with the student using respect, acceptance, and reassurance.

**Stage 3 – IDENTIFY MAJOR PROBLEMS,** allows for the student to vent about the precipitating event, and helps the student rank the problems by harm or potential threat.

**Stage 4 – DEAL WITH FEELINGS,** uses active listening skills and communicates warmth, respect, reassurance, and non-judgmental validation.

**Stage 5 – EXPLORE ALTERNATIVES,** uses the calmness and rationality of the crisis worker, since the student is often distressed and unable to function clearly. Ideally the student and the crisis worker can join collaboratively; however, often the crisis worker may need to initiate discussion of adaptive coping mechanisms.

**Stage 6 – DEVELOP ACTION PLAN**, develops and implements actions to help restore the student to balance and functionality. Reasonableness, encouragement, and supportiveness are essential ingredients in successful implementation.

**Stage 7 –FOLLOW-UP,** completes the crisis resolution and sets times to meet (daily, weekly or monthly) to gauge the student's success in functioning.

Greenstone & Leviton (2002) (see Table 6) have a similar crisis intervention plan that calls for six major components along with some practical suggestions.

**Table 6. Greenstone & Leviton's (2002) model.**

1. **IMMEDIACY** – Work "to relieve anxiety, prevent further disorientation [and] ensure that sufferers do not harm themselves or cause harm to others" (p. 8).

2. **CONTROL** - Work to "be clear about what and whom you are attempting to control, enter the crisis scene cautiously, [and] be clear in your introductory statements, do not promise things that might not happen. . . . direct and arrange the pattern of standing or sitting to gain the victim's attention, guide the sufferer with your eyes and voice rather than through physical force, use physical force only as a last resort and only if you are trained and authorized, [and] remove the victim from the crisis situation" (pp. 8-10).

3. **ASSESSMENT** - Work to "evaluate on the spot. . . make the evaluation quick, accurate, and comprehensive. . . focus your assessment on the present crisis and events. . . what are the precipitating events. . . ask short direct questions. . . one at a time. . . allow enough time for the victim to answer. . .allow the crisis to be the victim's crisis. . .assess actual and symbolic meaning. . .listen for what is not being said. . . allow the victim to speak freely and to ventilate feelings. . . see the crisis as temporary. . .[and] return control to the victim as soon as possible" (pp. 10-13).

4. **DISPOSITION** – Work to "help the victim identify and mobilize personal resources. . . mobilize social resources. . .hold out hope that solutions are possible. . .develop options. . . [and] help the parties to the crisis make an agreement" (p. 13).

5. **REFERRAL** – Much preplanning is needed for this component. As a crisis worker, you need to have a comprehensive list of referral sources (agencies, community professionals, doctors, lawyers, clergy, hospitals, transporters, and law enforcement) with hours of operation, telephone numbers, and names, always accurate and available to you for immediate use. Provide the information (if a minor to the parent or guardian) clearly and in writing, asking for verification of information.

6. **FOLLOW-UP** – Work to determine whether follow up procedures have been done, providing further help or re-referrals if necessary.

Myer (2001) worked to expand the concept of assessment as paramount in effective intervention in his "Triage Assessment Model." This assessment begins by listening to the crisis story to determine the catalyst and the student's view. Next, assessment takes place within three domains: **affective** (identify and rank anger/hostility, or anxiety/fear, or sadness/melancholy); **cognitive** (identify and rank whether there is perceived physical, psychological, social/relationship, or moral/spiritual transgression); and **behavioral** (identify and rank behaviors as either approach, avoidance, or immobility). There are always reactions to crisis in these three domains and it is vital to work to determine and **rank severity of impairment** in each area. Next, crisis workers are encouraged to begin to **use appropriate interventions** in the domains that appear with most impairment: affective (awareness, support, and catharsis), cognitive (clarifying, delimiting and ordering), or behavioral (guiding, protecting, and mobilizing).

*Age-Specific Interventions in the Schools*

A key piece to remember is that crisis is in the eye of the person perceiving it. It is paramount that the crisis worker suspend judgmental thoughts concerning the appropriateness of the student's reactions to the crisis. Working to understand the crisis and validate the reactions from the student's perspective is essential. Students often exhibit behaviors as a direct result of their emotional states. In school situations, these behaviors may often be the first things seen and attended to. School personnel need to be careful not to immediately discipline behaviors toward compliance without an understanding of what the student really needs (Kohn, 1996).

Table 7 provides interventions appropriate for the schools to help the student regain balance and pre-crisis levels of stress (Greenstone & Leviton, 2002, pp. 68-72).

**Table 7. Age appropriate interventions for students recovering from crisis.**

Interventions for preschoolers (1-5 years)
- play reenactment
- verbal and physical comforting and attention
- expression of feelings and concerns
- suggestion of comforting home bedtime routines and support

Interventions for school age students (5-11 years)
- patience and tolerance
- play reenactment, discussing emotions
- discussion about crisis experience with peers and adults with expectations that occur in crisis
- temporary relaxation of expectations in school and home
- opportunities for undemanding structure and routine

Interventions for preadolescent students (11-14 years)
- group activities geared toward resuming routine
- same-age activities
- undemanding but structured routine
- individual attention and consideration

Interventions for adolescent students (14-18 years)
- letter writing
- participation in the community
- discussion of feelings and concerns
- temporary reduction of expectations
- encouragement of discussion of crisis fears with family

## A Special Look at Suicide

One of the most devastating things that can happen in crisis is loss of life. When that loss of life is a student's, everyone involved asks what could have been done to prevent it, or why the signs were not seen. For youth 10-24 years of age, unintentional injury, suicide and homicide are the leading causes of death. Most completed suicides occur between ages 12 and 14 and attempts increase in the late teens with boys being five times more likely to commit suicide (National Center for Health Statistics, 1998). Professional school counselors need to be able to assess the danger of suicide or homicide and know the steps to take in these emergency situations. Importantly, if a professional counselor reasonably suspects that a student may take his or her own life or the life of someone else, referral and/or commitment is vitally necessary.

While this topic certainly warrants more expanded coverage, Table 8 provides the basic steps in the assessment of suicide or homicide risk needed to determine the level of risk (compiled from Farberow, Heilig, & Litman, 1968; Gliatto & Rai, 1999: Gould & Kramer, 2001):

**Table 8. Basic steps in addressing suicidal or homocidal intent.**

Step 1: Assess for predictors:

A. sex and age
B. previous attempts
C. familiarity with someone who has attempted or completed suicide
D. use of drugs and/or alcohol
E. depression and/or medical conditions
F. warning signs, such as suicide talk, giving away personal items, sudden change in behavior and patterns, preoccupation with death (in music or reading)
G. sexual orientation issues (gay, lesbian, bisexual and transsexual adolescents have more self-harm and suicidal thoughts and behaviors)

Step 2: Determine the seriousness of the intent:

A. solicit suicidal or homicidal thoughts
B. determine whether there is a plan and solicit details to determine feasibility with the higher risk in very specific details and actions. Regarding homicide, if specific individuals are named, there is a duty to protect and warn.
C. determine lethality -check out the means and access – a gun is the most dangerous and if a loaded gun is kept available in the home, there is high risk

Step 3: Determine life stressors and life resources. If life is lately filled with many stressors and few supports, the likelihood of completed suicide is greater.

If there is any risk of suicide or homicide, always consult with supervisors or experienced clinicians before releasing a student from your office. Never leave such a student unattended. ALWAYS bring in another individual to assist and consult. Should a moderate or high risk of suicide or homicide be detected, know the steps necessary in your community for referral for further assessment or to hospitalize if necessary. Have these emergency names, numbers, and modes of transport readily available.

Some short-term interventions are:

1. Write up a safety contract with the student, specifying actions when ideations occur.
2. Make plans to remove the means.
3. Make others aware and get the support of family and significant others such as clergy or community resources.
4. Contact mental health counselors for increased visitation or advise existing therapist.
5. Further suicide assessment instruments can be used for more information, or refer for psychiatric evaluation.
6. Call police if imminent danger is suspected.

## Summary/Conclusion

In summary, Table 9 provides *"A Dozen Things to Remember in Crisis Work."*

**Table 9. A dozen things to remember in crisis work.**

1. Work to keep yourself grounded and healthy, and your skills effective and developed.
2. Remember to understand the crisis through the perception of the person in the crisis. Actively listen to the story.
3. Work to establish rapport and trust.
4. Plan ahead with appropriate and adequate referral source information, allocated space for intervention, and an accessible model of intervention.
5. Remember to be holistic. Observe and assess the physical, behavioral, emotional, and cognitive manifestations.
6. Begin work where there is most impairment.
7. Determine whether the effects are long-lasting and if referral for PTSD assessment is needed.
8. Remember to keep a multicultural awareness of the student's expressions of emotions, perspectives, and behaviors.
9. Remember that student behaviors are often the most immediately noticeable. Ask yourself what the student needs rather than fall into the compliance/conformance trap.
10. Make yourself an expert in suicidology. Know what to assess, how to do it, and how to refer in lethal cases.
11. Never work in isolation. Involve the student's support system and always involve your consultant/supervisor.
12. Continue to develop and practice your art.

## References


American Psychiatric Association. (2000). *Diagnostic and statistical manual of mental disorders-fourth edition-text revision. (DSM-IV-TR)*. Washington, DC: Author.

Corsini, R. J. (1981). *Innovative psychotherapies*. New York: Wiley Interscience.

Cournoyer, B. R. (1996). Converging themes in crisis intervention, task-centered and brief treatments approaches. In A. R. Roberts (Ed.), *Crisis management & brief treatment* (pp. 3-15). Chicago: Nelson-Hall Publishers.

Farberow, N. L., Heilig, S. M., & Litman, R. (1968). *Techniques in crisis intervention: A training manual.* Los Angeles: Los Angeles Suicide Prevention Center.

Girdano, D. A., Everly, G. S., & Dusek, D. E. (1993). *Controlling stress and tension: A holistic approach.* Englewood Cliffs, NJ: Prentice-Hall.

Glaitto, M. F., & Rai, A. K. (1999). Evaluation and treatment of patients with suicide ideation. *American Family Physician*. Retrieved March 1, 2000 from http://www.aafp.org/afp/990301ap/1500.html

Gould, M. S., & Kramer, R. A. (2001). Youth suicide. *Suicide and Life-Threatening Behavior, 31,* 6-30.

Greenstone, J. L., & Leviton, S. C. (2002). *Elements of crisis intervention: Crises and how to respond to them.* Pacific Grove, CA: Brooks/Cole.

Hendricks, J. E., & McKean, J. B. (1995). *Crisis intervention: Contemporary issues for on-site interveners.* Springfield, IL: Thomas.

James, R. K., & Gilliland, B. E. (2001). *Crisis intervention strategies.* Belmont, CA: Brooks/Cole.

Janosik, E. H. (1984). *Crisis counseling: A contemporary approach.* Monterey, CA: Wadsworth Health Sciences Division.

Kohn, A. (1996). *Beyond discipline: From compliance to community.* Alexandria, VA: Association for Supervision and Curriculum Development.

Lindemann, E. (1944). Symptomatology and management of acute grief. *American Journal of Psychiatry, 101*, 141-148.

Lindemann, E. (1956). The meaning of crisis in individual and family. *Teachers College Record, 57*, 310.

Mitchell, J. T., & Everly, G.S. (1993). *Critical incident stress debriefing (CISD): An operations manual for the prevention of traumatic stress among emergency services and disaster workers.* Ellicott City, MD: Chevron Publishing Corporation.

Myer, R. A. (2001). *Assessment for crisis intervention: A triage assessment model.* Belmont, CA: Brooks/Cole.

Myer, R. A., & Hanna, F. J. (1996). Working in hospital emergency departments: Guidelines for crisis intervention workers. In A. R. Roberts (Ed.), *Crisis management & brief treatment* (pp. 3-15). Chicago: Nelson-Hall Publishers.

New York Office of Mental Health. (2002). *Age-related reactions of children to disasters.* Retrieved May 19, 2002 from http://www.omh.state.ny/us/omhweb/crisis/crisiscounseling3.html

Pederson, P. (1987). Ten frequent assumptions of cultural bias in counseling. *Journal of Multicultural Counseling and Development, 15,* 16-24.

Roberts, A. R. (1996). Epidemiology and definitions of acute crisis. In A. R. Roberts (Ed.), *Crisis management & brief treatment* (pp. 3-15). Chicago: Nelson-Hall Publishers.

Rogers, C. (1957). *Client-centered therapy.* Boston: Houghton Mifflin.

Seyle, H. (1956). *The stress of life.* New York: McGraw-Hill.

# Chapter 87

# Systemic Crisis Intervention in the Schools

*Fran Steigerwald*

## Preview

Systemic crisis intervention needs to be seriously addressed system wide, both in the school and the community. Many crises affect large numbers of people and must be addressed systemically in order to facilitate optimal recovery for everyone, as well as to effectively solve problems and facilitate needed changes to prevent further incidents. Development of a comprehensive crisis plan is a large undertaking, but many of the elements are generic and can be universally incorporated, along with adaptations that need to be made for specific system needs. Understanding these components and having a plan in place to quickly activate can be the difference between extended problems and effective solutions.

A junior high school student commits suicide. A kindergarten student disappears and is suspected to be kidnapped. A family on vacation with their three elementary children is killed in an airplane crash. Gang slogans and activity have sprung up in the school hallways. A suspected gay student has been beaten up behind the school. Two 15-year-olds overdosed over the weekend. Four seniors are fatally injured on prom night in a car accident involving alcohol. A drive-by shooting kills the star basketball player. Five girls report being fondled and groped in the hallway by sixth grade boys. In addition to these many possible school-life crises, 25 real incidents of school shootings occurred in the United States, from 1996-2002, causing the media to call school violence a "deadly pattern" (Family Education Network, 2002).

Schools have installed metal detectors, used armed police, have policies of zero tolerance, and insisted on mesh book bags in order to help control the violence. But still crises seem an uncontrollable part of school life. What can be controlled is the knowledgeable and quick response of the school's professionals to crises, in order to prevent further exacerbation, trauma, and harm. All the above scenarios require a systemic crisis plan, which is comprehensive, well-planned, mobilizes many resources, and operates quickly.

## What Is Systemic Crisis Intervention

Systemic crisis intervention is based in systems theory, which emerged in the 1940's. Goldenberg and Goldenberg (1998) summarized the development of systems theory as a new way to look at a problem, event, situation, or organization from the perspective of the interaction of all the components and of how the entire unit operates. Later, family therapy applied these concepts and elaborated the movement from looking at individual characteristics to interactions among individuals. The study became the system. Previously, scientific thinking was infused with "linear causality: A causes B, which acts upon C, causing D to occur" (p. 21). The circular causality of systems work stresses reciprocity. Forces do not move in one linear direction, but rather are influenced by and are influencing other components in the system. Systems theory is more holistic, understanding that the whole is greater than the sum of its parts, and that each part continually impacts and is mutually affected by the others.

Systems theory offers distinct advantages to effectively solving problems and crises in schools. Carns and Carns (1997) stated:

> Initially, it is helpful to envision the school district as a supra or mega system, the individual schools as systems, the individual classrooms as subsystems, and even the small social or task groups within the classroom as smaller subsystems. Each child brings his or her interactional patterns and ways of relating to others in his or her own family system into the school subsystems. (p. 220)

Solutions are seen as the responsibility of all the members involved, rather than one person's duty. The maintenance of positive change is more possible and effective with multiple input and change occurring at the interactional level. Keys and Lockhart (1999) proposed that a multisystemic approach be taken by professional school counselors, expanding the systems to include school, home, peer group, and community. "To achieve such broad-based change, schools, families, and communities must engage in collaborative problem solving that engages the multiple expertise of members of each system" (p. 107).

The stated crises that began this chapter do not impact just one individual. Many people are affected and many need to be considered in crisis intervention, and many resources need to be mobilized in crisis intervention. The National Education Association (2002) stated that in crises, communication is often the problem:

> The overall communication objective in a crisis is to quickly adjust. . . the school community position from one of response and reaction to one of relative control, and an ability to take proactive steps toward healing and a return to learning. (p. 4)

An important piece to remember is that in a crisis that has gained public attention, the crisis can be perpetuated by the mishandling of a situation by a member of the school community. System-wide, school and community involvement in the plan outlining expected roles and duties can only help the crisis situation.

## A Systemic Approach to Individual Crisis

In systemic intervention, the professional school counselor knows that the problem does not reside in the student alone, but in the student's interactions with others in the system. It may be determined that this student was bullied and harassed on the playground, or that in the morning the student overheard his parents speaking of divorce. Resolution involves intervention with all the involved parties and resources.

Several techniques to assess and intervene systematically are important to know. Mapping can be done with the student, parents or persons the professional school counselor determines to be close to the student. Minuchin (1974) and Minuchin & Fishman (1981) developed the concept of mapping in family work. It is a type of diagramming that examines through drawing the family structure and patterns of interaction, observing distances, connections, coalitions, repetitive sequences, and boundaries. Creative questioning by the professional school counselor elicits vital information regarding open and closed systems, negative or positive feedback loops, enmeshed or disengaged subsystems, boundaries, and power.

This same tool can be extended to include the classroom, teachers, school, and community. This more global approach has been referred to as ecosystemic mapping. Here diagrams include the larger social system and outer world of the child. Utilizing community organizations and institutions, as well as the child/family/classroom/ school community, problematic symptoms and resources can be identified (Sherman & Fredman, 1986).

Cerio (1995) discussed other techniques that professional school counselors can use, such as worldview, hierarchy, and triangles. In *worldview*, the professional school counselor works to illicit the values that influence the interactions of the students with parents and others in their environment. A clash of values between home and school can create a problem. Examining the *hierarchical structure* often leads to an understanding of the power and influence dynamics as well as getting a clearer picture of the roles that are played out in the system. *Triangulation* refers to the process of involving a third party to take sides against another. Triangle work looks at the interaction of three members or parties as a way of resisting, sabotaging, or impeding change, since alliances influence the other member in the triangle and increase the degree of difficulty of arriving at and agreeing to solutions. Cerio summarizes these techniques with five basic questions that a professional school counselor should ask to get a systems perspective:

1. What are the world views of the family and the school personnel?
2. What are the positions of the family members and school personnel in the family-school hierarchy?
3. What subsystems are involved with the problem?
4. What is the nature of the boundaries of the subsystems?
5. What triangles are in play related to the problem? (p. 43)

Individual crises can benefit from systems intervention by assessing the crisis and formulating the interventions from a more holistic perspective.

## A Systemic Approach to School-Wide Crisis

Systemic counseling is needed when the school or school system is more visibly affected by the crisis, such as with a student suicide or homicide. Here many parts of the system will be impacted. Best friends, neighbors, classmates, fellow students, and friends of friends all form concentric circles of closeness around the victim and all experience some stress from the crisis. A general plan needs to be in place prior to the crisis to mobilize resources as needed and to involve the community for effective prevention/intervention action.

A comprehensive guide to systemic crisis intervention is needed and the many aspects involved in such a plan need to be formulated and available for immediate action. Professional school counselors can assist in the formulation and utilization of such plans or can be instrumental in beginning the dialogue to formulate such a plan.

### *A Comprehensive School Crisis Plan*

James and Gilliland (2001) explained that comprehensive crisis plans take a great deal of time and resources, but are essential to effectively respond to crises. Plans all need to involve generic elements, so utilizing an available outline as a template is helpful. But these plans also need to be specific to the school community's particular needs and demands. Beginning with a needs assessment is vital. James and Gilliland suggested a two-tiered team, the first involving the school-community resources for the larger planning picture, and a second tier composed of building response teams with information on the physical plant and its occupants. Some suggested roles for the crisis response team are the crisis response coordinator, the crisis intervention coordinator, the media liaison, the security liaison, the community/medical liaison, the parent liaison, crisis interveners, and the resource person.

James and Gilliland suggested the following elements be spelled out in a crisis response plan: **physical requirements** set-up for counseling, communications, operations, information, first-aid, and break centers; **logistics** involving how communication will flow, procedural checklists, provisions, and building plans; and the **crisis response** by getting and verifying the facts, assessing the impact to determine the degree of mobilization, providing triage assessment to determine who is most affected and needs immediate intervention, providing psychological first-aid, having a model of intervention in place, providing crisis interviews, and finally the briefing, debriefing, and demobilizing phase.

In a school-wide crisis, the systemic crisis intervention plan is a very comprehensive project that involves the entire community. The National Education Association (NEA) (2002) provides information and guidance for developing and using a crisis plan. Their *Crisis Communications Guide and Toolkit* (http://www.nea.org/ crisis) can take the professional school counselor and a crisis planning team through assessment of the system's needs, developing a crisis response team and plan, and building local, state, and national crisis networks. The toolkit is organized into three main sections: being prepared before a crisis; being responsive during a crisis; and being diligent in moving beyond crisis.

In the first section, the NEA provides assistance by giving guiding principles for crisis response and prevention plans. These plans: must be inclusive and collaborative among school community, staff, administrators, teachers, associations, law enforcement, fire department, mental health agencies, PTA's, and other community partners; must have as a goal to be supportive of students and staff; must provide strategies for information dissemination of the plan to all involved and know that members know what to do in case of an emergency; and must be practiced and updated. This section also provides a checklist to assess how the system measures up to meeting crisis needs in terms of policy and procedure, operations, and aftermath.

In the second section, critical response actions are outlined and organized by the action to be taken each day and the media or communications challenges that may need to be addressed. Day one is focused on response. Day two is focused on information. Day three and beyond is focused on communication. Detailed responses are given in this useful resource, from reminders to mobilize resources to follow-up letters that need to be sent.

In the third section, attention is given to support for long-term healing, building partnerships, striving to achieve a "new normal," and dealing with the media. Information on handling donations and memorials and managing anniversaries and physical reminders is outlined.

> Victims of a crisis experience a real need to return to normal. It is a commonly expressed desire and although almost everyone articulates this need, they fail to achieve it. "Normal" as they once knew it is forever gone and changed. For many the recognition that such a "normal" is unattainable can be debilitating. As a result, counselors and crisis survivors find the concept of "a new normal" to be very reassuring and accurate. (NEA, 2002, p. 6)

## Critical Incident Stress Debriefing (CISD) Model

"Critical Incident Stress Debriefing is a form of structured psychological debriefing conducted in small groups. It was originally developed. . . as a direct, action-oriented crisis intervention process designed to prevent or mitigate traumatic stress" (Mitchell & Everly, 1993, p. 3). CISD was first formulated and used with emergency and public service personnel, but its use has expanded and it is now used with most populations that have experienced a natural disaster, accident, trauma, or event critical enough to tax the coping skills of the people involved. It has been used successfully world-wide and with all ages, including school-aged children. Most areas of this country have trained CISD personnel available to assist commercial, industrial, and community groups.

When a crisis hits a school community, systematic crisis intervention assumes that all members of the community are affected to some degree and need attention. Students and their parents can be the beneficiaries of CISD work. However, often the professional staff, teachers, and crisis personnel are overlooked because all the focus is upon the students. The caregivers also need care. Burn-out is especially severe if caregiver needs in a crisis are unattended. CISD is one way to provide staff, faculty, crisis workers, and witnesses an effective way to help them cope.

CISD was the result of study and research by Mitchell and Everly (1993). "CISD is a crisis intervention process designed to stabilize cognitive and affective processes and to further mitigate the impact of a traumatic event" (p. 15). Some of the basic principles of CISD are that:

1. it is not therapy and should only be done by a team of people specifically trained in CISD,
2. it is a group process with the purpose of reducing stress and enhancing recovery,
3. not all problems will be solved, referrals may be necessary,
4. a person can attend a meeting and not speak and still gain benefit,
5. it is best to have the participation voluntary, but often attendance is required for all to benefit,
6. CISD generally should take place after 24 hours and before 72 hours of the crisis (with variations depending upon the event),
7. CISD teams are "multi-organizational and multi-jurisdictional in structure" (p. 15), and
8. CISD should be taken as one option of critical incident stress management.

Chapter 86 provided in this book, "Crisis Intervention in the Schools," should be consulted for a basic understanding of the symptomology and signs of stress on people. It is important to prepare people who have suffered from a crisis or trauma to know that many physical, affective, cognitive and behavioral manifestations are "normal" under the circumstances. There is a specific stage in the CISD intervention when this material needs to be shared with the participants.

The CISD response team for a regional response is usually made up of about 40 people, with about 12 mental health professionals, and the rest being peer support personnel, made up of community workers in emergency or stress-related fields, such as nursing, law enforcement, or first response teams. Once the need for CISD has been determined, team membership is formed from this community pool and is composed of three to five members depending on the number and nature of the participants. A clergyman trained in CISD can also be present to act as a listener and a guide, although preaching or praying is not a part of CISD. The optimal number of participants is 4 - 20, but up to 30 participants can be handled if the time is lengthened to give everyone an opportunity to share. Detailed descriptions of each member's duties, preparation and set-up, and procedures for the debriefing are very specific and prescribed. The normal time required for an intervention is anywhere from one to four hours. During each stage, participants as a whole are asked directed questions to help tell their story. They usually take turns responding. People are allowed to pass if they choose not to say anything. Each stage has specific questions to move the process along. Leaders typically do not provide feedback after individuals share.

> The overall strategy for a CISD team during a debriefing is to start at the point which is easiest to discuss and then move gradually into more emotionally intense discussions. After handling the intense materials the group is gradually brought back out of the intense discussion to the less intense until the discussion finally concludes. (p. 86)

Table 1 presents a description of the seven stages of CISD (Mitchell & Evely, 1993, p. 144). Post-debriefing activities include one-on-one time with members who, during the CISD intervention, expressed or exhibited a need for extra attention. This connection can be a supportive word or a suggested referral for therapy. This one-on-one time can occur during refreshments following the CISD intervention. A post-debriefing meeting for the intervention team itself must occur to provide good mental health and prevent against stress overload for the team. Professional school counselors need to know how to access a CISD team if the need should arise, or seek out specialized training or community support to start a CISD project. Knowledge and skill enhancement through CISD training and participation can greatly benefit a professional school counselor's sense of competency at times of crisis.

**Table 1. Seven stages of CISD.**

| *Stage* | *Description/Purpose* |
|---|---|
| 1. Introduction | To introduce team members, explain process, set expectations. |
| 2. Fact Phase | To describe the traumatic event from each participant's perspective on a cognitive level. |
| 3. Thought Phase | To allow participants to describe cognitive reactions and to transition to emotional reactions. |
| 4. Reaction Phase | To identify the most traumatic aspect of the event for the participants. |
| 5. Symptom Phase | To identify personal symptoms of distress and transition back to the cognitive level. |
| 6. Teaching Phase | To educate regarding what are normal reactions and adaptive coping mechanisms, i.e., stress management. Provide cognitive anchor. |
| 7. Re-Entry Phase | To clarify ambiguities and prepare for termination. |

*The NOVA Model*

The NOVA model (National Organization for Victim Assistance, 1997) has been used successfully with older students in group crisis intervention. It is similar to the CISD model, but requires less structure and allows for more interactions between the facilitator and the participants. It generally lasts about two hours long and should be large enough to provide good interaction, but small enough to be able to identify for assessment the students who may need further help. The NOVA Model session includes:

1. introductions and safety and security statements;
2. descriptions of physical, emotional, and cognitive reactions at the time of the event;
3. ventilation and validation of emotional upheaval;
4. descriptions of the aftermath and present reactions or feelings;
5. ongoing facilitation of validation, refraining from judgment, and drawing and bonding students together to normalize thoughts and feelings;
6. questions about the future with a discussion of coping strategies;
7. referral sources;
8. summarization to reaffirm experiences; and
9. post-group sessions (30 minutes) to distribute handouts, answer questions, or follow-up.

This more informal group process is used to help all students affected by the crisis, and also should highlight those students who need further assessment and assistance.

## Summary/Conclusion

In summary, following are ten things to remember in systemic crisis intervention:

1. A systems approach to crisis is more holistic than individual work alone.
2. A systems approach to crisis broadens the scope of assessment and available resources.
3. Communication is key in resolving systemic crises.
4. Systems intervention helps with the realization that problems reside in the interactions.
5. Being able to utilize systems techniques, such as mapping, discovering subsystems and boundaries, hierarchy, worldview, and triangulation work, enhance individual crisis intervention.
6. A comprehensive plan involving school and community needs to be in place before a crisis occurs.
7. The professional school counselor plays a vital role in the formulation and implementation of such a plan.
8. Physical requirements, logistics, and crisis responses all need to be planned out.
9. Training in a systemic crisis intervention model (e.g., CISD, NOVA) is important for the professional school counselor.
10. Always remember to attend to the needs of the caregivers, professionals, and crisis workers.

## References


Carns, A. W., & Carns, M. R. (1997). A systems approach to school counseling. *The School Counselor, 44,* 220-226.

Cerio, J. (1995). Systems troubleshooting for school counselors. *The Journal for the Professional Counselor, 10(2),* 39-47.

Family Education Network. *A time line of recent worldwide school shootings.* Retrieved July 1, 2002 from http://www.infoplease.com/ipa/A0777958.html

Goldenberg, H., & Goldenberg, I. (1998*). Counseling today's families.* Pacific Grove, CA: Brooks/Cole.

James, R. K., & Gilliland, B. E. (2001). *Crisis intervention strategies.* Belmont, CA: Brooks/Cole.

Keys, S. G., & Lockhart, E. J. (1999). The school counselor's role in facilitating multisystemic change. *Professional School Counseling, 3,* 101-107.

Minuchin, S. (1974). *Families and family therapy.* Cambridge, MA: Harvard University Press.

Minuchin, S., & Fishman, H. (1981). *Family therapy techniques.* Cambridge, MA: Harvard University Press.

Mitchell, J. T., & Everly, G. S. (1993). *Critical incident stress debriefing: An operations manual for the prevention of traumatic stress among emergency services and disaster workers.* Elliot City, MD: Chevron Publishing Corporation.

National Education Association. (2002). *Crisis communications guide & toolkit.* Retrieved June 20, 2002, from http://www.nea.org/crisis/b1home.html.

National Organization for Victim Assistance. (1997). *Community crisis response team training manual* (2nd ed.). Washington, DC: Author.

Sherman, R., & Fredman, N. (1986). *Handbook of structured techniques in marriage and family therapy.* New York: Brunner/Mazel.

# Chapter 88

## Parent Involvement in Schools

*Henry L. Harris & Doris Rhea Coy*

### Preview

This chapter will focus on various aspects of parent involvement in schools including the different categories of parent involvement, barriers preventing parent involvement in schools, recommended actions to increase parent involvement, and brief descriptions of successful parent involvement programs along with Internet resources.

Each year millions of students receive formal education in our nation's elementary and secondary public schools. During the 1999-2000 academic year, 26 million students were enrolled in pre-kindergarten to 6th grade, 20 million were in 7th-12th grade, and 0.6 million were considered non-graded students (National Center for Educational Statistics, 2002). Throughout the educational process, many of these students will flourish academically and socially while others may encounter a variety of obstacles that make school a more challenging experience. However, one of the most significant factors that can help students cope with such challenges and reach their full potential, regardless of school location and school size, is parent involvement.

The interest and support that parents provide children has traditionally been recognized as a crucial element for student educational success (Berger, 1995). According to Epstein (1987), when parents are actively involved their children's potential for school success at all grade levels was enhanced. A report released by the U.S. Department of Education (1998) contended that years of research demonstrated significant differences in learning achievement occur when students have dependable family members, teachers, and the community involved in their education. Following are some facts to consider regarding parent involvement (USDOE, 1998):

- The overwhelming majority of students (90%) who make A and B grades suggested they received encouragement from their parents to do well in school.
- 72% of students aged 10-13 indicated they would like to have more discussions about homework with their parents.
- Truancy, excessive time spent watching television, and having an assortment of reading materials in the home explained close to 90% of the difference in 8th grade math test scores across low performing and high performing states on the National Assessment of Educational Progress.
- 50% of students liked school more and made mostly A's when their fathers were involved.
- Fathers with low involvement compared to those highly involved in schools are more likely to have students who repeat a grade (15% versus 7%) or suspended or expelled from school (18% versus 10%).
- Most teachers believed parent involvement in education needs to be the number one priority.
- 40% of parents across the U.S. believed they were not devoting enough time to their children's education.

While numerous positive benefits of parent involvement have been demonstrated, the level of parent involvement decreases as students progress from elementary through middle and high schools. Parents, school officials, and communities must learn to build cooperative educational partnerships if students are to be provided with necessary educational skills.

## Categories of Parent Involvement

According to Feurstein (2000), parent involvement included a variety of parenting behaviors including discussing homework with children, attending Parent-Teacher Organization/Association (PTO/PTA) meetings, serving as assistants in the classroom, or participating as school volunteers. Dimock, Donoghue, and Robb (1996) discussed methods for helping school officials create effective family/school partnerships, including: (1) school choice, (2) decision-making through formal structures, (3) teaching and learning, (4) effects on the physical and material environment, and (5) effective communication.

The first type of parent involvement, *school choice*, refers to parents making the decision about the actual school their children will attend. It is assumed that when parents are given the power to make decisions about the choice of school their children will attend, they will choose more successful schools and become more involved. The second type of parent involvement, *decision-making through formal structures*, stems from the belief that parents and school officials will develop plans calling for a cooperative partnership in the administration of schools. Parents have inclusive roles on advisory councils, advocacy groups, school review boards, and various other committees.

The third category, *parent involvement in teaching and learning*, include parent activities ranging from helping children with homework to participating in the school as a volunteer. The fourth type of parent involvement, *effect on the physical and material environment,* refers to efforts made by parents to ensure their children have a safe, comfortable, physical and material environment. This includes matters such as school safety, maintenance of school property and learning resources. The fifth type of involvement addressed the significance of *effective communication* between parents and schools. The authors contend that how information is delivered between schools and parents is critical in establishing a positive, cooperative relationship.

The California State Board of Education (as cited in Epstein & Dauber, 1991) added a sixth type of involvement entitled *collaboration and exchanges with community organizations.* Schools, parents, community businesses, and other agency groups are directly or indirectly involved in sharing the responsibility of educating students. School programs that provide different forms of health care, after school services, and other programs that enhance and support the learning process of students are elements of this type of involvement.

## Parent Involvement Barriers

### *The Problems of Mistrust and Race*

Given the significance of parent involvement, there are a number of important factors contributing to the absence of parent involvement in schools. Anderson (1999) contended that some parents and teachers have a difficult time working together because they do not trust each other. Parents are sometimes perceived as outsiders lacking basic educational skills needed to help children learn. This could cause some parents to develop negative feelings and attitudes toward school personnel. Parents may not understand the kind of role the school would like them to fill regarding their involvement at home and school. Parents may also question whether school officials are sincerely concerned about the educational welfare of their children (Eccles

& Harold, 1993).

Race may be another element contributing to mistrust. School officials must understand the socio-political history of parents who have children of color attending schools. Some may not completely trust school personnel for a number of reasons, including lack of a diverse, understanding teaching staff. Frequently, parents of minority students have personal experiences with schools related to controversial issues such as biased testing or racial tracking.

*Language and Poverty*

School officials should be aware of how language could be a barrier limiting parent involvement. According to Sue and Sue (1999), Euro-American culture places a huge emphasis on a person's ability to understand and speak English. As a result individuals who are bilingual or from lower class backgrounds who do not use Standard English while communicating may be unfairly treated or perceived as inferior.

Many American families today are deeply impacted by poverty and economically disadvantaged students are at a greater risk for experiencing a variety of academic, socio-emotional, behavioral and health problems that can negatively impact their long-term development (McLoyd, 1998). Thus, it is crucial for schools to encourage parents from low-income families to become involved in their children's education. School officials should also be aware that some parents are living from paycheck to paycheck. In order to survive, these parents hold multiple jobs with rigid work schedules preventing frequent participation in school-related events.

*Teachers and Parents*

Epstein (1987) noted that the majority of teachers have had very little training working or consulting with parents. Leitch and Tangri (1988) reported a number of teachers perceived parent involvement barriers including: parents not having realistic expectations about the school's role; parents' inability to help their children with school work; parents' belief system that their children's education was not important enough to take time off from work; parental jealousy of teachers along with teacher suspicion of parents who are involved; lack of responsiveness and interest on the part of experienced teachers serving as role models; and absence of activities to attract parents into the schools.

Parents may see themselves as barriers because of economic differences, work-related responsibilities, and health problems (Leitch & Tangri, 1988). Some parents may have had negative experiences during their educational years and feel intimidated by school personnel, sometimes believing that teachers, professional school counselors, or administrators only call parents to deliver negative news about their children or blame them personally for the problems their children are experiencing at school (Eccles & Harold, 1993).

## Recommended Actions to Increase Parent Involvement

School officials should seriously explore ways to overcome barriers and develop a school environment that facilitates parent involvement. Chavkin and Garza-Lubeck (1990) originally outlined six critical steps needed for successful parent involvement programs and within this chapter two additional steps are included. The steps consist of: (1) motivation; (2) accurate assessment; (3) training of staff; (4) community outreach programs; (5) networking with community businesses and agencies; (6) parent-teacher partnerships; (7) role of school boards; and (8) role of the professional school counselor.

The first step required is motivation. School officials must be highly motivated and have a genuine desire to create a parent involvement initiative that welcomes parents from all racial, ethnic, and economic backgrounds to become valued partners in the education of students. School officials must have the desire, ability, and willingness to establish open lines of communication with parents. Effective communication happens when all participants involved have a clear understanding and interpretation of each others' messages. School officials typically communicate with parents using informal contacts, written notes, home visits, telephone calls, and parent/school official meetings (Hornby, 2000).

Motivation also calls for flexibility as demonstrated by scheduling programs during times more convenient to parents, providing daycare to younger siblings for major school programs, alternating conference times to accommodate the work schedules of parents, and offering to bring some school related functions to the site of major employers (Stouffer, 1992) or community settings. School officials should persevere and avoid becoming overly discouraged or frustrated, especially when great efforts to attract parents to schools yield low participation rates. This is a long-term process and results are not always immediately seen.

Step two calls for an accurate assessment of parent involvement. This helps establish accurate information reflecting the interest level and needs of the community. The assessment process could include methods such as informal observations, town-hall meetings with parents and school officials, examining preexisting data (e.g., number of parents attending PTA meetings, looking at the current number of parent volunteers, previous school history), reviewing current policies regarding parent involvement programs, organizing focus groups, mailed surveys, random telephone surveys, and local radio call-in programs (Pryor, 1996). When accurate knowledge is developed, specific programs can be designed to better address concerns.

Step three calls for continuous training and staff development, a vital component of successful parent involvement programs. In-service training could initially begin by exploring school officials' views of parent involvement and past experiences. School officials should be made aware that some parents (e.g., parents who lack education, have low incomes, are from culturally diverse backgrounds) may feel unwelcome in the educational environment and avoid schools. Workshops addressing these types of issues could prove beneficial in helping school officials become more aware of their own personal biases and also help them develop a better understanding of individuals from culturally different groups.

Step four involves school officials venturing out into the community in an attempt to establish a relationship with the various members of the community. Recreational facilities, churches, and cultural gatherings provide unique opportunities for educators to familiarize themselves with key community members who also may be able to further assist them in developing strong parent-school relationships (Chavkin & Garza-Lubeck, 1990). Employers should also be targeted during this step and be encouraged to use family- and student-friendly business practices such as providing leave time for parents to volunteer in school or attend conferences, and, when possible, offer parent training and childcare. Employers could potentially benefit by having better public and community relations, improved worker morale and loyalty, and a more qualified workforce of the future (USDOE, 1996).

Step five involves schools networking with social services agencies. Chavkin and Garza-Lubeck (1990) suggested that helping to arrange services for families in need is a significant part of the effort required to involve parents. Student achievement and attendance is based on more than just instruction because factors such as health, housing, transportation, nutrition, and clothing play influential roles in determining student success.

Step six focuses on the quality of parent-teacher partnerships. Parents and teachers must, for the benefit of the children and the success of the school, work to create effective home/school partnerships. Teachers and parents must be trained to work together. Teachers would like parents to: attend PTA meetings, inform teachers about home situations affecting students, reinforce school programs at home by reading or supervising homework, read and acknowledge letters sent home, teach students what is expected of them at school, and have realistic expectations about their children's capabilities (Hornby, 2000).

Parents would like teachers to: consult more frequently and genuinely listen to the parents' point of view, treat all students with respect, and have a more approachable attitude. Parents would also like teachers to make allowances for individual differences in students, regular and informed reports about their children's progress, and use parents as a resource in the school (Hornby, 2000). Parents and teachers must be willing to develop open lines of communication with one another and start perceiving each other as partners rather than adversaries.

Step seven focuses on the role of the school board in helping to encourage parent involvement. Devlin-Sherer and Devlin-Sherer (1994) suggested that school boards could be more proactive in promoting parent involvement by: influencing administrators to establish meaningful parent involvement programs; requiring administrators to create realistic plans for parent involvement that would be reviewed periodically; helping to establish and promote guidelines for parent involvement initiatives; and encouraging schools to create a school-community newsletter detailing parent involvement activities. Effective school boards seek to employ key administrators who want to create ways that school quality can be enhanced through parent involvement.

Step eight involves the role of the professional school counselor in facilitating parent involvement. Brown (1999) suggested professional school counselors could involve parents more by becoming advocates for parents and students (especially when students are being unfairly treated by the educational system) by regularly consulting with parents and offering a variety of parent education classes. Good communication skills (e.g., listening, paraphrasing, clarifying, interpreting, and reflecting feelings) are valued tools needed to work effectively with parents. Professional school counselors, because of their unique training, could offer workshops to bolster parent communication skills.

## Programs Designed to Improve Parent Involvement

Table 1 provides a brief description of eight highly successful programs that could be easily modified by individual schools desiring to improve parent involvement. Table 2 provides useful Internet resources to bolster parent involvement.

## Summary/Conclusion

Helping students from diverse backgrounds gain a quality education is one of the most important tasks facing America. Parents must become more actively involved in their children's education. Parents must attempt to provide their children, regardless of circumstances, with a nurturing environment conducive to academic success. Professional school counselors, teachers, administrators, and other staff members must equally strive to do more to encourage parent involvement, especially from fathers and parents from low-income families. Schools must work to eliminate barriers preventing parent involvement and realize that most parents would like to become full partners in the educational process. Finally, parents, school professionals, and members of the community should understand that it really does "take a village" to educate a child.

**Table 1. Effective parent involvement programs.**

1. *Good News Cards* were printed postcards with a list of school-related events on the front. Teachers were encouraged to write positive messages about students in their class and mail them home to parents (Loucks, 1992).
2. *Parent/Student Switch Day* involved a process in which students were excused one day from class only if a parent volunteered to take their place at school. The parent was responsible for following the student's daily schedule (with some exceptions) (Loucks, 1992).
3. *Newsletters* inform parents about various topics, including: homework strategies, reports about special school projects, teacher features, and parenting tips. The newsletters should be well-designed and sent out to parents monthly or quarterly, depending on school needs (Loucks, 1992).
4. *Teacher in the Round* required parents to pick up their children's report card at school during a variety of set times. This provided parents with the opportunity to personally meet face to face with the teacher and other school officials (Loucks, 1992).
5. *Parent Classes* were offered at school and focused on topics such as how to help students with homework, tutoring strategies, parenting skills, drug education, and improving communications skills (Loucks, 1992).
6. *Soliciting Parent/Family Volunteers* was a method consisting of a checklist of volunteer opportunities sent home to parents. The list included helping in the library, duplicating copies, tutoring, chaperoning events, and speaking to classes. Incentives, such as a pizza party, to classes with high return rates, were offered (Loucks, 1992).
7. *Lunch with Professional School Counselors* was a program designed by professional school counselors that involved going to the parents' places of employment. The program provided parents a convenient and non-threatening chance to speak with professional school counselors about important information concerning the educational and career planning needs of their children. Employers sensed a real need and asked professional school counselors to see all employees, including those from second and third shifts (Evans & Hines, 1997).
8. *Visiting the Factory*. Ridgeview, Inc. is a hosiery and sock manufacturer located in Catawba County, NC, home of the nation's highest percentage of working moms. The employees holding assembly line jobs found it difficult to take time off to visit their children's schools. As a result, local professional school counselors came to the factory once a month and spent approximately 15 minutes with each parent. Since the plan began, professional school counselors reported no truancy or absentee problems, and also reported more involved fathers (U.S. Department of Education, 1996).

**Table 2. Internet resources.**

The Children's Partnership: Children and Technology
http://www.childrenspartnership.org/bbar/ctech.html
The Children's Partnership On-line - Parent's Online Resource Center
www.childrenspartnership.org/prnt/prnt.html
Family Involvement Partnership for Learning - Parents and Families
www.ed.gov/Family/BTS/covpg.html
How Schools Can Support Family Involvement in Education
www.ed/gov/Family/schoola.html
Kids Can Learn
http://www.kidscanlearn.com
Learning Partners
www.ed.govpubs/parents/LearnPtnrs/
National Coalition for Parent Involvement in Education(NCPI)
www.nul.org/resource.html
National Parent Information Network (NPIN)
http://npin.org/
Parent's Handbook
www.eduplace.com/math/res/parentbk/phs1.html
Partnership for Family Involvement in Education
www.pfie.ed.gov
Publications for Parents, including the partnership for Family Involvement in Education
www.ed.gov/pubs/parents
Steps You Can Take to Improve Your Children's Education
www.ed.gov/Family/families.html

## References


Anderson, S. A. (1999). How parental involvement makes a difference in reading achievement. *Reading Improvement, 60,* 61-86.

Berger, E. H. (1995). *Parents as partners in education: Families and schools working together.* Englewood Cliffs, NJ: Prentice-Hall.

Brown, D. (1999*). Improving academic achievement: What school counselors can do.* Greensboro, NC. ERIC Document Reproduction Service No. ED 435 895.

Chavkin, N. F., & Garza-Lubeck, M. (1990). Multicultural approaches to parent involvement: Research and practice. *Social Work in Education, 13*(1), 22-34.

Devlin-Sherer, R., & Devlin-Sherer, W. L., (1994). Do school boards encourage parent involvement? *Education, 114,* 535-542.

Dimock, C., O'Donoghue, T., & Robb, A. (1996). Parent involvement in schooling: An emerging research agenda. *Compare, 26*, 5-20.

Eccles, J. S., & Harold, R. D. (1993). Parent-school involvement during the early adolescent years. *Teachers College Record, 94,* 568-587.

Epstein, J. L. (1987). What principals should know about parent involvement. *Principal, 66,* 6-9.

Epstein, J. L., & Dauber, S. L. (1991). School programs and teacher practices of parent involvement in inner-city elementary schools and middle schools. *The Elementary School Journal, 91*, 289-305.

Evans, J. E., & Hines, P. L. (1997). Lunch with school counselors: Reaching parents through their workplace. *Professional School Counseling, 1,* 45-48.

Feurstein, A. (2000). School characteristics of parent involvement: Influences on participation in children's schools. *Journal of Educational Research, 94*, 29-41.

Hornby, G. (2000). *Improving parent involvement.* New York: Cassell Wellington House.

Leitch, M. L., & Tangri, S. S. (1988). Barriers to home school collaboration. *Educational Horizons, 66,* 70-74.

Loucks, H. (1992). Increasing parent/family involvement: Ten ideas that work. *NASSP Bulletin, 4*, 19-23.

Pryor, C. (1996). Techniques for assessing family school connections. *Social Work in Education, 18,* 85-94.

McLoyd, V. C. (1998). Socioeconomic disadvantage and child development. *American Psychologist, 43,* 185-204.

National Center for Educational Statistics. (2002). *The condition of education.* Washington, DC: U.S. Government Printing Office.

Stouffer, B. (1992). We can increase parent involvement in secondary schools. *NASSP Bulletin, 4*, 5-8.

Sue, D. W., & Sue, D. (1999). *Counseling the culturally and ethnically different client* (3rd ed). New York: John Wiley & Sons.

U.S. Department of Education. (1996). *A new understanding of parent involvement: Family-work-school.* Washington, DC: U.S. Government Printing Office.

U.S. Department of Education. (1998). *America goes back to school: Key facts on community involvement in children's learning*. Washington, DC: U.S. Government Printing Office

# Chapter 89

## Community Outreach Initiatives

*Cheryl Holcomb-McCoy*

### Preview

This chapter describes the professional school counselor's role in community-empowered schools. Practical suggestions as to how professional school counselors can play a pivotal role in developing and maintaining school-community linkages are listed. A discussion of how community involvement in schools affects student success is provided.

A community-empowered school is one in which administrators, professional school counselors, teachers, staff, students, parents and members of the community feel that they have a stake in the success of that school. By having a shared stake in a school's success, it is believed that the needs of students, families, and society will be better met. Much of the impetus for community-empowered schools stems from educational reform initiatives which hope to not only improve the lives and futures of students but also strengthen neighborhoods and communities. Despite common reservations about the involvement of community members in the day-to-day management of schools, the long-term advantages of sustained school-community partnerships and community-empowered schools have been well-documented (Hatch, 1998; Lewis, 1997; Murnane & Levy, 1996). The foundation of the work of successful community outreach initiatives, therefore, consists of building relationships among parents, educators, community leaders, and public officials. These relationships, in turn, foster increased involvement and shared norms among the people who are essential to school change.

In response to this movement toward community- empowered schools, many professional school counselors have accepted the challenge of playing a major role in developing school-community linkages or community outreach initiatives. The American School Counselor Association (ASCA) and the Council for the Accreditation of Counseling and Related Program (CACREP) have even suggested that professional school counselors have the skills necessary to promote school-community partnerships. With that said, this chapter is designed to offer professional school counselors direction for promoting community outreach initiatives or partnerships. For the sake of clarity, community outreach initiatives will be used interchangeably with school-community partnerships.

### Why Community Outreach Initiatives?

One of the most important factors in producing rapid increases in test scores and overall student achievement is community involvement (Hatch, 1998). Over the last twenty years, many schools have opted to create outreach initiatives such as community mental health clinics, parent education programs, weekly chats among teachers and parents, and community wide safety campaigns as an effort to involve community members in the schooling of its youngsters.

As a result, these same schools have frequently experienced a dramatic increase in state mandated test scores and reading levels. Beyond changes in curriculum and instruction and other school restructuring activities, the power of community involvement for improving student learning is great and can transform the culture of a school.

Common patterns among schools that have experienced a drastic increase in student achievement suggest that community involvement contributes to improvement in the:

- physical conditions, resources and constituencies that support learning;
- attitudes and expectations of parents, teachers, and students; and
- depth and quality of the learning experiences in which parents, teachers, and students participate.

## Components of Community Outreach Initiatives

According to Colbert (1996), successful school-community initiatives or partnerships are associated with four guiding principles:

1. Coordinate and integrate Epstein and Salina's (1993) School and Family Partnership Types model,
2. Make community initiatives an integral part of the school's organizational and operating structure,
3. Identify and use effective parent and teacher models, and
4. Maintain ongoing monitoring and evaluation of all community initiatives.

According to Colbert (1996), the first principle is important because it ensures that community outreach initiatives are relevant to various types of partnerships as delineated by Epstein and Salinas (1993). Epstein and Salinas purported that there are six types of partnership activities in schools: (1) parenting skills, understanding of child development, home conditions for learning and the school's understanding of its families; (2) communications from school-to-home and from home-to-school about programs and student progress; (3) the organization, schedules, and use of volunteers at and for the school, and the opportunities and schedules for audiences at school for student events; (4) family involvement in learning activities at home, including homework, class work, curriculum-related interactions, and decisions; (5) family involvement in school decisions, committees, school-based management, advocacy, and other practices of participation; and (6) community collaborations and resources for students, the school, and families. Colbert believed that community initiatives should be varied across these types of partnerships and that one initiative may be relevant to more than one of the types.

The second principle suggests that community outreach initiatives should be an integral part of the school's organizational and operating structure. For instance, informing parents of new instructional strategies and engaging parents in activities that can enhance their student's learning are strategies that make outreach an ongoing component of a school's day-to-day existence. To do this, there should be planned and well-coordinated events where curriculum-related matters are relayed among parents, school operational groups, and a school's curriculum committee.

The third principle, identifying and using effective parent and teacher models, suggests that community outreach initiatives should strive to highlight parenting and teaching models or practices that foster healthy development of children. For instance, teachers and parents who exemplify exceptional skills and strategies would be enlisted as trainers or models for other teachers and parents. A means for identifying model parents and teachers must be determined by school personnel in order to achieve this principle.

Finally, it is critical that community outreach initiatives be closely monitored and evaluated. Ongoing feedback provides the information needed in order to continue or discontinue the initiative. Evaluation procedures and designs must be decided upon before implementation.

In addition to the preceding four guiding principles, efforts to establish effective community outreach activities require new school policies and processes in order to meet the needs of all students, families, schools, and communities. According to Taylor and Adelman (2000), schools must make the following procedural changes to ensure effective school-community partnerships:

- Create shared decision-making and appropriate degrees of local control and private sector involvement. There must be guaranteed roles for the involvement of staff, families, students, and community members in the decision-making process of schools.
- Create change teams and agents to carry out daily activities associated with systemic change. Establishing a school-based, resource-oriented team, properly constituted with school, home, and community representatives is a first step. This team leads and steers efforts to maintain and improve a multifaceted and integrated approach to community outreach.
- Establish institutionalized mechanisms to manage and enhance resources for community outreach activities. These mechanisms should include ways to analyze, plan, coordinate, integrate, monitor, evaluate, and strengthen ongoing efforts.

According to Giles (1998), a critical component of successful community outreach initiatives was the perception or belief of the initiators. Giles suggested that the initiators of school-community partnerships must view the school and its surrounding community as a part of an interdependent social ecology that is only understood as a whole, rather than independent parts. In her observations, successful outreach initiatives address the strengths and difficulties in a school and community. Also, Giles suggested that successful initiatives involve the engagement of not only those parents who seek to get involved but of parents who are less likely to become involved in school-related activities (e.g., minority parents, low-income parents). As a means to get all parents involved, Giles suggested that outreach efforts begin with an activity where parents can reflect critically upon the education of their children. This accomplishes more than activities such as parent education workshops where educators and mental health professionals often view parents as patients in need of treatment. These "patient-like" activities, according to Giles, keep parents isolated from each other and dependent on the expertise of educators.

Another author, Heckman (1996), indicated that regular meetings with parents, students, teachers, counselors, administrators, and community leaders is a critical component of successful outreach initiatives. Parents, community members, and educators must meet together to identify common concerns, decide on which to focus, and then develop strategies for addressing them. By meeting regularly, parents learn more about their supportive role in their child's education and teachers learn more about the lives of the students in their classrooms. Furthermore, community leaders, who are often left out of these dialogues, have an opportunity to offer their support and resources to resolve critical problems in the school.

## Implications for Professional School Counselors

The process for developing and facilitating community outreach is consistent with educational reform and comprehensive developmental school counseling programs that require professional school counselors to develop the skills to provide leadership in addressing educational goals. The primary emphasis for professional school counselors is to take on a leadership role in coordinating the efforts of diverse groups (e.g., parents, teachers, community members, staff, administration) when developing and implementing community outreach initiatives. Professional school counselors might use their expertise to facilitate discussions between these diverse school and community groups and to restructure their method of communicating with each other. For instance, professional school counselors might revise the method used for teachers to communicate with parents and for parents to communicate with teachers. Such a restructuring of communication methods could enhance the information channels between parents and teachers and develop a sense of trust between the school and community.

In addition to taking on a leadership role in the initiation of community outreach activities, professional school counselors can:

- Collaborate with other school personnel and community members in order to develop a working group or committee that will initiate and monitor community outreach initiatives.
- Coordinate monthly or weekly meetings or chats with groups of parents and community members. The chats should consist of parents of all groups and community institutions represented in the school and community.
- Acknowledge the role of "power" in school-community partnerships. Professional school counselors should become knowledgeable of how to conduct a "power analysis" that identifies the self-interests of different groups and individuals in a particular education bureaucracy. In other words, the purpose of implementing a power analysis is to uncover the influence of various groups in the decision-making process in a particular school. These analyses frequently reveal the absence of parents and community members in educational decision-making. Professional school counselors, if knowledgeable of this process, should enlighten educators regarding power's influence on the way students are educated and the involvement of families in the educational process.
- Assist with the monitoring and evaluating of community outreach initiatives. Professional school counselors should be able to use educational outcome data such as achievement scores, attendance, and drop-out rates to determine the effectiveness of community outreach initiatives. Also, professional school counselors should be involved in evaluating less tangible outcomes of their outreach efforts such as students' attitudes toward learning and the school climate.
- Actively promote collaborative leadership in all community outreach activities. Successful community outreach is dependent upon trust between the community and school personnel. Therefore, by promoting collaborative leadership in which the responsibilities of leadership are shared among administrators, teachers, professional school counselors, parents, and community leaders, a sense of trust is fostered among the school community.
- Attend workshops and training sessions that focus on community outreach and school reform. Meeting with other professional school counselors, educators, and community leaders who are interested or involved in community outreach reinforces and encourage the maintenance of outreach programs.
- Conduct interviews or conversations periodically (at least 10 per year) with parents and community members to discuss community and school needs.
- Coordinate "neighborhood walks" for teachers and other school personnel each year. These walks, in which parents, community members, and educators gather at the school and then go out to visit families and businesses, provide an opportunity for community members and educators to discuss their concerns for the school and community.

## Summary/Conclusion

Professional school counselors can play a pivotal role in enhancing the ways schools and communities connect. By focusing on linking communities and schools, school culture, quality of relationships among educators, parents, and students, and student educational outcomes will invariably change for the better. Further, since schools alone cannot solve all the problems they encounter, community outreach initiatives go beyond the school and draw upon the power of community institutions (e.g., families, churches, civic groups). Professional school counselors, like schools, are unable to address all of the problems on their student caseload. By accepting a leadership role in the development of a community-empowered school, they can improve the lives of students and aspects of life in the community that impact student education.

## References

Colbert, R. D. (1996). The counselor's role in advancing school and family partnerships. *School Counselor, 44,* 100–105.

Epstein, J. L., & Salinas, K. C. (1993). *School and family partnerships: Questionnaires for teachers and parents.* Baltimore: Johns Hopkins University, Center on Families, Communities, Schools, and Children's Learning.

Giles, H. C. (1998). *Parent engagement as a school reform strategy.* ERIC Document Number ED 419031.

Hatch, T. (1998). How communities contribute to achievement. *Educational Leadership, 55,* 16-19.

Heckman, P. E. (1996). *The courage to change: Stories from successful school reform.* Thousand Oaks, CA: Corwin Press.

Lewis, A. (1997). *Building bridges: Eight case studies of schools and communities working together.* Chicago: Cross City Campaign for Urban School Reform.

Murnane, R. J., & Levy, F. (1996). The first principle: Agree on the problem. In R. J. Murnane, & F. Levy (Eds.), *Teaching the new basic skills: Principles for educating children to thrive in a changing economy.* New York: The Free Press.

Taylor, L., & Adelman, H. S. (2000). Connecting schools, families, and communities. *Professional School Counseling, 3,* 298-308.

# Chapter 90

## The Professional School Counselor as Resource and Services Broker

*Stuart F. Chen-Hayes & Inez G. Ramos*

### Preview

Professional school counselors advocate both inside and outside elementary, middle, and high schools for the best possible academic, college, career, emotional, personal, and social resources for students, educator colleagues, parents, guardians, and other stakeholders. This chapter provides specific knowledge and skills in how to broker resources effectively and ensure that school counseling services reach everyone in the school to create and maintain a comprehensive developmental school counseling program.

Professional school counselors can play a pivotal role in assisting students, families, and educators as collaborative team players skilled in the art of advocacy. As such, professional school counselors can help families and educators access accurate information and broker resources and services for students. This skill can be developed through hands-on experience in collaboration and teamwork (Bemak 2000; Keys, 2000). However, there is no manual on how to navigate the intricate webs of social service systems, school district systems, and local, county, city, state, and national educational systems. Most social service and educational systems have both traditional print brochures and online websites, but using the Internet or print information alone is not a substitute for developing and maintaining the unique personal and informal relationships that allow for brokering resources and services for all students, families, and educators.

*Advocacy* can be defined as empowerment of people, or the ability to deliver information, resources, services, and the necessary skills to use them successfully. With professional school counselors evidencing expert abilities in listening and influencing skills (Ivey & Ivey, 2003), advocacy for all students, families, and educators requires finding the best information, resources, and services. Professional school counselors must be expert collaborators to advocate and broker academic, career, and personal/social development information and counseling resources and services (Bemak, 2000; Campbell & Dahir, 1997; Dahir, Sheldon, & Valiga, 1998; Erford, House, & Martin, 2003; Keys, 2000; Keys, Green, Lockhart, & Luongo, 2003).

The professional school counseling literature evidences multiple recent examples of professional school counselors as transformative advocates in delivering and brokering school counseling services as well as community and family resources and services: in e-mail mentoring programs (Thompson & Brown, 2000), as agents of systemic change (Chen-Hayes & Erford, 2003; Littrell & Peterson, 2001), as advocates against sexual harassment in schools (Stone, 2000), as collaborators on a school district-based mental health services team with community and family agencies (Keys, 2000), through interagency and interdepartmental collaboration (Bemak, 2000), as collaborators in ensuring school safety through coordination of programs ensuring all students receive appropriate mental health services (Porter, Epp, & Bryant, 2000), and in school-home-community models of collaboration and advocating for legislators to support school-community partnerships (Taylor & Adelman, 2000).

So with the recent examples of scholarship in professional school counseling related to brokering resources and services, how can professional school counselors put theory into practice? There are many ways of accessing services and resources. The traditional way involves building a repertoire of resources and services through networking with other professionals. Sharing and exchanging information is the quickest way to access services and resources both in person and over the Internet. Word of mouth information keeps professional school counselors, school social workers, and school psychologists up to date. Another way of accessing resources and services is utilizing the media. Traditional and ethnic-community focused newspapers, specialty magazines, regular and cable-access television stations, billboards and advertisements, hospital and mental health center publications, houses of worship publications, community-based organization publications, political publications, and the Internet can be important outlets for resources and services.

Use of computer technology may be the quickest tool available to professional school counselors to broker resources and services effectively. There are numerous websites and search engines on the Internet of interest to professional school counselors (Sabella, 1999). Professional school counselors can focus on websites in areas that match the ASCA national standards: academic development, career and college development, and emotional/personal/social issues. Creating lists of sites in each of these areas on a school counseling program homepage linked to the school's homepage provides a terrific way to assist students, families, and educators in accessing academic, career/college, and emotional/personal/ social resources and services quickly and effectively. In addition, professional school counselors can list available community referral sites for tutoring, learning assistance, mentoring, mental health, career/college, bilingual support, and social services referrals. Professional school counselors, in their advocacy role as brokers of resources and services, can enhance their effectiveness by developing personal contacts and professional relationships in each of these areas to benefit all students, families, and educators.

As professional school counselors gain information, they can share it with students, parents and guardians, and educational colleagues and administrators via a school counseling or school home page/website, school newsletter, bulletin boards, school counseling brochure, and flyers posted around the school and sent home to parents/guardians. An important parallel academic and social advocacy role for professional school counselors in brokering resources and services is to also promote the school counseling profession (Bailey, Getch, & Chen-Hayes, 2003; VanZandt & Hayslip, 2001).

But professional school counselors aren't expected to have all the answers; often parents and guardians are excellent sources of information. Parents and guardians can increase staff and educator knowledge about cultural and ethnic traditions and values. They also know about informal and formal gathering centers where diverse groups go for help. Parents and guardians have much to teach staff and educators about their families' values and belief systems. This helps build trust and credibility (Sue & Sue, 2002) when addressing various counseling and human development issues in schools and communities.

Another source of community resource and services information includes places of worship and faith-based communities. Many families turn to spiritual and religious gathering places in times of distress or celebration. Such venues play an important role in the community and often have multiple resources and services available to students and families or know how to access those resources and services. Therefore, it is important to know where the places of worship are in one's community and have a working relationship with staff and knowledge of informational publications, advertising resources, and services.

In addition, the offices of local, state, and national politicians and school board members provide attention to constituents and are often the source of new legislation and/or funding for various community and school-based projects. Knowledgeable constituents and professional school counselors can work together as allies to ensure that all community members receive the resources and services they deserve. Politicians are especially good at challenging red tape when students, families, and educators find themselves stuck in bureaucracy. Most politicians do not get re-elected unless they have expertise in improving the quality of life for voters in their districts. As Sue & Sue (2002) indicated, counseling is a sociopolitical act. The same can be said of brokering resources and services: professional school counselors perform sociopolitical action on behalf of students and families when partnering with politicians.

Professional school counselors are more effective when they know how to advocate inside and outside the school and district communities on behalf of students, families, staff, and educators. To become skilled in accessing resources and services, professional school counselors cannot work in a vacuum or play "Lone Ranger" any longer (Erford et al., 2003). The best way is to befriend school and community leaders by networking inside and outside the school, the district, and the community. Professional school counselors build collaborative relationships by attending professional development workshops and multidisciplinary meetings at school, on the district level, and in community-based agencies, organizations, hospitals, or mental health centers. Take advantage of opportunities to interface with professionals inside and outside of schools to share and exchange information and resources related to academics and learning, career and college development, and emotional, personal and social needs. Develop a directory of services that can be accessed either in person, through a school counseling program brochure or pamphlet, or via the school's website.

Many communities have nonprofit organizations funded by the public sector, such as community centers in urban and suburban districts and cooperative extension programs in rural districts. Professional school counselors can develop a relationship with these community–based organizations (CBOs) which serve as a clearinghouse of community resources and service information. In addition to meeting district leaders and school board representatives, professional school counselors need to know their community board, township, county, and similar organization officials. Also, professional school counselors can develop working relationships with local community colleges and universities to partner for early access to college and university courses and for materials for students and their families. College advising and awareness and the multitude of resources and services available to students and their families can be highlighted prior to kindergarten (Schneider & Chen-Hayes, in press) and needs to be continuously reinforced throughout elementary, middle, and high school levels by professional school counselors. An outstanding one-stop resource for college searches, college planning, taking college placement exams, and paying for college is the College Board, www.collegeboard.com.

There are many additional resource references in online and print formats available to professional school counselors. The United Way and/or local counties usually publish a resource directory of all the social service organizations in their jurisdictions, and the national United Way website gives instant access to many local community agencies by clicking on their "Find My United Way" icon (www.unitedway.org). All states and most large cities publish resource books and pamphlets online and in print formats. For example, the Department of Education in New York City publishes many resource books and online information at their website (www.nycboe.net), as does the New York State Department of Education (www.nysed.gov) to help students, families, educators, and administrators access resources, services, and information.

Federal and state agencies publish resource guidebooks in print and online. Of particular interest for professional school counselors are publications from the U.S. Department of Education (www.ed.gov) and the Department of Health and Human Services (www.hhs.gov). Education-based union websites are also an excellent source of information on current issues affecting students, families, and educators including the American Federation of Teachers (www.aft.org) and the National Education Association website (www.nea.org). For outstanding data to demonstrate how to increase student achievement and challenge the myth that poor and working class children and youth and children and youth of color cannot learn at high levels, The Education Trust's website is full of excellent data, power point slides, and multiple publications. It also has an entire section devoted to their Transforming School Counseling Initiative (TSCI) (www.edtrust.org).

Finally, counselor education and school counseling programs are beginning to teach the skills in how to broker resources and services and advocate for all students and families. Counselor education programs are encouraged to add specific components supporting advocacy and brokering of resources and services to pre-practicum, practicum, and internship courses and fieldwork.

## Summary/Conclusion

High expectations for student success are found in the call for outcomes-based evidence from data-driven educational and school counseling programs. These programs are accountable for ensuring academic achievement at high levels for all students (Erford et al., 2003). Professional school counselors have joined the accountability and results-based movement to ensure all students, families, and educators succeed through increased advocacy and brokering of resources. Professional school counselors effectively advocate on behalf of all students when staying informed of local, state, and national information sources and services to address student academic, career, and personal/social needs.

## References

Bailey, D. F., Getch, Y. Q., & Chen-Hayes, S. F. (2003). Professional school counselors as social and academic advocates. In B. T. Erford (Ed.), *Transforming the school counseling profession* (pp. 411-434). Columbus, OH: Merrill/Prentice-Hall.

Bemak, F. (2000). Transforming the role of the counselor to provide leadership in educational reform through collaboration. *Professional School Counseling, 3*, 323-331.

Campbell, C. A., & Dahir, C. A. (1997). *Sharing the vision: The national standards for school counseling programs.* Alexandria, VA: American School Counselor Association.

Chen-Hayes, S. F., & Erford, B. T. (2003). Living the transformed role. In B. T. Erford (Ed.), *Transforming the school counseling profession* (pp. 449-454). Columbus, OH: Merrill/Prentice-Hall.

Dahir, C. A., Sheldon, C. B., & Valiga, M. J. (1998). *Vision into action: Implementing the National Standards for School Counseling Programs.* Alexandria, VA: American School Counselor Association.

Erford, B. T., House, R., & Martin, P. (2003). Transforming the school counseling profession. In B. T. Erford (Ed.), *Transforming the school counseling profession* (pp. 1-19). Columbus, OH: Merrill/Prentice-Hall.

Ivey, A. E., & Ivey, M. B. (2003). *Intentional interviewing and counseling: Facilitating client development in a multicultural society* (5th ed.). Pacific Grove, CA: Brooks/Cole-Thomson Learning.

Keys, S. G. (2000). Living the collaborative role: Voices from the field. *Professional School Counseling, 3,* 332-338.

Keys, S. G., Green, A., Lockhart, E., & Luongo, P. F. (2003). Consultation and collaboration. In B. T. Erford (Ed.), *Transforming the school counseling profession* (pp. 171-190). Columbus, OH: Merrill/Prentice-Hall.

Littrell, J. M., & Peterson, J. S. (2001). Transforming the school culture: A model based on an exemplary counselor. *Professional School Counseling, 4,* 310-319.

Porter, G., Epp, L., & Bryant, S. (2000). Collaboration among school mental health professionals: A necessity, not a luxury. *Professional School Counseling, 3,* 315-322.

Schneider, G., & Chen-Hayes, S. F. (2004). College begins in pre-K: Creating academic access, equity, and success for all students and their families through a model pre-K developmental school counseling program. In B. T. Erford (Ed.), *Professional school counseling: A handbook of theories, programs & practices.* Greensboro, NC: CAPS Press.

Stone, C. B. (2000). Advocacy for sexual harassment victims: Legal support and ethical aspects. *Professional School Counseling, 4,* 23-30.

Sue, D. W., & Sue, S. (2002). *Counseling the culturally diverse* (4th ed.). New York: Wiley.

Taylor, L., & Adelman, H. S. (2000). Connecting schools, families, and communities. *Professional School Counseling, 3,* 298-307.

Thompson, A. L., & Brown, L. L. (2000). A collaborative e-mail mentoring program for elementary school students. *Professional School Counseling, 4,* 71-74.

VanZandt, Z., & Hayslip, J. (2001). *Developing your school counseling program: A handbook for systemic planning* (2nd ed.). Belmont, CA: Wadsworth.

# Chapter 91

## College Begins in Pre-K: Creating Academic Access, Equity, and Success for All Students and Their Families through a Model Pre-K Developmental School Counseling Program.

*Gabrina Schneider & Stuart Chen-Hayes*

### Preview

This chapter demonstrates how professional school counselors can advocate for pre-K children and their families through a model developmental school counseling program created at Babies Prep School in Manhattan, NY, for pre-K children with disabilities. The goal is to create an atmosphere of high expectations for all students and pre-K staff to ensure an outstanding start for academic access, equity, and success for all students at the earliest ages. This program aims to interrupt the systemic barriers that confront the pre-K staff and parents and guardians working with the students. Once the systemic barriers are acknowledged and challenged, professional school counselors can develop academic, career/ college, and emotional, personal, and social resources for pre-K children and their families through ongoing staff and parent/guardian training workshops.

The Education Trust's motto is "College begins in kindergarten." These authors respectfully disagree. If professional school counselors are given the ability (or seize the opportunity) to create developmental school counseling programs for pre-K students and their families, then the goal of college and the need for academic and interpersonal success skills for all students and their families can begin in pre-K. Professional school counselors can be advocates for the academic, career, college, and personal/social success of the youngest students and their families by developing and implementing comprehensive developmental pre-K school counseling programs. The first author developed such a program in her work as a pre-K professional school counselor at an early intervention school for students with developmental disabilities. This chapter gives specific suggestions for how all professional school counselors can develop resources and programs that ensure equity, access, and school success for all students beginning in pre-K.

Developmental school counseling programs need to be created and implemented for pre-K children, parents and guardians, and school staff to set a tone of high expectations and equally strong support for academic, career/college, and emotional/personal/social equity, access, and success. Not only do pre-K students develop their learning skills preparing for elementary school, but this is a critical time to teach parents and guardians and educational staff how to advocate for all students within the educational system and at home. With college costs at record highs and no end in sight, pre-K is an excellent time to discuss parent and guardian hopes and dreams for their children and how they need to begin thinking about college, including financing a college education in the earliest (pre-K) years.

The school counseling literature addresses pre-K programs in both systemic and individual programs. Entire pre-K-12 comprehensive developmental school counseling programs have been developed and implemented at the state level (South Carolina Department of Education,

1999; Texas Education Agency, 1998). At the same time, individual pre-K programs highlighting the elementary school counselor's role in providing services for pre-K students and their families have also been illustrated in the literature (Bacon & Dougherty, 1992; Hohenshil & Brown, 1991). Similarly, theoretical pieces have been developed on the importance of working with pre-K students with disabilities and their families (Gerler & Myrick, 1991; Telzrow, 1991) and how early intervention program services call for professional school counselors to use family systems and early childhood development theories in intervention and empowerment of pre-K students and families (Fine & Gardner, 1991; Hoffman, 1991). The professional school counselor has an essential role to play in closing the achievement gap and assisting educators in ensuring high level coursework and college preparatory expectations for poor and working class children and youth and for children and youth of color (Johnson, 1996). The professional school counselor must shift functions from a purely individual focus to being an academic and social advocate on a systemic level with poor and working class African American, Latino/a and other children and youth of color to challenge barriers of racism and classism (Bailey, Getch, & Chen-Hayes, 2003).

In many cases, funding for pre-K services is often based on an early intervention model of services for students with disabilities and their families. The first author created a comprehensive developmental pre-K school counseling model for pre-K children with developmental disabilities and their parents and guardians. This model program focused on the professional school counselor's role in developing equity, advocacy, and success for all students and their families so that each could succeed at high levels in school and eventually apply to and complete college.

Ultimately, only teamwork and collaboration on the part of all adults involved made the program successful and helped all students to overcome the barriers that inhibited them from achieving academic and interpersonal success. While entering and graduating from college — over a decade or two into the future - may seem a distant idea, all adults involved in pre-K children's lives must overcome the barriers that hinder our students from achieving academic and interpersonal success goals that could limit their college-bound opportunities.

## Systemic Barriers to Overcome

Multiple barriers can impede the growth of pre-K students with developmental disabilities. These barriers often affect how the adults who teach and support pre-K students interact with pre-K students as well as their future expectations for students with disabilities. Numerous barriers were encountered by family members, staff and teachers. The barriers faced by parents, guardians and other family members include:

- lack of knowledge about the child's disability, and therefore a lack of how to properly advocate for school-based services that assist with high-level learning and achievement;
- frustration of going through a difficult time with their child's disability without anyone to help, support, understand, or share the experience;
- not being aware of the N-16 (newborn to college) education process that their child will go through and fear of how to intervene in a series of educational systems due to lack of knowledge or skills in interacting with the N-16 system;
- lack of time to enjoy interactions with their child or significant others due to an overfocus on the stressors of life due to living with a child with a developmental disability.

Barriers faced by the pre-school staff included:

- lack of awareness, knowledge, and skills in noticing and affirming, let alone understanding, the importance of cultural, linguistic, and family diversity;

- lack of knowledge about technology, including computers, that help to facilitate learning, teaching, and supporting pre-K students and their families;
- lack of collaboration and teamwork skills and their importance for successful learning and behavioral outcomes with pre-K students and their families;
- lack of self-reflection on their roles as educators and how their awareness, knowledge, and skills directly effect the pre-K student's learning experience.

Barriers faced by pre-school teachers included:

- poor writing and grammar skills that impede student advocacy as demonstrated in poorly written or disempowering Individualized Education Plans (IEPs);
- little or no knowledge about how to write an empowering IEP to advocate for pre-K students and their families.

Overcoming these barriers was essential to ensure a comprehensive developmental pre-K school counseling program and was embraced by all members of the school community.

## Creating Change through Parent/Guardian and Staff Development Workshops

Workshops for training adults in developing advocacy skills and high expectations for the learning and interpersonal success of all students were developed for the three main groups of adults working with the children: (1) parents, guardians, and family members, (2) preschool staff who are not teachers, and (3) teachers. The developmental pre-K school counseling program provided adults with the necessary tools to help overcome any systemic or individual barriers that might prevent the students from achieving, learning, and developing interpersonal skills to help them succeed throughout elementary, middle, and high school and successfully gain access to college and meaningful career paths. This developmental school counseling program workshop model was inspired by the Education Trust's Transforming School Counseling Initiative model, which focused the professional school counselor's role and mission toward leadership, advocacy, teamwork and collaboration, use of data for assessment of equity, and counseling and coordination (Erford, House, & Martin, 2003). The goal was for the pre-K professional school counselor to assist in closing the achievement gap through academic and social advocacy, particularly toward students and families of nondominant socioeconomic and racial identities (Bailey, Getch, & Chen-Hayes, 2003).

Key to the success of these workshops was the ethical guidelines and standards of practice of the American Counseling Association (ACA, 1997) and the American School Counselor Association (ASCA, 1992). To be most effective and demonstrate cultural competence at all times, all adults needed to respect diverse values, cultures, ethnicities, races, and spiritual identities of the students, family members, and staff. Sensitivity toward, and consideration of, a student's cultural identity demonstrated trust and credibility (Sue & Sue, 2003) on the part of school staff and teachers. In addition, staff and educators were encouraged to demonstrate basic multicultural and linguistic competencies through awareness, knowledge, and skills of culturally and linguistically diverse students, families, and their educational colleagues and staff (Arredondo et al., 1996). Due to the high number of families that spoke Spanish in the school, as well as a number of staff whose first language was Spanish, all workshops were conducted in two languages when possible and the use of a translator was also encouraged at times when workshops were delivered in English. All written materials were also translated into Spanish. Another way that collaboration within the developmental school counseling program was encouraged involved the use of and openness to all different groups and organizations in the Manhattan community neighborhood of the Upper West Side near Babies Prep School. The professional school counselor facilitated the empowerment of clients in culturally diverse populations by advocating for the development of coalitions among local community groups and organizations that shared common goals even though their constituencies came from different cultural, ethnic, and linguistic backgrounds (Lewis, Lewis, D'Andrea, & Daniels, 1998).

## Parent and Guardian Workshops

The first workshops were presented to parents/guardians and other family members of students and focused on teaching parents and guardians how to advocate for themselves and their children in educational and social services settings to challenge ableism, the use of prejudice multiplied by power against persons with disabilities to keep them from accessing resources. Teaching the members of student's families was recognized as important empowerment so that all parents and guardians had the knowledge of what their rights were as family members of students with disabilities, to build upon their expertise as parents and guardians of students with disabilities, and to give them advanced knowledge about their children's disabilities to make them the experts in working with both educational and social services systems. Use of a social justice advocacy approach in these workshops increased the parents' and guardians' personal power and fostered sociopolitical change reflecting greater responsiveness to the student's personal needs in terms of academic and social success (Bailey et al., 2003; Lewis et al., 1998).

The second workshop done with the parents, guardians, and family members sought to create and implement a regular school newsletter. This newsletter was created by staff with the idea of having parents, guardians, and family members of students maintain and improve it. This publication encouraged family members to inform, educate, and advocate for themselves and for their children. The newsletter became a stepping-stone for the family and friends of the students to become powerful advocates and social action participants. The different sections were designed to include topics such as: powerful stories of struggle that individual families have endured and learned; technological resources such as useful websites; technological advances in assisting children and families with disabilities; poems and creative stories of success and resisting ableism; parenting tips for children with disabilities; nutrition issues; and tips on academic, career, college, and personal/social success for all ages. By sharing newsletter responsibility with parents and guardians, they were empowered to create and educate on their own, increasing their presence and position as an integral part of the social interactions of the school. By becoming a part of the school in such a visible and empowering manner, the school staff promoted, as Homan (1999) stated, distribution of authority and responsibility.

The third workshop done with parents and guardians was focused on issues specific to negotiating the Committee on Preschool Special Education (CPSE) and Individualized Education Program (IEP) processes. Annually, students have an IEP written for them. The IEP consists of evaluations as well as goals that the student is expected to meet by the end of the school year. An IEP often also includes requests for specialized student services such as physical, speech, or occupational therapy, in addition to educational objectives. After the IEP is written collaboratively by the teacher and occupational, physical, and speech therapists who work with the student, a meeting between the child's parents/guardians and school and district staff is called to explain the goals and decide whether the goals and requested services are appropriate for the student.

For parents and guardians these meetings can be intimidating and confusing, especially if parents and guardians are not given explanations for the purpose of the meetings and the technical language that is often used by staff during the meetings. A workshop that explained the different IEP components helped parents and guardians understand how to advocate for or against the various goals, types of services, and specific parent/guardian tasks needed to successfully assist a student with disabilities. The information presented to parents and guardians in this workshop allowed them to take a more active role in the CPSE meeting and play a larger role in assisting in the decision-making about their child's annual goals. This information-giving and decision-making skills workshop exemplified what Homan (1999) defined as empowerment. When people feel greater worth and control they see how they can participate in and influence life circumstances.

The final workshop for parents and guardians was a regular series on educational issues arising from the various disabilities. The more knowledge that parents and guardians have about the disabilities and how to successfully manage and monitor the conditions, the greater the likelihood for academic and social success for their children. Many families of children with disabilities are not able to advocate for or even understand their children if they do not comprehend what their children are experiencing. This workshop also provided resources for families through outside organizations and local, state, and national disability groups that have funds, toys, resources, and ideas to help families raise children. This introduction to other resources widened the school's community collaboration and used collective power to promote advocacy and change.

Assessment and measurement of the design and success of these workshops occurred through an ongoing needs assessment. In the beginning of the transformation of Babies Prep School, the school director and the professional school counselor both noticed a drop in family involvement. They created a questionnaire that asked parents and guardians for suggestions to increase group and workshop adult attendance and participation. The needs assessment revealed that the time that prior workshops had been held made it difficult for parents and guardians to attend. The staff decided that instead of having parents and guardians have to find babysitters, staff would care for students during workshop time so that parents and guardians would be more likely to attend. The needs assessment also gave feedback that many Spanish-speaking family members were feeling left out even with the use of the translator. Once workshop facilitators realized they were speaking too fast for the translator to keep up, the pace slowed and the translator and family members were able to hear all of the information successfully. After these adjustments were made, attendance soared. As a result, staff members and family members became closer and more involved in reciprocal relationships and parents and guardians participated more and were more vocal.

## Staff Workshops

In the best-performing pre-school programs, like other top schools, professional school counselors do not work alone. All educators play a role in creating an environment that promotes the achievement of the identified academic, career, and personal/social goals and outcomes for students as evidenced in the ASCA *National Standards for School Counseling Programs* (Campbell & Dahir, 1997). The professional school counselor facilitates communication and establishes linkages for the benefit of students, teachers, staff, administration, families, student services personnel, agencies, businesses, and other members of the community. In keeping with these guidelines and national school counseling standards, the preschool staff workshops addressed professional development for the entire preschool staff to create a better learning environment and optimal academic and social success for students.

The first workshop developed and implemented was on multicultural competencies beginning with cultural awareness, knowledge and skills (Arredondo et al., 1996) for students, teachers, staff, and parents and guardians. To respect and affirm all members of the school community, everyone at the preschool needed to learn about different cultures, traditions, life situations, and worldviews (Herring, 1997; Sue & Sue, 2003). Just as staff learned the importance of creating a safe environment for students with disabilities, staff also realized the need to create safety for a pre-school staff comprised of differing cultures, ethnic and racial identities, and world views. The cultural competency workshop was designed to be ongoing and included segments specific to self-awareness (sharing about one's own cultures, ethnic and racial identities, and world view) and ending oppressions, such as racism (including definitions and how staff can use their roles to end oppression on individual, cultural, and systemic levels in the school).

The next staff development workshop was designed to build collaboration and teamwork skills. Working as an effective team only increased the success of students and families. The staff development workshop on teaming and collaboration focused on two major areas: collaboration and bettering communication skills between staff members. Homan (1999) stated that teamwork is an ideal way to make change as it allows for a creative exchange of ideas, lessens disconnections, and helps everyone become motivated toward team success.

The final staff development workshop was on technology skills and computer training. As Sabella (1999) stated, many professional school counselors often fear technology. At the preschool, many staff were interested in having more training in how they could use technology to assist them in their jobs. This staff development workshop included training in all areas of computers, including basic operational skills, typing lessons, and learning how to navigate the Internet. The professional school counselor began the technology and computer training workshops and quickly discovered that other staff members wanted to use their skills to help educate all staff. Because the school utilized Applied Behavior Analysis (ABA), a data-driven model of special education services, the school used staff knowledge of computer technology to transfer ABA data from paper to computers, conserving resources and time that were used instead to assist students and families.

All professional school counselors and other leaders need to believe that their staff has powerful potential. The success of the workshops resulted from the director's and the professional school counselor's shared view that staff was capable of greatness and would rise to the challenge of high expectations for success for all students. Before the transformation, many staff were excluded from meetings and workshops. This gave these staff members the feeling that they were not valuable to the school. Involving all staff in these workshops and encouraging staff to run their own workshops had a positive impact. More staff became part of the transformation, and staff members became closer with parents and guardians due to their participation in different groups. Staff members became team members, and everyone understood the importance of everyone else's role. Staff members, enjoying their increased appreciation and significance, reported enjoying their jobs more. Students reaped the benefits because staff recognized, as team members, what their part was in achieving high levels of success for all students and families in the program.

## Teacher Workshops

The final set of workshops was developed for the teachers. To continue the transformation toward a school that advocates for all students to have a better education and successful futures, teachers also needed to grow and develop their educational awareness, knowledge, and skills. A strong bond between teachers and their students' families was crucial, as evidenced by multiple early childhood research studies. David & Galinsky (1988) referred to teacher-caregivers as supplements to assist family members as a type of extended family. To keep this bond strong, workshops and open communication lines were vital.

The first teacher workshop was on grammar and writing skills, since teachers were responsible for significant amounts of paperwork. Many teachers were having some difficulty writing, in part because of the advanced technical language used in Applied Behavior Analysis and special education, and many had significant grammatical mistakes. If teachers are not clear in their writing about specific disability issues and how to effectively resolve them, they cannot be effective in conveying to parents and guardians what they need to do to be effective in working with children at home.

The next teacher workshop was on the Individualized Education Plans (IEP) that teachers must write for all students. Until this workshop was developed, teachers had never been instructed in how to write effective IEPs, which meant that some teachers would not be able to name the goals they could set or the services they could assist in delivering to the students. This workshop covered each of the basic components of writing an IEP, and how to work collaboratively with families to utilize the IEP for everyone's knowledge and benefit and ensure that teachers and family members were clear on how to use the IEP for maximizing the student's success in school and at home.

The last teacher workshop focused on the importance of respecting all cultures, ethnic and racial identities, and world views within the classroom and through teaching techniques. This workshop was an ongoing process whereby teachers and the professional school counselor reflected on the teaching and learning process as it applied to all students and their families. Understanding how learning is influenced by the myriad of cultural forces in society helped teachers and schools create positive learning environments and academic success for students (Nieto, 1999). Fortunately, teaching in a setting with students with disabilities where it is understood that there is always more than one way to teach a student creates a learning base in which teachers are already open to learning accommodations, making an effective bridge for using multicultural education and learning theories.

Measuring the success of the teachers' workshops resulted from the volume of data and written results from student learning. It was discovered that when teachers feel more confident in their writing skills they spend more time writing and are more interested in it. Different district personnel who oversee IEP meetings involving students, parents, guardians, and teachers have seen the difference as well. The school's educational staff and paperwork is more professional than in the past and compares quite favorably to other preschools. Most importantly, as teachers and families developed a better understanding of what they were requesting and why, they became advocates for better services, and the districts have been more generous in what they have to offer students and families.

## Summary/Conclusion

The professional school counselor's collaborative role in successfully transforming a preschool into a place of advocacy and success for all students in areas such as academic achievement, career development, and interpersonal development, included these key steps:

1. Develop teachers, staff, parents, and guardians who will act as powerful, culturally and technologically competent advocates for every student.
2. Learn the systemic barriers that impede each team member's part in acting as powerful success advocates for every student.
3. Deliver learning and teaching workshops and services to overcome these systemic barriers to teacher, staff, parent, and guardian effectiveness.
4. Measure workshop effectiveness and success through informal and formal surveys and needs assessments.

These steps begin the cycle of successfully persuing learning outcomes for all the pieces that create student success by challenging the systemic barriers erected by adults. Remembering that this cycle is an ongoing process is key. As Dahir, Sheldon, & Valiga (1998) stated, program development, implementation, and evaluation are never-ending, and the journey toward educational success for all students becomes the destination.

## References

American Counseling Association. (1997). *Code of ethics and standards of practice.* Alexandria, VA: Author.

American School Counselor Association. (1992). *Ethical standards for school counselors.* Alexandria, VA: Author.

Arredondo, P., Toporek, R., Brown, S. P., Jones, J., Locke, D. C., Sanchez, J., & Stadler, H. (1996). Operationalization of the multicultural counseling competencies. *Journal of Multicultural Counseling and Development, 24,* 42-78.

Bacon, E. H., & Dougherty, A. M. (1992). Consultation and coordination services for prekindergarten children. *Elementary School Guidance and Counseling, 27*(1), 24-32.

Bailey, D. F., Getch, Y. Q., & Chen-Hayes, S. F. (2003). Professional school counselors as social and academic advocates. In B. T. Erford (Ed.), *Transforming the school counseling profession* (pp. 411-434). Columbus, OH: Merrill/ Prentice-Hall.

Campbell, C. A., & Dahir, C. A. (1997). *Sharing the vision: The national standards for school counseling programs.* Alexandria, VA: American School Counselor Association.

Dahir, C. A., Sheldon, C. B., & Valiga, M. J. (1998). *Vision into action: Implementing the national standards for school counseling programs.* Alexandria, VA: American School Counselor Association.

David, J., & Galinsky, E. (1988). *The preschool years: Family strategies that work from experts and parents.* New York: Time Books.

Erford, B. T., House, R., & Martin, P. (2003). Transforming the school counseling profession. In B. T. Erford (Ed.), *Transforming the school counseling profession* (pp. 1-19). Columbus, OH: Merrill/Prentice-Hall.

Fine, M. J., & Gardner, P. A. (1991). Counseling and education services for families: An empowerment perspective. *Elementary School Guidance and Counseling, 26*(1), 33-44.

Gerler, E. R., & Myrick, R. D. (1991). The elementary school counselor's work with prekindergarten children: Implications for counselor education programs. *Elementary School Guidance and Counseling, 26*(1), 67-75.

Herring, R. D. (1997). *Counseling diverse ethnic youth: Synergetic strategies and interventions for school counselors.* Fort Worth, TX: Harcourt Brace.

Hoffman, L. R. (1991). Developmental counseling for prekindergarten children: A preventive approach. *Elementary School Guidance and Counseling, 26*(1), 56-66.

Hohenshil, T. H., & Brown, M. B. (1991). Public school counseling services for prekindergarten children. *Elementary School Guidance and Counseling, 26*(1), 4-11.

Homan, M. S. (1999). *Promoting community change: Making it happen in the real world.* Pacific Grove, CA: Brooks/Cole.

Johnson, R. (1996). *Setting our sights: Measuring equity in the school change.* Los Angeles: The Achievement Council.

Lewis, J. A., Lewis, M. D., Daniels, J. A., & D'Andrea, M. J. (1998). *Community counseling: Empowerment strategies for a diverse society* (2nd ed.). Pacific Grove, CA: Brooks/Cole.

Nieto, S. (1999). *The light in their eyes: Creating multicultural learning communities.* New York: Columbia.

Sabella, R. (1999). *Schoolcounselor.com: A friendly and practical guide to the World Wide Web.* Minneapolis, MN: Educational Media Corporation.

South Carolina State Department of Education. (1999). *The South Carolina comprehensive developmental guidance and counseling program model: A guide for school counseling programs, prekindergarten-twelfth grade.* Columbia, SC: Author.

Sue, D. W., & Sue, S. (2003). *Counseling the culturally diverse* (4th ed.). New York: Wiley.

Telzrow, C. F. (1991). Prekindergarten children with special needs. *Elementary School Guidance and Counseling, 26*(1), 22-32.

Texas Education Agency. (1998). *A model developmental guidance and counseling program for Texas public schools: A guide for program development pre-K-12th grade* (3rd ed.). Austin, TX: Author.

# Chapter 92

# Transition Programming for Professional School Counselors

*Patrick Akos*

## Preview

Research has demonstrated both risk and opportunity for students during normative school transitions. Professional school counselors, in collaboration with others, have an opportunity to provide programming that can influence the developmental paths and academic success of students. A brief summary of research is presented along with recommendations for programming.

Transitions are crucial turning points in one's life. Regardless of the type of transition, most have inherent risk and opportunity. Starting something new usually causes most people stress and anxiety and taxes coping abilities. At the same time, a new start affords an opportunity to establish new relationships and achieve new potential.

Professional school counselors are quite familiar with non-normative transitions. Non-normative transitions are unexpected changes that occur in one's life. Loss of a parent or guardian or the breakup of a family or a relationship are common examples of when professional school counselors intervene. Often these events create unexpected transitions for students and families and require school counseling assistance with grieving, managing emotions, facilitating closure, and/or developing coping skills. Most professional school counselors also prepare students and practice new ways to adjust and thrive in the new situation. As developmental specialists, professional school counselors understand the difficulty associated with an unexpected change and expend great energy to repair and foster students' adjustment and coping abilities.

While they receive much less attention, normative transitions can also be influential events in development and similarly carry extensive risk and opportunity. More importantly, normative transitions are both planned and predictable. Hence these normative transitions are opportunities for proactive intervention by professional school counselors. Normative transitions include, but are not limited to, the transition into school, moving from elementary to middle to high school, and moving from high school to post-secondary education or work. Mid year transfers are another student transition that professional school counselors often help with, yet transfers are not normative, planned, or completed by the majority of students. The major normative school transitions provide professional school counselors a significant opportunity to plan proactive prevention to facilitate development and success in school for all students.

One example of an opportunity for such interventions is school entry. Several large-scale studies, such as the Head Start Transition Study (Ramey & Ramey, 1999), the National Education Longitudinal Study (Meisels, 1999), and the NICHD Study of Early Child Care (Kagan & Neuman, 1998) have investigated the importance of school entry to academic and social outcomes. In fact, most states have focused policy on preschool education and more than 50% of elementary schools have programs targeted to pre-kindergarten children (Rimm-Kauffman & Pianta, 2000). While home environments play a large role in school readiness, professional school counselors may assist in developmental readiness assessment and conduct a variety of interventions to help with separation anxiety. The emerging research has demonstrated that several important child factors (e.g., temperament, language abilities, cognitive readiness), contextual factors (e.g., class size, peer relationships, the family processes), and the complex developing interactions between both are influential sources for later school success. Rosenkoelter (1995) recommends systemic (e.g., peer, family, school, community) collaboration with frequent contacts, agreed upon goals, and a focus on supporting the child's development of skills as a means to support the positive transition. Resources for professional school counselors to use in programming include *The Transition into Kindergarten* (Pianta & Cox, 1999), *Entering Kindergarten* (U.S. Department of Education, 2001), and *Even Start: Facilitating Transitions to Kindergarten* (Riedinger, 1997).

Another well recognized and researched normative transition includes the transition from school to work or post-secondary school. Both the Perkins Act in Title IIIE (Tech Prep) and the School to Work Opportunities Act of 1994 legislate career development activities for students (Ettinger & Perry, 1993). Career development is a traditional part of school counseling and outcome research in school counseling has established the effectiveness of career interventions (Whiston, 2003). Additionally, the American School Counseling Association's National Standards have recommended career development as a core outcome for school counseling programs (Campbell & Dahir, 1997). Many high schools have career development counselors and career centers preparing students for school to work and post-secondary education. In fact, colleges and universities increasingly have extensive orientation programs to acclimate students to the college environment. In addition to general career development and college preparation, the Individuals with Disabilities Education Act (IDEA) legislates transition planning for special education students starting at age 14. IDEA specifies outcome-oriented practices to promote movement from school to post-school activities. Professional school counselors, due to career development training, are valuable collaborators with special education professionals in information dissemination, career assessment and planning, job exploration, and school or work placement. Wandry, Pruitt, Fox, and Anderson (1998) have called for "transition teams" including professional school counselors, special education professionals, and a variety of community agencies to meet to effectively create transition plans appropriate for students with Individualized Educational Programs. Numerous programming resources exist including *Transition Planning for Secondary Students with Disabilities* (Flexer, 2001), *Counseling Employment Bound Youth* (Herr, 1995), and *Enhancing Linkages to Postsecondary Education: Helping Youths make a Successful Transition to College* (Bragg, 1999).

Less research has examined effective ways to promote student development and success between elementary, middle, and high school. The transition from elementary to middle school represents a noteworthy rite of passage. The distinctive aspects of the transition from elementary to middle school include both the vast contextual differences and the dual timing of personal and school transitions. This difference between elementary school organization and procedures and those in the middle school are extensive. Multiple teachers, larger school buildings, block scheduling, lockers, and new and different peers characterize the move to middle school. While this contextual change occurs, significant personal change occurs with puberty. Dramatic physical, emotional, and cognitive change is more abrupt during preadolescence than any other time (other than infancy). Finally, the timing of the two transitions together has shown to lead to some detrimental consequences.

Developmental psychologists, for the most part, have demonstrated the influence that the transition to middle school has on students. Research has demonstrated that students exhibit decreases in self-esteem, academic achievement, and motivation (Aspalgh, 1998; Harter, 1981; Simmons & Blyth, 1987; Wigfield, Eccles, Mac Iver, Reuman, & Midgley, 1991). Additionally, the transition to middle school has been associated with increases in behavior problems (Wigfield et al., 1991) and increases in psychological distress (Chung, Elias, & Schneider, 1998).

Several theorists have proposed useful theories to understand transitional outcomes. Fenzel (1989) described role strain, or how individuals experience concepts like role ambiguity, role overload, lack of control, and conflict in the transition to a new environment. Koizumi (2000) conceptualized anchor points to describe information, knowledge, skills, or people in the environment that students use to evaluate and structure their experience. Most notable, Ecceles et al. (1993) has suggested that a poor person-environment fit explains many of the outcomes for the transition to middle school. Several of her published reports suggest that preadolescent developmental needs (e.g., autonomy, peer support) are not met in most junior high/middle school environments (e.g., more controlling teachers, less decision making for students, more competition and ability grouping).

Although the contextual differences between middle and high school are less than those from elementary and middle school, seemingly more is at stake upon moving to high school. MacIver and Epstein (1991) suggested that most middle schools provide four to five bridge activities between the elementary and middle school, yet in the transition to high school, only two to three bridge activities were reported. The distinctive aspects of the transition from middle to high school involve the academic transition and the implications of unsuccessful transitions. Students often choose academic tracks that impact not only the next four years of high school, but also their future post-secondary and work options. For example, eighth grade students in North Carolina choose an academic Course of Study that offers so little flexibility that students who switch after freshman year must often complete another year of high school to meet graduation requirements.

Students and parents report the majority of concerns about high school include academic themes such as homework and academically rigorous teachers (Akos & Galassi, 2002). These academic concerns and implications are supported in the research literature. Similar to the transition to middle school, reports have demonstrated declines in grades and attendance (Alspaugh, 1998; Barone, Aguirre-Deandreis, & Trickett, 1991; Mizelle & Irvin, 2000; Reyes, Gillock, Kobus, 1994) with the transition to high school. For both transitions, several research reports have documented a variety of student, parent, and teacher concerns with moving between levels of schooling (Akos, 2002; Akos & Galassi, 2002; Maute, 1991; Mitman & Packer, 1982). For example, students have reported concerns about homework, bullies, and lockers (Akos, 2002; Akos & Galassi, 2002; Mitman & Packer, 1982) for the transition from elementary to middle school and keeping friends, getting good grades, and knowing how to study (Maute, 1991) for the transition to high school. Parents have also reported concerns about homework, peer pressure, and fitting in for both transitions (Akos & Galassi, 2002). Last, teachers have reported concerns about student peer pressure, fitting in, and getting along with others for both transitions (Akos & Galassi, 2002).

## Implications for Professional School Counselors

Professional school counselors are presented with a unique challenge. Predictable, planned, and major normative transitions occur for students moving to and from middle school. These transitions have been shown to result in significant (and mostly negative) outcomes. These transition opportunities provide professional school counselors with a chance to proactively address or ameliorate the negative outcomes associated with transition and promote school success and optimal developmental trajectories.

Since transitions occur between levels of schooling, decisions regarding who should be responsible for transition programming are not always clear. Elementary school counselors play a large role in preparing students to move and high school counselors are significant to high school entry. Usually, feeder schools offer proactive interventions, while receiving schools provide both preventative and enrichment services to help students get adjusted to the new building. Middle school counselors have the dual responsibility of both a feeder and receiving school. In fact, because middle school is often viewed as a transition time itself (from childhood to adolescence), middle schools should invest significant time and energy into transition programming.

Another challenge in transition programming is the wide variety of tasks that occur, not all directly related to a traditional definition of school counseling. Transitional tasks may include preparing student schedules, securing medical records, determining student bus schedules, grouping students for teams, tracking students for academic curriculum, and curriculum articulation between levels of schooling. The wide and diverse set of tasks often results in segmentation and duplication of services.

There are very few published reports that examine the effectiveness of transition programming. The existing reports document "shadow" programs for students (Ferguson & Bulach, 1994), education and peer support (Reyes et al., 1994), peer counseling and tutoring (Leland-Jones, 1998), group counseling in combination with parent and teacher support (Greene & Ollendick, 1993), social skills and drama curriculum (Walsh-Bowers, 1992), and significant school restructuring such as teams and teacher advisories in high school (Felner et al., 1993). Findings ranged from no effects (Reyes et al., 1994) to general student satisfaction, improved achievement, behavior and attendance, and more positive school environments. Further research is needed on the common interventions used in transition programming (e.g., scheduling presentations, school tours, orientation programs), but this increasing accumulation of research on school transitions presents several implications for professional school counselors.

## Transition Programming Recommendations

### *A Year-long Dynamic or Developmental Transition Program*

Results of the research on student perceptions suggest that student's needs during a transition change over time and a transition program needs to be responsive to developmental changes (Akos, 2002; Maute, 1991; Mitman & Packer, 1982). For example, students in elementary school report parents are more helpful than teachers, yet after they transition into middle school they report teachers are more helpful than parents (Akos, 2002). It may be useful to construct programming responsive to the student's perceptions and developmental needs. It may also be most useful to conceptualize a transition program from January to December to help students prepare for and adjust to the new school. In doing so, students receive assistance for an extended period of time and the responsibility for helping students during transition falls to both feeder and receiving schools. For example, elementary school counselors may provide transition groups (Akos & Martin, 2002) and/or deliver coping skills in 5th grade classrooms to help prepare students for the move to middle school. Common articulation activities during the spring also include scheduling presentations, school tours, and ambassador or "shadow" programs. In the summer and fall, middle schools may prepare students through enrichment programs and fall orientation programs to induct students to the middle school. The year-long structure attends to both the development of students and the collaboration between levels.

### *Collaboration with Teachers, Administrators, and School Staff between Levels of Schooling*

Although professional school counselors in feeding and receiving schools may collaborate, other school staff is essential to comprehensive transition programs. Professional school counselors between levels of schooling often meet to discuss students at risk, but it is equally fruitful that support staff (e.g., nurses, ESL coordinators, special education coordinators), administrators, and teachers communicate to facilitate a smooth transition. For example, Mizelle and Mullins (1997) recommend teacher shadowing between levels with processing meetings to discuss differences between the schools, classroom, and curriculum. In this way, transitional tasks not directly linked to professional school counselors, such as curriculum articulation, can be initiated. Often this complex task involves teachers from multiple feeder and receiving schools, as well as central office personnel coming to consensus on curricular issues. These policies are usually district-wide and have direct implications for transitions for all schools in a district. This activity aligns well with the new ASCA *National Model*, offering an opportunity for leadership and advocacy district wide (Hatch & Bowers, 2002). Additionally, research (Akos, 2002) suggested that student questions about the new school most often concern rules and procedures.

*Administrators and teachers are crucial for information dissemination to both students and parents*

Much of the transition research (Ecceles et al., 1993) also points to the classroom environment and teacher relationships as influential to transition outcomes. For example, Fenzel (1989) and Mizelle and Mullins (1997) speculate that the middle school concept (e.g., teaching teams, advisory) eliminates many of the negative outcomes attributed to the transition. Also, most of the published transition programs significantly involve restructuring the environment (e.g., teaming, teacher advisory) of the receiving school. It is therefore crucial that professional school counselors collaborate with school personnel, especially teachers, on orientation programming and restructuring efforts.

*Inclusion and Programming Specifically for Parents and Families*

MacIver and Epstien (1991) discovered that parents are more active participants in the education of their child when involved in transition programs. As research has shown the benefits of parent participation in student achievement (Hess & Holloway, 1984), the transition to a new school seems to be an important opportunity to generate parent involvement. It is also significant that students, especially Hispanic students, mention parents as sources of help during the transition between levels of schooling (Akos, 2002; Akos & Galassi, 2002). It may be useful to engage parents in the spring prior to the transition with school newsletters, parent meetings, and course scheduling. Later, receiving schools can utilize parent volunteers as part of orientation planning or conduct parent/teacher meetings or potluck dinners as part of early open houses to welcome and connect new parents to the school.

*Intentional Peer Program*

One developmental need common to students in both middle and high school transitions is the intense peer focus and desire for peer connection. Students report peers as a positive aspect and the most influential source of help during transitions to middle and high schools (Akos, 2002; Akos & Galassi, 2002; Diemert, 1992). Research (Eccles et al., 1993) also speculates that the negative outcomes associated with transition are partly due to the upheaval of peer networks. Professional school counselors can utilize the developmental influence of peers to provide accurate information and easily accessible help for students through group counseling, peer mentoring or tutoring, or "shadow" or buddy programs.

*Intentional Extracurricular Programs and Activities to Connect Students to School*

Connection or belongingness to school has been shown to be an important contribution to student adjustment and academic success (Osterman, 2000). Professional school counselors can facilitate these connections with activity fairs, information brochures, or student activity or club presentations to students new to the building. Often, sixth and ninth grade students have limited options for school-sponsored sports or clubs. Professional school counselors can advocate for inclusion of sixth or ninth grade students in extracurricular programs, no-cut policies, and school-sponsored activities specifically for new students. For example, it may be beneficial for schools to sponsor fifth and sixth grade or eight and ninth grade school dances to help students bridge the transition and feel connected to school.

*Broad Programming for All Students and Specific Programming for At-risk Students*

Primarily with prevention and the influence of comprehensive guidance programs, professional school counselors seek to serve all students in the school. Transition programming is an excellent example of providing large scale services for all students. For example, most schools provide an orientation program for new students. It may be useful to conceive of orientation as a process whereby schools work with students to accommodate different adjustment timetables. In fact, professional school counselors should direct services to students who may be having or who demonstrate more difficulty in transitioning. The current research on school transitions does not allow for a means to predict who may struggle most in the transition, although some research has investigated demographic and school variable factors in transition outcomes. Although the research is not conclusive, many speculate that female students, low achievers, and urban, minority students may be more at risk during the transition to middle school (Eccels et al., 1993; Seidman, Allen, Aber, Mitchell, & Feinman, 1994). It may be beneficial for professional school counselors to determine a way to identify students who struggle due to the transition. For example, using cumulative folders from the previous school, professional school counselors can identify students who exhibit a pronounced drop in grades or increases in behavior problems or absences. It may be useful to provide small group sessions for new students and individual counseling to those students who demonstrate significant declines and those who appear least connected to the new school.

## Summary/Conclusion

As professional school counselors help students with unexpected life changes, it is important that they capitalize on the influential and significant normative changes between levels of schooling. District configurations vary and each transition represents a new opportunity to affect the developmental path for students. While most professional school counselors engage in transition activities, it is useful to provide leadership and advocacy for transition programs that include collaboration between levels and staff, inclusion of parent and peer programming, and evaluation of transition related interventions.

## References


Akos, P. (2002). Student perceptions of the transition from elementary to middle school. *Professional School Counseling, 5*, 339-345.

Akos, P., & Galassi, G. (2002). *School transitions as viewed by students, parents, and teachers.* Unpublished manuscript.

Akos, P., & Martin, M. (2002). Preparing students for middle school in transition groups. *Journal for Specialists in Group Work.* Manuscript in press.

Alspaugh, J. W. (1998). Achievement loss associated with the transition to middle school and high school. *The Journal of Educational Research*, *92*, 20-25.

Barone, C., Aguirre-Deandreis, A. I., & Trickett, E. J. (1991). Mean-ends problem-solving skills, life stress, and social support as mediators of adjustment in the normative transition to high school. *American Journal of Community Psychology, 19,* 207-225.

Bragg, D. (1999). *Enhancing linkages to postsecondary education: Helping youths make a successful transition to college.* Washington, DC: U.S. Dept. of Education, Office of Educational Research and Improvement.

Campbell, C. & Dahir, C. (1997). *Sharing the vision: The national standards for school counseling programs.* Alexandria, VA: American School Counseling Association.

Chung, H., Elias, M., & Schneider, K. (1998). Patterns of individual adjustment changes during middle school transition. *Journal of School Psychology, 36*, 83-101.

Diemert, A. (1992). *A needs assessment of fifth grade students in a middle school.* Acton, MA: Author. (ERIC Document Reproduction Service No. ED 362 332)

Eccles, J. S., Wigfield, A., Midgley, C., Reuman, D., MacIver, D., & Feldlaufer, J.(1993). Negative effects of traditional middle schools on students' motivation. *The Elementary School Journal, 93*, 553-574.

Ettinger, J., & Perry, N. (1993). School to work programs and the school counselor. In G. Walz & J. Bleuer (Eds.), *Counseling efficacy: Assessing and using counseling outcome research.* Ann Arbor, MI: ERIC-CAPS.

Felner, R., Brand, S., Adan, A., Mulhall, P., Flowers, N., Sartain, B., & Dubois, D. (1993). Restructuring the ecology of the school as an approach to prevention during school transitions: Longitudinal follow-ups and extensions of the School Transition Environment Project (STEP). *Prevention in Human Services, 10,* 103-136.

Fenzel, M. (1989). Role strains and the transition to middle school: Longitudinal trends and sex differences. *Journal of Early Adolescence, 9*, 211-226.

Ferguson, J., & Bulach, C. (1994). *The effect of the shadow transition program on the social adjustment of Whitewater Middle School.* Eric Document Reproduction Service 380 878.

Flexer, R. (2001). *Transition planning for secondary students with disabilities.* Upper Saddle River, N.J.: Merrill/Prentice Hall.

Greene, R., & Ollendick, T. (1993). Evaluation of a multidimensional program for sixth graders in transition from elementary to middle school. *Journal of Community Psychology, 21,* 162-176.

Harter, S. (1981). A new self-report scale of intrinsic versus extrinsic orientation in the classroom: Motivational and informational components. *Developmental Psychology, 17,* 300-312.

Hatch, T., & Bowers, J. (May/June, 2002). The block to build on. *School Counselor, 39*(5), 12-19.

Herr, E. (1995). *Counseling employment bound youth.* Greensboro, NC: ERIC Counseling and Student Services Clearinghouse.

Hess, R. D., & Holloway, S. D. (1984). Family and school as education institutions. In R. D. Parke (Ed.), *Review of child development research* (Vol. 7, pp. 179-122). Chicago: University of Chicago Press.

Kagan, S., & Neuman, M. (1998). Lessons from three decades of transition research. *Elementary School Journal, 98*, 365-379.

Koizumi, R. (2000). Anchor points in transitions to a new school environment. *The Journal of Primary Prevention, 20*, 175-187.

Leland-Jones, P. (1998). Improving the transition of sixth-grade students during the first year of middle school through a peer counselor mentor and tutoring program. (Doctoral dissertation, Nova Southeastern University, 1998). *Dissertation Abstracts International.*

MacIver, D. J., & Epstein, J. L. (1991). Responsive practices in the middle grades: Teacher teams, advisory groups, remedial instruction, and school transition programs. *American Journal of Education 99,* 587-622.

Maute, J. K. (1991). *Transitions concerns of eighth-grade students in six Illinois schools as they prepare for high school.* Unpublished doctoral dissertation, National-Louis University, Evanston, IL.

Meisels, S. (1999). Assessing readiness. In R. Pianta & M. Cox (Eds.), *The transition to kindergarten: Research, policy, training, and practice* (pp. 39-66). Baltimore, MD: Paul Brooks Publishers.

Mitman, A. L., & Packer, M. J. (1982). Concerns of seventh-graders about their transition to junior high school. *Journal of Early Adolescence, 2,* 319-338.

Mizelle, N. B., & Irvin, J. L. (2000). Transition from middle school to high school. *Middle School Journal, 31,* 57-61.

Mizelle, N., & Mullins, E. (1997). Transitions into and out of middle school. In J. Irving (Ed.), *What current research says to middle level practitioners* (pp. 303-316). Columbus, OH: National Middle School Association.

Osterman, K. F. (2000). Students' need for belonging in the school community. *Review of Educational Research, 70,* 323-367.

Pianta, R., & Cox, M. (1999). *The transition to kindergarten.* Baltimore: Brooks Publishing Co.

Ramey, C., & Ramey, S. (1999). Beginning school for children at risk. In R. Pianta & M. Cox (Eds.), *The transition to kindergarten: Research, policy, training, and practice* (pp. 217-252). Baltimore: Paul Brooks Publishers.

Reyes, O., Gillock, K., & Kobus, K. (1994). A longitudinal study of school adjustment in urban, minority adolescents: Effects of a high school transition program. *American Journal of Community Psychology, 22,* 341-369.

Reidinger, S. (1997). *Even start: Facilitating the transition into kindergarten.* Washington, DC: U.S. Dept. of Education, Office of Educational Research and Improvement.

Rosenkoetter, S. (1995). *It's a big step: A guide for transition to kindergarten.* Topeka, KS: Kansas Coordinating Council on Early Childhood Developmental Services. (ERIC Document Reproduction Service No. ED 385 087)

Rimm-Kaufmanm, S,. & Pianta, R. (2000). An ecological perspective on the transition to kindergarten: A theoretical framework to guide empirical research. *Journal of Applied Developmental Psychology, 21,* 491-511.

Seidman, E., Allen, L., Aber, J., Mitchell, C., & Feinman, J. (1994). The impact of school transitions in early adolescence on the self-system and perceived social context of poor urban youth. *Child Development, 65,* 507-522.

Simmons, R., & Blyth, D. (1987). *Moving into adolescence: The impact of pubertal change and school context.* Hawthorne, NY: Aldine de Gruyter

U.S. Department of Education, National Center for Educational Statistics. (2001). *Entering kindergarten: A portrait of American children when they enter school.* Washington, DC: U.S. Government Printing Office.

Walsh-Bowers, R. (1992). A creative drama prevention program for easing early adolescents' adjustment to school transitions. *The Journal of Primary Prevention, 13,* 131-147.

Wandry, D., Pruitt, P., Fox, R., & Anderson, G. (1998). Special educators and school counselors: An emerging team in transition services. *B.C. Journal of Special Education, 21,* 95-111.

Whiston, S. (2003). Outcome research on professional school counseling services. In B. T. Erford (Ed.), *Transforming the school counseling profession.* Upper Saddle, N.J.: Merrill/Prentice-Hall.

Wigfield, A., Eccles, J. S., Mac Iver, D., Reuman, D., & Midgley, C. (1991). Transitions during early adolescence: Changes in children's domain specific self-perceptions and general self-esteem across the transition to junior high school. *Developmental Psychology, 27,* 552-566.

# Chapter 93

## Preventing Professional School Counselor Burnout

*Kelly Murray*

### Preview

Burnout and attrition from the field of school counseling is quite high. It is a condition that emerges as a function of the complex interplay of environmental stressors and individual differences. Burnout is a slow and corrosive condition that causes fatigue, cynicism, lack of motivation and possibly depression.

As a professional school counselor or school counselor in training, you may have wondered about burnout and even questioned whether you may be suffering some of the symptoms associated with burnout. Burnout is a term often read and learned about during a training program. Because of professional training it may be relatively easy to spot in other people. However, when it is the professional school counselor herself who is tired and feeling ineffective, it is often rationalized as being part of the job. In reality, burnout and attrition from the field of school counseling is quite high. A study of academicians and practitioners conducted by Wood, Klein, Cross, Lammers and Elliott (1985) looked at symptoms of burnout and depression and discovered that 63% of participants reported having an awareness of colleagues whose work is affected by their impairment while 32% of the participants admitted having feelings of burnout or depression that affected their own work. A 1994 study by Grosch and Olsen suggested that the average counselor has a productive life span of 10 years before burnout becomes a substantial factor. Some studies have described the prevalence of depression in psychiatrists to be at 60% to 90% (Swearingen, 1990; Wood et al., 1985).

Burnout is a slow, corrosive condition that tends to get progressively worse over time. This is especially true for the professional school counselor who will often overlook his own needs in order to be available to others. As the professional school counselor continues to ignore or deny the extent of his burnout, symptoms get slowly worse and more pervasive.

In the past, definitions for burnout have been vague and all encompassing. Although there has been a good deal of research on burnout for human service workers, there has been relatively little research on burnout for professional school counselors. The research that does exist for professional school counselors shows that the professional school counselor has a job that is often stressful, intense, and unrelenting. The demands placed upon a professional school counselor are often plentiful and varied. They are called upon to work with students who present with a host of issues, the families and parents of these students, administrators, teachers, other mental health professionals, and other school officials. The professional school counselor may work in many different domains and wear many hats. Professional school counselors are relied upon to make critical decisions about students which may affect those students for the rest of their lives.

Wise (1985) reported that professional school counselors often experience a variety of on-the-job stressors. Such stressors are reported to be an over-abundance of work, insufficient pleasure at work, inadequate structure and poor management, poor relationships with supervisory personnel, meager recognition for efforts, and the feeling of lacking control of one's situation. Also reported as stressors are a lack of time, excessive caseloads, being unable to catch up on backlogs of work, and a lack of support. Several other areas reported as unsatisfactory among professional school counselors were unavailability of adequate testing and interview facilities, lack of funding to attend conventions, lack of inservice training, lack of opportunity for advancement and promotion, and isolation from peers (Niebrugge, 1994). An important contributor to burnout is the absence of the opportunity to experience completion and follow through with students with whom professional school counselors work. In many circumstances the child or the counselor moves on, and therefore, the counselor is unable to determine if the work she has done with the child has been truly effective. The lack of opportunity for the professional school counselor to conduct ongoing follow up with a particular student can cause the counselor to view her work as ineffective and unrewarding (Freudenberger, 1977). The stress and anxiety associated with these many demands may be intense and may take their toll on the professional school counselor.

Burnout has been defined as a reaction to chronic problems in coping with stress (Cherniss, 1980). Maslach and Jackson (1986) reported that burnout is a three dimensional construct. The first component is described as *emotional exhaustion*. Frequently, professionals report feelings of being tired and overwhelmed with work demands. As emotional resources are expended, professionals feel they are no longer able to give of themselves at a psychological level. In this component the professional school counselor may feel overwhelmed by his job demands. The second component involves *depersonalization*. Professionals suffering from burnout develop impersonal attitudes and become indifferent in responding to students. They may have negative feelings and attitudes toward students. This distancing of others can lead professional school counselors to believe their student's deserve their afflictions. The last component of burnout is a *reduced sense of personal accomplishment* that is often manifested in feelings of incompetence and helplessness toward helping students.

Huberty and Huebner (1988) conducted a national survey of burnout among school psychologists. The major correlates of burnout identified in this study included clarity of role definitions, time pressures that result from excessive demands (e.g., heavy caseloads), external pressures beyond their control (e.g., teacher pressure), and internal pressure regarding how school psychologists perceived themselves (e.g., personality conflicts).

Huebner (1993) reported that results of several of his studies showed three sources of stress for school psychologists: (1) organizational factors such as role ambiguity, role conflict and role overload, (2) interpersonal factors such as poor supervisors and lack of positive feedback, as well as a low degree of peer support, and (3) intrapersonal factors including inadequate preparation for the job and personality characteristics such as workaholism and Type A behavior, lack of commitment to work, low self-esteem, empathy, external locus of control, job-related expectations, and attributional style.

## Symptoms of Burnout

Burnout can have serious and pervasive consequences for professional school counselors and the students they serve. Individual differences in burnout reactions emerge as a function of the complex interplay of environmental stressors and individual differences. Kottler (1993) described burnout as the single most common personal consequence of practicing therapy. He believes that it is not a question of who will experience burnout, but how long the next episode will last. According to Kottler, symptoms of burnout include an unwillingness to discuss work in social and family circles, a reluctance to check messages or return calls, and an unseemly delight in canceled appointments. Daydreaming and escape fantasies occupy the professional counselor's thoughts. Cynicism, loss of enthusiasm and spontaneity, procrastination, physical fatigue, and lack of family and social involvement predominate. Frequently there is also a reluctance to admit that a problem exists. The use of alcohol and other drugs has also been linked with burnout among several groups of helping professionals.

Kahill (1988) groups the symptoms of burnout into five major categories. The first reported category is physical. Burnout has been associated with general physical health and illness, as well as some somatic complaints, such as sleep disturbance. The second category of symptoms is emotional. Some of the most commonly reported emotional symptoms are emotional depletion, irritability, anxiety, guilt, depression and helplessness. Kahill found that burnout is most closely associated with depression. The third category of burnout symptoms is behavioral. A number of unproductive behaviors are associated with burnout. Such behaviors include job turnover, poor job performance, absenteeism and substance abuse. The fourth category of symptoms is interpersonal and usually affects clients, friends, and family members. The final category of symptoms is attitudinal. Negative attitudes and cognitions may develop toward clients, work, family, oneself, and life.

The quality of support systems available to the helping professional has also been correlated to burnout. The supervisor can be a major source of stress or a significant figure in the prevention and management of burnout. Supervisors who respond effectively to professional school counselor needs increase feelings of confidence, competence and control. Professional school counselors whose supervisors are not counselors may be at high risk of burnout, since such supervisors may possess neither the technical expertise nor the requisite emotional sensitivity to provide support related to some of the unique problems of professional school counselors (Lynch, 1999).

Inadequate preparation for the job is also a crucial intrapersonal variable in burnout. Among professional school counselors, age has also been consistently associated with burnout. Modest inverse relationships have been reported indicating that the likelihood of burnout decreases as age increases. This relationship suggests that professional school counselors eventually succeed in effecting the development of job satisfaction through changes in personal aspirations and needs, or in the job itself, or they leave the profession (Huebner, 1993).

Burnout is described by Schaufeli, Maslach, and Marek (1993) as not an endpoint, but a process. If the trend is not corrected, symptoms that began in a minor way may lead to serious depression, substance abuse, and other severe emotional distress that can be expected to lead to critical impairment.

## Steps to Minimize and Eliminate Burnout

So, what are some steps that can be taken to minimize or, better yet, eliminate burnout? Corey (1996) offered advice to look within yourself to determine what choices you are making (and not making) to keep yourself alive. This can go a long way in preventing what some people consider to be an inevitable condition associated with the helping professions. It is crucial to recognize that you have considerable control over whether you become burned out. Although you cannot always control stressful events, you do have a great deal of control over how you interpret and react to these events. It is important to realize that you cannot continue to give and give while getting little in return. There is a price to pay for always being available and assuming that you are able to control the lives and destinies of others. Become attuned to the subtle signs of burnout, rather than waiting for a full-blown condition of emotional and physical exhaustion to set it. Develop your own strategy for keeping yourself alive personally and professionally. Table 1 lists a number of suggestions for preventing burnout (Corey, 1996), while Table 2 provides a list of resources to help professional school counselors deal with job stress burnout.

**Table 1. Suggestions for preventing burnout (Corey, 1996).**

1. Evaluate your goals, priorities, and expectations to see if they are realistic and if they are getting you what you want and need.
2. Recognize that you can be an active agent in your life.
3. Find other interests besides work, especially if work is not meeting your important needs.
4. Think of ways to bring variety into your work.
5. Take the initiative and start new projects that have personal meaning, and do not wait for the system to sanction this initiative.
6. Learn to monitor the impact of stress on the job and at home.
7. Attend to your health through adequate sleep, an exercise program, proper diet, and meditation or relaxation.
8. Develop new friendships that are characterized by a mutuality of giving and receiving.
9. Learn how to ask for what you want, though don't always expect to get it.
10. Learn how to work for self-confirmation and for self-rewards, as opposed to looking externally for validation.
11. Find meaning through play, travel, or new experiences.
12. Take the time to evaluate the meaningfulness of your projects to determine where you should continue to invest time and energy.
13. Avoid assuming burdens that are properly the responsibility of others. If you worry more about your clients than they do themselves, it would be wise for you to reconsider this investment.
14. Take classes and workshops, attend conferences, and read to gain new perspectives on old issues.
15. Rearrange your schedule to reduce stress.
16. Learn your limits, and learn to set limits with others.
17. Learn to accept yourself with your imperfections, including being able to forgive yourself when you make a mistake or do not live up to your ideals.
18. Exchange jobs with a colleague for a short period, or ask a colleague to join forces in a common work project.
19. Form a support group with colleagues to share feelings of frustration and to find better ways of approaching the reality of a difficult job situation.
20. Cultivate some hobbies that bring pleasure.
21. Make time for your spiritual growth.
22. Become more active in your professional organization.

## Summary/Conclusion

Burnout and attrition from the field of school counseling is quite high and the symptoms of burnout can be insidious. Burnout is often slow and tends to get worse over time. This is especially true if the professional school counselor ignores or overlooks his own needs. It can be relatively easy to rationalize the symptoms of burnout as being "just part of the job." With heavy caseloads, long hours, a population that presents with difficult and plentiful issues and potential lack of resources, a professional school counselor's job can be extremely stressful, intense and unrelenting. Burnout symptoms can be serious and pervasive. It is imperative for the professional school counselor to be aware of what the definitions of burnout are and how to spot it in oneself and colleagues. Engaging in self-care and prevention is also essential to decrease the risk of burnout and minimize symptoms.

**Table 2. Resources to help professional school counselors deal with job stress and burnout.**

***Burnout: Symptoms, Antecedents, and Assessments***

Cherniss, C. (1980). *Professional burnout in human service organizations*. New York: Praeger.

Cordes, C. L., & Dougherty, T. W. (1993). A review and an integration of research on job burnout. *Academy of Management Review, 18,* 621-656.

Farber, B. A. (1991). *Crisis in education: Stress and burnout in the American teacher.* San Francisco: Jossey-Bass.

Golemiewski, R. T., & Munzenrider, R. F. (1988). *Phases of burnout: Development in concepts and applications*. New York: Praeger.

Grosch, W. N., & Oleson, D. C. (1994). *When helping starts to hurt: A new look at burnout among psychotherapists*. New York: W. W. Norton & Co.

Grosch, W. N., & Oleson, D. C. (1995). Therapist burnout: A self psychology and system perspective. *Innovations in Clinical Practice, 14,* 439-454.

Heubner, E. S. (1993). Professionals under stress – A review of burnout among the helping professions with implications for school psychologists. *Psychology in the Schools, 30,* 40-49.

Schaufeli, W. B., Maslach, C., & Marek T. (Eds.) (1993). *Professional burnout: Recent developments in theory and research.* Washington, DC: Taylor & Francis.

***Burnout: Interventions and Prevention***

Cherniss, C. (1995). *Beyond burnout: Helping teachers, nurses, therapists, and lawyers recover from stress and disillusionment.* New York: Praeger.

Figley, C. R. (1995). *Compassion fatigue: Coping with secondary traumatic stress disorder in those who treat the traumatized.* New York: Brunner/Mazelm.

Gold, Y., & Roth, R. A. (1993). *Teachers managing stress and preventing burnout: The professional health solution.* Washington, DC: Falmer Press.

Grosch, W. N., & Oleson, D. C. (1995). *Prevention: Avoiding burnout.* In M. B. Sussman (Ed.), *A perilous calling: The hazards of psychotherapy practice.* John Wiley & Sons: New York.

Jaffe, D. T., & Scott, C. D. (1988). *Take this job and love it: How to change your work without changing your job.* New York: Simon & Schuster.

Paine, W. S. (Ed.) (1982). *Job stress and burnout: Research, theory and intervention perspectives.* Beverly Hills, CA: Sage Publications.

Pines, A., & Aronson, E. (1988). *Career burnout: Causes and cures.* New York: Free Press.

Pines, A., Aronson, E., & Kefry, D. (1981) *Burnout: From tedium to personal growth.* New York: The Free Press.

Richardson, A. M., & Burke, R. J. (1995) Models of burnout: Implications for interventions. *International Journal of Stress Management, 2,* 31-43.

Spicuzza, F., & de Voe, M. W. (1982). Burnout in the helping professions: Mutual aid groups as self-help. *Personnel & Guidance Journal, 61,* 95-99.

***Agencies, Organizations, and Advocacy Groups***

*American Institute of Stress (AIS)*: A nonprofit organization that serves as a resource and clearinghouse for information on stress-related matters. The Institute's services include newsletter reprints, monographs, and abstracts: 1-800-24-RELAX.

*American Psychological Association (APA) Help Line:* Call APA's help line at 1-800-964-2000 for information on resources and helping professionals in your area (choose the first option).

***Internet Resources***

*Center for Anxiety and Stress Treatment:* Address: http://www.stressrelease.com; Phone: (619) 542-0536. This site has a variety of resources that aid in stress reduction, including tips and techniques for reducing stress at work.

*Pathways to School Improvement:* Address: http://ncrel.org/ncrel/sdrs/pathways.htm. This is an award-winning, multimedia homepage with an entire section devoted to professional development, complete with online videos and lectures on school reform and successful staff improvement and growth.

*Teachers Helping Teachers:* Address: http://www.pacificnet.net/~mandel/; Phone: (818) 780-1281. This is a networking site for teachers to ask and answer questions about the teaching field. They can also get information about special issues, such as burnout and job stress.

---

## References

Cherniss, C. (1980). *Staff burnout: Job stress in the human services*. Beverly Hills, CA: Sage Publications.

Corey, G. (1996). *Theory and practice of counseling and psychotherapy*. Pacific Grove, CA: Brooks/Cole.

Freudenberger, H. J. (1977). Burnout: Occupational hazard of the child care worker. *Child Care Quarterly*, *6* (2), 90-99.

Grosch, W. N., & Olsen, D. C. (1994). *When helping starts to hurt: A new look at burnout among psychotherapists*. New York: Norton.

Huberty, T. J., & Huebner, E. S. (1988). A national survey of burnout among school psychologists. *Psychology in the Schools, 25,* 54-61.

Huebner, E. S. (1993). Professionals under stress: A review of burnout among the helping professions with implications for school psychologists. *Psychology in the Schools, 30,* 40-49.

Kahill, S. (1988). Symptoms of professional burnout: A review of the empirical evidence. *Canadian Psychology, 29,* 284-297.

Kottler, J. (1993). *On being a therapist*. San Francisco: Jossey-Bass.

Maslach, C., & Jackson, S. E. (1986). *Maslach Burnout Inventory manual* (2nd ed.). Palo Alto, CA: Consulting Psychologists Press.

Niebrugge, K. M. (1994). *Burnout and job dissatisfaction among practicing school psychologists in Illinois*. Paper presented at the Annual Meeting of the National Association of School Psychologists, Seattle WA.

Schaufeli, W., Maslach, C., & Marek, T. (1993). *Professional burnout: Recent developments in theory and research*. Washington, DC: Taylor & Francis.

Swearingen, C. (1990). The impaired psychiatrist. *Psychiatric Clinics of North America*, *13*, 1-11.

Wise, P. S. (1985). School psychologists' rankings of stressful events. *Journal of School Psychology*, 23, 31-41.

Wood, B., Klein, S., Cross, H., Lammers, C., & Elliott, J. (1985). Impaired practitioners: Psychologists' opinions about prevalence, and proposals for intervention. *Professional Psychology: Research and Practice, 16*, 843-850.